Gerald —
Trusting this may prove
as useful as it
appears formidable,
we remain, sir,
yr. obt. servants
— Merry Xmas
Don & Betty

LITERARY CRITICISM

A SHORT HISTORY

WILLIAM K. WIMSATT, JR.
& CLEANTH BROOKS

YALE UNIVERSITY

LITERARY CRITICISM

A SHORT HISTORY

ALFRED A. KNOPF
NEW YORK

1957

L.C. catalog card number: 57-5286
© WILLIAM K. WIMSATT, JR., *and* CLEANTH BROOKS, *1957*

THIS IS A BORZOI BOOK, PUBLISHED BY ALFRED A. KNOPF, INC.

FIRST EDITION

TO RENÉ WELLEK

INTRODUCTION

IT IS NOT LIKELY THAT A PERSON WHO ENTERTAINS EVEN A MODEST prejudice against the kind of history writing which appears in this book will have his mind changed by introductory apologetics. Still some preliminary advertisement of aims may be only fair—and may even be generally helpful to a receptive reading. The first principle on which we would insist is that of continuity and intelligibility in the history of literary argument. Plato has a bearing on Croce and Freud, and vice versa. Or, all three of these theorists are engaged with a common reality and hence engage one another through the medium of that reality and either come to terms or disagree. Literary problems occur not just because history produces them, but because literature is a thing of such and such a sort, showing such and such a relation to the rest of human experience. True, languages and cultures, times and places, differ widely. The literary historian will always do well to nurse a certain skepticism about the thoroughness with which he may be penetrating the secret of his documents. But then he has to worry too about an opposite danger of being merely and overly skeptical. There are techniques of caution and neutrality which put the historian somewhat in the position of the student who, having his difficulties with a Latin or German reading examination, is content to put down a translation that does not make sense. He writes as if he is not convinced that the foreign language does make sense. Our own notion of how to write a history of literary ideas is just the opposite of that. The history is bound to be an interpretation, in part even a translation. In part it will even be built on reasonable guesses. The least it can do is make sense.

And that connects closely with a second of our main notions about method; namely, that a history of literary ideas can scarcely escape being written from a point of view. It seems to us that on a strictly neutral plan there can be in fact no history of literary ideas at all, nor, for that matter, any direct history of literature. At least not any history that hangs together. This book, we hope and believe, both grows out of and illustrates and contributes to a certain distinct point of view. It is the history of one kind of thinking about values, and hence it could not have been written relativistically, or indifferently, or at random. It contains much praise and blame, both implicit and explicit. There are even senses, complimentary we believe, in which it could be called "polemic" or "argumentative." It is nevertheless, we contend, a true history. Call it *An Argumentative History of Literary Argument in the West.*

The reader will now readily conceive yet another of our notions: namely, that in a history of this sort the critical *idea* has priority over all other kinds of material. The present "short" history does not attempt a grand assemblage of information (though information of the right kind and in the right amount, we believe, is here). Neither encyclopedism nor the Saintsburyan gigantically conversational range has been our purpose, but a series of narrative focusses precisely on ideas. In some chapters, especially in those concerning the neo-classic age, the argument runs directly along thematic lines. Other chapters, especially those concerning classical antiquity, are developed around certain heroic figures—Plato, or Aristotle, or Longinus. Still even in these chapters, the idea, not the hero, is always paramount. Hence it happens that we have attempted no complete account of any one philosopher or literary man (much less any complete survey of disciples or other minor figures). We have used the little figures, and even the great figures, as they came in handy to our narrative. Hence also we have been little interested in proving the consistency, we have been little dismayed by the frequent inconsistencies, of our great literary theorists. Where we have here and there noticed inconsistencies (as, let us say, in Addison's account of imagination, or in Arnold's account of classic grandeur and the "touchstones"), the point has been made not so much against the author as against a collection of ideas which have often been credited with more coherence than they actually exhibit. Or it has been made simply for the sake of gaining the expository advantage of contrast. By and large, as notably with Plato in the first chapter, we have preferred the idea in full bloom and have made no attempt to harmonize the smaller contradictions, real or apparent, which are always to be found in the canon of a prolific author. When the main ideas of an author have been leveled off or averaged in with all the marginal variations, the result is not a story with parts, contours, accents, climaxes, but a dead level of neutrality—the melted wax doll. The principle applies with equal force to themes and eras in intellectual history. Statistical scrupulosity in the study of "ideas" tends of course toward a smudge. This truth was never more clearly betrayed than in the following recommendation of minute history by a late distinguished American scholar:

> One of the surest evidences of a better understanding of an individual or a period is that sharp lines disappear, strong lights and shadows are modified, uniqueness and isolation melt away, the man is seen to be more like other men, the age like other ages.[1]

The present writers, despite their confidence in the continuity and real community of human experience through the ages,[2] are confident also

[1] R. D. Havens, "Changing Taste in the Eighteenth Century," *PMLA*, XLIV (June, 1929), 534-5.

[2] Some variations on the theme of the "universal" perhaps relevant to the present paradox are to be found near the end of Chapter 15.

of differences—of levels, depressions, and eminences—of the difference between Elizabethan England and Augustan Rome, of that between Chaucer and Pope, and of that between Pope and Blackmore, Dryden and Rymer.

The examples just mentioned invite allusion to one further methodological notion and one which is perhaps not very immediately entailed by what we have so far been saying. We have finally to confess what may seem to some of our more severely idealist friends a principle of distinct impurity in our method. Our book is not a history of general aesthetics (though a few quite limited excursions into the aesthetic ambient have been ventured). On the other hand, it is not a history of literary technicalities or techniques, of prosody or grammar. Yet if we had had to make a choice between a more markedly aesthetic direction and a more grammatical, it is the latter (in the full classical sense of the term "grammatical") which we should have chosen. That is, we have written a history of ideas about verbal art and about its elucidation and criticism. The ultimate object of our regard then, though seen at a remove, through the eyes of the critic and the theorist of criticism, has been poetry or literature. So much literary criticism and theory and so much of the best has been written by the men of letters. Often, whether consciously or not, they have written their general theories as a comment on their own best performances in poetry, and on the *kinds* of poetry which were most dear to them. The theory, furthermore, has been both stated and exemplified by the poems, and undoubtedly both poetry and theory have interacted in several ways. To show that the history of literary theory has been no more than a series of temporary explanations directed toward poetic vogues of the moment and hence that the name of "poetry" enjoys only a long record of equivocality, would be the final triumph of the neutrally and pluralistically minded investigator. Such (need it be said?) has scarcely been our aspiration. On the other hand, to show that through all the ambiguous weave and dialectical play of the successive concrete situations which make the history of poems and theory, the sustaining truth continues and may be discerned and its history written—this would seem to be an appropriate enough goal for the historian who believes that he has in fact a coherent, a real and unequivocal subject matter. To tell the story pure, as a series of internally driven developments of ideas or patterns of abstractly significant oppositions and resolutions, will have advantages for the philosopher. But to tell it more or less impurely, bringing in the colors of the literary milieu and allowing critical episodes to take shape out of the milieu, will have some advantages for the student of literature. In a few sentences of the Epilogue which concludes this book we have tried to sketch a view of how the several literary genre conceptions dominant in several ages—dramatic, epistolary, heroic, burlesque, and lyric—will if studied carefully open up not so many diverse views into multiplicity and chaos but so many complementary insights into the one deeply rooted and perennial human truth which is the poetic principle.

As our chapter titles will suggest, the substance of the book includes Greek and Roman classicism, Renaissance, Augustan, romantic, and Victorian English criticism, and 20th-century English and American. In addition, there are excursions or inter-chapters or sections of chapters dealing with the Middle Ages and with main episodes in modern Italian, French, German, and Russian criticism. The book tries to follow the main lines of the critical heritage and then draw in the story toward the end to the immediate arena of the modern English-speaking world.

Any history of any subject has to begin somewhere—a matter perhaps of some embarrassment. Where it begins will be determined not only by the availability of certain documents but by the views of the author concerning the real nature of his subject. The present history might have lingered longer near its beginning than it actually does with certain proto-glimpses of literary critical consciousness in the Western tradition—invocations by the early Greek poets Homer and Hesiod to the Muses and assertions of an aim to teach or to charm, phrases of some pith and relevance concerning craft and genius or the fate of man, from early and all but lost lyric poets, from law-givers, dramatists, and pre-Socratic philosophers. The history as it actually begins, in our first chapter, plunges immediately, with only a few preliminary words, into an early Platonic dialogue, the *Ion*. This is the earliest extant Western writing that addresses itself deliberately, formally, and exclusively to the general matter of literary criticism. Furthermore this dialogue treats the topic of literary criticism in a way which the present writers conceive to be the correct way—that is, by asking a difficult question about the kind of knowledge which a criticism of a poem, or a poem itself, can lay claim to. What does a poem say that is worth listening to? What does criticism say? The entire course of literary theory and criticism, from the time of Plato to the present, has in effect been occupied with producing more or less acute versions of those questions and more or less accurate and telling answers. Plato's *Ion* is a thoroughgoing, radically naive, inquiry into the nature of poetic composition as a department of verbal meaning and power. It has also the advantage to the historian that it is a dialogue— that is, its arguments are put not purely and schematically but in dramatic form. There are two speakers and at least two points of view. The historian of critical ideas who takes such ideas in any degree tentatively, yet seriously, could scarcely find himself beginning on more congenial ground.

The supplementary passages which appear after most of the chapters in the book are intended to supply in part historical and theoretical dimensions which could not be conveniently handled in the narrative and in part illustrations or problems (some of them comic) which the meditative reader may enjoy placing for himself in relation to the themes of the narrative. Passages following a given chapter may stand either in harmony with one another or in opposition, and in various relations to the content of the chapter.

Quotations from Greek and Latin and from modern foreign languages appear for the most part in already available translations, which are appropriately acknowledged. But here and there the authors have for one reason or another attempted their own, perhaps rather free, translations. These appear for the most part without further advertisement.

This book would perhaps never have been begun except for a suggestion made to the authors a few years back by two friends, George W. Stewart and John Nerber. The authors wish to record their debt and express their gratitude.

The whole work has been written by a method of fairly close collaboration not only in the general plan but in the execution of each part. The authors have read and criticized each other's work closely and repeatedly at various stages. The substantial responsibility for the chapters is, however, to be divided as follows: Chapters 1–24, and 32, W. K. Wimsatt, Jr.; Chapters 25–31, Cleanth Brooks.

The parts of the book by W. K. Wimsatt, Jr., owe an obvious large debt to a Yale graduate English seminar, Theories of Poetry, inaugurated many years ago by Albert S. Cook, and conducted subsequently by F. A. Pottle and T. W. Copeland. To those founders, and especially to F. A. Pottle, and to the students in the course since 1942 and to those in its more recent undergraduate parallel, Introduction to Criticism, the author makes a grateful acknowledgement.

Cleanth Brooks did part of his work on the book while holding a Fellowship of The John Simon Guggenheim Memorial Foundation. He wishes to acknowledge the kindness of the Foundation and to express his thanks.

For various kinds of assistance in research and preparation of typescript, the authors express their thanks to Robert B. Brown, Richard J. Browne, James Cook, Harold Cogger, Mrs. D. W. Gordon, John Oates, Michael Pertschuk, Mrs. David Underdown, and Donald Wheeler.

A more or less pervasive debt in several chapters to a manuscript book by H. M. McLuhan concerning the ancient war between dialecticians and rhetoricians is here gratefully acknowledged and is underscored by the quotation, following Chapter 4, of two substantial excerpts from published essays by Mr. McLuhan.

To their colleagues Bernard Knox, Maynard Mack, John Palmer,

John Smith, and René Wellek, the authors are indebted for reading and criticism of various chapters in early drafts, and to Charles Feidelson, Charles C. Walcutt, and Father Walter J. Ong, S.J., for various kinds of critical advice. More than to any other single scholar, they are indebted for general theoretical and historical help to René Wellek. Not only his published but his yet unpublished works and his advice in conversation have done much to promote the writing of the modern chapters.

To Margaret and Tinkum, for labors expert, various, and unremitting, the authors join in affectionate expression of gratitude.

To Marshall Waingrow the authors owe special thanks for a skillful reading of the entire page proof. Alfred Stiernotte made the index.

Two fairly extended passages of Chapter 32, the Epilogue, follow an essay "Criticism Today: A Report from America," published by W. K. Wimsatt, Jr., in *Essays in Criticism*, VI (January, 1956), 1–21. Our thanks are due to F. W. Bateson, the editor.

ANNOTATIONS AND SOURCES

This book is annotated lightly. The notes aim at giving a guide to verifying our treatment of sources and a minimal clue to further reading. Certain works which have general relevance for the whole book or for major sections of it are brought together in the following list. At various places in the annotation, some of these works are cited by abbreviated titles or simply by names of their authors. The reader will easily understand such references on consulting the list.

Meyer H. Abrams, *The Mirror and the Lamp*. New York: Oxford University Press, 1953

Raymond M. Alden, ed., *Critical Essays of the Early Nineteenth Century*. New York: Charles Scribner's Sons, 1921

J. W. H. Atkins, *English Literary Criticism*. I, *The Medieval Phase*. Cambridge: At the University Press, 1943; II, *The Renascence*. London: Methuen & Co. 1947; III, *The Seventeenth and Eighteenth Centuries*. London: Methuen & Co., 1951

J. W. H. Atkins, *Literary Criticism in Antiquity*, vols. I and II. Cambridge: At the University Press, 1934

Charles S. Baldwin, *Ancient Rhetoric and Poetic*. New York: The Macmillan Company, 1924

Medieval Rhetoric and Poetic. New York: The Macmillan Company, 1928

Renaissance Literary Theory and Practice. New York: Columbia University Press, 1939

Walter J. Bate, *From Classic to Romantic, Premises of Taste in Eighteenth-Century England*. Cambridge, Mass.: Harvard University Press, 1946

Walter J. Bate, ed., *Criticism: The Major Texts.* New York: Harcourt, Brace and Company, 1948

Albert C. Baugh, *A History of the English Language.* New York: D. Appleton-Century Company, 1935

Albert C. Baugh *et al.*, *A Literary History of England.* New York: Appleton-Century-Crofts, 1948

Bernard Bosanquet, *A History of Aesthetic.* London: Swan Sonnenschein & Co.; New York: Macmillan & Co., 1892

Aisso Bosker, *Literary Criticism in the Age of Johnson.* Groningen: J. B. Wolters' Uitgevers-Maatschappij, 1930; revised edition, 1953

René Bray, *La Formation de la doctrine classique en France.* Dijon: Maurice Darantière, 1927

Edgar de Bruyne, *Études d'esthétique médiévale*, vols. I, II, III. Brugge (België): "De Tempel," 1946

E. F. Carritt, *Philosophies of Beauty from Socrates to Robert Bridges.* Oxford: Oxford University Press, 1931

Alexander F. B. Clark, *Boileau and the French Classical Critics in England (1660–1830).* Paris: Librairie Ancienne Édouard Champion, 1925

Ronald S. Crane *et al.*, *Critics and Criticism Ancient and Modern.* Chicago: The University of Chicago Press, 1952

Benedetto Croce, *Aesthetic as Science of Expression and General Linguistic*, trans. Douglas Ainslie, 2nd ed. London: Macmillan and Co., 1922

John F. D'Alton, *Roman Literary Theory and Criticism.* London and New York: Longmans, Green and Co., 1931

Willard H. Durham, ed., *Critical Essays of the Eighteenth Century.* New Haven: Yale University Press, 1915

T. S. Eliot, *The Use of Poetry and the Use of Criticism, Studies in the Relation of Criticism to Poetry in England.* Cambridge, Mass.: Harvard University Press, 1933

Allan H. Gilbert, ed., *Literary Criticism Plato to Dryden.* New York: American Book Company, 1940

Katherine E. Gilbert and Helmut Kuhn, *A History of Esthetics.* New York: The Macmillan Company, 1939; Bloomington: Indiana University Press, 1953

Theodore M. Greene, *The Arts and the Art of Criticism*, 2nd ed. Princeton: Princeton University Press, 1947

Werner Jaeger, *Paideia: The Ideals of Greek Culture*, trans. Gilbert Highet, vols. I, II, III. New York: Oxford University Press, 1939–44

Leah Jonas, *The Divine Science, The Aesthetic of Some Representative Seventeenth-Century English Poets.* New York: Columbia University Press, 1940

Thomas Munro, *The Arts and Their Interrelations.* New York: The Liberal Arts Press, 1949

William V. O'Connor, *An Age of Criticism 1900–1950.* Chicago: Henry Regnery Company, 1952

Melvin Rader, ed., *A Modern Book of Esthetics, An Anthology.* New York: Henry Holt and Company, 1935, 1952

William Rhys Roberts, *Greek Rhetoric and Literary Theory.* New York: Longmans, Green and Co., 1928

George Saintsbury, *A History of Criticism and Literary Taste in Europe,* vols. I, II, III, 4th ed. Edinburgh and London: William Blackwood & Sons, 1949

Mark Schorer *et al.,* eds., *Criticism: The Foundations of Modern Literary Judgment.* New York: Harcourt, Brace and Company, 1948

Joseph T. Shipley, ed., *Dictionary of World Literature: Criticism—Forms —Technique.* New York: The Philosophical Library, 1943

G. Gregory Smith, ed., *Elizabethan Critical Essays,* vols. I and II. Oxford: Oxford University Press, 1937

James H. Smith and Edd W. Parks, eds., *The Great Critics, An Anthology of Literary Criticism.* New York: W. W. Norton & Company, 1951

Joel E. Spingarn, ed., *Critical Essays of the Seventeenth Century,* vols. I, II, III. Oxford: At the Clarendon Press, 1908–9

Joel E. Spingarn, *A History of Literary Criticism in the Renaissance.* New York: Columbia University Press, 1899

Robert W. Stallman, *Critiques and Essays in Criticism, 1920–1948, Representing the Achievement of Modern British and American Critics.* New York: The Ronald Press Company, 1949

Alba H. Warren, Jr., *English Poetic Theory, 1825–1865.* Princeton: Princeton University Press, 1950

René Wellek, *A History of Modern Criticism: 1750–1950.* I, *The Later Eighteenth Century;* II, *The Romantic Age.* New Haven: Yale University Press, 1955

René Wellek, *The Rise of English Literary History.* Chapel Hill: The University of North Carolina Press, 1941

René Wellek and Austin Warren, *Theory of Literature.* New York: Harcourt, Brace and Company, 1949

Morton D. Zabel, ed., *Literary Opinion in America.* New York: Harper & Brothers, 1951

Titles of learned and critical journals are sometimes abbreviated in the notes, as follows:

AJP   *The American Journal of Philology*
ELH   *ELH: A Journal of English Literary History*
JEGP *The Journal of English and Germanic Philology*
JHI   *Journal of the History of Ideas*

MLN	*Modern Language Notes*
MLQ	*Modern Language Quarterly*
MLR	*The Modern Language Review*
MP	*Modern Philology*
PQ	*Philological Quarterly*
SP	*Studies in Philology*
PMLA	*Publications of the Modern Language Association of America*
RES	*The Review of English Studies*
TLS	*The Times Literary Supplement*

CONTENTS

PART III

PART IV

PART V

LITERARY CRITICISM:
A SHORT HISTORY

PART ONE

CHAPTER I

SOCRATES AND THE RHAPSODE

§ *Early poets as critics,* The Frogs, *poetry in the scales—*
II. Plato's Ion, *character of a rhapsode, character of Soc-*
rates, some embarrassing questions and unfortunate an-
swers, the magnet and the iron rings, a light, winged and
holy thing, poetry as inspiration, rhapsode vs. charioteer,
pilot, and general, poetry as information—III. other works
of Plato: Meno, Phaedrus, *contradictory passages about*
inspiration, Republic *and* Laws, *poetry and morals, poetry*
feeds and waters the passions, showing poets the gate,
quarrel between poets and philosophers, Homer tells lies,
poetry as imitation, the merely dramatic sense, the meta-
physical sense, the painter and the three beds, the cine-
matic cave, the line and the four grades of knowledge—
IV. Platonic "ideas," Phaedo, *anamnēsis,* Symposium,
Phaedrus, *"love" and the "beautiful," the classic Platonic*
theme, varied senses of to kalon, Philebus, *Xenophon's*
Memorabilia, Greater Hippias—*V. reality and mathemat-*
ics, ratio, logos, geometry of the five elements, visual art,
Philebus, *mixed pleasures,* Sophist, *eikastic and phantastic,*
skiagraphia, "dynamic symmetry," illusion and formalism,
Cratylus *and the image of Cratylus* §

BECAUSE POETS HAVE A STRONG TENDENCY TO FORM OPINIONS ABOUT THEIR
craft and to use these opinions as part of the message of their
poems, we are likely to find literary theory of a sort as far
back as we can find poems. When Homer begins his epics with an invocation to the muse, he is uttering a theory about his poems—namely, that
they are written, or had better be written, with the help of divine inspiration—and this is an idea which has played a considerable role in the sub-

3

sequent history of poetics. During the several centuries that elapse between Homer and Plato, the first philosopher of literature whose ideas we shall examine with any care, other Greek writers, Hesiod, Solon, Simonides, Pindar and the rhetoricians and dramatists of the fifth century, made various critical remarks—that poetry is charming, that poetry is instructive, that it comes natural to a genius, that it has to be learned by art, that it is like painting, that it consists in a clever use of words— and to these opinions we shall here and there have occasion to allude in retrospect.

In Athens towards the close of the fifth century, after the great Periclean age, the comic dramatists, who made satirical criticism of life in general their business, had some sharp things to say about literature. Especially Aristophanes, and his special literary target was the modernist tragic dramatist Euripides. The earliest piece of extended literary criticism which survives from classical antiquity is an agon or debate in the *Frogs* of Aristophanes (405 B.C.), where Dionysus, patron and god of the theater festivals, has descended into Hades for the purpose of bringing back to earth the recently departed Euripides, but in the end actually makes the award to the good old-fashioned writer Aeschylus. The announced standards of criticism are "skill in the art" and "wise counsel for the state." The latter of these is perhaps the more important, but the actual decision of Dionysus seems to rest not so much on an appeal to either standard as on the fact that Aeschylus is the poet who takes his fancy. Some specific poetic traits are amusingly criticized—the wild and whirling magniloquence of Aeschylus (his "hippalectors" [1] and "trage-laphs" [2]), the sentimental fondness of Euripides for lame beggars as heroes. But the thing that a critically inclined person may remember most vividly is a certain directness in the form of argument. Scales are brought out, and the poets are weighed against each other line for line.

> DIONYSUS: Now, then, each repeat a verse.
> EURIPIDES: "I wish that Argo with her woven wings."
> AESCHYLUS: "O streams of Spercheius, and ye pastured plains."
> DIONYSUS: Let go!—See now—this scale outweighs that other. Very considerably.
>
> —lines 1381-5 [3]

Although this is a parody of critical procedure, one might take it as a symbol of what is often most refreshing in early critical documents—a certain frontal naiveté, an immediate shrewdness of inquiry which the inheritors of criticism have long since, and by necessity, obscured in their more sophisticated formulations. To be able to speak about

[1] Horse-cocks, gryphons.
[2] Goat-stags, fantastic animals such as were known on Eastern carpets.
[3] Translation of J. Hookham Frere.

Homer's epics, not as the remote and venerable source of a classical tradition 3,000 years old, but as heroic poetry currently recited at popular festivals, and to be able to speak about tragedy and comedy as social and religious forms of art which had developed only within a preceding half century of Athenian prosperity—these were great advantages to the freelance speculator on general problems of human existence who is the central figure in the next critical work which we are to consider.

II

PLATO's *Ion* was written sometime in the first decade of the fourth century, a few years later than the death of his master Socrates in 399. Like the agon in the *Frogs* of Aristophanes, this piece of criticism takes the dramatic form. It is a philosophic dialogue, the scene being at Athens a short time before the close of the Peloponnesian war and the temporary eclipse of Athenian democracy. The interlocutors are Socrates and the rhapsode Ion, the latter just returned from Epidaurus, where he has won first prize at a festival in honor of Asclepius. A rhapsode (as we conceive him, and indeed largely on the evidence of this dialogue) was a person who might be described, in terms of our own culture, as a sort of combined actor and college teacher of literature. He gave public recitations from the *Iliad* and the *Odyssey*, especially of the more exciting passages; and he undertook to deliver critical and moral lectures. He must have drawn large audiences (even if we take the 20,000 mentioned in the dialogue as a great exaggeration), and he sometimes succeeded in moving these audiences very deeply, even to tears. He appeared in rich attire, perhaps wearing a golden crown, and he received a handsome pecuniary reward. He is representative of the older, literary, and unsystematic Greek education (*paideia*).

Socrates as he confronts Ion in this dialogue may be taken as representing a spirit of criticism which was increasing with the sad experiences of the city state. A mere sophist in the *Clouds* of Aristophanes, as he appears in his *phrontistērion* or "thinkery," corrupting a youth to turn against his father, Socrates is transformed into a subtle philosopher and relentless enemy of ignorance as he appears in the dialogues of Plato. In a friendly and restrained yet insistent way, Socrates, as if seeking to know something of our literary professor's trade secrets, succeeds in asking him some uncomfortable questions and in eliciting some unfortunate answers. Ion admits, for instance, that although there are many poets, and although they speak often on the same topics, he himself is skilled only in reading Homer, and he is interested only in Homer. He drops off into a doze when somebody talks about any other poet. Enough comes out to make it appear that anything Ion has to say about Homer is scarcely said with the help of what Socrates would call art and knowledge (*technē kai epistēmē*). Ion has no rational technique, for a technique or art is a unified thing (*holon*). Or, as we might say, the term "poetry" if it means anything intelligible is a univocal term, not a quibble. Anybody who can criticize one poet ought to be able to criticize another.[4]

A general tendency of the Socratic argument to thrust at the poet himself through his punier representative the rhapsode [5] culminates midway of the dialogue in a celebrated speech which likens the poet to a magnet radiating a kind of divine power (*theia dunamis*) out through a chain of iron rings, the rhapsode and his audience. Both poets and rhapsodes utter what they do by a divine dispensation, a form of madness.

> For the poet is a light and winged and holy thing, and there is no invention in him until he has been inspired and is out of his senses, and the mind is no longer in him: when he has not attained to this state, he is powerless and unable to utter his oracles.—534 [6]

This passage has, during later centuries, sometimes been used for the purpose of invoking Plato as a witness in the cause of poetry. Shelley, for instance, translated the *Ion* and in his own *Defense of Poetry* echoed this passage. Yet it is perhaps worth noting that Ion himself is reluctant to accept this version of his talents.

> That is good, Socrates; and yet I doubt whether you will ever have eloquence enough to persuade me that I praise Homer only when I am mad and possessed; and if you could hear me speak of him I am sure you would never think this to be the case.—536

And in fact the heavy reiteration by Socrates of the idea that the poet is out of his mind or senses—not acting by art, not his own master—does not seem an unequivocal compliment. One might easily come away with the impression that this is a lame alternative to the rational explanations

---

[4] At the end of Plato's *Symposium*, Socrates, having outlasted all the other guests in an all-night drinking party, is seated, as dawn breaks, with the tragic poet Agathon on one hand and the comic poet Aristophanes on the other, forcing them to admit, drowsily, that since poetry is *one* art, a comic poet should be able to write tragedies, and a tragic poet comedies. Despite literal interpretation by the Platonists, this looks like an ironic counterpart of the argument from fact to theory in the *Ion*. In the *Symposium*, Socrates, starting with a theory, urges it against the well-known contrary fact: that poets do *not* work by a scientific technique.

[5] Craig LaDrière, "The Problem of Plato's Ion," *Journal of Aesthetics and Art Criticism*, X (September, 1951), 26–34, elaborates the view that the dialogue is aimed not at poetry itself but only at the art of criticism.

[6] Quotations from Plato's *Dialogues* in this chapter are in the translation of Benjamin Jowett, the third edition, revised, first published in 1892. The Fourth Edition of the *Dialogues*, revised by order of the Jowett Copyright Trustees, 4 vols., Oxford, 1953, does not make substantial changes in any of the passages which we quote.

which Socrates has apparently tried so hard to elicit. A second series of questions, leading to the conclusion of the dialogue, is not calculated to minimize such an impression.

SOCRATES: Then which will be a better judge of the lines which you were reciting from Homer, you or the charioteer?

ION: The charioteer.

SOCRATES: Why, yes, because you are a rhapsode and not a charioteer.

ION: Yes.

SOCRATES: And the art of the rhapsode is different from that of the charioteer?

ION: Yes.

SOCRATES: And if a different knowledge, then a knowledge of different matters?

ION: True.

SOCRATES: You know the passage in which Hecamede, the concubine of Nestor, is described as giving to the wounded Machaon a posset, as he says,
"Made with Pramnian wine; and she grated cheese of goat's milk with a grater of bronze, and at his side placed an onion which gives a relish to drink." [*Iliad* XI, 639–40]
Now would you say that the art of the rhapsode or the art of medicine was better able to judge of the propriety of these lines?

ION: The art of medicine.—538

Socrates drives the inquiry along for some time in this manner, obtaining admissions about the rhapsode's incompetence in one art after another, until at length he is in a good position to raise the question whether any art at all remains the peculiar possession of the rhapsode himself.

SOCRATES: . . . Do you, who know Homer so much better than I do, Ion, select for me passages which relate to the rhapsode and the rhapsode's art, and which the rhapsode ought to examine and judge of better than other men.

ION: All passages, I should say, Socrates.

SOCRATES: Not all, Ion, surely. Have you already forgotten what you were saying? A rhapsode ought to have a better memory.

ION: Why, what am I forgetting?

SOCRATES: Do you not remember that you declared the art of the rhapsode to be different from the art of the charioteer?

ION: Yes, I remember.

SOCRATES: And you admitted that being different they would have different subjects of knowledge?

ION: Yes.

SOCRATES: Then upon your own showing the rhapsode, and the art of the rhapsode, will not know everything?

ION: I should exclude certain things, Socrates.

SOCRATES: You mean to say that you would exclude pretty much the subjects of the other arts. As he does not know all of them, which of them will he know?

ION: He will know what a man and what a woman ought to say, and what a freeman and what a slave ought to say, and what a ruler and what a subject.

SOCRATES: Do you mean that a rhapsode will know better than the pilot what the ruler of a sea-tossed vessel ought to say?—539–40

So the argument swings back to where it was before. We observe that a momentary attempt by Ion to move into an area which we might call something like "general human nature" is quickly checked by Socrates with a question which insists on the technical or scientific. At the conclusion of the dialogue Ion is reduced to the comic position of maintaining that his being a rhapsode implies at least that he would be also a good general—perhaps because, as Plato explains in Book X of the *Republic*, the reading of Homer was traditionally supposed to have something to do with the art of warfare.

In the starkest and least reducible sense the questions put to Ion amount to these: What does poetry tell us? What is the source of the poet's power? And, though this is left more obscurely implicit: What is the relation between the poet's source and the nature of what he actually says? At the beginning of his *Theogony* the poet Hesiod had qualified the traditional appeal to the Muses with a voucher for their veracity. The Muses had actually appeared to him and said:

> Many feigned things (*pseudea*) like to the truth we know how to tell; yet we know how, when we are willing, to tell what is true.—*Theogony*, 27 ff.[7]

By a kind of joke or sleight of argument Socrates combines a partly negative answer (poetry and rhapsody—in their own right and as such

---

[7] Cf. W. C. Greene, "The Greek Criticism of Poetry, a Reconsideration," in *Perspectives of Criticism*, ed. Harry Levin (Cambridge, Mass., 1950), p. 21.

—do not tell us anything scientific) with a positive answer about the divine origin of poetry and rhapsody. One of the traditionally respectable accounts of poetry (Not only had Homer and the other poets invoked the Muses, but Pindar, for instance, had maintained that poetry proceeds from genius, *phua*, rather than art, *technē*) is put in such a context as to suggest a certain emptiness. Either Ion has been teasing, Socrates implies, and deceitfully refusing to reveal his rationally understood professional secrets, or else there is nothing rational for him to reveal. He is either dishonest or divinely mad. The cross-examination has carefully kept out of sight whatever may be the rhapsode's type of actual professional discourse, the external manifestation of his "madness" —though from the start Ion has been eager to give an exhibition of that. Overlooking a degree of unfairness in the procedure of Socrates, we may say that we are invited by this dialogue to consider at least two principles which are not on the face of the matter absurd: 1. Being able to compose poetry is not the same as being able to give a rationale of it; 2. poetry is not concerned with making scientific statements.

III

IT IS possible to point out places in the dialogues of Plato where he seems to treat poetic inspiration very respectfully. In the *Meno* (98–99), for instance, a useful kind of "right opinion" (rather than "knowledge") is conceded to statesmen, interpreters of oracles, seers, and "all poetic persons"—and all these are divinely inspired. And in the *Phaedrus*, although poets rank only sixth in a hierarchy of the elite (248), and although the chief aim of the dialogue is to assert the philosophic or dialectical responsibility of rhetoricians, there is more than one hint that a philosopher is the better for a dash of madness. As for the poet, the *Phaedrus* contains a very strong statement of his dependence on divine madness—in a passage (245) which may be looked on as reversing the ironic emphasis of the parallel passage in the *Ion*.[8] But a history of arguments about poetry will have to claim some license to look rather for ideas in full bloom than for the person behind the ideas. It is another kind of job to try to harmonize all the statements in the dialogues of Plato.

After the *Ion*, the place where we find Plato's mistrust of poetry

[8] See R. G. Collingwood, *The Principles of Art* (Oxford, 1938), pp. 46–7, for a good instance of the argument that Plato was really a friend of the arts. We proceed here on the assumption that the student of poetry need not be really much concerned to enlist Plato on the side of poetry, nor much discomfited to believe that on the whole Plato disapproved of poetry. Plato may conveniently be taken as the representative of an impressive and fairly coherent system of anti-poetic. From early times, the attack upon poetry has often enough been made in his name.

expressed in the simplest and most practical terms is the passage on the "musical" education of the "Guardians" in Books II and III of the *Republic*, a work, be it remembered, of Plato's mid-career and maturity. Here, and again in Book X of the *Republic*, in a more metaphysical context, and in the *Laws*, the compromise *Republic* of Plato's old age, we encounter his well-known objection to the moral effects of poetry. Poetry "feeds and waters the passions," creating division and unsteadiness in the heart, or frivolous laughter, and producing the opposite of civic virtue. The Guardians of the Republic will in fact have the duty of showing poets the gate.

> And therefore when any one of these pantomimic gentlemen . . . comes to us, and makes a proposal to exhibit himself and his poetry, we will fall down and worship him as a sweet and holy and wonderful being; but we must also inform him that in our State such as he are not permitted to exist; the law will not allow them. And so when we have anointed him with myrrh, and set a garland of wool upon his head, we shall send him away to another city. For we mean to employ for our souls' health the rougher and severer poet or story-teller, who will imitate the style of the virtuous only, and will follow those models which we prescribed at first when we began the education of our soldiers.—III, 398

A passage of similar tenor in the *Laws* speaks of an ideal, civic-minded poet, a man "more than fifty years old," a safe one for composing patriotic songs. But such a one was not to be found among the actual poets—Homer, the tragedians, the writers of comedy.

> We are ready to acknowledge that Homer is the greatest of poets and first of tragedy writers; but we must remain firm in our conviction that hymns to the gods and praises of famous men are the only poetry which ought to be admitted into our State. For if you go beyond this and allow the honeyed muse to enter, either in epic or lyric verse, not law and the reason of mankind, which by common consent have ever been deemed best, but pleasure and pain will be the rulers in our State. . . . But that she may not impute to us any harshness or want of politeness, let us tell her that there is an ancient quarrel between philosophy and poetry.—*Republic* X, 607

The quarrel between the poet and the philosopher is the deep end of the quarrel between the poet and the moralist. If poetry produces immoral results, this happens not without certain causes in the nature of poetry itself—one of these, for instance, is the very fact that poetry deals with a variety of motives and feelings, the good and the bad, pleas-

ure and pain. In Books II and III of the *Republic* it appears that poetry
is engaged in fictions—often, moreover, in wicked fictions—wicked
lies. Homer and Hesiod and the dramatists, instead of representing God
as good and the source of all good (instead of telling the truth about
which Hesiod's Muses boasted), give us an anthropomorphic, wrangling, deceitful, and revengeful crowd of deities. These poets show
heroes as emotional and cowardly, wicked men as prosperous, and just
men as wretched. Earlier exegetes, forsooth, had invented a pretty way
of defending these impieties by saying that they were "allegorical."
They were supposed to conceal an acceptable message at a more abstract
level.

At this stage of the argument appears the incidental concept of "imitation" (*mimēsis*)—which, with a certain modification, becomes in later
passages the center of Plato's poetics. Certain poems, he observes in
Book III, simply tell what happened; others actually imitate what happened—dramas, of course—and these are the most dangerous ones, because the most contagious. A man who is to play a serious part in life
cannot afford to imitate any other kind of part. (Let the slaves and hired
strangers, he says in *Laws* VII, 817, act our comedies for us.) It is needless to try to guess how consciously Plato's view had developed by the
time he wrote his second discussion of poetry in the *Republic*, that of
Book X (it was written perhaps some years after Books II and III). In
any case the concept of imitation [9] has now become markedly more
pejorative and is furthermore now applied to poetry as if it were inseparable.

> Speaking in confidence, for I should not like to have my words
> repeated to the tragedians and the rest of the imitative tribe—
> but I do not mind saying to you, that all poetical imitations are
> ruinous to the understanding of the hearers, and that the know-
> ledge of their true nature is the only antidote to them.—595

The reasoning is made clearer in a very explicit analogy between a poet
and an illusionist painter of a bed.

> And the painter too is, as I conceive. . . . a creator of appear-
> ances, is he not?
>
> Of course.
>
> But then I suppose you will say that what he creates is untrue.
> And yet there is a sense in which the painter also creates a bed?
>
> Yes, he said, but not a real bed.

[9] Richard McKeon's exposition of the analogical series of meanings enjoyed by
the term *mimēsis* in Plato's works ("Literary Criticism and the Concept of Imitation in Antiquity", MP, XXXIV, August, 1936, 1–35) tends to soften the application
of the term to poetry in these contexts, but the pejorative implications can scarcely
be dismissed.

And what of the maker of the bed? were you not saying that he too makes, not the idea which, according to our view, is the essence of the bed, but only a particular bed?

Yes, I did.

Then if he does not make that which exists he cannot make true existence, but only some semblance of existence; and if any one were to say that the work of the maker of the bed, or of any other workman, has real existence, he could hardly be supposed to be speaking the truth.

Beds, then, are of three kinds, and there are three artists who superintend them: God, the maker of the bed, and the painter?

Yes, there are three of them.

God, whether from choice or from necessity, made one bed in nature and one only; two or more such ideal beds neither ever have been nor ever will be made by God.

And what shall we say of the carpenter—is he not also the maker of the bed?

Yes.

But would you call the painter a creator and maker?

Certainly not.

Yet if he is not the maker, what is he in relation to the bed?

I think, he said, that we may fairly designate him as the imitator of that which the others make.

Good, I said; then you call him who is second [1] in the descent from nature an imitator?

Certainly, he said.

And the tragic poet is an imitator, and therefore, like all other imitators, he is twice removed from the king and from the truth?

That appears to be so.—596–7

With the allusion to the ideal bed, the work of God, we are involved in the Platonic metaphysics of transcendental reality, a system of ideas which needs to be clarified by reference to two passages which inter-

---

[1] The words in Plato's text are actually "third" and "thrice," but their meaning depends on the classical or inclusive method of counting.

vene in the *Republic* between the discussion of poetry in Books II–III
and that in Book X. One is the allegory in Book VII of the cinematic
cave in which men sitting on a bench with their backs to an opening
and a great fire beyond, see only the shadows of a sort of passing puppet
show cast on the wall before them. Such is our own experience of what
we think to be reality. The other passage is the more technically instructive figure of the "line," in Book VI, with its four ascending phases
of knowledge: the lowest *eikasia*, or sensory imaging (of the surface of
things and their shadows—the aspects of the bed which can be painted);
the second, *pistis* (faith), a kind of trustful apprehension of the solid yet
mutable things of our world (beds and horses); the third, on the upper
side of a major central division, *dianoia*, discursive understanding of
mathematicals or geometric figures; and at the top, *noēsis*, intuitive and
true knowledge of permanent beings, the forms or ideas (*eidē*).[2] For
the moment let us not attempt to say more precisely what these last are.

I V

PLATO's doctrine of ideas is perhaps most often known in its rather vague
relation to the "beautiful" (*to kalon*) and to love (*erōs*), and in this relation chiefly through three other dialogues, the *Phaedo*, the *Symposium*
and the *Phaedrus*. In the first of these, the conversation on immortality
held by Socrates with his friends on the day he is to drink the hemlock,
we find the doctrine of *anamnēsis*[3] (Wordsworthian otherworldly recollection) as an explanation of how we come to be possessed at all of ideas
more perfect than the things of our worldly experience. As for beautiful
things, they are indeed beautiful "by reason of beauty"—that is, by participating in the beautiful—but beauty is named only as one among other
kinds of perfection (75a–d; 100c–e). The discourse is ascetic rather than
aesthetic, stressing preparation for immortality by philosophic discipline.
But in the *Symposium* and the *Phaedrus*, the preparation, or approach,
is that of the lover, by way of mortal beauty. The lover graduates, in
the *Symposium* (210–12), from single beautiful bodies to all beautiful
bodies, from bodies to forms, and from forms to practices and notions,
until he contemplates "the vast sea of beauty"; and in the *Phaedrus* (249,
265–6, 277), he graduates from bodily beauty not only to ideal beauty
but to "wisdom, goodness, and the like," all the hierarchy of ideas. The
lover becomes in effect the philosopher.

[2] Both *dianoia* and *noēsis* come under the generic head of *epistēmē* (knowledge), what Socrates found wanting in Homer and Ion. Both *eikasia* (the awareness
of images, *eikones*) and *pistis* come under the generic head of *doxa* (mere opinion)
and both refer to the world of becoming, *ta gignomena*.

[3] See too the *Meno*, 82–5, where Socrates elicits geometrical reasoning from
a slave boy.

An honest reading of these and other passages in Plato can scarcely blink the fact that the bodily beauty alluded to is that of the boy lover. (*Orthōs paiderastein* reads one phrase of the *Symposium*, 211, rendered by an eminent Victorian translator as "true love.") Pederasty was a Spartan cult, supposed to induce military virtue, and, as the first two speeches of the *Symposium* and the temptation of Socrates described in the same dialogue by Alcibiades make sufficiently clear, it had a vogue among Athenian intellectuals during Plato's boyhood. "Love is of generation," says the *Symposium* (206), "of birth in beauty." "Souls which are pregnant conceive wisdom and virtue" (209). The beautiful notions begotten through this love make a clear enough contrast to the results of heterosexual love.[4] Without wholly endorsing the charge of one writer on this theme,[5] that these dialogues have been the "sulphurous breviary" of homosexual literary cults in all succeeding ages, we incline to say that the general warmth and color of the dialogues, the brilliant use of allegorical imagery like that of the soul as charioteer and the higher and lower passions as his pair of horses in the *Phaedrus*, and the vivacious drama of the conversationalists at the banquet—Aristophanes, Agathon, Alcibiades, Socrates—on the attractive theme of love, have helped a great deal to make the aspect of Platonism that relates to "love" and "beauty" best known and best liked among literary students during every Renaissance. Yet these topics have furnished not so much a workable theory about the nature of poetry as inspirational subject matter for literary treatment—the "Idees on hie . . . which Plato so admyred" in Spenser's *Hymne of Heavenly Beautie* or the conception of Platonic pure love in the Fourth Book of Castiglione's *Courtier*.

The term "beauty" (*to kalon*) is used in the Platonic dialogues to refer rather loosely to a wide range of natural objects, artifacts, institutions, and ideas. In the *Philebus* (64e) we have the relatively helpful concept of beauty as measure and proportion (*metriotēs kai summetria*) and the distinction (51c) between the beautiful in itself and the relatively beautiful. In the *Memorabilia* of Xenophon (III, 8; IV, 6) Socrates produces the concept of the beautiful as the convenient (i.e. the "functional"—a dung basket, if well made, is beautiful; a golden shield, if not well made, is ugly). And the dubiously Platonic *Greater Hippias* presents him in his most sustained effort to face the difficult problem. He disposes easily of such too concrete suggestions by the sophist as that a beautiful horse or a beautiful maiden may be adduced to define the

[4] In the *Phaedo*, as Socrates prepares for the draught of hemlock, the women of his family are admitted to see him, but briefly and grudgingly toward the close of the day.

[5] John Jay Chapman, *Lucian, Plato, and Greek Morals* (Boston, 1931), p. 133. Cf. the more sober account by Warner Fite, *The Platonic Legend* (New York, 1934), Chap. VIII, "Platonic Love." Plato censures this kind of *eros* in *Republic* III, 403 and *Laws*, 636.

concept of the beautiful (*parthenos kalē kalon*), or that whatever is gold is beautiful. (What about the chryselephantine statue of Athena? says Socrates. Why didn't Phidias make it all gold?) Canvassing the problems of the convenient, the appropriate, and the useful—in fact, the whole difficult problem of terminal and instrumental values—he arrives at the tentative (and far from ridiculous) conclusion that the beautiful may be that which is beneficially pleasurable (*hēdonēn ōphelimon*) through the senses of sight and hearing (419). But the idea of the "beneficial" persists in betraying the instrumentalism of the concept. The conclusion is that the discourse has been useless. And even these efforts at definition are not very precisely reflected in the *Symposium* or in the other classic places where Plato discusses beauty and love.

V

LET us turn back, toward a colder side of Plato's theory of ideas which we have already hinted. The presence of the hypothetical *mathēmatika*, the geometric forms, at the third level of the scale of knowledge in Book VI of the *Republic* might lead one to wonder whether any more purified element of the mathematical is implicit in the highest level, that of the pure forms. A pronounced attention to mathematics and geometry as one stage of the Guardian's education, in Book V of the *Republic*, might suggest the same speculation. Students of the Platonic text and of other evidence about Plato's thought, especially the criticisms of Aristotle, do in fact distinguish two strains in his theory of ideas. One is the Socratic or logical, the argument that our use of general terms and class conceptions entails the existence of real and transcendent unities corresponding to these conceptions. It is an argument which receives heavy criticism, apparently from Plato himself, in the *Parmenides* and other late dialogues. The second is a more subtle ontological attempt to get at the permanent and necessary structure of reality, a development of Pythagorean number theory in which Plato distinguishes between the continuous and boundless stuff of our sensory experience, the indeterminate world of becoming, and a real or rational world of limit, that is, of *ratios* between both unit numbers and geometric lines. The word for the rational principle is *logos*—the same word that appears in the crucial definition of geometric ratio in the Fifth Book of Euclid. At the level of *mathematicals* or geometric figures, one may have, let us say, a multiplicity of isosceles triangles, all of different sizes and hence participating in the diversity and indefiniteness of material extension. The final oneness, or what they have in common, is their ratio, something intelligible though unimaginable. As Aristotle was to put it:

> Further, besides sensible things and Forms he says there are the
> objects of mathematics, which occupy an intermediate position,
> differing from sensible things in being eternal and unchange-
> able, from Forms in that there are many alike, while the Form
> itself is in each case unique.—*Metaphysics* I (A), 6.[6]

What may be difficult for us to conceive is that the theory posits
such a number or ratio as the real idea behind each of the ordinary and
immediately concrete names which we give to objects. As a modern interpreter has put it:

> The idea of man is not the general term which designates all
> perceived men. The idea of myself is not what I sense when I
> consider myself introspectively. The idea of fire is not the gen-
> eral term (or any notion in the mind of which the general term is
> a symbol) referring to all cases of perceived fire. Nor is the idea
> of fire that notion given by a definition which distinguishes fire
> from all other factors in the universe, in terms of perceived prop-
> erties. All the so-called concepts which we use in ordinary dis-
> course, and which most modern philosophers have in mind when
> they refer to Plato's theory of ideas,—all such notions are not
> ideas, in the Platonic meaning of the term. They are merely
> nominalistic terms referring to factors in "the class of the mixed."
> Ideas are purely in the class of the limit and they cannot be il-
> lustrated by pointing to anything immediately sensed. . . .
> "ideas," whether they be the idea of the fire, the idea of myself,
> or the idea of the good, are ratios which only an analytical math-
> ematical symbolism can express and only the pure scientific intel-
> lect can grasp.[7]

Perhaps the most easily grasped evidence that Plato really thought this
way is to be found in his late cosmological dialogue the *Timaeus*,
(53–6), where, taking advantage of the fact that there are five, and only
five, kinds of regular polyhedra, he assigns a basic structure, the real
idea, to each of what were then supposed to be the four primary elements: fire, earth, air, water, and to a fifth imagined element, "ether."
Fire, as we might guess from its volatility and sharpness, has for its
mathematical the regular pyramid or tetrahedron, and for its "idea" the
ratio of magnitudes which defines the tetrahedron. Earth, as the most
solid and least movable element, has the cube or hexahedron; and so
forth with perhaps less plausibility, according to the lightness and number of faces of the octahedron (air), the icosahedron (water), and the

---

[6] See *post* Chapter 2, p. 22, n. 1.

[7] F. S. C. Northrop, "The Mathematical Background and Content of Greek
Philosophy," in *Philosophical Essays for Alfred North Whitehead* (New York, 1936),
pp. 32–3. By permission of Longmans, Green & Co., Inc.

dodecahedron (ether).[8] Until very recent times the five regular solids were known as the Platonic bodies. The better part of the soul, Plato said in *Republic* X (602), trusts to measure and calculation. In the *Theaetetus* (143b) he said that God himself is a geometer (*geōmetrein*). He is said to have inscribed over the entrance to his school: "Let no one ignorant of geometry enter" (*Ageōmetrētos mēdeis eisitō*).[9]

One will be perhaps likely to think that this side of Plato's theory, hyperintellectual and even frigid, must have seemed even to him far less relevant to the nature of literature than the more visionary conceptions which we have described somewhat earlier. It is possible, however, that through another group of arts which were highly cultivated in Greece during Plato's time—the visual—at least a remote kind of relevance may be inferred. One of Plato's later dialogues, the *Philebus*, is a discussion of pleasure and knowledge in which he attempts for one thing to distinguish what he calls mixed pleasures (those that follow on pain or are somehow dependent on it—and here he puts the pleasures of tragedy and comedy) from certain kinds which he considers more pure and hence more nearly related to the good. One passage of this dialogue has often been produced in our day as a charter from antiquity for theorists of "significant form" in the visual arts.

> I do not mean by beauty of form such beauty as that of animals or pictures, which the many would suppose to be my meaning; but, says the argument, understand me to mean straight lines and circles, and the plane or solid figures which are formed out of them by turning-lathes and rulers and measures of angles; for these I affirm to be not only relatively beautiful, like other things, but they are eternally and absolutely beautiful, and they have peculiar pleasures, quite unlike the pleasures of scratching. And there are colours which are of the same character, and have similar pleasures.—51[1]

Let us place in conjunction with this a tabular view of the imitative arts digested from several places in another late dialogue, the *Sophist* (219, 235, 264, 266). The sophist himself, viewed by Plato as a special kind of

[8] *Timaeus*, 53c–56c. Francis M. Cornford, *Plato's Cosmology, The Timaeus of Plato Translated with a Running Commentary* (London, 1937), pp. 210–22. The assignment of the dodecahedron to ether is not explicit in Plato but was apparently made so in early Platonic commentary. See the quotation from Plutarch's *On the E at Delphi* (XI) in Cornford, p. 220; Paul Shorey, *What Plato Said* (Chicago, 1933), p. 408; *Epinomis* 981, 984.

[9] Adolph Busse, ed., *Commentaria in Aristotelem Graeca*, XVIII (Berlin, 1900), 118, the commentary of Elias. Cf. Aristotle: "Mathematics has been turned by our present day thinkers into the whole of philosophy" (*Metaphysics*, I, 9).

[1] Cf. E. F. Carritt, in *Philosophies of Beauty* (Oxford, 1931), pp. 29–30; Herbert Read, *Art Now* (New York, 1933), p. 101; R. H. Wilenski, *The Meaning of Modern Sculpture* (London, 1933).

imitator or deceiver, is the object of definition, but some incidental light
is cast in another direction.

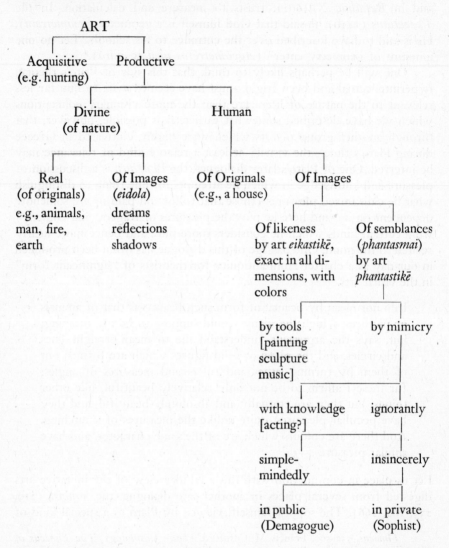

The part of the table which specially concerns us is the division between
eikastic (or realistic) images and phantastic (or imaginative). Here Plato
seems to be attempting to deal, though perhaps not very decisively, with
a question which is prominent in ancient theory of art, that of illusion.
There is a passage in the *Iliad* of Homer—often quoted by historians of
literary theory—where the shield made by Hephaestus for Achilles is described with great admiration—the images with which it was adorned
were so life-like that the furrows of a ploughed field, though wrought

from the gold, seemed black. During the lifetime of Plato himself Greek
visual art seems to have been moving rapidly in the direction of naturalism and illusionism. Art historians of the formalist school like to tell us
that even the Great Period of Greek sculpture (that of the pediments of
the Temple of Zeus at Olympia, for instance, or the Periclean Parthenon
at Athens) is a degeneration from a more formal (and Egyptian) antiquity. Visual art was already tending toward the Rogers-ware style of
Hellenistic narrative and genre sculpture (the dying Gaul, the old market woman). Later documents of antiquity, especially the *Natural History* of Pliny the Elder, record such instances of illusionist virtuosity in
Plato's day as that of Zeuxis, who painted grapes so well that they attracted birds,[2] or that of Parrhasius, who painted drapery that appeared
to move. These achievements seem to have arisen out of one of the chief
developments during the fifth century in theatrical design, that of *skiagraphia* (shaded painting) or perspective scenery. At the same time the
formal and geometrical element of visual art continued very prominently
in the architecture by which Plato was surrounded. Modern investigation
has fairly well demonstrated that the art of Greek vases and temple architecture was based on the principle of "dynamic symmetry"—the com-
mensurability of area rather than of line and above all the commensu-
rability generated by extreme and mean ratio, the "Golden Section." [3]

The relation between illusion and formalism in Plato's day was
scarcely simple—as may be instanced even in the "fantastic" art mentioned by Plato in the *Sophist* (235e). Painters and sculptors, he points
out, strive for the proportion that will *appear* beautiful. Those who carve
colossal figures, for instance, make the upper parts larger so that from
the ground they will be seen in usual proportions. A Byzantine Greek
chronicler has preserved the story that when Phidias produced his statue
of Athena in competition with that of a rival, the people were ready to
stone Phidias when the statue was seen lying on the ground.[4] Such proportioned illusion as this Plato classes with the work of the sophist. Yet
even the architectural formalism of Plato's day depended on the same
adjustments—as in the well-known entasis or swell of the temple columns,
in virtue of which they look straight as one sees them from below.

Let us move toward a close of this discussion by placing side by
side two more Platonic passages, the first from an early dialogue about
verbal images or names, the *Cratylus*.

[2] Pliny, *Natural History*, XXXV, 36, 60: ". . . *uvas pictas tanto successu ut in
scaenam aves advolassent.*" See Pierre-Maxime Schuhl, *Platon et L'Art de Son Temps*
(Paris, 1933).

[3] Among a number of works on this subject by Jay Hambidge, see especially
Dynamic Symmetry, The Greek Vase (New Haven, 1920), *The Parthenon and
Other Greek Temples, Their Dynamic Symmetry* (New Haven, 1924), *Practical
Applications of Dynamic Symmetry* (New Haven, 1932).

[4] Tzetzes, *Historiarum Variarum Chiliades*, VIII, 353–69, ed. T. Kiessling
(Lipsiae, 1826), pp. 295–6.

> I should say . . . that the image, if expressing in every point the entire reality, would no longer be an image. Let us suppose the existence of two objects: one of them shall be Cratylus, and the other the image of Cratylus; and we will suppose, further, that some God makes not only a representation such as a painter would make of your outward form and colour, but also creates an inward organization like yours, having the same warmth and softness; and into this infuses motion, and soul, and mind, such as you have, and in a word copies all your qualities, and places them by you in another form; would you say that this was Cratylus and the image of Cratylus, or that there were two Cratyluses?—432

The second, from the attack on poetry in Book X of the *Republic*.

> Then the imitator . . . is a long way off the truth, and can do all things because he lightly touches on a small part of them, and that part an image. For example: A painter will paint a cobbler, carpenter, or any other artist, though he knows nothing of their arts; and, if he is a good artist, he may deceive children or simple persons, when he shows them his picture of a carpenter from a distance, and they will fancy that they are looking at a real carpenter.—598

The minimal conclusion to be drawn from all the evidence would seem to be that Plato has confronted the very difficult problem of the relation between formalism and illusionism in art and, in line with the austerity and subtlety of his basic mathematical view of reality, has expressed his mistrust of the realistic trends of his day and has cast a perennially influential vote in favor of some kind of visual formalism.[5] If this part of his theorizing does not go far in telling us about the nature of poetry, at least it offers a prototype for theories of "stylization" or "detachment" which have never since in the history of poetics been altogether submerged. In what is no doubt its excess of detachment Plato's theory offers an approach by contrast to—as indeed it was historically the point of departure for—the more empirically weighted and warmer theory which we shall encounter in the next chapter.

[5] Plato's formalism seems not to extend to auditory art. See his rules for moral fitness in modes of music, *Republic* III, 398–400, and his censure of "the bare sound of harp and flute," *Laws* II, 669.

CHAPTER 2

ARISTOTLE'S ANSWER: POETRY AS STRUCTURE

§ *Aristotle's* Poetics *in relation to his major works, relation between Plato and Aristotle on universals, the mathematical, the biological, entelechy, the Socratic problem of
classes—II. theoretical and practical sciences, the* Ethics
and Politics, *poetry and information, the artistic norm—
III. the universal, the probable,* mimēsis, homoiōma, *internal action, music, figures and colors,* opsis, *the ideal (to
beltion, hoia einai dei)—IV. growth of tragedy, norms of
size and order,* peripeteia, anagnorisis, desis, lusis, *wholeness, beginning, middle, end—V. cohesion of causes,* Pos-
terior Analytics, *the logic of the syllogism, dramatic logic,*
Oedipus, *organic unity, Aristotle's six elements of tragedy,
reality of the poetic object* §

PLATO'S PUPIL ARISTOTLE CAME TO THE ACADEMY IN THE YEAR 367 OR
eighteen years before Plato's death at the age of 80 in 349. Fourteen
years later, in 335, Aristotle founded his own school the Lyceum.
It was apparently towards the end of his career that he produced his
treatise in three books on *Rhetoric* and in some way was responsible for
an essay or compilation of notes, in twenty-six chapters, the celebrated
Poetics. Even if it were to happen that at this late date classical scholars
changed their opinion about the authorship of the *Poetics,* one would
still turn, for the explication of these condensed and partly chaotic hints,
to the system of Greek philosophy which most readily connects with
them, the major works of Aristotle, especially his *Metaphysics, Ethics,*
and *Politics.* The *Poetics* is a work of the type which Aristotle himself
called "acroamatic"—to be interpreted only with the help of other and
larger works. The difference between Aristotle and Plato on poetry is a
fulfilment of their difference on ideas or universals, and the *Rhetoric*

21

and *Poetics* are parts of a larger answer to Plato. Plato is a teacher and opponent who often appears, or is often just out of sight, in the arguments of Aristotle, and especially in historical parts of the *Metaphysics*.

> . . . having in his youth first become familiar with . . . the Heraclitean doctrines (that all objects of sense are ever in a state of flux and there is no knowledge about them), Plato held these views even in later years. Socrates, however, was busying himself about ethical matters and neglecting the world of nature . . . he fixed thought for the first time on definitions. Plato accepted his teaching but held that the problem applied not to objects of sense but to entities of another kind—for this reason, that common definitions could not be definitions of any objects of sense, as these are always changing. The "entities of another kind," then, he called Ideas, and objects of sense, he said, were all named after Ideas and in virtue of a relation to these; for the many objects of sense exist by participation in the Ideas that have the same name as they.—*Metaphysics* I (A), 6 [1]

> . . . if the Forms exist and "animal" is present in "man" and "horse," it is either one and the same in number, or different. (In formula it is clearly one, for he who states the formula will go through the same formula in either case.) If then there is a "man-in-himself" who is a "this" and exists apart, the parts also of which he consists, e.g. "animal" and "two-footed," must indicate "thises," and be capable of separate existence and substances.—*Metaphysics* VII (Z), 13

> Again, if the Forms are numbers, how can they be causes? Is it because existing things are other numbers, e.g. one number is man, another is Socrates, another Callias?
>
> —*Metaphysics* I (A), 9

It is perhaps best for our purpose to attempt to express the difference between Plato and Aristotle in their view of universals as broadly and as simply as possible. It derives from the fact that whereas Plato, as we have seen, was mathematical, transcendental, and rigorously abstract, Aristotle (whose father, Nicomachus—if a biographical note be relevant—was court physician to Amyntas II of Macedonia—and who was himself

---

[1] Works of Aristotle, other than the *Poetics* and *Rhetoric*, are quoted in this and the following chapter mainly from the Oxford translation, completed in 1931, and largely reprinted in *The Basic Works of Aristotle*, ed. Richard McKeon (New York, Random House, 1941). In the passage from *Metaphysics* I (A), 6 above, the term "sensibles" in the Oxford translation is altered by the present writers to "objects of sense." Some shorter quotations from various Aristotelian works are borrowed from the commentary of S. H. Butcher on the *Poetics*. (Cf. *post*, p. 25, n. 2.)

The Oxford Translation of Aristotle is quoted by permission of the Delegates of The Clarendon Press.

a naturalist and collector of specimens for King Hermias of Atarneus and Assos in Syria) was biological, natural, empirical, and concrete. We shall not go far wrong if we form the habit of imagining behind the universal of Aristotle, rather than a geometric figure like a triangle, some living animal, say a horse. If there was change here, from colthood to death and decay, it was yet possible to say that *something* had changed. (Even if something which is cold becomes hot, a potency has been realized, and potency resides in something.[2]) There is also, especially in a biological object, direction in change, a purpose or *entelechy*, the full self of the object as realized in the object—the horse rather than the colt. "What each thing is when fully developed, we call its nature."[3] Or: ". . . a thing is more properly said to be what it is when it has attained to fulfilment than when it exists potentially."[4] Recurrence in generation also has something to do with it. When a tree is made into a bed, and if the bed then happens to be planted—if anything comes up at all, it will not be a bed but a tree.[5] "Man is born from man, but not bed from bed." The *ousia* or essence, the *eidos* or form, which, as we have seen, was the object of knowledge at the top of Plato's line—but which was apparently transcendental and separate from the horses and beds which are crudely and trustfully known at a lower level by *pistis* (a kind of "animal faith")—is brought down by Aristotle into the things themselves as the dynamic principle of their being which continues through change in a certain direction. The *form* must be in the thing as one of its causes.

> When we are dealing with definite and ordered products of Nature, we must not say that each *is* of a certain quality because it *becomes* so, but rather that they *become* so because they *are* so and so, for the process of becoming attends upon being and is for the sake of being, not *vice versa*.[6]

The Platonic term *ousia* as it appears in Aristotle attracts both "substance" and "essence" for its English translations. The *to ti ēn einai*—the "being what a thing was"—is a relative of *ousia* so close as to be nearly indistinguishable from it. "When we say *what* a thing is, we do not say 'white' or 'hot' or 'three cubits long,' but a 'man' or 'a god.'"[7] Aristotle carries on the Socratic or logical, rather than the Pythagorean or mathematical, strain in Plato's thinking; but he re-enforces this strain ontologically by grounding it more deeply in things themselves, as their vital principle of unity in change. In the *Parmenides* of Plato the younger Socrates, as he is dramatically presented, suffers some embarrassment at

[2] *Metaphysics* IX (Θ); *Physics* I.
[3] *Politics* I, 1.
[4] *Physics* II, 1.
[5] *Physics* II, 1.
[6] *On the Generation of Animals* V, 1.
[7] *Metaphysics* VII (Z), 1.

the questions of the Eleatic Parmenides about the number of things which have *forms*—that is, about the kinds of forms themselves and their number. About some kinds Socrates is sure: there are forms of universal categories such as likeness and difference, of ethical qualities such as justice and goodness, of mathematicals, of elements (fire, air, water, earth), and of natural species, such as man and horse. But about such transitory or inferior classes as, say, mud or hair, the argument is less decided. It is not clear that Aristotle has completely or triumphantly solved this problem. But at least his biological and hence structural emphasis tends to center the concept of form on more complex and stable living things —organic substances. His emphasis falls upon the qualifications which a thing must have in order to be a thing at all, a *this* or a one.[8]

II

THE transition from the more metaphysical areas of Aristotle's thought to his *Poetics* and *Rhetoric* is stepped down or cushioned for us by a distinction again characteristic of the empiricism of Aristotle in reaction against the rational severity of Plato. This is the general distinction which Aristotle makes between theoretical science and a varied range of "practical" philosophies and "productive" arts—or, more briefly, between the demonstrably certain and the arguably probable. The distinction was not pejorative and exclusive, as it tended to be for Plato, but tolerant and inclusive—extending to each kind of discipline a charter to work with the kind of evidence and within the degree of precision which could as a matter of fact be exacted of its peculiar materials. As the ontological and epistemological dialogues of Plato have their themes reflected in the vast museum of his political masterpiece the *Republic*, so the metaphysical, logical and scientific works of Aristotle shade off into his *Ethics*, or philosophy of rational activity along the path of the "mean," and his *Politics*, a more historical inquiry into that activity as it derives from man's role as a member of society. "Man is naturally a social animal" (*Anthrōpos phusei politikon zōon*).[9] Book VIII of the *Politics* deals with education, and more specifically, Chapters 5 and 7 of this Book, with the value of visual, musical, and verbal arts. With the value of poetry, says Aristotle, I have dealt more fully in my *Poetics*. We may think of both his *Poetics* and his *Rhetoric* as expansions of this area of the *Politics* and may safely work on the hypothesis that for Aristotle, as for Plato, poetry is an art to be understood, and praised or blamed, only in its relation to the whole human being of whom it is both the instrument and the reflection.

[8] Cf. *post* Chapter 7, the neo-Platonic development of this conception.
[9] *Politics* I, 2.

Such a basic assumption, however, does not prevent Aristotle from looking at poetry in its own perspective as a thing having its own peculiar character. One of the most interesting passages in the *Poetics*—though it is but an incidental excursion—occurs in Chapter XXV when Aristotle in the course of rejecting several pedantries of criticism apparently prevalent in his day (the reliances, no doubt, of the caviller Zoilus [1] and his friends) alludes to a kind of hyper-literalism, a scientific and informational criterion, such as might easily be imputed to the Socrates of Plato's *Ion*. One may distinguish, says Aristotle, between faults which affect a poem as such and those which do not.

> . . . if the failure is due to a wrong choice—if he has represented a horse as throwing out both of his off legs at once, or introduced technical inaccuracies in medicine, for example, or in any other art—the error is not essential to the poetry.[2]

Or, to shift the example to the sister mimetic art of painting: "Not to know that a hind has no horns is a less serious matter than to paint it inartistically." With the word *inartistically* Aristotle may be thought to have begged the question, and in a sense no doubt he has. In somewhat the same sense all the other poetic theory which we are to consider in this book will do the same—in the sense, that is, that a certain nuclear area of the indefinable will never be reduced by the theory; a scientific or completely analytic definition of poetry has never been achieved. What is *artistically?* What is art? What does an art of words tell us?

III

AMONG the parts of the *Poetics* which have been most often quoted by later theorists are the dicta that poetry is a more philosophic and more serious thing (*philosophôteron kai spoudaioteron*) than "history," that it deals with the universal (here is the direct retort to Plato) while history deals with particulars, that it cares not for what *has* happened but for

---

[1] Zoilus, a critic who flourished about 350 B.C., was the author of a work in nine books probably entitled *Homeromastix* (*A Whip for Homer*).

[2] The *Poetics* of Aristotle is quoted in this and the following chapters from the text and for the most part from the translation of S. H. Butcher, *Aristotle's Theory of Poetry and Fine Art*, 4th Edition, London, 1907. Cf. *ante* p. 22, n. 1. Other editions and English translations which may be very profitably consulted are: *Aristotle on the Art of Poetry*, trans. Ingram Bywater (Oxford, 1909); Allan H. Gilbert's translation of the text according to Gudeman's edition, 1934, in Gilbert's *Literary Criticism, Plato to Dryden* (New York, 1940); Seymour M. Pitcher, "Aristotle on Poetic Art," *The Journal of General Education*, VII (October, 1952), 56–76; L. J. Potts, *Aristotle on the Art of Fiction* (Cambridge, 1953). The last is a highly accomplished translation which confers perhaps more continuity and readability on Aristotle's notes than any other attempt in English. Butcher's translation is quoted by permission of Macmillan & Company Ltd and St. Martin's Press.

what may happen (ch. IX), and that it prefers impossible probabilities (*adunata eikota*) to improbable possibilities (*dunata apithana*).[3] But how can what is impossible be probable? Probable, plausible, or harmonious, by certain approximate laws of spirit, value and desire, we might say, rather than by rules of physical science and measurement. Or, by certain internal laws set up by a work of art for itself, rather than by laws of scientific external reference.

The main effort of the Aristotelian tradition in criticism has been to reconcile such statements with the fact that one of the central terms in Aristotle's system—as might be expected from his proximity to Plato and his purpose of rebuttal—is the term *imitation* (*mimēsis*). A term which meant for Plato removal from reality and distortion (at least when he applied the term to art) is manipulated by Aristotle to mean something apparently better than reality—though we may have difficulty in understanding this. In more scientific contexts Aristotle seems to conceive the mimetic relation between practical art and nature as one of assistance in a teleological process. "Art imitates nature" (*hē technē mimeitai tēn phusin*). This statement occurs not in the *Poetics* but in the *Meteorology* (IV, 3) and refers to the help given to digestion by cookery.[4] Art gives nature a boost in her seeking of the goal. Again: "Every art and educational discipline aims at filling out what nature leaves undone" (*pasa gar technē kai paideia to prosleipon bouletai tēs phuseōs anaplēroun*—*Politics* IV [VII], 17). Or again: "Art finishes the job when nature fails, or imitates the missing parts" (*hē technē ta men epitelei ha hē phusis adunatei apergasasthai, ta de mimeitai*—*Physics* II, 8). To go a little further, art in having aims and working by a plan or idea, parallels the work of nature. Nature makes a horse; an artist makes a bed.[5]

It is not precisely these meanings, however, which explain what is meant by the preliminary statements in the *Poetics* that the several arts such as music, dancing, painting, and poetry are all *imitative*. In the end one may decide to try for a synthesis of meanings, but primarily the term *mimēsis* in the *Poetics* must be taken as referring not to some kind of aid or parallel to nature but to the making of a likeness or image of nature. An equivalent term is *homoiōma*, one used instead of *mimēsis* in an important passage of the *Politics* (VIII, 5) which speaks of rhythm and melody as an imitation of passions. From certain allusions to portraiture and to other painting in the *Poetics* one might for a moment suppose that the Aristotelian concept of *mimēsis* was of a very literal and external sort, something like the *technē eikastikē* of Plato in the *Sophist*. On the

[3] Ch. XXIV. Cf. XXV: *pros te gar tēn poiēsin hairetōteron pithanon adunaton ē apithanon kai dunaton.*
[4] In the Socratic argument against verbal art (as we shall see, *post* Chapter 4 p. 63), cookery is not an art at all, but a sophistical knack, the false counterpart of medicine.
[5] Cf. *Metaphysics* VII, 9.

other hand music and dancing too are counted in the *Poetics* (as in the *Politics*) as forms of imitation, and the peculiar object of poetic imitation is said in the *Poetics* to be "men in action," their characters, passions, and deeds or experiences (*ēthē, pathē, praxeis*).[6] Aristotle, in short, means that poetic imitation is an imitation of inner human action. The word *homoiōma* in the *Politics* seems to mean a very full imitation, an embodiment, or a "symbol," as it might be called today, of "anger and gentleness . . . courage and temperance, and all the qualities contrary to these." And it is noteworthy that the objects of no other senses, not even the objects of sight, are thought to share this directly emotive and moral quality. "Figures and colors are not imitations, but signs (*sēmeia*), of moral habits, indications which the body gives of states of feeling." As, for example, when a person blushes or grows pale or grimaces. These remarks in the *Politics* may help to explain why at a few places in the *Poetics* Aristotle alludes to the dramatic element of *opsis* or spectacle in a slighting way,[7] as a matter of machinery and costuming rather than poetry, hardly a matter for criticism. Aristotle's emphasis in the *Poetics* falls very clearly on the imitation *in words* of a sort of objects peculiarly suitable for that sort of imitation—namely, human action, passion, and character.

Again, the possible objects of poetic imitation are said in the *Poetics* to be not only men as they are in real life, but men either better (*beltionas*) or worse than they are (ch. II)—and not only things as they were or are, but things as they ought to be (*hoia einai dei*), or as they are said or thought to be (XXV).

> . . . if it be objected that the description is not true to fact, the poet may perhaps reply,—'But the objects are as they ought to be': just as Sophocles said that he drew men as they ought to be; Euripides, as they are.—XXV

> Again, it may be impossible that there should be men such as Zeuxis painted. 'Yes,' we say, 'but the impossible is the higher thing (*beltion*); for the ideal type must surpass the reality.'
> —XXV

The term *beltion* ("better thing" or "higher reality") is a part of Aristotle's general metaphysics of form, growth, direction, or ideal. "Nature," he says in the treatise *On the Parts of Animals* (IV, 10), "makes the best (*to beltiston*) of the materials at her disposal." And in that *On the Generation of Animals* (I, 4): "Nature works either through mechanical necessity (*to anagkaion*) or through a drive toward the ideal (*to beltion*)." But what ideal, we might ask, is presented in the *mimēsis*

---

[6] *Poetics* I–II. Cf. *Problems* XIX, 27: "Though it has no words, music nevertheless has ethical character."

[7] *Poetics* VI, VII, and XIV.

of poetry? Shall we be able through the conception of the ideal to show how poetry as an image is also an imitation in the sense, earlier defined, of a process auxiliary to nature? Shall we say that poetry (taken in the educational sense of the *Politics*) assists or parallels the forces of man's moral nature by offering images of the ideal? If we do say this, we shall come very close to putting a didactic clause in our definition of poetry —closer than Aristotle himself seems to wish. But to say otherwise may terminate in another embarrassment, that of the circular definition. The expression *hoia einai dei* ("things as they ought to be"), says Butcher in his admirable commentary (p. 151), must be taken not in a moral but simply in an aesthetic sense. And with this he confirms the apparently tautological statement of Aristotle that the only *artistic fault* is to paint the animal *inartistically*.

IV

IN A characteristic biological analogy Aristotle sums up the history of tragedy as a genre.

> Tragedy, having passed through many phases, reached its natural form, and there it stopped.[8]

The stages of growth in a single organism, from colt to horse, are paralleled in the history of Greek drama from Dionysiac ritual dithyrambics to the tragedies of Sophocles—after which progress ceases. It is possible for the thinker of historical bent to make too much of the fact that Aristotle was an inductive observer and hence to be too confident in assuming that Aristotle's description *a posteriori* of what had been accomplished in the Greek drama of the fifth century was without any implication of value.

Among the simplest norms one might propose for a play is that it should be of a certain size—not too long, so that the mind cannot entertain it (an animal a mile long could not be seen and so would scarcely be called beautiful), but on the other hand, not too short, so as to preclude certain internal relations. The play must in fact be of a certain *magnitude* (*ti megethos*)—because it must be of a certain structure and proportions. "Beauty depends on magnitude and order" (*to gar kalon en megethei kai taxei estin—Poetics* VII).[9] In a simpler and restrictive sense

---

[8] *Poetics* IV: *pollas metabolas metabalousa hē tragōdia epausato epei esche tēn autēs phusin.*

[9] Cf. *Politics* VII, 4: "Beauty is realized in number and magnitude. . . . To the size of states there is a limit, as there is to other things, plants, animals, implements. . . . For example a ship which is only a span long will not be a ship at all, nor a ship a quarter of a mile long. . . . In like manner a state when composed of too few is not. . . . self-sufficing; when of too many . . . it is not a state, being almost

the action of a tragedy is not longer than one day (*hupo mian periodon hēliou*).[1] In the positive sense, of structure and magnitude, the action must be large enough to admit a change from evil to good or from good to evil (VII)—and, one might add, large enough to display both good and evil adequately. A "complex" action is better than a simple—"complex" being that which includes a *peripeteia* or sudden turn and, as the mechanism of this turn, an *anagnōrisis* or recognition. It is characteristic of Aristotle's thought that these terms, formal in one respect and linking closely with other more formal terms, are in another respect full of implications about the ideal content of tragedy, and in that connection we shall return to them in our next chapter.

The terms *peripeteia* and *anagnōrisis* and also the terms *desis* (complication), *metabasis* (change of fortune—standing in a generic relation to *peripeteia*), and *lusis* (unravelling or denouement) [2] may be looked on as variously intermediate between the sheerly formal and the contentual. The most purified formal terms which Aristotle uses are perhaps *holos* and *teleios;* the action, he says, must be not only of a certain size but whole and complete.[3] The echo from the *Physics* is quite close.

> For thus we define the whole—that from which nothing is wanting, as a whole man or a whole box. . . . "whole" and "complete" are either quite identical or closely akin. Nothing is complete (*teleion*) which has no end (*telos*); and the end is a limit.
> —*Physics* III, 6

The discussion of the whole in the *Poetics* postulates the further formal conceptions of an end (*teleutē*), a beginning (*archē*), and a middle (*meson*). The interdependence of these three formal concepts and that of the *whole* is nicely stated in the *Metaphysics:*

> Of quanta that have a beginning and a middle and an end, those to which the position does not make a difference are called totals, and those to which it does, wholes. V, 26.

---

incapable of constitutional government. For who can be the general of such a vast multitude, or who the herald, unless he have the voice of a Stentor." In *Metaphysics* XIII, 3, beauty consists in symmetry, order, and proportion, and is illustrated by the mathematical sciences in a special degree.

[1] *Poetics* V. The phrase in the context refers clearly to internal length (plot) rather than to external length (duration), although a careless variation in meaning of *mēkos* (size) in V, 4, and VII, 6 and a synonymous use of *chronos* (time) for one of the meanings have raised some doubt among the commentators. For the unities of time and place, see also Chapter II, 3.

[2] *Poetics* XVIII. In Chapter XII occurs the more superficial distinction of the quantitative parts of a play: "Prologue, Episode, Exodos, Choric song; the last being divided into Parodos and Stasimon." This is thought by some to be a non-Aristotelian interpolation.

[3] *Poetics* VII.

A beginning, says the *Poetics*, is that which requires nothing to have come before it; a middle is that which naturally follows something and precedes something else; an end is that something else. Abstract as the terms are, almost truistic as they may appear to us, the heirs of the whole Aristotelian tradition, they yet involve a certain richness of meaning, and they even raise a few problems. That which requires nothing to have come before it will of course not be found very patly in a drama. The beginning of any story is likely to concern a man or a family and hence to imply at least such antecedents as ancestors (who may or may not be mentioned in a prologue or retrospective narration).[4] The acceptable sense of the statement that a story must have a beginning would seem to be that the story must start more or less where its antecedents may be taken for granted, that is, where they are generic rather than specifically relevant. And this has a very special meaning with reference to the stock materials of Greek tragedy, the favorite stories of Thebes or the house of Atreus. These indeed, says Aristotle, are usually the best, because they have the advantage of having really happened and so must be at least probable. One may add—for it is an idea which readily follows —that these stories have the advantage of getting off to a fast start. A comic poet of Aristotle's time complained:

> Your tragedian is altogether the most fortunate of poets. First his plot is familiar to the audience before a line is uttered—he need only give a reminder. If I just say "Oedipus," they know all the rest: his father was Laius, his mother, Jocasta, the names of his sons and daughters, what he has done and what will happen to him. . . . We comic playwrights have no such resources.[5]

It was in virtue of such a well-stocked tradition of fabulous fact that Horace could later give his classic advice about beginning with the siege of Troy, not with the birth of Helen and her sister and brothers (*nec gemini ab ovo, in medias res*). Yet the Horatian *in medias res* stands in a curiously oblique relation to Aristotle's *meson*—which is an actual middle of a plot, not a beginning. And the paradox cannot be resolved if the Aristotelian terms are taken with chronologically complete and measured reference to the external world.

V

THE terms *beginning, middle,* and *end* emphasize a specially close cohesion of causes. Not everything that happens in the life of one man,

---

[4] Antecedent events introduced in this way are called by Aristotle *ta exōthen* (externals) and are considered as part of the *desis* (XVIII).

[5] Antiphanes, *Poiēsis*, fr. 191, quoted in Gilbert Norwood, *Greek Comedy* (London, 1931), p. 49.

says Aristotle, can be included in one story. Without attempting to force
what is mainly a verbal resemblance to the *major, minor,* and *middle*
terms of the Aristotelian syllogism, one may yet turn to Aristotle's *Pos-
terior Analytics* for an instance of how the logic of deduction or the
syllogism relates to inductive, or as one might say, dramatic reasoning.

> Quick wit is a faculty of hitting upon the middle term instan-
> taneously. It would be exemplified by a man who saw that the
> moon has her bright side always turned towards the sun, and
> quickly grasped the cause of this, namely that she borrows her
> light from *him*; or observed somebody in conversation with a
> man of wealth and divined that he was borrowing money, or that
> the friendship of these people sprang from a common enmity.
> In all these instances he has seen the major and minor terms and
> then grasped the causes, the middle terms.
>
> —*Posterior Analytics* I, 34

Aristotle proceeds to reduce the reasoning about the sun to syllogistic
form somewhat as follows:

> The moon is lighted from the sun. (minor premise)
> That which is lighted from the sun has its bright side
>   sunward. (major premise)
> Therefore: The moon has its bright side sunward.

The syllogistic reduction we observe is a reversal of the actual experience and act of learning. It is a reformation of a certain order derived
from raw experience. One may draw a parallel: a man looks up at the
moon and speculates how it comes to be so and so; a man witnesses the
tragedy of Oedipus and speculates on its significance, the reasons why it
should be so and so. One difference between the astronomical act of
learning and that which takes place in the presence of tragedy will be
that in the latter we have what Aristotle considers not the demonstrably
certain middle terms of a science but the probable terms of a practical
art. From the play we could derive not strictly a "syllogism" but an
"enthymeme," a counterpart of the syllogism in the realm of probability.[6] Another difference might be that the more complicated chain of
events in a drama would yield not one but several middle terms, so that
we should have the kind of chain of suspended syllogisms known as the
Aristotelian sorites. Again, as it is characteristic of poetry to refrain from
generalizations or from giving away any messages, we might expect not
to find the major premise of our syllogism—though on the other hand
Greek tragedy might provide an exception in that its choruses and frequent gnomic utterances serve a highly generalizing purpose. At any rate
if we find a drama, let us say *Oedipus the King* by Sophocles (a play

[6] Cf. *post* Chapter 4, p. 67, n. 5.

which Aristotle seems to regard as something like his ideal),[7] if we find this a coherent and orderly structure, we shall tend to carry away from it some dominant impression. And this might be reduced or depoetized, with great overemphasis on the element of generalization, somewhat as follows:

> Oedipus commits patricide and incest.
> He who commits patricide and incest is a criminal, brings a
>   curse on his country, and is doomed to punishment.
> Therefore: Oedipus is a criminal, brings a curse on his country,
>   and is doomed to punishment.

The precise interpretation of the play which we embody in our syllogism is not essential to the general theory. The reader may write in his own middle term or terms (corresponding to whatever he infers about the source of illumination in *Oedipus*). The point of emphasis here is the implicitly reasonable or consistent pattern, the inductive and imaginative cohesion of the dramatic parts, beginning, middle, and end, and in turn the smaller parts of these.

The kind of oneness implied not only in Aristotle's general theory of organic form but in his theory of verbal mimesis is the oneness of a thing which has heterogeneous, interacting parts. The concept is illustrated by a striking analogy in the *Politics* (II, 2):

> Is it not obvious that a state may at length attain such a degree
> of unity as to be no longer a state?—since the nature of a state is
> to be a plurality, and in tending to greater unity, from being a
> state, it becomes a family, and from being a family, an individ-
> ual. . . . Again, the state is not made up only of so many men,
> but of different kinds of men; for similars do not constitute a
> state. It is not like a military alliance. The usefulness of the latter
> depends upon its quantity . . . but the elements out of which a
> unity is to be formed differ in kind.

"The parts of the action," says the *Poetics* (VIII), "stand together." Aristotle's speculations begin with the observation of life, but they do not end in atomistic analysis. He sees the whole as more than the sum of its parts if only in that it includes the relations among the parts.

To make a final application of these notions to the literary object, let us say that rightly understood Aristotle asks us to distinguish between what is really a verbal object (a unity, a thing, and hence an analogue of substantial being) and what only pretends in certain superficial ways to be so. The unity of the verbal object is one which penetrates to many levels and one which requires the complement of all these

[7] See *Poetics* XI, XIII, XV, XVI, XXIV, XXVI.

levels—as perhaps Aristotle indicates in his list of the six elements of
tragedy: *muthos* (plot), *ēthos* (character), *dianoia* (thought)—these, he
says, are the "matter"; [8] *lexis* (diction), *melos* (song)—*these* are the "medium";[8] *opsis* (spectacle)—this is the "manner."[8] The integration of
these six is not a thing to be lightly supposed, nor, for that matter, is
the legitimacy of the triple distinction: matter, medium, manner—on
these issues we shall have occasion to say more. For the moment we assume that the integration, which we discuss now mainly with reference
to plot, will in the fullness of fact include the other five elements. Let
us put our stress for the moment upon the unity and reality of the play,
as distinct from, but analogous to, that of objects in other areas of our
experience.

> A sentence or phrase may form a unity in two ways—either as
> signifying one thing, or as consisting of several parts linked to-
> gether. Thus the Iliad is one by the linking together of parts, the
> definition of man by the unity of the thing signified.
>
> —*Poetics* XX

A passage in the *Metaphysics* (VII, 4) makes it clear, indeed, that the
oneness of a thing signified, man, for instance, was for Aristotle a oneness of greater metaphysical dignity than the oneness of verbal composition.

> . . . we have a definition not where we have a word and a
> formula identical in meaning (for in that case all formulae or
> sets of words would be definitions; for there will be some name
> for any set of words whatever, so that even the *Iliad* will be a
> definition), but where there is a formula of something pri-
> mary. . . .

Nevertheless, the unity of the verbal composition, "by the linking together of parts," has a worth of its own—quite different from that of
the other kind of verbal unity, the more abstract unity of definition or
statement. *Oedipus the King* is more than its title, and it is more than a
certain number of scenes placed together under one title—just as an
actual man is more than his name or his definition, and, within the world
of physical substances, is more of a thing than a number of cardboard
boxes wrapped together and identified with a label. The *Oedipus* has a
far more cohesive actuality and substantiality than, for instance, the
entries for a year in the *Anglo-Saxon Chronicle* or a chapter of Xenophon's *Anabasis*. It has a great deal more than certain other Greek plays,
notably than some by Euripides, a dramatist to whom Aristotle refers

---

[8] For the relation of these terms to the term "form" as that appears throughout
this history, see *post* Chapter 32, Epilogue, pp. 747–8.

with markedly less approval. The *Andromache* of Euripides, for example, falls in half (if not into smaller parts) and might easily be viewed as fragments of at least two unfinished plays stuck together by means of the title and certain other abstract indexes. Its unity is somewhat illusory. *Oedipus*, on the contrary, not only presents a certain unified and significant image of reality, but is itself a form of reality.

CHAPTER 3

ARISTOTLE: TRAGEDY AND COMEDY

§ *The tragic focus, definition of tragedy, catharsis—II.
plot and character, spectacle, the ideal tragic hero—III.
hamartia (three interpretations), Aristotelian vs. Socratic
ethics, good and bad luck, theological blunders,* Oedipus—
IV. peripeteia and anagnōrisis *as dramatic content—V.
definition of comedy, comic catharsis, Old Comedy and
New, lampooning vs. general significance, label names,
comic types in Aristotle's* Ethics, *Theophrastan Characters, the comic universal, tragic and comic* hamartia—*VI.
tragic and comic antinomies, importance of Aristotle's
answer to Plato, a double concern for the universal, escape
from both Thracian and Boeotian theory, Abbé Bremond,
mystery vs. criticism* §

W E HAVE BEEN USING THE TERM "TRAGEDY" ALMOST AS IF IT WERE
synonymous with "poetry." Aristotle does the same, or at least
he devotes a large part of his *Poetics*, Chapters VI–XIX, to
talking about tragedy. Not only had tragedy evolved, as we have seen,
through several phases to its entelechy or full form, but this same evolution was in a broader sense the evolution of poetry to *its* full form, which
was no other than that of tragedy. Epic, which Aristotle treats in the last
four chapters of the *Poetics*, had been a phase in the genesis of tragedy, it
might be discussed in much the same terms, and—though this seems to
have run contrary to the prevailing opinion—it was inferior to tragedy
because less concentrated, less ideal. Dithyramb was a more recent ritual approach to tragedy, surviving in lyric and choral parts, which ought
to be closely integrated with the action. The philosophy of lyric as such
does not appear in the *Poetics*. The didactic is clearly not countenanced
—the physics of Empedocles being adduced as an instance of what is

35

verse but not poetry. The literary genres as such make a post-Aristotelian chapter of critical history. But it may be observed here that the dominance of one genre or another at different periods of critical history may strongly affect whole systems of criticism and may afford the insights through which they make their most permanent statements. The Aristotelian poetics is the poetics of the drama and especially of tragedy. We now quote the celebrated definition of tragedy from Chapter VI. Tragedy is:

> an imitation of an action that is serious, complete, and of a certain magnitude; in language embellished with each kind of artistic ornament, the several kinds being found in separate parts of the play; in the form of action, not of narrative; through pity and fear (*di' eleou kai phobou*) effecting the proper purgation (*katharsis*) of these emotions.

One of the most debated clauses of this definition is the last, concerning catharsis. It will be noted that just as Aristotle is in the main intent on answering Plato in metaphysical terms—putting his poetic "universal" against Plato's imitation of an imitation—so here he has thrown out a brief answer in emotive terms to Plato's argument that poetry inflames the passions and weakens moral fiber. Perhaps Aristotle said more about catharsis in a lost second part of his *Poetics*. In the section of the *Politics* on education there is a parallel statement about the benefit of music in working off emotions of religious frenzy. "When hereafter we treat of poetry," he says, "we will treat the subject with more precision" (*Politics* V [VIII], 7). The exegetes of Aristotelian catharsis have chiefly devoted their efforts to arguing the question whether the term "catharsis" is a medical, Hippocratic metaphor implying the purgation or expulsion of something harmful, the emotions themselves—or is a religious or moral metaphor, implying the purification or aesthetic depersonalization of our usually selfish emotions of pity and fear. (Various intermediate theories, of tempering or moderation, appeared in the late Renaissance, and will claim our attention in a later chapter.) The first or hygienic view, though cruder, appears to be what Aristotle meant—if we may judge from what he says of music in the *Politics* and from the usual syntax of the noun *katharsis* with an objective genitive of the harmful thing purged away (rather than of the other thing purified and retained), as in the phrase of Plato's *Phaedo*, *katharsis tis tōn toioutōn pantōn* (i.e. *hēdonōn kai phobōn*),[1] which may be Aristotle's model.[2] The second or

---

[1] *Phaedo* 69: "Truth is in fact a kind of purgation of all such [pleasures and fears]."

[2] A third argument may be found in the fact that Aristotle's *Rhetoric* (II, 5, 8) speaks of pity and fear as naturally related. This seems to tell against the view (Butcher, p. 265) that these emotions are specially brought together in tragedy so that they may purify each other of sentiment and selfishness.

lustratory view is that adopted by Butcher in his influential essay. It connects more readily with normal modern views about the dignity of the tragic experience and its enlargement of our souls; it is doubtless nearer not only to what most of us would like to say but to the truth. It has at least the advantage of making the enjoyment of tragedy occur while we are witnessing it, rather than in a sounder sleep when we get home, a relief after emotional orgy. But both views concern after all not what tragedy says or what tragedy is so much as what tragedy may do to us; they lie rather in the realm of experimental psychology than in that of literary criticism. They treat "pity and fear" as a reference to something in the audience rather than to something (scenes or elements) in the play, "scenes of pity and fear," as the phrase may justly be rendered.

II

ANOTHER question vigorously debated by the exegetes has concerned the statement (*Poetics* VI) that the plot (*muthos*) is the soul and first principle (*archē kai psuchē*) of tragedy. A shift of interest to character as a thing somehow appearing apart from or prior to plot is associated historically with the rise of romantic criticism and the drama of soul-analysis through reverie and soliloquy. Today a rigorously minded classical critic may write an essay [3] rebuking Shakespearian studies for overlooking a central Aristotelian principle and indulging too much in thoughts about Shakespeare's characters. But in an earlier chapter of the *Poetics* Aristotle says that poetry imitates men not only in their actions but in their characters and feelings. And he says too that *ēthos* as well as *muthos* is one of the six elements of tragedy. One might be content to say that—whatever the possibly successful imbalances of character or of action in drama, and they are doubtless many—there can be no basic consideration of character and action separately. Or, one might say, plot without character is a puzzle, as in a detective story; character without plot is a series of conversations or soliloquies, as in some romantic closet dramas. "What is character but the determination of incident?" asks Henry James. "What is incident but the illustration of character?" "If a woman stands with her hand on a table and looks at me a certain way it is an incident."[4]

Perhaps not enough has ever been said about Aristotle's slight regard for the sixth element of tragedy in his list, *opsis*, the optical part or spectacle. Mere scene-shifting, he considers it, and scarcely a concern of

---

[3] E. E. Stoll, "Poetry and the Passions: An Aftermath," *PMLA*, LV (December, 1940), 979–92.

[4] Henry James, *The Art of Fiction*, ed. L. N. Richardson (New York, 1941), p. 86.

criticism.[5] He seems to concur in Plato's disapproval of animal mimicry and artificial thunder claps (*Republic* III, 396) and is thus the second critic of antiquity to take up the long fight by men of good sense against the usurpation of the stage by vaudeville, operatic diversions, and slapstick—"Cato's long wig" and "Flowered gown," Pinkie and the chicken swallowed whole. It is better,—says Aristotle, "to depend on an artistic handling of the story." We ought to get the effect from simply hearing (or reading). This may be an armchair view and rather extreme—but it has the advantage of stressing the verbal and poetic element of drama, that which is most stable and permanently eligible for criticism.

In our last chapter we have considered *to beltion*, or the ideal aim of nature's working in the Aristotelian scheme of universals, as that aim is reflected or paralleled in the human work, the poem, taken as itself a structural entity. It is more difficult—though equally important—to consider how the Aristotelian ideal may relate to nature as an object which the poem represents or imitates. Perhaps Aristotle meant, in an affective sense, that poetry helps our nature towards its norm (catharsis aids nature's ethical purposes as cooking aids digestion). And he does seem to say that nature as imitated in poems is chosen with some kind of reference to ethical values. But this reference, whatever it may be, scarcely seems to be the same thing as measurement by an ethical norm.

Tragic poetry, says Aristotle, may represent men as better than they are, or as they are. Sophocles represented them as better; Euripides, as they are. Poetry, he says again, defending tales of the marvellous against literalistic criticism, may even plead that it is giving us things as they are said to be or as they are thought to be. So far as rewards and punishments are concerned—and they are a great concern in tragedy—distributive justice, to each according to his desert, is a weak dramatic form, a concession to the audience. It appears in comedy. Another weak form is that which only shows the villain suffering an appropriate downfall. It is difficult to entertain any very intense feelings about such an outcome.

The moral bent of the theory comes out more distinctly in the exclusion of two other cases, that where the virtuous man suffers adversity (this produces only shock—*to miaron*), or that where the villain prospers (this is against our moral sense or human feeling—*to philanthrōpon*). Tragedy appears in the nicely balanced and complicated instance where a man of strong character—and of eminent worldly position, like

[5] *Poetics* VI. We have already noticed (*ante* Chapter 2, p. 27) the opinion expressed in the *Politics* that the objects of vision, color, and figure, have a much weaker claim than music to serve as symbols of ethical experience. In a passage near the beginning of the *Poetics* (Ch. IV) concerning the pleasure we experience in recognizing the picture of a person we know, the emphasis seems to be on the universality of the mimetic pleasure: it occurs even in such a simple instance as that of portraiture.

Oedipus or Thyestes—suffers downfall as a result of some error (*di'
hamartian tina, di' hamartian megalēn*). And yet he is undeserving
(*anaxios*) of so great a downfall (so we may pity him); and he is a man
much like ourselves (*homoios*), so we may experience fear at the spectacle of his downfall.[6]

III

A LARGE difference of opinion about Greek tragedy may be epitomized in a difference about the term *hamartia*. Etymologically, this
means the missing of a mark with bow and arrow, an unskillful but not
morally culpable act. And according to one school of thought *hamartia*
in Greek drama is mainly an accent upon a larger tragedy of fate, man's
larger suffering, unpredictably and without measure, at the hands of the
gods, and man's stoic endurance.[7]

> As flies to wanton boys, are we to the gods;
> They kill us for their sport.

But the term may also be thought to have implications of moral responsibility (it means *sin* in the Greek of the New Testament). And according to another school, *hamartia* is the crux of a deeply moral (and even
Christian) kind of tragedy, the story of man's culpable weakness and
his due punishment. Classic Greek literature, from Homer to the tragedians, is full of human character and will engaged in responsible action.
Even Antigone, when she hangs herself in the sealed cave, does not elude
the criterion. Imagine in the same predicament the much-enduring
Odysseus—or remember his courageous and ingenious tactics when a
prisoner in the cave of the Cyclops.[8]

But again another, though a somewhat more difficult, notion is possible—one which may do more justice to the uneasy tension between
willing and knowing observable in some Greek plays, notably in *Oedipus
the King*, and may at the same time be more consonant with the hints
of Aristotle when the latter are taken in relation to the main tenor of
his thought. Error arises only through ignorance, Socrates had argued
again and again, and most eloquently in the *Protagoras* (352). It is not

---

[6] In another chapter of the *Poetics*, XV, the tragic character must be good
(*chrēston*), appropriate (*harmotton*), true to life (*homoion*), and consistent (*homa-
lon*). The second, third, and fourth, if they may be distinguished, make the classical
doctrine of character decorum. Cf. *post* Chapter 5.

[7] Seymour M. Pitcher, "Aristotle's Good and Just Heroes," *PQ*, XXIV (January,
1945), 1–11; (April, 1945), 190–1; C. M. Bowra, *Sophoclean Tragedy* (Oxford, 1944),
Ch. V.

[8] Lane Cooper, *Aristotelian Papers* (Ithaca, 1939), "The Villain as Hero"; and
"Ἁμαρτία Again—AND AGAIN," *The Classical Journal*, XLIII (October, 1947),
39–40.

really possible to know what is correct and to do otherwise. But the psychology of Aristotle's *Ethics* is more complicated. Concerned, as so often, to rebut or to qualify the view of Plato or Socrates, he argues in Book VII of the *Nicomachean Ethics:*

> Now we may ask . . . how a man who judges rightly can behave incontinently. That he should behave so when he has knowledge, some say is impossible; for it would be strange—so Socrates thought—if when knowledge was in a man something else could master it and drag it about like a slave. For Socrates was entirely opposed to the view in question, holding that there is no such thing as incontinence; no one, he said, when he judges acts against what he judges best—people act so only by reason of ignorance. Now this view plainly contradicts the observed facts, and we must inquire about what happens to such a man. . . .
>
> . . . . since there are two kinds of premises, there is nothing to prevent a man's having both premises and acting against his knowledge, provided that he is using only the universal premise and not the particular; for it is particular acts that have to be done. . . .
>
> But now this is just the condition of men under the influence of passion; for outbursts of anger and sexual appetites and some other such passions, it is evident, actually alter our bodily condition, and in some men even produce fits of madness. It is plain, then, that incontinent people must be said to be in a similar condition to men asleep, mad, or drunk.—VII, 2–3

Somehow or other, experience teaches us, it is possible to know the better and do the worse. (*Video meliora, proboque. Deteriora sequor.*)[9] But the degrees of responsibility may be very elusive of definition.

> Now when (1) the injury takes place contrary to reasonable expectation, it is a *misadventure* (*atuchēma*). When (2) it is not contrary to reasonable expectation, but does not imply vice, it is a *mistake* (*hamartēma*) (for a man makes a mistake (*hamartanei*) when the fault originates in him, but is the victim of accident when the origin lies outside him). When (3) he acts with knowledge but not after deliberation, it is an *act of injustice* (*adikēma*)—e.g. the acts due to anger or to other passions necessary or natural to man; for when men do such harmful and mistaken acts (*blaptontes kai hamartanontes*) they act unjustly, and the acts are acts of injustice, but this does not imply that the doers are unjust or wicked; for the injury is not due to

[9] Ovid, *Metamorphoses* VII, 20.

vice (*mochthēria*). But when (4) a man acts from choice, he is
an *unjust man* and a vicious man.—*Ethics* V, 8

A close affinity between (3) in this list, the act of passion, and (2), the
act of culpable negligence, is further suggested in the continuation of
the passage quoted just above from Book VII.

. . . incontinence . . . is blamed not only as a fault (*hamartia*)
but as a kind of vice (*kakia*).[1] VII, 4

In yet another passage (*Ethics* III, 1) even rooted and wicked ignorance,
(4) in the list above, is alluded to as *hamartia*. *Hamartia* (error) and its
concrete equivalent *hamartēma* (an erroneous act) and the cognate verb
hamartanein seem to connote an area of senses shading in from a peri-
phery of vice and passion to a center of rash and culpable negligence.[2]
Both V, 8 and III, 1 of the *Ethics* include very helpful descriptions of
the latter.

. . . those done in ignorance are *mistakes* (*hamartēmata*) when
the person acted on, the act, the instrument, or the end that will
be attained is other than the agent supposed; the agent thought
either that he was not hitting anyone or that he was not hitting
with this missile or not hitting this person or to this end, but a
result followed other than that which he thought likely (e.g.,
he threw not with intent to wound but only to prick), or the
person hit or the missile was other than he supposed.—V, 8

A man may be ignorant, then, of who he is, what he is doing,
what or whom he is acting on . . . and to what end (e.g. he
may think his act will conduce to someone's safety). . . . of
what a man is doing he might be ignorant, as for instance people say, "it slipped out of their mouths as they were speaking,"
or "they did not know it was a secret," as Aeschylus said of the
mysteries, or a man might say he "let it go off when he merely
wanted to show its working," as the man did with the catapult.
Again, one might think one's son was an enemy, as Merope did,
or that a pointed spear had a button on it, or that a stone was
pumice-stone; or one might give a man a draught to save, and
really kill him; or one might want to touch a man, as people do
in sparring, and really wound him.—III, 1

Or—if we may take a very slight liberty of interpolation—one might meet
an old man and his retinue at a cross-roads, fall into an altercation, and

---

[1] *Kakia* seems to be approximately equivalent to the *mochthēria* (vice) mentioned in *Ethics* V, 8 and distinguished from *hamartia* in *Poetics* XIII.

[2] Butcher, pp. 320–1, points out a passage in *Oedipus at Colonus*, ll. 966 ff., where
hamartia and *hamartanein* shift in successive lines from the connotation of the volun-
tary to that of the involuntary.

end by killing them all—and one might be ignorant that the old man was one's father. Or one might serve the people of a foreign state by solving a riddle and one might be rewarded with the hand of their queen—and one might be ignorant that the queen was one's mother. "The doing of an act that is called involuntary in virtue of ignorance of this sort," says the *Ethics* (III, 1), "must be painful and involve repentance." It is upon "ignorance of particulars" that "pity and pardon depend." [3]

The matter in question may be even further illustrated by another Aristotelian distinction, that made in the *Physics* between what he called the *spontaneous* (the mechanically determined natural event) and *chance* (the stroke of good or evil fortune).

> Chance (*tuchē*) and what results from chance are appropriate to agents that are capable of good fortune and of moral action generally. Therefore necessarily chance is in the sphere of moral actions. This is indicated by the fact that good fortune (*eutuchia*) is thought to be the same, or nearly the same, as happiness, and happiness to be a kind of moral action, since it is well-doing.
>
> . . . spontaneous events (*hosa apo tou automatou*) are said to be "from chance" if they have the further characteristics of being the objects of deliberate intention and due to agents capable of that mode of action.—*Physics* II, 6

The moral application is developed in passages of the *Rhetoric* concerning the psychology of praise and blame.

> Since praise is founded on actions, and acting according to moral purpose is characteristic of the worthy man, we must endeavour to show that a man is acting in that manner, and it is useful that it should appear that he has done so on several occasions. For this reason also one must assume that accidents and strokes of good fortune are due to moral purpose; for if a number of similar examples can be adduced, they will be thought to be signs of virtue and moral purpose.—I, 9 [4]

[3] Another class of actions treated in Aristotle's *Ethics* (III, 1) as perhaps involuntary are those "done from fear of greater evils or for some noble object." One might perform such an action, for example, "if a tyrant were to order one to do something base, having one's parents and children in his power, and if one did the action they were to be saved, but otherwise would be put to death." The concept of the involuntary defined here, though it does not seem to be central to the *hamartia* discussed in the *Poetics* and *Ethics*, would be clearly available in discussing such a tragic fault as Agamemnon's sacrifice of Iphigenia to gain a favoring wind for the expedition against Troy.

[4] Passages of Aristotle's *Rhetoric* quoted in this chapter and the following are reprinted by permission of the publishers from *Aristotle . . . The "Art" of Rhetoric*, translated by John Henry Freese, The Loeb Classical Library, Cambridge, Mass.: Harvard University Press, 1939.

Or, as the poet Simonides had already put it:

> . . . a man . . . cannot but be evil if he be overtaken by hope-
> less calamity; for any man is good in good fortune and bad in
> bad, and take it all in all, they are best who are loved by the
> gods.[5]

Fortes fortuna juvat. God helps him that helps himself. The darker side
of this wisdom has perhaps always been the one more likely to receive
literary treatment, even though the treatment may be comic. Chekhov's
Cherry Orchard, for instance, provides a diminished figure from Greek
tragedy in the melancholy, unlovable, and unlucky philosopher servant
Epihodof, whose "Twenty Misfortunes a Day" (if he opens a door, the
knob comes off in his hand; if he plays billiards, he rips the cloth) are
clearly a part of his miserable character. In Greek thought what we encounter is no doubt a primitive notion of Providence: If the gods superintend all things, then both good and bad luck must somehow be their
doing, and for sufficient reason. A modern version will be psychological
—a Freudian theory of unconsciously deliberate slips, cultivated bad
luck, accident-prone persons.[6]

To be responsible for mistakes which are partly unavoidable is bad
enough in any area of human activity—it must be worst, and overwhelming, when the area is that of man's relation to the supernatural.
An Ancient Mariner shoots a friendly albatross with his crossbow
(*hamartia* by hitting the mark) and brings down an appalling punishment on himself and on all his shipmates. When an elderly female novelist complained to Coleridge that the poem did not have any moral, he
answered that in his opinion it had "too much." And he went on to say
that it should have been altogether without moral like the Arabian Nights
story of the merchant who threw date shells down a well putting out, by
ill luck, the eye of a genie's son. The genie rose from the well and claimed
in retaliation the merchant's life.

It is in this department of man's blundering, that which is committed against the supernatural and is hence boundless in its import and
consequences—that we shall have to place the *hamartia* of Aristotle's
ideal Greek tragedy, *Oedipus the King*. In the partly analogous Hebrew
tragedy of *Job*, the meaning announced at the end by the Voice from
the Whirlwind is that Job's sufferings have not been strictly determined
by the extent of his own sins. The same meaning is implicit in the *Oedipus*, but the tilt of the emphasis is toward a responsibility, which though
it could never have been satisfactorily discharged, Oedipus was yet not

[5] "Eulogy to Scopas," in *Lyra Graeca*, trans. J. M. Edmonds (London: Loeb
Classical Library, 1924), vol. II, fr. 19. The fragment is preserved in the *Protagoras*
of Plato, 339, 347.

[6] See Freud, *The Psychopathology of Everyday Life*, trans. A. A. Brill (New
York, 1914).

free to evade. If on the one hand Oedipus is predestined to destruction, on the other hand, the particular time, features, and fullness of his suffering are determined ironically by the kind of militant scepticism which he shares with his mother, and by his own violent efforts to get free. The rashness which may be traced in his early actions—the flight from Corinth and the murder of Laius—only prefigures the hasty, ill-tempered, and irreverent steps of his inquisition on the day of downfall.[7]

I V

WE HAVE talked in our last chapter about Aristotle's theory of poetry as a theory of poetic form. But it is a theory of form only in the sense by which *form* has plenary implications for what may be thought of, from another point of view, as poetic content. Two precise and technical Aristotelian concepts, already mentioned briefly in our last chapter, serve very well to show the interdependence of the two sides of the theory. *Peripeteia* (sudden reversal) and *anagnōrisis* (recognition) are the pivots of the complex action (*peplegmenē praxis*) preferred by Aristotle; they are a formal necessity in the well-developed whole of a certain size, the action with beginning, middle, and end, where good and evil are adequately set against each other. At the same time, *peripeteia* and *anagnōrisis* are key incidents in the serious story (*muthos*) of the upright protagonist, his *hamartia*, and his suffering. *Peripeteia* is an acute form of *metabasis* or change from good to bad. In the light of Aristotle's examples (the messenger from Corinth comes to cheer Oedipus but clinches the revelation of horror; Danaus leads off Lynceus for the purpose of executing him but is himself executed—) it would seem that *peripeteia* means something very much like a reversal of expectation or frustration of purpose, an "unexpected catastrophe resulting from a deed unwittingly done." [8] *Peripeteia*, says one classical scholar, is a kind of irony of action. Irony of words, so frequent also in Greek tragedy and so telling, occurs "when words, are caught up by circumstances and charged with a fuller meaning than the speaker meant." Irony of action occurs when "deeds are caught up out of an agent's grasp and charged with a meaning the very opposite" of what was meant.[9] *Anagnōrisis*, when used, as it may be, in close junction with *peripeteia*, is the hero's realization of the truth, the full meaning of the deed done in error. There

---

[7] For a detailed exposition of the play as a "critique of rationalism," see Cleanth Brooks and Robert B. Heilman, *Understanding Drama* (New York, 1948), pp. 573 ff.

[8] Atkins, I, 91; F. L. Lucas, "The Reverse of Aristotle," *Classical Review*, XXXVII (1923), 98–104; and his *Tragedy in Relation to Aristotle's "Poetics"* (London, 1928), pp. 91 ff.

[9] Atkins, I, 92; W. Lock, "The Use of περιπέτεια in Aristotle's *Poetics*," *Classical Review*, IX (1895), 251–3.

are six kinds, says Aristotle, of which the most effective is not that of the scar discovered in the bath (as on the return of Odysseus to Ithaca) or that deliberately contrived by one of the characters (as when Orestes makes himself known to Iphigenia) but that which grows naturally from the very workings of the plot—and the example is that of the messenger in *Oedipus*. *Peripeteia* and *anagnōrisis*, we suggest, are but the due developments and complements of *hamartia;* they are the surprising, but natural, aftermath of the partly responsible act of error. The reversal, says Aristotle, should follow its antecedents in a way that is probable or necessary—but it is much better if the way is also surprising. If there were no surprise—that is, if the downfall were clearly predictable or acceptable from the start as the only plausible outcome of the protagonist's fault—we should have not *hamartia* as it may be accurately conceived, but the fully vicious act of the villain. *Peripeteia* and *anagnōrisis* are requirements for the action of a certain magnitude—an action large enough to exhibit the development of a character through confidence, error, recognition and suffering. These two technicalities are specifications for the kind of moral consequence, crossed by surprise, which makes the cohesive beginning, middle, and end, the whole and unity of Aristotle's formal theory. "It may perhaps be," said a later Greek writer in the Aristotelian vein, "that nature has a liking for contraries and evolves harmony out of them and not out of similarities. . . . The arts . . . apparently imitate nature in this respect." [1]

V

WHAT of comedy? Opposite and complement of tragedy, the other half of Greek drama, it is so different a half, and may seem in its marked physical response of laughter so different from all the rest of poetry as to resist being assimilated into any general poetics either of form or of content. Like catharsis, comedy is a topic upon which Aristotle may have said more in a second part of his *Poetics*.[2] It is a topic to which he refers several times in the extant part of the *Poetics*, but rather casually, as if comedy were a minor genre, a reverse or grotesque of serious poetry. This was the kind of poetry that would deal with men as worse than they are (II) or at least as uglier than they are. Plato in the *Philebus* (48–50) had thought the comic response a kind of malicious joy or emotion of self-enhancement at the spectacle of obnoxious characters (those who in real life could hurt us) made innocuous on the stage. Aristotle, with a more kindly insight, is concerned about the pain which those who

[1] *De Mundo*, Chapter 5 (trans. E. S. Forster [Oxford, 1914], 396ᵇ).
[2] Cf. *Rhetoric* III, 18; I, 11; *Poetics* VI.

exhibit deformities may themselves be imagined to suffer or not to suffer. The well-known definition runs as follows:

> Comedy is, as we have said, an imitation of characters of a lower type,—not, however, in the full sense of the word bad, the ludicrous (*to geloion*) being merely a subdivision of the ugly (*to aischron*). It consists of some defect (*hamartēma*) or ugliness which is not painful (*anōdunon*) and not destructive [3] (*ou phthartikon*). To take an obvious example, the comic mask (*to geloion prosōpon*) is ugly and distorted, but does not imply pain.—V

A recently too much celebrated document, the *Tractatus Coislinianus*,[4] a late peripatetic deductive parallel to the chapters of the *Poetics* on tragedy, adds to our definition a cathartic clause.

> Comedy is an imitation of an action that is ludicrous and imperfect . . . through pleasure and laughter effecting the purgation of the like emotions.

This seems a plausible guess. It is supported by our finding in Aristotle's *Ethics* (X, 6) the thesis that happiness consists not in amusement but in rational activity, and by the fact that both Plato and Aristotle include laughter among the politically dangerous emotions. Plato in both the *Republic* (III, 388–395) and *Laws* (VII, 816–17; XI, 934–6) looks on the act of comic mimesis as a dangerous contagion; he would man the comic stage with slaves and hired strangers. Aristotle remarks in his *Politics* (VII, 7) that "the legislator should not allow youth to be spectators of iambi or of comedy until they are of an age to sit at the public tables or to drink strong wine." [5] This kind of catharsis for comedy would be homeopathic (the purging of laughter by working it off) and would be neatly symmetrical with Aristotle's answer to Plato concerning the tragic catharsis. At the same time, it is at least possible to construct another theory of comic catharsis along lines suggested in Plato's *Philebus*, where, as we have noted, laughter is release from the mental pain of envy, and in a passage of Aristotle's *Rhetoric* (II, 3) asserting that "We

---

[3] The example of the comic mask which follows seems to refute those who would translate this "destructive to others."

[4] Called so from the De Coislin Collection in the Bibliothèque Nationale at Paris, from which it was printed by J. H. Cramer in his *Anecdota Graeca* in 1839. The manuscript is of the tenth century A.D.; the contents date apparently from about the first century B.C. See Lane Cooper, *An Aristotelian Theory of Comedy* (New York, 1922), p. 10.

[5] Among the "Characters" of Aristotle's successor Theophrastus is the Ruffian or Reckless Man who "is not ashamed, even while sober, to exhibit himself in the lascivious dance, or to play a part in comedy unmasked." For a recent exposition of this view of comic catharsis, see J. C. Ransom, *The World's Body* (New York, 1938), "The Cathartic Principle," pp. 188–9.

are placable when we are in a condition opposed to angry feeling, for example, at a time of sport or laughter or festivity." [6] But this would be allopathic catharsis and not symmetrical with the tragic. The present writers are content to leave this problem where it stands.

A more specifically critical problem is posed in the *Poetics* by a series of statements in which Aristotle draws a comparison between the "Old," lampooning, or Aristophanic comedy (for the sake of convenience it may be said to have ended with the Athenian downfall of 404) and the "New" or Menandrian comedy (dating after the conquest by the Macedonians in 338). Tragedy had originated in Dionysiac ritual dithyrambics; comedy had originated with the leaders of phallic songs in the *kōmoi* or village Dionysiac revels (IV). Back of each at another remove stood Homer.

> Homer . . . first laid down the main lines of Comedy, by dramatizing the ludicrous instead of writing personal satire. His Margites bears the same relation to Comedy that the Iliad and Odyssey do to Tragedy. . . . lampooners became writers of Comedy, and the Epic poets were succeeded by Tragedians.
> —IV

Lampoon, however, seems to have been a deviation from Homer in the wrong direction toward personality; lampoon was not all it should be.

> As for the plot, it came originally from Sicily; but of Athenian writers Crates was the first who, abandoning the "iambic" or lampooning form, generalized his themes and plots.—V

> In comedy . . . the poet first constructs the plot on the lines of probability, and then inserts characteristic names;—unlike the lampooners who write about particular individuals.—IX

Aristotle's conception of comedy seems even better satisfied by later Hellenistic new comedy and the Roman translations of Terence and Plautus than by the sentimental intrigues found actually in the Middle Comedy and the New Comedy of his own day. It may seem rash to say [7] that he did not appreciate the hilarity of the older lampooning comedy. But at least he must have thought comedy had been moving in the right direction. His remarks about comedy are better illustrated by almost any play of Plautus than by the masterpieces of Aristophanes.

In tragedy, he says, the poet took the already legendary name and rewrote the already known story around it. In comedy he took "characteristic" names (*ou ta tuchonta onomata*). The phrase is an emendation by Butcher, but seems eminently plausible. The plays of Plautus and Terence and the fragments and titles of Greek New Comedy and Mid-

---

[6] Lane Cooper, *op. cit.*, pp. 66–70.
[7] With Butcher, p. 380.

dle Comedy yield a large and various collection of label names [8]—racial names of slaves, like *Cario* or *Syrus*, type names like *Monotropos* (Hermit) or *Polypragmon* (Busybody), compound suggestions like *Philocomasium* (Village Revel Girl), *Artotrogus* (Breadnibbler), *Pamphile* (All-dear), or the monstrosity *Pyrgopolynices* (Conqueror of Towered Cities). Such names illustrate in a nicely definable and tabloid form a difficult poetic choice, that between naturalism (truth to life) and significance. Shall a playwright sacrifice reality for the easy symbolism of the label name, or shall he sacrifice significance for the convincing realism of a name which is as pointless as most of those in real life? Or shall he escape the dilemma by using a common noun, a "citizen," a "tapster," a "slave," a "messenger," or a "soldier," a "1st man in blue serge," a "2nd man in blue serge" (the names of minor dramatic characters from Aeschylus to our own day)?

Both Greek comedy and Greek tragedy decided mainly for the significant name, that of the type or that of the known historic person, the difference between the two being a part of the difference between the meaning of the comic character and that of the tragic. In the *Ethics* of Aristotle virtue is reasonable activity along a line of moderation, on both sides of which are the vices of extremity. A slant toward comic theory is quite pronounced in the description (IV, 8; II, 7) of the tasteful or ready-witted gentleman joker (*eutrapelos*) [9] and the extremes between which he stands, the uncultivated boor, an enemy of jokes (*agroikos*), and the buffoon (*bōmolochos*), who tries to be funny at all costs. One may see the difference between good and bad taste in wit, says Aristotle, "in the old and the new [1] comedies; to the authors of the former indecency (*aischrologia*) of language was amusing; to those of the latter innuendo (*huponoia*) [2] is more so." Again, we encounter (IV, 7) the admirably mock-modest or Socratic man (*eirōn*) and his antitypes the humbug, he who assumes modesty about trifles, and the boaster (*alazōn*), obvious precursor of the Hellenistic *Alazōn* and the Plautine Miles Gloriosus.[8] But if comedy deals with inferior examples of humanity, how, one might speculate, is the ironic man, a tenant of the

---

[8] The term "charactonym" has been recently suggested to fill a kind of gap in English critical vocabulary (Thomas E. Berry, in *Word Study*, XXV, December, 1949, 1).

The plays of Plautus contain more of these significant names than of the opposite kind.

[9] Cf. *Rhetoric* II, 12, wit (*eutrapelia*) as "cultured insolence."

[1] I.e., Middle.

[2] The *Tractatus Coislinianus* uses the terms *loidoria* and *emphasis* for the same contrast.

[8] The buffoon, the ironist, and the impostor are named as specific comic types in the *Tractatus Coislinianus*. A near equivalence between *eirōneia* and *huponoia* is indicated in a passage of the *Rhetoric* (III, 18), where the gentleman, or ironist, who jokes to amuse himself, is set against the buffoon (*bōmolochos* again), who tries too hard to amuse others.

virtuous mean, to be taken as a comic type? How is *huponoia*, the conversational style of the gentleman, to be associated with "New Comedy"
or with any form of comedy at all? The answer is perhaps not explicit
in ancient documents but may be suggested in the speculation that comedy has always required in addition to its gulls and butts such critical
agents as the clever slave and planner, the gentleman commentator and
wit. It might almost be a definition of a certain more sophisticated kind
of comedy to say that it arises from the opposition of mixed characters
or sets of mixed characters, composites who serve reciprocally as butts
and critics.

Aristotle treats virtues no less than vices as clearly conceptualized
types, but he has a tendency to see the vices more vividly. The tendency
is continued and accentuated by his pupil and successor Theophrastus,
in whose *Characters*[4] we find such contrasting pairs as the obsequious
man (*areskos*) and the surly (*authadēs*), the boaster (*alazōn*) and the
mock-modest (*eirōn*), and with these such companions in unattractive-
ness as the loquacious and the garrulous, the flatterer and the complai-
sant, the penurious, the avaricious, and the mean. Theophrastus gives us
a nosology, a gallery of nasty persons. Greek ethical theory and comic
theory are strongly alike in finding vice, much more than virtue, susceptible of fixed portraiture. The names of six out of the thirty Theophrastan Characters are the same as titles of lost plays by Menander.[5]
And Menander is said to have been the pupil of Theophrastus.

These correlations between vice and comedy may be taken as the
reverse of the truth that virtue is not only a mean but a course of conduct which requires such positive qualities as strength of purpose and
courage, and which is best seen in a dynamic form, in motion toward an
object. The comically evil character stands still, despite warnings and
punishments, and his "sufficient destiny" is simply to go on revealing
himself.[6] "Greek tragedy . . ." says Butcher, "combines in one harmonious representation the individual and the universal. Whereas comedy
tends to merge the individual in the type, tragedy manifests the type
through the individual" (p. 388). This may not be so easy a distinction
as it sounds. But at least we can say that in tragedy we start with a known
individual, Oedipus or Agamemnon, and see what he comes to—at what
being and meaning he arrives through a certain development. In comedy
(or at least in Greek New Comedy) we start, on the other hand, with
the defined meaning, and it remains defined or fixed. We only more or
less fill it out with examples. (It is a mechanism which we employ to-

---

[4] *Ethikoi charaktēres*, they were called by Diogenes Laertius, the earliest
extant writer of antiquity to refer to them. See *The Characters of Theophrastus*,
trans. R. C. Jebb (London, 1870).

[5] *Menander*, ed. F. G. Allinson (London: Loeb Classical Library, 1921), p. xiii.
Cf. Butcher, pp. 377–9.

[6] Cf. Maynard Mack, ed. *Joseph Andrews* (New York, 1948), pp. xiii–xiv.

ward some more complex overall end.) And this is partly because, just as Aristotle says, comedy deals with the inferior—and hence with a kind of human character which may at least be supposed to occur very readily in everyday life. The Aristotelian notion of the tragic protagonist as king or at least as man of eminence was complemented more explicitly, with an opposite notion for comedy, perhaps by Aristotle himself in a lost dialogue *On Poets*, perhaps by his pupil Theophrastus,[7] certainly by later theorists. "Imitatio vitae," Cicero was to call comedy, "speculum consuetudinis, imago veritatis." [8]

Tragedy and comedy show different, though understandably different, relations to the Aristotelian universal. One hinge of this unity and difference is *hamartia*. (The nearly synonymous *hamartēma* is the name of the comic flaw in Aristotle's definition of comedy.) Tragedy takes *hamartia* literally but magnifies its punishment—and is thus fearful and pitiful. Comedy distorts *hamartia* by caricature, reduces punishment to discomfiture and mortification, and is thus ridiculous. The victorious general Agamemnon returns to Argos with the captive princess Cassandra; Pyrgopolynices, the braggart captain, arrives at Ephesus with the captured slave girl Philocomasium. In the second half of the *Miles Gloriosus*, when Pyrgopolynices is tricked into attempting a marriage with a harlot supposed to be his next-door neighbor's wife, we are at least in the general region of the Oedipus transgression. But where the tragic heroes suffered death and self-inflicted blindness, the braggart soldier meets the catastrophe of an ignominious beating and responds by bellowing out a confession of his several errors.[9] In the fragmentary *Perikeiromenē* (*She Who Got Sheared*) of Menander, the girl describes the rape of her locks by the sailor lover with the verb *hubrizein*,[1] cognate with the tragic name (*hubris*) for man's eruption out of his proper sphere. These parallels are consistent with what has been observed as a broader degeneration during the fifth and fourth centuries in Greek concepts of character, from the *authadeia* which with Aeschylus was Promethean self-will to the mere "surliness" which adequately renders the term in the *Character* by Theophrastus,[2] from *eirōneia* as a philosophic strategem in the Platonic dia-

---

[7] Atkins I, 159; A. P. McMahon, "On the Second Book of Aristotle's *Poetics* and the Source of Theophrastus' Definition of Tragedy" and "Seven Questions on Aristotelian Definitions of Tragedy and Comedy," *Harvard Studies in Classical Philology*, XXVIII (1917), 1–46; XL (1929), esp. 100–3. The argument rests on statements made by the fourth-century grammarians Diomedes and Donatus.

[8] Cicero, *De Re Publica* IV, 13, quoted by Donatus, *Excerpta de Comoedia* (Atkins II, 38).

[9] Pyrgopolynices might also be profitably compared with the romantically successful bully fellow Hercules in the *Alcestis* of Euripides, or the mock Hercules Dionysus in the *Frogs* of Aristophanes.

[1] Act IV, l. 600 (Loeb *Menander*, p. 256): Glycera: [*eis allas koras*] *hubrizetō to loipon*.

[2] Cf. G. Gordon, "Theophrastus and His Imitators" in *English Literature and the Classics* (Oxford, 1912), p. 53.

logues and a gentlemanly form of modesty in Aristotle's *Ethics* to the
chicanery of the Theophrastan Dissembler: "A man of this sort (*ho de
eirōn*) approaches his enemy with professions of friendship; he flatters
those against whom he is plotting mischief; and he condoles with them
in the way of their calamity."

VI

THE division of Greek drama into comic and tragic and Aristotle's
corresponding theory would seem to represent a tension of principles
that extends into literature and life perhaps not so deeply as some recent
speculators have maintained, but deeply enough. We reduce the following table of mutually dependent "antinomic symbols" from Mr. Albert
Cook's *The Dark Voyage and the Golden Mean, A Philosophy of Comedy.*[3] Under one or the other of these two opposed but interdependent
headings we have nearly all that may be conceived in the realm of human interests.

TRAGEDY	COMEDY
The Wonderful	*The Probable*
Imagination	*Reason*
Ethics	*Manners*
The Individual	*Society*
The Extreme (Christianity)	*The Mean (Aristotle)*
Symbol	*Concept*
Death	*Politics, Sex*
Good and Evil	*Conformity or Expulsion*
The Handsome Actor	*The Ugly Actor*
The Pariah Artist	*The Diplomatic Artist*
Failure	*Success*
Soliloquy	*Aside*
The Superhuman	*The Subhuman (beast, machine)*
Aristocrat	*Bourgeois*
Paradox	*Contrast*

We venture to add this tentative thought: that the two sides of this interesting dichotomy may be more closely interdependent in literature
than in life—that a certain union of the two may well be near to the
center of whatever is universal in poetry.

Aristotle, by his formal analysis of the two dominant genres of Greek
literature, made a respectable effort to rebut Plato's arguments against
poetry and to answer the business-like and Rotarian questions of Socrates
in the *Ion*. The answer is perhaps not ironclad, but it has at least one
important virtue, namely, that it tends to shift the emphasis of inquiry

[3] Cambridge, Mass., 1949. Our table is selected and adapted from pp. 28 and
50–1.

away from what poetry may *say,* or tell us, in a practical or even in a philosophic sense, toward what poetry may embody or in itself *be.* And this the answer accomplishes through its *double* concern for the universal—that is, its concern both for what is imitated or reflected in the poem and for the poem itself as a form or kind of being in which the imitation is realized. As Aristotle's theory is a theory of imitation, it is a theory of reference (what the poem *is* never really escapes entanglement with what the poem *says*); it is a theory of a universal and an ideal in the field of reference, and this ideal tends to be the ethical man. Still this ideal is never quite that. The theory never quite says that the poetic worth of the imitation is to be decided directly in terms of the practical ideal. Whether poetry is something which charms (as Homer and the Thracians had said) or something which teaches (as Hesiod and the Boeotians said) [4] was an inherited issue which Aristotle met not head on but by the oblique device of saying that poetry is something which pleases us by being an image and by being at the same time very serious and very philosophic (*philosophōteron kai spoudaioteron*).

We conclude our account of Aristotle's debate with Plato by alluding to the spirited judgment of a modern French critic, the Abbé Henri Bremond in his *Prière et Poésie.* His first chapter, *"Platon et la Poésie Exilée,"* speaks well enough for present purposes in its title. From the second chapter, *"Aristote et la Poésie Dépoétisée,"* we attempt the following translation of an apologia put in the mouth of Aristotle.

> As for the meaning which is captured in a poem, though it may have been as it were divinely discovered through that *theia dunamis* of which professor Socrates tells us, it remains nevertheless intelligible and as a result definable. If a doctor is able to enumerate the parts of a human skeleton, it hardly follows that he is open to censure for not being interested in life. He follows his anatomical bent; I follow mine as logician. You profess to deplore the fact that I have put poetry under "the absolute yoke of reason." But it is not quite clear to me where you get that idea. That fantastic line about "sole reason," the first principle of all poetic beauty, is not to be found in my own writings so far as I know. . . . It is not as if I had overlooked, as you seem to suppose, that specific and ineffable quality which constitutes the poetic experience. It is simply that I am not concerned with it—unless in that famous statement of mine about catharsis [5]—a somewhat obscure expression, I admit, but one

[4] Atkins I, 80–1; W. C. Greene, "The Greek Criticism of Poetry" in *Perspectives of Criticism,* ed. Harry Levin (Cambridge, Mass., 1950), p. 21.

[5] As a matter of fact Aristotle makes some casual acknowledgements of poetic inspiration. In the *Poetics* (XVII) he calls one kind of poet *euphuēs* and another *manikos;* in the *Rhetoric* (III, 7) poetry is an inspired thing (*entheon hē poiēsis*).

from which they will someday derive a thoroughgoing mystical poetics.

And the Abbé's comment on this:

> He tells the truth. There is no metaphysic, either right or wrong, in his *Poetics*. There is no other heresy than that of silence—the most dangerous of all—Aristotle's sin of omission, his disappearing trick. He has not written a single sentence from which one might convict him of setting aside the traditional view of the poet's inspiration and identifying poetic knowledge with rational. But then he has not written a sentence either—except to be sure that about catharsis—from which one might even suspect the contrary. To remain silent is to consent. Aristotle has kept his silence—silence forever to be deplored—silence pregnant with catastrophe, pregnant, if I may so express myself, with Boileau.[6]

This seems the place for a candid assertion that our own view as theorists of poetry is something like that which Aristotle is made to confess. We argue that criticism, if it is to occur at all, must be like that. It must be rational and aim at definitions, whether it can or cannot quite achieve them. But what is left over and above definition, we argue furthermore, is still an objective quality of poems, knowable if indefinable, and distinguishable from that other realm, the dark well of mystery and inspiration [7]—which is the poet's alone. If these two areas, the knowable yet indefinable individuality of the poem, and the unknowable or incommunicable mystery of the poet's inspiration, are alleged to show limits to the critic's activity, we concede the point. The first area, the individuality of the poetic utterance, may tease the critic's ambition. He would conquer it if he could though this is not required of him. With the second, the inspiration, he is scarcely concerned.

---

[6] Henri Bremond, *Prière et Poésie* (Paris, 1926), Chapter II, translated by permission of Burns Oates & Washbourne Ltd., London.

[7] A more recent, and to the present time perhaps the largest and most brillant celebration of this "translucid spiritual night" is Jacques Maritain's *Creative Intuition in Art and Poetry* (New York: Pantheon Books, 1953). Mr. Maritain, so far as he would grant any significance at all to the concerns of the present narrative, would say that they are the concerns of "art," not of "poetry." There is a partial sense in which he would be perfectly right.

SUPPLEMENT

I connect the essential distinction between tragedy and comedy with two opposing impulses deeply rooted in human nature. Until we can find a way of reconciling the antinomy in our nature we are all torn between the desire to *find* ourselves and the desire to *lose* ourselves. It is on some such antithesis as this that Coleridge based his whole philosophy and in particular his theory of imagination.

We are impelled to preserve and accentuate and glory in our separate lives; we believe that every member of our species has his particular and distinct destiny; there are even atheists who cannot bring themselves to believe in the possibility of their own extinction. This natural pride of man and in man I believe to be the psychological foundation of tragedy. . . .

But if there is a proper human pride, there is also a proper human modesty; and the two are never, I think, far from each other. We cherish our separateness jealously; but we need also to merge it in the life of the world into which we were born, to mix with other people, to adjust our own wills and even our characters to the *milieu* in which by choice or necessity we live and to the general laws of nature. This second impulse is surely as healthy and strong as the other, and it is found in men of the most vigorous and robust character; Blake, for instance, cries in one of his most moving lines

"O why was I born with a different face?"

We cannot be satisfied with the mere assertion of our individuality; we must recognize a destiny other than our individual destinies: the *destiny of our race*. From one point of view every sparrow is infinitely important; from another the greatest man is completely unimportant. These two truths are complementary, and perhaps neither has much meaning without the other. This is one of the great paradoxes of the Christian religion; but one does not need to be a Christian to recognize its truth.

—L. J. Potts, *Comedy* (London, 1949), pp. 16–18, by permission of Hutchinson & Co. (Publishers) Limited, London

It may be said that whereas tragedy deals with the unusual but normal, comedy deals with the abnormal but not unusual. The abnormality of comic characters is not absolute; we should feel that they are capable of behaving normally if they would. But it is the main concern of the comic writer to discriminate between what is normal and abnormal in human behaviour; he is detached from his subject-matter in a sense in which other artists are not. He needs not merely a strong feeling for normality, but also a clear notion of it. It is therefore necessary for him to be in some measure a moral philosopher; for the norm is a philosophical concept. The usual, or average, is not; it can be calculated statistically from observed facts. But normality, like the cognate concepts of health and sanity, is not a fact, nor a complex of facts, nor even a simplification of facts; it is an idea, and exists only in the mind that has brought itself to bear on all the relevant facts. There is not one norm of human behaviour, but many: some of them widely divergent and even contradictory. Jane Austen's norm differs drastically in some respects from Chaucer's or Fielding's. But all comic writers must have a norm in view. To detect eccentricity you must have a centre: that is to say a consistent, if not consciously worked out, standard of character and conduct.

—L. J. Potts, *Comedy*, pp. 46–7

Greek tragedy is the tragedy of necessity: i.e., the feeling aroused in the spectator is "What a pity it had to be this way"; Christian tragedy is the tragedy of possibility, "What a pity it was this way when it might have been otherwise." . . . the hubris which is the flaw in the Greek hero's character is the illusion of a man who knows himself strong and believes that nothing can shake that strength, while the corresponding Christian sin of Pride is the illusion of a man who knows himself weak but believes he can by his own efforts transcend that weakness and become strong. . . .

A modern reader, accustomed to the tragedy of possibility, instinctively asks, "Where and when did he make the wrong choice?" and as instinctively answers, "He should not have listened to the prophecy in the first place, or, having done so, then he should never have struck the old man or anyone else, and should never have married Jocasta or anyone else." But such thoughts would never have occurred to Sophocles or his audience. Macbeth and Captain Ahab are wrong to listen to the prophecies about them, because they are equivocal, and each reads into his a possibility he is wrong to desire; the prophecy Oedipus hears is not only not unequivocal but something he is right to wish to avoid. When he kills the old man he feels no guilt, neither is he expected to feel any, and when he marries Jocasta there is nothing the matter with the relation as such. It is only when it turns out that, as a matter of fact, the former was his father and the latter is his mother that the guilt begins. . . .

Other Greek heroes are faced with the tragic choice between two evils: Agamemnon must either sacrifice his daughter or fail in his duty to the Greek Army; Antigone must be false either to her loyalty to her brother or to her loyalty to her city.

The tragic situation, of learning that one is a criminal or of being forced to become one, is not created by the flaw in the hero's character, but is sent him by the gods as a punishment for having such a flaw.

The pessimistic conclusion that underlies Greek tragedy seems to be this: that if one is a hero, i.e., an exceptional individual, one must be guilty of hubris and be punished by a tragic fate; the only alternative and not one a person can choose for himself is to be a member of the chorus, i.e., one of the average mass; to be both exceptional and good is impossible.

How does "Moby Dick" compare with this?

The hero, Captain Ahab, far from being exceptionally fortunate, is at the beginning, what in a Greek tragedy he could only be at the end, exceptionally unfortunate. He is already the victim of what the modern newspaper, which is Greek in this respect, would call a tragedy; a whale has bitten off his leg. What to the Greeks could only have been a punishment for sin is here a temptation to sin, an opportunity to choose; by making the wrong choice and continuing to make it, Ahab punishes himself.

—W. H. Auden, "The Christian Tragic Hero," *The New York Times Book Review*, December 16, 1945, p. 1, by permission of the author and *The New York Times*

It is . . . a strange and a rather embarrassing phenomenon that precisely the centuries which were thoroughly unconversant with such an enthusiastic and flying humanism produced great tragedy; while precisely those periods that had dedicated themselves entirely and without reserve to the possibility of progress and social surge failed again and again to hit off the true tragic note. Indeed, as one courses through these readings and commentaries of a half-generation ago on modern tragedy, one cannot quite get rid of the constant suspicion that *all* the evidence had been tampered with, subtly, better still, unconsciously. The facts had been rather badly twisted, so badly that as a consequence we are now in rapid danger of having our sense of the tragic completely perverted. The truth of the matter comes down to this: that it was our modern tragic literature and theory that alone inserted these strange concepts of exaltation and triumph (and did not write tragedy); while in other periods these notions have been remarkable for their absence, indeed for their rejection (yet tragedy was written). And though this writer hesitates to broach so scandalous a thesis, yet he cannot contain the suspicion that it was exactly this heresy of exaltation, and all the splendid adjectives out of which it was compounded, that was partly responsible in our times for our very great failure in the theater. . . .

We have but to try anything mightily and see what happens. In the end we come back to the decision of everyone of the great tragedies that, left to itself, the human will at the very height of its straining stands broken and defeated. . . . If, for example, we should picture the fact of defeat in terms of the metrical pattern of a production of the *Oedipus*, it should be in terms of the confident forward iambics of a machine of perfect dignity that bit by bit begins to disintegrate, in the end loses all sense of an ictus in the pattering, stuttering rows of consecutive short-syllabled feet of a blinded man, and in the very end does not even have the energy to complete the final iamb. It hangs in the air and there is nothing left. There is neither room nor energy for those artificial endings of defiance and mystical victory that we love to tack on to our tragedies. These things are lies, at least in the sense that there is no evidence for their possibility or validity. They are completely outside the *human* story and neither history nor theology can give any ground for them.

—William F. Lynch, "Confusion in Our Theater," *Thought, Fordham University Quarterly*, XXVI (Autumn, 1951), 346, 349, by permission of the editors of *Thought*

THE VERBAL MEDIUM: PLATO AND ARISTOTLE

§ *The verbal medium, "rhetoric" as verbal artifice, Sicilian
rhetoricians—II. Plato's* Phaedrus: *love, beauty, rhetoric,
the speech of Lysias (a bad speech badly written), the
mock speech of Socrates (style without truth), second
speech of Socrates (eloquent truth)—III. theoretical discussion by Socrates: dialectic,* psuchagogia, *Socratic ethic,
rhetoric as an ignorant "knack," rhetorical technicalities,
written vs. spoken words—IV. Isocrates, epideictic rhetoric, a florid* paideia—*V. Aristotle's* Rhetoric: *a practical
defence, rhetoric, dialectic, and the probable, ethical and
emotive arguments, verbal style, something superficial yet
significant, clarity, propriety, and the ornate, metaphor,
related figures—VI. Isocrates again, the power of words,
the Logos, grammar, dialecticians vs. rhetoricians, Ciceronian retrospect* §

W E HAVE BEEN TALKING ABOUT POETIC IMITATION AS IF IT WERE
a straight copy of its objects, or a vision of them through
plate glass; and in so doing we have minimized the possibility
of talking about the poem rather than about its objects, about what it
may *be* rather than about what it may *say*. In our first three chapters
we have heard a debate conducted upon grounds of maximum advantage
to the Platonic moral cause. Let us return now to the fact that Aristotle
treated plot, character, and thought—the *content* of drama—as only
some of its elements. Let us recall that he treated also, by a method of
separation which may have seemed to us at first glance rather crude,
two elements which he called the *medium*—language and music—and
that there was even another element which he called the *manner*—the
stage spectacle. Among these three elements, language stands out as a

thing basic to all literature. Language is an inevitable concern of literary criticism. And this fact invites us to canvass a part of ancient critical history which for want of a better name we shall call *Rhetoric*.

It is a commonplace of recent critical history to observe that ancient rhetoric, from its formal beginning near the end of the fifth century B.C. to its second sophistication in the early Christian centuries, was basically a practical art, concerned, that is, with the business of persuading judges in law courts, senators in assemblies, and congregations in churches. The counter facts which we insist on here are that this legal or political art came in Roman times to be practically equivalent to higher education, and that from first to last it dwelt characteristically upon verbal artifice. It was in this art rather than in that of poetics that words were most often deliberately studied, and its examples were drawn indiscriminately from poetry and prose. "The art of contention in speech," says Socrates in the *Phaedrus*,

> is not confined to courts and political gatherings, but apparently, if it is an art at all, it would be one and the same in all kinds of speaking, the art by which a man will be able to produce a resemblance between all things between which it can be produced.—261 [1]

The term *rhetoric* has, and has had from early times, the highly useful secondary sense: *a study of how words work*. It is primarily in this sense that we shall use the term throughout this book.

Corax and Tisias were Sicilian sophists who flourished about fifty years before the birth of Aristotle. They taught legal rhetoric in Syracuse and wrote the earliest recorded treatises on the art, but these have perished. One of their successors was Gorgias of Leontini, who came to Athens on an embassy in 427 and remained to instruct and fascinate the generation of young intellectuals and aesthetes portrayed in the *Clouds* of Aristophanes. A later Sicilian Greek historian has left this account of the matter:

> On arriving at Athens and being allowed to address the people, he [Gorgias] spoke on the theme of federation in a style of such exotic artifice that he cast a spell over his audience, euphuistically inclined as they were and devoted to the ideal of eloquence. He was the first to use the strikingly artificial figures of antithesis, isocolon, parison, homoeoteleuton, and sundry other embellishments of this kind, which came at that time as admired

[1] With one exception, indicated in a note, quotations from Plato's *Phaedrus* in this chapter are reprinted by permission of the publishers from the translation of H. N. Fowler, *Plato . . . Euthyphro, Apology, Crito, Phaedo, Phaedrus*, 1938, Loeb Classical Library, Cambridge, Mass.: Harvard University Press.

novelties, though now they seem rather ridiculously affected and precious.[2]

Gorgias and a fellow rhetorician Polus are the antagonists of Socrates in an early and lengthy Platonic attack on rhetoric, the dialogue entitled *Gorgias;* and the same rhetorical school is the subject of criticism in the mature, highly sophisticated and dramatic *Phaedrus,* a document which is not only the earliest substantial counter-rhetoric now surviving but is still one of the most formidable in all rhetorical history.

II

THE *Phaedrus* contains some of the best-known Platonic passages on love and beauty—ones which we have alluded to in an earlier chapter —most notably the illustrative oration by Socrates built on the elaborate allegory of the soul or intellective principle as charioteer, with difficulty driving his two horses, a noble steed of the higher desires and a balky beast of the lower passions, toward the empyreal sphere of divine forms. Classical scholars have disagreed as to whether this main motif of the dialogue shows sufficient relevance to an equally conspicuous second motif—an examination of the art of rhetoric. The relevance between the two motifs (and hence the unity of the whole dialogue) actually seems very close. It is the relevance of ideal illustration to a theory of an art ideally conceived. A main assumption of the whole dialogue is the Socratic principle that virtue is knowledge, and, springing from this, the main argument is that a worthy rhetoric—one aimed at the highest good—will be, not a way of fooling people in law courts, but an approach to knowledge, or an embodiment of it—a kind of inspired philosophy. The theme of love and beauty, which Plato believed to be the only adequate theme of philosophy, was the only one which he could have employed for the full illustration of the thesis.

The argument begins adroitly with an enthusiastic reading by Phaedrus, and a cool analysis by Socrates, of a shoddy speech—either an actual speech of the orator Lysias or a parody—an academic invective against ardent lovers.[3] The objections of Socrates are two: that the speech is wrongheaded (though he ironically professes not to urge this) and that its style is confused. Some sort of connection between these two facts is perhaps a main innuendo.

> SOCRATES: How now? Are you and I to praise the speech because the author has said what was called for, or is the sole

[2] Diodorus Siculus, *Historical Library* XII, 53.
[3] The homosexual meaning alluded to in our first chapter is to be assumed throughout this discussion.

point whether the expressions, taken singly, are clear, compact, and finely turned? If we must judge it by the substance, I readily give way to your opinion; the substance because of my ineptitude, escaped me. I paid attention to the rhetoric of it only, and this I doubted whether Lysias himself would consider adequate. If you will let me say so, Phaedrus, it seemed to me he said the same things over twice or thrice, perhaps because he wasn't very well supplied with things to say on a given subject, or perhaps he didn't bother about a point like that. And then it seemed to me that he was showing off in youthful fashion how well he could say the same thing over in two different ways.

PHAEDRUS: Nonsense, Socrates! What you call repetition is the peculiar merit of the speech. . . .[4]

The speech of Lysias is in fact a tediously overlapping enumeration of reasons against the eager lover and in favor of the person who is more calculating in his approach, or, as he is called, the "non-lover." At a later point in the argument (264) Socrates likens it to an inscription that was said to appear on the tomb of Midas the Phrygian. Any line of it could be put first or last.

> A bronze maiden am I; and I am placed upon the tomb of
>   Midas.
> So long as water runs and tall trees put forth leaves,
> Remaining in this very spot upon a much lamented tomb,
> I shall declare to passers by that Midas is buried here.

Some of the distortions of style which the basically careless structure of thought has forced upon the writer—the "two different ways" of saying the same thing to which Socrates alluded—may be more apparent in the Greek than in English translations where efforts of translators to tidy up have missed the point.

> For lovers repent (*ekeinois . . . metamelei*) of the kindnesses
> they have done when their passion ceases; but there is no time
> when non-lovers naturally repent (*metagnōnai prosēkei*).—231

Here the translator's logical repetition of *repent* covers up the pointless "elegant variation" of the Greek. The following example is more faithful to the Greek text.

> And besides, lovers consider the *injury they have done to their
> own concerns* on account of their love, and the benefits they
> have conferred, and they add *the trouble they have had*, . . . ;

[4] *Phaedrus* 234–5. We quote the translation by Professor Lane Cooper, *Phaedrus, Ion, Gorgias* (London, 1938), p. 15, by permission of the Oxford University Press, Inc., New York.

but non-lovers cannot aver *neglect of their own affairs* because
of their condition, nor can they take account of the *pains they
have been at in the past.*—231

The italicized phrases tease a very simple meaning into coy but drab
variations. The gist of the matter is that this is a bad speech, and that
it is badly written. And both these things are true, implies Socrates,
because the author does not know what he is talking about.

The next step in the dramatically conceived argument is accomplished by a second speech on the same theme—one delivered by Socrates, *ex tempore*, with his head wrapped up for shame, in the character
of a crafty lover who tries to gain favors by pretending to be a non-
lover. It is a better speech than the first, because it begins with a definition of love (as desire) and proceeds, in a style which is at least orderly, to expound the evil of being ruled by that force. Socrates even
makes a pretense of being in a kind of dithyrambic frenzy and winds
up his speech with a hexameter.[5] But the whole argument is negative,
at the expense of the lover, and stops without saying a word in actual
favor of the non-lover—because, of course, nothing can be said in his
favor. Whereas the first speech and the critique of it has suggested the
union or even identity of bad, ignorant thinking and bad style, the second
speech exhibits the severe handicap imposed upon himself by the person
who in a sense knows the truth but who pretends not to know it—
and leads "his hearers on with sportive words" (262).

Almost immediately Socrates is stricken with remorse at having
participated in a blasphemy and, in the manner of a man who not only
knows the truth but is inspired to speak in its defence, launches into
his palinode, the prolonged and eloquent allegorical discourse upon
love, beauty, and immortality to which we have already alluded. Despite
its enthusiasm and lavish invention, the speech is well ordered, beginning with a fourfold celebration of *mania* (244-245) or inspired madness and pursuing the theme of the soul's immortality in the figure
of the charioteer and his two horses. This figure itself might be taken
as a symbol of orderly composition and division.

The rhetorical significance of the three speeches on love becomes
unmistakable in the comparison of their merits and the theoretical discussion which follows.

But I do think you will agree to this, that every discourse must
be organised, like a living being, with a body of its own, as it
were, so as not to be headless or footless, but to have a middle
and members, composed in fitting relation to each other and to
the whole.—264

[5] *Phaedrus* 238, 241. Aristotle is apparently thinking of these passages when in
his *Rhetoric* (III, 7) he alludes to the ironic use of emotive language in the *Phaedrus*.

The second speech of Socrates is described apologetically as figurative, plausible, perhaps expressive of some truth—a "sportive jest."

> . . . but in these chance utterances were involved two principles, the essence of which it would be gratifying to learn, if art could teach it.
>
> PHAEDRUS: What principles?
>
> SOCRATES: That of perceiving and bringing together in one idea the scattered particulars, that one may make clear by definition the particular thing which he wishes to explain; just as now, in speaking of love, we said what he is and defined it whether well or ill. Certainly by this means the discourse acquired clearness and consistency.
>
> PHAEDRUS: And what is the other principle, Socrates?
>
> SOCRATES: That of dividing things by classes; where the natural joints are, and not trying to break any part, after the manner of a bad carver.—265.
>
> Now I myself, Phaedrus, am a lover of these processes of division and bringing together, as aids to speech and thought; and if I think any other man is able to see things that can naturally be collected into one and divided into many, him I follow after and "walk in his footsteps as if he were a god." And whether the name I give to those who can do this is right or wrong, God knows, but I have called them hitherto dialecticians.—266

In short, rhetoric, so far as it is anything at all but a sham, is philosophy. To be able to define and divide, the rhetorician has to be able to think; he has to know the truth. There would seem to be some hedging on the part of Plato in this dialogue—as to whether the truth to be known is the cognitive content, the doctrine, about which the rhetorician would persuade his hearers, or another kind of truth, the psychological truth about their individual temperaments, which he must know if his discourse is to be a successfully administered persuasion (*psuchagōgia*).—271.

> He must understand the nature of the soul, must find out the the class of speech adapted to each nature, and must arrange and adorn his discourse accordingly, offering to the complex soul elaborate and harmonious discourses, and simple tales to the simple soul.—277.

But the emphasis of the dialogue is very largely upon the question *what* is to be said, not upon the question *to whom*, and the chief distinction is between the politico-legal rhetorician, who prefers "what seems to be true," or what is probable, to actual truth, and the philosophic rhetorician, who labors "not for the sake of speaking and acting before men, but that he may be able to speak and to do everything, so far as possible, in a manner pleasing to the gods." (273) In short, the main distinction is between professional rhetoricians as they are actually found to be, and the ideal rhetorician as he may be conceived to be. And here the Socratic identification of virtue with knowledge works relentlessly. If he who knows what is right will always do it, then he who does wrong (a sophistical rhetorician who uses his "art" to work evil) cannot know the right—or at least the so-called "art" by which he works evil cannot be a way of knowing it. As in the *Ion* the retreat was ironically from poetry as an art or form of knowledge to poetry as divine insanity (and indeed the same retreat occurs in the *Phaedrus* on several planes of irony and seriousness), so the specific resort imputed to rhetoric (a close relative of poetry) is from artful knowledge to the cheapness of a knack or trick (*tribē*). That is the only way to explain its undoubtedly effective, but subversive, performance.

> I seem, as it were, to hear some arguments approaching and protesting that . . . ["the art of speaking"] is lying and is not an art, but a craft devoid of art (*hoti pseudetai kai ouk esti technē all' atechnos tribē*). A real art of speaking . . . which does not seize hold of truth, does not exist and never will.—260

This explanation had been given a fancier (and no doubt to the rhetoricians an even more exasperating) shape in the earlier *Gorgias*, where the same key concept, *tribē* or knack, is applied in a four-point analogy. As the cheap knack of *cookery* is to the art of *gymnastic* in building health, and as *cosmetic* is to *medicine* in repairing health, so in the field of politics, *sophistic* is the meretricious rival of *legislation*, and *rhetoric* is that of *jurisprudence*.

At one place in the *Phaedrus* (267), Socrates makes a scornful review of contemporary rhetoricians and the niceties of their art (*ta kompsa tēs technēs*): Theodorus of Byzantium, with his introduction, narrative, testimony, proofs, probability, confirmation and further confirmation, refutation and further refutation; the "illustrious Parian" Evenus, with his covert allusion, indirect praises (*parepainoi*), and indirect censures (*parapsogoi*); Gorgias and Tisias, who make small things seem great and great things small, and new things old and old things new, and who invented conciseness (*suntomia logōn*) and measureless length on all subjects (*apeira mēkē peri pantōn*); Prodicus and Hippias of Elis; Polus, with his duplication (*diplasiologia*), sententiousness (*gnōmologia*), and figurativeness (*eikonologia*); Licymnius, with his beautiful diction (*euepeia*); Protagoras, with his correctness of diction (*orthoepeia*); the "mighty Calcedonian" Thrasymachus, with his genius for rousing audiences to wrath and for soothing them again, for devising or for refuting calumnies on any grounds whatsoever. On one piece of technique, that of summarizing a speech at the end, all seem to be agreed, though some call it recapitulation (*epanodos*), others something else. This is a section of the *Phaedrus* which might be transplanted almost verbatim into Benedetto Croce's expressionistic history of *Aesthetic*.

The ground of Plato's objection to rhetoric may be perhaps most deeply understood, near the end of the *Phaedrus*, in a distinction between written and spoken words, a distinction which is the more relevant to the argument because of the fact that Attic oratory made no pretense of being *ex tempore*. The written word, urges Socrates, is a static thing useful only to tell people what they already know, an amusement, a reminder for the forgetfulness of old age. But the spoken word is the true, vital, and dialectic word—it is written in the mind of the hearer and is able to defend itself in the process of question and answer.

> But the man who thinks that in the written word there is necessarily much that is playful, and that no written discourse, whether in metre or in prose, deserves to be treated very seriously (and this applies also to the recitations of the rhapsodes, delivered to sway people's minds, without opportunity for questioning and teaching), but that the best of them really serve only to remind us of what we know; and who thinks that only in words about justice and beauty and goodness spoken by teachers for the sake of instruction and really written in a soul is clearness and perfection and serious value, that such words should be considered the speaker's own legitimate offspring, first the word within himself, if it be found there, and secondly its descendants or brothers which may have sprung up in worthy manner in the souls of others, and who pays no attention to the other words,—that man, Phaedrus, is likely to be such as you and I might pray that we ourselves may become.
> —277–8 [6]

In this clear confirmation of the anti-mimetic doctrine of the *Republic*, we may see that in theory at least (or at least in this dialogue) Plato prefers the object imitated in his dialogues, the actual conversations as they may be supposed to have taken place, to his own highly artful or poetic embodiment of them in fixed words. And this may remind us that poetic quality does indeed reside in fixity, or determinacy, of words. Not only meter and rhyme and all the minute effects of a lyric but the

[6] Cf. Atkins, I, 148 on the niceties possible in written style and on the "deliberative" oratorical style as shadow-painting (*skiagraphia*).

dialogue and succession of scenes in a tragedy, the whole economy and precision of poetic power in words, depend on choice, limitation, and fixation, and hence are opposed to the fluid character of dialectic or of the bull session—though the latter, in virtue of its capacity to shift words, correct, repeat, rephrase, paraphrase, and in general adjust itself to the exigencies of debate, may in a sense fit closer to the truth of the matter which is discussed.

IV

IT WAS no less against literary than against oratorical interests that Plato was fighting. The close alliance of rhetoric and poetry as his enemies, seen more than once in the *Phaedrus*,[7] is suggested a final time in a closing allusion to the rhetorician Isocrates.

> I think he has a nature above the speeches of Lysias and possesses a nobler character; so that I should not be surprised if, as he grows older, he should so excel in his present studies that all who have ever treated of rhetoric shall seem less than children; and I suspect that these studies will not satisfy him, but a more divine impulse will lead him to greater things; for my friend, something of philosophy is inborn in his mind.—279

The fictional date of the dialogue is about 410 B.C., when Isocrates, the pupil of Gorgias, was making his first appearance on the scene. But the dialogue was written perhaps as late as 370,[8] at a time when Isocrates was the most eminent and affluent teacher of rhetoric at Athens and hence the chief rhetorical antagonist of the Platonic school. The *Art of Rhetoric* which Isocrates wrote survives only in a few fragments. But from several of his discourses, especially that *Against the Sophists* and the *Antidosis*, which deal with education—and from the style itself of his writing—we get an idea of the kind of campaign which he waged against law-court and assembly rhetoric and the debased form of ethical dialectic which he calls "eristic." Although he discountenanced the academic exercise on mythological topics or on paradoxical themes such as those affected by Gorgias and Protagoras—"that we cannot lie," or "that nothing exists"—or on such anticipations of Swift's broomstick as "humble bees" or "salt," the theory of Isocrates was literary rather than practically oratorical. The form of speech which he chiefly sponsored was the epideictic (the encomiastic or the invective declamation), and this was an oratory that had moved as far as possible away from the give and take of dialectic toward the fixity of a set piece or essay—

[7] See for instance, 258, 261.
[8] R. Hackforth, *Plato's Phaedrus* (Cambridge, 1952), pp. 3–8.

albeit an essay that would seem by our standards a rather florid one. The epideictic style, Aristotle would say in his *Rhetoric* (III, 12), is especially suited to written compositions; it aims at being read. Isocrates hoped that his *Antidosis* would prove a "monument more noble than statues of bronze." The rhetoric of Isocrates was a scheme of general education (*paideia*) which aimed at a liberal union of philosophy and persuasion, an understanding of elevated and large political topics, and withal an artistic verbal style, imaginative (*poiētikos*) and diverse. The "thoughts" of the graduate rhetorician were to be not only "dignified and original" but "adorned with a number of striking figures." What was desired was a kind of poetic prose oratory, or literary prose, something which would serve not only for statesmen but for critics of poetry, for historians, for writers of panegyric. Isocrates entertained a highly integrated view of life and letters; he conceived the former as greatly in need of the latter. The sum of his teaching was a genial, flowery, belletristic kind of humanism.[9]

V

THIS was one kind of answer both to the Sophists and to Plato. A rhetorician of later antiquity [1] reports that Aristotle's systematic treatise on the question, his *Rhetoric* in three books, was the outcome of a feud with Isocrates. The story says that during his first residence in Athens (367–347 B.C.) Aristotle sneered at the ideas of Isocrates and the method of their dissemination in bundles of speeches hawked by the booksellers. Yet the difference between the two as theorists of rhetoric is not so profound. Aristotle takes more examples from the orations of Isocrates than from the works of any other author. The difference between them might be summed up, without great distortion, in the statement that Aristotle, looking on rhetoric in a far more utilitarian way than Isocrates, is somewhat closer to being sophistical; as a philosopher, however, as a teacher of rhetoric in Plato's Academy, he is at the same time more systematic than Isocrates. The latter virtue is the one by which Aristotle gains the advantage of having his ideas preserved not in speeches but in a treatise.[2]

"Do you think we have reproached the art of speaking too harshly?" asks Socrates in the *Phaedrus*. "Perhaps she might say:

'Why do you talk such nonsense, you strange men? I do not compel anyone to learn to speak without knowing the truth,

[9] See Atkins, I, 124–8, 148, 154–5.
[1] Dionysius of Halicarnassus, *On Isocrates* 18; Atkins, I, 133.
[2] Aristotle's *Theodectia*, on style, and other works on rhetoric are lost. Atkins, I, 133, 135, 136.

but if my advice is of any value, he learns that first and then acquires me. So what I claim is this, that without my help the knowledge of the truth does not give the art of persuasion.'—260

It would not be unfair to say that Plato has here anticipated the gist of Aristotle's doctrine. "What makes the sophist," says Aristotle, "is not skill in argument, but [defect of] moral purpose." [3]

Aristotle's *Rhetoric* opens with the statement: "Rhetoric is a counterpart of dialectic." But the term *dialectic* has for Aristotle a softer meaning than for Plato—the meaning of a conversationally plausible inquiry rather than of a metaphysically compelling demonstration. Dialectic is a comfortable neighbor to rhetoric, on the higher side. Both dialectic and its practical counterpart, rhetoric, enjoy a kind of cushioning from the severity of theoretical science (mathematics, physics, metaphysics). Dialectic is the argumentative technique of the social, practical, deliberative and "alternative" sciences (ethics and politics). "It is the mark of an educated man" says Aristotle in his *Ethics*, "to look for precision in each class of things just so far as the nature of the subject admits; it is . . . equally foolish to accept probable reasoning from a mathematician and to demand from a rhetorician scientific proofs." [4]

Even that much would have been enough to protect rhetoric from the full brunt of the Platonic inquisition. But Aristotle does more. There is a moment in the first chapter of Book I when he seems bent on treating rhetoric rather rigorously within the limits of its probable arguments (its "examples" and "enthymemes"). [5] "Proofs," he says, "are the only things in . . . [rhetoric] that come within the province of art." And he is severe upon the previous compilers of handbooks who have devoted their attention chiefly to methods of arousing prejudice. Nevertheless, the argument begins to change even in the same chapter; there is a disposition to talk more about persuasion than about proof. The truth may be the truth, but it may need help before it is accepted. Not all persons are easy to persuade by reason. The orator should be able to prove opposites—like a logician—not for the sake of doing this,

---

[3] *Ho gar sophistikos ouk en tē dunamei all' en tē proairesei* (*Rhetoric*, I, 1).

[4] *Nicomachean Ethics* I, 3.

[5] The term "enthymeme" was used by Aristotle's successors, as it is by modern logicians, to refer to the elliptical syllogism. But for Aristotle, in his *Rhetoric* and in his logical writings, "enthymeme" is the name of the rhetorical syllogism, which is a *probable* argument for a *particular* conclusion. The enthymeme is thus distinguishable from two other kinds of syllogism, the dialectic syllogism, which is a probable argument for a general conclusion, and the apodeictic or scientific syllogism, which is a certain argument for a universal conclusion. See J. H. Freese, *Aristotle . . . the "Art" of Rhetoric* (London: Loeb Classical Library, 1939), p. 474, Glossary, s.v. *Dialektikē;* James H. McBurney, "Some Recent Interpretations of the Aristotelian Enthymeme," *Papers of the Michigan Academy of Science, Arts and Letters,* XXI (Ann Arbor, 1936), 489–500.

but just for understanding. All good things except virtue itself may be abused. The function of rhetoric is not so much to persuade as to find out the existing means of persuasion. Thus runs what would seem to be almost the dialogue of Aristotle with his own conscience, as he moves toward the empirical and anti-Platonic procedure of justifying rhetoric as it is found in fact to be. The second chapter begins by "defining rhetoric anew." "Rhetoric then may be defined as the faculty of discovering the possible means of persuasion in reference to any subject whatever." And we learn in this chapter that there are no fewer than four kinds of "artificial proof" [6] or means of persuasion: (1) the ethical or those depending on the moral character of the orator himself —by which he elicits confidence in himself; (2) the affective or those which appeal to the emotions of the audience (It was only the *exclusive* use of such proofs to which I alluded disparagingly in my first chapter, he explains); (3) valid arguments, which tend to establish the truth of whatever we are maintaining; and (4) apparent arguments, which only seem to establish it. The first two books of Aristotle's *Rhetoric* do in fact proceed in that pattern, the first Book telling about materials, or areas of argumentative probability, the second Book giving us mainly the psychology of good relations between speaker and audience. Aristotle has put a four-layered mattress between rhetoric and the inexorable or scientific truth—two of the layers being psychological, that is, relating to the character and feelings of the speaker and audience, one, the layer of probable cognitive arguments being at least nonscientific, and the fourth, the layer of apparent arguments, being feathered with actual deception. Aristotle thus defends rhetoric on approximately the same grounds as those on which Plato condemns it.

These Aristotelian graduations away from the strictness of scientific demonstration are not the immediate stuff for a rhetoric of verbal surface. But they do provide the underlying contour of such a rhetoric. They enable or make plausible a fifth and a sixth graduation—verbal style (*lexis*) and structure or architecture (*taxis*), the subjects of Aristotle's third book. About Aristotle's conception of *taxis* Plato could not have complained, though he might have related this (the organic order, beginning, middle, and end named in the *Phaedrus*) more intimately to "dialectic." But *lexis* is the apex and epitome of the difference between Plato and Aristotle as rhetoricians, and not so much the details of what Aristotle said about *lexis* as the very fact that he thought it reasonable to devote twelve chapters to the topic.

"We have therefore next to speak of style; for it is not sufficient to know what one ought to say,—but one must also know how to say it, and this largely contributes to making the speech appear of a certain

---

[6] I.e., artful, as distinguished from the inartificial or ready-made, such as witnesses, tortures, contracts.

character" (III, 1). It is almost as if this matter of style should be grouped with the newly acknowledged and even more external art of delivery (a kind of acting, *hupokrisis*), a thing that has to be conceded, not as right but as necessary, owing to the corruption of politicians and judges. Just a little more can be said for style:

> . . . it does make a difference, for the purpose of making a thing clear, to speak in this or that manner; still, the difference is not so very great, . . . all these things are mere outward show for pleasing the hearer; wherefore no one teaches geometry in this way.[7] III, 1

It is a cautiously divided account of style, giving due recognition to clarity and purity (*esti d' archē tēs lexeōs to hellēnizein*—the first principle of style is to use good Greek [8]) and in general to propriety, but at the same time showing considerable respect for the elevated and ornate, for a certain strangeness or departure from the ordinary which (like a foreigner among our fellow citizens) appears more distinguished (III, 2 and 5).

One of the most interesting technical features [9] of the discussion is a marked concern for metaphor. The section of his *Poetics* (Chs. XXI–XXIV) devoted to the element of tragedy which Aristotle calls diction or style, *lexis*, is mentioned four times in the first two chapters of Book III of the *Rhetoric*. If we turn back to the *Poetics*, we find the often-quoted statement that to be a master of metaphor is the greatest poetic gift, because metaphor shows an eye for resemblances, and metaphor cannot be learnt from anyone else.[1] We find also the definition: "Metaphor consists in assigning to a thing the name of something else," and the four classes of metaphoric reference: from genus to species, from species to genus, from species to species, and by propor-

---

[7] He continues: ". . . . written speeches owe their effect not so much to the sense as to the style. The poets, as was natural, were the first to give an impulse to style; for words are imitations, and the voice also, which of all our parts is best adapted for imitation, was ready to hand; thus the arts of the rhapsodists, actors, and others, were fashioned. And as the poets, although their utterances were devoid of sense, appeared to have gained their reputation through their style, it was a poetical style that first came into being, as that of Gorgias." In the *Poetics* (XXIV) appears the rather frigid statement: "The diction should be elaborated in the pauses of the action, where there is no expression of character and thought. For . . . character and thought are merely obscured by a diction that is over brilliant."

[8] Under this head comes a censure of ambiguity (*amphiboloi*), III, 5.

[9] The statements in III, 8 that prose should have rhythm but not meter (*rhythmon dei echein tōn logōn, metron de mē*) and that the best rhythm for prose is the paeonic, are Aristotle's attempt to reconcile the Pythagorean and Platonic doctrine that number confers order and limit (see the literary application in *Philebus* 23) with the fact that the "rhythm" or movement of good prose is not really a matter of number or measure.

[1] A thought repeated in *Rhetoric* III, 2.

tion.[2] Somewhat more specific, if miscellaneous, remarks on the same subject appear in the *Rhetoric*. "It is metaphor above all that gives perspicuity, pleasure, and a foreign air" (III, 2). "It must be appropriate and not far-fetched," but not too obvious either (III, 11). It can make things look either better or worse—as when a pirate calls himself a "purveyor" or an actor calls himself an artist, or someone else calls the actor a flatterer of Dionysus. A metaphor is like a riddle. Metaphors should mostly be "derived from things that are beautiful." "It does make a difference, for instance, whether one says 'rosy-fingered morn,' rather than 'purple-fingered,' or, what is still worse, 'red-fingered'" (III, 2). A climax to these obiter dicta and to the whole treatment of *lexis* occurs in Chapters 10 and 11, where metaphor is joined with figures of parallel sound and sense and with various verbal deceptions or jokes shading into paronomasia or pun.

> "And he strode on, under his feet—chilblains," whereas the hearer thought he was going to say "sandals."

> The more special qualities the expression possesses, the smarter it appears; for instance, if the words contain a metaphor, and a metaphor of a special kind, antithesis, and equality of clauses, and actuality.

"Actuality" or vividness (*energeia*) [3] is perhaps better taken as a term for summing up the effect of rhetorical figures than as a name for another figure on the same footing. But we may say that Aristotle has here very shrewdly observed a close relation among rhetorical features which are not always or easily seen as so closely related—the logic of parallel and distinction, the apparently alien pun or trick with sounds, and mediating these extremes the imaginative force of metaphor. He has thus come not far from supplying an accurate formula for a long tradition of poetical wit.

> Here Britain's statesmen oft the fall foredoom
> Of foreign Tyrants and of Nymphs at home;
> Here thou, great ANNA! whom three realms obey,
> Dost sometimes counsel take—and sometimes Tea.

---

[2] Proportion is defined in *Ethics* V, 3 as "an equality of ratios, implying four terms at least." See *Rhetoric* III, 4: "If the goblet is the shield of Dionysus, then the shield may properly be called the goblet of Ares."

[3] Roman rhetoricians (Dionysius of Halicarnassus, *De Lysia*, VII; Longinus, *Peri Hupsous*, XV; Quintilian, *Institutio Oratoria* VIII, 3, 62) use the term *enargeia* in approximately the same sense. Cf. W. Rhys Roberts, *Longinus on the Sublime* (Cambridge, 1935), pp. 197–8.

VI

THE important thing about both Aristotle and Isocrates as rhetoricians is, in brief, that they affirm the power of the word—Aristotle the more systematically and analytically, Isocrates the more eloquently. This is the point at which to make a brief return to Isocrates for the sake of introducing some of his enthusiastic conceptions. According to Isocrates eloquence is creative process (*poiētikon pragma*), the source of civilization, of laws and arts, and of most other human blessings, the mark which distinguishes men from the brutes, the instrument and test of wisdom. It is the adorner and transformer of experience, making old things new and new things old, the big little and the little big. It is an expression of intelligence, a reflection of character, an outward image of a true and virtuous soul (*psuchēs agathēs kai pistēs eidōlon*).[4] The rhetorical doctrine made current by Isocrates had been heard before from sophists and much earlier had had a more lyric orientation, as in the myth of Orpheus taming savage men and beasts by his music, and that of Amphion charming stones with his poetry and building the Theban walls.[5] It had been aligned with such verbal and poetic interests as the allegorical interpretation of Homer rejected by Plato in Book III of the *Republic* or the semi-facetious etymological reasoning about the right sense of words, the natural relation between words and things, in Plato's *Cratylus*. The Stoic Zeno's *Homeric Problems* would later establish the school of allegorical criticism for the post-Aristotelian or Hellenistic age;[6] the natural expressiveness of language would be defended by the school of Analogists among the Alexandrian grammarians and critics.[7] A commonplace of antiquity, especially among the Stoic philosophers,[8] was a doctrine which we may call simply that of the *Logos*—the word as the expression and hence the mold and determination of reason and intelligence: in a mathematical sense, as in the logos of Euclid, in grammatical, etymological, symbolic, exegetic, rhetorical, and moral senses—in the grand and synthesizing sense that eloquence and wisdom are inseparable. The relation of this doctrine to literary criticism may be hinted by allusion to the earliest extant Greek *Grammar*, the sixteen pages of the second-century Dionysius Thrax, a standard for centuries, in which we ascend through six stages, from accurate reading aloud and interpretation of figures of speech, to the crown of

[4] *Against the Sophists* 12; *Nicocles* 5–9; *Antidosis* 254; *Panegyricus* 8; all cited in Atkins, I, 125–6.

[5] Atkins, I, 13, 29, 127.

[6] Atkins, I, 187.

[7] Atkins, I, 184; II, 17.

[8] E. Vernon Arnold, *Roman Stoicism* (Cambridge, 1911), esp. pp. 128–49.

all, the criticism of poetry. The *Grammaticus* of this age was scarcely the figure for a mid-19th-century *Grammarian's Funeral*. He was the professionally qualified *poetarum interpres*.[9] Finally, the doctrine of the *Logos* with all that it implied was a doctrine less dear even to poets and grammarians than to statesmen. It was one of the main theoretical supports of a life devoted to public leadership. "I am grateful to the Stoics," said Cicero, "for this reason: that they alone of all the philosophers have declared eloquence to be virtue and wisdom."[1] The debate about rhetoric which we have been considering is but an early chapter, though an important one, of a controversial history which continues through later antiquity, the Middle Ages, and the Renaissance. The ancient quarrel between the philosophers and the poets to which Plato alludes in the *Republic* was the same in principle as a later and much longer quarrel between dialecticians (in the Platonic sense, philosophers tending toward science) and rhetoricians.[2] On the side of the dialecticians one might align in one consistent team: Plato, Abelard, Occam, Ramus, Descartes. On the side of the rhetoricians, poets and grammarians: Aristotle, Cicero, Quintilian, Augustine,[3] John of Salisbury, Bonaventure, and Richard Hooker.[4] The following retrospective passages in the *De Oratore* of Cicero define the role of Socrates in the long debate and the importance of the whole incident in which Plato, Isocrates, and Aristotle were the other chief participants.

> It was Socrates who . . . separated the ability to think wisely
> from the ability to speak gracefully, though these are naturally
> united—Socrates! the philosopher whose genius and varied con-

[9] Atkins I, 182–3; J. E. Sandys, *A History of Classical Scholarship* (Cambridge, 1921), I, 6–11; Richard McKeon, "The Philosophic Bases of Criticism," in R. S. Crane, *Critics and Criticism*, p. 507.

[1] "*Stoicis hanc habeo gratiam, quod soli ex omnibus eloquentiam virtutem ac sapientiam esse dixerunt*" (quoted in Arnold, *Roman Stoicism*, p. 149). Cf. J. S. Watson, *Cicero on Oratory and Orators*, 1890, p. 210; *De Oratore* III, 18.

[2] The Stoic philosopher Zeno made a comparison (recorded in Cicero's *Orator* XXXII, 113) between the concise form of dialectic utterance, a "closed fist," and the expanded expression of rhetoric, an "open palm." The fact that Stoic philosophers promoted the doctrine of the Logos (or verbal power) but at the same time favored a concise and severe dialectic style must be looked on as an anomaly arising characteristically enough out of the complex issue concerning verbal style and content. Cf. *post* Chapter 12, our account of Ramism and 17th-century rhetoric.

[3] The theological aspect is well illustrated in this passage from the *Adversus Praxean* of Tertullian (about A.D. 213): "This reason is His own thought; this is what the Greeks call 'Logos,' which word we translate also by 'speech.'. . . To understand it more easily, take knowledge from yourself, I pray you, as from 'the image and likeness' of God. . . . See, when you silently meet with yourself in the process of thinking, that this very process goes on within you by reason meeting you along with word at every movement of your thought, at every beat of your understanding. Whatsoever you think is word; whatsoever you understand is speech" (*Tertullian Against Praxeas*, trans. A. Souter, London, 1920, pp. 36–7, Par. 5).

[4] See H. M. McLuhan, "Edgar Poe's Tradition," *Sewanee Review*, LII (January–March, 1944), 24–33.

versation Plato's dialogues have committed to immortality, but who himself has left us nothing in writing. Hence arose that divorce of the tongue from the heart (*discidium illud . . . quasi linguae atque cordis*), that absurd, needless, and deplorable conception, that one set of persons should teach us to think, and another should teach us to speak.—*De Oratore* III, 16

The ancients, till the time of Socrates, used to combine the whole of their study and science pertaining to morality, to the duties of life, to virtue, and to civil government, with the art of speaking; but afterward, the eloquent being separated by Socrates from the philosophic, and the distinction being continued by all the followers of Socrates, the philosophers despised eloquence, and the orators philosophy. . . . the followers of Socrates excluded the pleaders of causes from their own ranks, and from the common title of philosophers—though the ancients had been of the opinion that the faculty of speaking and that of understanding were allied in a marvellous harmony.—*De Oratore* III, 19 [5]

Aristotle . . . said it was disgraceful that he should remain silent and let Isocrates do all the speaking. He therefore undertook to equip that philosophy of his with due illustrations and ornament and to connect the knowledge of things with skill in speaking. This of course came to the notice of that sagacious monarch Philip, who summoned Aristotle as a tutor for his son Alexander. Let the boy get from the same teacher instructions in behavior and in language.

Now, if anybody desires to call that philosopher who instructs us fully in things and words an orator, he may do so without opposition from me; or if he prefers to call that orator whom I describe as having wisdom united with eloquence a philosopher, I shall make no objection. . . . If I had to choose one of the two, I should prefer uneloquent good sense to loquacious folly. But if it be inquired which is the more eminent excellence, I give the palm to the learned orator, and if you will admit that this person is also a philosopher, there is an end of controversy; but if you insist on distinguishing the orator from the philosopher, the philosopher will be inferior— for the equipment of a complete orator includes the knowledge of the philosopher, but the knowledge of the philosopher does not necessarily include the eloquence of the orator.—*De Oratore* III, 35 [6]

[5] Adapted from J. S. Watson, *Cicero on Oratory and Orators* (New York, 1890), pp. 209, 212.
[6] Adapted from J. S. Watson, p. 233.

SUPPLEMENT

This tradition [the oratorical] has been a continuous force in European law, letters, and politics from the time of the Greek sophists. It is most conveniently referred to as the Ciceronian ideal, since Cicero gave it to St. Augustine and St. Jerome, who in turn saw to it that it has never ceased to influence Western society. The Ciceronian ideal as expressed in the *De Oratore* or in St. Augustine's *De Doctrina Christiana* is the ideal of rational man reaching his noblest attainment in the expression of an eloquent wisdom. Necessary steps in the attainment of this ideal are careful drill in the poets followed by a program of encyclopedic scope directed to the forensic end of political power. Thus, the *doctus orator* is, explicitly, Cicero's sophistic version of Plato's philosopher-king. This ideal became the basis for hundreds of manuals written by eloquent scholars for the education of monarchs from the fifth century, through John of Salisbury and Vincent of Beauvais, to the famous treatises of Erasmus and Castiglione.

So far as America is concerned, this was a fact of decisive importance, since Virginia, and the South in general, was to receive the permanent stamp of this Ciceronian ideal. . . . It is thus no accident that the creative political figures of American life have been moulded in the South. Whether one considers Jefferson or Lincoln, one is confronted with a mind aristocratic, legalistic, encyclopedic, forensic, habitually expressing itself in the mode of an eloquent wisdom.

New England is in the scholastic tradition, and profoundly opposed to "humanism." Briefly, the theocratic founders of Harvard and rulers of New England were Calvinist divines, fully trained in the speculative theology which had arisen for the first time in the twelfth century—the product of that dialectical method in theology which is rightly associated with Peter Abelard. Unlike Luther and many English Protestants, Calvin and his followers were schoolmen, opposed to the old theology of the Fathers which Erasmus and the humanist-Ciceronians had brought back to general attention after the continuous predominance of scholastic theology since the twelfth century. To the humanists nobody could be a true interpreter of Scripture, a true exponent of the *philosophi Christi*, who had not had a full classical training. So Catholic and Protestant schoolmen alike, were, for these men, the "barbarians," the "Goths of the Sorbonne," corrupting with "modernistic" trash (the schoolmen were called the *moderni* from the first) the eloquent piety and wisdom of the Fathers. (The Fathers were called the "ancients" or *antiqui theologi*.)

Harvard . . . originated as a little Sorbonne, where in 1650 the scholastic methods of Ockham and Calvin, as streamlined by Petrus Ramus, were the staple of education. Logic and dialectics were the basis of theological method, as of everything else at Harvard. Here rhetoric was taught, not for eloquence, but in order to teach the young seminarian how to rub off the cosmetic tropes of Scripture before going to work on the doctrine with dialectical dichotomies. Ramus taught a utilitarian logic for which he made the same claims as pragmatists do for "scientific method." In fact, Peirce, James, and Dewey could never have been heard of had they not been nurtured in the Speculative tradition of the scholastic theologians Calvin and Ramus.

—H. M. McLuhan, "Edgar Poe's Tradition," *The Sewanee Review*, LII (January–March, 1944), 25–8, selected passages, by permission of the author and *The Sewanee Review*

Until Gutenberg, poetic publication meant the reading or singing of one's poems to a small audience. When poetry began to exist primarily on the printed page, in the seventeenth century, there occurred that strange mixture of sight and sound later known as "metaphysical poetry" which has so much in common with modern poetry.

The printed page was itself a highly specialized (and spatialized) form of communication. In 1500 A.D. it was revolutionary. And Erasmus was perhaps the first to grasp the fact that the revolution was going to occur above all in the classroom. He devoted himself to the production of text-books and to the setting up of grammar schools. The printed book soon liquidated two thousand years of manuscript culture. It created the solitary student. It set up the rule of private interpretation against public disputation. It established the divorce between "literature and life."

We have long been accustomed to the notion that a person's beliefs shape and color his existence. They provide the windows which frame, and through which he views, all events. We are less accustomed to the notion that the shapes of a technological environment are also idea-windows. Every shape (gimmick or metropolis), every situation planned and realized by man's factive intelligence, is a window which reveals or distorts reality. Today when power technology has taken over the entire global environment to be manipulated as the material of art, nature has disappeared with nature-poetry.

From the point of view of its format, the press as a daily cross-section of the globe is a mirror of the technological instruments of communication. It is the popular daily book, the great collective poem, the universal entertainment of our age. As such it has modified poetic techniques and in turn has already been modified by the newer media of movie, radio, and television. These represent revolutions in communication as radical as printing itself.

James Joyce was the first to seize upon newspaper, radio, movie, and television to set up his "verbivocovisual" drama in *Finnegan's Wake*. Pound and Eliot are, in comparison with Joyce, timid devotees of the book as art form.

In cognition we have to interiorize the exterior world. We have to recreate in the medium of our senses and inner faculties the drama of existence. This is the work of the *logos poietikos*, the agent intellect. In speech we utter that drama which we have analogously re-created within us. In speech we make or *poet* the world even as we may say that the movie parrots the world. Languages themselves are thus the greatest of all works of art. They are the collective hymns to existence. For in cognition itself is the whole of the poetic process. But the artist differs from most men in his power to arrest and then reverse the stages of human apprehension. He learns how to embody the stages of cognition (Aristotle's "plot") in an exterior work which can be held up for contemplation.

It is only common sense to recognize that the general situation created by a communicative channel and its audience is a large part of that in which and by which the individuals commune. The encoded message cannot be regarded as a mere capsule or pellet introduced at one point and consumed at another. Communication is communication all along the line. One might illustrate from sports. The best brand of football played before fifty people would lack something of the power to communicate.

What we have to defend today is not the values developed in any particular culture or by any one mode of communication. Modern technology presumes to attempt a total transformation of man and his environment. This calls in turn for an inspection and defense of all human values. And so far as merely human aid goes, the citadel of this defense must be located in analytical awareness of the nature of the creative process involved in human cognition. For it is in this citadel that science and technology have already established themselves in their manipulation of the new media.

—H. M. McLuhan, "Sight, Sound and the Fury," *The Commonweal*, LX (April 9, 1954), 7–11, selected passages, by permission of the author and *The Commonweal*

ROMAN CLASSICISM: HORACE

§ *Hellenistic criticism—II. the context of the* Ars Poetica *—III. its meaning: literary genres,* Platonic *forms, Aristotelian decorum, formulas and examples, imitation of models—IV. nature and convention, the audience—V. theory and practice in Horace, a modern problem: imperfection vs. objectivity—VI. (literary ideas in the* Satires *and other* Epistles) *satire and comedy as poetry, the language of poetry, usage, the* callida junctura—*VII. mediocrity in poems—VIII. the structure of the* Ars Poetica, *Peripatetic topics: matter and form, hedonism and didacticism, poet and poem, divine inspiration, genius and technique— IX. Augustan studio advice* §

MORE THAN TWO CENTURIES OF HELLENISTIC CIVILIZATION LIE between Aristotle and the literary theorist who is next to claim our attention, the Roman poet Horace. This period, during which we hear of literary studies no longer in Athens, but in the capital of the Attalids at Pergamum and in that of the Ptolemies at Alexandria, is not celebrated for important literary theory. The reason is, in one sense, simply that the writings have disappeared. The history has to be pieced out inferentially from titles of lost works, from later writers like the geographer Strabo, the biographer Plutarch, or the encyclopedist Diogenes Laertius, and from certain very recently recovered papyrus fragments. Yet the reason for the paucity of documents in turn would seem to be that the Hellenistic period produced no literary theory which could compare in seriousness with that of the fourth century in Athens and no literary art which could compare with that of the Periclean or that of the Homeric age. It is a period known for historically rigorous studies, formalism, and technicalities, and at the same

time for extreme aestheticism, literary novelties, and *préciosité*. It is
known for genre naturalism and at the same time for romantic fantasy.
It was the heyday not only of the grammarian, the scholiast, the philologist, but also of the epigrammatist, the idyllist, the "Asiatic" rhetorician.[1]
The communal interest in religious and patriotic issues which during
more ancient times had produced the great genres of drama and epic
dwindled during the Hellenistic age to an esoteric and merely literary
cultivation of smaller forms—epigram, elegy, idyll, pastoral, didactic,
epyllion. Scholar poets developed the utmost nicety in exploring the
byways of myth. When Apollonius of Rhodes published about the middle of the third century the four books of his romance epic *Argonautica*,
his former instructor Callimachus, the epigrammatist and scholar, led the
critics of the day in censure of its long-windedness. "I hate the cyclic
poem," said Callimachus, "the common road which everyone uses."
And he said also: "a big book is a big nuisance" (*mega biblion mega
kakon*).[2] The portrait of the age on the historico-critical side can be
suggested in the production by Callimachus of the massive bio-bibli-
ographical catalogue of the Alexandrian Library, *Lists of Illustrious
Writers and Their Works*, in 120 volumes.[3] The century is celebrated
for the editing and textual criticism of Homer and of the dramatists and
lyric poets, the most learned laborers in this field having been Zenodotus
(325–234 B.C.), the first librarian of the Alexandrian Museum, and his later
contemporaries Eratosthenes, Aristophanes of Byzantium, and Aristarchus. Aristarchus, who centuries later was to be known as the first
"critic" in antiquity (the antitype of Aristotle's equally eponymous contemporary the snarling critic Zoilus), earned his fame by a program
of studying Homer in the light of the Homeric age, dialect, and idiom.
In place of the allegorical or symbolic defence (still employed by the
Stoics in the tradition of Zeno), he introduced the concepts of racial
childhood, the naively heroic, and the poet as their faithful reporter.[4]
Another way of summing up the Alexandrian period in polite letters is
to say that it was one of tension between history and criticism, a prolonged Quarrel of Ancients and Moderns, which, even dimly known as
it is, forecasts some of the main issues of much later critical history.

---

[1] Hegesias of Magnesia, who flourished about the middle of the third century,
was the champion of the oratorical school known to modern scholars as the First
Sophistic.

[2] Atkins, I, 177–9.

[3] Of the same order were a treatise *On Comedy* in eleven books by Lycophron
and *The Old Attic Comedy* in twelve volumes by Eratosthenes. The forty-volume
History of the Graeco-Roman world by Polybius (c. 210–125 B.C.) was a pioneer
effort to trace philosophic, political, and social causes.

[4] During the same century Euhemerus of Messina maintained that the Homeric
gods were apotheosized primitive benefactors of mankind—and thus gave his name
to the "euhemeristic" tradition of mythic interpretation.

II

AT THE death of Theophrastus in 287 B.C., the texts of Aristotle's works are said to have passed to a disciple who hid them from the bibliomania of the Attalid kings in a cave at Scepsis in the Troad. There they lay unknown until about 100 B.C., when they were taken back to Athens. From Athens they were taken by the Roman general Marius to Rome in 86 B.C.[5] The Peripatetics meanwhile carried on in their own fashion, formalizing and fixing the system which Aristotle had sketched. One of these was Neoptolemus, a grammarian-poet of Parium in Bithynia, whose name is connected with that of Horace by the scholiast Porphyrio in the third century A.D. Horace, says Porphyrio in his introductory note to the classic *Ars Poetica*, "epitomized the precepts (*congessit praecepta*) of Neoptolemus of Parium—or at least the most important of them." The assertion has been verified in modern times by the recovery at Herculaneum of some charred papyrus scraps containing a partial digest of Neoptolemus in passages from a work *On Poems* (*Peri Poematōn*) by a first-century Epicurean philosopher Philodemus of Gadara.[6] The connection with Horace is made biographically plausible by the fact that the papyri were recovered from the villa of Lucius Piso Caesonius, Roman consul in 58 B.C. and father of Lucius Calpurnius Piso, who in turn was consul in 15 B.C. and father of the two young men to whom Horace addressed his epistle on the art of writing. It has been easy for historians to imagine the youthful Horace as member of a literary coterie attending the "garden school" at Naples, where Philodemus was a professor, or gathering at the Herculanean villa of the consul Caesonius to discuss with Philodemus the opposed philosophies of Peripatetic utilitarianism and Epicureanism.

The *Epistola ad Pisones* (in the next century dubbed *Ars Poetica* by Quintilian, VIII, 3) is a slick piece of writing, produced by Horace apparently toward the end of his life (65–8 B.C.) after he was the established author of the four books of *Odes*, one of *Epodes*, two of *Satires*, and two of *Epistles*. The whole poetic career of Horace is part of an Augustan and patriotic reaction against Alexandrian belletristic trends and at the same time against Patrician antiquarianism. But there is a great difference in ethical and metaphysical resonance between the *Ars* of Horace and the *Poetics* of Aristotle or the *Phaedrus* of Plato.

---

[5] Atkins, I, 167. The authorities are Strabo, *Geography* XIII, 1; Plutarch, *Life of Sulla;* Diogenes Laertius, *Lives of the Philosophers*, chapters on Aristotle and Theophrastus.

[6] Atkins, I, 170; II, 54; and L. P. Wilkinson, *Horace and His Lyric Poetry* (Cambridge, 1945), pp. 87 ff. The work of Philodemus *On Poems* appears in the edition of C. Jensen, *Philodemos über die Gedichte (fünftes Buch)*, Berlin, 1923.

In the rugged days of the Republic, when high political aims governed taste in literature, Cicero had said: "If I had twice as long to live, I should have no time to read lyric poetry." [7] And the soldier dictator Caesar had said: "Avoid a curious word as you would a rock." [8] But Horace practised his art in the day of aristocratic and imperial patronage and polish, when there was need not so much for powerful speeches to decide political issues as for elegant poems to celebrate ancestral grandeur, military triumph, peaceful and benevolent sway. The poetry and criticism of Horace was part of an Augustan classical movement— back toward the high seriousness, if not the moral intensity, of Greek classical art. At the same time Horace had become a refined poet under the Epicurean influence of the school at Naples and along with the neoteric and Hellenizing coteries of the mid-century. He emerged from an Alexandrian atmosphere which may be symbolized equally by Catullus' lament of Lesbia for her sparrow and the sojourn of Cleopatra at Rome for the two years preceding the assassination of Caesar. What- ever earnest pleading Horace does is that of a poet for the poet's cause, as in the two long epistles of his Second Book, to Augustus and to Florus. His opponents are not politicians, sophists, or philosophers, but his fellow poets and various kinds of literary pretenders—the poetasters, criticasters, buffoons, libellers, aesthetes, and fops. "The Socratic dia- logues (*Socraticae chartae*)," says Horace, "will provide you with ideas." His specialty is not the deep question or the tenacious train of reasoning, but the tacit assumption and upon this the neatly erected formula. Yet he is, in a way that is curiously his own, eminently worth while.

III

THE main thing assumed in the criticism of Horace is the normative value of the literary "species," [9] the genre, kind, or type, and of the companion principle designated by the term "propriety"—*to prepon* in Aristotelian criticism, *decorum* in Latin.[1] The ultimate reference for both genre and decorum was the Greek doctrine of ideas or forms, either in the Platonic or in the Aristotelian version. The Platonic, or supposedly Platonic, perfect idea of a thing had by the time of Horace developed a literary application which may be conveniently illustrated in these passages from Cicero's *Orator*.

> When that great artist [Phidias] was working on a statue of Jupiter or Minerva, he was not trying to copy an actually exist- ing model but was intent on some vision of perfect beauty

[7] Seneca, *Epistles* XLIX, 5; Atkins, II, 44.
[8] Aulus Gellius, *Noctes Atticae* I, 10; Atkins, II, 53.
[9] As it was accurately called in English criticism of the 18th century.
[1] Cicero, *Orator* XXI.

(*species pulchritudinis eximia quaedam*). By that he directed
his hand and chisel. And just as visible forms and figures each
participate in a certain perfection or excellence, an intelligible
ideal by reference to which the artist transcends mere ocular
experience, so eloquence has its ideal, which we conceive in
our minds and attempt to copy in audible words. These forms
of things were called *ideas* by that eminent philosopher, that
master of thought and speech, Plato. He said that they were an
innate part of our minds and did not, like all other things,
suffer beginning and end, flux and lapse, continual passage from
one state to another. It follows that whatever topic a person
undertakes to discuss rationally and methodically, he ought to
reduce it to its ultimate and proper character and form.

I confess that I myself have learned whatever I may know
about the art of oratory not from the workshops of the rhetoricians but from the spacious walks of the Academy.—*Orator*
II–III, 9–10, 12

A fairly specific encouragement for such a literary doctrine had actually been given by Aristotle in those passages of his *Poetics* where
he said that tragedy having passed through many stages of growth
(*pollas metabolas metabalousa*) had reached its final and perfect stage,
and where he said that characters should be true to life and internally
consistent—or in those passages of the *Rhetoric* where he insisted that
style should be appropriate to theme, or where he spoke of the differences between poetic and prose style and of the three main oratorical
styles (matching the three main types of oratorical purpose), forensic,
deliberative, epideictic. By the time of Horace, such notions had undergone a marked development in the subdivision and multiplication of
fixed literary types and had acquired a nearly legislative prestige. Instead of the three literary genres, epic, tragedy and comedy, which are
mainly treated by Aristotle, we have in the time of Horace a spectrum
of genres including epic, tragedy, comedy, lyric, pastoral, satire, elegy,
and epigram.[2] The aim of criticism was to expound for each of these
types an *operis lex*[3] and its corollaries.

Horace begins his *Ars Poetica* with the negatively Aristotelian example of a mixed species, a beautiful woman sporting a fishtail, and
after laughing at this, adds his sufficiently generalized but nonetheless

[2] Cf. Horace, *Satires* I, 10; *Epistles* II, 2; *Ars Poetica* 73; J. F. D'Alton, *Roman
Literary Theory and Criticism* (London, 1931), Ch. VI.

[3] *Ars Poetica* 135. The edition of Horace mainly consulted here is that of
the Loeb Classical Library: *Satires, Epistles and Ars Poetica*, ed. H. Rushton Fairclough, Cambridge, Mass., 1936; *The Odes and Epodes*, ed. C. E. Bennett, Cambridge,
Mass., 1934. For a few longer passages, the "imitations" of Alexander Pope appear in
lieu of translations. The prose paraphrases of shorter passages are the work of the
present authors.

memorable advice about purple patches and unity. "Make it anything at all, so long as it hangs together" (*Sit quod vis, simplex dumtaxat et unum*). A long middle section of the poem, devoted in a rambling fashion to the history and rules of literary genres, manages to formulate a good many very explicit instructions:

Five acts, no more, no less.
Neve minor neu sit quinto productior actu
fabula. 189

Only three speakers at a time.
. . . *nec quarta loqui persona laboret.* 192

Scenes of butchery offstage.
ne pueros coram populo Medea trucidet. 185

Plunge right in.
Semper ad eventum festinat et in medias res. 148

Hexameter verse for war poems.
Res gestae regumque ducumque et tristia bella
quo scribi possent numero, monstravit Homerus. 73–4

Along with such rules come the more interesting gallery of capsule character types, from carefree boy to crotchety old man, " full of difficulties and complaints, the encomiast of days gone by" (*difficilis, querulus, laudator temporis acti,* 173)—and the formulas for historical figures, like the well-known thumbnail sketch of Achilles: "restless, wrathful, ruthless, fierce" (*impiger, iracundus, inexorabilis, acer,* 121). A very reasonable corollary of the doctrines of decorum and genre had been a shift from the Aristotelian *mimēsis* of nature to the fully classical and traditional kind of imitation,[4] that of models, a matter nicely epitomized by Horace:

Be Homer's works your study and delight,
Read them by day, and meditate by night.

vos exemplaria Graeca
nocturna versate manu, versate diurna.—268–9

IV

WE HAVE already suggested that it is one thing to make neatly turned pronouncements of this sort—perhaps even with semi-playful amusement

---

[4] George Converse Fiske, *Lucilius and Horace* (Madison, 1920), Chapter I; Richard McKeon, in *MP*, XXXIV (August 1936), 1–35. The imitation of models was consistent with the notion, occasionally expressed in classical antiquity and in the later age of neo-classicism, that primary topics of literary imitation had already all been imitated. Thus: *nullumst iam dictum quod non dictum sit prius* (Terence, *Eunuchus*, l. 41); *omnis ad accessus Heliconis semita trita est* (Manilius, *Astronomica* III, Prol.). Cf. *post* Ch. 10, pp. 178–81; Ch. 12, pp. 234–5; Ch. 15, pp. 326–7.

in the so tidy control of a situation—another to entertain a profound rationale in support of them or to be able to expound this. One question which modern scholars have asked about the critical assumptions of Horace is whether the notion of *decorum* entertained by him refers to something intrinsic to the nature of things or to something established by human convention.[5] This question can hardly be answered without one's taking some notice of a more general and more important question—that of how conventions in general are related to nature. Does the convention of a man's opening a door for a lady, or the salutation *dear* at the beginning of a letter, have any rightness in nature? Are these any better than others that might be imagined? There is little direct evidence of what Horace thought about this difficult question. His criticism does, however, offer a good example of the thorough interpenetration of nature and convention in the classical literary tradition. One recent way of stating the matter has been to say that the decorum of Horace is something affectively and socially oriented—toward the taste and standards of the aristocratic theater audience of his day rather than toward an Aristotelian or natural objectivity.[6] Does not the *Ars Poetica* allude to this audience repeatedly?

> Both highbrow and lowbrow will raise the loud guffaw.
> *Romani tollent equites peditesque cachinnum.*   113

> Take my advice—I know what your public wants.
> *Tu quid ego et populus mecum desideret audi.*   153

> The orchestra will be harder to please than the peanut gallery.
> *offenduntur enim, quibus est equus et pater et res,*
> *nec, si quid fricti ciceris probat et nucis emptor,*
> *aequis accipiunt animis donantve corona.*   248–50

But such an argument, we venture to suggest, lays too much theoretical stress on what can more plausibly be taken as only the most convenient and dramatic way of impressing young literary aspirants with the ideas of success and failure. The peanut gallery may cheer. The literati will laugh. Such are always among the possible rewards of trying to write poetry. But rewards do not constitute definitions. Horace himself has implied as much, in his *Epistle to Augustus*, where he despises the playwright's dependence on a public, and in his tenth *Satire*, where he asserts the sophistication of his satirical standard.

> Never mind what the mob thinks—"fit audience find, though few."

[5] Craig LaDrière, review of Wolf Steidle, *Studien zur Ars Poetica des Horaz*, 1939, in *American Journal of Philology*, LXIII (April, 1942), 241–3.
[6] R. S. Crane, review of Paul F. Saintonge *et al.*, *Horace: Three Phases of His Influence*, Chicago, 1936, in *Philological Quarterly* XVI (April, 1937), 162–3.

> . . . *neque te ut miretur turba labores,*
> *contentus paucis lectoribus.*   73–4

"Let but Plotius and Varius approve of these verses. . . ." Horace appeals to an audience selected not by social or political standards but just by literary standards—to his fellow poets and his literary friends, to Maecenas and the other patrons and arbiters of the day. This procedure may be close to the fallacy which in our day C. S. Lewis has amusingly imputed to T. S. Eliot,[7] of crowning and mitring himself king and pope of pointland. (On Eliot's view that only a poet can judge of poetry, it must be only as a poet that he knows that his judges are poets and hence competent judges of his own poetry.) But it is a procedure which is the opposite of sociological. It is the opposite of an appeal to any decorum, or convention, established merely by the taste of the Roman gentlemen.

V

ANOTHER difficulty in interpreting Horace (rather a biographical than a strictly critical difficulty) may arise if we observe that some of his neatly turned dicta are not very readily squared with his own practice as a poet. His *Odes* and *Epodes*, for instance, are far too varied and original in their union of meter and matter to be accountable to such rules of the *Ars Poetica* as those which say that anger should be expressed in iambs, that only gods, sporting events, young love and the banquet should be treated in lyric meters. There is no place in the *Ars Poetica* for a facetious lyric like the Horatian *Integer vitae*, beginning with its over-confident claims for the man of sterling character ("he needs no barbaric armory"—*non eget Mauris jaculis*) and ending with the poet's lighthearted determination to keep thinking fondly of his Dulcinea no matter what happens (*dulce ridentem Lalagen amabo, dulce loquentem*). A scholar writing early in this century, and perhaps in a mood of over-responsiveness to the triumphant aesthetic of Benedetto Croce, has defended the practice of Horace against the theory of Horace in the following manner:

> It was the settled practice of the Renaissance that classical poetry should be regarded as the achievement of objective perfection; a practice which has had the most disastrous consequences. The very name of the "humanities" forbids that they be tried by the criterion of impeccability. . . . a genuine poem is not a machine, and is always subjective.

. . .

[7] *A Preface to "Paradise Lost"* (Oxford, 1942), pp. 9–11.

> *Integer vitae* has long been felt to present difficulties. It begins
> like a hymn with the more or less solemn proclamation of the
> poet's inviolability, and ends with . . . gaiety.[8]

The alignment of ideas implicit, or even largely explicit, in this passage
makes a curious antithesis. *Objectivity, perfection* or *impeccability*, and
the machine go together as unpoetic and apparently almost equivalent,
and in the opposite or poetic scale, *subjectivity* (and implicitly *imperfection*) and *spontaneity*. By such a division the only term which gains
anything is *imperfection*, and this is a gain which poetry may not be
grateful to find transferred to itself. The charm of the lyric *Integer
vitae* for this critic lies in the supposed fact that its ending is an afterthought, "purely decorative," connected to the beginning by very slight
ties (though he says that this ending is "appropriate to the theme").
The difficulty might not have occurred had the critic noticed that *Integer vitae* does not in fact begin with the solemnity of a hymn (though
it has been mistakenly set to hymn music) but with a playful exaggeration which is perfectly in keeping with its conclusion—and with its
even more preposterous middle stanza, about a wolf that fled from the
poet in the Apulian woods. It is perhaps stretching the evidence to say
with another modern interpreter that the theory of decorum expounded
by Horace is flexible enough to account entirely for his own practice.

> An organic, a vital, coherency, a beauty neither less nor more
> dependent on the adaptation (not ruthless subjugation) of
> means to ends than is the beauty of the creations of Nature
> herself, is the ideal pointed to by the school of criticism prop-
> erly called Classic.[9]

Such a view does, however, have the advantage that it avoids the critical
nonsense of applauding Horace for imperfections.

> I am annoyed when I come across mistakes in a classic like
> Homer. *indignor quandoque bonus dormitat Homerus.—Ars
> Poetica* 359

And such a view finds added support when we survey not only certain
passages in the *Ars Poetica* which tell against taking the rules too
seriously but other more casually critical passages in the *Satires* and
Epistles.

VI

THERE are places, we might say, where the conservative critical theory
of Horace frays out or blurs into his actual practice, places where he is

---

[8] Roy Kenneth Hack, "The Doctrine of Literary Forms," *Harvard Studies in
Classical Philology*, XXVII (1916), 35–6.

[9] A. Y. Campbell, *Horace, A New Interpretation* (London, 1924), p. 256.

less on guard as a theorist and mainly on the alert to catch every shade
of advantage in writing the poet's apologia. Thus in the *Epistle to Augustus* he defends the innovating poets of his own circle against the
archaizing snobbery and faddism of the patrician audience. And this involves him in the view that the classics were in their own day innovations.

> Had ancient times conspired to disallow
> What then was new, what had been ancient now?
> *Quod si tam Graecis novitas invisa fuisset*
> *quam nobis, quid nunc esset vetus?*   90–1

And we have the curious side look at Horace's theory of decorum which
is provided through *Satires* I, 4 and 10, where he appears as if struggling,
though scarcely in any theoretical anguish, with the opposed facts that
satire had been a parvenu, a latter-day genre and a low one, but that to
have invented it, as Lucilius did in the second century, was a great thing.
Horace considers himself to be less than the inventor (*inventore minor*), though at the same time he can be scornful of Lucilius for his
lack of polish and proud of himself for having added this quality. As
Aristotle distinguished the abusive fun of Old Comedy from the witty
innuendo of the New, Horace prefers the liberal polite jest and the
shaded style, by turns grave and gay (*modo tristi, saepe jocoso*), to the
harsher and coarser, the careless, satire of Lucilius written two hundred
lines at a breath, "standing on one foot." (*In hora saepe ducentos, ut
magnum, versus dictabat stans pede in uno.* I, 4, l.10.) A fairly strict theory of decorum begins to operate no doubt where Horace gives up the
defence of both himself and Lucilius as poets, saying that satire is after
all not poetry at all—not noble enough—just words put together in verse
though they might as well be in prose (*sermoni propiora*, I, 4, l.42).[1] The
name for his satires is in fact "Talks," "Causeries"—*Sermones*.[2] To support this humility, Horace is even willing to countenance the question,
raised by some others, whether comedy is or is not poetry—for it lacks
fire and force both in words and matter (*quod acer spiritus ac vis nec
verbis nec rebus inest.* I, 4, ll. 45–6). There is evidence in the *Epistle to
Augustus*, however, and in the *Ars Poetica*, that Horace actually considered comedy when it was polished, like that of Menander and Terence
(scarcely that of Plautus), to be real poetry. Satire too, if we allow ourselves the indulgence of speculating about what Horace most sincerely
thought, probably stood a little higher in his estimation than the tactical

[1] Cf. H. R. Fairclough, "Horace's View of the Relations between Satire and
Comedy," *American Journal of Philology*, XXXIV (1913), 186, 190; G. L. Hendrickson, "Horace, Serm. I, 4: A Protest and a Programme," *American Journal of
Philology*, XXI (1900), 121–42.

[2] Lucilius had used the term *sermones* of his own satires (Fairclough, *loc. cit.*,
pp. 187, 191). In *Satire* II, 6, l. 17 Horace is content to be inspired by a *musa pedestris*.

modesty of his apologia would indicate. He concludes his confession
with an evasion. "Some other time we'll see whether this kind of writing
is true poetry or not" (*alias justum sit necne poema . . . genus hoc
scribendi.* I, 4, ll. 63–5).

The least rigid of all Horatian doctrines is that concerning the low
and the lofty in language. Here we see the idea of decorum placed in
the most softening and concessive light. Horace pays his notable respects
to dignity and splendor of diction in a passage of his *Epistle to Florus*
often quoted in neo-classic times—for instance, as the motto of Samuel
Johnson's *Dictionary:*

> at qui legitimum cupiet fecisse poema,
> cum tabulis animum censoris sumet honesti;
> audebit, quaecunque parum splendoris habebunt
> et sine pondere erunt et honore indigna ferentur,
> verba movere loco, quamvis invita recedant
> et versentur adhuc intra penetralia Vestae;
> obscurata diu populo bonus eruet atque
> proferet in lucem speciosa vocabula rerum,
> quae priscis memorata Catonibus atque Cethegis
> nunc situs informis premit et deserta vetustas;
> adsciscet nova, quae genitor produxerit usus.
>   —*Epistle* II, 2, ll. 109ff.

In the adaptation of Pope:

> But how severely with themselves proceed
> The men who write such Verse as we can read?
> Their own strict Judges, not a word they spare
> That wants or force, or light, or weight, or care,
> Howe'er unwillingly it quits its place,
> Nay tho' at Court (perhaps) it may find grace:
> Such they'll degrade; and sometimes, in its stead,
> In downright Charity revive the dead;
> Mark where a bold expressive phrase appears,
> Bright thro' the rubbish of some hundred years;
> Command old words that long have slept, to wake,
> Words, that wise Bacon, or brave Raleigh spake;
> Or bid the new be English, ages hence,
> (For Use will father what's begot by Sense).

It is a plea for coinages and revivals almost the opposite in emphasis from
those cautious words of Pope in his own *Essay on Criticism* recommend-
ing the mean between the old-fashioned and the new-fangled.

> In words, as fashions, the same rule will hold;
>   Alike fantastic, if too new, or old;

> Be not the first by whom the new are tried,
> Nor yet the last to lay the old aside. II, 333 ff.

In *Satire* I, 10 Horace has his fun at the expense of the affected neoterics who salted their Latin with Greek (*At magnum fecit, quod verbis Graeca Latinis miscuit*, 20), but in the *Ars Poetica* he recognizes the principle (later rampant in vernacular poetics of the Renaissance) that a language may be enriched by adaptations from one older and more impressive:

> Newly coined words will get by if they are taken from the Greek, a few at a time.

> *et nova fictaque nuper habebunt verba fidem, si*
> *Graeco fonte cadent parce detorta.* 52-3

Yet Alexander Pope probably considered the passage quoted above from his *Essay on Criticism* Horatian enough in spirit—and he was not far wrong. The double principle of decorum and fertility which appears in the last line of Johnson's *Dictionary* motto (*quae genitor produxerit usus*) may not express the emphatic idea of the whole passage, but it still expresses something central to Horace's view of language, an implicit key or point of control. Horace takes the middle way, that of living speech. Both with regard to obsolescence, the passing away of fine old words, and with regard to revivals, the norm is usage.[3] Usage is the final court of appeal.

> Many words that have perished will be reborn, and many will perish that now live respected—if Usage says so. Usage is judge and law and rule of speech.

> *multa renascentur quae jam cecidere, cadentque*
> *quae nunc sunt in honore vocabula* (the hexameter falls with a wistful cadence), *si volet usus,*
> *quem penes arbitrium est et jus et norma loquendi. Ars Poetica*
> 70-2

The Horatian doctrine of usage—steering between Attic purism on the one hand and on the other aristocratic archaizing and macaronic Hellenizing—defines the vital speech of a satirist, a social poet of everyday words (*sermoni propiora*). This is the more remarkable when we consider the degree of formal codification at which contemporary rhetoric had arrived. Such a view of the poetic idiom owes something, no doubt, to the kind of humility which is seen also in the Horatian apology, or

[3] In the third-century debate between Analogists and Anomalists to which we have referred above (Chapter 4), Horace would have been among the latter, the sceptics about any natural fitness of words for things.

mock apology, for the satiric genre. The view can scarcely be separated either from the realist theory of comedy coming down from Aristotle [4] and expressed for Augustan Rome in the Ciceronian phrases (preserved by Donatus) *comoedia . . . imitatio vitae, speculum consuetudinis, imago veritatis.* [5] In his Epistle to Augustus (168–70) Horace advances in defence of comedy the argument that, although its everyday materials are easy enough to come by, yet the comic writer's task is an especially exacting one because his descriptions of life are so easily held to account (*habet Comoedia tanto plus oneris, quanto veniae minus*). Despite the fact that the *Ars Poetica* says so much about epic and drama, even noting satyr plays and stage music,[6] and despite the modest claim for satire which we have quoted, the satire and epistle and the conversational lyric are the Horatian genres. It is through these that the more general insights of Horace into poetry are focussed—as those of Aristotle were focussed through the theatrical genres of tragedy and comedy. For in a wider sense Horace does define the idiom of all poetry. As a modern poet has put it, in all solemnity:

> The word neither diffident nor ostentatious,
> An easy commerce of the old and the new,
> The common word exact without vulgarity,
> The formal word precise but not pedantic.[7]

Add to this conception of idiom another conception, casually asserted by Horace, that of "order and juncture"—the "cunning juncture" of words (*series juncturaque, callida junctura*—*Ars Poetica*, 242, 47), and we recognize the precept of the cliché-breaker, the mind persistently on the verge of metaphor.

> I'll give a twist to the familiar that will make anybody think he could do the same—but he will waste his perspiration if he tries.

> *ex noto fictum carmen sequar, ut sibi quivis*
> *speret idem, sudet multum frustraque laboret ausus idem.*   240–2

VII

ONE of the most widely read amateurs of criticism in recent times, G. E. B. Saintsbury, called Horace's *Ars Poetica* a treatise *De Medio-*

[4] Cf. *ante* Chapter 3.

[5] Atkins, II, 38; H. R. Fairclough, *American Journal of Philology*, XXXIV, 183. Cf. *ante* Chapter 3, p. 50.

[6] A fact which has been taken to argue the construction of the *Ars Poetica* upon a Hellenistic model (Atkins, II, 71–2).

[7] T. S. Eliot, *Little Gidding*, V.

critate. To inquire into the justice of this disparagement would be to raise again, as with Hack, the question whether perfection (of precisely turned idiomatic speech) is the contrary of poetic force and a check upon it or is not rather its appropriate channel and its only realization. But Saintsbury's *mot*, set against certain conspicuous features of Horace's poem, may remind us of another perennial question for criticism. An academic wit of our own day has observed that pretty good poetry is like pretty good eggs. In the 18th century, when James Boswell once argued, for the sake of argument, that "poetry of a middle sort was entitled to some esteem," Samuel Johnson retorted that since poetry is a luxury and there is no necessity for our having it at all, it can have no value unless exquisite.[8] The perennial inclination of both critic and poet toward a kind of perfectionism, perhaps snobbishness, which sets them apart from producers and critics in other fields, even in some of the other arts, poses, besides social and editorial problems, a difficult critical problem. If there is some sort of absolute difference between the poem which is really a poem and that which is not—if there are no middle grounds, as there are with most human values, no shades of goodness, grace, and nourishment—why is this so? Is it so? We shall see the opposite implication in some of the most metaphysical defences of aesthetic value. The point here is that the tradition of perfectionism has one of its most insistent formulas in the *Ars Poetica* of Horace—not only in the whole drift of the treatise, its plenary range of decorums, but in the celebrated dictum: "Neither gods nor mortals—nor booksellers—have any use for the middling poet."

> *mediocribus esse poetis*
> *non homines, non di, non concessere columnae.* 372-3

If Horace's treatise was *De Mediocritate*, this was surely not according to his own conception. And it is in fact only by the odd equation "Perfection=Mediocrity" that one can make it so. Nevertheless, it is one of the curiosities of critical history, perhaps symptomatic of a deeply founded and irreconcilable paradox, that this equation has often been assumed—and not necessarily in opposition to high ideals but apparently in support of them. We shall see a classical source of the equation in our next chapter.

VIII

IF ONE were looking for an ironic illustration of the doctrine of genres, it could most readily be found in the fact that classical scholars have seriously debated the question whether the *Ars Poetica* is to be taken as

[8] Boswell's *Life*, April 10, 1775.

a theoretical treatise (a formal *poetics*), or as an introductory and practical guide (an *isagoge*), or, its haphazard sequence of topics considered,
as merely an *epistle* to a friend.[9] As a critical question this may be readily
dismissed for its utter vacuity. It may have some historical or genetic
sense—what genre would Horace, if asked, have said that he was writing? The fact is that the poem presents a rather random structure—it
tends itself to be an instance of beautiful woman shading into fish
(. . . *in piscem mulier formosa superne*). It can scarcely be invoked to
illustrate its own dictum:

> a place for everything and everything in its place.
> *ut iam nunc dicat iam nunc debentia dici.*   43

"Horace still charms with graceful negligence and without method talks
us into sense." [1] So far as one can discern an overall order, it is roughly
this: Lines 1–72 present a miscellaneous bundle of topics: *purple patches,
unity, brevity, writing within one's own powers, order of ideas, verbal
usage,*—all of which might be conceived under some such head as *poesis*,
the qualities that go into poems, the common sinews. Lines 73–294 speak
of various genres, their history, decorum, and rules—the form of the
whole poem itself—*poema*. Lines 295–476 tell some jokes about poets
and give some partly jocular good advice about what to do and what not
to do in being a poet; they present a miscellaneous bundle of ideas about
poeta. This threefold division is one of the main resemblances which
Horace is thought to show to the Peripateticism of Neoptolemus rather
than to the more simplified Epicureanism of Philodemus. It is a division
deriving from two distinctions which had been made by theoretical critics with increasing explicitness from early times: that between the matter (or statement) of poetry and its poetic "form," and that between the
poem and the poet. The first of these distinctions we have seen entertained by Aristotle, but with a restraint dictated by his basic view that
the residence of forms is only in concrete things. The threefold arrangement of Neoptolemus, his *poiēsis* (matter), *poiēma* (form), *poiētēs* (poet)
—was more clearly divisive—though of course Neoptolemus, like most
Hellenists, asserted that "matter" and "form" were alike important.[2] As
the emphasis fell on "form" or on "matter", one other thing had usually
been decided in Hellenistic criticism—the question whether the function
of poetry is hedonistic or didactic—whether the correct view is the Io-
nian and Homeric, that the aim of poetry is pleasure through enchantment, or the Boeotian and Hesiodic, that it is teaching. Stoic philosophers
held more or less consistently to the contentual or didactic view. Profes-

---

[9] R. K. Hack, *loc. cit.,* pp. 9–10.
[1] Scaliger was to call the poem "an art written without art." Heinsius transposed
passages to improve it. *Atkins,* II, 69.
[2] Atkins, I, 170–3.

sional scholars and critics, like Heracliodorus and Eratosthenes, dwelt on diversion and the enchantment of beautiful words. But Horace's model Neoptolemus adopted what we may call a Peripatetic compromise, Aristotelian in spirit but more specific than Aristotle,[3] the doctrine that the aim of poetry is twofold, to charm and at the same time to be a useful teacher.[4] It is this adjustment of the issue, the hedonistic-pedagogic compromise, which we find in one of the passages of the *Ars Poetica* most often quoted by posterity. "Either a poet tries to give good advice, or he tries to be amusing—or he tries to do both. . . . A mixture of pleasure and profit appeals to every reader—an equal administration of sermon and tickle."

> *Aut prodesse volunt aut delectare poetae*
> *aut simul et iucunda et idonea dicere vitae.*   333-4

> *omne tulit punctum qui miscuit utile dulci,*
> *lectorem delectando pariterque monendo.*   343-4

The second main distinction which enters into the threefold division of the *Ars Poetica*, that between poem and poet, is one with which we have already been concerned in several earlier places—in alluding to the personal invocations of the muse by Homer and Hesiod, in discussing the semi-ironic retreat by Socrates from the analysis of poetry to the *theia moira* (divine dispensation) or magnetic irradiation of the poet himself. The *Odes* of Horace offer enough evidence that the poet's divine inspiration was still a current concept—if perhaps largely a tacit myth or poetical figure. But divine inspiration bears a close resemblance to another mysterious thing, that which is often called "genius" or a natural gift. A different version of the antithesis poet-poem occurs in Pindar's contention that poetry is nature (*phua*, not *technē*), in Aristotle's passing tribute to the mad poet and to the genius (*Poetics* XVII), in the remarks dropped in his *Rhetoric* to the effect that certain things are to be learned either by native insight or by technical training (I, i; III, i), and in the four requirements for good rhetoric named by Isocrates: native ability (*phusis*), practice (*epimeleia*), technical knowledge (*epistēmē*), and imitation of models.[5] An intimate correspondence between the character of the verbal artist and the worth of his utterance was a reiterated doctrine of antiquity which received such neat epitomes as the Stoic definition of an orator, "a morally good verbal technician"

---

[3] Aristotle, despite the cathartic clause in his theory, had indicated that the aim of each kind of fine art is to give the pleasure proper to it (*Poetics* XIV).

[4] Atkins, I, 175-7. Cf. the Lucretian figure of bitter medicine in the honeyed cup (*De Rerum Natura* I, 936-50) and the ancient definition quoted in Strabo's *Geography* I, 2: poetry is "a primitive philosophy guiding our morals, our tastes, and our actions."

[5] Atkins, I, 127-8.

(*vir bonus dicendi peritus*),[6] or the statement of the younger Seneca
that a man's oratory could be no better than his life (*talis hominum
oratio qualis vita*).[7] It is this branch of the doctrine, rather than that referring to divine inspiration, which appears in the Peripatetic arrangement: *poiēsis, poiēma, poiētēs*. But apparently *poiētēs*, on any terms, lent
himself much less readily to formal analysis than did his product.
Neoptolemus is able to observe that native gifts (*dunamis hē poiētikē*)
as well as technical skill (*technē*) are requisite. He can distinguish between the technically skilful writer and the born poet.[8] And this was
about all anybody had been able to say about the poet himself as distinct
from his poems. Perhaps even this distinction between genius and technique was no more than a translation of the initial distinction, from
which it stemmed, that between poet and poem. A fragment ascribed to
Simylus,[9] a didactic poet, probably of the Hellenistic period, reduces the
issue to absurdity by asserting that neither genius (*phusis*) nor art
(*technē*) is any good alone, nor both together without practice (*meletē*),
good luck (*kairos euphuēs*) and a well-disposed critic (*kritēs*).

IX

THE *Ars Poetica* of Horace is a climax to all this history in the neat compression of his statement about a choice that was no choice at all. "People like to ask whether a good poem comes natural or is produced by
craft. So far as I can see, neither book-learning without a lot of inspiration nor unimproved genius can get very far. The two things work together and need each other."

> *Natura fieret laudabile carmen an arte,*
> *quaesitum est: ego nec studium sine divite vena*
> *nec rude quid prosit video ingenium; alterius sic*
> *altera poscit opem res et coniurat amice.*   408–11

For Horace neither the distinction between poem and poet nor that between *ars* and *ingenium* was very rigorous, as may be seen indeed in the
number of rather mixed statements which he contrived to make about
the poet, a few of them even in the first two sections of the *Ars*, sections
which are ostensibly concerned with poetry and poems. Shortly after
the advice about brevity running the danger of obscurity (*brevis esse
laboro, obscurus fio*), comes that about knowing our own limitations

[6] Preserved from a lost treatise on rhetoric by the elder Cato (Atkins, II, 16).
The same source gives us the memorable advice about content and form: *rem tene,
verba sequentur.*
[7] *Letters to Lucilius*, CXIV, 16; Atkins, II, 168, 325. Such ideas were given a
reverse twist by Epicurus: the wise man would "live poems" rather than write them.
[8] Atkins, I, 173.
[9] Preserved by Stobaeus (A.D. c. 500) in his *Florilegium*; Atkins, I, 180. The
fragment is quoted by Ben Jonson in his *Discoveries*.

(*Sumite materiam vestris, qui scribitis, aequam viribus*, 38–9). After the history of the tragic and comic genres, comes "patience and revision" (*limae labor et mora*, 291).[1] Almost the whole third section of the poem is of course not theory of poetry at all but theory of being a poet (if we may take the liberty of turning some of Horace's satirical descriptions into terms of advice): Don't be a Bohemian; a bath won't wash off your inspiration. Read Socrates and get wisdom. Too bad for your poetic chances if you have been exposed to the standard Roman commercial education. Be careful, but not paralysed with scruples (*non ego paucis offendar maculis*). Aim at the top (*mediocribus esse poetis . . .*) Don't force your inspiration (*Tu nihil invita dices faciesve Minerva*). Don't rush into print (*nonumque prematur in annum*). Remember the glorious history of poetry, its sacred function. Don't take the praise of your friends and retainers too seriously. Get the advice of an honest critic— and follow it. Be steady, the best poet is not the mad one. The conclud- ing paragraph of Horace's eipstle, an almost Rabelaisian portrait of the crazy poet—victim of the itch (*scabies*), of the king's disease (*morbus regius*), of some frantic hallucination (*fanaticus error*), or of lunacy (*iracunda Diana*), or perhaps a man who has defiled ancestral ashes or disturbed a consecrated spot—shows how far the sophisticated Augustan age had moved away from the ancient theory of the poet as a vessel of Dionysiac enthusiasm.[2] The Horatian view of poetic inspiration lies in the field of author-psychology and professional strategy.

The *Ars Poetica* of Horace is a nice mélange of objective and crit- ical rules with snatches of studio wisdom. Keep your pencils sharpened, carry a pocket notebook, drink a pint of beer with lunch, go walking in the country, listen to the muse when she speaks, recollect your emotions in tranquillity, revise carefully, take your time in publishing. It is no der- ogation from such statements to say that they are not strictly parts of criticism. In the *Ars Poetica* of Horace they are, despite the random structure of the poem, not actually in great danger of being confused with criticism. One of the advantages of the aphoristic style is that its ideas tend to stay detached and clean. The implications of a given *dictum* do not operate very far in any direction.

---

[1] The oft-quoted "*si vis me flere, dolendum est primum ipsi tibi*," 102–3, is not in its context a genetic rule. It refers to the roles of tragic characters, Telephus or Peleus.

[2] Cf. Persius, Prologue to *Satires;* Lucian, *Discussion with Hesiod.*

SUPPLEMENT

THE SONNET

Sir,— The sonnet has a universally accepted rhythm, beat, rhyme and number of lines. The rules apply not only to English sonnets but to those of all cultivated lands. You do our nation and yourselves, as a critical literary journal, a real disservice when (October 13) you accept the line "My moon is brought down from the sky in kindness" as a sonnet line, without any comment or reproof to the author who perpetrates it. However charming Mr. Warner's poems from which you quote may be as lyrics, the one you quote without comment as a sonnet is simply not a sonnet. In these days of weak and gagged critics, we look to your paper for a cultivated criticism to arrest the decay of English letters by ardent but lazy and conceited young writers who do not take the trouble to learn the elements of their craft.

Marie Carmichael Stopes

—*The Times Literary Supplement*, London, November 3, 1945, p. 523, quoted by permission of *The Times*

Analysis

Last Tuesday morning a young lady employed as a reader by one of the local book publishers turned in a report on the manuscript of a novel she had been reading. She had this to say about one of the leading characters: "I do not think this man should be identified as a bookmaker. He seems too uncouth, even sporty, a character to be wholly convincing as a craftsman."

—*The New Yorker*, December 2, 1944, by permission; © 1944 The New Yorker Magazine, Inc.

The unskilful poet will portray a dolphin living in the woods and a wild boar on the ocean. (*Delphinum silvis adpingit, fluctibus aprum.*)

—Horace, *Ars Poetica*, l. 29

The fishes got stuck in the tops of the elms, where the doves usually sat. and frightened deer were swimming on the flood.

> (*Piscium et summa genus haesit ulmo*
> *Nota quae sedes fuerat columbis*
> *Et superjecto pavidae natarunt*
> *Aequore dammae.*)

—Horace, *Odes*, I, 2, 9–12

He is to consider himself as a Grotesque painter, whose works would be spoiled by an imitation of nature, or uniformity of design. He is to mingle bits of the most various, or discordant kinds, landscape, history, portraits, animals, and connect them with a great deal of flourishing, by heads or tails, as it shall please his imagination, and contribute to his principal end, which is to glare by strong oppositions of colours, and surprise by contrariety of images.

Serpentes avibus geminentur, tigribus agni.   Horace.

His design ought to be like a labyrinth, out of which nobody can get clear but himself. And since the great Art of all Poetry is to mix Truth with Fiction, in order to join the *Credible* with the *Suprising;* our author shall produce the Credible, by painting nature in her lowest simplicity; and the Surprising, by contradicting common opinion. In the very Manners he will affect the *Marvellous;* he will draw Achilles with the patience of Job; a Prince talking like a Jack-Pudding; a Maid of honour selling bargains; a footman speaking like a philosopher; and a fine gentleman like a scholar. Whoever is conversant in modern Plays, may make a most noble collection of this kind, and, at the same time, form a complete body of modern *Ethics and Morality.*

—Alexander Pope and friends, *Peri Bathous: or of the Art of Sinking in Poetry* (1728), Chapter V, "Of the true Genius for the Profund, and by what it is constituted"

CHAPTER 6

ROMAN CLASSICISM: LONGINUS

§ *date and context of* Peri Hupsous—*II. elevation (the sublime), ekstasis, the five "sources": great ideas, passion, figures, diction, synthesis, little actually said about the first two—III. political and ethical differences between the Augustan and Imperial eras, interest in the poet's soul, imitation as inspiration, the five sources not co-ordinate, the "diagonal distinction"—IV. development of verbal rhetoric in the Hellenistic and Roman eras—V. Longinian rhetorical technicalities, devices for reconciling them with elevation and passion, correctness vs. grandeur—VI. variety of criteria considered in* Peri Hupsous, *universality, physical grandeur, Petronius, anticipations of heroic drama and Kant—VII. occasional subtleties, synthesis as rhythm or as verbal ordonnance, Sappho's Ode, "synaesthesis," Longinian decorum of transport* §

THE HORATIAN INTEREST IN THE AUTHOR NO DOUBT OWED SOMETHING to the Epicurean and anti-rhetorical teaching of Philodemus of Gadara, the professor to whom Horace may have been exposed in his youth. Viewed in that way the ideas of Horace become part of a critical trend, a "romantic" concern for the poet's inspiration which, if we may generalize somewhat broadly, came to its climax only in the second half of the next century. This climax is recorded for us not in the writing of a school but in the single extraordinary essay entitled *Peri Hupsous*, to which (or to the major part of the essay which survives) the name of an otherwise unknown "Longinus" has become attached. An alignment with the age of Horace is specially suggested by the fact that Longinus refers (Chapter III) with the deference of an old pupil or epigonist to another Gadarine or Epicurean philosopher, Theodorus, and

97

even more by the fact that the main argument of the essay is directed against a certain Caecilius of Calacte, a rhetorician and a friend of the famous rhetorical critic Dionysius of Halicarnassus, who flourished at Rome during the Augustan period.[1] A certain slant of the essay toward the *somnia Pythagorea* of neo-Platonism has led one recent commentator[2] to return to the accepted Renaissance view that Longinus was Cassius Longinus, philosopher-rhetorician of the third century, friend of Plotinus, teacher of Porphyry at Athens, and unfortunate counsellor of the rebellious Palmyran Queen Zenobia. But the internal evidence, especially the range of quotations and allusions, from Homer to Caecilius and other Augustan rhetoricians, sufficiently argues for a Greek rhetorician at Rome in the first century.[3] The text of the *Peri Hupsous* is a discovery of the 16th century—in the first edition by Robortello at Basel in 1554. No reference to the essay from either classical or medieval times survives.

II

UNDERTAKING to improve on the work of the Augustan Caecilius, Longinus insists that Caecilius has said little about the sources, or components, of what both authors call *hupsos*,[4] a quality of "elevation" in writing, of intensity or eloquence, the "sublime," as it was much later to be called. It could appear in prose or in poetry, in the oratory of Demosthenes, the dialogues of Plato, the epic narrative of Homer, the Greek drama, the lyric poetry of Sappho, the opening of the Hebrew Lawgiver's *Genesis*: " 'God said'—what? 'Let there be light, and there was light; let there be land, and there was land' " (IX). The range of the author's reading and his capacity for enthusiasm are among the most striking characters of the essay. A strong interest in the emotional response of the poetic audience is indicated by a distinction between rhetoric and poetry made in the first chapter: "The effect of elevated language upon

[1] Caecilius was a member of the reigning school of Apollodorus, the more doctrinaire champions of rhetorical rule. See Atkins, II, 214.

[2] R. A. Scott-James, *The Making of Literature* (London, 1936), ch. VIII, "The First Romantic Critic," pp. 81–3.

[3] W. Rhys Roberts, *Longinus on the Sublime* (Cambridge, 1935), Introduction. We quote the translation of Roberts throughout this chapter, by permission of the Cambridge University Press.

[4] Other similar expressions used by the author are *ta huperphua, ta megala, ta megathē, to megalophuēs, hē hupsēgoria, to thaumasion, to hupertetamenon*. The term *bathos*, used in Chapter II, is apparently a synonym (though taken waggishly by Alexander Pope as an antonym and hence given its modern English meaning). Cf. Atkins, II, 253; Roberts, Appendix B; St. Paul, *Romans* XI, 33–6; *Ephesians* III, 13–21. The earliest English translations were *Of the Height of Eloquence*, by John Hall, 1662, and *Of the Loftiness or Elegancy of Speech*, by John Pulteney, 1680. After the translation by Boileau in 1674 the term "sublime" prevailed. Cf. A. F. B. Clark, *Boileau and the French Classical Critics* (Paris, 1925), pp. 371–5.

an audience is not persuasion but transport." And transport (*ekstasis*) [5] has been one of the ideas principally associated with Longinus by posterity. The chief theoretical challenge of the essay, however, lies in a certain peculiarity to be observed in the basic layout of the whole upon a five-fold division of the "sources" of "elevation." These five, announced and briefly defined in chapter VIII, are: (1) the power of forming great conceptions (*noēseis*), (2) inspired and vehement passion (*sphodron kai enthousiastikon pathos*), (3) formation of figures (*schēmata*), (4) noble diction (*phrasis*), (5) dignified and elevated "composition" (*sunthesis*). It is a regrettable matter that we do not actually hear as much about the first two of these sources, great conceptions and vehement passions, as we should like and as we may be led to expect from the plan announced in chapter VIII. The emotions, we learn in a later chapter (XLIV), were to be treated in another, now unknown, essay. And one of the most distressing lacunae in the Paris manuscript, that of six leaves from the second quaternion (KE), occurs in the very midst of the discussion about great conceptions.[6] "Sublimity is the echo of a great soul" (*hupsos megalophrosunēs apēchēma*). And after a few more lines, *Desunt sex folia*. Nevertheless it is clear enough that "sources" (1) and (2), conceptions and passions, refer to the state of the poet's soul more emphatically than to anything in poems themselves. They are both parts of greatness of soul, both, as Longinus puts it, on the side of nature, whereas "sources" (3), (4), and (5), figures, diction, and composition, are on the side of art.

III

ONE of the differences between Horace and Longinus is the difference between the ethical and patriotic Augustan era (conducive, it seemed, to great poetry) in which Horace wrote and the later corrupt and discouraging times to which Longinus in the closing chapter of his essay attributes a decline in poetic power and eloquence. It was common for philosophers during the reign of Vespasian to look back wistfully (*laudatores temporis acti*) to Republican institutions, to argue that democratic freedom had nurtured genius, and to impute a contemporary decline in oratory to political servitude. Longinus, like other literary men,[7]

[5] In Chapter XV vivid poetical images (*phantasiai*) aim at enthrallment (*ekplēksis*).

[6] A fact which might seem remarkable, that in a manuscript of which more than a third is missing, the forty-four chapter numbers remain, is explained by the further fact that the chapter headings are in a later hand than that of the scribe who wrote *Parisinus 2036*, the primary surviving manuscript, of the tenth century. This manuscript lacks actually eight leaves at the place mentioned, but the first and last are supplied from another manuscript. See Roberts, pp. 166, 169.

[7] "Similar speculations" may be "traced in the writings of the two Senecas, Petronius, Tacitus, and Velleius Paterculus; and to these discussions later contributions were to be made by Quintilian and the younger Pliny" (Atkins, II, 215).

though agreeing with the philosophers about the literary decline, professed to have more confidence in the restorative power of enlightened autocracy. He puts the argument against autocracy in the mouths of the philosophers and for his own part lays the blame for decline on ethical rather than political causes, on the prevailing vices of the day, love of money and pleasure, insolence, and lawlessness—the general atrophy of man's immortal part, the soul. "It is not possible that men with mean and servile ideas . . . should produce anything that is admirable and worthy of immortality." Such an interest in the causes of poetic decline was the legitimate complement of his profound interest in the cultivation of the poet's soul as the way to sublimity. "Homer enters into the sublime action of his heroes." He "shares the full inspiration of the combat" (IX). In the first chapter of the essay a point of complaint against the Augustan critic Caecilius is that he has, "strangely enough," failed to tell how "we may succeed in raising our own capacities to a certain pitch of elevation." And one of the most distinctive features of the Longinian system is a special version of the Roman doctrine of imitation. What Horace was content to understand as a technical imitation of classic models becomes for Longinus something far more exciting, a powerful illumination and inspiration enjoyed through submission to the ancient masters. As the Pythian priestess is impregnated with prophetic knowledge by a divine afflatus which rises through the floor of the Delphic chamber, so modern devotees of the ancient poets experience a kind of inspirational effluence from those mighty souls (XIII).

To turn our attention once again to all *five* sources of the sublime and try to see these in a single perspective: the basis of division, a logician might say, is not single. (1) and (2), thoughts and emotions, are coextensive, not co-ordinate, with (3), (4), and (5), the rhetorical features. The quintuple division does not in reality constitute a single logical classification coextensive with the sources of the sublime. The Longinian preoccupation with the genius of the poet (as it is managed in the essay alongside of the rhetorical themes) suggests a question whether the two ancient distinctions which we have considered in our last chapter, that between *poiēsis* (content) and *poiēma* (form) and that between either *poiēsis* or *poiēma* on the one hand and on the other *poiētēs* (the author), may not sometimes become confused. The more compact choice *natura . . . an arte* (*ingenium* or *studium?* natural gifts or studied art?) seems to be equally capable of referring either to two things in the poet, his native genius and his acquired art, or to two other things, no doubt reflections of the first, but properly enough attributed to the poem itself, its fidelity to some kind of nature and its artfulness or technique. The problem may be sketched by a table having four compartments, as follows:

	POET	POEM
NATURE	1 GENIUS	1 X SUBLIMITY, OR HIGHER REALITY, OR ANY QUALITY OF CONTENT IMPUTED TO THE POEM ITSELF
ART	2 EDUCATION	2 X TECHNIQUE

A literary psychologist or a teacher of composition might well wish to inquire whether 1 or 2 in this table is the more important for the making of a poet, and whether they produce respectively and separately 1x and 2x or (what is more plausible) combine—both causes producing each effect. But a theorist looking at literature itself may be more concerned with inquiring whether 1x and 2x can actually be distinguished within a poem, and if they can, which is the more important, and what the relation is between the two. The last question may be par excellence the question confronting the literary theorist. What it is more relevant to stress at the present moment, however, is the possibility that a theorist might slide into yet another distinction, one which seems to harbor a certain duplicity and invalidity. This might conveniently be called the "Diagonal Distinction." It is indicated by the dotted line in the table. Two distinctions in one, we may say, by which the agile theorist is able to move out of an area of difficulty and reappear in another area with a solution which does not legitimately avail for the first. As if a theoretical rhetorician on being pushed to the wall about extravagance of conceits or figures in his favorite author were to answer: "Well, I excuse them on the grounds of the author's genius, the high seriousness of his message, and his intense emotion. Lesser persons, you and I, couldn't get away with them. But he obviously can. It is because he has the ideas and passions of a great soul. He uses his figures sincerely."

IV

BUT it may be well at this point to back away and return to the *Peri Hupsous* from another angle, observing that this essay is after all a rhetorician's essay, the third and fourth sources of elevation—that is, diction and figures—filling a very large part of what survives (Chapters XVI–XL). The chapters on these two sources, much more than the casual and graceful dicta of Horace on words, require for their understanding that one remember the degree of formal codification at which Graeco-Roman rhetoric had arrived. The history of that rhetoric was one which closely paralleled the history of the Horatian genre concepts.

The victory of verbal rhetoric which we have described in an earlier chapter had not occurred without serious cost through the encouragement which it gave to a hyper-development of rhetorical machinery. Where Isocrates had named [8] and Aristotle (*Rhetoric* III, 13) had grudgingly accepted four main parts of a speech: *proem, narrative, proof,* and *epilogue,* Cicero in his youthful summation of Hellenistic doctrine, the *De Inventione,* prescribes for the custom-built speech the following five: *exordium, narratio, argumentum, refutatio, peroratio.* The loose divisions of the art itself rather casually implied by Aristotle—*heurēsis* or finding of arguments (Books I and II of the *Rhetoric*), *taxis* or structure (Book III, Chapters 13–19), *lexis* or verbal style (Book III, Chapters 1–12), *hupocrisis,* acting or delivery (mentioned disrespectfully in Book III, Chapter 1)—have become in Cicero's *De Inventione* (I, 9) the clearly definable and formally distinct four heads: *inventio* (*heurēsis*), *dispositio* (*taxis*), *elocutio* (*lexis*), and *pronuntiatio* (*hupocrisis*), and at the same time a fifth and purely subjective head, *memoria,* has been added between *elocutio* and *pronuntiatio.* The kind of analytic interest shown by Aristotle in such technically namable figures as *parisōsis, paromoiōsis, antithesis, homōnumia,* and *metaphora* [9] had blossomed by the time of Horace into the manifold repertoire of the figures of speech and figures of thought (*figurae verbi, figurae sententiae; schēmata lexeōs, schēmata dianoiēs*). These were managed with diverse efforts at precision by numerous rhetoricians, by Cicero in his *De Oratore,*[1] by his contemporaries, the anonymous author of the Hellenistic *Ad Herennium* and the Greek litterateur Dionysius of Halicarnassus in his *Peri Suntheseōs Onomatōn* (*On Verbal Composition*), and during the next century by Demetrius in his *Peri Hermēneias* (*On Style*) and by Quintilian in Books VIII and IX of his *Institutio Oratoria.* Finally, the time of Horace and Cicero saw the firm establishment of three (or four) *kinds* of verbal style. Aristotle had said cautiously that it might be useful to think about three areas of prose style, appropriate more or less to the three recognized branches of oratory—forensic, deliberative, and epideictic.[2] With far greater confidence Cicero named the three now celebrated kinds of oratorical style: *genus vehemens, genus modicum, genus subtile* (*Orator* XXI). The author of the *Ad Herrenium* used the approximately synonymous terms: *gravis, mediocris, extenuata.*[3] The treatise *On Verbal Com-*

---

[8] Atkins, I, 132, says that Lysias first named these parts. Cf. R. C. Jebb, *Attic Orators from Antiphon to Isaeus* (London, 1893), II, 68.

[9] Balance of clauses, like sounds at beginning or end of clauses, antithesis, equivocation, metaphor.

[1] See *De Oratore* III, 36–54.

[2] Dionysius of Halicarnassus reports that the lost *Peri Lexeōs* of Theophrastus alludes to a mixed or middle style (Atkins, I, 156).

[3] *Ad Herennium* IV, viii.

position of Dionysius used a slightly different three: the elegant (*sunthesis glaphura*), the middle or common (*koinē*), and the severely plain (*austēra*); and the same author's *Essay on Demosthenes*, again a different three: the lofty or "sublime" (*charaktēr hupsēlos*), the middle (*mesos*), and the plain (*ischnos*). Demetrius is the only author who distinguishes not three styles, but four: the magnificent (*charaktēr megaloprepēs*), the elegant (*glaphuros*), the plain (*ischnos*), and the forceful (*deinos*).[4]

The three styles had been linked by Cicero with three great purposes of oratory: to prove (low style), to please (middle style), and to move or persuade (vigorous or lofty style).[5] Cicero distinguished the style of oratory in general from the styles of philosophy, sophistry, history, and poetry.[6] But during later centuries the three oratorical styles would be formally appropriated to three genres of poetry: to elegiac the low, to bucolic the middle, to epic the lofty.[7]

The whole Graeco-Roman system of verbal rhetoric receives its eclectic, serenely sophisticated, and classically retrospective statement about a century after Horace in Books VIII and IX of a kind of politician's and pleader's encyclopedia, the *Institutio Oratoria* in twelve books, by the lawyer and laureate rhetorician [8] Quintilian. In the century after that rhetoric moved once more, as in the century after Aristotle, with Hegesias of Magnesia, in the direction of perfumery, euphuism, Asiatic conceit. A chief authority was Hermogenes of Tarsus. The period is known to historians as the Second Sophistic.

V

THE "figures" noticed by Longinus tend to have to do with abnormalities of syntax and other peculiarities of structure: *asundeton* (absence of conjunctions), *huperbaton* (inversion), changes of number, person, tense, *periphrasis* (a roundabout way of saying something), rhetorical question. It may even seem to a modern reader something like an inversion of values to dignify these twists by the name of "figure" when the queen of figures (the chief rhetorical concern of Aristotle) metaphor, along with comparison and simile, is treated under the head of "diction." The whole distinction between the third and fourth Longinian sources

[4] See Charles S. Baldwin, *Ancient Rhetoric and Poetic* (New York, 1924), pp. 56–7; *Demetrius On Style*, ed. W. R. Roberts (Cambridge, 1902), p. 22; Donald Lemen Clark, "John Milton and 'the fitted stile of lofty, mean, or lowly,'" *Seventeenth-Century News*, XI (Winter, 1953), No. 4, *Milton Society Supplement*, 5–9.

[5] "*Quot sunt officia oratoris tot sunt genera dicendi: subtile in probando, modicum in delectando, vehemens in flectendo*" (*Orator* XXI).

[6] *Orator* XIX–XX.

[7] Cf. *post* Chapter 8, p. 146.

[8] Under Vespasian.

of the sublime, diction (*phrasis*) and figures (*schēmata*), is indeed one which may be difficult to explain, and its status is not improved by the nearly parallel or overlapping subdistinction which appears under the head of "figures" themselves: between those of expression (*lexis*) and those of thought (*noēsis*). A certain technical conventionalism marks the rhetorical analysis of Longinus, a limitation through dealing with inherited concepts. This can be seen too in other parts of the essay, for instance, under the head of "great thoughts," the first source of elevation, where we come upon such an anomaly as "amplification" (or padding out an idea). Nevertheless, Longinus is an extraordinary rhetorician—and for the reason that he is trying to put two sides of a problem together—one side, the technicalities and definitions of the rhetoric which was current, and the other side, a sense of something indefinable which he calls "elevation" and which he attempts actually to specify in a non-rhetorical dimension, that of the great soul and its thoughts and passions. Whether these latter are something observable in the poem itself—or something outside the poem which causes the poem—or again something which the poem causes in its audience—is not clearly indicated. At times therefore the equation between the passions of the soul and verbal rhetoric tends to take the form of a shortcircuit or, as we have suggested, a diagonal escape back and forth between tricky technique and passionate inspiration, artful poem and natural man. This is most evident in the several treatments of extravagance in figures and diction. What is it that makes us swallow a violent hyperbole (Ch. XXXVIII)? or a far-fetched metaphor (Ch. XXXII)? Nothing else but "strong and timely passion," or "deeds and passions which verge on transport." Such passion (ours or the poet's may not be clear) is a kind of lenitive and remedy (*panakeia*) for hyperbole and a palliative (*alexipharmakon*) for metaphor.[9] "Art (*technē*)," says Longinus in another place, "is perfect (*teleios*) when it seems to be nature, and nature hits the mark when she contains art hidden within her."[1] And one of the main points of apology in his opening chapters concerns the difficulty of conceiving an *art* for so natural and spontaneous a performance as the sublime (*ei estin hupsous tis ē bathous technē*). On the main premises of the essay one might well argue that works of nature are only enfeebled and wizened by rules of art (*tais technologiais kataskeleteuomena*). But Longinus undertakes precisely to defend art against such hypernaturalistic charges.

> While nature as a rule is free (*autonomon*) and independent in matters of passion and elevation, yet she is wont not to act at random and utterly without system (*amethodon*). Further, na-

[9] Cf. *alexēma* (Ch. XVI), a palliative for the figure of adjuration.
[1] Ch. XXII, on the figure of inversion or *huperbaton*.

ture is the original and vital underlying principle in all cases, but system (*methodos*) can define limits and fitting seasons, and can also contribute the safest rules for use and practice.   II

On the view suggested by such words as *panakeia* and *alexipharmakon*, however, we seem actually to have something more like nature blurring the vision, soothing our doubts and irritations, covering over and apologizing for the ineptitude of art. We may be moved to ask: What has art done for nature? Do the metaphors and hyperboles and other paraphernalia of art correspond somehow to nature in her phase of emotion? Do they provoke her emotions? Or do they express them? Longinus does not say any of these things—though to say any one of them might be a bolder critical statement than he actually makes and would reverse the direction of what actually seems to be a retreat from the analyzable rhetorical figures into a reservoir of emotive origins and effects which somewhat vaporously defies inspection.

This kind of choice appears under another form in a section of the essay which in later ages was to be among the most often echoed. Chapters XXXIII—XXXVI are a digression from the technical theme of metaphor for the sake of drawing a strong contrast between scrupulous technical correctness and a grandeur of soul which is conceived as careless.

> . . . I am well aware that lofty genius is far removed from flawlessness; for invariable accuracy incurs the risk of pettiness, and in the sublime, as in great fortunes, there must be something which is overlooked. It may be necessarily the case that low and average natures remain as a rule free from failing and in greater safety because they never run a risk or seek to scale the heights, while great endowments prove insecure because of their very greatness.

> . . . does Eratosthenes in the *Erigone* (a little poem which is altogether free from flaw) show himself a greater poet than Archilochus with the rich and disorderly abundance which follows in his train and with that outburst of the divine spirit within him which it is difficult to bring under the rules of law? Once more: in lyric poetry would you prefer to be Bacchylides rather than Pindar? And in tragedy to be Ion of Chios rather than—Sophocles?   XXXIII

> In reply . . . to the writer who maintains that the faulty Colossus is not superior to the Spearman of Polycleitus, it is obvious to remark . . . that in art the utmost exactitude is admired, but

that grandeur is admired in the works of nature; and that it is by
nature that man is a being gifted with speech. XXXVI

There is an obvious truth about all this (that if a poet writes a great
play, an *Oedipus* or a *Lear*, marred by a faulty line or even a faulty
scene, he has achieved more than if he wrote a good sonnet, even a *very*
good sonnet), but this obvious truth seems to get out of hand, in the author's enthusiasm, and to sweep him along to something very like an implication that mediocrity is on the whole apt to be flawless, and swash-
buckling genius strongly, if forgivably, inclined to make mistakes. A dis-
claimer to the effect that the blunders of Homer, Demosthenes, and
Plato add up to only "an infinitesimal fraction" of their works (XXXVI)
scarcely stems the main sweep of the argument, which reaches its flood
in statements such as those we have quoted, that the abundance of Ar-
chilochus is disorderly and lawless, that art and exactitude stand against
grandeur and nature, that great authors despise persistent accuracy
(XXXV). Two possibilities, that a mediocre writer might be full of
faults and partly because of these faults might be mediocre, and that a
great writer might be faultless (or rather that his greatness might be in
proportion to the fewness of his faults) are scarcely given enough
weight.[2] The single sublime and happy touch (XXXVI), a notion that
echoes one of the original emphases of the essay,[3] plays a greater role in
redeeming the mistakes of genius than any greatness or perfection
achieved through a whole structure. The discussion could scarcely
countenance the idea that in a large literary work (as in a large practical enterprise, say the building of a jet bomber compared to the building of a wheelbarrow) a relevant mistake—one that is really a mistake—
will be the more catastrophic. If we conceive both *perfection* and *grandeur* as qualities which ought to be resident in a poem itself, the antagonism suggested by Longinus seems bound to be troublesome. It is on the
whole perhaps easier to read this celebrated digression upon genius and
perfection as part of the author's prevailing tendency to seek a route of
escape from the technicalities of the poem itself (where his spirit with-
ers) to the great soul of the poet (in the idea of which he rejoices). The
alignment of *perfection*, not against any *grandeur* in the poem itself, but
against a godlike soul or "genius" in the author, is strongly invited. At a
later date, from the *Spectators* of Addison to the *Seven Lamps* of Ruskin,
this antithesis, with all the ambiguity of its bearing on the actual work
of art, was to enjoy, despite the protests of a few hard heads like Macaulay, a triumphant vogue in English criticism.

[2] There is indeed the statement that Lysias is inferior to Plato not only in degree of excellences but by reason of his faults (XXV).
[3] "Sublimity flashing forth at the right moment scatters everything before it
like a thunderbolt" (I).

VI

ONE of the most extraordinary features of the essay on *The Sublime* is the variety of criteria, the number of approaches to poetry, which it manages to include: not only the main three, the transport of the audience, the genius of the author, the devices of rhetoric—but in passing the democratic idea that great poetry is that which pleases all and always (VII)[4] and again a further variation on the subject-object relation, the most spectacular or operatic part of the essay (in Chapters IX and XXXV), the idea of physical grandeur as the counterpart of psychic. There may be some danger of our supposing that the author means that the sublime state of soul is to be measured by the magnitude of the external objects mentioned in a poem. For instance, by the battle of the gods in *Iliad* XX and XXI:

> You see, my friend, how the earth is torn from its foundations, Tartatus itself is laid bare, the whole world is upturned and parted asunder, and all things together—heaven and hell, things mortal and things immortal—share in the conflict and the perils of that battle.   IX

We are perhaps saved from an over-simple interpretation of this passage if we notice the warning that these things must be taken allegorically (*kat' allēgorian*), that Homer makes gods of men and men of gods, and that hence even superior to the battle of the gods are passages which represent the gods as pure and great and undefiled. But another and more eloquent passage, in Chapter XXXV (part of that digression on genius and accuracy), hangs out the fiery symbols more brightly and became to later ages one of the most attractive spots in the essay.

> . . . Nature has appointed us men to be no base or ignoble animals; but when she ushers us into the vast universe as into some great assembly, to be as it were spectators of the mighty whole and the keenest aspirants for honour, forthwith she implants in our souls the unconquerable love of whatever is elevated and more divine than we. Wherefore not even the entire universe suffices for the thought and contemplation within the reach of the human mind, but our imaginations often pass beyond the bounds of space, and if we survey our life on every side and see how much more it everywhere abounds in what is striking, and great, and beautiful, we shall soon discern the purpose of our birth. This is why, by a sort of natural impulse, we admire not

---

[4] Cf. XXXVI, and Atkins, II, 236. Sikes, *The Greek View of Poetry*, p. 236, quotes St. Vincent of Lerins (d. 304): *quod semper, quod ubique, quod ab omnibus.* See his *Commonitorium*, ed. R. S. Moxon (Cambridge, 1915), II, 3.

the small streams, useful and pellucid though they be, but the
Nile, the Danube, or the Rhine, and still more the Ocean. Nor
do we view the tiny flame of our own kindling (guarded in lasting purity as its light ever is) with greater awe than the celestial
fires though they are often shrouded in darkness; nor do we
deem it a greater marvel than the craters of Etna, whose eruptions throw up stones from its depths and great masses of rock,
and at times pour forth rivers of pure and unmixed subterranean fire. In all such matters we may say that what is useful or
necessary men regard as commonplace, while they reserve their
admiration for that which is astounding.

Here, it is true, Longinus is talking a language of teleology and religious
psychology. He is speaking directly about the place of man in the universe, rather than making rules for literary composition. But in the context of the whole essay the passage might easily be given a direct literary
application. It has been easy to assimilate to another famous piece of
first-century literary exhortation, that of the old Bohemian poet Eumol-
pus in the *Satyricon* of Nero's Arbiter Elegantiarum, Petronius. *Praeci-
pitandus est liber spiritus.* This is a plea for Homeric machinery and supernatural excitement (*ambages deorumque ministeria*), after the mere
military realism of Lucan's *Civil Wars.* Put Petronius and Longinus together, and you have something like the spirit with which Dryden was
to defend Heroic Plays in 1672 and a little later opera. Take the Longinus of *Peri Hupsous*, Chapter XXXV, alone ("Wherefore not even the
entire universe suffices for the thought and contemplation within the
reach of the human mind, but our imaginations often pass beyond the
bounds of space . . ."), and we have a very good start toward the "sublime" in Kant's *Critique of Judgment* in 1790.

VII

THE same quest for the indefinable, no doubt, gives the rhetorical analysis itself here and there a more subtle turn. It is the mark of a rhetorician
who knows the difficulties and the limits of his metier to observe that
sublimity must "leave in the mind more food for reflection than the
words seem to convey" (VII), and that "the very fact that there are
some elements of expression which are in the hands of nature alone, can
be learned from no other source than art" (II). Among the preliminary
statements of the first chapter, close to that about the "transport" of the
audience, occurs a statement that "Elevation (*hupsos*) consists in a certain distinction and excellence of expression" (*akrotēs kai exochē tis
logōn*).[5] The author of a recent essay on Longinus has suggested that

[5] Cf. XXX: "Beautiful words are in very truth the peculiar light of thought."

the key to understanding this "excellence" lies in the fifth source of "elevation," that is, composition (*sunthesis*), or "harmony," as the term may perhaps be translated.[6] *Sunthesis* had been distinguished by Aristotle (*Rhetoric* III, 5) from simple diction or single words, though his observations under the two heads show not much difference. *Sunthesis* seems to have been emphasized by at least one Hellenistic critic, Heracleodorus.[7] And the term, as we have seen, appears in the title of one of the best poetico-rhetorical treatises of the century preceding Longinus, the *Peri Suntheseōs Onomatōn* of Dionysius, though there it seems to have a fairly generic and perfunctory meaning, simply the "management" of words. Longinus himself devotes relatively little space, Chapters XXXIX–XL, to his fifth source, and he appears to mean by the term *sunthesis* the special feature of verbal order which is usually called *rhythm*.[8] From this alone not a great deal might be deduced, at least not a very comprehensive theory of verbal ordonnance—not very much about any indefinable exactitudes of style or dynamic interdependence between style and content. But one other and more celebrated passage of the *Peri Hupsous* may be adduced to support such an emphasis. Chapter X, on the choice and combination of striking materials, contains the passage which speaks of the dazzling intensity and complexity of Sappho's Ode to Anactoria.

> Are you not amazed how at one instant she summons, as though they were all alien from herself and dispersed, soul, body, ears, tongue, eyes, colour? She unites contradictions. She is, at one and the same time, hot and cold, in her senses and out of them. She is either terrified or at the point of death. The effect desired is that not one passion only should be seen in her, but a concourse of the passions (*pathōn de sunodos*). All such things occur in the case of lovers, but it is, as I said, the selection of the most striking of them and their combination into a single whole that has produced the singular excellence of the passage.

This is a long way from the figures of thought and diction in the *Ad Herennium* or in Book VIII of Quintilian's *Institutio* and even from the acute observations of Aristotle on metaphor and pun. It is a kind of statement which may be extrapolated in various directions—perhaps even in that suggested by another recent commentator,[9] who sees the Longinian *ekstasis* as an adjustment, harmony, or gratifying integration

---

[6] Allen Tate, "Longinus and the 'New Criticism,'" in *The Forlorn Demon* (Chicago, 1953), pp. 131–51.

[7] Atkins, I, 174.

[8] Chapter I explicitly prefers the momentary lightning flash of sublimity to the "hard-won result . . . of the whole texture of the composition" (*tou holou tōn logōn huphous molis*).

[9] T. R. Henn, *Longinus and English Criticism* (Cambridge, 1934).

of impulses, much like that to which Messrs. Ogden and Richards once gave the name of "synaesthesis." [1] In any event Longinus must be saluted as a lover of great literature who knew something about how to cope with what was for him the very palpable, in fact inescapable, barbed wire of contemporary rhetoric. As Horace had subdued the theory of poetic words to a decorum of urbanity, conversation, idiom and satire, Longinus heightened it to a decorum of transport.

SUPPLEMENT

I never got my lips in the Horse's spring, and I can remember dreaming no dreams on either peak of Parnassus—not for such reasons do I suddenly come forth a poet. The Heliconian ladies and the waters of Pirene that produce the library pallor are not my dish. I leave these to the gentlemen whose busts are graced with the ivy tendrils. I venture out among the holy professional poets like a half-citizen at a village festival. What teaches the parrot his "Polly-want-a-cracker" and the magpie to ape being a man? That master of arts, that generous dispenser of genius—the Belly. Most skilful in removing obstacles to speech! If only they could take in the lovely, meretricious flash of money, what poets and poetesses, ravens and magpies, you would hear—singing the pure Horse nectar.

—Persius, Prologue to the *Satires*

What I should like to stress is the fact that in creative intuition we have the primary rule to which, in the case of the fine arts, the whole fidelity, obedience, and heedfulness of the artist must be committed. I also should like to stress the fact that between this primary, primordial, primitive rule and all other rules of making, however indispensable they may be, there exists an essential difference, so to speak infinite, as between heaven and earth. All other rules are of the earth, they deal with particular ways of operation in the making of the work. But this primary rule is a heavenly rule, because it deals with the very conception, in the bosom of the spirit, of the work to be engendered in beauty. If creative intuition is lacking, a work can be perfectly made, and it is nothing; the artist has nothing to say. If creative intuition is present, and passes, to some extent, into the work, the work exists and speaks to us, even if it is imperfectly made and proceeds from a man

c'ha l'habito de l'arte a man che trema,

—who has the habit of art and a hand which shakes.

At the summit of artistic activity, and for one who has long traveled along the road of the rules, finally there is no longer any road. For the sons of

[1] C. K. Ogden and I. A. Richards, and James Wood, *The Foundations of Aesthetics* (New York, 1925), pp. 75-6.

God are under no law. Just as finally the unique law of the perfect soul, according to the saying of St. Augustine (not literally of him, but it does not matter), is "*ama et fac quod vis*"—love and do what you want—so the unique rule of the perfect artist is finally: "Cling to your creative intuition, and do what you want."

—Jacques Maritain, *Creative Intuition in Art and Poetry* (Bollingen Series XXXV, I, New York, 1953), Chapter II, p. 60, by permission of Pantheon Books Inc.

But the inner and most important distinction between the Sublime and Beautiful is, certainly, as follows. (Here, as we are entitled to do, we only bring under consideration in the first instance the sublime in natural Objects; for the sublime of Art is always limited by the conditions of agreement with Nature.) Natural beauty (which is self-subsisting) brings with it a purposiveness in its form by which the object seems to be, as it were, pre-adapted to our Judgement, and thus constitutes in itself an object of satisfaction. On the other hand, that which excites in us, without any reasoning about it, but in the mere apprehension of it, the feeling of the sublime, may appear as regards its form to violate purpose in respect of the Judgement, to be unsuited to our presentative faculty, and, as it were to do violence to the Imagination; and yet it is judged to be only the more sublime.

The mind feels itself *moved* in the representation of the Sublime in nature; whilst in aesthetical judgements about the Beautiful it is in *restful* contemplation. This movement may (especially in its beginnings) be compared to a vibration, i.e. to a quickly alternating attraction towards, and repulsion from, the same Object.

Bold, overhanging, and as it were threatening, rocks; clouds piled up in the sky, moving with lightning flashes and thunder peals; volcanoes in all their violence of destruction; hurricanes with their track of devastation; the boundless ocean in a state of tumult; the lofty waterfall of a mighty river, and such like; these exhibit our faculty of resistance as insignificantly small in comparison with their might. But the sight of them is the more attractive, the more fearful it is, provided only that we are in security; and we readily call these objects sublime because they raise the energies of the soul above their accustomed height, and discover in us a faculty of resistance of a quite different kind, which gives us courage to measure ourselves against the apparent almightiness of nature.

—Immanuel Kant, *Critique of Judgement* (1790), trans. J. H. Bernard (2d ed., London, 1931), pp. 102–3, 120, 125, by permission of Macmillan & Company Ltd.

Kant wrote in terms which presaged a Wagnerian view of the Rhine on a foggy night.—Student paper, 1950

THE NEO-PLATONIC CONCLUSION: PLOTINUS AND SOME MEDIEVAL THEMES

§ *place of Plotinus in critical history—II. the philosophy of his* Enneads, *its relevance to aesthetics: unity and being, the good and the beautiful, ugliness and evil, matter, negation, beauty and reality in* Enneads I, vi *and* V, viii—III. *problems posed by Plotinus: unity and simplicity in relation to diversity, Stoic symmetry and brightness, beauty of parts, light, vision, intelligibility, subject and object, the problem of various beautiful forms, the two pieces of stone—IV. St. Augustine,* beate contemplari, *harmony of number, "angelic imagination," unity in spite of diversity,* obiter dicta *suggesting the contrary, symbols in Scripture —V. Aquinas, substantive ontology and theology (conflict of neo-Platonism and Christianity), "beauty" as a Divine Name, as form and intelligence,* quae visa placent, tria requiruntur, *splendor of form, beauty distinguished from the good, aesthetic detachment, analogy, beauty a transcendental, beauty and art, poetry in relation to logic and rhetoric—VI. Neo-Platonic aesthetic through the ages, the 19th century, James Joyce, cognitive and affective axes of theory* §

HISTORY OF TASTE AND LITERARY CRITICISM HAS LITTLE TO SAY ABOUT the thinker with whom we conclude our account of classicism. He is a theorist of *to kalon* in its purest sense rather than of *mimēsis* or of the *utile* and the *dulce*. All the other classical theories which we have seen have been considered by a great modern aesthetic philosopher [1] to be less than "aesthetic," defective either through simple hedonism or through hedonism joined with didacticism; but the theory we are now to look at is considered by the same philosopher to be something *more* than aesthetic, a mystical "excess" or ascent into the boundless, beyond criticism. Not only peripatetic definition, genre, and technicality, so friendly to the comic and satiric mirror of daily life, but their source in Aristotelian realism are now of vastly diminished account. Plotinus, the founder of the Roman school of neo-Platonism, who came to Rome from the school of Alexandria in 244 and died at Rome in 270, was a man who was able to hurl back sorceries upon those of a jealous rival; his presiding spirit, evoked by an Egyptian priest in the Temple of Isis at Rome, turned out to be a divinity; and several times in his life he experienced the trance of mystic communion with the Absolute. When he was asked to sit for a portrait, he replied: "Is it not enough to have to bear the mere simulacrum (*eidōlon*) of reality in which nature has wrapped me, without consenting to perpetuate the image of an image, as if that were worth contemplating?" It is through an emphasis on divinity, on the Divine One, as the radiating source and constitutive principle of all Being, that neo-Platonism, and especially the philosophy of Plotinus, makes its peculiar contribution to aesthetics.

II

THE philosophy of Plotinus is contained in his six *Enneads*, or sets of nine essays each, which after the death of Plotinus his disciple and biographer Porphyry arranged and edited in an order of ascent from ethical and aesthetic matters up to the absolute or One. It is a philosophy of Being through emanation (*tolma*) from, and return (*epistrophē*) to, the Divine One. There is this world, an appearance, as for Plato, and there is the reality which is Yonder. The grades of a kind of trinity, Soul (*psuchē*), intelligence (*nous*), and Oneness (*to hen*), occur as microcosmic and macrocosmic counterparts: in the individual things of this world, in the whole world, and in the Yonder. (In effect a kind of stratified or hierarchical universe is projected from our introspective awareness of our own consciousness.) An analogy to the generations of the Hesiodic theogeny, the Uranian, Chronian, and Olympian, was noticed of course by Plotinus but barely countenanced. The divine soul, looking toward the world, dreams it up or creates and sustains it. Looking toward intelligence, this soul reflects the ideas of Intelligence, the forms of the world. And Intelligence, looking up toward the One, is transcended in the One, the very principle of form or Being, the first

[1] Benedetto Croce, *Aesthetic*, trans. Douglas Ainslie (London, 1922), pp. 65, 156.

thing (*to prōton*), and hence the good (*to agathon*). The One is so pure and simple and primal [2] that we ascend to a concept of it only by the way of abstraction or negation.

> But possess yourself of it by the very elimination of Being and you hold a marvel.—*Ennead* III, viii, 10 [3]

The more empirical aspects of this reasoning and its most immediate relevance to aesthetics appear in passages of the following tenor:

> It is in virtue of unity that beings are beings. This is equally true of things whose existence is primal and of all that are in any degree to be numbered among beings. What could exist at all except as one thing? Deprived of unity, a thing ceases to be what it is called: no army unless as a unity: a chorus, a flock, must be one thing. Even house and ship demand unity, one house, one ship: unity gone neither remains.
>
> Take plant and animal; the material form stands a unity; fallen from that into a litter of fragments, the things have lost their being; what was is no longer there; it is replaced by quite other things—as many others, precisely, as possess unity.
>
> —*Ennead* VI, ix, 1

> Where the Ideal-Form has entered . . . it has rallied confusion into co-operation: it has made the sum one harmonious coherence: for the Idea is a unity and what it molds must come to unity as far as multiplicity may.
>
> And on what has thus been compacted to unity, Beauty enthrones itself, giving itself to the parts as to the sum. . . . Thus for an illustration, there is the beauty conferred by craftsmanship, of all a house with all its parts, and the beauty which some natural quality may give to a single stone.—*Ennead* I, vi, 2

But if One is Being and the Good and the Beautiful, and if nothing can even be unless it is one, how do we explain the operation of an apparently contrary principle in the world of physical things with which we are most familiar? What makes so much failure, evil, and ugliness? How are such things even conceivable? Philosophers have devised three kinds of answer to this question: the dualistic or Manichaean, which says that evil is an independent, positive, active principle fighting the

---

[2] "Yet again, the One is prior to the intelligence. For the intelligence, though unmoved, is yet not unity: in knowing itself it is object to its own activity" (Proclus, *Institutio Theologica*, 20).

[3] The *Works* of Plotinus are quoted throughout this chapter from the translation of Stephen MacKenna, 5 vols., London, 1917–1930, by permission of Faber and Faber Limited and Pantheon Books Inc. Proclus is quoted from E. R. Dodds, *Select Passages Illustrating Neo-Platonism* (London, 1923), by permission of The Macmillan Company.

good (Ahriman the Persian god of darkness against Ormazd the god of light); the neutral or Spinozistic, which says that good and evil are relative to our own pleasures and sufferings only and that the substantial and ultimate reality is beyond Good and Evil; and the Neo-Platonic and Christian scholastic, which says that evil per se is really nothing, but that it manifests itself as an absence of something where something ought to be. If we conceive that the form or unity or being of a given something has to work against or upon, or dominate, something else, we may readily slip a little way toward Manichaean dualism and conceive that something else to be "matter," a kind of potentiality or thing inconceivably nothing in itself if we try to conceive it purely—but nevertheless a principle of negation and evil. This is approximately the form which the theory of evil according to Plotinus assumes. Matter (*hulē*), said Plotinus, is multiplicity, the principle of falling apart and being nothing, the negative or nothingness which the One conquers into form and being. We may conceive unity (form or reality) and its opposite, matter, to be like a pair of intersecting cones—as in the world system of W. B. Yeats.[4] Each vanishes to a point at the base of the other. Again, invoking a Plotinian metaphor of the luminous (about which we shall have more to say within a few pages), we may conceive the universe as a series of concentric rainbows, the One in the center as pure white light, radiating through circles of increasingly dark color, to blackness at the outer limit. Matter is the last, lowest, and least emanation of the creative power of the All-Soul—the fringe or fraying-out limit at which the transmission of ideas and unity and the generative power of the soul come to a halt. (In the sphere of individual moral consciousness an analogy to "matter" appears in the concept of "environment," so far as that checks our purely rational or autonomous acts.[5]) Plotinus came near to making matter a kind of recalcitrant and obstructive low-grade stuff—a clay or powder—hence a positive principle of amorphousness.

> An ugly thing is something that has not been entirely mastered
> by pattern, that is by reason, the matter not yielding at all points
> and in all respects to Ideal-form.—*Ennead* I, vi, 2

A later Athenian Neo-Platonist, Proclus (who has been called the Aristotle of the movement), was to put the doctrine of evil as negation in a safer form.

[4] "If we think of the vortex attributed to Discord by Empedocles as formed by circles diminishing until they are nothing, and of the opposing sphere attributed to Concord as forming from itself an opposing vortex, the apex of each vortex in the middle of the other's base, we have the fundamental symbol of my instructors" (William Butler Yeats, *A Vision*, London, 1937, p. 68). "My instructors used . . . a double cone or vortex, preferring to consider subjectivity and objectivity as intersecting states struggling one against the other" (p. 71).

[5] *Ennead* I, viii, 7, 15.

> If Evil be wholly independent of God, then there is plurality of First Principles, Good and Evil arising from two several sources. . . . we can neither introduce a Form of things evil, nor yet consider Matter to be their cause. . . . Accordingly, we must . . . represent them [evils] as a side-product of certain partial and dispersed causes. . . . If a body is infected with Evil it doubtless embraces diverse elements which do not observe their just relative proportions, and thus, because every part would have the mastery, distemper is generated as a side-product.
> —*In Rempublicam*, 358

We find Plotinus in the earlier of two essays which he wrote on beauty,[6] *Ennead*, I, vi, strongly inclined, like his master Plato, to depreciate physical beauty, or at best to value it as an approach to the real beauty of intelligence in the Yonder.

> He that has the strength, let him arise and withdraw into himself, foregoing all that is known by the eyes, turning away forever from the material beauty that once made his joy. When he perceives those shapes of grace that show in body, let him not pursue: he must know them for copies, vestiges, shadows, and hasten away towards That they tell of. For if anyone follow what is like a beautiful shape playing over water—is there not a myth telling in symbol of such a dupe, how he sank into the depths of the current and was swept away to nothingness?
> —*Ennead* I, vi, 8

> Therefore the Soul must be trained—to the habit of remarking, first, all noble pursuits, then the works of beauty produced not by the labour of the arts but by the virtue of men known for their goodness: lastly, you must search the souls of those that have shared these beautiful forms.—*Ennead* I, vi, 9

This we might say is the *Symposium* of Plato revisited. Perhaps the tone is even more lofty—and somewhat more severe. Yet it required little more than a shift of accent for Plotinus to distinguish himself from the Gnostic puritans of that era, the philosophers who were carrying the distinction between matter and formal reality to the point of making apparent natural beauty an actual ugliness and evil.

[6] The identity of Being, Good, and Beauty, and of Negation, Evil and Ugliness is to be assumed throughout the discussion. "We may even say that Beauty *is* the authentic-Existents and Ugliness is the Principle contrary to Existence: and the Ugly is also the primal evil; therefore its contrary is at once good and beautiful, or is Good and Beauty: and hence the one method will discover to us the Beauty-Good and the Ugliness-Evil. . . . the Intellectual-Principle . . . is preeminently the manifestation of Beauty; through the Intellectual-Principle Soul is beautiful."—*Ennead* I, vi, 6

Evil is not alone: by virtue of the nature of Good, the power of Good, it is not evil alone: it appears necessarily, bound around with bonds of Beauty, like some captive bound in fetters of gold.—*Ennead* I, viii, 15

What geometrician or arithmetician could fail to take pleasure in the symmetries, correspondences and principles of order observed in visible things? . . . Surely no one seeing the loveliness lavish in the world of sense—this vast orderliness, the Form which the stars even in their remoteness display—no one could be so dull-witted, so immovable, as not to be carried by all this to recollection, and gripped by reverent awe in the thought of all this, so great, sprung from that greatness.

—*Ennead* II, ix, 16

And if nature may be countenanced—as an excellent mirror or image —what of art? It would have been greatly to our discomfort had so radical a philosopher of unity and being as Plotinus not written in *Ennead* V, viii (one of his later essays if the chronology of Porphyry is correct) a defence of worldly beauty which was catholic enough to find room even for the products of art.[7] This he manages by saying that artists, far from being at a disadvantage, as on the Platonic view of double removal from reality, actually enjoy a more than usual divine radiation of *nous*, a more than usually full participation in the Divine Intelligence and realization of the beautiful reality of the Yonder. It is a simple exchange of basic analogies, and in the rarefied atmosphere of the Plotinian context it may seem almost arbitrary. But it makes the difference between two worlds of literary theory.

Still the arts are not to be slighted on the ground that they create by imitation of natural objects; for, to begin with, these natural objects are themselves imitations; then, we must recognize that they [the arts] give no bare reproduction of the thing seen but go back to the Ideas from which nature derives, and, furthermore, that much of their work is all their own; they are molders of beauty and add where nature is lacking. Thus Pheidias wrought the Zeus upon no model among things of sense but by apprehending what form Zeus must take if he chose to become manifest to sight.—*Ennead* V, viii, 1

If we are willing to give this passage the benefit of some 1,400 years' anachronism, to place it momentarily in a context shining back from, let us say, the Germany of the Schlegels and the England of Coleridge

---

[7] The concession is made more cursorily in the paragraph of II, ix from which we have just quoted.

and Shelley (and such a procedure can be by no means contrary to the spirit of a really critical and theoretical inquiry), we may agree with those historians who have already proclaimed Plotinus as the earliest systematic philosopher of the creative imagination.[8]

III

ENNEAD V, viii is a remarkable essay in general aesthetics, not only for its Platonic eloquence and lofty metaphysics, but for certain more analytic problems which it is likely to pose to a thoughtful reading. We have seen that the emphasis of the Plotinian system lies upon a kind of unity which we can conceive as the triumph of an ordering principle over multiplicity and diversity of parts. It is even difficult to conceive this triumph except as occurring through and in virtue of the diversity of the parts. The Plotinian term "simple" (*haplous*), a modern editor of Plotinus explains, may describe either *absence* of *internal differentiation* (as with the simplicity or unity of a pebble) or precisely the opposite, a high degree of *internal differentiation*—in other words, organic unity (as with the unity of a living body).[9] The kind of unity and intelligibility enjoyed by the Plotinian object of knowledge is furthermore not that of a species, but that of an individual, and of an individual so intensely organized as to be microcosmic, an implication of the whole universe.

> Each member shall remain what it is, distinctly apart; yet all is to form, as far as possible, a complete unity so that whatever comes into view shall show as it were the surface of the orb over all, bringing immediately with it the vision, on the one plane, of the sun and of all the stars with earth and sea and all living things as if exhibited upon a transparent globe.
>
> —*Ennead* V, viii, 9

Yet the system of Plotinus, in another of its emphases, transcends, as we have seen, the heterogeneity of this world in an ascent to a divine One that is so simply One as to be conceivable only by the method of abstraction and negation. As the mind turns from this abstracted and

---

[8] The specifically aesthetic idea and the same example occur also in the *Life of Apollonius of Tyana* written in the same century by Flavius Philostratus. "For imitation will fashion what it has seen, but imagination goes on to what it has not seen, which it will assume as the standard of reality. . . . If you have envisaged the character of Zeus, you must see him with the firmament and the seasons and the stars, as Pheidias strove to do in this statue." VI, 19. The passage is part of an argument that Greek plastic art rose above the animal symbolism of the Egyptians to an expression of divinity in the human form. Flavius Philostratus of Tarsus (c. A.D. 172–245) was a sophist who taught rhetoric at Athens and Rome.

[9] Dodds, pp. 45–6, notes to *Ennead* VI, vii, 13–15.

severe concept back to the diverse and composite world of nature and art, certain perplexities may arise.

Among the criteria of beauty known to later antiquity two of the most respected were those emphasized by Stoic philosophers and lit-terateurs: symmetry and brightness of color.[1] But how *could* symmetry be part of the definition of beauty? Think, says Plotinus, what that doctrine leads us to.

> Only a compound can be beautiful, never anything devoid of parts; and only a whole; the several parts will have beauty, not in themselves, but only as working together to give a comely total. Yet beauty in an aggregate demands beauty in details; it cannot be constructed out of ugliness; its law must run throughout.—*Ennead* I, vi, 1 [2]

> All the loveliness of color and even the light of the sun, being devoid of parts and so not beautiful by symmetry, must be ruled out of the realm of beauty. And how comes gold to be a beauti-ful thing? And lightning by night, and the stars, why are these so fair?—*Ennead* I, vi, 1

Such questions may be translated all too easily into the language of the practical literary critic. How many lines of a poem, we might ask ourselves, do we read before we begin to form some opinion of its merit? How many scenes of a play, before knowing whether we enjoy it? Certain short phrases have, or seem to have, poetic power— the sudden flashes of the sublime about which Longinus spoke—the sure "touchstones" or sovereign fragments by which Matthew Arnold in a distant post-Platonic age would propose the ordering of criticism. Our choice between a holistic view of art and a connoisseurship of the *disjecta membra* may not be able altogether to escape the fact that in one of its most natural, primitive, and perennial uses, the term *beautiful* does apply to simple and bright and smooth objects—gold rather than rusty iron, a polished topaz rather than a lump of mud. The Stoic doctrine of charming color may seem, when confronted with such ex-amples, not very profoundly integrated with that of symmetry. If nowadays we refuse to entertain any such conception as that earlier Greek one of *kosmos*[3]—the word "purple" or the word "topaz" as a

---

[1] Cicero, *Tusculan Disputations* IV, 13. Cf. Aristotle, *Metaphysics* XIII, 3: "The essential characters composing beauty are order, symmetry, and definition."

[2] Cf. the statement of Coleridge, written not without influence of Neo-Platonic reading, but shaded too by the Kantian distinction between the beautiful and the agreeable: A poem is a species of composition which proposes "to itself such delight from the *whole*, as is compatible with a distinct gratification from each component part" (*Biographia Literaria*, XIV).

[3] Cf. Lane Cooper, "The Verbal 'Ornament' (KOSMOS) in Aristotle's Art of Poetry," *Classical and Mediaeval Studies in Honor of Edward Kennard Rand*, ed.

valuable ornament in a poem—or to adopt the thought of the sophist Hippias in the Platonic dialogue, "Gold is what is beautiful,"—nevertheless we do to some extent inevitably recognize the affinity between the beautiful and the brilliant. We do so, for instance, in the very metaphors we choose for commending works of art—bright or brilliant or clean or clear, we are likely to say, not muddy, or dirty or drab.

The reconciliation which Plotinus himself effects between simple brightness and complex intelligible order as criteria of beauty is based on a metaphor that runs through all Platonic philosophy, beginning with the great image of the dark cave and the fire of knowledge in the *Republic* and the analogy of sun and eyesight to truth and intelligence.

> The beauty of colour is also the outcome of a Unification. It derives from shape, from the conquest of the darkness inherent in matter by the pouring-in of light, the unembodied, which is a Rational-Principle and an Ideal-Form.
>
> Hence it is that fire itself is splendid beyond all material bodies, holding the rank of Ideal Principle to the other elements, making ever upwards, the subtlest and sprightliest of all bodies, as very near to the unembodied; itself alone admitting no other, all the others penetrated by it: for they take warmth but this is never cold; it has colour primally; they receive the Form of colour from it: hence the splendour of its light, the splendour that belongs to the Idea. And all that has resisted and is but uncertainly held by its light remains outside of beauty, as not having absorbed the plenitude of the Form or colour.—*Ennead*, I, vi, 3

In the Persian dualistic system, the god of light, Ormazd, is the principle of good; the god of darkness, Ahriman, the equally positive principle of evil. It is one of the insights of the Platonic Western mind to make darkness a negation, brightness an analogue of all that is positive—knowledge, form, being, Divinity.

> O Light eternal who only in thyself abidest, only
> thyself doest understand, and to thy self, self-
> understood, self-understanding, turnest love and smiling! [4]

L. W. Jones (New York, 1938), pp. 61–77. "Further, add words for fine raiment, as 'purple,' and armor, as 'corslet,' 'glaive,' and 'hauberk,' and all the noble names for things that delight the senses, particularly sight and hearing, as Aristotle notes, but also touch, taste, and smell, and delight the higher sensibilities, and for things with which men and women adorn themselves, their servants, their animals, their houses, public buildings, ships; 'jewel' and the names of jewels—'beryl,' 'topaz,' 'amethyst,' 'diamond,' 'coral,' 'pearl,' and 'ruby'; words for incense and perfume—'frankincense,' 'spices,' and 'myrrh'; beautiful words from music, 'music' itself, 'melody,' 'harmony,' 'choral,' 'canticle,' 'alleluia,' and the names of instruments, the harp, the flute. . . ." (pp. 70–1).

[4] *Paradiso*, XXXIII, 124–6, trans. Philip H. Wicksteed.

O luce eterna, che sola in te sidi,
sola t'intendi, e, da te intelleta
ed intendente te, ami ed arridi!

Hail holy Light, offspring of Heaven first-born,
Or of the Eternal coeternal beam.

Lo! thy dread Empire, CHAOS! is restored;
Light dies before thy uncreating word;
. . .
And universal darkness buries all.

The idea of brightness as intelligible form is closely connected with
another classical aesthetic idea—found, for instance, in Plato's *Philebus*
and *Hippias Major* and again in *Enneads* I, vi, 1—that Beauty is discerned
chiefly by the senses of sight and hearing [5]—these being the highest or
most intellectual senses and those through which we derive our most distinct ideas of pattern and, more abstractly and metaphysically, of "form."
Plotinus takes it for granted that sight comes first. "Beauty addresses itself
chiefly to sight."

Again the refined sensory experience of sight allies itself readily
with the idea that human knowledge arises from some kind of interdependence between object and organ. "Thought and thing depend upon
and correspond to each other."

Never did the eye see the sun unless it had first become Sunlike,
and never can the soul have vision of the First Beauty unless itself be beautiful.—*Enneads* I, vi, 9

Like alone sees like. Or as modern students of neo-Platonism, quoting
Blake, are likely to put it.

The sun's light when he unfolds it,
Depends on the organ that beholds it.

Or, quoting Goethe:

Did not the eye partake of sun,
Sun would be darkness to our seeing;
No splendour could from the divine be won
Were God not part of mortal being.[6]

In the higher reaches of Plotinian thought, the idea of the brilliant intelligibility of all being blends into the idea that being *is* pure intelligibility

[5] Cf. Aristotle, *Politics* VIII, 5, and *ante* Chapter 2, pp. 26–7.
[6] Ludwig Lewisohn, *Goethe: The Story of a Man* (New York, c. 1949), II, 74,
Lewisohn's translation from Goethe's *Zahme Xenien*, III, by permission of Farrar,
Straus and Cudahy, Inc.

or is composed of ideas. "It is hard to work down to crude matter beneath all that sheathing of idea." [7]

Perhaps one of the chief questions about beauty which the system of Plotinus is likely to provoke a modern reader to ask will run somewhat as follows: Are all the perfect forms (*eidē*) equally good and beautiful? And if not, how do we know which sensible forms have more beauty than others? Is a peacock more beautiful than a goose? Is a worm or a warthog more beautiful than certain objects undoubtedly lower in the hierarchy of complex unities but more usually called beautiful, say a block of lapis lazuli or even a finely cut diamond? Plotinus himself has written two contrasting passages which present the problem succinctly. One, from *Ennead* I, vi, 2, we have quoted above:

> . . . there is the beauty, conferred by craftsmanship, of all a house with all its parts, and the beauty which some natural quality may give to a single stone.

The following appears in *Ennead* V, viii, 1:

> Suppose two blocks of stone lying side by side: one is unpatterned, quite untouched by art; the other has been minutely wrought by the craftsman's hands into some statue of God or man, a Grace or a Muse, or if a human being, not a portrait but a creation in which the sculptor's art has concentrated all loveliness.
>
> Now it must be seen that the stone thus brought under the artist's hand to the beauty of form is beautiful not as stone—for so the crude stone would be as pleasant—but in virtue of the form or idea introduced by art. This form is not in the material; it is in the designer before it enters the stone.

The stone as something already existent is a being and has a form of its own, a unity and beauty. But then to expound the stamping of form on the formlessness of sheer matter, we adopt the analogy of the image finely imposed upon the simple and unadorned piece of material. Form upon form. And how beautiful was the original form? And is something of it not lost in the carving? The theory of Plotinus does not start as a theory of beauty, much less as a theory of art or poems. It is a theory of the world and God, of all being and all knowing, and only as an incident

---

[7] *Ennead* V, viii, 7. *Ennead* I, vi, 3 bears a marked resemblance to the notion of closure or psychic completion of forms found today in Gestalt psychology and in general aesthetics. "So with the perceptive faculty: discerning in certain objects the Ideal-form which has bound and controlled shapeless matter, opposed in nature to Idea, seeing further stamped upon the common shapes some shape excellent above the common, it gathers into unity what still remains fragmentary, catches it up and carries it within, no longer a thing of parts, and presents it to the Ideal-Principle. . . ."

or an analogy does it find a place for art. The opposite procedure, to start by explicitly attempting a theory of art and to move away from that to a general epistemology,—that is, to try to explain art or beauty or poetry by a principle so broad that it explains everything else too—is a reversal, or mirror imaging, of neo-Platonism which appears in some forms of modern idealism and aesthetic and perhaps testifies to the toughness of the paradox posed by Plotinus.[8]

IV

THE ideas of Plotinus, though perhaps least likely of all ideas about aesthetics to be widely known or respected today, have had their subsequent career and their analogues—especially among Christian philosophers from about the time of Plotinus himself to the late middle ages. St. Augustine for instance had read Plotinus in a Latin translation, and as he shared with Plotinus the aim of combatting the several forms of dualism and Puritanism prevalent in the third and fourth centuries (he was frequently engaged, for instance, *Contra Manichaeos*), he gives us some rather close echoes of the neo-Platonic philosopher.

> Without unity nothing could exist. To be is no other than to be one; the more unity a thing has, so much the more being does it possess . . . no material object is really one because a body as such is indefinitely divisible, potentially, if not actually.[9]

> Any beautiful object whatsoever is more worthy of praise in its totality as a whole than in any one of its parts. So great is the power of integrity and unity that what pleases as a part pleases much more as a unified whole.[1]

The Plotinian affinity between subject and object is argued by Augustine at both the sensory and spiritual levels. The senses enjoy whatever is proportioned to them by simple reason of the principle that agreement always produces pleasure.[2] And the full aesthetic pleasure of delighted contemplation (*beate contemplari*) occurs in the presence of objects which are in harmony not only with the senses but with the whole na-

---

[8] See *post* Chapter 23, Benedetto Croce.

[9] *De Moribus Ecclesiae Catholicae et de Moribus Manichaeorum* II, vi. Translations from Augustine in this paragraph are adopted from Immanuel Chapman, *Saint Augustine's Philosophy of Beauty* (New York, 1935); see esp. pp. 59, 61, 63. See the same author's "Some Aspects of St. Augustine's Philosophy of Beauty," *Journal of Aesthetics and Art Criticism*, I (Spring, 1941), 46–51. The Latin texts of St. Augustine may be consulted in J. C. Migne's *Patrologia Latina*, vols. XXXII and XXXIV (Paris, 1841, 1845).

[1] *De Genesi Contra Manichaeos* I, xxi.

[2] *De Vera Religione* I, xxxix; *De Musica* VI, xiii.

ture of man, especially with the mind as the ruler and interpreter of the senses.[3] In Augustine's treatise *De Musica* a line from a hymn by St. Ambrose, *Deus creator omnium*, furnishes the more analytic concepts— funneled as it were towards unity—of number, form, and order.[4] The heading of Book VI of the *De Musica*, "The ascent from rhythm in sense to the immortal rhythm which is in truth,"[5] synopsizes the argument by which Augustine, returning to Pythagorean and Platonic ideas about number, performs for the aesthetic of sound a service analogous to that performed by Plotinus for the aesthetic of bright colors. Like Plotinus and even more like Socrates arguing the doctrine of recollection (*anamnēsis*) in the *Phaedo* and *Meno*, Augustine is at a loss to know how we derive from our actually imperfect material experiences the normative concepts of order and perfection. He maintains that we do not. Such criteria are supplied to our minds, or infused, directly by divine gift.[6]

The argument is marked by a certain etherealism, an appeal to what a modern literary critic might call the "angelic imagination."[7] The quest for beauty is rather an argument from divine postulates than an attempt to ascend from human experience. Or at any rate it is ordered by a devotion to harmony and unity which in many places seems to entertain little respect for the multiplicity and resistance of the secular principle. The supreme good of the spirit is *monas*, a state of freedom from the discords incident to human life, even from the division intrinsic to sex. Moral evil is *duas*, two-ness, the failure to submit to the power of the One.[8] From such principles it follows more or less plausibly—though perhaps not with strict necessity—that among geometrical figures an equilateral triangle is more beautiful than a scalene, a square even more beautiful than an equilateral triangle, and a circle the most beautiful figure of all.[9] One likes the doors and windows of a house to be arranged symmetrically.[1] Here is a critical spirit which if not militantly anti-dramatic seems at least largely indifferent to whatever aesthetic claims may be enjoyed by the principle of division or conflict. Like Plotinus, Augustine seems to understand beauty as arising through a unity which occurs in spite of, or aside from, the diversity of parts. Certainly this beauty does not arise *through*, or at least not in virtue of, that diversity.

It may be with some surprise that we encounter certain remarks which Augustine let fall in other connections. A work of art, he will say

[3] *De Ordine* II, xii.
[4] *De Musica* VI, ii.
[5] W. F. Jackson Knight, *St. Augustine's De Musica* (London, 1949).
[6] *De Vera Religione* I, xxx–xxxi.
[7] Allen Tate, *The Forlorn Demon* (Chicago, 1953), esp. p. 37; William F. Lynch, "Theology and the Imagination," *Thought*, XXIX (Spring, 1954), esp. p. 76.
[8] *De Ordine* II, xv–xix; Gilbert and Kuhn, pp. 133–4, citing K. Svoboda, *L'Esthétique de St. Augustine et ses Sources*, Brno, 1933.
[9] *De Quantitate Animae* I, ix.
[1] *De Ordine* II, xi.

in one place, has its own truth, and just in virtue of its being a particular species of falsehood. An artist cannot be true to himself unless he is in a sense a maker of lies.[2] Again: Rightly attuned souls will look at all things in their contexts. Beauty cannot bear scrutiny in isolation. Augustine is indeed able to countenance something very much like an artistic theory of harmony *through* contrast, beauty *in* variety: Poets use even barbarisms and solecisms to "season" their poetry; sweet music is made sweeter by the consonance of differing voices; a drama needs clowns and villains to bring out the virtue of the heroes.[3]

One problem which somewhat puzzled Augustine concerned the appearance of symbols in the Scriptures. Why was it pleasant to linger in symbols? to prefer the outer show to the inner and pure meaning? Was it commendable? The more remote or difficult the divine symbol (the lion, the panther, the bear, the worm), the more difficult perhaps the problem. Another writer of the patristic era, the Pseudo-Dionysius, speaks (almost in what nowadays we might call "metaphysical" terms) of incongruity, shock and stimulus to the mind in unravelling mystery.[4] Augustine himself engages in a meditation which comes close to stating, if not so close to solving, one of the main problems of literary criticism in every age.

> I feel greater pleasure in contemplating holy men, when I view them as the teeth of the Church, tearing men away from their errors. . . . It is with the greatest pleasure too that I recognize them under the figure of sheep that have been shorn. . . . But why I view them with greater delight under that aspect than if no such figure were drawn from the sacred books, though the fact would remain the same, is another question, and one very difficult to answer. Nobody, however, has any doubt about the facts, both that it is pleasanter in some cases to have knowledge communicated through figures, and that what is attended with difficulty in the seeking gives greater pleasure in the finding.[5]

V

NINE hundred years later than Augustine, Thomas Aquinas turned the preoccupation of Christian metaphysics from the Platonic realm yonder

---

[2] *Soliloquia* II, x. Cf. *Confessions* III, vi; Gilbert and Kuhn, p. 126.

[3] *De Ordine* II, iv. Gilbert and Kuhn, p. 138, point out that Plotinus had said: "Take away the low characters and the power of the drama is gone; they are part and parcel of it."

[4] *De Coelesti Hierarchia* II ("*Quod apte res divinae atque coelestes dissimilibus etiam signis explicentur*"), v (in *Patrologia Graeca*, ed. J. C. Migne, III, 143-6). Cf. Gilbert and Kuhn, p. 154-5.

[5] *De Doctrina Christiana* II, vi, quoted by Gilbert and Kuhn, pp. 153-4, from *Nicene and Post-Nicene Fathers*, 1st Series, II (Buffalo, 1887), 537. Cf. Migne, *Patrologia Latina*, XXXIV, 38-9.

of forms to an Aristotelian, immediately experienced world of natural substances. It was a world, however, which pointed upwards (like a cathedral, says Henry Adams) to a transcendentally substantive and personal God.[6] Between the dreaminess of Plotinian pantheistic immanence and the concrete, particular, historical claim of Christianity there was a difference which was bound to develop sooner or later theoretical differences at the aesthetic as well as at the metaphysical and theological levels. The Plotinian theory of emanation, a theory of continuity between Creator and created, a shading of values, is supplanted in the Christian Aristotelianism of Aquinas by an emphatic distinction between God and his works. Our apprehension of God, the source of the beautiful, is not by any kind of either spiritual or abstractive suffusion, as, for instance, of light from an inner stage seen through a gauze curtain, but by a clear apprehension of, and reasoning from, the separate works of His hand. The philosophy of the first ten or twelve centuries of the Christian era had been, for that matter, not only a Platonic attack on materialism (at some moments even carried to the extreme of "iconoclasm" [7]) but alternatively, in certain phases, a realistic (and in that sense a materialistic) defense of this world against the Gnostic and Manichaean rarefactions of value.[8] A certain kind of beauty, a serenely abstracted and ordered cosmos of neo-Platonism (in which abstraction itself was spirituality and divinity)—like the columns of a Greek temple distant upon a hill in a luminous mist—was cut across and wrecked by the concretely historical, bloody and suffering claim of Christianity. A fourth-century Roman philosopher, Eunapius, called it a "fabulous and formless darkness mastering the loveliness of the world." [9] And a modern Irish poet has echoed:

> The Roman Empire stood appalled:
> It dropped the reins of peace and war
> When that fierce virgin and her Star
> Out of the fabulous darkness called.[1]

Yet we may be disappointed if we look to Aquinas or to other theologians of the high Middle Ages for any new and more concrete theory of beauty, of fine art in general, or of poetry. In the aesthetic remarks of Aquinas—remarks occurring mainly at three places in his

[6] See the elaboration of this image by Henry Adams, *Mont-Saint-Michel and Chartres* (Boston, 1927), p. 382.

[7] Cf. Bosanquet, *A History of Aesthetic*, pp. 132–9.

[8] Cf. Etienne Gilson, *The Philosophy of St. Thomas Aquinas*, trans. Edward Bullough (London, 1937), Ch. 17, esp. p. 354; Thomas Gilby, *Poetic Experience* (New York, 1934), pp. 23–4.

[9] Eunapius, *Vita Maximi*, quoted by E. R. Dodds, *Select Passages Illustrating Neoplatonism* (London, 1923), p. 8.

[1] W. B. Yeats, "Two Songs from a Play," *Collected Poems* (New York, 1942), p. 246, by permission of The Macmillan Company.

Summa Theologiae[2] and in his opuscular commentary on the *Divine Names* of Dionysius—we have a discussion of "beauty" precisely as a "Divine Name." "Beauty" belongs to form and intelligence, and hence pre-eminently to the contemplative life.[3] If we try to take Aquinas in the most secular or natural way we can—looking at what he says about the objects in this world which are the analogical starting points for our knowledge of Divine beauty and at what he says about the human experience of perceiving beauty, we find a kind of tabloid and laconic, even casual, codification of the principles with which we are familiar in the earlier centuries of neo-Platonism. Beautiful things, he says, are those which are apprehended with pleasure—*quae visa placent*—and thus he parallels Augustine in giving his simplest definition of the beautiful a subjective accent. As with Augustine and Plotinus, we are once more in the presence of a basic assumption of radical harmony between man the knower and the external universe which he knows—and in some parts of which he takes a special delight. The beauty of a beautiful object consists not merely in a self-enclosed character but in a corresponding external relation of fitness to the knowing subject, a relation of knowability. All knowledge, and especially knowledge of the beautiful, and pleasure in the beautiful, arise by a kind of union between subject and object.[4]

As for that object itself, the cognitive counterpart of aesthetic pleasure, it must have three qualities (*tria requiruntur*): wholeness or perfection (*integritas sive perfectio*), due proportion or harmony (*debita proportio sive consonantia*), and brilliance (*claritas*). The term "harmony" may sound sufficiently broad, but it is worth noting that in this passage Aquinas seems to be thinking chiefly about the kind of "harmony" that obtains between an image and what it images. This requirement for beauty, he says, is found in the Son because he is the "express image of the Father" (*inquantum est imago expressa Patris*).[5] No doubt the Stoic

---

[2] *Summa Theologiae* I, 5, 4, ad 1m (*quae visa placent*); I, 39, 8 (*tria requiruntur*); I–II, 27, 1, ad 3m (*sensus maximi cognoscitivi*). Works of Aquinas are conveniently consulted in *Sancti Thomae Aquinatis . . . Opera Omnia*, ed. Vernon J. Bourke, vols. I–XXV (New York: Musurgia Publishers, 1948–50). This is a photographic reproduction of the edition at Parma, 1852–73.

[3] "*Et ideo in vita contemplativa, quae consistit in actu rationis, per se et essentialiter inventur pulchritudo.*" *Summa Theologiae* II–II, 180, 2, ad 3m.

[4] "*Sensus delectantur in rebus debite proportionatis, sicut in sibi similibus. . . . Et cognitio fit per assimilationem, assimilitudo autem respicit formam*" (*Summa Theologiae* I, 5, 4, ad 1m). Concerning the peculiarly subjective and emotive kind of knowledge called by neo-Thomists "knowledge through connaturality" or "knowledge through effective connaturality," see Thomas Gilby, *Poetic Experience* (New York, 1934), p. 21; Jacques Maritain, *Creative Intuition in Art and Poetry* (New York, 1953), pp. 117–25. See de Bruyne I, 26 and III, 23 on musical and visual harmonies between man and the universe in different phases of medieval aesthetics.

[5] *Summa Theologiae* I, 39, 8. Echoing Aristotle and other ancient writers, Aquinas adds that an image is said to be beautiful if it perfectly represents even an ugly object (*Unde videmus quod aliqua imago dicitur esse pulchra, si perfecte repraesentat rem, quamvis turpem*). It is perhaps permissible to reflect further that if an image

criterion of bright color occurs to Aquinas with a special recommendation in the light of the cathedral art with which he was familiar, the Byzantine mosaic, the rose-stained glass of nave or apse,[6] the bright painting of the school of Cimabue. "Bright colored objects," remarks Aquinas, "are said to be beautiful." Yet neo-scholastic commentators hasten to assure us, and plausibly, that such *claritas* is but the accent of perfection in the structural concept. They produce from an opusculum written either by Aquinas or by his master Albertus the phrase *resplendentia formae*— "the splendor of form shining upon the proportioned parts of matter, or upon diverse powers or actions." [7] In Aquinas, as in most of the theological and aesthetic writers of his century, and notably the Franciscans, we find the Plotinian and Platonic philosophy of light more radiant than ever. *Claritas, splendor, resplendentia, fulgor, lux, lumen*—such words recur throughout theological writing with almost as much frequency as words relating to *form* itself or to unity and being.[8] And we are not surprised to read in this context, as we have read before in Plato, Plotinus, and Augustine, that sight and hearing are the senses which preeminently open on beauty, because they are the preeminently intellectual senses (*maxime cognoscitivi*).[9]

---

is proportioned to an object (even an ugly object), the image by that very fact will have its own, internal, proportion or harmony, corresponding to the degree of harmony which the object must have in order to be an object at all. See the interesting speculation of Dorothy Sayers on "Trinitarian" aspects of poetic creation, *Unpopular Opinions* (London, 1946), p. 37, "Towards a Christian Aesthetic." John A. Duffy, *A Philosophy of Poetry Based on Thomistic Principles* (Washington, D.C., 1945), pp. 28–9, lists a number of passages on beauty in which Aquinas uses such terms as *consonantia, ordo, proportio* in a more directly internal sense to mean relation or location of parts (*situs partium*).

[6] Cf. Robert Grinnell, "Iconography and Philosophy in the Crucifixion Window at Poitiers," *Art Bulletin*, XXVIII (September, 1946), 171–96.

[7] *Opusculum de Pulchro et Bono* I, 6, 2. Cf. Jacques Maritain, *Art and Scholasticism*, trans. J. F. Scanlan (New York, 1943), pp. 25, 160; Leonard Callahan, *A Theory of Esthetic, According to the Principles of St. Thomas Aquinas* (Washington, D.C., 1927), pp. 31, 89, 126, quoting *Opuscula Selecta S. Thomae Aquinatis* (Paris, 1908) XXI, *De Pulchro et de Bono*: "[Pulchrum] congregat omnia, et hoc habet ex parte formae cujus resplendentia facit pulchrum. . . . Secundum autem quod forma resplendet super partes materiae, sic est pulchrum habens rationem congregandi. . . . Ratio pulchri in universali consistit in resplendentia formae super partes materiae proportionatas, vel super diversas vires, vel actiones."

[8] Gilbert and Kuhn, p. 141. For an extended account of the pervasive 13th-century neo-Platonic and Biblical philosophy of light—an aesthetic of light, mystical, physical, and cosmological—see de Bruyne III, 3–29, "*L'esthétique de la lumière.*" See Robert Grosseteste, *On Light*, trans. Clare C. Kiedl (Milwaukee, 1942).

[9] "*Illi sensus praecipue respiciunt pulchrum qui maxime cognoscitivi sunt, scilicet visus et auditus rationi deservientes: dicimus enim pulchra visibilia et pulchros sonos; non enim dicimus pulchros sapores aut odores*" (*Summa Theologiae* I-II, 27, 1, ad 3m). The opinion of Aquinas seems, however, by no means rigid. Other passages (*Summa Theologiae* I, 91, 3, ad 3m; *In Libris Aristotelis De Coelo et Mundo Expositio* II, 14) suggest that he looked upon the human pleasure in smelling flowers as close to the beautiful when compared with an animal's pleasure in smelling food. See John A. Duffy, *A Philosophy of Beauty* . . . , p. 62.

Beauty is thought to be apprehended in a kind of reposeful contemplation (*pulchrum . . . cuius ipsa apprehensio placet*) [1] and in that sense is different from the good (*bonum*),[2] which is the object of appetite. The conception is much better known to modern aestheticians under its Kantian name of "disinterest." There may be difficulties here, relating to the fact that the very act of knowing is a kind of possessing, so that "possession" in the sense of control or ownership, though less often requisite for aesthetic knowing than for other kinds of knowing, is scarcely the crux of the argument. We know the picture that we see in the art gallery (or in our own collection), and we know the apple that we eat, and it is these two kinds of knowledge or possession that must be compared—the amorphic and even destructively internal possession of the apple and the more coolly distanced ocular union with the picture. The pleasure afforded by a thing we call beautiful—whether a natural object or a product of art—would seem to differ from other pleasures in being more steady and cumulative and more surely held by the mind, and more charged with symbolic intimations. In the case of the overtly symbolic or referential arts at least, and especially in that of verbal arts, it is easy to make a distinction between those, the rhetorical, whose end is persuasory and dynamic (to move us toward their referents) and those others, the poetic —sometimes nowadays called the "autotelic"—arts, which seem to absorb the interest of their referents and hold it in themselves by a kind of symbolic suspension.

One of the most striking technical feats of Thomist aesthetic consists in its being able to confront rather squarely that paradox of the two stones —plain beauty and excellently carved beauty—which was bequeathed by Plotinus. This is accomplished through one of the central concepts of the metaphysics, that of "analogy," the very concept by which the whole world of created reality is kept both dependent upon and apart from God. Both above and below, beauty is in everything. It is a transcendental, surpassing "all limits of kind or category." It is always relative to the individual form.[3] It is predicated differently (that is, analogously) of each beautiful object in the wide variety of objects to which we give that

---

[1] *Summa Theologiae* I–II, 271, ad 3m. Cf. *In Librum Beati Dionysii de Divinis Nominibus Expositio* IV, v, 356: "*Quamvis autem pulchrum et bonum sint idem subiecto, quia tam claritas quam consonantia sub ratione boni continentur, tamen ratione differunt: nam pulchrum addit supra bonum, ordinem ad vim cognoscitivam illud esse huiusmodi*" (ed. Fra Ceslai Pera, O.P., Turin and Rome, 1950, p. 115).

[2] Yet the distinction again is hardly rigid. *Summa Theologiae* II–II, 145, 2, "*Utrum honestum sit idem quod decorum*," argues that moral good is spiritual beauty: "*Et ideo honestum est idem spirituali decori. Unde Augustinus dicit . . . 'Honestum voco intelligibilem pulchritudinem, quam spiritualem nos proprie dicimus.'*"

[3] "*Pulchritudo quodamodo dicitur per respectum ad aliquid. Alia enim est pulchritudo spiritus et alia corporis, atque alia hujus et illius corporis*" (*In Librum Beati Dionysii de Divinis Nominibus Expositio* IV, v, 339; ed. cit., p. 113).

name. As one neo-Thomist,[4] with his eye on the logical and semantic difficulties involved, has put it: we use an ordinary, literal specific term like "man" in a way that does not admit the idea of more or less and in a way that is standard or univocal. Jack is not less a man than Jim, and each is a man in just the same way and for just the same reason. But it is clear that the contrary is true of a term like "beauty." Beauty is indeed everywhere, and it is more or less. And in each case (and most clearly in each case of expressive art) beauty is of a different kind or occurs for a different reason. The details always have to be taken into account in some special way. As another neo-Thomist has said wittily: "The lack of a head or an arm is a serious defect in a woman but of much less account in a statue—whatever disappointment M. Ravaisson may have felt at being unable to *complete* the Venus of Melos." [5]

For such reasons, the discussion of the term "beauty" in Aquinas is not closely related to, and is not at all dependent upon, the discussion of the term "art," however close or inevitable the association between the two terms may have come to seem in later times. Art in the Middle Ages is just the right way of making whatever anybody happens to be making (*recta ratio factibilium*)—each artifact according to its own plan, in a hierarchy, a cathedral being worth more than a cowshed, but each one right (and beautiful) in its own way. In this hierarchy there were, from a modern point of view, certain curious placements—painting in the same class with saddle-making, for instance, because saddles were painted.[6] The physical, servile, or mechanical arts in general (not only saddle-making and shoe-making but sculpture, architecture, and painting) were on a plane inferior to that of the seven liberal arts named in the canon of the encyclopedist Martianus Capella: grammar, rhetoric, logic, dialectic, music, arithmetic, geometry, and astronomy. And these in turn were, of course, inferior to the theological arts. The medieval conception viewed from its lower end (the root of any functionalist theory of art) has been neatly epitomized in our century by the neo-Thomist sculptor and theorist Eric Gill in the title of his book *Beauty Looks After Herself*. "To make a drain pipe," he says in another book, "is as much the work of an artist as it is to make paintings or poems." [7] Properly speaking, there are no fine arts in such a system. The neo-Thomist philosopher Jacques Maritain offers us his own version of the two stones of Plotinus when he says that what we now call the fine arts are right ways of making which are some-

---

[4] Thomas Gilby, *Barbara Celarent* (London, 1949), pp. 78–9.

[5] Jacques Maritain, *Art and Scholasticism*, trans. J. F. Scanlan (New York, 1943), p. 27. The joke is not altogether spoiled by the fact that this Hellenistic statue was not made à la Rodin, and that it *would* actually be completed by the restoration of its arms. See R. H. Wilenski, *The Meaning of Modern Sculpture* (London, c. 1933), p. 66.

[6] Gilbert and Kuhn, pp. 157–8.

[7] *Art* (London, 1935), p. 4.

how specially directed to the splendid rightness of beauty—a species is in a peculiar way turned back upon its transcendental genus.[8]

And in all this what of poetry? The literary student will by now have missed any conspicuous mention of poetry either under the Thomist head of beauty (what especially affects the senses of sight and hearing) or under that of art (a discipline of honest making). We hear that the Middle Ages, following such ancient writers as Quintilian and Augustine, were likely to treat poetry as a pendant to logic, or to rhetoric. (The Dutch Meistersingers called themselves rhetoricians, for poetry was a "secondary rhetoric.") Or in deference to Aristotle's dictum, repeated by Aquinas, that one cannot think logically without framing images, poetry might be made a propaedeutic to logic.[9] The student who inquires about poetry in the system of Aquinas himself will search the texts to find poetry treated only here and there, either as a problem in semantics—the locale of a kind of subrational metaphoric evasion (to be distinguished from theological analogy) [1]—or as an art of verbal reasoning lower even than sophistic or rhetoric (that is, at the bottom) in a scale which has Aristotelian metaphysical demonstration at the top.[2]

> Poetic knowledge concerns matters which through a deficiency in their truth cannot be laid hold of by the reason; hence the reason has to be beguiled by means of certain similitudes. Theology, on the other hand, deals with matters which are above reason. So the symbolic mode is common to both types of discourse; neither type is suited to reasoning.[3]

VI

THE train of sceptical and scientific thinking which began with Galileo and Descartes was not friendly to the kind of aesthetic we have been

[8] *Art and Scholasticism* (New York, 1943), pp. 33-4. See his later adjustment of this view—beauty an "end beyond the end" of "poetry," a "transcendental correlative"—in *Creative Intuition in Art and Poetry* (New York, 1951), pp. 167-71.

[9] Gilbert and Kuhn, p. 157. Cf. Aristotle, *De Anima* III, 7; Aquinas, *In Boethii de Trinitate* 6, 2, ad 5m.

[1] Cf. Walter J. Ong, "Wit and Mystery: A Revaluation," *Speculum*, XXII (1947), 324.

[2] Cf. Walter J. Ong, "The Province of Rhetoric and Poetic," *Modern Schoolman*, XIX (1942), 25, quoting Aquinas, *In I. Analytica Posteriora*, lectio 1.

[3] "*Ad tertium dicendum, quod poetica scientia est de his quae propter defectum veritatis non possunt a ratione capi; unde oportet quod quasi quibusdam similitudinibus ratio seducatur: theologia autem est de his quae sunt supra rationem; et ideo modus symbolicus utrique communis est, cum neutra rationi proportionetur.*" *Commentum in Primum Librum Sententiarum Magistri Petri Lombardi, Prologus*, q.1, a5, ad 3m. See M.-D. Chenu, O.P., *Introduction à l'Étude de Saint Thomas D'Aquin* (Montreal, 1950), pp. 93, 144, for a succinct statement of the opposition between the Aristotelian and scholastic scientific Latin style of Aquinas and the Platonic and Augustinian poetical styles of irony, metaphor, and symbol.

sketching, at least not to its ontological supports, Platonic or Thomistic. Yet as early as the late 17th century and notably in the *Monadology* and related essays and letters of Leibniz, an idealistic reaction set in which was not without affinities for neo-Platonism and which, if pursued through German aesthetics of the later 18th century to the flowering of German and English criticism,[4] would provide a chain of statements about beauty through unity and order[5] with which one might amply continue our history. The kind of "organic" unity acclaimed by Coleridge and the Germans, with its strongly pantheistic implications about the organic structure of the universe and the union in knowledge and being of subject and object, will be a part of our theme in later chapters (17 and 18). By the end of the 19th century, several forms of idealism had become available for litterateurs of a metaphysical bent. They might turn to various romantic and neo-Platonic forms—or, just after 1900, to Crocean expressionism. It was a distinct anachronism, however, that the novelist James Joyce should at about that date allow an acquaintance with scholastic philosophy gained in his school days with the Jesuits in Clongowes and Dublin to determine the character of the rather elaborate exposition of an aesthete's creed which occurs toward the end of *A Portrait of the Artist as a Young Man*.[6] An account of this retrospective and romanticized piece of scholasticism may serve appropriately as a conclusion to the present chapter and to the present section of our history. In a rather florid, even pompous, yet sufficiently accurate style of schoolroom metaphysics Stephen Dedalus expounds to his friend Lynch a series of freely rendered Thomistic theses.

> You see I use the word *arrest*. I mean that the tragic emotion is static. Or rather the dramatic emotion is. The feelings excited by improper art are kinetic, desire or loathing. . . . The arts which excite them, pornographical or didactic, are therefore improper arts. The esthetic emotion . . . is therefore static. The mind is arrested and raised above desire and loathing.—*Portrait*, p. 205

> Aquinas . . . says that is beautiful the apprehension of which pleases. p. 207

. . .

---

[4] See a convenient summary by James Benziger, "Organic Unity: Leibniz to Coleridge," PMLA, LXVI (March, 1951), 24–48.

[5] See for instance Coleridge's three essays "On the Principles of Genial Criticism," *Biographia Literaria* (ed. J. Shawcross), II, esp. p. 239.

[6] "The lore . . . was only a garner of slender sentences from Aristotle's Poetics and Psychology and a *Synopsis Philosophiae Scholasticae ad mentem divi Thomae*." The *Synopsis* is apparently not to be identified with any school book actually used by Joyce. The quotations from *A Portrait of the Artist* which follow in our text are from the Viking Compass Edition, New York, 1956, by permission of The Viking Press, Inc.

. . . all people who admire a beautiful object find in it certain relations which satisfy and coincide with the stages themselves of all esthetic apprehension.   p. 209

Aquinas says: *Ad pulcritudinem tria requiruntur integritas, consonantia, claritas.* . . . Do these correspond to the phases of apprehension? p. 211

The synthesis of immediate perception is followed by the analysis of apprehension. Having first felt that it is one thing, you feel now that it is a thing. You apprehend it as complex, multiple, divisible, separable, made up of its parts, the result of its parts and their sum, harmonious. That is *consonantia*.   p. 212

. . . you make the only synthesis which is logically and esthetically permissible. You see that it is that thing which it is and no other thing. The radiance of which he speaks is the scholastic *quidditas*,[7] the *whatness* of a thing. . . . The instant wherein that supreme quality of beauty, the clear radiance of the esthetic image, is apprehended luminously by the mind which has been arrested by its wholeness and fascinated by its harmony is the luminous silent stasis of esthetic pleasure.—p. 213

We have Aquinas, we might say, with inverted emphasis, or the *tria* of required objective qualities seen upside down in the deep pool of the poet's imagination. It is an idealistic modification which rings very naturally against the background of the preceding century. The other form of idealism, the Platonic or purely symbolic, by which beauty is "a light from some other world, the idea of which matter was but the shadow," is explicitly rejected by Stephen (pp. 249–50). "That is literary talk." And to complete the account, it is worth noting that in Joyce's earlier and longer version of the *Portrait* entitled *Stephen Hero*, the idea of "claritas" has a somewhat different accent.

> *Claritas* is *quidditas*. After the analysis which discovers the second quality the mind makes the only possible synthesis and discovers the third quality. This is the moment which I call epiphany. First we recognize that the object is *one* integral thing, then we recognize that it is an organized composite structure, a *thing* in fact: finally, when the relation of the parts is exquisite, when the parts are adjusted to the special point, we recognize that it is *that* thing which it is. Its soul, its whatness, leaps to us from the vestment of its appearance. The soul of the commonest object,

---

[7] As Stephen expounds the matter, this radiance is more like scholastic *haecceitas* or individuality. *Quidditas* is actually the Aristotelian specific universal, the essence of the main class to which the individual belongs. See Aquinas, *On Being and Essence*, ed. A. A. Maurer (Toronto, 1949).

the structure of which is so adjusted, seems to us radiant. The object achieves its epiphany.[8]

There is more about discovery here, less about a phase of apprehension and feeling. More about the soul of the object, less about the imagination of the artist. With its now current Joycean word *epiphany*, the passage may strike us as more clearly like Joyce himself and significantly less like Stephen Dedalus, rebellious aesthete, scribbler of *fin de siècle* verses, "priest of the eternal imagination."

Taken as a dual statement and dramatically ambiguous emphasis on the relation between object and response in the experience of the beautiful, the aesthetic of Stephen Dedalus may be thought of as epitomizing and holding unresolved a choice that has haunted not only aesthetics but general epistemology since early times. The answers we have been hearing up to now have borne far more heavily on object than on response or feeling. We have yet to hear the opposite case in any strength. By way of anticipating some of the main themes of the history which lies ahead of us and of indicating their relation to what has gone before, one might draw a diagram of two radically opposed axes of aesthetic theory, thus:

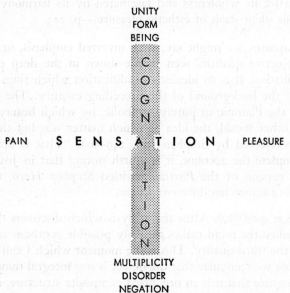

UNITY
FORM
BEING

PAIN   S E N S A T I O N   PLEASURE

C O G N I T I O N

MULTIPLICITY
DISORDER
NEGATION

The classical theories of antiquity range themselves along the vertical axis, with Plotinus one of the most systematic classical spokesmen but at the same time the most subjectively idealistic. We have had so far no instance of a theory lying simply along the horizontal axis—though the

[8] *Stephen Hero* (New York, 1944), p. 213. Copyright 1944, 1955 by New Directions and reprinted by permission of the publisher, New Directions.

affective clause—*quod placet*—is somewhat prominent with Aquinas. The era of fully horizontal theory does not appear until the 18th and 19th centuries. In the *Portrait* Stephen guards against one form of affectivism, the exclusively sensate.

> The desire and loathing excited by improper esthetic means are really not esthetic emotions not only because they are kinetic in character but also because they are not more than physical. Our flesh shrinks from what it dreads and responds to the stimulus of what it desires by a purely reflex action of the nervous system. Our eyelid closes before we are aware that the fly is about to enter our eye.—p. 241

Some of the most refined theories of aesthetic value which have appeared since the date of the *Portrait* have been attempts to raise the horizontalism of sensate and purely emotive theory into an alignment with the cognitive. Modern aesthetics may be thought of, provisionally, as operating along a line drawn at some intermediate angle of our diagram.

SUPPLEMENT

Eryximachus spoke as follows: . . . . medicine may be regarded generally as the knowledge of the loves and desires of the body, and how to satisfy them or not; and the best physician is he who is able to separate fair love from foul, or to convert one into the other; and he who knows how to eradicate and how to implant love, whichever is required, and can reconcile the most hostile elements in the constitution and make them loving friends, is a skilful practitioner. Now the most hostile are the most opposite, such as hot and cold, bitter and sweet, moist and dry, and the like. And my ancestor, Asclepius, knowing how to implant friendship and accord in these elements, was the creator of our art, as our friends the poets here tell us, and I believe them; and not only medicine in every branch, but the arts of gymnastic and husbandry are under his dominion. Any one who pays the least attention to the subject will also perceive that in music there is the same reconciliation of opposites; and I suppose that this must have been the meaning of Heracleitus, although his words are not accurate; for he says that The One is united by disunion, like the harmony of the bow and lyre. Now there is an absurdity in saying that harmony is discord or is composed of elements which are still in a state of discord. But what he probably meant was, that harmony is composed of differing notes of higher or lower pitch which disagreed once, but are now reconciled by the art of music; for if the higher and lower notes still disagreed, there could be no harmony,—clearly not. For harmony is a symphony, and symphony is an agreement; but an agreement of disagreements while they disagree there cannot be; you cannot harmonize that which disagrees. In like manner rhythm is compounded of elements short and long, once differing and now in accord; which accordance, as in the former instance, medicine, so in all these other cases, music implants, making love and unison to grow up among them; and thus music, too, is concerned with the principles of love in their application to harmony and rhythm. Again, in the essential nature of harmony and rhythm there is no difficulty in discerning love which has not yet become double. But when you want to use them in actual life, either in the composition of songs or in the correct performance of airs or metres composed already, which latter is called education, then the difficulty begins, and the good artist is needed.

    —Plato, *Symposium*, 186–7, trans. Benjamin Jowett

Do love and harmony arise through diversity, or in spite of diversity?

PART TWO

PART TWO

CHAPTER 8

FURTHER MEDIEVAL THEMES

§ *metaphysics of beauty reviewed, harmony, light, number (the quadrivium), applications to literature, metrical discussions, Latin and vernacular (metrum, rhythmus, rhyme)—II. the trivium, rhetoric as verbal technique, Martianus Capella,* dictamen, *Geoffrey of Vinsauf, "colors," Chaucer's application, importance to him of conventions—III. logic vs. grammar, Servius on Vergil, identifying the figures—IV. allegory, the world as God's book, Aquinas, symbolism of things and words, Dante's Letter, the four levels, Fulgentius on Virgil—V.* The Owl and the Nightingale, *Chaucer on "moralitee," Aquinas on secular literature and the Scriptures, Dante's* Convivio, figura, *the Medieval grotesque—VI. Boccaccio on theology and poetry, Platonism in Church Fathers, Augustine's* Confessions, *the Middle Ages devoted to theology, not literary criticism* §

OUR LAST CHAPTER HAS PICKED OUT CERTAIN POINTS OF INTEREST IN the history of a theme which runs rather evenly through a vast period of European literary history, the thousand years or more which extend from the twilight of pagan antiquity in the fifth century, A.D., to the Renaissance of antique learning in the fifteenth. That theme was the metaphysical aesthetic of beauty in unity, order, and being. It had, as we have noted briefly, two metaphoric developments: the aesthetic of Platonic and Biblical luminosity (the beauty of brightness seen as the analogue of clear knowledge and of the clearly knowable) and the aesthetic of numerical and musical harmony (the beauty of ordered sound, related to the Pythagorean and Platonic beauty of the numerically ordered ground of being). Both these metaphoric dimensions might have been illustrated much more fully not only from scholastic metaphysicians but from other writers more directly concerned with the liberal arts—poets, grammarians, and rhetoricians. The aesthetic of numerical harmony, we ought to note, is in fact involved in all four branches of the Quadrivium or higher medieval school curriculum: arithmetic, geometry, music, and astronomy (the last including in its purview the "music of the spheres"). This aesthetic, we are told by a recent historian,[1] reached its climax in a very quantitatively minded 12th century. The succeeding century, more metaphysically and qualitatively minded, was that in which Aquinas made the remarks about integrity, harmony, and brilliance to which we have already alluded, and in which a school of writers including Grosseteste, Bonaventure, and the unknown author of a *De Intelligentiis*, produced a far more pervasively physical and cosmological account of light as the fundamental form and energy of all being, the source and form of all beauty—from the mineral realm dull but susceptible of polish and glitter, out through water, air, fire, the moon, and the other heavens to the crystalline sphere and the empyrean. "Light is the most beautiful, the most delightful, the very best of all material things."[2] Light is "the beauty and perfection of all material things."[3]

A history of literary theory ought to *try* to discern the theoretical working of such overall mystiques as that of light and number during the Middle Ages in their most specific connections with literature. Such an aim, however, may not carry very far. These philosophies were perhaps not likely to foster any specific code of the literary man (an Horatian *Ars*) or the literary philosopher (a *Poetics*). What the historian of medieval ideas may call with some justice a "collective spiritual life of gigantic proportions" does seem to have produced during the Middle Ages, along with the metaphysical and cosmological strains of luminist philosophy which we have seen, an equally pronounced literary tradition. The tradition, however, is not properly a theoretical one. It is a tradition of literary content—it can be described approximately in lists of nouns, adjectives, and verbs referring to light and brightness and radiant beauty. The literary historian gives us, for example, the roseate effulgence at the end of the *Commedia*, the play of sunlight on the helms, weapons, shields and gonfalons at Roncevalles—

> *E Durandal, cum ies et clere et blanche!*
> *Cuntre soleil si reluis et reflambes!*—

[1] De Bruyne III, 3–29, "*L'Esthétique de la Lumière.*"

[2] Bonaventure, *Commentaria in Librum Sapientiae* VII, 10 (*Opera Omnia*, 1882, VI, 153); De Bruyne III, 23.

[3] Grosseteste, *De Luce seu de Inchoatione Formarum* (Ludwig Baur, *Die Philosophischen Werke des Robert Grosseteste, Bischofs von Lincoln*, Münster, 1912, p. 56); De Bruyne III, 28.

or the clear light of moon and stars ("*Clere est la lune, les esteiles flambent*") over the same objects. He gives us of course the white skin of "Bele Erembors" or "Bele Yolanz," the golden hair, the bright eyes, the vermeil, the roses and lilies of all the other ladies, even some of the knights, in the romances.[4] But we all know that poetry, even medieval poetry, can be written about dark things too. There is nothing here relevant to a general formal principle of poetry. Perhaps the features of Gothic architecture to which we have partly alluded in Chapter 7, its *verticalisme* joined with its *luminisme*,[5] the lofty window openings and the stained glass, come closer to showing a formal relation between the medieval aesthetic of light and the working of an actual art.

The aesthetic of proportion and number, as we have perhaps already suggested, was more likely to connect with, or even to start from, technical problems of musical art. Yet even such technicalities may give us relatively thin ideas about a poetics. St. Augustine, as we have seen, derived his metaphysics of beautiful number and order from a single line of a hymn by St. Ambrose—or from his contemplation of such geometrical entities as triangle, square, and circle. In his *De Musica* we find a theology of harmonious order connected with a technical prosody written on classical quantitative principles. Boethius, the Roman senator of the early sixth century whose mournfully anti-aesthetic *De Consolatione Philosophiae* was a classic of the Middle Ages and Renaissance, was also a theorist of numerical harmony who wrote a *De Musica* and a *De Arithmetica*. In these we read once more that unity, number, and proportion are the Divine principles of all being, and that music is their universal expression, alike in the most cosmic and the most humanly technical senses. The music made by human instruments is an imitation of the music of the world, the harmony of the four elements. "How could the swift movement of that celestial machinery proceed in silence? The sound may not come to our ears—this happens for a number of reasons—but the extreme velocity with which those great bodies are whirled about cannot fail to generate some sound."[6]

Later on, metrical speculation, such as that in the letters of the Bishop Sidonius Apollinaris or that in the *Ars Metrica* of the Venerable Bede,[7] is couched in terms which were very largely decided by one of the great technical changes involved in the emergence of vernacular literature from Latin, the change from quantitative, non-accentual verse (*metrum*, or

[4] De Bruyne III, 11–16, citing in part Emile Legouis, *Défense de la poésie française, à l'usage des lecteurs anglais* (London, 1912).

[5] De Bruyne III, 10.

[6] *De Musica* I, ii. "*Qui enim fieri potest ut tam velox coeli machina tacito silentique cursu moveatur? Et si ad nostras aures sonus ille non pervenit, quod multis fieri de causis necesse est, non poterit tamen motus tam velocissimus ita magnorum corporum, nullos omnino sonos ciere.*" The *De Musica* of Boethius may be consulted in J. C. Migne, *Patrologia Latina*, LXIII (Paris, 1847). Cf. De Bruyne I, 12–13.

[7] Saintsbury I, 384; Atkins, *English Criticism* I, 45–6.

meter proper) to accentual verse (*rhythmus*), the new form of Latin hymns and their later parodies in Goliardic songs and of vernacular poetry, both sacred and profane. The transition from Latin quantitative theory to the inductively discovered new rhythms—the new accentual swing, and the new *magic* of rhyme (curious deflection from the prose *logic* of homoioteleuton)—was doubtless a challenge of considerable gravity to theoretically minded litterateurs of those centuries. For us today, looking back from the other side of the whole vernacular and romantic diversification (both medieval and modern), it is relatively easy to see that rules of phonetic form in poetry arise in each age from the concrete nature of a spoken language. It worries us little that we have to accept somewhat different phonetic materials in our approximate scansion of Virgilian hexameter, of Chaucerian rhyme royal, of Racinian Alexandrine. The problem is one which we may well consider as subsumed under the more general conflict between neo-classic theories of decorum and romantic experimental violations—the general conflict with which the 16th century was to be engaged so busily.

II

MEDIEVAL literary criticism and theory, where it appears as such, is connected less often with the higher part of the school curriculum (the Quadrivium and its mathematical implications) than with the lower, the Trivium, the three grade-school subjects, Grammar, Logic, and Rhetoric.[8] Most obviously, and perhaps least profoundly, criticism appears all through late antiquity and the middle ages as Rhetoric. Rhetoric, as we have seen, was from the start, in the theory of Isocrates or Aristotle, concerned equally with verse and prose examples and was never far removed from the purposes of a technical poetics. If we consider style—diction, figures of syntax and word order, metaphor, and "ornament" of all kinds —in a means-end relation to the practical, hortatory purposes of forensic or parliamentary speeches, then we have "rhetoric" in the double sense— verbal artifice in the cause of legal or political results. But if we consider the same details in a part-whole relationship to the more cognitive, the more dramatic, features of a verbal composition—love, honor, war and the expression of human feeling about these things—then we have, crude or refined, what is implicitly poetics—a study of verbal meaning at its several interacting levels. The difference between the Middle Ages and Classical Antiquity in the management of such rhetorical poetics was mainly a diminution of whatever classical tendency there had been to philosophize or understand the repertory of figures and a corresponding

[8] See Paul Abelson, *The Seven Liberal Arts, A Study in Mediaeval Culture* (New York, 1906).

increase in the formalizing, stereotyping, and prescriptive tendency—a thickening of the atmosphere of artificiality, euphuism, flowers, incense, ornament. The models were for the most part late Hellenistic (like the pseudo-Ciceronian treatise *Ad Herennium*) or Second Sophistic (Latin derivations from the second-century Hermogenes). The role of Rhetoric as sweet adorner may well be illustrated from a celebrated, though perhaps to our eyes fantastically allegorical and conceited, treatise on the seven liberal arts (of Quadrivium and Trivium) which stands conveniently at the exit from antiquity. The *De Nuptiis Mercuriae et Philologiae* of the fifth-century African Martianus Capella celebrates the wedding of wit and learning—that is, of the inventive or imaginative faculty and the faculty of learning and understanding. Whatever the actual performance, the title is an epitome and promise of all that a literary scholar presumably might desire. The seven arts appear as Muses, to be recommended by Mercury to Philologia his bride. The book on Rhetoric opens with a flourish of trumpets (*Interea sonuere tubae . . .*) and Rhetoric steps forth:

> a stately woman of lofty stature, and confidence greater than common, but radiantly handsome, helmed and crowned, weaponed both for defence and with flashing arms wherewith she could smite her enemies with a thundering coruscation. Under her armpits, and thrown over her shoulder in Latian fashion, was a vest, exhibiting embroidery of all possible *figures* in varied hue, while her breast was baldricked with gems of the most exquisite colour. As she walked her arms clashed, so that you would have thought the broken levin to rattle—with explosive handclaps, like the collision of clouds, so that you might even believe her capable of wielding the thunderbolts of Jove. For it is she who, like a mighty queen of all things, can direct them whither she will and call them back whenever she chooses, and unbend men to tears or incite them to rage, and sway the minds of civic crowds as of warring armies. She brought beneath her sway the senate, the rostra, the courts at Rome.[9]

In short, rhetoric is a powerful form of incitation and subdual; it works with an armory of flashing devices. The thousand years of Medieval Europe are, as Saintsbury observes, a period of human history which has scarcely been paralleled in its cultural continuity—and especially in respect to the rhetorico-poetical tradition. The encyclopedic pageant of Martianus is an allegory which remains appropriate for the whole period. In the Carolingian age rhetoric appears notably in the service of

---

[9] Translated by Saintsbury I, 351–2. Cf. *De Nuptiis Philologiae et Mercurii*, V, 426 ff (Adolfus Dick, ed. *Martianus Capella*, Leipzig, 1925, pp. 211–12).

the flowery diplomacy of court letter-writing (*dictamen*) [1]—another application in the doubly "rhetorical" form of suasive verbal artifice. During the late 12th and the early 13th centuries, the poetical application,
which had always been ready (and which by the end of the Middle Ages
would flourish elegantly in the school of French poets called the "*Grands
Rhétoriqueurs*"), broke out in a "new poetics" among French and English international scholars—in the *Ars Versificatoria* of Matthew of Ven-
dôme, for instance, or the *Poetria Nova* and the *De Coloribus Rhetoricis*
of the Norman Englishman Geoffrey of Vinsauf. The main model for
these treatises was the pseudo-Ciceronian *Ad Herennium*.

The list of ornaments in Vinsauf's *Poetria* includes sixty-three, divided into difficult ornaments or tropes and easy ornaments or "colors."
Colors (or figures) are in turn divided into those of speech (*figurae
verborum*) and those of thought (*figurae sententiarum*). The distinctive
features of the system are the formal definition of the figures, the prescription of the contexts in which each is at home, and the practical
illustration. For example, "Apostrophe" is a turning toward, or address
to, some absent thing or person or some abstraction personified. It is good
for amplifying a theme. King Richard Coeur de Lion was mortally
wounded on a Friday. To express your grief, deliver a reproachful
series of addresses, to that very day Friday, to the soldier who was
guilty of the blow, and so on.

> With grievous words express your hour of grief.
> . . .
> O Vendreday, O tearful, bitter blight,
> Not day but night, and Venus turned to venom.
> You gave the wound. . . .[2]

Within one figure of course others can be contained. A 13th-century
manuscript of the *Poetria Nova* glosses the passage just quoted as follows:

> Note that in the expression *Venus . . . venenum* appears the
> verbal color known as agnomination, which may be defined as
> an echo of one word by another which differs only in a single
> letter or in certain syllables or letters. See the chapter on verbal
> colors.[3]

---

[1] John C. Mendenhall, *Aureate Terms* (Lancaster, 1919), p. 21.
[2] *Temporibus luctus his verbis exprime luctum:*
   . . .
   O Veneris lacrimosa dies! O sidus amarum!
   Illa dies tua nox fuit et Venus illa venenum.
   *Illa dedit vulnus. . . .—*ll. 368 ff.
Edmond Faral, *Les Arts Poétiques du XIIe et du XIIIe Siècle* (Paris, 1924), p. 208.
[3] Karl Young, "Chaucer and Geoffrey of Vinsauf," *Modern Philology*, XLI
(February 1944), 175: "*Nota quod dicendo illa Venus fuit venenum utitur colore*

In the complicated and sometimes perverse history of the literary self-consciousness perhaps nothing ever goes to waste—not a vanity is given in vain—no aridity or pomposity appears which may not be ploughed under to sprout again and bloom in its own way another season. The systems of technical stereotyping, the "conventions" of rhetorical figure and of literary genre, as well as those of making love and war, which characterize the Middle Ages, may appear as simple and flat conventions in the work of one poet, but in another they may be an intricate repertory of starting points for fun and feeling. The medieval poet spoke not a dialect more restricted or jejune than that of a liberated and naturalistic age (the language of a Sandburg chanting the fog over Chicago or slabs of the sunburnt West) but on the contrary the language of a highly civilized and sophisticated living past. Chaucer, the medieval poet most familiar to modern English readers, will come readily enough to mind in his diverse dramatic adaptations of fixities—his ironically slanted portraits of superlative persons in the Canterbury Prologue, his echoes of the liturgy in the Prioress's Tale, of patristic and French satirical misogyny in the Wife of Bath's Prologue, of courtly love, of romance, of Arthurian legend, of the vulgar fabliau, of uncounted other literary and social conventions in all that he wrote. The rules of the rhetorical prescribers too afforded him many an oddly tilted detail—one of the examples most easily recognizable today being, in fact, a reference to the *New Poetry* of Vinsauf. A cock is carried off by a fox on a Friday. Now here would be a chance to illustrate the working of those rules.

> O Venus, that art goddesse of plesaunce,
> Syn that thy servant was this Chauntecleer,
> And in thy servyce dide al his poweer,
> Moore for delit than world to multiplye,
> Why woldestow suffre hym on thy day to dye?
>   O Gaufred, deere maister soverayn,
> That whan thy worthy kyng Richard was slayn
> With shot, compleynedest his deethe so soore,
> Why ne hadde I now thy sentence and thy loore
> The Friday for to chide, as diden ye?

---

verborum qui dicitur anominacio, et provenit quando de nomine ad idem nomen acceditur commutacione vel addicione unius litere vel silabarum aut literarum, ut patebit in capitulo de coloribus verborum."

Atkins, *English Criticism*, I, presents a helpful summary of Vinsauf's ornaments (pp. 201-3) and tries to disentangle the terms *trope, color,* and *figure* (pp. 108-9). A number of duplicate devices seem to occur, and the lines drawn between the main classes must seem to a modern reader tenuous in the extreme.

This is part of the history of applied rhetoric.[4] It is not a direct or sober examination of the classico-medieval rhetorical claim. In its implications, however, it may perhaps be read as a substitute for a kind of rhetorical theory which in that age does not seem to have been written.

III

THE relation of the other two parts of the medieval Trivium, Grammar and Logic, to literary criticism has been for succeeding ages far less apparent, and it was indeed more submerged even in the Middle Ages. The second part of the Trivium, Logic (or Dialectic), the methodology of metaphysics and science, may be conceived as a lurking antipoetics, the inheritor of the dialectic bias which we have noted as far back as the pre-Platonic "quarrel between the philosophers and the poets," and to which we shall turn again in a chapter on the rhetorical issues of the 17th century (Ch. 10). By the same token, medieval "Grammatica," handed down by such authorities as the late classical treatises of Donatus and Priscian and the Book on Grammar in the *Wedding* of Martianus, undoubtedly carries on, though at a level largely taken for granted beneath tangled technicalities, the method of poetic and polysemous interpretation which we earlier noted in Stoic philosophers and Hellenistic grammarians. The late classical and medieval grammarians are on the side of the poets, but in a way which they themselves scarcely understand and which they are never concerned to argue or expound. The actual performance borrows, on its most obviously literary side, much from rhetoric—the difference being that instead of prescribing figures in advance of occasions, the grammarians, in their role as practical explicators, dissect the parts of an existing text and, with an air of justifying something, tag these parts with the names of the rhetorico-poetical repertory. Thus in the greatest Latin commentary on Virgil, that of the fifth-century variorum editor Servius, we read that when Virgil says *Arma virumque, arma*, meaning "war," is a trope called "metonymy," and the order of the two words is an inversion called "hyperbaton." When Virgil borrows and alters a phrase from Ennius, Servius points out that the figure is "acyrologia." When Virgil describes the Libyan harbor where the ships of Aeneas take refuge (*Est in secessu longo locus . . .*), the figure is not "topographia" (which is *rei verae descriptio*) but "topothesia" (*fictus secundum poeticam licentiam locus*).[5]

[4] See J. M. Manly, "Chaucer and the Rhetoricians," *Proceedings of the British Academy*, XII (1926), 95–113. "But that some of Chaucer's freest and most delightful work should contain twice as much rhetoric as some of his least inspired compositions is a puzzle that demands investigation" (p. 108). ". . . he came more and more to make only a dramatic use of these rhetorical elements" (p. 110).

[5] Saintsbury I, 334–9. See p. 340 for Servius on the three styles.

IV

WHERE grammar came closest to an adequate rationale of literary criticism was not, however, in such feats of technical classification but in a somewhat differently slanted, though also anciently inherited, conception: namely, that allegorical and etymological meanings were naturally present in poetic texts and deserved explication. For here grammar was allied as a method to a view which we have already noted in ancient philosophers, in Church fathers as exegetes of the Scriptures, and in medieval theologians, the view according to which the created world in its radiant order and hierarchy is God's symbolic book. The world is the shell or cover (*cortex*) of an inner meaning (*nucleus*), the veil over a hidden meaning, the entrance to such a meaning, the lower symbol of a higher meaning.[6] Or, as the Franciscan St. Bonaventure put it, in a union of symbolist theory with the aesthetic of the luminous:

> It is clear that the whole world is like a mirror, bright with reflected light of the divine wisdom; it is like a great coal radiant with light.[7]

If all this was true, if the world was God's book, the objects which composed the world were a kind of dictionary of God's meanings, and when God himself wrote a verbal book (the Bible), He would write not only a word language but the directly symbolic language of the objects which He mentioned. Thus St. Thomas Aquinas near the outset of his *Summa Theologiae*:

> The author of Holy Scripture is God, in Whose power it is to signify His meaning, not by words only (as man also can do), but also by things themselves. So, whereas in every other science things are signified by words, this science has the property that the things signified by the words have themselves also a signification. Therefore the first signification whereby words signify things belongs to the first sense, the historical or literal. That signification whereby things signified by words have themselves also a signification is called the spiritual sense, which is based on the literal, and presupposes it.[8]

[6] Gilbert and Kuhn, pp. 147–50; D. W. Robertson, Jr., "Historical Criticism," *English Institute Essays 1950* (New York, 1951), pp. 10–13; E. R. Curtius, *European Literature and the Latin Middle Ages*, trans. W. R. Trask (New York, 1953), pp. 319 ff.

[7] "*Et sic patet quod totus mundus est sicut unum speculum plenum luminibus praestantibus divinam sapientam, et sicut carbo effundens lucem.*" Etienne Gilson, *The Philosophy of St. Bonaventure* (New York, 1938), pp. 229–30.

[8] *Summa Theologiae*, I, q.1, art. 10, ad 3m., trans. Anton Pegis, in *The Basic Writings of St. Thomas Aquinas* (New York, 1945), I, 16, by permission of Random House, Inc. The article goes on to name the three kinds of spiritual sense, allegorical, moral, and anagogical.

There is some serious concern here, with Aquinas as with other school-men, about a natural and proper revelatory symbolism of objects (water, the sun, Jerusalem) as distinct from the mere symbolism of words and their metaphoric manipulation—the latter department (if we may antici-pate a more modern emphasis) being in a special way the concern of poetry. But one may say that the recognition of symbolism in general was a strain of medieval thinking (grammatical, aesthetic, and theological) which, without much advertisement as such, had deep, if ambiguous, im-plications for the theory of poetry. The classic appearance of symbolistic doctrine in medieval writing upon a literary subject is that in Dante's Letter to Can Grande della Scala (prefixed to the *Paradiso*),[9] in which he is concerned explicitly to set forth the levels of meaning in his own *Commedia*. Following the lead of the Scriptural exegetes, he finds in, or has put into, his own works not only a literal meaning, the story of his journey with Virgil through Hell and Purgatory and his ascent with Beatrice through the Heavenly spheres, but three higher levels of mean-ing, the allegorical (or worldly symbolic meanings), the anagogical (or other-worldly), and the tropological (or personal and moral). This we might say is Scriptural method put to the explication and vindication of religious poetry written by natural inspiration. With more difficulty the same thing could be done for fully secular and even for pagan poetry. As in Platonic times and earlier the defenders of Homer had invoked the allegorical way (often extravagantly and pedantically, but by a ra-tionale basically correct), so late classical and medieval defenders of pagan fable, and especially of Virgil's *Aeneid*, relied largely on that way—with the support where possible of the subsidiary way of etymol-ogy. Thus the *Expositio Virgiliana*, written probably in the sixth century by the African grammarian Fulgentius, finds Virgil in his *Eclogues* a prophet, priest, musician, physiologist, and botanist, in his *Georgics* an astrologer, haruspex, physiognomist, and physician, and in his *Aeneid* something like a universal philosopher. The *Aeneid* is an allegory of the course of human life: the wanderings of the first three books are the tales that amuse childhood; the love affair of the fourth and the athletic exercises of the fifth typify phases of youth; the descent into Hades of the sixth is a profound study of the whole nature of things; the rest is the contest of active life. In the same way words and syllables are pressed to yield their meanings allegorical and etymological. *Achates* is "Graece quasi *aconetos* id est tristitiae consuetudo." In a *Mythologiae* attributed to the same author, *Teiresias* is derived from the Greek *theros* and *aeon*,

---

[9] The authorship of the Epistle to Can Grande has been questioned by mod-ern scholars, apparently on plausible grounds (see Helmut Hatzfeld, "Modern Literary Scholarship as Reflected in Dante Criticism," *Comparative Literature*, III (Fall, 1951), 296, citing Luigi Pietrobono, "L'Epistola a Can Grande," *Giornale Dan-tesco*, XL (1937), 1–51. For the purpose of our argument, it is not essential that the epistle should have been written by Dante.

meaning "eternal summer," and *Ulixes* is "quasi-*olon xenos* id est omnium peregrinus."[1]

V

In a 13th-century vernacular poem which has been called the earliest literary criticism in English, the allegorical *conflictus* entitled *The Owl and the Nightingale,* the case for didactic aims in poetry (the hidden moral and religious lessons in the symbolic husk) can no doubt be heard, at least by an interested ear, as the owl argues the merits of his own austere song; at the same time the hedonistic argument for the new kind of Troubadour love lyric seems audible in the nightingale's counter plea.[2] Toward the end of the next century, Chaucer, in the same varied burlesque of medieval stereotypes (the tale of the cock and the fox) where he makes the notable use of Vinsauf's rhetoric which we have seen, is slyly scanning didactic ambitions when he has the Nun's Priest conclude with the excellent advice:

> Now, goode men, I prey yow herkneth alle:
> Lo, how Fortune turneth sodeynly
> The hope and pryde eek of hir enemy!
> . . . .
> . . . .
>   Lo, swich it is for to be recchelees
> And necligent, and truste on flaterye.
>   But ye that holden this tale a folye,
> As of a fox, or of a cok and hen,
> Taketh the moralite, goode men.
> For seint Paul seith that all that writen is,
> To oure doctrine it is ywrite, ywis;
> Taketh the fruyt, and lat the chaf be stille.

The medieval schoolmen themselves were likely to make an emphatic distinction between secular literature and the Scriptures. Modern students of medieval poetic theory have perhaps not taken seriously enough such a passage as that in his *Quaestiones Quodlibetales* where Aquinas says in effect that it is wrong to look in secular poetry for any allegorical, any tropological, any anagogical meanings. The only kind of meaning to be found in secular poetry is literal meaning. *In nulla scientia, humana industria inventa, proprie loquendo, potest inveniri nisi*

---

[1] Saintsbury I, 392–5; Smith and Parks, 130–2. Cf. *Fabii Planciadis Fulgentii V.C. Opera,* ed. Rudolfus Helm (Leipsic, 1898), pp. 44, 48, 83–4, 92.

[2] This interpretation, at any rate, is plausibly urged by Atkins. See *English Criticism* I, 143–5, and Atkins's edition of the poem, 1922.

litteralis sensus; sed solum in ista Scriptura cujus Spiritus sanctus est auctor, homo vero instrumentum.[3] This may sound forbidding. It may at first sound like an oppressively simple view of the whole nature of poetry. It may indeed run counter to the aspirations of a certain modern kind of historical rereading of medieval poems.[4] On the other hand it might be argued that the dictum of Aquinas fits, or at least is adaptable to, the needs of a strictly critical historicism very well. It must be clear for one thing that by the term *literal* in this passage the medieval philosopher did not mean to rule out of secular poetry the range of natural metaphoric and analogical meanings which are obviously there. (The places where Aquinas speaks of metaphor in poetry and compares it to metaphor in Scripture have been often enough quoted by recent students.) *Literal* in this passage of scholastic philosophy seems to be opposed quite strictly to the other three, divinely intended, levels, the allegorical, the tropological, and the anagogical. Human poetry might very well *refer* to these levels of meaning, or point to them, and in some way involve them. Dante and many other medieval poets would show that this could be done, and would easily theorize around any difficulties. But the human poet, not being at the divine level, could hardly speak down from it with a real message about divine meaning.

If we take the passage about the four meanings in Dante's *Letter to Can Grande* along with an earlier passage, in his *Convivio* (or *Banquet*), on kinds of meaning and kinds of allegory, we find that he wished to distinguish the thing he attempted in the *Convivio*, a mere "allegory of poets," abstractive, didactic, and platonically thin, from what he attempted in the *Commedia*, an "allegory of theologians," or at least something like that, a more concrete and historically dramatic kind of allegorizing, which by the use of individually named historical figures (Beatrice rather than Lady Philosophy) turned the methods of the inspired Scriptures into a special kind of secular poetry. Without forgetting the objection of Aquinas, and without overlooking the fact that Dante's poem is not after all a history but a fiction (a *bella menzogna*), we may yet conceive that his theorizing corresponds approximately to a certain contribution which the poets of the Middle Ages, and especially Dante, made to the technique of realistic narrative. In the Scriptural situation known to exegetes as *figura* or typology, an individual historical person or thing of the Old Testament (Adam, Rahab, or Jerusalem) is seen as standing for or prophesying an individual person or thing in the

---

[3] *Quaestiones Quodlibetales* VII, q.6, a.16; cf. the answer to the second objection to this article.

[4] See, for instance, H. Flanders Dunbar, *Symbolism in Medieval Thought* (New Haven, 1929), p. 20 ("Every symbol should be understood at one and the same time in all of these significations") and p. 459, the poem as "cryptographic code"; D. W. Robertson, Jr. and Bernard F. Huppé, *Piers Plowman and Scriptural Tradition* (Princeton, 1951), e.g. pp. 5–6, 240.

New Testament (Christ, or the Christian Church). An eminent modern authority on medieval literature has seen a profound difference between such "figurism and other similar forms of thinking" such as "allegorism or symbolism." In the other forms, "at least one of the two elements combined is a pure sign" (that is, a fictitious thing, a rose or a lady, supposedly valued only in as much as it stands for something else, love or wisdom). "But in a figural relation both the signifying and the signified" are "real and concrete historical" things.[5] And in Dante's *Commedia* something like a fictitious parallel to this incarnational figurative meaning may perhaps be observed. The realism of his persons as he makes them appear to exist in the places of the other world sets up strangely solid fields of relational meaning between these translated souls and the persons they have been in secular history and the Bible. The Old Testament persons appear as acted out analogies or concrete realizations of figurisms traditionally attached to them.

Under a related aspect, the whole exegetical tradition had the effect of strongly promoting the downfall of the classically separate decora of comedy and tragedy.[6] The grotesquerie, the mingling of the sublime with the low and the funny, of which we find representative examples in the *Comedy* of Dante or in miracle and mystery plays and in cathedral architecture, expressed a spirit and rationale which are close to the Scriptural interpretations of which we have been speaking—the hospitable harlot Rahab seen as a type of the Christian Church, the scarlet thread which she lets down from the window seen as a type of Christ's blood. In virtue of such occasional literary pronouncements as those of Dante and the theological pronouncements that stand behind them, the literary situation in the Middle Ages—the unique poetic achievement—has at least an implicitly shadowed, and a profound, relation to the history of literary theory.

VI

THE strain of theological criticism which we have been describing appears most boldly perhaps in Boccaccio's extended defense of poetry

[5] Erich Auerbach, "Typological Symbolism in Medieval Literature," *Yale French Studies*, No. 9 (Spring, 1952), p. 6. Cf. the same author's *Mimesis*, trans. Willard R. Trask (Princeton, 1953), pp. 73, 195, 201. Cf. Charles S. Singleton, "Dante's Allegory," *Speculum*, XXV (January, 1950), 79–83 (reprinted in his *Dante Studies 1, Commedia, Elements of Structure*, Cambridge, Mass., 1954).

[6] The medieval lack of interest in these classical genres and their norms is clear, for instance, in a formula for tragedy starkly simplified from the Aristotelian. "Tragedie," says Chaucer's Monk, "is to seyn a certeyn storie, As olde bookes maken us memorie, Of hym that stood in greet prosperitee, And is yfallen out of Heigh degree Into myserie, and endeth wrecchedly. And they been versified communely Of six feet, which men clepen *exametron*."

in the fourteenth and fifteenth books of his *De Genealogia Deorum*, a work of which the very title sufficiently suggests the symbolist and allegorical contents, and in a passage of his *Trattatello* or short *Life of Dante* which 19th-century professors, W. J. Courthope in his *Life of Alexander Pope* (*Works*, V, 50) and Saintsbury in the first volume of his *History of Criticism* (p. 457) pounce upon as showing "the very head and front of that Renaissance side of him which is so undeniable."

> I say that theology and poetry can be called almost the same thing, when they have the same subject; I even say that theology is none other than the poetry of God. What else is it than a poetic fiction when the Scripture in one place calls Christ a lion, in another a lamb, and in another a worm, here a dragon and here a rock, and many other things that I omit for the sake of brevity? What else do the words of Our Savior in the Gospels come to if not a sermon that does not signify what it appears to? It is what we call—to use a well-known term—allegory. Then it plainly appears that not merely is poetry theology but that theology is poetry. And surely if in so important a matter my words deserve little reliance, I am not disturbed by it; for I put my trust in Aristotle, an excellent authority in any important matter, who affirms he found that the poets were the first to write theology.—Chapter xxii [7]

Saintsbury is surely correct in his insistence that this is not the main and not the authorized voice of Christian medievalism. This and the Virgilian allegorical defences are to be looked on rather as recurrent efforts of humanism to save secular poetry from a neglect and even disapproval which after all was a plausible enough accompaniment of the Christian Church's struggle with the classical pagan world and the surrounding barbaric world of the Middle Ages. Along with much else that the Church Fathers owe to Plato there are not a few passages which show the accent of Book X of the *Republic*. The following from St. Augustine's *Confessions* are eloquent instances.

> I was forced [by the so-called grammarians] to learn the wanderings of one Aeneas, forgetful of my own, and to weep for dead Dido, because she killed herself for love; the while with

---

[7] Gilbert, p. 211, his translation emended in one phrase. Cf. Charles G. Osgood, *Boccaccio on Poetry, being the Preface and the Fourteenth and Fifteenth Books of Boccaccio's "Genealogia Deorum Gentilium"* (Princeton, 1930). The reference to Aristotle is not to his *Poetics* but to his *Metaphysics* III, 4. Saintsbury compares Boccaccio to Maximus Tyrius as expounded *supra* in the same volume, *History of Criticism* I, 117. Cf. Tasso on theology and poetry, in Gilbert, p. 476.

Allan H. Gilbert's translations from Italian critics are quoted here and in the next chapter from his *Literary Criticism Plato to Dryden*, New York, 1940, by permission of the American Book Company.

dry eyes, I endured my miserable self dying among these things, far from Thee, O God my life.—I, 13

Did I not read . . . of Jove the thunderer and the adulterer? both, doubtless, he could not be; but so the feigned thunder might countenance and pander to real adultery. . . . As if we should have never known such words as "golden shower," "lap," "beguile" . . . or others in that passage, unless Terence had brought a lewd youth upon the stage, setting up Jupiter as his example of seduction. . . . And then mark how he excites himself to lust as by celestial authority. . . . Not one whit more easily are the words learnt for all this vileness; but by their means the vileness is committed with less shame. Not that I blame the words, being, as it were, choice and precious vessels; but that wine of error which is proffered us in them by intoxicated teachers.—I, 16

To Carthage I came, where there sang all around me in my ears a cauldron of unholy loves. . . . Stage-plays also carried me away, full of images of my miseries, and of fuel to my fire. Why is it, that man desires to be made sad, beholding doleful and tragical things, which yet himself would by no means suffer? yet he desires as a spectator to feel sorrow at them, and this very sorrow is his pleasure. What is this but a miserable madness? for a man is the more affected with these actions, the less free he is from such affections.—III, 1–2

And now I was chief in the rhetoric school, whereat I joyed proudly, and I swelled with arrogancy. . . . in that unsettled age of mine, learned I books of eloquence, wherein I desired to be eminent, out of a damnable and vainglorious end, a joy in human vanity.—III, 3–4 [8]

At the same time, a second point, made implicitly in the *Confessions*, and noted by Saintsbury in his *History of Literary Criticism*, seems worth repeating here. The seductions of secular literature were far from being the most dangerous which a St. Augustine had to think about. We shall not get from him or from his age the grounds of a literary theory such as may be found in so systematic an attack on literature as that of Plato—the philosopher of an age when other disciplines, notably poetry and sophistry, made not only practical but serious theoretical claims to the office of *paideia*. Book Ten of St. Augustine's *Confessions* closes with a discourse on worldly pleasures which contains not a single reference to literature. The pleasures of literature are

---

[8] *The Confessions of St. Augustine*, revised from a former translation by the Rev. E. B. Pusey, D.D. (Oxford, 1838).

apparently not important enough to be named in a list of either the main sensory or the main intellectual temptations. "The boy had been charmed by Virgil and Terence—wicked charms he acknowledges—but the man, though he certainly does not mean to deny their wickedness, has simply put them away as childish things." [9]

Let us say, in summation, that the Middle Ages—where we have lingered not long and over no single important critical figure—were not in fact ages of literary theory or criticism. They were ages indeed of great literary creativity, when romance and the lyric of both secular and religious love were born, when drama was reborn, when fable, satire, fairy tale, allegory and narrative in a dozen other forms flourished, enriching the ground for a luxuriant future criticism. But the direction of theoretical thinking in these ages was elsewhere—to the metaphysical as that leads to speculative theology or joins with Scriptural revelation. In short it was an age of theological thinking in a theologically oriented and theocratic society. Such a society does not characteristically promote the essentially humanistic activity of literary criticism—an activity which we may describe provisionally and in this context as the self-conscious discipline of man's verbal imagination, of his achievements in rhythmic and metaphoric expression, of his natural inventions in the sphere of ethical and religious symbol.

[9] Saintsbury I, 380. For similarly rigorous views of secular literature (*daemonum cibus*) on the part of Tertullian (*De Spectaculis*), Jerome, and Gregory, see Gilbert and Kuhn, pp. 120–3; Atkins, *English Criticism*, I, 17. See the following page of Atkins for examples of a contrary or more liberal attitude, especially on the part of the Greek Fathers Origen, Clement, and Basil.

CHAPTER 9

THE SIXTEENTH CENTURY

§ *Italian editing of classic texts, four other kinds of critical work—II. lines of speculation: justification of vernaculars, poetic diction, quantitative meters, attack on rhyme—III. more substantive problems: rules of Aristotle vs. romance materials, unities of action, time and place, Scaliger, Castelvetro, Virgil-worship—IV. Gothic innovations, defences by Cinthio and others, Minturno on "errant" poetry, problem of mixed genres—V. Tasso and Mazzoni on the fantastic, allegorical theory, mythology, the supernatural, forward glance at Boileau and Granville—VI. the moral status of poetry debated, Gosson's attack, Sidney's Defense, its style and sources, main features: Horatian, Aristotelian, Platonic, opinions of English literature, ambiguous solution of the moral problem, statements about creative imagination in Shakespeare, Bacon, Sidney §*

LITERARY THEORY AND CRITICISM RECEIVED A NEW EMPHASIS IN ITALY during that phase of the general Renaissance which was speeded by the western movement of Byzantine manuscripts after the fall of Constantinople (1453) and the multiplication of texts after the invention of printing. The *Ars Poetica* of Horace had been more or less known throughout the Middle Ages.[1] But the *Poetics* of Aristotle (master document of the theorizing which was to come in the 16th century) had lain, even in the later Middle Ages,[2] almost unknown in Latin translations from the abridged Arabic version of Averroes. And so we mark

[1] It is mentioned, for instance, in the sixth century by Isidore of Seville, in the 12th by John of Salisbury (in his humanistic treatise the *Polycraticus* I, 8), and in the 13th by Dante.
[2] It had been for that matter little known in antiquity. It is not mentioned by Horace, Cicero, or Quintilian. Aristotelian literary ideas in later antiquity were Peripatetic and Hellenistic.

with interest the first complete Latin translation, by Giorgio Valla, at Venice in 1498; the first Greek text, in the Aldine *Rhetores Graeci*, in 1508; the first juxtaposition of Latin and Greek texts, by Alessandro de' Pazzi, in 1536; the first critical edition (with a Latin commentary) by Francisco Robortello, in 1548; and the first Italian translation, by Bernardo Segni, in 1549. A text "abandoned and neglected for a long time," said Segni. "Buried for a long time in the obscure shadows of ignorance," wrote Bernardo Tasso, the father of the epic poet. And Robortello in the edition of 1548: "*Jacuit liber hic neglectus, ad nostra fere haec usque tempora.*"[3] A few years after his edition of the *Poetics*, Robortello brought out his equally celebrated first edition of the Longinian *Peri Hupsous* (1554)—the Greek text with a Latin commentary. The *Institutio Oratoria* or rhetorical and literary encyclopedia of Quintilian had been known to literary men during the Middle Ages only in fragmentary versions. But the complete text had been rediscovered by the famous literary detective Poggio at the monastery of St. Gall in 1417 and had been edited by Cardinal Campano in 1470.[4] Editions such as these and larger editions of classic philosophers and poets, such as the Aldine editions at Venice of Homer, Plato, Aristotle, and the *Rhetores Graeci*, helped to bring on a Renaissance of furious theoretical activity, an era of criticism which remains one of the most conspicuous in literary history. Yet for several reasons—the difficulty of the Italian and Latin texts, the often very local emphasis of the controversies, and the derivative and authoritarian character of the critical principles invoked—the writings of the era have long been only obscurely known to the student of English poetry and poetics.

In addition to such critically edited classical texts as we have just noted, there were four other main genres in which the critical writing of the Italian Renaissance luxuriated. (1) There was the poetic or versified *Art* (in the manner of Horace), of which the best known example is the Latin *De Arte Poetica* in three books published in 1527 by the Italian Bishop Marco Girolamo Vida—to be far outshone in the later 17th century by the French *Art Poétique* of Boileau (1674) and in the early 18th century by the English *Essay on Criticism* of Alexander Pope (1711). (2) There was the deliberately scientific and ambitiously professed treatise on poetics (in the manner of what Aristotle's notes might be thought to represent): for example, the Latin *De Poeta Libri Sex* published in 1559 by the Bishop of Ugento Antonio Minturno and later (1564) supplemented by his Italian *L'Arte Poetica;* or—most massive, most celebrated, and most reactionary, of all such treatises—the *Poetices Libri Septem* of the Frenchman Julius Caesar Scaliger, published posthumously in 1561. (3) There was the apologetic essay, either

---

[3] Spingarn, pp. 11–18.
[4] J. E. Sandys, *A History of Classical Scholarship* (Oxford, 1891), II, 103.

specifically directed against purists and classicists, and in the cause of a vernacular literature, like the *Deffence et Illustration de la Langue Francoyse* of Joachim du Bellay in 1549; or generally directed against moralists and other main enemies of poetry, like a youthful oration of Scaliger's, *Contra Poetices Calumniatores Declamatio*,[5] or the much better known English epitome of Renaissance poetics, the *Defense of Poesie* or *Apologie for Poetrie*, by Sir Philip Sidney, published in 1595. (4) There was the preface or special treatise in retort to classical objections against some particular romantic form or vernacular style—for example, Giraldi Cinthio's defence of his own tragedy *Orbecche* (1541) and of Ariosto's romance epic (1549), Tasso's *Discorsi* (1594) in defence of his *Gerusalemme Liberata*, Mazzoni's two defences of the *Divina Commedia* (1572 and 1587), and Guarini's *Compendio della Poesia Tragicomica* (1601). Italian apologetics of this species found echoes in such English prefaces as that of Sir John Harington prefixed to his translation of Ariosto (1591) and that of George Chapman prefixed to the *Seven Books* of his *Iliad* (1598).

II

SOME of the most important and persistent preoccupations of the 16th-century literary theorists have perhaps been suggested even in the enumeration of types which we have just made. Beginning with the most local and concrete critical issues and moving towards those of more general import, let us now venture to set forth briefly certain main lines of Renaissance literary speculation. One of the most local and special issues had received its classic treatment as early as about 1300 in Dante's Latin essay defending vernacular poetry, the *De Vulgari Eloquentia*. As the earlier Middle Ages had needed a revision in prosodic theory to meet the fact of the shift from quantitative, classical meters to the accentual rhythms of hymn and song, so the later Middle Ages faced a broader revision in theory to justify the increasingly palpable fact of the vernacular literatures. And long after the fact had been accomplished, theoretical scruples could be revived by professors of newly discovered classical theory and could be given new twists which corresponded to changes of balance in the classical-vernacular relationship. Where Dante is concerned mainly to assert the dignity and poetic availability of the emergent vernacular, and to distinguish certain more refined classes of words within it, in the mid-16th century the *Deffence* of Du Bellay leans heavily upon the possibility that the vernacular may be enriched by plunder and adaptation of all the finest vocabulary of the classics. "Visit the ancients

[5] In his *Epistolae et Orationes*, 1600; see Vernon Hall, "Scaliger's Defense of Poetry," *PMLA*, LXIII (December, 1948), 1125–30.

and strip them of their wealth," Vida had said repetitiously, in each part of his *De Arte Poetica*,[6] developing the late classical doctrine about the imitation of models in a direction of which we shall have more to say in Chapter 10. In the next generation, however, the distinguishing feature of an English defense of vernacular, E. K.'s Epistle prefixed to the *Shepheardes Calender*, is a reversal of Du Bellay's thesis in that E. K. applauds the Spenserian enrichment of the language from native, if rustic, dialect sources, rather than from the "inkhorns" of humanistic pedants who were practising the theory of Du Bellay with all too great a will. These shifts in the argument about vernacular show its tendency to be refined into an argument essentially about what came within a few centuries to be known as "poetic diction"—a tendency strongly manifest even in Dante's *De Vulgari Eloquentia* as he divides the noble and exalted "curial" vernacular into words *rustic* (ignoble) and *urban*, then subdivides the *urban* into the *childish*, the *feminine* (both ignoble), and the *masculine*, and then again subdivides the *masculine* into words *shaggy* and *rumpled* (ignoble) and words *combed out* and *glossy* (the final distillation or noblest poetic residue).[7] At this level (that concerning "poetic diction" rather than the rights of vernacular and classic) the debate, whether or not profound, is perennial. It is one to which we shall return (Chapter 16) at the classic locus for the history of English poetic diction, the Wordsworthian revulsion from the post-Spenserian diction that became standardized in the 18th century.

It remains to round off our present topic by observing that the earlier medieval contest between classical and vernacular prosodies had an aftermath during the 16th century in a succession of misguided attempts by Italian, French, and English litterateurs to cultivate quantitative vernacular meters.[8] (In England the coterie, known as the Areopagus, included, besides Drant, Harvey and others, so bright a star as Sidney.) It is difficult to imagine anything more thoroughly self-refuting than the example of this workmanship offered by Webbe in his *Discourse of Poesie* (1586), the song in Spenser's Fourth Eclogue turned into sapphics.[9] A related phenomenon was the classically-minded attack on rhyme (as a "monkish" and "beggarly" barbarism) which extended

---

[6] I, 409; II, 542 ff (. . . *te plurima Achivos Consulere hortamur veteres, Argivaque regna Explorare oculis, et opimam avertere gazam In Latium*); III, 244 (*passimque avertite praedam*).

[7] *De Vulgari Eloquentia*, ed. Aristide Marigo (Firenze, 1938), Book I, Chapters xvii–xix, pp. 142–61. Dante's theorizing is made comprehensible, if not attractive, by the fact that he has in mind among his own works the Platonic lyrics of his *Vita Nuova* and not the grandly mixed vocabulary of his later *Commedia*. Cf. Erich Auerbach, *Mimesis*, trans. Willard Trask (Princeton, 1953), pp. 185–7.

[8] Saintsbury II, 46, sees "the beginning of that pestilent heresy" in the *Versi e Regole della Nuova Poesia Toscana* of Claudio Tolomei, 1539.

[9] Smith, *Elizabethan Essays*, I, 286 ff. Cf. G. L. Hendrickson, "Elizabethan Quantitative Hexameters," *Philological Quarterly*, XXVIII (1949), 238 ff.

from the later 16th century even into the early 18th, many years after the structural triumph of rhyme in the Augustan couplet. The reasons for the success and necessity of English rhyme, especially in lyric and in witty satirical verse, lie in such practical differences between the vernacular and the classical languages as that between stress and quantity, and in the absence from the vernacular of the classical morphology and hence the relative ease of avoiding the logical (and antimetrical) figure of *homoioteleuton* (similar endings). Yet an age which theorized with the classical part of its mind was bound to find fault with a difficult and often cramping technique which had indeed flourished first in the "monkish" ages, and to dream of a return to a supposed classic state of majesty—plain and regular, like the columns of the Greek temples. Rhyme, says Richard Puttenham, a courtier theorist in the great age of Elizabeth, "is all the sweetness and harmony of our vulgar poesie." [1] But at the same time he says it was brought into Greek and Latin by "barbarous souldiers out of the Campe." This was typical and casual enough. The better known and more deliberate attacks are that of Campion in his *Observations in the Art of English Poesie* (1602) (answered by Daniel in *A Defence of Rhyme*, 1603?) and the later note prefixed by Milton to *Paradise Lost*—perhaps at the request of a publisher apprehensive about the side-effect of a current courtly controversy in which rhyme had so able a defender as John Dryden. Milton avoided the difficulty of carrying rhyme through the vast, discursive effort of his epic. A "troublesome and modern bondage" he called it, used by some poets "much to their own vexation, hindrance, and constraint to express many things otherwise, and for the most part worse than else they would have expressed them." The court controversy concerned drama, perhaps the weakest ground on which a champion of rhyme could choose to stand. Yet this controversy had, as we shall note later on,[2] a special theoretical interest in connection with the larger Renaissance issue of dramatic verisimilitude.

III

MORE substantive problems too—of genres, of decorum and rules— were from the beginning the characteristic concern of the 16th-century critics. The world of medieval and early Renaissance fable, romance,

---

[1] Puttenham's *Arte of English Poesie* (1589) is a neo-rhetorical treatise characterized by the flamboyance of its diagrams of "figure" poems and by its quaintly native reduction of the classical figure terminology (*antitheton*, the "quarreller"; *traductio*, the "tranlacer"; *paradoxon*, the "wonderer"; *micterismus*, the "fleering frumpe"). Book I, Chapters V–VII and Book II, Chapters V–IX, contain his comments on rhyme. See the edition by Gladys D. Willcock and Alice Wallser (Cambridge, 1936), pp. 10–15, 76–84.

[2] Chapter 10, pp. 188–90.

and burlesque lay between the classic age and the new poets and theorizers. If they undertook to write the old forms (tragedy, or comedy, or
Virgilian epic), it was difficult not to find the new materials (Christian,
feudal, Gothic, romantic, in a word, "European") equally with the new
vernacular media, an obstacle to a perfect return. How strictly interpret
the rules of Aristotle? How far stretch or relax them? How far improve
or tighten them up? Such are the issues which inspire Giraldi Cinthio's
Address to the Reader defending his own *Tragedy of Orbecche*, 1541,
his *Apology* for his tragedy *Dido*, 1543, his treatise *On the Composition of Comedies and Tragedies*, 1543, or Giangiorgio Trissino's *Poetica*,
1529–1563, a work in part apologetic for his own epic *Italy Liberated
from the Goths* and for his tragedy *Sofonisba*. In somewhat the same
vein with these instances of special pleading appear the treatises of Antonio Minturno, his *De Poeta*, 1559, and *L'Arte Poetica*, 1564. All these
works and many others reexamine—without special illumination—such
prime Aristotelian and Horatian topics as character and plot in tragedy,
the difference between tragedy and comedy, happy and unhappy conclusions, the *deus ex machina*, pity and fear, purgation. The most signal
victory for the Aristotelian rules—or the greatest extension of their authority and increase in their stringency—was that by which the unity
of action so much stressed by Aristotle and the unity of time to which
he undoubtedly alluded (in his phrase *hupo mian periodon hēliou*) became the now famous three unities of action, time, and place, the *unités
Scaligeriennes* of French classical drama in the next century. Sufficiently
indicated by Scaliger in his *Poetics* of 1561, they were hammered home
by Lodovico Castelvetro in his *Poetica D'Aristotele Vulgarizzata et
Sposta* of 1570 (the Greek text translated and heavily annotated in Italian).[3] Castelvetro, a progressive critic who kept stage and audience firmly
in mind, argued with admirable practical solicitude that unity of time, the
limitation of the drama to one day, was a necessity by reason of the
bodily needs of the audience. (. . . *il quale io no veggo che possa passare
il giro del sole, siccome dice Aristotele, cioè ore dodici, conciosiacosaché
per le necessità del corpo, come è mangiare, bere, disporre i superflui pesi
del ventre e della vesica, dormire e per altre necessità, non possa il popolo
continuare oltre il predetto termine così fatta dimora in teatro*.) [4] This
kind of time, we may observe in passing, external or theater time, rather
than internal or plot time, was not really what Aristotle had in mind (a
matter for scene shifters only, he said—and the Greek tragedies came
three to a day, with a satyr play afterwards). The problem of internal

---

[3] See H. B. Charlton, *Castelvetro's Theory of Poetry* (Manchester, 1913); F. M.
Padelford, *Select Translations from Scaliger's Poetics* (New York, 1905).
[4] Quoted by H. Breitinger, "*Un passage de Castelvetro sur l'unité de lieu*,"
Revue Critique d'Histoire et de Littérature, Nouvelle Série, VII (27 December, 1879),
478–80. Cf. Castelvetro, *Poetica D'Aristotele*, Basil, 1576, p. 109 (II, 7). Breitinger
quotes the edition of Vienna, 1570, p. 60.

unity of time—how far it is entailed by unity of action and how far in turn it entails unity of place—is a real critical problem to which we shall have good occasion (Chapter 10) to return.

Such was the more reactionary outcome of the conflict between Aristotle and modernity—the outcome for which 16th-century literary criticism has been best known and least liked. Everyone knows about the neo-classic deference to authority and prescription and the concurrently wholehearted acceptance of the classical code for the imitation of the best models. In the words of Saintsbury's convenient simplification:

> The poet is to look first, midmost, and last to the practice of the ancients. . . . The ancients have anticipated almost everything, and in everything that they have anticipated have done so well that the best chance of success is simply to imitate them. The detailed precepts of Horace are never to be neglected; if supplemented, they must be supplemented in the same sense.[5]

What is called "Virgil Worship," the elevation of Virgil over Homer or the narrowing of the epic model to Virgil alone—flagrant instances of which appear in Vida's verse *Art* and, perhaps the most notorious, in Scaliger's *Poetics*—was a nationalistic, rather than a strictly critical, phenomenon. Still the resulting debate lasted long, in England for instance, from Chapman's Preface to the *Iliad* in 1598 (defending Homer against Scaliger of course) to the essays and clubbable conversations of the 18th century—where we find Dr. Samuel Johnson also on the side of Homer.

I V

But criticism in the 16th century might be at many moments uneasy in its submission—it might be even energetic in stretching, rather than tightening, the rules—and this especially when it had to say something about the undoubted (if irregular) masterpieces which were being contrived during that era in the Gothic mode: romantic and heroic epics (with tinges of burlesque), modifications of pastoral, and other hybrids of classical and medieval decora. Pronounced instances of a critical trend may be seen in the defence of Ariosto's "variety" by Cinthio in his treatise *On the Composition of Romances* (1549), in Tasso's *Discourses on the Heroic Poem* (1594) written to defend the theme of love in his own *Jerusalem Delivered*, in Mazzoni's two discourses (1572, 1587) defending the delightful "teaching" of Dante's mixed poetry and politics in the *Comedy*, and in Guarini's *Compendium of Tragicomic Poetry* (1601) written to defend his own "Pastoral Tragicomedy" *Il Pastor Fido*. ("Pastoral tragi-

---

[5] Saintsbury II, 217.

comedy purges with pleasure the sadness of the hearers.") [6] One of the happiest instances (through a sort of metaphoric argument about content and form which it contains) is a defence of Ariosto epitomized for the unfriendly purpose of refutation by Antonio Minturno in his *L'Arte Poetica* of 1564.[7]

VESPASIANO: Since we have gone so far in our reasoning, just what is the romance?

MINTURNO: I shall not deny that it is an imitation of great and illustrious actions that are worthy of epic poetry. But certainly the word is strange, and in the Spanish as well as in the Provençal I believe it refers to the vulgar tongue. . . . because they dealt in that language with the actions and the loves of knights more than with any other subject, the compositions made on that theme were called romances. The same word passed into Italy, because our writers began to imitate the romantic and classical compositions of the barbarians. And since our authors, as Cicero teaches us, always improve what they find in others, they make also the poetry of the romances more graceful and beautiful, if in truth it is to be called poetry.

VESPASIANO: Why is it not worthy of this name? Is not M. Ludovico Ariosto a most excellent poet, as he is a most noble writer of romance?

MINTURNO: Yes, indeed, nor do I judge that a lower estimate should be made of him. But I cannot affirm that his romances and those of others contain the kind of poetry that Aristotle and Horace taught us.

VESPASIANO: Of what consequence is it that the romance is not such poetry but another kind taken over from the Ultramontanes and made more splendid and more beautiful by the Italians, if the world is pleased with it and accepts and receives it with delight?

MINTURNO: I do not wonder about the common crowd. . . . But I cannot but be greatly astonished that there are some learned men, well versed in good literature and of excellent abilities, who (as I understand) acknowledge that there is not in the ro-

[6] Gilbert, pp. 262, 373–4, 378, 381, 484, 524.
[7] A treatise *Della Toscana Poesia*, written as a complement of his earlier Latin work on the poet in six books.

> mances the form and the rule that Homer and
> Vergil follow, and that Aristotle and Horace
> command as appropriate, and who nevertheless
> labor to defend this error. Nay more, since that
> sort of composition gives the deeds of *errant
> knights*, they obstinately affirm not merely that
> it is not fitting to' write poetry in the manner of
> Vergil and Homer, but even that it is desirable
> that *poetry* also should be *errant*, passing from
> one manner to another, and binding various things
> in one bundle.[8]

Erratic form to express erratic materials. If we think of the classical
genres and their corollary rules of decorum as the patterns according to
which poetry was supposed to succeed in being like the several most
important kinds of reality, we may say that in all the ramifications of
their manifold debate over Aristotelianism—down to the articles concerning rhyme and meter—the theorizers of the 16th century were debating
(by a highly codified and rather crabbed convention) nothing else than
the degree of correspondence which should obtain between art and reality. Is a mixed genre (let us say tragicomedy) an offence against reality?
Certainly not in one sense: it is not an offense against realism or naturalism, because events in life do tend to occur mixed, the sad and the happy
and funny close together. But if we are willing to speak of such occurrences with an accent on our responses to them—if we confer on "reality"
something of an implication of ideality in its easiest sense—we may arrive
at a situation where in a very crude and preliminary way we have to say
that to mix tears and laughter is unreal. In real life a sad event tends to
concentrate or purify our sad feelings to the point where we either do
not notice, or may even resent, anything gay or hilarious. If such mixtures or alterations are to be received kindly on the stage, clearly some
sophistication must be at work—ideality at a special remove. On this
point no very explicit theory appears to have been entertained during the
period of which we speak. But about the ideality of poetry in still a third
sense (fairly broad and obvious)—the sense of poetic fantasy and invention in contrast to the ordinariness of actual life—there are some more
or less enlightened Aristotelian and Platonic speculations.

V

TASSO, for instance, in his *Discourses* of 1594, though he avers that poetry
should be true (*icastic*), not false (*phantastic*), and that the "marvelous"

---

[8] Gilbert, pp. 277–8, translating Minturno, *L'Arte Poetica* (Naples, 1725), Book I,
p. 26a–b. The italics are ours.

should be "credible," says at the same time that poetry is not the piddling truth of particular facts, but is something which is *like* the truth of the universal.[9] Even the opposite emphasis, the full plea for invention, might appear. Thus, for instance, Mazzoni in his treatise *On the Defense of the Comedy* (1587):

> . . . poetry, because of paying more attention to the credible than to the true, ought to be classed as a subdivision of the rational faculty, called by the ancients sophistic.

> . . . phantasy is the true power over poetic fables, since she alone is capable of those fictions which we of ourselves are able to feign and put together. From this of necessity it follows that poetry is made up of things feigned and imagined, because it is founded on phantasy.

The metaphysics of Mazzoni's view of art appears (though somewhat obscurely) in this passage of his Introduction:

> Those arts that have as their object the image, or idol, have an object for the construction of which there is no other end than to represent and to imitate; hence they are properly called imitative. . . . they are distinguished from the other arts that are not called imitative in that the latter have objects that are good for some other use and some other end. . . . when we concluded above that the image is the object of the imitative arts we did not mean that sort of image that comes into being without human artistic activity . . . but that which has its origin from our art, which usually springs from our phantasy and our intellect by means of our choice and will, as an image in pictorial art or in sculpture. . . . this species of image is that which is an adequate object of human imitation, and . . . when Aristotle said in the beginning of the *Poetics* that all the species of poetry were imitative, he meant that imitation which has for its object the image that springs entirely from human artifice. . . . Plato in the *Sophist* has left a statement that imitation is of two sorts. One of these he has named icastic; it represents things that are truly derived from some work already existing. . . . The other, which he called phantastic, is exemplified in pictures that are made by the caprice of the artist.[1]

Allow for a certain blurring of Platonic terminology here, a double (or triple) service for the word *image*, to mean both object in nature (the

---

[9] Gilbert, pp. 477, 479, 494.

[1] Gilbert, pp. 359, 360, 367, 387. Mazzoni's *Della Difesa della "Commedia" di Dante* (Books I–III published in 1587, Books IV–VII, in 1688) appears actually to have been composed by Tuccio dal Corno from materials supplied by Mazzoni.

image of a divine idea) and object in our fancy, made manifest only in the external imitation (which is a third sort of image), and we have a defense of fantasy thoroughly grounded in a transvalued Platonic theory of imitation. Not that poetry *must* be false in the factual, historical sense, but that it may be, and that even when it is false it has its peculiar kind of truth.

Such a defense of poetry was highly compatible with another, which we have already observed in the Middle Ages, the allegorical defense of pagan fables. And we must suppose this latter (or rather the whole issue of the relation of theology and poetry, as we have noted it in Boccaccio's *Life of Dante* and *De Genealogia Deorum*) to have been always close to the critical consciousness of the later age. Harington's *Apologie* prefixed to his Ariosto is an English text which names the "literal," "moral," and "allegorical" levels of poetic meaning—applying these to the myth of Perseus and Andromeda in a passage for which modern scholarship has shown the direct source to be the neo-Platonic philosopher Leo Ebreo's *Dialoghi d'Amore*.[2] One of the most radical 16th-century pleas, much like the earlier one of Boccaccio, appears in the *Discourses* of Tasso.

> . . . it is not strange that the poet should be almost the same as the theologian and the dialectician . . . . divine philosophy, or theology as we prefer to call it, has two parts, and each of them is adapted and fitted to one part of our mind, which is composed of the divisible and the indivisible, not merely according to the opinion of Plato and of Aristotle, but of the Areopagite, who wrote in the epistles to Pope Titus in the *Mystic Theology*, and elsewhere, that that part of occult theology that is contained in the signs, and has the power of making one perfect, is fitting to the indivisible part of our soul, which is the intellect at its purest. The other, eager for wisdom, which brings proofs, he attributes to the divisible part of the soul, much less noble than the indivisible. Thence it leads to the contemplation of divine things; and to move readers in this way with images, as do the mystic theologian and the poet, is a much more noble work than to teach by means of demonstration, which is the function of the scholastic theologian. The mystic theologian and the poet, then, are far more noble than any of the others, even though Saint Thomas in the first part of the *Summa* put poetry in the lowest order of teaching.[3]

[2] See the text in Smith II, 201–2; and cf. Douglas Bush, *Mythology and the Renaissance Tradition in English Poetry* (1932), p. 70; R. Elbrodt, "Sir John Harington and Leone Ebreo," *MLN*, LXV (1950), 109–10; Margret G. Trotter, *TLS*, December 30, 1944, p. 631.

[3] Gilbert, p. 476, from *Discourses on the Heroic Poem*, Book II, [10]. Gilbert quotes Aquinas, *Summa Theologiae* I, 1, 9: "It is objected that sacred teaching should not use metaphors. . . . to proceed by various similitudes and representations

As the age of scientific reason succeeded to that of humanistic imagination, and the standard of measured literalness to that of analogical insight,
such allegorical defenses were to fall more and more below the critical
horizon. Even Tasso argued against the intrusion of classical mythology
in modern poems, on the ground that it jarred with verisimilitude.

> . . . if we . . . have recourse to the same ones as were invoked
> by the ancients, by that plan we are deprived of the probable
> and the credible. . . . I speak of the enchanted rings, the flying
> horses, the ships turned into nymphs, the ghosts that interfere in
> battles, the burning sword, the garland of flowers, the forbidden
> chamber . . . . if these miracles, or prodigies rather, cannot be
> brought about by the power of nature, it is necessary that the
> cause be some supernatural force or some diabolical power, and
> if we turn to the deities of the pagans, we for the most part give
> up the lifelike and the probable, or rather I would say the credi-
> ble . . . . but in the ancient poets these things should be read in
> another frame of mind and with another taste, as it were, not
> merely as things received by the people but as those approved by
> their religion.[4]

In the next century, Boileau in his *Art Poétique*, written just a few
years after the publication of Milton's *Paradise Lost*, came to a conclusion in one sense opposite to that of Tasso, yet inspired by a similar
latent critical principle. Boileau argued that the one form of supernaturalism to be avoided by the epic poet was the Christian, for spiritual truth
was bound to be so deformed by imagistic embodiment as to lack conviction. (And despite the signal instance of Milton, the history of Christian epic poetry in the 17th century, both French and English, largely
substantiates the apprehension of Boileau.) During the rather brief 17th-
century defense of "heroic" drama, the supernatural is justified, with quotations from Petronius and Longinus, largely in terms of the power to
amaze and shock. After that, the theoretical contest between realism and
the fantastic-supernatural flutters down progressively to the criterion of
this-world naturalism. A degenerate phase of the controversy may be illustrated from a note to the poem called *An Essay on Unnatural Flights
in Poetry* (1701) by Pope's friend George Granville.

> The Poetic World is nothing but Fiction; Pernassus, Pegasus,
> and the Muses, pure imagination and Chimaera. But being, how-
> ever, a system universally agreed on, all that shall be contriv'd

---

is proper to poetry, which is the humblest branch of knowledge. . . . I answer that
it is proper for Sacred Scripture to set forth in metaphors divine and spiritual things
under the similitude of corporeal things." Cf. *ante* Ch. 7, p. 131; Ch. 8, pp. 147–8, 150.
   [4] Gilbert, p. 479; *Discourses*, II, [13].

or invented upon this Foundation according to Nature shall be reputed as truth: But what so ever shall diminish from, or exceed, the just proportion of Nature, shall be rejected as False, and pass for extravagance, as Dwarfs and Gyaunts for Monsters.[5]

That is to say: the poetic world is a classical canon of fantasy which is agreed to be according to nature because it is a classical canon—Pegasus and the Muses, not romantic Dwarfs and Gyaunts. This may not seem a great improvement over the more scholastic arguments from the principle of analogy relied on by Boccaccio and Tasso.

VI

WE MAY add one more theme—that concerning the moral status of poetry—to our account of poetics in the 16th century, and at the same time bring this account to an appropriate conclusion, if we refer now to an essay, the *Defence of Poesie* by Sir Philip Sidney, which is both the English locus of closest contact with Italian criticism and a brilliant epitome of what was best in the spirit of that criticism. The utilitarian defense of poetry by an Englishman appears quite early in the century with Sir Thomas Elyot's *Boke of the Governour*, 1530, in which chapters X and XII of Book I (the education of a public servant described by a public servant) maintain that Homer and Virgil can teach the young man not only moral lessons but arms, politics, and horse-breeding.[6] (The pre-Platonic directness of this apology—as if the rhapsode Ion were speaking —was perhaps possible only because it came before the great vogue of Aristotle's *Poetics*.) A less pragmatic idea about the civilizing value of literature was one of the basic premises of Renaissance humanism and of the Renaissance theory of education—in the *Adagia* of Erasmus, for instance, or the treatises of Ludovicus Vives.[7] Throughout Italian criticism of the century (in Trissino, Minturno, Cinthio, Mazzoni, for instance, and in almost all other writers) the accepted formula is morally didactic, the Horatio-Aristotelian instruction and pleasure,[8] with countless inconclusive variations on the relation between the two. (Castelvetro, with a practical concern for the recreation of the common spectator, was one of the earliest to make an emphatic disavowal of the didactic view—a dis-

---

[5] Cf. *post* Chapter 15, pp. 335-6.

[6] Gilbert, pp. 234, 236.

[7] A symptomatic though decidedly minor instance may be cited for English humanism in the treatise *De fructu qui ex doctrina percipitur* by Henry VIII's officer Richard Pace.

[8] Cf. Marvin T. Herrick, *The Fusion of Horatian and Aristotelian Literary Criticism, 1531-1555* (Urbana, 1946). Ch. IV, "The Function of Poetry."

avowal that would gain ground with French 17th-century critics.[9]) At the same time the Platonic charge of immorality might readily enough be brought against poetry—especially when English moralists (for example, Roger Ascham in his *Scholemaster*) associated poetry with Italianate license in manners or dress, or when Puritan writers turned their attention to the theater. One of the most pungent of the latter—and today one of the best known of all those who engaged in the long pamphlet war that began in England shortly after the start of the London professional theater in 1571—was Stephen Gosson, by turns a writer for the theater himself, a student at a Catholic seminary in Rome, and an Anglican clergyman, parson at Great Wigborow in Essex and at St. Botolph's, Bishopsgate. The gist of his rattling, tart, Euphuistic double protest, against the moral influence of plays themselves and of the deplorable bordello company which flocked to the theater, may be told almost sufficiently in the garrulous title of his *School of Abuse: Containing a pleasant invective against Poets, Pipers, Players, Jesters, and such like Caterpillars of a Commonwealth: Setting up the Flag of Defiance to their mischievous exercise, and overthrowing their Bulwarks, by Prophane Writers, Natural Reason, and common experience: A Discourse as Pleasant for them that favor learning, as profitable for all that will follow virtue.* "Because I have been matriculated myself in the school where so many abuses flourish," writes Gosson in one of his characteristically eloquent passages, "I will imitate the dogs of Egypt, which coming to the banks of Nilus to quench their thirst, sip and away, drink running, lest they be snapped short for a prey to crocodiles."

> . . . you are no sooner entered but liberty looseth the reins and gives you head, placing you with poetrie in the lowest form, when his skill is shown to make his scholar as good as ever twanged: he prefers you to piping, from piping to playing, from play to pleasure, from pleasure to sloth, from sloth to sleep, from sleep to sin, from sin to death, from death to the Devil, if you take your learning apace, and pass through every form without revolting.[1]

This pamphlet appeared in 1579, with a dedication "To the right noble Gentleman, Master Philip Sidney, Esquire." It was a moment when Sidney, returned from his educational travels in Switzerland and Italy, standing loosely attached to Elizabeth's court under the patronage of Leicester, and in companionable relation to Spenser and the gentlemen of

[9] See, for instance, the Abbé d'Aubignac, Corneille in his *Discours de l'utilité . . . du poème dramatique*, and St. Evremonde. Their ideas may be looked on as embryonic of far later theories of aesthetic autonomy. Cf. René Bray, *La formation de la doctrine classique en France* (Dijon, 1926), p. 727.

[1] (London: The Shakespeare Society, 1841), p. 14. We have modernized the spelling.

the Areopagus, was engaged in the literary occupations, his sonnets to Stella and his romance *Arcadia*, by which in the short time that remained before his death at Zutphen he became the brilliant symbol of the courtly literary spirit of England. Largely from Gosson's dedication and from an allusion to this by Spenser in a letter dated from Leicester House to the Cambridge scholar Gabriel Harvey, but in part also from certain moments in Sidney's argument and certain snatches of parodied Euphuistic style which seem echoes of Gosson,[2] Sidney's *Defence of Poesie*, though written perhaps as late as 1585, has been traditionally considered a retort to Gosson. It circulated in manuscript among the literati during Sidney's life and was soon quoted in the best critical places—in Puttenham's *Arte* of 1589, in Harington's *Apologie* of 1598. In the year 1595 it had the advantage of being published simultaneously by two printers, Ponsonby and Olney, under two titles, *The Defence of Poesie* and *An Apologie for Poetrie*. It is a kind of formal beginning of literary theorizing by the English man of letters, and a brilliant enough one—written in the high, enthusiastic, occasionally a-syntactic style of the gifted amateur champion, headlong to outdazzle the lowness and myopia of professional moral grumblers. The essay reflects and telescopes not only the continental criticism of the century but a certain amount of classical Greek and Roman as well. Passages have been assigned to Minturno, Scaliger, and Castelvetro. And latterly the original sources of neo-classic criticism and anti-criticism, Aristotle's *Poetics* and Plato's *Republic*, Book X (perhaps in Latin translations such as Pazzi's of Aristotle and Ficino's of Plato), have been urged as the true fountains of Sidney's learning.[3] It is certain that he read little Greek, and it appears likely to us that he was better acquainted with contemporary interpretations of classical criticism than with the latter itself. But it all matters little. Sidney wrote, not a pedant's encyclopedia, but a gentleman's essay.

High points of interest in the essay include a preliminary double definition of poetry, from Aristotle and from Horace, a now famous statement that the poet's tale "holds" children from play and old men from the chimney-corner,[4] an adaptation of Aristotelian doctrine making poetry a union of philosophy and history and giving it the highest literary palm after the *Scriptures*, an invocation of Plato as a witness for poetry (following so reputable an authority as Scaliger, Sidney overrates the Socratic concessions to poetic frenzy in the *Ion*), and a section where Sidney ap-

---

[2] The opposition between Sidney's simplified Ramist rhetoric and the parody of patristic symbol-reading in the Euphuism of Gosson is part of a theme which we develop in Chapter 12.

[3] Cornell March Dowlin, "Sidney's Two Definitions of Poetry," in *MLQ*, III, (December, 1942), 573–81.

[4] "With a tale, forsooth, he cometh unto you, with a tale which holdeth children from play, and old men from the chimney-corner" (ed. A. S. Cook, Boston, 1890, p. 23). This passage is borrowed from Sidney by Harington.

plies Scaligerian and Horatian norms to English poetry. He protests against the slack unity of academic tragedies (excepting *Gorboduc*) and the clatter of wooden swords in battle endings. He mentions Spenser's *Shepheardes Calender* with respect, admits the stirring of his heart at the old ballad of Chevy Chase, and looks back with wistful respect and wonder at Chaucer—"that he in that misty time could see so clearly." We may look on these latter details of Sidney's *Defence* as constituting an early landmark in the progress of English literary self-consciousness and literary history—a topic to which we shall have occasion to return in later chapters.[5]

To look a little more closely at the theoretic content of Sidney's moral defense of poetry: one should note in the first place that the second of Sidney's preliminary definitions is such as to make the moral *content* of poetry (that is, vices and virtues correctly evaluated) a part of its essential requirement—as indeed his first definition names the purpose of poetry explicitly as teaching.

> Poesy, therefore, is an art of imitation, for so Aristotle termeth it in his word *mimēsis*, that is to say, a representing, counterfeiting, or figuring forth; to speak metaphorically, a speaking picture, with this end,—to teach and delight.[6]

> . . . it is not riming and versing that maketh a poet . . . but it is that feigning notable images of virtues, vices, or what else, with that delightful teaching, which must be the right describing note to know a poet by.[7]

Yet in the second place, at a much later point in the essay, when he is facing Platonic objections and is hence forced into reasoning about the moral requirement and how to reconcile it with the stark fact that much fine poetry is immoral, Sidney says something different: The phenomenon of immoral poetry ("amorous conceits," "lust," "vanity," "scurrility" in poetry) means "not . . . that poetry abuseth man's wit, but that man's wit abuseth poetry." He could have said (though to say so would have contradicted easily observable facts, and he did not say it) that immoral poetry was, by his earlier definition, no poetry at all. He preferred to raise the question how poetry, which is defined as something moral, can be *in fact* either moral or immoral. His answer—in terms of the ideal conceived as what is most real—should not be dismissed too lightly, though it perhaps gives mere logic some difficulty.

> Nay, truly, though I yield that poesy may not only be abused, but that by being abused, by the reason of his sweet charming force, it can do more hurt than any other army of words, yet

[5] See especially Chapters 11 and 24.
[6] Cook, p. 9.
[7] Cook, p. 11.

shall it be so far from concluding that the abuse should give reproach to the abused, that contrariwise it is a good reason, that
whatsoever, being abused, doth most harm, being rightly used—
and upon the right use each thing receiveth his title—doth most
good.[8]

Many volumes of subsequent debate have perhaps not adjusted this delicate conflict of values any more satisfactorily. One might summarize the
problem by saying that Sidney, like most of those who have maintained
that poetry is (and ought to be) moral, has not been able to resolve an
ambiguity of the word *ought* as used in the formula. Is this a poetic
"ought," or is it in fact only a moral "ought"? In the second sense "ought
to be moral" is a tautology—since moral is what all our works ought to
be. Is the thesis about the morality of poetry a truism in the realm of
morals, or does it lie actually in the realm of poetics? Does it actually
relate to the poet's craft?

But it is when we back off from the too explicit question about
morals posed by the uncomfortable Gosson and allow ourselves to hear
Sidney echoing some of those safer, because more generalized, Renaissance doctrines of ideality to which we have lately referred, that we have
the Sidney who is dearest to the English literary tradition. In late antiquity, we remember, there had appeared the Plotinian doctrine of the
poet's intimate access to the transcendent forms, and the example of the
divinely conceived Phidian Zeus, which Plotinus shared with the *Vita
Apollonii* of Philostratus. These approaches to a theory of creative imagination have their notable counterparts in Renaissance English. There is,
for example, that passage in Shakespeare's *A Midsummer Night's Dream*
where the "poet's eye, in a fine frenzy rolling, Doth glance from heaven
to earth, from earth to heaven, ... the poet's pen . . . gives to airy
nothing A local habitation and a name." [9] There is that in Bacon's *Proficience and Advancement of Learning* where "reason doth buckle and
bowe the mind unto the Nature of things," poetry "doth raise and erect
the Minde, by submitting the shewes of things to the desires of the
mind." "Therefore it was ever thought to have some participation of
divinesse." [1] And Sidney himself contributes two of the brightest in our
florilegium of such sententiae: the brief refutation of a stock charge, ". . .
the poet . . . nothing affirmeth, and therefore never lieth," and a metaphor of the zodiac's range and fire, which, framed in its needed context, we present as the tailpiece and conclusion of our procession from
antiquity to the earliest flourishing of English critical self-consciousness.

---

[8] Cook, p. 38.

[9] In the context (*Midsummer Night's Dream*, V, i, 1–28), where the poet is
grouped with the lunatic and the lover, these words are perhaps not to be taken
quite so solemnly as they often have been.

[1] *Proficience and Advancement of Learning*, Book II, paragraph 43.

There is no art delivered unto mankind that hath not the works of nature for his principal object. . . . Only the poet, disdaining to be tied to any such subjection, lifted up with the vigor of his own invention, doth grow, in effect, into another nature, in making things either better than nature bringeth forth, or, quite anew, forms such as never were in nature, as the heroes, demigods, cyclops, chimeras, furies, and such like; so as he goeth hand in hand with nature, not enclosed within the narrow warrant of her gifts, but freely ranging within the zodiac of his own wit. Nature never set forth the earth in so rich tapestry as divers poets have done; neither with pleasant rivers, fruitful trees, sweet-smelling flowers, nor whatsoever else may make the too-much-loved earth more lovely; her world is brazen, the poets only deliver a golden.[2]

SUPPLEMENT

The error here lies obviously in applying to these verses a rhythm which, if it lay not wholly outside the consciousness of their composers, at all events lay quite outside their habit and intention. A more reasonable procedure in the face of such grotesque effects would have been to hazard the query, whether such a reading or pronunciation can possibly have been contemplated by Sidney, Harvey, and the rest. An approach to such an inquiry was made by McKerrow, who asked "what is the rhythm of a hexameter?" but unfortunately he did not pursue his quest farther, and replied with the acquiescent words, "I doubt not that they read hexameters then as they are read in schools now, 'árma virúmque canó, Trojaé qui etc.'," that is with scansion rhythm. But this throws us back to the point of view of Southey, Ellis, Saintsbury and the rest, the improbability of which we have observed.

But let us reverse the procedure and see where it leaves Virgil and Ovid and Lucan on this same charge of false accents with respect to their own language. For if it is a sound conclusion that Sidney, in order to obtain hexameter rhythm, must have intended his line "núrs inwárd maladíes" to be read with distorted accents as marked, then it is equally true that Virgil made the same demand of his Roman readers in writing *Italiám fató profugús*, in defiance of the Latin rule, that no word, unless followed by an enclitic, may be accented on the last syllable. The conclusion to which such a comparison leads scarcely requires the specific formulation, that neither the Roman nor the English poet intended or entertained any thought that his verses should be read otherwise than with natural accents proper to his own language.

Where, then, unless a well defined metrical ictus is observed, is the rhythm, the characteristic beat of the hexameter? In the case of the English example

[2] Cook, pp. 7–8.

we may well ask. As for the Virgilian line the answer is easier. The poet himself and the reader whom he contemplates, possessing by nature and by training from earlier poetry a feeling for syllabic quantity, would recognize from the mere succession of long and short syllables the underlying rhythm, undisturbed by the true accents of the several words. The English reader of Sidney's day on the other hand, reproducing by artifice what the ancient reader possessed by birth, and untrained by any past usage to recognize long and short syllables, can scarcely have felt any discernible rhythm in the vague and uncertain quantities of many lines which Sidney or Stanyhurst presented to the readers of their day as quantitative hexameters.

Neither the Elizabethan composer nor his reader approached the hexameter with a preconceived notion of, or feeling for, the rhythmical movement of the whole line, or of that "tune" so to speak, which in the modern hexameter, of Longfellow for example, is so familiar. "Scanning" of course was known and practiced for the instruction of schoolboys and for "proving" their compositions, but it was not then or later looked upon as a legitimate literary rendering of the line. To be sure a good many verses occur in the compositions of Sidney and Harvey which correspond more or less accurately to the scanning scheme of dactyls and spondees, but, as we shall see, they occur rather by accident than by design. The only fixed rhythmical feature of the Latin hexameter line in agreement with the scanning pattern was the accentual cadence of the last two feet *primus ab oris* (-uu/-u), in which word accent and syllabic quantity usually coincide. This regular recurrent cadence became from an early time so fixed a mark of the verse, that in crude popular epitaphs and in late and medieval verses it is often the index of an author's intention or ambition to construct a hexameter, when little else corresponds to the requirements of the classical verse.

But this general absence of a well defined rhythmical movement throughout the verse was not missed either by the composer or by his reader. Both had inherited the century old habit of reading Latin verse simply by the word accents, and they carried this usage over naturally from Latin into the new English counterpart. The poet himself was of course conscious of his painstaking and orderly sequence of dactyls and spondees, and in the privacy of his closet may well have "scanned and proved" their correctness; but surely it was no part of his purpose that his readers should share that consciousness.

—G. L. Hendrickson, "Elizabethan Quantitative Hexameters," *Philological Quarterly*, XXXVIII (April, 1949), 241–3, by permission of the editors

Professor Hendrickson's thesis, that the quantitative pattern of the experimental verse written by Sidney and other Elizabethans was not expected either to conform to or to twist out of shape the natural English accentual rhythm, seems unquestionable and is a valuable clarification. The aesthetic problem which remains might be put thus: In what way were the English readers expected to be conscious of the quantitative dactyls and spondees? In what way did Latin readers of Virgil feel "from the mere succession of long and short syllables the underlying rhythm, undisturbed by the true accents of the several words?"

CHAPTER 10

ENGLISH NEO-CLASSICISM: JONSON AND DRYDEN

§ *Jonson as playwright: humours, characters, satire, moral intent—II. Jonson's* Timber, *its sources, its literary ideas—III. the imitation of classical models distinguished from plagiarism and illustrated, Jonson's classicism summarized—IV. French neo-classicism, Corneille's essays on drama—V. Sorbière's attack on England, Dryden's* Essay of Dramatic Poesy: *the setting, the identity and stances of the four speakers, Neander's radicalism, his Examen of Jonson's* Epicoene—*VI. the argument about rhyme, its relation to verisimilitude and the unities, rhyme in English drama and in French, Dryden's conversion to Shakespearian blank verse, the unities of different types of stages—VII. contrast between Dryden and Corneille, Dryden's gentlemanly dialectic, varieties of scepticism in his day, his probabilism* §

THE SOURCES OF SIDNEY'S "DEFENCE" WERE CLASSICAL, BUT THE SPIRIT was not very sternly classical. Sidney sends up the joyous fireworks of the Italianate Renaissance. His colors are enthusiastic, neo-Platonic, ideal purple and gold. The motion is soaring. He is essentially a theorist of the exuberant imagination. A far more severe classicism, squared off on the norms of objective ethical imitation, may be observed in Ben Jonson, next in line of the English men of letters who have had notably critical preoccupations. Jonson was a man of the public theaters whose genius lay in the salty, astringent, and prickly comico-satiric department of classicism. He wrote middling classical tragedies (*Sejanus, Catiline*) but rubbed both the city and general humanity down well with salt in comedies either native or Italian in setting (*Every Man in his Humour, Bartholomew Fair, Volpone*). These he planted solidly on the classical unities, and in their ethical technique he united the medieval physiological heritage, the simplified character as a "humour," or an affectation of "humour," [1] with the Plautine label type (a braggart soldier, a clever servant, an avaricious and jealous husband, a gay young man, a town gull, a country gull). He showed withal a strong trace of the Theophrastan "character," a genre newly restored to the tradition by the editing of the continental scholar Isaac Casaubon, in 1592 and 1598, and appearing, simultaneously with Jonson's plays, in the English *Characterisms* (1608) of Bishop Joseph Hall and *Characters* (1614) of Sir Thomas Overbury.

Jonson wrote a kind of native [2] classicism which it has been difficult for any audience since the mid-18th century really to enjoy—obscene yet moralizing, caustic, thorny, vulgar, immediate, Londinian and topical (and so now obscure). It was Roman satiric technique applied to London vice, and a solid instance of the Augustan principle of "imitation" or recreation of the classic model. This was a time when London, the manifold and sophisticated metropolis, was producing a mushroom growth of social literature. The epigram, little known in the West since the time of Martial and imperial Rome, was now cultivated again, and so was Juvenalian satire. As Sophocles and Aristophanes had been followed by Theophrastus and his pupil Menander, Shakespeare was followed by Jonson and by Hall.[3]

The theory that comic and satiric literature has a moral rather than a libelous intent (a theory which perhaps to some extent actually guided Jonson's comic performance) often breaks out explicitly in his Prologue, Epilogue, or Induction, or in editorializing speeches by his characters. Cicero, says the Moderator Cordatus in *Every Man out of His Humour* (III, i), would have a comedy to be:

> *Imitatio vitae, Speculum Consuetudinis, Imago veritatis,*[4] a thing throughout pleasant and ridiculous, and accommodated to the correction of manners.

---

[1] Henry L. Snuggs, "The Comic Humours: A New Interpretation," *PMLA*, LXII (March, 1947), 114–22, argues convincingly that the comic humours of Jonsonian drama were not actually the temperaments defined in the physico-psychological tradition but the pseudo-humours of affected eccentricity.

[2]
> Our scene is London, 'cause we would make known,
> No country's mirth is better than our own;
> No clime breeds better for your whore,
> Bawd, squire, imposter, many persons more,
> Whose manners, now call'd humours, feed the stage.
> —Prologue to *The Alchemist*

Here is an early phase in the development of a kind of national pride upon which we shall have occasion for further comment in Chapter 11.

[3] E. C. Baldwin, "Ben Jonson's Indebtedness to the Greek Character-Sketch," *MLN*, XVI (1901), 385–96.

[4] Henry L. Snuggs, "The Source of Jonson's Definition of Comedy," *MLN*, LXV (1950), 543–4, shows an intermediate source in Minturno, *De Poeta*. Cf. *ante* Chapter 5, p. 89.

Along with this comfortable view of the comic purpose went the self-righteous confidence of the author in his own character,[5] something which had come down from Aristotelian instructions to the orator about self-advertisement, from the dictum of Cato that a good orator has to be not only skilled in speaking but a good man (*vir bonus dicendi peritus*),[6] and from the Horatian portrait of the upright satirist. As Milton would put it in the *Apology for Smectymnuus*:

> He who would not be frustrate of his hope to write well here-after in laudable things, ought himself to be a true poem.[7]

II

JONSON's more formal critical utterances included an indifferent blank verse translation of Horace's *Ars Poetica*, an *Ars* of his own which may have been lost when his library burned in 1623,[8] a few pungent *obiter dicta* upon English contemporaries (as "that Donne for not keep-ing of accent deserved hanging") made when he walked to Scotland in 1619 and conversed with the poet Drummond, and one other thing—most important by far of all. This is the book published posthumously in the 1641 folio of the *Works* and given the title *Timber: or, Dis-coveries; Made upon Men and Matter: As they have flow'd out of his daily Reading; or had their refluxe to his peculiar Notion of the Times.* As the title suggests, the work is a stock book of established classical ideas collected and translated, somewhat at random, by a practising man of letters for his several purposes. The resemblance between a few of the passages and certain passages of Jonson's verse[9] points toward one of these purposes. A group of essays in the political vein looks like materials for a letter to the king on the regal function. Certain passages of literary satire are the kind a man might copy or translate to soothe his own ran-cor at the stupidity of his enemies. Several other sections, the most con-tinuously developed and the most directly concerned with literature, have somewhat the look of lecture notes, and the recent discovery of a

[5] Cf. Eugene M. Waith, "The Poet's Morals in Jonson's *Poetaster*," *MLR*, XII (March, 1951), 13–19.

[6] Atkins, II, 16.

[7] *The Student's Milton*, ed. Frank A. Patterson (New York, 1941), p. 549. The dramatic application of this doctrine and hence its real critical significance are hand-somely illustrated in the biographical prefaces at the start of Books III, VII, and IX of *Paradise Lost* (cf. John S. Diekhoff, "The Function of the Prologues in *Paradise Lost*," *PMLA*, LVII, September, 1942, 696–704) and again in Alexander Pope's apol-ogies for his satiric career, especially in the *Epistle to Arbuthnot*.

[8] Cf. Leah Jonas, *The Divine Science* (New York, 1940), p. 16.

[9] Cf. No. 101, "*Amor nummi*," and No. 103 with *The Staple of News*, III, ii, and III, i; *Discoveries A Critical Edition*, ed. Maurice Castelain (Paris, 1906), pp. XXII–XXIII. Jonson told Drummond that his method of composing was to write out his thoughts first in prose and then translate them.

legal document which seems to show Jonson's residence about 1623 to have been Gresham College has led to the plausible speculation that he exercised the deputy function of Professor of Rhetoric in that College.[1] Modern scholarship has discovered classical and Renaissance sources (in Cicero, Petronius, Quintilian, and the two Senecas, in Erasmus, Machiavelli, Vives, Bacon and a host of others) for about four-fifths of the material which makes up Jonson's *Timber*. The most sustained classical literary discussion is that on poetry, tragedy, and comedy, which runs through the last eleven numbers.[2] The second half of this, on tragedy and comedy, is mostly derived, not from the Italian sources upon which Sidney had relied, but from more northern ones, from the *De Tragoediae Constitutione* and the *Ad Horatii de Plauto et Terentino Judicium Dissertatio* of the Dutch professor Daniel Heinsius and from the Bohemian Jesuit Jacobus Pontanus.[3] One longish part on prose style and letter writing (Nos. 124–126) is taken directly from an English rhetorical treatise then circulating in manuscript among the cognoscenti, the *Directions for Speech and Style* of the diplomatist John Hoskins.[4] Those parts of Jonson's *Timber* which are concerned with literary criticism constitute about two thirds of the whole. Shall we argue that these, by the simple fact of their having been chosen and put together by Jonson, represent his critical inclinations and hence may be discussed as if they were his own? Perhaps we may. At any rate, here we have a good anthology of classical and Renaissance doctrine reduced to pithy Senecan English:[5] that "ready writing makes not good writing; but good writing brings on ready writing" (No. 115); that poetry (*poesis*) requires not only "goodness of natural wit" but "exercise," "imitation," "study," and "art" (No. 130); that comic poetry[6] is nearest to oratory because most variously gifted to portray and to stir the "affections of the mind" (No. 130); that "the Episodes, and digressions in a Fable, are the same that housestuffe, and other furniture are in a house" (No. 134). Except for the last solid section (Nos. 127–136) of poetic and dramatic theory, the emphasis of *Timber* is on epistolary and oratorical style, on the manly virtues of brevity, perspicuity, vigor, discretion (No. 125), on

---

[1] C. J. Sisson, "Ben Jonson of Gresham College," *TLS*, September 21, 1951, p. 604; and the comment of George B. Johnston, *TLS*, December 28, 1951, p. 837. See Ralph Walker's rearranged edition, *Discoveries* (Syracuse, 1953).

[2] The numbers 1–37 were inserted by Gollancz (1898) and are retained by Castelain.

[3] J. E. Spingarn, "The Source of Jonson's Discoveries," *MP*, II (April, 1903), 1–10; Allan H. Gilbert and Henry L. Snuggs, "On the Relations of Horace to Aristotle in Literary Criticism," *JEGP*, XLVI (July, 1947), 240–4.

[4] John Hoskins, *Directions for Speech and Style*, ed. Hoyt H. Hudson (Princeton, 1935), pp. xxvii–xxviii.

[5] Jonson expresses his admiration of Bacon's style in Nos. 71 and 72. Swinburne, rediscovering *Timber* in 1889, rated its style better than that of Bacon.

[6] We shall have occasion in the next chapter to quote what must seem to modern ears the curious treatment of comedy in No. 131.

the author's practical problems and the rules of thumb which a veteran practitioner has found useful, on *poeta* rather than on *poema*. A few opinions about English writers form a notable incident in the early history of English literary self-consciousness.

> As *Livy* before *Salust, Sydney* before *Donne;* and beware of letting them taste *Gower,* or *Chaucer* at first, lest falling too much in love with Antiquity, and not apprehending the weight, they grow rough and barren in language onely. . . . *Spencer,* in affecting the Ancients, writ no Language: Yet I would have him read for his matter.—No. 116

> *Lucretius* is scabrous and rough in these; hee seekes 'hem: As some do *Chaucerismes* with us, which were better expung'd and banish'd.—No. 119 [7]

III

PROBABLY the classical doctrine which Jonson's *Timber* most illuminates is that concerning the imitation of models. That the exuberance and invention of the English Renaissance was consistent with a steady interest in classic models is a fact of which we may remind ourselves by thinking simply about such well-known phenomena as the sources of Shakespeare's plays and the numerous translations produced by the Englishmen of that age (Golding's *Ovid*, Harington's *Ariosto*, Chapman's *Homer*, Fairfax's *Tasso*, Florio's *Montaigne*, the works of the "Translator General" Philemon Holland).[8] Jonson's *Timber* relates to this spirit of the age in two ways—both through precept, and, as we have already more than hinted, very notably through example. Perhaps some of the precepts may seem in conflict with others. One of the five main ways to *poesis*, as we have noted, is "imitation."

> . . . to bee able to convert the substance or Riches of another *Poet,* to his owne use. To make choise of one excellent man above the rest, and so to follow him, till he grow very Hee; or so like him, as the Copie may be mistaken for the Principall.
> —No. 130

At the same time Jonson's *Timber* contains a number of severe animadversions regarding servile prostration before the ancients ("Nothing is

[7] See No. 64, on Shakespeare, quoted *post*, p. 180. (Jonson's statements about Shakespeare's "small Latin and less Greek" and his being "not of an age, but for all time" appear in the commendatory poem prefixed to the First Folio; that Shakespeare "wanted art" appears in the *Conversations with Drummond*.)

[8] Cf. F. O. Matthiessen, *Translation An Elizabethan Art* (Cambridge, Mass., 1931).

more ridiculous, then to make an Author a *Dictator* as the schools have done Aristotle." "Whiche of the Greekelings durst ever give precepts to Demosthenes?").[9] And like his ancient models Horace and Martial, Jonson has a stern sense of indignation at the kind of literary imitation which may be called robbery.[1] It was Martial who had introduced the term *plagiarius* (kidnaper) into Latin literature. Jonson in his *Poetaster* (1601) and Bishop Hall in his *Satires* (1608) use "plagiary."[2] Jonson himself, Dryden was to say,[3] is a "learned plagiary." But this phrase, applied to Jonson's acknowledged use of ancient sources, was a joke, for the concept of plagiarism was an ethical and social one, concerned with stealing another man's fame and profit. It was not a critical concept, as it has nearly become for a later age which has merged patent office legalism with aesthetic standards of inspiration and voyantism. "Plagiarism," one of Jonson's editors has remarked, "is an invention of the 19th century."[4]

The borrowed and translated fragments of Jonson's *Timber* exhibit as much care, force, and accuracy of style as if they had been his own most preciously individual thoughts. The reason is that he did not make a distinction of literary value in favor of his own thoughts and *against* those which he found in Quintilian and Cicero. Literary work was not primarily personal expression but objective imitation, either of nature straight or of nature through the model. And the use of models entailed their assimilation and invited their improvement.

> Not, as a Creature, that swallowes, what it takes in, crude, raw, or undigested; but, that feeds with an Appetite, and hath a Stomacke to concoct, devide, and turne all into nourishment. Not, to imitate servilely, as *Horace* saith . . . but to draw forth out of the best, and choisest flowers, with the Bee, and turne all into Honey.—No. 130[5]

The following passage of *Timber* on the subject of memory might surely be said to have the ring of intimate self-revelation.

> *Memory* of all the *powers* of the mind, is the most *delicate* and *fraile;* it is the first of our *faculties* that Age invades. *Seneca,*

[9] Nos. 123, 130.

[1] Writers who refuse the help of imitation (No. 65) include not only those who despise models but those who steal without acknowledgment and those who steal and protest originality—making a "false venditation of their own naturals." "Such are all the Essayists, even their master Mountaigne."

[2] Harold O. White, *Plagiarism and Imitation during the English Renaissance* (Cambridge, 1935), pp. 120-1, 133-4. Cf. Austin Warren, *Crashaw* (Baton Rouge, 1939), pp. 102-3.

[3] *Essay of Dramatic Poesy,* in *Essays,* ed. W. P. Ker, I, 43.

[4] Schelling, quoted by Castelain, p. XXIII.

[5] Cf. *post* p. 218-20 the use made by Swift of the symbol of the bee and the spider in expounding the difference between "ancients" and "moderns."

the father, the *Rhetorician*, confesseth of himselfe, hee had a miraculous one; not only to receive but to hold. I my selfe could in my youth, have repeated all, that ever I had made; and so continued, till I was past fortie; Since, it is much decay'd in me. . . . Whatsoever I pawn'd with it, while I was young, and a boy, it offers me readily, and without stops: but what I trust to it now, or have done of later yeares, it layes up more negligently, and oftentimes loses.—No. 56

Yet Jonson is here following rather closely the passage in Seneca the Elder to which he alludes.[6] (Perhaps because it fitted his own case literally, perhaps because by intimations in his own experience he saw a general truthfulness in it.) Or take one of the best known paragraphs in *Timber*, the sketch of Shakespeare.

DE SHAKE-
SPEARE
NOSTRATI.
I remember, the Players have often mentioned it as an honour to *Shakespeare*, that in his writing (whatsoever he penn'd) hee never blotted out line. My answer hath beene, would he had blotted a thousand. Which they thought a malevolent speech. I had not told posterity this, but for their ignorance, who choose that circumstance to commend their friend by, wherein he most faulted. And to justifie mine owne candor, (for I lov'd the man, and doe honour his memory (on this side Idolatry) as much as any). Hee was (indeed) honest, and of an open, and free nature; had an excellent *Phantsie;* brave notions, and gentle expressions: wherein hee flowed with that facility, that sometime it was necessary he should be stop'd: "*Sufflaminandus erat,*" as Augustus said of Haterius. His wit was in his owne power; would the rule of it had beene so too. Many times hee fell into those things, could not escape laughter: as when he said in the person of *Caesar*, one speaking to him; "*Caesar, thou dost me wrong.*" Hee replyed, "*Caesar did never wrong, but with just cause;*" and such like, which were ridiculous. But hee redeemed his vices, with his vertues. There was ever more in him to be praysed, then to be pardoned.—No. 64

AUGUSTUS
IN HAT.

Here Jonson advises us that a source for at least some of his phrasing is Seneca—a passage in the *Controversiae* (IV, Preface, 7–11) of Seneca the Elder concerning a poet named Haterius. But would we think that the part about inspiration and control—which is fitted so neatly into the context, framing the illustration from Shakespeare's *Julius Caesar*

[6] *Controversiae, Liber* I, 2–3.

—had been written originally sixteen hundred years earlier, about a minuscule Latin poet?

> *In sua potestate habebat ingenium, in aliena modum. . . . saepe*
> *incidebat in ea, quae derisum effugere non possent. . . . Redi-*
> *mebat tamen vitia virtutibus et persaepe plus habebat quod*
> *laudares quam cui ignosceres.*

To the neo-classical mind the earlier discovery of this individual reality seemed not to diminish its fitness for the case of a contemporary. Nor did earlier exploitation of a general truth preclude its genuine and living modern realization.[7]

Jonson's stout and craftsmanly common sense about imitation, shown even more convincingly in his practice than in his precepts, may be taken as the key to a theory of poetry which stressed hard work—imitation, practice, study, art (and with these but one poor pennyworth of *ingenium*)—a theory too which stressed poems squared off by the norm of reality. This theory celebrated the mobility and power of poetry, but it included no hymn to spontaneity or to what today we think of as the creative imagination. It included no statement even remotely parallel to that of Sidney about the free range of wit within its zodiac or that of Bacon about poetry submitting the shows of reality to the desires of the mind. Some deviation or wavering from the classic norm may appear in Jonson's treatment of such a minor article as that prescribing the unity of place—and we have seen that he is guilty of defying the authority of the antique critics. But he is the first English man of letters to exhibit a nearly complete and consistent neo-classicism. His historical importance is that he throws out a vigorous announcement of the rule from which in the next generation Dryden is to be engaged in politely rationalized recessions. One basic problem which Jonson leaves us pondering (the same as that posed implicitly once before, by a strong appreciator of poetic inspiration, Longinus) might be formulated as follows: Does an aesthetic norm of objective reality entail a *genetic* theory of conscious and strenuous artistic effort? If a poet is to give us a truthful account of general human nature, does this poet have to be a learned consumer of midnight oil, a graduate in grammar, logic, and rhetoric, and in the higher liberal disciplines? Or on the other hand: Does an aesthetic norm of personal expression entail a genetic theory of untrammeled and unstudied inspiration? If a poet is to tell the truth as he himself most really and deeply experiences it, does he have to be a rebel against tradition and conventional education, a Bohemian, long-haired, and unwashed, a defiler of ancestral ashes? [8]

[7] Cf. *Timber* No. 116 ("If you powre a glut of water . . .") with Quintilian, *Institute* I, ii, 26; and *Timber* No. 11 ("What a deale of cold business . . .") with Quintilian XII, xi, 18.

[8] Cf. Horace, *Ad Pisones*, 296–7, 470.

IV

DURING the time between Sidney's *Defense of Poesie* and the beginning of John Dryden's long critical career (with the Dedication of his tragi-comedy *The Rival Ladies* in 1664) the seat of continental critical author-ity shifted from Italy to France. In the Frenchified courtly literary circle of Restoration England, 1660–1688, the most effective outside in-fluence was contemporary French classicism—the spirit which reached its zenith in the dramas of Corneille and Racine. One difference between this French classicism and the earlier Italian classicism was that the best creative works associated with the earlier movement were those written without concern for the code, or at least in expansion of it (*Orlando Furioso, Gerusalemme Liberata, Il Pastor Fido*), whereas the best French classicism seemed actually the product of the code or at least a conscientious attempt to demonstrate it. Neo-classicism in 17th-century French poetry was apparently a dynamic and generative force. At the same time its critical utterances tended to be cranky. Corneille's first masterpiece, *Le Cid* (1637), was a remarkably classical play, a close re-alization, for instance, of the three *unités Scaligeriennes* (henceforth *Corneliennes*). Yet he himself came to look on it as one of his more re-laxed efforts.[9] *Le Cid* was meanly disparaged in the *Observations* of Scudéry and in Chapelain's *Sentiments de l'Académie* during the noto-rious imbroglio known to French historians as *La Querelle du Cid*. In the Abbé d'Aubignac's *Pratique du théâtre*, 1657, Corneille was treated to a fine blend of censure and faint praise. Corneille's own critical de-fenses appear in the *Examens* which he prefixed to each of his plays in the collected edition of 1660 and in the three *Discours* contained in the same volumes, *De l'Utilité et des Parties du Poëme Dramatique, De la Tragédie et des Moyens de la Traiter selon le Vraisemblable ou le Nécessaire*, and *Des Trois Unités*. These documents show the neo-classic conscience torturing itself and explaining its lapses in a way that is scarcely urbane and when seen from outside may look even a little comic.[1]

When Aristotle says the plot must be constructed *kata to eikos ē to anagkaion* (according to probability or necessity), he means, thinks Corneille, either probability of versimilitude (the way things are likely to work in nature) or—in case that is inconvenient—the "necessity"

[9] *"Bien que ce soit celui de tous mes ouvrages réguliers ou je me suis permis le plus de licence, il passe encore pour le plus beau auprès de ceux qui ne s'attach-ent pas à la dernière sévérité des règles"* (*Examen* of *Le Cid, Oeuvres*, ed. Charles Marty-Laveaux, 1862, III, 91).

[1] Cf. Pierre Legouis, "Corneille and Dryden as Dramatic Critics," in *Seven-teenth Century Studies Presented to Sir Herbert Grierson* (Oxford, 1938), pp. 269–78.

imposed by dramatic requirements, the exaction of the rules. Improbable that Don Rodrigue could fight two mortal combats of honor and a battle against the Moors in the space of twenty-four hours or a little more—but necessary to the economy of Corneille's classic design in the *Cid* (*c'est l'incommodité de la règle*).[2] Was unity of place really plausible (verisimilitudinous) in the *Cid* if the Moors had to be supposed invading Seville on a high tide when in fact the Guadalquivir perhaps had no such tide? The French audience would not object to this disregard of geographical truth, since they could at least conceive the phenomenon from their experience of the Seine at Paris.[3] There was a more legitimate subtlety in Corneille's explanation of his abstract or unspecified treatment of locality (*le lieu théâtral*), a vague neutral ground, an antechamber into which apartments of divers inmates of the same palace open, or even a kind of unidentified space where actors by taking only a few steps move from one part of a city to another.[4] And there was no doubt a great measure of truth in his contention that one formal "embellishment" in which he specialized, the *liaison des scènes* (whereby each group of characters, within an act, supplied some for the next group, or scene, so that the stage was never vacant), had been increasingly dictated by his own successful practice and by the steadily more finical taste of the audience themselves, rather than by ancient authority or by *a priori* theoretical conceptions. In any case, however, freedom was quickly narrowing in "from precedent to precedent." The *Discourses* and *Examens* of Corneille represent a very advanced state of neo-classic exactitude and ingenuity.

V

It happened that in the year 1663 a Frenchman named Samuel Sorbière visited England on some sort of quasi-diplomatic or journalistic mission and on returning to France did the undiplomatic thing of publishing an account of his *Voyage*[5] in which he made highly uncomplimentary remarks about English science and about the English stage.

---

[2] For the sake of compactness we here conflate general principles from Corneille's *Discours* on tragedy and specific instances from his *Examen* of *Le Cid*.

[3] *Examen* of *Le Cid*, *Oeuvres*, III, 97–8.

[4] "*Ainsi, par une fiction de théatre, on put s'imaginer que don Diegue et le Comte, sortant du palais du Roi, avancent toujours en se querellant, et sont arrivés devant la maison de ce premier lorsqu'il recoit le soufflet qu'il oblige à y entre pour y chercher du secours*" (*Examen* of *Le Cid*, *Oeuvres*, III, 100).

[5] *Relation d'un Voyage en Angleterre où sont touchées plusieurs choses qui regardent l'état des Sciences, et de la Religion, et autres matières curieuses* (Paris, 1664). See George Williamson, "The Occasion of 'An Essay of Dramatic Poesy,'" *MP*, XLIV (August, 1946), 1–9.

These comedies of theirs would not be received quite so well
in France. Their poets play hob with the unity of place and the
rule of twenty-four hours. Their comic plots run for twenty-
five years. The first act gives you the marriage of a Prince, and
immediately afterwards come the travels and exploits of his
son.[6]

Sorbière succeeded in provoking one reply, both on scientific and on
literary grounds, from the historian of the English Royal Society, Thomas
Sprat. And it was not long after the incident that John Dryden, courtly
poet and dramatist,[7] having apparently stocked his mind with the
critiques of Corneille, retired to the country during the plague years
of 1665 and 1666 and wrote his dialogue published in 1668, *An Essay of
Dramatic Poesy*,[8] the most ambitiously constructed critical document of
his career and the most important for general literary theory.

Taking advantage of one of the most notable international relations
of the day, the naval battle fought in the Channel between the British
and the Dutch on June 3, 1665, Dryden imagines the four gentlemanly
and witty interlocutors of his dialogue as drifting in a barge softly down
the Thames past Greenwich (for the sake of better hearing the guns).
The literary discussion in which they find themselves soon involved (an
international engagement at another level)[9] comes about at random
through some remarks about certain extravagant Clevelandish poems
which have recently appeared in celebration of public events. As the
conversation progresses, an interest in two somewhat similar oppositions, that between classicism and modernity and that between the Elizabethan generation (the "last age") in English letters and the present,
tends to entangle and temporarily to obscure the lines of the argument.

---

[6] "*Mais les Comedies n'auroient pas en France toute l'approbation qu'elles ont
en Angleterre. Les Poëtes se mocquent de l'uniformité du lieu, & de la regle des
vingt-quatre heurs. Ils font des comedies de vingt-cinq ans, & apres avoir representé
au premier acte le mariage d'un Prince, ils representent toute d'une suite les belles
Actions de son fils, & luy font voir bien du pays*" (*Relation*, Cologne, 1669, p. 129,
quoted by Williamson, p. 2).

[7] He became Poet Laureate in 1668 and Historiographer Royal in 1670 (D.
Nichol Smith, *John Dryden*, Cambridge, 1950, p. 11).

[8] Dryden's *Essay of Dramatic Poesy* makes about a dozen direct allusions to
Corneille's criticism, all but one or two apparently to the *Discours des Trois Unités*.
The *Essay* shows also a considerable debt to Ben Jonson, as will be in part sug-
gested during the course of our discussion. Lord Bolingbroke was to tell Joseph
Spence that Dryden said he had got more from the Spanish critics than from the
Italians and French and all others together (Saintsbury II, 332; Ker I, lxvi), but the
meaning of this remains doubtful. For more detailed accounts, see Ker I, 288 ff and
Amanda M. Ellis, "Horace's Influence on Dryden," *PQ*, IV (January, 1925), 39–60;
Frank L. Huntley, *On Dryden's "Essay of Dramatic Poesy"* (University of Michigan
Press, 1951), pp. 2–6. Dryden's *Essays*, ed. W. P. Ker, 2 vols., Oxford, 1926.

[9] Cf. Charles Kaplan, in *The Explicator*, VIII (March, 1950), No. 36.

But in the main: the speaker who first develops his view at length, Crites (standing perhaps for Dryden's brother-in-law Sir Robert Howard,[1] a dramatic collaborator with Dryden and one who had already published arguments on rhyme in drama and the unities), expounds the extreme classic view, that the Greeks and Romans fully discovered and illustrated those reasonable and perennial rules to which the modern drama can do no better than conform. In the really minor issue between the "last age" and the present in England, he maintains the superiority of the "last age" in making plays but is nearly ready to recognize the new degree of correctness in versification achieved by Waller and Denham. The recent advance of English versification to a state of nearly classic perfection is an assumption so solidly established for the other speakers in the dialogue as not to be of main moment to the argument. The second person to speak at length, Eugenius (plausibly to be taken as Dryden's friend Charles Sackville, Lord Buckhurst,[2] great-grandson of that Thomas Sackville who was co-author of *Gorboduc*, the first "regular" English tragedy in 1561), takes the negative position that the ancient poets failed badly in their illustration of the rules prescribed by their critics. The implication is that the moderns[3] have actually best illustrated the rules —but there is little effort to adduce positive evidence for this view. Then thirdly, Lisideius (whose name seems like an anagram of Sidleius, or Sir Charles Sedley,[4] a younger wit of the day), accepting the same premises as Crites and Eugenius, that the classical rules for decorous imitation of nature are indeed the fundamentals of correct dramatic creation, advances the argument by finding the locus of perfect realization not in the contemporary English drama (as may have been implied by Eugenius) but in the French. Thus Dryden gives preliminary free rein to three leading kinds of classicism, letting them talk themselves out, and it is not until this late point in the *Essay* that the main pivot of the argument occurs—with the entrance of Neander (the new man, Dryden of course, whose name so nearly makes a convenient anagram). A definition of a play to which all four speakers have agreed has been formulated at the outset by Lisideius:

[1] But see *post* p. 188; G. R. Noyes, "Crites in Dryden's *Essay of Dramatic Poesy*," *MLN*, XXVIII (June, 1923), 333 ff; and Frank L. Huntley, "On the Persons of Dryden's *Essay of Dramatic Poesy*," *MLN*, LXIII (1948), 88–95.

[2] Despite the actual historical presence of this nobleman in the fleet fighting the Dutch and the song "To all you ladies now at land" which he wrote on board his ship.

[3] Eugenius is a new thinker, a scientist. "If natural causes be more known now than in the time of Aristotle, . . . it follows that poesy and other arts may, with the same pains, arrive still nearer to perfection" (Ker I, 44).

[4] Dryden dedicated *The Assignation* to him in 1673, calling him the Tibullus of his age. Huntley, *On Dryden's "Essay . . . ,"* p. 11, suggests that "Lisideius" may be a play on an Anglicized pronounciation of *Le Cid*.

> A just and lively image of human nature, representing its pas-
> sions and humours, and the changes of fortune to which it is
> subject, for the delight and instruction of mankind.[5]

The other arguments have all rested on the first term in this definition,
the word "just." That is, they have all tried to set a value on drama according to the degree of its versimilitude. The strategy of Neander (the
champion of the English against the French) is now to redirect the argument toward the idea of liveliness and toward humours and passions.
He pushes the argument in such a way as to raise a question about the
relation of the term "justice" to the second term of the definition—*liveliness*. He asks, in effect, whether justice in an imitation of human life
can occur at all unless through liveliness—that is, through lifelikeness.

> 'Tis true, those beauties of the French poesy are such as will
> raise perfection higher where it is, but are not sufficient to give
> it where it is not: they are indeed the beauties of a statue, but
> not of a man, because not animated with the soul of Poesy,
> which is imitation of humour and passions.[6]

Dryden has some fun here with the French unity of place (where the
characters stand still and "the street, the window, the house, and the
closet, are made to walk about" [7]), and with the French declamatory
speeches. (Frenchmen are more frivolous and airy and need to be sobered
by their theatre; the English, more sullen, need entertainment.) One of
Corneille's statements in favor of practice at the expense of the rules is
quoted with approval. "Il est facile aux speculatifs d'estre severes."
Neander is willing to come out for the more unkempt, boyish, and
rowdy features of English drama—the roll of drums and clash of swords
at the finale which Sir Philip Sidney in one of the stern moments of his
Defence had ridiculed (*Quodcumque ostendis mihi sic, incredulus odi*)
and which had been a joke to Ben Jonson:

>   with three rusty swords,
> And help of some few foot-and half-foot words,
> Fight over *Yorke* and *Lancaster's* long jars.
>   —Prologue to *Every Man in his Humour*

"Whether custom has so insinuated itself into our countrymen, or nature has so formed them to fierceness," says Neander, "I know not; but
they will scarcely suffer combats and other objects of horror to be taken
from them."[8]

"The great work of Dryden in criticism," says T. S. Eliot, "is that
at the right moment he became conscious of the necessity of affirming

[5] Ker I, 36.   [7] Ker I, 77.
[6] Ker I, 68.   [8] Ker I, 74.

the native element in literature." [9] And at least he did succeed in blending an English accent with the French accent which had for the time being become a necessity.

> He who writ this, not without pains and thought,
> From *French* and *English* theatres has brought
> Th' exactest rules, by which a play is wrought.
>
> The Unities of Action, Place, and Time;
> The scenes unbroken; and a mingled chime
> Of *Johnson's* humour, with *Corneille's* rhyme.
>   —Prologue to *Secret Love*, 1668

The sketches of the dramatists of the "last age" in Dryden's *Essay* are among the dearest moments in the history of national self-appreciation.

> [Shakespeare] was the man who of all modern, and perhaps ancient poets, had the largest and most comprehensive soul. . . . when he describes any thing, you more than see it, you feel it too. Those who accuse him to have wanted learning, give him the greater commendation: he was naturally learn'd.

> [Beaumont and Fletcher] understood and imitated the conversation of gentlemen much better; whose wild debaucheries, and quickness of wit in repartees, no poet can ever paint as they have done.

> [Ben Jonson was] the most learned and judicious writer which any theatre ever had. . . . If I would compare him with Shakespeare, I must acknowledge him the more correct poet, but Shakespeare the greater wit. Shakespeare was the Homer, or father of our dramatic poets; Johnson was the Virgil, the pattern of elaborate writing; I admire him, but I love Shakespeare. [1]

To show that classical rules, so far as they may be convenient, can be and have been cherished by the English, Neander chooses for an extended *Examen* one of the most regular plays of Ben Jonson, *Epicoene or the Silent Woman*. The comic action of this play occurs in two houses (actually four houses and an alley) in London and all within a few hours (between the late rising of gallants and an afternoon dinner party) and on "a signal and long-expected day." The main character, or humour (Morose, a rich old uncle, who cannot tolerate noise), is both delightful

---

[9] *Use of Poetry*, p. 14.

[1] Ker I, 79–83. "The account of Shakespeare may stand as a perpetual model of encomiastick criticism" (Samuel Johnson, *Life of Dryden*, *Works*, 1787, II, 378). Johnson, says D. Nichol Smith, "knew the pedigree of his own preface. Dryden's *Essay* had struck the note and set the method of the best criticism of Shakespeare for the next hundred years" (*John Dryden*, Cambridge, 1950, p. 20).

and plausible [2] (and besides, Jonson had known such a man—here the rationale teeters). And the "intrigue" (the marrying of the Morose uncle to a Silent Woman who at the wedding party becomes a chatterbox and after due torture of Morose is next discovered to be a boy—whereby Sir Dauphine releases his uncle and is rewarded with a fortune), the "intrigue," says Neander, is "the greatest and most noble of any pure unmixed comedy in any language." If we could fully understand that word "noble," we might understand much which is perhaps now obscure to us in the neo-classic view of comedy. [3]

VI

FINALLY, Dryden's *Essay*, with Neander still in charge, veers off toward its conclusion with a protracted wrangle over a question which both Dryden and his brother-in-law had before this argued in print. (On him incidentally Dryden now plays a mean trick, for Crites, whom we may plausibly accept as Howard, is made to argue Howard's real life view that rhyme is not appropriate in serious plays and is made by Neander to seem wrong, but at the same time he has in the first part of the *Essay* been assigned the losing view that the ancients surpassed the moderns—which was not Howard's view in real life.) The dispute was to be continued in the following year in a Preface by Howard and in Dryden's *Defence of an Essay of Dramatic Poesy*. Only the main lines are of interest—but they are curiously so. Howard argued against rhyme in the dialogue of serious plays on the ground that rhyme was unreal, not the way people really talk. And Dryden argued for it on the ground that:

> A serious play . . . is indeed the representation of Nature, but 'tis Nature wrought up to an higher pitch. [4]

> A play is supposed to be [not "a composition of several persons speaking ex tempore," but] the work of the poet. [5]

---

[2] Dryden here makes an attempt to explain the variety in unity of so complex a "humour" as Shakespeare's Falstaff. "I need but tell them, that humour is the ridiculous extravagance of conversation, wherein one man differs from all others. . . . As for Falstaff, he is not properly one humour, but a miscellany of humours or images, drawn from so many several men: that wherein he is singular in his wit. . . . among the English . . . by humour is meant some extravagant habit, passion, or affection, particular . . . to some one person, by the oddness of which, he is immediately distinguished from the rest of men" (Ker I, 84–5). Cf. *post* Chapter 11, p. 205.

[3] See *post* Chapter 11, pp. 204–13. See *OED*, "noble," A. II 8.

[4] Ker I, 100 (*Essay of Dramatic Poesy*).

[5] Ker I, 114 (*Defence*).

At the same time, however, and in the same documents Howard was pooh-poohing the unities of time and place on the ground that they aimed at an impossible verisimilitude through exact coincidence of theater time and space with plot time and space. The argument is a rather full anticipation (wrapped though it is in Howard's bungling manner) of a far more celebrated instance which was to appear a hundred years later, in Samuel Johnson's *Preface to Shakespeare.*

> He that can take the stage at one time for the palace of the *Ptolemies*, may take it in half an hour for the promontory of *Actium*. Delusion, if delusion be admitted, has no certain limitation. . . . Time is, of all modes of existence, most obsequious to the imagination; a lapse of years is as easily conceived as a passage of hours.[6]

Dryden argued the opposite: he upheld the unities because he thought they tended, successfully enough, toward verisimilitude. We have then an odd opposition in which Howard rejects rhyme because it is further from reality than blank verse but rejects the unities because they are only a pointless approximation to a reality which cannot be attained—whereas Dryden upholds the unities for their verisimilitude but upholds rhyme for its transcendence of a verisimilitude which is not the real aim of the drama. The tastes of both Howard and Dryden may perhaps be made consistent if one suggests for each a different, though not explicitly entertained, general principle. Howard, that is, apparently desired a relaxation of formalities (and hence, though he may not have known it, of dramatic intensity). Dryden on the contrary desired to maintain the formalities. And each was misled in his theorizing by the then current but partly irrelevant issue of verisimilitude.

What degree of formality, and what kind, is possible for a given theater in a given language? The history of the 17th-century drama in France and England shows that certain qualities of the French language, its relative absence of tonic stress and its undulatory long Alexandrine, made possible for Corneille a certain style which the accentuated English language and its pentameter made at least exceedingly difficult for Dryden. The English rhymed heroic couplet was to have its successes, but not in heroic drama. The rhetorical declamations of Dryden's plays were moving toward an idiom of epigrammatic, moral and reflective poetry; the movement was towards satire and Popean epistle. Among the several conversions for which Dryden's career is noted was one *from* rhyme and *to* blank verse in his later serious dramas. In the Prologue to the last of his heroic dramas, *Aurengzebe*, 1675, "Our Author. . . . to confess a truth (though out of time) Grows weary of his long-lov'd Mistress, Rhyme." And the style of the best of his serious

[6] *Works* (1787), IX, 259-60.

plays, *All for Love*, 1677, is blank verse, as nearly on the Shakespearian model as his genius and his classical inclinations would permit. "In my style," he writes in the Preface, "I have professed to imitate the divine Shakespeare; which that I might perform more freely, I have disencumbered myself from rhyme." [7]

As for the unities, it is to be observed that the peculiarities of the French stage in the time of Corneille and those of the English stage in the time of Shakespeare and again in that of Dryden go a long way to determine the argument. Every stage is both one place and several places —one sitting room with several corners or groups of chairs (more or less set off as separate places according to the needs of the action), or one city square or street with several houses. The stage designer's problem of unity (before it is complicated by a temporal succession of scenes on the same stage) is a problem of the relation between an overall space and its components. How abstract and conventional (and hence how flexible), or how concrete and natural (and hence how inflexible) shall this be?

The three arches of the Hellenistic arcade stage, representing formally and hence freely three entrances from three places at indeterminate distances apart, was a medium decor from which one might diverge in several directions—toward the advanced abstraction or formal freedom of the Elizabethan architectural and symbolic façade (something arrived at apparently through the influence of other visual arts—the monument and the tableau) or at the other extreme toward the highly illusionistic Vitruvian perspective contrived by wings and painted backdrops on the Italian stage during the 16th century. The latter was a very reasoned attempt to make the several places which were simultaneously present (and successively needed for the action) appear as parts of one larger outdoor place—typically a city street or square—one place in the sense that in nature it could really all be seen at once by a human eye. [8] And then, thirdly, there was a kind of stage which had departed wildly and naively from such norms, toward a simultaneous ocular realization of several places widely distant on the earth's surface and beyond—the *maisons* (mansions) of the French medieval mystery stage: Paradise, Nazareth, the Temple, Jerusalem, the Palace, the Golden Gate, the sea of Galilee, Limbo and Hell.

By an inopportune anachronism the theater of the Hôtel de Bourgogne, at which the classical plays of Corneille and his early contemporaries were acted, had inherited the machinery of the medieval dramatic society called the Basôche or Confraternitée de la Passion. As a

[7] "Not that I condemn my former way, but that this is more proper to my present purpose" (Ker I, 200).

[8] See George R. Kernodle. *From Art to Theatre, Form and Convention in the Renaissance* (University of Chicago Press, 1944), esp. Chaps. IV, V, VI, VIII.

result the evolution of stage and plot toward the perspective ideal and its companion classical unities produced some curious intermediate phases.[9] Imagine, for instance, two towns or even two distant quarters of the same town joined in a kind of perspective synthesis. Corneille's free treatment of such paradoxes under the rubric of the indeterminate place, or *lieu theatral*, was in effect a movement toward something like the fluid or merely geometric space of the Elizabethan façade and apron, with its entrance right and left, its balcony representing anything above, its curtained recess representing anything within or discoverable. With an increased use of the *ferme* or movable shutter on the French stage and at the same time the moving forward and enlargement of the proscenium, the theater of the seventeenth century developed toward the more complicated realism of successive different scenes—though not toward the dispersion of these in time and space such as may be found in Shakespeare's *Antony and Cleopatra* and other global or cosmic Elizabethan plays. The French ideal of concentration was fully achieved perhaps once, a few years after Dryden's *Essay*, in Racine's *Bérénice*, 1670, where the whole action (summed up by Racine in the words of Suetonius: *Titus Reginam Berenicen dimisit invitus invitam*) takes place during about two hours and a half in one small chamber. This ideal, or its approximation, is what has actually prevailed in the modern European theater, where today an *Antony and Cleopatra* or a *Marco's Millions* is an anomalous intrusion of a structure more familiar in the novel.

As for the unity of time, two inversely proportional verisimilitudes seem always to have troubled the dramatist. If the play's plot time is compressed into the Aristotelian single day or into Racine's even smaller compass, thus approaching or attaining the verisimilitude of the actual two hours of the theater, this achievement is likely to impair the plausibility of the strenuous series of exertions and the reversal of fortune required for a dramatic action [1]—the several armed conflicts of Don Rodrigue, or the firm faith and sudden suspicion of Othello. On the other hand, the extension of time and space required to accommodate a large and various action moves inevitably away from the verisimilitude of the theatrical two hours. A concentration of psychological effort within a vaguely defined period has been found on the whole a smaller affront to our sense of the real than the jamming together of many visible acts of violence during a period so sharply defined as a day or a little more.

---

[9] Ker I, xlv.

[1] "If a Tragedy is to be composed from the last story [that of Ceyx and Alcyone] it should not begin with the departure of Ceyx, for as the whole time for stage-representation is only six or eight hours, it is not true to life to have a storm arise, and the ship founder, in a part of the sea from which no land is visible" (Scaliger, *Poetics*, III, 97). In an era where air travel from Paris to London in a time much shorter than one "period" of the sun is an everyday matter, requirements for unity of space on the stage may well be expected to undergo some change.

VII

NEANDER and his three friends at the end of the *Essay of Dramatic Poesy* come quietly to shore at the foot of Somerset Stairs and, having amicably agreed on hardly anything, part with mutual courtesy for their several destinations. One of the chief contributions of Dryden to English criticism is the conversational pace, the gentlemanly tone (though it sometimes masks ironic mayhem), the cool and judicial posture. Corneille wrote lofty and fiery tragedies of honor but attached to them quibbling criticisms—crabbed vindications of literary honor. Dryden's plays, produced for the most part in the pragmatic, craftsmanly spirit of one who aims to hit the public taste or who is satisfied that he has "swept the stakes," (or who will even cynically confess: "I knew they were bad enough to please" [2]) are less impressive, but in their very defects they were the occasions for the casually graceful causerie of his Prefaces, Dedications, and other defences. The *Essay of Dramatic Poesy* exemplifies that kind of pseudo-Platonic dialogue which during the next seventy-five years became one of the most prevalent neo-classic forms in England.[3] Neander, however, differs from Socrates in having not only less dialectical tenacity and subtlety but also less triumphant pugnacity. Neander is Socrates become a gentleman, an *honnête homme*. His opponents have their say at length, and his own replies, though wittily pointed, are not insistent or humiliating. A remarkable feature of Dryden's critical mind is his capacity to retain, along with a steady concern for the reasoned justification of taste, an openness to contrary argument almost approaching scepticism. Among several somewhat different principles of scepticism prevalent in Dryden's day, one was scientific and positivistic, what we find in the work of Hobbes and in the activities of the Royal Society, of which Dryden himself, with other literary men, was for a time a member.[4] Another principle—a form of reaction to the scientific —was Pyrrhonist, antirational, fideist. Dryden apparently cultivated in himself a degree of resemblance to the more fashionable modes of doubt. In the *Defence of the Essay*, for instance, he says:

> My whole discourse was sceptical, according to that way of reasoning which was used by Socrates, Plato, and all the Academics of old, . . . and which is imitated in the modest inquisitions of the Royal Society. . . . You see it is a dialogue sus-

[2] Dedication of *The Spanish Friar*, 1681 (Ker I, 246).

[3] Eugene R. Purpus, "The Plain, Easy, and Familiar Way: the Dialogue in English Literature 1660–1725," *ELH*, XVII (March, 1950), 47–58.

[4] See Louis I. Bredvold, *The Intellectual Milieu of John Dryden* (Ann Arbor, 1934), Chaps. II and III; R. F. Jones, "Science and Criticism in the Neo-Classical Age of English Literature," *JHI*, I (October, 1940), 387–8; H. O. White, "Dryden and Descartes," *TLS*, December 19, 1929, p. 1081; cf. *TLS*, January 2, 1930, p. 12.

tained by persons of several opinions, all of them left doubtful, to be determined by the readers in general.[5]

Dryden's basic critical attitude, nevertheless, would seem to have been not so much scepticism as a kind of reaction to scepticism which we may call "probabilism," the source of which, transmitted in certain contemporary treatises of logic, was the Aristotelian way of practical reasoning to which we have referred in an earlier chapter. It is the mark of an educated man, Aristotle had said, to seek in each field of knowledge the degree of precision which is available there. In the practical sciences, ethical and political, and in the practical art of rhetoric, knowledge is not of the same sort as in the demonstrations of physics, metaphysics, and mathematics. It is this distinction which Dryden apparently wishes to give us in the following passage of his *Defence of the Essay*.

> Hitherto I have proceeded by demonstration; . . . having laid down, that Nature is to be imitated, and that proposition proving the next, that then there are means which conduce to the imitating of Nature, I dare proceed no further positively; but have only laid down some opinions of the Ancients and Moderns, and of my own . . . which I thought probable.[6]

SUPPLEMENT

Seen from the perspective of a brief jaunt around Western Europe, that good old proscenium arch seems in general to be mighty small—and shrinking. Everywhere you see or hear about open stages. Everywhere, at least during the summer, the theatre leaves the darkness of the picture frame and moves outside into the sunlight—in front of palaces, into church courtyards, in village squares, on hillsides. It seems to be searching by instinct if not by design for the kind of stage it had in periods of greatest achievement: a platform in space.

And what of the proscenium? It remains, but perhaps a little less sure of itself. So recently a liberal, it has in the normal course of events become a conservative. Once so obviously the normal relation between actor and audience, it has become one of many norms, many relationships. Hardy the architect who would today design a theatre without adequate provision for varying, enlarging, breaking through—if not entirely eliminating—that artificial dam through which the theatre tends to spill.

. . .

[5] Ker I, 124.

[6] Ker I, 123. See the lucid statement of Dryden's probabilism by Hoyt Trowbridge, "The Place of the Rules in Dryden's Criticism," *MP*, XLIV (November, 1946), 84–96.

Granted that something magical is missing when there is no red velour curtain, no background splendor or technical virtuosity. But there is some other kind of magic lurking about these actors who have three dimensions and not two-and-a-half; Prospero would have liked this island that appears and disappears in space.

Someone is always asking: What about their backs? The questioner is the same fellow who, when the movie close-up was invented, prophesied that women and children would scream when they saw their decapitated heroes before them. With equal logic, what about their faces? Is a face per se necessarily more interesting or revealing than a back? Would Phidias agree? Or Michelangelo?

The open stage, four-sided or three-sided, or in a corner of a room, is no passing fancy. It represents for the theatre the same search, the same tendencies which have taken place in the past half-century in the arts of sculpture, painting and architecture and which we have termed "modern." Like the other arts, the theatre sometimes turns to simplicity, to essentials, to the primitive. Like the other arts, it tries to extend itself beyond rigid framework; it looks for fluidity and freedom; it gropes for organic form just as much as does the Lever House, a Finnish armchair, or a Fourth Street ashtray. Between Frank Lloyd Wright and Stanislavsky, after all, there is not so much difference. The key to both lies in their faith that inner life dictates outer form.

Most specifically, the theatre's continuing experiment with the open stage represents, alongside the other arts, a concern with revealing and utilizing instead of concealing the nature of its material.

A theatre building lasts longer than an ashtray or a chair. But is that any reason why it should be any less "modern"?

No one tears down theatres for esthetic reasons, only for parking lots. So that good old proscenium arch remains—a respectable though illegitimate grandchild of Renaissance painting and Baroque elegance. Not exactly crumbling either. But—watch out for falling plaster.

—Alan Schneider, "Shrinking Arch," *The New York Times*, Sunday, July 25, 1954, Section 2, Drama . . . , by permission of the author and *The New York Times*. Mr. Schneider was Artistic Director of Arena Stage, Washington, D.C., 1952–54

Discovery in the Works Accounts of the startling evidence that Shakespeare's stage at Court was placed *in the middle of the Hall* has established a novel and revealing point. Not only was his platform not provided with a front curtain: it was moreover not set against any scenic wall or background whatever. With this plastic rather than pictorial kind of stage, the only fluent method of production feasible is that of the traditional "multiple" or "simultaneous" setting of fixed "mansions" or "scenes" common to the European stage of the Renaissance.

Hardest perhaps for our modern minds to give up is the preconception of a backdrop: to realize, instead, that spectators were *behind* the stage, on the fourth side, as in a circus. But now we *know* that at Court Shakespeare's plays were produced completely "in the round." What then of the production at the public theaters such as the Globe? Were they utterly different? Or has our fixed modern idea of a "background" blinded us to the fact that here too there was no "scenic wall," that the Globe productions also were completely "in the round"?

Once we lay preconception aside, it is curious to see how the proof that the public stage, like that at Court, was a complete circus stage has been staring us in the face unregarded. The De Witt drawing has always shown spectators on the fourth side, behind the stage. As W. J. Lawrence pointed out, "Of the four known views of early non-scenic theatres, three show incontestably that spectators sat in elevated boxes at the back of the stage"—a position from which it is physically impossible to see the "inner stage" of the theorists. Henslowe at the Rose Playhouse mentioned "the room over the tire-house," and contemporary references to this "lords' room" for spectators at centre-back "over the stage" are common. This audience on the fourth side refuses to be argued out of existence to make hypothetical and remote inner and upper stages possible. It is a fact, as it is at Whitehall. Clearly, the Elizabethans meant what they said when they called their playhouses "amphitheatres," when they spoke of the "cirque" and "the Globe's fair Ring," and when they imagined "lines drawn from the circumference of so many ears, whiles the Actor is the Center."

Those responsible for the theory of an inner stage have managed to close their eyes not only to Shakespeare's common sense as a producer and to the undeniable presence of high-paying spectators behind the stage, but also to the economics of the theatre. A theory which would tuck crucial action away in a recess beyond the sight-line both of the lords' room and of the adjacent arcs of "this wooden O," "this throngèd round, . . . this fair-fill'd Globe," ignores the all-important box-office. The "inner stage" proposition would receive short shrift from any business manager. His advice would be, "Don't be foolish. Keep the action out on the stage, as it is shown in the De Witt picture, where it can be seen from all the surrounding galleries. The only way to make money is to fill the house."

—Leslie Hotson, "Shakespeare's Arena," *The Sewanee Review*, LXI (Summer, 1953), 356–7, by permission of *The Sewanee Review*

CHAPTER II

DRYDEN AND SOME LATER SEVENTEENTH-CENTURY THEMES

§ *the heroic norm, English heroic plays, Dryden's theory, burlesque resistance—II. courtly wit vs. "mechanic humour,"* Epilogue *to* Conquest of Granada, *comic theory,* Preface *to* An Evening's Love, *shift from "humour" to manners, the conversational norm, "fallacy of imitative form," passage from Virginia Woolf's* Orlando*—III. aim of comedy, delight vs. instruction, Poetic Justice, French influences, Dryden, Rymer, Dennis, Addison's* Cato, *poetic injustice, Rapin and catharsis sentimentalized—IV. satire as painless execution, the classical defence of satire and comedy: agelastic (Sidney and Jonson), urbane (Molière and Pope), problem of moral aim vs. libel, general vs. local truth—V. Molière's refinement, English "humours," Jonson to Sterne, Temple's* Of Poetry, *a 19th-century reaction, Meredith's lecture on the* Comic, *relation of the comic to the serious in the classical tradition, Fielding's* Covent Garden Journal*—VI. Dryden's later years, translation, his view of Chaucer, Augustan sense of superiority, ancients vs. moderns, progress and cycles, Latin vs. English, translation and imitation, Pope, principle of allusion and burlesque* §

At about the same time as he was writing his *Essay of Dramatic Poesy* Dryden signed a contract with the King's Theater to write three plays a year. Shortly afterwards he became Poet Laureate and Historiographer Royal and entered upon the palmiest phase of his career. In a critical sense this phase had two main features: it was heroic and it was courtly, and in neither of these ways was it modest.

196

Both the theory and to some extent the practice of heroic poetry were the outcome of a theory of ideal literary genre which had waxed in the later 16th century.[1] Thus Sir Philip Sidney:

> There rests the heroical, whose very name, I think, should daunt all backbiters. For by what conceit can a tongue be directed to speak evil of that which draweth with it no less champions than Achilles, Cyrus, Aeneas, Turnus, Tydeus, Rinaldo? who doth not only reach and move to truth, but teacheth and moveth to the most high and excellent truth; . . . But if anything be already said in the defense of sweet poetry, all concurreth to the maintaining the heroical, which is not only a kind, but the best and most accomplished kind of poetry. For, as the image of each action stirreth and instructeth the mind, so the lofty image of such worthies most inflameth the mind with desire to be worthy, and informs with counsel how to be worthy.[2]

The term "poem" (which since the time of Wordsworth and Keats has meant for us a short piece of verse, characteristically, let us say, an ode or sonnet) meant in Dryden's time par excellence a long story in verse (an epic or heroic poem) or a drama like an epic. (D'Avenant argued that the epic should be fashioned after the drama in five main parts;[3] Dryden argued that the narrative epic was the correct model for the mighty drama.) A shorter poem was likely to be dubbed a "paper of verses."[4] Nobody in Dryden's day would have understood (or at least nobody would have admitted understanding) Edgar Allan Poe's typically romantic thesis that a long poem is a contradiction in terms and that such an apparently successful long poem as Milton's *Paradise Lost* is really a collection of short poems, intense moments, held together by prose.[5] As tragedy was the norm of Aristotle's theory, and epistolary

---

[1] The theory begins at least as early as Vida's *De Arte Poetica*. See B. J. Pendlebury, *Dryden's Heroic Plays* (London, 1913), pp. 9 ff; C. V. Deane, *Dramatic Theory and the Heroic Play* (London, 1930).

[2] *A Defense of Poesy*, ed. A. S. Cook (Boston, 1890), p. 30. Cf. Scaliger, *Poetics* III, 96: "In epic poetry, which describes the descent, life, and deeds of heroes, all other kinds of poetry have . . . a norm, so that to it they turn for their regulative principles."

[3] Letter to Hobbes prefixed to *Gondibert*, 1651. D'Avenant's letter and Hobbes's answer, the earliest full-bloom pronouncements in English of heroic theory, first appeared, together, at Paris in 1650.

[4] See Howard, Preface to *Four Plays* (D. D. Arundell, *Dryden and Howard*, Cambridge, 1929, p. 8) and Dryden, *Essay of Dramatic Poesy*: "Blank verse is acknowledged to be too low for a poem, nay more, for a paper of verses; but if too low for an ordinary sonnet, how much more for Tragedy, which is by Aristotle, in the dispute betwixt the epic poesy and the dramatic, for many reasons he there alleges, ranked above it?" (Ker I, 101).

[5] But cf. Dryden's opinion: Milton "runs into a flat of thought, sometimes for a hundred lines together . . ." (*Original and Progress of Satire*, Ker II, 29); and cf. *post* Chapter 20.

satire implicitly that of Horace's best insights, so the heroic epic was the more or less explicit norm of poetry in the latter part of the 17th century (and was a rather unhappily dilated focus for critical theory). Witness not only the numerous original epic attempts and the epic translations of the century but the epic straining of even such a topical poem as Dryden's *Annus Mirabilis* and the dreams of strong poets like Dryden and Pope about writing a British epic. Heroic poets, says the Earl of Mulgrave in his *Essay upon Poetry*, 1682, are "gigantic souls;" the heroic poem is the "chief effort of human sense." And Dryden was sure that the heroic poem not only always had been but always would be "esteemed . . . the greatest work of human nature." [6] As late in his career as 1697 (long after the passion for heroic *drama* had cooled) he opened the Dedication of his translated *Aeneis* with the sentence: "A HEROIC POEM, truly such, is undoubtedly the greatest work which the soul of man is capable to perform."

Partly as a result of such ideas, partly as a result of grandiose political trends (which doubtless underlay the literary doctrine), and in some small part through the Puritan interdict of the stage which drove the poet Davenant in 1656 to adopt in lieu of a real play the expedient of a musical and recitative spectacle (*The Siege of Rhodes*), the English heroical play was born. At its most glorious the heroical play was an amalgam of Marlovian and Cornelian passion drama, of Fletcherian romantic melodrama, of French nine-volume pastoral romance, of masque and Italian opera. It was Homeric and Aristotelian in its aim at action, largeness, and elevation; it was Virgilian and Heliodoran [7] in its tender concern for the union of a pair of lovers and the founding of an illustrious house. It urged the themes of love, honor, and civic virtue, in high places, and with furious confusion and rivalry, before an exotic and pseudo-historical setting, to the continuous fanfare of trumpets and clash of arms on nearby plains.

The English heroic drama consisted most conspicuously of Dryden's five plays of this kind, from *The Indian Queen*, written in collaboration with Howard and produced in 1664, to *Aurengzebe*, produced in 1677. Heroic theory, Dryden's justification for the magnitude, the uproar, and the constant oratorical altitude at which he found himself moving, appears in his *Essay of Heroic Plays*, prefixed to his two-part heroic play *The Conquest of Granada*, 1672, and in his *Apology for Heroic Poetry and Poetic Licence* prefixed to his operatic rhymed rendition of Milton's *Paradise Lost*, *The State of Innocence and the Fall of Man*, a work printed in 1677, though never acted. Heroic theory was a coarse

---

[6] *Apology for Heroic Poetry and Poetic Licence*, Ker I, 181.

[7] See Sidney's and Scaliger's statements about the *Theagenes and Chariclea* of Heliodorus compared by Cornell M. Dowlin, "Sidney and Other Men's Thoughts," *RES*, XX (October, 1944), pp. 257-71.

parody of Aristotelian epic theory: the Homeric hero inflated to a colossus and paragon of prowess, honor, and passion, the element of the wonderful (*to thaumaston*) magnified both in the direction of the amazing and in that of the admirable, and the element of fear, in the direction of terror. Withal a dash of Longinianism and Petronianism [8] was convenient to justify the liberal introduction of the supernatural (ghosts and heavenly signs) to the main end of hair-raising. Were it not for Dryden's unparalleled aplomb, which makes him at all times amusing, it might be a sorry shock to find his hand lent to this task.

> But I have already swept the stakes; and, with the common good
> fortune of prosperous gamesters, can be content to sit quietly;
> to hear my fortune cursed by some, and my faults arraigned by
> others, and to suffer both without reply.[9]

Critical resistance to heroic insensibility in England was furnished not so much by reasoned argument as by ruthless burlesque, the first effort being that of Buckingham and his friends in *The Rehearsal*, 1671, which hit Dryden himself and may in part have provoked his defences. Later, came the retrospective sortie of Fielding, *The Tragedy of Tragedies; or the Life and Death of Tom Thumb the Great*, 1731, which parodies every element of inflation in English drama from Shakespeare to Addison.[1]

II

THE second main character of Dryden's thinking in this period, his standard of courtly wit, though it merged easily with the heroic, yields perhaps a nicer critical question—a question about reality, and about ideality and imitation, as these grow out of a social circumstance. This standard has to do mainly with comedy rather than with heroics, but as even in his heroic plays Dryden aimed at and even achieved the refinement of wit, and as his complacency about the heroic plays was closely bound up with his successful arrival in the court circle, it happens that his most blatant pronouncement on the courtly theme (and the most succinctly turned, because in verse) is attached to the Second Part of *The Conquest of Granada* in the form of an Epilogue. We quote this admirably conceited poem in its entirety.

> They, who have best succeeded on the stage,
> Have still conform'd their genius to their age.

---

[8] Petronius is quoted in *Of Heroic Plays* (Ker I, 152); Longinus is cited in the *Apology for Heroic Poetry and Poetic Licence* (Ker I, 181).

[9] *Of Heroic Plays*, Ker I, 159.

[1] And later still (1779) *The Critic* of Sheridan.

Thus *Johnson* did mechanic humour show,
When men were dull, and conversation low.
Then, *Comedy* was faultless, but 'twas coarse:
Cobb's tankard was a jest, and *Otter's* horse.[2]
And, as their *Comedy*, their love was mean;
Except, by chance, in some one labour'd scene,
Which must atone for an ill-written play:
They rose, but at their height could seldom stay.
Fame then was cheap, and the first comer sped;
And they have kept it since, by being dead.
But, were they now to write, when critics weigh
Each line, and ev'ry word, throughout a play,
None of them, no, not *Johnson* in his height,
Could pass, without allowing grains for weight.
Think it not envy, that these truths are told;
Our poet's not malicious, though he's bold.
'Tis not to brand 'em that their faults are shown,
But, by their errors, to excuse his own.
If *Love* and *Honour* now are higher rais'd,
'Tis not the poet, but the age is prais'd.
Wit's now arriv'd to a more high degree;
Our native language more refin'd and free.
Our ladies and our men now speak more wit
In conversation, than those poets writ.
Then, one of these is, consequently, true;
That what this poet writes comes short of you,
And imitates you ill (which most he fears),
Or else his writing is not worse than theirs.
Yet, though you judge (as sure the critics will),
That some before him writ with greater skill,
In this one praise he has their fame surpast,
To please an age more gallant than the last.

Or, as Dryden found himself compelled to put it in his immediately subsequent prose *Defence* of this Epilogue:

Now, if they ask me, whence it is that our conversation is so much refined? I must freely, and without flattery, ascribe it to the court; and, in it, particularly to the King, whose example gives a law to it. His own misfortunes, and the nation's, afforded him an opportunity, which is rarely allowed to sovereign princes,

[2] Cobb is a poor water-carrier in Jonson's *Every Man in his Humour;* Otter is a braggart but hen-pecked captain in Jonson's *Epicoene,* who has a favorite tankard named "Horse."

I mean of travelling, and being conversant in the most polished courts of Europe.

Gentlemen will now be entertained with the follies of each other.[3]

The application of this taste to a theory of the comic appears in the Preface prefixed by Dryden in 1671 to his comedy *An Evening's Love* but actually representative of the more refined concept of comedy which by 1671 he was able to embody in his best comic effort *Marriage-à-la-Mode*. The burden of the argument is that Ben Jonson was good at the realism of humours but was unequal to wit. Jonson's technique consisted in the faithful imitation of low-grade material, "the natural imitation of folly." This required some "judgment," to be sure, in order to tell when folly was faithfully imitated, but no creative wit. The new way of comedy, that which Dryden would illustrate, was to be a "mixed way," part humours, part wit, with an accent on the pleasant theme of amorous intrigue. The repartee of witty gentlemen was a department in which Dryden specially plumed himself—though modesty devised the compensatory confession that he found himself lacking in the "judgment" necessary to follow Jonson's way of the humour. An insistence that wit could not, as might be sometimes thought, transcend the principle of propriety inherent in the humour—that is, that various kinds of witty characters must be fitted with variously appropriate kinds of witty speech—may be said to have turned somewhat the edge of the argument which Dryden was urging.[4]

[3] Ker I, 176–7. The servility that at moments accompanied this view may be sampled in Dryden's motto to *Marriage-à-la-Mode* ("*Quicquid ego sum . . . . tamen me cum magnis vixisse, invita fatebitur usque invidia*") and in the Dedication of that play to Rochester: "I am sure, if there be anything in this play, wherein I have raised myself beyond the ordinary lowness of my comedies, I ought wholly to acknowledge it to the favour of being admitted into your lordship's conversation. . . . Wit seems to have lodged itself more nobly in this age, than in any of the former; and people of my mean condition are only writers, because some of the nobility, and your lordship in the first place, are above the narrow praises which poesy could give you. . . . Your lordship has but another step to make, and from the patron of wit, you may become its tyrant."

The readiness of such talk to collapse into irony may be seen in the opening paragraphs of the mock-modest debate about rhyme with Sir Robert Howard in Dryden's *Defence of an Essay* and (after his being slighted by Rochester) in the passage on gentleman wits in the Preface to *All for Love*, 1678. "And is not this a wretched affectation, not to be contented with what fortune has done for them, and sit down quietly with their estates, but they must call their wits in questions, and needlessly expose their nakedness to public view?" (Ker I, 196).

[4] The transition from the English comedy of humours to the comedy of manners involved among other critical problems that concerning the difference between the supposed individuality of the humour (asserted by Dryden in his discussions of Falstaff; see *ante* Chapter 10) and the social or class implications of the "manners," and that concerning the difference between an opaque butt or target of ridicule (the

The social influences at work in Dryden's theory, the snobbery and complacence of the courtier poet, the dawning signs of linguistic Augustanism, the character of Dryden's actual comic production (a mélange of Fletcherian romance, humor of courtly affectation, and wit of bawdy lovemaking), markedly inferior to the best of Ben Jonson—these should not obscure for us the quite basic critical issue involved in the shift from the comedy of Jonsonian humors toward the comedy of Restoration manners, and in Dryden's rationalization of his part in this. Throughout the English Augustan age, from Dryden to Samuel Johnson, a certain kind of ease and naturalness in writing, partly initiated by Dryden himself in his critical discourses (but so various a thing as to include the coffee-house pace of Defoe, the green-room frippery of Cibber, the affable chatter of Addison) is supposed by historians to have run parallel with an ideal of correctness and elegance that was being cultivated in the actual conversation of cultured society. Literary historians have been inclined, in effect, to agree with Dryden, that English written prose during the period in question improved greatly through the imitation of English conversation. But what shall our theory be? If naturalness is desirable in a novel or play, why is a novel or a play preferable to the daily run of natural conversation? Was Lord Chesterfield or Bishop Atterbury a model talker because he sounded like Addison? Or was Addison a good essayist because he sounded like Chesterfield or Atterbury, or like what one heard everyday in the boudoir or coffee-house? Low realism ("mechanic humour"), we may suppose, is less difficult to write than high realism (the wit of Benedick and Beatrice, Millamant and Mirabell, Diana of the Crossways). Drab realism may be at times merely neutral, but it has at least a tendency toward the formless and subrational, and hence toward producing the problem for criticism which one 20th-century American critic has sharply focussed in the phrase "fallacy of imitative form." If a fullness of imitative embodiment is what poetry must achieve, and that through its form, can this form survive the imitation of negative or formless materials? [5] So far as concerns social conversation and its imitation in literature, a conclusion which to the present writers seems eminently plausible has been dramatized as follows by Virginia Woolf in a passage of her fantastic history of modern English literary taste, *Orlando*.

> About the third time Orlando went . . . [to one of Lady
> R.'s assemblies] a certain incident occurred. She was still under

---

Jonsonian humour) and the witty character *with* whom the audience laughs. The latter question is nearer to Dryden's drift in the Preface to *An Evening's Love*. The more delicate situation which arises when two main characters are reciprocally partial butts and partial wits has been alluded to *ante* Chapter 3.

[5] On the other hand, of course, stands the question: Can the fullness of this form, its quality of embodiment, survive the imitation of the highly rational, the scientific or metaphysical?

the illusion that she was listening to the most brilliant epigrams in the world, though, as a matter of fact, old General C. was only saying at some length, how the gout had left his left leg and gone to his right, while Mr. L. interrupted when any proper name was mentioned. "R.? Oh! I know Billy R. as well as I know myself. S.? My dearest friend. T.? Stayed with him a fortnight in Yorkshire"—which, such is the force of illusion, sounded like the wittiest repartee, the most searching comment upon human life, and kept the company in a roar; when the door opened and a little gentleman entered whose name Orlando did not catch. Soon a curiously disagreeable sensation came over her. To judge from their faces, the rest began to feel it as well. One gentleman said there was a draught. The Marchioness of C. feared a cat must be under the sofa. It was as if their eyes were being slowly opened after a pleasant dream and nothing met them but a cheap washstand and a dirty counterpane. It was as if the fumes of some delicious wine were slowly leaving them. Still the General talked and still Mr. L. remembered. But it became more and more apparent how red the General's neck was, how bald Mr. L.'s head was. As for what they said—nothing more tedious and trivial could be imagined. Everybody fidgeted and those who had fans yawned behind them. At last Lady R. rapped with hers upon the arm of her great chair. Both gentlemen stopped talking.

Then the little gentleman said.

He said next.

He said finally.*

Here, it cannot be denied, was true wit, true wisdom, true profundity. The company was thrown into complete dismay. One such saying was bad enough; but three, one after another, on the same evening! No society could survive it.

"Mr. Pope," said old Lady R. in a voice trembling with sarcastic fury, "you are pleased to be witty." Mr. Pope flushed red. Nobody spoke a word. They sat in dead silence some twenty minutes. Then, one by one, they rose and slunk from the room. That they would ever come back after such an experience was doubtful.[6]

* These sayings are too well known to require repetition, and besides they are all to be found in his published works.

In Dryden's day the matter was put as follows by Congreve in his Letter to Dennis *Concerning Humour in Comedy*, 1695.

[6] Virginia Woolf, *Orlando* (New York: Harcourt, Brace and Company, Inc., 1928), Chapter IV, pp. 200–2. By permission of Harcourt, Brace and Company, Inc., and Leonard Woolf.

If this Exactness . . . were to be observed in Wit as some would have it in Humour, what would become of those Characters that are design'd for men of Wit? I believe if a Poet should steal a dialogue of any Length from the Extempore discourse of the two Wittiest Men upon Earth, he would find the Scene but coldly receiv'd by the Town.[7]

III

DRYDEN was inclined to take the aim of comedy not very seriously. Comedy, he observed, begets "malicious pleasure," testified by laughter.[8] "The chief end of it is divertisement and delight. . . . the first end . . . is delight, and instruction only the second."[9] And he was inclined to wink at—nay participate cheerfully in—the obscenity[1] of the Restoration comedy of manners. He drew a rather sharp distinction between the moral responsibility of comedy and that of tragedy, especially in the matter of instruction through the spectacle of rewards and punishment.

> Comedy is not so much obliged to the punishment of faults which it represents, as Tragedy. For the persons in Comedy are of a lower quality, the action is little, and the faults and vices are but the sallies of youth, and the frailties of human nature, and not premeditated crimes.[2]

With regard to serious drama Dryden was already in tune with a latter-day species of classical didacticism which became a fixation toward the end of the century.

The theme of "Poetic Justice"[3] begins to appear in Dryden's critical defences of the late 1670's: his *Apology for Heroic Poetry*, 1677, his Preface to *All for Love*, 1678, and that to his improved version of *Troilus and Cressida*, 1679. In these essays Dryden exhibits the influence of cer-

---

[7] Spingarn III, 247.

[8] *Essay of Dramatic Poesy*, Ker I, 85.

[9] *Preface to An Evening's Love*, Ker I, 143.

[1] A quality which at the end of his life, after the storm raised by Jeremy Collier, he could recognize and even connect with one of its main causes, the Stuart court.

> But sure a banished court, with lewdness fraught,
> The seeds of open vice returning brought. . . .
> The poets, who must live by courts or starve,
> Were proud, so good a government to serve;
> And mixing with buffoons and pimps profane,
> Tainted the stage for some small snip of gain.
> —Epilogue to Beaumont and Fletcher's *Pilgrim*, 1700

[2] Preface to *An Evening's Love*, Ker I, 143.

[3] On the general question whether poetry should mainly teach or mainly please, Dryden's varied career exhibits all the usual Renaissance devices and modifications. See, for instance, Ker I, 113, 142, 196, 209; II, 128.

tain French critics who had recently published notable works: Boileau, whose Horatian *Art Poétique* and translation of Longinus had both appeared in 1674; René Rapin, whose *Réflexions sur la Poétique d'Aristote* appeared in the same year and was translated by an English critic of a fanatically classic temper, Thomas Rymer; and René le Bossu ("the best of modern critics," says Dryden), whose *Traité du Poëme épique,* 1675, was the most authoritative summation of 17th-century epic theory, a kind of dried essence of epic, as a romantic historian has termed it, or recipe for epic *in vacuo.* French influence meant a tightening of Dryden's classicism all along the line. It meant far less indulgence of the English foibles and irregularities than we saw in the *Essay of Dramatic Poesy,* and, along with a continuing expression of esteem for the "divine Shakespeare" (especially in the matter of his characterizations),[4] a complacent opinion that Dryden himself was improving upon Shakespeare in language, in regularity of plot, and in the administration of "justice." In the story of Antony and Cleopatra both Dryden and Shakespeare had enjoyed a great initial advantage.

> I mean the excellency of the moral: for the chief persons represented were famous patterns of unlawful love; and their end accordingly was unfortunate. All reasonable men have long since concluded, that the hero of the poem ought not to be a character of perfect virtue, for then he could not, without injustice, be made unhappy.[5]

But the end of the chief persons in the story of Troilus and Cressida, as Shakespeare managed it, had been not so felicitously "unfortunate." "The chief persons, who give name to the tragedy," complains Dryden, "are left alive; Cressida is false, and is not punished." It is later in the same Preface that he uses the full term "poetical justice," [6] introduced by Rymer the year before in his *Tragedies of the Last Age,* and soon to become a commonplace of criticism.[7] In the closing scenes of Dry-

---

[4] The appreciation of the brutish character of Caliban (Preface to *Troilus and Cressida,* Ker I, 219) is a classic spot of 17th-century Shakespeare criticism. And the effort to reconcile Falstaff's complexity with the canon of consistency in character-drawing (I, 215) is a marked advance in theoretical precision over the account of the same character in the *Essay of Dramatic Poesy.* Cf. *ante* Chapter 10, p. 188.

[5] Preface to *All for Love,* Ker I, 191. ". . . nor yet altogether wicked," continues Dryden, "because he could not then be pitied. I have therefore steered the middle course; and have drawn the character of Antony as favourably as Plutarch, Appian, and Dion Cassius would give me leave."

[6] Preface to *Troilus and Cressida,* Ker I, 203, 210.

[7] The conception, always a dangerous likelihood in the Aristotelian poetic tradition (especially in view of the adjacent doctrine of distributive justice in Aristotle's *Ethics*), may be found adumbrated in many earlier authors—in Jonson, for instance, and Sidney. M. A. Quinlan, *Poetic Justice in the Drama* (Notre Dame, 1912) quotes the Parliamentary Act of 1543 tolerating only such plays as presented "the rebuking and reproaching of vices and the setting forth of virtue." Cf. Spingarn, *Essays* I, lxxiii, lxxxvi.

den's *Troilus and Cressida,* Cressida stabs herself, Troilus kills Diomede,
and Achilles, coming along with his Myrmidons, kills Troilus—a far
enough cry from the cynical half-light of Shakespeare's closing scene,
where Ulysses and Thersites lead Troilus beside a tent and he overhears
the conversation in which Cressida gives Diomede the sleeve. It was not
Dryden, however, nor even Thomas Rymer, but in the next generation
Pope's antagonist John Dennis, of the neo-Longinian sensibility, who
raised the loudest voice for Poetic Justice—in a controversy which
reached its climax over the suicide of Addison's patriotic protagonist
Cato.[8]

Poetic Justice was an exaggeration of the Aristotelian punishment of
the flaw in the character of the tragic protagonist. But the doctrine could
thrive only through a certain lack of interest in what Aristotle said about
the greatness of the protagonist and about the infelicity of distributive
justice, or the mixed ending, in tragedy—punishment for the wicked,
reward for the just. A conspicuous exhibit in the history of Poetic Justice is Nahum Tate's mixed ending for *King Lear,* in which Cordelia
marries Edgar. Yet, like most other moral conceptions of poetry, Poetic
Justice is not adequately treated by a summary dismissal. The question
is at least a complicated one, for it concerns not only evil and punishment but virtuous inclinations and sympathy, and conflict of sympathies.
"Though I might use the privilege of a poet," says Dryden, "to introduce . . . [Octavia] into Alexandria, yet I had not enough considered,
that the compassion she moved to herself and children was destructive
to that which I reserved for Antony and Cleopatra." [9] Even in Shakespeare's version of the story, the casual and gross injustice with which
Antony treats Octavia may somewhat obstruct our view of Antony as a
protagonist worthy of tragic sympathy. And then on the other hand
there is such a case as that of Addison's Cato. It is not easy to argue,
against Dennis, that the Stoic death of the champion of republican virtue
is really the downfall of a tragically erring figure. Innocent suffering, or
poetic injustice, as it appears in *Cato* and is defended by Addison in advance in *Spectator* 40, has a close relation to the tide of generally tender
feelings, the commiseration and compassion, that would run so strong
through the whole of the 18th century. The intensity of the neo-classic
crusade to see that the sinful protagonist suffered the death-penalty—
and that no innocent character did—may obscure for us a reactionary
but equally simplistic trend of that time toward the luxury of pity for
innocence injured. The cases had much in common, for in either the
Aristotelian tension was resolved. And in either the Aristotelian catharsis

---

[8] See *Spectators* 39 and 40, by Addison, and 548, attributed to Addison, and
the several replies of Dennis including his *Remarks upon Cato, a Tragedy,* 1713
(*Works,* ed. E. N. Hooker, Baltimore, 1939–1943, I, 40; II, 7, 19, 49, 435–42, 446–57).

[9] Ker I, 192.

of undesirably soft emotions (pity and fear) slides conveniently into a new and sentimentalized version of catharsis—such as that which Dryden in the Preface to his *Troilus and Cressida* adapts from Rapin: not catharsis (or "abatement") of fear and pity, but abatement of such aggressive and evil emotions as pride and anger through the *feeding and watering* of the soft-hearted emotions of fear and pity.[1] Thus the most nearly amenable classic doctrine became, by a sufficient deflection, an authority on the side of the coming ethics of benevolent feeling.[2]

I V

It is one of Dryden's claims to an urbane, if at times rather faltering, good sense that he was not one of the most earnest promoters of Poetic Justice—like Rymer or Dennis. He only lent himself to it. As we have already observed, he took his comic art even more lightly, resting his apologia on the easy grounds of pleasure and diversion. As for his burlesque and hurting satires, *MacFlecknoe* and *Absalom and Achitophel*, he doubtless looked on them honestly as what they were—masterly exhibitions of the art of personal assault and partisan politics. His theory of satire appears later, in the long essay entitled *The Origin and Progress of Satire* prefixed to his translation of Juvenal and Persius in 1693.

> . . . the nicest and most delicate touches of satire consist in fine raillery. . . . How easy it is to call rogue and villain, and that wittily! But how hard to make a man appear a fool, a blockhead, or a knave, without using any of those opprobrious terms!. . . . Neither is it true, that this fineness of raillery is offensive. A witty man is tickled while he is hurt in this manner, and a fool feels it not. . . . there is . . . a vast difference betwixt the slovenly butchering of a man, and the fineness of a stroke that separates the head from the body, and leaves it standing in its place. A man may be capable, as Jack Ketch's wife said of his servant, of a plain piece of work, a bare hanging; but to make a malefactor die sweetly was only belonging to her husband.[3]

This view of fine satire as a form of painless execution could doubtless be shown to have its resemblance to Dryden's idea of the comic. In the

---

[1] "Rapin, a judicious critic, has observed from Aristotle, that pride and want of commiseration are the most predominant vices of mankind; therefore, to cure us of these two, the inventors of Tragedy have chosen to work upon two other passions, which are fear and pity" (Ker I, 210). Cf. Baxter Hathaway, "John Dryden and the Function of Tragedy," *PMLA*, LVIII (September, 1943), 665-73.

[2] See *post* Chapter 14.

[3] Ker II, 92-3.

relaxed theory of comedy which we have already noted, Dryden stood even further apart from his age than in his relative casualness about Poetic Justice.

Dryden's views are hardly the ideal ground from which to launch a discussion of English neo-classic theory. Yet because there is no other single theorist of the period who provides that ground, we choose to enter here upon the following brief elaboration. Other comic writers and other satirists, from Ben Jonson to Pope and Fielding, were mightily preoccupied with a kind of satirist's apology which we have already noted in Jonson. We may summarize it roughly as follows: The satirist meant to hurt nobody, least of all any innocent person; he named nobody, but aimed at the universal; his charter was to lash vice and folly, to correct manners, to uphold morality. In times so low that men were not afraid to be known as knaves, they were yet ashamed to be laughed at as fools. Hence the satirist's special power and opportunity—in fact his duty—which he performed with an obvious gusto. In tragic justice grand crimes were punished by death. In comic and satiric justice mean vices and the folly which went with them were punished by scornful ridicule.

There is some evidence from the earlier part of this period that the view of comedy as a moral agent may have been quite grim. Thus Sir Philip Sidney in his *Defence:*

> I speak to this purpose, that all the end of the comical part be not upon such scornful matters as stir laughter only, but mixed with it that delightful teaching which is the end of poesy. And the great fault, even in that point of laughter, and forbidden plainly by Aristotle, is that they stir laughter in sinful things, which are rather execrable than ridiculous; or in miserable, which are rather to be pitied than scorned.[4]
>
> [4] *Defense of Poesy*, ed. A. S. Cook, p. 51.

And Ben Jonson in a passage of his *Timber* translated from an agelastic interpretation of Aristotle's *Poetics* by the Dutch theorist Heinsius:

> Nor is the moving of laughter alwaies the end of *Comedy*, that is rather a fowling for the peoples delight, or their fooling. For, as *Aristotle* saies rightly, the moving of laughter is a fault in Comedie, a kind of turpitude, that depraves some part of a man's nature without a disease. As a wry face without paine moves laughter, or a deformed vizard.—No. 131 [5]

[5] Compare Heinsius: "*Nec movere risum sane constituit Comoediam, sed plebis aucupium est, et abusus. Nam Ridiculum, ut recte Aristoteles, vitium est et foeditas, doloris expers; quae partem in homine aliquam corrumpit absque morbo. Sicut foeda et detorta facies, si nullo cum dolore id fiat, risum movet*" (*Ad Horatii de Plauto et Terentino judicium*, quoted in *Timber*, ed. Castelain, pp. 133-4). And compare Aristotle, *Poetics* V. The fault in human nature which Aristotle took as the object

Jonson must have made his audience laugh, in order to make his living. Yet the starkness of his plays, the saltiness and grit, a certain holystoning of the sensibility often quite distressing even if funny, doubtless might be argued to show some correspondence to the version of Aristotle which he chose to adopt from Heinsius.

Later on, the tone of the comic writer's apology is more easy. He admits being funny and claims laughter as his moral technique. Molière, even though under official censure for the immorality of *Tartuffe*, Pope, though beset by Grubstreet in a war of libels, conduct their self-defenses with urbanity and wit. The satire so obviously rejoices in the skilful administration of punishment that it is difficult to accept with complete seriousness the concern avowed for "healing." These ideas, like so many others of the age, were epitomized often and neatly by Alexander Pope— sometimes with casual aplomb, as in his *Epistle to Augustus*, where paraphrasing the Horatian thumbnail history of poetry, he slips in the couplet:

> Hence Satire rose, that just the medium hit,
> And heals with Morals what it hurts with Wit.

Sometimes with feelings of tender self-regard, as in his *Epistle to Arbuthnot*, where he brings in his filial piety and the good influence of his parents. And once, with fierce conviction and political self-righteousness, in the *Epilogue* to his *Satires*.

> Yes, I am proud; I must be proud to see
> Men not afraid of God, afraid of me:
> Safe from the Bar, the Pulpit, and the Throne,
> Yet touched and shamed by Ridicule alone.
> O sacred weapon! left for Truth's defence,
> Sole Dread of Folly, Vice, and Insolence!

The special élan of Pope's *Epistle to Arbuthnot* arises in large part from the ironic alternations of slaughterous portraiture with the author's professions of childlike innocence.

> Yet soft by nature, more a dupe than wit,
> *Sappho* can tell you how this man was bit.

One may observe in passing that the neo-classic satirist's protestation of moral, and denial of slanderous, intent, poses very vividly the Aristotelian distinction between general poetic meaning and historical particularity. Although Pope and Warburton maintained that the names in the *Dunciad* did not matter, because the types were perennial,[6] the

---

to be imitated in comedy (the ridiculous, *to geloion*) is taken by Heinsius as a fault in comedy itself, the laughable, *ridiculum*. Jonson heavily underscores this interpretation with the phrase "the moving of laughter is a fault in Comedie."

[6] Cf. Fielding, *Joseph Andrews*, Bk. III, Ch. 1.

fact that Grubstreet was then and there swarming with dunces was what provoked the poem, and living dunces were hit—some less fairly than others. It was surely not immoral for Molière to satirize the pious fraud (*faux dévot*), but then Molière could scarcely help implying something about the prevalence of frauds among pious persons in the France of Louis XIV. The practical truth and moral value of all such implicit indictments (or their untruth and immoral libel) depended on statistical factors which lay outside the scope of literary criticism and of moral philosophy too.

V

THE kind of generalized moral criticism which was the professed aim of 17th-century comedy and satire is to be found at its most refined in a few plays of Molière—*Le Tartuffe, Le Bourgeois Gentilhomme, L'Avare,* and above all *Le Misanthrope.* English comedy of manners along the same lines—and sometimes it was copied rather closely from Molière— suffers from two main defects, the Horneresque indecency which later elicited Lamb's defence [7] and Macaulay's censure, and the English fondness for the "humour," a kind of bumptiousness which was never completely sophisticated even in the smartest Restoration comedies. Toward the end of the century this very indigenous form of the laughable settled into a national institution, a phenomenon of actual English life, a supposedly superior source of comedy, and a matter of national pride. Thus Temple in his essay *Of Poetry,* 1690:

> . . . our English [comedy] has . . . excelled both the modern and the Ancient, . . . by Force of a Vein Natural perhaps to our Country, and which with us is called . . . Humour, a Word peculiar to our Language too, and hard to be expressed in any other. . . . This may proceed from the Native Plenty of our Soyl, the unequalness of our Clymat, as well as the Ease of our Government, and the Liberty of Professing Opinions and Factions. . . . Thus we come to have more Originals, and more than appear what they are; we have more Humour, because every Man follows his own, and takes a Pleasure, perhaps a Pride, to shew it. . . . We are not only more unlike one another than any Nation I know but we are more unlike our selves too at several times. . . . our Country must be confest to be what a great Foreign Physitian called it, The Region of Spleen, which may arise a good deal from the great uncertainty and many suddain changes of our Weather in all Seasons of the Year. . . .

[7] By a theory which posited a more than Kantian degree of detachment in our experience of such comedy.

There are no where so many Disputers upon Religion, so many Reasoners upon Government, so many Refiners in Politicks, so many Curious Inquisitives, so many Pretenders to Business and State-Imployments, greater Porers upon Books, nor Plodders after Wealth. And yet no where more Abandoned Libertines, more refined Luxurists, Extravagant Debauchees, Conceited Gallants, more Dabblers in Poetry as well as Politicks, in Philosophy, and in Chymistry. I have had several Servants far gone in Divinity, others in Poetry; have known, in the Families of some Friends, a Keeper deep in the *Rosycrucia Principles*, and a Laundress firm in those of *Epicurus*.[8]

The English "humour" was softening. What had been in the plays of Ben Jonson prickly, gross, and smelly now became quaint, merely eccentric, cozy, a harmless or lovable tendency of national character. A tribe of "originals" flourished: the bluff squire, the angular and brambly spinster, the cove, the codger, the dodger, Uncle Toby with his hobby horse, Aunt Betsey Trotwood, Mr. Micawber. Without passing judgment on this art of comfortable caricature, we may observe that along with the Augustan trend toward burlesque (of which we must say more before the end of this chapter) this kind of comic art was mainly to blame for the fact that the most brilliant essay in English on the ethical value of comedy was to be written only in the latter 19th century as an expression of classical reaction against what its author considered the hoydenish parochialism of English laughter. George Meredith's lecture *On the Idea of the Comic and the Uses of the Comic Spirit in Literature*[9] was delivered in 1877, and except for the fact that it relates closely to a concept of comedy both expounded and to some extent illustrated in several of his own novels (*The Ordeal of Richard Feverel, The Egoist, Diana of the Crossways*),[1] it was an anachronism—an unlimited celebration of French classical comedy and something like a master statement of the values achieved in that form.

There are, announces Meredith, two extreme spirits which are anti-comic—that of the Puritanical enemies of Comedy, the non-laughers or *agelasts* (here conceivably one might have to place Heinsius and the Ben Jonson of *Timber*) but no less that of the bellyshaking *hypergelasts*, the riotous Bacchanalians. (In Aristotle's *Ethics* indeed one found the boorish enemy of fun and the buffoonish and chronic fun-maker set on each side of the gentlemanly and discreetly ready wit. Meredith's terms, aside from their etymology, have a clear classical coloration.) Within the area of the literary laughable he distinguishes from comedy both satire

[8] Spingarn III, 103–6. Cf. Congreve, Letter to Dennis *Concerning Humour in Comedy* (Spingarn, III, 252); E. N. Hooker, "Humour in the Age of Pope," *Huntington Library Quarterly*, XI (August, 1948), 361–85.

[9] See the edition by Lane Cooper, *An Essay on Comedy* (New York, 1918).

[1] See J. W. Beach, *The Comic Spirit in George Meredith* (New York, 1911).

(prideful, egoistic, self-vindicatory, sentimental, working on a storage tank of bile) and humour, so beloved of the British (bumptious and cheerful, "laughter holding both his sides," comforting his victim with the hearty slap on the back). Meredith's lecture is a plea for the corrective and civilizing agency of wit and especially of feminine wit.[2] Shrewdly he read a tribute to the saving grace of woman's charity and laughter in even such minor fragments of the plays of Menander as were then known. He traced the same theme in the Roman echoes of Terence's she-comedies, *The Mother-in-Law*, and *The Woman of Andros*, then in the comedies of Molière and par excellence in *The Misanthrope*—where the heroine Célimène, coquette and gossip, sweetheart and foil to the cynical Alceste, soars in the end as the sweetly transcendent critic of his surliness, his self-gratulatory spirit of satire, and his morose impulse to retirement. English plays which attempted to follow this chastely tempered pattern of bitter-sweet, sad-and-funny—Wycherley's *Plain Dealer*, for instance, with its theme of gross infidelity, its tarpaulin-and-brandy-smelling hero, its farrago of irrelevant humours and *Twelfth Night* girl in boy's clothes—pointed all too readily the contrast which Meredith was interested to draw at the expense of his countrymen. Such a view of comedy had some difficulty in the accommodation of irregular or romantic comic geniuses like Aristophanes, Rabelais, and Shakespeare—a feat accomplished only by local brilliance of phrasing and at the cost of some inconsistency in Meredith's total argument. But in his main stress he comes as close as anyone ever has to laying out a definition of high and quintessential comedy as a literary genre—a golden center of the comic target, the kind of moral and social quality, non-didactic, non-satiric if one insists, sympathetic, yet clearly critical, which had been the province of the most exquisite in the classical way of comedy.[3]

The rather severe and ethically serious theory of comedy to be traced from Aristotle to Meredith did not often if ever reach the point of saying that comedy is a strangely chameleon obverse, or mocking counterpart, of the tragic. The theory did not notably seek to associate comedy with the peripeteia and its complement of verbal irony so conspicuous in Sophoclean tragedy, nor did it make much of the insight hinted in Aristotle's analogous use of the terms *hamartia* and *hamartēma* in his definitions of the tragic and the laughable. Still the low style, the *genus tenue* of comedy and of Horatian epistle and satire, was not conceived as something merely frivolous or frolicsome. In our next chapter

[2] Compare the following by Lord Chesterfield: ". . . the conversations of our mixed companies here . . . if they happen to rise above bragg and whist, infallibly stop short of everything either pleasing or instructive. I take the reason of this to be, that (as women generally give the tone of conversation) our English women are not near so well informed and cultivated as the French; besides that they are naturally more serious and silent" (*Letters*, January 23, 1752).

[3] See the classical vein admirably renewed in our own day by L. J. Potts, *Comedy*, London: Hutchinson's University Library, 1949.

we shall have something to say about the role played in the theory of this era by the ambiguous native term "wit." At this point, we may relevantly remark that the double orientation of this term was toward the two poles of the smartly amusing and the imaginatively creative. It would be somewhat of a simplification, but not a grossly unfair one, to say that the main effort of the "wits" of Pope's age, so far as it was a theoretical effort, was directed to asserting the serious value of the laughable. The point was made by Swift and Pope but perhaps never so explicitly as by their successor Henry Fielding (the last of the English comic wits in the classical tradition) in a passage of his *Covent Garden Journal* with which we may conclude this section of our history.

> It is from a very common but a very false Opinion, that we constantly mix the Idea of Levity with those of Wit and Humour. The gravest of Men have often possessed these qualities [of Wit and Humour] in a very eminent Degree, and have exerted them on the most solemn Subjects with very eminent Success. These are to be found in many Places in the most serious Works of Plato and Aristotle, of Cicero and Seneca. Not only Swift, but South hath used them on the highest and most important of all subjects. In the sermons of the Latter, there is perhaps more Wit, than in the Comedies of Congreve.—No. 18, March 3, 1752 [4]

VI

THE last twenty years of Dryden's long career were devoted increasingly to translation and to critical writing apropos of his translation. And so at the close of the 17th century Dryden brings us back again to an emphasis upon which we dwelt at the beginning, with Ben Jonson, that on the imitation of classical models. Dryden produced translations of Ovid's *Epistles*, 1680, of the *Satires* of Juvenal and Persius, 1693, of the French painter Du Fresnoy's *De Arte Graphica*, 1695, of Virgil's *Eclogues*, *Georgics*, and *Aeneid*, 1697, and of selections from Homer, Ovid,

[4] A complementary Augustan insight was that dulness could appear in the form of smartness or frivolity. Fielding continues: "True indeed it is that Dulness appears in her own Form, and in her proper Dress, when she walks abroad in some critical Essay on a grave Subject; and many millions of Reams have in all Ages been sacrificed to her by her Votaries in this Manner; but she doth not always preserve this solemn Air. She often appears in public in Essays of Entertainment . . . and sometimes in Print, as well as on the Stage, disguises herself in a Jack-pudding Coat, and condescends to divert her good Friends with sundry Feats of Dexterity and Grimace. The late ingenious Dr. Swift . . . likens these two different Appearances of Dulness to the different Qualities of small Beer in the Barrel, and small Beer in the Bottle. The former of which is well known of all Things the most vapid, insipid and heavy; but the latter is altogether as airy, frothy, brisk and bouncing." Cf. *Dunciad* IV, 239–40: "Ah, think not. Mistress! more true Dulness lies In Folly's Cap, than Wisdom's grave disguise."

Boccaccio, and Chaucer which in the last year of his life, 1700, he published under the title of *Fables*.

Perhaps the best known of the critical essays attached to these
translations, the last and one of the mellowest expressions of Dryden's
fluent old age, is the Preface to the *Fables*. And the most notable feature
of this is the generous appreciation of Chaucer which Dryden managed
in spite of a quaintly confident inability to scan his verses. Chaucer is
"the father of English poetry," "a perpetual fountain of good sense."
Yet his verses have only the "rude sweetness of a Scotch tune;" "some
thousands" of them are "lame for want of half a foot." He lived "in the
infancy of our poetry." [5] Here we have both a milestone in one kind of
Augustanism, the superior notion that the rudeness of the past ought to
be translated into the elegance of the present, and at the same time a very
sympathetic reading of an archaic idiom, an outstanding exercise of what
today is likely to be called the "historic sense." Dryden, let us reflect,
was writing six years after the publication of the following lines by
Addison in the *Sixth Miscellany*.

> . . . Chaucer first, a merry bard, arose,
> And many a story told in rhyme and prose,
> But age has rusted what the poet writ,
> Worn out his language and obscur'd his wit:
> In vain he jests in his unpolish'd strain,
> And tries to make his readers laugh in vain.
> —*Account of the Greatest English Poets*, 1694

And thirty-seven years before Pope's *Epistle to Augustus*:

> Chaucer's worst ribaldry is learn'd by rote,
> And Beastly Skelton Heads of houses quote.

Dryden and Pope's translations from Chaucer and Pope's *Satires of Dr.
Donne Versified* illustrate this side of Augustanism. The Augustan feeling of superiority to archaic English poetry sat comfortably enough
with respectful submission to the classical ancients. "Still green with
bays each ancient Altar stands." And hence Augustanism was at odds
with the kind of scientific or Royal Society modernism which often (as
in the argument of Eugenius in Dryden's *Essay*) came over into the
literary battle between the Ancients and Moderns. This battle,[6] translated

[5] Ker II, 257–9. Cf. Edmund Waller, *Of English Verse*: "Chaucer his sense can
only boast; The glory of his numbers lost!" The correct versification of Waller in
English was made parallel to that of Malherbe in French when Dryden chose the
English equivalents for French examples in Soames's translation of Boileau's *L'Art
poétique*, 1683. In the Preface to the 1690 edition of Waller's *Poems*, his claims were
stated in an extravagant way by Francis Atterbury. Waller became the "parent of
English verse and the first that showed our Tongue had Beauty and Numbers in
it." Wellek, *Rise*, pp. 35–6.

[6] See R. F. Jones, *Ancients and Moderns: a Study of the Background of the
"Battle of the Books,"* St. Louis, 1936; Wellek, *Rise*, pp. 39 ff.

from France to England in a series of attacks and counterattacks, from Temple's *Essay Upon the Ancient and Modern Learning*, 1690, to Swift's *Battle of the Books*, 1704, was an intricate confusion of several issues, among them these two: (1) whether there is progress in literature, as in science; (2) whether, if there is progress, it is continuous from antiquity steadily onward, or is cyclical,[7] through alternate ages of barbarism and polished Augustanism. A belief in cycles was not inconsistent with a belief in the overall decline of poetry from antiquity to modern times— a progress from Ennius to Virgil and Horace, from Chaucer to Dryden, but the old height not to be reached again. In part this was due to the rapidity of the shifts in the linguistic ground under one's feet. Bacon had written his important works in Latin or translated them into Latin or let somebody else do it. Most English poems of great repute in this age and of convenient length (and some much longer) [8] were translated by somebody into Latin. And as late as the time of Pope it made good sense to lament the insubstantiality of the idiom upon which one had to rely.

> Poets that lasting marble seek
> Must carve in Latin or in Greek;
> We write in sand. . . .[9]

Marble, let it be understood (this seems a legitimate implication of the argument all along), is better for sculpture than sand for two reasons: not only does it wear better but one can do more with it to begin with. And thus arises the need not only to bring the archaic and ragged English writers (Chaucer and Donne) into line with whatever Augustan perfection of form has been achieved in English but also (and this is the heroic task) to translate the more monumental values of antique literature into the modern idiom—not only in order that the less learned may read more readily, but also in order that the more learned may have the pleasure of following the translator in the course of his creative analogizing. The translations from the classics in the era of Dryden and Pope would seem to have been directed by a conjunction of two literary theories: one, as we have seen, that heroic poetry is the most desirable kind (though apparently an almost impossible feat in the modern age of decline); and the other, that translation and "imitation" are quite possible in such and such ways.

Dryden's role in the history of English translation was described in the next century by Samuel Johnson as follows:

[7] Cycles of culture are discussed in Bouhours' *Entretiens*, 1671, and Fontenelle's *Dialogue des morts*, 1683.

[8] Sir Francis Kynaston translated the first two books of Chaucer's *Troilus and Criseyde* into rhymed Latin: *Amorum Troili et Creseidae Libri Duo Priores Anglico-Latini*, Oxford, 1635. Christopher Smart's *Poems on Several Occasions* (London, 1752) includes *De Arte Critica; a Latin Version of Mr. Pope's "Essay on Criticism."*

[9] Waller, *Of English Verse.* Cf. Pope, Preface to *Works*, 1717.

> Dryden saw very early that closeness best preserved an author's sense, and that freedom best exhibited his spirit; he therefore will deserve the highest praise, who can give a representation at once faithful and pleasing, who can convey the same thoughts with the same graces, and who when he translates changes nothing but the language.—*Idler* 69, 1759

Dryden himself in one of his early statements on the subject, the Preface to his *Ovid*, had distinguished grades of translation thus:

> All translation, I suppose, may be reduced to these three heads.
>
> First, that of metaphrase, or turning an author word by word, and line by line, from one language into another. . . . The second way is that of paraphrase, or translation with latitude, where the author is kept in view by the translator, so as never to be lost, but his words are not so strictly followed as his sense; and that too is admitted to be amplified, but not altered. . . . The third way is that of imitation, where the translator (if now he has not lost that name) assumes the liberty, not only to vary from the words and sense, but to forsake them both as he sees occasion; and taking only some general hints from the original, to run division on the groundwork, as he pleases.[1]

Dryden announces as his own standard the mean, "paraphrase," but he confesses that he may sometimes have taken more liberty. Both the theory and the practice of Dryden presage something which is far more plainly legible in the first half of the next century in the Horatian imitations of Pope and the Juvenalian imitations of Samuel Johnson. To take but one instance, Pope's *Epistle to Augustus* is an imitation of the corresponding Horatian epistle in a sense quite far advanced beyond that in which Ben Jonson's character of Shakespeare in *Timber* is an imitation of the happy model which he had found in Seneca's sketch of Haterius. With Jonson the parallel between Haterius and Shakespeare is of small consequence. If we attend to it at all, it is only a small joke, almost irrelevant to the tone and pattern of Jonson's sketch. But with Pope not only parallel, but adaptation, and even recognizable deviation are the essential techniques. It is a technique of discrepant or ironic analogy—Augustan London matched fairly enough against Augustan Rome, but George Augustus II matched lamely and insultingly against Oc-

---

[1] Ker I, 237. Similar distinctions may be found in English writing of an earlier date—as far back, for instance, as the *Scholemaster* of Roger Ascham. Dryden takes the term "imitation" in the special sense in question from Cowley. He notes the practice of this kind of translation in Cowley's Pindaric and Horatian Odes and in Denham's Second *Aeneid*.

tavius Augustus—ridicule accomplished by eulogy. "A vile Encomium doubly ridicules: There's nothing blackens like the ink of fools." In short the difference between the Jonsonian and the Popean stages of classical imitation is that between mere borrowing from a source and the strategy of allusion, a difference of all the more theoretical import if we consider the pervasive and Protean role of allusion in the poetry of all sophisticated ages.

The aesthetic of imitation in the age of Dryden and Pope merges with another principle, that of parody and burlesque—forms of literature which were at the same time techniques of intricate allusion and symptoms of decline from the heroic. They were symptoms too of the freedom of the poetic spirit even when it appears most dedicated to the rules.[2] If it was not possible to be the English Homer or the English Virgil or even adequately to translate the highly serious works of those authors, it was both possible and delightful to use their range of meaning and the mammoth authority of their very presence in the mind of the age to construct smaller but brightly reflecting models, either in the mode of rococo delicacy or in that of the harrowing grotesque. It may have been play—the elevated person putting on the mask for the visit to the bazaar of ordinary life—but it was crafty and potent play. In these modes of composition the poet enjoyed all the advantages which "imitation" can afford. He was an objective imitator in the fullest way—in a way, however, which during every age lies at least latent in the triangular relationship of poet, contemporary world, and literary past.

SUPPLEMENT

The work by Mr. Pound which has laid itself most open to this kind of attack, *Homage to Sextus Propertius*, is not included in the volume under consideration here. At the same time, though it is strictly not a translation of Propertius so much as what a Restoration poet would have called an "Allusion to Propertius" or "Imitations of Propertius," it perhaps provides the best starting-point for a general consideration of Mr. Pound's achievement as a verse translator. The academic critics of this poem are right, of course, in dis-

[2] Cf. Austin Warren, "The Mask of Pope," *Sewanee Review*, LIV (Winter, 1946), 19–33. Fielding in his Preface to *Joseph Andrews* finds it incumbent upon him to distinguish between mere burlesque and the truly comic imitation of nature which he professes. For about seventy-five years various forms of play and irresponsibility may have been a chief outlet for the poetic impulse—not only the burlesques of Pope, Swift, and Fielding, but the Spenserian parody of Shenstone (increasingly tender in its revisions), Smart's whimsical mad play with the Scriptures, Percy's condescension to the ballads, Chatterton's forged medievalism. Cf. R. D. Havens, "Assumed Personality, Insanity, and Poetry," *Review of English Studies*, New Series, IV (January, 1953), 26–37.

covering howlers in it. They could discover comparable howlers in Marlowe's very beautiful versions of Ovid, and it may be admitted that Mr. Pound's knowledge of Latin is nearer to that of an eager undergraduate (an under- graduate impatient with grammar and in love with the *idea* of poetry) than to that of a university lecturer. At the same time, the academic critics of *Homage to Sextus Propertius* have largely missed Mr. Pound's point. We can see what he is doing in this poem most clearly if we look at passages where there are no howlers, but where, for the sake of bringing out a latent irony in Propertius, Mr. Pound deliberately distorts his strict sense. Thus the elegiac couplet,

> *a valeat, Phoebum quicumque moratur in armis!*
> *exactus tenui pumice versus eat,* [*Elegies* III, i, 7–8]

which is literally, in Butler's version, "Away with the man who keeps Phoebus tarrying among the weapons of war! Let verse run smoothly, polished with fine pumice," becomes in Mr. Pound's variation:

> Out-weariers of Apollo will, as we know, continue their Martian generalities.
> We have kept our erasers in order.

Mr. Pound obviously here does understand the literal sense of the Latin. But for his own purposes, he is "pointing up" that sense. He is not using Propertius as a *mere* stalking-horse. He is, in the lines just quoted, striving by a slight distortion of the literal sense of his original to bring over much more vividly than Butler does its tone and feeling. He brings in "Martian" to remind us that after all it is a Latin poet he is starting from. On the other hand, he brings in the modern word "generalities" and the word "erasers" (which probably sug- gests typewriter erasers to us more immediately than fine pumice) to remind us that the reason why he is imitating, or alluding to, Propertius, is that Proper- tius has contemporary relevance. We are to reflect not only that Propertius did not want to write war-poetry but that Mr. Pound did not fancy himself as a poet of the school of Newbolt and Kipling.

> —"The Poet as Translator," review of *The Translations of Ezra Pound*, with an Introduction by Hugh Kenner (London, 1953) in *Times Literary Supplement*, London, September 18, 1953, p. 596, by permission of *The Times*

Upon the highest corner of a large window, there dwelt a certain spider, swollen up to the first magnitude by the destruction of infinite numbers of flies, whose spoils lay scattered before the gates of his palace, like human bones before the cave of some giant. The avenues to his castle were guarded with turnpikes and palisadoes, all after the modern way of fortification. . . . it was the pleasure of fortune to conduct thither a wandering bee, to whose curiosity a broken pane in the glass had discovered itself, and in he went; where, expatiating a while, he at last happened to alight upon one of the out- ward walls of the spider's citadel; which, yielding to the unequal weight, sunk down to the very foundation. . . . the bee had acquitted himself of his toils, and, posted securely at some distance, was employed in cleansing his wings, and disengaging them from the ragged remnants of the cobweb. By this time the spider was adventured out, when, beholding the chasms, the ruins, and dilapidations of his fortress, he was very near his wit's end; he stormed and swore like a madman, and swelled till he was ready to burst.

'Not to disparage myself,' said he, 'by the comparison with such a rascal, what art thou but a vagabond without house or home, without stock or inheritance, born to no possession of your own, but a pair of wings and a dronepipe? Your livelihood is an universal plunder upon nature; a freebooter over fields and gardens; and, for the sake of stealing, will rob a nettle as easily as a violet. Whereas I am a domestic animal, furnished with a native stock within myself. This large castle (to show my improvements in the mathematics) is all built with my own hands, and the materials extracted altogether out of my own person.'

'I am glad,' answered the bee, 'to hear you grant at least that I am come honestly by my wings and my voice; for then, it seems, I am obliged to Heaven alone for my flights and my music; and Providence would never have bestowed on me two such gifts, without designing them for the noblest ends. I visit indeed all the flowers and blossoms of the field and the garden; but whatever I collect thence enriches myself, without the least injury to their beauty, their smell, or their taste. Now, for you and your skill in architecture and other mathematics, I have little to say: in that building of yours there might, for aught I know, have been labour and method enough; but, by woeful experience for us both, 'tis too plain, the materials are naught, and I hope you will henceforth take warning, and consider duration and matter as well as method and art. You boast, indeed, of being obliged to no other creature, but of drawing and spinning out all from yourself; that is to say, if we may judge of the liquor in the vessel by what issues out, you possess a good plentiful store of dirt and poison in your breast; and, though I would by no means lessen or disparage your genuine stock of either, yet I doubt you are somewhat obliged, for an increase of both, to a little foreign assistance. Your inherent portion of dirt does not fail of acquisitions, by sweepings exhaled from below; and one insect furnishes you with a share of poison to destroy another. So that, in short, the question comes all to this— Whether is the nobler being of the two, that which, by a lazy contemplation of four inches round, by an overweening pride, feeding and engendering on itself, turns all into excrement and venom, producing nothing at all, but flybane and a cobweb; or that which, by an universal range, with long search, much study, true judgement, and distinction of things, brings home honey and wax.'

This dispute was managed with such eagerness, clamour, and warmth, that the two parties of books, in arms below stood silent a while, waiting in suspense what would be the issue, which was not long undetermined: for the bee, grown impatient at so much loss of time, fled straight away to a bed of roses, without looking for a reply, and left the spider like an orator, collected in himself and just prepared to burst out.

It happened upon this emergency, that Aesop broke silence first. . . . he . . . swore in the loudest key, that in all his life he had never known two cases so parallel and adapt to each other, as that in the window, and this upon the shelves. . . . 'For, pray, gentlemen, was ever anything so modern as the spider, in his air, his turns, and his paradoxes? He argues in the behalf of you his brethren and himself, with many boastings of his native stock and great genius, that he spins and spits wholly from himself, and scorns to own any obligation or assistance from without. Then he displays to you his great skill in architecture, and improvement in the mathematics. To all this the bee, as an advocate retained by us the Ancients, thinks fit to answer—that, if one may judge of the great genius or inventions of the Moderns by what they have produced, you will hardly have countenance to bear you out in boasting of either. Erect your schemes with as much method and skill as you please; yet if the materials be nothing but dirt, spun out of your own entrails (the guts of modern brains), the edifice will conclude at last in a cobweb, the duration of which, like that of other spiders' webs, may be imputed to their being forgotten, or neglected, or hid in a corner. For anything else of genuine that the Moderns may pretend to, I cannot recollect; unless it be a large vein of wrangling and satire, much of a nature and substance with the spider's poison; which, however, they pretend to spit wholly out of themselves, is improved by the same arts, by feeding upon the insects and vermin of the age. As for us the Ancients, we are content with the bee to pretend to nothing of our own, beyond our wings and our voice, that is to say, our flights and our language. For the rest, whatever we have got, has been by infinite labour and search, and ranging through every corner of nature; the difference is that, instead of dirt and poison, we have rather chosen to fill our hives with honey and wax, thus furnishing mankind with the two noblest of things, which are sweetness and light.'

—Jonathan Swift, *The Battle of the Books,* 1704

CHAPTER 12

RHETORIC AND
NEO-CLASSIC WIT

§ *Crocean view of 17th-century rhetoric, Ramus and
Talon: rearrangement of rhetoric and dialectic, relation
of poetry to dialectic and rhetoric, Arcadian Rhetoric,
euphuism, ambiguous import of Ramism, Cicero and Professor Howell—II. scientific plain style in England, Glan-
ville, The Royal Society, Wilkins and Sprat, Swift's satire
—III. "wit" vs. "judgment," Dryden, Hobbes, Locke,
Addison ("mixt wit"), Augustan vs. metaphysical poetry,
lag between poetry and theory, Puttenham's figures—IV.
Alexander Pope,* Essay on Criticism, *classical "imitation"
again, literary theory as influence, content, and norm,
Vida, Boileau, the mob of English gentlemen, synopsis
of Pope's* Essay—*V. Pope's ideas: "Nature" universal and
social, reason and authority, rhetorical rules, "representative" verse, Pope's tour de force, diction, Horace's rule
of idiom vs. poetic diction—VI. "wit" again, a genteel
slang word, Pope's artful use of its meanings, the norm of
salon conversation, a social question, Tories and high
churchmen vs. middle-class dissenters, Blackmore, "wit,"
"nature," and "dress," the inevitable residuum, Samuel
Johnson's retrospect, "familiarity" and "surprise," "sheer
wit" and repartee, Corbyn Morris—VII. the 17th-century
double shift, in style and theory, ambiguity of theory,
Sprat, Pascal, Swift, Newman; Pope, Dryden, Gildon,
Blackmore—VIII. end of ancient rhetorical tradition in
18th century, simultaneous new concept, Giambattista
Vico died 1744, contrasted to Hobbes, Pope's* Dunciad
IV, 1743, negative celebration of the "word" §

T HE STRONGLY BIASED SURVEY OF CRITICAL HISTORY WHICH FORMS THE
second part of Benedetto Croce's *Aesthetic* probably did a great
deal to establish the 17th century in the mind of the early 20th
as the moment of a rhetorical event that had been long overdue—the
breakdown of the elaborate system of verbal artifice which had endured
under the name of "rhetoric" from classical times into the Renaissance.
According to this view, the last and most preposterous phase of classical
rhetoric occurs during the early 17th century in such baroque developments as Gongorism and Marinism on the continent and in the English
parallel known as "metaphysical wit," the extravagant ingenuity in metaphor, pun, and paradoxical conceit attained by the poets Donne, Herbert,
and Crashaw, and by such sermon writers as Donne and Andrewes.
After this phase there was no further scope for the elaboration of ornamental rhetoric. The system collapsed.

Subsequent research has produced a good deal of evidence tending
to show the part played in England by post-Baconian science and the
Puritan spirit of economic and practical tidiness in clearing the ground
for what was conceived as a desirable unification of language and real
knowledge. Whatever the justice of the Crocean evaluation, it is safe to
say that the 17th century was a critical period in the long struggle—more
or less continuous since pre-Platonic times—between the custodians of
pure idea and pure fact, dialecticians and scientists, on the one hand, and
on the other, the custodians of the riches of the "word," grammarians,
rhetoricians, critics, exegetes.

A preliminary *cause célèbre*, though probably more symptomatic of
the main unrest of the age than a sufficient or even a necessary influence
for the rhetorical events which followed, had been the educational reform
promoted by the French logician Peter Ramus, whose life work was a
sustained attack on what he considered the perversions of latter-day
Aristotelianism. His program included a broad revision of the traditional
rhetoric, carried out with the assistance of his colleague and special authority in that department, Omer Talon. Among the most influential
books during the later 16th century and the first half of the 17th century
in France and England were undoubtedly the now little-known *Dialectique* (1555) and *Dialecticae Libri Duo* (1556) of Ramus and the
companion *Institutiones Oratoriae* (1544), in a later version entitled *Rhetorica*, of Talon.[1] Ancient Stoic philosophers had made a distinction be-

---

[1] See Wilbur Samuel Howell, "Ramus and English Rhetoric," *Quarterly Journal
of Speech*, XXXVII (October, 1951), 301–2. The date of Talon's subsidiary work is
to be explained by the fact that both the *Dialectique* and *Dialecticae Libri Duo*
were condensations of earlier works by Ramus. His *Dialecticae Institutiones* or *Dialecticae Partitiones* and his *Aristotelicae Animadversiones* appeared in 1543. See also

tween the "closed fist" of dialectic and the "open palm" of rhetoric.[2] With Ramus and with his English followers of the 17th century, both dialectic and rhetoric came heavily under the "clunchfist"[3] of method.

One of the first principles of Ramist reasoning was a clean separation of each liberal discipline from every other—with no overlapping. Ramus could not tolerate, for instance, the fact that the intellectual activities of "invention" and "disposition" had traditionally appeared not only in dialectic (or logic) but in rhetoric. His revision of the art of rhetoric began with a radical reassignment of the anciently established five parts of the art of rhetoric—Invention, Disposition, Elocution, Memory, and Delivery. He took invention, disposition, and memory[4] away from rhetoric and gave them securely and univocally to dialectic, leaving to rhetoric proper only elocution (that is, style) and delivery. Since the last of these is a matter of externalization (the actor's part), rhetoric proper might be conceived as consisting only of style. And that, furthermore, was to be a relatively simple style. For everywhere Ramus was a purist and simplist. In dialectic he reduced the traditional complexities of "invention" to ten topics or commonplaces of argument, and (under the head of distribution) he treated the syllogism only in its most elementary forms.[5] In rhetoric he treated style as a repertory of "tropes" and "figures," with greater emphasis on the latter. "Tropes" included what we today might call the metaphoric and the ironic qualities of meaning— what medieval rhetoricians called "difficult" ornaments. "Figures" were various artful or unusual ways of expression—apostrophe, exclamation, hesitation, concession, understatement and the like, and also various repetitive or echoing patterns of words ("turns," as Dryden would later call them)—all these being the "easy" ornaments of the medieval rhetorician. There were (and are) of course rather close ties—of ironic and metaphoric insinuation—between the "tropes" of such a system and the "figures." But Ramist rhetoric did not reach the levels of analysis where such connections might have been discussed.

One striking feature of this rhetorical situation lay in the close relation of *poetry*, as Ramus saw it, both to rhetoric and to dialectic. The Ramist dialectic was implicitly the Platonic anti-rhetoric of the *Phaedrus* returning against the long successful Aristotelian answer. The main plea was for a revitalized dialectic, a more direct and intuitive union of mind

---

P. A. Duhamel, "The Logic and Rhetoric of Peter Ramus," *Modern Philology,* XLVI (February, 1949), 163–171.

[2] Cicero, *Orator* XXXII. "*Zeno quidem ille a quo disciplina Stoicorum est manu demonstrare solebat quid inter has artis interesset; nam cum compresserat digitos pugnumque fecerat, dialecticam aiebat eiusmodi esse; cum autem deduxerat et manum dilataverat, palmae illius similem eloquentiam esse dicebat.*" Cf. *ante* Chapter 4.

[3] See *Oxford English Dictionary*, s.v. *clunchfist:* "1662 Fuller *Worthies* I, 189, The Clunch-fist of Logick (good to knock a man down at a blow)."

[4] Duhamel, *loc. cit.,* p. 164, n. 12.

[5] Duhamel, pp. 166, 169.

with "argument," the steady unfolding of natural and concrete implications and of necessary and logically compelling dichotomies—without
the interference of deductive abstraction (the "false secondary power by
which we multiply distinctions").[6] Ramism had a strong leaning toward
the immediacy and warmth of the poetic argument. It conceived an
"argument" not as a statement or series of statements, but simply as any
term, idea, image, or quality—any *thing*, in short, when seen in the light
of some significance.[7] The system was strongly "practical" in that it
stressed example more than theory. Both in their dialectical and in their
rhetorical works the Ramists freely adduced examples from the poets.
The Lawiers Logike (1588) of Abraham Fraunce, translated and digested
from Ramus's *Dialecticae Libri Duo*, uses, side by side, illustrations from
English law and from Spenser's *Shepheardes Calendar*. A companion volume, Fraunce's *Arcadian Rhetorike*, translated from Talon's *Rhetorica*,
is in effect a rich anthology of examples from Homer, Virgil, Sidney,
Spenser, Tasso, Du Bartas, and other continental poets.[8] Sidney's Arcadian figures became standard Ramist rhetorical illustrations in England.

Sidney's Arcadian rhetoric is likely to seem florid enough to a 20th-
century reader. A recent close analysis of this rhetoric has, however,
suggested its rather heavy dependence on certain devices of word order
(*figures* or *schemes*—such as isocolon, parenthesis, anaphora, antithesis)
rather than on the metaphoric and ironic range of the *tropes*. In short,
Sidney's rhetoric was what would have been called by a medieval writer
in the *Ad Herennium* tradition a rhetoric of "easy ornaments." [9] Another Elizabethan style which would have been called "easy" in the same
tradition was that of Lyly in his *Euphues*, no matter how great its modern
reputation for artificiality. The dominant artifice of Euphuism was structural (in parallel, antithesis, and transverse alliteration), and its numerous
images, far fetched though they were from natural history and myth,
were seldom truly metaphoric, seldom ironic or in any way subtle. The
fact that Stephen Gosson (the Puritan enemy of poetry) wrote in a
Euphuistic style which was more elaborate than that of the courtier
Sidney, who was provoked, perhaps by Gosson himself, to the *Defence
of Poesie*, constitutes a paradoxical crisscross which well illustrates the
concrete complexity of the historic situation.[1] But this is perhaps only a

---

[6] Wordsworth, *Prelude* II, 214-17.

[7] P. A. Duhamel, "Milton's Alleged Ramism," *PMLA*, LXVII (December, 1952),
1035-53. Cf. Rosemond Tuve, "Imagery and Logic: Ramus and Metaphysical Poetics," *JHI*, III (October, 1942), 383-4.

[8] Howell, *loc. cit.*, p. 305. See *The Arcadian Rhetorike by Abraham Fraunce*,
ed. E. Seaton, Oxford, 1950. Cf. Thomas Blount, *Academie of Eloquence*, 1654.

[9] P. A. Duhamel, "Sidney's *Arcadia* and Elizabethan Rhetoric," *SP*, XLV (April,
1948), 134-150.

[1] Comparable crosscurrents appear in antiquity. Stoics of the third century B.C.
hold the doctrine of the *logos*, the creative word, yet favor plain style, the closed
fist. Seneca the Younger champions philosophy but holds for the union of eloquence

facet of the larger paradox that the technically simplified rhetoric pro-moted by Ramus and Talon, the "Arcadian" rhetoric, should soon come to be taken as the very embodiment of rhetorical floridity.[2] The explana-tion of this latter fact lies in the principle that a pure rhetoric (that is, a rhetoric of elocution detached from invention and disposition—of style detached from sense), no matter how simplified or restricted, is inevi-tably an excessive and artificial rhetoric. Far more "difficult" writers than either Lyly or Sidney—Shakespeare, for instance, or Donne—employ the whole range of both figures and tropes without being "flowery."

The Ramist reshuffling of the three intrinsic parts of ancient rhet-oric—invention, disposition, and elocution—that is, the translation of the term "rhetoric" from a name embracing all three of these parts to a name of merely the third, was a procedure of highly ambiguous import. It might mean, on the one hand, that a person decided: "Invention and disposition, the two substantial sinews of argument, are really parts of logic. Rhetoric in fact is mainly logic. What good rhetoric wants is a severe and honest style of adherence to argument. The elocution is the trimmings—or the clippings. Save them who will." This in fact was the kind of 17th-century thinking represented in the aphorism of Pascal, "*La vraie éloquence se moque de l'éloquence,*"[3] and no less in the plain-ish, anti-metaphysical, anti-baroque style which in England during the third quarter of the century would appear in pulpit eloquence, in the scientific writing of the Royal Society, and even in literary prose, for instance, in the lucidly conversational idiom of Dryden.

But at the same time, a person caught in the consequences of the Ramist rhetoric and logic might conceivably entertain a different train of reflections, somewhat as follows: "The art of rhetoric, as distinct from philosophy and science, has after all been always a matter essen-tially of style. Leaving the content and structure of argument, therefore, to the logician, the scientist, the theologian, let me discuss rhetoric in its pure form, that of the figures and tropes and of external pronunciation." And this in fact is what may be heard in many places. Professor Perry Miller quotes the following Commencement theses on rhetoric proposed at Harvard College during the latter part of the 17th century.

---

and wisdom. Quintilian champions rhetoric against philosophy, but writes, and argues for, a plainish style. The same ambiguous allegiance in the contest between rhetoric and thinking is shown in the Ciceronian mean between Asianism and At-ticism and the later development of the Silver Latin or Senecan curtly brilliant artifice. Cf. *ante* Chapter 4.

[2] Cf. *ante* Chapter 6, p. 103, n. 4.

[3] *Pensées* VII, 34. Cf. Montaigne, "*Le parler que j'aime, c'est un parler simple et naif, tel sur le papier qu'à la bouche . . .*" (*Essais*, I, xxvi). Cf. the statements of Nashe, Puttenham and Jonson, quoted by F. W. Bateson, *English Poetry and the English Language* (Oxford, 1934), p. 39.

Rhetoric differs as a species from logic.

The principal constituents of rhetoric are elocution and pronunciation.

Elocution is the place of the flowers of rhetoric, pronunciation
the expiration of the odors.[4]

Whichever way one interpreted the Ramist mandate, a serious cleavage
in the art of verbal expression was the result. The new Platonic philosophy, like the old, was the enemy of a kind of verbal power which,
whatever its relation to science or philosophy, is close to the interests of
both oratory and poetry. In Roman classical times the complaint of
Cicero, the champion of eloquence, against Socrates, the dialectician, was
that the latter had succeeded in dividing the mind and the tongue, the
man who knew from the man who spoke. In a strikingly parallel fashion
a modern professor of public speaking (Professor Wilbur S. Howell of
Princeton) looks back on the reform effected by Ramus and reports:
". . . it tended to separate the investigative responsibilities of speakers
and writers from their presentational responsibilities . . . as if one set
of men could do the thinking for society, and quite another set, the
speaking." [5]

II

DURING the latter half of the 17th century, re-enforcements to plain-style
philosophy from Cartesian and empirically scientific quarters largely
took over the program. At least it is true that in England the scientific
was the most obvious influence upon literary men and is the most easily
described. The contrast between the baroque, Brownian way of writing
and the new severe scientific style may be conveniently shown in a passage which Joseph Glanvill, author of the Cartesian and anti-Aristotelian *Vanity of Dogmatizing*, 1661, revised for a version of that work
which appeared after his admission to the Royal Society. In 1661 Glan-
ville was no doubt proud of the following:

[4] Perry Miller, *The New England Mind* (New York, 1939), p. 323.

[5] W. S. Howell, *loc. cit.*, pp. 309-10. Professor Howell adds that at that moment
in history "social pressures were at work to bring these responsibilities together."
"Talaeus's rhetoric, with its exclusive emphasis upon these routines [tropes and
figures, voice and gesture], had increasingly less and less to say to the brave young
science of the seventeenth century, whereas that science meanwhile wanted nothing
so much as a theory of communication suitable to the transfer of experimental
knowledge from scientist to scientist and from scientist to public." For the reasons
indicated above, we suggest that the system of Ramus taken as a whole made its
own contribution toward the development of the plain scientific style and even
more toward that of the plain preaching style. Cf. Miller, *op. cit.*, Ch. XII, "The
Plain Style;" Walter J. Ong, "Peter Ramus and the Naming of Methodism," *JHI*,
XIV, 2 (April 1953), pp. 235-48.

If after a decoction of *hearbs* in a Winter-night, we expose the
liquor to the frigid air; we may observe in the morning under
a crust of Ice, the perfect appearance both in *figure*, and *colour*,
of the *Plants* that were taken from it. But if we break the *aqueous Crystal*, those pretty images dis-appear and are present[ly]
dissolved. Now these *airy Vegetables* are presumed to have
been made, by the reliques of these *plantal emissions* whose
avolation was prevented by the *condensed inclosure*. And therefore playing up and down for a while within their liquid prison,
they at last settle together in their natural order, and the *Atomes*
of each part finding out their proper place, at length rest in
their methodical Situation, till by breaking the *Ice* they are disturbed, and those counterfeit *compositions* are scatter'd into
their first Indivisibles.[6]

But in 1676:

   . . . after a decoction of Herbs in a frosty Night, the shape of
the Plants will appear under the Ice in the Morning: which
Images are supposed to be made by the congregated *Effluvia* of
the Plants themselves, which loosly wandring up and down in
the Water, at last settle in their natural place and order, and so
make up an appearance of the Herbs from whence they were
emitted.[7]

The Royal Society too inspired the most resolute effort of the age to
reduce natural language to the abstractness, regularity, and reliability of
mathematical symbols, a basic English and symbolic logic of that age.
This was Bishop John Wilkins' *Essay Towards a Real Character and a
Philosophical Language*, 1668—a system of "integral" and "particle"
shorthand that proved far too cryptic to be manageable.[8] And again, the
Royal Society, in its *History* (1667), written by a literary and religious
man, the biographer of the poet Cowley, Bishop Thomas Sprat, gives
us one of the age's most unvarnished statements concerning what was
conceived as the ideal relation between things and words:

    [6] *Vanity of Dogmatizing*, 1661, p. 46. Cf. R. F. Jones et al., *The Seventeenth
Century* (Stanford, 1951), pp. 89–93. The five essays of Professor Jones reprinted in
this volume are pioneer investigations of first importance to the theme pursued in
this chapter.

    [7] *Essays*, 1676, p. 11. The second and largely unrevised edition of Glanville's
Vanity, published in 1664 and entitled *Scepsis Scientifica*, contains a dedicatory
"Address to the Royal Society" in which he makes an advance announcement of
his change of heart about style. In his *Essay Concerning Preaching*, 1688, he was to
say: "Plainness is a character of great latitude and stands in opposition, First to *hard
words:* Secondly, to *deep and mysterious notions:* Thirdly, to *affected Rhetoricians:*
and Fourthly, to *Phantastical Phrases*" (Spingarn, II, 273).

    [8] Cf. Francis Christensen, "John Wilkins and the Royal Society's Reform of
Prose Style," *MLQ*, VII (1946), 179–87, 279–90.

They have therefore been most rigorous in putting in execution, the only Remedy, that can be found for this *extravagance:* and that has been, a constant Resolution, to reject all the amplifications, digressions, and swellings of style: to return back to the primitive purity, and shortness, when *men* deliver'd so many *things*, almost in an equal number of *words*. They have exacted from all their members, a close, naked, natural way of speaking: positive expressions; clear senses; a native easiness: bringing all things as near the Mathematical plainess, as they can.[9]

The later burlesque version of this ideal, in the Third Book of *Gulliver's Travels,* during the visit to the scientific Academy of Lagado, conveys very well the implications to which a literary man was bound to object.

The other project was a scheme for entirely abolishing all words whatsoever, and this was urged as a great advantage in point of health as well as brevity. . . . An expedient was therefore offered, that since words are only names for things, it would be more convenient for all men to carry about them such things as were necessary to express the particular business they are to discourse on. . . . many of the most learned and wise adhere to the new scheme of expressing themselves by things.[1]

Words and things, *res et verba*, was a theme which had come echoing down rhetorical corridors since the days of the Ciceronian *ratio et oratio* and Quintilian's *Curam ergo verborum rerum volo solicitudinem esse.*[2] But the 17th-century preoccupation with the theme laid a new emphasis on the naked "thing." The words they would somehow get around. "Few words are best when once we go a-Maying."

III

Such depreciation of the word had intimate connections with a simultaneous decline in respect for something which was then usually called "wit," and which we may describe approximately as the inventive or imaginative side either of poetic writing or of pulpit eloquence. (In the latter sphere, the root of the matter was supposed to be the religious quality of "enthusiasm." This inspired vain imagination and was

[9] *History of the Royal Society,* 1667, p. 112. ". . . and preferring the language of Artizans, Countryman, and Merchants, before that, of Wits, or Scholars." Contrast the views of Dryden described *ante* Chapter 11.

[1] *Gulliver's Travels,* Book Three, Chapter 5, Section 4.

[2] See the excellent discussion of the 17th-century situation by A. C. Howell, "*Res et Verba:* Words and Things," *ELH,* XIII (June, 1946), 131-42.

equally to be mistrusted.[3]) The history of the highly indigenous term and concept "wit" in 17th-century England was a disguised double progress, both a shifting in the value normally attributed to poetry and an accommodative shifting in the definition of a term so rich with value associations that it could only by a violent wrench of speaking habits have been abandoned. Let us conceive "wit," [4] a term which etymologically means the faculty of knowing in general (with either mind or senses) and which about the time of Shakespeare comes to mean smart knowing, joking, or repartee, invention or ingenuity, and even poetic keenness or fancy. Then, as the idea of ingenuity, the metaphysical *discordia concors*, becomes for a time more firmly attached to the idea of poetry, "wit" in the days of Cowley and the youthful Dryden comes to be almost equivalent to poetry itself or to the main principle of poetry. It is almost synonymous with "imagination" and "fancy." It is defined analytically as the faculty of seeing difficult resemblances between largely unlike objects—and in practice it is the enforcement of such resemblances by all the verbal resources available. At this juncture, however, arises the complication of a growing philosophical and scientific stress on the desirability, not of conceiving resemblances between things (too much of that, on slender grounds, in the poets and orators already), but of discerning differences. In short, an emphasis on analysis rather than synthesis. And the faculty of analysis is called, in distinction from "wit," "judgment." Classical notions of decorum and fitness to nature are highly compatible with this philosophic "judgment." For a time philosophy (or science) and neo-classical humanism walk evenly together.

Bacon had described the two powers—that of perceiving resemblances and that of perceiving differences—in the Latin of his *Novum Organum* (I, 55) without recourse to either of the terms "wit" or "judgment." And it may be well if we try to think of those powers, or the concepts of them, taken neutrally, as relatively stable concepts behind a considerable activity of the term "wit," an effort as it were on the part of that agile term to keep up with the center of value which not only in philosophy but in poetry was shifting from the pole of imagination or seeing resemblances to that of judgment or seeing differences. "Imagination" and "fancy" had to stay more or less on one side of the polarity, and so did "judgment." But "wit," because of its near synonymity with "poetry," had to move as the implicit concept of good poetry moved. It is only thus that one can explain, from

---

[3] Donald F. Bond, " 'Distrust' of Imagination in English Neo-Classicism," *SP*, XXX (1933), 571–603; George Williamson, "The Restoration Revolt Against Enthusiasm," *SP*, XXX (October, 1933), 571–603.

[4] See W. L. Ustick and H. H. Hudson, "Wit, 'Mixt Wit,' and the Bee in Amber," *Huntington Library Bulletin*, VIII (October, 1935), 103–30; Murray W. Bundy, "Wit," in *Dictionary of World Literature*, ed. Joseph T. Shipley (New York, 1943).

the inside as it were, the successive uses of the term "wit" by single writers, like Dryden or Hobbes. In the Preface to his *Annus Mirabilis*, 1666, Dryden says:

> *Wit writing* . . . is no other than the faculty of imagination in the writer, which, like a nimble spaniel, beats over and ranges through the field of memory . . . , *Wit written is* . . . the happy result of thought, or product of imagination.[5]

In his *Defence of the Epilogue*, 1672, we find him canvassing a double definition of "wit." There is "wit in the stricter sense, that is, sharpness of conceit," a thing which Ben Jonson's comedy of "humour" does not have. At the same time:

> Ben Johnson . . . always writ properly, and as the character required; and I will not contest farther with my friends who call that wit; it being very certain, that even folly itself, well represented, is wit in a larger signification.[6]

Then later, in the *Apology for Heroic Poetry*, 1677, we find Dryden completely embracing the tamer alternative.

> . . . the definition of Wit . . . is only this: that it is a propriety of thoughts and words; or, in other terms, thought and words elegantly adapted to the subject.[7]

As Dryden's courtly friend the Earl of Mulgrave put it in his *Essay Upon Poetry*, 1682:

> 'tis the top of wit
> T'express agreeably a thing that's fit.[8]

The epistemological groundswell which accounts for this dancing of the literary coracles may be seen very well in the philosophers Hobbes and Locke. Chapter VIII of Hobbes's *Leviathan* furnishes the following complicated, if not self-contradictory, instance of the mid-century commotion among the ideas associated with the term "wit." To make it easier to trace the activity of the term in this passage, we present what appear to be the crucial statements in a numbered list:

[5] Ker I, 14. Even at this date, Dryden, who had already outgrown his own metaphysical period (that of the verses lamenting the death of Lord Hastings), was inclined to view imagination as a faculty that needed restraint. Cf. the parallel image of the spaniel in the Epistle Dedicatory of *The Rival Ladies*, 1664. "For imagination in a poet is a faculty so wild and lawless that like an high-ranging spaniel, it must have clogs tied to it, lest it outrun the judgment" (Ker I, 8).

[6] Ker I, 172.

[7] Ker I, 190.

[8] Spingarn II, 294.

1. Naturall Wit, consisteth principally in two things; *Celerity of Imagining*, (that is, swift succession of one thought to another;) and *steddy direction* to some approved end. . . .

2. Those that observe their similitudes, in case they be such as are but rarely observed by others, are sayd to have a *Good Wit;* by which, in this occasion, is meant a *Good Fancy*. But they that observe their differences, and dissimilitudes; which is called *Distinguishing*, and *Discerning*, and *Judging* between thing and thing; in case such discerning be not easie, are said to have *good Judgement*. . . .

3. In a good Poem, whether it be *Epique* or *Dramatique;* as also in *Sonnets, Epigrams*, and other Pieces, both Judgement and Fancy are required: But the Fancy must be more eminent; because they please for the Extravagancy; but ought not to displease by Indiscretion.

4. In a good History, the Judgement must be eminent. . . . Fancy has no place, but onely in adorning the stile. In Orations of Prayse, and in Invectives, the Fancy is praedominant. . . .

5. And in any Discourse whatsoever, if the defect of Discretion be apparent, how extravagant soever the Fancy be, the whole discourse will be taken for a signe of want of wit; and so will it never when the Discretion is manifest, though the Fancy be never so ordinary. . . .

6. Judgement therefore without Fancy is Wit, but Fancy without Judgement not.

In the following passages from Locke's *Essay Concerning Human Understanding* (1690) the clear reference of the term "wit" to a faculty of seeing resemblances is a reversion to earlier usage, but the spirit is none the less Hobbesian and anti-rhetorical; the role assigned to "wit" is not complimentary.

For *wit* lying most in the assemblage of ideas, and putting those together with quickness and variety, wherein can be found any resemblance or congruity, thereby to make up pleasant pictures and agreeable visions in the fancy; *judgment*, on the contrary, lies quite on the other side, in separating carefully, one from another, ideas wherein can be found the least difference, thereby to avoid being misled by similitude.—II, xi

Since wit and fancy find easier entertainment in the world than dry truth and real knowledge, figurative speeches and allusion in language will hardly be admitted as an imperfection or abuse of it. I confess, in discourses where we seek rather pleasure and delight than information and improvement, such ornaments as are borrowed from them can scarce pass for faults. But yet if we would speak of things as they are, we must allow that all the art of rhetoric, besides order and clearness; all the artificial and figurative application of words eloquence hath invented, are for nothing else but to insinuate wrong ideas, move the passions, and thereby mislead the judgment; and so indeed are perfect cheats. . . . —III, x

In one of his *Spectator* essays on "wit," No. 62, Joseph Addison, making some parade of acquaintance with the first of these passages from Locke, is confident that this, rather than Dryden's later equation of wit with propriety, is the correct account. Unlike Locke, Addison starts with the assumption that "wit" is a term of honor, but his approval is ingeniously qualified. With his introduction of the categories "False Wit" (consisting merely in resemblance between words—as in puns, anagrams, rhymes, acrostics, figure poems and the like) and "Mixed Wit" (consisting partly in resemblance between words and partly in resemblance between ideas—as, for example, in the "flames" and "ardors" of love in Cowley's *Mistress* [9]) Addison leans very heavily toward the side of "judgment." He gives us, within a metaphysical and neoclassical frame of reference, a shrewd enough anticipation of a technical question that in our own day has been much more urgently brought to the fore: To what extent and in what way is the auditory intimation of metaphoric insight a respectable poetic procedure? More directly: Isn't it true that poetry flourishes on puns? And how can this be defended?

The 17th-century campaign against imagination is sometimes said to have been directed against the extravagant or licentious use of that faculty or only against its use in certain places—in sermons, for example, or in scientific papers. And often enough attacks on imagination did include provisos that the author did not mean to censure the appearance of imagination in poetry, its native and appropriate place. The passage which we have quoted above from Hobbes might be put under this head.

---

[9] The conceits in Cowley's *Mistress* to which Addison refers—the cold eyes of the mistress as burning glasses, the secret message read by the flame of love—may well strike a modern reader as less clear examples of the pun than many in Donne or Herbert. We suggest that the punning effect of the Cowleyan conceit comes about as follows: An expression at some time metaphorical, such as "flame" of love, lapses into cliché; it becomes an entrenched and firmly authorized—though not an intensely realized—meaning. In a final stage, "flame" of love comes to mean something quite unrelated to "flame" of combustion, and one need not think at all of the latter when referring to the former. Then occurs the extravagant re-realization or galvanization of the original metaphoric sense through the Cowleyan conceit (reading a message by the flame of love), and the very extravagance of the realization, or testing, of the dormant metaphor suggests that Cowley has taken unfair advantage of an authoritative cliché metaphor—or perhaps of a mere phonetic accident—"flame[1]" and "flame[2]."

There were even active defenses of poetic imagination by literary men.[1] But so pervasive a change in epistemological assumptions and in norms of prose communication as that which we have been discussing could scarcely take place without affecting the adjacent art of poetry. Even nowadays, with all our revival of respect for Augustan English poetry, we hardly dispute the view that this was more regularly ordered, more restrained, decorous, and *prima facie* a more prosaic, mode of composition than Metaphysical or Elizabethan poetry. There is that much truth in the now discredited statement of Matthew Arnold that "Dryden and Pope are classics of our prose."

On the other hand, there is a peculiar sense in which Augustan practice, more than theory, escaped the rigor of the scientific mood. The achievement of Dryden and Pope was that they used the guise of an apparently level and rationalized, even prosaic, discourse to accomplish poetic expression of a certain character. Though Pope's imaginative forces may seem somewhat soberly drawn up and cautiously limited to the obvious, the ordered parallels and contrasts of his verse have their own way of framing and forcing implicit metaphoric alignments and ironic confrontations. Pope and Dryden and no less Swift (whose insidiously plain prose may be taken as a counterpart of the Augustan prosaic verse) are the grand rhetoriqueurs of the close of an age of rhetoric that had its antecedents in classical antiquity. Pope's verse stands near the end of the tradition, not as an instance of decline, but as the most intense neo-classic realization of the verbal artifice described in Aristotle's *Rhetoric* [2] and the socially idiomatic nicety intimated by Horace.

The age of Pope witnessed a strange lag between poetry and theory—a success for poetry which consisted in its being a hundred years behind the most advanced theory. The numerous and varied figures (mixed wit and false wit), antithesis, metaphor, pun and quasi-pun, Gothic rhyme, alliteration, turn, tranlacer, and agnomination, which actually mark the highly artful poetry of Alexander Pope, are scarcely alluded to in the reigning poetic treatise of his day, the *Art of Poetry* by Edward Bysshe.[3] In his burlesque critical work *Peri Bathous, or of the Art of Sinking in Poetry*, Pope himself betrays a decided relish for ridiculing the figures. For an enthusiastic account of many of the Popean figures and the specific recommendation of them as poetic techniques we must go back as far as the Elizabethans, to Fraunce's *Arcadian Rhetorike*, for instance, or to Puttenham's quaintly phrased repertoire:

[1] See the articles by Donald F. Bond and George Williamson cited *ante* p. 229.

[2] Cf. *ante* Chapter 4, p. 70. For an account of the rhetoric involved in Pope's "poetry of statement," see Maynard Mack, "Wit and Poetry and Pope: Some Observations on His Imagery," in *Pope and his Contemporaries, Essays Presented to George Sherburn* (Oxford, 1949), pp. 20–40.

[3] Bysshe's *Art* appeared first in 1701 and went through numerous editions during Pope's lifetime.

Mezozeugma, or the Middlemarcher
Sillepsis, or the double supply
Parison, or the figure of even
Traductio, or the tranlacer
Antitheton, or the quareller
Ploche, or the doubler
Ironia, or the drie mock
Meiosis, or the disabler
Micterismus, or the fleering frumpe
Charientismus, or the privie nippe
  ("These be souldiers to the figure *allegoria*
  and fight under the banner of dissimu-
  lation.")
Paradoxon, or the wonderer
Synecdoche, or the figure of quick conceit
Noema, or the figure of close conceit [4]

But even Puttenham, with his uneven collection of jokes and conceits and the theoretical hints which he musters to introduce them, falls far short of providing anything like an adequate rationale of either Renaissance or Augustan poems of any sort. The significance of Puttenham is that he testifies to a climate of ideas in which the poetic relevance of these rhetorical and conversational, ironic and jesting, artifices was safely to be assumed.

IV

But we have reached a point in our account of wit and rhetoric in the neo-classic age where some expansion of that theme is needed. A consideration of so important a figure as Alexander Pope requires, for one thing, the re-introduction into our argument and the reaccentuation of the theme of classical "imitation." Pope's most ambitious critical work, his verse *Essay on Criticism*, is written squarely in the tradition of the Horatian *Ars Poetica*. It is thus an "imitation" of a literary genre complicated by the fact that literary theory itself is the theme of the work to be executed. Let us dwell on this point momentarily by asserting that a literary theory which operates as an influence on the writing of a poem ought to be distinguished more often than perhaps it is from a literary theory which manages to appear in the poem itself. And both of these ought to be distinguished from yet a third thing, the theory which is unified with a work by being really exemplified or carried out in that work. Pope's *Essay* shows marked relations to the literary theory in all

[4] Atkins, *English Criticism*, II, 157, believes that the extensive treatment of the figures in Puttenham's *Arte* argues a date of composition before 1570.

three ways. He is not only influenced by the tradition and clearly enough
bent on talking *about* the tradition, but he is at the same time exemplifying
it—for he is writing a classical poem, an example of the Horatian *Ars*,
and an example which succeeds by its classical brilliance. The reason
for the relative inferiority of the most celebrated 16th-century Italian
re-enactment of Horace, the *De Arte Poetica* of Vida, is that Vida was
not enough of a poet to bring it off. He knew the rules very well, but
apparently not what they meant. And so his poem is memorable mostly
for a few of its echoes of Horace [5] and for its forthright nationalistic advice about plundering the Greek classics and worshiping Virgil.[6] Boileau's
Art Poétique, 1674, had been a far more amusing expansion of Aristotle
and Horace to encompass the several genres—epic, tragedy, comedy, pastoral, elegy, ode, sonnet, epigram, rondeau, ballade, madrigal, satire,
"vaudeville"—which were countenanced by French classicism. This poem
exhibited a certain interesting Gallic bias, as of classicism nationalized, and
a nicely reasonable wit. The clean Horatian and Aristotelian ring of
Boileau's formulas and their occasional satiric sting created his own kind
of authority.

La montagne en travail enfante une souris. III, 274

Qu'en savantes leçons votre muse fertile
Partout joigne au plaisant le solide et l'utile. IV, 87–8

Pour me tirer des pleurs, il faut que vous pleuriez. III, 142

Mais dans l'art dangereux de rimer et d'écrire,
Il n'est point de degrés du médiocre au pire. IV, 31–2

Toutefois aux grands coeurs donnez quelques foiblesses.
   III, 104

Conservez à chacun son propre caractère. III, 112

Il n'est point de serpent ni de monstre odieux,
Qui, par l'art imité, ne puisse plaire aux yeux. III, 1

Aimez donc la raison—I, 37

Que la nature donc soit votre étude unique,
Auteurs qui prétendez aux honneurs du comique. III, 359

Quelque sujet qu'on traite, ou plaisant, ou sublime,
Que toujours le bon sens s'accorde avec la rime. I, 27–8

Un sot trouve toujours un plus sot qui l'admire. I, 232

[5] See, for instance, I, 40 (*Atque tuis prudens genus elige viribus aptum*); III,
459–60 (*Non totam subito praeceps secura per urbem Carmina vulgabit*).
[6] Cf. *ante* Chapter 9, p. 161.

The highly finished resumés of classical norms, the jokes against the universal enemy, stupidity, the keen moral maxims, are bound to elicit admiration. Boileau's flash was followed within a few years by a series of similar efforts on the part of the English courtly critics, the "mob of gentlemen who wrote with ease": Rochester's *Allusion to the Tenth Satire of Horace* (in which Dryden is treated like the archaic crude poet Lucilius), 1680; Mulgrave's *Essay upon Poetry*, 1682; and Roscommon's translation of Horace's *Ars* and his *Essay on Translated Verse*, 1684. In Pope's day appeared the *Essay on Unnatural Flights in Poetry* by George Granville, 1701, Samuel Wesley's *Epistle to a Friend*, 1700, and other more or less lame instances of the genre. After Pope's precocious summation had appeared in 1711 there was nothing further for Englishmen to say in this area. By the title of this poem, not *An Essay on Poetry* but *An Essay on Criticism*, Pope appears to stand apart from the tradition in a new perspective. He appears to be raising the Art of Poetry to the second power. In actuality the notion of "criticism," when scrutinized, very readily becomes transparent, focussing telescopically on the more concrete matter of poetry itself, so that much of what Pope says is actually *De Arte Poetica*. At the same time his poem is never without the interest of a certain shimmer upon the surface through the implied dimension of criticism of criticism. The First Part of the poem, after the introductory wit, making the critic's job no less risky, responsible, and comically vulnerable than the poet's,

> 'Tis hard to say, if greater want of skill
> Appear in writing or in judging ill,   1–2

dwells on the theme of universal nature and the ancient models, sliding from that easily at the end to social observation upon the deplorable license of the last age. The Second Part enumerates causes of bad criticism, of which the greatest number are moral and psychological—pride, partisanship, snobbery, fashion, and the like ("Whatever nature has in worth denied, She gives in large recruits of needful pride"). But one of these causes—the bad habit of judging mere details, wit, diction, and verse, instead of whole poetic achievements—is of a very technical and objective sort. The discussion of it contains the heart of practical criticism in the *Essay*. The Third Part of the *Essay* is a history of the norms reflected in the first two parts, a recital of the great names of criticism—Aristotle, Horace, Quintilian, Longinus (who "is himself the great sublime he draws"), Boileau, Roscommon, and lastly, with a concluding dedication, Pope's boyhood monitor and promoter, the English gentleman critic, William Walsh. It was he who had repeatedly given Pope the advice that the last accomplishment left for an English poet was to be not only "great" but "correct."

V

THE theme of the present chapter is verbal rhetoric, but another theme of Pope's *Essay*, the prominent if elusive idea of "nature," claims some emphasis here, for Pope's main statement about rhetoric will turn out to be a prescription for some kind of improving conjunction or complementary interaction between the "wit" of rhetoric and the "nature" it deals with.

"Nature" (the object of artistic imitation) has for Pope three main features. First, Nature is a Platonic and Stoic universal order and superior reality:

> First follow Nature, and your judgment frame
> By her just standard, which is still the same.
> Unerring NATURE, still divinely bright,
> One clear, unchang'd, and universal light.
>
> —68–71

Secondly, Nature, the universal order, assimilates readily with man's effort to enforce or increase that order in his own affairs—that is, with his civilization and all its parts, his cities, institutions, businesses, and recreations. Pope's nature is the nature not only of Windsor Forest but of Hampton, Stowe, Twickenham, Drury Lane, Button's, and Grubstreet. It is the nature of socially ordered human conduct. Its antithesis is eccentricity or hyper-individualism. Another kind of nature, that known best to Rousseau and Wordsworth ("I heard a thousand blended notes, while in a grove I sate reclined . . .") was, to be sure, already well on the way in Pope's age. There are traces of it, primitivistic gleams, in Pope's *Essay on Man*. But it was not yet an open standard for poetry. That standard, and with it a hostile spotlight on the contrary element of civilization, was to come only after Pope's day—though not long after. Pope "stuck to describing *modern manners*," wrote Joseph Warton in 1782, "but these *manners*, because they are *familiar, uniform, artificial,* and *polished*, are, in their very nature unfit for any lofty effort of the Muse."[7]

Thirdly, Pope's idea of nature has the distinction of residing in a state of great harmony with the idea of the classical models. No other poet or theorist has expressed the reconciliation of these threateningly twin standards[8]—the rivals, modern reason and classic authority—with such persuasive aplomb.

[7] *Essay on the Genius and Writings of Pope* (London, 1808), II, 401–3.

[8] Homage to classical models, as we have already noticed, did not disable the theory of cultural cycles among the Augustans—that as Roman literature has been

Nature and Homer were, he found, the same.—135

Those RULES of old discover'd, not devis'd,
Are Nature still, but Nature methodiz'd.—88–9

Still green with bays each ancient Altar stands,
Above the reach of sacrilegious hands.—181–2

But to turn now to the rhetorical part of Pope's *Essay*, that concerning the technical reasons for bad criticism: it may be observed first that Pope seems guilty of a certain shifting between two pairs of coordinates, part-whole and aim-effect (or means-end).

In ev'ry work regard the writer's End,
Since none can compass more than they intend.—255–6

Survey the WHOLE, nor seek slight faults to find.—235

Here is an alternation of concepts which has often been paralleled—in certain 20th-century criticism, for instance, written along lines very much different from Pope's.[9] But the confusion straightens out in the ensuing passage on "wit," "diction," and "verse." The last of these topics is the occasion for a brilliant display of literary theory under two complementary aspects which we have mentioned above—that of assertion and that of exemplification. In a criticism preoccupied with the idea that poetry is an imitation of nature (and a loving if superior sister of other imitative arts—music and painting)[1]—it was reasonable to bestow a close attention on any poetic feature which could be shown to be not merely statement about nature but in some peculiar way direct imitation. The theme of "representative" verse, as Samuel Johnson was to term it, was a native of the classical climate. In his *Spectator* No. 253, reviewing Pope's *Essay*, Addison quotes the best-known antique locus, the passage by Dionysius of Halicarnassus praising the artful reality—the heavy labor and the sudden drop—of Homer's verses in which Sisyphus rolls up hill the continually relapsing stone. One of the most original passages in Vida's *De Arte Poetica* was a repetitive demonstration of six main metrically imitative effects: heavy, light, slow, fast, rough, smooth. The

---

refined from Naevius to Virgil, so English, from Chaucer to Dryden. Pope was on defensible, if somewhat ambiguous, ground when in the maturity of his satirical *Epistle to Augustus* he imitated Horace:
   Had ancient times conspir'd to disallow
   What then was new, what had been ancient now?   135–6
   [9] See *post*, Chapter 27 pp. 624–5, comment on I. A. Richards' *Principles of Literary Criticism*.
   [1] See *post* p. 274 and Robert J. Allen, "Pope and the Sister Arts," in *Pope and his Contemporaries, Essays Presented to George Sherburn* (Oxford, 1949). The passage on representative verse in the *Essay on Criticism* has a counterpart on music in *Dunciad* IV, 3–70, where Pope defends Handel's supposed mimetic re-enforcement of his chorus by cannon. "But soon, ah soon, Rebellion will commence, If music meanly borrows aid from sense."

parallel passage by Pope is much more economical and pointed. In a space of 29 lines Pope simultaneously states and illustrates some nine prosodic principles. Thus, the fault of hiatus, three times in one line:

> Tho' oft the ear the open vowels tire. . . .   345

(where just the opposite of Milton's natural rule of elision is called for in order to have enough syllables for the pentameter). Or the atomically structured monosyllabic line:

> And ten low words oft creep in one dull line.—347

Or stereotyped rhymes:

> Where-e'er you find "the cooling western breeze,"
> In the next line, it "whispers thro' the trees:"
> When crystal streams "with pleasing murmurs creep,"
> The reader's threaten'd (not in vain) with "sleep."—350-3

And then that attractive matter of "representation," comprising the last six of Pope's principles:

> 'Tis not enough no harshness gives offence,
> The sound must seem an Echo to the sense.—364-5

The "hoarse rough verse" for the "roaring torrent," the "smoother numbers" in which the "smooth stream flows," the heavy labor of Ajax ("The line too labors, and the words move slow"), and, most striking of all, the contrasting hexameters, one off-beat, spondaic, and slow, the other precisely and elliptically fast.

> A needless Alexandrine ends the song,
> That, like a wounded snake, drags its slow length along.—356-7

> Not so, when swift Camilla scours the plain,
> Flies o'er th' unbending corn, and skims along the main.—372-3

In a series of shrewd *Rambler* inquiries into metrical realism, Samuel Johnson was to indulge in too much skepticism about this Popean *tour de force*. There can scarcely be any question that Pope here demonstrates how the Alexandrine (so often used, along with the triplet, for special purposes in the narrative verse of Dryden [2]) is capable of exactly contrasting effects. It is no refutation of his doctrine to observe that such effects are always highly generic or schematic, taking their specific feel from the sense of the lines, as the chameleon takes its color from the grass. The precise limits of metrical imitation and the wider range of phonetic properties or "orchestrations" distinguished by modern schol-

---

[2] Cf. Pope's *Epistle to Augustus*, ll. 267-9: "Waller was smooth; but Dryden taught to join . . . The long majestic March, and Energy divine."

ars [3] (and indeed recognized in the repertory of Renaissance figures) would be an inquiry of more technical nicety than is needed for the present argument.

Concerning the second of the three technical details named above—"diction"—Pope's formula in the *Essay on Criticism* is a neat approximation to the Horatian rule of idiom which we have already quoted in Pope's words, in our chapter on Horace.[4] Be neither archaic nor new-fangled, use the living language of your day, avoid both the flat and the highfalutin. Some further specifications but also some complications appear when we explore other statements by Pope. "Shut, shut the door, good John! fatigu'd I said, Tye up the knocker, say I'm sick, I'm dead." The opening of the *Epistle to Arbuthnot* is a neat complement to one of the burlesque rules of the *Peri-Bathous*, that for "the Buskin or stately" style: "Will not every true lover of the Profund be delighted to behold the most vulgar and low actions of life exalted. . . ?" Instead of "Shut the Door," say "The wooden guardian of our privacy quick on its axle turn." On the other hand there are Pope's *Pastorals* and his Homer and the whole matter of "poetic diction." As Isaac Watts said and Samuel Johnson was to repeat, there was "scarcely a happy combination of words or a phrase poetically elegant in the English language" which Pope was not skilful enough to "insert" in his Homer.

To come then to the last, and most important, of our three technical details,—that is to say, "wit"—Alexander Pope's *Essay on Criticism*, if we view it in the perspective of 17th-century history already outlined in this chapter, is remarkable less for any theoretical contribution to the problem of "wit" that for his artful management of the large repertory of intimations which the term "wit" had acquired by his time. Poet, critic, salon joker—mind, thinking, speech—what is brilliant, inventive, poetic—what is critical, mocking, affected, specious, frivolous—such gradations and oppositions of meaning play in and out of the 46 occurrences of the key term "wit" in Pope's *Essay*.

> For wit and judgment often are at strife,
> Tho' meant each other's aid, like man and wife.—82–3
>
> Nay wits had pensions, and young Lords had wit.—539
>
> Some have at first for Wits, then Poets past,
> Turn'd Critics next, and prov'd plain fools at last.—36–7
>
> Pleas'd with a work where nothing's just or fit;
> One glaring Chaos and wild heap of wit.—291–2
>
> True wit is Nature to advantage dress'd;
> What oft was thought, but ne'er so well express'd.—297–8

[3] Wellek and Warren, pp. 164 ff.
[4] See *ante* Chapter 5, pp. 87–8.

"Wit" is a kind of genteel slang word in Pope's day—a handy instrument of "complex structure" capable of being managed so as to intimate a number of "equations" between the ideas which it implicates.[5] At the sociocritical level, Pope is slyly urging (though with all kinds of momentary ironies and reversals) the case for the aristocratic wit which Dryden had announced in the essays of his most courtly phase. The witty man of the salon, the master of elegance in conversation, gives us the best idea of what an appreciator and critic of poetry ought to be, and this composite figure, the salon conversationalist and critic, provides us in turn with our paradigm of the poet or at least of the gifts and outlook the poet ought to have. As the Tory gentlemen and high churchmen who constituted the party of wit in Pope's day were the political opponents and social superiors of the rising generation of middle-class dissenters, so the gentlemanly standard of wit aroused the partizans of middle-class sobriety and "good sense" to violent resentment.[6] Sir Richard Blackmore (Homer of the modern profound) published, among other attacks on "wit," his *Satyr Against Wit* in 1699. He was promptly answered by a combination of wits in the scurrilous volume entitled *Commendatory Verses* and was defended by his friends in a retaliation entitled *Discommendatory Verses*. The squabble was mean on both sides, but the main ideas of Blackmore are worth noticing. Wit as Blackmore saw it was not, as in the later phrase of Johnson, a principle of "vitality," but actually a principle of universal corruption. The influence of Will's Coffee House —"Dryden and his crew"—was debauching not only literature but all virtue, public and private,—business, arts, the church, the legal profession. Wit was soft, loose, degenerate, insane; it wanted the traditional "noble roughness" of the British temper.

> Felonious *G*[*arth*] pursuing this Design,
> Smuggles *French* Wit, as others Silks and Wine.

The rhetoric of the remedy proposed was founded on images of solid commercial virtue.

> If once the Muses Chequer would deny
> To take false Wit, 'twould lose its currency.

Let Congreve, Southerne, Wycherley, and especially Dryden, be melted down and coined into new, sound wit (good sense) and a safe national balance be deposited in a new Bank of Wit administered by Sheffield and other more conservative lords.

---

[5] William Empson, " 'Wit' in the *Essay of Criticism*," *Hudson Review*, II (Winter 1950), 559–77.

[6] See Robert M. Krapp, "Class Analysis of a Literary Controversy, Wit and Sense in Seventeenth-Century English Literature," *Science and Society*, X (Winter, 1946), 80–92.

These are good men, in whom we all agree,
Their Notes for Wit are good Security.[7]

So a form of rhetoric had a social tone and implied a social content. The deepest matter and meaning of Pope's poems was tied in to what was considered by the bourgeois men of sense as the frivolity and immorality of a brilliant form. And this depth of correspondence is what we should hope to find in any period where we could sample first-class literature. But here we have more to do with Pope's expressed theory. The last quotation in the series from Pope above is his famous definition of "wit" and hence of poetry, his epigrammatic reconciliation of the terms "wit" and "nature" by the mediation of the third term "dress," a reconciliation which may be said to resound with all the social implications of the view of nature which Pope entertained. This aphorism no more describes the "meaning" of Pope's own poetry in its fullness than the phrase "emotion recollected in tranquillity" does that of Wordsworth. But since a conspicuous part of Pope's meaning does lie in a high degree of verbal brilliance (a feature perfectly in keeping with and indeed impossible without an internal or abstract meaning of a certain witty sort), the aphorism has seemed to the post-romantic mind an all-too-apt expression of the superficiality of neo-classic rhetorical practice. The statement, both as specific theory of Augustan poetry and as general theory, is in fact disappointing. It is a kind of minimum classical stand, a last-ditch defense of wit-theory after a century more or less of the empirical assault. It is the wittily summarized dilemma of the classic mind in confrontation with the scientific, a reflection of the tightened poetic defense, the apparently prosaic and stripped-down wit of the neo-classic retreat from the metaphysical.

To give Pope's aphorism its due, on the other hand, one can hardly pretend that it does not offer us a sort of token, or temporary expression, for a paradoxical idea which is always residual in attempts to rationalize poetry—the ultimate surrender of theory in its attempt to reduce poetic meaning to the kinds of rational or philosophic meaning on which in some sense and in part it does depend. The element of "dress" (so repugnant under that figure to the romantic mind) is never quite squeezed out of poetic theory except by a rigorous extreme of idealistic symbolism. Samuel Johnson was to object that Pope's definition of wit depressed it "below its natural dignity," "reduced it from strength of thought to happiness of language." But Johnson himself, suffering along with the rest of his generation from an even more advanced phase of the scientific division between argument and elocution (and so rejecting energetically the metaphysical *discordia concors*), could offer as substitute only a defi-

[7] Richard Boys, *Sir Richard Blackmore and the Wits* (Ann Arbor, 1949), pp. 7-13.

nition close to the terms of "familiarity" and "surprise" provided by the psychological aesthetics of the century. He found "more noble and adequate" than Pope's view the compromise view of wit as "that which though not obvious is, upon its first production, acknowledged to be just." [8]

In Johnson's day the word "wit" was well on the way to becoming only a relic of serious criticism. Johnson was writing in retrospect. The ambiguous reference to the poetically imaginative and the nimbly amusing which "wit" had enjoyed from Elizabethan times was split during the neo-classic age into the meaning of "propriety" which we have observed and a second and lighter meaning of "sheer wit" or repartee in comedy.[9] As the wit which was equated with poetry (the respectable wit of propriety) sank before certain kinds of pre-romantic imagination, the wit of the comic became associated with more disagreeable and trivial forms of laughter, with raillery, ridicule, and nasty satire. (Satiric criticism, as we have suggested in Chapter 11, was at the same time softening into the roly-poly kind of "humour.") During the 18th century such associations seem to have gained ground, until the term "wit" assumed something like the vague and degraded meaning which is still popular in the 20th century—a form of the ludicrous more smart than humour. The definition framed by the literary gentleman Corbyn Morris in his *Essay Towards Fixing the True Standards of Wit, Humour, Raillery, Satire, and Ridicule*, 1744, might seem not unpromising:

> Wit is the Lustre resulting from the quick Elucidation of one Subject, by a just and unexpected Arrangement of it with another Subject.—p. 1

But it soon appears (pp. 3–4) that the quality of being "quick" and "unexpected" is what distinguishes "wit" from both "simile" and "metaphor," and then come the examples.

> Upon the Restoration Mr. Waller presented a congratulatory Copy of Verses to King Charles; His Majesty, after reading them, said,—Mr. Waller, these are very good, but not so fine as you made upon the PROTECTOR:—to which Mr. Waller return'd,—Your Majesty will please to recollect that we Poets always write best upon FICTIONS.—p. 7

In short, wit appears as joke or repartee.

---

[8] Johnson minimizes the Addisonian idea of surprise, yet relies on it. See his *Life of Cowley*, in *Lives of the Poets*, ed. G. B. Hill (Oxford, 1905), I, 19–20 and Appendix F. In the couplet following that to which Johnson objected Pope had written: "Something, whose truth convinc'd at sight we find, That gives us back the image of our mind."

[9] Spingarn, *Essays* I, lviii.

VII

To RETURN to Pope: the fact that neo-classic performance itself remained more complicated than the neo-classic theoretical assertion points up a principle which we may now urge a little more insistently than earlier in this chapter: namely, that in the 17th-century decline of rhetoric celebrated by Croce, at least two main things took place. (1) There was a shift in *theory* of style from the extravagance of Renaissance Aristotelianism and Ciceronianism to the theory of the Royal-Society era that words should be strictly tied down to things. And (2) at the same time there was a shift from certain Baroque forms of flamboyance (as in the actual prose of Browne or the verse of Donne) either to a fully plain form (like the scientific prose of the Royal Society) or to a superficially plain form (like the conversational verse of Dryden and Pope). It is of great importance to note that these two shifts (one of theory and one of performance) were not identical, nor even inevitably tied together, nor in a step-for-step relation—especially if we take the theoretical shift broadly as a shift from a theory of ornamentalism to a theory of stylistic integration. Within certain limits it has been possible, at various times in literary history, for either kind of theory (ornamental or integrational) to refer to either kind of style (flamboyant or simple). Most obviously, it has been possible for one of the theories, that of integrated style, to have a very wide range of applications. When Sprat in his *History of the Royal Society* spoke of "so many things almost in an equal number of words," he had in mind a use of words so severely limited to a certain kind of human experience (the scientifically factual) that he was content to make no demand whatever on a considerable range of important linguistic powers—the metaphysical, the moral, the poetic, the rhetorical. Such levels of meaning were inevitably irrelevant and merely ornamental in the program of research and reporting which the Royal Society was mapping out for itself. Sprat, that is, hardly meant the same thing as Pascal (a scientist of different affiliations) when the latter said, "*La vraie éloquence se moque de l'éloquence.*" Again, Sprat hardly meant the same thing as Swift (the satirist of Royal-Society thing-speech) when the latter wrote, "Proper words in proper places, make the true definition of a style." [1] And again, probably neither Pascal nor Swift had arrived at the advanced stage of expressionism which in the 19th century permitted so traditionally minded and patristically eloquent a writer as Cardinal Newman to write:

> Thought and meaning are inseparable from each other. Matter and expression are parts of one: style is a thinking out into lan-

[1] *A Letter to a Young Clergyman, Lately Entered into Holy Orders,* 1721.

guage. . . . When we can separate light and illumination, life and motion, the convex and the concave of a curve . . . then will it be conceivable that the . . . intellect should renounce its own double.[2]

To explore the issue for a moment in the opposite direction: it may be worth while to compare the turn and emphasis of Pope's couplet definition of wit with certain more awkward betrayals. That of Dryden, for instance, in the Preface to his *Fables:*

Words are the colouring of the work, which, in the order of nature, is last to be considered. The design, the disposition, the manners, and the thoughts, are all before it.[3]

Or that of Gildon in his *Complete Art of Poetry*, 1718:

As for your Ladyship's *fine Things*, and *fine Language*, to prefer them to more charming, and more essential excellencies, wou'd be as ridiculous, as to prefer your Ladyship's *Dress* to your *Person*.[4]

Or the debasing definition of the anti-wit Blackmore:

Wit is a Qualification of the Mind, that rises and enlivens cold Sentiments and plain Propositions, by giving them an elegant and Surprising Turn.[5]

An expression of ornamentalist theory when it takes a form like Pope's couplet means something a little different from what a less guarded expression means. And the general theory of ornamentalism means one thing when applied to the verse of Blackmore and another when applied to that of Pope himself.

VIII

THE large part of a century that follows the effort of Pope, before the rise of romantic theory, produces, as we have already suggested, only a more or less dismal continuation of the ornamentalist view concerning

[2] "Literature, a Lecture in the School of Philosophy and Letters," 1858, in *The Idea of a University* (London, 1907), pp. 276–7.

[3] Ker II, 252. L. I. Bredvold, *Selected Poems of Alexander Pope* (New York, 1926), pp. xvi–xvii, quotes the opinion of the French academician LeBrun that "design imitates all *real* things, whereas color only imitates that which is accidental." Cf. *post*, Chapter 13, p. 264.

[4] Durham, p. 36. Cf. Samuel Wesley, *Epistle to a Friend* (London 1700), p. 15: "Style is the dress of thought."

[5] *Essay upon Wit, in Essays Upon Several Subjects*, 1716, p. 191, quoted by Boys, *op. cit.*, p. 10. Cf. the edition of Blackmore's *Essay* by Boys (Ann Arbor, 1946).

metaphor and related figures. The ancient defense of the dignity of verbal powers was slowing to a standstill. At the same time, let us note it here, a new concept of verbal power was in the early phases of development, although this concept, because of geographical and cultural distances, seems to have had for about a hundred years no direct influence upon any English man of letters. Modern scholarship has been interested to discover in certain late 17th-century Italian criticism antecedents of "pre-romantic" ideas which appeared during the 18th century in England. In a broader perspective, the most important new critical idea of the early eighteenth century was that concerning metaphor and its relation to the rise of human institutions which was announced in the *New Science* of the Neapolitan professor Giambattista Vico, published first in 1725. Vico was a reactionary against 17th-century rationalism. Where the English empiricist Hobbes imagined primitive man as thinking just like Hobbes himself (in a scientifically calculating way) and coming to abstract conclusions about the desirability of social conventions, and where Sprat, as we have seen, believed in a "primitive purity and shortness," by which words matched things in a terse economy, the Italian jurisconsult and rhetorician conceived man in the early phases of human culture, the patriarchal and the heroic, as groping dimly and imaginatively, through symbols, myths, and nascent metaphors, toward the abstract speculations which in later phases of civilization bring on the anemia of spirit and decrepitudes which we know. It was a form of primitivism and a theory of history which not only for 19th-century historiographers but for neo-idealist philosophers and theorists of poetic imagination was to seem increasingly important in retrospect.

Vico died in 1744 at about the age of 74. It is a less striking coincidence that his younger but rhetorically archaic British contemporary Alexander Pope should have died in the same year than that in 1743 Pope should have published his Greater *Dunciad*. The revised Fourth Book of the *Dunciad*, especially in its sublimely chaotic and profoundly dark conclusion, is a burlesque celebration of the "word," so radical, so metaphysical, Platonic, and Patristic, that it goes far to return the neo-classic argument to a place in its history where it connects with the remote sources of Vichian and romantic symbolism. The Fourth *Dunciad*, a climactic afterthought to the rest of the poem (and a grand climax to Pope's whole career) presents a vast levee of courtiers before the throne of Dulness, "bard and blockhead side by side," a throng of crank patrons, virtuosos, pedagogues, scholars, tutors, and publicists, all the false educators by whom the mind of youth and that of more mature imbecility are formed. Even at the outset the event is made safe by the knockout and imprisonment of two ancient guardians of sense (members of the classical trivium).

> There foam'd rebellious *Logic*, gagg'd and bound,
> There, stript, fair *Rhet'ric* languish'd on the ground;
> His blunted Arms by *Sophistry* are born,
> And shameless *Billingsgate* her Robes adorn.

In the chiaroscuro nightmare which follows, as the champions advance to the throne, they repeat no theme more often than that of the "word" and its abuses.

> . . . Since Man from beast by Words is known,
> Words are Man's province, Words we teach alone. 149–50

> Confine the thought, to exercise the breath;
> And keep them in the pale of Words till death. 159–60

> Give law to Words, or war with Words alone. 178

> 'Tis true, on Words is still our whole debate. 219

> First slave to Words, then vassal to a Name. 501

The concluding crescendo of the poem is an extraordinary recapitulation in negative of the rhetorico-metaphysical tradition.

> *Wit* shoots in vain its momentary fires,
>
> *Art* after *Art* goes out, and all is Night.
>
> *Physic* of *Metaphysic* begs defence,
> And *Metaphysic* calls for aid on *Sense!*

The last lines reach out for the utmost metaphysical and theological implications of the "word," not only the human but the divine creative act, the "logos." Not only grammarian, rhetorician, and poet, but Academician, Church Father, neo-Platonist, scholastic theologian, and aesthetician of "light," have contributed to the edifice of humanistic intelligence which appears in the darkly brilliant subverted image of this denouement.

> Lo! thy dread Empire, CHAOS! is restor'd;
> Light dies before thy uncreating word.

SUPPLEMENT

But in order to discover with perfect clearness and precision the importance of literature, both in its original destination, and in the power which it certainly exerts on the worth and welfare of nations, let us for a moment consider it under both of these aspects. And, in the first place, let us regard the true nature and object, the wide extent, and original dignity of literature. Under this name, then, I comprehend all those arts and sciences, and all those mental exertions which have human life, and man himself, for their object; but which, manifesting themselves in no external effect, energise only in thought and speech, and without requiring any corporeal matter on which to operate, display intellect as embodied in written language. Under this are included, first, the art of poetry, and the kindred art of narration or history; next, all those higher exertions of pure reason and intellect which have human life and man himself for their object, and which have influence upon both; and, last of all, eloquence and wit, whenever these do not escape in the fleeting vehicle of oral communication, but remain displayed in the more substantial and lasting form of written productions. And when I have enumerated these, I imagine I have comprehended almost everything which can enter into the composition of the intellectual life of man.—With the single exception of reason,—and even reason can scarcely operate without the intervention of language—is there anything more important to man, more peculiar to him, or more inseparable from his nature than speech? Nature indeed could not have bestowed on us a gift more precious than the human voice, which, possessing sounds for the expression of every feeling, and being capable of distinctions as minute, and combinations as intricate, as the most complex instrument of music, is thus enabled to furnish materials so admirable for the formation of artificial language. The greatest and most important discovery of human ingenuity is writing; there is no impiety in saying that it was scarcely in the power of the Deity to confer on man a more glorious present than LANGUAGE, by the medium of which he himself has been revealed to us, and which affords at once the strongest bond of union, and the best instrument of communication. So inseparable indeed are mind and language, so identically one are thought and speech, that although we must always hold reason to be the great characteristic and peculiar attribute of man, yet language also, when we regard its original object and intrinsic dignity, is well entitled to be considered as a component part of the intellectual structure of our being. And although, in strict application and rigid expression, thought and speech always are, and always must be regarded as two things metaphysically distinct,—yet there only can we find these two elements in disunion, where one or both have been employed imperfectly or amiss. Nay, such is the effect of the original union or identity that, in their most extensive varieties of application, they can never be totally disunited, but must always remain inseparable, and every where be exerted in combination.

However greatly both of these high gifts, which are so essentially the same,—these, the proudest distinctions of human nature, which have made man what he is, may be in many instances misdirected and abused; still our innate and indestructible sense of the original dignity of speech and language, is sufficiently manifest, from the importance which we attach to them, in the formation of all our particular judgments and opinions. What influence the art of speaking has upon our judgment in the affairs of active life, and in all the relations of society,—what power the force of expression every where exerts over our thoughts, it would be superfluous to detail. The same considerations which govern us in our judgment of individuals, determine us also in our opinions concerning nations; and we are at once disposed to look upon that people as the most enlightened and the most polished, which makes use of the most clear, precise, appropriate, and agreeable medium of expression: insomuch, that we not unfrequently allow ourselves to be biassed even to weakness by the external advantage of diction and utterance, and pay more attention to the vehicle than to the intrinsic value of the thoughts themselves, or the moral character of those from whom they proceed.

—Friedrich von Schlegel, *Lectures on the History of Literature, Ancient and Modern* (1811), trans. J. G. Lockhart (Philadelphia, 1818), I, 10–13, Lecture I.

Because of its peculiar insistence on remaining concreted within the act of apprehension itself, a poem resists the very abstraction by which we would understand it. Abstraction, in one way or another, destroys it, dissolves it away. So we must content ourselves largely with simply apprehending the poem by reading or hearing it read, and as for any strict understanding of a poem, we must content ourselves with thinking and talking *around* it. Thomas does not put it in exactly the same words, but when he speaks of its 'deficiency of truth,' he is concerned with the same thing about a poem which prompts Mr. Archibald MacLeish to observe that 'A poem should not mean/ But be.'

Yet it would be inaccurate to say that we have no understanding at all of poetry. We do find ourselves able to think about it, which means that somehow or other our understanding is concerned with it. What we are doing is approaching it by a kind of indirection—this fact is attested to by the constant resort to metaphor which the most rigorous discussion of poetry seems inexorably to demand. A poem seems unable to forego this minimum of concretion even in being discussed. And in so far as it will not submit fully to abstraction but must retain the concretion of metaphor, it escapes reason. Not that it is against reason, anti-rational. Reason is an imperfect way of getting at a thing: it implies a special approach, it produces understanding only under certain conditions, and those things which are not amenable to these conditions simply escape it.

Hence poetry really demands too much of the reason in its insistence both that it be understood, and that it be understood somehow without resort to abstractions. From this fact arises the strain, which Thomas supposes as a matter of common observation, the state of tension in which poetry leaves reason. Plato had some warrant, after all, for barring poets from his republic: they do violence to and unsettle the reason on which his political order was to have been based.

In this connection Thomas says nothing specifically about the use of conceit. But the implications of his view are plain. If poetry implies a sort of rational derangement, an unmanagableness, a non-integration on the rational level in the face of a unity perceptible in other ways (the unity of impression, the unity of perception in a poem), *the superlative derangement inherent in the conceit*, which by operating through devices such as paradox maintains a sense of order in disorder and disorder in order, *stands as a kind of paragon of procedure in a poetic economy*.

Perhaps the most familiar instance of wit in St Thomas Aquinas's poetry is a couplet in the vesper hymm *Pange Lingua* written for the office of Corpus Christi, where it still occurs in the Roman breviary:

> *Verbum caro panem verum*
> *Verbo carnem efficit.*

This multi-dimensional conceit is a variant of one of the paradoxes consequent upon the Incarnation of the Word of God, and in availing himself of it, Thomas is tapping a source which lies at the innermost heart of Christian doctrine. . . . This is the same theology of the Word which has proved a limitless source of conceits not only for mediaeval theologians but also for patristic rhetoricians, for seventeenth-century Englishmen, and for contemporary poets interested in the metaphysical tradition. St Thomas is moving over ground to which wit poetry has never relinquished its claim. One conceit, for instance, is to be found in all the three groups of writers just mentioned. St Augustine uses in a sermon the paradox of the *Verbum infans*, Who was not only the infant Word, the child Jesus, but, to take the Latin *infans* in its full etymological force, the unspeaking Word. A strange and startling paradox, but an unmistakable dogmatic fact, that the Word of God initiates His personal mission among men in the inarticulate role of a child. The identical paradox is remarked later by Lancelot Andrewes in a sermon on the Incarnation: 'What, *Verbum infans*, the Word of an infant? The Word, and not to be able to speak a word.' And from Andrewes' world, that of the English 'metaphysicals,' the same conceit makes its way into Mr. T. S. Eliot's *Gerontion*.

> —Walter J. Ong, "Wit and Mystery: A Revaluation in Mediaeval Hymnody," *Speculum*, XXII (July, 1947), 326–7, 316–17, by permission of the author and The Mediaeval Academy of America

As the art of discourse or speaking, or of teaching, dialectic or logic had a definite connection with the audile and with words as sounds, with the definite personalist and existentialist implications which attach to a world of voices. Ramus arrives on the scene at the time this dialectic is being "simplified" in an operation which is among the most complicated and critical and central in the whole history of the human mind and out of which grows preoccupation with method and the whole modern mechanistic-minded world, for it must not be forgotten that, in theory and to a great extent in fact, dialectic or logic controlled all the other arts or sciences or curriculum subjects. This simplification of logic is connected with the humanists' determination to provide something adapted to the capacities of children, for humanism is pupil-centered, whereas the northern universities, essentially teachers' unions, were teacher-centered, tending to see their pupils not in terms of the pupils' capacities here and now, but as aspirant pedagogues. But the simplification is even more deeply related to a widespread and mysterious shift from the audile to the visile in the whole way of thinking about cognition and the nature of man. At the end of this shift, by the eighteenth century, God will become in the minds of many curiously mute, and by that fact depersonalized, a mere mechanic, a celestial architect, a mason, whose laws concern not the human consciousness but the ranging of objects in space. Man's notion of what he himself is will undergo a corresponding shift in emphasis.

Ramism is above all, although not exclusively, a manifestation of the subtle and apparently irresistible shift sacrificing auditorily oriented concepts for visually oriented ones which sets in with medieval scholasticism and on which most of the characteristic manifestations of the modern as against the ancient world depend. This shift is intimately connected with the scholastic emphasis on a logic which, as against more purely Aristotelian logic, was a kind of logistic, and on physics—a bad physics, but physics nevertheless, taught to millions of schoolboys from the thirteenth to the sixteenth century and later on a scale the ancient world had never even approximated. The shift is equally connected with the scholastic build-up of the teaching profession. It is connected with the invention of printing, with the emergence of book titles in their postincunabular form, with the development of a sense of format for communication encouraged by printing, with the humanists' attitude toward language—a thing controlled by the *written* word, the word committed to space, not by *living* speech—as well as with the belief that all revelation was contained in a book.

The shift manifests itself in Ramism particularly in Ramus's complete divorce between dialectic and rhetoric. For Ramus appears on the scene just when dialectic (or logic) was shifting from an art of discourse, as Cicero had had it and as Ramus's Latin definitions nominally have it, to an art of thinking or reasoning. As an art of discourse, dialectic had suggested an interplay of personalities, a give and take in an existentialist situation. As an art of thinking, it was carried on in the privacy of one's own head and in a fashion more and more diagrammatic, with greater and greater reliance on spatial analogies and a more or less overt desire to dispense with words as words, since these annoyingly hint that in some mysterious way thinking itself is always carried on in the presence—at least implicit—of another. The meaning of the well-known Ramist tables of dichotomies is to be sought here in the drift toward spatial analogies of any and all sorts. With dialectic separated from rhetoric as a kind of intellectual diagrammatics, rhetoric is left in absolute control of the world of sound as sound. But even here, the spatial imagination gains control, and rhetoric comes to be described as a kind of ornament conceivable in mechanico-spatial terms.

—Walter J. Ong, "Ramus and the Transit to the Modern Mind," *The Modern Schoolman*, XXXII (May, 1955), 307-9, copyrighted. By permission of the author and *The Modern Schoolman*.

ADDISON AND LESSING: POETRY AS PICTURES

§ *philosophy of sensation, Hobbes, Locke—II. Addison,*
Spectators *on imagination, a medley of themes: art and*
nature, pleasant and unpleasant, primary and secondary,
imagination and wit, ease and difficulty, nature's wit,
notion of sight compared with the neo-Platonic, lower
senses and the understanding—III. the rationalist alterna-
tive, Cartesianism, esprit géométrique, *seeing the world*
as it really is, without colors, guaranteed external causes
of beauty, gross or corpuscular, Burke, Lord Kames, the
sublime, immediacy and compulsion, Abbé Dubos on the
merits of a stew, Leibniz, Baumgarten, clear though con-
fused ideas (sensuous), the je-ne-sais-quoi, internal aes-
thetic sense, Hutcheson—IV. "aesthetic," the "fine arts,"
Batteux *and the Encyclopedists, parallels between the arts,*
ancient hints: Aristotle, Simonides, Cicero, Horace, Du
Fresnoy's De Arte Graphica, *two meanings of* ut pictura
poesis, *literary influence on painting, Aristotelian critique*
of Poussin's "Fall of Manna," painting the passions, paint-
erly influence on literature, toward sensation and land-
scape, Claude and Rosa, James Thomson, landscape gar-
dening—V. virtuoso and Hellenizing trends, Spence's
Polymetis, *Count Caylus, Winckelmann, Lessing's La-*
okoon, *the sculptural group and Virgil, difference be-*
tween painting and poetry before Lessing, time and space,
actions and objects, 18th-century nature poetry, Lessing's
insight, Goethe's praise, limitations of Lessing, moving
pictures, enargeia, *artificial and natural signs, drama,*
Homeric lines on Agamemnon's sceptre—VI. poetry and
music, the 16th century academies, music serves poetry:
Campion, Milton and Lawes, poetry serves music: operas,
Dryden, Tate, Purcell, the era of the music odes, Dryden's

ONE OF THE CRITICAL CATCHWORDS MOST OFTEN REPEATED IN OUR time has been "dissociation of sensibility," a term adapted from Remy de Gourmont [1] by T. S. Eliot in 1921 and used by Mr. Eliot to describe the aesthetic frame of mind which he believed to have developed in the latter half of the 17th century with the lapse of metaphysical poetry and the rise of rationalism and prosaism, and, at a later stage, of sentimentalism. In some areas the "dissociation" may be noted more easily than in others. Something like it perhaps appears, for instance, in the drama, that is, in the ethical declamatory and heroic tendencies of neo-classic tragedy and in the attendant decline of what is today called poetic imagery. On the other hand, the kind of witty discursive poetry and the burlesque narrative developed by Dryden and Pope were forms of seeming acquiescence in the laws of prose which actually sustained, as we have suggested in our last chapter, a peculiar kind of poetic interest. The full effects of 17th-century philosophy on creative writing, and especially on verse writing, were not felt until the mid-18th century. In the early part of the century perhaps the effects may be most readily observed in the areas of epistemology and aesthetic theory. It would appear that in this age both feeling and the act of valuing were theoretically detached from a certain something—an Aristotelian structure of ideas, a substantive belief about God, man, and the universe—and were either left floating free of reference or were attached to another area of experience provided or newly emphasized in another vision of reality—the new vision of the empirical and sensational.

One of the most convenient concentrations of the new epistemology in its British beginnings is that very opening section of Hobbes' *Leviathan*, the eighth chapter of which we have already quoted for

[1] Cf. F. W. Bateson in *Essays in Criticism*, I (1951) 302–12. Bateson argues persuasively that Eliot himself meant by the term "sensibility," not emotion, but sensation and at the same time, a union of thought and sensation. Later writers have taken "dissociation of sensibility" to mean a split between thought and emotion. "The sentimental age" is on Eliot's view a second stage.

the sake of the somewhat confused semantics of its dealings with "wit." In his first and second chapters Hobbes states with an appropriate forthrightness the simple epistemological grounds of his world view.

> Chapter I. *Of* SENSE. . . . The cause of Sense, is the Externall Body, or Object, which presseth the organ proper to each Sense, either immediatly, as in the Tast and Touch; or mediately, as in Seeing, Hearing, and Smelling. . . . All which qualities called *Sensible,* are in the object that causeth them, but so many several motions of the matter, by which it presseth our organs diversely. Neither in us that are pressed, are they anything else, but divers motions. . . . But their apparance to us is Fancy, the same waking, that dreaming. . . . Sense in all cases, is nothing els but original fancy.

> Chapter II. *Of* IMAGINATION. . . . after the object is removed, or the eye shut, wee still retain an image of the thing seen, though more obscure than when we see it. And this is it, the Latines call *Imagination,* from the image made in seeing; and apply the same, though improperly, to all the other senses. But the Greeks call it *Fancy.* . . . IMAGINATION therefore is nothing but *decaying sense;* and is found in men, and many other living Creatures, as well sleeping, as waking.

> . . . when we would express the *decay,* and signifie that the Sense is fading, old, and past, it is called *Memory.* So that *Imagination* and *Memory,* are but one thing, which for divers considerations hath divers names.

There is not much to add to this. Later on, Locke's *Essay Concerning Human Understanding,* 1690, urged the distinction between the primary qualities of our sensory experience (those that were really *in* things—bulk, shape, and movement) and the "secondary" (those that were only in our eyes, noses, and ears—color, smell, and sound). In this way, Locke greatly furthered the subjective and phenomenalistic drift of the sensationalist philosophy. Even more than Hobbes, Locke broke down the metaphysical rallying point of substance, and provided the complete set-up for the startling coup of Berkeley—the merging of primary and secondary qualities in the same status (*esse* is *percipi*), by which, overnight, sensationalism was inverted into idealism.

II

IN A celebrated series of *Spectator*[2] papers *On the Pleasures of the Imagination* (Nos. 411–421, appearing in June and July of 1712) Joseph

[2] Joseph Addison, *The Spectator,* ed. Henry Morley, 3 vols. (London, 1883).

Addison made his acknowledgement (as he had done in his paper on "mixed wit") to the *Essay* of Mr. Locke. The *term* "imagination" in Locke's *Essay* had, as we have seen, largely the pejorative sense associated with the malefactor "wit." Nevertheless, the newly brightened *meaning* of "imagination" as that term appears in Addison's *Spectators* is to a large extent determined by the sensationalism of Hobbes and Locke.

The ten *Spectator* papers on the imagination present some difficulties to exposition largely through their complicated inconsistency, the medley of aesthetic theses which they complacently recite. In Nos. 414 and 418, for instance, we discover in effect the following account of the pleasures of artistic *imitation*. Artistic imitation is more pleasant the more it resembles nature, but at the same time nature is more pleasant the more it resembles art—as when clouds or veins of marble display the shape of trees or other objects. Art improves on nature, though at the same time it cannot compete with nature. Artistic imitation is the more pleasant if it contains a touch of emotion—as when a portrait of a beautiful human countenance shows a melancholy cast. But in this miscellany of observations, nothing is so typical of the contemporary aesthetic trend as Addison's distinction between pleasant and unpleasant objects of imitation. Artistic imitation, even of an unsavory object like a dunghill, gives pleasure through fidelity of resemblance.[3] But, all other things being equal (complete fidelity of imitation, that is, obtaining), an imitation of a pleasing object is more pleasing than an imitation of an unpleasing object. Thus: the bowers and fruits and sweet gales in Book IV of *Paradise Lost* are a more pleasing poetic imitation than the brimstone and pitchy fires of Hell in Book I. This statement is central. It develops in all literalness the implications of Addison's first paper of the series (No. 411), in which the "primary" pleasures of the imagination are defined as simply those experienced upon our actually seeing certain natural objects,[4] and the "secondary" pleasures are defined as those experienced in our seeing good representations (surrogates) of the same kinds of objects.[5]

Addison's theory of the secondary pictorial imagination is the clas-

[3] As Aristotle, Plutarch, Aquinas and others had observed.

[4] The thesis holds also for certain artificial objects, like architecture, as appears later (No. 415).

[5] The three kinds of natural objects which qualify for the definition are, let us note in passing, the beautiful, the great, and the uncommon, approximate types of the three aesthetic genres more distinctly discriminated later in the century, the beautiful, the sublime, and the picturesque. The third of these, the "uncommon" (the "novel" or "surprising" in Addison's definition of "wit") is a detail which has a strong affinity for more overt forms of 18th-century affectivism.

The terms "primary" and "secondary" of Addison's distinction, though apparently inspired by the Lockean distinction between the "primary" and the "secondary" qualities of our general experience, exhibit no very closely analogous meaning.

sical theory of imitation reduced to its most stark and literal form, the imitative object or ikon performing its most servile and secondary role —that of the photograph on the bureau which reminds the lonely student of the distant sweetheart. If we compare Addison's *Spectators* on the imagination with his earlier series on "wit," especially No. 62, on "wit," "mixt wit," and "false wit," we can observe the rising new "imagination" and the declining old "wit" moving for a moment in conjunction, though in opposite directions. The series on imagination deals with a resemblance between art objects and extrinsic nature. The series on wit deals with a kind of resemblance which is internal to a poetic composition—a resemblance between two parts of a metaphor, between two ideas or two word sounds. A literary student might well attempt an inquiry whether there is any rationale by which the two kinds of resemblance (internal and external to the poem) may be approximated to each other. If the structure of a poem is such that we may look on the whole (a kind of reflecting structure of metaphorically arranged parts) as a tacit larger metaphor or symbol of other areas of reality than those explicitly mentioned in the poem, then Addison's remarks on the secondary or imitative imagination may invite being subsumed (and to some extent tested) under the general head of "wit."

One of the reasons why Addison praises the pleasures of the secondary imagination (and we shall develop this idea further in a few pages) is the easiness and persuasiveness of these pleasures—no cudgelling of the brain needed to respond to a picture of a flower or of a beautiful flower girl, or to notice a camel in the clouds. At the same time (even though Addison sets some store by the element of surprise in almost any kind of artistic pleasure),[6] the main burden of the papers on wit is a protest that some forms of wit—the mixed and the false—are fantastic, far-fetched, over-ingenious. It would seem to be not only the purely verbal trick but the difficult metaphysical trick —the metaphors yoked together by violence—which Addison dislikes.[7] "The pleasures of the fancy are more conducive to health, than those of the understanding, which are worked out by dint of thinking, and attended with too violent a labour of the brain" (No. 411). The examples of "mixt wit" (the message writ in juice of lemon read by the heat of love's flames, the lady's eyes felt as burning glasses of ice) which Addison adduces from Cowley's *Mistress* will perhaps be more readily seen as instances of extravagant metaphorical conceit than as the partial puns which Addison himself professes to see.[8] The contrast, though it is not overtly developed, between the two kinds of resem-

[6] Cf. Clarence D. Thorpe, "Addison and Some of his Predecessors on 'Novelty,'" *PMLA*, LII (December, 1937), 1114–29.

[7] Cf. Robert L. Morris, "Addison's *Mixt Wit*," *MLN*, LVI (December, 1942), 666–8.

[8] See *ante* Chapter 12, p. 232.

blance, the metaphoric, intellective, difficult metaphysical, and the literal, pictorial, easy "imaginative," invites us to look on the latter as the wit of the new epistemology—nature's wit in shaping a cloud like a camel, the artist's wit in making a portrait remind us of a lovely girl.[9]

Addison's argument in *Spectator* No. 411 that the sense of sight is by far the most richly dowered in pleasures of the imagination is almost a metaphysical argument (almost neo-Platonic and scholastic). But the margin by which it fails to be such an argument is important. The older argument for the aesthetic superiority of sight, and of hearing (the *sensus maxime cognoscitivi*), worked (through analogy) in the direction of form and intelligibility. The new argument worked (literally) in the direction of diversified pleasurable excitements. A medieval theorist would have said, for instance, that the art of painting looked (through the analogy of brilliance) toward the mind. A later 18th-century literary theorist, writing in a highly Addisonian vein, would propose explicitly: "the Poet writes principally to the eye." [1] The sense of sight (aside from the fact that in the Lockean and Addisonian system it enjoyed only a secondary and subjective status) suffered the limitation of being but another sense of touch—long-range and hypersensitive, "more delicate and diffusive." Addison's main thesis, unmistakable despite the cul-de-sacs with which his papers are amusingly varied, is that the pleasures of the imagination are the pleasurable sensations stimulated in ourselves directly by certain external causes or indirectly by reasonably close imitations of or substitutes for such causes.[2] "The Pleasures of the Imagination, taken in the full Extent," explains Addison, "are not so gross as those of Sense, nor so refined as those of the Understanding" (No. 411). But the word "sense" in this sentence has abruptly acquired the special meaning of "lower sense" (touch, taste, or smell presumably), for nothing in Addison's system can be clearer than that the pleasures of the imagination all proceed from the sight, and that sight is a "sense."

---

[9] In *Spectator* No. 62 Addison includes "external mimicry" among the forms of false wit. In No. 416 the secondary pleasures of imitative art are explained as arising from the exercise of our faculty of comparing and are explicitly associated with wit. In No. 418 the pleasure arising from the description of an unpleasant object like a dunghill is said to be "more properly called a pleasure of the understanding than of the fancy."

[1] Erasmus Darwin, *The Botanic Garden* (London, 1791), Part II, p. 48 (Interlude to Canto I, *The Loves of the Plants*). And a German theorist Wilhelm Heinse (1746–1804) would say: "Painting and sculpture serve first of all lust." Gilbert and Kuhn, p. 311.

[2] "My Design being first of all to Discourse of those Primary Pleasures of the Imagination, which entirely proceed from such Objects as are before our Eyes; and in the next place to speak of those Secondary Pleasures of the Imagination which flow from the Ideas of visible Objects, when the Objects are not actually before the Eye, but are called up into our Memories, or formed into agreeable Visions of Things that are either absent or Fictitious" (No. 411).

III

Yet not "so refined" in its pleasures as the Understanding. And not so difficult. The main reason for the new sensationalist trend in theory of the arts (the heavy investment in sweet and grand stimulations) lay, as we have already suggested, in the fact that the other side of contemporary philosophy, its rationalistic and supposedly superior side, was too sterile and discouraging. The same Hobbes who had laid out the easy definition of "imagination" as decaying sense had also said this:

> We must consider that although sense and memory of things, which are common to man and all living creatures, be knowledge, yet because they are given us immediately by nature, and not gotten by ratiocination, they are not philosophy.[3]

It was of course possible for a literary theorist to pursue not the Addisonian alternative but actually this rational line. It was done less in England than in Cartesian France, where some critics of Addison's day had the disillusioning candor to style themselves *géomètres*, or to boast of their *esprit géométrique*. Consider, for instance, the statement of the Homeric critic Terrasson:

> The way to think about a literary problem is that pointed out by Descartes for problems of physical science. A critic who tries any other way is not worthy to be living in the present century. There is nothing better than mathematics as a propaedeutic for literary criticism.[4]

For the literary man of the other temper, the British empiricist, the threat of that cold mathematical realm of reality—the "unearthly ballet of bloodless categories"—was all too imminent—the tissue of colorful ocular pleasures by which he protected himself all too flimsy. Addison himself, in *Spectator* No. 413, on final causes, the reasons why God has made the world beautiful, writes a passage which reveals with shocking clarity how forcefully the Lockean epistemology of subjective secondary qualities, and the Newtonian corpuscular universe which causes the experience of such qualities by its incessant bombardment

---

[3] *Elements of Philosophy*, I, i, 2, quoted by D. G. James, *The Life of Reason* (London, 1949), pp. 54–5.

[4] *Dissertation Critique sur L'Iliade d'Homère*, 1715, Preface, p. 65. "*Toutes les critiques que Perrault, Fontenelle, La Motte dirigent contre les Oeuvres particulières des anciens sont fondées sur ce principe. Ce que je ne comprends pas ne saurait être raisonnable*" (Gustave Lanson, "*Sur l'Influence de la Philosophie Cartesienne sur la Littérature Française*," *Revue de Metaphysique et Morale*, IV, 517–50, quoted by Austin Warren, *Alexander Pope as Critic and Humanist* [Princeton, 1929] p. 17).

of our sensoriums, had laid hold of the "imagination" of the age. Suppose we had to *see* the world as it *really* is—without its colors.

> Things would make but a poor Appearance to the Eye, if we
> saw them only in their proper Figures and Motions: And what
> Reason can we assign for their exciting in us many of those
> Ideas which are different from any thing that exists in the
> Objects themselves, (for such are Light and Colours) were it
> not to add Supernumerary Ornaments to the Universe, and
> make it more agreeable to the Imagination? . . . what a rough
> and unsightly Sketch of Nature should we be entertained with,
> did all her Colouring disappear, and the several Distinctions of
> Light and Shade vanish.[5]

British critics, on the whole, escaped the geometric urge. They did exhibit nevertheless a strong desire to account for aesthetic experience by fixed external *causes,* either grossly observable, or corpuscular. As Burke was to put it in his youthful *A Philosophical Inquiry into the Origin of Our Ideas of the Sublime and Beautiful* (1757):[6] "Beautiful objects" are "small," "smooth," gently curved, "delicate," "clean and fair" (III, xiii–xviii).[7] "Beauty is, for the greater part, some quality in bodies acting mechanically upon the human mind by the intervention of the senses" (III, xii). "Beauty acts by relaxing the solids of the whole system" (IV, xix). With a more pictorial emphasis on the observed object, Henry Home, Lord Kames, would write in his *Elements of Criticism* (1762):

> Such is our nature, that, upon perceiving certain external objects, we are instantaneously conscious of pleasure or pain: a
> gently-flowing river, a smooth extended plain, a spreading oak,
> a towering hill, are objects of sight that raise pleasant emotions:
> a barren heath, a dirty marsh, a rotten carcase, raise painful emotions.

> Elevation touches the mind no less than grandeur doth; and,
> in raising the mind to elevated objects, there is a sensible
> pleasure: the course of nature, however, hath still a greater influence than elevation; and therefore, the pleasure of falling with
> rain, and descending gradually with a river, prevails over that

[5] Addison refers to the Eighth Chapter of the Second Book of Mr. Locke's *Essay.*

[6] "Second Edition with an Introductory Discourse concerning Taste, and Several Other Additions," 1759. We quote the edition of Glasgow, 1818.

[7] "Observe that part of a beautiful woman, where she is, perhaps, the most beautiful, about the neck and breasts; the smoothness; the softness; the easy and insensible swell; the variety of the surface, which is never, for the smallest space, the same; the deceitful maze, through which the unsteady eye slides giddily, without knowing where to fix, or whither it is carried" (III, xv). "An air of robustness and strength is very prejudicial to beauty" (III, xvi).

of mounting upward. But where the course of nature is joined with elevation, the effect must be delightful: and hence the singular beauty of smoke ascending in a calm morning.[8]

The sublime, as it had been hinted long ago by Longinus and recently developed in a trend of criticism to be noticed further in our next chapter, was particularly susceptible to this kind of causative explanation. "The noise of vast cataracts," says Burke, "raging storms, thunder, or artillery, awakes a great and awful sensation in the mind." "A low, tremulous, intermitting sound . . . is productive of the sublime" (II, xvii, xix).[9] The philosophy of the aesthetic according to its guaranteed external causes was perhaps not very unfairly summarized in a joke recorded by A. W. Schlegel: According to Burke, "the Beautiful is a tolerably pretty strumpet, and the Sublime is a grenadier with a big moustache."[1]

Such a definitive location of aesthetic objects allied itself quite readily with a concept of sensational immediacy and compulsion—a stage beyond the mere idea of easiness. "Of the emotions thus produced," said Kames, "we inquire for no other cause but merely the presence of the object."
And Addison:

It is but opening the Eye, and the Scene enters. The Colours paint themselves on the Fancy, with very little Attention of Thought or Application of Mind in the Beholder. We are struck, we know not how, with the Symmetry of any thing we see, and immediately assent to the Beauty of an Object, without enquiring into the particular Causes and Occasions of it.[2]

And Burke:

The appearance of beauty as effectively causes some degree of love in us, as the application of ice or fire produces ideas of heat or cold.—*Enquiry* III, ii

[8] *Elements of Criticism*, 1805, I, 30 (Chap. 2); I, 22 (Chap. 1). Compare Mark Akenside's didactic blank verse poem, *The Pleasures of Imagination*, 1744.
[9] The list extends through Sections iii–xx. John Dennis, *The Grounds of Criticism in Poetry*, 1704, draws up a similar list of objects which inspire the lofty emotion of terror: Gods, Daemons, Hell, Spirits, and Souls of Men, Miracles, Prodigies, Enchantments, Witchcraft, Thunder, Tempests, Raging Seas, Inundations, Torrents, Earthquakes, Volcanoes, Monsters, Serpents, Lions, Tygers, Fire, War, Pestilence, Famine.
[1] A. W. Schlegel, *Vorlesungen über Schöne Litteratur und Kunst* (Heilbronn, 1884), I, 63: "*Man hat ganz treffend eingewandt: nach Burke sey eine nur leidlich artige Buhlerin schön, und ein Grenadier mit einem grossen Schnurrbarte erhaben.*" The translation, perhaps a slight improvement on the original, is Saintsbury's, III, 400.
[2] *Spectator* No. 411. No. 409 compares a taste in writing to a taste in tea.

The Abbé J. B. Du Bos in his *Réflexions critiques sur la poésie et sur la peinture*, 1719, drew a parallel between the pleasures of the aesthetic taste and those of cookery.

> Do we stop to reason about the merit of a stew? Do we appeal
> to geometric principles of flavor, or attempt a scientific descrip-
> tion of ingredients, or debate about their proportion—before
> we decide if the stew is good or bad? [3]

Do we indeed? The force of such a question was one powerful per-
suader to a strictly sensuous theory of the aesthetic.

Continental philosophers in the Cartesian heritage, Leibniz in his *Meditationes de Cognitione, Veritate, et Ideis*, 1684, and Baumgarten, in his *Philosophical Thoughts on Matters Connected with Poetry*, 1735,[4] made a special contribution to the dissociation of sensibility when they formulated the theory that beauty is experienced not in Cartesian clear *and* distinct ideas, but in ideas that are clear though *confused*, that is, in "sensuous" ideas (images). Clear but confusedly sensuous ideas (that is, ideas which are distinguishable from one another but not internally analyzable) constitute one form of the ineffable. The theory of the ineffable, the nameless object of "taste" (the Leibnizian *je-ne-sais-quoi*, in more amateurish terms the "grace beyond the reach of art")[5] is strongly in the ascendant at the birth of modern aesthetics, and along with it, let us add, the theory of an "internal" aesthetic "Sense," no less simple and ultimate than the external senses, no less autonomous, no less infallible. "Nor does there seem any thing more difficult in this matter, than that the Mind should be always determin'd to receive the Idea of *Sweet*, when Particles of such a Form enter the Pores of the Tongue."[6]

IV

THE term "aesthetic," which has been creeping into our discussion of the last few pages, can be justified here in part by its etymology and its Platonic meaning of a sheerly sensate, phenomenal or phantasmal, kind of experience. A poetics of sensational pleasure is, in that simple sense, necessarily an "aesthetic." But there is another and a more pre-cisely historical sense which does much to justify the use of the term

---

[3] *Réflexions* II, xxii.
[4] See *Reflections on Poetry, Alexander Gottlieb Baumgarten's Meditationes philosophicae de nonnullis ad poema pertinentibus*, trans. Karl Aschenbrenner and William B. Holther (Berkeley and Los Angeles, 1954).
[5] Samuel H. Monk, "A Grace Beyond the Reach of Art," *JHI*, V (1944), 131–50.
[6] Francis Hutcheson, *An Inquiry into the Original of our Ideas of Beauty and Virtue*, 1725, VI, x. Cf. Clarence D. Thorpe, "Addison and Hutcheson on the Imagi-nation," *ELH*, II (1925), 222–9.

"aesthetic" in referring to the poetics conditioned for Addison by the epistemology of Locke and Hobbes. During this age, as we have remarked a few lines above, arose the modern concept of general "aesthetics," the general philosophy of the higher arts. Poetry, as we have seen, had been discussed in antiquity at times under the rubric of the fine or the beautiful (*to kalon*), but more readily, along with rhetoric, under the rubric of art or technique (*technē*), and again in the Middle Ages chiefly under the latter. It remained for the Renaissance, with the aid of a neo-Platonic historical appeal, to shift the emphasis in speaking of the arts very pronouncedly toward the concept of the fine, the ideal, the beautiful, and at the same time to begin viewing several of the "imitative" arts as members of one general and literally unified category. A medieval accent on the intellectuality of such verbal arts as poetry and rhetoric (and along with them music, because of its mathematical component) was in the Renaissance gradually modified so as to admit to equal standing visual arts such as painting and sculpture. These had once been looked on as lower, because they were physical arts, manual or handicraft, like shoemaking. We find Italian painters of the 16th century, for instance, much concerned to argue that the manual character of their effort was outweighed by the intellectual. Painting demanded a knowledge of mathematics, especially in perspective, and of other sciences. Like poetry, it could achieve a moral end, for it could show human gesture and facial expression.[7] The argument could also become comic. Leonardo, in his comments *Della Pittura*, makes an invidious distinction between the art of the sculptor (laborious, with sweat and fatigue, and covered with stone dust) and that of the painter (elegantly and easily at work in his studio with brush and colors).[8]

During the 16th and 17th centuries appear various momentary and partial alignments of arts and sciences according to one principle or another. A sharp differentiation between arts and sciences appears to have been an event that had to wait on the late 17th-century quarrel between Ancients and Moderns. Meanwhile, however, in Italy during the 16th century had arisen the term *Arti del Disegno* and in France during the 17th century the corresponding term *Beaux Arts*, both terms meaning in the main the newly unified and newly respected arts of visual appeal, painting, sculpture and architecture—though sometimes poetry and music were included. By the early 18th century, habits of thinking about groups of the "imitative" and idealizing arts were closely approaching the concept of the "Fine Arts" which was to become so widely honored and so much taken for granted during the 19th and

---

[7] Thomas Munro, *The Arts and Their Interrelations*, p. 32.

[8] Munro, pp. 32–3, citing J. P. Richter, *The Literary Works of Leonardo da Vinci* (London, 1880), Vol. I, No. 654. See a longer quotation by Jacques Maritain, *Art and Scholasticism* (New York, 1942), p. 156.

20th centuries. The Abbé Du Bos' *Réflexions critiques sur la poésie et sur la peinture* of 1719 says a good deal not only about painting and poetry but also about sculpture, engraving and music, and in the English translation of this work in 1748 the word *Music* is added to the title. This was one milestone. But to the Abbé Charles Batteux, in his *Les beaux arts réduits à un même principe* of 1746, seems to go the credit of having first defined and rationalized almost exactly the modern category. The common principle was "imitation of beautiful nature," and the arts included were music, poetry, painting, sculpture, and the dance. Succeeding writers, notably the encyclopedists (Montesquieu, Diderot, D'Alembert) took up and broadcast the ideas of Batteux, substituting for the dance architecture—and the grouping most often encountered today was established.[9] Meanwhile, the German Leibnizian philosopher Alexander von Baumgarten, whose early work on *Poetry* we have already mentioned, had constructed the first sensuous philosophy of the fine arts and had given it the name *Aesthetics*.[1]

Such broadly inclusive theorizing came accompanied by a new kind of urge to draw parallels between the arts and to describe and criticize one art in terms of another. A visually centered sensationalist aesthetic such as we have noted in Addison's *Spectators* might plausibly enough promote a discussion of poetry in terms taken from sculpture or painting. And it happened too that antiquity provided a few hints for such a parallelism:—the equal mention in Aristotle's *Poetics* of music, dancing, and painting as forms of *mimēsis;* an even more ancient *mot* of Simonides, repeated by Plutarch (that painting is mute poetry, poetry a speaking picture); the general defence of the arts by Cicero in his speech for a poet threatened with banishment (*habent omnes artes quoddam commune vinculum*); and most persuasive of all the three words of Horace—so easily taken out of context[2] and then so easily misinterpreted: *ut pictura poesis*.[3] By the latter half of the 17th century the phrases of Horace and Simonides had accumulated through repetition

[9] Paul O. Kristeller, "The Modern System of the Arts: A Study in the History of Aesthetics," *JHI*, XII (October, 1951), 496–527; XIII (January, 1952), 17–46. See esp. XII, 497–524 ("Beaux Arts"), 525–7 (Ancients and Moderns); XIII, 18–23 (Du Bos and Batteux and the Encyclopedists). D'Alembert's *Discours préliminaire* to the *Encyclopédie* I (1751), 117, makes the substitution of architecture for the dance: "*La peinture, la sculpture, l'architecture, la poésie, la musique et leurs différentes divisions composent la troisième distribution générale, qui naît de l'imagination et dont les parties sont comprises sous le nom de beaux-arts*" (Kristeller, XIII, 23).

[1] His work of that title appeared in 1750.

[2] *Ut pictura poesis: erit quae, si propius stes, te capiat magis, et quaedam, si longius abstes* (ll. 361–2). That is, *some pictures are murals, and some miniatures—and so with poems.*

[3] The authority of the phrase had perhaps always threatened. Saintsbury (I, 398) points out that Venantius Fortunatus in an epistle to Syagrius of Autun introduces an elaborate "shaped" poem and argues for this combination of visual and verbal art "by a twist of the Horatian tag."

and debate a considerable weight of authority. Thus in the opening lines of a popular poetical treatise (paralleling Horace's *Ars Poetica* and Boileau's *Art Poétique*) the *De Arte Graphica* by the French painter Charles Alphonse Du Fresnoy:

> *Ut pictura poesis erit; similisque Poesi*
> *Sit Pictura; . . . .*
>
> *. . . . muta Poesis*
> *Dicitur haec, Pictura loquens solet illa vocari.*

> A poem is like a picture; so a picture ought to try to be like a poem. . . . a picture is often called silent poetry; and poetry a speaking picture.

This poem was translated into English by no less a man of letters than Dryden in 1795 and given a lengthy theoretical Preface containing a "Parallel Between Poetry and Painting." The plot of a poem, for instance, is, as Aristotle had suggested, like the line drawing or sketch for a painting. The diction and imagery are like the colors (the outline "to advantage" filled).[4]

The theory in the phrase *ut pictura poesis* worked in complementary directions between the arts of painting and poetry: It worked for a literary influence on painting and a judgment of painting in literary terms; and at the same time for a painterly influence on literature and a corresponding kind of judgment.[5] The first of these influences is not directly a matter of literary criticism; but it may be examined as a highly instructive parallel. For the theory was not only technical (concerned with colors, outlines, ways of painting clouds, shadows, and light, and of grouping figures) but very broadly humanistic—historical and heroic. That is, both poetry and painting were said to aim at imitation: the most proper subject of imitation was human nature, and not ordinary but ideal or heroic human nature. The models for either painting or poetry might be found alike in the classics. More precisely, the

---

[4] Cf. *ante* Chapter 12, p. 245. When Augustan theorists took an anti-rhetorical stand, that is, when they wished to stress their dedication to the main design or grand total meaning and their relative contempt for the stylistic niceties, they found this analogy quite convenient.

"The words are the colouring of the work, which, in the order of nature, is last to be considered. The design, the disposition, the manners, and the thoughts, are all before it. . . . Words, indeed, like glaring colours, are the first beauties that arise and strike the sight; but, if the draught be false or lame . . . then the finest colours are but daubing."—Dryden, Preface to *Fables*, 1700 (*Essays*, ed. Ker, II, 252–253)

Cf. L. I. Bredvold, *Selected Poems of Alexander Pope* (New York, 1926), pp. xvi–xvii, parallel quotations from the French academicians Félibien and Le Brun and from Gildon and Pope. The Lockean assignment of color to the subjective secondary status worked in fairly close harmony with Platonic neo-classic tendencies toward the abstract universal. Cf. *post* Chapter 15.

[5] William G. Howard, "*Ut Pictura Poesis*," *PMLA*, XXIV (1909), 46–123; Cicely Davies, "*Ut Pictura Poesis*," *MLR*, XXX (1935), 159–69.

models for historical, or narrative, painting (the highest genre, as epic was the highest in poetry) might be found in the literary classics. The painter had to be not only accomplished in his technique of color and shape, but "learned" in the important subject matters—classical mythology and Christian Scriptures. A critique of Nicholas Poussin's Biblical painting "The Fall of Manna in the Desert" by the French Academicians is a remarkable illustration. Here was the graphic telling of an action, single, of sufficient size and completeness, in a mode highly compatible with the rules laid down in Aristotle's *Poetics*. It had a beginning (the downcast state of those Israelites who had not yet noticed the manna), a middle, with a peripeteia or turning point (the descent of the manna and the looking up of certain Israelites to see it), an end or denouement (the gathering and eating of the manna by certain others). So the element of time was caught and rendered in space, and so were cause and effect, the reasons for emotions and the expression of them.[6]

Another highly developed part of humanistic painting theory, one to which we have alluded briefly at the opening of this chapter, related precisely to the visual symptoms by which human emotion is betrayed. The French Academicians in general made this their concern, but none more systematically than the official painter to Louis XIV, Charles Le Brun, in his treatise entitled *Expression des passions*. As a recent writer has happily phrased it, this work put "Descartes' psychology . . . virtually on the tip of the young painters' brushes."[7] A translation of the work that appeared in London as late as 1813, with twenty copper engravings, gives, for example, the following caption for the picture of "Sadness."

> The dejection that is produced by sadness makes the Eye brows rise towards the middle of the forehead more than towards the Cheeks; the Eye ball appears full of perturbation; the white of the Eye is Yellow, the Eye lids are drawn down and a little swell'd; all about the Eyes is livid; the Nostrils are drawn downward; the Mouth is held open and the corners are drawn down; the head carelessly leaning on One of the Shoulder[s]; the face is of a lead Colour the lips of pale.[8]

[6] Rensselaer W. Lee, "Ut Pictura Poesis: The Humanistic Theory of Painting," *The Art Bulletin*, XXII (December, 1940), esp. 223–5.

[7] Brewster Rogerson, "The Art of Painting the Passions," *JHI*, XIV (January, 1953), 75. Rogerson's account (pp. 68–94) extends to the arts in general—for not only painting but all such visual and auditory arts as poetry, oratory, acting, and music were arts of "painting" the passions. He points out that the theory of expressive signs involved runs back through the Renaissance, appearing prominently, for instance, in Leonardo's remarks on painting and in Lomazzo's handbook of 1585, and that it finds its classical authority in Aristotle's *Rhetoric* III, 1 and 7, and in Quintilian's *Institutes* XI, iii, 61 ff.

[8] Rogerson, *loc. cit.*, p. 76. Cf. Edmund Burke's account of what beauty does to the beholder, quoted *post* Chapter 14, p. 299.

We are now in a position to notice a curious contrast between the influence of literary norms on painting and the influence of painting norms on literature. Whereas the influence of literature on painting was broadly intellectual and humanistic, the reciprocal influence of painting on literature was in the long run if not anti-intellectual and anti-humanistic at least markedly non-humanistic and sensational. At its best, the new influence was part of a blandly urged general movement of human nature (toward landscape) which was in progress throughout the 18th century, a substitution of landscape for the older ethical structure of values as the objective counterpart of human emotions.[9] It was not in the heroic historical pictures of French and Italian painters that the poets had a great deal to learn (the historical pictures were learned from poetry itself), but in pictures where the painters were not so closely rivaling earlier poets, that is, in landscapes—the serenely classical ones by Claude (with their human elements static and remote—a group of fishing peasants by a stream, a boat in a bay, a shepherd with his flock, the porticos of temples on hilltops rising out of valley mists) or the wild and ragged ones by Salvator Rosa (the crags, the brown and blasted heaths and twisted trees, the torrents, and the ruined Gothic arch or tower). A distinct reflection of these painting styles appears throughout English topographical and descriptive poetry of the 18th century.[1] On the theoretical side, the classic quotation is from James Thomson's allegorical, Spenserian description of the castle of Indolence.

> Sometimes the Pencil in cool airy Halls
> Bade the gay Bloom of vernal Landskips rise,
> Or Autumn's varied Shades imbrown the Walls:
> Now the black Tempest strikes the astonish'd Eyes;
> Now down the Steep the flashing Torrent flies;
> The trembling Sun now plays o'er Ocean blue,
> And now rude Mountains frown amid the Skies;
> Whate'er *Lorrain* light-touched with softening Hue,
> Or savage *Rosa* dash'd, or learned *Poussin* drew.
>
> —I, xxxviii

A fair example of the execution, the actual significance for poetry of the liaison with painting, is this Claudian perspective across the landscaped estate of Hagley Park—from the last edition of Thomson's *Spring* during his lifetime (1744):

> Meantime you gain the Height, from whose fair Brow
> The bursting Prospect spreads immense around;

[9] Cf. H. M. McLuhan, "Tennyson and the Analogy of the Picturesque," *Essays in Criticism*, I (July, 1951), 262–82.

[1] See Elizabeth W. Manwaring, *Italian Landscape in Eighteenth Century England* (London, 1927).

And snatch'd o'er Hill and Dale, and Wood, and Lawn
And verdant Field, and darkening Heath between,
And Villages embosom'd soft in Trees,
And spiry Towns by dusky Columns mark'd
Of rising Smoak, your Eye excursive roams . . .
To where the broken Landskip, by degrees,
Ascending, roughens into ridgy Hills;
O'er which the *Cambrian* Mountains, like far Clouds
That Skirt the blue Horizon, doubtful, rise.—ll. 950–62

Modern scholarship has labored the point that Italian and French painting affected the actual landscaping of 18th-century English gardens and
parks, an outdoor movement in which not only Lyttelton, the owner of
Hagley, but Alexander Pope and other poets took an important part.

V

FRIENDLY relations between poetry and the visual arts were also much
assisted during the 18th century by antiquarian, virtuoso, and Hellleniz-
ing trends of the day. One of these was the "illustration" of classical
literature by classical sculpture, reliefs, and medals—as in the encyclopedic dialogue *Polymetis*, 1747, the work of the Oxford Professor of
Poetry and friend of Pope, Joseph Spence. There was also the fresh
illustration of classical poetry by living draughtsmen and at least an
implicit judgment in favor of this poetry according to its capacity to
inspire such illustration—as in the Count Caylus' *Tableaux Tirés de
l'Iliade, de l'Odysée de Homère et de l'Enéide de Virgile*, 1754–1758.
Such matters were the theme of the archeologist Winckelmann's *Gedan-
ken über die Nachahmung der griechischen Werke in der Malerei und
Bildhauerkunst*, 1755. The instructive frontispiece of this book, in an edition of 1756, shows the learned painter at work on a sacrifice of Iphigenia,
Agamemnon holding his cloak to his eyes; on the ground at the painter's
feet are scrolls bearing versions of the story by Sophocles and Aeschylus,
and in the painter's left hand is the play by Euripides at the passage:
"Putting his cloak before his eyes" (*hommatōn peplon protheis*). The
appearance of the three books just mentioned precipitated in 1766 the
most notable act of theorizing upon our theme to occur during the 18th
century, the *Laokoon* [2] of G. E. Lessing.

    The German critic's protest against the extravagance of the hu-
manistic *ut pictura poesis* gets under way with some bickering about a
Hellenistic sculptural group dug up on the site of Hadrian's villa in
1506 and lodged in the Vatican Museum. Why is the mouth of the priest
Laokoon, entoiled in mortal struggle with the two serpents, not wide

---

[2] *Laocoon*, trans. William A. Steel, Everyman's Library (London, 1930).

open in a shout of agony? Because, said **Winckelmann**, the Greek ideal of emotional restraint admirably forbade it. Because, says Lessing, a gaping cavity is a formal defect in a sculpture, and because the moment of the half-open mouth, short of the climax, is a highly "significant and fruitful" moment.[3] Students of antiquity had long considered the question whether or not the sculptural group was modeled upon the similar passage in the Second Book of Virgil's *Aeneid*. There were those who believed it highly probable that the "honour of the invention and first conception" belonged to Virgil. Lessing would agree with the sequence but reverse the honors. Why does Virgil's description of the incident differ in several important respects from the sculpture? Because, says Lessing, the sculptors, coming after Virgil, saw fit to improve upon him. There is no other way to explain the facts. With the sculptural model to work from, Virgil would have had no reason to deviate.[4]

Here we observe Lessing entangled (though like Laocoon uttering a half-suppressed cry of anguish) in the coils of the very critical assumption which the later chapters of his long essay so adroitly almost throw off. When he comes (Chapter XI) to consider the imbecilities of the Count Caylus, the attempts to exploit the greatness of Homer through pictures ("how much more perfect" the artist's "delineations will prove the more closely he clings to the very smallest circumstances noticed by the poet"), Lessing deals with the real critical issue, if not definitively, at least very acutely.

The difference, says Lessing in effect, between poetry and painting (Chapter XVI) is more important for criticism than the resemblance between them. He was not the first to have said something like this. In the somewhat remote past Leonardo, with an insistence on the direct and natural appeal of paint to the eye, *virtu visiva,* had drawn a clear distinction, albeit all in favor of his own art. Both the 17th and the 18th century are full of casual protests against the prevailing trend toward assimilation. "*Les mots et les couleurs ne sont choses pareilles,*" says La Fontaine. "*Ni les yeux ne sont les oreilles.*"[5] Within the more immediate era of 18th-century theorizing the Abbé Du Bos had distinguished between the real imitations ("signes naturels") of painting and the arbitrary symbols ("signes artificiels") of poetry.[6] In the fifth part of his

[3] Chapters I–III. *Fixierte Blitz* Goethe was to call this piece of sculpture, with a slightly different emphasis on the single moment. See Margarete Bieber, *Laocoon* (New York, 1942).

[4] Chapters V–VI. The Laocoon, a composition in six pieces of stone by three Rhodian sculptors, Athenodorus, Polydorus, and Agesander, is dated by modern archeologists about 50 B.C.

[5] *Conte du Tableau.* See Atkins II, 329, for an instance of the distinction in antiquity.

[6] *Réflexions* I, xl. Cf. E. N. S. Thompson, "The Discourses of Sir Joshua Reynolds," *PMLA,* XXXII (September, 1917), 342, on Johnson, Shaftesbury, and James Harris.

Inquiry (a work which Lessing long pondered translating) Burke had taken some pains to assert that words are not pictorial substitutes for the visible world.[7] Yet Lessing is the first to write an extended argument in an accent that establishes the importance of the question. The difference between poetry and painting, he says, is a basic difference, that between a medium of time and a medium of space. A medium of space can present corporeal objects directly and vividly; the same medium can present the actions of such bodies only indirectly and through images of the bodies themselves. Conversely, a medium of time can present actions directly and vividly, but can present bodies only indirectly and through actions. Certain passages of 18th-century nature poetry (for example, a flower stanza from Von Haller's *Alpen*—a few English examples might have been found in Thomson's *Seasons*) are adduced to show the opaque effect of over-thick painting—static and minute attention to the corporeal object.[8] Poetry ought to describe not objects as such but objects in action—not the color and shape of Helen but the effect of her beauty upon the lascivious graybeards of Troy. Writing as he does in the face of the classical doctrine, and that freshly sanctioned by the new empirical aesthetics, Lessing must be credited with a keen theoretical insight. An idea of his originality and daring may be got from the retrospect of Goethe.

> One must be a youth to realize the effect exercised upon us by Lessing's *Laokoon,* which transported us from the region of miserable observation into the free fields of thought. The long misunderstood *ut pictura poesis* was at once set aside; the difference between art and poetry made clear; the peaks of both appeared separately, however near each other might be their bases. . . .[9]

Yet some reservations seem in order. A certain incompleteness of critical reorientation may perhaps be seen here and there in Lessing's argument. There is, for example, his curious recommendation that poetry should get around troublesome descriptive spots by the device of reducing them to some kind of narration. See how Homer does the shield of Achilles—an elaborate description but all conveyed in the process of the fabrication of the shield by Vulcan. See how Homer describes the bow of Pandarus, all through an account of how a goat was hunted and killed to yield the horns of which the bow was made. See how Anacreon describes the lovely boy Bathyllus—by the exquisite con-

[7] In *Spectator* No. 416, Addison expresses the contrary view—that words can call up more lively images than nature itself.

[8] Cf. *post,* Chapter 15, p. 315, the recommendation of particulars by Joseph Warton and other English critics of the mid-century.

[9] *Wahrheit und Dichtung* VIII, quoted by James Sime, *Lessing* (London, 1877), I, 304; Cf. Goethe, *Werke,* XXVII (Weimar, 1889), 164.

trivance of having his portrait made by a painter. In short, Lessing's conception of the difference between painting and poetry, when put under the pressure of a practical application, seems to amount to a distinction between still pictures and moving pictures. He offers us an urgent invitation to speculate what would have happened to his theory if his experience of artistic media had been broadened by an acquaintance with the cinema. His notion of the moving pictures that make up poetry would perhaps better correspond to the now archaic and naive phases of the modern cinematic art than to the advantages of verticality or associational depth which have been explored in more recent techniques.[1]

Lessing's theory leans all too clearly toward vividness or illusionism, the *enargeia*, the *phantasiae* of the ancient rhetoricians, though in a footnote he astutely identifies those very figures with 18th-century poetical pictures.[2] The fact that he actually countenanced this aesthetic norm, while perhaps believing that he was severe upon it, is suggested not only in *Laokoon* but in some moments of his dramatic theory. He was a pioneer German dramatic critic and a rebel against French neo-classicism. He had an ideal of intensity for poetry, and especially for drama, which he explained by starting with that distinction between natural and artificial signs which we have already cited from the Abbé Du Bos. Thus in a letter written to a friend about the reception of the *Laokoon*:

> Poetry must try to raise its arbitrary signs to natural signs: that is how it differs from prose and becomes poetry. The means by which this is accomplished are the tone of words, the position of words, measure, figures and tropes, similes, etc. All these make arbitrary signs more like natural signs, but they do not actually change them into natural signs; consequently all genres which use only these means must be looked upon as lower kinds of poetry; and the highest kind of poetry will be that which transforms the arbitrary signs completely into natural signs. That is dramatic poetry.[3]

That is to say: the directness of drama, the mimetic use of language as the speech of dramatic persons, is more poetically important than the poet's management of language, his rhythms, and his figurative imagination. A passage in the *Laokoon* which Lessing permitted himself to indulge in almost as if it were a joke gives perhaps a better clue to the power which he actually displayed as dramatic critic in his celebrated *Hamburg Dramaturgy*. In his discussion of the Homeric lines on the

[1] Cf. Sergei Eisenstein, *The Film Sense*, trans. Jay Leyda (New York, 1947), *passim*, and especially "montage," pp. 3–12, 30–6, 43–6.
[2] Chapter XXV.
[3] Letter to Nicolai, May 26, 1769, about a review of *Laokoon* by Garve, quoted by Wellek, *History*, I, 164–5, from Lessing's *Sämtliche Werke*, ed. K. Lachmann and F. Muncker (Leipzig, 1886–1924), XVII, 290–1.

sceptre of Agamemnon he seems partially at a loss to explain their power. Somewhat diffidently and apologetically, he assumes the manner of a Hellenistic grammarian—or perhaps of some future pedant-exegete— and writes the following reverie:

> It would not surprise me if I found that one of the old com- mentators of Homer had admired this passage as the most per- fect allegory of the origin, progress, establishment, and heredi- tary succession of the royal power amongst mankind. True, I should smile if I were to read that Vulcan, the maker of this sceptre, as fire, as the most indispensable thing for the preserva- tion of mankind, represented . . . the satisfaction of those wants which moved the first men to subject themselves to the rule of an individual monarch; that the first king, a son of Time (*Zeus, Kroniōn*), was an honest ancient who wished to share his power with, or wholly transfer it to, a wise and eloquent man, a Mercury . . . that the wily orator, at the time when the infant State was threatened by foreign foes, resigned his su- preme power to the bravest warrior. . . . I should smile, but nevertheless should be confirmed in my esteem for the poet to whom so much meaning can be attributed.—Chapter XVI

VI

BUT *ut pictura poesis* was part of something larger, a general ground swell toward assimilating the arts which a *Laokoon* could scarcely have much success in checking. A companion movement which should be noticed here, though more briefly, was that toward unifying the arts of poetry and music, the restoration of that primitive harmony and sister- hood which had been noted with approval by Plato and illustrated by such classical figures as Orpheus and Timotheus and in the Old Testa- ment by David. The modern separation of music and poetry was an actuality which had begun to emerge during the 16th century with the specialized development of instrumental music. But even during the same period a theoretical drive toward unifying these arts had begun with the musical academies (Baïf's *Académie de Poésie et de Musique* most notably in France and in Italy the Florentine *Camerata*).[4] This was a reaction, towards simplicity and naturalism, against the contrapuntal intricacies of polyphonic music in the medieval tradition. The movement continued and gained strength through the 17th century as part of the same humanistic yearning for emotive imitation which we have sampled

[4] See James E. Phillips, "Poetry and Music in the Seventeenth Century," in *Music & Literature in England in the Seventeenth and Eighteenth Centuries* (Los Angeles: William Andrews Clark Memorial Library, 1953), pp. 2–18.

in the theory of poetry and painting. The formula "poetry plus melody equals music" meant first, in the 16th and early 17th centuries, that music was to serve the higher, more intellectual and imitative purposes of poetry. The proposed ideal was a single melodic line closely matching the verbal line, note for syllable, quantity for quantity, and aiming even at some degree of story-telling, that is, a harmony of notes and "modes" with passions and motions, with heights and depths of verbal meaning.

> If the subject be light, you must cause your music to go in motions which carry with them a celerity or quickness of time . . . ; if it be lamentable, the note must go in slow and heavy motions. . . . Moreover, you must have a care that when your matter signifieth ascending, high heaven and such like, you make your music ascend; and . . . where your ditty speaks of descending, lowness, depth, hell and other such, you must make your music descend. For as it will be thought a great absurdity to talk of heaven and point downward to the earth: so it will be counted great incongruity if a musician upon the words *He ascended into heaven* should cause his music to descend.[5]

Thomas Campion's songs and his theoretical aim (to "couple" his "words and notes lovingly together"), Milton's *Comus* and the music of Henry Lawes [6] are examples which will readily occur to the student of English poetry.

Later, in the second half of the 17th century, the subserviency of music to poetry was reversed. Poetry came actually to be written to meet the requirements of musical setting. Witness the operas of Dryden, or the tame libretto of Tate's *Dido and Aeneas*, for the music of Purcell. The poetry, Dryden complained in his Preface to *Albion and Albanius*, 1685, must "please hearing rather than gratify understanding." "The same reasons which depress thought in an opera have a stronger effect upon the words." The trend of the times is manifest in the social and musico-dramatic forms which were increasingly popular—opera, oratorio, song, ballad, hymn, and the great Pindaric ode for music, which began in 1683 with the London Musical Society's annual performance of an ode celebrating the powers of music and paying honor to the patron saint of Christian music, St. Cecilia.[7] Dryden's two poems for St. Cecilia's Day are magnificent instances of that genre of poetry which came to be written as an invitation to an exercise of powers by the

[5] Thomas Morley, *A Plain and Easy Introduction to Practical Music*, 1597, quoted by Bertrand H. Bronson, "Some Aspects of Music and Literature in the Eighteenth Century," in *Music & Literature* . . . , p. 31.

[6] Cf. Willa M. Evans, *Henry Lawes, Musician and Friend of Poets* (New York, 1941), pp. 90–109.

[7] Cf. Robert M. Myers, "Neo-Classical Criticism of the Ode for Music," *PMLA*, LXII (June, 1947), 399–421.

musical composer. A series of stanzas from the first of these poems, the
"Song for St. Cecilia's Day, 1687," will illustrate the poetic range.

III

The trumpet's loud clangor
    Excites us to arms
With shrill notes of anger
    And mortal alarms.
The double double double beat
    Of the thundering drum
Cries: "Hark! the foes come;
Charge, charge, 'tis too late to retreat."

IV

The soft complaining flute
In dying notes discovers
The woes of hopeless lovers,
Whose dirge is whisper'd by the warbling lute.

V

Sharp violins proclaim
Their jealous pangs, and desperation,
Fury, frantic indignation,
Depth of pains, and height of passion,
    For the fair, disdainful dame.

On the side of the music, it may be observed that Handel's setting of
this Song, for Soprano and Tenor, Chorus and Orchestra, 1739, is "about
fifteen times" longer than a plain reading of the words. The word "warbling," for instance, is extended over six bars of vocalization, with "lute-
like 'warbling' in the bass accompaniment." [8] In this baroque elaboration, all those gains of the 16th-century humanists against medieval poly-
phony were sadly voided—as John Wesley would complain in a pamphlet
entitled *Thoughts on the Power of Music* and Dr. John Brown (1763)
in his *Dissertation on the Rise, Union, and Power, the Progressions, and
Corruptions, of Poetry and Music.*[9]

The effort on the side of poetry was carried into the 18th century
with less success by Pope[1] and petered out in poems like Collins' *The*

---

[8] Bertrand H. Bronson, "Some Aspects of Music and Literature in the Eighteenth Century," in *Music & Literature*, pp. 32, 38, 40.
[9] Bronson, *loc. cit.*, p. 47, Wesley; Phillips, *loc. cit.*, p. 19, Brown.
[1] *Ode for Music on St. Cecilia's Day*, 1713. At a later date (*Dunciad* I, 40) Pope
would allude to "soft sing-song on Cecilia's day." His *Epistle to Augustus* and his
Fourth *Dunciad* express the Aristotelian and intellectualist contempt of a literary
man for the merely acoustic and emotive tendencies of Italian opera and for the
concurrent optical excess or spectacularism of the stage.

Passions: An Ode for Music (1747) and Gray's *Ode for Music, Irregular* (1768). The end was indicated by the burlesque *Cantata* of Swift and Bonnell Thornton's *An Ode on St. Cecilia's Day, Adapted to the Ancient British Music, viz. the Salt-Box, the Jew's Harp, the Marrow-bones and Cleavers, the Humstrung or Hurdy-gurdy* (1749).[2] The serious odes show us the painting of the passions in all the virtuosity of "vivid"[3] allegorical image and metrical representation of movement. Dryden's second poem, *Alexander's Feast*, so highly esteemed by himself and by several succeeding generations of critics, is without question the most flamboyantly successful demonstration of the technique. Its rapidly shifting succession of passionate announcements and appropriate rhythmical variations surely go far to justify the place it has long held in the repertoire of school declamations.

By the mid-18th century, English theorists were a highly vocal chorus, though today quite obscurely known—Avison, Mason, Jones, Beattie, Brown, Webb, Harris, and others. They picked up and carried along the theme of poetry and music at about the time when *ut pictura poesis* was beginning to falter—and when the norm of classical imitation, in literary art at least, was beginning to shift toward that of romantic emotion and expression. This school of theorists contrived to recognize three main kinds of resemblance between music and poetry:

1. Technical and formal. (The verbal "matter" of poetry was said to correspond to the harmony of music; the subject or story, to the melody; the meter, to the measure.)
2. Imitative. (In the choral works of Bach and Handel, the voices rise, with the mention of hills, descend with the valleys. Bach's "Clavier-piece" imitates a post-horn and in Mozart's *Marriage of Figaro* horns express cuckoldry.)
3. Expressive. (Music expresses classes of passions—joy, grief, love. "To imitate the passions was to describe them in music; the pleasure of music was the pleasure of the passions themselves.")[4]

Correspondences of the second kind, the most distinctly recognizable, were looked on with some suspicion by the critics and were called

[2] Robert M. Myers, *loc. cit.*, pp. 410–11; A. D. McKillop, "Bonnell Thornton's Burlesque Ode," *Notes and Queries*, CXCIV (July 23, 1949), 321–4.

[3] Cf. Earl Wasserman, "The Inherent Values of Eighteenth-Century Personification," *PMLA*, LXV (June, 1950), 444–8.

[4] See the valuable articles by Herbert M. Schueller, "Literature and Music as Sister Arts: An Aspect of Aesthetic Theory in Eighteenth-Century Britain," *PQ*, XXVI (July, 1947), 193–205; " 'Imitation' and 'Expression' in British Music Criticism in the Eighteenth Century," *Musical Quarterly*, XXXIV (October, 1948), 544–66; "The Pleasures of Music: Speculation in British Music Criticism, 1750–1800," *JAAC*, VIII (March, 1950), 155–171; "The Use and Decorum of Music as Described in British Literature, 1700 to 1780," *JHI*, XIII (January, 1952), 73–93; "Correspondences Between Music and the Sister Arts, According to 18th Century Aesthetic Theory," *JAAC*, XI (June, 1953), 334–59.

musical "puns." Comparative theorists of the day considered poetry to be the highest art, because it could say things. Painting was second. Music, third. Vocal music was preferred to instrumental. That is, the norm of imitation was (so far as formal commitments went) preferred to norms of sensory pleasure, of the geometric or formal, or even of direct emotive expression. The genres of opera, oratorio, and song were hailed as steps toward an ideal reunion of poetry and music, a restoration of music to its primitive and correct status as the handmaid of poetry. There were some Aristotelian echoes in this discussion (as in Thomas Twining's notable edition of the *Poetics*, 1789) and doubtless a faintly quadrivial strain, some sound across the centuries from the Pythagorean, Platonic, and medieval aesthetic of harmonious numbers.

VII

BECAUSE of its basic assumption that the aim of the arts is a direct imitation of nature, 18th-century theory was in the curious position of seeing literature as the contentual norm of painting and music, and at the same time of seeing either painting or music as the technical norm of literature. For literature was clearly in possession of objects for imitation but was handicapped by having really no paint (no natural sensory signs) or none to speak of; painting itself was in a favorable middle position, having both definable objects and natural signs; while music (when pure and not allied to vocal art) was in the odd position of having a persuasively direct sensory medium but no controllable correspondence between the medium and any definite objects.[5]

Despite the analytic glance of a Lessing here and there, the tide of theory and taste moved toward a synthesis, inevitably to be made easier by the metaphysical ascendancy of idea over material in the romantic era. In the mid-18th century occur such phenomena as the Abbé Castel's Clavecin de Couleurs and speculations such as Diderot's on transfer of sense experience,[6] and in the early 19th century the references of German literary philosophers to architecture as frozen music, to poetry as music for the inner ear and painting for the inner eye. The verbal synaesthesis which is epidemic in romantic poetry and is advertised later, quite self-consciously, in such doctrinaire poems as those of Baudelaire

[5] The lesson of Professor Calvin Brown's *Music and Literature, a Comparison of the Arts* (Athens, Georgia, 1948) would seem to be that music owes more to literature than it is able to repay.

[6] See Irving Babbitt, *The New Laokoon* (Boston, 1910). The story of the man born blind who identified the color scarlet by the sound of a trumpet, first published in Locke's *Essay* (from the communication of the Irish philosopher Molyneux), reverberated through the century. Cf. Marjorie Nicolson, *Newton Demands the Muse* (Princeton, 1946), pp. 83–5.

and Rimbaud on "correspondences," the Pre-Raphaelite experiment,[7] the Wagnerian *Gesamtkunstwerk*, the birth of ballet, the hero of Huysmans' *A Rebours* playing his fugues on a taste organ of spigots inserted in kegs of liqueurs, all these are typical of a trend (a mélange and confusion of the arts) which as late as 1910 provoked the Harvard humanist Irving Babbitt to write his summation and alarm entitled *The New Laokoon*. The vogue during recent centuries of what Tolstoy in a reactionary treatise characterizes as upper-class voluptuary art has been a vogue of sensory pleasures analogized and merged, and it has moved climactically away from objects of imitation toward media and hence toward the imitation of media by one another.

> When the center of life disappears, the arts of poetry become the art of poetry. And in an advanced stage of the evil, in the nineteenth century and today, we get the *mélange des genres*, one art living off another, that the late Irving Babbitt so valiantly combated without having understood the influences that had brought it about. Painting tries to be music; poetry leans upon painting; all the arts "strive toward the condition of music"; till at last seeing the mathematical structure of music, the arts become geometrical and abstract, and destroy themselves.[8]

VIII

The Abbé Charles Batteux had, as we have seen, reduced all the arts to a single principle, and his unified view of the fine arts taken up by Diderot and D'Alembert in the *Encyclopédie*, proved widely influential during the second half of the century. Batteux's single "principle" was the classical principle of "imitation." But no matter what the principle, the unification of the arts was a fertile ground for subsequent attempts at more or less scientific division and subdivision. Where Lessing was concerned only with the modest project of separating poetry from painting (time from space), his contemporary and critic J. G. Herder distinguished painting (the art of the eye), music (the art of the ear), and sculpture (the art of touch). And from these arts poetry differed yet

---

[7] Compare, for instance, D. G. Rossetti's painting *The Blessed Damozel* with his poem of the same title. "Whether this interpenetration of poetry and painting is of advantage to either, may admit of question. . . . The sonnets of 'The House of Life' have appeared to many readers obscure and artificial, the working out in language of conceptions more easily expressible by some other art. . . . Such readers are apt to imagine that Rossetti suffers from a hesitation between poetry and painting. . . . The method proper to one art intrudes onto the other; everything the artist does has the air of an experiment; he paints poems and writes pictures" (Henry A. Beers, *A History of English Romanticism in the Nineteenth Century*, New York, 1901, p. 307).

[8] Allen Tate, *Reactionary Essays* (New York, 1936), p. 55.

again. It was the only immediate art of the soul, the music of the soul—
not work, but energy.[9] J. G. Sulzer's *Allgemeine Theorie der Schönen
Künste*, 1771–1774, an alphabetically arranged encyclopedia, divided the
fine arts somewhat simply by media: color, body, tone, words. In his
aesthetic entitled *The Critique of Judgment*, 1790, Kant arrived at a
three-fold basic division of the arts corresponding to three characters
of spoken communication, word, gesture, and tone: 1. arts of speech
(*redende Künste*), poetry and rhetoric; 2. arts of shaping (*bildende
Künste*), architecture, sculpture, painting; 3. arts of beautiful sensory
pattern (*Künste des schönen Spiels der Empfindungen*), music and color
design.[1] This became an important landmark. Still it was but a limited
model for the brilliant efflorescence of "systems" which marks the subsequent history of general aesthetics—in the work of Hegel and a host
of other 19th- and 20th-century continental writers. The system of the
English aesthetician Sidney Colvin may be consulted in his article "Fine
Arts" in the *Encyclopedia Britannica*, 11th edition, 1910. The most recent system to appear is perhaps that of Etienne Souriau in his *La
Correspondance des Arts*, 1947.[2]

The modern activity of classifying the arts has been an attempt to
put certain traditionally distinguished arts into more or less neatly
bounded areas in a pattern having two basic dimensions. These dimensions are, unavoidably: (1) the dimension of physical medium—under
the aspects of time and space; and (2) the dimension of intellectual
reference—positive and negative, that is, symbolic and non-symbolic.
Attempts to add other basic dimensions[3] or to refine too far on the subdivisions of these two have produced overlapping or have created areas
of unoccupied abstraction. Such attempts have only accentuated the ir-
reducibly concrete character of works of art. In the symbolic dimension a useful division seems to be that (defined so early by the Abbé
Du Bos) between more or less natural symbols (pictures) and more or
less artificial symbols (words). But a great obstacle to tidiness in the
whole system arises from the fact that in the physical dimension so
radical a thing as movement appears in both space and time—so that arts
of movement in space (dancing, drama, opera) are inevitably also time

---

[9] Robert T. Clark, Jr., "Herder's Conception of 'Kraft,'" *PMLA*, LVII (1942),
737–52. Herder's distinctions appeared in his *Plastik*, 1778.

[1] Kristeller, *loc. cit.*, XIII, 43 n., 278, explains Kant's *Farbenkunst* (mentioned
also by Herder and by Mendelssohn) with reference to the Abbé Castel's color piano.
For the moment we are not concerned with Kant's more radical preliminary distinctions between science and skill, between mercenary art (*Lohnkunst, Handwerk*)
and free art, between the merely pleasing (*angenehm*) and the beautiful (*schön*).
Cf. *post* Chapter 17, p. 371.

[2] See the excellent survey in Thomas Munro's *The Arts and Their Interrelations* (New York, 1949), Chap. V.

[3] As: utilitarian and non-utilitarian (table utensils, sculpture); made with or
without tools (sculpture, dancing).

arts, though not the only time arts. There are also time arts of pure sound (either symbolic or non-symbolic—poetry or music). The element of symbol (natural, artificial, or combined) may obviously be joined with the elements of space, time and movement in a variety of complexes, from the simplicity of song to the hetereogeneity of opera. It is, in short, impossible to construct a classification both basic and abstract and yet precise enough to isolate the several arts as they are traditionally and concretely marked off from one another.[4]

Our own effort to construct such a classification produces a table of the following sort.

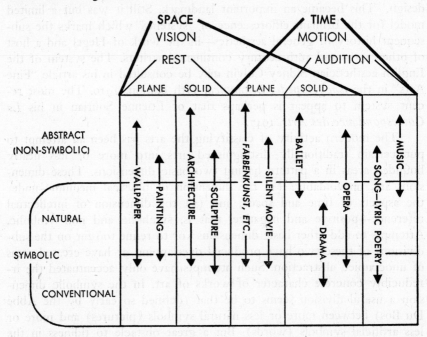

The construction or the perusal of a table like this has no very immediate relation to literary criticism. The exercise may, however, have some merit. It may have the merit of persuading us that some differences are more basic than others—as that between symbolic and non-symbolic, that between space and time, or that between natural resemblance and conventional sign. It may further remind us that art works are always concrete, that classifications are abstract, and that there are

[4] Etienne Souriau attempts to avoid the difficulty by making symbolic and non-symbolic his only two-fold division and multiplying across that the enumeration of the several media in one spectrum. Thus to the visual media of line, color, and volume he adds "luminosity." In the symbolic zone of his wheel he has a space for cinema, but in order to fill the corresponding non-symbolic space he has to make use of "luminous projections"; in the non-symbolic space corresponding to literature he has to introduce "pure prosody."

differences between the concrete arts which are better bridged meta-phorically than literally. A theorist of poetry, being inevitably a person who subscribes to metaphoric and analogical ways of thinking, is in a good position to avoid both the fault of running the arts confusedly to-gether by metaphors which become literal and the opposite fault of cut-ting the arts off from one another too completely by the denial of all such relations. There are poetic dimensions which can never be described except metaphorically, and to keep open, if only tentatively, the time-honored metaphoric avenues may do something to prevent theoretical discussion from declining into the literalism of a quasi-scientific seman-tics.

SUPPLEMENT

On the Camera Obscura

Yield *Raphael*, Titian yield, whose mimic strife
Would warm th' unwilling Canvas into life;
Colours more true shall in my Landskip glow,
If equal to my Theme my Numbers flow;
The Cloud-topt Summit, or enamel'd Lawn,
Woods, Rivers, Seas, by Nature's Pencil drawn;
By Art contracted shall Assistance bring,
And from their blended Charms a fair Creation spring.
Thro' the small Portal, see a gath'ring Ray,
To the dark Room transmit a doubtful Day!
Spontaneous Beauties fill th' extended Scroll,
Reflected Streams with silent Motion roll.

—from *The Museum*, published by Robert Dodsley, No. 13, September 12, 1746, pp. 492–3

When taken out, the plate [of the Daguerreotype] does not at first appear to have received a definite impression—some short processes, however, develop it in the most miraculous beauty. All language must fall short of conveying any just idea of the truth, and this will not appear so wonderful when we reflect that the source of vision itself has been, in this instance, the designer. Perhaps, if we imagine the distinctness with which an object is reflected in a positively perfect mirror, we come as near the reality as by any other means. For, in truth, the Daguerreotyped plate is infinitely (we use the term advisedly) is *infinitely* more accurate in its representation than any painting by human hands. If we examine a work of ordinary art, by means of a power-ful microscope, all traces of resemblance to nature will disappear—but the closest scrutiny of the photographic drawing discloses only a more absolute truth, a more perfect identity of aspect with the thing represented. The variations of shade, the gradations of both linear and aerial perspective are those of truth itself in the supremeness of its perfection.

—*Alexander's Weekly Messenger*, Philadelphia, December 15, 1840, reprinted by Clarence S. Brigham, *Edgar Allan Poe's Contributions to Alexander's Weekly Messenger* (Worcester, Mass., 1943), p. 21. Poe's authorship seems likely.

The analogy anciently suggested in the phrase ut pictura poesis *is a very hard one to keep down; it is revived with a varied accent according to the bent of each age. Mr. Allen Tate, in the essay from which we have quoted above, draws an interesting parallel between the poetry of John Peale Bishop and some features of 20th-century surrealism in painting.*

PERSPECTIVES ARE PRECIPICES

Sister Anne, Sister Anne,
Do you see anybody coming?

> I see a distance of black yews
> Long as the history of the Jews.

> I see a road sunned with white sand
> Wide plains surrounding silence. And

> Far off, a broken colonnade
> That overthrows the sun in shade.

Sister Anne, Sister Anne,
Do you see nobody coming?

> 　　　　　　　A man
> Upon that road a man who goes
> Dragging a shadow by its toes.

> Diminishing he goes, head bare
> Of any covering even hair.

> A pitcher depending from one hand
> Goes mouth down. And dry is sand

Sister Anne, Sister Anne,
What do you see?

> His dwindling stride. And he seems blind
> Or worse to the prone man behind.

Sister Anne! Sister Anne!

I see a road. Beyond nowhere
Defined by cirrus and blue air.

I saw a man but he is gone
His shadow into the sun.

From *Now with His Love* by John Peale Bishop; copyright 1933 by
Charles Scribner's Sons and used with their permission.

*As Bishop himself was to suggest in a lecture delivered partly as a response to
Tate's essay,[5] a painting may do more than merely refer to time in the way it
does when it shows a season or a time of day, a calendar or a clock. A painting
may achieve something more like a direct presentation of the experience of
time. This it can do by the use of perspective (a technique not merely of
versimilitude but of temporal metaphor),[6] and by the use of successively placed
and postured figures, as in a battle scene of raised, falling, and thrusting lances
or swords, or in a Fall of Manna. Or fantastically, as in certain Siennese narrative paintings showing the same person simultaneously at different points on
a road.[7] By a technique approximately the counterpart of this, that is, by patterns of repetition and diminishment (the refrain of Bishop's* Perspectives*),
by a degree of overt reference to spatial features, and by certain associations
with a style of painting, that of Salvador Dali in the present instance, the poet
may achieve something curiously like a realization of space in the time art of
words.*

Although each art has . . . its own specific order of impressions, and an
untranslatable charm, while a just apprehension of the ultimate differences of
the arts is the beginning of aesthetic criticism; yet it is noticeable that, in its
special mode of handling its given material, each art may be observed to pass
into the condition of some other art, by what German critics term an *Anders-
streben*—a partial alienation from its own limitations, through which the arts
are able, not indeed to supply the place of each other, but reciprocally to lend
each other new forces.

Thus some of the most delightful music seems to be always approaching
to figure, to pictorial definition. Architecture, again, though it has its own
laws—laws esoteric enough, as the true architect knows only too well—yet
sometimes aims at fulfilling the conditions of a picture, as in the *Arena* chapel;
or of sculpture, as in the flawless unity of Giotto's tower at Florence; and
often finds a true poetry, as in those strangely twisted staircases of the
chateaux of the country of the Loire, as if it were intended that among their

[5] "Poetry and Painting," *The Sewanee Review*, LIII (Spring, 1945), 247–58.
[6] "The conquest of perspective by the great Western painters was no mere
display of erudition or of virtuosity in imitation. It was what Oswald Spengler
calls it, the creation of a spiritual space, 'wide and eternal,' which responds to the
imperious need of Western man for a symbol of distance and the infinite" (Melvin
Rader, *A Source Book of Modern Aesthetics*, Introduction, p. xii).
[7] Lessing refers to such pictures with disapproval. He is dealing with essentially
the same problem as the 17th-century theorists of stage unity when they were confronted with the Italian perspective stage and the French medieval *maisons*. The
question of what constitutes a true unity in painting—harmony of line and color,
coherence of story, continuity of background, consistency of perspective, or mere
adjacency of lines and colors—is one which we leave for the theorist of painting.

odd turnings the actors in a theatrical mode of life might pass each other unseen; there being a poetry also of memory and of the mere effect of time, by which architecture often profits greatly. Thus, again, sculpture aspires out of the hard limitation of pure form towards color, or its equivalent; poetry also, in many ways, finding guidance from the other arts, the analogy between a Greek tragedy and a work of Greek sculpture, between a sonnet and a relief, of French poetry generally with the art of engraving, being more than mere figures of speech; and all the arts in common aspiring towards the principle of music; music being the typical, or ideally consummate art, the object of the great *Anders-streben* of all art, of all that is artistic, or partakes of artistic qualities.

All art constantly aspires towards the condition of music. For while in all other kinds of art it is possible to distinguish the matter from the form, and the understanding can always make this distinction, yet it is the constant effort of art to obliterate it. That the mere matter of a poem, for instance, its subject, namely, its given incidents or situation—that the mere matter of a picture, the actual circumstances of an event, the actual topography of a landscape—should be nothing without the form, the spirit, of the handling, that this form, this mode of handling, should become an end in itself, should penetrate every part of the matter: this is what all art constantly strives after, and achieves in different degrees.

—Walter Pater, "The School of Giorgione," in *The Renaissance* (Modern Library edition), pp. 110–11

GENIUS, EMOTION, AND ASSOCIATION

§ *resumé of "dissociation"—II. inspirationalism, neo-Longinianism, Boileau, the sublime in England, external grandeur, Dennis and Addison, Gothic irregularity, Pope, untrammeled genius vs. correctness, Addison, Reynolds, Ruskin, Macaulay's objection—III. originality, Edward Young, "imitation" damned, "pleasures of the pen," Johnson on Homer and Virgil, athletes who died young—IV. "ecstasis," Dennis, "enthusiastick emotion," Aristotelian catharsis, as purgation, as sublimation, as moderation (1) Stoic, (2) sentimental, Rapin, Dryden, Dennis, Steele, Addison, Johnson—V. pleasures of painful emotion, mimetic and didactic explanations, affective explanations: safety and self-congratulation, Hobbes and Lucretius, the unselfish alternative, Descartes, merger with sentimental catharsis —VI. "sympathy," Sterne and Adam Smith, Kames, Blair, Cowper to a young lady, illusionism, everyday life, simplicity, George Campbell, Coleridge—VII. genealogy of the Man of Feeling, tearful literature, reputation of Pope's Elegy, pure emotion dark, opposition between wit and passion, Dennis, Hume, Johnson, Warton on Pope, "sublime and pathetic" poets, "ethical" poets—VIII. Burke again, physiological and affective theory of beauty, the problem of verbal art, picture or passion, "expression," —IX. the Lockean special sense of association, the Humean and Hartleyan general sense, flattening of a distinction —X. kinds of application: the garrulous dramatic, the Shandean whimsical, the synecdochic, pregnant particulars, "associational response," putting the world back together again, "imagination," Adam Ferguson, "coalescence," Abraham Tucker—XI. association of values, Alison, Hazlitt, Coleridge, Hobbes, Gerard and Tucker. Coleridge on Hartley, "gift of spreading the tone," Hazlitt, J. S. Mill's essays on poetry, 1833* §

W E HAVE NOTED THAT A CERTAIN MISTRUST OF THE MEANINGS CON-
veyed by poems, especially by witty or imaginative poems, had
grown during the later 17th century with the growth of
scientific philosophy. The epistemological charter of the new philosophy,
the Hobbesian and Lockean sensationalism, had inspired its own kind of
substitute for the moral, political, and religious values which the older
defences of poetry had been likely to rely upon. In the place of Sidney's
"feigning notable images of virtues [and] vices," appeared Addison's
ocular pleasures, the "beautiful," the "grand," and the "novel." Here was
a tendency to assign to poetry a new and simpler province, less pretentious, more soothing, and more easily amusing. This at least had the
advantage of suggesting that poetry was something by itself, an innocent
pleasure set aside from both the sterner prerogatives and the heavy responsibilities which the didactic view would confer upon it. We shall
have occasion in a later chapter to notice these ideas from the retrospective advantage of the 19th-century doctrine of autonomous or gratuitous
aesthetic value—*l'art pour l'art*. Meanwhile we may observe certain other
ways in which the apology for poetry during the age of reason retreated
from the area of rational truth claimed by the scientific and rationalist
forces. These ways may be broadly described as retreats into the area of
feeling and emotion, or into an area of feeling and emotion conceived
as pure and prior to, or separate from, the objects of knowledge which
had previously been considered their grounds. The term "dissociation of
sensibility," to which we have referred already, at the start of our last
chapter, is a coinage which aptly suggests that situation—a dissociation
of the feeling and responding side of human consciousness from the side
of knowing and rational valuing. There were two emotive directions in
which the dissociation could work—toward the inspirations of the author
of poetry, and toward the responses of his audience.

II

The inspiration of the poet had been since early classical times a
main reliance of those who would account for the element of the mysterious in poetry. The muse invoked by Homer or Hesiod personified
the magnetic frenzy ironically ascribed by Socrates both to the unscientific bard and his enraptured critic. In later antiquity the treatise of
"Longinus" *On The Sublime* centered these ideas less in the divine inspiration than in the great soul—the great thoughts and emotions—of
the poet himself. And the modern career of Longinus, which began with
the first edition by Robortello in 1554 and reached its influential phase
with the translation of Boileau, *Du Sublime*, in 1674, was a strain of

classicism very well qualified to promote a subjective and inspirationalist trend in contemporary poetics. Such a trend was in part to be expected from the introspective implications of the available new psychology, in the tradition of Descartes' *Treatise on the Passions of the Soul*, and also, as we have been saying, from the mere pressure of the rationalist objections to the traditionally cognitive or "imitative" premises of criticism. But inspirationalism as it appears in actual literary theory at this period takes a strong local coloration from Longinianism. Criticism was still nominally under the authority of the classics; it was a great point in favor of a literary thesis to have classical countenance or to be able to assume a classical form. By a slight oversimplification, we may think of Longinus as the Trojan horse in the camp of neo-classicism.

The term "sublime" in French criticism, shortly before the work of Boileau, had been applied to diction and had meant something like *préciosité* or a metaphysical affectation of nicety. And Boileau's main point in his classic Preface (the effort which established the modern term "sublime" for French and English criticism) was that the sublime so well described by Longinus resided not in nicety of terms but in grandeur of conception—a grandeur which had to be expressed, not preciously, but strongly, and which was capable of being expressed in only a few simple words. The example cited by Longinus from the opening of the "Hebrew Lawgiver's" *Genesis* lent itself most impressively to Boileau's new conception.

> By the "sublime" Longinus did not mean what orators call "the sublime style;" he meant the element of the extraordinary in discourse, the marvellous, the striking, that in virtue of which a work exalts, ravishes, transports. The sublime *style* needs lofty language; but the *sublime* may appear in a single thought, a figure, a phrase . . . *Le souverain arbitre de la nature d'une seule parole forma la lumière*: there is the sublime *style* for you. . . . But, *Dieu dit: Que la lumière se fasse; et la lumière se fit.* This extraordinary expression . . . is genuinely sublime; it has something divine about it.[1]

[1] *Oeuvres Complètes*, ed. Daunou (Paris, 1839), II, 311–12. Cf. A. F. B. Clark, *Boileau and French Classical Critics in England* (Paris, 1925), pp. 371–9; Samuel Monk, *The Sublime* (New York, 1935), pp. 30–1. An accent on simplicity of diction can be derived not so much from the words of Boileau himself as from his Biblical example and the interpretation of that by French and English readers. See Monk, p. 33, the protest of Huet that the style was too simple, and the following from Robert South, Sermon XVI, "A Discourse against Long and Extempore Prayers," first published in 1694 (*Sermons*, Oxford, 1842, I, 335): "Was it [this way of speaking] not authorized and ennobled by God himself in his making of the world? Was not the work of all the six days transacted in so many words? There was no circumlocution or amplification in the case; which makes the rhetorician Longinus, in his book of the Loftiness of Speech, so much admire the height and grandeur of Moses's style in the first chapter of Genesis."

Boileau was later somewhat hard pressed by French critical opponents, and in

In England the importance of Boileau's sublime was the launching of a term and a text rather than of a single clearly defined idea. English critics made mainly two things of the sublime, and each of these was an exaggeration of hints contained in memorable Longinian passages which we have quoted in an earlier chapter. For one thing, looking chiefly at the passage in Chapter XXXV of Longinus, on the Nile, the Danube, the Rhine, the Ocean, the celestial fires, the craters of Etna ("whose eruptions throw up stones from its depths and great masses of rock, and at times pour forth rivers of . . . pure and unmixed subterranean fire"), the critics erected a theory of the external objects which are sublime— namely, the big, the irregular, the surprising, and frightening. In our last chapter we have touched on this topic apropos of the 18th-century preoccupation with the externally definable sensational stimulus.[2] But certain features of the external sublime deserve to be specially noted in the present context. One of these was what might be summed up in the phrase "dangerous bigness." This was a bigness especially of landscape objects, the Alps, for instance, over which Dennis made a journey in 1688 and was impressed with "a delightful Horrour, a terrible Joy." Addison later made a similar journey with similar feelings,[3] and in a *Spectator* he wrote:

> . . . of all Objects that I have ever seen, there is none which affects my Imagination so much as the Sea or Ocean. I cannot see the Heavings of this prodigious Bulk of Waters, even in a calm, without a very pleasing Astonishment. But when it is worked up in a Tempest, so that the Horizon on every side is nothing but foaming Billows and floating Mountains, it is impossible to describe the agreeable Horrour that rises from such a Prospect.[4]

---

a series of twelve *Réflexions sur Longin*, the last three published posthumously, he arrived at the modified view that the sublime could in effect be a medley of all five of the Longinian sources—great thought and passion and (on the side of technique or rhetoric) words, figures, and harmonious composition.

[2] Cf. *ante* p. 255.

[3] C. D. Thorpe, "Two Augustans Cross the Alps: Dennis and Addison on Mountain Scenery," *SP*, XXXII (1935), 463–82.

[4] No. 489. In another *Spectator* (No. 592) Addison gives a humorous report on this kind of sublime as artificially arranged in the theater. "I look upon the Playhouse as a World within itself. They have lately furnished the Middle Region of it with a new Sett of Meteors, in order to give the Sublime to many modern Tragedies. I was there last Winter at the first Rehearsal of the new Thunder, which is much more deep and sonorous than any hitherto made use of. . . . They are also provided with above a Dozen Showers of Snow, which, as I am informed, are the Plays of many unsuccessful Poets artificially cut and shredded for that Use."

Another passage worth consulting here is that in which Samuel Johnson gives his estimate of the lines describing Dover Cliff in *King Lear* (Boswell, *Life*, 16 October, 1769). "No, Sir; it should be all precipice—all vacuum. The crows impede your fall. The diminished appearance of the boats, and other circumstances . . . do not impress the mind at once with the horrible idea of immense height."

Here was an aspect of the sublime which seems to have blended very readily with ideas of grandeur such as we shall discuss mainly under the head of neo-Platonic universality in our next chapter. A second main feature of the external sublime, relating obviously to bigness and danger, was that of wildness, shagginess, or Gothic irregularity. And this was a landscape feature which more easily even than bigness became a companion and external counterpart of the great and original soul of the poet. Thus Pope, in a liberalizing part of his *Essay on Criticism*:

> In prospects thus, some objects please our eyes,
> Which out of nature's common order rise,
> The shapeless rock, or hanging precipice.
> Great Wits sometimes may gloriously offend,
> And rise to faults true Critics dare not mend.
> —ll. 156-60

And with this we have, in fact, the second of the two main things which English criticism made of the Longinian sublime—a philosophy of untrammeled great "genius." Longinus himself, we may recall, had gone rather far in conferring upon such ideas as "perfection," "precision," and "regularity" a pejorative cast and in setting these against the idea of poetic genius. Addison in several of his *Spectators* was able to make the doctrine more precise and naive.

> At the same time that we allow a greater and more daring Genius to the Ancients, we must own that the greatest of them very much failed in, or, if you will, that they were very much above the Nicety and Correctness of the Moderns.—No. 160

> I must . . . observe with Longinus, that the Productions of a great Genius, with many Lapses and Inadvertencies, are infinitely preferable to the Works of an inferior kind of Author, which are scrupulously exact and conformable to all the Rules of correct Writing.—No. 291

> There is sometimes a greater Judgment shown in deviating from the Rules of Art, than in adhering to them; and . . . there is more Beauty in the Works of a great Genius who is ignorant of all the Rules of Art, than in the Works of a little Genius, who not only knows, but scrupulously observes them.
> —No. 592

Later in the century Reynolds was to report:

> So far, indeed, is the presence of genius from implying an absence of faults, that they are considered by many as its inseparable companions.[5]

[5] *Discourses Delivered to the Students of the Royal Academy.* The Eleventh Discourse, 1782, par. 2. Cf. *ante* Chapter 6, pp. 105-6; Chapter 11, p. 202, the similar theme of "imitative form."

This was the bizarre critical doctrine (according to which poetic form consists in imperfection) inherited with distaste by Macaulay in his review of Moore's *Byron,* and with an anachronistic gusto by Ruskin in the chapter of his *Stones of Venice* (II, 6) where the handwrought irregularity of Gothic architecture is praised in contrast to the machine-made "perfection" of modern glass beads. Macaulay's views are perhaps an adequate summation of the issue:

> Wherein especially does the poetry of our times differ from that of the last century? Ninety-nine persons out of a hundred would answer that the poetry of the last century was correct, but cold and mechanical, and that the poetry of our time, though wild and irregular, presented far more vivid images and excited the passions far more strongly than that of Parnell, of Addison, or of Pope. In the same manner we constantly hear it said that the poets of the age of Elizabeth had far more genius, but far less correctness, than those of the age of Anne. It seems to be taken for granted that there is some incompatibility, some antithesis, between correctness and creative power. We rather suspect that this notion arises merely from an abuse of words, and that it has been the parent of many of the fallacies which perplex the science of criticism.
>
> What is meant by correctness in poetry? If by correctness be meant the conforming to rules which have their foundation in truth and in the principles of human nature, then correctness is only another name for excellence. If by correctness be meant the conforming to rules purely arbitrary, correctness may be another name for dulness and absurdity.[6]

III

THE most quotable expression of the Longinian philosophy of original genius to appear in 18th-century England was the essay entitled *Conjectures upon Original Composition* published in 1759 by the aged poet of melancholy *Night Thoughts,* Edward Young.

> A *genius* differs from a *good understanding,* as a magician from a good architect; . . . Hence genius has ever been supposed to

[6] Alden, p. 346. Macaulay's bullseye appeared in the *Edinburgh Review* for June, 1831. Cf. A. W. Schlegel, *Lectures on Dramatic Literature* (1809–11), XXIII (Bate, p. 423): "If the formation of a work throughout, even in its minutest parts, in conformity with a leading idea; if the domination of one animating spirit over all the means of execution, deserves the name of correctness (and this, excepting in matters of grammar, is the only proper sense of the term); we shall then, after allowing to Shakespeare all the higher qualities which demand our admiration, be also compelled, in most cases, to concede to him the title of a correct poet."

partake of something divine. *Nemo unquam vir magnus fuit, sine aliquo afflatu divino.*[7]

While he adopts and magnifies the Longinian notion that true poetic imitation is the intercourse of the aspiring poet's mind with the master spirits of the past,[8] Young flatly rejects the doctrine that it is a good thing to study the classic models. His essay is a vigorous recommendation of the *cacoethes scribendi*, a sustained celebration of the "pleasures of the pen," the "sweet refuge" of original composition. "The more composition," he says, "the better." "How independent of the world is he, who can daily find new acquaintance . . . in the little world, the minute but fruitful creation, of his own mind?"[9] In bold strokes Young lays down the poetic criteria of chronological novelty and loyalty to the self's own productions—no matter what their quality.

> We read *Imitation* with somewhat of his languor, who listens to a twice-told tale: Our spirits rouze at an *Original;* and all throng to learn what news from a foreign land: . . . tho' it comes, like an *Indian* prince, adorned with feathers only, having little weight.[1]

The study of great models is not only *not* helpful but actually baneful, because:

> They *engross* our attention, and so prevent a due inspection of ourselves; they *prejudice* our judgment in favor of their abilities, and so lessen the sense of our own; and they intimidate us with this splendor of their renown.[2]

It is a paradoxical fact that the ancients themselves "had no merit in being *Originals.*" In those days it was impossible to be otherwise. "They could *not* be *Imitators.*"[3] Young is presumably here thinking back to the really first, but now altogether forgotten, ancients. The actually known ancients may very well be holding their honors only through our own ignorance.

> . . . they tho' not *real,* are *accidental Originals;* the works they imitated, few excepted, are lost.[4]

If we suppose Young's manifesto to be representative of a thickening climate of literary opinion, we shall not be surprised when, about twenty years later, that far more severe critical thinker, Samuel Johnson, lets fall the following *obiter dictum.*

[7] *Conjectures,* ed. Edith Morley (Manchester, 1918), p. 13. See Gilbert and Kuhn, p. 342, n. 45, on 20th-century studies of the *Geniebegriff.*

[8] Cf. Elizabeth Nitchie, "Longinus and the Theory of Poetic Imitation in Seventeenth and Eighteenth Century England," *SP,* XXXII (1915), 580–97.

[9] *Conjectures,* pp. 4–5.

[1] *Conjectures,* p. 7.

[2] *Conjectures,* p. 9.

[3] *Conjectures,* p. 10.

[4] *Conjectures,* p. 8.

'We must consider (said he) whether Homer was not the greatest poet, though Virgil may have produced the finest poem. Virgil was indebted to Homer for the whole invention of the structure of an epick poem, and for many of his beauties.'[5]

Dryden, in his elegantly blunt way, had once said of the Elizabethan writers:

> Fame then was cheap, and the first comer sped;
> And they have kept it since, by being dead.

This gross mistake had at least the merit of proceeding on the assumption that literary worth was something that might suffer by comparison with superior worth. On the new theory, of genius and originality, the only way to be sure of having any worth (a kind of inescapable and hence unmeritorious worth) was to be in on the threshold of literary history, to get there first, even if with the least. For all improvements on the beginning would inescapably suffer the handicap of not being first. Thus literary creators were accorded in effect that variety of honor, in most cases necessarily sentimental and archaic, which the world can afford for its inventors—an Archimedes, a Fulton, a Watt, the brothers Wright —athletes who died in good time, runners whom renown did not outrun. Why would not Homer's poems, on Edward Young's view, be subject to the same discount in value as the first steamboat or the first airplane if put into competition with the machines of 1950? Simply because of the peculiar fiat, the confusion in critical thinking between poet and poem, by which during this period in critical history the first became equivalent with the best.

IV

THE neo-Longinian great soul was never far from an attendant concept, that of emotion. Yet emotion is a thing more externally manifest than the secret inspiration of poetry, and it is better observed in the audience than in the poet. In the neo-classic era, as in the ancient, emotion characteristically attaches itself to the audience; it is discussed under the head of the results or aims of poetry. The affective side of ancient Longinianism, the emotion of the sublime, had been called "transport" (*ekstasis*). The affective side of neo-Longinianism was "enthusiasm" or "passion," a kind of emotion raised by reason above pettiness to the grandeur of a

---

[5] Quoted by Boswell in *Life of Johnson*, 22 September, 1777.

Even Dryden had been guilty of this sort of thinking on the Homer-Virgil question. See his Preface to *Fables*, 1700 (*Essays*, ed. Ker, II, 251–4). He furthermore gave great credit to Chaucer for inventing the *Wife of Bath's Tale* and the *Nun's Priest's Tale* (p. 255).

religious experience. "Vulgar Passion," according to John Dennis, is aroused by external "Objects;" "Enthusiastick emotion," by "Ideas in Contemplation." [6] This was a kind of thinking that later might easily be turned to the account of the wild genius of the poet himself. Yet in this earlier phase of neo-Longinianism the emphasis was not actually there. Dennis is a classically oriented critic; he holds the exalted and religious emotion up for some scrutiny and stresses its rational transcendence in a way that clearly concerns the semi-public realm of the collective reader's bosom.

In another place—in the diluted strain of Aristotelianism that continued during the later 17th and the 18th centuries—one finds a kind of affectivism appearing more clearly under a classic sanction. As far back as Dryden's heroic and French classical period—or even in the earlier Preface by Milton to his classical drama *Samson Agonistes*—we can detect a softer tone in the English account of catharsis than would be familiar to a person who had read only the documents of antiquity. Catharsis, we may remember, in the Aristotelian construction *tēn tōn toioutōn pathēmatōn katharsin*, referred in a very practical, downright and medical way to a supposed capacity of tragic drama to cleanse our minds of painful and unhealthy emotions. Yet through religious and lustratory metaphoric interpretation the notion was susceptible of being sublimed to mean something like a purifying and exalting of the emotions themselves. This interpretation seems to have appeared even during later antiquity, in neo-Platonic thought. But its hyper-development, to the eclipse of purgative Aristotelianism, was a modern accomplishment. The first step in a fairly plausible evolution was to say—as we may notice, for instance, the Dutch critic Daniel Heinsius saying, and later Milton—that purging the emotions meant tempering or moderating them, to a just proportion in our temperamental equilibrium. From there a later step would be the extreme already mentioned, the exaltation of pity and fear to the heights of unselfish contemplation, a zenith reached in the post-romantic 19th century. Or, by a kind of sidestep, the theory might arrive—and did even during the 17th century arrive—at the position of saying that the emotions of pity and fear aroused by tragedy were beneficent because they neutralized *other* and dangerous passions —such as anger, ambition, or greed.

These are plausible variations on the cathartic theme. Yet a great significance lies in the matter of *what* emotions "catharsis" is thought to moderate. The homeopathic moderation of pity and fear (like the Aristotelian purgation) is anti-emotional. In its 17th-century form it was

[6] John Dennis, *The Grounds of Criticism in Poetry*, 1704, in *Works*, ed. E. N. Hooker, I, 338–9. Cf. the excellent statement by Norman Maclean concerning Dennis and other writers in the same vein, e.g., Bishop Lowth in his *De Sacra Poesi Hebraeorum*, 1753 ("From Action to Image: Theories of the Lyric in the Eighteenth Century," in *Critics and Criticism Ancient and Modern*, ed. R. S. Crane, pp. 438–9).

neo-Stoic and allied to the sort of severe statement exemplified in Spinoza's *Ethics,* where passion is "Human Bondage."

> Pity, in a man who lives under the guidance of reason, is in itself bad. The good effect which follows, namely our endeavour to free the object of our pity from misery, is an action which we desire to do solely at the dictation of reason; only at the dictation of reason are we able to perform any action, which we know for certain to be good; thus, in a man who lives under the influence of reason, pity in itself is useless and bad.[7]

On the other hand, the allopathic theory that pity and fear moderate *other* less desirable passions was on the side of emotional development and would run quite naturally into 18th-century sentimentalism. By a partial suppression of Rapin's view in his *Réflexions sur la Poétique d'Aristote* (1674), Dryden in his Preface to *Troilus and Cressida* (1679) arrived at an early English statement:

> Rapin, a judicious critic, has observed from Aristotle, that pride and want of commiseration are the most predominant vices in mankind; therefore, to cure us of these two, the inventors of Tragedy have chosen to work upon two other passions, which are, fear and pity. . . . When we see that the most virtuous, as well as the greatest, are not exempt from [such] . . . misfortunes, that consideration moves pity in us, and insensibly works us to be helpful to, and tender over, the distressed; which is the noblest and most godlike of moral virtues.[8]

The triumphant progress of the argument may be illustrated at pleasure from the aestheticians and essayists of the next hundred years: from Dennis, for instance ("Tragedy . . . has been always found sufficient to soften the most obdurate Heart"); from Steele ("The contemplation of distresses . . . softens the mind, and makes the heart better. It extinguishes the seed of envy and ill will . . . corrects the pride of prosperity"); from Addison ("Diversions of this kind . . . soften insolence, sooth affliction, and subdue the mind to the dispensations of providence").[9] The casually axiomatic status of the doctrine, and a version of it which tries to include Stoic moderation, may be shown by quoting another of Samuel Johnson's off-the-cuff pronouncements:

[7] *Ethics, Chief Works,* trans. R. H. Elwes (London, 1887), II, 221, quoted by Baxter Hathaway, "John Dryden and the Function of Tragedy," *PMLA,* LVII (September, 1943), 668.

[8] Ker I, 210. Rapin had argued that the play not only increases sensibility in those who are deficient in it, but moderates it in those who have too much (Hathaway, p. 668).

[9] *The Critical Works of John Dennis,* ed. E. N. Hooker (Baltimore, 1939), I, 164; Steele, *Tatler* No. 82; Addison, *Spectator* No. 39. See Hathaway, pp. 666–7 for more complete quotations and further authorities.

'But how are the passions to be purged by terrour and pity?'
(said I, with an assumed air of ignorance, to incite him to talk
. . .). Johnson, 'Why, Sir, . . . The passions are the great mov-
ers of human actions; but they are mixed with such impurities,
that it is necessary they should be purged or refined by means
of terrour and pity. For instance, ambition is a noble passion; but
by seeing upon the stage, that a man who is so excessively
ambitious as to raise himself by injustice, is punished, we are
terrified at the fatal consequences of such a passion. In the same
manner a certain degree of resentment is necessary; but if we see
that a man carries it too far, we pity the object of it, and are
taught to moderate that passion.' [1]

V

Such reasonings pertained to the moral effects of tragedy and were
aimed at an emotive moral justification. They could be more or less
closely tied in with a more cognitive and a more aesthetic kind of argument which we have touched upon in an earlier chapter, the didactically
aesthetic plea that our pleasure in witnessing the painful events of a
tragedy arises from our use of the mind in learning, as well as our use
of the will in approving, a moral pattern of actions and sanctions, a pattern of "poetic justice." [2] But the aesthetic justification of tragedy was
on the whole more difficult than the moral. How can it be that the
human mind actually takes pleasure in the contemplation of suffering,
the evocation of painful emotions? Another classical answer was the
mimetic:—that our pleasure in the imitation of a disagreeable or a painful
object (a dunghill [3] or a murder) arises just from the skill of the imitation
and the exercise of our minds in seeing the likeness. Both these types
of explanation, the ethical and the simply mimetic, had been developed
from hints in Aristotle by the Italian writers of the 16th century, were
handed on by Corneille and other French writers of the 17th century,
and during the 18th century in England were still more or less available.

Meanwhile, however, certain explanations of a different sort had
originated in 17th-century psychology and had made some headway.
One of these was a theory of safe feelings and self-congratulation on
the part of the spectator as he realized the merely mimetic and playful
character of the drama and his own detachment from the sufferings portrayed. "We consider tragedy at the same time as Dreadful and Harmless," said Addison.—"The Pleasure we receive [is] from the sense of our

[1] Boswell, *Life of Johnson*, April 12, 1776.
[2] See *ante* Chapter 11, pp. 204–6.
[3] Addison's example in *Spectator* No. 414; see *ante* Chapter 13, p. 255.

own safety." [4] "The movement of our melancholy passions is pleasant,"
said Edward Young, "when ourselves are safe: We love to be at once,
miserable, and unhurt." [5] This had a root in the self-regarding philosophy
of Hobbes and was an analogue to the idea of self-enhancement which
appears in the Platonic and Hobbesian theory of laughter and to that
increase of self-confidence and expansion of soul in the presence of the
"sublime" described by Addison and Burke and later refined theologically in the "Dynamic sublime" of Kant.[6] The theory also had an antique
source in a passage by Lucretius which was often quoted by the literary
theorists.

> There is a pleasure in looking out over the great ocean when
> a storm rages across it and seeing some vessel in distress, not
> because we are glad that somebody else is suffering, but because
> we have our own feet safely on the shore. There is a pleasure
> in watching the struggle of armies upon a battlefield—so long as
> we ourselves are standing out of danger.[7]

But a second affective explanation of tragic pleasure which had
arisen during the 17th century was a less clearly selfish one, and during
an era so consciously goodhearted as the 18th century, this was bound to
engulf the selfish Hobbesian. According to Descartes, sensory pain is
something that presses inward on our vital spirits, but emotion is an
outward motion, a form of responsory exercise and assertion, in itself
pleasurable, healthy, and in general good (the opposite of lethargy)—
so long as painful impressions are not so strong as to overwhelm us, and
so long as our inner state of soul is positive and strong enough to launch
the vigorous response.[8] The mimetic character of drama tended of course
to accomplish the necessary softening of the painful impression; and the
ethical nature of tragedy was friendly to the inner calm and strength.
The Cartesian theory of the emotional workout had from the start the

---

[4] *Spectator* No. 418.

[5] *Conjectures*, ed. Morley, p. 41.

[6] Cf. *post* Chapter 17, p. 371, the Kantian sublime; and Chapter 25, psychological
theories of laughter.

[7] *Suave, mari magno turbantibus aequora ventis,*
e terra magnum alterius spectare laborem;
non quia vexari quem quamst jucunda voluptas,
sed quibus ipse malis careas quia cernere suave est.
suave etiam belli certamina magna tueri
per campos instructa tua sine parte pericli.
Lucretius, *De rerum natura*, II, 1–6. Cf. Baxter Hathaway, "The Lucretian 'Return
upon Ourselves' in Eighteenth-Century Theories of Tragedy," *PMLA*, LXII (September, 1947), 672–89.

[8] Earl R. Wasserman, "The Pleasures of Tragedy," *ELH*, XIV (December,
1947), 283–307. The present treatment of 18th-century tragic theory is substantially
indebted to Professor Wasserman's essay, which may be consulted for copious illustration of nearly all the points made here. See also A. O. Aldridge, "The Pleasures
of Pity," *ELH*, XVI (March, 1949), 76–87.

strongest affinity for the sentimental version of Aristotelian "catharsis" which we have already described. The latter was a theory of the moral function of tragedy; the former a theory of tragic pleasure; but they were natural complements. They may be seen, for instance, early in the 18th century, coming together in the words of Shaftesbury's *Inquiry Concerning Virtue or Merit:* ". . . the moving our passions in this mournful way, the engaging them in behalf of merit and worth, and the exerting whatever we have of social affection, and human sympathy, is of the highest delight." [9]

VI

BOTH in hard ethical theory and in literary art—in *The Theory of Moral Sentiments* by Adam Smith and in *A Sentimental Journey* by Laurence Sterne [1]—the finest thing in the world during the age of reason was "sympathy." For sympathy was not selfish, it was both Cartesian emotive self-development, and moreover it was ethical but not in a cold reflective sense; it was a spontaneous overflow of our best, our softest, warmest, most benevolent feelings, the loving and social impulses never so fully elicited as at the intuition of our fellow beings in distress. It was a good thing for us that they *were* in distress. It was good for us to go out of ourselves in this way, and to be aware of the fact. And it was pleasant. The pleasure of tragedy, said Lord Kames, arises from "an appetite after pain," "an inclination to render one's self miserable." [2] The pleasure of tragedy, said another Scotch theorist, Hugh Blair, is a "luxury of woe." [3] A young lady who had uttered a "Prayer for Indifference" was rebuked by the poet Cowper in the following definitive stanzas.

> 'Tis woven in the world's great plan,
> And fixed by Heaven's decree,
> That all the true delights of man
> Should spring from Sympathy.

. . .

[9] *Characteristics*, ed. J. M. Robertson (London, 1900), I, 297–8, quoted by Hathaway, p. 666. We may note also the theory of Hume (*Of Tragedy*, 1757): Any passion (even a contrary passion, provided it be not too strong) will strengthen another. The secret of tragic pleasure, therefore, is that our admiration for the mimetic art of the representation is buoyed and enhanced by the surge of more painful emotions—as flowery essences in a perfume, one might say, are embodied more effectively in musk. See Hume, *Essays and Treatises* (Edinburgh, 1804), I, 236. Cf. J. Frederick Doering, "Hume and the Theory of Tragedy," *PMLA*, LII (December, 1937), 1130–4. Cf. Burke, *Inquiry* (1757), I, xv.

[1] Kenneth MacLean, "Imagination and Sympathy: Sterne and Adam Smith," *JHI*, X (June, 1949), 399–410.

[2] *Essays on the Principles of Morality and Natural Religion* (Edinburgh, 1751), p. 14.

[3] *Lectures on Rhetoric and Belles Lettres* (Philadelphia, 1829), p. 515. The *Lectures* were first published in 1783.

'Tis Nature bids, and whilst the laws
Of Nature we retain,
Our self-approving bosom draws
A pleasure from its pain.

Thus grief itself has comforts dear
The sordid never know;
And ecstasy attends the tear
When virtue bids it flow.

For when it streams from that pure source
No bribes the heart can win,
To check, or alter from its course,
The luxury within.[4]

The earlier stages of sentimental theory had remained more or less compatible with classicism. But full-grown "sympathy" was strongly anti-classical. Sympathy allied readily with the neo-Longinian free genius soaring above the trammels of the rules, and hence sympathy worked against the Aristotelian conception of mimetic decorum. Sympathy pleaded persuasively for a kind of illusionistic naturalism. A really tragic happening, argued Burke,[5] for instance a public execution of a criminal, is more moving than the most horrible figment of the stage. And so sympathy worked also against the Aristotelian person of high estate and in favor of every-day life, the shopkeeper protagonist of bourgeois drama. At the same time, sympathy was too simple to accommodate the Aristotelian tension of pity and fear. The "mixture of good and odious qualities" in a protagonist, said yet another Scotch theorist, the rhetorician George Campbell, tears the mind "opposite ways at once, by passions which, instead of uniting, repel one another." Such a mixture is "shocking and disgustful." [6] The tragedy of sympathy was a tragedy of simple pity, without fear, a tragedy of "innocent misfortune," without moral, without "poetic justice." It was an illusionistic tearjerker, the Kotzebuian tragedy with which Coleridge was to be so much disgusted.[7] In the year of the *Lyrical Ballads*, a minor theorist achieved the following happy summary of both the genetic and affective sides of the sympathetic complex.

[4] *Addressed to Miss Macartney on Reading the Prayer for Indifference* (1762), ll. 45–60.

[5] *Inquiry* I, xv. The announcement that a great criminal was about to be executed in a neighboring square would immediately empty any theater in which even the most sublime of tragedies was being performed. Boswell will bear Burke witness.

[6] *The Philosophy of Rhetoric* (1776), I, 327.

[7] *Biographia Literaria*, ed. Shawcross, II, 159. It works on our "sluggish sympathies by a pathos not a whit more respectable than the maudlin tears of drunkenness."

An untutored genius, having strong conceptions, a heart that can enter into the feelings of a fellow heart, quick in catching the most striking features of distress, judgment to select a happy tale of virtuous suffering, and simplicity to follow nature in her plain walk, will in the fabrication of tragedy reach its highest excellence.[8]

VII

THE Man of Feeling and his "genealogy,"[9] the sympathetic and tearful tendencies in the literature of the later 17th and the 18th centuries—especially in novels and in the kind of ethical comedy that replaced the immodest satire of manners—these constitute a phase of literary history which was both a record and a cause of a deep turn in the minds of our ancestors, towards an attitude which we today are likely to betray in some of our most spontaneous habits of speech—as when we say that we "feel" a thing to be so rather than "think" it, or when we speak of a "sensitive" rather than a "perceptive" person or mind. Feeling, sad feeling, melancholy musing, pensive meditation, were among the most pervasive strains of the 18th-century music and of the thinking about it. The classically generic term "pathetic" (meaning what arouses *any* kind of emotion) gradually assumed during this period the more special modern English meaning of the tenderly moving and pitiful. Not long after Pope's death it became possible to say that among the poems on which his reputation would principally depend was his early exercise in the "pathetic" mode *Eloisa to Abelard*.[1] Even so tough-minded a person as the philosopher David Hume knew Pope's *Elegy to the Memory of an Unfortunate Lady* by heart, and so did many others.[2] The pleasures of melancholy, the pleasures of pity, the pleasures of tragedy, the pleasures of the painful, the pleasures of the unpleasant—these, as we have been seeing, were the reiterated paradoxes of 18th-century aesthetic theory. And this is a matter of some general theoretical interest.

When emotion is attached to extremely simplified motives or when it is cut away from concrete motives altogether, it becomes emotion of great purity and intensity; it is likely to be dark rather than light, it is likely to be painful even if at the same time pleasurable. It is the "ro-

[8] George Walker, "On Tragedy and the Interest in Tragical Representations," *Memoirs of the Literary and Philosophical Society of Manchester*, V (1798), 332–3, quoted by Wasserman, p. 306.

[9] Cf. R. S. Crane, "Suggestions toward a Genealogy of 'The Man of Feeling,'" *ELH*, I (1934), 205–30.

[1] Joseph Warton, *An Essay on the Genius and Writings of Pope* (London, 1806), I, 330.

[2] Cf. Geoffrey Tillotson, ed. *The Rape of the Lock and Other Poems* (London 1940), p. 336.

mantic agony." Again, joy does not feed on joy, as melancholy feeds on melancholy. And melancholy, as a romantic inheritor of the tradition would write, may feed on both. "Ay, in the very temple of delight Veil'd Melancholy holds her sovran shrine." It is perhaps a truth of 20th-century psychology, perhaps only a truism, to say that melancholy tends to be automatic and morbid. Dark emotions drive toward purity.

On the other hand, cheer and wit go handily together. Cheer is sociable and extrovert: 18th-century theorists recognized this principle when they removed the "man of wit," the poet of social poetry, from the ranks of genius. Back in 1679 Dryden had said that "no man is at leisure to make sentences and similes, when his soul is in an agony."[3] And Dennis a little later had asserted that the production of similes was an exercise of the mind "utterly inconsistent" with intense grief.[4] Hume in his essay "Of Simplicity and Refinement in Writing" found wit and passion "entirely incompatible."[5] Johnson's classic objection to Milton's *Lycidas* was that it "is not to be regarded as the effusion of real passion; for passion runs not after remote allusions and obscure opinions."[6] The most sustained insistence on the theme occurs no doubt in the two volumes of Joseph Warton's *Essay on Pope* published, with so long an interval for meditation between them, in 1756 and 1782. In the Dedication of the first volume, to Edward Young, Warton not only divides real poets from mere "men of wit" and "mere versifiers," but with equal decision elevates a class of "sublime and pathetic" poets (Spenser, Shakespeare, Milton—"at proper intervals" Otway and Lee) above a second class of more moderately gifted ("ethical") poets (Dryden, for instance, Donne, Denham, Cowley, Congreve).[7] The main argument of Warton's *Essay*, culminating at the end of the second volume, is that Pope is "the great poet of Reason, the First of Ethical authors in verse." He has written "nothing in a strain so truly sublime, as the *Bard* of Gray."[8] In one of his most pointed passages, Warton asserts that "WIT and SA-TIRE are transitory and perishable, but NATURE and PASSION are eternal."[9] Pope, he asserts, "stuck to describing *modern manners;* but

[3] Preface to *Troilus and Cressida*, in *Essays*, ed. Ker, I, 223.

[4] Preface to *The Passion of Byblis*, 1692, in *Works*, ed. E. N. Hooker, I, 2, 424.

[5] *Essays Moral, Political, and Literary*, ed. T. H. Green and T. H. Grose (London, 1898), I, 242: "It is a certain rule, that wit and passion are entirely incompatible. When the affections are moved, there is no place for the imagination."

[6] Johnson, *Lives of the Poets*, ed. G. B. Hill, I, 163. Cf. J. H. Hagstrum, *Samuel Johnson's Literary Criticism* (Minneapolis, 1953), pp. 45–6.

[7] Otway, Lee, and Congreve were dropped from the listing in the edition of 1782, and Donne was demoted to a mere man of wit. Hoyt Trowbridge, "Joseph Warton's Classification of English Poets," *MLN*, LI (December, 1936), 515–18.

[8] *Essay on the Genius and Writings of Pope* (London, 1806), II, 403–5. In Warton's satire *Ranelagh House*, 1744, Pope in the Elysian fields is found not among the poets but among the philosophers.

[9] *Essay*, 1806, I, 330.

those *manners*, because they are *familiar, uniform, artificial*, and *polished*, are, in their very nature, unfit for any lofty effort of the Muse." [1]

VIII

IN OUR last chapter we have noticed that according to the philosophical view of Edmund Burke "beauty is, for the greater part, some quality in bodies acting mechanically upon the human mind by the intervention of the senses" (III, xii). "Beauty," he said, "acts by relaxing the solids of the whole system" (IV, xix). And the external symptoms of this relaxation were to be described with considerable precision.

> When we have before us such objects as excite love and complacency, the body is affected, so far as I could observe, much in the following manner: The head reclines something on one side, the eyelids are more closed than usual, and the eyes roll gently with an inclination to the object; the mouth is a little opened, and the breath drawn slowly, with now and then a low sigh; the whole body is composed, and the hands fall idly to the sides. All this is accompanied with an inward sense of melting and languor.—IV, xix [2]

In the fifth part of his *Philosophical Inquiry* Burke turns directly to the problem of verbal art and states the alternatives which lay before an age of anti-metaphysics. In effect: *Aut pictura poesis, aut passio.* He is mistrustful of the first alternative, the Addisonian, for he feels certain that words do not really excite very good pictures, neither words like "honour," "justice," "liberty," nor even words like "blue," "hot," "man," or "horse." So there is no other choice than *passio.*

> Poetry and rhetoric do not succeed in exact description, so well as painting does: their business is, to effect rather by sympathy than imitation; to display rather the effect of things on the mind of the speaker, or of others, than to present a clear idea of the things themselves.—V, v

Our "Passions are affected by words from whence" we "have no ideas." Our highest range of words, "compound" abstractions like "virtue," "liberty," "honour," are:

> in reality but mere sounds; but they are sounds, which being used on particular occasions, wherein we receive some good or suffer some evil . . . produce in the mind whenever they are afterwards mentioned, effects similar to those of their occasions.
>
> —V, ii

[1] *Essay*, 1806, II, 402.   [2] Cf. *ante* Chapter 13, p. 265.

We arrive thus at the idea that a poetry of emotion "cannot with strict propriety be called an art of imitation." As other writers of the time were putting it, poetry, along with music, is a kind of passionate "expression." [3] We arrive also at another idea, one which, along with "sensation" and "emotion," played a persuasive role in the new aesthetic thinking of the age. That is, "association." "Association," we may observe provisionally, was for the age of reason something which acted as a kind of intermediate justification of emotions—a form of mechanical operation softened and subtilized to shade off into what had once been conceived of as thinking.

IX

THE first main sense attached to the term "association of ideas" when it was launched by John Locke in the fourth edition of his Essay, 1700, was very much like that which the word now has for the ordinary user. It meant a connection between ideas which has occurred a number of times or some one memorable time, yet is not thought of, or should not be thought of, as always or necessarily occurring. A boy eats a surfeit of mince pie and gets sick. Twenty years later the man associates mince pie with a feeling of nausea. A man meets a girl several times at a certain restaurant, and after that he never goes there without thinking of her. She used a certain perfume; the smell of it later on will remind him of her. This way of connecting things seemed to Locke unsound in principle. He contrasted it to the way of thinking which seeks out the underlying and reliable connections between things—i.e., the laws of nature.

Locke himself, however, by his insistence on the phenomenal (rather than the real or substantial) character of much of our experience, did a great deal to develop the Hobbesian "train of ideas" toward the full doctrine of association announced by Hume in his *Treatise* of 1739 (the source of his later and more influential works) and by David Hartley in his *Observations on Man*, 1749. This kind of association was in effect an extension of the other until it covered the whole field of our knowledge; association was on this view not an accidental and occasional way of connecting things, but the basic principle of all connections—a "transcendental"—the principle by which our sensations, all of them, happen to occur in certain bundles and establish in our minds certain patterns of expectancy. I have a more or less casual and infirm association of a cer-

---

[3] See Wellek, *Rise*, pp. 51–2, citing James Harris *Three Treatises*, 1733; Charles Avison, *Essay on Musical Expression*, 1752; James Beattie, *Essays on Poetry and Music*, 1776; and Sir William Jones, "Essay on the Arts Commonly Called Imitative" (1772) in his *Poems Consisting Chiefly of Translations from the Asiatick Languages* (2d ed., London 1777), p. 207. Music and poetry are "expressive of the passions and operate on our mind by sympathy."

tain person with a certain place or a certain old hat, and only a somewhat firmer association of his head with his shoulders, of the sun with light and heat, of summer time with the ripening of fruit, and so on. The several Aristotelian principles of association—that is, likeness and difference, cause and effect, contiguity in space and time—with which Hume began his discussion (cf. *Treatise* I, i, iv.)—were at a stroke reduced by Hartley to a single mechanical principle of contiguity in time (either "synchronous" or "successive"). Hartley made that contiguity a character not of things as known by the human subject but of sensory vibrations and of their "miniature" reproductions (vibratiuncles) in the "medullary" substance of the brain. For each unit or simple item of experience, a vibration of a certain sort and a vestigial remainder of it. If several of these experiences happened to occur together often enough, the recurrence of a single one of the group stimulated from outside would set up a reminiscential jangle of the others.[4] Hume, by a subtler technique of introspection (without Hartley's externalizing clatter of mechanization), pushed the principle of mere association to its ultimate, reducing all real knowledge to unitary discrete phenomenal moments and thus exploding not only external substances and causes but the internal substance or self which we usually think of as the receptacle of knowledge or as the knowing agent. As his argument might be rephrased by a modern positivist: The Cartesian "cogito, ergo sum" takes too much for granted. "Descartes is only the name of a series of mental phenomena."

The new concepts of "association," the Humean and Hartleyan, in effect washed out the earlier Lockean kind of "association" by making it no different from any other connection between things. If fire and cooking, heart and blood, sunlight and leaves, are only associations,

[4] Hartley, *Observations*, 1749, Part I, Chapter I, Section ii, Propositions 9–10, pp. 58–66. The human body was viewed as "a kind of barrel-organ . . . set in motion by the external forces of the world" (Leslie Stephen, *English Thought in the Eighteenth Century*, 1927, II, 64). The physiological aspect of this theory of association is anticipated in Descartes' flow of "animal spirits" into traces in the brain— with wider and easier traces worn for pleasure than for pain. Cf. Addison, *Spectator* No. 417. As Coleridge would later point out, the physiological elaboration is irrelevant to the psychological and aesthetic problem. "The wise Stagyrite speaks of no successive particles propagating motion like billiard balls (as Hobbs); nor of nervous or animal spirits, where inanimate and irrational solids are thawed down, and distilled, or filtrated by ascension, into living and intelligent fluids, that etch and reetch engravings on the brain, (as followers of Des Cartes, and the humoral pathologists in general); nor of an oscillating ether which was to effect the same service for the nerves of the brain considered as solid fibres, as the animal spirits perform for them under the notion of hollow tubes (as Hartley teaches)—nor finally (with yet more recent dreamers) of chemical compositions by elective affinity, or of an electric light at once the immediate object and the ultimate organ of inward vision, which rises to the brain like an Aurora Borealis, and there disporting in various shapes (as the balance of plus and minus, or negative and positive, is destroyed or re-established) images out both past and present" (*Biographia Literaria*, Chapter V, ed. Shawcross, I, 71–2).

then association in the sense of a kind of accidentally pertinacious cohesion of ideas is no longer distinguishable. By the subsumption of a special into a more generic sense, a distinction has been levelled off; a certain flattening of experience and vocabulary has been at least attempted. The difficulty with the attempt is to some extent indicated by the fact that "association" as it survives in usual discourse today still has the sense of the Lockean coinage. We associate persons with places, but not their heads with their shoulders.

During the 18th century, however, "association" was in the air. It was a smart term in the vocabulary of moral and aesthetic theorists and litterateurs. It was a system of gently persuasive laws of connection between our ideas (analogous to Newton's more exact but equally pervasive physical laws) by which Hume hoped to advance moral philosophy to the stage where some century earlier physical science had moved ahead of it. A number of variations would be played on the two main senses we have defined, the sense of accidental connection, and the sense of the principle behind all connections. The history of association in 18th-century literary theory is a history of such variations and of several merging relations between the two radical senses.

X

In a quite simple form, for instance, Shakespearian criticism might invoke the phenomenon of superficial or accidental association to explain how faithfully the speech of certain characters—Dame Quickly or Juliet's nurse—imitates the incoherent reality of garrulous and rambling conversation, or of partially irrelevant retort. Association was thus subsumed under the principle of dramatic interpretation.

> Falstaff: What is the gross sum that I owe thee?
> Dame Quickly: Thyself and thy money too.[5]

A similar meaning of association—perhaps better exploited by creative writers than by theorists—might be synopsized as a thesis that the sequences of ideas which pass through our minds are not so rigorously determined by laws of logic or the structure of external nature as we

[5] Walter Jackson Bate, *From Classic to Romantic* (Cambridge, Mass., 1946), pp. 96, 105, 123, citing Lord Kames, *Elements of Criticism* (Edinburgh, 1762), and Alexander Gerard, *Essay on Genius* (1774). The present account of association is substantially indebted to Bate's chapter on the subject. See too Gordon McKenzie, *Critical Responsiveness* (Berkeley, 1949)—p. 139 concerns Falstaff's Hostess; Martin Kallich, "The Association of Ideas and Critical Theory: Hobbes, Locke, and Addison," *ELH*, XII (1945), 290–315; "The Associationist Criticism of Francis Hutcheson and David Hume," *SP*, XLIII (October, 1946), 644–67; and Walter J. Ong, "Psyche and the Geometers: Aspects of Associationist Critical Theory," *MP*, XLIX (August, 1951), 16–27.

might hope, but are nevertheless determined in ways that make curious sense and may be studied with profit. We may learn many unsuspected things about the human being and his world if we study his habits of "association." One of the most subtly sustained 18th-century illustrations of this principle is the pedantically talkative and humorous novel *Tristram Shandy*, in which the hero is not born until the third volume and disappears from the story after the sixth of the total nine. Various absurdities and accidents of his pre-nativity and early infancy are affectionately developed as critical or nearly critical events in the shaping of a character and career—the fact that his mother a few moments before he was conceived remembered to ask his father whether he had wound the clock, the bungle of a servant girl at his christening by which the name Tristram was made out of Trismegistus, the later carelessness of the same girl in holding the child under a window sash from which the leaden weights happened to have been removed to make toy cannon for his Uncle Toby. Sterne was whimsical. By a technique of apparently disordered and meandering fancy, he was concerned to build a comic contrast between associational causes and the more reliable patterns of deliberation and predictability which we usually suppose to hold our world together. He was thus antimetaphysical while escaping the embarrassment of being too seriously and scientifically associational.[6]

The 18th-century theorist, however, was on the whole working very seriously. He was less concerned with whimsy or with intuitive flashes of mind-reading than with the achievement of a grammarian's or a mechanist's reliable map of the whole of our thinking. One such application of associationism proceeded upon what in ancient times might have been called the principle of "synecdoche," or part for whole. The 18th century saw a growing theoretical concern—especially on the part of critics like Joseph Warton who relished nature description in poetry and on the part of certain Scottish rhetoricians—for the concrete particular, the kind of thing to be found in the drama of Shakespeare, or in the Bible, or in the seasonal paintings of Thomson, as distinguished from the supposed generalizations of Pope's ethical *Essays*.[7] The associational way of explaining the force of skilfully chosen particulars in description was to say that certain particulars were extremely potent in evoking a cloud of further particulars in the imagination of a reader. As Addison had put it in *Spectator* No. 417:

---

[6] Cf. D. W. Jefferson, "*Tristram Shandy* and the Tradition of Learned Wit," *Essays in Criticism*, I (July, 1951), 239, 244-5; Kenneth MacLean, *John Locke and English Literature of the Eighteenth Century* (New Haven, 1936); *Tristram Shandy*, ed. James A. Work (New York, 1940), Introduction, pp. xlix-li.

[7] See *ante* Chapter 13, p. 264, the relation of this interest to the parallel between poetry and painting, and *post* Chapter 15, p. 316, the conflict with the neoclassic universal.

. . . any single Circumstance of what we have formerly seen often raises up a whole Scene of Imagery, and awakens numberless Ideas that before slept in the Imagination; such a particular Smell or Colour is able to fill the Mind, on a sudden, with the Picture of the Fields or Gardens, where we first met with it, and to bring up into View all the Variety of Images that once attended it. Our Imagination takes the Hint, and leads us unexpectedly into Cities or Theatres, Plains or Meadows.

Happy powers of association! A striking complement to all this was the principle that the particular gets all of its significance or at least most of it from the other particulars that cluster around it in our memories (helping us to co-ordinate and interpret it),[8] and further that the significance of any particular for a given person will depend on the other particulars which that given person happens to associate with it. The name for this interpretation and valuing of particulars was "associational response." The fruits of an individual's past experience constitute his readiness or power of associational response.[9] And "objects stand in order when their situation corresponds with that of our ideas." [1]

At the same time a different emphasis (complementary to the subjective concept of "response") was possible, and toward the end of the century this began to emerge as one of the main lessons of associationism. By a kind of inversion of the synecdochal viewpoint, one might observe that, after all, association was a potent faculty for making combinations, for seeing objects, not thin and meager as they are rendered by abstraction, but in the whole richness of their concrete significance or of some particular significance they may have in a given situation. Association under this aspect might be a way of putting back together the world which had been fragmented into atoms or moments of discrete experience by the Humean *dis*sociation. It might be that we ought to set less store by reason and logic, our rationalist abstractive powers, and a great deal more by our entire mental and emotional workings, our total minds, even our instincts. These might give us a world of solid and extremely valuable reality. Under this aspect the name "association" gave way to the name "imagination." Imagination, said the common-sense moral philosopher Adam Ferguson, conceives a thing

with all its qualities and circumstances . . . in respect to all their relations of similitude, analogy, or opposition; whereas, in ab-

[8] Abraham Tucker, *The Light of Nature Pursued* (1768–1778), II, 18, observes that little children are uneasy when hungry but are not experienced enough to know what they want; they push the food away from them (Bate, *Classic to Romantic*, p. 111).

[9] Bate, *Classic to Romantic*, p. 112, citing Hume and also Priestley's Introduction to an edition of Hartley's *Theory of the Human Mind*, 1775.

[1] Bate, *Classic to Romantic*, p. 103, quoting Abraham Tucker.

stractions, we should consider subjects, or *parts* of subjects, in
some *limited* point of view, to which our reasoning or thought
in that instance is directed.[2]

A related emphasis was that on "coalescence," an aspect of the associative imagination which today we discuss under such names as "synthesis," "fusion," or "integration." Wordsworth and J. S. Mill would use
the term "mental chemistry." The English associationist Abraham
Tucker in his *Light of Nature Pursued*, 1768, was the first to stress the
uniqueness of the object produced by the associational coalescence. Not
an addition or juxtaposition of simple qualities in complex ideas, as in
the Lockean epistemology, but a fusion into a special and irreducible
whole—this is the process by which we know syllables composed of
letters, words composed of syllables, and a lump of sugar as a white,
sweet, hard, and angular somewhat.[3]

XI

But let us return to the theme of emotion and value—or of value explained by emotion—from which our account of association began and
with which, if we are to be faithful to the subtlest and most persistent
meaning of association for aesthetic theory, we ought to conclude. If
our power of combining and of enjoying ideas was in any event a free,
plastic, fluent, even whimsical power of "association," what might this
power not be capable of when loosened and encouraged by the genial
heat of emotion?

One fairly simple way in which association dealt with value was
the attempt to explain our pain or pleasure in some things by shoving
these things back on their associations with other things, which might
or might not be more basic. Why do we consider such colors as bright
blue and gold beautiful? Because, said the Scotch aesthetician Archibald
Alison, we associate these with the clothes and furniture of the opulent,
comfortable, and titled persons who wear blue coats with gold braid.
And on the contrary the colors "of the Earth, of Stone, of Wood, etc.
have no kind of Beauty, and are never mentioned as such. . . . The
colours in the same manner, which distinguish the ordinary dress of the
common people, are never considered as Beautiful." [4] Why do we enjoy

[2] *Principles of Moral and Political Science* (Edinburgh, 1792), I, 104, "Imagination"; cf. Dugald Stewart, *Elements of the Philosophy of the Human Mind*
(Edinburgh, 1792), 477–8, "Of Imagination" (Bate, *Classic to Romantic*, pp. 113–
17). Cf. Bate, "The Sympathetic Imagination in Eighteenth-Century English Criticism," *ELH*, XII (June, 1945), 144–64.

[3] Cf. Bate, *Classic to Romantic*, pp. 118–20.

[4] Archibald Alison, *Essay on The Nature and Principles of Taste*, 1790, quoted
by J. H. Muirhead, *Coleridge as Philosopher* (New York, 1930), p. 196. For a helpful
account of Alison, see Martin Kallich, "The Meaning of Archibald Alison's *Essays
on Taste*," *PQ*, XXVII (October, 1948), 314–24.

ourselves when out for a day in the country? Because, explained a later essay by Hazlitt, we had a good time sporting in the country as children, and on returning to the country we still invest it with these pleasures by association.[5] As homesick poet, and even at moments as metaphysician, Coleridge would subscribe to the same view:

> I had found
> That grandest scenes have but imperfect charms
> Where the eye vainly wanders, nor beholds
> One spot with which the heart associates
> Holy remembrances of child or friend.
> —*Lines Written at Elbingerode in 1799*

This kind of value association had been invoked earlier in the 18th century, by Francis Hutcheson and others, to explain individual aberrations from the true standard of taste. The main 18th-century drift, however, was toward giving it the full sanction of theoretic approval.

The desires and interests of a human being, his *patterns* of response to the objects of his experience, one might easily enough reflect, have a great deal to do with determining the pattern of his associations so far as these may differ from what might be considered the stereotyped or merely normal, the logically or scientifically directed. It was just this thought which occurred with special force to Scottish "Common-Sense" theorists and others in the later 18th century. The aesthetic and ethic of feeling, the Shaftesburyan "moral sense," appeared as if specially designed to complete the doctrine of association and bring out happily all its implications. Emotions, or more broadly feelings, were precisely the norm by which association in ethics and in aesthetics could be distinguished from association in physical science.[6] Toward the end of the century and in the early nineteenth, the union was firmly and contentedly established—"as the rose blendeth its odor with the violet, —solution sweet."

Back in 1651 Hobbes had been of the opinion that "wit" is a "swift succession" of thoughts to "some approved end," and that the reason why some men are more quickwitted than others lies in "the difference of men's passions; that love and dislike, some one thing, some another" (*Leviathan*, I, viii). In 1774 Alexander Gerard's *Essay on Genius* makes the common-sensical observation that our passions tend to keep our minds running in certain directions. For instance, a man who is extremely angry about something.

> can scarce avoid thinking of the person who has offended him,
> and of the injury he has done him, recollecting everything he

[5] *On the Love of the Country.*

[6] Associationism as an all-inclusive basis not only for psychology but for ethics was first formally proposed in 1731 by John Gay, the cousin of the poet (Bate, *Classic to Romantic*, p. 100). It was of course a part of Hartley's system.

can dishonourable to that person, . . . and in a word dwelling on everything immediately relating to his anger.[7]

A passion, said Gerard, "preserves us from attending to foreign ideas, which would confound our thoughts and retard our progress." Passion promotes unity of thinking. And not only "passions" in the sense of strong excitement but all the quieter kinds of feeling and interest. In his *Light of Nature Pursued* Tucker meditates on how a person going to market to buy oats for his horse meets a wagon on the way and is reminded, not of turnpikes, roads, or commerce, but of the fact that the owner of the wagon is a farmer who might have some oats for sale more cheaply than at the market.[8] Such is the magnet-like power of our imagination when informed by a desire for some satisfaction.

These pronouncements of the philosophers went a long way, if not all the way, in anticipating the things that both German philosophers and the great English romantic poets were later on to say about emotion in the high tide of their revulsion from the mechanistic phases of association theory. "Hartley's system totters," wrote Coleridge to Southey in 1803. Why did Hartley's system totter? Because "association depends in a much greater degree on the recurrence of resembling states of feeling than trains of ideas."

> I almost think that ideas never recall ideas, as far as they are ideas, any more than leaves in a forest create each other's motion. The breeze it is runs thro' them—it is the soul or state of feeling.[9]

And this was not only a doctrine that concerned the emotions but one which appealed *to* them. "A metaphysical solution [like Hartley's] that does not instantly tell you something in the heart is grievously to be suspected." The literary theory of both Coleridge and his friend Wordsworth, a theme to which we shall return in later chapters, is marked by frequent and notable utterances about such topics as "predominant passion" in poetry, the "union of deep feeling with profound thought," the "gift of spreading the tone," "emotion recollected in tranquillity."[1] The bearing of this associationist victory for feeling and emotion on the metaphysical point of reference, from which theory had been moving so steadily away, may be handily consulted in an essay by Hazlitt on "Wit and Humour," the introduction to his *English Comic Writers*

[7] Alexander Gerard, *Essay on Genius* (1774), p. 163; cf. Bate, *Classic to Romantic*, p. 124. Gerard's *Essay on Taste* first appeared in 1759.

[8] Abraham Tucker, *Light of Nature Pursued* (1768–1778), I, 246; cf. Bate, *Classic to Romantic*, p. 126.

[9] Coleridge to Southey, August 7, 1803 (*Letters*, 1895, I, 428). Cf. Muirhead, *Coleridge as Philosopher*, p. 199.

[1] *Biographia Literaria*, Chapters IV, XV; Preface to *Lyrical Ballads*.

of 1819. Hazlitt was a kind of Addisonian spokesman of the romantic age, a very knowledgeable educator who blurted out secret meanings in quite plain prose. As Addison had often been influenced by Locke, so Hazlitt in his theorizing about aesthetic principles was influenced by Abraham Tucker, whose *Light of Nature Pursued* he abridged and edited in 1807.[2] In his essay on "Wit and Humour" Hazlitt proposes that "wit principally aims at finding out something that seems the same, or amounts to a momentary deception where you least expected it, viz. in things totally opposite"—but that "imagination may be said to be the finding out something similar in things generally alike, or with like feelings attached to them."[3]

During the mid-19th century the prime role of emotion as a principle of association or of artistic unification is not so much a discovery or matter of argument as an assumption that may be reproclaimed with more or less éclat. The statements in J. S. Mill's *Autobiography* and in his two essays on poetry published in the year 1833 represent a memorable dramatization of the problem and of the sentimental associationalist resolution. As a young man Mill passed through the stages of the 18th-century association philosophy; he "entered the whirlpool."

> The very excellence of analysis (I argued) is that it tends to weaken and undermine whatever is the result of prejudice: that it enables us mentally to separate ideas which have only casually clung together; and no associations whatever could ultimately resist this dissolving force, were it not that we owe to analysis our clearest knowledge of the permanent sequences in nature; the real connexions between Things, not dependent on our will and feelings; . . . Analytic habits may thus even strengthen the associations between causes and effects, means and ends, but tend altogether to weaken those which are, to speak familiarly, a *mere* matter of feeling.[4]

What then of poetry? Poetry is clearly not analysis and on the record of the past two hundred years or so seems not especially flattered by analysis. Mill's own view of analysis seems not likely to reverse the trend. By a kind of wilful flip-flop in his evaluation of one part of the analytic doctrine, he marks out the honors of poetry. "Whom, then," he asks in the second of his essays dealing precisely with the problem of poetry, "Whom, then, shall we call poets?" And he replies:

[2] W. C. Bullitt, "Hazlitt and the Romantic Conception of the Imagination," *PQ*, XXIV (October, 1945), 351.

[3] *Lectures on the English Comic Writers* (Philadelphia, 1819), p. 38.

[4] *Autobiography* (New York, 1874), pp. 137–8, quoted by Walter J. Ong, "J. S. Mill's Pariah Poet," *PQ*, XXIX (July, 1950), 333–44.

Those who are so constituted, that emotions are the links of association by which their ideas, both sensuous and spiritual, are connected together.[5]

With these words Mill succeeded in reformulating briefly, to his own satisfaction, a supposition which for about a hundred years had been becoming more and more normal in critical thought, and which has very largely continued until our own day to operate as a latent premise in theoretical discussions of the value of poetry. It would be difficult to find a person who has theorized to any extent about his literary preferences without at some time, under the stress of analytic objections, having fallen back on the plea that some poem which he admires is not constructed on a principle of logical unity, or of narrative unity, but simply and sufficiently on one of emotional unity.[6]

SUPPLEMENT

It is likewise necessary for a Man who would form to himself a finished Taste of good Writing, to be well versed in the Works of the best *Criticks* both Ancient and Modern. I must confess that I could wish there were Authors of this kind, who beside the Mechanical Rules which a Man of very little Taste may discourse upon, would enter into the very Spirit and Soul of fine Writing, and shew us the several Sources of that Pleasure which rises in the Mind upon the Perusal of a noble Work. Thus although in Poetry it be absolutely necessary that the Unities of Time, Place and Action, with other Points of the same Nature, should be thoroughly explained and understood; there is still something more essential to the Art, something that elevates and astonishes the Fancy, and gives a Greatness of Mind to the Reader, which few of the Criticks besides *Longinus* have considered.

Our general Taste in *England* is for Epigram, Turns of Wit, and forced Conceits, which have no manner of Influence, either for the bettering or enlarging the Mind of him who reads them, and have been carefully avoided by the greatest Writers, both among the Ancients and Moderns. I have endeav-

[5] Mill's first essay on poetry, "What is Poetry?" appeared in the *Monthly Repository* for January, 1833; his second essay, "The Two Kinds of Poetry," in the same journal for October, 1833. He reprinted the two together, with slight revisions, as "Thoughts on Poetry and Its Varieties," in his *Dissertations and Discussions: Political, Philosophical, and Historical* (New York, 1874–82); see I, 106. And cf. Ong, *loc. cit.*, pp. 334, 339. For some complications and qualifications in Mill's theory, see Alba Warren, pp. 69–77.

[6] "Continuity of interest" is a less emotively committed term which psychologists in the positivist tradition have used to designate a principle of associative order which to a large extent is taken for granted by the modern mind. G. F. Stout, *Manual of Psychology*, 3d. ed, p. 558, quoted by Muirhead, *Coleridge as Philosopher*, p. 200.

oured in several of my Speculations to banish this *Gothic* Taste, which has taken possession among us. I entertained the Town, for a Week together, with an Essay upon Wit, in which I endeavoured to detect several of those false Kinds which have been admired in the different Ages of the World; and at the same time to shew wherein the Nature of true Wit consists. I afterwards gave an instance of the great Force which lyes in a natural Simplicity of Thought to affect the Mind of the Reader, from such vulgar Pieces as have little else besides this single Qualification to recommend them. I have likewise examined the Works of the greatest Poet which our Nation or perhaps any other has produced, and particularized most of those rational and manly Beauties which give a Value to that Divine Work. I shall next *Saturday* enter upon an Essay *on the Pleasures of the Imagination*, which, though it shall consider that Subject at large, will perhaps suggest to the Reader what it is that gives a Beauty to many Passages of the finest Writers both in Prose and Verse. As an Undertaking of this Nature is entirely new, I question not but it will be received with Candour.

—Joseph Addison, *Spectator* 409, June 19, 1712

The father of English poetry, like that of the Grecian, lived in a period little favourable to simplicity in poetry, and several meannesses occur throughout his works, which, in an age more refin'd, or more barbarous, he must have avoided. We see among the *worthie* acts of *Duke* Theseus,

> *How he took the nobil cite after,*
> *And brent the walls and tore down roof and rafter.*

And, among the horrid Images which crowd the temple of Mars,

> *The child stranglid in the cradil,*
> *The coke scaldid for alle his long ladil.*

That state of equipoise between horror and laughter, which the mind must here experience, may be rank'd among its most unpleasing sensations.

—J. Hookham Frere, in *The Microcosm* (Windsor, 1787), No. IX, January 29, 1787. The "microcosm" reflected in this periodical work was the world of Eton College. Frere was in his seventeenth year.

The *Association* of Ideas above hinted at, is one great Cause of the apparent Diversity of Fancys in the *Sense of Beauty*, as well as in the external Senses; and often makes Men have an aversion to Objects of *Beauty*, and a liking to others void of it, but under different Conceptions than those of *Beauty* and *Deformity*. And here it may not be improper to give some Instances of some of these Associations. The *Beauty* of *Trees*, their *cool Shades*, and their *Aptness* to conceal from Observation, have made *Groves* and *Woods* the usual Retreat to those who love *Solitude*, especially to the *Religious*, the *Pensive*, the *Melancholy*, and the *Amorous*. And do not we find that we have so join'd the Ideas of these Dispositions of Mind with those external Objects, that they always recur to us along with them. The Cunning of the *Heathen Priests* might make such obscure Places the Scene of the fictitious Appearances of their *Deitys;* and hence we join Ideas of something *Divine* to them. We know the like Effect in the Ideas of our Churches, from the perpetual use of them only in religious Exercises. The faint Light in Gothick Buildings has had the same Association of a very foreign Idea, which our Poet shews in his Epithet.

> A Dim religious Light.

In like manner it is Known, "That often all the Circumstances of *Actions* or *Places,* or *Dresses* of Persons, or *Voice,* or *Song,* which have occur'd at any time together, when we were strongly affected by any Passion, will be so connected that any one of these will make all the rest recur." And this is often the occasion both of great Pleasure and Pain, Delight and Aversion to many Objects, which of themselves might have been perfectly indifferent to us: but these *Approbations,* or *Distastes* are remote from the Ideas of *Beauty,* being plainly different Ideas.

—Francis Hutcheson, *An Inquiry into the Original of Our Ideas of Beauty and Virtue* (London, 1725), pp. 76–77 (Sec. 6, par. 11)

In Collins' *Ode to Evening* we find a melancholy which at moments, as in the description of the bat, verges on disorder, and which at all times is far too profound to arise from an evening landscape alone. . . . Collins' bat is not mad nor a sufficient motive for madness, but it is used to express a state of mind irrelevant to him. It is as if a man should murder his mother, and then, to express his feelings, write an *Ode to Thunder.* Or rather, it is as if a man should murder his mother with no consciousness of the act, but with all of the consequent suffering, and should then so express himself. A symbol is used to embody a feeling neither relevant to the symbol nor relevant to anything else of which the poet is conscious: the poet expresses his feeling as best he is able without understanding it. . . . Shelley's *Ode to the West Wind,* and in a measure Keats' *Ode to the Nightingale,* are examples of the same procedure; namely, of expressing a feeling, not as among the traditional poets in terms of its motive, but in terms of something irrelevant or largely so, commonly landscape. No landscape, in itself, is an adequate motive for the feelings expressed in such poems as these; an appropriate landscape merely brings to mind certain feelings and is used as a symbol for their communication. The procedure can be defended on the grounds that the feeling may be universal and that the individual reader is at liberty to supply his own motive; but the procedure nevertheless does not make for so concentrated a poetry as the earlier method, and as an act of moral contemplation the poem is incomplete and may even be misleading and dangerous.

—Yvor Winters, *Primitivism and Decadence* (New York, 1937), pp. 36–7. Reprinted from *In Defense of Reason* (pp. 50–1) by Yvor Winters by permission of the publisher, Alan Swallow. Copyright 1937 and 1947 by Yvor Winters.

. . .

LADY BLUEBOTTLE: Well, now we break up;
  But remember Miss Diddle invites us to sup.
INKEL: Then at two hours past midnight we all meet again,
  For the sciences, sandwiches, hock, and champagne!
TRACY: And the sweet lobster salad!
BOTH: I honour that meal;
  For 'tis then that our feelings most genuinely—feel.

—Lord Byron, *The Blues, Eclogue the Second*, ll. 154–9

THE NEO-CLASSIC UNIVERSAL: SAMUEL JOHNSON

§ *enargeia, particularity, Longinus, Quintilian, Pope, Spence, Joseph Warton on Thomson, Kames, James Campbell—II. ut pictura poesis again, ideal form, Dryden's Du Fresnoy,* Pope's Essay on Criticism, *neo-classic senses of "nature," Lovejoy, the universal, Cartesian and Newtonian reason, authority of the ancients, "Nature methodized," literary genres, decorum, character types,* Peri Bathous, *the social accent, the unnatural, outdoor nature, Samuel Johnson and Fleet Street, Wordsworth—III. Johnson on species and grandeur:* Rasselas, Preface to Shakespeare, Life of Cowley, Rambler 36; *Sir Joshua Reynolds:* Idlers, Discourses, *passage like Bacon; complexity and inconsistency of Johnson's views—IV. Johnson on genius, catharsis, the pathetic, the sublime, poetry and religion, the beautiful, the vast and the general, Longinus vs. Quintilian, Johnson's rationalism and empiricism, classical and anti-classical details of his criticism: couplet verse, dramatic structure, pastoral conventions, tragi-comedy, unities, his affectivism, regard for the audience, distinction between laws of nature and convention—V. Johnson on plagiarism and models, on genius as general capacity, scope of his writing, "the common voice of the multitude," specialized diction vs. general (synopsis of Renaissance theory and Augustan), Johnson on particular detail, personal morality and introspection vs. social philosophy and history, the life-and-letters method, uniformity of the state of man, truth of fact, distrust of "imagination," scepticism about "representative" verse—VI. nine meanings of the "universal"—VII. classic and neo-classic preoccupation with* art *and* nature: *anthology of short passages* §

VIVIDNESS (ENARGEIA) APPEARS IN CLASSICAL TREATISES AS A QUASI-cognitive figure, a rhetorical merit which tends to be definable best in terms of the imaginative excitement which it is said to induce in an audience. In the treatise of Longinus, the conception is treated under the head of images (*phantasiai*).

> At the present day the word [*phantasia*] is predominantly used in cases where, carried away by enthusiasm and passion, you think you see what you describe, and you place it before the eyes of your hearers.—XV

Aristotle (*Rhetoric*, III, xi) had suggested that vividness is likely to appear along with such more definable figures as metaphor, antithesis, and parallel. The most extended classical attempt to give the figure a cognitive basis is that of Quintilian in Book VIII, Chapter 3 of his *Institute*, where he dwells on the merit of multiplying descriptive particulars.

> The mere statement that the town was stormed, while no doubt it embraces all that such a calamity involves, has all the curtness of a dispatch, and fails to penetrate to the emotions of the hearer. But if we expand all that the one word "stormed" includes, we shall see the flames pouring from house and temple, and hear the crash of falling roofs and one confused clamour blent of many cries; we shall behold some in doubt whither to fly, others clinging to their nearest and dearest in one last embrace, while the wailing of women and children and the laments of old men that the cruelty of fate should have spared them to see that day will strike upon our ears. Then will come the pillage of treasure sacred and profane, the hurrying to and fro of the plunderers as they carry off their booty or return to seek for more, the prisoners driven each before his own inhuman captor, the mother struggling to keep her child, and the victors fighting over the richest of the spoil.[1]

Such testimonies were to be quite convenient to English theory of the 18th century. Alexander Pope, citing Longinus in a footnote to his translation of the *Iliad*, pointed out that Homer deals not only in the "great and noble" but in the minutely observed detail.[2] Pope's friend Spence, in an *Essay on Pope's Odyssey* (1726–1727), invoked the state-

---

[1] Reprinted by permission of the publishers from Quintilian, *Institutio Oratoria*, III, 249, translated by H. E. Butler, Loeb Classical Library, Cambridge, Mass.: Harvard University Press, 1943.

[2] George Sherburn, "The *Dunciad*, Book IV," in *Studies in English . . . The University of Texas, 1944* (Austin, 1945), p. 184, quoting Pope's note to *Iliad* VI, 595.

ment by Quintilian as a classical sanction for the same thing.[3] And so too did Joseph Warton in his *Essay on the Genius and Writings of Pope*,[4] though here the general argument was at the expense of Pope's *Pastorals* and in favor of the more minutely descriptive poetry of Thomson's *Seasons*.

> Thomson was blessed with a strong and copious fancy; he hath enriched poetry with a variety of new and original images, which he painted from nature itself, and from his own actual observations: his descriptions have, therefore, a distinctness and truth, which are utterly wanting to those poets who have only copied from each other, and have never looked abroad on the objects themselves. . . . Innumerable are the little circumstances in his descriptions, totally unobserved by all his predecessors.—I, 40-2

> The judicious addition of circumstances and adjuncts is what renders poesy a more lively imitation of nature than prose.
> —I, 11

> A minute and particular enumeration of circumstances judiciously selected, is what chiefly discriminates poetry from history, and renders the former, for that reason, a more close and faithful representation of nature than the latter.—I, 47

Warton thought that contemporary literature showed many symptoms of "departing from these *true* and lively and *minute* representations of Nature, and of *dwelling in generalities*."[5]

The doctrine of particularity became something like a rhetorical standard during the latter half of the 18th century, especially in the work of Scottish rhetoricians and associational aestheticians. Thus Lord Kames in his *Elements of Criticism*:

> . . . avoid as much as possible abstract and general terms. . . . images, which are the life of poetry, cannot be raised in any perfection but by introducing particular objects.[6]

And George Campbell in his *Philosophy of Rhetoric* (1776):

> . . . the more general any name is as it comprehends the more individuals under it, and consequently requires the more ex-

[3] *An Essay on Pope's Odyssey*, Part II (Oxford, 1727), "Evening the Fourth," p. 122. "There is a *Poetical Falsity*, if a strong Idea of each particular be not imprinted on the Mind; and an *Historical*, if some things are passed over only with a general mark of Infamy or Dislike. It was in *Quintilian* I first met with this Observation. . . ."

[4] Edition of 1806, II, 168.

[5] II, 168.

[6] *Elements of Criticism*, 2d. ed. (Edinburgh, 1763), I, 307, Ch. 4.

tensive knowledge in the mind that would rightly apprehend it, the more it must have of indistinctness and obscurity.[7]

> Nothing can contribute more to enliven the expression, than that all the words employed be as particular and determinate in their signification, as will suit with the nature and the scope of the discourse. The more general the terms are, the picture is the fainter; the more special they are, it is the brighter.[8]

The rule of thumb concerning particular descriptive writing is so well established in the textbook code of our own century in America and England that it scarcely needs illustration for anybody who has ever been either a pupil or a teacher in a high school or college freshman course in composition. The descent of the rule from the 18th century through such 18th-century rhetoricians as Archbishop Whately and the Scottish logician and moralist Alexander Bain is not a part of the story which this book aspires to tell.

Particularity was part of an 18th-century reaction against the neo-Platonic classical tradition. The aim of our chapter is to describe the terminus and the last enfeebled exaggeration of that theoretically anti-particularist tradition.

II

ONE feature of the doctrine of ideal form was its great readiness to embrace both the arts of language and those of picturing. This was part of the parallelism *ut pictura poesis* and illustrated most of the general weaknesses of the parallel. There is scarcely any general theory of literary value (unless the opposite theory of particularization) which will translate so easily into painters' terms. The climax of the tradition and its grandest claim appeared, as we shall see, in the shoulder-to-shoulder pronouncements of the giant litterateur Samuel Johnson and his friend the portrait painter Sir Joshua Reynolds. One of the earliest strong statements in English was that by Dryden in the Preface to his translation (1795) of the French painter Du Fresnoy's *Art of Painting*. In part Dryden quoted from the Italian neo-Platonist Bellori.

> Nature always intends a consummate beauty in her productions, yet through the inequality of the Matter, the Forms are altered.

[7] *Philosophy of Rhetoric*, 2d. ed. (London, 1801), II, 103, Bk. II, Ch. 7.
[8] II, 136. Cf. Scott Elledge, "The Background and Development in English Criticism of the Theories of Generality and Particularity," *PMLA*, LXII (March, 1947), esp. 176–81; and Houghton W. Taylor, "Particular Character": an Early Phase of a Literary Evolution," *PMLA*, LX (March, 1945), 161–74.

. . . For which Reason, the artful Painter, and the Sculptor, imitating the Divine Maker, form to themselves, as well as they are able, a Model of the Superior Beauties.[9]

Pope in his *Essay on Criticism* stated the thesis in the literary context:

> Unerring Nature, still divinely bright,
> One clear, unchang'd, and universal light,
> Life, force, and beauty, must to all impart,
> At once the source, and end, and test of Art.
>   —I, 68–73

> In some fair body thus th' informing soul
> With spirit feeds, with vigour fills the whole.
>   —I, 76–7

One ingratiating feature of this doctrine of the universal-ideal as found in Dryden and Pope, a derivative amalgam of Platonic, Aristotelian and Roman Stoic ideas, was its accommodating vagueness. Recent students of the history of ideas, in a somewhat overanalytic enthusiasm, have found themselves able to distinguish an indeterminate number of senses or "uses" of the term "nature" as it appears during the neo-classic age in English and continental writers. Yet the senses thus distinguished are not all strictly co-ordinate. They are not on the same footing and do not actually make the problem as unmanageable as one might fear. In Professor Lovejoy's early article on the subject, "Nature as Aesthetic Norm" (1927),[1] some of the 37 senses which he distinguished refer to the external world of nature, some to the artistic imitation, some to the artist's genius, some to the responses of the audience. Of those which refer to the external world, some refer to separate objects in that world, some to rules or principles, and some to the whole world order, the total embodiment of the principles. We have in short a set of complementary and analogical senses intrinsic to the subject-object relation of human knowledge and to the process of abstracting principles from concreteness. The main neo-classic emphasis was on the idea that there is a world order, both as a total embodiment,[2] as a set of principles, and as a realm of more or less knowable and predictable objects of various classes. Among these classes of objects the most important for

[9] *Art of Painting* (London, 1795), p. v. Cf. L. I. Bredvold, "The Tendency toward Platonism in Neo-Classical Esthetics," *ELH*, I (September, 1934), 91–119.

[1] A. O. Lovejoy, "Nature as Aesthetic Norm," *MLN*, XLII (November, 1927), 444–50. The same writer in "The Parallelism of Deism and Classicism," *MP*, XXIX (February, 1932), 283 ff., refers to 60 odd senses or uses; and Harold S. Wilson, "Some Meanings of 'Nature' in Renaissance Literary Theory," *JHI*, II (1941), 430–48, refers to 35.

[2] The plenitude, continuity, and gradations of the Great Chain of Being, as A. O. Lovejoy points out, constituted a system rife with implications of fecundity, variation, and romantic diversification.

the artist's study were human beings themselves, in their several sub-
classes, and in their institutions and productions. Lovejoy's sense I. E 17,
"the universal and immutable in thought, feeling, and taste," is referred
by him to the artist's public, but it referred equally and reflexively in
the Augustan mind to the most important objects of the artist's imitation.

As the classical idea of nature worked its way out in the aesthetic
speculations of Pope and his contemporaries, it took on certain highly
significant local colorations. For one thing, the idea of the uniformity
and universality of nature appeared now strongly re-enforced by Cartesian and geometric standards of clear reason, and by Newtonian concepts of a mechanically ordered universe.

We have alluded in an earlier chapter to the geometric spirit which
flourished among French critics. At the same time, the most agile literary
men of the age were able to reconcile this new scientism and modern
spirit of "reason" with the older principle of authority or reverence for
the ancient models. The literary rules were said not to supplant, but to
methodize nature. And as the central concept was that of a universal
truth, the reconciliation of reasonable rules and ancient authorities was
not in fact so difficult. What is permanent is bound to have been known
to the ancients, and vice versa. "These rules of old discovered, not
devised, Are Nature still, but Nature methodized."

> When first young Maro in his boundless mind
> A work t' outlast immortal Rome design'd,
> Perhaps he seem'd above the Critic's law,
> And but from Nature's fountains scorn'd to draw:
> But when t' examine ev'ry part he came,
> Nature and Homer were, he found, the same.
>
> —I, 130–5

As once long before, in the age of Cicero and Horace, so now again
the idea of the universal made its practical literary appearance in close
association with the implemental ideas of literary genre and of decorum
for various kinds of detail, notably for character-drawing. Pope's theoretical assumptions about character types, for instance, are clearly seen
in the irony of the following passage from his *Peri Bathous*, a recital
upside-down of a classical code which includes not only Longinian but
Horatian and Aristotelian clauses.

> Since the great Art of all Poetry is to mix Truth with Fiction,
> in order to join the *Credible* with the *Surprising*; our author
> shall produce the Credible, by painting nature in her lowest
> simplicity; the Surprising, by contradicting common opinion.
> In the very Manners he will affect the *Marvelous*; he will draw

Achilles with the patience of Job; a Prince talking like a Jack-pudding; a Maid of honour selling bargains; a footman speaking like a philosopher; and a fine gentleman like a scholar. . . .

Nothing seemed more plain to our great authors, than that the world had long been weary of *natural things.*—Ch. V

We have already suggested that the Augustan concept of "nature" had a strongly social cast. It was a nature of man's creations, his civilization, cities, estates, temples, palaces, drawing rooms, boudoirs, theaters, debates, conversations, and literature. It included, but it was not centered in, the kind of "nature" which nowadays we mostly mean by the term "nature" and which we experience chiefly on picnics—the Rousseauistic and Wordsworthian nature of the outdoors and of the unspoiled, spontaneous and primitive man who might be supposed to inhabit the outdoors. The *un*natural for Pope was a deviation from a norm; for romantic naturalists the unnatural would actually be the restraint imposed by a norm [3] (a meaning, incidentally, that grew plausibly enough out of the 17th-century trend in favor of reason, "good sense" (*le bon sens*), or "common sense," as opposed to mere authority).[4] One fled from authority to the outdoors. It is not difficult to illustrate the antithesis, especially in its indoor-outdoor, city-country, aspect, from statements by the leading English men of letters. It is standard procedure to quote Samuel Johnson's preference for the vista of Fleet Street over any rural landscape or his meditation at Anoch in the Western Islands:

> I sat down on a bank, such as any writer of romance might have delighted to feign. I had indeed no trees to whisper over my head, but a clear rivulet streamed at my feet. The day was calm, the air soft, and all was rudeness, silence, and solitude. Before me, and on either side, were high hills, which, by hindering the eye from ranging, forced the mind to find entertainment for itself.

And by contrast, Wordsworth's avowal: "One impulse from a vernal wood May teach you more of man, Of moral evil and of good, Than all the sages can." Or Byron's "High mountains are a feeling, but the hum Of human cities torture." It is a fairly easy matter to connect this shift in appreciation with the neo-Longinian vast and irregular, and with the

---

[3] This romantic idea is of course to be found in Pope too. "The great secret how to write well, is to know thoroughly what one writes about, and not to be affected . . . to write naturally." "Arts are taken from nature; and after a thousand vain efforts for improvements are best when they return to their first simplicity." Joseph Spence, *Anecdotes*, ed. S. W. Singer (London, 1820), pp. 11–12, 291.

[4] Cf. Austin Warren, *Alexander Pope as Critic and Humanist* (Princeton, 1929), pp. 17–18.

taste in painting, in landscape gardening, and in loco-descriptive poetry
which we have earlier noted.

III

BUT our present theme is rather the natural as the universal. And here
the critics of the last classical generation, the Johnsonian, offer us a definition that has both the advantage for the historian and the disadvantage
to itself of being somewhat over-formally drawn. Three of Samuel
Johnson's least escapable statements on the theme are the often-quoted
tulip passage in the discourse of the philosopher Imlac in *Rasselas* (1759),
that on character in his *Preface to Shakespeare* (1765), and that on metaphysical wit in his *Life of Cowley* (1781).

> The business of the poet . . . is to examine, not the individual,
> but the species; to remark general properties and large appear-
> ances; he does not number the streaks of the tulip, or describe the
> different shades in the verdure of the forest. He is to exhibit in
> his portraits of nature such prominent and striking features, as
> recall the original to every mind; and must neglect the minuter
> discriminations, which one may have remarked, and another have
> neglected, for those characteristics which are alike obvious to
> vigilance and carelessness. . . . He must divest himself of the
> prejudices of his age or country; he must consider right and
> wrong in their abstracted and invariable state; he must disregard
> present laws and opinions, and rise to general and transcendental
> truths, which will always be the same.—*Rasselas*, Ch. X

> [Shakespeare's] characters are not modified by the customs of
> particular places, unpractised by the rest of the world; by the
> peculiarities of studies or professions, which can operate but upon
> small numbers; or by the accidents of transient fashions or tem-
> porary opinions: they are the genuine progeny of common hu-
> manity, such as the world will always supply, and observation
> will always find. His persons act and speak by the influence of
> those general passions and principles by which all minds are agi-
> tated, and the whole system of life is continued in motion. In
> the writings of other poets a character is too often an individual;
> in those of Shakespeare it is commonly a species.
>
> *Preface to Shakespeare* [5]

Great thoughts are always general, and consist in positions not

[5] Cf. Fielding's statement about his own comic characters the lawyer and Mrs.
Slipslop, in *Joseph Andrews*, Part III, chapter 1.

limited by exceptions, and in descriptions not descending to minuteness.

The fault of Cowley, and perhaps of all the writers of the metaphysical race, is that of pursuing his thoughts to their last ramifications, by which he loses the grandeur of generality; . . . all the power of description is destroyed by a scrupulous enumeration.—*Life of Cowley*, paragraphs 58, 133 [6]

Let us add to this gallery some of the statements made by Johnson's friend and pupil in aesthetic discourse, Sir Joshua Reynolds. First some samples from three essays which he contributed to Johnson's periodical series of 1759, *The Idler*.

The *Italian* attends only to the invariable, the great and general ideas which are fixed and inherent in universal nature; the *Dutch*, on the contrary, to literal truth and a minute exactness of detail, as I may say, of nature modified by accident. The attention to these petty peculiarities is the very cause of this naturalness so much admired in the *Dutch* pictures, which, if we suppose it to be a beauty, is certainly of a lower order.—No. 79

In consequence of having seen many [individuals of the same species] the power is acquired . . . of distinguishing between accidental blemishes and excrescences which are continually varying the surface of nature's works, and the invariable general form which nature most frequently produces, and always seems to intend in her productions. . . . Every species of the animal as well as the vegetable creation may be said to have a fixed or determinate form towards which nature is continually inclining . . . . perfect beauty is oftener produced by nature than deformity; I do not mean than deformity in general, but than any one kind of deformity.—No. 82

Then from his annual *Discourses* (1769–1790) as President of the Royal Academy, these rules for the serious painter:

[6] *Rambler* No. 36 includes in the following succinct statement the two important words "species" and "grandeur." "Poetry cannot dwell upon the minuter distinctions, by which one species differs from another, without departing from that simplicity of grandeur which fills the imagination; nor dissect the latent qualities of things, without losing its general power of gratifying every mind by recalling its conceptions." In his last *Rambler*, Johnson states what he believes to be the relation of the theory to his own practice as a prose essayist. "I have never complied with temporary curiosity, nor enabled my readers to discuss the topick of the day; I have rarely exemplified my assertions by living characters; in my papers, no man could look for censures of his enemies, or praises of himself; and they only were expected to peruse them, whose passions left them leisure for abstracted truth, and whom virtue could please by its naked dignity."

The sentences quoted above from the *Life of Cowley* are closely associated in their context with a neo-Longinian notion of the sublimely vast. Cf. *post*, p. 324.

He will leave the meaner Artist servilely to suppose that those are the best pictures which are most likely to deceive the spectator. He will permit the lower painter, like the florist or collector of shells, to exhibit the minute discriminations, which distinguish one object of the same species from another; while he, like the philosopher, will consider Nature in the abstract, and represent in every one of his figures the character of its species.
—*Discourse* III [7]

In the same manner as the historical Painter never enters into the detail of colours, so neither does he debase his conceptions with minute attention to the discriminations of drapery. It is the inferior style that marks the variety of stuffs. With him the clothing is neither woollen, nor linen, nor silk, satin, or velvet; it is drapery; it is nothing more.—*Discourse* IV

It is of course possible to show that both Johnson and Reynolds uttered a variety of other critical statements and even at times contradicted or came close to contradicting the emphatic rule of the universal. Thus in one of his latest *Discourses*, Reynolds, having apparently read Bacon's well-turned compliment to the poetic imagination in the *Proficience and Advancement of Learning*,[8] introduces the following variation upon his own basic distinction between naturalistic detail and the grandeur of generality.

Apply to that reason only which informs us not what imitation is—a natural representation of a given object—but what it is natural for the imagination to be delighted with.

It is allowed on all hands, that facts and events, however they may bind the historian, have no dominion over the poet or the painter. With us, history is made to bend and conform to this

[7] A person concerned to drive home the difficulties involved in taking the species as aesthetic norm could do no better than quote certain other passages of this *Discourse*. "In the human figure . . . the beauty of the Hercules is one [beauty], of the Gladiator another, of the Apollo another; which makes so many different ideas of beauty. It is true, indeed, that these figures are each perfect in their kind, though of different characters and proportions; but still none of them is the representation of an individual but of a class." "I should be sorry, if what is here recommended should be at all understood to countenance a careless or undetermined manner of painting. For though the painter is to overlook the accidental discriminations of Nature, he is to exhibit distinctly, and with precision, the general forms of things."

The marginalia which about 1808 William Blake wrote in a copy of Reynolds' *Discourses* include the following pungent comments: "Real effect is making out of Parts, and it is Nothing Else but that." "Sacrifice the Parts: What becomes of the whole?" "Minute Discrimination is not accidental. All Sublimity is founded on Minute Discrimination." "Distinct General Form cannot exist. Distinctness is Particular, Not General." "To Generalize is to be an Idiot." "This Man was Hired to Depress Art."

[8] See *ante* Chapter 9, p. 171.

great idea of art. And why? Because these arts, in their highest province, are not addressed to the gross senses; but to the desires of the mind, to that spark of divinity which we have within, impatient of being circumscribed and pent up by the world which is about us.—*Discourse* XIII

As for Samuel Johnson, he is the Great Cham of 18th-century English literary criticism, a mammoth personality who was more capacious than any abstract dimension of critical theory. We surround him here with the atmosphere of the classic universal because his championship of that view is a late climax in its history and appears to be his distinctive contribution to 18th-century English criticism. As a late classical giant, however, he is even more interesting for the complexity and sometimes inconsistent detail of his views. Near the close of our discussion of neo-classicism, it will be appropriate to dwell for a few pages on this curiously rounded, or squared out, figure.

I V

JOHNSON participated heavily in the rationalistic and psychological trends which we have described in our last chapter. We have already seen, for example, his acquiescence in the doctrine of genius and originality. (If Homer did not write as good a poem as Virgil, he was yet a better poet, because he came first.) [9] We have seen his off-the-cuff sentimental answer to the ancient question about catharsis. He thought of Shakespeare as a pathetic, tender, and domestic poet, and his devotion to the pathetic differed from the prevailing attitude of his age mainly in that he refused to merge the pathetic with that other emotive keynote, the sublime. Johnson's surrender to the sublime itself was limited by his shrewd and orthodox realization that it was in effect a new form of religion—rhapsodic and worshipful of outdoor nature. He lived at a time when in fact it was impossible for poetry and religion to come together without the dilution of one or the other. His response was an attitude of contempt for the services of poetry in the cause of religion. "Devotional poetry" was simply "unsatisfactory."

The paucity of its topics enforces perpetual repetition, and the sanctity of the matter rejects the ornaments of figurative diction. It is sufficient for Watts to have done better than others what no man has done well.

"The good and evil of Eternity," he said, summing up the limitations of *Paradise Lost*, "are too ponderous for the wings of wit."

Yet Johnson was at one with his age in recognizing the sublime as a

[9] Cf. *Rambler* No. 121, on the evils of imitating.

category distinct from the beautiful. (The beautiful for Johnson was something close to the rhetorically elegant. Milton was sublime, Pope beautiful.) [1] The sublime plays a pronounced, if somewhat disguised, role in Johnson's thought as an adjunct or ambiguous equivalent of the universal. The grandeur of generality is something inclusive, not only in the sense of being universally valid or true, but in that of being big, reaching out and taking in all. Thus, in his remarks on the metaphysical poets:

> Nor was the sublime within their reach . . . ; for they never attempted that comprehension and expanse of thought which at once fills the whole mind, and of which the first effect is sudden astonishment, and the second rational admiration. Sublimity is produced by aggregation, and littleness by dispersion. Great thoughts are always general.[2]

The ancestry of this alliance between the vast and the general becomes clearer if we revert now to a difference between the two ancient critics Quintilian and Longinus on the rhetorical merit of vividness (*enargeia*). Both believe in it. But whereas Quintilian, as we have seen, recommends in its support the meticulous description, Longinus notes the danger of falling into meanness.

> When Theopompus had dressed out in marvelous fashion the descent of the Persian king upon Egypt, he spoilt the whole by some petty words. . . . With his wonderful description of the whole outfit he mixes bags and condiments and sacks, and conveys the impression of a confectioner's shop. . . . He might have described the scene in broad outline . . . and with regard to the preparations generally have spoken of 'waggons and camels and the multitude of beasts of burden carrying everything that ministers to the luxury and enjoyment of the table.'—XLIII

We have observed that the classicism of the later 17th and the 18th centuries was supported by strains of scientific rationalism which in the end undercut the authoritarian element in classicism and placed new and disastrously heavy stresses upon its claims to being reasonable. Johnson was a resolutely reasonable classicist—not in the *a priori* mood of the French *géomètres* but with the experimental resolution of the English Baconians. The amateur empiricism which Johnson practised with chemical retorts and in such simple experiments as the plucking of his own hairs to see how long they would take to grow back [3] was matched in literary criticism by his constant appeals from literary convention to a

---

[1] See J. H. Hagstrum, "Johnson's Conception of the Beautiful, the Pathetic and the Sublime," *PMLA*, LXIV (March, 1949), 134–157, reprinted in his *Samuel Johnson's Literary Criticism* (Minneapolis, 1952), ch. VII, pp. 129–52.

[2] *Life of Cowley*, par. 58.

[3] Boswell, *Life of Johnson*, ed. Hill-Powell. III, 398, n. 3.

general knowledge of life and literature. "Reason," he says, "wants not Horace to support it."[4] And, "There is always an appeal open from criticism to nature."[5] Johnson's theory of literary criticism was something analogous to deism in contemporary theology.

It is true that he had rather rigorous ideas about metrical accuracy (His ear seems to have been open only to the couplet), and there is a pair of *Ramblers* in which he talks harshly about *Samson Agonistes* on the Aristotelian grounds that it has a beginning and end but no middle. But Johnson was not at heart a critic according to the neo-classic species. He never wrote anything approximating Addison's series of *Spectators* appraising *Paradise Lost* according to the categories laid down by neo-Aristotelianism. His notorious disgust at *Lycidas* was part of a pre-romantic preference for nature over the formal species and the conventions of the pastoral. In his Shakespeare *Preface* he not only defended the "mingled" genre of tragicomedy, but in a passage which we have quoted in an earlier chapter he gave memorably vigorous expression to that rejection of the unities of time and place (as no true illusions) which had been under way in English criticism since early in Dryden's day.[6]

The appeal to nature and reason has with Johnson a strong equalitarian orientation, toward the common audience and their spontaneous vote. Though he believes that "reason and nature are uniform and inflexible," such uniformity as he in fact discovers is often in the psychology of the persons whom the poet addresses, rather than in any norm beyond and superior to themselves. Johnson's anti-classic revolt erupts with some energy rather early in his critical career, in three of his *Ramblers*, Nos. 125, 156, and 158, devoted to an inquiry into the binding force of the literary rules.

> Definitions have been no less difficult or uncertain in criticism than in law. Imagination, a licentious and vagrant faculty, unsusceptible of limitations, and impatient of restraint, has always endeavoured to baffle the logician, to perplex the confines of distinction, and burst the enclosures of regularity. There is therefore scarcely any species of writing of which we can tell what is its essence, and what are its constituents; every new genius produces some innovation, which when invented and approved, subverts the rules which the practice of foregoing authors had established.—No. 125

Both the tone of lament and that of applause seem rather studiously absent from this passage. It is a hard-headed report on the facts. But the

---

[4] *Preface to Shakespeare, Works* (1787), IX, 248.
[5] *Life of Dryden, Lives of the Poets*, ed. G. B. Hill (Oxford, 1905) I, 423.
[6] T. M. Raysor, "The Downfall of the Three Unities," *MLN*, XLII (1927), 1–9. Cf. *ante* Chapter 10, p. 189.

writer's sympathy becomes clear enough before he is done. He is in the course of launching a fully committed attack on the "arbitrary edicts of legislators" (No. 158), the hardening into law of rules derived from over-rated classic models, and the general failure of critics to distinguish between laws of nature and mere conventions.[7]

> Some [laws] are to be considered as fundamental and indispensable, others only as useful and convenient; some as dictated by reason and necessity, others as enacted by despotick antiquity; some as invincibly supported by their conformity to the order of nature and operations of the intellect; others as formed by accident, or instituted by example, and therefore always liable to dispute and alteration.—No. 156

Among the more fixed and obligatory rules of drama, Johnson recognizes the unity of action and the single hero. Among the more obviously legitimate targets for dissent are the unity of time, the rule against tragicomedy, the rule of five acts, and the limit of three persons together on the stage. The superior rule by which Johnson would test all such accidents of custom and prejudice is, as we have suggested, a principle graded through "reason," "nature," and "experience" in such a way as to terminate rather candidly now and then in an appeal to the pleasures of the voting audience.

> . . . any man's reflections will inform him, that every dramatick composition which raises mirth, is comick. . . . If the two kinds of dramatick poetry had been defined only by their effects upon the mind, some absurdities might have been prevented.
> —No. 125

The affectivism of such remarks is, however, a relatively casual commitment with Johnson, the consequences of which he seems scarcely to entertain.[8]

V

But to turn back toward the main line of our dealing with Johnson: the principle of the neo-classic universal is something which works its way through his objective theorizing with great consistency. The titles of two of his essays, *Rambler* No. 143, "The Criterions of Plagiarism,"

---

[7] Cf. Joseph E. Brown, *The Critical Opinions of Samuel Johnson* (Princeton, 1921), pp. 221–6, "Rules."

[8] The "absurdities" which he has in mind in the above passage, for example, are those committed, not by critics, but by poets (like Dryden in *Don Sebastian*) when they mix the heroic with "unseasonable levity." The argument quickly leads into a plea for classical decorum which may not fit so well with Johnson's statements elsewhere in favor of the tragi-comic license.

and *Adventurer* No. 95, "Apology for Apparent Plagiarism, Sources of Literary Variety," go far to suggest the degree of Johnson's fidelity to the classical canon of model objectivity which we have examined some chapters back in its Jacobean phase. For a man with Johnson's advanced conception of the universal, plagiarism was something which a good poet could scarcely avoid. *Rambler* No. 36, on pastoral, offers the following concrete illustration.

> The range of pastoral is indeed narrow, for though nature itself, philosophically [i.e. scientifically] considered, be inexhaustible, yet its general effects on the eye and on the ear are uniform, and incapable of much variety of description. . . . However, as each age makes some discoveries, and those discoveries are by degrees generally known, as new plants or modes of culture are introduced, and by little and little become common, pastoral might receive, from time to time, small augmentations, and exhibit once in a century a scene somewhat varied.[9]

This emphasis was logically compatible with the large credit which we have seen Johnson conceding to the Homeric original genius, though it was far from compatible with that mania for continuing original genius in which Edward Young's *Conjectures* were more characteristic of the age. Johnson had a view of "genius" itself which, in a way related to the Lockean *tabula rasa*, was quite consistent with his respect for the abstract universal. Genius was a general sort of mental superiority, a power of invention capable of being turned in any direction.[1] "I am persuaded," said Johnson in one of his moments of more advanced self-complacency, "that, had Sir Isaac Newton applied to poetry, he would have made a very fine epic poem. I could as easily apply to law as to tragic poetry." [2] He would undertake to write a preface or dedication for a book of any kind—Percy's *Reliques*, Rolt's *Commercial Dictionary*, John Payne's *Tables of Interest*, William Payne's *Elements of Trigonometry*.

We have commented on the affective side of Johnson's respect for the general opinion—the "common voice of the multitude, uninstructed by precept and unprejudiced by authority" (*Rambler* No. 52). The apparently comfortable relation of this concept to the doctrine of the universal is no less to be noted. "About things on which the public thinks long it commonly attains to think right." [3] "In the character of his

---

[9] Compare Warton, *Essay on Pope* (1806), I, 86–7: "The Works of those who profess an art, whose essence is imitation, must needs be stamped with close resemblance to each other. . . . Descriptions, therefore, that are faithful and just, MUST BE UNIFORM AND ALIKE." Cf. Hurd, "A Discourse on Poetical Imitation," in his edition of Horace's *Epistola ad Augustum* (London 1751), pp. 133–4.

[1] See *Idler* No. 40; *Life of Cowley*, in *Lives of the Poets*, ed. G. B. Hill, I, 2; Joseph E. Brown, *The Critical Opinions*, pp. 118–23, "Genius."

[2] Boswell, *Journal of a Tour to the Hebrides*, 15 August, 1773.

[3] *Life of Addison*, in *Lives*, ed. G. B. Hill, II, 132.

Elegy I rejoice to concur with the common reader." [4] "That cannot be unpoetical with which all are pleased." [5] Everybody could recognize a tulip. And the species tulip we must suppose was precisely something which everybody could recognize.

One of the most practical operations of the universal was in the area of diction. In the high Renaissance the taste had been in favor of the local color and baroque individuality of specialist vocabularies. Terms of mining, founding, and gold working, of marine, hunting, and falconry, Ronsard had especially recommended. The time was to come, beginning perhaps about the date of Falconer's *Shipwreck* (1762), and running through the whole 19th century and our own, when localization was again the norm. But Johnson was a late spokesman for an era in which the specialized or technical vocabulary was an accidental, bastard, and vulgar lingo. Addison censured Milton for using "larboard," "Doric," "pilasters," "cornice," "ecliptic," "eccentric" (*Spectator* No. 297). The minor critics of the time may almost all be quoted to the same effect. Boileau was 46 years old but spoke of himself in a poem as 40, and Dennis commended him, "for poetry admits of no odd Numbers above Nine." [6] Both Pope [7] and Johnson objected to Dryden's parade of special knowledge in *Annus Mirabilis*.

> Some the *gall'd* ropes with dawby *marling* bind,
> Or sear-cloth masts with strong *tarpawling* coats.

"I suppose," says Johnson, "here is not one term which every reader does not wish away."

> It is a general rule in poetry that all appropriated terms of art
> should be sunk in *general* expressions, because poetry is to speak
> an universal language.[8]

The norm of style which Johnson was expounding was close to the metaphysics and the science of his age. It was recommended by the French naturalist Buffon as a "care in naming things only in the most

[4] *Life of Gray, Lives* III, 441.

[5] *Life of Milton, Lives* I, 175. Hume's appeal to the verdict of time in questions of art ("Of the Standard of Taste") was a contemporary parallel to Johnson's view. Longinus and Castelvetro are two earlier critics who entertain a clear respect for the universal suffrage. In the next century Tolstoy's peasant standard is the *reductio ad absurdum*.

[6] Dennis, *Miscellanies in Prose and Verse*, 1693, p. 50. See Spingarn, *Essays*, II, 333.

[7] Letter 23 in *Works*, ed. W. Elwin and W. C. Courthope, VI, 107. In the second volume of his *Essay on Pope*, 1782 (1806, II, 170), Joseph Warton writes in the new spirit, defending familiar words like "market-place," "alms-house," "seats," "spire." But in the Dedication of his *Virgil*, 1753, he had regretted the georgic necessity of using such coarse and common words as "plough," "sow," "wheat," "dung," "ashes," "horse," "cows." These would disgust "many a delicate reader."

[8] *Lives* I, 433–4.

general terms." With that and a delicate taste, one achieved "nobility" of style.

It may be with some dismay—yet it should be also with an improved sense of the difficult problem which 18th-century neo-classicism was trying to solve—that one comes upon Johnson's frequent statements in favor of something like literary particularity. Some of these are miscellaneous and casual. He did not like the "general and undefined" drawing of human nature in the plays of Nicholas Rowe.[9] No more did he like a "general" and "indefinite" encomium in epitaphs. And he said of these: "There are no rules to be observed which do not equally relate to other compositions." [1] He thought that as Pope had never seen America, he did well by not writing his projected American pastorals.[2] Toward the end of his life it is possible that Johnson shows the influence of the Wartonian doctrine of particulars. The *Life of Thomson*, 1781, might be expected to reflect Warton's *Essay on Pope*, and perhaps it does, with a certain dipping of the standard in recognition of Thomson's nature pencilling.

But there is a deeper strain of particularism which is with Johnson both early and late and tied in closely with one of his most basic inclinations, that toward introspection and personal morality rather than social philosophy or the history of princes. This particularism is part of his interest in biography, in the "life and letters" method, of which William Mason's *Gray* in 1777 was the first classic example, and Johnson's *Lives* and Boswell's *Life of Johnson* greater examples, and for which Johnson and his friends in their conversations and journals were continually and consciously at work producing materials. "I esteem biography," said Johnson, "as giving us what comes near to ourselves, what we can turn to use." [3] He wrote two essays, *Rambler* No. 60 and *Idler* No. 84, in development of the theme.[4]

> The general and rapid narratives of history, which involve a thousand fortunes in the business of a day, and complicate innumerable incidents in one great transaction, afford few lessons applicable to private life, which derives its comforts and its wretchedness from the right or wrong management of things, which nothing but their frequency makes considerable.—*Rambler* No. 60

Johnson conceives that his preference here is related consistently enough to the master principle of the universal—"there is such an uniformity in

[9] *Lives* II, 76.
[1] *Works* (1787), IX, 443.
[2] *Works* (Oxford, 1825), VI, 39–40, 42.
[3] Boswell, *Journal of a Tour to the Hebrides*, 21 August, 1773.
[4] Cf. Bergen Evans, "Dr. Johnson's Theory of Biography," *RES*, X (1934), 301–10.

the state of man, considered apart from adventitious and separable decorations and disguises." But the passage might stand very well as epigraph to a treatise on the anti-Aristotelian, anti-aristocratic poetic theory of the 18th-century drama. That theory, as we have seen, was a lover not only of sentiment but of naturalistic detail. The more true to life a story was, the better, the more convincing, the more sympathetic. Such connections undoubtedly lie behind Johnson's well-known and somewhat scandalous dedication to truth of fact.

> A story . . . should be a specimen of life and manners, but if the surrounding circumstances are false, as it is no more a representation of reality, it is no longer worthy our attention.[5]

> The value of every story depends on its being true. A story is a picture of either an individual or of human nature in general: if it be false, it is a picture of nothing.[6]

As a 20th-century neo-humanist has observed, such passages would seem to cut the Johnsonian grandeur of generality off from any commerce with fiction. It is difficult to see where poetry can come in. In dealing with poetry Johnson frequently enough paid his respects to the power of make-believe or fantasy—a power which he called "invention." But the term "imagination" meant for Johnson characteristically either (1) the normal 18th-century power of vivid picturing (or perhaps combining pictures—*Idler* 44), or (2) on the other hand, something verging on the pathological, a tendency to vagrant invention, seductive reverie, castles in Spain, day-dreaming. He speaks of the "Luxury of Vain Imagination" (*Rambler* 89), the "seducements of imagination" (*Rambler* 134), the "Dangerous Prevalence of the Imagination" (*Rasselas*, Chapter 44).[7] He resolves for his own part "to reclaim imagination" (*Prayers and Meditations*, September 18, 1760). In a *Rambler* which we have already quoted (No. 25), the same sort of derogatory phrasing seems to apply specifically to the faculty of poetic invention. "Imagination, a licentious and vagrant faculty . . . has always endeavoured to baffle the logician, to perplex the confines of distinction." We confront here in part of course a matter of semantics. The word "imagination" bore for Johnson a different burden from that which it has borne for the post-Coleridgean world. But in part also, and in large part, we are involved with the fact that in the Johnsonian world there was small place for that later burden.[8]

---

[5] Hester Lynch Piozzi, *Anecdotes* (2d. ed., 1786), p. 18.

[6] Boswell, *Life of Johnson*, 16 March, 1776.

[7] Cf. Irving Babbitt, "Dr. Johnson and Imagination," *On Being Creative*, Boston, 1932; R. D. Havens, "Johnson's Distrust of the Imagination," *ELH*, X (September, 1939), 243-55.

[8] There have been some efforts lately to attribute to Johnson an almost Coleridgean view of imagination as reconciliation and transvaluation, the combination of the familiar and the unfamiliar, the *discordia concors*. See J. H. Hagstrum, *Samuel*

In an earlier chapter we have noticed the reduced and uncertain status enjoyed by the term "wit" as it was used by Johnson and his contemporaries, the degraded condition of metaphor, and the general ornamentalism of stylistic theory. In recent years Johnson has earned a dry rebuke for his failure of response to Denham's metaphysical comparison between the flow of the Thames and that of poetic discourse.[9] A certain myopic literalism was undoubtedly one of the limitations of his critical theory and practice. His scepticism about the "representative" or directly imitative powers of verse (*Ramblers* 92, 94) is another case in point. This was shrewd, and within limits Johnson argued on a sound principle, that verse directly imitates very little. But a stubborn lack of interest in presentational analogy seems to prevent Johnson from hearing the fact that Pope had written one hexameter slow ("That like a wounded snake drags its slow length along") and one hexameter fast ("Flies o'er th' unbending corn and skims along the main").

VI

WHAT then of the grandeur of generality? In Johnson the literary theorist we confront a system of ideas (in part rigidly consistent, in part rather manifestly inconsistent, in part at least paradoxical) which constitutes a massive summary of the neo-Platonic drive in literary theory and of its difficulties. Johnson's occasional downright contradictions do not make him a worse theorist than many another; they do make him an exceptionally revealing one. It would be difficult to say exactly what neo-classic theory as a whole, or what any particular neo-classic theorist, meant by the standard of universality. Let us move toward a conclusion of our account of the neo-classic era by looking at several things which the theory might or could mean. The nine meanings which follow are related to one another not so much by semantic or dictionary fact (which is not always the most important) but by a logic of resemblances, analogies and relations. We should say that:

1. An idea is general (or universal) when it is viable from one mind to another. Even a strictly singular idea—*Socrates*, for instance—is general in this way. (And even the most highly individual and personal romantic poem has to be general in this sense. It has to be intelligible and negotiable.)

2. An idea is general in a more special way if it is viable for a great many persons, or for the average person, or for a natural person un-

Johnson's Literary Criticism (Minneapolis, 1952), Chapter VIII, and W. B. C. Watkins, "Dr. Johnson on the Imagination: a Note," *RES*, XXII (April, 1946), 131–4.

[9] Allen Tate, "Johnson on the Metaphysical Poets," *The Forlorn Demon* (Chicago, 1953), pp. 114–15.

corrupted by civilized sophistications. Such an idea seems to be most often conceived by the theorist as being *very* simple. We have noted Samuel Johnson's participation in this form of primitivism.

3. An idea is general when it is applicable to several individuals. The idea expressed by any common noun is general, for example, *philosopher*.

4. An idea is general, again in a more special way, if it is *more* general (or generic) as opposed to more limited or specific. *Man* is more general than *philosopher*, and *animal* is more general than *man*. The more general an idea is in this sense the more "abstract" it may also be said to be. The more ready it is, at least, to be turned into a second-stage abstraction—e.g., *animality*.

5. An idea is general if it refers to objects which generally exist, i.e., which are statistically common. A high degree of such generality does not necessarily go along with a high degree of that just described under 3., though much neo-classic discussion seems to assume that it does. There are more bald-headed philosophers wearing spectacles than there are philosophers with green hair—but the latter idea is the less specific of the two. This distinction may be put in terms of neo-classic literature as follows: There is fantasy and there is realism, and either form can be more specific or less specific. There is *Gulliver's Travels*, and there is *Rasselas*. There is Defoe's *Journal of the Plague Year*, and there is the *Rambler*.

6. An idea is general if it is at the specific or substantive level conceived by Aristotle and the schoolmen. This is the Aristotelian species, the medieval *propria idea*, the essential answer to the question: What is it? "When we ask what it is," says Aristotle, "we do not say white or hot, or four cubits long, but a man or a god." "The essence of Socrates," says Aquinas, "is the essence of man." Post-Lockean logic runs against it, but this concept is actually implicit in almost all ordinary discourse, and it may be necessary to the very idea that there are individual subsistent things, distinct from one another. Quiddity is something like a limit of change beyond which a thing becomes a different thing. It is the highest level [1] of stable differentiation between classes of things. The history of the neo-classic universal suggests a close connection with this Aristotelian quiddity—though it was often idealized into a kind of Platonic unreality. Johnson and Reynolds often employ the word *species*. One thing, however, which must be obvious is that neither poetry nor painting is confined either, in detail, to alluding to species (tulips rather than streaks) or, in whole works, to presenting a species or any subspecies (essential man, or essential gladiator). If the species or the subspecies were the norm, then all paintings of human beings, or all

[1] Cf. Mortimer Adler, "The Hierarchy of Essences," *The Review of Metaphysics*, VI (September, 1952), 3-30.

paintings of certain classes of human beings, would have the same aesthetic value. This seems a sure enough principle, even though it solves no critical problem. Ruskin's critique of Reynolds in a chapter of *Modern Painters* (III, i) touches a fundamental truth about poetry in the observations:

> Instead of finding . . . the poetry distinguished from the history by the omission of details, we find it consist entirely in the *addition* of details. . . . yet it cannot be simply that addition which turns the history into poetry. For it is perfectly possible to add any number of details to a historical statement, and to make it more prosaic with every added word.

7. An idea is general if it is large and inclusive—if it contains, for instance, the whole universe. Platonism has always tended to promote the generically universal to the status of the inclusive universal. *Being*, for instance, is a term which covers both ideas. Platonism has always tended to the sublime—the big, the overwhelming, the awesome. Despite Johnson's religious misgivings about the secular sublime, his version of the grandeur of generality was, as we have seen, an ambiguous junction of neo-Platonic largeness with the Aristotelian species.

8. An idea is general if it represents what is necessary—either *a priori*, like the Pythagorean theorem, or *a posteriori* (which shades off into the probable), like the law of gravity or the fact that every living man must have a head. This kind of generality may be considered as a development of 4. above, and as preparing the way for 9.

9. An idea is general if it represents what is perfect, or ideal, and hence, in the direction of structure and purpose, most real—that which tends to fulfil a possibility, capability, or potentiality of some being. A man who is a philosopher or who has profound religious experience may be statistically less common than his opposite, but there is a sense in which he is more completely a man. The Aristotelian *to beltion* comes in here, and the kind of idealism reflected in the passage from Reynolds' Thirteenth *Discourse* quoted earlier in this chapter.

None of these senses of the general or the universal will completely explain or justify the neo-classic theory. None of these is by itself a sufficient account of poetry. By and large the neo-classic universal centered too simply in the area of 3., 4., and 5. (the logical and scientific universals). These concepts were too literally taken as sufficient, and they were confused with one another. In the opinion of the present writers, 8. and 9. (the universals of structure and coherence) look more directly toward poetry and suggest a circuit of ideas which will include 1.—the intelligible and negotiable individual.

VII

THE neo-classic theory of general truth was an attempt to say what kind of reality is given in art, an attempt to relate and even to identify the real and the ideal. Yet the human ideal must be always in some sense fictitious. And fiction stretches out to embrace fable. Art, in the classic tradition, professed to render reality through a trick of presenting something either better or more significant than reality. But the trick obviously and quite often involved the unreal. Four antitheses: realism *vs.* fantasy, history *vs.* fiction, particular *vs.* universal, real *vs.* ideal, were subsumed in a medley of ways by the classic tradition under the basic antithesis nature *vs.* art. We have noticed how some of these antitheses clustered in the critical thinking of Samuel Johnson. And in our enumeration of senses for the term "general" we have suggested some of the logical dangers inherent in the whole situation. We may perhaps fittingly close not only this chapter but our narrative of neo-classicism with a brief anthology of passages touching with various accents on the most persistent preoccupation of all classic and neo-classic criticism, the puzzling relation between nature and art.

> Do you mean that a rhapsode will know better than the pilot what the ruler of a sea-tossed vessel ought to say?—Plato, *Ion* 540

> Not to know that a hind has no horns is a less serious matter than to paint it inartistically.—Aristotle, *Poetics* XXV

> And he tells lies and mixes true and false in such a way that the middle is consistent with the beginning and the end with the middle.—Horace, *Ars Poetica*, ll. 151–2

> For (as I never cease to say) the deeds and passions which verge on transport are a sufficient lenitive and remedy for every audacity of speech.—Longinus, *On the Sublime*, XXXVIII

> The poet is not a recorder of facts in verse; historians take care of facts much better. The poet's job is, by a technique of mystery, by invocations of the supernatural, by a boldly fictive elaboration of ideas, to release the free spirit of poesy—so that what he writes sounds like the prophetic utterance of a soul aflame, not like a scrupulous statement of fact testified to by witnesses.—Petronius, *Satyricon*, 118

> We have known of festivals without pipes and dances; but never of a poem without its fabulous or fictitious element.
> —Plutarch, *How to Study Poetry* 16c

The arts are not to be slighted on the ground that they create by imitation of natural objects; for, to begin with, these natural objects are themselves imitations; then, we must recognize that they give no bare reproductions of the thing seen but go back to the Ideas from which Nature itself derives.

—Plotinus, *Ennead* V, viii

He goeth hand in hand with nature, not enclosed within the narrow warrant of her gifts, but freely ranging within the zodiac of his own wit.

—Philip Sidney, *Apologie for Poetrie*, c. 1580–4

When Aristotle said in the beginning of the *Poetics* that all the species of poetry were imitative, he meant that imitation which has for its object the image that springs entirely from human artifice. . . . Plato in the *Sophist* has left a statement that imitation is of two sorts. One of these he has named icastic; it represents things that are truly derived from some work already existing. . . . The other, which he called phantastic, is exemplified in pictures that are made by the caprice of the artist.

—Jacopo Mazzoni, *On the Defense of the Comedy*, 1587, Introduction

Poesie was ever thought to have some participation of divinesse, because it doth raise and erect the Minde, by submitting the shewes of things to the desires of the Mind, whereas reason doth buckle and bowe the Mind unto the Nature of things.

—Francis Bacon, *Advancement of Learning*, 1605

For he knows poet never credit gained
By writing truths, but things like truths, well feigned.

—Ben Jonson, Prologue to *Epicoene*, 1609

We shall tolerate flying Horses, black Swans, Hydra's, Centaur's, Harpies and Satyrs; for these are monstrosities, rarities, or else Poetical fancies, whose shadowed moralities requite their substantial falsities.

—Sir Thomas Browne, *Pseudodoxia Epidemica* (1646), V, 19

If I am not deceived, a play is supposed to be the work of the poet, imitating or representing the conversation of several persons.

—John Dryden, *A Defence of an Essay of Dramatic Poesy*, 1668

An heroic poet is not tied to a bare representation of what is true . . . but . . . he may let himself loose to visionary objects, and to the representation of such things as depending not on

sense, and therefore not to be comprehended by knowledge, may give him a freer scope for imagination.
                    —John Dryden, *Of Heroic Plays,* 1673

The Poetic World is nothing but Fiction; Pernassus, Pegasus, and the Muses, pure imagination and Chimaera. But being, however, a system universally agreed on, all that shall be contriv'd or invented upon this Foundation according to Nature shall be reputed as truth: But what so ever shall diminish from, or exceed, the just proportions of Nature, shall be rejected as False, and pass for extravagance, as Dwarfs and Gyants for Monsters.
—George Granville, *An Essay upon Unnatural Flights in Poetry,* 1701

As no Thought can be justly said to be fine, unless it be true, I have all along had a regard for Truth; except only in Passages that are purely Satirical, where some Allowance must be given: For Satire may be fine, and true Satire, tho' it be not directly and according to the Letter, true: 'tis enough that it carry with it a Probability or Semblance of Truth.
            —Edward Bysshe, *The Art of Poetry,* 1702, Preface

A strict Verisimilitude . . . [is] not requir'd in the Descriptions of this visionary and allegorical kind of Poetry, which admits of every wild Object that Fancy may present in a Dream, and where it is Sufficient if the moral meaning atone for the Improbability.—Alexander Pope, *The Temple of Fame,* 1715

The task of an author is, either to teach what is not known, or to recommend known truths by his manner of adorning them.
                    —Samuel Johnson, *Rambler* 3, 1750

The muses wove, in the loom of *Pallas,* a loose and changeable robe, like that in which *Falsehood* captivated her admirers; with this they invested *Truth,* and named her *Fiction.*
                    —Samuel Johnson, *Rambler* 96, 1751

Poetry is the art of uniting pleasure with truth, by calling imagination to the help of reason.
            —Samuel Johnson, *Life of Milton,* 1779 (*Lives,* I, 170)

PART THREE

PART THREE

POETIC DICTION: WORDSWORTH AND COLERIDGE

§ *"poetic diction" as a critical problem—II. sketch of English poetic diction: the Spenserian strain, the neoclassic: Latinism, adjectives, periphrase, high and low style (Addison, Pope, Johnson), rise of the concept "poetic diction," Dryden to Gray—III. the classical protest (Horace, Jonson, Dryden, Pope, Goldsmith, Swift), the romantic protest (more radical), the anonymous poetic style circa 1797, the diction of the* Lyrical Ballads, *Wordsworth's argument in the* Advertisement *and* Preface: *"very language of men," "low and rustic persons," "men in a state of vivid sensation"—IV. Coleridge's critique: distinction between words and manner of combining words, between hackneyed image and nonsense, relation of learning to poetry, Wordsworth's ventriloquism—V. history of poetic diction since Wordsworth: Taylor in 1834, Pre-Raphaelite diction, 20th-century imagistic, realistic, and metaphysical reactions, significance of the debate between Wordsworth and Coleridge—VI. antecedents of Wordsworth's primitivism: continental ideas, Homeric theories, the noble savage, Ossian and other forgeries, Duck and other worker poets, Byron's ridicule, the reaction to aristocratic neo-classicism (Swift, Johnson, Goethe, the "bourgeois standard"); varieties of primitivism since Wordsworth: Tolstoy's peasant norm, Saxonism theoretical and practical, concept of false primitives, Celticism, folk speech and argots—VII. who invents good new words?—VIII. poetic diction and the language of poetry, intrusion of the chronological norm, social and commercial requirement of originality (T. S. Eliot, Gertrude*

Stein), *the "Cliché Expert," Gourmont, ingenious and*
original clichés, Gene Fowler's Barrymore, H. W. Fowler
on misapplied quotations—IX. "old saws with new teeth,"
New Yorker *sophistication vs. schoolboy style, tradition*
and usage, Milton to Pope, Dante to Gray, Wordsworth
and 18th-century nature poetry, Blake and Elizabe-
thanism §

A T A LATER POINT IN THIS NARRATIVE (CHAPTER 29) WE SHALL HAVE occasion to consider the question how far a close verbal analysis of poetry may fall short of doing justice to the more massive structural features of such works as novels, epics, dramas. Literary criticism of the mid-20th century in America has been raising that question with an insistence which might even be taken at this point as a discouragement to our dignifying the episode of 18th-century "poetic diction" and the Wordsworthian condemnation of it with very much notice. Both "poetic diction" and the reaction against it, however, stand out conspicuously in critical history, and we choose to dwell upon them with some deliberation. The concept of "poetic diction" is at least a handy one both for the theorist and for the literary historian. It has at least the advantage that it reduces to a nearly definable and testable form a good many other problems of literary criticism. "Poetic diction" is a good small-scale model of the larger problems.

II

THE issue of poetic diction had been growing upon the English literary consciousness steadily since about the time of Chaucer, that is, since the beginning of Renaissance English literature, and with special intensity since the time of Spenser. A new linguistic consciousness, the new linguistic expansiveness of the Renaissance nation, promoted the learned enrichment of vernacular expression and produced a plethora of words.[1] A somewhat different, but closely related, spirit of self-conscious artistry promoted a specifically poetic diction. Such a diction grew rapidly with the tradition of an important poetry in an important language and the development and refinement of this poetry through several generations of poets and critics.

Precisely what kinds of poetic diction were invented and handed on by the succession of English poets and translators—by Spenser, Fair-

---

[1] Cf. F. W. Bateson, *English Poetry and the English Language* (Oxford, 1934).

fax, Sylvester, Sandys, Milton, Dryden, Pope, Thomson, Collins, Gray? This is a complicated question. One may distinguish minor and major strains. Some kinds of poetic diction (like the Petrarchan flowers that flourished in the lesser Elizabethan sonneteers and were twined with graceful levity by Spenser and Sidney, or the rustic dialect words of Spenser's *Shepheardes Calender*) did not continue into the neo-classic era. Others grew stronger and were consolidated in the English tradition continuously up to Wordsworth's time. Without making a long excursion into what is a matter rather of directly poetic than of critical history, the historian of poetic theory may well note some of the main kinds of poetic diction which became fixed in the 18th-century complex. Slightly to one side perhaps belongs the archaic, melancholy, and variously romantic strain invented by Spenser for the *Faerie Queene*[2] and lavishly repeated in the 18th-century Spenserian imitations. A more distinctly classical diction can be described under three main grammatical headings: (1) With regard to etymology, the most pronounced trend was the continuation of Renaissance Latinism, especially as this was helped by the rise of scientific or "philosophic" ideas and vocabulary and by Ovidian and Virgilian meanings in the translations of Dryden and his predecessors. (2) With regard to parts of speech, the most pronounced trend was the increase of adjectives, both Latin derivatives and a large crowd of scientific and poetic coinages bearing the English termination -y.[3] The growth of empirical observation during all this period had an understandably inflationary effect upon descriptive language. (3) With regard to syntax and logical relation, the most pronounced trend was the coupling of the adjective with the noun in a kind of glossy stock phrase, or periphrase, which was sometimes epithetical and redundant, in the Homeric style, sometimes more abstractly definitional (by genera and properties) in a way that is nowadays said to have reflected a philosophy and science of orderly classes in a stable cosmos.[4]

[2] Cf. Ernest De Selincourt, ed. *The Poetical Works of Edmund Spenser* (Oxford, 1932), Introduction, pp. lxi–lxii; F. M. Padelford, "Aspects of Spenser's Vocabulary," *PQ*, XX (July, 1941), 279–83; E. E. Stoll, *Poets and Playwrights* (Minneapolis, 1930), p. 193.

[3] George Gordon, *Shakespeare's English*, S. P. E. Tract No. 39 (Oxford, 1928), p. 274; John Arthos, *The Language of Natural Description in Eighteenth-Century Poetry* (Ann Arbor, 1949), Appendix C.

[4] Cf. Geoffrey Tillotson, *Essays in Criticism and Research* (Cambridge, 1942), p. 84, on "Physico-theological nomenclature"; John Arthos, *The Language of Natural Description*, Chapters IV and V. Other correlatives of 18th-century poetic diction may perhaps be named. The closure and symmetry of couplet verse, for instance, may often have demanded the trochaic or dactyllic adjective. Cf. Thomas Quayle, *Poetic Diction* (London, 1924), Chapter II, p. 29, quoting Shenstone's *Essays*. Personification, as found in the poetry of Johnson, Collins, or Gray, is a kind of abstraction which may be viewed as a special type of poetic diction. Cf. Bertrand H. Bronson, "Personification Reconsidered," *ELH*, XIV (September, 1947), 163–177; Earl R. Wasserman, "The Inherent Values of Eighteenth-Century Personification," *PMLA*, LXV (June, 1950), 435–63.

The definitional type of periphrase stood in a fairly close relation to the standard of universality and abstraction which we have discussed in our last chapter. And the taste for the universal entailed, as we have suggested, a certain mistrust of particularity, the imputation to this of lowness, meanness, or vulgarity. The classical high, middle, and low styles which we have seen transferred by late classical theory from oratory to poetry (becoming the epic, georgic, and eclogue styles) [5] appear by the mid-18th century to have been simplified into the polar concepts of the lofty and the low. Thus Addison could be guilty of saying:

> Since it often happens that the most obvious Phrases, and those which are used in ordinary Conversation, become too familiar to the Ear, and contract a kind of Meanness by passing through the Mouths of the Vulgar, a Poet should take particular Care to guard himself against Idiomatick Ways of Speaking.
>
> —*Spectator* No. 285

And Pope:

> It must also be allowed that there is a majesty and harmony in the Greek language, which greatly contribute to elevate and support the narration. But I must also observe, that this is an advantage grown upon the language since Homer's time: for things are removed from vulgarity by being out of use; and if the words we could find in any present language were equally sonorous or musical in themselves, they would still appear less poetical and uncommon than those of a dead one, from this only circumstance, of being in every man's mouth.[6]

And Samuel Johnson, in a *Rambler* passage on Shakespeare, erected one of the most notorious monuments to the lofty taste.

> Words become low by the occasions to which they are applied, or the general character of them who use them. . . .
> > Come, thick night!
> And pall thee in the dunnest smoke of hell,
> That my keen knife see not the wound it makes;
> Nor heaven peep through the blanket of the dark,
> To cry, Hold, hold!
>
> . . . the efficacy of this invocation is destroyed by the insertion of an epithet now seldom heard but in the stable, and *dun* night may come or go without any other notice than contempt. . . .

[5] See *ante* Chapter 6, p. 103; Chapter 8, p. 146.
[6] Postscript to Pope's translation of the *Odyssey*. Cf. James Sutherland, *A Preface to Eighteenth Century Poetry* (Oxford, 1948), p. 85.

[the] sentiment is weakened by the name of an instrument used by butchers and cooks in the meanest employments. . . . Who, without some relaxation of his gravity, can hear of the avengers of guilt *peeping through a blanket?—Rambler* No. 168

The following positive defense of a special poetic diction is provided by Gray.

The language of the age is never the language of poetry; except among the French, whose verse, where the thought and image does not support it, differs in nothing from prose. Our poetry, on the contrary, has a language peculiar to itself, to which almost everyone that has written has added something by enriching it with foreign idioms and derivations: nay, sometimes words of their own composition or invention. Shakespeare and Milton have been great creators this way; and no one more licentious than Pope or Dryden, who perpetually borrow expressions from the former.[7]

The precise terms "diction" and "poetic diction" seem to have arisen somewhat earlier, in the high Augustan era. Dryden uses "diction" with an apology for Latinism, in the preface to *Sylvae*, 1685. The first person to use the term "poetic diction" is apparently Dennis, in his *Advancement and Reformation of Modern Poetry* (ch. V), 1701. In his Preface to the *Iliad*, 1715, Pope wrote: "We acknowledge him [Homer] the father of poetical diction."[8] As with so many other classic themes, Samuel Johnson wrote a retrospective last word.

There was . . . before the time of Dryden no poetical diction. . . . Those happy combinations of words which distinguished poetry from prose had been rarely attempted; we had few elegancies or flowers of speech.[9]

III

Two kinds of protest against poetic diction have occurred: that of the classicist, hostile to pedantry and affectation, appealing to polite idiom, the educated spoken word; and that of the romantic, hostile to the same things, but appealing to the primitive, the naive, the directly passionate, the natural spoken word. The first of these protests occurs intermittently

[7] To Richard West, April 4, 1742, *Letters*, ed. Leonard Whibley, I, 98. Cf. Lord Chesterfield's recommendation of "poetic diction" to his son seven years old (*Letters*, October 26, 1739).
[8] Thomas Quayle, *Poetic Diction*, p. 7; F. W. Bateson, *English Poetry and the English Language*, p. 71.
[9] *Life of Dryden*, *Lives* (ed. G. B. Hill), I, 420.

throughout the classical and Renaissance eras. It is the voice of Horace (*usus quem penes arbitrium est et jus et norma loquendi*), of Ben Jonson ("Pure and neat Language I love, yet plaine and customary"),[1] of Dryden in his preface to *Annus Mirabilis* (" 'Tis not the jerk or sting of an epigram . . . nor the jingle of a more poor paronomasia"), of Pope in his *Essay:*

> False eloquence, like the prismatic glass,
> Its gaudy colours spreads on ev'ry place;
> The face of Nature we no more survey,
> All glares alike, without distinction gay.
>
> II, 311–314

It is the latter-day voice of Goldsmith, in his *Life of Parnell*,[2] complaining about the "pristine barbarity" of contemporary Spenserians and Miltonists.

The classical protest is more or less unremitting, but it is at the same time moderate, good-tempered, hardly revolutionary. The same Goldsmith who accuses the archaizers of "vainly imagining that the more their writings are unlike prose the more they resemble poetry" will write an essay entitled "Poetry Distinguished from Other Writing." "Certain words" are "particularly adapted to the poetical expression." Jonathan Swift was a consistent classical champion of good prose sense and the idiomatic norm, but the following passage from his satiric *Apollo's Edict*, 1721, illustrates the ambiguity of the classic stand:

> Your tragick Heroes shall not rant,
> Nor Shepherds use *poetick* Cant:
> Simplicity alone can grace,
> The Manners of the rural Race.

Perhaps Swift avails himself of an ironic intimation in that closing periphrase. The "shepherds" become the "rural race" in the course of sixteen syllables saying that they have no right to such a title. Or does Swift accept a certain amount of poetic diction without noticing it? The question evaporates out of the poem itself into the obscure region of Swift's conscious or unconscious intentions.

The final and successful revolt against classical "poetic diction" was more violent—a protest of the second type, primitive, naive, "vegetally"

---

[1] *Timber* No. 118.

[2] *The Miscellaneous Works of Oliver Goldsmith* (London: Globe Edition, 1919), p. 483. "These misguided innovators have not been content with restoring antiquated words and phrases, but have indulged themselves in the most licentious transpositions and the harshest constructions, vainly imagining that the more their writings are unlike prose, the more they resemble poetry."

And see Samuel Butler, *Hudibras*, Part II, Canto I, ll. 591–632.

radical,[3] the first of its kind, at least in English literature, and a thing distinctive of a new social and philosophic era. It is worth while remembering that in the statements which we are about to quote, Wordsworth was reacting immediately not so much against Spenser, Milton, and Pope,[4] the poets who had created English poetic diction, as against his own now anonymous contemporaries who wrote the mélange of dictions which was then poetic staple. The following from the *Monthly Magazine*, for February, 1797, specializes in periphrastic elegance.

> For thee the fields their flowery carpet spread,
> And smiling Ocean smooths his wavy bed;
> A purer glow the kindling poles display,
> Robed in bright effluence of ethereal day,
> When through her portals bursts the gaudy spring,
> And genial Zephyr waves his balmy wing.
> First the gay songsters of the feather'd train
> Feel thy keen arrows thrill in every vein.

From the same issue of the *Monthly* comes this example of the ameliorated pensiveness which had descended in the tradition of Milton's minor poems:

> Oh, far removed from my retreat
> Be Av'rice and Ambition's feet!
> Give me, unconscious of their power,
> To taste the peaceful, social hour.
> Give me, beneath the branching vine,
> The woodbine sweet, or eglantine,
> When evening sheds its balmy dews,
> To court the chaste, inspiring muse.[5]

Beside these let us set down some short examples of the verse which Wordsworth ventured to print in the *Lyrical Ballads* of 1798 and which he defended in his *Advertisement* and in his *Preface* to later editions.[6]

[3] Kenneth Burke, "The Vegetal Radicalism of Theodore Roethke," *Sewanee Review*, LVIII (Winter, 1950), 76, argues that all movements toward a new style are movements toward the "infantile," a way of re-expressing the basic things.

[4] "To this day I believe I could repeat, with a little previous rummaging of my memory, several thousand lines of Pope" (*Letters of the Wordsworth Family*, ed. W. Knight, Boston, 1907, III, 122). The statement is part of a comment made by Wordsworth, in 1836 or later, on Hazlitt's *Spirit of the Age* and recorded in the manuscript *Memoirs* of Barron Field.

[5] Both examples are quoted in Marjorie L. Barstow, *Wordsworth's Theory of Poetic Diction* (New Haven, 1917), pp. 62–3.

[6] The texts of 1800, 1802, 1805 may be conveniently consulted in *Wordsworth, Representative Poems*, ed. Arthur Beatty (New York, 1937), pp. 676–704.

"How many are you then," said I,
"If they two are in Heaven?"
The little Maiden did reply,
"O Master! we are seven."

Few months of life has he in store
As he to you will tell,
For still, the more he works, the more
His poor old ancles swell.
My gentle reader, I perceive
How patiently you've waited,
And I'm afraid that you expect
Some tale will be related.

I heard a thousand blended notes,
While in a grove I sate reclined,
In that sweet mood when pleasant thoughts
Bring sad thoughts to the mind.

And Susan's growing worse and worse,
And Betty's in a sad *quandary*
And then there's nobody to say
If she must go, or she must stay:
—She's in a sad *quandary*

In his *Advertisement* of 1798 Wordsworth called these poems experimental, and he said they were "written chiefly with a view to ascertain how far the language of conversation in the middle and lower classes of society is adapted to the purposes of poetic pleasure." He feared his readers would think he had been "too low" and "too familiar," but he contrasted with his own style "the gaudiness and inane phraseology of many modern writers." [7] In his *Preface* some of the statements are even more downright. He is proud of having uttered "little of what is usually called poetic diction." His purpose has been "to imitate, and, as far as possible, to adopt the very language of men." [8] He asserts "that there neither is, nor can be, any essential difference between the language of prose and metrical composition." [9] His objection to poetic diction is that it is not true to nature—either to external nature or to human nature in

[7] Coleridge, *Biographia*, Chapter I, speaks of the "glare and glitter of a perpetual yet broken and heterogeneous imagery . . . an amphibious something."

[8] Cf. his later note to *Simon Lee the Old Huntsman:* "The expression when the hounds were out, 'I dearly love their voice,' was word for word from his own lips."

[9] The phrasing is that of 1802, a slight alteration from that of 1800.

its responses to the external. "I have at all times endeavored to look steadily at my subject; consequently, I hope that there is in these poems little falsehood of description, and that my ideas are expressed in language fitted to their respective importance." He seems to believe too that even honest expressions can become bad poetry just by being repeated. "I have . . . abstained from the use of many expressions, in themselves proper and beautiful, but which have been foolishly repeated by bad poets, 'till such feelings of disgust are connected with them, as it is scarcely possible by any art of association to overpower." On the genetic side the *Preface* contains a strong statement of the reasons why the language of "low [1] and rustic" persons is likely to be poetic:

> . . . because such men hourly communicate with the best objects from which the best part of language is originally derived; and because, from their rank in society and the sameness and narrow circle of their intercourse, being less under the influence of social vanity, they convey their feelings and notions in simple unelaborated expressions. Accordingly, such language, arising out of repeated experience and regular feelings, is a more permanent, and a far more philosophical language, than that which is frequently substituted for it by poets.

Yet this *Preface* contains a few statements which look like attempts to qualify Wordsworth's main view concerning the "very language of men," the language of "low and rustic" persons. For he speaks also about "a selection of the real language of men in a state of *vivid sensation*," about "a certain *colouring of imagination*, whereby ordinary things should be presented to the mind in an *unusual way*." [2] He wishes to make ordinary situations "interesting" by tracing in them the laws of human nature "as far as regards the manner in which we associate ideas in a *state of excitement*." "All good poetry," as every reader of the *Preface* will remember, "is the spontaneous overflow of *powerful feelings*." [3]

---

[1] "Low" becomes "humble" in 1832.

[2] 1802.

[3] The italics in these quotations are ours. In the same year, 1800, Wordsworth's letter to the critic John Wilson develops his theory as follows: "Please whom? or what? I answer, human nature as it has been and ever will be. But, where are we to find the best measure of this? I answer, from within; by stripping our own hearts naked, and by looking out of ourselves towards men who lead the simplest lives, and most according to nature; men who have never known false refinements." But he says also: "It is not enough for me as a Poet, to delineate merely such feelings as all men *do* sympathize with; but it is also highly desirable to add to these others, such as all men *may* sympathize with, and such as there is reason to believe they would be better and more moral beings if they did sympathize with." Wordsworth's argument is aimed against the distaste felt by Wilson and his friends for *The Idiot Boy*.

IV

THE simplism and primitivism of Wordsworth's poems, and even more of his theoretical views, provoked a considerable volume of immediate protest from his reading public. But the critic who spoke with the shrewdest authority was Coleridge, after a lapse of seventeen years, in his reminiscential *Biographia Literaria*. Coleridge's argument about poetic diction may be summarized under three main heads.

(1) He said that if Wordsworth, in arguing that the language of "metrical composition" is essentially the same as that of prose, meant only that poetry and prose have the same vocabulary, or dictionary, on which to draw, he was uttering a truism. Coleridge concluded that Wordsworth really meant that the poetic manner of combining words was no different from that of prose. And this, he retorted, was patently false.[4] (It is perhaps worth observing that Wordsworth may not in fact have made it quite clear whether he excluded either of the meanings defined by Coleridge—and that it is not necessary, either for justice to Wordsworth, or for the purposes of literary history, to suppose that he had brought himself to the point of facing a sharp distinction.)

(2) Coleridge argued that if a given image or figure (for instance, the "image" of Phoebus as the sun) is used badly by a given poet (for instance, Gray in a sonnet criticized by Wordsworth), the reason for the badness is not that the figure is a repetition of what other poets have done, but that it is in some way a violation of "grammar, logic, psychology," "good sense," or "taste"—the *"rules* of the IMAGINATION."[5]

> . . . it is a bad line, not because the language is distinct from that of prose; but because it conveys incongruous images, because it confounds the cause and effect, the real *thing* with the personified *representative* of the thing; in short, because it differs with the language of GOOD SENSE! That the "Phoebus" is hackneyed and a school-boy image, is an *accidental* fault, dependent on the age in which the author wrote.—II, 58

Another poet might be found, for instance Spenser, who had used the Phoebus image well.[6]

---

[4] Cf. Thomas M. Raysor, "Coleridge's Criticism of Wordsworth," *PMLA*, LIV (June, 1939), 496–510.

[5] Chapter XVIII, (*Biographia*, ed. J. Shawcross, II, 64–5).

[6] Coleridge's master at Christ's Hospital, the Reverend James Bowyer, had been in the habit of saying that "in the truly great poets . . . there was a reason assignable, not only for every word, but for the position of every word" (Chapter I; I, 4).

(3) Coleridge argued that education, and not the lack of it, tends to make a poet. Uneducated men are disorderly in their writing; they lack "surview." If the peasantry of Wordsworth's Westmoreland and Cumberland spoke a pure and vigorous language, this came not from uninstructed communion with nature, but from a spirit of independence and from a solid religious education and acquaintance with the Bible and hymnbook.

One kind of speech (socially defined) could not be more *real* than another.[7] But in a given instance it might be either more or less poetic. In his appreciation of Wordsworth's own poetic performance, Coleridge noted that Wordsworth suffered the difficulties of a ventriloquist in his undue liking for the dramatic form. Either a rustic speaker was invested with a Wordsworthian authority of utterance, or an opposite fault appeared, matter-of-factness, circumstantiality, and a downright prosaism.[8] "I've measured it from side to side; 'Tis three feet long, and two feet wide." It is not possible for a poet, urged Coleridge, especially not for a lyric poet, "to imitate truly a dull and garrulous discourser, without repeating the effects of dullness and garrulity." [9]

V

THE episode of the *Lyrical Ballads* was of course far from settling the business of poetic diction in English. Before many years had passed, a reviewer of Wordsworth's poems would raise his voice to accuse even Wordsworth of having fostered his own kind of poetic diction, more dangerous than the old, because more "covert and surreptitious," more "insidious." A new set of "stock words" seemed to this reviewer to be sprinkled through the "fugitive" poetry of the day "with a sort of feeling senselessness"—words, for instance, like *wild, bright, dark, lonely, light, dream*. The principle of their use was sentimental association lending color to a "pretext of conveying sense"—"in a manner which Mr. Wordsworth's prefaces will be found to explain." [1]

A recent historian of English poetic language has noted the progressive "deliquescence" of diction in English poetry (the development of a

---

[7] Chapter XVII (II, 39).

[8] Chapter XXII (II, 101, 109).

[9] Chapter XVII (II, 36). Cf. Letter to Southey, July 29, 1802 (*Letters*, ed. E. H. Coleridge, I, 386): "Here and there a daring humbleness of language and versification, and a strict adherence to matter of fact, even to prolixity. . . ."

[1] [Sir Henry Taylor], "Wordsworth's *Poetical Works*," *Quarterly Review*, LII (1834) 318-19. Cf. Theodore Spencer, "Antaeus, or Poetic Language and the Actual World," *ELH*, X (September, 1943), 182-3. Taylor means that Wordsworth's defense of his own diction offers the rationale of a new poetic diction. A close parallel appears between Taylor's argument and Wordsworth's own indictment of earlier poetic diction. See especially the Appendix to the *Lyrical Ballads*. 1802.

certain moonlight norm) during the Tennysonian and Pre-Raphaelite era.[2] In our own century we have experienced several waves of reaction to that era, the imagism of Pound, the realism of Masefield, the metaphysical inclusiveness of Eliot. Nothing is likely to seem more axiomatic to the student of poetry today than statements to the effect that "The poetry of a people takes its life from the people's speech and in turn gives life to it," [3] that "the language which is good enough for labor and love and marriage, for birth and death, and the friendly breaking of bread, is good enough . . . for the making of poetry." [4]

Nevertheless, the debate between Wordsworth and Coleridge was a significant event in English literary history. It is part of the first romantic revolt against poetic diction in English and it is a more or less adequate monument to two questions: one genetic—Among what kinds of people does poetic language originate? The other critical—How is "poetic diction" in the sense of something undesirably artificial to be distinguished from the valid language—the idiom—of poetry?

VI

The primitivism of Wordsworth was something which had numerous relations with his immediate background, though some of these are only vaguely implicit. Vico was a fountainhead of which he was certainly unaware. It is not necessary to inquire how directly he was in touch with Herder and other continental writers on the theme of *Volkspoesie*, or with theories of the bardic composition of Homer's epics in English writers like Blackwell, Kames, and Blair.[5] More concrete phenomena are the archaic forgeries of the 18th century (the Ossianic epics of Macpherson, the Rowleyan balladry of Chatterton), the cult of the "noble savage," the "child of nature," and the pathetically exploited worker poets—Stephen Duck the thresher, Henry Jones the Irish bricklayer patronized by Lord Chesterfield, James Woodhouse the shoemaker, Anne Yearsley the milkmaid (Lactilla) who developed airs and fell out with Hannah More.[6] The vogue was recorded in the ridicule of Byron.

[2] F. W. Bateson, *English Poetry and the English Language* (Oxford, 1934) pp. 108–15.

[3] T. S. Eliot, *The Use of Poetry and the Use of Criticism* (Cambridge, Mass.: 1933), p. 5.

[4] Harriet Monroe, quoted in Marguerite Wilkinson, *New Voices* (New York, 1931), p. 113.

[5] Cf. Wellek, *Rise*, p. 87; and Wellek's review of Vico's *Autobiography, PQ*, XXIV (1945), 166–8. Wordsworth's acquaintance with the Abbé Delille and other French georgic poets of the 18th century, shown in his early poems *An Evening's Walk* and *Descriptive Sketches*, is discussed by Arthur Beatty in his *Wordsworth, Representative Poems* (New York, 1937), pp. 31–3, 673.

[6] C. B. Tinker, *Nature's Simple Plan* (Princeton, 1922), pp. 92–103. One difference between Wordsworth and his forerunners of the 18th century was that with

When some brisk youth, the tenant of a stall,
Employs his pen less pointed than his awl,
Leaves his snug shop, forsakes his store of shoes,
St. Crispin quits, and cobbles for the muse,
Heavens! how the vulgar stare! how crowds applaud!
How ladies read, and literati laud!

. . . .

Let poesy go forth, pervade the whole,
Alike the rustic, and mechanic soul!
Ye tuneful cobblers! still your notes prolong,
Compose at once a slipper and a song.[7]

Wordsworth's primitivism was part of a general reaction, setting in well before his own day, against the aristocratic side of neo-classicism. We have seen that Dryden believed the right language of poetry—the very model of correct poetry—to be the language of the king and court. Pope believed the same, at least of the Elizabethan age.[8] About George II he had much difficulty.[9] Swift[1] and Johnson were severe upon the imbecilities of society talk. Johnson spoke of "female phrases," "fashionable barbarisms."[2] It was possible, perhaps usual, during all this time, for the anti-aristocratic tendency to rest short of sheer primitivism in what Marxist criticism would later call the bourgeois standard. Thus Goethe, giving explicit utterance to an idea that was no doubt often implicitly entertained: "A middle rank is much more favorable to talent [than a noble rank], so we find all great artists and poets in the middle classes."[3]

The period from Wordsworth to the present day has been notable for the variety and complexity of its archaizing and primitivistic trends. Some of these, like the peasant standard arrived at by Tolstoy, have had no direct relation to the language. Others, like the theoretical Saxonizing of English essayists and scholars (Macaulay, for instance, and Furnivall), or the practical Saxonizing of the Homeric translator Francis Newman,[4] are quite obviously in the area of "poetic diction." We encounter now, in

the latter the preference for nature did not reach the crisis of diction. That was what Wordsworth had against them. The supposedly primitive or natural poets of the 18th century were not distinguished for a Wordsworthian simplicity of language. They used all the ornaments. The point was precisely that they were able to do this. That apparently was thought to reveal something about origins, about natural inspiration.

[7] *English Bards and Scotch Reviewers*, ll. 765 ff.
[8] See his *Preface* to Shakespeare.
[9] See his *Epistle to Augustus*.
[1] See his *Tatler* No. 230.
[2] *Idler* No. 77.
[3] *Conversations*, February 24, 1825. Cf. Wordsworth's phrase "language of conversation in the middle or lower classes of society."
[4] Cf. *post* Chapter 20, p. 443.

contrast to the 18th-century beginnings, a primitivism rather formidably equipped with archeological and philological apparatus. A later special development has been a certain esoteric removal of the primitive locus. This means admitting the existence of fake primitives or bourgeois poseurs (like Robert Burns or Longfellow) but at the same time asserting the existence of a genuine peasant wisdom, an oral tradition from the foundations of the world. This was once in rapport with aristocratic and learned wisdom (the hut with the castle and the cloister) but has now been split off by the wedge of bourgeois culture and is withering away. Theorizing of this kind has had a Celtic and visionary orientation.[5]

So far as any view of poetic origins prevails very explicitly today, it is still likely to be the primitivistic. Our large literature in the departments of dialect, folk speech, argot and slang, is one testimony to a settled primitivistic interest among scholars. And this interest sometimes raises curious problems concerning not only compilation but evaluation. To select one instance from the many: a writer in the magazine *American Speech* argues that during World War II there were two kinds of soldier slang—a small number of terms really invented by soldiers and truly expressive (*shack up, sweat out, latrine rumour, chew ass*), and a much larger number of fake terms invented by newspaper writers, USO workers, and entertainers (*armoured cow,* for canned milk, *scandal sheet,* for payroll, *misery pipe,* for bugle, *homing device,* for furlough, *handgrenades,* for hamburgers, *tire patches,* for pancakes). In the same way there are two kinds of jazz slang—the genuine expressions of jazz musicians and fans (*Tailgate, solid, jam, riff, gutbucket, barrelhouse*), and the spurious inventions of publicity agents, masters of ceremonies, and popular music magazines (*God box,* for organ, *skin-beater,* for drummer, *syringe,* for trombone, *sliver sucker,* for clarinetist, *doghouse,* for bass fiddle, *gitter* or *git box,* for guitar).

In each case the terms especially invented by persons not familiar through experience with the daily life of soldiers or musicians bear the mark of their artificial origins. They seldom

---

[5] See W. B. Yeats, "What is Popular Poetry?" in *Ideas of Good and Evil* (London, 1903), pp. 1-15. The classic philological discussion is that concerning the origin of the medieval vernacular lyric, Troubadour and Minnesang poetry. Did its origins lie in courtly scholarship or in folk minstrelsy? See Leo Spitzer, "The Mozarabic Lyric and Theodor Frings' Theories," *Comparative Literature,* IV (Winter, 1952), 1-4, 17-22. "Where within primitive lyricism should we then place the narrative-lyrical love songs of women inferred from the *jarchas* (= *refrains*)? Obviously in that pre-Christian framework of collective, improvised dancing songs of women in springtime which G. Paris, followed therein by Frings, recognized to be at the base of all lyrics in the Romance and Germanic vernaculars." "We are brought ultimately to visualize a primitive world of women dancing and chanting stanzas of love provided for them by the poets (a *Glückslaut* or *Klage* "im Munde des Mädchens, aber von einem Mann, dem Dichter, hineingelegt"), who thus achieve a vicarious pleasure. . . . Such a collaboration of the two sexes is no *creatio ex nihilo.* . . ."

serve a denotive purpose, are laborious, and lack the expressive
quality of the terms that have been born of the life experience
of the participants themselves.

At the same time, however, this writer notes that jazz musicians and
fans tend to discard their own vocabulary when it is taken over by
commercial users.[6] In this kind of inquiry, which is inferred from which?
The quality of the term from its origin, or the origin from the quality?

VII

THE question about the origins of poetic language seems to allude to a
language upon which some sort of special poetic virtue has been conferred before it reaches the poet himself. We are forced to conceive
poetic language as a kind of pre-poetically potent vocabulary or vigorous
mode of expression. At the same time the history of poetic diction strongly
suggests that the main inventors of poetic diction have been professional
poets themselves—Spenser, Milton, Dryden, Pope. Who does make up
the good new words and phrases—those that add something to our expressive stock and are fitted to survive? Do these occur first in works of
creative literature, or in miscellaneous non-literary places? [7] Did the
primitive bard write the best poetic language? And if he did, was he
an unusually primitive, or an unusually advanced, member of his tribe?
Is a modern poet an unusually advanced, or an unusually primitive,
member of modern society?

If a dramatic clause be invoked—that is, if we observe that the
language of any social class is proper when a writer is representing that
class—the inquiry may appear to be translated into something quite
different. And indeed it is true that the supposed speaker of any poem
is always dramatic, and is always to be conceived as some kind of person, and often as a person not learned or poetically skillful. Nevertheless—as we have heard Coleridge remark about the experiments of
Wordsworth—a direct imitation of the uncouth speaker does run a special
risk of lapsing into realistic disorder and insignificance. This may be
much like what a modern critic has called the "fallacy of imitative form,"
or like what Dryden called "mechanic humour" in the correctly low-life

[6] Morroe Berger, "Some Excesses of Slang Compilers," *American Speech*, XXI
(October, 1946), 196–8.
[7] Cf. Max J. Herzberg, "Who Makes Up the New Words?" *Word Study*, XXIV
(October, 1948), 1–9. The modern professionals quoted by Mr. Herzberg make very
modest claims as linguistic innovators. As any new expression which becomes a part
of the language has to appear in print in order to be recorded, it seems at least
likely that a professional phase occurs early in the life of each neologism. But do
professional journalists make up their own new words or overhear them in oral
discourse?

imitations of Ben Jonson. It is possible also to have correctly tedious imitations of high life. Johnson and Swift were right about this. Anybody who has ever tried to collect brilliant or pungent expressions either at cocktail parties or at diners along truck routes must have been struck by the prevalence of the brassier kind of clichés and the reiterated simplisms of blasphemy.

VIII

IN THE end the only question of critical significance is the second of the two which we have framed above: How is poetic diction in the sense of something false and undesirable to be distinguished from the valid language of poetry? Yet it may not be easy to isolate this critical question. In addition to the concept of origins as we have just attempted to describe it, there is yet another, an intermediate kind of concept, that of chronological staleness, the hackneyed, which is usually associated with that of poetic diction and tends greatly to obscure the critical discussion of the latter. The theoretical issue of poetic diction seemed to Wordsworth an issue between artifice and nature.[8] To Coleridge it seemed more like an issue between propriety and impropriety, congruity and incongruity. In effect he applied the classic norm of decorum. Both Wordsworth and Coleridge assigned a relatively slight role to the chronological concept of the "hackneyed." Yet the notion of the hackneyed, the stereotype, the cliché, today enjoys a strongly established place in habits of critical thinking. It is likely to be among the first appeals of a theorist called upon to explain why poetic diction is undesirable.

The most obvious sense in which the poet is bound to bear the burden of originality is that which relates originality to the social and commercial conditions of success in literature. There is no practical point in repeating the classics, or in repeating their style. Even if some classic had failed to get written on schedule (in its own era) and even if it could be written instead today, the expectancies and demands of publishers and readers preclude the success of the performance. The undergraduate joker who types out a selection of the less well-known sonnets of Shakespeare and submits them over his own name to a New York press does so in full expectation of being rejected.[9] This massive and immovable fact about markets and readers is one of the grounds which supports a kind of statement that often proceeds with great authority from the successful literary person. Thus T. S. Eliot:

> It is exactly as wasteful for a poet to do what has been done already, as for a biologist to rediscover Mendel's discoveries. The French poets in question have made "discoveries" in verse

[8] Cf. Meyer Abrams, *The Mirror and the Lamp* (New York, 1953), p. 120.
[9] Cf. David Daiches, *A Study of Literature* (Ithaca, 1948), pp. 127-8.

of which we cannot afford to be ignorant, discoveries which are not merely a concern for French syntax. To remain with Wordsworth is equivalent to ignoring the whole of science subsequent to Erasmus Darwin.[1]

And Gertrude Stein:

> The whole business of writing is the question of living in that contemporariness. Each generation has to live in that. . . . what I am trying to make you understand is that every contemporary writer has to find out what is the inner time-sense of his contemporaries. The writer, or painter, or what-not, feels this thing more vibrantly, and he has a passionate need of putting it down; and that is what creativeness does.[2]

But the critical problem of poetic diction and the cliché requires a somewhat more precise handling than that. One of the minor comic figures of our time is the "Cliché Expert," who in an early appearance was made to "take the stand" and testified along these lines.

> Q—Mr. Arbuthnot, you are an expert in the use of the cliché, are you not?
>
> A—Yes sir, I am a certified public cliché expert.
>
> Q—Would you answer a few questions on the use of the cliché in ordinary speech and writing?
>
> A—I should be only too glad to.
>
> Q—Thank you. Now just for the record—you live in New York?
>
> A—I like to visit New York but I wouldn't live there if you gave me the place.
>
> Q—Then where do you live?
>
> A—Any old place where I hang my hat is home sweet home to me.
>
> Q—What is your age?
>
> A—I am fat, fair, and forty.
>
> Q—And your occupation?
>
> A—Well, after burning the midnight oil at an institution of higher learning, I was for a time a tiller of the soil. Then I went down to the sea in ships. I have been a guardian of the law, a poet at heart, a prominent clubman and a man about town, an eminent— [3]

[1] 1918. Quoted by N. H. Pearson and W. R. Benét, *The Oxford Anthology of American Literature* (New York: Oxford University Press, Inc., 1939), p. 1636.

[2] Gertrude Stein, "How Writing is Written," a talk before the students at Choate School in 1935 (cf. *The Choate Literary Magazine*, XXI, ii, 5–14), in N. H. Pearson and W. R. Benét, *The Oxford Anthology of American Literature*, pp. 1446–51.

[3] Frank Sullivan, "The Cliché Expert Takes the Stand," *The New Yorker*, August 31, 1935, pp. 15–16.

Here is an ironic frame of reference which makes a series of sorry expressions amusing. But what makes each of the expressions in itself so sorry? Not merely the fact that it is a cold potato, a stereotype (any word in the dictionary enjoys the same status), but the further fact that the expression has a certain special character, even if tame and drab. It attempts to stand up and make a little joke, and the joke is out of place. When the cliché expert took the stand, the context was all against him. There could hardly be any chance for his embroideries, even for the plainest of them. "Fat, fair, and forty" is not an answer for the witness stand.

"In the true notion of the *cliché*," says a French critic, "incoherence has its place by the side of triteness." [4] The logic of the situation would suggest that even ingenuity and originality are no sure proofs against the cliché. The highly ingenious periphrases often employed at certain levels of journalism have a cold ring, like echoes, even though we cannot say of what. A popular biography of a famous actor, for instance, yields a reviewer the following grounds of patronizing complaint.

> For Mr. Fowler, Broadway is inevitably "this street of fickle luster," a distiller a "maker of spirituous delicacies," and Shakespeare "Stratford's first gentleman;" cigarette-smoking is "bronchial debauchery," hair on the chest "torsorial upholstery," and the men's washroom "ammoniac grottos" equipped with "cracked and homely porcelains." When he wants to convey the idea that some white mice were multiplying rapidly, he says that the "snowy rodents were fruitful;" and when Barrymore sets out to play Hamlet, or take on "the Danish assignment," Mr. Fowler says that he "announced . . . his decision to draw on the black tights of the classic Scandinavian." [5]

Some of the expressions quoted here are no doubt clichés in the ordinary chronological sense. Others, however, seem unusual. The real character of their offensiveness (or presumable offensiveness) does not lie in their newness or oldness, but in the difficulty one has in conceiving an excuse for them. There is enough information in the expressions themselves and in their translations by the reviewer to suggest a certain inevitable silliness. They may be saved only on the principle of dramatization—and perhaps even then only at some expense to their author. "The fuzzy

[4] Remy de Gourmont, "Of Style or Writing" (from his *Decadence*, trans. W. A. Bradley, New York, 1921), in *Essays in Modern Literary Criticism*, ed. Ray B. West, Jr. (New York, 1952), p. 62. Cf. Gourmont, *Esthétique de la langue française* (Paris, 1905), pp. 301–38, "*Le Cliché.*"

[5] Edmund Wilson, review of Gene Fowler, *Good Night, Sweet Prince*, in *The New Yorker*, XIX (January 22, 1944), 58; also in Edmund Wilson, *Classics and Commercials* (New York: Farrar, Straus and Company, 1950).

raffish style of this book," says the reviewer, "has its special appropriateness to the subject: it is a literary equivalent for the atmosphere in which the events take place. What we get here is the folklore of the Barrymores."

Bad poetic diction includes a wide range of non-meanings—from the fuzziness or lack of focus that may characterize the whole work of a minor and derivative poet to such grossly misapplied cliché quotations as those noticed by H. W. Fowler in his *Modern English Usage*.[6] A person who actually remembers what goes on in the first act of *Hamlet* will not be guilty of a jocular statement that the Ten Commandments are rules which by and large have been "more honored in the breach than in the observance."

IX

ONE might experiment with the conception that all language is an arsenal of clichés, some expressions, like *man* and *tree*, being only more ordinary and more solidly established than some others,[7] like *umbrageous, prelusive, fleecy kind*, and *finny tribe*. The usual rule of thumb is that a poet should avoid clichés. But a higher rule is that he should be a master of clichés—at all levels. The mastery of the cliché may be illustrated sharply, if simply, in a kind of twisted echo phrase which has been called the "cliché extended."

> At the drop of a brass hat.
> To gild the lily with radiator paint.[8]

> A penny saved is a penny to squander.
> A man is known by the company that he organizes.[9]

Or the autological expression, which itself sums up the principle:

> Old saws fitted with new teeth.[9]

Such echoes themselves, of course, are not proof against the cliché use. The final worth always depends on a larger context. "Put a beetle in alcohol, and you have a scarab; put a Mississippian in alcohol, and you have a gentleman." This piece of local-color wit has a kind of shoddy

---

[6] *S.v.* "quotation." Cf. Eric Partridge, *A Dictionary of Clichés* (New York, 1940), Introduction.

[7] There is such a thing as failure to achieve the established clichés of a language. One may have a sense of something like this in reading one of the classics turned into "Basic."

[8] George Arms, "Clichés, Extended and Otherwise," *SRL*, XXIX (November 30, 1946), 9.

[9] Ambrose Bierce, *The Devil's Dictionary, s.v.* "saw," in *Collected Works* (New York, 1911), VII, 310–11.

value which is greatly enhanced in Faulkner's *Sanctuary* through the fact that it echoes the utterance of Gowan Stevens, the collegiate slicker and lady-killer.[1]

Nowadays one may identify a genre of lightly sophisticated magazine poems whose main logic is the slight tilt which they give to a pattern of cliché vocabulary, or the dainty jangle of cross-purposes which they create between intersecting patterns.

> Every soldier is his own architect, a specialist
> In the small home constructed reasonably
> Along pretty traditional lines, complete with
> Smiling wife at ease on screened verandah.[2]

And on the other hand:

> For nineteen years I lived a carefree life
> And pain and toil and grief I never knew.
> Although the world rushed madly on to strife,
> My thoughts of national welfare were but few.[3]

It is not necessary to quote more of either poem to establish the contrast: the simple, unaltered reproduction of clichés by the schoolboy veteran about to tell his experiences on being inducted into the army; and the adroitly proffered series of not-quite clichés from the areas of business and advertising in a competent report from the front on the soldier's day dreams. The first poem is an exercise in a limited kind of whimsy—but within its limits, and in contrast to the second, it shows the difference between dead and live language.

Language gains depth and resonance only by being used, and hence some of the most complete and poetically significant uses of words are just those that occur within a poetic tradition. Beside Milton's

> No light, but rather darkness visible
> Served only to discover sights of woe

we put Pope's

> Of darkness visible so much be lent,
> As half to show, half veil, the deep intent.

Gray was glad to call attention to the origin of

> The curfew tolls the knell of parting day

in Dante's

> . . . *squilla di lontano,*
> *Che paia 'l giorno pianger, che si muore.*

[1] *Sanctuary* (New York, 1931), p. 29.
[2] W. W. Gibson, "The Architects," *The New Yorker*, XX (October 1, 1944), 28. Permission the author; © 1944 The New Yorker Magazine, Inc.
[3] Freshman poem.

A recent examination of mid-18th-century English poetry has defined the "major vocabulary" of that poetry as a complex of quite simple words relating to the age's dominant interest in landscape symbols of optimistic divinity. This vocabulary yields the following synthetically typical line:

> Rise, fair day, before the eyes and soul of man.[4]

The poetry of Wordsworth, coming as an artistic climax and renewal, rather than rejection, of this tradition, is in a sense a poetry that turns very simply to nature and the human soul—yet, inescapably, it does this through words, and not entirely through the simple range of words represented in the line just quoted. Wordsworth's poetry is a sound realization and a deepening of certain nature symbols already available to his age in more or less cliché simplifications. It is a dramatization of those symbols by bringing them into contact with select terms from both higher and lower ranges,[5] from the metaphysical and Johnsonian Latinate range and from the range of low, country words.

> Once again I see
> These hedge-rows, hardly hedge-rows, little lines
> Of sportive wood run wild: these pastoral farms,
> Green to the very door; and wreaths of smoke
> Sent up, in silence, from among the trees.

> And I have felt
> A presence that disturbs me with the joy
> Of elevated thoughts; a sense sublime
> Of something far more deeply interfused,
> Whose dwelling is the light of setting suns.

A more directly literary—a more artificial—form of such dramatization was no less a part of the romantic movement in English literature. Thus William Blake, in his juvenile *Poetical Sketches.*

> My silks and fine array,
>   My smiles and languish'd air,
> By love are driv'n away. . . .
>   . . .

---

[4] Josephine Miles, *The Primary Language of Poetry in the 1740's and 1840's* (Berkeley, 1950), pp. 174, 222.

[5] In his *Prelude; or Growth of a Poet's Mind* (VI, 109–12) Wordsworth, speaking, not with complete fairness, of his own early compositions, alludes to a weakness of trading in "classic niceties,"

> The dangerous craft of culling term and phrase
> From languages that want the living voice
> To carry meaning to the natural heart.

I'll pore upon the stream,
Where sighing lovers dream,
And fish for fancies as they pass
Within the watery glass.

Whether on chrystal rocks ye rove,
    Beneath the bosom of the sea
Wandring in many a coral grove,
    Fair Nine, forsaking poetry!

In these wryly graceful adaptations of an earlier idiom that had come down through the 18th century in Percy's *Reliques* and other collections, Blake gives an advanced demonstration of what it means to be a cliché expert.

SUPPLEMENT

The poet who takes his art seriously will come to his task in a spirit of honest self-criticism. He will not flinch at throwing out whatever words are lacklustre or lack-weight or in any way undeserving—though such words have a way of hanging on hard. A good poet will dig up long forgotten treasures of vocabulary and put them into circulation again, brilliantly old-fashioned terms which lie hidden in the junkpiles of neglect. He will be on the alert to take advantage of the newest creations of shifting usage. His utterance will be urgent and clear, like the spring torrent; he will pour out a wealth of words, he will enrich his mother tongue. At the same time he will cut through stylistic brambles and make smooth and wholesome the paths of meaning; he will be forceful. And all the while, he will make what he is doing look as easy as play, though it keeps his wit on the rack—as he dances through his roles, now Satyr, now boorish Cyclops.—Horace, *Epistle* II, ii, ll. 109–25

A poet ought to avoid the least taint of what we may call low-breeding (*vilitas*) in his vocabulary; he has to assume a style that marks him off from ordinary speakers—let him carry it off with an Horatian "distaste for the crowd and aloofness" (*odi profanum et arceo*). At the same time he has to be careful not to let his wit stick out like an extraneous ornament; it ought to be closely woven into the texture of his argument. Witness Homer! and the Lyrists! and Roman Virgil! And the verbal magic (*curiosa felicitas*) of Horace. . . . The mighty business of a civil war will be a crushing job for any but an exceedingly well educated poet. Civil and military exploits as a matter of fact are hardly to be managed in verse; prose history takes care of them much better. The business of poetry . . . is a free effusion of the spirit . . . through devices of mystery, through divinely contrived interventions, through the torment of wit into forms of fable. Poetry should sound, not like a solemn deposition of fact under oath, but like the utterance of a prophetic mind . . . wildly thrown out, as on first inspiration, without tidying touches.

—Petronius Arbiter, *Satiricon*, Chapter 118

When I travelled, I took a particular Delight in hearing the Songs and Fables that are come from Father to Son, and are most in Vogue among the common People of the Countries through which I passed; for it is impossible that any thing should be universally tasted and approved by a Multitude, tho' they are only the Rabble of a Nation, which hath not in it some peculiar Aptness to please and gratify the Mind of Man. Human Nature is the same in all reasonable Creatures; and whatever falls in with it, will meet with Admirers amongst Readers of all Qualities and Conditions. *Molière*, as we are told by Monsieur *Boileau*, used to read all his Comedies to an old Woman who was his House-keeper, as she sat with him at her Work by the Chimney-Corner; and could foretel the Success of his Play in the Theatre, from the Reception it met at his Fire-side: For he tells us the Audience always followed the old Woman, and never failed to laugh in the same Place.

I know nothing which more shews the essential and inherent Perfection of Simplicity of Thought above that which I call the Gothick Manner in Writing, than this, that the first pleases all Kinds of Palates, and the latter only such as have formed to themselves a wrong artificial Taste upon little fanciful Authors and Writers of Epigram. *Homer*, *Virgil*, or *Milton*, so far as the Language of their Poems is understood, will please a Reader of plain common Sense, who would neither relish nor comprehend an Epigram of *Martial*, or a Poem of *Cowley*: So, on the contrary, an ordinary Song or Ballad that is the Delight of the common People, cannot fail to please all such Readers as are not unqualified for the Entertainment by their Affectation or Ignorance; and the Reason is plain, because the same Paintings of Nature which recommend it to the most ordinary Reader, will appear Beautiful to the most refined.

—Joseph Addison, *Spectator* No. 70, May 21, 1711

One touch of Nature may make the whole world kin, but two touches of nature will destroy any work of Art. If, on the other hand, we regard Nature as the collection of phenomena external to man, people only discover in her what they bring to her. She has no suggestions of her own. Wordsworth went to the lakes, but he was never a lake poet. He found in stones the sermons he had already hidden there. He went moralising about the district, but his good work was produced when he returned, not to Nature but to poetry. Poetry gave him "Laodamia," and the fine sonnets, and the great Ode, such as it is. Nature gave him "Martha Ray" and "Peter Bell," and the address to Mr. Wilkinson's spade.

—Oscar Wilde, *The Decay of Lying*, in *Intentions* (London, 1913), p. 19

In writing *The Playboy of the Western World*, as in my other plays, I have used one or two words only that I have not heard among the country people of Ireland, or spoken in my own nursery before I could read the newspapers.

A certain number of the phrases I employ I have heard also from herds and fishermen along the coast from Kerry to Mayo, or from beggar-women and ballad-singers nearer Dublin; and I am glad to acknowledge how much I owe to the folk-imagination of these fine people. Anyone who has lived in real intimacy with the Irish peasantry will know that the wildest sayings and ideas in this play are tame indeed, compared with the fancies one may hear in any little hillside cabin in Geesala, or Carraroe, or Dingle Bay. All art is a collaboration; and there is little doubt that in the happy ages of literature, striking and beautiful phrases were as ready to the story-teller's or the playwright's hand, as the rich cloaks and dresses of his time. It is probable that when the Elizabethan dramatist took his inkhorn and sat down to his work he used many phrases that he had just heard, as he sat at dinner, from his mother or his children. In Ireland, those of us who know the people have the same privilege. When I was writing "The Shadow of the Glen," some years ago, I got more aid than any learning could have given me from a chink in the floor of the old Wicklow house where I was staying, that let me hear what was being said by the servant girls in the kitchen. This matter, I think, is of importance, for in countries where the imagination of the people, and the language they use, is rich and living, it is possible for a writer to be rich and copious in his words, and at the same time to give the reality, which is the root of all poetry, in a comprehensive and natural form. In the modern literature of towns, however, richness is found only in sonnets, or prose poems, or in one or two elaborate books that are far away from the profound and common interests of life. One has, on one side, Mallarmé and Huysmans producing this literature; and on the other, Ibsen and Zola dealing with the reality of life in joyless and pallid words. On the stage one must have reality, and one must have joy; and that is why the intellectual modern drama has failed, and people have grown sick of the false joy of the musical comedy, that has been given them in place of the rich joy found only in what is superb and wild in reality. In a good play every speech should be as fully flavoured as a nut or apple, and such speeches cannot be written by anyone who works among people who have shut their lips on poetry. In Ireland, for a few years more, we have a popular imagination that is fiery and magnificent, and tender; so that those of us who wish to write start with a chance that is not given to writers in places where the springtime of the local life has been forgotten, and the harvest is a memory only, and the straw has been turned into bricks. January 21st, 1907.

—J. M. Synge, Preface to *The Playboy of the Western World*, Boston: J. W. Luce Co., 1911, quoted by permission of Random House, Inc., New York.

The historian of the English language may attach to the word inkhorn *in its Elizabethan context meanings which are no part of Synge's meaning when he uses the word in the Preface here quoted. Synge's mistrust of city language as a literary model can be paralleled, with a different evaluative accent, in a passage quoted earlier in this book (Chapter 11) from Congreve. The aristocratic norm of poetic utterance is in the end true to itself only in aiming to improve on the salon, whereas the peasant norm in being truest to itself drives toward some kind of fidelity to the actual.*

GERMAN IDEAS

§ *early German theory, French classicism, Gottsched, the efforts of Breitinger and Bodmer, Lessing's* Hamburg Dramaturgy, *Herder's radical new interests—II. the historical point of view, Italians, Boileau, Dryden, Shakespeare and Spenser criticism, Vico's* New Science, *comparative studies, the folk—III. rise of term "romantic," A. W. Schlegel, Madame de Staël, nature vs. self, Schiller's* Über naive und sentimentalische Dichtung, *Schelling on pagan and Christian, F. Schlegel, classic beauty, romantic energy, Goethe's reminiscence, Hegel's three stages, Schiller's* Spieltrieb, *Jean Paul—IV. transcendental reconstruction, Novalis on science, the importance of Kant,* Critique of Judgment, *the beautiful and the sublime, the former distinguished from pleasure, interest, and concept, "purposiveness without purpose," symbolism, severe formalism of Kant's view—V. shift from epic and dramatic norms to lyric, Herder, sense media, energy, "music of the soul," synaesthesis, A. W. Schlegel, architecture as music, Schopenhauer, music and will, poet as creator, metaphor and the birth of speech, Herder* Über den Ursprung der Sprache, *later distinction between symbol and allegory —VI. poetry as spiritual regeneration, "myth," F. Schlegel's Discourse, Schelling, poetry as philosophy, as absolute reality, Novalis, Fichte, elevation of criticism, poetry as creative dreaming, poetry as fullness, mechanism vs. organism—VII. rationale of the comic, A. W. Schlegel's defence of puns and irony, Jean Paul's* Vorschule, *"infinite incongruity," "humor" and the sublime, F. Schlegel on irony, self-transcendence, the Byronic and dark, metaphysical versions, Heine, K. F. W. Solger, irony the principle of art, Hegel: irony is "Satanic impertinence" —VIII. Goethe on the debt of German literature to English, Kant and English empirical ideas, the German transformation, good for English theory* §

363

Though the issue of poetic diction had, as we have suggested, its continental affinities, Wordsworth and Coleridge fought out their quarrel here pretty much on native grounds. It is hardly necessary to go to the contemporary continent to understand English poetic diction of the 18th century and the reaction against it. Certain much larger critical issues centering around what may be called a new idea of poetic "imagination" were, however, more inevitably tied in with continental romanticism. Wordsworth and Coleridge and Shelley did not arrive at their highly important statements in this area without having learned something from abroad, and especially from the Germans.

German literary theory, caught at its outset, during the latter 17th and early 18th centuries, in the rigors of French classicism (see the systematic genre prescriptions of Gottsched's[1] *Versuch einer kritischen Dichtkunst*, 1730) or engaged in the merely emancipatory (Miltonic, Addisonian, neo-Longinian, and pictorialist) counter-efforts of the Swiss professors Breitinger and Bodmer,[2] began with Lessing and some of his friends to rouse itself and threaten more radical announcements. The next two generations of German litterateurs, in league with transcendental philosophers and aestheticians, were to take over the critical leadership which had passed in its classical phases through Italy and France and during the middle part of the 18th century was held by the British empiricists.

Lessing himself in his series of dramatic reviews in the *Hamburg Dramaturgy*, written shortly after the *Laokoon*, turned a destructive scorn on the Voltairean heroic inflation of French classical drama[3] and did much to modulate Cornelian admiration and Voltairean astonishment into the softer norm of 18th-century pity.[4] Yet Lessing was a classical critic, a "new Preceptist," as Saintsbury has called him, a kind of Prot-

[1] He has been called the "German Johnson," but, as Saintsbury (II, 552) points out, the resemblance between the two ends with the fact that each was a neo-classic stalwart. We have observed Johnson's small respect for the genres.

[2] In their imitation of the *Spectator* entitled *Diskurse der Maler* (started in 1721), in four great manifestos: Bodmer's *Von dem Wunderbaren in der Poesie* (1740) and *Über die poetischen Gemählde der Dichter* (1741) and Breitinger's *Von der Natur* (1740) and *Kritische Dichtkunst* (1740), and in Bodmer's translations of Homer, *Paradise Lost*, and English ballads. See Wellek, *History* I, 147.

[3] See, for instance, the comparison in his paper No. 11 between the ghost in *Hamlet* and that in *Semiramis*. "Voltaire's ghost steps out of his grave in broad daylight, in the midst of an assembly of the royal parliament, preceded by a thunderclap. . . . Shakespeare let only Hamlet see the ghost. . . . The spectre operates on us, but through him rather than by itself. . . . At his [Voltaire's] ghost many are frightened, but not much." *Selected Prose Works of G. E. Lessing*, trans. E. C. Beasley and Helen Zimmern (London: Bohn's Standard Library, 1890).

[4] See *Hamburg Dramaturgy* No. 14, on bourgeois tragedy, and Nos. 48, 79, on pity. J. E. Gillet, "A Note on the Tragic 'Admiratio,'" *MLR*, XIII (1918), 233–8, traces the shift from earlier Renaissance "wonder" and "fear" to sympathetic "admiration" and "pity" and the development of these latter in the period from Corneille to Lessing.

estant Aristotelian, one who claimed to be looking back past Voltaire, Corneille, Scaliger, the neo-classic distorters, to the pure classic idea. He did not "hesitate to admit" that he considered the *Poetics* of Aristotle to be as "infallible as the *Elements* of Euclid." "I would dispose of his authority easily enough if I could dispose of his reasons." [5] We have seen how his attempt upon the neo-classic *ut pictura poesis* left that doctrine fundamentally untouched. The degree of romanticism that shows in Lessing consists in the humanitarian and compassionate shading of his ethical views on tragedy.

Between Lessing and the next major figure in the rise of German critical theory, J. G. Herder, a rather distinct line will be drawn by a reader inclined to recognize some antithesis between the "classic" and "romantic." In the voluminous criticism of Herder—for instance, in such representative works as his *Fragmente zur deutschen Litteratur* (1767) and his *Kritische Wälder* (1769),—we find a group of radically new concerns centering in the relations of poetry to race, geography, and history, and in the creative and symbolic powers of verbal expression.[6] These were germinal and explosive ideas.

The criticism of the Italian Renaissance—the annotated editions of the classics, the formal treatises, the "defences" of poetry—had been a relatively deliberate and stolid performance, circumspectly, even legalistically, argued by the savants of that day. The new renaissance of German romanticism was an eruption of notes, fragments, letters, conversations, pamphlets, prize essays, lectures, and systems, enthusiastically thrown out by poets, novelists, translators, oracular professors, and transcendental philosophers. Where the 16th-century Italians had translated Aristotle, the Germans now translated Shakespeare and made him one of the main inspirations. At the same time, Goethe played the role of a contemporary demi-urge and seemed to his fellows the very incarnation of the theories they were developing.[7] Among literary expressions of first importance appear the various essays of Goethe and his retrospectively dramatic *Conversations*.[8]

II

ITALIAN criticism of the 16th century had looked back with reverence to at least one medieval text, the *Commedia* of Dante, and had been

---

[5] *Hamburg Dramaturgy*, No. 74. Cf. Nos. 101–4.

[6] See Wellek, *History* I, Chapter 9. The notes to the present chapter do not attempt to make explicit acknowledgement of all that is owing to the first two volumes of René Wellek's *History of Modern Criticism: 1750–1950*. The debt is especially large in the passages referring to Herder. The chapter owes much also to Gilbert and Kuhn's *History of Esthetics* and to the help of Richard J. Browne in verifying citations from the German sources.

[7] See especially *Über die bildende Nachahmung des Schönen*, 1788, by Goethe's admirer and fellow traveler in Italy, Karl Phillip Moritz.

[8] Published by J. P. Eckermann in 1836.

much concerned to vindicate the new Ariostan form of epic which had developed out of medieval romance and burlesque. Then this kind of Gothicism had suffered a relative eclipse during the era of French neo-classicism. Boileau's scorn for the Italian tradition was representative.

> *Évitons ces excès; laissons a l'Italie*
> *De tous ces faux brillans l'éclatante folie.*[9]

But at least as early as Dryden's appreciation of Chaucer in the Preface to his *Fables* (1700) a similar vein of archaic taste had begun to appear in English criticism. It ran through the 18th century in Shakespeare and Spenser criticism and in some other notable places like Bishop Hurd's *Letters on Chivalry and Romance*, 1763. There were strong developments in a kind of antiquarianism which was to have special import for methods of literary scholarship.[1] At the same time, a general broadening and deepening of historical interest worked into more exalted notions about the nature of literature. One early continental source, though during the romantic period it was not influential,[2] was the *New Science* of Vico (1725) expounding the patriarchal and monarchic origins of society and along with these the metaphoric and symbolic origins of human thought and institutions.[3] Similar trains of ideas appear in 18th-century books on Homer,[4] such as those in English by Thomas Blackwell (1735) and Robert Wood (1769), leading up to Friedrich Wolf's thesis that the Homeric epics are put together from a number of smaller poems handed down by oral recitation.[5] From the time of Herder on, the appreciation of various folk and Gothic literatures and the comparative study of ancient, eastern, and modern foreign literatures (the criticism of literature by age and race)[6] were strongly established, and these interests profoundly affected theories about the nature of literature as the expression of, or the power that shaped, human cultures or human nature in general. Friedrich Schlegel only accented an already pervasive view when he called poetry the most specifically human energy, the central document of any culture. Developments were partly nationalistic, even chauvinistic (as with the poet Klopstock). Ideas of German

---

[9] *Art Poétique*, I, 43-4.

[1] See *post* Chapter 24.

[2] Vico was scarcely known outside of Italy before Michelet's translation published in 1829.

[3] A devious connection between Vico and Herder has been shown in the notes of the Italian scholar Cesarotti attached to the pseudo-primitive Scottish *Ossian* in the German version by Denis which Herder read. Robert T. Clark, Jr., "Herder, Cesarotti and Vico," *SP*, XLIV (October, 1947), 645-71.

[4] Cf. *ante* Chapter 16, p. 350.

[5] *Prolegomena in Homerum*, 1795.

[6] Herder's main effort on this theme is his Prize Essay of 1773 on the *Causes of the Decline of Taste in Different Nations*. But there is much elsewhere in Herder about climate, landscape, racial customs, politics, and the like.

folk, German literature, and German destiny were rampant. The critics reached out for Shakespeare [7] as a translatable and adoptable expression of the national spirit—even as the 16th-century Italians had exclaimed: "Plunder the ancients and bring home the spoils."

III

ONE historical question with which the German critics were much occupied was that concerning the difference between "classic" and "romantic." The term "romantic" had come a long way from its early neo-classic uses—largely either neutral or pejorative—relating to medieval adventure stories written in the romance languages. During the 18th century the term had gained so much ground that it now became available to the German critics as an honorific, if problematic, name of a central and dynamic literary conception.[8] The Jena professor and Shakespeare translator A. W. Schlegel [9] devoted the first of his Vienna *Lectures on Dramatic Art and Literature* (1808) to rebuking neo-classic exclusiveness and pleading for a "universality of true criticism."

> The groundwork of human nature is no doubt everywhere the same; but in all our investigations, we may observe that, throughout the whole range of nature, there is no elementary power so simple, but that it is capable of dividing and diverging into opposite directions. The whole play of vital motion hinges on harmony and contrast. Why, then, should not this phenomenon recur on a grander scale in the history of man? In this idea we have perhaps discovered the true key to the ancient and modern history of poetry and the fine arts.[1]

Those who have adopted this idea have given "to the peculiar spirit of *modern* art, as contrasted with the *antique* or *classical*, the name of *romantic*." Schlegel's popularization of the "romantic" idea was further broadcast over Europe by Madame de Staël in her *De L'Allemagne*. Coleridge began to use the term and the distinction in his lectures of 1811. "Romanticism" was a highly self-conscious literary movement.

[7] Both Lessing and Herder were main agents for "inoculating" the Germans with Shakespeare (Saintsbury III, 359).

[8] Cf. René Wellek, "The Concept of 'Romanticism' in Literary History," *Comparative Literature*, I (Winter, 1949), 1–23.

[9] The most widely successful propagandist of German romanticism. He was known in England as "our national critic," the "one clear voice out of Germany." He delivered in all four great series of public lectures on literary theory. The *Über schöne Literatur und Kunst*, 1801–03, was superior to, if not more widely known than, the *Über dramatische Kunst und Literatur*.

[1] *A Course of Lectures on Dramatic Art and Literature*, trans. John Black and A. J. W. Morrison (London, 1846), p. 21.

The German critics conceived classical art to be a direct, objective, and happily unsophisticated communion with nature, and romantic (or modern) art to be a view of nature complicated, somewhat unhappily, by various phases of reflexiveness and subjectivity. As long as nature had been sound on the inside of man, he could look at it outside him simply and without tampering. When nature in modern times had gone wrong inside him, he looked on nature outside with nostalgic projections; he invested it with a shimmer of his own yearning personality. Modern art, said Goethe's younger friend, the poet-philosopher of Jena, Friedrich Schiller, in his definitive essay *Über naive und sentimentalische Dichtung* (1795), is a striving toward an ideal synthesis (of intellect and feeling) which is in its very nature unrealizable, but which is nevertheless a higher thing than the once perfect, now irrecoverable, naive.[2] Schelling, in his *Philosophie der Kunst*,[3] dwelt on the harmony between man and nature which had found adequate symbols in pagan mythology, and on the breach between man and God which it was the dialectical role of Christianity to create, and the resulting unsatisfied, infinite yearning of which modern literature was fated to be the inadequate allegory. Friedrich Schlegel, closely echoing the ideas of Schiller, talked about a *progressive Universalpoesie*.[4] Classic art was conceived by the German critics as "beauty;" romantic art as "energy." Classic was universal and ideal; romantic was individual and "characteristic." Classic was plastic (like sculpture), finite, closed, pure in genre. Romantic was picturesque (like painting), infinite, open, mixed.[5]

In a late polemical statement aimed against the French romantics Goethe said:

> I call the classic *healthy*, the romantic *sickly*. In this sense, the *Nibelungenlied* is as classic as the *Iliad*, for both are vigorous and healthy. Most modern productions are romantic, not because they are new, but because they are weak, morbid, and sickly; and the antique is classic, not because it is old, but because it is strong, fresh, joyous, and healthy.[6]

[2] Schiller divided modern "sentimental" poetry into three kinds, according to modes of feeling: satire, which looks down on reality from the height of the ideal; elegy, which mourns the loss of the ideal; idyll, which imagines a past or future ideal as real.

[3] Composed in 1802–03 and circulated in manuscript, though not published until 1859. His *System des Transcendentalen Idealismus* appeared in 1800.

[4] *Athenaeum* No. 116, in Jakob Minor, ed. *Friedrich Schlegel; seine prosaischen Jugendschriften* (Vienna, 1906), II, 220. Cf. Victor Lange, "Friedrich Schlegel's Literary Criticism," *Comparative Literature*, VII (Fall, 1955), 297.

[5] See, for instance, A. W. Schlegel, *Lectures on Dramatic Art and Literature* (London, 1846), pp. 22–7, 340–3, Lectures I and XXII; and René Wellek's account of these passages and of parallel passages in the Berlin Lectures of 1801–04 (*History* II, 48, 58–9).

[6] *Conversations*, April 2, 1829, trans. John Oxenford. See the selections in Bate, *Criticism: the Major Texts*, pp. 400–05.

He was in a somewhat creatively reminiscent mood when he made the following statement—but it will serve here as a summary dramatization of the antithesis we have been describing.

> The idea of the distinction between classical and romantic poetry, which is now spread over the whole world, and occasions so many quarrels and divisions, came originally from Schiller and myself. I laid down the maxim of objective treatment in poetry, and would allow no other; but Schiller, who worked quite in the subjective way, deemed his own fashion the right one, and to defend himself against me, wrote the treatise upon *Naïve and Sentimental Poetry*. He proved to me that I myself, against my will, was romantic, and that my *Iphigenia*, through the predominance of sentiment, was by no means so classical and so much in the antique spirit as some people supposed.

> The Schlegels took up this idea, and carried it further, so that it has now been diffused over the whole world; and everyone talks about classicism and romanticism—of which nobody thought fifty years ago.[7]

From a neutrally retrospective standpoint, one might observe that German romantic poetry and criticism were hardly at all primitive or "natural" in the sense that English nature poetry was. German romanticism was historical, Hellenic, actually classic, in an appeal not to Aristotle, but to Homer and the tragic dramatists. It was a spirited and vastly aspiring revision of Winckelmannian classicism. The main paradox of the romantic mind was that it yearned for a primitive or direct nature, yet was compelled to do this through the medium of its own historical awareness and introspective virtuosity.

A further phase in the dialectic of classic versus romantic is marked by Hegel's massively systematic revision of romantic theory, his *Lectures on Aesthetics* (1835) or, as the work is now known in English, *Philosophy of Fine Art*. Hegel divides all art into three stages: first symbolic—where, as in the Egyptian pyramids and temples, the activity of spirit or idea only half struggles forth from the mass of matter; second classic—where, as in Greek sculpture, idea (form) and matter are perfectly fused; and third romantic—where, as in modern music, painting, and (above all) poetry, spirit overflows and envelops matter in self-conscious fulness.[8] There was more moral energy here, less beauty, than in the classic. As Schiller had put it, all art arises out of two impulses and balances these variously—the finite material impulse (*Stoff-*

[7] *Conversations*, March 21, 1830.

[8] G. W. F. Hegel, *The Philosophy of Fine Art*, trans. F. P. B. Osmaston (London, 1920), I, 1–5, "Introduction to Second Part."

trieb) and the infinite impulse of the idea (*Formtrieb*). The reconciliation of these is the free "play" of the whole human person (*Spieltrieb*).[9] The novelist Jean Paul Richter in his *Vorschule der Ästhetik* (1804) spoke of two extremes, the materialist and the empty idealist (or nihilist), both of which missed the mean of true form and art.[1] It would not be a great exaggeration to say that all German romantic criticism was devoted to the problem of how literature reconciles sensory experience and ideas (the "particular" and the "universal" of Warton's and Johnson's thinking). Their criticism was hence, at higher levels of speculation, devoted to the problem of how literature reconciles the worldly with the transcendental, the external and dubious material object with the spiritually reliable and self-aware subject, the outer world of "nature" and scientific observation with the inner world of schemes and of will and morals,[2] the contingent world of *history* with the necessary world of *system*.

I V

ALL these antitheses and their attempted resolutions may be described as arising in the due course of historic process out of the empirical and analytic trends of the 17th and 18th centuries. They were the romantic reconstruction, in transcendental terms, of the world successively and resolutely abstracted apart by the Cartesian and the British empirical analyses. German romanticism was a retort to scientism, a program for poetic re-establishment of the analytically dissolved harmony between man and nature and between the parts of man's own consciousness. The most lyric and most visionary of the Jena circle of theorizers, Friedrich von Hardenberg (Novalis), in his essay *Christendom or Europe*, wrote a memorable version of the charge that science was ruining all. Science was making "the infinite creative music of the universe into the dull clappering of a gigantic mill driven by the stream of chance and floating upon it, a mill, without architect and without miller, grinding itself to pieces, in fact a *perpetuum mobile*." [3]

The whole aesthetic trend owed a great deal to Immanuel Kant, whose "Copernican revolution" had recalled thinking from the atomically and externally oriented analyses of Hume and centered it reflexively on an active and unifying creativity of the knowing subject.

[9] Friedrich Schiller, *Letters upon the Aesthetical Education of Man*, Letters XII-XV, in *Essays Aesthetical and Philosophical* (London: Bohn's Standard Library, 1916, *Schiller's Works*, vol. VI), esp. pp. 60-2, 67, 69-72.

[1] *Vorschule*, No. 69, at end, in *Jean Pauls Sämtliche Werke* (Historisch-Kritische Ausgabe, Weimar, 1935), I, ii, 234.

[2] Cf. Schiller, *op. cit.*, pp. 60-3.

[3] Quoted by Carlyle in his essay on "Voltaire," 1829. See his *Critical & Miscellaneous Essays* (Boston, 1860), II, 75-6.

Kant's *Critique of Judgment*, 1790, was a happily aesthetic afterthought, making an intermediate ground and connection between his earlier philosophy of science or *Critique of Pure Reason* and his philosophy of the moral imperative or *Critique of Practical Reason*. His account of *Judgment* was a decisive statement in the history of modern general aesthetics and at once exerted a strong influence upon literary aesthetics. It has a direct reflection in the essays of Schiller, and it is the ghostly paradigm, in *a priori* lines, of many more highly colored utterances by the poets and literary professors. On the one side, Kant had mapped the world of necessary physical events: conditioned by time and space, the spectacles of our sensory intuition (*Anschauung*), unified by imagination (*Einbildungskraft*), ordered according to the categories of scientific understanding (*Verstand*), and in the end only somewhat tentatively and hopefully affirmed under the sanction of the absolute (or thing-in-itself), the soul, the world whole, and God, ideas which were provided by our highest *a priori* faculty, the reason (*Vernunft*). On the other side, the free moral world of our choices, according to the categorical imperative. And then, after a while, the mediational concept of the aesthetic values, the beautiful (*das Schöne*) and the sublime (*das Erhabene*), both subjective. The latter, the more subjective of the two, was an a-prioristically elevated version of the feelings of awe (in the presence of great magnitude) and of self-congratulatory expansion (in safe recoil from the fear of wild natural energy) which had been described empirically by 18th-century British writers and especially by Burke. These feelings yielded Kant the "Mathematical Sublime" and the "Dynamic Sublime." [4] The beautiful, however, was something higher than accidental and private sense pleasure (*das Angenehme*), had a universal claim on human recognition, and was a norm though not a strictly definable norm (it was "without concept"). The appreciation of it was not "interested" in any possessive or practical way.[5] It was a form of order with which nature was "favored" by our own act of knowing, though we looked on it, unlike the subjectively experienced sublime, as something out there, in nature. It was a "purposiveness without purpose" (*Zweckmässigkeit ohne Zweck*). That is, it was not a teleology toward a nameable further end (like nourishment or shelter), but a highly satisfactory fitting of experience precisely to our own faculty of experiencing, to the progress of our knowledge. Our satisfaction in the presence of the beautiful was a feeling of unification, a harmonious interplay of sense and mind, a perfect freedom from scientific and utili-

---

[4] Among the fruits of the Kantian sublime may be listed A. W. Schlegel's view (*Lectures on Dramatic Art and Literature*, III) of tragic endurance as a form of self-assertion, for its own sake, in the face of fate, and the similar view of Schiller.

[5] That is, Kant asserted the "autonomy" of the *aesthetic*, distinguishing it from *pleasure*, from *emotion* and *interest*, and from didactic *knowledge*.

tarian necessity. At the same time the beautiful was "the symbol of the morally good."

> In the faculty of taste the judgment does not find itself, as in judging by experience, constrained by empirical laws; it legislates for itself on the objects of so pure a satisfaction, just as reason legislates autonomously on the faculty of desire in morality. And owing to this capacity in ourselves and to the capacity in external nature to harmonize therewith, the judgment finds in itself a reference to something in us and also outside us, which is neither physical necessity nor moral freedom but is allied to the supersensible conditions of freedom. In this supersensuous reality, the theoretical faculty and the practical faculty are mutually and mysteriously interwoven.[6]

Kant's idea of beauty was severe; it related (so far as human making was concerned) almost exclusively to the formal, decorative, and abstract: to Greek designs, foliation on wallpaper, arabesques (things which "mean nothing in themselves"), music without words. The "charms" of direct sensuous pleasure might fuse with beauty,[7] and beauty *might* be combined with perfect natural forms and purposive human artifacts (the good, the ideal), but in neither of these cases was beauty pure. Beauty allied to the good was not "free beauty" (*pulchritudo vaga*) but dependent beauty (*pulchritudo adhaerens*). The two might help *us* by being together, but strictly speaking neither helped the other. It is worth noting that here was a system which conceived Homer and Shakespeare as less aesthetically pure than wallpaper.

V

CERTAIN technical literary notions which were often repeated by the German critics form a very coherent pattern. This was the time, for instance, when modern literary criticism completed one of its major shifts in preference among the literary genres. The 17th-century norm had been, as we have seen, heroic and epic. That of Lessing, in the third quarter of the 18th century, had been dramatic and Aristotelian. Lessing's high regard for the action, the Aristotelian "fable," was a form of classical objectivity that had a fairly close connection with his preference for the colorlessly ideal forms of sculpture over the mere

---

[6] E. F. Carritt, *Philosophies of Beauty* (Oxford, 1931), p. 123. Cf. *Kant's Critique of Judgement*, trans. J. H. Bernard, 2d ed. revised (London, 1931), p. 251. Our account above uses the terminology of Carritt's translated selections.

[7] Carritt, p. 116; Bernard, pp. 81–2.

phenomenalism of colored painting.[8] Lessing, as we have seen,[9] believed drama to be the most poetic form of literature, and for the reason (related to a distinction made earlier in France by DuBos) that the ordinarily "artificial" signs of language become "natural" signs in drama. They are the direct imitation of persons speaking. But even in the early writings of Herder—and consistently with a general turn of interest from the external world to the knowing and expressing self—we find the notion that not the drama but the lyric is the most poetic kind of poetry, the most direct, free, and unlimited making of the poetic mind. "Lyrical poetry is the perfect expression of an emotion or representation in the highest euphony of language."[1] We have already sampled, apropos of Hegel's division of art into symbolic, classic, and romantic, the more or less normal later romantic view that poetry in general is the expression of mind using itself directly as medium; it is the very energy of mind.

Herder was dissatisfied[2] with the distinction made in *Laokoon* between painting as an art of space and verbal narrative as an art of time (still pictures and moving pictures, as we have suggested earlier). The real difference, said Herder, is that the physical arts work each by its peculiar sense, the ear, the eye, the touch (sculpture is the art of touch),[3] but poetry works by no sense. It is the direct *energy* of the shaping spirit, "immediate of the soul," the "music of the soul."[4] The old *Laokoon* had been written against an external, pictorial analogy between media. The *New Laokoon* of 1910 would look back over a century and a half in which the strong sway of the fascinating spirit had driven toward a general synaesthesis of media or an assimilation of all media to spirit itself and toward their reobjectification in the most intangible

[8] "Mere color and transitory expression have no ideal because Nature has proposed to herself nothing definite in them" (Hugo Blümner, ed. *Laokoon*, Berlin, 1880, 399—cf. 469—notations by Lessing, cited by F. O. Nolte, *Lessing's Laocoon*, Lancaster, Pa., 1940, p. 37).

[9] *Ante* Chapter 13, p. 270.

[1] *Terpsichore*, Part II, in *Werke*, ed. Suphan, XXVII (Berlin, 1881), 171. The earliest fragments of Herder include two sketches for a history of ode and lyric. "The firstborn child of emotion, the origin of poetry, the germ of life, is the ode" (*Werke*, XXXII, 1899, 62).

[2] *Erstes Kritisches Wäldchen*, 1769.

[3] See his *Plastik*, 1778. Cf. *ante* Chapter 13, p. 276.

[4] *Kritische Wälder* I and IV, in *Werke* III, 144, 157; IV, 166. The idea of energy (*energeia*) as a force to be distinguished from its product, a work (*ergon*), may be found in Aristotle, *Metaphysics* IV, 3–8. James Harris, *Three Treatises*, 3d. ed. (London, 1752), pp. 33 ff., uses the terms *energy* and *production*. Cf. Robert T. Clark, Jr., "Herder's Conception of 'Kraft,' " *PMLA*, LVII (1942), 737–52.

The idea of poetry as verbal music is developed by Ludwig Tieck and W. H. Wackenroder, *Phantasien über die Kunst*, ed. Jakob Minor in *Deutsche National-literatur* (Berlin and Stuttgart, n.d.), CXLV, 55–98, esp. 88. Novalis, echoing Diderot, thought of poetry as either inner music or inner painting, "freely modified by the nature of feeling." *Fragmente und Studien*, VI, 21; IX, 3; X, 60, in *Novalis Schriften*, ed. Paul Kluckhohn (Leipzig, n.d.), II, 323; III, 63; III, 290.

or immaterial of media, music. Even so massively solid a thing as architecture might be looked upon as "frozen music." The following statement by A. W. Schlegel summarizes the trend.

> We should once more try to bring the arts closer together and seek for transitions from one to the other. Statues perhaps may quicken into pictures, pictures become poems, poems music, and (who knows?) in like manner stately church music may once more rise heavenward as a cathedral.[5]

In the voluntaristic idealism of Schopenhauer—where the blind *nisus* of will is the noumenal ground of experience—music was to become the fullest and most subtly modulated revelation of that will itself. "The other arts speak only of Shadows." Music "is a copy of the will itself." [6] It has been a commonplace of modern aesthetics—though now somewhat discredited—that music is the center and ideal of all the arts.

If poetic words are the direct energy of spirit, they do not merely present meaning, they create it. Poetry is an "imitation," not of nature, but of the creating, naming Godhead.[7] The poet is a "second creator, *poietes*, maker." This is nowhere more obviously true than in metaphors. The metaphor is conceived as presiding, along with music, at the very birth of speech, of ideas, and of human institutions. Thus Herder in his prize essay of 1770 *Über den Ursprung der Sprache:* The earliest language was a "dictionary of the soul, it was at the same time mythology and a marvelous epic of the actions and speeches of all beings— a constant fable with passion and interest." [8]

> A certain savage sees a lofty tree, with its majestic crown, and is awestruck: the crown rustles! That is stirring godhead! The savage falls prostrate and worships! Behold the history of sensuous Man . . . and the easiest transition to abstract thought! [9]

---

[5] *"Die Gemählde,"* *Athenaeum* II (Berlin, 1799), 49–50, quoted in Irving Babbitt, *The New Laokoon* (Boston, 1910), pp. 124–5. See p. 125 for relations between A. W. Schlegel and Diderot in the "confusion" of the arts, and p. 61 on the claims of F. Schlegel, Schelling, and Görres to authorship of the phrase "Architecture is frozen music."

[6] *World as Will and Idea*, trans. R. B. Haldane and J. Kemp, 7th ed. (London, 1927), I, 333.

[7] Herder, *Über Bild, Dichtung, und Fabel*, 1787, in *Zerstreute Blätter, Dritte Sammlung* (*Werke*, XV, 526).

[8] Herder, *Abhandlung über den Ursprung der Sprache*, 1772 (*Werke*, V, 51–3). The theory implies rejection of at least three earlier theories of the origin of language: the theory of divine inspiration, the rationalistic theory of deliberate human compact, and Condillac's sensualistic theory which derived language from brutal cries. Herder's idea of the poet as maker is rather closely anticipated in Shaftesbury's *Moralists*, Part III, end of section 2.

[9] *Werke*, V, 53. "*Jener Wilde sahe den hohen Baum mit seinem prächtigen Gipfel und bewunderte: der Gipfel rauschte! das ist webende Gottheit! der Wilde fällt nieder und betet an! Sehet da die Geschichte des sinnlichen Menschen, das*

Primitive man thinks in symbols, allegories, and metaphors. Combinations of these make fable and myth. And so far as modern man is a poet, he is primitive. Later theory (formulated first by Goethe [1] in 1797 and repeated by Schelling in his *Philosophie der Kunst* and by A. W. Schlegel in his *Dramatic Lecture* on Aeschylus) modified this vocabulary, if not the ideas behind it, by making a very insistent distinction between what was considered the merely conceptualized and finite meaning of "allegory" and the metaphorically full-bodied and infinite meaning of "symbol."

VI

THERE are passages in Herder which suggest that human history shows a uniform degeneracy from the glories of the age of poetry to the civilized weakness of the age of reason,[2] and that, having entered on the age of reason, the human race was committed to further technical progress and hence to the extinction of imagination.[3] But a more optimistic view was more prevalent—namely, that poetry was a new means of spiritual regeneration. With the Schlegels, poetry, and especially metaphor, is a perennial mother speech, a promise and vehicle of future human perfection. An even more formidable concept, that of "myth," comes into its own with several pronouncements by Friedrich Schlegel and the philosopher Schelling. The "main difference between the ancient poets and the modern," says Schlegel in his *Dialogue on Poetry*, is that the moderns "have no mythology. But let me add that we are not far from having one, or rather, that it is time we should make a serious effort to produce one." [4] In the *Discourse on Mythology* which forms part of the *Dialogue*, he issues a ringing invitation to a new world view, a new "synthetic" mythology, a "great mythological poem," which is to rise from some source in modern idealist philosophy or natural science.[5] And Schelling carried this theme even further in an elaborate

---

dunkle Band, wie aus den Verbis Nomina werden—und den leichtesten Schritt zur Abstraktion!" Cf. Ernst Cassirer, *Language and Myth*, trans. Susanne Langer (New York, 1946), p. 85.

[1] In his *Über die Gegenstände der bildenden Kunst;* and later in his *Maximen.*

[2] See, for instance, *Fragmente einer Abhandlung über die Ode,* c. 1765? (*Werke*, XXXII, 69).

[3] For similar views see Vico (with regret) and Fontenelle (with sentiments of welcome to the new age) in his *Traité de la Poésie en Général.* And see the debate between Shelley and Peacock, *post* Chapter 19.

[4] *Gespräch über die Poesie*, 1800, in Jakob Minor, ed. *Friedrich Schlegel: seine prosaischen Jugendschriften* (Vienna, 1906), II, 358, quoted in translation by Victor Lange, "Friedrich Schlegel's Literary Criticism," *Comparative Literature*, VII (Fall, 1955), 301.

[5] *Rede über die Mythologie*, 1800, in Minor, II, 357–63; see Lange, *loc. cit.*, p. 302. "What distinguishes Schlegel's thinking from Herder's," says Lange, "is that . . . at this time, he rejects any temptation to resort to a mere re-creation of past mythological substance."

deification of natural "potencies." Ideas were images of divinity when taken as ideas. When taken as real, they were no less than gods. Thus: the "point of absolute difference" between self and the outer world was Jupiter; the ideal world was Apollo; the formative principle embodied in iron was Vulcan; water, the formless principle, was Neptune.[6] In the aspirations of romantic poetical philosophy, the classic pantheon was always eminent. Schlegel[7] and Schelling were prophetic of a kind of mythology which materialized much more vividly during the later 19th century in the work of Comte, Wagner and Nietzsche.

Poetry conceived along these lines would be a kind of philosophy, the most creative and highest philosophy. It would take the place of ordinary philosophy. Poetry—art—was the supreme fact. "Poetry," wrote Novalis in one of his *Fragments*, "is a genuine absolute reality. This is the gist of my philosophy. The more poetical, the more true."[8] Such speculations soared the more wildly when the subjective idealism of Kant (where the sway of the human intellect was limited to appearances) was stepped up by his followers to the phase of absolute idealism —where all reality is the production of selfhood—of inner, conscious, self and outer, unconscious, self, in conflict with each other (as with Fichte) or reconciled in a higher aesthetic and philosophic self (as with Schelling). There were tensions here between the claims of art and those of philosophy, perhaps most sensitively felt by Schelling, who at first made art the sufficient "organon" of philosophy, an eternal revelation, an infinite satisfaction, but in the absolute phase of his idealism[9] later conceived that, although art mythologized and reflected the absolute, philosophy alone could conceptualize and understand it. A distinctive feature of Friedrich Schlegel's diffusely oracular system was his elevation of criticism itself to a metaphoric and creative status equal to that of the poetry which was its object.[1] The critic must illuminate the original exercise of the poet by transcending it. "Poetry," he said, "can only be criticized by poetry,"[2] and the dictum was honored throughout Europe for more than a century in a flourishing tradition of impressionistic criticism.[3]

Nothing could have been less realistic or less naturalistic than the full romantic theory. Poetry as creative dreaming was one of the most

---

[6] *Philosophie der Kunst*, I, B.1, in *Sämtliche Werke* (Stuttgart and Augsburg, 1859), I, 5, 402ff.

[7] Schlegel's essay *Über die Sprache und Weisheit der Inder*, 1808, was to have a considerable influence on the later study of comparative mythology (Lange, *loc. cit.*, p. 303).

[8] *Fragmente und Studien* VI, 468 (*Schriften*, ed. Kluckhohn, II, 411).

[9] In his *Philosophie der Kunst*, written in 1802–03.

[1] Schlegel called his own elaborate review of *Wilhelm Meister* (1798) an *Übermeister* (Lange, *loc. cit.*, p. 296).

[2] Minor, II, 200, quoted by Lange, p. 296.

[3] Cf. *post* Chapter 22, p. 496.

satisfactory conceptions of the era—like the creative dreaming of the Plotinian world soul. In his unfinished novels *Heinrich von Ofterdingen* (about the youth of a medieval Minnesinger) and *Die Lehrlinge zu Sais* (containing the Märchen of *Hyazinth und Rosenblut* or insight through spiritual love) Novalis offers both statement and illustration of his yearning for a single pregnant and reconciling fantasy.[4] Dreaming, said Jean Paul, is involuntary poetry.[5] The photographic naturalism of the later 19th century ("romanticism on all fours") and the direct emotional display which came to represent spontaneity had far less in common with Schiller and the Schlegels and Novalis than with anti-classical phenomena of the earlier 18th century—the emotivism which we have already described in England (in Germany *Sturm und Drang*) and the realism which went with it—the view of "truth" that may be found in Lessing, in Samuel Johnson, in Diderot.

A poetry which is to be truly philosophical will have to be a rounded image of the human spirit. It will have an imaginative fairness and fullness. True simplicity (*Einfachheit*), said Jean Paul, dwells in the organic whole, not in parts. During the era of rationalistic enlightenment, the imagery most often implicit in theories of poetry had been mechanical—imagery of a verbal force working to produce clear impressions on our mental tablets or to pile up handsome aggregations of atomic parts into literary "compositions." The new German imagery of aesthetic theory was botanical and zoological—an imagery of the spontaneously unfolding and articulated self-conscious spirit, in a word, of organism. The poem sprang like a flower from the poetic genius. Organism, said Schelling in his *Philosophie der Kunst*, is the highest "potency" of nature. (Art, the analogue of organism, is the highest potency of the absolute.) In his system of antitheses between classic and romantic, A. W. Schlegel assigned "mechanical" form to the classic,[6] "organic" to the romantic, and though this was not meant as an altogether derogatory judgment upon the "mechanical," the distinction

[4] Cf. Eugene E. Reed, "Novalis' *Heinrich von Ofterdingen* as *Gesamtkunst-werk*," PQ, XXXIII (April, 1954), 200–11.

[5] *Sämtliche Werke* (Berlin, 1841), XIII, 262, "Briefe und bevorstehender Lebenslauf," postscript to the fifth letter.

[6] At least he managed to suggest that "mechanical" form is what is found in the neo-classic (*Lectures on Dramatic Art*, London, 1846, p. 340, Lecture XXII). "Form is mechanical when, through external force, it is imparted to any material merely as an accidental addition without reference to its quality; as, for example, when we give a particular shape to a soft mass that it may retain the same after its induration. Organical form, again, is innate; it unfolds itself from within, and acquires its determination contemporaneously with the perfect development of the germ. We everywhere discover such forms in nature throughout the whole range of living powers, from the crystallization of salts and minerals to plants and flowers, and from these again to the human body. In the fine arts, as well as in the domain of nature—the supreme artist, all genuine forms are organical, that is, determined by the quality of the work." Cf. Wellek, *History* II, 48, 59.

was one way of honoring the expansive aspiration of a romantic mode which under such aspects as the mixture of its genres might suffer momentary disadvantages in comparison with the purity of the classic.

VII

A HIGHLY distinctive feature of German romantic theory was its concern to develop, under the sanction of such major premises as we have been describing, a rationale of the comic. Rational statements, thought Jean Paul, are one-sided.[7] Sober statements, or painful statements, or tearful statements might well seem to have the same defect. The relation of tragedy to comedy became an important issue, and there was a general tendency to set the comic up and dignify it, either as a separate, yet highly significant, laughable genre of verbal art, or as an integral side of the serious. A moderate version of the argument appears in A. W. Schlegel's defence of puns ("sportive word-play") as a small-scale model of the whole poetic structure, a kind of fullness and directness in verbal representation,[8] and in his guarded view that "irony," though it has no place at all in the "proper tragic," yet permeates the whole fabric of Shakespeare's plays and almost the whole range of literature upward from the "avowed raillery of comedy." [9] More radically, other German critics developed various concepts of the laughable into specific technical literary implementations of the paramount concept of transcendence. Jean Paul (known to English students best as the model of Carlyle's gigantic agility in the laughing style and as a source for

[7] Cf. *Vorschule der Ästhetik*, No. 69 (*Jean Pauls Sämtliche Werke*, 1935, I, ii, 234).

[8] "An imagination which has been powerfully excited is fond of laying hold of any congruity in sound which may accidentally offer itself, that by such means it may, for the nonce, restore the lost resemblance between the word and the thing. . . . We do not mean to say that all playing upon words is on all occasions to be justified. This must depend on the disposition of mind, whether it will admit of such a play of fancy, and whether the sallies, comparisons and allusions, which lie at the bottom of them, possess internal solidity" (*Lectures on Dramatic Art*, XXIII, on Shakespeare).

[9] "Shakespeare makes each of his principal characters the glass in which the others are reflected. Nobody ever painted so truthfully as he has done the facility of self-deception, the half self-conscious hypocrisy towards ourselves, with which even noble minds attempt to disguise the almost inevitable influence of selfish motives in human nature. The secret irony of the characterization commands admiration as the profound abyss of acuteness and sagacity; but it is the grave of enthusiasm. We arrive at it only after we have had the misfortune to see human nature through and through. . . . Shakespeare . . . makes, as it were, a sort of secret understanding with the select circle of the more intelligent of his readers or spectators; he shows them that he had previously seen and admitted the validity of their tacit objections; that he himself is not tied down to the represented subject, but soars freely above it; and that if he chose, he could unrelentingly annihilate the beautiful and irresistibly attractive scenes which his magic pen has produced" (*Lectures on Dramatic Art*, XXIII).

some of Meredith's ideas in his lecture on the *Comic Spirit*) devoted
Chapter VI of his *Vorschule* to a theory of comic *contrast* in the vogue
prevalent after the statement of Kant.[1] The contrast between the stupidity of the comic action and the ordinary human good sense which
the spectator projects upon or "lends" to the comic figure constitutes,
in Jean Paul's view, an "infinite incongruity" (*unendliche Ungereim-
theit*).[2] We have a lively freedom of choice among three series of
thoughts, our own insight, that of the stupid comic figure, and that part
or aspect of our insight which we lend. Our intellect toys with these
possibilities; it plays and dances back and forth in a delightful freedom.[3]
Only man has follies; and only man can recognize them. But on a
still higher plane, Jean Paul conceives a phase of the laughable upon
which he confers a name dedicated in English theory to an earthier
usage—that is, "humor." "Humor" becomes an inverted and sympathetically laughable form of the sublime (treading "in the low buskin
of comedy" but carrying the tragic mask in her hand), a measure of
the finite against the infinite.

> If man, like ancient theology, glances down from the world be-
> yond on the terrestrial world, the latter looks small and vain;
> if he measures the infinite world with the small one, as humor
> does, connecting them with each other, then laughter arises,
> wherein is sorrow and greatness.[4]

Humor annihilates not the single object but finiteness as such—merely
by setting it in opposition to the idea.

One kind of climax to such laughing sympathies appears in the
essays of Friedrich Schlegel on the theme of "irony." [5] It was possible
to play and dance not only in comparing the stupidity of the comic
character and our own projected shrewdness, but in comparing phases
of our own stupidity and shrewdness, superior evolutions of the self,
moments in that "transcendence of self" developed by Fichte in the
higher reaches of the subject-object dialectic. Irony was a succession of
contrasts between the ideal and the real, a technique by which the
"transcendental ego" was capable of mocking its own convictions and
its own productions. It was ultimate self-parody. It remained aloof from
fixation or satisfaction at any level of insight. It was an avenue to the

[1] To be sampled in English, for instance, in Hazlitt's lecture on "Wit and Humor," introducing his series on the *English Comic Writers*, 1819.

[2] *Vorschule*, No. 28 (*Werke* I, ii, 97).

[3] Cf. Edward V. Brewer, "The Influence of Jean Paul Richter on George Meredith's Conception of the Comic," *JEGP*, XXIX (April, 1930), 243-56.

[4] *Vorschule*, No. 33 (*Werke* I, ii, 116). Kierkegaard's later two-phase transcendence was to move from the aesthetic to the moral (via "irony") and from the
moral to the religious (via "humor"). See his *Concluding Unscientific Postscript*,
trans. David F. Swenson (Princeton, 1944), p. 448.

[5] *Athenaeum* Nos. 37 and 116 (J. Minor, *op. cit.*, II, 209, 220-1).

infinite, the expression of man's appetite for the boundless; it was expansiveness, it was megalomania. Life at its most incandescent phase destroyed itself as it created.

At the hands of romantic poets, this irony might be very dark, sardonic, misanthropic; the hero stood with cloak pulled round his shoulder thrust out to the cold blast—a Byronic and Poesque figure. "Hot baths of sentiment," says Irving Babbitt, "were followed by cold douches of irony." [6] In its more obvious and emotive phases romantic irony was an engine of self-protection and self-enhancement—the device which the amateur employs when he speaks of his masterpiece as a trifle.

But other phases were hyper-metaphysical. In the essays of the pre-symbolist poet Heine, for example, and in the system of the aesthetician K. W. F. Solger, irony was subtilized until it became coextensive with all art; it was the very principle by which art triumphs over nature, spirit over matter. Looking at even the cruder kind of irony from a metaphysical point of view, Solger accuses it of "conferring a semblance of existence upon nothingness in order to annihilate the latter more easily." Solger conceives the finer irony as an almost mystical energy of artistic insight. It is the creative act by which idea or essence steps into the place of and annihilates phenomenal reality. It is the translation of the world of experience into the artist's ideal dream. The idea, expression of the infinite, surpasses the poverty of its medium. Irony is a transcendental means of contemplative "enthusiasm," a union of impulse and rational lucidity, a poise between the extremes of ecstasy and disenchantment. "Without irony there is no true art." [7] By such stages one emerges again onto the high, transcendentally illuminated plateau of Schiller's impulse of free play (*Spieltrieb*), the reconciliation of *Stoff* and *Form*, the aesthetic equipoise. Hegel, who, like Jean Paul, employed the term "humor" and meant by it something much like what Friedrich Schlegel and Solger meant by "irony," delivered an appraisal which has often been quoted. This activity, he observed, implies the "perversion and overthrow of all that is objectively solid in reality."

> It works through the wit and play of wholly personal points of view, and if carried to an extreme amounts to the triumph of the creative power of the artist's soul over every content and every form.[8]

It is "Satanic impertinence."

[6] *Rousseau and Romanticism* (Boston, 1919), Ch. VII.

[7] Maurice Boucher, *K. W. F. Solger, Esthéthique et philosphie de la présence* (Paris, 1934), pp. 107–10; Kurt Weinberg, *Henri Heine, "romantique défroqué," héraut du symbolisme français* (Paris and New Haven, 1954), pp. 122–5.

[8] *Philosophy of Fine Art*, trans. F. P. B. Osmaston (London, 1920), II, 386; Subsection III, ch. 3, 3, b.

VIII

ONE of Goethe's best-known pronouncements concerns the debt of the Germans to the English.

> Our own literature is chiefly the offspring of theirs! Whence have we our novels, our tragedies, but from Goldsmith, Fielding, and Shakespeare? And in our own day, where will you find in Germany three literary heroes who can be placed on a level with Lord Byron, Moore, and Walter Scott? [9]

Not only German poets and novelists but German literary theorists of the romantic period owed a considerable debt to English writers, though in the latter area the English writers were for the most part less distinguished. We have alluded to the correspondence between Kant's sublime and the empirical ideas of Burke's *Inquiry*.[1] Historians of aesthetic thoery point out how Kant's doctrines about "beauty" are only a reduction to systematic form (though "what a systematic form was that!")[2] of ideas widely current in 18th-century England. In Shaftesbury and Hutcheson, for instance, one finds the disinterestedness of aesthetic pleasure; in Kames, the same disinterestedness and the notion that judgments of taste are immediate; in Addison, the pleasures of the imagination conceived as something intermediate between those of sense and those of understanding.[3]

In the important area of comic theory the Germans had less sufficient antecedents in England than in France, where the leading critical mind of the 18th century, Diderot, after a career of largely *larmoyant* thinking had turned at the end, in his *Paradoxe sur le comédien*, to a view of acting and poetry that laid strong stress on the moment of self-awareness, the ironic reserve of passion. But in general England provided better anticipation of the more solemn themes. The primitivistic ideas of Herder and his successors concerning *Volkspoesie*, lyricism, rhythmic expression, emotion, and the birth of language, were fostered, for one thing, by the very impostures of primitivism, chiefly the Ossianic, that came out of England. The same ideas were available too and were known

---

[9] *Conversations*, December 5, 1824.

[1] A similar correspondence appears in Addison's *Spectator* No. 420, where he speaks of the pleasure to be derived from expanding our imagination by degrees. Kames's use of St. Peter's at Rome and of the pyramids as examples of the sublime is a curious anticipation of Kant's use of the same examples in contradiction to his own principle that works of human art cannot participate in the sublime. See E. F. Carritt, "The Sources and Effects in England of Kant's Philosophy of Beauty," *The Monist*, XXXV (April, 1925), 315 ff.

[2] Gilbert and Kuhn, p. 323.

[3] E. F. Carritt, *loc. cit.* Muratori, the Italian neo-classic critic, had conceived the aesthetic imagination as the harmonious union of the understanding and the imagination in general. (Gilbert and Kuhn, p. 322; cf. E. F. Carritt, *Philosophies of Beauty*, p. 63.)

to Herder in English Homeric theorists and in general aesthetic theorists like Shaftesbury, John Brown, "Hermes" Harris, Hugh Blair, Percy, the Wartons, and Edward Young. And in England the lyric norm had been in serious preparation throughout the 18th century not only in the writings of the theorists but in the practice of numerous "Great Ode" and elegy writers.[4]

The work of the British aestheticians, literary theorists, and writers on genius lay ready for the German transformation. The transformation, the stepping up, was nevertheless a matter of great moment. What was empirical, descendental, down-looking, matter-of-fact in the British pioneering, became with the Germans metaphysical, transcendental, ideal, and absolute. Theories of how human feelings and trains of consciousness *happen* to work became theories of what art *is*, what poetry *is*, and the *is* implied an *ought to be*. This was in a sense a return to classical and neo-Platonic lines of thought, but with a change that made these lines acceptable to a generation that had undergone the disillusioning experience of the "enlightenment." German classico-romantic literary theory bears the same kind of relation to British mid-18th-century aesthetics and criticism as Kant bears to Hume. The *disjecta membra* of experience, subject and object, and parcels of each, were re-assembled by force of spirit—in a philosophy of life that placed human creation, or art, either at or near the pinnacle. The new synthesis and the new faith had a new subjective richness resulting from the long analytic and skeptical decomposition which had preceded. The new idealism was more epistemological than any preceding idealism. It may be true that such thinking, when it occurred in the department of literary criticism, was not always so close as it should have been to its literary object. Saintsbury has taken pleasure in pointing out some mistakes of the Germans in the interpretation of Shakespeare and other Elizabethan texts, even a certain aloofness from the texts, as in the case of Goethe's *Hamlet* criticism in *Wilhelm Meister*. This, says Saintsbury, might have been written about a translation of Shakespeare. It is a commonplace of literary history to observe the heavy schematism of the German critical effort and to believe that the German critics were less

---

[4] See Norman Maclean, "From Action to Image: Theories of the Lyric in the Eighteenth Century," in *Critics and Criticism*, ed. R. S. Crane, pp. 408–60. Eighteenth-century English instances of a desire to push even drama toward a lyric norm may be noted. Kames complained that the Greek drama had more action than feeling. It had "no sentiments except of the plainest kind . . . no intricate or delicate situation to occasion any singular passion; no gradual swelling and subsiding of passion: no conflict between different passions" (letter to Mrs. Montague, June 17, 1771, quoted in Helen W. Randall, *The Critical Theory of Lord Kames*, Northampton, 1944, p. 111). (Cf. *post*, Chapter 20, Hugo, Newman, and Arnold on dramatic norms.) The orientalist Sir William Jones by a simple dichotomy rejected "imitation" in favor of lyric feeling. "The finest parts of poetry, music and painting, are expressive of the passions, and operate on our minds by sympathy. The inferior parts of them are descriptive of natural objects, and affect us chiefly by substitution" (*Poems*, London, 1777, p. 207).

lovingly and immediately in touch with the letter of the literary work than the English literary men of the same generation. Yet the latter took what they could of German philosophy, gratefully, and were improved by it. What came out of British empiricism came back raised to a power where it actually met the critical needs of the literary mind or some of those needs.

IMAGINATION: WORDSWORTH AND COLERIDGE

§ *semantics of "imagination" and "fancy" from 17th century to romantic era, Wordsworth's Preface to* Poems, *1815: elevation of both "imagination" and "fancy," Coleridge's objections, his concern with psychology rather than poems, essential agreement between Wordsworth and Coleridge—II. Coleridge's progress from association to idealism, tabloid treatment of imagination and fancy* (Biographia XIII), *German sources and parallels: Schelling's Oration, Kant, Coleridge's system: Understanding, Reason, Primary and Secondary Imagination, coalescence of inner and outer, creation—III. superior idealism of the artist, symbols, nature and the spiritual life, within us and abroad, various other statements by Coleridge:* Treatise on Method, Semina Rerum, Philosophical Lectures, Anima Poetae, Dejection, *emphasis on coadunation, Schelling, In-Eins-Bildung, reconciliation of opposites* (Biographia XIV), *genesis of* Lyrical Ballads, *"a constitutional malady" —IV. meter and passion, Shakespeare's characters,* Venus and Adonis, *imitation as "mesothesis," Schelling again, transcendental principle and landscape applications, Coleridge on topography, on sonnets, intimate combinations (symbols) vs. formal similes (allegory), "pathetic fallacy," omission of overt statement, reduction of disparity—V. "fancy," Wordsworth's examples, Coleridge on* Venus and Adonis, *on "wit," on metaphysical poets* (Biographia I, XVIII), *canonical content, pantheism, philosophy and poetry, modern objections, Coleridge on "pleasure and truth," difficulties, poems about romantic imagination, Shelley, Coleridge—VI. continuation of 18th-century genius, sublimity, emotion, vagueness, Coleridge at the waterfall, Wordsworth's Preface of 1815, Longinianism, numbers consolidated, Johnsonian generality again, infinity and obscurity, emotive congruity, Wordsworth's statements (1800 and 1815), Coleridge: letter to Southey, Biographia on Shakespeare, "predominant passion," "unity of interest"* §

D
URING THE 17TH CENTURY THE TERMS "IMAGINATION" AND "FANCY" had often enough been used in a vaguely synonymous way to refer to the realm of fairy tale or make-believe. Yet here and there (as in the opening of Hobbes's *Leviathan*) the term "imagination" had tended to distinguish itself from "fancy" and settle toward a meaning centered in the sober literalism of sense impressions and the survival of these in memory. This was in accord with medieval and Renaissance tradition, where *imaginatio* and *phantasia* had all along been fairly close together, but where, so far as a distinction of this kind had been made, it was *phantasia* which meant the lighter and less responsible kind of imaging.[1] In the light of 17th-century reasonableness, "fancy" suffered the decline in reputation which we have discussed in an earlier chapter. But "imagination" (when it did not mean "fancy") held its own and even slid into a new place of respect in sensationalist aesthetics. It followed that during the 18th century, whenever the distinction between "imagination" and "fancy" was being made—and it often was—honors were likely to fall to the term "imagination." A certain softness and warmth and depth of good feeling grew around the term "imagination" in its Addisonian sense; it stayed close to the heart of 18th-century poetry. A corresponding coldness and brittleness and a suggestion of unreliable frolic invested the related but opposed term "fancy." As 18th-century "imagination" moved through the stages of association theory to which we have alluded in an earlier chapter, the honors accorded the two terms were now and then reversed—"fancy" assuming the higher role of reference to a more creative mental power, imagination, the humbler reference to the mind's more reportorial kinds of drudgework.[2] But such an assign-

---

[1] Cf. Murray W. Bundy, *The Theory of Imagination in Classical and Mediaeval Thought (University of Illinois Studies in Language and Literature,* XII, May–August, 1927, Nos. 2–3), p. 266: "Mediaeval usage was, on the whole, unfavorable to any recognition of the creative capacity of *imaginatio. Phantasia* implied the loftier functions, the greater freedom—but at the same time the greater liability to error."

[2] See John Bullitt and Walter Jackson Bate, "Distinctions Between Fancy and Imagination in Eighteenth-Century English Criticism," *MLN,* LX (1945), 8–15. Earl R. Wasserman, "Another Eighteenth-Century Distinction Between Fancy and Imagination," *MLN* (January, 1949), 23–5, calls attention to the reversal of the usual roles of the terms in Arthur Browne's *Miscellaneous Sketches: or, Hints for Essays,* 1789. A. W. Schlegel's later assignment of *Einbildungskraft* to the lower and *Fantasie* to the higher role corresponds with the minority English usage.

ment of honors was a little noticed exception. The relative dignity of the two *terms* "imagination" and "fancy" was so well established in English usage by the end of the 18th century that no matter what revised *meanings* Wordsworth and Coleridge and others might assign to them, it was almost inevitable that the superior *term* should be "imagination."

An early and somewhat haphazard attempt on the part of Wordsworth to discriminate between imagination ("Impressive effects out of simple elements") and fancy ("Pleasure and surprise . . . excited by sudden varieties of situation and accumulated imagery") appears in a note to "The Thorn" in the 1800 edition of *Lyrical Ballads*. But the first word in the major critical discussion by Wordsworth and Coleridge occurs in the *Preface* to the *Poems* of 1815, when Wordsworth breaks out in an excited correction of William Taylor's *British Synonyms Discriminated*, 1813. Taylor had unfortunately written:

> A man has imagination in proportion as he can distinctly copy in idea the impressions of sense: it is the faculty which *images* within the mind the phenomena of sensation. A man has fancy in proportion as he can call up, connect, or associate, at pleasure, those internal images (*phantazein* is to cause to appear) so as to complete ideal representations of absent objects. Imagination is the power of depicting, and fancy of evoking and combining. The imagination is formed by patient observation; the fancy by a voluntary activity in shifting the scenery of the mind. The more accurate the imagination, the more safely may a painter, or a poet, undertake a delineation, or a description, without the presence of the objects to be characterized. The more versatile the fancy, the more original and striking will be the decoration produced.

That summed up a century more or less of settled usage and compromise opinion. Wordsworth's objection was in part simply that the terms, as an antithetic pair, were turned upside down. "Imagination," not "fancy," should be used to refer to the creative or poetic principle. Furthermore, and this was really the critical issue (though how far Wordsworth distinguished the merely semantic from the critical may be questioned), the very distinction between the two terms was made at too low a level. The higher power (what Taylor called "fancy") had to be something better than the mere power of wilfully (capriciously) "evoking or combining" images—"shifting the scenery of the mind"—making "decorations." There was a "higher" creative power than that. And this was the "imagination."

> Fancy does not require that the materials which she makes use of should be susceptible of change in their constitution, from her

touch; and, where they admit of modification, it is enough for her purpose if it be slight, limited, and evanescent.

The law under which the processes of Fancy are carried on is as capricious as the accidents of things, and the effects are surprising, playful, ludicrous, amusing, tender, or pathetic, as the objects happen to be appositely produced or fortuitously combined. Fancy depends upon the rapidity and profusion with which she scatters her thoughts and images; trusting that their number, and the felicity with which they are linked together, will make amends for the want of individual value: or she prides herself upon the curious subtilty and the successful elaboration with which she can detect their lurking affinities.[3]

(Even fancy was far from being the uncreative or unoriginal thing, the mere juggler, which William Taylor would have made it.) But imagination! Imagination was a "conferring," an "abstracting," a "modifying," an "endowing" power. The imagination "unites" and "coalesces." It "shapes and creates." [4] In the language of his friend Charles Lamb, the imagination

draws all things to one. . . . it makes things animate or inanimate, beings with their attributes, subjects with their accessories, take one colour and serve to one effect.[5]

Imagination

. . . recoils from everything but the plastic, the pliant, and the indefinite. . . . When the Imagination frames a comparison . . . a sense of the truth of the likeness, from the moment that it is perceived, grows—and continues to grow—upon the mind; the resemblance depending less upon outline of form and feature, than upon expression and effect; less upon casual and outstanding, than upon inherent and internal, properties: moreover, the images invariably modify each other. . . . the Imagination is conscious of an indestructible dominion;—the Soul may fall

[3] Wordsworth's *Preface* of 1815 is quoted from *Wordsworth's Literary Criticism*, ed. Nowell C. Smith (London, 1925), pp. 155–65.

[4] Imagination is "that intellectual lens through the medium of which the poetical observer sees the objects of his observations, modified both in form and colour; or it is that inventive dresser of dramatic *tableaux*, by which the persons of the play are invested with new drapery, or placed in new attitudes, or it is that chemical faculty by which elements of the most different nature and distant origin are blended together into one harmonious and homogeneous whole" ("Conversations and Reminiscences Recorded by the (Now) Bishop of Lincoln," Wordsworth's *Prose Works*, ed. Grosart, III, 465; cf. R. D. Havens, *The Mind of a Poet*, Baltimore, 1941, p. 208).

[5] Wordsworth quotes Lamb's essay "Upon the Genius of Hogarth." See Lamb's *Works* (1811), I, 96.

away from it, not being able to sustain its grandeur; but, if once felt and acknowledged, by no act of any other faculty of the mind can it be relaxed, impaired, or diminished.

In short, where the 18th century had been content with a distinction between a faithfully reportorial imaging faculty, and an unfaithful, or playfully inventive fancy, Wordsworth raised the level of the whole distinction. Simple reproduction interested him not at all. He distinguished two modes of imaging, both inventive.[6] The difference was that one was frolicsome, and inferior, the other was totally serious, and superior.

It was this concession to fancy, though it was only incidental to Wordsworth's aim of elevating the imagination, that became a point of grievance with Coleridge. In Chapter XII of his *Biographia*, he comes down on Wordsworth's venture with a heavy hand.

> If, by the power of evoking and combining, Mr. Wordsworth means the same as, and no more than, I meant by the aggregative and associative, I continue to deny, that it belongs at all to the imagination; and I am disposed to conjecture, that he has mistaken the co-presence of fancy with imagination for the operation of the latter singly.[7]

In Chapter IV of the *Biographia*, after giving Wordsworth the grand credit of having originally inspired his own whole theory of the imagination,[8] Coleridge had already drawn a patronizing distinction between Wordsworth's purpose of considering only the "influences" or "effects" of fancy and imagination "as they are manifested in poetry," and his own more psychologic purpose of investigating "the seminal principle"—that is, the process of imaginative creation, rather than poems themselves.[9] It is our own view that Coleridge did not differ vitally from Wordsworth about "imagination," and that the two may well be considered together,[1]

[6] "To aggregate and to associate, to evoke and to combine, belong as well to the Imagination as to the Fancy." Wordsworth here ventures to object to an opinion expressed by Coleridge in an article contributed to Southey's *Omniana* (London, 1812), II, 13.

[7] *Biographia Literaria*, ed. John Shawcross (Oxford, 1907), I, 194.

[8] "I was in my twenty-fourth year, when I had the happiness of knowing Mr. Wordsworth personally, and while memory lasts, I shall hardly forget the sudden effect produced in my mind, by his recitation of a manuscript poem. . . . It was the union of deep feeling with profound thought; the fine balance of truth in observing, with the imaginative faculty in modifying the objects observed; and above all the original gift of spreading the tone, the *atmosphere*, and with it the depth and height of the ideal world around forms, incidents and situations, of which, for the common view, custom had bedimmed all the lustre, had dried up the sparkle and the dew drops" (*Biographia*, Chapter IV: I, 58–59).

[9] I, 58–64.

[1] For a development of the difference between them, see Clarence D. Thorpe, "The Imagination: Coleridge *versus* Wordsworth," *PQ*, XVIII (January, 1939), 1–18.

although Coleridge no doubt may be conveniently accepted as the more articulate and more theoretical spokesman of the two.

II

In Chapters V–IX of the *Biographia*, Coleridge traces the growth of his mind from Hartleyan associationism to neo-Platonic and then to German transcendental idealism. Chapter XII lays down in ten Theses the Fichtean and Schellingian phase of ideal realism in which at the moment he finds himself. All this is undertaken in preparation for the grand purpose of expounding "the nature and genesis of the imagination," the literary topic which was laid aside—for want of proper groundwork—at the end of his skirmish with Wordsworth in Chapter IV. Chapter XIII is the well-known Shandean spoof. The tortured exposition abruptly and whimsically gives way to so "completely" convincing a letter of complaint from "a friend" that our author is content to drop the argument and state his "main result" in the following tabloid.

> The IMAGINATION then, I consider either as primary, or secondary. The primary IMAGINATION I hold to be the living power and prime Agent of all human Perception, and as a repetition in the finite mind of the eternal act of creation in the infinite I AM. The secondary Imagination I consider as an echo of the former, co-existing with the conscious will, yet still as identical with the primary in the *kind* of its agency, and differing only in *degree*, and in the *mode* of its operation. It dissolves, diffuses, dissipates, in order to recreate; or where this process is rendered impossible, yet still at all events it struggles to idealize and to unify. It is essentially *vital*, even as all objects (as objects) are essentially fixed and dead.

> FANCY, on the contrary, has no other counters to play with, but fixities and definites. The Fancy is indeed no other than a mode of Memory emancipated from the order of time and space; while it is blended with, and modified by that empirical phenomenon of the will, which we express by the word CHOICE. But equally with the ordinary memory the Fancy must receive all its materials ready made from the law of association.[2]

[2] I, 202. For similar but briefer Coleridgean definitions of "imagination" and "fancy," see *Coleridge's Miscellaneous Criticism*, ed. T. M. Raysor, p. 387. For Coleridge's comparison of imagination to delirium (an all-inclusive coloring of the mind) and fancy to mania (a specially channelled response), see *Biographia*, Chapter IV (I, 62) and Shawcross's note (I, 225–6) quoting *Table Talk*, June 23, 1834, and *Aids to Reflection*, Bohn edition, p. 173. Coleridge recognized combinations of imagination and fancy, or shadings between the two. In *Miscellaneous Criticism*, p. 38, Spenser has "fancy under conditions of imagination. He has an imaginative fancy, but he has not imagination."

Does Coleridge mean the same thing that Wordsworth means in the more informal and literary statement of the 1815 Preface? Or does Coleridge mean something far more profound? The question is complicated by the presence of German ideas in Coleridge's mind.

It is not the issue of plagiarism [3] (though that is present for the biographer of Coleridge) which we would here pursue, but the relation of his theory to certain presiding metaphysical notions of his time, and especially to the notions of Kant and Schelling. It is true that a number of clear and even detailed borrowings by Coleridge from the Germans are to be noted, but let us say in advance that the importance of his debt is not always in proportion to its flagrance or its definability.

The lecture *On Poetry or Art* of 1818, for instance, is a fairly close paraphrase of Schelling's Academy Oration *On the Relation of the Formative Arts to Nature* (1807), and this has an importance to which we shall return in a few pages.[4] One of the most amusing betrayals of Coleridge's way with sources is his coinage of the term *esemplastic* (unifying or coadunative) in Chapters X and XIII of the *Biographia* on the model of Schelling's *In-Eins-Bildung* and apparently with the mistaken notion also that the term is authorized by the German word *Einbildungskraft*.[5] One of Coleridge's clearest debts to Kant appears in his *Principles of Genial Criticism* (1814), where both doctrine and examples, concerning pleasure, taste, beauty, and disinterest, are taken directly from Kant's *Critique of Judgment*. Yet this aesthetic borrowing has no very important relation to Coleridge's own literary aesthetic. The main relation of Coleridge's literary theory to Kant is a vaguer one, and lies in the direction not of the *Critique of Judgment* but in that of Kant's general epistemology and ontology in the *Critique of Pure Reason*. "The writings of the illustrious sage of Königsberg, the founder of the Critical Philosophy," says Coleridge in Chapter IX of the *Biographia*, "more than any other work, at once invigorated and disciplined my under-

---

[3] In Chapter IX of the *Biographia* Coleridge makes a more or less convincing disavowal of "ungenerous concealment or intentional plagiarism," though he admits that his doctrines are likely to show a remarkable coincidence with those of Schelling. "I regard truth as a divine ventriloquist. I care not from whose mouth the sounds are supposed to proceed, if only the words are audible and intelligible" (*Biographia* I, 105). And in *Anima Poetae* under the year 1804 (Boston, 1895, p. 89): "In the preface of my metaphysical works, I should say, 'Once for all, read Kant, Fichte, etc., and then you will trace, or, if you are on the hunt, track me.' Why, then, not acknowledge your obligations step by step? Because I could not do so in a multitude of glaring resemblances without a lie, for they had been mine, formed and full-formed, before I ever heard of these writers." An early instance of the charge of plagiarism against Coleridge appears in De Quincey's article "The Plagiarisms of S. T. Coleridge" in *Blackwood's Magazine* for March, 1840.

[4] See *Biographia*, I, 95, 243, for another free translation from Schelling.

[5] *Biographia Literaria*, I, 107, 195, 249; *Anima Poetae* (Boston, 1895), p. 199; *Letters* (1895), I, 405-406; marginalia to J. G. E. Maass, quoted in Sarah Coleridge, ed. *Biographia Literaria* (1847), I, 173. Cf. Patrick L. Carver, "Evolution of the Term Esemplastic," *MLR*, XXIV (1929), 329.

standing." It may be worth adding that the ideas concerned had been rather widely foreshadowed throughout the neo-Platonic tradition, a tradition in which Coleridge was deeply versed, and one in which Kant himself stood as the theistic and transcendental champion of the age against Spinozan immanentism and pantheism.[6]

We may see the relation of Coleridge's "imagination" and "fancy" to German ideas better if we set beside the definitions already quoted from Chapter XIII of the *Biographia* the following passage, defining two Kantian terms, "Understanding" (*Verstand*) and "Reason" (*Vernunft*), from an early essay by Coleridge in *The Friend:*

> By understanding, I mean the faculty of thinking and forming judgments on the notices furnished by the sense, according to certain rules existing in itself, which rules constitute its distinct nature. By the pure reason, I mean the power by which we become possessed of principles—the eternal verities of Plato and Descartes, and of ideas, not images.[7]

And along with this let us set down the development of these ideas, perhaps not quite consistently, in Coleridge's later religious and philosophic work entitled *Aids to Reflection.*

> 1. Understanding is discursive. 2. The Understanding in all its judgments refers to some other Faculty as its ultimate Authority. 3. Understanding is the Faculty of *Reflection.*

> 1. Reason is fixed. 2. The Reason in all its decisions appeals to itself, as the ground and *substance* of their truth. (Hebrews vi, 13.) 3. Reason of Contemplation. Reason indeed is much nearer to SENSE than to Understanding: for Reason (says our great HOOKER) is a direct aspect of Truth, an inward Beholding, having a similar relation to the Intelligible or Spiritual, as SENSE has to the Material or Phenomenal.[8]

---

[6] René Wellek, *Immanuel Kant in England*, pp. 115 ff., points out that Coleridge's manuscript *Logic* is largely an elaborate exposition of the *Critique of Pure Reason*, with architectonics, tables of categories, and antinomies taken over literally. The direct relation of this fact to literary matters is no doubt slight. Wellek says (p. 114), "Of the major writings of Coleridge least of Kant's immediate influence is to be found in the *Biographia Literaria.*" Various borrowings by Coleridge from Schiller's *Naive and Sentimental Poetry*, Jean Paul's *Vorschule*, A. W. Schlegel's *Dramatic* lectures, are pointed out by T. M. Raysor in his editions of Coleridge's *Miscellaneous Criticism* and *Shakespeare Criticism.* Shawcross (I, 231) notes that Coleridge's history of association psychology in Chapters V and VI of the *Biographia* is drawn in part from J. G. E. Maass, *Versuch über die Einbildungskraft*, 1797. See also Wellek, *History* II, 151–3.

[7] *Complete Works*, ed. W. G. T. Shedd (New York, 1853), II, 164.

[8] *Aids to Reflection* (London, 1913), p. 148, "On the Difference in Kind of Reason and the Understanding." Joseph W. Beach, *The Concept of Nature in Nineteenth Century Poetry* (New York, 1936), p. 321, believes that Coleridge's dis-

Let four terms, then, "Primary Imagination"↔"Understanding," "Secondary Imagination"↔"Reason," stand as a kind of ascending series, with affinities between the first (or lower) and the second (or upper) pair indicated by the sign ↔. And let "Fancy" ride as a kind of side effort or false parallel to "Secondary Imagination." The Platonic sensory knowledge (*eikasia*), more or less the equivalent of the Kantian immediate sensory intuition (*Anschauung*), does not appear in the Coleridgean system, but so far as it might be distinguished in itself it would be conceived as a shadowy beginning which is substantiated or shaped up into the world of our everyday external experience (horses and houses) by the faculty of Primary Imagination (*Einbildungskraft*) working in accord with the schemes or laws of the scientific Understanding. This "Imagination" is a primary creative act, a willed activity of spirit, a self-consciousness, a "self-realizing intuition," joining and coalescing the otherwise separated parts of our self, the outer unconscious, and the inner conscious, the object and the subject. To support this part of the interpretation, we turn back to the Theses of *Biographia*, Chapter XI and to certain Kantian passages in Chapter VII.

> There are evidently two powers at work, which relatively to each other are active and passive; and this is not possible without an intermediate faculty, which is at once both active and passive. (In philosophical language, we must denominate this intermediate faculty in all its degrees and determinations, the IMAGINATION.[9]

The two powers between which the Imagination mediates are the "subject" and "object" of Chapter XII and the two opposing and counteracting forces described in the involved Schellingian terms of Chapter XIII before it is interrupted by the letter from the friend.[1] Primary Imagination is a human creative act which we may take as a type of and participation in the Divine act, though we are told that Coleridge later deleted that clause in a copy of the *Biographia*—"a repetition in the finite mind of the eternal act of creation in the infinite I AM."

---

tinction is derived, with some misunderstanding, merely from Kant's Preface to his *Critique of Pure Reason*.

Neo-Platonic and Christian writers were accustomed to make a similar distinction between the terms *scientia* and *sapientia*. See, for instance, Augustine, *De Trinitate*, XII, 25. Cf. Aristotle's distinction, in *De Anima*, between the passive and the active intellect.

[9] I, 86.

[1] Cf. Clarence D. Thorpe, "The Imagination: Coleridge *versus* Wordsworth," *PQ*, XVIII (January, 1939), 8.

III

EVERY human being, then, is, so far as he perceives anything at all, a creator and an idealizing agent. What then about the special role of the artist (the poet or maker)? What more can *he* do? What kind of "imagination" does *he* enjoy?

> . . . in common language, and especially on the subject of poetry, we appropriate the name to a superior degree of the faculty, joined to a superior voluntary control over it.[2]

We conceive the "Secondary Imagination," a higher plastic power. This reworks the perceptual products of primary imagination into concrete expressions (symbols) of those "ideas"—the self, the absolute, the world, and God—which are otherwise, conceptually, given by that superior part of the transcendental mind the Reason. Nature, especially as seen by the poet, symbolizes the spiritual life of man and hence too that higher life in which the spiritual life of man participates, "the one life within us and abroad." The ideas of such a life were, as Kant conceived them, framed by the Reason only as regulative hypotheses. But for Coleridge (as for the German post-Kantians, Schelling, Fichte, and Hegel), these ideas were realities (*noumena*) and the Reason was the faculty of philosophic insight into them—as Secondary Imagination gave them symbolic embodiments.[3] Kant had distinguished this imagination, under the name of the "aesthetic," from the "productive" (Coleridge's "primary Imagination") and from the "reproductive" (Coleridge's "fancy").

Various other writings of Coleridge give more poetically colored and less difficult accounts of that higher meaning of nature which he conceived it to be the role of poetic imagination to create and in creating know.

> Certainly the Fine Arts belong to the outward world, for they all operate by the images of sight and sound, and other sensible impressions; and without a delicate tact for these, no man ever was, or could be, either a Musician or a Poet; nor could he attain to excellence in any one of these Arts; but as certainly he must always be a poor and unsuccessful cultivator of the Arts

[2] Chapter VI (I, 86).

[3] Coleridge's *Preliminary Treatise on Method*, 1818, assigns to aesthetics a "middle position" between physics, which deals with sensory facts by hypothetical constructions, and metaphysics, which is concerned with "laws" apprehended through the *Ideas* of the reason (J. H. Muirhead, *Coleridge as Philosopher*, New York, 1930, Chapter VII, pp. 197–8). Cf. Shawcross, ed. *Biographia Literaria*, I, lvii–lviii.

if he is not impelled first by a mighty, inward power, a feeling, *quod nequeo monstrare, et sentio tantum;* nor can he make great advances in his Art, if, in the course of his progress, the obscure impulse does not gradually become a bright, and clear, and living Idea! [4]

If the artist copies the mere nature, the *natura naturata,* what idle rivalry! . . . Believe me, you must master the essence, the *natura naturans,* which presupposes a bond between nature in the higher sense and the soul of man. . . . In the objects of nature are presented, as in a mirror, all the possible elements, steps, and processes of intellect antecedent to consciousness, and therefore to the full development of the intelligential act; and man's mind is the very focus of all the rays of intellect which are scattered throughout the images of nature.[5]

To have a genius is to live in the universal, to know no self but that which is reflected not only from the faces of all around us, our fellow-creatures, but reflected from the flowers, the trees, the beasts, yea from the very surface of the waters and the sands of the desert. A man of genius finds a reflex of himself, were it only in the mystery of being.[6]

In looking at objects of Nature while I am thinking, as at yonder moon dim-glimmering through the dewy window-pane, I seem rather to be seeking, as it were *asking* for, a symbolical language for something within me that already and forever exists, than observing anything new. Even when that latter is the case, yet still I have always an obscure feeling as if that new phenomenon were the dim awaking of a forgotten or hidden truth of my inner nature.[7]

Or the emphasis might fall sadly on the waning or loss of that inner power of investiture.

> O Lady! we receive but what we give,
> And in our life alone does Nature live:
> Ours is her wedding-garment, ours her shroud!
> And would we aught behold, of higher worth,
> Than that inanimate cold world allowed
> To the poor loveless ever-anxious crowd,
> Ah! from the soul itself must issue forth

[4] *Preliminary Treatise on Method,* 1818, III, 21 (ed. Alice D. Snyder, London, 1934, pp. 62–3).
[5] *On Poesy or Art,* in *Biographia,* ed. Shawcross, II, 257–8.
[6] *The Philosophical Lectures (1818–19),* ed. Kathleen Coburn (New York, 1949), p. 179.
[7] *Anima Poetae* (Boston, 1895), p. 115.

A light, a glory, a fair luminous cloud
  Enveloping the Earth—
And from the soul itself must there be sent
  A sweet and potent voice, of its own birth,
Of all sweet sounds the life and element! [8]

All these statements about the meaning of art and the meaning of nature refer to a kind of union between the two. They could all be developed under the aspect of union, the Schellingian emphasis on coalescence, on reconciliation. And it is precisely this emphasis that is the most distinctive feature of Coleridge's theory. This, though it was a tenet of absolute idealism, was capable of working out, and in Coleridge's thinking to some extent did work out, into a dualistic and variously applicable theory of poems. Reconciliation of what? Primarily and generically of the two sides of self, conscious and unconscious, subject and object—and of certain related abstract entities. *In-Eins-Bildung,* said Schelling, *des Einem mit dem Vielen. In-Eins-Bildung des Realen und Idealen.*[9] Or, to give the antithesis a warmer color, *In-Eins-Bildung* (coadunation) of *man* and *nature.* Coleridge's lecture *On Poesy or Art* (1818) is in parts a close paraphrase of Schelling's oration *On the Relation of the Formative Arts to Nature.*

> Art itself might be defined as of a middle quality between a thought and a thing, or, as I have said before, the union and reconciliation of that which is nature with that which is exclusively human. It is the figured language of thought, and is distinguished from nature by the unity of all parts in one thought or idea.[1]

In a passage of the *Biographia* much celebrated recently, Coleridge writes his most enthusiastic and expansive account of the aesthetic "reconciliation."

> Imagination. . . . reveals itself in the balance or reconciliation of opposite or discordant qualities: of sameness, with difference; of the general, with the concrete; the idea, with the image; the individual, with the representative; the sense of novelty and of freshness, with old and familiar objects; a more than usual state of emotion, with more than usual order; judgement ever awake and steady self-possession, with enthusiasm and feeling profound or vehement; and while it blends and harmonizes the natural and the artificial, still subordinates art to nature; the

[8] Cf. Wordsworth's *Ode: Intimations.* . . . "There was a time when meadow, grove, and stream. . . ."
[9] Shawcross, I, 249.
[1] *Biographia Literaria,* II, 254-5.

manner to the matter; and our admiration of the poet to our sympathy with the poetry.[2]

The weaving back and forth of Coleridge's syntax and the variation of his phrasing may tend to obscure the generic alignment of the eleven (partially overlapping) pairs of opposites which we now repeat in tabular form.

Imagination reconciles (balances, or harmonizes):

A		B
1. sameness	with	difference
2. general	"	concrete
3. idea	"	image
4. representative	"	individual
5. familiarity	"	novelty
6. order	"	emotion
7. judgment	"	enthusiasm
8. artificial	"	natural

Imagination subordinates:

A		B
1. art	to	nature
2. manner	"	matter
3. admiration of the poet	"	sympathy with the poetry

Column A will come under the head of the "subject," the "human;" Column B under that of the "object," "nature." In the first part of the same chapter Coleridge had given a nice example of reconciliation between familiarity and novelty, treated in such a way as to suggest the intimate relation of these reconcilable opposites with another and more difficult pair, the inner human spirit and the outer transcendental or supernatural. The example is so engaging an incident of English literary history as almost to preclude the possibility of cavil.

> During the first year that Mr. Wordsworth and I were neighbors, our conversations turned frequently on the two cardinal points of poetry, the power of exerting the sympathy of the reader by a faithful adherence to the truth of nature, and the power of giving the interest of novelty by the modifying colors of imagination. The sudden charm, which accidents of light

[2] Chapter XIV (II, 12). Alice D. Snyder, *The Critical Principle of the Reconciliation of Opposites as Employed by Coleridge* (Ann Arbor, 1918), p. 28, was apparently the first modern writer to quote this passage. She was followed by T. S. Eliot in his essay on Marvell (1921), by I. A. Richards in his *Principles of Literary Criticism* (1924). Cf. René Wellek, in *The English Romantic Poets*, ed. T. M. Raysor (New York, 1950), p. 109.

and shade, which moonlight or sun-set diffused over a known and familiar landscape, appeared to represent the practicability of combining both. . . . In this idea originated the plan of the "Lyrical Ballads;" in which it was agreed, that my endeavours should be directed to persons and characters supernatural, or at least romantic; yet so as to transfer from our inward nature a human interest and a semblance of truth sufficient to procure for these shadows of imagination that willing suspension of disbelief for the moment, which constitutes poetic faith. Mr. Wordsworth, on the other hand, was to propose to himself as his object, to give the charm of novelty to things of every day, and to excite a feeling analogous to the supernatural, by awakening the mind's attention from the lethargy of custom, and directing it to the loveliness and the wonders of the world before us.[3]

Coleridge's interest in opposites and their reconciliation was, says Miss Snyder, "a constitutional malady." And she is able to present a very miscellaneous set of topics—foam islands shaping and reshaping below a waterfall, a tooth-ache and the forgetting of it, a cone of loose sand rising and sinking at the bottom of a spring, the movement of ghostlike crowds through the sepulchral fixities of London streets—all of which provoke in Coleridge reflections on this theme.[4]

I V

ONE might expect that the doctrine of reconciliation would be a wide and varied sanction for poetic moods and genres and that it would have a varied and subtle application in Coleridge's practical criticism. Certain more precise technical modulations do appear, for instance the treatment in *Biographia,* Chapter XVIII, of meter as a balance between passion and organization, or in the notes on *The Tempest* an observation about the individuality of Shakespearian women despite their essential sameness, in the notes on *Hamlet* a comment on the tragi-comedy of a semi-feigned madness.[5] In his lecture "Shakespeare, a Poet Generally" (corresponding in part to Chapter XV of the *Biographia*) Coleridge executes a rhapsodic analysis of a couplet from *Venus and Adonis.*

> Look! how a bright star shooteth from the sky;
> So glides he in the night from Venus' eye.

[3] Chapter XIV (II, 5–6). Wellek, *History* II, 177, notes the anticipation of Coleridge's celebrated "willing suspension of disbelief" by Moses Mendelssohn, *Rhapsodie über die Empfindungen,* 1761, and *Morgenstunden,* 1785.

[4] Snyder, pp. 20 ff., quoting *Anima Poetae* (Boston, 1895), pp. 7, 14, 44; *Works,* IV, 434.

[5] Cf. Snyder, pp. 29–30, 37, 48–9.

> How many images and feelings are here brought together with-
> out effort and without discord, in the beauty of Adonis, the
> rapidity of his flight, the yearning, yet hopelessness, of the en-
> amoured gazer, while a shadowy ideal character is thrown over
> the whole!

In other places, he makes a highly reflexive application of the
doctrine of reconciliation to the work of art itself conceived as a non-
illusory object.

> Imitation, as opposed to copying, consists either in the inter-
> fusion of the SAME throughout the radically DIFFERENT,
> or of the different throughout a base radically the same.[6]

> Imitation is the mesothesis of Likeness and Difference. The dif-
> ference is as essential to it as the likeness; for without the differ-
> ence, it would be Copy or fac-simile.[7]

We have been bringing ourselves, however, to the point of asking
an important question about the limits of this doctrine of imaginative
reconciliation and hence about the whole theory of poetic imagination
entertained by Coleridge and, in fairly close concert, by Wordsworth.
Was their theory in fact a general theory of poetry? Or was it not
rather a theory slanted very heavily toward a particular kind of poetry,
one in which they themselves, and especially Wordsworth, excelled?
(The latter status would not have precluded a fairly wide extension of
the theory, even by Coleridge and Wordsworth if they had been sufficiently interested.) Let us return for a moment to that lecture of
Coleridge's on *Poesy or Art*, so intimately related to Schelling's oration
On the Relation of the Formative Arts to Nature.

> Now so to place these images, totalized, and fitted to the
> limits of the human mind, as to elicit from, and to superinduce
> upon, the forms themselves the moral reflexions to which they
> approximate, to make the external internal, the internal external,
> to make nature thought, and thought nature,—this is the mystery
> of genius in the Fine Arts.[8]

Or, we might quote here again that passage which we have quoted just
above from Chapter XIV of the *Biographia*, about light and shade, moonlight or sunset "over a known and familiar landscape." In such passages
we are confronted in a special way with the important difference between Primary Imagination and Secondary Imagination. We are asked
to focus a special attention upon the distinction between the first (a

[6] *Biographia*, Chapter XVIII (II, 56).
[7] *Table Talk*, *Works*, VI, 468. Cf. Snyder, p. 52.
[8] *Biographia Literaria*, II, 258.

basic and universal power of knowing) and the second (a special power of artistic knowing—yet *not in principle different* from the first). This difficult paradox has haunted all idealistic theory of art from Plotinus to Croce and Susanne Langer. In this crucial instance (crucial because Coleridge and Wordsworth as poet-philosophers did have an eye closely on poems and wished to remain close to them) it may be doubted if the theory succeeds in making the transition from general epistemology to poetics without a leap that largely abandons the epistemology as a formal principle. The theory, at least in some phases, seems to have in mind especially a kind of poetry which will somehow, either by some kind of dramatic figuration, or perhaps by a merely contentual reference, be the appointed representative of the basic philosophy. Yet this poetry, for all that, may not be a sufficient demonstration or illustration of the theory. It is one thing to say that all our knowledge is a "self-realizing intuition" which reconciles subject or conscious self with object or nature. (It is impossible to write a poem which will specially illustrate this transcendental principle. How could any one expression better illustrate or embody it than any other?) It is a vastly different thing to say that the forms of nature are, or are capable of being, suited to moral reflections—or that the latter can be, in any peculiar way, elicited from or superinduced upon the former. This is a very special showing of how "nature" is "thought," and "thought" is "nature." (It may be quite possible to illustrate this in a special kind of poem.)

And so we have such more special statements of preference by Coleridge as that in Chapter XV of the *Biographia*. Images become poetic "when a human and intellectual life is transferred to them from the poet's own spirit, 'Which shoots its being through earth, sea, and air.' "

> Behold yon row of pines, that shorn and bow'd
> Bend from the sea-blast, seen at twilight eve.

In these lines, he says, "There is nothing objectionable, but also nothing to raise them much above the level of a "book of topography" or a "descriptive tour." But the "same image" can be raised to a "semblance of poetry" by being altered thus:

> Yon row of bleak and visionary pines,
> By twilight glimpse discerned, mark! how they flee
> From the fierce sea-blast, all their tresses wild
> Streaming before them.[9]

Or we have the following in the Introduction to the volume of sonnets which Coleridge edited in 1796.

[9] *Biographia*, II, 16–17. Cf. Coleridge's lecture *Shakespeare, a Poet Generally*.

Those sonnets appear to me to be the most exquisite in which moral sentiments are deduced from and associated with the scenery of Nature. They create a sweet and indissoluble union between the intellectual and the material world.[1]

Or this in a letter to Southey of 1802.

A poet's heart and intellect should be *combined*, intimately combined and unified with the great appearances of nature. . . .[2]

In this letter, Coleridge is intent on making a distinction between such "intimate" combinations and certain other combinations, or loose mixtures, such as have to be made explicit by "dim" moralizing analogies and "formal similes."[3]

We have similar statements by Wordsworth (with a more genetic accent): that "images and sentiments" should be "wedded" naturally in the mind; images should rise to the mind unsought for, like "exhalations."[4] "The subject and simile should be as much as possible lost in each other," especially in lyric poetry.[5]

In short, we have a theory of "animating" imagery, of romantic anthropomorphism, what Ruskin not many years later termed the "pathetic fallacy" (and one may echo the term without the least hint of derogation), the fallacy, the fiction, of portraying the face of nature so as to invest it with reflections of our own mind and feelings and hence with

---

[1] *Biographia*, I, 207.

[2] *Letters* (Boston, 1895), I, 403.

[3] Coleridge here verges on the distinction between "symbol" and "allegory" which he was later to make after the example of Goethe and other Germans (cf. *ante* p. 375). "An allegory is but a translation of abstract notions into a picture-language, which is itself nothing but an abstraction from objects of the senses; the principal being more worthless than its phantom proxy, both alike unsubstantial, and the former shapeless to boot. On the other hand a symbol . . . is characterized by a translucence of the special [the species] in the individual, or of the general [the genus] in the special, or of the universal in the general; above all by the translucence of the eternal through and in the temporal" (*The Statesman's Manual*, in *Works*, ed. W. G. T. Shedd, New York, 1884, I, 437). Coleridge and the Germans lay a negative stress on "allegory" which in its broadest application the word will perhaps not bear. If we set aside this semantic difficulty, however, we may recognize in the distinction itself a valid effort to discriminate between various abstractly asserted kinds of imagery and that kind (conveniently called "symbol") which a recent critic of *The Ancient Mariner* has aptly described as "massive," "focal," and "not arbitrary" (R. P. Warren, *The Ancient Mariner*, New York, 1946, p. 76). But Coleridge apparently had no very intent gaze upon the "symbol." In other places he speaks of the symbol as being a part of the whole which it represents, and he seems to be thinking of synecdoche. (See *Miscellaneous Criticism*, p. 99, and *Aids to Reflection*, London, 1913, p. 173 n.) He is sometimes willing to shade his opinion of allegory or to stretch a point to save a poet from the odium of allegorical imputation. *Don Quixote* is "substantial living allegory" (*Miscellaneous Criticism*, p. 102), and Dante is only quasi-allegorical (*Miscellaneous Criticism*, p. 150).

[4] "Letter to Mathetes," *Prose Works*, ed. Grosart, I, 318. Cf. *Prelude*, IV, 113–14.

[5] *Letters of William and Dorothy Wordsworth: The Later Years*, ed. Ernest De Selincourt (Oxford, 1939), I, 158–9.

expressions of the divinity which is the "one life within us and abroad." And this was in fact the way Goethe and Schiller defined modern or "sentimental" poetry. A brilliant host of symbolic nature poems by Blake, by Coleridge, by Keats, by Shelley, and above all by Wordsworth, illustrate the theory and justify it. No poetry before had shaded overt statement of spiritual or psychological meaning (the "still, sad music of humanity," the presence "whose dwelling is the light of setting suns") so curiously, so dramatically, and with such sleights and duplicities of meaning, into the metaphoric intimations of the literally described landscape ("the soft inland murmur," the "one green hue," the "wreaths of smoke . . . as . . . of vagrant dwellers in the houseless woods.") "A puddle," says Hazlitt, speaking of Wordsworth's *Excursion*, "is filled with preternatural faces."

The theory of imagination elaborated by Coleridge, and less precisely but in substantially the same way, by Wordsworth, was an excellent description of their own best poetry in its formal, structural, and metaphoric aspect. One might redescribe this structure approximately in these terms: It is a structure which makes only a restrained use of the central overt statement of similitude which had been so important in all poetry up to that time.[6] Both tenor and vehicle are wrought in a parallel process out of the same material. The landscape is both the occasion of subjective reflection or transcendental insight and the source of figures by which the reflection or insight is defined. In such a structure, finally, the element of tension in disparity may not be prominent. The interest derives not from our being aware of disparity in stated likeness, but in the opposite activity of our discerning the design and the unity latent in a multiform sensuous picture. This is no doubt a form of "reconciliation." At the same time there are certain clearly anti-"metaphysical" tendencies here—the absence of overt definition, the reduction of disparity, the play of phenomena on the one hand and of "spirit" on the other, rather than of entities conceived substantially.

V

THIS is the place to recall that inferior faculty which at the outset was set apart from "imagination"—the "fancy," with its fixities and definites, its capricious, light, playful, and coldly asserted way of connecting these. Wordsworth's examples of "fancy" are Shakespeare's description of Queen Mab, a rather silly couplet by Chesterfield,

[6] Wordsworth's examples of "imagination" in his 1815 Preface are drawn chiefly from his own poems and from Milton. The longest example of his own poetry, from *Resolution and Independence*, is actually framed as an overt similitude—yet, as he himself observes, it is a very subtly complicated "modification" of a natural phenomenon into a human meaning.

> The dews of the evening most carefully shun,
> They are the tears of the sky for the loss of the sun,

and a far from silly, if lighthearted, minor "metaphysical" poem by Charles Cotton, an *Ode Upon Winter*.

> a magazine
> Of sovereign juice is cellared in;
> Liquor that will the siege maintain
> Should Phoebus ne'er return again.

Wordsworth speaks of this poem with considerable affection and even admiration (for the "extreme activity of intellect" displayed and the "correspondent hurry of delightful feeling"). "Though myself a water drinker, I cannot resist the pleasure of transcribing what follows." But the patronage is apparent, and the second-rate status of "fancy" is never for a moment questioned. Coleridge's example of fancy, which does not appear in the *Biographia*, but in the lecture on *Shakespeare, a Poet Generally*, is a quatrain from *Venus and Adonis*.

> Full gently now she takes him by the hand,
> A lily prisoned in a jail of snow,
> Or ivory in an alabaster band:
> So white a friend ingirts so white a foe.[7]

Coleridge's more severe animadversions upon this kind of thing were likely to occur in the immediate context of the word "wit" rather than in that of "fancy." But a close relation is plain enough. In Chapter I of the *Biographia* he observes that "Our faulty elder poets [from Donne to Cowley] sacrificed the passion and passionate flow of poetry, to the subtleties of intellect, and to the starts of wit . . . the heart to the head." They indulged in "the most fantastic out-of-the-way thoughts," though "in the most pure and genuine mother English."[8] In Chapter XVIII a rather bad passage from Cowley's *Pindaric Odes* is rebuked in the following terms:

> . . . such language and such combinations are the native produce neither of the fancy nor of the imagination; . . . their opera-

---

[7] Coleridge here defines "fancy" ("the faculty of bringing together images dissimilar in the main by some one point or more of likeness") in a way that goes far to invite the quantitative interpretation which I. A. Richards makes of the difference between "imagination" and "fancy." The difference seems to lie in the *number* of "links of relevance between the units." A great number adds up to mutual modification (*Coleridge on Imagination*, pp. 78–9). Richards admits (p. 19) that he writes "as a Materialist trying to interpret . . . the utterances of an extreme Idealist." Cf. Wellek, in *Romantic Poets*, ed. T. M. Raysor (New York, 1950), p. 110. Both Coleridge and Wordsworth clearly insist in their main arguments that the difference between "imagination" and "fancy" is one "of kind."

[8] I, 15.

tion consists in the excitement of surprise by the juxta-position and *apparent* reconciliation of widely different or incompatible things. As when, for instance, the hills are made to reflect the image of a *voice*. . . . this compulsory juxta-position is not produced by . . . any sympathy with the modifying powers with which the inner genius of the poet had united and inspirited all the objects of his thought . . . it is therefore a species of *wit*, a pure work of the *will*, and implies a leisure and self-possession both of thought and of feeling, incompatible with the steady fervor of a mind possessed and filled with the grandeur of its object.[9]

The truth is that romantic nature poems are all poems of a certain symbolic furniture and of a certain philosophy—the philosophy of immanence or pantheism which appears in Coleridge's *Aeolian Harp* and in Wordsworth's *Tintern Abbey*, and the related idealism of Coleridge's *Dejection*. For Coleridge, as for the Germans, there was a powerful temptation to equate philosophy and poetry. It is notorious that he proposed to write an essay on poetry which would "supersede all the books of metaphysics, and all the books of morals too." It would be in reality a "disguised system of morals and politics." [1] In his chapter of the *Biographia* on Shakespeare, he says, "No man was ever yet a great poet, without being at the same time a profound philosopher." [2] This was Coleridge's dabbling in that grandiose absorption of metaphysics into *Dichtung* and *Kunst*, or into a philosophy of these, such as we have noted among the Germans. The modern intuitional critic will object to this as an over-conceptualization of poetry.[3] The modern "Aristotelian" will say, in his own language, that such a theory of poetry is not a theory of the poetic object as something specifically different from anything else, that the theory deals only with the poetic process and furthermore assimilates this to metaphysics and to other non-poetic mental processes.[4] To which it may be added that Coleridge himself, in Chapter XIV of the *Biographia*, offers his own definition of the poem as a "composition" having "for its *immediate* object pleasure not truth," [5] but that

---

[9] II, 68.

[1] *Letters* (1895), I, 338, 347 (to Sir Humphry Davy, October 9, 1800, and February 3, 1801).

[2] Chapter XV (II, 19). Cf. Letter to Sotheby, September 10, 1802 (*Letters*, 1895, I, 4-3): Bowles "has no native passion because he is not a thinker."

[3] Cf. A. E. Powell, *The Romantic Theory of Poetry, An Examination in the Light of Croce's Aesthetic* (London, 1926), pp. 111, 117-21. A. C. Bradley, *Oxford Lectures on Poetry* (London, 1950), p. 172, makes the same case concerning Shelley.

[4] R. S. Crane, *et al.*, *Critics and Criticism* (Chicago, 1951), *passim*.

[5] Alba Warren, p. 133, cites the Victorian critic E. S. Dallas's appropriate observation that Coleridge's "pleasure" and "truth" are "objects" of two different orders, subjective and objective. It is scarcely possible to choose either one as an alternative to the other.

by this definition he would have had trouble discriminating between a poem by Wordsworth and one by Bowles. It was only when the general norms of content—passion and thought—were invoked that he could tell a good poem from a bad one.

A difficulty that has always been rather prominent for romantic scholarship lies in the fact that romantic poems do so pronouncedly *contain* and *assert* the philosophy of nature and of art which is supposedly also their formal principle. What the writers in the classical *Ars Poetica* tradition might try to do here and there, as in Pope's little series of handsprings on the theme of sound and sense, the romantic writers may approximate in a whole poem, and more subtly—and this, presumably, one would say they were led to do and were able to do because of the intimate union which they conceived to obtain between art and nature. The theory was endlessly reflexive and self-conscious. The assertion of the romantic poetics seems always to lurk not far from the embodiment in the poems and to be needed for the deciphering of the latter. Romantic poems tend to be about romantic imagination. Shelley's *West Wind* and Wordsworth's *Prelude* are triumphant instances of how the assertion may be dramatized and assimilated into structure. Coleridge's *Ancient Mariner*, which may be read as a poem about imagination, gets along with so little assertion that its theme has perhaps not even been suspected until very recently. The assertion (the content) of a poem is, however, never the same as the embodiment (the poem itself, the achievement), and the first never assures us of the second.

VI

A CONFUSION between poetic theory as operative in poems and poetic theory as their stated content is most often a feat of the historian and critic, rather than of the original theorist or the poet. Yet in his very bias toward illustrating a certain theory the poet-theorist may have done more mischief. The very division between fancy and imagination promoted by Wordsworth and Coleridge, though it was intended as a division between bad and good form in poetry, was responsible for a certain exclusiveness in their view of the thoughts and emotions (the range of psychological materials) which were available for poetry. Nothing too definite, nothing too precisely thoughtful (as tending toward mere scientific understanding), nothing too cool, too playful, too witty. Nothing too "metaphysical." Despite the sharp break with the 18th century which Wordsworth and Coleridge believed themselves to be making and which tradition has credited them with making, their theory of poetic imagination was on its genetic side a continuation of 18th-century "genius," and, with regard to the content of poetry, it prescribed certain items inherited from the 18th-century reaction against metaphysical and neo-classic "wit." These items were the "sublime" and its components the emotive and the vague.

The repeated story of Coleridge at the waterfall [6] and his superior amusement at touristic confusions of the sublime, the beautiful, the pretty, and the picturesque, suggests a great concern to discriminate the "sublime" (in stricter 18th-century and Kantian fashion) from other departments of landscape and hence presumably from other departments of poetry. Yet, when discussing "imagination," both Wordsworth and Coleridge actually place either the "sublime," or its components the emotive and the vaguely grand, very near the center of the complex of qualities by which the imagination and hence poetry are defined.

> The grand storehouses of enthusiastic and meditative Imagination [7] . . . are the prophetic and lyrical parts of the Holy Scriptures, and the works of Milton; . . . . I select these writers in preference to those of ancient Greece and Rome, because the anthropomorphitism of the Pagan religion subjected the minds of the greatest poets in those countries too much to the bondage of definite form; from which the Hebrews were preserved by their abhorrence of idolatry. This abhorrence was almost as strong in our great epic Poet. . . . However imbued the surface might be with classical literature, he was a Hebrew in soul; and all things tended in him toward the sublime. [8]

The Longinianism of the following passage, though not explicit, will hardly be questioned.

> The Imagination also shapes and *Creates;* and how? By innumerable processes; and in none does it more delight than in that of consolidating numbers into unity, and dissolving and separating unity into numbers,—alternations proceeding from, and governed by, a sublime consciousness of the soul in her own mighty and almost divine powers. [9]

[6] The story appears four times in the works of Coleridge himself: *Coleridge's Shakespeare Criticism*, ed. T. M. Raysor (Cambridge, 1930), I, 182; II, 62–63, 352; and *Biographia*, ed. Shawcross, II, 225 (*Genial Criticism*); and once in the *Journals of Dorothy Wordsworth*, ed. W. Knight (London, 1910), I, 195. In *Genial Criticism* Coleridge says the cataract is "in the strictest sense of the word, a sublime object." In Dorothy Wordsworth's *Journal* and in other versions he seems to consider the term "majestic" equally accurate. Cf. C. D. Thorpe, "Coleridge on the Sublime," in *Wordsworth and Coleridge, Studies in Honor of George M. Harper*, ed. Earl L. Griggs (Princeton, 1939), pp. 192–219.

[7] We omit the phrase ". . . of poetical, as contra-distinguished from human and dramatic Imagination," for we are not concerned to tax Wordsworth with this antithesis. "Of human and dramatic Imagination," he says, "the works of Shakespeare are an inexhaustible source."

[8] Preface to 1815, in *Wordsworth's Literary Criticism*, ed. N. C. Smith, p. 162.

[9] N. C. Smith, pp. 160–1. Cf. *Peri Hupsous*, Chapter XXIV: "The conversion of plurals into singulars sometimes conduces in a marked degree to elevation." Words-

In nothing did Wordsworth and Coleridge agree more wholeheartedly than in their association of the "imagination" with the vast, the infinite, the "shadowy ideal character." "Imagination recoils from everything but the plastic, the pliant, and the indefinite." [1] "Imagination [is given] to incite and support the eternal." "The Secondary Imagination . . . dissolves, diffuses, dissipates, in order to recreate." One receives the impression that the spiritual, the divine meaning at which they would get is something nearly identical with the generality, the abstraction. There is something much more Johnsonian here than one might have expected. This is one meaning of the statement sometimes encountered that Coleridge strove to unite with the "organic vitalism" of his day the "traditional rationalistic values of classicism." [2] Wordsworth's later conversations on the theme of imagination seem to have dwelt pretty heavily on "universal ideas or abstractions" embodied in "individual forms" or given a "local habitation." Crabb Robinson, one reporter of such conversations, adds:

> Wordsworth represented, much as unknown to him the German
> philosophers have done, that by the imagination the mere fact
> is exhibited in connection with infinity.[3]

That is, by universal ideals and abstractions, Wordsworth seemed to mean infinity. And for both Coleridge and Wordsworth infinity was not far from obscurity. Coleridge wished to habituate "the intellect to clear, distinct, and adequate conceptions concerning all things that are the possible objects of clear conception." But only in order to put these aside and hence be able

> to reserve the deep feelings which belong, as by a natural right
> to those obscure ideas that are necessary to the moral perfection

---

worth knew both Longinus and his English counterpart John Dennis (*Correspondence of Crabb Robinson with the Wordsworth Circle*, ed. E. Morley, I, 78; undated letter to Southey in N. C. Smith, p. 224). DeQuincey reports that both Wordsworth and Coleridge "had an absurd 'craze' about" Dennis (*Critical Works of Dennis*, ed. E. N. Hooker, II, lxxiii). For the literalness with which Wordsworth pursued this notion of numbers consolidated into unity, see not only the examples from Milton following the passage of the 1815 Preface just quoted but his *Letter to Lady Beaumont*, 1817, defending his sonnet "With ships the sea was sprinkled far and nigh" ("The mind can have no rest among a multitude of objects" . . .), and his "forty feeding like one" ("Written in March," 1802); cf. DeQuincey's comment, concerning "sublime unity," in his essay "On Wordsworth's Poetry," *Tait's Magazine*, September, 1845 (Alden, pp. 336–7).

[1] "You will know that you are dealing with imagination when the edges of things begin to waver and fade out" (F. A. Pottle, "The Eye and the Object in the Poetry of Wordsworth," in *Wordsworth, Centenary Studies*, ed. Gilbert T. Dunklin, Princeton, 1951, p. 38).

[2] W. J. Bate, in *Perspectives of Criticism*, ed. Harry Levin (Cambridge, Mass., 1950), p. 154.

[3] Extracts from Crabb Robinson's *Diary*, 1815 and 1816, quoted by Shawcross, *Biographia Literaria*, I, 227–8.

of the human being, notwithstanding, yea, even in consequence, of their obscurity—to reserve these feelings, I repeat, for objects, which their very sublimity renders indefinite, no less than their indefiniteness renders them sublime: namely, to the ideas of being, form, life, the reason, the law of conscience, freedom, immortality, God! [4]

The 18th-century notion of sublimity as a subjective experience of genius had gotten along well enough with the emerging principle of association by emotive congruity. The latter principle was so well installed in critical thinking by the time of Wordsworth and Coleridge that they could hardly have avoided taking advantage of it. It is true that they did this with delicacy. Wordsworth in his 1800 Preface, after twice invoking the "spontaneous overflow of powerful feelings," adds the tempering phrase "emotion recollected in tranquility," [5] and he touches the same note in his verse.

> And *then* my heart with pleasure fills
> And dances with the daffodils.

> The music in my heart I bore
> Long after it was heard no more.

In one of his later letters he professes: "I have never given way to my own feelings in personifying natural objects without bringing all that I have said to a rigorous after-test of good sense." [6] Like the Germans, both Wordsworth and Coleridge must be largely exculpated as transmitters of 18th-century sentimentalism. Nevertheless the critical theory of each contains some striking statements of the emotive principle. Thus in the 1800 preface:

> Another circumstance must be mentioned which distinguishes these Poems from the popular Poetry of the day; it is this, that the feeling therein developed gives importance to the action and situation, and not the action and situation to the feeling.[7]

"The appropriate business of poetry, . . ." he says later, "and her *duty*, is to treat of things not as they *are*, but as they *appear*; not as they exist in themselves, but as they *seem* to exist to the senses, and to the *passions*." [8] "You feel strongly," he writes to a minor poet; "trust to

---

[4] *The Friend*, I. Essays: Introductory, Essay XIV (London: Bohn's Standard Library, 1906, p. 66).

[5] N. C. Smith, pp. 15, 34.

[6] Letter to W. R. Hamilton, December 23, 1829, *Letters . . . Laters Years*, I, 436–7.

[7] N. C. Smith, p. 16.

[8] *Essay Supplementary to the Preface*, 1815 (N. C. Smith, p. 169).

those feelings, and your poem will take its shape and proportions as a tree does from the vital principle that actuates it." [9]

And Coleridge:

> Association depends in a much greater degree on the recurrence of resembling states of feeling than trains of ideas. . . . A metaphysical solution [like Hartley's] that does not instantly tell you something in the heart is grievously to be suspected. . . . I almost think that ideas never recall ideas, any more than leaves in a forest create each other's motion. The breeze it is runs thro' them—it is the soul or state of feeling. If I had said no one idea ever recalls another, I am confident that I could support the assertion.[1]

What first struck Coleridge about Wordsworth's poetry was

> the union of deep feeling with profound thought . . . and above all the original gift of spreading the tone, the atmosphere and with it the depth and height of the ideal world. . . .[2]

And apropos of Shakespeare:

> Images become proofs of original genius only so far as they are modified by a predominant passion.[3]

He speaks of "modifying a series of thoughts by some one predominant thought or feeling." In the preceding chapter, his phrase is "a tone and spirit of unity." [4] In his dramatic criticism, Coleridge likes to speak about the ruling passion of a character (Capulet or Lear), and, like A. W. Schlegel, he replaces the old unities of time, space, and action by a "unity of interest." [5]

If the Wordsworthian formula "emotion recollected in tranquillity" be taken in an approximately hylo-morphic way, one may suppose that "emotion" refers to a kind of poetic content, and tranquil "recollection" to the control or shaping of this content—the formal poetic principle. In the Coleridgean formulas which we have just quoted, however, the emphasis is reversed. Emotion appears, or attempts to appear, as the organizing principle. The difference is crucial. As organization is a form of intelligibility, it is a basic question of poetic theory whether in fact

---

[9] *Letters . . . Later Years*, I, 537.

[1] Letter to Southey, August 7, 1803 (*Letters*, 1895, I, 428).

[2] *Biographia Literaria*, Chapter IV (I, 59).

[3] *Biographia*, Chapter XV (II, 16).

[4] *Biographia*, II, 12.

[5] *Shakespearean Criticism*, ed. T. M. Raysor, I, 50, 212-13, 216; II, 73-4, 131. Cf. *post* Chapter 20, E. A. Poe. Both in the *Biographia* and throughout his Shakespearian criticism Coleridge connects poetical figures and meter closely with strong passion. See *Shakespearean Criticism*, I, 96, 206, 209, 218; II, 78, 103.

emotion as such can become the formal or organizing principle of a poem without the disappearance of the principle.

SUPPLEMENT

                                        Nor should this, perchance,
Pass unrecorded, that I still had loved
The exercise and produce of a toil,
Than analytic industry to me
More pleasing, and whose character I deem
Is more poetic as resembling more
Creative agency. The song would speak
Of that interminable building reared
By observation of affinities
In objects where no brotherhood exists
To passive minds. My seventeenth year was come
And, whether from this habit rooted now
So deeply in my mind, or from excess
In the great social principle of life
Coercing all things into sympathy,
To unorganic natures were transferred
My own enjoyments; or the power of truth
Coming in revelation, did converse
With things that really are; I, at this time,
Saw blessings spread around me like a sea.
Thus while the days flew by, and years passed on,
From Nature and her overflowing soul,
I had received so much, that all my thoughts
Were steeped in feeling; I was only then
Contented, when with bliss ineffable
I felt the sentiment of Being spread
O'er all that moves and all that seemeth still;
O'er all that, lost beyond the reach of thought
And human knowledge, to the human eye
Invisible, yet liveth to the heart;
O'er all that leaps and runs, and shouts and sings,
Or beats the gladsome air; o'er all that glides
Beneath the wave, yea, in the wave itself,
And mighty depth of waters. Wonder not
If high the transport, great the joy I felt,
Communing in this sort through earth and heaven
With every form of creature, as it looked
Towards the Uncreated with a countenance
Of adoration, with an eye of love.
One song they sang, and it was audible,

Most audible, then, when the fleshly ear,
O'ercome by humblest prelude of that strain,
Forgot her functions, and slept undisturbed.

—William Wordsworth, *The Prelude* (1850),
II, 376–418.

Next, in the serpent we approach the source of a group of myths, world-wide, founded on great and common human instincts, respecting which I must note one or two points which bear intimately on all our subject. For it seems to me that the scholars who are at present occupied in interpretation of human myths have most of them forgotten that there are any such things as natural myths; and that the dark sayings of men may be both difficult to read, and not always worth reading; but the dark sayings of nature will probably become clearer for the looking into, and will very certainly be worth reading. And, indeed, all guidance to the right sense of the human and variable myths will probably depend on our first getting at the sense of the natural and invariable ones. The dead hieroglyph may have meant this or that—the living hieroglyph means always the same; but remember, it is just as much a hieroglyph as the other; nay, more—a "sacred or reserved sculpture," a thing with an inner language. The serpent crest of the king's crown, or of the god's, on the pillars of Egypt, is a mystery; but the serpent itself, gliding past the pillar's foot, is it less a mystery? Is there, indeed, no tongue, except the mute forked flash from its lips in that running brook of horror on the ground.

—John Ruskin, *The Queen of the Air*, Lecture II

The fancy sees the outside, and is able to give a portrait of the outside, clear, brilliant, and full of detail.

The imagination sees the heart and inner nature, and makes them felt, but is often obscure, mysterious, and interrupted, in its giving of outer detail. . . . hear Hamlet:

Here hung those lips that I have kissed, I know not how oft.
Where be your gibes now, your gambols, your songs, your flashes of
merriment that were wont to set the table on a roar.

There is the essence of lip, and the full power of the imagination. . . . In Milton it happens, I think, generally . . . that the imagination is mixed and broken with fancy, and so the strength of the imagery is part of iron and part of clay:

Bring the rathe primrose, that forsaken dies,	*Imagination.*
The tufted crow-toe and pale jessamine,	*Nugatory.*
The white pink, and the pansy freaked with jet,	*Fancy.*
The glowing violet,	*Imagination.*
The musk rose, and the well-attired woodbine,	*Fancy,* vulgar.
With cowslips wan that hang the pensive head,	*Imagination.*
And every flower that sad embroidery wears.	*Mixed.*

—John Ruskin, *Modern Painters*, Volume II (1846), Section II,
Chapter iii

Pope starts with an abstraction or a generalization concerning human nature and then looks for a correlative in the world of nature apart from man. His habit of observation of external nature is not detailed and precise; indeed, he thinks it unimportant whether the "facts" of nature which he alleges in his illustrations are really facts or superstitions. The natural history of Pliny and the old bestiaries are as much grist to his mill as the latest papers of the Royal Society. He appears also to me to have at times no clear, detailed, and consistent mental picture of his own figures. To illustrate: in the couplet near the beginning of the *Essay on Man,*

> The latent tracts, the giddy heights explore
> Of all who blindly creep or sightless soar,

he means, I suppose, moles and birds of some sort. . . . he appears to be making use of the ancient and medieval notion that all birds except the eagle blind themselves by looking at the sun. Surely, by Pope's time it was generally known that the high-flying birds are not "sightless"; that on the contrary they have telescopic vision. . . . Or consider a famous passage from the Second Dialogue of the *Epilogue to the Satires* . . . :

> Ye tinsel Insects! whom a Court maintains,
> That count your Beauties only by your Stains,
> Spin all your Cobwebs o'er the Eye of Day!
> The Muse's wing shall brush you all away. 220–23

"Tinsel" to me means "shining or glittering like cheap metal foil," and my natural image of a "tinsel insect" would be some kind of beetle ("this Bug with gilded wings"). But the word can mean no more than "pretentiously showy" and so may not have been intended to identify the kind of insect Pope has in mind. "Stains," however, can hardly mean anything else than moths or butterflies ("Innumerable of stains and splendid dyes, As are the tiger-moth's deep-damask'd wings"). But the trouble with that is that Pope's insects spin cobwebs, which no butterfly or moth can do. I think we shall do Pope no injustice if we conclude that his insects have the combined characteristics of beetles, moths, and spiders, and hence do not belong to any order known to naturalists. . . .

May I remind the reader again that this essay is descriptive, not judicial? Wordsworth is right in maintaining that many of Pope's images are "false" from the naturalistic point of view, but I should be willing to argue that they are appropriate for the kind of poetry Pope was writing. In the metaphor just discussed, a general idea of insect-ness is what Pope wants, and he can produce it better by eclecticism than by sharp individuation.

—Frederick A. Pottle, "The Eye and the Object in the Poetry of Wordsworth," in *Wordsworth, Centenary Studies Presented at Cornell and Princeton Universities,* ed. Gilbert T. Dunklin (Princeton: Princeton University Press, 1951), pp. 34–6. The essay is copyrighted 1950 by Yale University Press.

PEACOCK VS. SHELLEY: RHAPSODIC DIDACTICISM

§ *romantic theory vs. rationalism, Coleridge and Words-worth, hopes for reunion, "false secondary power," Eng-lish empirical and utilitarian philosophy, decline in prestige of poetry (Sprat, Diderot), poetry as "magic," as painting, as insanity (Macaulay), poetry useless (Bentham)—II. Peacock's* Four Ages: *superficially cyclic, assault on Lake School, modern primitivism, bumptious rhetoric, Shelley's retort, "Reason" and "Imagination," echoes of Plato, Shel-ley's early naturalism, later idealism, ontologic and epis-temologic, plastic power of poetry, an enthusiastic celebra-tion (anthology of passages from* Defense*), parallels in* Ode to the West Wind, *romantic* Ars Poetica, *emphasis on moral power, similarity to Sidney, profound difference, Aristotle vs. Kant, imagination the absolute—III. Blake, apocalyptic humanism, a literalist of the imagination, Wordsworth's error, outward creation as dirt—IV. inter-national events, social and economic pressures, popular reversion to classical notions, religious and patriotic re-viewing, contrast to didacticism of revolution, summary: poetic autonomy during the 18th century, hedonistic di-rection, romantic theory more ambiguous, 19th-century dual continuation in England: art for art's sake, new didacticisms, rhapsodic and classical, atmospheric influence of Kant—V. De Quincey, journalistic flourishes on Ger-manic themes, "The Poetry of Pope" (1848), "literature of knowledge," "literature of power," Carlyle, early essays, on poetry and science, enfeeblement of poetry, true poet as visionary,* On Heroes. . . (1840), *from divinity to poet, poet as universal Great Man, generals as poets, Plato's* Ion *again* §

THE GERMAN AND ENGLISH ROMANTICISM WHICH WE HAVE SEEN IN our last two chapters was a late reaction, or a slowly reached culmination of reactionary trends, against the claims of scientific rationalism which had begun to show strength during the latter 17th century. The attitude of protest against scientific encroachment which we illustrated by a passage from Novalis might have been noted too in Wordsworth and Coleridge. The passage in Coleridge's *Aids to Reflection* on the subject of "understanding" associates this lower faculty quite clearly with geometrical, mechanical, and other abstractively scientific modes of thought. In other places Coleridge shared with German Nature philosophers the pious hope that science might some day graduate from its mechanistic bent and become reconcilable with an aesthetic view of the world. Wordsworth's best known thought upon the subject appears in the passage of his 1802 Preface where he laments the contemporary separation of science from everyday life and its consequent repugnance to poetry, but allows himself the hope that at some future day a reunion all round may occur.[1] Wordsworth's allusion, in the *Prelude*, to the abstractive reason as a "false secondary power by which we multiply distinctions" and his lyric phrase "meddling intellect" are also well known.[2] But less well known is the completeness with which he could apply these notions to science—as in his later allusion to the "dull eye, dull and inanimate" of science,[3] and his reported remark that science "waged war with and wished to extinguish Imagination," and that he would much rather be a "superstitious old woman" than a scientist ignorant of theology.[4]

It was not as if Wordsworth and Coleridge were engaged with windmills. True, the scientists and inventors of the age were more intent on making discoveries about electricity and steam than on disparaging poetry. The German metaphysicians and aestheticians radiated an authoritative encouragement in the direction of the poetic endeavor. Deep in the mind of the age, however, and solidly settled lay the heritage of the enlightenment—a good hardpan of complacency about the advances of science and its extensive promises. The ideas of German philosophers which invaded England found the ideas of native utilitarian philosophers like Bentham and James Mill very firmly and respectably in possession.

Exhortations by earlier empirical philosophers about what *ought* to be the effect of science on poetry had passed during the latter 17th and

---

[1] Cf. D. G. James, *Scepticism and Poetry* (London, 1937), p. 167. "Such a transfiguration," says James, "is as undesirable as it is impossible, an absurd fiction created for an eloquent argument."

[2] *Prelude*, II, 214-17; *The Tables Turned*, in *Lyrical Ballads*.

[3] *Excursion* IV, 124-5.

[4] R. P. Graves, *Life of William Hamilton* (Dublin, 1882-89), I, 313. The remark is dated August, 1829.

18th centuries, especially among the French, into announcements, more often with a tone of congratulation than with one of regret, that the effect was in the process of being accomplished.[5] Sprat, for instance, in his *History of the Royal Society*, 1672, had described poetry as a technique of primitive pedagogy, now outmoded. "When the Fabulous Age was past, philosophy took a little more Courage; and ventured to rely upon its own strength, without the assistance of Poetry."[6] Fontenelle, in his *Traité de la Poésie en Général* (written apparently in the last quarter of the 17th century though not published until 1751), was well content to witness the end of the age of fable and the retirement of nature and emotion (the essentials of poetry) before the march of civilization. And Diderot in his *Salon de 1767*:

> Poetry always contains a pinch of untruth. The philosophic spirit gives us the habit of noting this untruth, and goodbye poetic illusion, goodbye poetic effect.[7]

In England the idea that poetry is magic might seem during the 18th century a comfortable one, a sufficient compliment to poetry.

> True Poesy is *magic*, not nature; an effect from causes hidden or unknown.[8]

The extent to which this idea is susceptible of a patronizing interpretation—and at the same time the deliquescence of another 18th-century idea, *poesis* as *pictura*—may be observed in the following remarkable passage occurring near the outset of Macaulay's essay on Milton, 1825.

> Perhaps no person can be a poet, or can even enjoy poetry, without a certain unsoundness of mind, if anything which gives so much pleasure ought to be called unsoundness. . . . By poetry we mean the art of employing words in such a manner as to produce an illusion in the imagination, the art of doing by means of words what the painter does by means of colours. . . . Truth, indeed, is essential to poetry; but it is the truth of madness. The reasonings are just; but the premises are false. After the first

[5] The theme appears of course even in classical times. Cf. Atkins, II, 323, on Plutarch's *Why the Pythia does not now give Oracles in Verse*, 406 E. "So, as language also underwent a change and put off its finery, history descended from its vehicle of versification, and went on foot in prose, whereby the truth was mostly sifted from the fabulous. Philosophy welcomed clearness and teachability in preference to creating amazement, and pursued its investigations through the medium of everyday language" (Plutarch's *Moralia*, trans. F. C. Babbitt, vol. V, London, 1936).

[6] *History of the Royal Society of London* (London, 1722), p. 6.

[7] "*Il y a dans la poésie toujours un peu de mensonge. L'esprit philosophique nous habitue à le discerner; et adieu l'illusion et l'effet*" (*Oeuvres*, ed. Tourneur-Assézat, XI, 136).

[8] Maurice Morgann, *Essay of the Dramatic Character of Sir John Falstaff*, ed. W. A. Gill (London, 1912), p. 70.

suppositions have been made, everything ought to be consistent; but those first suppositions require a degree of credulity which almost amounts to a partial and temporary derangement of the intellect. Hence of all people children are the most imaginative. They abandon themselves without reserve to every illusion. . . . Such is the despotism of the imagination over uncultivated minds.

In a rude state of society men are children with a greater variety of ideas. It is . . . in such a state of society that one may expect to find the poetical temperament in its highest perfection. In an enlightened age there will be much intelligence, much science, much philosophy, abundance of just classification and subtle analysis, abundance of wit and eloquence, abundance of verses, and even of good ones; but little poetry. Men will judge and compare; but they will not create. They will talk about the old poets, and comment on them, and to a certain degree enjoy them. But they will scarcely be able to conceive the effect which poetry produced on their ruder ancestors, the agony, the ecstasy, the plenitude of belief. The Greek Rhapsodists, according to Plato, could scarce recite Homer without falling into convulsions. The Mohawk hardly feels the scalping knife while he shouts his death-song. The power which the ancient bards of Wales and Germany exercised over their auditors seems to modern readers almost miraculous. Such feelings are very rare in a civilized community, and most rare among those who participate most in its improvements. They linger longest amongst the peasantry.

Poetry produces an illusion on the eye of the mind, as a magic lantern produces an illusion on the eye of the body. And, as the magic lantern acts best in a dark room, poetry affects its purpose most completely in a dark age.[9]

Poetry in brief is a combination of painting and insanity. In the same spirit and with even more authority Bentham was plastering the arts with the epithets *anergastic* (no-work-producing) and *aplopathoscopic* (mere-sensation-regarding). "The game of push-pin," he said, "is of equal value with the arts and sciences of music and poetry."[1]

[9] Macaulay's review of Milton's *De Doctrina Christiana*, August, 1825, paragraphs 14–17 (*Essays*, Everyman's Library, 1907, I, 154–5). Cf. Hazlitt's opinion that the "Necessary advances of civilization are unfavorable to the spirit of poetry" (*Works*, ed. P. P. Howe, V, 9) and that the "greatest poets, the best painters, appeared soon after the birth" of the technological arts "and lived in a state of society, which was, in other respects, comparatively barbarous" (*Works*, IV, 161). Cf. "The Age of Brass," *TLS*, August 11, 1950, p. 50.

[1] Alba Warren, *English Poetic Theory 1825–1865* (Princeton, 1950), pp. 66–7.

II

MACAULAY'S too, too solid comment is a serious counterpart to a more notorious, if only whimsical, essay which had appeared five years earlier. This was *The Four Ages of Poetry*, by Shelley's friend the neo-pagan satirical novelist Thomas Love Peacock. Aside from the fact that it is the most sustained account in English of the conflict between poetry and science as it stood in the era of the romantic poets, Peacock's essay is notable for two things: a superficially cyclic account of the history of culture and poetry, and springing out of that a triumphantly unfair assault on contemporary English poetry, especially that of the Lake School. The four ages of poetry in the antique world were, says Peacock, the iron age (when poetry was rude panegyric of rude but real heroes), the golden age from Homer to Sophocles (when poetry was ancestral retrospect—the infancy of history), the silver age of civilization (when poetry was either heroic imitation, the epic of Virgil, or social criticism, the comedy of Aristophanes, the satire of Horace), and the brass age, the second childhood of poetry (a degenerate attempt to regain the primitive). The cause of the steady deterioration of poetry in the ancient world had been the rise of historical and philosophic thinking. First the empire of fact, then the empire of thought had been withdrawn. In the modern world, a second four-phase cycle had occurred: the age of medieval romance, the age of Ariosto and Shakespeare, the age of Dryden and Pope, and now the latest and most ridiculous phase in the history of poetry, that of modern primitivism, the second age of brass, the "patriarchs" of which appear in that "egregious confraternity of rhymesters . . . the lake Poets."

> While the historian and the philosopher are advancing in, and accelerating, the progress of knowledge, the poet is wallowing in the rubbish of departed ignorance, and raking up the ashes of dead savages to find gewgaws and rattles for the grown babies of the age. Mr. Scott digs up the poachers and cattle-stealers of the ancient border. Lord Byron cruises for thieves and pirates on the shores of the Morea and among the Greek islands. Mr. Southey wades through ponderous volumes of travels and old chronicles, from which he carefully selects all that is fake, useless, and absurd, as being essentially poetical; and when he has a commonplace book full of monstrosities, strings them into an epic. Mr. Wordsworth picks up village legends from old women and sextons; and Mr. Coleridge, to the valuable information acquired from similar sources, superadds the dreams of crazy theologians and the mysticism of German metaphysics, and favors

the world with visions in verse, in which the quadruple elements of sexton, old woman, Jeremy Taylor, and Immanuel Kant are harmonized into a delicious poetical compound.

A poet in our times is a semi-barbarian in a civilized community. He lives in the days that are past. His ideas, thoughts, feelings, associations, are all with barbarous manners, obsolete customs, and exploded superstitions. The march of his intellect is like that of a crab, backward.

. . . as if there were no such things in existence as mathematicians, astronomers, chemists, moralists, metaphysicians, historians, politicians, and political economists, who have built into the upper air of intelligence a pyramid, from the summit of which they see the modern Parnassus far beneath them, and, knowing how small a place it occupies in the comprehensiveness of their prospect, smile at the little ambition and the circumscribed perceptions with which the drivelers and mountebanks upon it are contending for the poetical palm and the critical chair.[2]

Peacock's waggishly provocative and bumptious rhetoric gives a vivid enough image of a closing phase in the long process by which the four ages, golden, silver, iron, brazen, of classical myth,[3] were settling into the three (theological, metaphysical, scientific) of 19th-century Comtean positivism. Except for the transvaluation, the accent of rejoicing rather than lament as science is supposed to deprive poetry of its dominion, this evolutionary account of poetic and cultural origins is the same as that which appears in Vico, in the Germans from Herder on, in Rousseau, and in 18th-century British primitivists like Monboddo and John Brown. And substantially the same account appears in the excited retort which Peacock elicited from Shelley.[4]

Shelley's *Defense of Poetry* [5] is not remarkable for metaphysical pre-

[2] Text in P. B. Shelley, *A Defense of Poetry*, ed. A. S. Cook (Boston, 1891), pp. 47–61; available also in *Peacock's Four Ages of Poetry, Shelley's Defense of Poetry, Browning's Essay on Shelley*, ed. H. F. B. Brett-Smith (Oxford, 1945).

[3] Cf. Ovid, *Metamorphoses*, I, 89–127. *Aurea prima sata est aetas. . . . subiit argentea proles, auro deterior. . . . Tertia post illas succesit aënea proles. . . . de duro est ultima ferro.*

[4] Professor Wellek points out that Shelley's immediate source appears to be French. Shelley speaks of the "Celtic" conquerors of the Roman Empire and the predominance of the "Celtic" nations after the fall of Rome. Such a confusion between Celtic and Teutonic occurs in Paul-Henri Mallet, the Swiss propagandist of things Nordic, and among the Celtomanes of the late 18th century, but in English it had been refuted by Bishop Percy, the translator of Mallet (René Wellek, "DeQuincey's Status in the History of Ideas," *PQ*, XXIII, July, 1944, 267).

[5] It was finished and sent to Charles Ollier (the publisher of Peacock's *Four Ages*) by March 20, 1821. With the failure of Ollier's *Miscellany* and then of Hunt's *Liberal*, to which the manuscript had been transferred, it was not published until 1840, in Mrs. Shelley's volume of *Essays, Letters from Abroad, Translations, and*

cision. The opening paragraph expounds a distinction between "Reason" (Coleridgean "Understanding") and "Imagination" (Coleridgean "Secondary Imagination" plus Coleridgean "Reason") along lines so simple as to be almost reminiscent of 17th-century arguments about "judgment" and "wit." [6] The essay contains two or three fairly close echoes of Plato's *Ion* and *Symposium,* both of which Shelley had been recently translating. The most significant of these passages (though Shelley's echo brings over nothing of the jocular spirit by which the words of Socrates in the *Ion* are protected) is perhaps the following:

> The sacred links of that chain have never been entirely disjoined, which descending through the minds of many men is attached to those great minds, whence as from a magnet the invisible effluence is sent forth, which at once connects, animates, and sustains the life of all.[7]

The general course of Shelley's philosophic career had been from French naturalism and necessitarianism (*Queen Mab,*[8] 1813), through a phase of Platonic or ontologic idealism[9] (perhaps more Wordsworthian than actually philosophic—*Mont Blanc* and the *Hymn to Intellectual Beauty,* 1816) to the psychologic or epistemologic idealism (more characteristic of his era) in the *Poems* of 1822.

> Thought
> Alone, and its quick elements, Will, Passion,
> Reason, Imagination, cannot die;
> They are, what that which they regard appears,
> The stuff whence mutability can weave
> All that it hath dominion o'er, worlds, worms,
> Empires, and superstitions.[1]

Fragments. In being edited for the *Liberal,* the essay was pruned of its direct references to Peacock.

[6] Cf. *Defense,* ed. Cook, p. 35. Reason is the "calculating faculty."

[7] "This is the language of Plato" (Shelley, at bottom of folio MS. d1. See A. H. Koszul, *Shelley's Prose in the Bodleian Manuscripts,* London, 1910, p. 88, n. 3). Shelley's translation of the corresponding passage in the *Ion* runs as follows: ". . . it is a divine influence which moves you, like that which resides in the stone called magnet by Euripides, and Heraclea by the people. . . . Do you not perceive that your auditor is the last link of that chain which I have described as held together through the power of the magnet. . . ." (*Essays, Letters* . . . 1840, I, 281). In his Preface to the *Symposium* Shelley says that he translated this dialogue from the 9th to the 17th of July, 1818. The only evidence for the date of his translating the *Ion* is a letter to Peacock, February 15, 1821, in which he alludes to reading it.

[8] Of course not *simply* a naturalistic poem. See *Queen Mab,* VI, 32 ff., where "soul" is the only element.

[9] On the sources of Shelley's Platonism, see James A. Notopoulos, "Shelley and Thomas Taylor," *PMLA,* LI (July, 1936), 502-17; *The Platonism of Shelley* (Durham, 1949), pp. 29-77, Ch. III, "The Direct Platonism of Shelley."

[1] *Hellas,* ll. 795-801. Cf. especially *Epipsychidion* and *Adonais.* In her Preface to the 1840 volumes of Shelley's prose Mrs. Shelley became authority for the notion that "Shelley was a disciple of the Immaterial Philosophy of Berkeley." And it is

It would be difficult to show that any one of these philosophies operates decisively in the poetics of the *Defense*, or that any is altogether absent. Even French naturalism may be said to be represented in the conception of poetic origins to which we have alluded just above. Strains of 18th-century primitivism mingle throughout with a Germanically colored romantic excitement about the immediately spiritual and morally plastic power of the poet.

> The savage (for the savage is to ages what the child is to years) expresses the emotions produced in him by surrounding objects in a similar manner; and language and gesture, together with plastic or pictorial imitation, become the image of the combined effect of those objects and his apprehension of them. Man in society, with all his passions and his pleasures, next becomes the object of the passions and pleasures of man; an additional class of emotions produces an augmented treasure of expression; and language, gesture, and the imitative arts, become at once the representation and the medium, the pencil and the picture, the chisel and the statue, the chord and the harmony.—p. 3

> Their language is vitally metaphorical; that is, it marks the before unapprehended relations of things and perpetuates their apprehension.—p. 4

> But poets, or those who imagine and express this indestructible order, are not only the authors of language and of music, of the dance, and architecture, and statuary, and painting; they are the institutors of laws, and the founders of civil society, and the inventors of the arts of life, and the teachers who draw into a certain propinquity with the beautiful and the true that partial apprehension of the agencies of the invisible world which is called religion.—p. 5

. . .

---

true that Shelley seems to have picked up a good deal of whatever philosophy he had from Sir William Drummond's Berkeleyan handbook of modern philosophy, *Academical Questions* (London, 1805). Yet in one of the few scraps of direct evidence which Shelley left, his fragmentary essay or jottings *On Life*, he follows a Berkeleyan phrase "Nothing exists but as it is perceived" in the same paragraph with the Fichtean monistic pronouncement "The words *I, YOU, THEY*, . . . are merely marks employed to denote the different modifications of the one mind" (*Shelley's Literary and Philosophical Criticism*, ed. John Shawcross, London, 1909, p. 56). See Joseph Barrell, *Shelley and the Thought of his Time* (New Haven, 1947), p. 122, n. 50; cf. pp. 28, 160, 197. And see G. S. Brett, "Shelley's Relation to Berkeley and Drummond," *Studies in English by Members of University College* (Toronto, Canada, 1931); Hans Liedtke, *Shelley durch Berkeley und Drummond beeinflusst* (Greifswald, 1933). Shelley apparently never read Kant. Barrell believes that Drummond taught both Shelley and Peacock (in *Nightmare Abbey*) to scorn the Critical Philosophy. Cf. René Wellek, *Immanuel Kant in England 1793–1838* (Princeton, 1931), pp. 181–2.

> Poetry in a more restricted sense expresses those arrangements of language, and especially metrical language, which are created by that imperial faculty whose throne is curtained within the invisible nature of man. And this springs from the nature itself of language, which is a more direct representation of the actions and passions of our internal being, and is susceptible of more various and delicate combinations, than color, form, or motion, and is more plastic and obedient to the control of that faculty of which it is the creation.—pp. 6–7

What is unique about the essay, and wherein it triumphs, is the overall rhythm of its enthusiasm and the glowing cascade of images which celebrate the magnificent theme.

> Man is an instrument over which a series of external and internal impressions are driven, like the alternations of an ever-changing wind over an Aeolian lyre, which move it by their motion to ever-changing melody.—p. 2

> . . . the mind in creation is as a fading coal, which some invisible influence, like an inconstant wind, awakens to transitory brightness; this power arises from within, like the color of a flower which fades and changes as it is developed, and the conscious portions of our natures are unprophetic either of its approach or its departure. Could this influence be durable in its original purity and force, it is impossible to predict the greatness of the results; but when composition begins, inspiration is already on the decline, and the most glorious poetry that has ever been communicated to the world is probably a feeble shadow of the original conceptions of the poet.—p. 39

> Poetry is the record of the best and happiest moments of the happiest and best minds. We are aware of evanescent visitations of thought and feeling. . . . It is as it were the interpenetration of a diviner nature through our own.—p. 40

> Poetry redeems from decay the visitations of the divinity in man.—p. 41

> It strips the veil of familiarity from the world, and lays bare the naked and sleeping beauty which is the spirit of its forms.
> —p. 42

> The most unfailing herald, companion, and follower of the awakening of a great people to work a beneficial change in opinion or institution, is poetry.—pp. 45–6

Poets are the hierophants of an unapprehended inspiration; the mirrors of the gigantic shadows which futurity casts upon the present; the words which express what they understand not; the trumpets which sing to battle and feel not what they inspire; the influence which is moved not, but moves. Poets are the unacknowledged legislators of the world.—p. 46 [2]

Shelley's *Defense* is written in the vein of his *Ode to the West Wind*, a poem which is a plenary instance of the romantic *Ars Poetica*, where overt enunciation of the cosmic and daemonic poetics is not only supported by imagery but is merged in tumultuous swirls of it and carried in headlong versification.

> Make me thy lyre, even as the forest is:
> What if my leaves are falling like its own!
> The tumult of thy mighty harmonies
>
> Will take from both a deep, autumnal tone,
> Sweet though in sadness.[3] Be thou, Spirit fierce,
> My spirit! Be thou me, impetuous one!
>
> Drive my dead thoughts over the universe
> Like withered leaves to quicken a new birth!
> And, by the incantation of this verse,
>
> Scatter, as from an unextinguished hearth
> Ashes and sparks,[4] my words among mankind!
> Be through my lips to unwakened earth
> The trumpet of a prophecy! [5]

[2] "Earlier laudators of poetry had said the same thing, but it did not mean the same thing; Shelley (to borrow a successful phrase from Mr. Bernard Shaw) was the first, in this tradition of Nature's M.P.'s" (Eliot, *Use of Poetry*, p. 16).

[3] Cf. *Defense*, ed. Cook, p. 35: "Sorrow, terror, anguish, despair itself, are often the chosen expressions of an approximation to the highest good. . . . tragedy delights by affording a shadow of that pleasure which exists in pain. This is the source also of the melancholy which is inseparable from the sweetest melody."

[4] Cf. *Defense*, ed. Cook, p. 11, "a spark of inextinguishable thought"; p. 33, "a spark, a burning atom of inextinguishable thought."

[5] Strains of Shelley's poetic theory, especially in its political and moral aspects, occur throughout his poetry—in *Queen Mab* and *Prometheus*, for instance, in *Mont Blanc*, the *Hymn to Intellectual Beauty*, the *Ode to Naples*, the *Ode to Liberty*. Cf. Melvin Solve, *Shelley, His Theory of Poetry* (Chicago, 1927), pp. 32 ff.

The "undisciplined overflowing of the soul," the "attempt to imitate the untamable wildness" (Preface to Shelley's *History of a Six Weeks Tour*, 1817) which we encounter in this poetry of Shelley's presents a nice problem concerning the formal (i.e., ordered) embodiment of tumult in poetry. As for the genetic question, Shelley speaks against deliberate art in the *Defense* ("I appeal to the greatest poets of the present day whether it is not an error to assert that the finest passages of poetry are produced by labor and study," p. 39). But his record here is not consistent. In the Preface to *Prometheus*, for instance, he confesses that the finest passages of the poem have been the product of laborious revision. Cf. *ante* Chapter 10, p. 181, the relation between genesis and product, ordered or disordered, in the context of Jonson's classical views.

The most definable theoretic tenet in all this looks much like a renewal of one of those practical functions defined in Ciceronian rhetoric, to "persuade" (*persuadere, flectere*). Shelley's emphasis is quite clear.

> A man, to be greatly good, must imagine intensely and comprehensively; he must put himself in the place of another and of many others; the pains and pleasures of his species must become his own. The great instrument of moral good is the imagination; and poetry administers to the effect by acting upon the cause. Poetry enlarges the circumference of the imagination by replenishing it with thoughts of ever new delight. . . . Poetry strengthens the faculty which is the organ of the moral nature of man.—p. 14

> The imagination is enlarged by a sympathy with pains and passions so mighty, that they distend in their conception the capacity of that by which they are conceived; the good affections are strengthened by pity, indignation, terror and sorrow, and an exalted calm is prolonged from the satiety of this high exercise of them into the tumult of familiar life.—p. 18

As Sir Philip Sidney had said, poetry is a feigning "notable images of virtues, vices, or what else, with . . . delightful teaching." Poetry combines the truths of philosophy with the persuasive vividness of history. How, one might be tempted to ask, does Shelley's *Defense* differ from Sidney's? A number of close parallels may be noted. The term "poet," say both Sidney and Shelley, is derived from the verb "to make" (*poiein*); poets are the earliest authors; they are teachers of religion and prophets (or are "called" prophets, as Sidney puts it). Poetry is rhythmic, but rhyming and versification do not make a poet. Aristotle has defined the difference between poetry and history. But great historians and philosophers (the philosopher Plato, for instance) have been poets. A few of Sidney's phrases—"Plannet-like Musick," "low-creeping" objections to poetry—are reborn in Shelley's "planetary music" of poetry and "low-thoughted envy" of contemporaries.[6] The difference between the two *Defenses*, nevertheless, could scarcely be more profound. It lies as deep as the difference between Aristotle and Kant. It amounts to this: that Sidney in all his talking about the teaching and persuading power of poetry would never dream that poetry was teaching or persuading any doctrine which it did not discover in some legislatively competent authority outside itself, either scriptural revelation or ethical philosophy. With Shelley just the opposite is true. When he talks about poetry getting at the motives for good action, touching the heart by enkindling the im-

[6] See *Defense*, ed. Cook, p. xix; ed. H. F. B. Brett-Smith, p. xx.

agination, he may sound for a moment almost pre-Cartesian, forensic, homiletic. The words are, nevertheless, part of an appeal for a vastly creative and autonomous power. There is no appeal to any other authority. The limits of the power come not from outside it but from within. Or, there are no limits. There is no specifically doctrinal commitment. Thus:

> A poet therefore would do ill to embody his own conceptions of right and wrong, which are usually those of his place and time, in his poetical creations, which participate in neither. By this assumption of the inferior office of interpreting the effect, in which perhaps after all he might acquit himself but imperfectly, he would resign a glory in the participation of the cause.
>
> —p. 14

> Milton has so far violated the popular creed (if this shall be judged to be a violation) as to have alleged no superiority of moral virtue to his God over his Devil. And this bold neglect of a direct moral purpose is the most decisive proof of the supremacy of Milton's genius.—p. 31

It is in this spirit that Shelley writes his Preface to *Prometheus* (1820): "Didactic poetry is my abhorrence; nothing can be equally well expressed in prose that is not tedious and supererogatory in verse." [7] The autonomously moral and religious power of poetry stands out much more prominently in Shelley's view than in that of Wordsworth or Coleridge. The Kantian "Reason" which Coleridge, following Fichte and Schelling, improved from a hypothetically constructive to a gnostic faculty does not appear in Shelley's system. The honor conferred upon poetic imagination, though nebulous, is the highest possible. In general import, if not in metaphysical precision, and doubtless not by any direct indebtedness, Shelley's poetic is close to that of Schelling in the "absolute" phase of his idealism and to the mythopoeia of Friedrich Schlegel.

III

ONLY one English poet of this era furnishes a companion theory to Shelley's, and that is Blake, whose apocalyptic humanism, proclaimed in such notations as those collected by modern editors under the title *A Vision of the Last Judgment* and in the gigantic sprawling myths of his

---

[7] A few contrary admissions are to be found in less formal utterances. In a letter of 1811 to Miss Hitchener he said that a large part of *Queen Mab* was overtly didactic. "My opinion is that all poetical beauty ought to be subordinate to the inculcated moral." In a letter of January 1819 he confessed to Peacock: "I consider poetry very subordinate to moral and political science."

canonical prophetic books, can hardly be pressed into literary or even general aesthetic service. Blake connects less with the literary tradition than with cabbalistic and visionary theories of knowledge. He is a "literal realist of imagination" [8] who takes down what is dictated to him by the "Authors in Eternity." [9] Imagination is "the real and eternal World of which even this Vegetable Universe is but a faint shadow." [1] To such an idealism not only the scientific view of nature but nature itself in any simple and external sense is repugnant. Blake, even more than Wordsworth, Coleridge, or Shelley, was an antagonist of scientism—explicitly, repeatedly and contemptuously. Nevertheless, there were moments when he could not quite stomach a nature poet like Wordsworth—or at least not Wordsworth's theory of his own achievement. Blake annotated Wordsworth's 1815 *Poems* thus: "I do not know who wrote these Prefaces: they are very mischievous & direct contrary to Wordsworth's own Practice." "Natural Objects always did & now do weaken, deaden & obliterate Imagination in Me. Wordsworth must know that what he writes valuable is Not to be found in Nature." [2]

> Error is created. Truth is Eternal. Error, or Creation will be Burned up, & then, and not till Then, Truth or Eternity will appear. It is Burnt up the Moment Men cease to behold it. I assert for My Self that I do not behold the outward Creation & that to me it is hindrance & not Action; it is as the dirt upon my feet, No part of Me.[3]

IV

INTERNATIONAL threats (first the republicanism of the French Revolution, then the imperialism of Napoleon) which prevailed during the era of English romantic poetry, and the economic and social troubles internal to England, produced at the level of popular criticism and reviewing, a wholesale resumption of something like the classical didactic mode of criticism, an impassioned appeal to patriotic, religious, and moral norms in the judgment of contemporary poems. "To devote poetry to religious purposes," a reviewer might say, "is to restore it to its original purpose." [4] "It is time," another might say (reviewing Coleridge's *Fears*

[8] W. B. Yeats, "William Blake and His Illustrations to *The Divine Comedy*," in *Essays* (New York, 1924), p. 14.

[9] Blake, *Poetry and Prose*, ed. Geoffrey Keynes (London, 1948), p. 869. ". . . a Grand Poem. I may praise it since I dare not pretend to be any other than the secretary; the Authors are in Eternity" (letter to Thomas Butts, July 6, 1803).

[1] *Jerusalem IV, To the Christians*, in *Poetry and Prose*, 1948, p. 535.

[2] *Poetry and Prose*, 1948, pp. 821-2.

[3] *A Vision of the Last Judgment*, in *Poetry and Prose*, 1948, pp. 651-2.

[4] William S. Ward, "Some Aspects of the Conservative Attitude Toward Poetry in English Criticism 1798–1800," *PMLA*, LX (June, 1945), 386–98. The quotation is from *The Christian's Pocket Magazine*, December, 1819.

in Solitude, during the Alarm of Invasion), "to enthrone reason on the summit of Parnassus; and make poetry the strengthener as well as the enlivener of the intellect;—the energetic instructor as well as the enchanting amuser of mankind." [5] Others might re-activate neo-classic scruples about the relation between instruction and pleasure.

> Poetry has been commonly supposed, indeed, to aim more at the gratification than the instruction of its votaries, and to have for its end rather delight than improvement; but it has not, we think, been sufficiently considered, that its power of delighting is founded chiefly on its moral energies.[6]

The vocabulary of these avowals might sometimes sound like an echo from the ranges of liberal criticism, whose peaks we have examined in Shelley and Blake. There was, however, little consonance between the two. Popular criticism always had in mind a didacticism and exhortation in the service of the tradition—the Church, the state, and the mores. The didacticism of Shelley and Blake, as was necessary for a theory of poetic creativity which had outrun all traditional theological associations, was a didacticism of revolution.

The defence of poetry against the claims of scientism had been during the 18th century an exploratory action, feeling its way toward the formulation of some kind of poetic autonomy. If scientific philosophy maintained that poetic statements did not satisfy scientific criteria, the answer was to be that poetry proceeded according to other criteria. In some way poetry proceeded according to its own criteria. And these were for the most part aligned with principles of sensory ("imaginative") and emotive pleasure. The autonomy was—at least implicitly—hedonistic. The later romantic development in the theory of creative "imagination" afforded, however, a more complex and ambiguous base from which the English defence of poetry during the 19th century could proceed. For one thing, the defence might and did continue along the line of an autonomy oriented toward pleasure—art for art's sake—a theme which we shall notice in a later chapter. But it might also, as we have just been seeing, wax into the assertion of a new, and autonomous, didacticism (more or less revolutionary). And this didacticism had at least two main phases, the rhapsodic (Shelleyan) and a later more calmly classical and cognitive (the Arnoldian—to be seen in our next chapter). The dual defence of poetry during the 19th century—the hedonistically autonomic, and the didactically autonomic—was a thoroughly plausible outcome and illustration of the ambivalent poise achieved in the continental defence of poetry by the end of the 18th century and taken over

---

[5] Ward, *loc. cit.*, p. 392, quoting *Monthly Review, or Literary Journal*, May, 1799.
  [6] Ward, *loc. cit.*, p. 395, quoting *Edinburgh Review*, November, 1820.

by Coleridge and Wordsworth. Kant's beautiful symbols of moral value, his purposiveness without purpose, his judgment by feeling, are a sufficient promise of the whole development. We are speaking of Kant as typical of the thought of an era. Only the vaguest and most atmospheric acquaintance with German ideas (in the case of Shelley a direct dash of Fichte, a general modern philosophical education in Drummond's *Academical Questions*), an awareness of the ideas of Coleridge, or a feeling of sympathy with the neo-Platonic tradition, would be the genetic requirement for a given English literary man's participation in the movement. "Bliss was it in that dawn to be alive."

V

WE MOVE toward a conclusion of this chapter and advance chronologically in the 19th century with quotations from two other authors, both more distinguished for general literary power than for clean lines in literary theory. Coleridge's friend De Quincey was given to ostentatious hints about his understanding of the metaphysics of Kant and performed various journalistic flourishes on the theme of German romantic literature and Germanic neo-Hellenism.[7] His essay of 1848 in the *North British Review* on Alexander Pope contains one of his chief claims to be remembered as a literary theorist—his distinction between a "literature of knowledge" and a "literature of power."

> The function of the first is to *teach;* the function of the second is to *move;* the first is a rudder, the second an oar or a sail. The first speaks to the mere discursive understanding; the second speaks ultimately, it may happen, to the higher understanding or reason, but always through affections of pleasure and sympathy. Remotely, it may travel towards an object seated in what Lord Bacon calls "dry light";—but proximately it does and must operate—else it ceases to be a literature of power—on and through that *humid* light which clothes itself in the mists and glittering iris of human passions, desires, and genial emotions. . . . there is a rarer thing than truth,—namely *power*, or deep sympathy with truth.

> What do you learn from a cookery-book? Something new, something that you did not know before, in every paragraph. But would you therefore put the wretched cookery-book on a

---

[7] René Wellek, "De Quincey's Status in the History of Ideas," *PQ*, XXIII (January, 1944), 250–5, 256 ff. For more about De Quincey's literary aesthetics, see Sigmund K. Proctor, *Thomas De Quincey's Theory of Literature* (Ann Arbor, 1943); John E. Jordan, *Thomas De Quincey Literary Critic* (Berkeley, California, 1952).

higher level of estimation than the divine poem? What you owe to Milton is not any knowledge, of which a million separate items are still but a million of advancing steps on the same earthly level; what you owe is *power*,—that is, exercise and expansion to your own latent capacity of sympathy with the infinite, where every pulse and each separate influx is a step upwards, a step ascending upon a Jacob's ladder from earth to mysterious altitudes above the earth.

> It is certain that, were it not for the literature of power, . . . ideals would often remain amongst us as mere arid notional forms; whereas, by the creative forces of man put forth in literature, they gain a vernal life of restoration, and germinate into vital activities. The commonest novel, by moving in alliance with human fears and hopes, with human instincts of wrong and right, sustains and quickens those affections. Calling them into action, it rescues them from torpor. And hence the preëminency over all authors that merely *teach*, of the meanest that moves, or that teaches, if at all, indirectly by moving.[8]

The throbbing utterance, the allusion to "discursive understanding" and the "higher understanding or reason," put this on the grand level of romantic theory. It sounds sufficiently like the emotive didacticism of Shelley. At the same time if we read it in the context of Coleridge's religious influence upon De Quincey and De Quincey's theocratic social views united with Tory politics in the belief that the British Empire was the torch-bearer of Christian progress,[9] the passage may sound not unreconcilable with the moralistic popular reviewing which we have quoted from the era of thirty to fifty years before.

In his early miscellaneous essays, Thomas Carlyle was one of the most powerful and most accurate transmitters of German aesthetic philosophy to England. His program included energetic announcements of the antagonism between poetry and science and of the paramount claim which poetry laid to all the truth that mattered. The "polish and languor," the "external glitter and internal vacuity," of 18th-century literature he blamed squarely on the analytic science of the era. He noted a continuing prevalence of the enfeeblement even in his own day.

> We enjoy, we see nothing by direct vision; but only by reflection, and in anatomical dismemberment. Like Sir Hudibras, for every Why we must have a Wherefore. We have our little *theory* on all human and divine things. Poetry, the workings of genius itself, which in all times, with one or another meaning,

[8] Alden, pp. 340–3. Twenty-five years earlier De Quincey had made the same distinction in his *Letters to a Young Man.*

[9] Wellek, *loc. cit.,* pp. 253–4.

has been called Inspiration, and held to be mysterious and in-
scrutable, is no longer without its scientific exposition. The
building of the lofty rhyme is like any other masonry or brick-
laying: we have theories of its rise, height, decline and fall,—
which latter, it would seem, is now near, among all peoples.[1]

The power of the true poet, whenever in history it did appear, was quite
another thing.

> The true Poet is ever, as of old, the Seer; whose eye has been
> gifted to discern the godlike Mystery of God's Universe, and
> decipher some new lines of its celestial writing; we can still call
> him a *Vates* and Seer; for he *sees* into this greatest of secrets,
> "the open secret"; hidden things become clear; how the Future
> (both resting on Eternity) is but another phasis of the Present:
> thereby are his words in very truth prophetic; what he has
> spoken shall be done.[2]

Carlyle's lectures *On Heroes, Hero-Worship, and the Heroic in History* were delivered in May, 1840. The diminishing sequence of roles
assigned to the hero in the six lectures—The Hero as Divinity, as
Prophet, as Poet, as Priest, as Man of Letters, as King—represents both
Carlyle's assurance in man's heroic destiny and at the same time a degree
of acquiescence in the philosophy of decline, in the view that civilized
advance means the decay of genius and greatness.[3] The poet is not the
prophet, not the divinity. The opening of the lecture on the Hero as
Poet surveys several phases in the power of the spirit to triumph against
science.

> The Hero as Divinity, the Hero as Prophet, are productions of
> old ages; not to be repeated in the new. They presuppose a cer-
> tain rudeness of conception, which the progress of mere scien-
> tific knowledge put an end to. There needs to be, as it were, a
> world vacant, or almost vacant of scientific forms, if men in
> their loving wonder are to fancy their fellow-man either a god
> or one speaking with the voice of a god. Divinity and Prophet
> are past. We are now to see our Hero in the less ambitious, but
> also less questionable, character of Poet; a character which does

[1] "Signs of the Times," in *Works* (1896–99), XXVII, 76. See Alba Warren,
pp. 79–84.

[2] "Death of Goethe," *Works*, XXVII, 377. Cf. René Wellek, *Immanuel Kant in
England* (Princeton, 1931), pp. 183–202.

[3] See René Wellek, "Carlyle and the Philosophy of History," *PQ*, XXIII (January, 1944), 55–76, for the uncertain kind of resemblance which obtains between
Carlyle's views and the several forms of historical method available in Germany,
France, or England at that day. Wellek argues that Carlyle's ethical normalism and
divinatory impulsiveness are closer to Germanic forms of "historism" and literary
nationalism than to French naturalistic and sociological trends.

not pass. The Poet is a heroic figure belonging to all ages; whom all ages possess, when once he is produced, whom the newest age as the oldest may produce;—and will produce, always when Nature pleases. Let Nature send a Hero-soul; in no age is it other than possible that he may be shaped into a Poet.

But:

I confess, I have no notion of a truly great man that could not be *all* sorts of men. The Poet who could merely sit on a chair, and compose stanzas, would never make a stanza worth much. He could not sing the Heroic warrior, unless he himself were at least a Heroic warrior too. I fancy there is in him the Politician, the Thinker, Legislator, Philosopher;—in one or the other degree, he could have been, he is all these. So too I cannot understand how a Mirabeau, with that great glowing heart, with the fire that was in it, with the bursting tears that were in it, could not have written verses, tragedies, poems, and touched all hearts in that way, had his course of life and education led him thitherward. The grand fundamental character is that of Great Man; that the man be great. Napoleon has words in him which are like Austerlitz Battles. Louis Fourteenth's Marshals are a kind of poetical men withal; the things Turenne says are full of sagacity and geniality, like sayings of Samuel Johnson.

Admitting not so much as Macaulay in his essay on Milton (that poetry flourishes best in a dark age), claiming not so much as Shelley in his *Defense* (that poets actually perform as legislators), Carlyle is shrewd enough to see the age-old paradox with which he is saddled, energetic enough to bounce it off as of small consequence. "Louis Fourteenth's Marshals are a kind of poetical men withal." On the high tide of Carlyle's plausible eloquence, an ancient moment in the history of the quarrel between rhapsode and dialectician is re-enacted with the victory reversed. One of the passages of Shelley's *Defense* most strongly reminiscent of Plato's *Ion* is that in which the Christian and chivalric poets of the early Middle Ages are credited with having created "forms of opinion and action . . . which, copied into the imaginations of men, became as generals to the bewildered armies of their thoughts." [4] In Plato's *Ion*, the rhapsode, after being pushed gradually into a corner with admissions that he was unfitted to discourse on such professional topics as medicine, charioteering, fishing, and piloting, gave utterance at the very last, under extreme pressure of the Socratic dialectical skill, to the desperate opinion that he might after all have been a successful general of the armies.

[4] *Defense*, ed. Cook, p. 25.

SUPPLEMENT

For the tides are the life of God in the ocean, and he sends his angel to trouble the great DEEP.

For he hath fixed the earth upon arches & pillars, and the flames of hell flow under it.

For the grosser the particles the nearer to the sink, & the nearer to purity, the quicker the gravitation.

For MATTER is the dust of the Earth, every atom of which is the life.

For MOTION is as the quantity of life direct, & that which hath not motion, is resistance.

For Resistance is not of GOD, but he—hath built his works upon it.

For the Centripetal and Centrifugal forces are GOD SUSTAINING and DIRECTING.

For Elasticity is the temper of matter to recover its place with vehemence.

For Attraction is the earning of parts, which have a similitude in the life.

For the Life of God is in the Loadstone, and there is a magnet, which pointeth due EAST.

For FRICTION is inevitable because the Universe is FULL of God's works.
For the PERPETUAL MOTION is in all the works of Almighty GOD.

For Newton nevertheless is more of error than of the truth, but I am of the WORD of GOD.

> —Christopher Smart, *Jubilate Agno*, p. IX, ll. 7–16, 35–6, 45 (written in 1759), quoted from *Rejoice in the Lamb, A Song from Bedlam*, ed. William Force Stead (London, 1939), pp. 83–6, by permission of the editor and Jonathan Cape Limited

His [Thomas Taylor's] first three books, *The Mystical Initiations* (translations of the Orphic hymns, 1787), *Concerning the Beautiful* (a translation from Plotinus, 1787), and *The Philosophical and Mathematical Commentaries of Proclus* (two volumes, 1788–89), provoked immediate criticism in the *Monthly Review* and were apparently widely discussed. . . . A volume containing *The Cratylus, Phaedo, Parmenides and Timaeus* of Plato (1793), following hard upon the *Phaedrus* (1792), was hailed by a writer in the *Analytical Review* as a good beginning toward "a grand *desideratum* in English literature," the translation of all Plato's works. Taylor's efforts, however, were turned for the moment to other tasks, of which the most important were translations of Pausanias's *Description of Greece* (1794), *Five Books of Plotinus* (1794), and *The Fable of Cupid and Psyche* by Apuleius (1795).

These many books, filled as they all were with neo-Platonic ideas, gained Taylor a wide notoriety, if not esteem. For he was militant in thrusting his mystical, polytheistic neo-Platonism before the eyes of a sober and unsympathetic eighteenth-century audience, who in turn ridiculed him as an insane fanatic. The materialism of the age and the concern of classical scholarship at the time with merely textual criticism aroused in Taylor a scorn which he freely expressed. In an eloquent plea for the study of Platonism, appended to his translation of the Orphic hymns, he called on his countrymen to resist these illiberal influences:

> The waters of Thames, heavy laden with the wealth of merchandize, and sonorous with the din of trade, may devolve abundance in a golden tide; but we must remember that the Daemon of commerce is at the same time advancing with giant strides, to trample on the most liberal pursuits, and is preparing with his extended savage arm, to crush the votaries of truth, and depopulate the divine retreats of philosophy. Rise then ye liberal few, and vindicate the dignity of ancient wisdom. Bring truth from her silent and sacred concealments, and vigorously repel the growing empire of barbaric taste; which bids fair to extinguish the celestial fire of philosophy in the frigid embraces of philology, and to bury the divine light of mind, in the sordid gloom of sense.—*The Mystical Initiations*, London, 1787, p. 226

This blunt indictment of contemporary civilization did not increase Taylor's popularity, though it attracted notice. Nor did the remedy which he proposed impress the eighteenth century with his sanity, though it made him famous. If London were found too far sunk in "barbarous ignorance," Taylor advised, the "liberal few" should fly to

> the regions of intellect, those fortunate islands of truth, where . . . we may find a retreat from the storms and tempests of a corporeal life. Let us build for ourselves the raft of virtue, and departing from this region of sense, like Ulysses from the charms of Calypso, direct our course by the light of ideas, those bright intellectual stars, through the dark ocean of a material nature, until we arrive at our father's land. For there having divested ourselves of the torn garments of mortality, as much as our union with body will permit, we may resume our natural appearance; and may each of us at length, recover the ruined empire of his soul.—*The Mystical Initiations*, pp. 226–7

—Frank B. Evans III, "Thomas Taylor, Platonist of the Romantic Period," *PMLA*, LV (December, 1940), 1067–8, by permission of the Modern Language Association of America

THE ARNOLDIAN PROPHECY

§ *feeling and image c. 1795, the lyric norm, a French incident: Hugo's* Cromwell *and* Hernani, Coleridge *and Poe on the long poem, Mill on mere stories, Newman's Evangelical critique of Aristotle, Keble's* Praelectiones, *pre-Freudian intimations, "spasmodic" poetry, Aytoun, Tennyson—II. Arnold's brusque resistance, Preface to 1853, all depends on the subject, the "grand style," bad influence of Shakespeare on Keats—III. an altered classicism, Essays, First Series, continental sources, Joubert (clarity and truth), Heine (Philistinism), British parochialism,* The Modern Element in Literature, *"Wragg is in custody,"* The Literary Influence of Academies, *English proposals for linguistic authority, Samuel Johnson, The Oxford Dictionary, Arnold's suave anachronism—IV. English violence and individualism, French intelligence and form, poetry and "natural magic,"* On the Study of Celtic Literature, *"moral profundity," vivid disparagement of Shelley, Byron, Coleridge, Keats,* On Translating Homer, *against Teutonizing, "the object as in itself it really is,"* The Study of Poetry, *"truth and high seriousness"—V. difficulties with Arnold: 1. shift from substance to norm of style, "touchstones," 2. high seriousness, mistrust of "lighter kinds of poetry," what Chaucer lacks, Gray patronized, Burns merely ironic, 3. misunderstanding of anachronism,* Merope, *literal view of translating, 4. poetry a "criticism of life," detachment vs. application, "laws of poetic truth and poetic beauty"—VI. poetry to replace religion and philosophy,* Culture and Anarchy, *"sweetness and light,"* Literature and Science, *a new kind of emotivism—VII. other idealist voices, Emerson, James, "The Genteel Tradition," the new humanism in America, P. E. More, humanism with religion, Irving Babbitt, "insight" and "inner check"* §

EELING AND IMAGE CAME THROUGH THE EIGHTEENTH CENTURY, AS WE
have seen, in close liaison, and they enjoyed at the dawn of the new
era a high estate together. Feeling was somewhat indiscriminately
treated as either something that welled up in the poet himself or (it
made little difference) something that was discernible in the poem or in
its images. Among the poetic genres, lyric had moved into the normative
place. Or the broader and simpler concept of "poem" (or "poetry," in
the soul of the poet) was the norm—it mattered not what "order of
composition" the poet elected. The notion of untutored, and hence genuine, utterance was not likely to be far absent from poetic discussion.
Let us re-focus momentarily on the situation about 1795 by quoting a
letter from a poetess, "The Swan of Lichfield," Anna Seward.

> Our very peasants show that the seeds of poetry exist in the
> rude soil of their minds. Awaken their passions or excite their
> wonder, and you will often hear them speaking in metaphor,
> which is the poetic essence.[1]

Not that anybody said much directly against the classic fable, the story,
the structural base of the long poem, but at the same time not much was
urged in favor of that element.[2] Poetic theory had passed in the course
of the centuries from a classic or Aristotelian focus on drama, through
a heroic focus on epic (and then an implicit or hidden focus on satire
and burlesque) to the romantic focus on lyric, the songlike personal
expression, the feeling centered in the image. The romantic age as the
age of lyric is a well enough recognized phenomenon—especially in England.

We have already observed certain lyrist features of the German high
theorizing. In France during the 1820's occurred an incident in the history of dramatic literature which may perhaps be relevantly mentioned
in this context. A classically regulated French drama, for reasons generated out of both revolutionary republicanism and Napoleonic and

---

[1] *Letters of Anna Seward* (Edinburgh, 1811), III, 320, October 1, 1793, quoted
by Norman Maclean, "From Action to Image: Theories of the Lyric in the Eighteenth Century," in Crane, *Critics and Criticism*, p. 460.

[2] Cf. Donald M. Foerster, "The Critical Attack upon the Epic in the English
Romantic Movement," *PMLA*, LXIX (1954), 432-47. "Thus, a writer in the *Reflector*
elevates Ferdusi almost to Homer's level despite the fact that the Persian poet had
paid little attention to those 'minuter excellences' of the epic, the fable and the three
unities; and in the same breath that he says that *Paradise Regained* is really 'a drama
of primal simplicity' and the *Odyssey* is not 'a legitimate epic,' Hallam calls it pure
'pedantry' to speak of the *Orlando Furioso* as a romance rather than an epic simply
because it lacks a principal hero and a continuity of action. . . . A particular form
was not often required; nor did an 'epic' seem to need a great action or a single action,
a principal hero or a mighty hero, a race of gods or any other invisible agency. All
that was demanded by many critics was a narrative thread which one could detect
here and there in a poem of some length" (pp. 435-6).

Bourbon conservatism, had kept up a show of authority for much longer than might now seem understandable in the general retrospect of merely literary history. The revolt came with Hugo's Preface to *Cromwell*, 1827, and with *Hernani*, his first acted play, 1830. This was, to be sure, not officially a lyric movement. But it introduced not only a new taste for enjambed Alexandrines, for a diction coextensive with greater areas of life, and for a juxtaposition of the grotesque with the sublime, but, in part to accommodate the latter ideal, a taste for a profusion of sub-plot and extra incident and for incidentally and lyrically developed characters. The movement was away from the tighter Aristotelian structure. If an audience expected to enjoy anything richer than the traditional pseudo-Racinian austerity, argued Hugo in his Preface to *Cromwell*, the new romantic poet would have to hold the stage for somewhat longer than two hours. He would need no less than the whole evening (all the time usually given to the farce and comic opera which came after the tragedy to relieve it). But such a poet would give a money's worth of character portrayal (an entire hero, with all his genius, beliefs, conflicting passions, tastes, habits, and the crowd of figures who mill around him) as well as the panorama of a whole struggling epoch (its customs, laws, manners, spirit, insights, superstitions, happenings, and people). A gigantic spectacle! (*On conçoit qu'un pareil tableau sera gigantesque.*) A stage crowded with figures of all sizes and shapes. (*Il y aura foule dans le drame.*) [3] One conceives too that an art formed on the principle of a vast assemblage of diversely interesting parts will tend to promote a certain looseness of relationship among such parts and in the parts themselves a certain extravagance of local coloring.

"A poem of any length," Coleridge had said, "neither can be, or ought to be, all poetry." [4] He was echoed about thirty years later by Poe in words which have become even better known: "I hold that a long poem does not exist. I maintain that the phrase, 'a long poem,' is simply a flat contradiction in terms." [5] A modern editor of Poe has paid him an accurate compliment in saying that this pronouncement was "essentially a demand that the poets of his time be themselves and admit that epic themes . . . did not in fact excite their poetic faculties." "What really interested them were emotions of melancholy, nostalgia, puzzled yearning, and the like that could find their proper expression . . . in lyrics of moderate length." [6] In an earlier chapter we have noted J. S. Mill's inheritance of the associational doctrine of feeling—which in full the-

---

[3] Victor Hugo, *"Préface de Cromwell" and "Hernani,"* ed. John R. Effinger, Jr. (Chicago, 1900), pp. 98–9, near the end of the *Préface*.

[4] *Biographia Literaria*, Chapter XIV (ed. Shawcross, II, 11).

[5] *The Poetic Principle*, first paragraph.

[6] W. H. Auden, *Edgar Allan Poe, Selected Prose and Poetry* (New York, 1950), p. xii.

oretical consciousness he adopted as alternative to the utilitarian and scientific rigors of his early training. And so:

> Lyric poetry, as it was the earliest kind, is also, if the view we are now taking of poetry be correct, more eminently and peculiarly poetry than any other: it is the poetry most natural to a really poetic temperament, and least capable of being successfully imitated by one not so endowed by nature.[7]

Mill distinguished [lyric] poetry from certain other and less intense kinds of emotive writing, novels and dramas, mere stories or *imitations* of life. These made an appeal to immature and shallow minds.[8]

A particularly instructive instance in the history of lyric feeling is that of John Henry Newman when he delivers his opinion in an early essay (1829) on no less a topic than Aristotle's *Poetics*.[9] Newman's Evangelical background puts him comfortably in possession of the same attitudes that Mill had to arrive at by struggle. He observes that Aristotle admires *Oedipus the King* for its plot and structure. That is to say, Aristotle conceives a play as "an exhibition of ingenious workmanship." But true poetry is spontaneous expression, the "free and unfettered effusion of genius." Newman goes to Greek drama in order to "listen to harmonious and majestic language, to the voices of sorrow, joy, compassion, or religious emotion,—to the animated odes of the chorus."

> A word has a power to convey a world of information to the imagination, and to act as a spell upon the feelings; there is no need of sustained fiction, often no room for it.

Newman's argument is a plenary participation in the Longinian double antithesis. The difference between plot and lyric passages is closely tied up with the difference between cold calculation on the part of the author and spontaneous effusion. Within a few years after his essay on poetry, Newman, moving along lines quite different from those of his literary criticism, had reached the opinion that the Evangelicals had landed Protestantism in a bondage to the "feelings." "His many attacks on the Evangelical system," observes a modern commentator, "are an attempt to rescue Evangelicals from a bondage he was willing to keep poets in."[1]

Newman's friend John Keble, Professor of Poetry at Oxford from

---

[7] "Thought in Poetry and its Varieties," in *Dissertations and Discussions* (London, 1859), I, 85. First published in 1832. Cf. *ante*, p. 308.

[8] Cf. Alba Warren, p. 71. Mill parallels Wordsworth's protest against "gross and violent stimulants," the melodrama of storm-and-stress novels.

[9] "Poetry with Reference to Aristotle's Poetics" appeared in the *London Review*, January, 1829. Cf. Alba Warren, pp. 35–45.

[1] Geoffrey Tillotson, "Newman's Essay on Poetry," in *Perspectives of Criticism*, ed. Harry Levin (Cambridge, Mass., 1950), pp. 161–195.

1831 to 1841, is a priestly poet and theorist whose *Praelectiones Academicae*, collected and published in 1844, turn on the same mistrust of "art," "execution," external medium, and plot construction, the same regard for the poet's spontaneous outburst of inmost feeling. The epigraph to his printed lectures is the image of the rhapsode and the magnetic ring from the *Ion* of Plato. Keble's emotivism invites a specially curious inspection in that it combines Aristotelian cathartic reminiscences with pre-Freudian intimations. He conceives poetry as an indirect strategy, an expression under "certain veils and disguises," whereby sensitive distraught souls may without blame find release from suffering. "It is the function of Poetry to facilitate, yet without prejudice to modest reserve, the expression of glowing motion." [2] The subtitle of his lectures is *De Poeticae Vi Medica*.

A distinct correlation with such minor but characteristic theorizing of the early Victorian era may be observed in the school of violently emotive and pseudo-Elizabethan dramatizing which erupted in the 1840's and was extinguished in the parody by W. E. Aytoun, *Firmilian: A "Spasmodic" Tragedy*, in 1854. Tennyson's *Maud* (1855), a "monodrama" of cloudy "madness," swirling around an all but undescribed action, participates in the spasmodic phase of English poetry. Matthew Arnold's two earliest volumes of poems, in 1849 and 1852, were touched by the same spirit and suffered some disadvantage in competing with it. [3]

II

ARNOLD emerges suddenly, however, the most imposing figure in English mid-Victorian criticism, not as a part of the lyric-spasmodic movement, but in a brusque classical resistance to it. The Preface to his *Poems* of 1853, [4] pitched in the high and confident tone of which he was to become increasingly master, announces the rationale of a valiant negative gesture, that of omitting from the volume of 1853 the long poem which gave the volume of 1852 its title, *Empedocles on Aetna*. Not because it is a poem on an ancient subject, says Arnold, though many may think this a sufficient reason. But because the dark emotions of the protagonist lead to no outcome. "Suffering finds no vent in action." The situation is

---

[2] *Keble's Lectures on Poetry 1832–1841*, trans. E. K. Francis (Oxford, 1912), I, 19–24, 36. See Alba Warren, pp. 46–9; Meyer Abrams, pp. 145–8.

[3] See Arthur Hugh Clough, in the *North American Review*, LXXVII (July, 1853), 4, anonymously reviewing Arnold's *Strayed Reveler* and *Empedocles* along with other volumes of verse including the Glasgow "mechanic" Alexander Smith's spasmodic *Life Drama*. Cf. Lionel Trilling, *Matthew Arnold* (New York, 1939), pp. 146 ff.

[4] The volume appeared in October.

monotonous and morbid. (Empedocles, it will be remembered, concludes his suffering by jumping into Aetna.) It is an ancient story, but it exhibits a modern and merely emotive development. The historical figure Empedocles himself is not a good hero for a poem, not a great example of Greek thought and feeling.

> Into the feelings of a man so situated there entered much that we are accustomed to consider as exclusively modern; . . . The calm, the cheerfulness, the disinterested objectivity have disappeared: the dialogue of the mind with itself has commenced; modern problems have presented themselves; we hear already the doubts, we witness the discouragement, of Hamlet and of Faust.

There is some wavering, some slithering of logic in Arnold's plea. In reaction against recent notions that "the poet must leave the exhausted past," [5] against "spasmodic" champions of "present import," "interest," and "novelty," and no less against the whole contemporary concept of "an era of progress, an age commissioned to carry out the great ideas of industrial development and social amelioration," Arnold wants to say that the "modernness or antiquity of an action . . . has nothing to do with its fitness for poetical representation." "The date of an action . . . signifies nothing." But it comes out pretty clearly before he is done that the great, "permanently" interesting actions, those that involve "permanent problems" and excite the "permanent passions," are all or nearly all to be found in the grand mythic repertories with which Greek epic and tragic writers were concerned. These endure. The occurrences of modern life are transitory. They have an immediate interest, but it is meretricious.

> The Greeks felt, no doubt, with their exquisite sagacity of taste, that an action of present times was too near them, too much mixed up with what was accidental and passing, to form a sufficiently grand, detached, and self-subsistent object for a tragic poem.

Arnold's Preface is an impressive exercise of hauteur at the expense of the thesis that literature has to be up to date.

But even more radically, the Preface is a countercheck quarrelsome to the prevailing lyric trend, a re-affirmation of the classic norm of the

---

[5] The complaint had been argued more picturesquely during the 17th-century quarrel of the ancients and the moderns. Cowley refers to "The cold-meats of the Ancients," "the threadbare tales of Thebes and Troy" (Preface to *Poems*, 1656; cf. Atkins, II, 173). In our own century the theme is well known. "The more progressive modern poets . . . discard not only archaic diction but also shop-worn subjects of past history or legend, which have been through the centuries a treasure-trove for the second-rate" (Harriet Monroe, ed. *The New Poetry, An Anthology*, New York 1927, p. vi).

fable. The "theory and practice alike" of the ancients, the "admirable treatise of Aristotle, and the unrivalled works of their poets, exclaim with a thousand tongues":

> 'All depends upon the subject; choose a fitting action, penetrate yourself with the feeling of its situations; this done, everything else will follow.'

"They regarded the whole; we regard the parts. With them, the action predominated over the expression of it." Hence the admirably severe style—the "grand style"—of the Greeks. And hence the dangerous influence on modern English poets of Shakespeare, a writer who had, along with his skill in managing "action," "situation," and "character," a further great gift, which, alas! could and did lead even him "astray." That was his power of "expression." "Here has been the mischief." Our modern poets, Keats and others, have been imitating the "attractive accessories," the "richness of imagery," not the central shaping power, the architecture.[6]

> We have poems which seem to exist merely for the sake of single lines and passages; not for the sake of producing any total impression. We have critics who seem to direct their attention merely to detached expressions, to the language about the action, not to the action itself.[7]

III

THE moderns, one might reflect, had been having it all their own way for nearly a century. It was time somebody spoke up for the ancients,

---

[6] A year before Arnold's Preface of 1853, a lesser if more systematic theorist, Eneas S. Dallas, had published his *Poetics: An Essay on Poetry*, containing a discussion of drama which reveals far more starkly than Arnold's plausibly written argument some of the commitments of a pantomimic regard for the element of dramatic action. "For looking at dramatic speeches in their true light, as the means of imitating character and life, not as a means of as it were by slanting mirrors throwing opinions among an audience, and far less as a running commentary on the whole play, it will be seen that if they convey anything different in kind from what may be conveyed, however feebly, by dumb show, they swerve from dramatic fitness, or at least are more than dramatic." Eneas S. Dallas, *Poetics: An Essay on Poetry* (1852), Book III, pp. 131–2. Cf. Alba Warren, pp. 137–8, and p. 139. Warren neatly locates the Dallas-Arnold fallacy under the rubric "assimilation of the drama to the visual arts."

[7] Arnold's tone becomes distinctly Augustan. "This over-curiousness of expression is indeed but the excessive employment of a wonderful gift—of the power of saying a thing in a happier way than any other man. Nevertheless, it is carried so far that one understands what M. Guizot meant, when he said that Shakespeare appears in his language to have tried all styles except that of simplicity. He has not the severe and scrupulous self-restraint of the ancients, partly no doubt, because he had a far less cultivated and exacting audience. . . . He is therefore a less safe model." "Others abide our question. Thou art free."

even if in overbearing tones, with a kind of kid-gloved arrogance. Not since Lessing perhaps had so keenly whistling a blade been tried on the wind in the classic quarter. But a classicism which had passed through that century of German idealism and German romantic Hellenism was bound to show a profound difference in its commitments. As the Platonism of Sidney stands in relation to that of Shelley, so the Aristotelianism of Lessing to that of Arnold.

Arnold's essays published in the *Cornhill* and other magazines, during the years immediately after he became Professor of Poetry at Oxford in 1857, and collected in 1865 as the first series of his *Essays in Criticism* show his classicism at perhaps its most level development, in the coolest and clearest light. He has gone to continental sources. One of these is the French Catholic, and conservative and Platonic *penseur* Joseph Joubert—a French Coleridge, as Arnold calls him, of less richness and power than the English Coleridge, but of more delicacy and penetration.

> Clearness is so eminently one of the characteristics of truth, that often it even passes for truth itself.

> Ignorance, which in matters of morals extenuates the crime, is itself, in matters of literature, a crime of the first order.

> In literature the one aim of art is the beautiful.

> To accustom mankind to pleasures which depend neither upon the bodily appetites nor upon money, by giving them a taste for the things of the mind, seems to me, in fact, the one proper fruit which nature has meant our literary productions to have.

Another is the German Jewish poet, self-exiled in France, arch-ironist and anti-romantic, Heinrich Heine, from whom Arnold takes up the weapons of a "life and death battle" against the *Philistine*. Arnold's hard-hitting repetitions succeeded in establishing this piece of German student lingo as the right name for the British middle-brow enemy of the noble and lovely.

> *Philistinism!*—we have not the expression in English. Perhaps we have not the word because we have so much of the thing. At Soli, I imagine, they did not talk of solecisms; and here, at the very headquarters of Goliath, nobody talks of Philistinism.[8]

---

[8] *Heinrich Heine*, in *Essays in Criticism, First Series* (London, 1902), p. 162. Cf. the last paragraph of Arnold's Preface to the *First Series*, the apostrophe to Oxford, "Adorable dreamer, whose heart has been so romantic! who hast given thyself so prodigally . . . only never to the Philistines"; and *Joubert* (*First Series*, p. 304), "the great apostle of the Philistines, Lord Macaulay." As early as 1827 Carlyle was using the term "Philistine" in his essays, and in *Sartor Resartus*, 1831, appears "Philistinism." See these words in *The Oxford English Dictionary on Historical Principles*.

Arnold displays a fine scorn for British homebred humour and parochial complacency. He assumes the same kind of anti-domestic and classical superiority of taste as we have witnessed already in the comic theory of George Meredith. It is true that he has a great interest in the national spirit, and, like fashionable thinkers on the continent (Taine and others) to whom we shall allude in later chapters, he believes in the race, the milieu, and the moment, in short, in the cultural determination of literature.

> For a literary masterpiece, two powers must concur, the power of the man, and the power of the moment, and the man is not enough without the moment.[9]

But Arnold reverses the revolutionary and sociological emphasis of the continental thinkers. With him it is not as if the march of the historical process were bound to be working into something superior or more real. Just the opposite. The English spirit he is so much interested to define is a mixed potential in the blood and in the culture,[1] capable of being very badly developed in a bad modern age. In his inaugural lecture at Oxford, delivered in 1857 and entitled *The Modern Element in Literature*, Arnold appears as a strenuous champion of cultural classicism. He enjoys a high degree of confidence that the age of Sir Walter Raleigh in England was but poorly lighted, infested with footpads, over-dressed, and, compared with the age of Thucydides in Athens, naively incompetent to write history. (Distinct, though transvalued, reminiscences of the Peacockian frame of mind are to be noted in his remarks on the deficiencies of Roman literature—the Lucretian depression and ennui, the Virgilian "sweet, touching sadness," the Horatian want of "seriousness.") The progressive vulgarization of English middle-class culture since the Elizabethan age is a theme to which Arnold never tires of returning.

> . . . this paragraph on which I stumbled in a newspaper . . . :
> "A shocking child murder has just been committed at Nottingham. A girl named Wragg left her workhouse there on Saturday morning with her young illegitimate child. The child was soon afterwards found dead on Mapperly Hills, having been strangled. Wragg is in custody."

[9] *The Function of Criticism at the Present Time* (First Series, p. 4).

[1] "If we had been all German, we might have had the science of Germany; if we had been all Celtic, we might have been popular and agreeable; if we had been all Latinised, we might have governed Ireland as the French govern Alsace, without getting ourselves detested. But now we have Germanism enough to make us Philistines, and Normanism enough to make us imperious, and Celtism enough to make us self-conscious and awkward; but German fidelity to Nature, and Latin precision and clear reason, and Celtic quick-wittedness and spirituality, we fall short of" (*On the Study of Celtic Literature and on Translating Homer*, New York, 1883, p. 132, *On the Study of Celtic Literature*, VI).

Nothing but that. . . . how eloquent, how suggestive are those few lines! "Our old Anglo-Saxon breed, the best in the whole world!"—how much that is harsh and ill-favoured there is in this best! *Wragg!* If we are to talk of ideal perfection, of "the best in the whole world," has any one reflected what a touch of grossness in our race, what an original shortcoming in the more delicate spiritual perceptions, is shown by the natural growth amongst us of such hideous names. Higginbottom, Stiggins, Bugg! [2]

Among the essays of the 1862 collection, the continental orientation of Arnold's critique stands out nowhere more remarkably than in *The Literary Influence of Academies*. Arnold here throws backward a last glance in the English tradition of wistful regard for the French and Italian academies. The proposals for reducing, refining, and "ascertaining" the Augustan language, the plans for legislative authority and for dictionaries, which appear from the time of the Royal Society on (in essays by Defoe, Addison, Swift, and numerous smaller busybodies and grammarians), had continued up to and even after the time of the greatest English effort to accomplish such dreams, the *Dictionary* of Samuel Johnson published in 1755.[3] But Johnson himself in his Preface had growled out something about the establishment of an academy . . .

which I, who can never wish to see dependence multiplied, hope the spirit of English liberty will hinder or destroy.

And he had followed this up with equally heavy lunges in his *Life of Swift* (". . . an academy; the decrees of which every man would be willing, and many would have been proud to disobey") and in his *Life of Roscommon* ("In this country an academy could be expected to do but little. . . . We live in an age in which it is a kind of public sport to refuse all respect that cannot be enforced. The edicts of an English Academy would probably be read by many, only that they might be sure to disobey them").[4] The idea of a legislated norm of correct linguistic usage was never at home in England. The great Oxford dictionary actually conceived and begun during Arnold's lifetime was a project of a far different order, part of the empirical and investigative spirit of the age. The authority which it sought to establish was strictly a historical

---

[2] *The Function of Criticism at the Present Time (First Series,* p. 23).

[3] See Albert Baugh, *A History of the English Language* (New York, 1935), Chapter IX, "The Appeal to Authority 1650–1800"; Sterling A. Leonard, *The Doctrine of Correctness in English Usage, 1700–1800* (Madison, 1929); Allen Walker Read, "Suggestions for an Academy in England in the Latter Half of the Eighteenth Century," *MP,* XXXVI (November, 1938), 145–56.

[4] The passage on academies was added to the 1781 *Life of Roscommon* when Johnson constructed this by expanding a sketch published in the *Gentleman's Magazine* in 1748.

authority. But Arnold enjoyed a tall and successful aloofness from the historizing spirit of his times. He broadcast his criticism with a suave assurance that made him seem anything but a gauntly anachronistic and mistaken prophet. "Dryden and Pope," he was to say in one of his later and most notorious pronouncements, "were classics of our prose." It would have been difficult for an Englishman of Arnold's time to participate more fully in the English Augustan spirit than Arnold does in his *Literary Influence of Academies* and *Function of Criticism in the Present Time.* Yet he did this with a difference. Swift in his Proposal to Lord Oxford ("Swift's petty proposal," Johnson called it) and in other essays on the theme had managed to sound no better than the sharp schoolmaster, a sensible, salutary, birch-rod influence, grammatical, philological, precisian. Arnold elevated the academy for which the Augustans had yearned into a vantage point of Olympian vision, a regulator of culture in the lofty creative sense which the German philosophy had by this time made plausible. In place of the Germanic and Carlylean throb of lyric freedom, it is true that he wanted the serenely normative and tempering light from classic France. He spoke of a "sensitiveness of intelligence" which is ready to defer to "authority." [5] But the nature of that authority! Without being very precise about it, he made it sound like a very wise and ultimate thing, something which in other essays he called "culture" and put even higher than religion.

IV

YET an accent of uncertainty appears here and there in Arnold's account of relations between the reasonable classic norm and the individual, nonconformist claims which are likely to be made by poetry—and especially, it would appear, by modern poetry. He entertains a notion that poetry proceeds from a certain honest energy. The English have plenty of this, and hence they do write poetry; for the same reason they write a violent, Corinthian polemic prose; and they write as individuals. The French on the contrary have intelligence and something called "form," and hence they write fine prose (not poetry—poetry has nothing to do with "form"), and they go beyond individual eccentricities, to produce not only prose but schools of prose.[6]

Poetry also has affinities for "magic." The concept takes the form of "natural magic," or "Celtic magic," in Arnold's retrospective expedition into 18th-century Celtomania, the lectures of 1865–1866 entitled *On the Study of Celtic Literature.* "Magic is the word to insist upon,—

[5] *First Series,* p. 49.
[6] *The Literary Influence of Academies (First Series,* pp. 50-2).

a magically vivid and near interpretation of nature."[7] (In its insistence
not only on magic but on melancholy, Arnold's pontification was to play
a part in determining the color of the actual Celtic revival in Ireland a
few decades later.)[8] In some contexts, "natural magic" is Arnold's rendering of the "object" ("nature," the familiar landscape under the charm
of moonlight) which stood on one side of the Coleridgean reconciliation
of subject and object. The other half of the formula, the "subject," the
human and moral kind of meaning, something much more congenial to
Arnold, he called "moral profundity." Keats, Shakespeare's imperfect
disciple, had an excess of natural magic, not enough moral profundity.
Wordsworth had mainly moral profundity. Shakespeare had both qualities to the full.[9]

Arnold's mixed regard for the major English poets of the preceding
generation produced some of the most highly colored images which he
has left us—Shelley a "beautiful and ineffectual angel, beating in the
void his luminous wings in vain,"[1] Byron in the act of carrying across
Europe "the pageant of his bleeding heart,"[2] Coleridge a "poet and
philosopher wrecked in a mist of opium,"[3] Keats's letters the "love letters
of a surgeon's apprentice."[4] The reason for Arnold's dislike of these
poets was partly biographical,[5] and to that extent it was purely moral.
He gives his most considered poetic reasons in the case of Byron: Byron
had personality, talent, sincerity, strength, energy—but he lacked "matter," that is, a serious moral meaning.[6]

Arnold always has less difficulty in knowing what to admire in the
classics. His Oxford lectures *On Translating Homer*, 1861, a disdainful
reaction against the Teutonized, or Saxo-Norman,[7] translation by Francis
William Newman, urge a conception of Homer as "eminently rapid,"

---

[7] *On the Study of Celtic Literature and On Translating Homer* (New York,
1883), *On the Study of Celtic Literature*, VI, p. 122; cf. pp. 102, 126, 128.

[8] John V. Kelleher, "Matthew Arnold and the Celtic Revival," in *Perspectives
of Criticism*, ed. Harry Levin (Cambridge, Mass., 1952), pp. 197–227.

[9] *Keats* (Second Series, p. 119). Cf. *Maurice de Guérin* (First Series, pp. 81–2).

[1] *Second Series*, pp. 203, 252, in both *Shelley* and *Byron*.

[2] *Stanzas at the Grande Chartreuse.*

[3] *Second Series*, p. 203, again apropos of Byron.

[4] *Second Series*, p. 103.

[5] And especially in the case of Shelley. Arnold's distaste is a response to unsavory aspects of Shelley's life which had recently been both revealed and defended
in Dowden's biography (*Second Series*, pp. 206 ff.).

[6] *Second Series*, p. 193.

[7] The 19th-century Teutonizing camp included such scholars as the Early English Text Society founders F. J. Furnivall and R. C. Trench, the historian E. A.
Freeman and the poets William Barnes and Gerard Manley Hopkins. Macaulay's essay on Boswell's *Johnson* contains a good instance of the trend. Cf. Austin Warren,
"Instress of Inscape," in *Gerard Manley Hopkins by the Kenyon Critics* (Norfolk,
1945), pp. 82–6. For some 17th-century instances of Teutonizing and a protest
against it, see Joseph Glanvill, *An Essay Concerning Preaching*, 1678, in Spingarn,
Essays, II, 274.

"eminently plain and direct," "eminently noble." [8] The argument is ruled in large measure by a concept of calm objectivity that is closely consonant with the theme of the classic action defined in 1853. Homer composes "with his eye on the object." [9] He thus participates in a virtue which the same lectures define as the main requirement (lacking in the eccentric English) of a good criticism—a "simple lucidity of mind," a capacity "to see the object as in itself it really is." [1]

The concept of a loftily objective aim carries through Arnold's career into his last important general pronouncement on poetics, the essay entitled *The Study of Poetry* which appears as introduction to T. H. Ward's *English Poets* in 1880 and is reprinted as the first of the *Essays in Criticism, Second Series*, in 1888. The Aristotelian phrase *philosophōteron kai spoudaioteron* is cue for the Arnoldian phrase "truth and high seriousness," expressing twin requirements of substance, failing in either of which a very good poet may fall far short of greatness. These requirements are found in the work of the few greatest poets, Homer, Dante, Milton, Shakespeare. Certain other ideas which appear in the essay of 1880 are taken up in the course of our next few pages.

V

"IF HE is not the greatest of English critics," says H. W. Garrod, "his make-up of being so is in itself a piece of greatness; and not to enjoy it is a piece of stupidity." [2] Fair enough. But if a further statement and summary of Arnold's position as developed by the end of his career be permitted a tone of moderate dissatisfaction, we would urge the following points.

1. His argument about Homer relies not only on an idea of dignified substance but rather heavily on another idea—one merely hinted in 1853—that of a classically objective style. Homer writes in the "grand style." This phrase, used in the Preface of 1853 apropos of the Greeks in general and repeated during Arnold's later years in two essays on Milton, expresses a stylistic (and somewhat chastened) version of the 18th-century Michelangelesque sublime.[3] "I think it will be found," he says in some *Last Words on Translating Homer*, "that the grand style

---

[8] *On the Study of Celtic Literature and On Translating Homer* (New York, 1883), p. 149.

[9] *Op. cit.*, p. 160. "Pope composes with his eye on the style."

[1] *Op. cit.* pp. 199–200. Arnold reiterates the phrase a few years later with heavy emphasis in the opening pages of his lecture on *The Function of Criticism* (*First Series*, pp. 1, 6). And Sophocles, it will be remembered, "saw life steadily, and saw it whole."

[2] *Poetry and the Criticism of Life* (Cambridge, Mass., 1931), p. 83.

[3] Trilling, *Matthew Arnold*, p. 173, points out Arnold's familiarity with Reynolds' *Discourses*.

arises in poetry, when a noble nature, poetically gifted, treats with simplicity or with severity a serious subject." [4] A similar concern not only for "substance" or "matter" but for "style" or "manner" runs through the important essay of 1880.[5] Both the substance and the style must have their "accent of high beauty, worth, and power." In this complication of his theory beyond the simple demand for the "excellent" subject of the 1853 Preface, there is a gain in critical insight—and not necessarily any contradiction. Yet one of Arnold's most memorable new terms in this essay is "touchstones." By this he means small pieces of poetry—"short passages, even single lines," a line of Dante, of Chaucer, of Shakespeare, two lines of Milton—unmistakable examples of great poetry, such as a critic ought to carry about with him and apply as norms in the estimate of other poetry. This open appeal to the chunklet, the sample piece of precious stuff, is a rather startling shift toward the norm of style and away from the initial classic thesis of 1853 that the "action is all." True, he says of his touchstone slightly misquoted from Chaucer ("O martyr souded in virginitee."): "A single line, however, is too little if we have not the strain of Chaucer's verse well in our memory." Still he is talking precisely about the "strain" of the *verse*. To make the touchstone test it would seem we do not have to know much if anything about the story of the little "clergeon."

2. On the other hand, the lofty purpose, the grand unified exclusive norm for poetry, the monolithic seriousness, which Arnold proclaims in 1880, is a consistent enough development from the Preface of 1853, where the requirement of the grand action is completed by a disparaging reference to comedy and the "lighter kinds of poetry." Comedy is good enough to take care of everyday materials, contemporary trifles. The "tragic poem," the poem with a seriously useful meaning (*pragmatic*, Arnold actually calls it in 1853, taking the expression from Polybius) requires the antique heroic subject matter. In 1880 Arnold has a more extended opportunity to betray his views on the comic modes of poetry. And we find that Chaucer is a poet of surpassingly fine style (a "divine liquidness of diction," a "divine fluidity of movement") and even of superior substance, in one sense (in his "large, free, simple, clear yet kindly view of human life"), but not in the full sense. He has truth, in short, but he lacks "high and excellent seriousness." Dryden and Pope, those two great "classics of our prose," were not "men whose criticism of life has a high seriousness," or even any "poetic largeness, freedom,

---

[4] *On the Study of Celtic Literature and On Translating Homer* (New York, 1883), p. 265.

[5] For an earlier gesture at a stylistic definition of poetry, see *Heinrich Heine* (*Essays, First Series*, p. 161): "Poetry is simply the most beautiful, impressive, and widely effective mode of saying things." Cf. later *Wordsworth* (*Second Series*, p. 128): "Poetry is nothing less than the most perfect speech of man, that in which he comes nearest to being able to utter the truth."

insight, benignity." The same low esteem of the Augustan mode works out in the patronizing estimate of Gray.[6] The basic lack of sympathy with the comic produces the meanly anaphoristic emphasis that the trouble with Burns' poetry lies in "Scotch drink, Scotch religion, Scotch manners." Burns' "genuine criticism of life" is merely "ironic." Arnold's stomach for literature suffers limitations of delicacy. "No one can deny," he says in the passage on Scotland, "that it is of advantage to a poet to deal with a beautiful world." And the retort of the 20th-century poet seems highly relevant: "It is an advantage to mankind in general to live in a beautiful world. . . . But the essential advantage for a poet is . . . to be able to see beneath both beauty and ugliness; to see the boredom, and the horror, and the glory." [7]

3. Despite a partial submission to the historistic trend of his age (his congratulation of Shakespeare, for instance, because he "applied freely in literature the then modern ideas"),[8] Arnold never seems to set a correct value on the formal principle of anachronism in poetry, the principle of rebirth in analogy and parody. The theoretical fault may be illustrated, *ad hominem*, in the Oxford Professor's cold fiasco *Merope: A Tragedy*, his most determined attempt as a poet to avail himself of one of those great classically permanent actions described in the Preface of 1853. The return to Messenia in that "period of transition from the heroic and fabulous to the human and historic age of Greece" is made in a spirit all too literal. The noted actress Helena Faucit tactfully shied away from Arnold's invitation to participate in this sort of thing. There were lessons in the metaphoric handling of the antique that Arnold had neglected to learn from Racine or Corneille, from Shakespeare's *Troilus and Cressida*, or from Chaucer's *Troilus and Criseyde*, the last of which one may be doubtful that he had ever read. The same kind of literal demand comes out in his theory of a Homeric translation (if not so flagrantly in the sample passages which he translates). Let the unhappy translator "not trust to his own judgment of his own work; he may be misled by individual caprices."

> Let him ask how his work affects those who both know Greek and can appreciate poetry; whether to read it gives the Provost of Eton, or Professor Thompson of Cambridge, or Professor Jowett here at Oxford, at all the same feeling which to read the original gives them. I consider that when Bentley said of Pope's translation, "It was a pretty poem, but must not be called

[6] F. R. Leavis, "Revaluations (XI): Arnold as Critic," *Scrutiny*, VII (December, 1938), 319-32.
[7] T. S. Eliot, *Use of Poetry*, p. 98. "The vision of the horror and the glory was denied to Arnold, but he knew something of the boredom."
[8] *Heine* (First Series, p. 176).

Homer," the work, in spite of all its power and attractiveness, was judged.[9]

Here again there were lessons of the neo-classic age which Arnold might have read more tolerantly. What Ascham in *The Scholemaster*, what Dryden in his Prefaces to Ovid and the *Sylvae*, said about "metaphrase," "paraphrase," "imitation," might not have provided Arnold with a ready-made and sufficient view. The older school of translation, like Arnold, was looking for a certain spirit, a certain "feeling." But in the freedom of their practice, verging on "imitation," lay an insight, or perhaps merely a habit derived from live classical studies, which was foreign to the age of Arnold. Arnold's arguments about translation (his stern rejection of Newman's effort in search of an idiom) illustrate the growth of the historical sense in his era but also the limitations of that sense as the age applied it to poetry. He was running parallel to the more or less well informed archeologizing of the Shakespearian stage which had begun in the time of Macready.

4. Another 20th-century critic has spoken of Arnold's essays as "higher pamphleteering,"[1] and yet another has called Arnold "rather a propagandist for criticism than a critic."[2] Very simply, very characteristically, and very repetitiously, Arnold spent his career in hammering the thesis that poetry is a "criticism of life." This led to a spectacular involvement in some of the difficulties that have always appeared for didactic theory. In the essay on *The Function of Criticism at the Present Time*, that function is described as the promotion of a lively circulation of the best ideas yet available to humanity,[3] and hence the production of a climate in which poetry can thrive. One "criticism" provides the set-up and encouragement for another "criticism," and the embarrassment of equating poetry with some kind of quasi-philosophic discipline is greatly accentuated. One recent authority[4] on Arnold's thought has interpreted his whole career as a tension between the impulse of detachment and that of practical application, between the Professor of Poetry and the Inspector of Schools. Arnold is frequently aware of the difficulty and attempts to qualify the phrase "criticism of life" as he applies it to poetry. He introduces into the predicate of his definition of "poetry" a safety device of circularity, a kind of short-circuit fuse. A tabular arrangement of the most definite avowals in several of his essays will show the dilemma.

[9] *On the Study of Celtic Literature and on Translating Homer* (New York, 1883), p. 144.

[1] F. R. Leavis, *Scrutiny*, VII, 321.

[2] T. S. Eliot, *The Sacred Wood* (London, 1920), p. 1.

[3] Literary criticism is "a disinterested endeavour to learn and propagate the best that is known and thought in the world, and thus to establish a current of fresh and true ideas" (*First Series*, p. 37).

[4] E. K. Brown, *Matthew Arnold, A Study in Conflict* (Chicago, 1938).

> The end and aim of all literature is . . . a criticism of life.
> —*Joubert*, 1864 (*First Series*, p. 303)

> Poetry is at bottom a criticism of life.
> —*Wordsworth*, 1879 (*Second Series*, p. 143)

> Poetry [is] a criticism of life under the conditions fixed for such a criticism by the laws of poetic truth and poetic beauty.
> —*The Study of Poetry*, 1880 (*Second Series*, p. 5; cf. p. 48)

> I have seen it said that I allege poetry to have for its characteristic this: that it is a criticism of life; and that I make it to be thereby distinguished from prose, which is something else. So far from it, that when I first used this expression, *a criticism of life*, now many years ago, it was to literature in general that I applied it, and not to poetry in especial. 'The end and aim of all literature,' I said, 'is, if one considers it attentively, nothing but that; *a criticism of life*.' And so it surely is; the main end and aim of all our utterance, whether in prose or in verse, is surely a criticism of life. We are not brought much on our way, I admit, towards an adequate definition of poetry as distinguished from prose by that truth; still a truth it is, and poetry can never prosper if it is forgotten. In poetry, however, the criticism of life has to be made conformably to the laws of poetic truth and poetic beauty.[1]
> —*Byron*, 1881 (*Second Series*, pp. 186–7)

VI

ARNOLD's didacticism reaches its mature and accurate formulation in the sentence so often quoted from the opening of the 1880 Essay:

> More and more mankind will discover that we have to turn to poetry to interpret life for us, to console us, to sustain us. Without poetry, our science will appear incomplete; and most of what now passes with us for religion and philosophy will be replaced by poetry.

("But now I only hear Its melancholy, long, withdrawing roar. . . . And we are here as on a darkling plain . . .") Arnold marks out a didactic function for poetry without any of the optimistic frenzy which buoyed the utterances of a Shelley or a Carlyle. He speaks with a level precision and a resolved firmness that make his prophecy all the more appalling. In the essays of broader cultural and quasi-religious scope which oc-

[1] The essay on Wordsworth includes lengthy disavowals of anything like an approval of the *doctrines* expressed in Wordsworth's poetry.

cupied his middle period, 1867–1877, especially in *Culture and Anarchy*, 1869, he had expounded in somewhat more detail the kind of new message—the "sweetness and light," the blend of Hebraic spirituality and obedience with Hellenistic critical spirit—which it should be the aim of "culture" and of poetic education to propagate. Religion had once done a fairly good job, but religion now seemed to Arnold to reside mainly in religious "organizations," and these were only "machinery." The highest promotion of the sweet, clear inner life would now be the job of "culture." The text would be the Greek classics.[2]

If we look at Arnold's most direct combat with science, a Cambridge lecture entitled *Literature and Science*, first printed in 1882, we discover the battle positions to be not so much different from those of the Peacock-Shelley incident. We see the names of the new generation of scientific bravos: Huxley, pronouncing a "funeral oration" on literary education at the opening of a college in Birmingham; Renan, Spencer, Darwin, and the liberal politician John Bright. A congress of elementary school teachers at Sheffield hears a proposal that the schools and the universities should come together on the common ground of natural science. On the ground of the dead languages, they can not. Arnold's rebuttal shares much with Shelley. It differs, however, in a more antiseptically confident tone, a quality of assurance that is even quasi-scientific. Arnold is on the stand to testify that literature is not, as Professor Huxley believes, merely *belles lettres*. Literature reaches out and begins with all knowledge, political, social, scientific—it is literally and inclusively "the best which has been thought and said in the world." Literature will be up with the latest scientific data. It will face even Mr. Darwin's proposition that the human ancestor was "a hairy quadruped furnished with a tail and pointed ears, probably arboreal in his habits." But literature (or the humane part of it, "humane letters") will go beyond all mere "instrument" knowledge and all merely "natural" knowledge; it will grasp knowledge in relation with the human "sense for conduct," the human "sense for beauty." Shelley's *Defense* had said much (in richly emotive terms) about "emotion," which was the efficient cause of moral action, even if it was not the faculty of moral definition. But there was no intimation in Shelley that ultimately there were not good enough grounds for the emotions of which he spoke. Arnold's more scientifically circumspect profession of faith does try to keep the tweezers between his truth-searching faculty and that highly desirable yet untruthful element of emotion.

> The middle age could do without humane letters, as it could do without the study of nature, because its supposed knowledge was made to engage its emotions so powerfully. Grant that the supposed knowledge disappears, its power of being made to en-

[2] Consult *Sweetness and Light*, the concluding Oxford lecture of 1867, which becomes the first chapter of *Culture and Anarchy*, 1869.

gage the emotions will of course disappear along with it—but the emotions will remain. Now if we find by experience that humane letters have an undeniable power of engaging the emotions, the importance of humane letters in man's training becomes not less, but greater, in proportion to the success of science in extirpating what it calls "medieval thinking." [3]

VII

ARNOLD was of course not the only voice of his kind to be heard during the long Victorian era. In America the ethical idealism of the New England litterateurs in the "classical" period, notably Emerson, is at least as traceable an influence as that of Arnold in the development of a "Genteel Tradition" [4] that has carried far into our own century. One of the most aesthetically acceptable—brilliantly cautious—statements of a moral perspective upon literature to appear during the whole period was that in the prefaces and other critical essays of Henry James. All art, he would say, is in basis moral. (He was speaking against Gautier's *l'art pour l'art*, and no less against the naturalism of Balzac.) [5] Both in art and in criticism, "the moral sense and the artistic sense lie very near together." "In each of the parts there is something of each of the other parts." [6]

> There is one point at which the moral sense and the artistic sense lie very near together; that is, in the light of the very obvious truth that the deepest quality of a work of art will always be the quality of the mind of the producer. In proportion as that mind is rich and noble, will the novel, the picture, the statue, partake of the substance of beauty and truth. To be constituted of such elements is, to my vision, to have purpose enough. No good novel will ever proceed from a superficial mind; that seems to me an axiom which, for the artist of fiction, will cover all needful ground. [7]

A medley of such voices was very friendly to the rise in academic America shortly after the turn of the century of a new humanistic and ethical school of criticism which, through the resounding efforts mainly of two champions, kept a hearing for about thirty years. It is true that

[3] *Literature and Science,* in *Four Essays on Life and Letters,* ed. E. K. Brown (New York, 1947), pp. 109–10.

[4] Cf. George Santayana, *The Genteel Tradition at Bay* (New York, 1931).

[5] *French Poets and Novelists* (London, 1919), pp. 14, 31–56, 116, essays on Baudelaire, Gautier, Balzac; *Notes on Novelists* (New York, 1914), pp. 122, 126, on Balzac.

[6] *The Art of Fiction,* in *Partial Portraits* (London, 1911), pp. 404–6, 392. Cf. Morris Roberts, *Henry James's Criticism* (Cambridge, Mass., 1929), p. 63.

[7] Beginning of last paragraph of *The Art of Fiction.*

Paul Elmer More in the Seventh volume (1910) of his long series of *Shelburne Essays* utters a lament for the deficiencies of a kind of "culture" which he tries to define by pairing Arnold with a much earlier English critic, the Deist Shaftesbury. "The fault," he says, "lay not in any intrinsic want of efficiency in the critical spirit, nor in any want of moral earnestness." "These men were lacking in another direction: they missed a philosophy which could bind together their moral and their aesthetic sense, a positive principle besides the negative force of ridicule and irony." Thus they left criticism open to subjectivism, impressionism, and moral anarchy.[8] Here was a tightening of the belt—or a promise of sharper teeth for the ethical tradition. In More himself, humanism enjoyed an overt alliance with religion and so of course was not the pure Arnoldian critique of life. But in More's Harvard colleague Irving Babbitt, the concepts of "insight" into the Higher Will through literary symbol and a consequent "inner check" upon romantic emotive expansiveness and naturalistic descendentalism ("romanticism on all fours") received a treatment which in the purity of its withdrawal from revealed religion[9] surpassed even the cultural dreams of Arnold. Babbitt's campaign in its negative phases, his attack on Rousseau, romanticism, and all that, is crowded with richly reported and bizarre incidents and luridly lit up with the flambeaux of his indignant rhetoric. His positive schemes, however, are more thinly delineated, his main illustrative appeals, to the drama of the Greeks, but sketchily intimated. Babbitt showed a heavy hand when late in his career he tried close dealing with an actual work of romantic English literature. His censure of Coleridge's imaginative control in *The Ancient Mariner* seems the all but fanatical result of a theory of literature that was not in fact literary. The twin detonations in 1930 of two anthologies, one for the new humanists and one against them, announced the end of a didactic critical movement which, adequately defined in Arnold's terms of 1880, had in the humanism of his successors moved no nearer to a distinct concern for literature.

SUPPLEMENT

The history of the creative arts is long
But the belief in art as the supreme
Criterion of experience is as new

[8] "Criticism," in *Shelburne Essays, Seventh Series* (New York, 1910), pp. 223-4. Cf. Zabel, *Literary Opinion in America*, p. 30.

[9] More defined Babbitt's kind of humanism as "the study and practice of the principles of human happiness *uncomplicated* by naturalistic dogmas on the one side and religious dogmas on the other" (*On Being Human*, Princeton, 1936, p. 18). Babbitt's parleying with Buddhism was a largely philosophic performance.

As the electric light. Our poets belong
In dangerous numbers to this strange persuasion.
Small wonder that they live like ghosts and perish
Without biographies; small wonder too
That they adopt an adjective for their name
And soberly defer to those who wear
The title of Intellectual. Poets by hosts
Spring fully armed from pure obscurity
To bay like demons at us and to slay
The man in front; our brawls are commonplaces.
. . . .
                                                   All rime more or less
Has a religious ancestry, for man,
The evidence says, is a believing being.
Nor does it follow that the civilized,
The secular and the profane in art must fail
For lack of faith—thus too the evidence.
What here pertains is the solicitude
Of modern artists for their missing gods,
Our attitude of nervous self-defence
Against the emotions roused by great belief,
Our purely literary use of Christ
In painting, prose and rime, our use of Christ
In any cynical neo-Christian sense
Or even with that perfunctory good-will
Which characterizes Tolerance.
. . . .
By now the plaints of Arnold are too stale
For repetition, yet it is curious
I think to make comparison of his lush
Nostalgia for the Age of Faith with ours
Which is nostalgia madly furious.
In part that deep Victorian melancholy
Is father to our more frantic abnegation
Of all the supernatural. Rime must refer
Anti-religiously to belief and nature,
Or else create the kind of nomenclature
Which hints at natural science.

—Karl Shapiro, *Essay on Rime* (New York, 1945), pp. 52-4, "The Confusion in Belief," copyright 1945 by Karl Shapiro. Reprinted by permission of Random House, Inc.

Poems by Alexander Smith, a volume recently published in London, and by this time reprinted in Boston, deserve attention. They have obtained in England a good deal more notice than is usually accorded there to first volumes of verse; nor is this by any means to be ascribed to the mere fact that the writer is, as we are told, a mechanic; though undoubtedly that does add to their external interest, and perhaps also enhances their intrinsic merit. It is to this, perhaps, that they owe a force of purpose and character which makes them a grateful contrast to the ordinary languid collectanea published by young men of literary habits; and which, on the whole, may be accepted as more than compensation for many imperfections of style and taste.

. . . .

We do not at all mean to prepare the reader for finding the great poetic desideratum in this present Life-Drama. But it has at least the advantage, such as it is, of not showing much of the *litterateur* or connoisseur, or indeed the student; nor is it, as we have said, mere pastoral sweet piping from the country. These poems were not written among books and busts, nor yet

> By shallow rivers, to whose falls
> Melodious birds sing madrigals.

They have something substantive and lifelike, immediate and first-hand, about them. There is a charm, for example, in finding, as we do, continual images drawn from the busy seats of industry; it seems to satisfy a want that we have long been conscious of, when we see the black streams that welter out of factories, the dreary lengths of urban and suburban dustiness,

> the squares and streets
> And the faces that one meets,

irradiated with a gleam of divine purity.

There are moods when one is prone to believe that, in these last days, no longer by "clear spring or shady grove," no more upon any Pindus or Parnassus, or by the shady side of any Castaly, are the true and lawful haunts of the poetic powers: but, we could believe it, if anywhere, in the blank and desolate streets, and upon the solitary bridges of the midnight city, where Guilt is, and wild Temptation, and the dire Compulsion of what has once been done—there, with these tragic sisters around him, and with Pity also, and pure Compassion, and pale Hope, that looks like Despair, and Faith in the garb of Doubt, there walks the discrowned Apollo, with unstrung lyre; nay, and could he sound it, those mournful Muses would scarcely be able as of old, to respond and "sing in turn with their beautiful voices."

Empedocles on Etna and other Poems, with its earlier companion volume, The Strayed Reveller and other Poems, are, it would seem, the productions (as is, or was, the English phrase) of a scholar and a gentleman; a man who has received a refined education, seen refined "society," had been more, we dare say, in the world, which is called the world, than in all likelihood has a Glasgow mechanic. More refined, therefore, and more highly educated sensibilities,—too delicate, are they, for common service?—a calmer judgment also, a more poised and steady intellect, the *siccum lumen* of the soul; a finer and rarer aim perhaps, and certainly a keener sense of difficulty, in life;—these are the characteristics of him whom we are to call "A."

—[Arthur Hugh Clough], review of "Recent English Poetry," *North American Review*, LXXVII (July, 1853), 1, 4-5, 12

CHAPTER 21

THE REAL AND
THE SOCIAL:
ART AS PROPAGANDA

§ *dialectic themes: the historical, the scientific, the realistic, the sociological, positivism and the future of art, study of origins, compromises with idealism—II. "realism," pictorial and literary, Courbet, Flaubert, the "democratic brush," transition to "naturalism," Zola, novelist as scientist, Le Roman Expérimental, later versions in America, Frank Norris, Responsibilities of the Novelist, environment, brutality, Gothic naturalism, a form of "romanticism"—III. early phases of Russian criticism, ideology of nationalism, Russian novelists, Belinsky and his disciples, realism and social relevance, hidden meanings, sequence of literary genres, disapproval of folk poetry, of pure art and pleasure themes, "The Destruction of Aesthetics," psychology and hygiene, paradox of determinism and revolutionary sacrifice—IV. Tolstoy, "the conscience of the world," What Is Art?, Christian anarchy, "infection," religious emotion of this age, pride, sex, ennui, "pleasure" arts caricatured, five-sense aesthetics, "counterfeit" art (Wagner's Nibelungen Ring), rejection of his own novels, peasant boys, Tolstoy's taste in pictures, great art and the plain man, impressionist pictures and symbolist poetry, obscurity and immorality, Baudelaire's Le Galant Tireur, Tolstoy on Shakespeare—V. Marxist criticism, class propaganda, deterministic origins, isolation of modern artist, bourgeois culture, mirror images, Christopher Caudwell, Illusion and Reality, 1937, Marxism and historical literary studies, party-line mimesis, society the work of art—VI. American phases, "muckraking," the 1930's, keeping up with "the vanguard of the Proletariat," Emerson and*

THE ARNOLDIAN PROPHECY WAS DIRECTED TOWARD THE FUTURE OF SOME autonomous poetic power—appealing for authority, so far as it made any such appeal, to the Hellenic and the Hebraic past. Poetry was not to take orders from, but to take the place of, modern philosophy and religion. Poetry was to tell science what science was working for. The fact was, however, that the most urgently didactic trend in European literary theory of the 19th century aimed at making poetry something far other than an autonomous power or an antique authority. This trend was already well under way in Arnold's time and was destined to arrive at its zenith in the English-speaking world during the earlier 20th century, at about the same time as the less aggressively launched campaign of neo-humanism. This was to be a didacticism committed to the exposition and advancement of a dogma that would receive its definition from a quite unpoetic authority. In its mature phase, it was to issue in a propagandism that far outdid in abstractive solidarity anything ever attempted by poetry in the ages of Christian humanism. In Arnold's day the movement was gaining most headway in continental places somewhat removed from his observation; and nearer home, in France, it was apparently not one of the things which most engaged his attention.

Four main emphases, closely inter-reliant, appear in the post-Hegelian literary thought of the mid-century continent. These are the historical, the scientific, the realistic, the sociological. In place of the Hegelian "spirit" which worked the dialectical play and counter-play of the historical process, post-Hegelianism produced the dialectic of purely material forces, the *mystique* of time and progress. Nevertheless, the idea of a certain kind of function and future for poetry fared not badly. Science with social programs was more inclusive in its tolerance than the simply rationalistic enlightenment of an earlier era. Science with such alliances could even perhaps make better offers than could metaphysical idealism. Whereas Hegel, the idealistic encyclopedist of the arts, had arrived at a view of metaphysical fulfillment which meant the end of art and prophesied for it no future at all, the French positivism of Saint-Simon, Proudhon,[1] and Comte, in a manner curiously akin to the vision

[1] *Du principe de l'art et de sa destination sociale*, 1865.

of Schelling, Friedrich Schlegel, or Shelley, assigned to art a gloriously continuing imaginative function in the phases of human advancement that were to succeed upon the outmoded eras of religion and metaphysics. At the same time, another sort of French positivism, that represented most notably by the literary philosopher and historian Taine, prescribed a rigorous study of literature in its origins (the determining forces of *race, milieu,* and *moment*). And this prescription in the long run had very noticeable effects upon the actual study of literature not only in France but abroad. To construct literary methodologies on the principle of an expansively propagandist future for poetry never became very practicable. But the richly various conditions under which literature had been produced in the past, the economic, the social, the religious, the total of influences on art which Taine called "moral temperature," these made an increasingly inviting field for the application of the "experimental" method.

So far as the definition of art itself was concerned, much was borrowed from German romantic idealism—even by Taine himself [2]—and by other French aestheticians of the romantic generation (Cousin, Jouffroy, and their successors) as they assumed various postures of moderation, compromise, or merger, in response to the increasingly historical, realistic, and social claims of the age.[3]

II

"Realism"—if we may use the term broadly to mean a reaction against a number of things that were thought in the mid-19th-century to be *unreal*, not only Gothic romance, picaresque adventure, and allegorical fantasy but classic composure and conservative morality—realism as an aesthetic norm comes into view not only for literary but for pictorial art at about the same time, in the exhibition by Courbet of 1855 and the publication of Flaubert's *Madame Bovary* in 1856. Flaubert's theory of realism was concerned with the professional procedures of a novelist. He conceived a scientific detachment, a coolness and care, in the observation of materials. He made a trip to Egypt to study the scenery for his novel *Salammbô*. "Flaubert, the son and brother of distinguished physicians," Sainte-Beuve would say, "holds his pen like a scalpel." [4] At the same time it can scarcely be said that the novels of Flaubert actually

[2] Cf. Iredell Jenkins, "Hippolyte Taine and the Background of Modern Aesthetics," *Modern Schoolman*, XX (March 1943), 141–56.

[3] Victor Cousin (1792–1867), Théodore Jouffroy (1796–1842), Victor de Laprade (1812–83), Jean-Charles Lévêque (1818–1900).

[4] *Causeries du Lundi* (1857–70), XIII, 363; from a manuscript chapter by René Wellek.

exhibit a very servile rendering of natural objects. "People believe I am taken with the real," he said—"whereas I detest it." [5] In the theoretical manifestoes which accompany the realist movement in painting, however, and notably in the codification of Courbet's friend Castagnary, there are no such sophistications.

> The painter of our own time will live our own life, with our own habits and our own ideas. He will take the feelings he gets from the look of things in our society, and give them back to us in pictures where we recognize ourselves and our own surroundings. It will not do to lose sight of the fact that we ourselves are both the subject and the object of art: art is the expression of ourselves for our own sake. [6]

"To make verses," says Courbet himself, in a way that happily shows us the bearing of the doctrine on literature, "is unfair; to speak in a fashion different from all the world, that is an aristocratic pose." [7] Courbet's critics spoke of his "scrupulous imitation of nature," the "signature of nature itself," his "democratic brush." [8] But the Courbet phase of French realism was regarded even by its promoters as a transitional moment. [9] Inherent in its sociological implications, the here and now democratic "truth" which it pursued, was the notion of the ordinary, and hence the notion of the monotonous, the meager, the drab, the underprivileged, even the seamy. And this realism rather quickly intensified into the phase called "naturalism." Of this phase the greatest exponent was Zola. Literary "realism" and "naturalism" constituted an aesthetic centered in the prose novel, which was the literary genre most directly dedicated to the social problems of the 19th century. The naturalistic novelist conceived himself as a scientific sociologist and psychologist, an experimentalist working with his hypotheses like a scientist in a laboratory. The object of the experiment was the social organism. One had to tell the truth about it, not fairy tales. One might admit only (when talking about the "constant evolution of the human spirit") that the eye of the observer did color the picture. The literary artist gave "a corner of

[5] Gustave Flaubert, *Correspondance*, III (Paris, 1892), 67–8. The statement is made apropos of *Madame Bovary*. "On me croit épris du réel, tandis que je l'exècre, car c'est en haine du réalisme que j'ai entrepris ce roman." Melvin Friedman, "Passages on Aesthetics from Flaubert's Correspondence," *Quarterly Review of Literature*, IV [1949], 390–400, gives us a translation of "the total . . . of Flaubert's comments on aesthetics." Cf. Gilbert and Kuhn, pp. 492.

[6] Jules Antoine Castagnary, *Salons* (*1857–70*), I (Paris, 1892), 187. Cf. Gilbert and Kuhn, pp. 481–3.

[7] Emile Gros-Kost, *Courbet, Souvenirs intimes*, 1880, p. 31.

[8] H. d'Ideville, *Gustave Courbet, Notes et documents sur sa vie et son oeuvre*, (Paris, 1878), pp. 107 ff. Gros-Kost and Ideville are quoted from Gilbert and Kuhn (pp. 481–2), to whom our account of Courbet is substantially indebted.

[9] Cf. Harry Levin, "What is Realism?" and Albert J. Salvan, "L'Essence du réalisme français," in *Comparative Literature*, III (Summer, 1951), 193–9, 218–3.

nature seen through a temperament."[1] Zola's theoretical treatise, *Le Roman Expérimental*, 1880, describes the setting up of the initial conditions, the release of the action (the life of a libertine, for instance, such as Hulot in Balzac's *La Cousine Bette*), then the patient observation by the scientist-novelist, leading to a sober knowledge,[2] rich in practical implications for the improvement of society.[3] The novelist aimed at nothing less than a supreme knowledge, how to be "master of good and evil, how to rule life, how to rule society."[4] Zola found an authoritative manual of instruction for his new literary procedure in the *Introduction à l'étude de la médecine experimentale* by Claude Bernard. Bernard was so much to the point that in taking over his ideas Zola needed to do little more than change the word "physician" to "novelist."[5]

> The experimental novel is a result of the scientific development which has occurred in this century; it is a continuation and complement to the science of physiology which in turn depends upon chemistry and physics; it substitutes for the study of man as an abstraction, man as a metaphysical entity, the study of the natural man, man as the subject of physico-chemical laws, a being determined by the influences of his environment.[6]

Or, as Zola expressed it in his "Plans" for a vast saga of determinism:

> Study men like simple elements and note the reactions.

> What matters most to me is to be purely naturalistic, purely physiological. Instead of having principles (royalism, Catholicism) I shall have laws (heredity, atavism). . . . I am satisfied to be a scientist, to tell of that which exists, while seeking the underlying reasons. . . . A simple exposé of the facts of a family by showing the interior mechanisms which direct them.[7]

[1] *Le Naturalisme au Théatre*, in *Le Roman Expérimental*, ed. Maurice le Blond (Paris, n.d.), p. 92.

[2] *Le Roman Expérimental*, ed. Maurice le Blond, p. 16: "*Dès qu'il a eu choisi son sujet, il est parti des faits observés, puis il a institué son expérience en soumettant Hulot a une série d'épreuves, en le faisant passer par certains milieux, pour montrer le fonctionnement du mécanisme de sa passion.*"

[3] P. 28. Gilbert and Kuhn, p. 484, quote by contrast the romantic nature worship and fetishism of Zola's *La Faute de l'Abbé Mouret:* "Oh good Earth, take me, thou that art the common mother, the sole source of life, thou the eternal, immortal, where the soul of the world circles. . . ."

[4] P. 28: "*Etre maître du bien et du mal, régler la vie, régler la société, résoudre à la longue tous les problèmes du socialisme.*"

[5] P. 1: "*Ce ne sera donc qu'une compilation de textes;—le plus souvent, il me suffira de remplacer le mot 'médecin' par le mot 'romancier,' pour rendre ma pensée claire et lui apporter la rigeur d'une vérité scientifique.*"

[6] P. 27.

[7] Matthew Josephson, *Zola and His Time* (New York, *The Book League Monthly*, I, 1, November, 1928), pp. 97–8, quoting Zola's manuscript Plans for *La Fortune des Rougon*, in the Bibliothèque Nationale, Paris.

Perhaps the most instructive later variations on the theme occur in America during the years around the turn of the century—where, in the utterances of Howells, for instance, we may observe scientific realism in moderately developed conflict with genteel idealism, or where Frank Norris shows that the lustiest pursuit of naturalism is capable of fantastic, even Gothic, realizations. Norris' *Responsibilities of the Novelist*, 1903, is the American counterpart of Zola's *Le Roman Expérimental* and the vindication of Norris' own novels, with their Zolaesque accumulation of careful detail, their studious concern for environment as the shaper of character, for disease, for brutality and violence. His canvas was crowded not only with weakness and misery but with primitive strong men and robustly animal women. Wheat workers clash with railroad management in a frontier contest of gigantic—nearly cosmic—proportions and implications. He combined an aim at disinterested, scientific objectivity with an evolutionary optimism about the collective future of mankind which it was difficult for readers of Herbert Spencer in that era to escape. And so his theory was not uncorruptly naturalistic. In an early essay he wrote:

> The naturalist takes no note of common people, common in so far as their interests, their lives, and the things that occur in them are common, are ordinary. Terrible things must happen to the characters of the naturalistic tale. They must be twisted from the ordinary, wrenched from the quiet uneventful round of every-day life and flung into the throes of a vast and terrible drama that works itself out in unleashed passions, in blood, and in sudden death.[8]

"Norris," says a recent historian, "knew that naturalistic fiction was a peculiar kind of adventure story. To write such stories, it helped to be able to think of modern business men as the descendants of the aggressive Anglo-Saxons carrying out their fighting instincts, not in war, but in trade." Naturalism, Norris came to believe, "is a form of romanticism, not an inner circle of realism."[9]

"Naturalism" had all along made a strong claim to be socially oriented. It showed a modern conscience for the plight of the working

[8] Editorial in the San Francisco *Wave*, quoted by Franklin Walker, *Frank Norris: A Biography* (New York, 1932), p. 83. Cf. Charles Child Walcutt, "Frank Norris and the Search for Form," *University of Kansas City Review*, XIV (Winter, 1947), 126–36; and "Frank Norris on Realism and Naturalism," *American Literature*, XIII (March, 1941), 61–3, convincing observations on Norris' failure to shape his novels consistently on a philosophy of scientific determinism. Moral responsibility was always breaking in.

[9] William Van O'Connor, *An Age of Criticism, 1900–1950* (Chicago, 1952), p. 42. Our account of Norris is substantially indebted to O'Connor. Cf. Norris, *The Responsibilities of the Novelist* (New York, 1903), pp. 214–15: "Zola has been dubbed a Realist, but he is, on the contrary, the very head of the Romanticists."

classes. It dealt with ordinary folk here and now, or with the kind of destiny and problems that most people experienced, not with moated castles, elfin knights, exotic love stories, border outlaws, or any other fantasies dreamed out of the now irrelevant feudal past or invoked from parts of the world still under the spell of that past. That is, naturalism was contemporary and socially didactic. But whether it was in any very strict sense "natural" or "true," or scientifically real or true, might all along have been considered another question—with obvious embarrassments to an affirmative answer. Courbet's paintings no less than Frank Norris' novels exhibit a much clearer relation to a philosophy and a spirit than to either the 19th-century fact of photography or to any physically determinable features of French peasant life or of Chicago industrialism.

III

IN Czarist Russia of the mid-19th-century,[1] a didactic theory of literature was strongly invited not only by political and social conditions but by the actual pre-eminence of a generation of socially conscious novelists. At the same time, Russian police censorship helped to make literary book reviewing a covert vehicle for much political, social, and moral criticism. The notion deeply inherent in German romantic literary historiography and in the ideology of romantic nationalism, that literature should be the expression of a national spirit (the symbol of the inner life of the nation, the national physiognomy), carried over into Russia in the writing of the first Russian critic to attain more than local importance, Vissarion Belinsky (1811–1848), and in that of his disciples who wrote during the decade following his death.[2] Marxist critics of the 20th century have looked back to Belinsky with reverence. The reviews and essays of Belinsky and his disciples deal with Pushkin, Gogol, Lermontov, Turgenev, Dostoevsky, and Tolstoy according to increasingly rigorous standards of realism and social relevance. These critics were on the lookout for empirical reality, for the moment in history, for social and national needs, and for corresponding responsibilities in literature. They merged the classical norm of the universal

[1] This account of pre-Tolstoyan Russian critics follows manuscript chapters of the third volume of Professor René Wellek's *A History of Modern Criticism*, now in progress. See his "Social and Aesthetic Values in Russian Nineteenth-Century Literary Criticism (Belinskii, Chernyshevskii, Dobroliubov, Pisarev)," in *Continuity and Change in Russian and Soviet Thought*, ed. Ernest J. Simmons (Cambridge, Mass., 1955), pp. 381–97. Examples of Belinsky's criticism may be found in *Selected Philosophical Works*, translated anonymously (Moscow, 1948) and of Dobrolyubov's in *Selected Philosophical Essays*, ed. J. Fineberg (Moscow, 1948).

[2] Nikolay Chernyshevsky (1828–89), Nikolay Dobrolyubov (1836–61), Dmitri Pisarev (1840–68).

with romantic theories of mythopoeia in a pressing demand that the literary artist create human types according to new patterns of social significance. They considered that the only real literature was the expression of the historically developing national spirit, the dialectic movement of the political and economic idea. That movement provided a norm for distinguishing between the eternal and the ephemeral in literature. The greatest authors were the ones most closely identified with the community and its evolution, those who divined the needs of their time, expressed its spirit, represented their contemporaries. Belinsky's disciple Dobrolyubov was the originator of the idea that novelists might do this independently of, or even contrary to, their conscious intentions. The function of criticism might be to explain hidden social meanings. At the genetic level, these critics shifted the responsibility for the work of art from the artist to his age. They made it a pure result of the historical process. They conceived it more and more as an expression relentlessly forced up out of the national consciousness under pressure exerted by the stream of history. They saw inevitable sequences of literary genres (as from lyric to epic to drama) both in national history and in the growth of individual poets.

On occasions they appeared as reactionaries against romantic primitivism and specifically against folk poetry as a thing socially implicated in a serf-civilization, a survival from an undesirable and irrecoverable past. They were apt also to speak severely against "pure art" or the pleasure art of erotic and convivial themes, dissolute adventures. Pisarev, the most rigidly naturalistic monist of the group, the author of a notorious paper entitled "The Destruction of Aesthetics" (1865), reduced aesthetics to psychology and hygiene, observing that "every healthy and normal person is beautiful." He would concede some usefulness to the art of drawing, but only for the illustration of scientific books. He said that no man of that generation who had genuine intelligence and talent could spend his life "piercing sensitive hearts with iambs and anapests." The main technical emphasis of this whole family of critics was on a faithful naturalistic reporting, a lifelike rendition of the social organism, the stages of its development. Belinsky spoke of Russian writers since Gogol as the "natural school."

Belinsky himself did not propose any simply didactic aim, like the overthrow of autocracy or the emancipation of the serfs—though he moved in this direction and his disciples moved further. Compared with the French positivists, Saint-Simon, Proudhon, Comte, these Russian critics had less to say about the glorious didactic future of art, more about immediate sociological realism, but their social emphasis had deeply and enduringly didactic implications. In the work of Belinsky's disciples, deterministic materialism, hedonistic utilitarianism, and enlightened egoism unite paradoxically with fervor for social reform and a revolutionary spirit of sacrifice and social optimism. They combine the view that any art which has ever been faithful to its historic moment has been for that reason right (even bad taste if pervasive enough expresses a spirit and a time) with a second view, sometimes not distinguished from the first, that the historic development of the mid-19th century is in itself a superior thing. Time and history take on the ambivalent character of an inevitable (blind and neutral) progression which is, however, in its present moment the only truth and is to be promoted with ardent loyalty.

I V

THE greatest Russian literary figure to participate in the 19th-century complex of socio-realistic theory and the writer whose pronouncements on art have impinged with most authority on the English literary mind, was undoubtedly Tolstoy—"the conscience of Russia" in his time, "the conscience of the world," "the conscience of humanity." [3] One might suppose offhand that Tolstoy could not very readily be assimilated to the materialistic trend of Russian social theory. He was in his middle age a violent convert to a certain kind of Christian thinking. A period of furious tractarian activity followed the production of the great novels. And it is a religious theory of literature that near the end of his life issues in his thunderously deliberate denunciation of all that he himself and all that European artists for 300 years had created. Tolstoy's *What Is Art?*, 1898, was published simultaneously in both Russian and English and was widely honored by English readers for its weight and elaboration and for its many passages of profound insight and passionate conviction. It pursued a religious argument—not, however, in the traditional sense. The religious feelings aroused in Tolstoy as he looks back over his career as liberal aristocrat and novelist run heavily counter to the established Christian institutions and to the whole cultural hierarchy related to them. The religion which appears in his tracts, beginning with *A Confession* in 1878,[4] and in all his essays on art, is a form of Christian anarchy, a wide and simple kind of religious feeling for the brotherhood of man and his common relation of sonship to God. Tolstoy's *What Is Art?* fits comfortably enough in the Russian complex, and Tolstoy too has his niche in the Marxist retrospect.

As a literary theorist, Tolstoy appears in the main tradition of emotive art theory developed during the 19th century along rather simple lines from the 18th-century concept which we have noted as late as the essays of Mill. But other versions of emotivism which appear during

[3] Cf. Ernest J. Simmons, *Leo Tolstoy* (Boston, 1946), p. 488; review by E. C. Ross, *Saturday Review of Literature*, XXX (January 18, 1947), 17.

[4] See Matthew Arnold's account of these in his long review of *Anna Karenina* included under the title *Count Leo Tolstoy* in *Essays in Criticism, Second Series*.

this era, and notably the expressionist theory of Véron,[5] have a more aesthetic orientation. Tolstoy's version is strongly anti-aesthetic. Art is to be known by its power of wholesome emotive "infection." He has a theory about the social function of art which invites comparison with the theories of Shelley and Comte. (Science, the pioneer thinker, is a little boat which takes kedge-anchors upstream to new positions; art is the windlass of moral energy which draws the barge up to the new positions. Chapter XX.) [6] And he more or less unwittingly accepts the paradox of the historically emergent new truth which we have noted among the earlier Russians.

There is a chapter (V) where Tolstoy first expounds his infection theory, and here he seems mainly to say that art transmits *emotion*. Then at the end of the same chapter he says that art transmits *religious* emotion. There are several other chapters (VI, IX, XI, XX) where he seems to say that art always transmits the genuine, the "fresh" religious emotion of any age. He uses such phrases as the "highest life-conception of a time" (XI), "the highest conception accessible to their age" (VI), "the highest level of life-comprehension" (IX). Finally, there is a chapter (XVI) where he says that the art of the *present* age must transmit only the progressive religious emotions of this age, those that relate to the universal brotherhood of man.[7]

Thus a problem arises (even though Tolstoy does not see it) concerning that which was once new but is now old.

> From the religious perception of the ancient Greeks flowed the really new, important, and endlessly varied feelings expressed by Homer and the tragic writers.—IX

> . . . good, supreme art; the Iliad, the Odyssey. . . . —X

> But the Christian idea changed and reversed everything, so that as the Gospel puts it, "That which was exalted among men has become an abomination in the sight of God." The ideal is no longer the greatness of Pharaoh or of a Roman emperor, not the beauty of a Greek nor the wealth of Phoenicia, but humility, purity, compassion, love.—XVI

> The artists of the Middle Ages, vitalized by the same source of feeling—religion—as the mass of the people, and transmitting

[5] Eugene Véron, *Aesthetics*, trans. W. H. Armstrong (London, 1897). Véron has optimistic evolutionary and secular millenarian views which are comparable to those of Tolstoy. "What shall we say, then, about the sentiments which are the true glories of our age,—charity, toleration, respect for womanhood, for childhood, and for human life? Pity for animals, is not that, too, a sign of the times?" (p. 353)

[6] See *What is Art? and Essays on Art*, trans. Aylmer Maude (Oxford: World's Classics, 1930).

[7] A second place is given to certain universally accessible, or folk, emotions— namely, merriment, pity, cheerfulness, and tranquillity (Ch. XVI).

. . . the feelings and states of mind they experienced, were true artists; and their activity, founded on the highest conceptions accessible to their age and common to the entire people—though for our times a mean art—was nevertheless a true one, shared by the whole community.—VI

European society [of the Renaissance] went back in their comprehension of art to the gross conception of the primitive Greeks, which Plato had already condemned.—VI

. . . rude, savage, and for us, often meaningless works of the ancient Greeks: Sophocles, Euripides, Aeschylus. . . .—XII

If by art it has been inculcated on people how they should treat religious objects, their parents, their children, their wives . . . and if this has been obeyed through generations by millions of people . . . then by art also other customs more in accord with the religious perception of our time may be evoked.—XX

Presumably the degenerate European art of Tolstoy's time would have been religious art in another era. And we are left with some question whether the religious perception of the new time is a genuine material for art because it is a better perception or because it is the latest.[8]

But Tolstoy is sufficiently compelling in his indictment of the effete emotions—the pride, sexual desire, and ennui which rule the upper-class patrons of the "pleasure arts" in his day. His walloping caricatures of metropolitan fashionable culture—the art show, the salon, the theater, the opera in rehearsal, art schools and art criticism—manage to suggest not only lavish waste and a measure of social injustice but a deplorable perplexity of aesthetic judgment and widespread vitiation of taste. He notices with scorn the new aesthetics of the lower senses—the five-sense aesthetics of gustatory, olfactory, and tactile pleasure which in that day was fulfilling the promise of 18th-century sensationalism and had some connection with the kinds of aesthetic autonomy then in vogue.[9] In short Tolstoy gives pointed expression to the difficult and permanent aesthetic problem whether a non-didactic or autonomous theory of art is bound to be merely a "hedonistic" or pleasure theory of art. He issues us an urgent invitation to ponder the validity of a café-society aesthetic devotion ranging from theater, orchestra, museum, and gallery, through opera and ballet, to the refinements of dinner with chartreuse, cigars, and music. *Aut prodesse . . . aut delectare*—Horace

[8] These paradoxes of post-Hegelian thinking are the paradigm for such quirks in later intellectual history as the appearance on the mid-20th-century American scene of the "premature" anti-communist, or the exclusive sanctity which the *Partisan* kind of liberalism confers upon the repentant Marxist.

[9] Cf. *post* Chapter 22, "Art for Art's Sake."

had given the poet his alternatives. Is there any other—aside from the merely mixed way of "winning all the votes" which Horace suggests? Must the interpretation of *delectare* incline to the frivolity of a merely sensate indulgence?

Tolstoy gives us another impressive set of negative judgments in a chapter (XI) on "counterfeit" art, under four main heads: "borrowing," "imitation," "striking," and "interesting." Or, in terms that may be nearer to our own minds: stock responses, local-color realism, pornography and horror, detective story plots. (Wagner's *Nibelungen Ring* is a model combination of the four ways!) Tolstoy is very pure, very austere, very acute in his opinion of what is not art, and very firm in his will to condemn it.

Yet his sternly exclusive standard would be even more impressive if he had left it less explicitly illustrated. For the application of the standard is horrifying in its sweep. The whole body of medieval, Renaissance, and modern European art—the work of Dante, Tasso, Shakespeare, Milton, Goethe, Raphael, Michelangelo, Bach, Beethoven, for instance (Chapter XII) [1]—is swept away, and with it the great novels of Tolstoy himself. He shows no compunction. "I belong," he says, "to the class of people whose taste has been perverted by false training" (XVI). He is willing to salvage only two of his simplest short stories: *God Sees the Truth but Waits*, the pathetic fable of a man railroaded to Siberia who, after growing old in the prison camp, discovers his enemy and forgives him; and *A Prisoner of the Caucasus*, a tender idyll, full of village and childhood colors, about a Russian officer captured by Tartars and helped to escape by a girl of the tribe. [2] Nearly forty years earlier Tolstoy had set up a school for peasant children in his ancestral estate at Yasnaya Polyana, and two boys Semka and Fedka had written for his school magazine stories which he called "in their way, equal to anything in Russian literature." It seemed to him "strange and offensive" that he "should hardly be able except at a happy moment of excitement to keep up with" these inspired peasant boys. [3] The simplicity, even sentimentality, of the aesthetic norm adopted by Tolstoy may be inspected in the half-tones which embellish Aylmer Maude's large edition of *What Is Art?*, [4] presenting examples of the pictorial art which Tolstoy at various places in his book selects for special commendation:—the peasant boy of Turgenev's story dreaming of the quail, the war widow

[1] Schiller, Hugo, Dickens, Harriet Beecher Stowe, Dostoevski, George Eliot, Cervantes, Molière, Gogol, Pushkin (Chap. XVI) have produced examples of art that *seem* good to Tolstoy, but he attaches no "importance" to his own taste.

[2] Tolstoy's Preface to another short story, Chekhov's *Darling*, argues, according to a principle we have noticed in the earlier Russian critics, that the author expresses a humanitarian meaning in his own despite.

[3] Aylmer Maude, *Life of Tolstoy*, vol. I, Chap. viii (World's Classics, c. 1930, I, 269–70).

[4] *Tolstoy on Art*, trans. Aylmer Maude (Boston, 1924).

weeping in the room behind the balcony overlooking the victory parade, the peasant girls giggling at a society huntsman, Russian peasants paying out money at a state liquor monopoly. In religious painting Tolstoy preferred N. N. Gay's drably natural *Last Supper* and *What is Truth?* to Manet's Pre-Raphaelite *Angels at the Tomb of Christ*. Millet's *The Man with the Hoe* is an object of his preference which his editor seems to have thought it needless to illustrate.

Tolstoy's exclusiveness raises the difficult aesthetic problem of "communication." Art for whom? [5] A "country peasant of unperverted taste" will detect the genuine work of art easily and unerringly (XIV). And Tolstoy seems to assume that the numerous peasantry are far more likely than the few genteel folk actually to have an unperverted taste. "Unperverted" *means* in fact uncomplicated, ordinary. "Good, great, universal, religious art may be incomprehensible to a small circle of spoilt people, but certainly not to any large number of plain men" (X). The democratic consumers' argument which we have noted here and there in the past, in Longinus, in Castelvetro, in Samuel Johnson, arrives at its fullest realization in Tolstoy.

He applies the norm of easy comprehensibility with special satisfaction against the immediately contemporary "decadent" art which he is most bent on condemning. The truth about this art—the pictures in the Paris impressionist and symbolist exhibitions of 1894, the poetry of Baudelaire, Mallarmé, Verlaine, Maeterlinck—was that it was not only luxurious and effete but also impertinently obscure. It tried to elevate inaccuracy, indefiniteness, lack of eloquence into marks of esteem. Tolstoy's heavily documented attack on symbolist poetry (Chap. X) takes in, along with a difficult sonnet by Mallarmé and a perhaps tenuously rewarding lyric by Maeterlinck, several much easier pieces, including a prose poem by Baudelaire which one finds it almost impossible to believe offered any resistance at all to Tolstoy's penetration. "*Eh bien! cher ange, je me figure que c'est vous! Et il ferma les yeux et il lâcha la détente. La poupée fut nettement décapitée.*" The loosely associated ideas of the obscure and immoral in Tolstoy's treatment of symbolist poetry strongly invite us to understand that the flippancy is morally chaotic and, just in that sense, obscure too.[6] The broad thesis

[5] In one place (XV) he wants to make the infectiousness of art depend on "individuality" of feeling, on clarity, and on sincerity. The artist is infected by his own production; writes for himself. Hence he expresses something individual and something which because of its individuality is clear to his audience. The least little stroke, says Tolstoy, makes the difference (XII). But it is difficult to relate this norm to his broad demands for the religious emotion. Cf. his introduction to Semenov's *Peasant Stories*.

[6] The view could hardly be maintained with complete consistency. Tolstoy's Introduction to the *Works of de Maupassant*, 1894, for instance, seems to take Maupassant's intelligibility for granted, though laboring his immorality (*What is Art?* World's Classics ed., pp. 21, 26, 33, 39).

suggested, though never quite stated, is that the fault of obscurity in art is a fault of immorality—and conversely that immorality is a kind of obscurity. Obscurity means obscurantism, confusion, nihilism, the invocation of chaos.

Tolstoy had been reading Shakespeare all his life, in at least three languages, Russian, German, English. At the age of 75, five years after *What Is Art?*, provoked by an English article on "Shakespeare and the Working Classes," he re-read the whole of Shakespeare and responded with a tirade.[7] G. Wilson Knight in an *English Association Pamphlet, Shakespeare and Tolstoy*,[8] has perhaps done as much as anyone to explain some part of Tolstoy's views by relating them to the "rocklike simplicity" of Tolstoy himself as a master of the realistic novel. The symbolic technique and verse conventions of the Elizabethan drama threw him off so badly that he was unable, for instance, to perceive that Shakespeare's characters speak at all differently from one another.

> [Shakespeare] is lacking in the chief, if not the sole, means of portraying character, which is individuality of language—that each person should speak in a way suitable to his own character. . . . All his characters speak, not a language of their own but always one and the same Shakespearian, affected, unnatural language, which not only could they not speak, but which no real people could ever have spoken anywhere.
>
> Lear raves just as Edgar does when feigning madness. Kent and the fool both speak alike. The words of one person can be put in the mouth of another, and by the character of the speech it is impossible to know who is speaking.
>
> The person [9] uttering these various thoughts becomes a mere phonograph of Shakespeare, deprived of any character of his own.

And the deplorable social values reflected in Shakespeare's writing—the feudal respect for kings and dukes, the disesteem of the working classes!

> The content of Shakespeare's plays . . . is the lowest, most vulgar view of life, which regards the external elevation of the great ones of the earth as a genuine superiority; despises the crowd, that is to say, the working classes; and repudiates not only religious, but even any humanitarian, efforts directed toward the alteration of the existing order of society.

The rejection both of Shakespeare's artful intentions and of his artless accomplishment comes near to being total.

[7] *Shakespeare and the Drama*, published in 1906, essay XVII in *Tolstoy on Art*, ed. Aylmer Maude (Boston, 1924).
[8] No. 88, April 1934.
[9] Hamlet.

The third and chief condition—sincerity—is totally absent in all Shakespeare's works. One sees in all of them an intentional artificiality; it is obvious that he is not in earnest but is playing with words.

Whatever people may say, however they may be enraptured by Shakespeare's works, whatever merits they may attribute to him, it is certain that he was not an artist, and that his works were not artistic productions. . . . Shakespeare may be anything you like—only not an artist.[1]

V

THE destruction of the idea "art for art's sake" and the reconstruction of art as a monitor and propagandist for the social process is the gist of Tolstoy's preachment, and this has been also the monotonous burden of subsequent Marxist criticism in Russia and the instructed echoes of this in English and American writing which sounded in the later 1920's and the 1930's. In Marxist writing the basic theme has received a fanatically detailed articulation according to the philosophy of dialectical materialism. Prominent features have been (1) an emphasis on class propaganda and revolutionary didacticism and on the ideological specifications of the total state; (2) a corresponding emphasis on the deterministic origins of art—the economic and social status (proletarian, bourgeois, pseudo-bourgeois, or aristocratic) of artists and artisans in various past eras. Party-line writers have occasionally paused to disclaim any simple deterministic view of art, and they have done this in the name of Marx himself, who said: "Certain periods of highest development of art stand in no direct connection with the general development of society, nor with the material basis and the skeleton structure of its organization." [2] Yet the general mood of Marxism and of other kinds of social criticism, even the most conservative, does not make much room for such refinements. Shakespeare appeared because "we were just in a financial position to afford" him; he "flourished in the atmosphere of buoyancy, exhilaration and the freedom of economic cares felt by the governing class, which is engendered by profit inflations." [3] Or, on

[1] To Tolstoy's credit stands the following contradictory anecdote. "Once, when his friend Chekhov came to see him when he was ill in bed, he pressed the latter's hand at parting and said, 'Good-bye, Anton Pavlovich. You know how fond I am of you and how I detest Shakespeare. Still, he did write better plays than you do'" (Aylmer Maude, *Tolstoy on Art*, Boston 1924, p. 19).

[2] Ralph Fox, *The Novel and the People* (1937), Chap. I, in Mark Schorer *et al.*, *Criticism, The Foundation of Modern Literary Judgment*, pp. 134-7.

[3] John Maynard Keynes, *A Treatise on Money* (New York, 1930), II, 154, quoted by Wellek and Warren, p. 102.

the contrary: "Shakespeare's tragic outlook on the world was consequential upon his being the dramatic expression of the feudal aristocracy, which in Elizabeth's day had lost their former dominant position." [4]

According to the Marxist theory, English poetry of the 19th century has in one way or another shown the growing isolation of the modern artist from the bourgeois machine culture in which he was for a time seductively protected, his increasing anarchic agony, and his effort to renounce the culture in ways which have been only mirror images of it. He has lacked a systematic revolutionary outlook, the real rationale of insurgency which would have made him something positive, an affirmatively proletarian artist. In the 20th century T. S. Eliot is said to make the last decadent gesture of the mentality which has turned away from the historico-social reality and sought refuge in the ivory tower of poetry and beauty pure. Among the Russians, the socialist Georgi Plekhanov in his *Art and Society*, 1912–1913 (English translation, 1936), and Leon Trotsky in *Literature and Revolution*, 1923, have elaborated this basic view of the modern poet's isolation from reality. And Christopher Caudwell in *Illusion and Reality*,[5] 1937, has made the applications to English literature. In a call to the barricades which echoed for twenty years, Lenin cried out: "Down with supermen-litterateurs. . . . Literature must become a component part of the organized, planned, unified Socialist party work." [6]

Seen from the genetic point of view, Marxist criticism has some curious affinities. The professional literary student will scarcely be horrified by the bourgeois origin of a given literature; he is not likely to evaluate writers according to the degree of their integration in a totalitarian process, or to believe that the Bohemian, the *poète maudit,* the untrammeled genius is necessarily an artistic bungler. Yet the Marxist program for literature—if one leaves out of account its hortatory violence—is able to take its place with some comfort as an application of the historical idea which purely literary scholars in the tradition of Thomas Warton and Hippolyte Taine have worked out so successfully, for their own purposes, during the past 200 years.[7] The specifically Marxist genetic approach takes its place quite gracefully as one of that numerous kind in literary studies which has attended to social and economic origins—to the mark upon his work made by the professional status of the dithyrambic tragedian, the *Minnesänger*, the court dramatist, the Grubstreet hack, or the affluent 19th-century periodical

---

[4] Anatoli V. Lunacharsky, in *The Listener*, December 27, 1934, quoted by Wellek and Warren, p. 102.

[5] See Chapter VI, "English Poets: The Decline of Capitalism," reproduced in Mark Schorer *et al.*, pp. 125–33.

[6] Quoted by W. V. O'Connor, *An Age of Criticism*, p. 115.

[7] Cf. *post* Chapter 24.

novelist.[8] It is less than a paradox that the Marxist critic, in all the severity of his logic, should have driven this method of the modern literary student to a conclusion that completely destroys the literary viewpoint.

Seen as a demand on the character of literature itself, Marxist criticism prescribes the broad picture of social reality, the novel of sound views, the social document, the party-line mimesis, the blue-print for social planning. And it equally proscribes the lyric cry, the personal relation, the individually intricate symbol, the detachment of contemplation, and any engagement that either bypasses or transcends the totalitarian social responsibility. It does not believe in the work of art. There is no good social art of the kind it prescribes. Under Marxism society itself "becomes the work of art." [9]

VI

IN AMERICA the idea of a socially activist literature appears during the first decades of the 20th century with the "muckraking" movement (of which Upton Sinclair's *Mammonart*, 1924, may stand as the sufficient symbol) and after that in the overtly Marxist criticism of the later twenties and the thirties—the work of such writers as Michael Gold, editor of the *New Masses*, Joseph Freeman, editor of the anthology *Proletarian Literature in the United States*, 1935, and V. F. Calverton, editor of the *Modern Quarterly*. Here we meet a barefaced rehearsal of the whole canon of Marxist ideas—much about the pessimism and decay of the middle class, the inferiority of the "bourgeois sexual code," the modern sell-out of human values to the "burgher," much about the "creative role" of the worker and the need of the novelist to keep up with "the vanguard of the Proletariat." We hear that the experiments of Joyce, Eliot, and Cummings are misguided and incommunicative, that on the contrary Emerson had confidence in the common man, that Whitman enjoyed a kinship with workers and farmers and had glimpses of a collective society.[1] A major monument was Vernon Louis Parrington's three-volume *Main Currents in American Thought* (1927–1930), where "thought" is equated with literature, and the sufficient principle of economic determinism receives a value shading that is "liberal" and "Jef-

[8] Cf. Wellek and Warren, pp. 93–5. Brander Matthews, "The Economic Interpretation of Literary History," in his *Gateways to Literature and Other Essays* (New York, 1912), is a good American instance of this kind of inquiry.

[9] Edmund Wilson, quoted by W. V. O'Connor, *An Age of Criticism*, p. 126.

[1] W. V. O'Connor, *An Age of Criticism*, pp. 119–24, quoting, among other works, Calverton's *The Newer Spirit* (1925) and *The Liberation of American Literature* (1932), Granville Hicks's "The Crisis in Criticism" in the *New Masses* (1933) and *The Great Tradition: An Interpretation of American Literature Since the Civil War* (1933), and Bernard Smith's *Forces in American Criticism* (1939).

fersonian." [2] Parrington gives us the following flowers of the economic and realist spirit in criticism.

> The problem of Poe, fascinating as it is, lies quite outside the main current of American thought, and it may be left to the psychologist and the belletrist with whom it belongs.[3]

> Hawthorne was the extreme and finest expression of the refined alienation from reality that in the end palsied the creative mind of New England.[4]

> In his subtle psychological inquires, . . . [Henry James] remained shut up within his own skull-pan.[5]

Marxism and the forms of social criticism more closely related to it have never had any real concern with literature and literary problems. In this country the cause enlisted some keen journalistic and literary minds. But a number of them, like Max Eastman as editor of *The Masses*, avoided sociology in their literary criticism. Eastman shied away from doctrinal and scientific claims for literature and worked up a theory of vivid sensory realization that belongs rather in the tradition of art for art's sake. Edmund Wilson in *Axel's Castle*, 1931, made gestures acknowledging the social responsibility of the artist but only as if in atonement for his having dwelt at such length among the mysteries of symbolism. As early as the anthology acclaiming *Proletarian Literature* in 1935, the editors of the *Partisan Review* were observing a flow of "gush" and "invective," in place of analysis, and the exercise of Marxism as a "sentiment" rather than a "science." James T. Farrell's *A Note on Literary Criticism*, 1936, is a critique by an "amateur Marxist" of the party-line simplifications. By 1939 it was possible for the *Partisan* editor Philip Rahv to write an essay under the title "Proletarian Literature: A Political Autopsy." [6] Marxist naturalism persists in American letters today less as a proclaimed cause than as a deeply rooted sympathy (a Gnostic utopianism) ready with each shift in political or literary dialectics to exert itself in a new stratagem. Perhaps the notion of "myth," despite its Germanic, Jungian, and quasi-religious orientation, is the latest of these.[7]

[2] Parrington's Introduction to the first volume and E. H. Eby's Introduction to the posthumous third volume, quoted in W. V. O'Connor, *An Age of Criticism*, pp. 119–20; see also p. 123, the passages next quoted from Parrington.

[3] *Main Currents in American Thought* (New York: Harcourt, Brace and Company, Inc., 1927–30), II, 58.

[4] II, 450.

[5] III, 241.

[6] *Southern Review*, IV (Winter, 1939), 616–28. Cf. Morton D. Zabel, *Literary Opinion in America* (New York, 1951), p. 36; Charles I. Glicksberg, *American Literary Criticism* (New York, 1952), pp. 46–52.

[7] Cf. *post* Chapter 31.

VII

THE main critical issue raised by the tradition of socio-realism—and this was apparent at least as far back as the indignation of Tolstoy over symbolist poetry—is that of "expression" and "communication." The bringing together of these two terms, one so strongly invoking the mind and inspiration of the artist, and the other so heavily entailing the receptivity and demands of the audience (what audience? communication to whom?), is today an especially important problem for the critic who believes in objective aesthetic values. But even the discussion of the problem (not to mention its solution) involves ideas of dramatic inclusiveness and artistic detachment which lie far beyond the range-finding sensitivity of the propagandist programs.

So far as the problem of poetic communication is peculiarly a social one, the opposing energies have been defined in our time with the most original insight by the philosopher Ortega y Gasset, in two complementary works. On the one hand he describes *The Revolt of the Masses*, a cultural phenomenon far more complicated than anything envisaged by the Marxist mind, and appearing in one of its aspects as a vast increase in the number and confidence of uneducated readers.

> Today we are witnessing the triumphs of a hyperdemocracy. . . . the present-day writer, when he takes his pen in hand to treat a subject which he has studied deeply, has to bear in mind that the average reader, who has never concerned himself with this subject, if he reads does so with the view, not of learning something from the writer, but rather, of pronouncing judgment on him when he is not in agreement with the commonplaces that the said reader carries in his head. If the individuals who make up the mass believed themselves specially qualified, it would be a case merely of personal error, not a sociological subversion. *The characteristic of the hour is that the commonplace mind, knowing itself to be commonplace, has the assurance to proclaim the rights of the commonplace and to impose them wherever it will.* . . . The mass crushes beneath it everything that is different, everything that is excellent, individual, qualified and select. Anybody who is not like everybody, who does not think like everybody, runs the risk of being eliminated.[8]

And on the other hand, there appears the exclusiveness and withdrawal of the modern artist in search of a fresh vision, a process which Ortega calls *The Dehumanization of Art*.

[8] *The Revolt of the Masses*, Chapter I (Mentor Book, 1952), p. 12. By permission of W. W. Norton & Company, Inc. The Spanish version appeared in 1930.

Romanticism was the prototype of a popular style. First-born of democracy, it was coddled by the masses.

Modern art, on the other hand will always have the masses against it. It is essentially unpopular; moreover, it is antipopular.

. . . . the split occurs in a deeper layer than that on which differences of personal taste reside. It is not that the majority does not *like* the art of the young and the minority likes it, but that the majority, the masses, do not *understand* it.

But such a thing cannot be done after a hundred years of adulation of the masses and apotheosis of the people. Accustomed to ruling supreme, the masses feel that the new art, which is the art of a privileged aristocracy of finer senses, endangers their rights as men. Whenever the new Muses present themselves, the masses bristle.[9]

Marxism considers modern vulgar art to be a feat of the bourgeoisie, and the revolt of the romantic artist to be a weak anarchic effort which mirrors in negative the same standards. The literary critic, or the metaphysician, of more classical perspective is likely to look on the Marxist alternative as itself a mirror revolution of socialized materialism against privately competitive materialism. In the crudity both of its determinism and of its inconsistent propagandism, the socio-realistic tradition of literary criticism has on the whole contributed little to an understanding of the relation which universality bears to individuality in artistic expression.

SUPPLEMENT

A laissez faire economy such as was dominant in the recent past is basically hostile to great art. "As in economics, so in art: laissez-faire within a capitalist economy (or within any economy) merely abandons art to the chances of unrestricted competition, and the devil take the hindmost. It means that art becomes one more commodity on the free market, and that to succeed it must practice all the wiles of salesmanship—mass appeal, sex appeal, adulteration, and the sacrifice of quality to cheapness." (Herbert Read, "Culture and Liberty," *Nation*, CLII, April 2, 1941, p. 438). On the other hand, a general-welfare-society, such as has been lately envisioned widely is, I believe, in principle, fertile soil for the realization of the ideal of art. . . .

[9] *The Dehumanization of Art and Notes on the Novel*, trans. Helene Weyl (Princeton: Princeton University Press, 1948), pp. 5–7. Cf. Q. D. Leavis, *Fiction and the Reading Public* (London, 1932).

Something of this sort, a beginning at least in certain directions, seems to have happened in Russia as it has struggled to its feet, following revolution, in recent decades. The arts there have had a position not unlike that in the best "organic" societies. They have been integrated with institutions enshrining a widely supported unity of belief. They have had not only official but immense popular support. The artist has been held in the highest esteem. His training has been anxiously attended to. He himself has enjoyed great respect and prestige. He has dedicated himself to the enrichment of the life of all the people. Commercialism between artist and audience has been eliminated and the disposition toward official interference, although certainly far from nonexistent, has been felt adversely far less than is commonly believed. The arts have been carried to the factories and farms and the remotest villages, and the great figures of art, such as the Pushkins and the Gorkys, are among the greatest national heroes. Nor have the arts been made the tool of merely "nationalistic" interests, although the relation of the arts to the life of the people has been kept immediate and evident. Traveling historical museums and theaters have penetrated into all parts of the country, the arts of all mankind have been displayed and studied, and sometimes a non-Russian artist has become as great a hero as the greatest of Russians, e.g., Shakespeare as great as Pushkin.

—D. W. Gotshalk, *Art and the Social Order* (Chicago: The University of Chicago Press, 1947), pp. 236–8. Copyright (1947) by the University of Chicago. A footnote on p. 238 cites as authorities for the view presented a generous selection of volumes dated in the 1930's.

CHAPTER 22

ART FOR ART'S SAKE

§ *aesthetic autonomy, early modern hints, German ideal-ism, an ambiguous ground, Benjamin Constant, Bourbon restoration, Madame de Staël, Cousin and Jouffroy, "Ger-man aesthetics," freedom, art for art's sake, a common-place—II. an atmospheric idea, E. A.* Poe, *blend of sources,* Philosophy of Composition, Poetic Principle, *diffuse Kantian elements, "Supernal Beauty," beauty an effect, different from passion and truth, the fate of M. Valdemar, importance of Poe—III. affinity for Baudelaire, beauty and evil, morality penetrates art, Poe and human anomaly, flowers of evil, "Epilogue," original sin, the "magic" of art,* Eloge du Maquillage, *art not illusion, Parnassian formalism—IV. aestheticism in England, Arnold's judg-ment, Swinburne's* Poems and Ballads *(1866), revolt from "middle class" moralism, "practical aestheticism,"* Wilde, De Profundis, *dandyism, "art," "beauty," "sensation," "passion,"* Pater, The Renaissance, *"gem-like flame," the-ory of moral subject matter (Ruskin), aesthetic counter theories: (1) "slim gilded feet," (2) indifference to subject, "negative capability" (Keats), Poe again, vita contempla-tiva—V. pure "form,"* Wilde, Intentions, *craftsmanship, verse technique, English "Parnassians," rondeau, ballade, etc., poetry and other arts again, Gautier's* Emaux et Camées, *Pater,* Améthystes *and* Intaglios, *Whistler's "Arrangement in Black and Gray," Roger Fry and Clive Bell, exclusiveness and abstraction, "significant form," warning for literary theory—VI.* Whistler, Gentle Art of Making Enemies, *nature imitates art,* Florentine Nights, *Wilde,* Decay of Lying *(anthology of passages), impres-sionist criticism, Lamb, Hazlitt, Sainte-Beuve, et al., soul among masterpieces, sensibility, Wilde,* The Critic as Artist, *the argument full circle: Arnold and Wilde the sons of F. Schlegel* §

475

THE REVOLUTIONARY VINDICATION OF POETRY BY GERMAN ROMANTICS and their followers resulted during the 19th century, as we have been seeing, in at least three main types of poetic theory which made claims upon ethics and politics. These were the Shelleyan and Carlylean rhapsodic retort to scientism, the Arnoldian neo-classic idealism, and the socio-realistic propagandism generated in Germany, Russia, and France. But the reassertion of poetic rights could take yet another turn, antithetic to the didacticism inherent in all those other three. Poetry— or art in general—might draw off by itself and be content with an emphatic assertion of autonomy—its own kind of intrinsic worth, to be understood and savored by its own devotees. It could be set up as a legitimate pursuit, apart from, and perhaps even in defiance of, the rival norms of ethics and politics.

This notion of art as a terminal value had appeared even during antiquity in the alternative offered the poet, *aut prodesse aut delectare*. It had gained a gradual and subtle emphasis in all those Renaissance versions of classic theory which reversed the usual formula to say that pleasing was somehow more important than teaching or was somehow the end aimed at through teaching. And such approaches to a theory of aesthetic autonomy gained greatly during the 18th century as literary theory first retreated from classical didacticism and then, after following Leibnizian and Lockean psychological lines, reacted against these too, shifting an emphasis on sensory and emotive pleasure toward various conceptions of "taste," inner sense, the absolute beauty of order and harmony, and pleasure without desire. The ideas of Shaftesbury, Hutcheson and other British aesthetic writers were paralleled in France and Germany by Diderot, Sulzer, Mendelssohn, and many others.[1] The transcendental synthesis of Kant's *Critique of Judgment* summarized all such trends and first lent weighty metaphysical authority to the pure aesthetic claim. The mythopoeic and symbolist doctrines of German idealist critics, by generally strengthening the position of art, provided an area of mobilization not only for the didactic claims which we have seen but for the characteristically 19th-century reaction to didacticism which moved under the aegis of art for art's sake. Either development was a more or less legitimate, if simplistic, move from the German positions. There was a fundamental uncertainty in the claim of art to create meanings, to mark out pathways of knowledge, which led perhaps inevitably toward multiple forms both of didacticism and of autonomism.

The French *littérateur* Benjamin Constant, attaching himself to

---

[1] Diderot's article *"Beau"* in the *Dictionnaire Encyclopédique*, 1751; J. G. Sulzer, *Allgemeine Theorie des Schönen Künste*, 1771–1774; Moses Mendelssohn, *Die Morgenstunden*, 1785. See Wellek, *History* I, 54, 149; and *ante* Chapter 13, pp. 276–7.

German literary circles in the year 1804, gives us in his *Journal intime* (not published until many years later) a casual glimpse of how the phrase "art for art's sake" may have begun to develop out of Kantian doctrine in Weimar-Jena discussions.

> Schiller calls. He is a man of keen mind in his art but almost wholly the poet. . . . I have a visit with [Henry Crabb] Robinson, pupil of Schelling's. His work on the *Esthetics* of Kant has some very forceful ideas. *L'art pour l'art* without purpose, for all purpose perverts art. But art attains the purpose that it does not have.[2]

With the return to Paris of intellectualist emigrés (among them Constant and his friend Madame de Staël) and the Bourbon restoration in 1814, began the era of a new and vaguely Kantian aesthetic in France. In the account of Kantian thought contained in Madame de Staël's *De l'Allemagne*,[3] first brought to Paris from England in 1813, in the exciting lectures of Victor Cousin at the Sorbonne during 1816–1818,[4] and in those of his pupil Jouffroy, the key ideas, or at least the key rubrics, of the new aesthetics were first popularized. On a tide of vaguely simplified Kantian thinking such terms as "German aesthetics," "Kant's aesthetics," "freedom," "disinterestedness," "pure art," "pure beauty," "form," and "genius" were floated into currency, and along with them the term "art for art's sake." It appeared in print perhaps for the first time in a journalistic skirmish of 1833.[5] In the Preface to his *Premières poésies*, 1832, Gautier, it is true, was able to pronounce his defiance of economists, utilitarians, utopians, Saint-Simonians, and all others of their purposeful kind without once invoking the term. ("What end does this book serve? It serves the end of being beautiful?") But in his article entitled *"Du Beau dans l'art,"* appearing in the *Revue des deux mondes* during 1847, *l'art pour l'art* seems to enjoy the status of a recently established commonplace—"cette formule devenue *célèbre par des polémiques.*"[6]

II

It is not, however, in the history of the term "art for art's sake" only, nor in the French school of aesthetic thinking only, that we may observe

---

[2] D. Melagari, *Journal Intime de Benjamin Constant* (Paris, 1895), p. 7, entry for February 10, 1804. Quoted by John Wilcox, "The Beginnings of *L'Art pour l'Art*," *JAAC*, XI (June, 1953), 360.

[3] *De l'Allemagne* (Paris, 1820), II, 290 ff. Wilcox, p. 365. The Paris edition appeared in 1814.

[4] Cousin's lectures were edited by his pupils from his class notes and printed twenty years later, 1836–42. See the exposition by Wilcox, pp. 367–8.

[5] Hippolyte Fortoul, in *La Revue Encyclopédique*, LIX, 109. Wilcox, p. 371.

[6] Wilcox, pp. 371, 376. Cf. Gautier's Preface to *Mademoiselle de Maupin*, 1834.

the development of that formula. The new idea spread out pervasively
and subtly; it was atmospheric. Shortly before the middle of the century, one of the most theatrical presentations occurs in the essays and
reviews of the American Gothic story-teller and poet Edgar Allan Poe.
Poe's critical origins were at first confusedly Coleridgean and Wordsworthian, with considerable borrowing from the English translation of
A. W. Schlegel's *Dramatic Lectures*.[7] He cherished ideas of lyric
brevity, unity of interest, "indefinite" pleasure, music, beauty. Later,
on reviewing a volume of the new phrenology, he picked up a physico-
psychological support for his sympathies, in the notion of a "Faculty of
Ideality—which is the sentiment of Poesy." After 1840 he apparently
became acquainted with Shelley's rhapsodic defence of romantic imagination. Only in his last efforts, the genetic tour de force entitled *The
Philosophy of Composition* (or how he went about thinking up *The
Raven*) and his last lecture, posthumously published in 1850, *The Poetic
Principle*, does the full luxuriance of Poe's opinion bloom.[8] We discover pronounced, if diffuse and vaporous, Kantian elements in Poe's
system: a division of the world of mind into pure intellect, taste, and
moral sense (with taste the intermediary between the other two); a
Kantian lack of esteem for mere reproduction of "beautiful" sounds,
colors, and odors; a general dreamy volume of enthusiasm for the
beautiful and the sublime and for the ethereal or supernal—for "Supernal
Beauty." (Tennyson[9] is the noblest poet who ever lived, because the
most "ethereal.")

> Inspired by an ecstatic prescience of the glories beyond the
> grave, we struggle, by multiform combinations among the
> things and thoughts of Time, to attain a portion of that Loveli-
> ness whose very elements, perhaps, appertain to eternity alone.

> *That* pleasure which is at once the most pure, the most elevat-
> ing, and the most intense, is derived, I maintain, from the con-
> templation of the Beautiful. In the contemplation of Beauty
> we alone find it possible to attain that pleasurable elevation,
> or excitement, *of the soul*, which we recognize as the Poetic

[7] Cf. Albert J. Lubell, "Poe and A. W. Schlegel," *JEGP*, LII (January, 1953),
1–12.

[8] See Poe's *Critical Essays*, ed. F. C. Prescott (New York, 1909), pp. xxx, 9–10;
Floyd Stovall, "Poe's Debt to Coleridge," *Studies in English*, No. 10, *The University
of Texas Bulletin*, July 8, 1930, pp. 70–127; Marvin Laser, "The Growth and Structure of Poe's Concept of Beauty," *ELH*, XV (March, 1948), 69–84.

[9] Poe's book reviews by and large look down upon the poetry of the 16th
and 17th centuries. Poetry began for him with Coleridge, Shelley, and Keats (Prescott,
p. xxix). The norm of lovely melancholy, developed so dramatically in *The Philosophy of Composition*, appears earlier in his Drake-Halleck review (*Southern Literary
Messenger*, April, 1836) along with the dogma that everything ludicrous is "utterly
at war with the Poetic Sentiment" and with the sentiments of the "mystical" and
the "august," which raise "fancy" to imagination (Laser, pp. 73–4).

Sentiment. . . . I make Beauty, therefore—using the word as inclusive of the Sublime—I make Beauty the province of the poem.[1]

But where is "beauty" located? Where but in the very experience of itself? "When, indeed, men speak of Beauty they mean, precisely, not a quality. . . . but an effect—they refer, in short, just to that intense and pure elevation of *soul* . . . which is experienced in consequence of contemplating 'the beautiful.' "[2] A certain amalgam or association of subject matters—the beautiful and the melancholy when these are "rhythmically created"[3] in a poem—produces in the reader that pleasurable elevation of soul which itself should justly be known as beauty.[4] Such devotion to "supernal beauty" entails a resolute disapproval of "passion" and, of course, a strict anti-didacticism.

> The manifestation of the [aesthetic] Principle is always found in *an elevating excitement of the Soul*—quite independent of that passion which is the intoxication of the Heart—or of that Truth which is the satisfaction of the Reason.

> For, in regard to Passion, alas! its tendency is to degrade, rather than to elevate the Soul.

> I allude to the heresy of *The Didactic*. . . . We Americans, especially, have patronised this happy idea; and we Bostonians, very especially, have developed it in full.[5]

There is much to Poe's credit in these latter Kantian clauses. Still the general picture is hazy. Ethereal vagueness and melancholy, evaporations of languorous and pallid loveliness wreathe the figure of Poe. His poems—*Ulalume, The Raven, Al Aaraaf, The City in the Sea, The Sleepers, Fairy-Land*—are softened and simplified counterparts of Coleridge's *Kubla Kahn, The Ancient Mariner, Christabel,* and *Youth and Age*. Poe's theoretical essays bear the same relation to chapters of Coleridge's *Biographia*. Neo-classic theory, in a way peculiar to itself, had rigidified or petrified, then dilapidated. Romantic theory did not do that. But in some of its inheritors it did liquefy or even vaporize. Poe's ideas are Kantian and Coleridgean aesthetic undergoing the fate of M. Valdemar. These writers deserved and got better epigonists. But Poe has become one of the most conspicuous, and his very existence

---

[1] *The Poetic Principle.*
[2] *The Philosophy of Composition.*
[3] "I would define, in brief, the Poetry of words as *The Rhythmical Creation of Beauty*" (*The Poetic Principle*). The emphasis on musicality and rhythm in Poe's last essays no doubt owes something to Shelley.
[4] See the analysis of this circularity by Charles C. Walcutt, "The Logic of Poe," *College English,* II (February, 1941), 438–44.
[5] *The Poetic Principle.*

says something of the era which they ushered in. It is possible to rate Poe up or down. It is difficult to avoid him. His criticism, said Henry James, is "probably the most complete and exquisite specimen of *provincialism* ever prepared for the edification of men." [6] He was, says T. S. Eliot, "not only an heroically courageous critic . . . but a critic of the first rank." [7]

III

It is a source of wonder to comparatists, but an inescapable fact, that the "exquisite provincialism" of Poe should have been highly relished by a spirit so sophisticated as Charles Baudelaire. The literary connection is underscored by the biographical: the sympathy to the degree of identification which Baudelaire felt for Poe, the reading of his own fate in Poe's supposedly aristocratic and feudal flight from American popular culture and in his supposedly ratiocinative discipline of mind so luridly contrasting to his nervous weakness, his dipsomania and wandering.

The title of Baudelaire's collected poems, *Les Fleurs du Mal*, stands as a ready brief symbol for the aesthetic devotion, the belief in beauty despite evil—in beauty through evil—which makes a large part in the reputation of Baudelaire. Yet Baudelaire was a critical essayist and journalist whose ideas one can hardly constrict within any of the simpler visions of art for art's sake. On the issue, baldly stated, whether art can escape the claims of morality, Baudelaire had a complex view. He alternates between the claim that his own poetry is *"un livre d'art pur"* and the opposite claim that it is a moral statement.[8] In other connections he comes out often enough against the current formulations of pure-art theory.

> The childish utopianism of the school of *art for art's sake*, in ruling out morals . . . was doomed to sterility. Art for art's sake was a flagrant defiance of human nature. On the authority of the higher and universal principles of life itself, we must convict the movement of heresy.[9]

> The feverish passion for art cankers and devours all else. And this . . . means the disappearance of art itself. The wholeness

[6] *Hawthorne* (New York, 1879), p. 62. James refers specifically to Poe's criticism of his American contemporaries.
[7] Review of *Israfel* by Hervey Allen, in *The Nation and Athenaeum*, XLI (May 2, 1927), 219.
[8] Marcel Françon, "Poe et Baudelaire," *PMLA*, LX (September, 1945), 841.
[9] *L'Art Romantique*, in *Oeuvres Complètes de Charles Baudelaire*, ed. Jacques Crépet, III (Paris, 1925), 184.

of the human being disintegrates. The specialization of a single faculty contracts toward nothingness.[1]

Morality does not appear with a formal title. Morality simply penetrates and blends itself with art as completely as with life itself. The poet is a moralist in spite of himself, simply through the overflowing abundance of his nature.[2]

Yet it would have been one thing for a Shelley, an Arnold, or a Tolstoy to have uttered statements like these; it was another thing for Baudelaire. Take them in the context of the essays in which they appear and of other essays by Baudelaire, and we see that here is a different enough accent from that of the didactic defenders of poetry. The accent, despite the concern for morals, is in a very special way on art itself. Perhaps the shade of emphasis comes from the cumulative coloring of passages rather than from any definitely abstract key terms.

It is imagination which has taught man the moral values of color, shape, sound, and perfumes. At the beginning of the world, imagination created analogy and metaphor. Imagination dissolves all creation. Remassing and reordering her materials by principles which come out of the depths of the human soul, imagination makes a new world, even a new realm of sensory experience. And as imagination has created this world (one may say this, I think, even in a religious sense), it is appropriate that the same faculty should govern it.[3]

Is there any such thing as a pernicious work of art? There is. It is one which distorts the patterns of living reality. . . . If a novel or a play is well made, it can be an invitation to nobody to deviate from the law of nature. The first requirement for a healthy art is a belief in an ordered whole of experience. I challenge anybody to show me a single work of imagination which satisfies the requirements of beauty and is at the same time pernicious.[4]

A passage from one of the three essays which Baudelaire wrote on Poe shows something of how the doctrine of moral order in art might relate to the artistic use of materials of a strikingly disordered sort. "That peculiar genius" of Poe's, Baudelaire writes, "that unique temperament enabled him—in a style at once impeccable and horribly compelling—to unfold the image of irregularity in the moral order. Let me repeat: no-

[1] *L'Art Romantique, Oeuvres*, III, 296.
[2] *L'Art Romantique, Oeuvres*, III, 382.
[3] *Salon de 1859*, in *Curiosités Esthétiques, Oeuvres Complètes* ed. Jacques Crépet, II (Paris, 1923), 274.
[4] *L'Art Romantique, Oeuvres*, III, 284.

body has had a more magical success in the portrayal of the human anomaly."[5] The magic of the anomaly, the burnished glow of perversion, the flowers out of evil, seem intrinsic to the Baudelairean vision of poetry as moral expression.

Epilogue

With heart at rest I climbed the citadel's
  Steep height, and saw the city as from a tower,
Hospital, brothel, prison, and such hells,

Where evil comes up softly like a flower,
  Thou knowest, O Satan, patron of my pain,
Not for vain tears I went up at that hour;

But, like an old and faithful lecher, fain
  To drink delight of that enormous trull
Whose hellish beauty makes me young again.

Whether thou sleep, with heavy vapors full,
  Sodden with day, or, new appareled, stand
In gold-laced veils of evening beautiful,

I love thee, infamous city! Harlots and
  Hunted have pleasures of their own to give,
The vulgar herd can never understand.[6]

The speaker asserts, without shame, his love for the infamous city, the enormous trull. Without shame? Yes, but not without something else, akin to shame, a luridly stated awareness that here is something shameful. There is more moral interest here than in certain simpler kinds of naturalistic celebration.

The German romantic and the Coleridgean versions of the creative power of poetry had moved toward closing the distance between art and nature, or toward elevating art into a higher and more ideal nature. Art was opposed to the artificial. In some instances the enterprise was to return art to the "nature" of a primitive unspoiled honesty. Such theory was part either of a radical optimism about the progress that could be made by the human imagination, or of an ironic self-assurance in the face of cosmic insufficiency. The romantic imagination did not believe in original sin. Nature was good. Quite the contrary with Baudelaire. The integration of which he speaks in some of the passages quoted above was to be a kind of preternatural transcendence—the "magic" of art—even if diabolical. The morality which Baudelaire conceives is something to

---

[5] *Edgar Poe, Sa Vie et Ses Oeuvres,* in *Histoires Extraordinaires par Edgar Poe, Oeuvres,* ed. Jacques Crépet, VIII (Paris 1932), xxviii–xxix.
[6] The translation of Arthur Symons.

which art may characteristically attain—but not naked nature. The poetry of Baudelaire despises vegetable fertility, clumps of trees and bushes. His ideal city has no plant life.

"Most false ideas about the beautiful," says Baudelaire in his essay *In Praise of Face Paint (Eloge du Maquillage),*[7] "arise from the false idea of morality current during the 18th century. In that age the foundation, source, and archetype of all good and all possible beauty was seen in Nature. In the universal blindness of the age the denial of original sin was a thing that passed without notice."

> Nature! That infallible goddess! It is she who has given us parricide and cannibalism and a thousand other abominations which it would be indelicate even to name. On the other hand we have philosophy (I mean right philosophy) and religion. It is these that tell us to take care of our parents when they are old and poor. (Nature, the voice of our self-interest, tells us to bludgeon them.) Take a critical look at what is natural, the actions and desires of the purely natural man. The view is ghastly. Absolutely everything that is beautiful and noble proceeds from reasonable reflection.

These general principles afford Baudelaire the opportunity to erect an extravagantly gilded little shrine around the civilized figure of the well made-up woman.

> It is the right of woman and her duty to give herself a magical finish, a supernatural lustre. She is expected to astonish and charm us. She is a kind of idol, and she ought to gild herself (*se dorer*) until she is a fit object of our adoration (*pour être adorée*).
>
> Rouge and mascara are the symbols of a heightened, a preternaturally intense mode of existence. The dark framing renders the gaze more profound and individual; it deepens the character of the eye as a window opened into infinity. The hectic color on the cheek increases the brilliance of the eye and creates in a feminine countenance of sufficient loveliness the mysteriously passionate look of the priestess.

Baudelaire is at pains to point out that he is not talking about art as mimesis. "I am not trying to assign art the sterile function of imitating nature." Even less, if possible, can there be any question of art as illusion. "There is no point at all in trying to hide cosmetic or make it pass unnoticed. It ought to proclaim itself—if not boastfully, at least with a de-

[7] This appeared in *Le Figaro*, December 3, 1863, as No. 11 in a series entitled *Le Peintre de la Vie Moderne*. The text may be found in *L'Art Romantique, Oeuvres Complètes,* ed. Jacques Crépet, III (Paris, 1925), 95–100.

gree of candor." Art, then, is a magical enhancement. But of what? The end of the argument may entail a certain contradiction of the initially dark view of nature. The anciently enlisted virgins of Crotona play a new role, it is true. But they have not been entirely eliminated from the theory. "Cosmetic artifice cannot improve ugliness. It can only serve what is to begin with beautiful." Baudelaire, in being less than a pure theorist of pure art, is one of the witnesses for the theory most worthy of our respectful attention.

With Baudelaire, the main fight for "art" in 19th-century France was won. After him, the simply aesthetic assertion fritters away into *Parnassien* formalism, the exoticism, the intricate versification of Leconte de Lisle or Théodore de Banville.[8] The main line of French poetry and poetics, with Verlaine and even more with Mallarmé, advances into subtler themes of musical intimation, ironic finesse, and symbol—above all else, symbol.[9] The simpler campaign of art for art's sake during the second half of the 19th century is carried with most flourish into the new territory of England.

I V

AESTHETICISM in England, says a recent writer, "was not a sudden development: the nature of the trend from Keats through Tennyson and Dante Gabriel Rossetti was, even in Arnold's mid-career, not unapparent to the critic who passed the judgment on the great Romantics. The insistence that poetry must be judged as 'criticism of life' is the same critic's reaction to the later Romantic tradition; it puts the stress where it seemed to him that it most needed to be put." [1] Arnold himself has left us such statements as the following in his Preface to Wordsworth (1879):

> Morals are often treated in a narrow and false fashion; . . . they grow tiresome to some of us. We find attraction, at times, even in a poetry of revolt against them; in a poetry which might take for its motto Omar Khayam's words: "Let us make up in the tavern for the time which we have wasted in the mosque." Or we find attraction in a poetry indifferent to them; in a poetry where the contents may be what they will, but where the form is studied and exquisite. We delude ourselves in either case; and the best cure for our delusion is to let our minds rest upon that

[8] The idea of art for art's sake can be seen, of course, in other places. It mixes with realistic theory, for instance, in the letters of Flaubert. See Gilbert and Kuhn, pp. 490–8.

[9] Cf. *post* Chapter 26.

[1] F. R. Leavis, *Scrutiny*, VII (December, 1938), 324–5.

great and inexhaustible word *life*, until we learn to enter into its
meaning. A poetry of revolt against moral ideas is a poetry of
revolt against life; a poetry of indifference towards moral ideas
is a poetry of indifference towards life.[2]

An abrupt separation of the artist from the "middle-class" world,
and from "middle-class" moralism [3]—or, as it might be conceived in a
somewhat different way, his revolt from subservience to the masses and
the norms of industrial civilization—was signalized in England by the
publication of Swinburne's *Poems and Ballads*, a volume read aloud with
excited devotion by Saintsbury and other undergraduate literati at Oxford
in the fall of 1866.[4] The "lithe limbs," the "strange, great sins," the
laus veneris, the dolors, were the more musically vague and voluptuous
counterpart in English of the evils which had recently flowered in France,
the paganism of Gautier, the satanism of Baudelaire. During the next three
decades the theoretical watchwords of the movement were sounded
most loudly by three authors: by Pater, by Whistler (who took legal
action against the moralist criticism of Ruskin), and by Wilde. The essays
of Wilde collected as *Intentions* in 1891 form perhaps the most imposing
theoretical monument.

On the side of "practical aestheticism," the artist's acting out of his
theory in his own life, the later phase shows us some repetitions and
some prettifications of the earlier. Baudelaire's explorations of vice, his
decline, and early death are matched in England by Wilde's perversion,
his trial, disaster, and death. "I treated art," he says in his *De Profundis*,
"as the supreme reality and life as a mere mode of fiction." [5] De Quincey's
essay "On Murder, Considered as One of the Fine Arts" is paralleled
from the life in Stevenson's "Villon, Student, Poet and Housebreaker"
and in the study "Pen, Pencil, and Poison" which Wilde includes in his
Intentions. A conspicuous feature of the movement is a kind of aesthetic
dandyism, an exquisiteness of dress and carriage no less than of the inner
life—men in velvet jackets and knee breeches, with a flower in the hand,[6]
women in lovely, flowing Pre-Raphaelite gowns. These pursue the voca-
tion of adoring beauty.

The theory of the art object itself during the English phase dwelt
intently on the terms "art" and "beauty." "Beauty" was something very
pure, very different from everything else. So was "art." "Beauty," said

---

[2] *Essays in Criticism, Second Series* (London, 1888), p. 144.
[3] In France, the enemies during this period were the positive philosophy of
Comte and the "bourgeois" society of the Second Empire.
[4] Cf. Dorothy Richardson, "Saintsbury and Art for Art's Sake in England,"
PMLA, LIX (March, 1944), 245–6.
[5] *De Profundis* (New York, 1950), p. 77.
[6] "With a poppy or a lily in your medieval hand" (W. S. Gilbert, *Patience*, in
Plays and Poems, New York, 1932, p. 200).

Wilde, "is the symbol of symbols. Beauty reveals everything, because it expresses nothing." [7] And: "All art is useless." [8] Art, said Whistler in his *Ten O'Clock Lecture* of 1888, is:

> selfishly occupied with her own perfection only—having no desire to teach—seeking and finding the beautiful in all conditions and in all times.[9]

Still the "beauty" of art for art's sake was far from being a cold or Platonic idea. It has to be reconciled somehow with two very hot ideas, near the center of the theory; namely, "sensation" and "passion"—or "sensation" intensified by "passion." (So far have we come from Kant and Poe!) The "hard, gem-like flame" of "ecstasy" with which we are asked to "burn" in the well-known Conclusion of Pater's *Renaissance* wears the aura of a flickering sensationalism—a philosophy of the fleeting moment—so scandalous to his contemporaries that this Conclusion was omitted in the second edition.

> Not the fruit of experience, but experience itself, is the end. A certain number of pulses only is given to us of a variegated, dramatic life. How may we see in them all that is to be seen in them by the finest senses? How shall we pass most swiftly from point to point, and be present always at the focus where the greatest number of vital forces unite in their purest energy?

The answer lies in the word "passion." "Great passions may give us this quickened sense of life. . . . Only be sure it is passion. . . . Of such wisdom, the poetic passion, the desire of beauty, the love of art for its own sake, has most." Or, as Wilde would put it:

> Emotion for the sake of emotion is the aim of art, and emotion for the sake of action is the aim of life.[1]

And this, explained Wilde, was the reason why "all art is immoral." The most recurrently anguished cry of the artist was against the claim of society in the voice of the moralist, against the pressure of the Philistine practical environment.[2]

A moral theory of art, we may note in passing, is intrinsically a theory about a subject matter. As the moral critic John Ruskin put it:

> The picture which has the nobler and more numerous ideas, however awkwardly expressed, is a greater and a better picture

---

[7] *The Critic as Artist,* in *Intentions* (London, 1913), p. 145.
[8] Preface to *Dorian Gray.*
[9] *The Gentle Art of Making Enemies* (New York, 1890), p. 136.
[1] *The Critic as Artist,* in *Intentions* (London, 1913), p. 169.
[2] See, for instance, Whistler, *The Gentle Art of Making Enemies,* p. 143: "Humanity takes the place of Art, and God's creations are excused for their usefulness."

than that which has the less noble and less numerous ideas, however beautifully expressed. No weight, nor mass, nor beauty of execution can outweigh one grain or fragment of thought.[3]

But the rebuttal by art-for-art's-sake was in some measure only a reflection of the same choice, a capture of a risky gambit pawn, a too easy triumph over moralistic rigor by the introduction of a rival rigor.

The only beautiful things . . . are the things that do not concern us. As long as a thing is useful or necessary to us, or affects us in any way, either for pain or for pleasure . . . it is outside the proper sphere of art. To art's subject-matter we should be more or less indifferent.[4]

The aestheticism of the 19th century had its own ideas about what is acceptable subject matter for art. This was roughly that complex of motifs at which we have already glanced in Poe and Baudelaire: the exotic and bizarre, the morbid and ugly, and the gilded and artificial.[5] And increasingly the dark area of this triad was acceptable only under an artifice of gilt. Art for art's sake—the art of the Yellow Book era— was an art of a "fiery-coloured world," [6] a world out of this world, out of the 19th-century socio-real and middle-class context. Beauty had "slim gilded feet." [7] This was one expression of the artist's isolation, the aristocratic exclusiveness of interest, the withdrawal into ivory-tower luxury, by which he was to earn so much contempt from socio-realist quarters.

At the same time, it is important to notice that such an exclusiveness was capable of a somewhat different emphasis. Wilde in the passage quoted above apparently means that there are some subject-matters which concern us, and some which do not, and the latter only are artistic. But a person could use nearly the same words and convey the different meaning that all subject matters, even those which concern us most acutely, should somehow be treated by the artist with detachment. "To art's subject-matter, we should be more or less indifferent." This would be a continuation and a degeneration of "negative capability," the anti-

---

[3] *Modern Painters*, Part I, Section I, Chapter 2. Ruskin differed from Arnold in that his interests were more confessedly practical and sociological, and again he differed from the French or Russian socio-realist critics in the direction of his thinking toward medievalism and the cultivation of a handicraft norm of values. But even more than Arnold, Ruskin stood in the public mind as a symbol of the moral critic. "The great arts," he said, ". . . have had, and can have, but three principal directions of purpose, first, that of enforcing the religion of men; secondly, that of perfecting their ethical state; thirdly, that of doing them material service" (*Lectures on Art*, New York, 1880, p. 37). Cf. Charles A. Yount, *The Reaction Against Ruskin in Art Criticism* (Chicago, 1941).

[4] Wilde, *The Decay of Lying*, in *Intentions*, pp. 16–17.
[5] Cf. William Gaunt, *The Aesthetic Adventure* (London, 1945), pp. 1–10.
[6] *The Critic as Artist*, in *Intentions*, p. 145.
[7] *The Critic as Artist*, in *Intentions*, p. 186.

partisan conception as entertained by Keats, the tolerance of "uncertainties, mysteries, doubts." "We hate poetry that has a palpable design upon us." [8] Art for art's sake may be seen as a kind of aesthetico-scientific detachment, an intellectual reaction against the romantic letting down of the hair and flood of personal emotion. Poe's *Philosophy of Composition*, making a parade of rational deliberacy and professional efficiency with regard to the most melancholy and lovely emotion a human being can experience, that for the death of a beautiful woman, combined an extremely exclusive view of subject matter with an aesthetic remoteness that would become typical. Art for art's sake has been described with some insight as a kind of return to the *vita contemplativa*, the *Bios Theōrētikos*, of the Christian ages. Schopenhauer's early exposition of such a notion lay for a while in obscurity but became popular toward the end of the century.[9] This approach to asceticism, in the literary men and painters at least, was a close kin of 19th-century medievalism— with the difference between the Middle Ages and the 19th century that the latter, especially under the rubric of art for art's sake, offered less to contemplate.

V

IN THE later era of art for art's sake, the argument sometimes became an appeal to a supposedly pure aesthetic element of "form." "Form," said Wilde, "is everything. It is the secret of life." "Start with the worship of form, and there is no secret in art that will not be revealed to you." [1] The term "form" might now and then be somewhat mysterious, but for one thing it had a close relation with the idea of craftsmanship so far as the latter was conceived as a quality discoverable in the art work itself. This meant in one sense, a literal sense, the craftsmanship of verse technique. Thus Wilde waxed ecstatic over the powers of rhyme.

> Rhyme . . . in the hands of the real artist becomes not merely a material element of metrical beauty, but a spiritual element of thought and passion also. . . . rhyme . . . can turn man's utterance to the speech of gods; rhyme, the one chord we have added to the Greek lyre.[2]

The matter may be plentifully, if more trivially, illustrated in the practice of the English "Parnassian" poets and translators (the "Rondelier" set) Payne, Lang, Dobson, Henley, Gosse—who followed Théodore de

[8] John Keats, *Letters*, ed. M. B. Forman, 2nd ed. (Oxford, 1935), pp. 72, 96: Nos. 32 and 44 (December 21, 1817, and February 3, 1818); cf. his advice to Shelley, p. 507: No. 227 (August 9, 1818).

[9] Gilbert and Kuhn, p. 472.

[1] *The Critic as Artist*, in *Intentions*, pp. 201–2.

[2] *The Critic as Artist*, in *Intentions*, pp. 102–3.

Banville in a devotion to French medieval and Renaissance poets (Villon, Charles d'Orléans, Marot, Ronsard) and the intricately fixed forms which they had perfected, *rondeau, ballade, villanelle, chant royal,* triolet.[3] "I intended an ode, And it turned to a sonnet."

But in another, and perhaps in the long run more significant, sense, the 19th-century pursuit of fine craftsmanship and "form" was working all along to establish a new kind of liaison, both literal and metaphoric, between poetry and the musical and visual arts.[4] The concept of poetry as "music" in the later 19th century arrived at a new subtlety, far refined beyond mimetic views of the 18th century, and in France this was a notable part of symbolist thinking.[5] The relation with visual art in the special mode of art for art's sake, going back perhaps to Hugo's *Les Orientales* (1829) and Gautier's *Emaux et Camées* (1853), was in a peculiar way more metaphoric and perhaps more fallacious. In a remark on his *Emaux et Camées* Gautier had written:

> This title . . . expresses the plan of treating tiny subjects in a severely formal way—like working on a gold or copper surface with brilliant enamels, or using a graver's wheel on precious stones, agate, cornelian, or onyx. Each piece would have to be as finely chased as an image for the cover of a jewel box or seal ring—something reminiscent of ancient medals such as painters and sculptors keep about their studios.[6]

In the same spirit Pater spoke of making language "a serious study, weighing the precise power of every phrase and word, as though it were precious metal."[7] *Améthystes, Rimes Dorées, Intaglios,* "Thoughts in Marble," *Proverbs in Porcelain, Ballades in Blue China* are characteristic of the period. They represent a passion for smooth surface and sharp outline, the poem as nearly as possible conceived as a thing, a hard shape, not a discourse. If this was an ideal difficult for literature to achieve, nevertheless the general aesthetic theory might look intently in that direction. Wilde praised purely decorative, or arabesque, art in virtue of its "deliberate rejection of Nature as the ideal of beauty, as well as of the imitative method of the ordinary painter."[8] During this era, visual art, reacting against the new claims of photography, tried to move closer to music, which was considered as a nearly pure form and hence an artistic ideal. The sufficient instance for the moment, if on the inten-

---

[3] See James K. Robinson, "A Neglected Phase of the Aesthetic Movement: English Parnassianism," *PMLA,* LXVIII (September, 1953), 733-54.

[4] Cf. *ante* Chapter 13.

[5] Cf. *post* Chapter 26, pp. 590-6.

[6] *Les Progrès de la Poésie Française depuis 1830,* in *Histoire du Romantisme,* 3d ed. (Paris, 1874), p. 322.

[7] *Marius the Epicurean,* Chapter VI (London, 1893), p. 71.

[8] *The Critic as Artist,* in *Intentions,* p. 200.

tionalist side, is Whistler's painting of his mother, bearing the title: "Arrangement in Grey and Black." [9]

The most flourishing descendant of art for art's sake during the early 20th century has been the school of pure "formalist" criticism in the graphic arts. Much more than any kind of literary criticism, this school has continued and accentuated the aesthetic trend not only toward purity of form but toward exclusiveness of appeal. "In proportion as art becomes purer," says Roger Fry, "the number of people to whom it appeals gets less. . . . It appeals only to the aesthetic sensibility, and that in most men is comparatively weak." [1] "The representative element in a work of art," says Clive Bell in his classic treatise entitled *Art*, "may or may not be harmful; always it is irrelevant." [2] And he tells us much of a "peculiar emotion provoked by works of art," "the aesthetic emotion," the correlative of which is something called "significant form."

> What quality is shared by all objects that provoke our aesthetic emotions? What quality is common to Sta. Sophia and the windows at Chartres, Mexican sculpture, a Persian bowl, Chinese carpets, Giotto's frescoes at Padua, and the masterpieces of Poussin, Piero della Francesca, and Cézanne? Only one answer seems possible—significant form. In each, lines and colours combined in a particular way, certain forms and relations of forms, stir our aesthetic emotions. [3]

The theory, despite a more overt tendency to tautology than is apparent in most art theories, might be a good enough theory if it could be compelled to answer the question whether lines and colors ever have their complete "significance" in a state purged entirely of our concrete optical experience—the resemblance of a circle to the sun and the moon and the wheel, the contrast between the geometrically ruled straight line and the whole world of organic nature. The problem, as we have suggested, may not have a very precise counterpart in literature, [4] yet it may offer some instruction, *a fortiori*, to literary theory. What is not quite possible in lines and colors may be even less possible in words. Again, the difference between aesthetic formalism and any ideas which the historian of metaphysics may be willing to impute to Kant will not quite eliminate the fact that this formalism (a theory of non-empirical, geometric art

[9] See Gaunt, *The Aesthetic Adventure*, p. 82, on Whistler's *Nocturnes*. Wilde said that "music is the perfect type of art" because it "can never reveal its ultimate secret" (*Intentions*, p. 148); and Pater: "All art constantly aspires towards the condition of music" (*The School of Giorgione*, in *The Renaissance*, Modern Library edition, p. 111).

[1] *Vision and Design* (London, 1920), p. 10.

[2] *Art* (New York, c. 1914), p. 25.

[3] *Art* (New York, c. 1914), p. 8.

[4] Twentieth-century Italian and French versions of "pure poetry" (syllables without sense) and Russian experiments in "trans-sense" language provide parallels.

values) stands in a fairly direct, if blurred line of descent from the Kantian *a priorism*.[5]

VI

IN THE didactic theories of the 19th century, art, even though it took a creative leadership, had to be somehow true to the way things basically are. In Arnold's formula—art is a "criticism of life"—the criticism would obviously have to be somehow faithful to, or limited by, its object. But art for art's sake, both early and late, wanted very much to say something nearly the opposite. Thus Whistler, in terms sufficiently reminiscent of Baudelaire:

> That Nature is always right is an assertion artistically as untrue as it is one whose truth is universally taken for granted. Nature is very rarely right, to such an extent even, that it might almost be said that Nature is usually wrong: that is to say, the condition of things that shall bring about the perfection of harmony worthy of a picture is rare.[6]

The mythopoeia of Schelling and Friedrich Schlegel and the Arnoldian neo-humanism, as well as some forms of the socio-realistic claim, were instances of a lofty view of the artist's power of reshaping reality. The morally didactic principle, the recognition of the artist's undoubted power over the wills and hearts of men, shaded off subtly into idealistic concepts of creative imagination or creative will. All along, too, the notion of art as creator was susceptible of receiving a more purely aesthetic, a more playful, twist. A French historian of romanticism and its effects on real life points out that the 19th century was filled with sins copied from the poets and novelists. For example, a plague of suicides that swept France during several decades of the mid-century followed a pattern of feeling set in romances like *Werther* and *René* and in the morbid verse and prose of writers like Petrus Borel, Philothée O'Neddy, and Alphonse Rabbe.[7] Heine in his *Florentine Nights*, 1836, shows how far the argument might sometimes facetiously venture when he maintains that the beauty of the Italian women is a clear instance of the influence of the fine arts on human physique. There may have been

[5] Formalist art critics frequently make an appeal to the mathematical elements in Plato's theory. Cf. *ante*, Chapter 1, p. 17.

[6] *The Gentle Art of Making Enemies*, p. 143.

[7] Louis Maigron, *Le Romantisme et les Moeurs* (Paris, 1910), Chapter II, "*Le Romantisme et le Suicide*," esp. pp. 314–15, 324, 332–3, 337, 347. "*En voici un, par exemple, Marcel V***, qui se vante d'avoir 'tout goûté, tout épuisé' de la vie conformément aux meilleurs principes romantiques. . . . Il relit Obermann, René, Joseph Delorme; et avant de se tuer, juge original de chanter un 'hymne à la Mort'* (p. 324). "*Je lègue à notre cher Club la petite bibliothèque de vous bien connue. A vous particulièrement j'ai réservé Werther, René, Obermann, les Oeuvres de Rabbe, et Jacques. . . . C'étaient mes bréviaires*" (p. 347).

a time when nature supplied models for art, but now it is the other way round. "A feeling for the beautiful has penetrated the whole people." "Spirit works on flesh." [8] More moderately, the theorist might observe that art teaches us what to see in nature, that it is characteristic of the human being, as Goncourt put it, "to see nothing in nature that is not a remembrance and recollection of art." [9]

The twin notions which we have just been sketching—that nature is inferior to art (so that art is forced to be untrue) and that art has power to anticipate and modify nature—are developed with fine paradoxical abandon by Wilde in his dialogue *The Decay of Lying* (1889). As to the matter of art and truth:

> My own experience is that the more we study Art, the less we care for Nature. What Art really reveals to us is Nature's lack of design, her curious crudities, her extraordinary monotony, her absolutely unfinished condition. Nature has good intentions, of course, but, as Aristotle once said, she cannot carry them out.[1]

> If something cannot be done to check, or at least to modify, our monstrous worship of facts, Art will become sterile, and beauty will pass away from the land.
>
> Even Mr. Robert Louis Stevenson, that delightful master of delicate and fanciful prose, is tainted with this modern vice, for we know positively no other name for it. There is such a thing as robbing a story of its reality by trying to make it too true, and *The Black Arrow* is so inartistic as not to contain a single anachronism to boast of, while the transformation of Dr. Jekyll reads dangerously like an experiment out of the *Lancet*.[2]

> Wordsworth went to the lakes, but he was never a lake poet. He found in stones the sermons he had already hidden there. He went moralising about the district, but his good work was produced when he returned, not to Nature but to poetry. Poetry gave him "Laodamia," and the fine sonnets, and the great Ode, such as it is. Nature gave him "Martha Ray" and "Peter Bell," and the address to Mr. Wilkinson's spade.[3]

. . .

[8] *Florentinische Nächte* (Vienna, 1945, Amandus-Edition), pp. 19–20, "*Erste Nacht.*" "*Die Natur hat hier den Künstlern das Kapital zurückgenommen, das sie ihnen einst geliehen, und siehe! es hat sich aufs entzückendste verzinst. Die Natur, welche einst den Künstlern ihre Modelle lieferte, sie kopiert heute ihrerseits die Meisterwerke, die dadurch entstanden. Der Sinn für das Schöne hat das ganze Volk durchdringen, und wie einst das Fleisch auf den Geist, so wirkt jetzt der Geist auf das Fleisch.*"

[9] Albert Cassagne, *La Théorie de l'Art pour l'Art en France* (Paris, 1906), p. 325.

[1] *Intentions* (London, 1913), p. 1.

[2] *Intentions*, pp. 8–9.

[3] *Intentions*, p. 19. A critique of Shakespeare introduced by Wilde (p. 21) makes a startling comparison to that which we have quoted from Tolstoy in our last chap-

As a method Realism is a complete failure, and the two things that every artist should avoid are modernity of form and modernity of subject-matter. To us, who live in the nineteenth century, any century is a suitable subject for art except our own. . . . it is only the modern that ever becomes old-fashioned. M. Zola sits down to give us a picture of the Second Empire. Who cares for the Second Empire now? [4]

They will call upon Shakespeare—they always do—and will quote that hackneyed passage forgetting that this unfortunate aphorism about Art holding the mirror up to Nature, is deliberately said by Hamlet in order to convince the bystanders of his absolute insanity in all art-matters.[5]

And secondly, the matter of art's priority to nature.

Where, if not from the Impressionists, do we get those wonderful brown fogs that come creeping down on our streets, blurring the gaslamps and changing the houses into monstrous shadows? To whom, if not to them and their master, do we owe the lovely silver mists that brood over our river, and turn to faint forms of fading grace curved bridge and swaying barge. The extraordinary change that has taken place in the climate of London during the last ten years is entirely due to a particular school of Art. You smile. Consider the matter from a scientific or a metaphysical point of view, and you will find that I am right. For what is Nature? Nature is no great mother who has borne us. She is our creation. It is in our brain that she quickens to life. Things are because we see them, and what we see, and how we see it, depends on the Arts that have influenced us. To look at a thing is very different from seeing a thing. One does not see anything until one sees its beauty. Then, and then only, does it come into existence. At present, people see fogs, not because there are fogs, but because poets and painters have taught them the mysterious loveliness of such effects. There may have been fogs for centuries in London. I dare say there were. But no one saw them, and so we do not know anything about them. They did not exist till Art had invented them.[6]

And if so much was true of art itself, what of art criticism? The notion of an art criticism for its own sake—of a criticism that was itself a kind of artistic exercise—was strongly invited. "Impressionistic" crit-

---

ter. From the viewpoint of art for art's sake one of Shakespeare's faults is "the over-importance assigned to character" in his later plays, his uncouthness and vulgarity, his "realism."

[4] *Intentions*, pp. 52–3.
[5] *Intentions*, p. 28.
[6] *Intentions*, p. 39.

icism of considerable brilliance had begun to appear in English at least as early as the work of Lamb and Hazlitt—Hazlitt's "gusto" and his *bravura* appreciation of *Elizabethan Literature* or *English Comic Writers*, Lamb's baroque whimsicalities concerning Shakespeare's tragedies or English "Artificial Comedy." We encounter there a use of metaphor, an overt personal reference, and a Longinian evocation of feeling such as cannot be matched in earlier English criticism. In a note on the *Revenger's Tragedy* Lamb confessed: "I never read it but my ears tingle, and I feel a hot blush overspread my cheeks." [7] And Hazlitt: "I say what I think: I think what I feel. I cannot help receiving certain impressions from things; and I have sufficient courage to declare (somewhat abruptly) what they are." [8] Later on Sainte-Beuve would say that for him criticism was only a way of "exhaling a hidden poetry in an indirect way." "Criticism as I intend it and want to practise it, is invention and perpetual creation." [9] The heyday of this kind of profession was not reached, however, until the end of the 19th century and the first three decades of the 20th, with critics like Anatole France and Jules Lemaître in France, Saintsbury and Quiller-Couch in England, and their cosmopolite disciples in America, Huneker, Mencken, Nathan, or Van Vechten—souls adventuring among masterpieces. The candor of Anatole France is perhaps best known. "To be quite frank, the critic ought to say: 'Gentlemen, I am going to speak about myself apropos of Shakespeare, apropos of Racine.'" [1]

At least three distinguishable propositions seem to be present in the philosophy of impressionist criticism and to call for notice if our account is to be accurate.

(1) That the most necessary, or the only necessary, equipment of the critic is his sensibility. The classic statement is that of Pater in the Preface to his Renaissance *Studies*.

> What is important . . . is not that the critic should possess a correct abstract definition of beauty for the intellect, but a certain kind of temperament, the power of being deeply moved by the presence of beautiful objects.[2]

[7] *Characters of Dramatic Writers Contemporary with Shakespeare*, 1808, in Charles and Mary Lamb, *Works*, ed. E. V. Lucas, I (London, 1903), 48.

[8] *Works*, ed. P. P. Howe, V (London, 1930), 175.

[9] *Portraits de Femmes* (1870), p. 411; *Portraits Littéraires* (1862-64), III, 546; from a manuscript chapter by René Wellek.

[1] *On Life and Letters, First Series*, trans. A. W. Evans (London, 1911), Preface, p. viii.

[2] See the comparable celebration of the "critic's sensorium," his "intimate personal relation" to the piece of literature, his "prizing" of "the fleeting mood, the passing poignant moment of enjoyment," his refusal "to feel twice alike about the same poem," by the Harvard Professor Lewis E. Gates, in his essay "Impression and Appreciation," in *Studies and Appreciation* (New York, 1900), pp. 208-9; cf. Zabel, p. 21.

"Temperament," said Wilde, "is the primary requisite for the critic—a temperament exquisitely susceptible to beauty." [3]

(2) That, as the artist himself is the person most susceptible to impressions of beauty, the artist himself is the only licensed critic. In his suit against Ruskin, Whistler complained:

> It is not only when criticism is inimical that I object to it, but also when it is incompetent. I hold that none but an artist can be a competent critic. [4]

(This idea comes echoing down even to our own time, in the opinion, for instance, of Mr. Eliot, who has been rebuffed by Mr. C. S. Lewis with the observation that the poet by this argument crowns himself "King of Pointland," for he can trust the judgment of those who acknowledge him a poet only in virtue of being a poet in order to judge them. It is true, notes Mr. Lewis, that good reasoning can be recognized only by a good reasoner; yet it is not true that good cooking can be recognized only by a good cook. [5] Poetry would appear to be a type of product—in part like reasoning, in part like cooking—which offers at least a considerable resistance to the theory that only a poet can be a critic.) [6]

(3) That a good critic, in virtue of his very criticism, is a true artist, or the truest artist. This is the extreme impressionistic theory of criticism. It is a theory of autotelic criticism, of criticism for its own sake, and perhaps it is a logical enough outcome of the original paradox of art for art's sake. The thesis was perhaps first distinctly propounded by Friedrich Schlegel. [7] It is developed by Wilde in a companion piece to *The Decay of Lying*, a long dialogue essay entitled *The Critic as Artist*.

> GILBERT: Yes: it has been said by one whose gracious memory we all revere, and the music of whose pipe once lured Proserpina from her Sicilian fields, and made those white feet stir, and not in vain, the Cumnor cowslips, that the proper aim of Criticism is to see the object as in itself it really is. But this is a very serious error, and takes no cognisance of Criticism's most perfect form, which is in its essence purely subjective, and seeks to reveal its own secret and not the secret of another. For the highest Criticism deals with art not as expressive but as impressive purely.

[3] *The Critic as Artist*, in *Intentions*, p. 194.
[4] *The Gentle Art of Making Enemies* (New York, 1890), p. 6.
[5] Cf. *ante* Chapter 5, p. 84. The relevance of such observations is of course perennial.
[6] C. S. Lewis, *A Preface to Paradise Lost* (London, 1942), pp. 9–10.
[7] Cf. *ante* Chapter 17, p. 376.

ERNEST: But is that really so?

GILBERT: Of course it is. Who cares whether Mr. Ruskin's views on Turner are sound or not? What does it matter? That mighty and majestic prose of his, so fervid and so fiery-coloured in its noble eloquence, so rich in its elaborate symphonic music, so sure and certain, at its best, in subtle choice of word and epithet, is at least as great a work of art as any of those wonderful sunsets that bleach or rot on their corrupted canvases in England's gallery.[8]

Hours ago, Ernest, you asked me the use of Criticism. You might just as well have asked me the use of thought. It is Criticism, as Arnold points out, that creates the intellectual atmosphere of the age. It is Criticism, as I hope to point out myself some day, that makes the mind a fine instrument. . . . Considered as an instrument of thought, the English mind is coarse and undeveloped. The only thing that can purify it is the growth of the critical instinct.[9]

This passage closes the cycle of aesthetico-impressionist thought in the appropriate way, showing how in the boundless realm of idealism aesthetic and didactic theory become one, or how impressionistic criticism can be assimilated to didactic art. If nature, reversing our usual conceptions, is to imitate art, then art, continuing the direction of reference, may well imitate criticism. Or one art, that which calls itself Art, will imitate, or at least be greatly influenced by, another art, that which calls itself criticism. This will be easier if criticism in turn calls itself Art. Thus Wilde and Arnold find themselves at one. Wilde and Arnold, the aesthete and the austere moralist, were both descendants of Schelling and Friedrich Schlegel. They were Victorian brothers. Both entertained not only a low opinion of the English mind but a vision of art and art criticism as free activities which were destined to bring about man's salvation from the bondage of philosophy and religion.

SUPPLEMENT

The theological consideration of the working idea clearly shows how foreign to art is the servile imitation of the appearance of nature, for art's most fundamental demand is that the work make apparent not something else already made, but the spirit from which it proceeds. As God makes created participa-

[8] *Intentions*, p. 140–1.
[9] *Intentions*, pp. 209–10.

tions of His being exist outside Himself, so the artist puts himself—not what he sees, but what he is—into what he makes. So anyone contemplating the myriad landscapes bearing God's signature at every revolution of light, or the features of any beast or man whatever, clearly sees that they are literally *inimitable* and that there is more humility in continuing in our own way the creative impulse than in striving to obtain a like effect in a picture.

The truth is, and it is the core of the mystery, that we have nothing but what we have received.

There is considerable truth in Wilde's paradoxes on lying; truth which, needless to say, has nothing to do with the shoddy Hegelianism with which he tricks it out. It is quite true that things are better in the mind than in themselves, that they acquire their full stature only when they have been expressed, and that they themselves pray to be assumed into the heaven of metaphysical or poetical thought, where they proceed to live outside time with a life which is universal. What would have become of the Trojan War without Homer? Unfortunate are the adventures which are never narrated.

But what Wilde, choked by the paper roses of his aestheticism, failed to understand is that our art does not derive from itself alone what it imparts to things; it spreads over them a secret which it first discovered in them, in their invisible substance or in their endless exchanges and correspondences. Take it out of "that blessed reality given once for all, in the centre of which we are situated," and it ceases to be. It transforms, removes, brings closer together, transfigures; it does not create. It is by the way in which he changes the shape of the universe passing through his mind, in order to make a form apprehended in things shine upon a matter, that the artist impresses his signature upon his work. He recomposes for each, *according as the poetry in him changes him*, a world more real than the reality offered to the senses.

So, because it is subjected in the mind of a man, the law of imitation, of resemblance, remains constant for our art, but in a sense purified. It must transpose the secret rules of being in the manner of producing the work, and it must be as faithful and exact, in transforming reality according to the laws governing the work to be done, as science in conforming thereto. What it makes must resemble not the material appearance of things, but some one of the hidden significances whose iris God alone sees glittering on the neck of His creatures—and for that very reason it will also resemble the created mind which in its own way discerned those invisible colours. Resemblance, but a *spiritual* resemblance. Realism, if you like, but transcendental realism.

—Jacques Maritain, "The Frontiers of Poetry," in *Art and Scholasticism*, trans. J. F. Scanlan (New York, 1942), pp. 95–6, quoted by permission of Charles Scribner's Sons

When poetry loses sight of the wonderful, it loses its significance and justification. Poetry cannot thrive in our trivial and commonplace world. The miraculous, the marvelous, and the mysterious are the only subjects that admit of a truly poetic treatment.

This conception of poetry is, however, rather a qualification and limitation than a genuine account of the creative process of art. Curiously enough the great realists of the nineteenth century had in this respect a keener insight into the art process than their romantic adversaries. They maintained a radical and uncompromising naturalism. But it was precisely this naturalism which led them to a more profound conception of artistic form. Denying the "pure forms" of the idealistic schools they concentrated upon the material aspect of things. By virtue of this sheer concentration they were able to overcome the conventional dualism between the poetic and the prosaic spheres. The nature of a work of art, according to the realists, does not depend on the greatness or smallness of its subject matter. No subject whatever is impermeable to the formative energy of art. One of the greatest triumphs of art is to make us see commonplace things in their real shape and in their true light. Balzac plunged into the most trifling features of the "human comedy." Flaubert made profound analyses of the meanest characters. In some of Émile Zola's novels we discover minute descriptions of the structure of a locomotive, of a department store, or of a coal mine. No technical detail, however insignificant, was omitted from these accounts. Nevertheless, running through the works of all these realists great imaginative power is observable, which is by no means inferior to that of the romantic writers. The fact that this power could not be openly acknowledged was a serious drawback to the naturalistic theories of art. In their attempts to refute the romantic conceptions of a transcendental poetry they reverted to the old definition of art as an imitation of nature. In so doing they missed the principal point, since they failed to recognize the symbolic character of art. If such a characterization of art were admitted, there seemed to be no escape from the metaphysical theories of romanticism. Art is, indeed, symbolism, but the symbolism of art must be understood in an immanent, not in a transcendent sense. Beauty is "The Infinite finitely presented" according to Schelling. The real subject of art is not, however, the metaphysical Infinite of Schelling, nor is it the Absolute of Hegel. It is to be sought in certain fundamental structural elements of our sense experience itself—in lines, design, in architectural, musical forms. These elements are, so to speak, omnipresent. Free of all mystery, they are patent and unconcealed; they are visible, audible, tangible. In this sense Goethe did not hesitate to say that art does not pretend to show the metaphysical depth of things, it merely sticks to the surface of natural phenomena. But this surface is not immediately given. We do not know it before we discover it in the works of the great artists. This discovery, however, is not confined to a special field. To the extent that human language can express everything, the lowest and the highest things, art can embrace and pervade the whole sphere of human experience. Nothing in the physical or moral world, no natural thing and no human action, is by its nature and essence excluded from the realm of art, because nothing resists its formative and creative process. "Quicquid essentia dignum est," says Bacon in his *Novum Organum* (Book I, Aphorism CXX), "id etiam scientia dignum est." This dictum holds for art as well as for science.

—Ernst Cassirer, *An Essay on Man* (New Haven, 1944), pp. 156–8, by permission of the Yale University Press

CHAPTER 23

EXPRESSIONISM: BENEDETTO CROCE

§ *nineteenth-century expressionism, context and origin of Croce's idealism, his Aesthetic, neo-idealism, Autobiography—II. the four activities of spirit, intuition-expression the aesthetic fact, externalization—III. resemblance of Croce to Plotinus, double concept of form and art, ugliness as failure of intuition, simple successful intuition vs. rich or full intuition, the analogy of bronze-casting—IV. duplicity in Croce's basic treatment of the affective, "feeling" in art, "lyrism" in his later theory (the* Britannica *article, the* Essence of Aesthetic*)—V. negative grounds of the system: rejection of the figures, genres, rules, analysis, etc., rejection of specific value terms—VI. Croce as a practical critic,* The Defence of Poetry, *"Poetic Personality" of the author (Shakespeare, Ariosto, and Corneille), Croce's anthological reading, neglect of plot and character, resemblance to Longinus—VII. balance sheet for and against the system, Croce's strength and influence* §

A RECENT STUDY ENTITLED *The Mirror and the Lamp* [1] SEES ONE OF the main trends of romantic poetics to have been a turning from Renaissance concepts of art as mechanically effected mimesis toward a new concept of art as organic creation. The mirror gave back the literal image of reality external to itself. The lamp threw out its own discovering and organizing rays into the void of darkness. A somewhat earlier study of the English romantic theory of poetry [2] had attempted to show that the concept of creative imagination entertained by Coleridge, Shelley and other poets was the same as the "aesthetic" concept

---

[1] M. H. Abrams, *The Mirror and The Lamp: Romantic Theory and the Critical Tradition* (New York, 1953).

[2] A. E. Powell, *The Romantic Theory of Poetry* (London, 1926).

elaborated a century later by Benedetto Croce.[3] The present writers, in undertaking some account of the Crocean aesthetic and in placing it at this juncture in their story, believe that Croce does actually achieve something like an ultimate definition and synthesis of the expressionistic art theory which first came clearly into view with the Germans and Coleridge and which was tested and matured through such 19th-century vicissitudes as in part we have been describing. Croce's aesthetic is a long way from looking like the preciously burnished perversions of a Baudelaire, the Whistlerian study in gray and black, the velvet-coated flippancies of a Wilde. Yet the theory is precisely an "aesthetic," a master theory of art for art's sake, a profound realization of all that might underlie and in part justify the 19th-century cry that art must be pure.

Croce's theory grows out of an initial preoccupation with the historico-social thinking which we have seen to be intrinsic to one sort of 19th-century didactic theory, and it is a partial resolution of the conflict between such theory and the starker versions of art for art's sake. His early studies, centering in the antiquities of Italy and especially of his native Naples, resulted soon in a conviction that the simple accumulation of factual knowledge was futile. He read Vico's *Scienza Nuova*. And there came a time in March, 1893, when "after a whole day of intense thought," he produced an essay entitled "History subsumed under the general concept of art." Shortly afterwards he complemented his historical studies by a period of concentration on economics and a studied rejection of Marxism.[4] In February and May of 1900 he read before the Accademia Pontaniana of Naples a memoir entitled *Fundamental Theses of an Aesthetic as Science of Expression and General Linguistic*, and this, with some amplifications, and the addition of a historical section, became his epoch-making *Aesthetic*, published in 1901. In later years Croce has stressed [5] the importance of his *Essence of Aesthetic* (or *Breviario*), four lectures read at the opening of the Rice Institute in 1912, and his *Encyclopedia Britannica* article "Aesthetic," by which he captured the term "aesthetic" in the English-speaking world for his own concept and system. We shall not overlook these statements. Yet the earlier *Aesthetic* not only opens up the system (and Croce's objections to all other systems) in far more detail but reveals in like detail some of the consequences of the system for literary study. This work joins with Croce's *Logic* and his *Philosophy of the Practical, Economic and Ethic* to compose his *Philosophy of the Spirit*. In his "opinion" this "exhausts the entire field of philosophy." [6]

[3] Croce in his *Conversazioni critiche*, Third Series (Bari, 1932), pp. 7–13, has some doubts about Miss Powell's understanding of his philosophy.

[4] *An Autobiography*, trans. R. G. Collingwood (Oxford, 1927), pp. 56–60.

[5] E. F. Carritt, *Philosophies of Beauty* (Oxford, 1931), p. 223, n. 1.

[6] Croce, *Aesthetic as Science of Expression and General Linguistic*, trans. Douglas Ainslie, 2nd ed. (New York, 1922–29), p. xxix, Croce's Preface of 1907. Croce's

In the Hegelian idealism there was something, a world or nature, on which spirit worked in a dialectical process. Marxism reduced this to a very thoroughly monistic working of material nature in and through itself. Croce, using as his entrance into the metaphysical realm no other than a literary observation, concerning the breakdown of classical rules and genres of art, arrives at an opposite, but equally thoroughgoing, monism of spirit. His criticism of the classical genres, he tells us in his *Autobiography*, enabled him to lay his finger "on the point at which 'nature,' the product of man's own spirit, is introduced into the pure spiritual world of art." Having "thus denied the reality of nature in art," he was led by degrees "to deny it everywhere and to discover everywhere its true character, not as reality but as the product of abstracting thought." [7] "Spirit" in the Crocean philosophy is the "absolute reality." Spirit "generates the contents of experience." [8] Some of these contents of experience, it is true, assume the character (by abstraction) of something external to the knowing spirit and (as we shall see) even become the means by which further acts of spirit are projected and made known to individual spiritual agents external to each other and to the immediate consciousness which we must suppose to be spirit for the philosopher of the system. But it is perhaps easiest just to say that Crocean neo-idealism is not interested in such embarrassments to its sweep. They are looked on as problems arising out of abstraction and hence ulterior to the concretely rich, vital and real intuitive knowledge which is the direct creation of spirit.

II

THERE are only four basic, essentially different activities or "moments" of spirit, four kinds of reality: two theoretical, or knowing activities; two practical, or volitional. They occur in the following order, each one supposing or needing all those that precede it: 1. intuition-expression (the primary imaginative act of individual characterization or forming); 2. conceptualization (the intellective and scientific knowledge of relations between individual intuitions); 3. volition in general (economic activity); and 4. volition of the rationally and universally conceived end—willing the true self of spirit (ethical activity—absolute freedom). These four ultimates, qualitatively and a-prioristically different from one another, take the place of such classical ultimates as the ideas of Plato, the sub-

Aesthetic is quoted throughout the present chapter from the translation of Ainslie by permission of the copyright holder, Mrs. G. C. Quinton. Ainslie's widely influential translation first appeared in 1909. It was republished in 1953 by The Vision Press, Peter Owen, London.
    [7] *An Autobiography*, trans. R. G. Collingwood (Oxford, 1927) p. 94.
    [8] J. A. Smith, *Encyclopedia Britannica*, 14th edition, VI, 732, "Benedetto Croce."

stantial forms of Aristotle, the categories and ideas of Kant. Only these four have abstract, absolute, conceptual, dialectical validity (Ch. IX, p. 73).[9] All other concepts are distinguished only quantitatively, temporarily, conveniently, and more or less arbitrarily, in the boundless realm of our empirical experience. "What is true in the natural sciences is either philosophy or historic fact" (Ch. III). The four sciences corresponding to the four cardinal activities of spirit are: aesthetic, logic, economics, and ethics.

The aesthetician, then, focuses on the first of the spiritual activities, intuition-expression. This is bounded at two levels, above by the abstracted concept, below by an "obscure region of the soul" (Ch. I, p. 9), unconscious or subconscious, something which Croce most often calls "impression," "sensation," or "matter." It is less a thing that really exists than a "notion postulated as a mere limit" (Ch. I, p. 6). It is not spiritual activity, but inchoate passivity, a formless nothing, a mere urge of something to be known, to be achieved, to be born.[1] Intuition-expression is individual character, it is form—always different in content, but always form. "The aesthetic fact, therefore, is form, and nothing but form" (Ch. II, p. 16). The system banishes all notion of art as illusion or as mechanical reproduction of, or substitute for, external beauty (Ch. II). It asserts that the notion of external physical beauty (either natural or artistic) is a "verbal paradox" (Ch. XIII). The natural world, be it remembered, exists only at the conceptual and abstract level.

It is of first importance to the system to insist that intuition-expression is *both* intuition *and* "expression," that no intuition can occur without expression. Knowing a thing is simply expressing it to oneself. There are really no mute inglorious Miltons, no geometricians who cannot draw a figure on the blackboard (Ch. I, p. 9). Let us ask ourselves: Do I know anything which I cannot put in words, draw, carve, hum as a tune, or express by some other sign? Try to tell someone what that something is? Try to draw a picture of it. The embarrassments are obvious. If I know anything which I cannot express, at least I cannot communicate it to anyone else or prove its existence to anyone else.

But this admission would scarcely be enough for Croce. He puts the acts of speaking or singing, of drawing or painting, under the aesthetically non-essential head of "externalization"—a merely practical, or willed, activity which may or may not follow on the internal and involuntary activity of intuition-expression. The physical work of art, the statue, painting, or verbal sound, is an external stimulus which for the qualified recipient will produce the same intuition-expression (aesthetic

[9] *Aesthetic*, trans. Douglas Ainslie, 1929.
[1] Though at moments Croce is able to speak of it as actually something. "Everyone speaks and should speak according to the echoes which things arouse in his soul, that is, according to his impressions" (Ch. XVIII, p. 150).

experience) as prompted the artist to externalize. "Artistic technique"
is no more than a complex of prior knowledge at the service of the
artist in his volitional activity of externalizing (Ch. XV). "Expression"
itself does not possess means.[2]

But looking inside ourselves again and reversing the direction of
inquiry, let us ask: Could I have a poem in my head without writing it on
paper or saying it aloud? Unless we are behaviorists enough to insist that
the essential thing in silent thinking is some unobserved twitching of
the throat muscles as the counterpart of audible speech, we will say we
could. But could I have a painting in my head without going through
the experimental act of smearing paint on canvas with a brush. Could
I really? Answers will differ. Beyond doubt, some painters will say yes.
Nevertheless, we would ordinarily think of a poem in the head, though
not written down, as a bird in the hand; but of a painting in the head,
though not painted, as a bird in the bush. Croce's insistence that there
is no difference between the two cases (that *aesthetic* is identical with
linguistic, Ch. XVIII) lies close to the heart of his secret, his strength,
and his weakness.

In favor of Croce's view we may reflect, provisionally, that not only
is it impossible to communicate to anyone else what we cannot put in
signs of some sort, but that whatever we know of that kind (and most
of us would surely claim to know something, even much, of that kind)
is, by the very fact that we cannot manage it in signs, likely to be somewhat vague, ill-formed, and unavailable even for our own thinking. Signs
do seem to help knowledge a great deal.

III

A FEATURE of Croce's system which has provoked some complaint from
his critics is his strong tendency to assert the equivalence of terms that
are ordinarily thought of as separate. "The entire aesthetic system of
Croce," says one of his Italian critics, "amounts to merely a hunt for
pseudonyms of the word 'art,' and may indeed be stated briefly and
accurately in this formula: art=intuition=expression=imagination=
fancy=beauty. And you must be careful not to take these words with
the shadings and distinctions which they have in ordinary or scientific

---

[2] So far as it has aesthetic relevance, what is sometimes loosely called a new
technique (a new kind of romance, a new style of light and shade in painting) is
really a new work of art. The technique is part of the vision. Yet perhaps Croce
slips for a moment when (Ch. XV, p. 112) he admits that certain theatrical methods
(the use of women on the stage, the use of machinery for changing scenes rapidly)
are in some more proper sense to be called "techniques." Rosalind as Katharine Hep-
burn is presumably a different aesthetic experience from Rosalind as boy actor.

language. Not a bit of it. Every word is merely a different series of syllables signifying absolutely and completely the same thing." [3] A counterpart of this sweeping principle of identity might be described as a subtly persistent principle of ambivalence. In this respect Croce's aesthetic is not unlike the few other most radical or metaphysical theories of both beauty and art which one encounters in ancient and modern times—and it is notably like the neo-Platonic identification of beauty with form, the principle of being, and the corollary Thomistic analogical transcendence of beauty. In such systems, what one might attempt to take as a special philosophy of art turns out to be a philosophy of all being, or of all knowledge. The circle defined is expanded to take in the whole horizon. The Plotinian form enjoyed by a piece of stone is beautiful in itself, but the example of an image exquisitely carved on the stone is used to give focus to the very idea of form. And the Crocean neo-idealism, despite a certain contempt for the mystical ad-libbing of Plotinus, is very much like the Plotinian idealism massively inverted; the *nous* "yonder" becomes the *nous* within, and all else is accordingly seen upside down. The Crocean concept of intuition-expression as the fundamental act both of all knowing and of the special kind of knowing called art involves a doubling almost identical with that of the two forms of stone in Plotinus. The difference between "history" and "art" in the Crocean system is the difference between fact and possibility. But within the general area of "art" itself a further distinction is demanded—a distinction between what is merely art in the sense of being not history and what is art in the sense of what is "generally called *par excellence* art." This is the difference between the art of a scribble on the blackboard or an everyday love letter, and on the other hand, the Art of the great masterpieces. And this difference is said to be merely quantitative and empirical; it is something to which philosophy is indifferent. Even the prose of a scientific discourse has its own character as an expressive effort, its own form. Ill-written=ill-thought (p. 24. Ch. III) is a Crocean equation of the most inclusive import.

> The artistic intuition differs from the ordinary not in intensity. The difference is not intensive but extensive.—p. 13

> The intuition of the simplest popular love-song, which says the same thing, or very nearly, as any declaration of love that issues at every moment from the lips of thousands of ordinary men, may be intensively perfect in its poor simplicity, although it be

---

[3] Giovanni Papini, *Four and Twenty Minds*, quoted by I. A. Richards, in *Principles of Literary Criticism* (New York, 1934), p. 255. We omit from Papini's equation two terms, "feeling" and "lyricism," because we have yet to note their place in Croce's thought.

extensively so much more limited than the complex intuition of
a love-song by Leopardi.—Ch. II, p. 13

The whole difference, then, is quantitative, and as such is indifferent to philosophy, *scientia qualitatum.*—p. 13

The limits of the expression-intuitions that are called art, as
opposed to those that are vulgarly called non-art, are empirical
and impossible to define. If an epigram be art, why not a simple
word? If a story, why not the news jottings of the journalist?
—p. 13

Why not indeed on Croce's major premises? What it all comes to is that
the "aesthetic" of Croce is after all not a philosophy of Art, but a philosophy of all intuitive knowing. Still the fact seems to be never clearly
admitted or even faced by Croce; it can be detected only by resolute
comparison of phrases obviously not meant to be compared. The steady
trend and rhetorical aim of Croce's *Aesthetic* is to suggest that the spiritual act of intuition-expression, as first broadly defined, is in fact the
central and necessary conception for a theory of Art.

The notion of fullness, completeness, success in the achievement of
intuition-expression plays an important role in the system. The "probable" in art is the same as the coherent. We strive with our intuitive
power to master the confusion of passive sensation, the welter of brute
impression, to objectify it and form it in the clear knowledge of spiritual
dominion. When we succeed completely, and only then, beauty appears.
Beauty is thus absolute, formal, unified, perfect. And it follows that the
anti-aesthetic fact is simply lack of intuitional form. Ugliness in art is a
hole in coherence.[4] Ugliness is embarrassment of intuitive activity; it is
multiplicity, failure of knowledge and reality.[5]

But a certain amount of sliding in the use of terms would appear to

[4] As art does not imitate any beauty already existing in the external world, neither does it imitate, nor can it be spoiled by dealing with, what would ordinarily
be called ugliness in the external world. The strong tendency of 20th-century art in
all media to include or even to center on what is ordinarily called both evil and
ugly in the external world is one correlative of the widely prevalent expressionist
aesthetic. Rembrandt's *Anatomy Lesson* gives place in the annual exhibition of 1950
to Hyman Bloom's *Female Corpse, Back View* (*Art News*, XLIX, May, 1950, 17).
This continues the classical and Renaissance opinion that even a dunghill if accurately represented is pleasing and the more modern debate of literary philosophers,
like Lessing (*Laocoon*, Chs. XXIII–XXV) or in the 19th century the Hegelian Karl
Rosenkranz (*Ästhetik des Hässlichen*, 1835) on the aesthetic relevance of the ugly.

[5] "If the ugly were *complete*, that is to say, without any element of beauty, it
would for that very reason cease to be ugly, because it would be without the contradiction in which is the reason of its existence. The disvalue would become nonvalue." Unsuccessful art works are said to have "merits," but not beauty. These "merits" are beautiful parts, or beautiful small wholes, in large failures, and furthermore
(though this may be more surprising) they can exist only in failures. The successful whole work, "being a complete fusion," has but one value. It has no beautiful
parts, no merits (Ch. X, pp. 79–80).

accompany the argument. The notion of the successful intuition harbors a certain duplicity. For there is in the first place the struggle of any given intuition, more simple or less simple, to clarify itself upon the welter of half-known impression. And there is in the second place the achievement of the complex and rich Art intuition in all its superiority over the simpler kind. And these two conceptions constantly blend. Thus:

> On the hither side of the lower limit is sensation, formless matter, which the spirit can never apprehend in itself as simple matter. This it can only possess with form and in form. . . . How often do we strive to understand clearly what is passing within us! We do catch a glimpse of something, but this does not appear to the mind as objectified and formed.—Ch. I, p. 5

But a few pages later:

> The world which as a rule we intuit is a small thing. It consists of little expressions, which gradually become greater and wider with the increasing spiritual concentration of certain moments. They are the words we say to ourselves, our silent judgments: "Here is a man, here is a horse, this is heavy, this is sharp, this pleases me," etc. It is a medley of light and colour, with no greater pictorial value than would be expressed by a haphazard splash of colours, from among which one could barely make out a few special, distinctive traits. This and nothing else is what we possess in our ordinary life; this is the basis of our ordinary action. It is the index of a book. The labels tied to things (it has been said) take the place of the things themselves. This index and these labels (themselves expressions) suffice for small needs and small actions. From time to time we pass from the index to the book, from the label to the thing, or from the slight to the greater intuitions, and from these to the greatest and most lofty.
> —Ch. I, pp. 9–10

> This passage is sometimes far from easy. It has been observed by those who have best studied the psychology of artists that when, after having given a rapid glance at any one, they attempt to obtain a real intuition of him, in order, for example, to paint his portrait, then this ordinary vision, that seemed so precise, so lively, reveals itself as little better than nothing.—p. 10

It is to be observed that the dialectical and absolute importance attached initially in the system to the sheer act of intuition-expression becomes by degrees transferred to a special sort of intuition-expression, that which is "greater and wider." The ordinary, slight intuitions are actually described in a way that makes them sound like cliché concepts—"indexes of a book," "labels tied to things." The greater and wider intuition, of the portrait painter, for instance, is then described as a "real intuition," and the "ordinary vision" sinks back into a status "little better than nothing"—i.e. into the status of sensation or impression. Yet in other passages of the book, where it suits him to be more consistent with his basic doctrine, Croce will say that any kind of intuition at all has an aesthetic worth equal to that of any other.

> Not only is the art of savages not inferior, as art, to that of civilized peoples, if it be correlative to the impressions of the savage; but every individual, indeed every moment of the spiritual life of the individual, has its artistic world; none of these worlds can be compared with any other in respect of artistic value.—Ch. XVII, p. 137

A double notion of "form" has extensive ramifications throughout the system. To take one example which may stand in general for the technical bearings of the difficulty: When Croce attempts to explain how it is that the intuition-expressions of Art do after all use a kind of conceptual language, an inheritance of ready-made forms and pre-fabricated bric-a-brac (words themselves, for instance, allusions, old saws, catch-words, aphorisms, and the like in poetry), he says that these elements do not enter into the new poem as forms but are first de-morphosed as it were, reduced and fused back into a state of mere "impression," formless stuff. An analogy from bronze-pouring seems ready to his purpose.

> He who conceives a tragedy puts into a crucible a great quantity, so to say, of impressions: expressions themselves, conceived on other occasions, are fused together with the new in a single mass, in the same way as we can cast into a melting furnace formless pieces of bronze and choicest statuettes. Those choicest statuettes must be melted just like the pieces of bronze, before there can be a new statue. The old expressions must descend again to the level of impressions, in order to be synthesized in a new single expression.—Ch. II, p. 20

But this analogy may not in fact read so smoothly. Do the conceptual materials (the old saws, catch words, and the like) which one finds in a poem really melt out of sight? Or don't they have to retain their form and meaning in order to operate poetically at all? To make the point in another way: there is a certain kind of form in the statuette—a kind that is absent in the "form*less*" pieces of bronze. But on the showing of Croce's own system, those pieces of bronze also have a form, the simpler intuition-expression which is the very form of our knowing them. And on an issue of intuition *versus* conception, there is no ground for discriminating between the statuette and the junk. The statuette does lose much more than the junk in being melted down. But that is an issue of Art *versus* general intuition. We are back with the Plotinian piece of stone, which always has form, but sometimes has form *par excellence* by having an image carved on it.

IV

CROCE's theory is in a sense the most resolutely cognitive of all modern art theories. His fundamental division of spiritual activity into the cognitive and the volitional enables him to proceed with great clarity and authority in his dismissal of the affective art theories which he groups under the headings "hedonistic" (Ch. XI) and "sympathetic" (Ch. XII). Nevertheless, the affective element is one which his system has always had to cope with, and one which comes to have a more prominent role in works written after his *Aesthetic*. To account for the fact that in the presence of works of art one experiences not just aesthetic knowledge but aesthetic *pleasure*, Croce proposes in his *Aesthetic* that each of the four radical spiritual activities, as it succeeds or fails, is accompanied by a "special activity, of non-cognitive nature, having its two poles, positive and negative, in *pleasure* and *pain*" (Ch. X, p. 74).[6] Aesthetic pleasure is simply the feeling of pleasure which accompanies our successful acts of intuition-expression. But let us realize clearly (and this may cost some effort) that *each* one of the four main spiritual activities is accompanied by this special volitional act (or overtone) called "feeling." Not only activities of knowing (poetic and scientific) but activities of volition themselves (economic and ethical) have their accompaniment of volitional pleasure and pain. Not only does the scientist experience delight in the knowledge of his discovery—*eureka*—but he must experience another delight in the success of his wishing to make the discovery. A certain clarity in the cognitive area has been obtained at the expense of a very odd double situation in the volitional area. This perhaps betrays some conflict between the cognitive effort of Croce's art theory and what turns out to be his equally resolute affectivism in general value theory —by which judgments of value "follow instead of preceding the affirmation of the will, and are nothing but the expression of the volition already experienced" (Ch. VI, p. 49). Working back from such empty acts of willing and feeling (which have to be valued themselves by their own echo acts of feeling), we rule out feeling from the aesthetic act by saying that although it accompanies the act it has nothing to do with the character of the act. To put the matter another way, Croce's affective duplicity in the *Aesthetic* is one cost of his attempt to keep practical

---

[6] In another paragraph (p. 75) he says that this activity is just the same as "that more elementary and fundamental practical activity which we have distinguished from the ethical," i.e., just the same as economic or volitional activity in general.

activity, economic and ethical feeling, too severely distinct from aesthetic activity. Perhaps the difficulty has never been completely overcome. The "incipient" or "imaginal" responses of a later psychological
theory of literature, for instance, or the purely contemplative pleasure
of an earlier metaphysics, may share somewhat the same embarrassment.
Yet there would appear to be something oddly maladroit and absent-
minded about this aspect of Croce's thought.

It is in certain other passages of the *Aesthetic*, where he is concerned with the danger of consulting either author or audience in their
moral activities, their feelings of guilt and innocence, that he makes his
best comments, negative though they may be, on "feeling."

> Many legends in the biographies of artists have sprung from
> this erroneous identification [between knowing and willing],
> since it seemed impossible that a man who gives expression to
> generous feelings should not be a noble and generous man in
> practical life; or that the dramatist whose plays are full of stab-
> bing, would not himself have done a little stabbing in real life.
> Artists protest vainly: *"Lasciva est nobis pagina, vita proba."*
> —Ch. VI, p. 53

> What are these apparent or manifested feelings, but feelings ob-
> jectified, intuited, expressed? And it is natural that they do not
> trouble and afflict us as passionately as those of real life, because
> those were matter, these are form and activity; those true and
> proper feelings, these intuitions and expressions.—Ch. X, p. 81 [7]

Croce has always been severe upon the mere display and indulgence of
feeling in poetry and upon the critical method of being interested in
authors themselves as feeling and willing beings.[8] Yet what, after all, of

[7] Three meanings of the term "feeling" are defined by Croce in his *Aesthetic*
(Ch. II, p. 18; Ch. X, p. 74): 1. the volitional activity of pleasure or pain with which
we have been dealing above; 2. feeling as passivity, matter, impression, inchoate
knowledge; 3. feeling as "pure intuition"—i.e., intuition in its character as non-conceptual and non-historical, neither scientific nor factual. In the passage of *Aesthetic*,
Chapter X quoted above, meanings 1 and 2 may be seen in fusion. In a passage which
we are about to quote from Croce's *Britannica* article, the use of the term "feeling"
in a shift from meaning 1 to meaning 3 is to be noted.

[8] Thus in an essay written as early as 1887: "It is not enough to feel. Feeling is
nothing if hand is not ruled by intellect. In the work of Gaspara, self-revelation
often remains a mere act of will, an intention. Gaspara sheds tears, but is not always
in command of enough magic to transform them into pearls" (Luigi Russo, *La Critica Letteraria Contemporanea*, Bari, 1946, I, 133).

For very strong statements against attending to the author himself (under any
practical aspect) instead of to his poetry, see Croce's opening Chapter on Shakespeare, *Ariosto, Shakespeare and Corneille* (New York, 1920), pp. 117 ff.; *The Poetry of Dante* (New York, 1922), pp. 27, 32; *Breviary of Aesthetics*, Rice Institute
Pamphlets (Houston, 1915), pp. 13–14; and *La Poesia* (1936), p. 297: ". . . *non im-
porta quel che il poeta si propone o vuol fare o crede di fare, ma unicamente quel
che esso fa.*"

feeling and its role in art? Does it have only the same minor role as do the feelings of pleasure attendant on a successful scientific conceptualization, or (in the awkward doubling which we have noted) those attendant on the success of our economic and ethical volitions? Even the impropriety of reading the dramatist's own feelings into his play about murder and incest does not obviate the fact that the element of feeling is a very prominent part of the poem. This line of inquiry can lead to a view arrived at by Croce only some years after the writing of his *Aesthetic* [9] —that Artistic intuition-expression is precisely the intuition-expression of "feeling." Not the tumult of feeling felt by an author in his practical life, not feeling simply spilled out, confessed à la Rousseau, or exposed to public view. But precisely feeling intuited and expressed, feeling objectified, embodied and made knowable in the artistic act—in the linguistic act of the poem. The new and more precise name now bestowed upon Artistic intuition-expression was "lyrism" (*liricità*). Thus in his *Britannica* article, "the basis of all poetry is the moral consciousness." But:

> The feeling is altogether converted into images, into this complex of images and is thus a feeling that is contemplated and therefore resolved and transcended. Hence poetry must be called neither feeling, nor image, nor yet the sum of the two, but "contemplation of feeling," or "lyrical intuition," or (which is the same thing) "pure intuition"—pure, that is, of all historical and critical reference to the reality or unreality of the images of which it is woven, and apprehending the pure throb of life in its ideality.[1]
>
> The lyric is not a pouring forth; it is not a cry or a lament; it is an objectification in which the ego sees itself on the stage, narrates itself, and dramatizes itself; and this lyrical spirit forms the poetry both of epic and of drama, which are therefore distinguished from the lyric only by external signs.[2]

[9] The Preface to the 1907 edition of the *Aesthetic* alludes to the "lyrical nature of art" (trans. Ainslie, 1929, p. xxix). The earliest emphatic development of the idea seems to be the paper on "The Lyrical Character of Art" delivered at the Heidelberg Congress of 1908. A translation of this appears in the first English edition of the *Aesthetic*, 1909. The Italian text may be found in *Problemi di estetica*, 1910. Cf. *Autobiography*, trans. Collingwood, 1927, p. 102, "the concept of intuition in aesthetic now elaborated into that of lyrism."

[1] The end of this passage seems to revert to the special sense of "feeling" as "pure intuition" defined in the *Aesthetic* (Ch. II, p. 18). But the main sense of "feeling" in these *Britannica* passages is clearly closer to the ordinary affective-volitional sense.

[2] *Encyclopedia Britannica*, 14th Edition, "Aesthetic," vol. I (1937), pp. 265, 268. Cf. *The Essence of Aesthetic* (London, 1921), pp. 32-3, "lyric" as synonymous with "art."

Croce has changed his definition of Art and of Art value by making feeling the required Art content or a prominent part of it. If we find a difficulty in squaring the new definition with his fundamental doctrine that to classify intuition-expressions in any way is to conceptualize and neutralize them, losing sight of the one aesthetically significant fact, the fullness and success of intuition-expression as "form," he will answer, no doubt, that the feeling itself is a kind of intensity or "throb" which has no specific coloration except from the cognitive character of the intuition-expression which it accompanies. On the plateau which he thus erects for himself, raising his early concept of the fullness and richness, the formal success, of the Artistic intuition more clearly into the strata of human ethical concerns, Croce is able to elaborate his views so as to accommodate much that appears more characteristically in other modern systems, those of the romantic Germans before him and those of his later expressionist and affectivist contemporaries. Thus in one of his *New Essays on Aesthetic* first collected in 1920 we find the doctrine of "lyrism" leaping exultantly into such affirmations as these.

> The particular throbs with the life of the whole intuition, and the whole exists in the life of the particular. Every pure artistic image is at one and the same time itself and the universe, the universe in this individual form and this individual form equivalent to the universe. In every word of the poet, in every act of his creative imagination, appears the whole of human destiny, all the hopes, illusions, sorrows and joys, the grandeur and misery, of the human state.

> To give to the contentual feeling an artistic form is to give it also the stamp of totality, the cosmic afflatus.

> Art is essentially free from practical interest, . . . because in art there is no suppression of any interest at all; rather art gives all our interests simultaneous free play in the image. It is only in this way that the individual image, transcending the particular and acquiring a value of totality, becomes concretely individual.[3]

Or in his Oxford lecture *The Defence of Poetry,* 1933, the following:

> The thoughts and actions and emotions of life, when sublimated to the subject-matter of poetry, are no longer the thought that judges, the action effectually carried out, the good and evil, or the joy and pain actually done or suffered. They are all now simply passions and feelings immediately assuaged and calmed, and transfigured in imagery. That is the magic of poetry: the union of calm and tumult, of passionate impulse with the con-

[3] *Nuovi saggi di estetica,* 3d ed. (Bari: Gius. Laterza & Figli, 1948), pp. 122–5, "Il Carattere di totalità dell' espressione artistica."

trolling mind which controls by contemplating. It is the triumph
of contemplation, but a triumph still shaken by past battle, with
its foot upon a living though vanquished foe. Poetic genius
chooses a strait path in which passion is calmed and calm is
passionate; a path that has on one side merely natural feeling,
and on the other the reflection and criticism which is twice removed from nature; a path from which minor talents find it but
too easy to slip into an art either convulsed and distorted by passion, or void of passion and guided by principles of the understanding. Then they are called "romantic" or "classical." [4]

V

LITERARY students have perhaps found their easiest sympathy with Croce,
and their most profitable instruction, in the negative starting points of
his polemic, and notably in his attack on such fixtures of the literary
tradition as the classical "figures" of speech and thought, the classical
literary species or genres and the rules of decorum long attached to these.
(The theoretical part of his *Aesthetic* is here vigorously supplemented
by his historical chapters.) All these classical technicalities, let it be remembered, had been taken at least implicitly, throughout centuries of
criticism, as conceptions of value and prescriptions for obtaining value.
To use a figure was to add an ornament to plainness and hence to score
a point (*punctum*) on the tally sheet of the *dulce*. To violate the decorum of a genre, as in experimenting with a new lyric meter or with the
hybrid of a pastoral tragi-comedy, was to court chaos or at least the
sharply raised eyebrow of the critical arbiter. But to the inviolable general rule Croce opposes the inviolable individual—the individual which
must not be touched by conceptual abstraction if it is to retain its aesthetic validity. (The beginning of his whole philosophy, as he himself
has confessed, was his criticism of the genres.)

Croce takes ruthless advantage of the inescapable fact that no literary
arbiter has ever succeeded in setting up a code which subsequent poets
have not with equal success subverted. Though the poet's materials and
even his forms in the grammatical and prosodic senses be conventional,
yet it is his rule of craft that he must do something different with them.
(Even if the little bronze image be not melted out of all identity, it must
at least be somewhat twisted.) The *verba . . . parce detorta*, the *callida
junctura* of Horace had long ago testified to this much. The most eloquent champion of genre theory in Croce's early days, Ferdinand
Brunetière, was scarcely setting up as a legislator; he was only joining

[4] *The Defence of Poetry: Variations on the Theme of Shelley*, trans. E. F. Carritt
(Oxford, 1933), p. 25, by permission of the Oxford University Press, Inc.

classical genre with Darwinism to create a frame of reference for the orderly exposition of literary history—*l'évolution des genres littéraires*. Something like that Croce himself would permit.[5] Yet such an exposition he would relegate to the dubious realm of literary history, a discipline which works "to some extent with generalizations and abstractions."

Croce's dogma is set sternly against all classification of expressions, all notions about the limits of a given art or about combinations of the arts (Ch. XV). It is set against anything like an intellectualization of the artistic meaning—against all analysis, all classification, all grammar,[6] all allegorizing, all rhetorical splits between "form" and "content," "ornament" and business, all conceptions of proper and "improper" ways of saying the same thing, all notions of homonym and synonym, and of literary translation. (If a metaphor is improper or an ornament external to the real meaning of an expression, why should it appear in the expression at all? If, on the other hand, it is really a proper part of the expression, why call it improper or ornamental?)

> Language is a perpetual creation. What has been linguistically expressed is not repeated, save by reproduction of what has already been produced. The ever-new impressions give rise to continuous changes of sound and meaning, that is, to ever-new expressions. To seek the model language, then, is to seek the immobility of motion.—Ch. XVIII, p. 150

> Language is not an arsenal of arms already made, and it is not a vocabulary, a collection of abstractions, or a cemetery of corpses more or less well embalmed.—p. 150

> We can elaborate logically what we have already elaborated in aesthetic form only; but we cannot reduce what has already possessed its aesthetic form to another form also aesthetic. Indeed, every translation either diminishes and spoils, or it creates a new expression, by putting the former back into the crucible and mingling it with the personal impressions of the so-called translator.—Ch. IX, p. 68

Croce makes a very damaging case not only against all the classic "paraphernalia" of criticism, but (and here the theory cuts to the quick

[5] "It may be asserted that the history of aesthetic productions shows progressive cycles. . . . When many are at work in a general way upon the same subject, without succeeding in giving to it the suitable form, yet drawing always more near to it, there is said to be progress, and when appears the man who gives it definite form, the cycle is said to be complete, and progress is ended" (Ch. XVII, p. 136).

[6] The "linguistic unit," says Croce, is the sentence: "Peteriswalkinginacountry-road." Any analysis of this into words, syllables, or syntax is an abstractive and more or less arbitrary act which does violence to its aesthetic integrity. One might be tempted to begin a critique of the Crocean system at just this point—with the question how one distinguishes a sentence from adjacent sentences of a linguistic discourse. And if such a distinction is valid, why not a distinction between words?

of even the modern critical consciousness) against every term that has ever taken on the least specific or technical coloring as a predicate in an attempt to define good poetry. Consider, he says, such opposed pairs of terms as *classical* and *romantic, symbolic* and *realistic*. Each of the four has been used as a term of positive valuing by a critic of a certain temper and can be used by us for the same purpose at a certain moment in a certain light—but blink your eyes, look again, and like the honeycomb cells of ambiguous perspective in the trick advertising sign, slanting now up, now down, the pair of critical terms will shift its value emphasis. *Classical* means either artistically perfect or coldly artificial; *romantic* means either warmly and truly expressive or sentimental and uncontrolled. *Realistic* means either mechanically imitative or vividly life-like; *symbolic* means either something that takes inspired liberties with reality or something that is stiffly allegorical. In short, any one of these terms can mean either *artistic* or *inartistic*. And no one of them, and no other critical term, has any privileged hold on the notion of the *artistic*. There is no such thing as specific, technical praise of an art work. All such terms when used for positive valuing—rhythm, meter, assonance, rhyme, metaphor, or what you please—are only synonyms for artistic form.[7] For neutral and scientific purposes you can move from the individual intuition into such abstractions, but you cannot move back again.

VI

THE total suppression of all critical discourse seems threatened. At the same time (and from Croce's own practice as a literary critic we may see this) he is scarcely in favor of such a suppression. He himself has defined the office of criticism as being to "discern and to point out exactly where lies the poetical motive." [8] Croce is always an interesting practical critic. He has given us some rather fine examples of a certain taste and of a certain critical idiom, the latter of which may or may not be exactly defined in the formula we have just quoted. Thus in his Oxford lecture *The Defence of Poetry*, the following exegesis of a single line by Racine.

It is a delusion to suppose that a verse delights us by any sounds with which it stimulates our ears to ecstasy. What it stimulates to ecstasy is our imagination, and thereby our emotion. There is a verse of Racine which Théophile Gautier used to scan and declaim with gusto, and which other disciples of preciosity are in the habit of reciting as absolutely unmeaning and yet, or rather

[7] Ch. IX, pp. 70–1.
[8] *Ariosto, Shakespeare and Corneille*, trans. Douglas Ainslie (New York, 1920), pp. 147.

for that reason, the only beautiful verse which the poet ever succeeded in writing:

La fille de Minos et de Pasiphaé

That is certainly beautiful, but not in virtue of the physical combination of its sounds. One might make infinite other combinations of such sounds without producing any effect of beauty. It is beautiful because these sounds, these syllables and accents, bring before us, in an instantaneous imaginative fusion, all that was mysterious and sinister, all that was divine and fiendish, all that was majestic and perverted, both in the person and in the parentage of Phaedra. And this is expressed by two epic names, that of the royal Cretan legislator and that of his incestuous wife, at whose side rises in our imagination, the brutal figure of the bull.[9]

Croce's criticism demonstrates a firm grasp on the nature of the verbal art expression (or in fact on the nature of all art expression as distinct from simply sensory pleasure). He has a fine flair for exploring the implicit meanings and hence the imaginative unity of poetic passages. Join with these facts his statements, already quoted, concerning the highly complex "totality" which he recognizes in a work of literary art—and we may be led to hope that in Croce has been discovered the patron theorist of the practical literary critic.

Yet a certain contradictory simplism may have been suggested in that definition of the critic's office which we have quoted—to "discern the poetical motive." And despite Croce's many eloquent pronouncements to the contrary, there is more than a hint here too of a genetic and biographical standard. Though he avoids the "Practical Personality" of Shakespeare, it is not, after all, the plays which he would take instead, but the "Poetic Personality." The classification of the spirit, the literary characterization (*caratteristica*), hovers between the single work and the author's whole output, the latter seeming to form some kind of necessary whole. Literary "history" is proper if it confines itself to the work of a single author, a single spirit, improper if it tries to include more.[1] "Criticism," wrote Croce in a letter not many months before his death, "does not require anything else than to know the true sentiment of the poet in the representative form in which he has translated it. Any other demand is extraneous to the question." [2]

"Sentiment" and "spirit" tend strongly, in Croce's thinking, to be

[9] *The Defence of Poetry*, p. 23, by permission of the Oxford University Press, Inc. See his glowing analysis of a passage from Virgil in the *Britannica* article.
[1] "*La riforma della storia artistica e letteraria,*" in *Nuovi saggi di estetica*, 3rd ed. (Bari, 1948), pp. 157 ff., cited by René Wellek, "Benedetto Croce," *Comparative Literature*, V (Winter, 1953), 76.
[2] Wellek, *Comparative Literature*, V, 77.

conceived as indivisible. They may flash out in a short lyric burst as well as in a whole work, perhaps more likely in the short burst. We recall the doctrine of the *Aesthetic* according to which unsuccessful works have, with reference to their wholeness, only "merits," not beauties, though each merit is in itself a beauty. One might have suspected Croce of an extreme fastidiousness with regard to nominal wholes, of a great readiness to look through long works for their most striking merits, their passages of "pure lyrism" (as Edgar Allan Poe thought a long poem a contradiction in terms and the best of "long poems" only a series of short poems linked by prose). And as a matter of fact this kind of anthological reading is quite prominent in Croce's criticism. He treats Goethe's *Faust*, for instance, almost as an album or commonplace book in which Goethe entered his feelings at various times.[3] He writes of Corneille:

> We care nothing for the canvas, but only for what of embroidery in the shape of poetry there is upon it.
>
> The poetry of Corneille, or what of poetry there is in him, is all to be found in the lyrical quality of the volitional situations, in those debates, remarks, solemn professions of faith, energetic assertions of the will, in that superb admiration for . . . personal, unshakable firmness. Here it is that we must seek it, not in the development of the dramatic action or in the character of the individual personages.
>
> We must insist that those four tragedies [*Le Cid, Horace, Polyeucte, Cinna*], like those that followed them, are not to be read by the lover of poetry otherwise than in an anthological manner.[4]

What might not at first come home to the unprepared reader is that Croce is not here speaking of what he supposes to be badly structured plays, in contrast to better structured, which it would be worth while reading as wholes. The truth is that he looks on the grosser architecture of any verbal work at all as a matter of very small moment, even of aesthetic irrelevance. He tends to associate structure with the mere intentions of the author, something to be known only abstractly and apart from the sentiment and imagination which is the poetry.[5] The structure of Dante's *Commedia* is what pertains to the "theological-political romance,"

---

[3] Wellek, *Comparative Literature*, V, 77.

[4] *Ariosto, Shakespeare and Corneille*, trans. Douglas Ainslie, pp. 407, 408, 414. Copyright, 1920, by Henry Holt and Company. Copyright, 1948, by Douglas Ainslie. By permission of the publishers.

[5] Wellek, *Comparative Literature*, V, 77, citing "*Recenti lavori tedeschi di critica del* Faust," in Croce's *Goethe*, 4th ed. (Bari, 1946), II, 101.

around which the actual poetry clings like luxuriant vegetation.[6] His statement concerning Shakespeare is perhaps the most shocking of all.

> Certainly, it would be possible to take one of the plays of Shake-
> speare, or all of them, one after another, and . . . to illustrate
> their aesthetic coherence and to point out the delicacy of treat-
> ment, bit by bit, scene by scene, accent by accent, word by
> word. . . . This insistence upon analysis and eulogy will be of
> special value to those who do not immediately understand of
> themselves. . . . But it does not form part of our object in writ-
> ing this treatise, nor does it appear to form part of the duty of
> Shakespearean criticism, for Shakespeare is one of the clearest
> and most evident of poets, capable of being perfectly under-
> stood by men of slight or elementary culture.[7]

It would seem to follow that when Croce in his *Britannica* article asserts
the unity of lyric, dramatic, and epic poetry, he does not mean that lyric,
dramatic and epic are three *different* ways of realizing the same poetic
quality (each having its own special features, approximate laws, and the
like) but that epic and dramatic are literally to be read as collections of
lyric passages framed together in a largely irrelevant structure of plot
and character. Despite all his disavowals, then, he takes his place as the
ultimate romantic critic, exhibiting a strong similarity to that far-off
harbinger, sometimes considered the first romantic critic, the author of
the *Peri Hupsous*, who also frankly confessed his belief that the poetic
ecstasy is a thing that occurs only in short spurts of energy, sudden
flashes.[8]

VII

IN TRYING to assess the Crocean system, one may be tempted to write
a kind of balance sheet. To the credit of the system, let it be set down
clearly that it is devoted to the discouragement of all didactic criticism,
all scientific, realistic, informational, and baldly mimetic norms, and also
the overtly intentionalistic, inspirational and biographical. It discourages
likewise all kinds of criticism according to the literary species and according to rules, or, as this is nowadays called (in the terminology

---

[6] *La Poesia di Dante*, 6th ed. (Bari, 1948), p. 59 (Wellek, *Comparative Literature*, V, 77).

[7] *Ariosto, Shakespeare and Corneille*, pp. 280–3.

[8] In the bewildering range of Croce's work one finds of course a certain number of statements in favor of conceptual criticism and of art as artifice or making,
and against merely impressionistic criticism. Critics, he says once, should be reminded of the prohibition posted in some German concert halls: "*Das Mitsingen ist
verboten.*" Wellek, *Comparative Literature*, V, 80–1, citing *Poesia popolare e poesia
d'arte* (1933) and *Nuovi saggi di esthetica*, 3rd ed. (Bari, 1948), pp. 223 ff.

promoted by Richards), criticism by technical presuppositions or general critical preconceptions. It discourages ornamentalism and every other separation of form from content, means from end. At the same time, if only certain clauses of the system are consulted (those concerning fullness, richness and unity of intuitions, harmony of interests and totality), then it will seem to encourage a study of literary parts in relation to wholes and a synthetic understanding of the art work. And lastly, the Crocean system more or less encourages the right kind of historical study, the reconstruction of the conditions, the vocabulary of ready meanings, which enter into the meaning of the work itself.

But on the other hand, and against the system, it must be set down that it inclines in some of its clauses to promote an exaggerated respect for the author himself (if not as a practical personality, yet as a poetic personality) and that in its emphasis on the unexternalized intuition it has favorably influenced (at least in the English-speaking world) the early 20th-century trend toward critical standards of sincerity, spontaneity, authenticity. In the same way, it has contributed its influence to the sway of critical impressionism. By the mere fact that it is a form of monistic expressionism and idealism, it has tended to undercut the notion of real values and hence to remove the background against which even an idealistic theory of art values must make its claims. Lastly, and this is the most serious complaint that must be made, in the zeal of his anathema against the classical paraphernalia, Croce moves on to prohibit in effect all critical analysis and hence all consideration of literary works as integrated objects or as complexes of meaning, and all distinctions between symbolic and literal structures of meaning. He forbids us in short to do anything for the critical enrichment of our intuitions. We are asked to remain content with the lightning flash. In the chapters of his *Aesthetic* on the history of art (XVI and XVII) he seems to face the fact that we can ultimately arrive at a better intuition of a whole through a conceptual analysis of its elements, but he does not like to extend this view into actual criticism—unless perhaps to the criticism of a short passage, a single line, like that of Racine's which he analyzes with such fervor. It is as if Croce can observe the fact of synthesis and contextual modification of elements within a small compass, but that the same thing in a wider perspective of plot, character, act and scene, forces the notion of abstractive conception upon him and leads him to speak of mere structural intentions and argumentative purposes. In insisting that the statuette must be melted to enter into a larger work of art, he forgets the gargoyle upon the cathedral—and he forgets that the small image if only it is allowed to retain its form can be *trans*formed by various juxtapositions with other objects and by the play of various lights upon its own shape.

The problems which we have been sketching are not the peculiar product of Crocean thinking. They are rather some of the most permanent problems of criticism, which Croce succeeds in bringing to a stage of acute even painful realization for the literary student who is faced with the practical need of talking about literary works. Croce perhaps more powerfully than any other modern aesthetician sums up and completes an era of idealistic and expressionistic thinking about art. He polarizes the philosophy of the art work as a uniquely individual organization and as an expression of spirit and hence a creation (ordered by its own laws) rather than an imitation (ordered by the laws of something external to itself). This philosophy, if one attempts to take it as all in all, is probably not enough to enable the survival either of art criticism or of art. Yet it is a pole of thought and reality which has always and unremittingly (whether critics were aware of the fact or not) exerted its energy toward the modification of too simple or too rigid norms of external reference or mimesis—just as those classical norms in turn, along with the affective norms which reach full discussion only in modern times, inevitably exert their own energy to subvert the monistic form of expressionism. We may venture the minimal and summary statement that today it has become almost impossible for the literary critic or historian to use classical conceptions of mimetic decorum or rhetorical affectivity without some tempering awareness of the Crocean critique.

Croce's influence in the English-speaking world has been most readily traceable in the names of his British translators and commentators, Collingwood, Carritt, Walkley, Carr, and in the work of expressionist aestheticians like the American C. J. Ducasse in his early phase, and more broadly in other aesthetic thinking, like Bosanquet's quasi-hedonist *Three Lectures on Aesthetic* of 1923, or even in thinking of a distinctly rival cast. A few years before they died, Croce and John Dewey confronted each other in the *American Journal of Aesthetics and Art Criticism,* the former making large claims of paternity upon the experiential and pragmatist aesthetic of the latter, and the latter irritably alluding to the pervasiveness of the concepts at stake. Literary critics have been on the whole less likely to advertise their indebtedness to Croce—though the "new criticism" sponsored in America by the historian J. E. Spingarn about 1910 was clamorously Crocean, and doubtless a number of acknowledgements might be cited as paralleling that made by the Scotch professor Lascelles Abercrombie in his *Theory of Poetry,* 1926—to Aristotle, Croce, and "common sense." The influence of Croce has been like that of Kant in the era 1800 to 1840 in France, of a pervasive and atmospheric kind, blending with a generally favorable climate of opinion so as not always to be clearly distinguishable.

SUPPLEMENT

In Richmond this month, the Virginia Museum of Fine Arts, instead of allowing the customary five-man jury to select its biennial of contemporary U.S. painting, has set a precedent that could be profitably followed by other and larger institutions the country over. To avoid what the Richmond director, Leslie Cheek, Jr., says of the previous juried exhibitions—"the selections inevitably represented compromises"—he invited, for the 1950 event, a one man jury and special director in the person of James Johnson Sweeney. Mr. Sweeney's philosophy and operating policy (with full power to select, invite and hang the exhibition) are set forth by him in the following pages.

. . . the *succès de scandale* of the first night was not an abstract painting at all, but a distinguished romantic realist, Hyman Bloom, with his *Female Corpse*. . . . Nobody seemed to take *that* as a metaphor, proving once more that most Americans can accept their symbolism in the form of anything, including trade-marks and jingling commercials, so long as it isn't symbolical realism. Even so, it would have been impossible to foresee the violence and the pathetic rage with which the Bloom was greeted. An editorial the next morning in the *Richmond Times-Despatch* went a long way toward a U.S. record for malapropism and bad taste: it began by disqualifying itself in ranking Mr. Sweeney's choice with its own evaluation of Joyce's *Ulysses*, "A tongue-in-cheek pretense of 'erudition' which must be seen to be properly deprecated." But it concluded with an attack on the Virginia Museum's source of income in state funds, implying that they could be cut off for showing "corpses"— which is serious business indeed.

The Bloom (any similarity in name to characters in James Joyce's *Ulysses* is entirely accidental) is, in the writer's opinion and that of many others, an important American picture. In its subject matter, of course, it shares some identity and apparently a momentary fate with that of Géricault's *Raft of the Medusa* and Courbet's *Burial at Ornans*. With them, it violates the sacred bourgeois tabu that the cadaver is never brought into the parlor except for the actual funeral party. And, with them, its fate will be to remain misunderstood until the metaphor is discovered beneath the superficial reality.

—Alfred M. Frankfurter, *Art News*, XLIX (May, 1950), 17, "Vernissage: One Man's Corpse"

Queries: Why is this only a bourgeois tabu? Why isn't it a good tabu? Who are the people who ordinarily bring the cadaver into the parlor? For what purposes? What is the metaphor he is talking about? Why isn't this just pretentious hot air? Is it? A look into Art News *for May, 1950, where Bloom's "Female Corpse, Back View, 1947" is reproduced on p. 18, might lead to a fruitful series of revelations and speculations concerning the "ugly" in graphic art.*

.   .   .

Let us now stop and restate the ideas which we are considering in relation to one another. The first is that the style of a poem and the poem itself are one; the second is that the style of the gods and the gods themselves are one; the third is that in an age of disbelief, when the gods have come to an end, when we think of them as the aesthetic projections of a time that has passed, men turn to a fundamental glory of their own and from that create a style of bearing themselves in reality. They create a new style of a new bearing in a new reality. This third idea, then, may be made to conform to the way in which the other two have been expressed by saying that the style of men and men themselves are one. Now, if the style of a poem and the poem itself are one; if the style of the gods and the gods themselves are one; and if the style of men and men themselves are one; and if there is any true relation between these propositions, it might well be the case that the parts of these propositions are interchangeable. Thus, it might be true that the style of a poem and the gods themselves are one; or that the style of the gods and the style of men are one; or that the style of a poem and the style of men are one. As we hear these things said, without having time to think about them, it sounds as if they might be true, at least as if there might be something to them. Most of us are prepared to listen patiently to talk of the identity of the gods and men. But where does the poem come in? And if my answer to that is that I am concerned primarily with the poem and that my purpose this morning is to elevate the poem to the level of one of the major significances of life and to equate it, for the purpose of discussion, with gods and men, I hope it will be clear that it comes in as the central interest, the fresh and foremost object.

—Wallace Stevens, *Two or Three Ideas*, Chapbook Published by the College English Association as a Supplement to *The CEA Critic*, XIII (October, 1951), pp. 4–5, by permission of the University of Pennsylvania Press

When gods and men turn into each other, curiously it is the poem (initially the medium for effecting such transvaluations) which begins to have a hard time maintaining its identity and calls out for salvaging. Wallace Stevens' subtly twisted essay in poetico-theology may be consulted as a plenary illustration of what occurs when the idealistic and fictional view of the world makes a present and urgent threat to take over.

CHAPTER 24

THE HISTORICAL METHOD: A RETROSPECT

§ *the idea of history, early bibliographies, history as de-cline, as progress, Ancients and Moderns, the rationalist stance—II. reactions,* Dryden, Gildon, *the medical analogy,* Thomas Warton *on* The Faerie Queene, Hurd, Letters on Chivalry and Romance, *the Gothic norm, French parallels,* Chatterton, Macpherson—III. Temple, *Of Ancient and Modern Learning, cyclic primitivism,* Vico, Hurd, *Eliza-bethan Dialogue,* Thomas Warton's *History, three ages of English literature,* Hazlitt's *Lectures on the English Poets,* Peacock *and* Shelley *again, romantic and classical dialectic—IV.* Warton *again, studying old poetry, Germanic com-plications, national spirit,* Carlyle, *French determinism,* Taine, *History of English Literature, race, milieu, and moment—V. scholarly achievements of 19th century, the personal and the genuine, scientific evidence, alliance of antiquarianism and genius, tough techniques and emotive interests, "expression"—VI. personal studies,* Schiller *and* Goethe, Taine's *devotion,* Sainte-Beuve, *Shandean depth,* Browning *and the* Shelley *letters,* Furnivall's *comment,* Percy's *folio, Mrs.* Brown *of Falkland, forged imagination,* Ossian, Skeat *and* Chatterton, Andrew Lang *and Sir Wal-ter* Scott, Bentley *and* Cicero—VII. aestheticism again, Oxford Hegelianism,* Leslie Stephen, John Morley, *Court-hope's History, the Cambridge History, decline in his-torical theory, art of praise,* Gosse *et al., literary scientism, Professor* Sherman *counting words, Johns Hopkins, the Modern Language Association of America, conflux of motives, the new era, Professor* Price's *address, vogue of* Taine *and* Brunetière, *science and the socio-real—VIII. recent complexities, History of Ideas, A. O.* Lovejoy, *ELH, affinities for literary criticism,* Geoffrey Tillotson,

the original meaning, F. W. Bateson, the elite audience,
dissatisfaction of the critic, Lionel Trilling, "The Sense of
the Past," "extra-aesthetic authority," contemporaneity,
dating and genuineness, tabloid of ambiguities §

IN SEVERAL EARLIER CHAPTERS [1] WE HAVE ALLUDED TO THE ROLE WHICH
the idea of history, or the consciousness of history, has played during modern times in determining conceptions of literature and of literary study. We have noticed the questions about literary progress which appeared in the quarrel between the Ancients and the Moderns during the latter 17th century, the notion of poetry as the evolving expression of racial or national history which occupied German romantic thought from the time of Herder on, and the Hegelian complication of historic process into dialectic idealism and the results of such philosophy during the 19th and 20th centuries, especially in Russian and French theories about the sociologically didactic function of literature. The present chapter aims at giving a somewhat more special account of how modern professional literary studies have developed in the direction of historical method.

In a very simple way historical method began to find an entrance into literary study through early modern attempts at writing literary chronicle—early nationalistic inclinations to look back over certain centuries and to catalogue authors, manuscripts, or printed books, as in the bibliographies of English literature compiled by Leland, c. 1545, Bale, 1548 and 1557, Tanner, 1748, or Mackenzie, 1708–22.[2] But such interests could not continue very long without becoming involved in complications.

The medieval and early Renaissance ages of criticism looked on literary norms as very safely fixed and enduring and on the history of literature—like that of civilization in general—as a decline from a Golden Age. The history of the world had exhibited a lamentable decline of "coherence."[3] But the early 17th century in England saw the rapid rise, under Baconian scientific auspices, of the idea that modern pigmy men might by standing on the shoulders of ancient giants reach even a little higher than they. The end of the century moved on the full sweep of

---

[1] Chapters 11, 17, 21, 22.

[2] See Wellek, *Rise*, pp. 4–5, 135. This chapter owes a great deal in various places not only to Professor Wellek's *Rise of English Literary History* and to various published essays of his which will be acknowledged in the notes but to two manuscript essays: "English Literary History during the Romantic Age" (read at the Indianapolis meeting of the Modern Language Association in 1941) and "English Literary Historiography in the Victorian Age" (read at the New York meeting of the Modern Language Association in 1944).

[3] Cf. Victor Harris, *All Coherence Gone* (Chicago, 1949).

the rationalist theory that history had been a steady progress from barbaric shadows toward the clear light of the new age. In literature, this
was the Modernist view of a direct clear progress from the medieval
quaintness of Chaucer toward the correctness in diction and verse of the
Augustans. France had taken somewhat of a lead and had provided a
model. Back toward the beginning of the century Malherbe had arrived
("enfin Malherbe vint") to purify French style. And at the end, Boileau,
though he battled against Modernist pretensions and claimed his authority
only "in right of Horace," could nevertheless be said to "reign." The
concept of a modern progress had to be more or less accommodated
(as we have seen, for instance, in Pope's *Epistle to Augustus*) inside a
wider panorama of the Ancient and Modern world. The cycle from
Chaucer to Pope was paralleled by the ancient Roman cycle from
Ennius to Horace. Still the Augustan emphasis was heavily on modern
perfection and on the limping steps which preceding generations had
taken toward this state. This was classicism stiffened by the Cartesian
accent. The same reasonable spirit which when operating by itself would
relegate poetry to a role of outmoded enchanter's gibberish, would when
it was allied with the literary spirit assert the principle of literary progress
and of modern supremacy in correctness. This Augustan attitude, so
well known nowadays to literary historians, was to survive throughout
the 18th century and, less conspicuously, even into the 19th. The Eliza-
bethanism of a Coleridge, a Hazlitt, or a Lamb was contemporary with
numerous antithetic expressions. Elizabethan prose, Nathan Drake would
say, was "quaint, uncouth and tedious, insufferably prolix." It was af-
flicted with a "barbarous and pedantic stiffness." [4] All poets before Surrey, said Surrey's editor of 1815, George F. Nott, "must be read in
reference to the particular age in which they lived. . . . But of this
allowance Surrey never stands in need." There is "hardly anything in
all his writings to remind us that he lived nearly three hundred years
ago." [5]

II

THAT was approximately the rationalist stance, or the classical stance as
fortified by the scientific spirit. But it had already, for over a hundred
years, been serving as a point of departure for several kinds of liberal

[4] *Essays, Biographical and Historical, Illustrative of the Tatler, Spectator and
Guardian* (1805), II, 3–4.

[5] *The Works of Henry Howard Earl of Surrey and of Sir Thomas Wyatt the
Elder* (London, 1815), I, ccliii. "Entire passages might be quoted which have all the
appearance of having been written in the purest times of modern literature; nor
could they be distinguished from the most finished periods of either Pope or Dryden. This is an improvement which reason and judgment must approve as one of
the highest importance to our literature."

reaction. The least aggressive kind might be described as merely a plea for tolerance, for giving the literature of ruder ages a square deal. Don't let a man be tried by the laws of a country of which he is not a citizen. Ignorance, in literature as in morals, is some extenuation of guilt. This, however, could easily turn into some such more liberal demand as— simply: Let us not dispute about the different tastes of different times and places! Or, again, with the cutting edge turned in a new direction: Perhaps it was the classic law-givers who were ignorant; they might have changed their minds if they had seen what we have seen.

> The climate, the age, the disposition of the people, to whom a poet writes, may be so different, that what pleased the Greeks would not satisfy an English audience.

> It is not enough that Aristotle has said so, for Aristotle drew his models of tragedy from Sophocles and Euripides; and if he had seen ours, might have changed his mind.[6]

Various scientific analogies might support the argument. Charles Gildon, answering an attack by William Walsh on the artificiality of modern love verses, first insinuates a relative aesthetic on the analogy of medical science:

> Our Physicians have found the Prescripts of *Hippocrates* very Defective; And as in Physic, so in Poetry, there must be a re- gard had to the Clime, Nature, and Customs of the People; for the Habits of the Mind as well as those of the Body, are in- fluenc'd by them; and *Love* with the other Passions vary in their *Effects* as well as *Causes*, according to each Country and Age; nay, according to the very Constitution of each Person affected.[7]

But later—shading tolerance into preference:

> Regard must be had to the *Humour, Custom,* and *Inclination* of the Auditory; but an *English* Audience will never be pleas'd with a dry, Jejune and formal Method that excludes Variety as the Religious observation of the Rules of *Aristotle* does.[8]

[6] Dryden, *Heads of an Answer to Rymer,* c. 1677, in *Critical and Miscellaneous Prose Works,* ed. Edmond Malone (London, 1800), I, ii, 305-6.

[7] *Miscellaneous Letters and Essays,* ed. Gildon (London, 1694), "An Essay and a Vindication of the Love-Verses of Cowley and Waller," p. 210, quoted by R. F. Jones, "Science and Criticism in the Neo-Classical Age of English Literature," *JHI,* I (October, 1940), 393. Jones cites Marchamont Nedham, *Medela Medicinae,* 1665, for the argument that diseases and remedies vary according to countries, times, and nations. Cf. Jones, *Ancients and Moderns* (St. Louis, 1936), p. 216.

[8] *Miscellaneous Letters,* p. 223, "To my Honoured and Ingenuous Friend Mr. Harrington, for the Modern Poets against the Ancients." In Thomas Killigrew's comedy *Chit-Chat,* 1719, a character remarks that he would as soon receive medical treatment by the rules of Hippocrates and Galen as see a play written by the rules of Aristotle and Horace (Jones, *JHI,* I, 395).

The argument for tolerance of various tastes and times might be used in favor of an earlier time (that of Chaucer or Shakespeare) when that time was criticized too rigorously by modern classical critics, or the same argument for tolerance might be used in favor of the modern times when that time was criticized too rigorously by the norms of classical antiquity. In this variation, the argument, though using comparative or relativistic premises, could actually swing into support of the classico-scientific notion of simple linear progress.

But the argument for the *earlier* time, the apology for Shakespeare or Chaucer as innocent violators of rules they never made, is that which had the greater immediate future. It was this which developed strongly during the 18th century as Thomas Warton and other writers took up apologetic themes invented two centuries earlier by Italian defenders of romance epic, but heard only now and then, as in an essay by Chapelain (*En Lisant les Vieux Romans*) [9] during the century of French classicism. Thus Warton in his *Observations on the Faerie Queene of Spenser*, 1754:

> In reading the works of an author who lived in a remote age, it is necessary, that we should look back upon the customs and manners which prevailed in his age; that we should place ourselves in his situation, and circumstances. . . . For want of this caution, too many readers view the knights and damsels, the turnaments and enchantments of Spenser with modern eyes, never considering that the encounters of Chivalry subsisted in our author's age . . . that romances were then most eagerly and universally read; and that thus, Spenser from the fashion of his age, was naturally dispos'd to undertake a recital of chivalrous achievements, and to become, in short, a ROMANTIC POET.[1]

> But it is absurd to think of judging either Ariosto or Spenser by precepts which they did not attend to. We who live in the days of writing by rule, are apt to try every composition by those laws which we have been taught to think the sole criterion of excellence. Critical taste is universally diffused, and we require the same order and design which every modern performance is expected to have, in poems where they never were regarded or intended. Spenser, and the same may be said of Ariosto, did not live in an age of planning. His poetry is the careless exuberance of a warm imagination and a strong sensibility. It was his business to engage the fancy, and to interest the attention by bold

[9] Cf. Victor M. Hamm, "A Seventeenth-Century Source for Hurd's *Letters on Chivalry and Romance*," *PMLA*, LII (1937), 820–8.
[1] *Observations* (1754), Section X, p. 217.

and striking images, in the formation, and the disposition of which, little labour or art was applied. The various and the marvellous were the chief sources of delight. Hence, we find our author ransacking alike the regions of reality and romance, of truth and fiction, to find the proper decorations and furniture for his fairy structure. Born in such an age, Spenser wrote rapidly from his own feelings, which at the same time were naturally noble. Exactness in his poem, would have been like the cornice which a painter introduced in the grotto of Calypso. Spenser's beauties are like the flowers in Paradise.[2]

Warton teeters from the accent of apology toward the accent of triumph. He wavers between saying that in order to read an old author we ought to know the customs, favorite books, and literary laws of the time when he wrote [3] and saying that if through better historical knowledge we do learn to read an old author, we may find that in him after all, rather than in our classically correct contemporaries, is the true spirit of poetry. How far this wavering represents an indecision on Warton's part (a conflict between the Augustan ideas in which he had been educated and the Spenserian poetry by which he felt himself attracted) or how far it was a strategy of getting a foot in the door before shoving, is a matter scarcely relevant to the present inquiry.[4] In the *Letters on Chivalry and Romance* published by Warton's friend and correspondent Bishop Richard Hurd in the same year (1762) as the second edition of Warton's *Observations*, the accent of apology [5] has become almost incidental to a far more excited manifesto in favor of the Gothic norm.

> The greatest geniuses of our own and foreign countries, such as Ariosto and Tasso in Italy, and Spenser and Milton in England, were seduced by these barbarities of their forefathers: were even charmed by the Gothic Romances. Was this caprice and absurdity in them, Or, may there not be something in the Gothic Romance peculiarly suited to the views of a genius, and to the

---

[2] Second edition, 1762, Section I (I, 21). Cf. the encomium of Chaucer, 1754, Section V, p. 142.

[3] For similar, if more generalized, statements of this part of the historical argument, see Samuel Johnson's *Miscellaneous Observations on Macbeth*, 1745, and *Preface* to Shakespeare, 1765.

[4] Cf. D. Nichol Smith, *Warton's History of English Poetry* (London, 1929), pp. 1–5, 27–9. Modern scholarship concerning Warton and his friend Hurd resounds with the question whether they were really "romantics" and rebels. See, for instance, R. D. Havens, "Thomas Warton and the Eighteenth-Century Dilemma," *SP*, XXV (1928), 50; Odell Shepard, "Thomas Warton and the Historical Point of View in Criticism," *JEGP*, XVI (1917), 153–63; Hoyt Trowbridge, "Bishop Hurd: A Reinterpretation," *PMLA*, LVIII (June, 1943), 450–65.

[5] See Letter VIII on examining a Gothic structure by Grecian rules.

ends of poetry, And may not the philosophic moderns have gone too far, in their perpetual ridicule and contempt of it? [6]

We are upon enchanted ground, my friend; and you are to think yourself well used that I detain you no longer in this fearful circle. The glimpse, you have had of it, will help your imagination to conceive the rest. And without more words you will readily apprehend that the fancies of our modern bards are not only more gallant, but, on a change of the scene, more sublime, more terrible, more alarming, than those of the classic fablers. In a word, you will find that the *manners* they paint, and the *superstitions* they adopt, are the more poetical for being Gothic.[7]

We arrive, then, at romantic primitivism—the notion that the poetry of uncivilized times, or poetry written about uncivilized times, is the most natural, the most directly human, the most powerfully emotional—pathetic and sublime—and is hence the best. It was about this time that in France Rousseau exploited the political and educational idea that human suffering proceeds from the artificiality of civilization. Diderot was saying that the more a people is civilized and polished, the less are its customs poetic. Everything civilized weakens and sweetens.[8] Condillac's *Traité sur l'Art d'écrire* (1775) draws a sharp contrast between the ages of vivid imagination and succeeding ages of analysis, taste and criticism. In England appeared the primitivistic forgeries of Chatterton (giving his age a stronger taste of the 15th century) and of Macpherson (giving the age what it wanted, a Homer of the Celtic dawn).[9] The issue of "poetic diction" (peasant or aristocratic?) which we have noted in the debate between Wordsworth and Coleridge was one of the more precise and grammatically defined issues produced by the trend of primitivism.

III

THE doctrine of primitivism was a stark contradiction to the Augustan notion of linear progress from barbarism. A simple view of progress was

[6] Letter I, p. 81. Cf. Letter VI, p. 108: Homer, had he had the opportunity, would have "preferred" the "feudal ages" for their "improved gallantry" and "the superior solemnity of their superstitions."

[7] Letter VI, p. 113. Cf. Letter XII, p. 154, "a world of fine fabling."

[8] *Oeuvres*, ed. Assézat-Tourneur, VII, 370.

[9] Macpherson's *Dissertation Concerning the Poems of Ossian*, published with *Temora* in 1763, observes that "The nobler passions of the mind never shoot forth more free and unrestrained than in the times we call barbarous. That irregular manner of life, and those manly pursuits, from which barbarity takes its name, are highly favorable to a strength of mind unknown in polished times. In advanced society, the characters of men are more uniform and disguised. The human passions lie in some degree concealed behind forms and artificial manners; and the powers of the soul, without an opportunity of exerting them, lose their vigor" (second paragraph).

countered by an equally simple view of effete decline. Some complication
of this procedure was, however, possible. The Augustan view itself, as
we have noticed, had required the contemplation of two classical or
Augustan ages, the ancient and the modern. In his essays *Of Poetry* and
Of Ancient and Modern Learning, 1690, Sir William Temple had given
this frame of reference a twist toward the primitivistic by arguing that
the modern situation was not a peak of poetical achievement but somewhere on a downslope toward effeteness. Such a complication was in
effect the meeting of the Augustan and the primitive notions and the
reduction of each, as purely conceived, to the status of an inferior extreme. Yet it was a complication too that was almost bound to favor the
primitive somewhat over the classical. For if poetry had risen, it could
have risen only from some state of uneducated rudeness, and if it had
ever declined, it could have declined only into some state of *over*civilized
effeteness. The scheme was bound to be viewed from its forward end
(no society of theorizers could possibly see themselves as sunk in barbarism). The theorizers were bound to look back to a less theoretical,
more imaginative, golden age. The earliest elaborate version of such a
cyclic primitivism is perhaps to be found in Vico's theory of the imaginative rise of human institutions (his ages of patriarch and myth, of king
and emblem, of society and law) expounded in the *Scienza Nuova* of
1725. Vico was not known in England during the 18th century. But his
ideas would not have been out of place. In one of Bishop Hurd's Elizabethan *Dialogues*, often printed along with his *Letters on Chivalry and
Romance*, occurs the following very adequate general statement.

> There is, I think, in the revolutions of taste and language, a cer-
> tain point, which is more favourable to the purposes of poetry,
> than any other. It may be difficult to fix this point with exact-
> ness. But we shall hardly mistake in supposing it lies somewhere
> between the rude essays of uncorrected fancy, on the one hand,
> and the refinements of reason and science, on the other.

> And such appears to have been the condition of our language in
> the age of Elizabeth. It was pure, strong, and perspicuous, with-
> out affectation. At the same time, the high figurative manner,
> which fits a language so peculiarly for the uses of the poet, had
> not yet been controlled by the prosaic genius of philosophy and
> logic.[1]

Both the simpler primitivistic contrast (between imagination and reason,
between elemental passion and social criticism) and some kind of cyclic

---

[1] *Hurd's Letters on Chivalry and Romance with the Third Elizabethan Dialogue*, ed. Edith J. Morley (London, 1911), pp. 71–2. The dialogue is the third of
Hurd's eight *Moral and Political Dialogues*, and the first of two dialogues on Elizabethan topics. The *Dialogues* were first published in 1759.

elaboration were 18th-century commonplaces which carried well through the theorizing of the romantic period. Thomas Warton's *History of English Poetry*, 1774–81, by far the most elaborate venture of its kind up to that date and an authority which remained standard for several generations, is permeated with an assumption that the growth of reason dries up the sources of imagination. The narrative is laid out on a conception of English literature as divided into three main ages, the archaic, the golden or Elizabethan, and the modern age of wit, toward which the Elizabethan declined.[2] This is a scheme which prevails in English literary history during the next half century, either in fairly literal repetitions, or in such modifications as that of Hazlitt in his *Lectures on the English Poets*, 1818, where he talks about the imagination of the Elizabethans, the fancy of the metaphysicals, the wit of the Restoration, the commonplaces of the 18th century.[3] In an earlier chapter [4] we have seen elaborate cyclic views joined with both primitivistic enthusiasm and anti-primitivistic satire in Shelley's *Defense* and in the *Four Ages* of his friend Peacock. Add to the Augustan phase of effete intellectualization a resurgence of poetry in the romantic era itself, and value this negatively as a pseudo-primitive relapse into barbarism, and we have the *Four Ages*. Value the romantic phase as a kind of promising spring-tide in cosmic legislation, and we have the historical conceptions underlying the *Defense*. Repetitions of the 18th-century pattern or protests against it appear in nearly all the English romantic essayists, in Coleridge, in De Quincey, in Carlyle.[5] At the same time, the romantic mind, both German and English, tended to reduce the phases of literary evolution to only two, a natural and an artificial, a romantic and a classical, conceived either as alternating without limit—a series of revolts against nature and of restorations—or as moving forward from the Homeric, directly natural or naive, in the irreversible dialectic of self-awareness or reflexive involution which we have noted in another earlier chapter.[6]

I V

BOTH in his *Observations on the Faerie Queene* and in his *History of English Poetry* Thomas Warton argues for the study of old, barbaric poetry mainly on the grounds that it records the "features" of a past

---

[2] Gray's scheme for a History of English Poetry, in a letter to Warton, 15 April, 1770 (first printed in the *Gentleman's Magazine*, February, 1783, pp. 100–1) gave Restoration and Augustan literature the name "school of France."

[3] See *Complete Works*, ed. P. P. Howe, VI (London, 1930), 83.

[4] Chapter 19.

[5] See René Wellek, "De Quincey's Status in the History of Ideas," *PQ*, XXIII (July, 1944), 264–5; "Carlyle and the Philosophy of History," *PQ*, XXIII (January, 1944), 63–4. Cf. Wellek, *Rise*, p. 193.

[6] Chapter 17.

time, "preserves the most picturesque and expressive representations of manners," "transmits to posterity genuine delineations of life." [7] During the romantic age the relation of literary study to historical antiquarianism becomes more complicated, participating in the Germanic conception that literature is the organic creation of a national mind, the expression of a certain society, age, and national spirit. Carlyle gives us the following vigorous formulation.

> The history of a nation's poetry is the essence of its history, political, scientific, religious. With all these the complete Historian of Poetry will be familiar: the national physiognomy, in its finest traits, and through its successive stages of growth, will be clear to him; he will discern the grand spiritual tendency of every period, which was the highest Aim and Enthusiasm of mankind in each, and how one epoch evolved in itself from the other. He has to record the highest aim of a nation, in its successive directions and developments; for by this the poetry of the nation modulates itself; this *is* the Poetry of the nation. Such were the primary essence of a true history of poetry. [8]

During the mid-19th century, French versions of this argument are the most prominent. They are less idealistic and patriotic than the earlier German versions, more sociological and deterministic. In what became the classic French instance with regard to England, Taine's *History of English Literature*, 1864, the aim of literary study is to uncover the environmental causes of literature—and these are conceived as falling under the now famous three main heads of *race, milieu,* and *moment.* That is, the study of literature is valuable because literature, even more than religion (which is a combination of poesy and credulity) and even more than philosophy (which is a mere dry abstraction from poetry) is the warmest and fullest revelation of the motives by which civilizations are determined. For the purpose of this study, poetry stands on the same level with all the other forms of direct human revelation, not only dramas and novels but letters, sermons, table talk, memoirs, "confessions." "The proper object of literature is to take note of sentiments." In fact literature cannot fail—it is rigorously determined—to take note of sentiments.

> And so for every kind of human production—for literature, music, the fine arts, philosophy, science, statecraft, industries,

[7] The phrases are taken from Warton's *History of English Poetry*, Preface, p. II. Cf. *Observations on the Faerie Queene*, 1762, Postscript, II, 323: "These compositions . . . preserve many curious historical facts, and throw considerable light on the nature of the feudal system. They are the pictures of ancient usages and customs; and represent the manners, genius, and character of our ancestors. . . ."

[8] *Essays* (Chapman and Hall edition, 1907), III, 225. Originally in the *Edinburgh Review*, vol. LIII (1831), no. 105, a review of William Taylor of Norwich's *Historic Survey of German Poetry*, 1831.

and the rest. Each of these has for its direct cause a moral disposition, or a combination of moral dispositions: the cause given, they appear; the cause withdrawn, they vanish; the weakness or intensity of the cause measures their weakness or intensity. They are bound up with their causes, as a physical phenomenon with its condition, as the dew with the fall of the variable temperature, as dilatation with heat.[9]

V

THE drive toward literary history had begun during the 18th century in observations and speculations that were primarily evaluative—that is, they had to do with a re-assessment of neo-classic norms and a turning back to look at primitive literatures with what was considered a greater fairness. Such fairness having been established, and along with it an attitude of some unfairness toward the classic spirit which had once held sway, speculation continued, as we have seen, in the direction of historical rather than explicitly evaluative goals. The pursuit of literary studies along such lines could not, however, fail to have profound implications concerning literary value. Both the goals themselves and the more and more efficient historical techniques which were developed in their pursuit tended to establish such implications. The mere presence of historical research as a method of ever-increasing efficiency tended to promote exhibitions of its worth. Expensive tools have to be used.

The notion of a rigorously historical study of literature had, it is true, a long neo-classic and classic ancestry. Yet this kind of study flourished during the 19th century as never before. It will be sufficient for present aims merely to allude to the union of Bentleian and Wolffian classical philology with Scriptural hermeneutics under the leadership of Wilhelm von Humboldt and Schleiermacher, the further transfer of these methods to modern literature in the *Encyklopädie und Methodologie der Philologischen Wissenschaften* of August Böckh, the Indo-Germanic philological and folklore triumphs of the brothers Grimm, and somewhat later in France the resuscitation of the epic cycles and romances by such French scholars as Léon Gautier and Gaston de Paris. Here was the exalted situation of primitive epic (plausible enough outcome of such 18th-century efforts as those of Hurd) against which Matthew Arnold raised a classical voice in 1881. In our chapter on Arnold we have alluded already to the contrast between the classical and critical spirit of Arnold and the contemporary rise of the empirical linguistic studies which launched the *Oxford English Dictionary on Historical Principles*. During the same era occurred the final purification of the Chaucerian canon by Bradley and Skeat, a work begun in the 18th-

[9] H. A. Taine, *History of English Literature*, trans. H. Van Laun (New York, 1886), Introduction, pp. 20, 18. Cf. esp. pp. 6–8, 10, 13–15.

century dawn by Tyrwhitt, and the multiplication of Shakespearian studies in every historical dimension. It is perhaps relevant to offer here the general observation that English literary scholarship tended to go against the grandiose generalizations, the dynamic aspirations, the sociological significance of the history writers in the German spirit. Resolute literary research avoided wider questions, suspended critical judgment, devoted all its energy to the accumulation of facts. The immediate value of these might be now and then difficult to see; still it would be rash to question their ultimate place in some construction of total learning.

The reversal of classical norms during the 18th century had meant not only a turning back to the primitive (as in itself a concept of value) but, as we have seen in Chapters 14 and 16, a new kind of respect for the original and genuine, and hence for the personal. Classical sophistication inevitably involved, or seemed to involve, a measure of "imitation" and artificiality. The really primitive, on the other hand, was necessarily a form of originality. And the really primitive could be discovered, in the last analysis, only by techniques of historical research. A certain wildness and abandon, a strength of color and emotion, might make out a *prima facie* case for the primitive. But the final test was scientific. Only scientific historical inquiry could justify an experience of pleasure in the emotion and the color.

The peculiar tone of 19th-century literary study, at least in England, would appear to result from a working union between two forces which one might offhand think of as quite disparate—the force of hardheaded, sceptical, factfinding, textual, bibliographical and biographical antiquarianism, and both augmenting this force and being augmented by it, the force of devotion to poetic genius, to the personality, originality, mind and emotion, virtues and vices, life, suffering and death of the literary creator. The concept of life and sufferings included all kinds of influences upon the creator, and hence no contradiction had to arise between personal study and more deterministic conceptions of national history, sociology, or politics. "Expression," as J. E. Spingarn has argued (with only a little exaggeration), was a motif common to all the forms of 19th-century theory. With the Germans and with their evangelists such as Mme. de Staël literature was an "expression of society." In the school of art for art's sake, from Victor Cousin on, "expression" in itself was the simple supreme law of art. In the variation given this philosophy by Sainte-Beuve and other men of letters, literature was the expression of personality. In the historical and deterministic critics deriving from Hegel, like Taine, literature was the expression of race, milieu, and moment. The "extreme impressionists," as Spingarn calls them, the later aesthetes like Pater and Wilde, thought of literature as the "exquisite expression of delicate and fluctuating sensations or impressions of life." [1]

[1] J. E. Spingarn, "The New Criticism," in *Criticism in America, Its Function and Status* (New York, 1924), pp. 19–20.

For all critics and theorists, literature was the expression of something. The norm of expression was the great co-ordinator, harmonizing the toughest and most scientific research techniques with the softest, most personal, and most emotive aesthetic interests.

VI

It is worth pointing out that the German romantic litterateurs, in their distinction between "classic" and "romantic" art, even Schiller in his germinal distinction between "naive" (direct and objective) classical art and "sentimental" (reflexive and subjective) romantic art, entertained no special reverence for authors themselves as persons to be consulted in the discrimination of one sort of art from another or even in the interpretation of the personal, sentimental, or romantic art. Thus Goethe in his *Conversations*:

> The Germans cannot cease to be Philistines. They are now squabbling about some verses, which are printed both in Schiller's works and mine, and fancy it is important to ascertain which really belong to Schiller and which to me; as if anything could be gained by such investigation—as if the existence of such things were not enough. . . . What matters the mine and thine? One must be a thorough Philistine, indeed, to attach the slightest importance to the solution of such questions.[2]

Literary critics of immediately succeeding generations, however (and one finds convincing examples both in France and in England), had no such scruples about the biographical application of the derivatively romantic theories to which they subscribed. Even Taine's vast schemes of cultural psychology were heavily grounded in a devotion to the individual, producing genius. The Introduction to his *History of English Literature* gets under way with the following nicely conceived imagistic strategy.

> What is your first remark on turning over the great, stiff leaves of a folio, the yellow sheets of a manuscript,—a poem, a code of laws, a declaration of faith? This, you say, was not created alone. It is but a mould, like a fossil shell, an imprint, like one of those shapes embossed in stone by an animal which lived and perished. Under the shell there was an animal, and behind the document there was a man. Why do you study the shell, except

---

[2] December 16, 1828. Cf. the complaint by Heine about the appeal to biographical information in reading his poetry and his sweeping rejection of the principle (*Correspondance*, I [Paris, 1867], 73 ff., June 10, 1823).

to represent to yourself the animal? So do you study the document only in order to know the man.[3]

And Sainte-Beuve, a critic moving along on the full tide both of the historical method and of the quasi-Kantian French movement of art for art's sake, exhibited in his numerous lectures and *causeries* the widest range of interest, understanding, and technique, but his most pronounced critical insight and most radical method, so far as he was a methodical critic, lay in the depth of his devotion to the personality of the author behind the work. The work existed mainly to provide him clues to the charting of that rich hinterland. No more deeply committed version of the biographical principle has perhaps ever been written than the following passage of his *Nouveaux lundis:*

> Literature, the literary product, is for me indistinguishable from the whole organization of the man. I can enjoy the work itself, but I find it difficult to judge this work without taking into account the man himself. I say without hesitation: *Like tree, like fruit.* Literary study thus brings me naturally to the study of morals.
>
> One has to ask oneself a certain number of questions about an author, and give answers to them (even though not out loud —and even though the questions may seem quite irrelevant to the nature of the works to be studied). Only after such questions can one be sure about the whole problem one faces. What did the author think about religion? In what way was he impressed by the contemplation of nature? How did he handle himself in the matter of women? How in the matter of money? Was he rich? Was he poor? What rules of living did he follow? What was his daily routine? And so on.—To sum it up: what was his master vice, his dominant weakness? Every man has one. Not a single one of the answers we give to these questions can be irrelevant to forming an opinion about the author of a book and about the book itself—that is, if we suppose we are dealing with something other than a treatise in pure geometry.[4]

[3] *History of English Literature,* trans. H. Van Laun (New York, 1886), Introduction, p. 1.

[4] *Nouveaux lundis* (Paris, 1865), III, 15, 28. The phrase *Like tree, like fruit* renders the French *tel arbre, tel fruit,* the inexplicit syntax of which is well suited to conveying the notion that here is something that will support Sainte-Beuve's line of argument. The Scriptural *arbor fructu cognoscitur,* which lies behind the French saying, points of course exactly in the opposite direction.

Sainte-Beuve wished to study an author in both his genealogy and his living family—in his father, his mother, his sisters and brothers, and even in his children (*Nouveaux lundis,* III, 18 ff.). He would study the author's childhood, his early environment, even the landscape in which he grew up. Taine, for instance, bore the impress of the gloomy Ardennes (*Nouveaux lundis,* VIII, 71).

From the mid-century in England we may take as a capital instance Browning's Introductory Essay to the Shelley letters published by Moxon in 1852. There are two kinds of poetry, wrote Browning, echoing faintly the utterances of the great Germans.[5] There is "objective" poetry, like that of Shakespeare, which does not depend on the personality of its author and does not require that we know anything about him. And there is "subjective" poetry, like that of Shelley, which is all compact of its author's personality and which takes on added richness and resonance with every iota of the author's personal record which we can discover. And so what extraordinarily good luck that these revelations of Shelley's mind have been preserved and are now made public!

> Such being the two kinds of artists [objective and subjective], it is naturally, as I have shown, with the biography of the subjective poet that we have the deeper concern. Apart from his recorded life altogether, we might fail to determine with satisfactory precision to what class his productions belong, and what amount of praise is assignable to the producer. . . . we must in every case betake ourselves to the review of a poet's life ere we determine some of the nicer questions concerning his poetry,—more especially if the performance we seek to estimate aright, has been obstructed and cut short of completion by circumstances,—a disastrous youth or a premature death. . . .

> The responsibility of presenting to the public a biography of Shelley, does not . . . lie with me: I have only to make it a little easier by arranging these few supplementary letters, with a recognition of the value of the whole collection. This value I take to consist in a most truthful conformity of the Correspondence, in its limited degree, with the moral and intellectual character of the writer as displayed in the highest manifestations of his genius.

One trouble with the argument, as all the world now knows, was that the supposed revelations of Shelley's mind were forgeries—throwing non-authentic light on Shelley's poems. Yet Browning we may suppose had his genuine access of pleasure and perhaps even an enhancement of insight into Shelley's art.[6] (There may well have been some insight,

---

[5] Cf. Meyer Abrams, *The Mirror and the Lamp* (New York, 1953), pp. 242–3, 375, n. 50, on the distinction between objective and subjective poetry as entertained by Friedrich Schlegel, Coleridge, De Quincey and others.

[6] See the statement of a recent editor: "The plain fact is that Browning wrote his essay as a foreword to a collection of spurious letters; but in this case the plain fact is less important than usual. Of the twenty-five letters in Moxon's publication of 1852, all but two were utter forgeries, pieced out with a few genuine phrases from Shelley's pen. . . . If here had been the only ground for the editor's enthusiasm, we

through whatever objective vision the forger himself enjoyed, and the forgeries to that extent were happy.) At any rate, Browning's venture was surely not to be written off as a failure in the cumulative history of romantic experience. One of the most scientific of Victorian philologists and one who was characteristically able to merge his science with a passion for the personal revelation, the distinguished Saxonist and Shakespearian F. J. Furnivall, makes, in an Introduction to the Browning Society reprint of the Introduction, published in 1881, the following boast of his own failure to be interested in Browning's poems:

> The interest [in Browning's Introductory Essay] lay in the fact, that Browning's "utterances" here are *his*, and not those of any one of the "so many imaginary persons" behind whom he insists on so often hiding himself, and whose necks I, for one, should continually like to wring, whose bodies I would fain kick out of the way, in order to get face to face with the poet himself, and hear his own voice speaking his own thoughts, man to man, soul to soul. Straight speaking, straight hitting, suit me best.[7]

The intense and precise labors of the Victorian philologists in the service of authenticity and other forms of factuality resulted in a great purification and straightening out of literary canons, and in large accesses of knowledge about the general education and reading habits of various authors. At the same time, the philologists were but moderately interested in the relation of their canonical and genetic discoveries to questions of evaluation and criticism. Furnivall and Hales, for instance, in their editing of the folio MS. from which Bishop Percy had taken his *Reliques of Ancient English Poetry* in 1765, pounced with much righteous scorn on the various prunings, normalizations, clarifications, and civilizations which Percy, not only an antiquarian but a critic, and faced with a real problem concerning the relation between antique fact and poetic value, had taken the liberty of imposing upon the old text. Furnivall and Hales performed their service of restoration and rehabilitation with unswerving rigor. It was an advantage to them not to be disturbed by any scruples about literary value such as had dis-

---

might well be startled at its strength. But it is clear that Browning paid very little attention to the letters he was introducing to the world" (H. F. B. Brett-Smith, *Peacock's Four Ages of Poetry, Shelley's Defence of Poetry, Browning's Essay on Shelley*, Oxford, 1945, p. xxiv).

[7] *Browning Society Papers*, No. 1, London, 1881. A note to this passage contains the further curious confession: ". . . if a reader is thick-headed, or can't spare time to study and think a poem out, should not a poet give him a helping hand by a 'mediate word'?" Quoted by Alba Warren, pp. 112–13. Cf. Warren, p. 90, Carlyle's mistrust of the poetic medium, his view of Shakespeare's works as only a poor glimpse of the man himself—"windows" opening dimly upon him.

turbed the Bishop—or rather it was their advantage to enjoy a serene
unification of scientific conscience with a belief that literary value was
always and essentially identical with primitive authenticity. They were
not coping with the question: Which of more than thirty versions of the
ballad of *Sir Patrick Spens* is the most artistic? It would not have occurred to them to raise the question raised by a recent American
scholar, whether Mrs. Brown of Falkland, Sir Walter Scott's informant
about the text of ballads, may not have showed as much artistry in the
recreative effort which went into her recording as had earlier recreators
(to whom she had listened as a young woman) in their own efforts.[8]

In that heyday of scientific and conscientious recovery of the English literary past, problems could, however, become curiously complicated by the existence of such forged monuments to sincere imagination as the enthusiastic primitivism of the 18th century had produced.
Here and there a stalwart taste, like that of Carlyle, J. S. Mill, or Herbert
Spencer, might hold out for the Homeric grandeur of Ossian, but by
and large the decline during the 19th century in the reputation of that
remote bard kept pace with the growing obviousness that the Celtic
magic was spurious. In another crucial instance, a special difficulty for
arbitrating between fact and value arose because there was ample opportunity for comparing the forged language with that which philology
could demonstrate to have actually prevailed in the literary era which
was mimicked. Skeat's essay on the 15th-century English style which
the ingenious Chatterton had scrambled together from 18th-century
glossaries was one of the clearest triumphs a modern philology might
win over the uncertainties which Warton, Ritson, and even Tyrwhitt
had to some extent shared with the juvenile hoaxer. "The plan of the
present edition," says Skeat, "will now be explained, and can be readily
understood. Given the problem, how to edit the Rowley Poems to the
most advantage? What must be the answer?" He was quite sure of
this answer:

> To do away with the needless disguises, and, on the supposition
> of their [the poems'] not being genuine, to give them as far as
> possible in modern English.

> The reader now has a chance, *for the first time*, of judging what
> the poems are really like, without being continually pulled up,
> sometimes three times in a line, by hard words which no amount
> of acquaintance with early MSS. will enable him to solve. The
> process of thus re-writing the greater part of the poems has
> been rendered easier by frequently substituting Chatterton's

[8] Bertrand H. Bronson, "Mrs. Brown and the Ballad," *California Folklore Quar-*
terly, IV (April, 1945), 129-40.

words in his *footnotes* for his words in the *text*. Thus, at p. 29, the second line in the original stands thus;

> Throwe halfe hys joornie, dyghte in *gites* of goulde;

but Chatterton's footnote explains *gites* by *robes*. It is therefore quite justifiable to substitute *robes;* indeed, we really thus approximate more closely to the true original text, viz. to the text as first conceived in the poet's brain before it was translated into the Rowleian dialect.

It is important to understand that Skeat undertook this normalization of Chatterton's text not simply as a way of attaining philological truth (at any aesthetic cost) but actually as a way of getting at true aesthetic value—so closely were the notions of philological truth and aesthetic value united in his philosophy.

What is the exact amount of merit to which Chatterton's genius attained, the reader can, in this edition, at last judge for himself. I only wish to say here that I have faithfully striven so to discharge my task as to protect the reader, on the one hand, from being misled by false old English, whilst endeavouring, on the other, to set forth Chatterton's thoughts to the best advantage. . . . That the public does not want *me* but *Chatterton*, is the fact I have endeavoured to keep steadily before me.[9]

Let us add one simple Chattertonian example to that which we have already supplied from Skeat's own Essay. The opening of Chatterton's *Bristowe Tragedie* reads:

> The feathered songster Chanticleer
> Han wound his bugle horn. . . .

Skeat duly corrects the second line to "Has wound his bugle horn" (without any advertisement of the fact) and so obliterates in the interest of grammar a part of whatever minor charm the tiny clarion of the line may have had.[1] Skeat's editing of Chatterton back to normal modern English is a turning of the knife in the wound; it accomplishes a kind of double forgery. The method carries out to the letter the

[9] W. W. Skeat, "Essay on the Rowley Poems," in *The Poetical Works of Thomas Chatterton*, ed. W. W. Skeat (London, 1872), II, xxxvii, xxxix, xlii. See the approving comment of Henry A. Beers, *A History of English Romanticism in the Eighteenth Century* (New York, 1899), p. 363. Skeat gets us "a little closer to the Rowley poems."

[1] For some 20th-century comments on Chatterton, written with a more Jabberwockian understanding of the relation between his faking and the exact nature of his poetic merit, see E. H. W. Meyerstein, *A Life of Thomas Chatterton* (New York, 1930), p. 176; Bertrand Bronson, "Thomas Chatterton," in *The Age of Johnson, Essays Presented to Chauncey Brewster Tinker* (New Haven, 1949), p. 246.

legitimate implications of the factual norm of authenticity and original-
ity; but it has the disadvantage that it leaves "Chatterton the Marvellous
Boy" with very little explanation of where he stands in the history of
English poetic achievement.[2]

Near the end of a long career as translator and popularizer of classical epic and as custodian of native balladry, Andrew Lang wrote a
book on the vexed question about the authenticity of the *Border Minstrelsy* which Sir Walter Scott had assembled from such authorities as
Mrs. Brown of Falkland and James Hogg the Ettrick Shepherd. And
what of Sir Walter's own role as a ballad maker? Of one thing Lang was
sure.

> If it [*Auld Maitland*] is a bad ballad, such as many people
> could compose, then it is not by Sir Walter.[3]

In short, authorship guaranteed quality, and by a legitimate manipulation of the hypothetical syllogism implied, quality was at least a necessary condition for the imputation of authorship. So far as this was a
focus on the literary work itself, rather than on external types of information about it, the argument might find its classical analogues. "I
wouldn't believe Cicero had written this way," said Bentley, "even if
Cicero himself should swear he had."[4] Cicero might have dreamed
he had written that way, or he might simply not have remembered not
having done so. So far as the emphasis is on the means of establishing
who wrote something, the preference in a given case for internal over
external evidence is neither peculiarly classical nor peculiarly post-
romantic.[5] But it will be noticed that Bentley's statement is a greater
hyperbole; it contemplates the extreme of discountenancing the very
testimony of the author himself about his own writing. The basic supposition on which Lang and his generation were working was the opposite. Clear, irrefutable external testimony that Sir Walter was the
author of a ballad would have elicited from Lang the admission that it

---

[2] On the genetic side, R. D. Havens, "Assumed Personality, Insanity and Po-
etry," *RES*, N.S. IV (1953), 26–37, discusses the resemblance of forger's mask to
Bedlam retreat in releasing such 18th-century poets as Chatterton, Macpherson, and
Smart from the inhibitions of the neo-classical poetic conscience.

[3] Andrew Lang, *Sir Walter Scott and the Border Minstrelsy* (London, 1910),
p. vi.

[4] The question at issue was whether the name of Hermagoras in Latin should
end in *as* or *a*. Quintilian quotes Cicero as using *a*. But: "*Repone hic paulisper, Hermagora inventor, & Hermagora habuisset; non sentis vocalium concursum vaste hian-
tem? Ego vero Ciceronem ita scripsisse ne Ciceroni quidem affirmanti crediderim*"
(Richard Bentley, *Epistola ad . . . Millium*, 1691, quoted in part in footnote to
Alexander Pope's *Dunciad* IV, 222). Cf. Bentley's *Emendationes in Menandri Re-
liquias* (Cambridge, 1713), p. [70].

[5] Cf. Thomas Warton's insistence on the internal and aesthetic evidence against
the authenticity of the Rowley poems (*An Enquiry into the Authenticity of the
Poems Attributed to Thomas Rowley*, London, 1782, p. 90).

was a good ballad. Criticism would be merely the finding of praise in support of the poetic value necessarily entailed by authenticity.

VII

DURING the latter part of the 19th century, the aesthetic movement which we have considered in Chapter 22 took a contemplative, static view of individual art works and so was anti-historical. Also anti-historical was the kind of non-dialectical Hegelian idealism which appeared at Oxford in A. C. Bradley's appreciation of Shakespearian tragedy and in the essays of W. P. Ker.[6] We have observed already that the more ambitiously systematic kind of literary history writing never enjoyed a real vogue in England. Still a modest tradition may be traced during the latter half of the century in works of Leslie Stephen, John Morley, and even so aesthetically removed a litterateur as Walter Pater.[7] This reached its climax and conclusion in W. J. Courthope's great *History of English Poetry*, published from 1895 to 1910. Courthope, reciting the history of the national imagination in close relation to political institutions, conceives a long dialectical conflict between individualism and collectivism—(the collective Middle Ages had been bad for literature, the harmoniously adjusted Renaissance very good, and the romantically individual modern time bad again). He was a master of the long vista into intellectual history.

The decades immediately following Courthope's *History* saw much activity in the simpler chronicle forms of English literary history (in this period the encyclopedic *Cambridge History of English Literature* was begun and completed), but at the same time there was a decline in speculative history-writing and in a theoretical concern for literary history.[8] The movement of art for art's sake, especially as it affected the criticism of such litterateurs as Gosse, Saintsbury, Raleigh, Quiller-Couch, or Garrod, led away both from history and from criticism to the creed of enthusiastic appreciation and in historical effort to the supposedly literal fidelity of the "photographer's plate." [9] A sceptical attitude toward scholarship became fashionable in England early in the

---

[6] Notably that on the "Philosophy of Art" in the Hegelian manifesto *Essays in Philosophical Criticism*, 1883, reprinted in Ker's *Collected Essays* (London, 1925), II, 231–68.

[7] See Stephen's *History of Thought in the Eighteenth Century*, 1876; Morley's *Studies in Literature*, 1891; Pater's *Plato and Platonism*, 1893. Literature, said Stephen, is the "noise of the wheels of history" (Frederick W. Maitland, *The Life and Letters of Leslie Stephen*, London, 1906, pp. 283–4).

[8] Just at the moment when general cultural history was spreading out into wider and wider cyclic panoramas—as in the works of Spengler and Toynbee.

[9] G. E. B. Saintsbury, *History of English Criticism* (Edinburgh, 1911), pp. 499, 521.

20th century and discouraged all but the less reflective kinds of anti-quarianism and the whimsical essay in the "art of praise." Within the field of critical writing in English, it has remained indeed for American scholarship during the 20th century to carry some of the anti-critical trends which we are about to describe to their most systematic extremes.

In America during even the first decades of the 20th century, academic literary criticism was less warmly colored by romantic personalism and the art of praising. Although a Bliss Perry, a William Lyon Phelps, and later a Henry Seidel Canby did appear and flourish, American literary study was much more inclined than the British to borrow rigors from the methods of German philology and in general to undertake a respectful emulation of feats being performed in the laboratories of physical science. The literary scientist tried to set up the rules of his experimental procedure with sober and neutral precision. Consider, for instance, Professor L. A. Sherman of the University of Nebraska. In a series of notes appearing in the periodical *Science* during 1889, he read that conclusions about the average number of words per sentence used by a given author should not be based on a sampling of fewer than many thousands of sentences. Inspired by this conception, he counted the number of words per sentence for all five volumes of Macaulay's *History of England* and demonstrated a "consistent numerical . . . average," of 23.43 words per sentence.

Here, then, in this 23.43 was the resultant of the forces which had made Macaulay's literary character.[1]

In 1876 the Johns Hopkins University had been founded expressly for the purpose of introducing upon the American scene the graduate seminar on the German model. In 1883 was organized the Modern Language Association of America, which in 1927 voted to change the original definition of its purpose, "the study of modern languages and literature," to a phrasing more consonant with what had long before become its actually dominant purpose, the "advancement of research in the modern languages and literatures." (It was only in 1950 that the members of the Association voted to add to their constitutional statement of purpose the word "criticism.") A new era of American literary studies was carried in triumphantly by a massive conflux of motives which might be named separately as (1) respect for German philology, (2) a native American desire for facts and scientific precision, (3) a social and moral readiness to fall in with the critical relativism invited by the study of literature in its causes and origins, (4) a growing democratic require-

---

[1] L. A. Sherman, "On Certain Facts and Principles in the Development of Form in Literature," *The University Studies of the University of Nebraska*, I (July, 1892), 350–3.

ment of mass production in the qualification of scholar-teachers, and (5) on the side of the warmer emotions a romantic nostalgia for the European past and the Middle Ages. The rigors of scientific antiquarianism were, as we have already suggested, far from incompatible with certain kinds of sentimentalism—both the personal devotions and gossip of biographical research and the various nationalistic limitations of view, the provincial specializations, which by the end of the 19th century had grown out of the romantic German stress on origins and the evaluation of literature as national or racial physiognomy.[2]

Great things were to be expected in America of the newly imported method, the dawn of a new intellectual life. The aspect of joy and celebration, of pioneer triumph, which came with the arrival of the new disciplines may be illustrated from the presidential address delivered by Professor Thomas R. Price of Columbia before the Annual Meeting of the Modern Language Association in 1901:

> . . . we must all feel a certain warmth and exhilaration. With that period of forty years . . . there has been a steady current of progress. . . . There has been, indeed, in this wide enthusiasm for the spreading and elevation of modern language instruction, an intellectual movement that may fairly be compared with the enthusiasm in the days of the Renaissance. . . . In country villages I found the same ardor for our special studies as in great universities. No man that has shared in this movement can fail to feel a noble joy.[3]

American literary scholars were on the whole more favorably impressed than were the British by deterministic and social thinking about literature along the lines that had been laid down by German and French historians, notably by Taine. The name of Taine and that of Brunetière (who had complicated and partly countered the deterministic view by adding to it the idea of the Darwinian evolution of literary genres)[4] were commonplaces of American journalistic criticism around the turn of the century.[5] In a more routine way, without reference to Taine or to other foreign authorities, and with only a more or less complete understanding of what went on, American literary research found wide scope in exercises relating literature to various kinds of influence—social, political, economic, climatic, national, regional, traditional, psychological, and genealogical—all that might be fitted under the most

[2] See René Wellek, "Literary Scholarship," in *American Scholarship in the Twentieth Century*, ed. Merle Curti (Harvard University Press, 1953), esp. pp. 111–17.

[3] *PMLA*, XVI (1901), 77–91, quoted by Wellek, *loc. cit.*, p. 112.

[4] See especially his *L'Evolution des genres dans l'histoire de la littérature*, 1890, and *Manuel de l'histoire de la littérature française*, 1897.

[5] See W. V. O'Connor, *An Age of Criticism 1900–1950* (Chicago, 1952), pp. 4–6, 51–3.

inclusive and most durable of Taine's three headings, the term "milieu." [6]

Let us attempt a brief retrospective statement which will locate the present topic in relation to that of the socio-real in literature which we have already discussed in Chapter 21. The ground of relation is the concept of science in literature. Two divisions of the concept may be distinguished, the creative and the historico-critical: 19th-century science as the religion of reason sponsored an advance from the realism of Flaubert to the highly theorized and self-conscious naturalism of Zola and Frank Norris (literature scientifically faithful to life), and at the same time another advance from the historical principles of literary study laid down by Taine to the literary evolutionism of Brunetière and then to the more generalized and readily available doctrine that literary criticism should be neutral and tolerant and should devote itself to discovering the natural forces by which literature is caused. There were easy enough connections between neutral determinism and sociological interests, and hence between historical science and certain new forms of didacticism. American literary scholarship during the 1920's and 1930's moved along lines that led quite smoothly into companionship with the proletarian criticism that flourished during the second of those decades. The case for literature as class propaganda and social criticism seemed very obvious. The academically established techniques stood clearly ready to support it. The association between the names of New England college professors and organs of doctrinaire liberal opinion like *The New Republic* became a normal phenomenon.

VIII

But the course of literary scholarship during the past twenty-five years both in America and in England has been remarkable for the variety and mixture of its historical and historico-critical drives. One of the most complicated contributions during this period from the historical side has been an American version of *Geistesgeschichte*,[7] the new school of the History of Ideas, initiated by Professor A. O. Lovejoy and represented in his numerous essays and in the *Journal of the History of Ideas* which he founded in 1940. A companion journal founded earlier (1933) by Hopkins professors, *ELH, A Journal of English Literary History*, has aspired to show the specific application of the same principles to the interpretation of English literature. Lovejoy and his colleagues

---

[6] See Edmund Wilson's essay "The Historical Interpretation of Literature," in *The Intent of the Critic*, ed. Donald Stauffer (Princeton, 1941).

[7] Wellek, *loc. cit.*, p. 119 points out that the form of *Geistesgeschichte* cultivated in Germany during recent decades was a reaction against positivistic philology. Among the few direct echoes of that movement in America was the hostile *Academic Illusions*, 1933, by Martin Schütze.

have quite openly confessed to being interested in literature only as it is a document of intellectual history, a "dilution" of "philosophical ideas." [8] These historians may be looked upon as frankly dismissing the discussion of literary values and hence as not being in aggressive conflict with that discussion. The technique of the History of Ideas when picked up by literary scholars themselves, however, has produced some new versions of the problems that were posed in their essentials during the 18th century by writers like Warton and Hurd. The history of ideas has turned out to have a special kind of affinity for literary criticism— the reason for this lying not in the emphasis of the discipline on history, but in its emphasis on ideas. Despite the atomistic treatment of "unit" ideas, like slogans or catchwords, which is a first principle of the school, ideas as such do tend to have implications and to be related in systems. It would be difficult, for instance, to expound Pope's *Essay on Man* in the light of Professor Lovejoy's essays on nature, deism, and classicism without implying something about the organization of ideas in the poem itself and hence about its unity and coherence. Much more than the classic types of textual, bibliographical, biographical and source study, the new reduction of "ideas" to historical study has tended to approach the contestable border lines where historical study and literary evaluation interact and must be reconciled. For ideas constitute the more universal and durable meaning of words—meaning as differentiated from momentary suggestion and from the mere denotation of local date, place, and other fact. Ideas are hence lexicography, the history of the meanings which inform and vitalize the poet's medium, his vocabulary. History of Ideas, if it has not created any critical problem which is on principle different from that created by Hurd's desire to re-appraise Gothic manners, has at least subtilized and universalized the problem.

But in the history of ideas, *whose* ideas are of most importance? The historical problem has been made somewhat more difficult in recent years not only by a growing interest in the history of poetic interpretation but by the emergence of a newly emphasized doctrine that the duty of the literary critic is to look only to the initial moment in any given history. A verbal expression will change in time, perhaps it will improve—but *illegitimately*. What a reviewer in the *Times Literary Supplement* called "an uncomfortably strict rectitude," a very pure attitude of reverence toward the historic moment at which the poet wrote and his first readers read, was illustrated vivaciously in the British critic Geoffrey Tillotson's *Essays in Criticism and Research*, 1942. "To read later emotions here and there into a poem," argued Professor Tillotson, "is a tedious error in criticism and worthy only of the insipidly fickle florilegist."

[8] *The Great Chain of Being* (Cambridge, Mass., 1936), p. 17.

The original meaning of a word in a great poem is the only one worth attending to. However delightful the meaning arising out of new verbal connotations, such meaning is irrelevant to the author's poem. He must stand by his poem as he meant it. . . . When Lady Anne Winchelsea wrote

> Nor will in fading silks compose
> Faintly the inimitable rose,

she meant that she disliked the common feminine pastime of embroidery since it can produce only a poor 'imitation' of an actual rose. But following on after the romantic poets and all the talk about pure poetry, those lines have accidentally taken on a beauty which did not exist for their author.[9]

Perhaps so. The wider implications of the argument, its actual stress on history in some public sense rather than on the author romantically *per se*, were more fully brought out only a few years ago by the British critic and historian F. W. Bateson of Oxford. Following up the success of an earlier inquiry into the linguistic determinations of literature (*English Poetry and the English Language*, 1934), this critic accomplishes a reversal of the usual bent of historical studies toward origins.[1] He is willing to think that the author himself and his inspirations can be related to the produced poem only somewhat dubiously and irrelevantly. Not so the audience for whom the author produced the poem and on whom it made its first impact. Here is a more objectively solid point of reference. Studies in literary reputation had appeared before this, and more than a little scattered attention had been paid to such first-hand evidence as that provided by the diaries and letters of novel readers and theater goers (Simon Forman in the day of Shakespeare, Samuel Pepys in the Restoration, Boswell, Fanny Burney, Horace Walpole, and all the memorialists and letter-writers of the 18th and 19th centuries). Bateson, however, has undertaken to manipulate such material into a distinct theoretical dimension. He offers us the proposition—fairly novel in its clarity—that the validity of the literary work is to be decided exactly by its measure of conformity to the understanding of some historically specific audience. Within a given age there will be not one audience but a number of audiences—according to class, sex, coterie, profession—and hence a number of possible frames of reference. Only one of these, however, will be right. The essential function of poetry is "the expression in language of the sense of social solidarity." And Bateson believes, "on the evidence of the poetry," that "at any one

---

[9] *Essays in Criticism and Research* (Cambridge, at the University Press, 1942), pp. xx–xxi. Cf. *TLS*, April 4, 1942, p. 174.
[1] F. W. Bateson, *English Poetry: A Critical Introduction* (London, 1950), pp. 69 ff.

period" there was "only one social group in England that was functioning healthily." If we modern readers want to understand a poem of the past, "we need to be able to identify ourselves as far as possible with its original readers, the poet's contemporaries, whose ideal response to the poem in fact constitutes its meaning." Here is milieu and moment with a sharply new twist.

Perhaps Bateson's argument offers as convenient a provocation as any for concluding our narrative of the historical method with some hint of the dissatisfaction which it may entail for the critic even in its most recent and subtle versions. A critic is a person who habitually finds himself puzzled to know on what grounds (the poem itself? or some testimony outside the poem?) he is expected to divine what are sometimes referred to as a poet's intentions. And in this matter Bateson is apparently at one with the critic. But may not a critic find himself equally puzzled to know on what grounds (poem or something outside the poem) he is expected to identify the readers the poet *intended* to address? Or how is the critic to decide who were the elite or "most intelligent" among the poet's actual first readers? And were these elite the poet's actual best readers? What of Dr. Johnson's response to the poetry of Gray? What of Milton's readers before Dryden's and Addison's criticism? What of the contemporary readers whom Gerard Manley Hopkins almost entirely lacked and did not seek? What of most readers of Eliot's *Waste Land* in 1922? Let the present writers be content to say here that they believe a critic ought to have in mind not just any response of a contemporary reader, or the average response, or even the response of any elite group, but in a more generally human sense an "ideal response." And in this of course we refuse the question, taking the onus off the shoulders of any empirically identifiable audience and placing it on the "meaning" of the poem itself.[2]

The American Professor Lionel Trilling's essay entitled "The Sense of the Past," as it is one of the latest, appears to us also one of the most delicate complications of the historical problem. "To suppose that we can think like men of another time," says Professor Trilling, "is as much an illusion as to suppose that we can think in a wholly different way." (As if points of view could be put in and out of our minds like lantern slides—and opaque ones at that.) Yet certain difficulties do attend upon our making the ideas of the past transparent for our own uses. "In cer-

---

[2] The view suggested here does not of course attempt to discountenance a dramatically conceived audience as reflected in the poem itself or in its tone—Marvell's coy mistress, Donne's metaphoric antagonist Death, Shelley's West Wind, or the audience of young ladies and their polite gentlemen admirers to whom Pope's *Rape of the Lock* (as distinguished, say, from his *Dunciad*) is immediately addressed. The critical reader of poetry, and especially the reader of a later age, constantly reads over the shoulder of a dramatic reader who is as much a fiction as the story of the poem or any of its rhetoric.

tain cultures," says Professor Trilling (and these include obviously our own), "the pastness of a work of art gives it an extra-aesthetic authority which is incorporated into its aesthetic power."

> Wordsworth's Immortality Ode is acceptable to us only when it is understood to have been written at a certain past moment; if it had appeared much later than it did, if it were offered to us now as a contemporary work, we would not admire it.[3]

Here it may be well to note the resemblance of the argument to that at which we arrived in concluding an earlier chapter,[4] on the technical problem of "poetic diction." Eliot's statement about the futility of repeating poetic achievements or Gertrude Stein's about the vital force of contemporaneity might as well appear in the present context as in the earlier. And so might the young joker who typed out some of Shakespeare's less well-known sonnets and submitted them to a New York press, with the result which need not be repeated here. Professor Trilling argues that a certain quality of pastness enters into some works of art with the lapse of time and becomes part of what we enjoy in them. But he seems to argue too—and this may be a somewhat different argument—that we excuse or accept certain masterpieces only because we know they were written in the past—as if we made allowances for the author's deficiency of scientific knowledge or social vision. Perhaps the truth is that we should find it so odd if a poet wrote in certain ways today that we could not help suspecting the poem somehow of being false. That is, any old-fashioned masterpieces that failed to get written in their own day will now never get written. And if they had been written, they would to some extent have changed the poetic tradition and hence would have changed the situation from which the modern poet must write. But none of these unquestionable facts about the genesis of poetry will quite justify the conclusion (which Professor Trilling in fact does avoid) that old masterpieces are to be taken only on tolerance, or that the only poems which are actually good reading today are contemporaneous ones. There is a passage in the *Practical Criticism* of I. A. Richards in which he argues that the date when a poem was written "cannot by itself settle its genuineness, in the sense of its sincerity." But it is good "presumptive evidence." A poet may well enough "write an entirely sincere poem in the manner of a different age, but on the whole the probability is strongly against it."[5] To the

---

[3] Lionel Trilling, *The Liberal Imagination, Essays on Literature and Society* (New York, 1953), pp. 182, 183, 184.

[4] Chapter 16.

[5] *Practical Criticism* (New York; 1935), p. 77. "It is impossible," writes Victoria Sackville West, "to imagine, even after allowing for changes of diction, a Gray's 'Elegy,' or an 'Ode on Intimations of Immortality,' still less a 'Prelude,' or a 'Paradise

ambiguous sense of the word "sincerity" in this passage—sincerity as warmness and innocence of purpose? sincerity as poetic power and achievement?—let us add a third shade of meaning (legitimate by historical and deterministic canons), sincerity as the poet's being in rapport with his age, and we have a tabloid of the whole ambiguously conceived ground which history and criticism are accustomed to dispute.

SUPPLEMENT

On examination mornings, he [Péguy] would ask the student next to him to wake him up in thirty minutes, after he had read the theme of the composition to be handed in. Then he would go to sleep as soundly as a child and upon being awakened would immediately set to work; and exactly on the dot, he turned in a flawless paper which almost always got the highest grade. There was never the slightest mistake in what he wrote and never a correction. Péguy did not believe it was right to make corrections. Whatever went through his mind in connection with the subject was immediately couched in that straightforward style which was already so convincing. Why, he thought, should he turn down a word or a group of words that had come to him as he wrote. They had a right to stand with all the other words on the page. They expressed something in him. He wasn't going to betray them by pretending that they never had been in his mind.

Péguy . . . wrote regularly, but he never knew what he was going to write when he sat down to his sheet of white paper. . . . Not a word was ever scratched out. If a word came to him, he argued, it had as much right to be written down as all its fellow-words in the book. It was there as a witness, like a pebble on the long road he travelled. Péguy considered that what he wrote had been dictated to him. When he wanted to praise a book, or a sentence in a book, he never said: 'It is good,' he said: 'It is dictated.'—Julian Green, Introduction to Charles Péguy, *Basic Verities, Prose and Poetry* (New York, 1943), pp. 17, 30, by permission of Pantheon Books, Inc.

The players have often mentioned it as an honour to Shakespeare, that in his writing, (whatsoever he penn'd) hee never blotted out line. My answer hath beene, would he had blotted a thousand. Which they thought a malevolent speech. I had not told posterity this, but for their ignorance who choose that circumstance to commend their friend by, wherein he most faulted.—Ben Jonson, *Timber: or, Discoveries* (1641)

Lost,' as the product of the twentieth century. . . . I do not believe that even a great poet, were one to arise, could or would move upon the place or breathe the air of Milton and Wordsworth. This is simply another way of saying that sublimity has gone out of fashion" (*Tendencies of Modern English Poetry*, quoted by H. W. Garrod, *Poetry and the Criticism of Life*, Cambridge, Mass., 1931, p. 13).

Rare Monkish Manuscripts for Hearne alone,
And Books for MEAD, and Rarities for Sloane.

—Alexander Pope, *Epistle to Burlington* (1731), ll. 9–10

Rarities! how could'st thou be so silly as not to be particular in the Raritys of *Sloane* as in those of the other five Persons? What knowledge, what Meaning, is conveyed in the Word *Raritys!* Are not some Drawings, some Statues, some Coins, all monkish Manuscripts, and some Books, *Raritys?* Could'st thou not find a Trisyllable to express some Parts of Nature for a Collection of which that learned and worthy Physician is eminent? Fy, fy; correct and write . . . *Butterflys* for SLOANE. *Sir Hans Sloane* is known to have the finest Collection of Butterflys in *England*, and perhaps in the World.

—Thomas Cooke, *The Comedian*, no. 2, May, 1732, p. 15 [Thomas Cooke was saluted by Pope in the *Epistle to Arbuthnot*, in *Dunciad* II, and in *Peri Bathous*.]

Rare Monkish Manuscripts for Hearne alone,
And Books for MEAD, and Butterflies for Sloane.

—Alexander Pope, *Epistle to Burlington* (1744), ll. 9–10

"Chamier once asked him," said Johnson, "what he meant by *slow*, the last word in the first line of *The Traveller*:
'Remote, unfriended, melancholy, slow.'
Did he mean tardiness of locomotion? Goldsmith, who would say something without consideration, answered 'Yes.' I was sitting by, and said, 'No, Sir; you do not mean tardiness of locomotion; you mean that sluggishness of mind which comes upon a man in solitude.' Chamier believed then that I had written the line as much as if he had seen me write it."

—James Boswell, *Life of Samuel Johnson*, 9 April, 1778

An editor of Goldsmith's poems, Austin Dobson, adds the remark: "It is quite possible, however, that Goldsmith meant no more than he said."

—*Poetical Works of Goldsmith*, Oxford, 1939, p. 167

Thomas Gray's *Elegy Written in a Country Churchyard* (1751) has been criticized adversely for being too personal a revelation of the poet's feelings about himself, especially in the Epitaph with which the poem concludes. On the other hand, the poem has been defended against this criticism by the following three lines of argument: (1) that the Epitaph represents Gray's feelings not about himself but about his close friend Richard West, who died in 1742; (2) that the Epitaph actually does not refer to Gray at all or to his friend, but, as may be seen if one reads the poem closely, to a rustic stone-cutter and epitaphic poet, addressed as "Thee" in stanza 24; (3) that the "me" of the first stanza, the "Thee" of stanza 24, and the Epitaph are all to be read, not in the traditional way, as representing Gray the man who is known in his letters to Walpole and other biographical documents, but in a more detached way, as representing a generalized *persona*, the anonymous poet who is the speaker of the poem. (For further light on these arguments, see Frank Ellis, "Gray's *Elegy:* the Biographical Problem in Literary Criticism," *PMLA*, LXVI, December, 1951, 971–1008.)

This problem in practical criticism is a trim realization of certain 18th-and 19th-century trends in theory about poems and poets. The second line of argument (2), a recent invention by Mr. Ellis, introduces a new degree of complication to the "diagonal" shift described in Chapter 6 apropos of Longinus.

.   .   .

It is not defence of the personalist drift, but explanation, that is needed. The personalist deviation is here to stay, not only in programme notes but in serious discussions of literature which, apparently unaffected by recent critical trends, continue to pour from the presses. For some it may be a racking experience to own that the personalist approach is still established as the dominant approach in most classrooms. But there it is, all the same.

However objectionable, the personalist approach manifests a persistency that itself clamours for explanation. If the urn really is the issue, why is it always in peril of being overlooked or tossed aside? If you so much as whisper that there is a jinnee in the urn, most onlookers will be only too willing to drop the urn without further ado. Broken, it will let the jinnee out, and they can ask him a few questions. While decrying the tendency to behave this way, we may be excused for asking what accounts for the presence of the tendency in the first place.

Man's deepest orientation is personal.

The assertion that in works of art it is the object itself which counts thus treads such crucial ground that it must be made with great honesty, which means with circumspection and humility. Not only the truth of the situation, but its awkwardness as well, must be faced. This awkwardness derives from the fact that, far fetched as it may seem when applied to less important works of art, the principle apparently holds that, in a valid but not exclusive sense, each work of art is not only an object but a kind of surrogate for a person. Anything that bids for attention in an act of contemplation is a surrogate for a person. In proportion as the work of art is capable of being taken in full seriousness, it moves further and further along an asymptote to the curve of personality.

—Walter J. Ong, "The Jinnee in the Well-Wrought Urn," *Essays in Criticism*, IV (July, 1954), 311, 315, 319, by permission of the editor.

PART FOUR

PART FOUR

TRAGEDY AND COMEDY: THE INTERNAL FOCUS

§ *Hegel's "lyrical" conception of tragedy: the ethical problem, conflict between rival "goods"—II. some modern variants of the Hegelian conception: A. C. Bradley and spiritual waste, Prosser Frye and the hero's guilt, J. W. Krutch and faith in the "greatness of man"—Arthur Schopenhauer's influence upon modern conceptions of tragedy: tragedy as affording insight into the blind striving of the Will—III. Nietzsche's "Musical" conception of tragedy: his distinction between an Apollonian and a Dionysian art: the origin of Greek tragedy in the festival of Dionysus, the union of the two gods in tragedy, Apollo speaks Dionysian wisdom—IV. tragedy as a harmonizing of discords: Nietzsche's stress upon the joyful wisdom of tragedy, upon tension in art generally—V. parallels and contrasts between Nietzsche's conception of tragedy and Bergson's conception of comedy: Bergson's notion that laughter springs from the discrepancy between the mechanical and the natural: sources of the comic in repetition, inversion, and reciprocal interference of series—Bergson's views on the social function of comedy, his relation to the "classical" view of comedy, his denial that comedy is a genuine art —VI. other psychological theories of laughter and the comic, Shaftesbury, Penjon, Kline, Kallen—VII. Freud's conception of wit as a device for conserving psychic energy: its aim to recover the lost euphoria of the child— VIII. the witty, the comical, and the humorous as distinguished by Freud: laughter as the sudden discharge of the conserved energy—IX. criticisms of Freud made by Max Eastman, and by Arthur Koestler: Freud's failure to distinguish the self-assertive and the self-transcending, integrative emotions—his concept of the "bisociative" treatment of phenomena: his argument that comedy, tragedy, and the process of scientific discovery all involve bisociative treatment of phenomena, and that since comedy and tragedy have the same "cognitive layout," they differ only in their specific emotional "charges" §*

EACH AGE TENDS TO FIND IN SOME ONE OF THE LITERARY GENRES THE norm of all literary art. The 17th century, we have seen, found the highest poetry to be embodied in the epic. The later 18th century saw in the lyric the "most poetic kind of poetry," [1] for men's interests had shifted, with the burgeoning Romantic movement, from an externally known world to the knowing and expressive self. Georg Wilhelm Hegel illustrates the new emphasis, not only in his philosophy of history, which is the story of spirit expressing itself through successive partial revelations until it finally achieves complete self-consciousness, but in his history of art as well. The first stage finds spirit almost overborne by matter, as in Egyptian art; then there comes the perfect balance between spirit and matter, as in Greek sculpture; and finally in modern art, spirit overflows and envelops matter.[2]

When men's minds are dominated by a lyric norm, their conceptions of the other genres are affected. Like metamorphosed rocks, the other genres, under the heat and pressure of lyricism, change their structure and appearance. Tragedy, for example, may be said to have become "internalized," even "lyricized." Terms like "struggle," "tension," and "resolution" shifted their meanings with the new conception of the problem. Consider, for example, how Aristotle characteristically handled the tragic protagonist's power of choice and his responsibility for that choice. The act that precipitated the downfall of the hero had to be more than a simple misadventure—an accident that simply "happened" to him; on the other hand, it had to be less than a calculated crime. The tragic protagonist could be neither passive victim nor obvious criminal. The problem of guilt and responsibility was thus a matter of central importance; but it is characteristic of Aristotle that this ethical problem is treated in the *Poetics* as a function of the plot. That is, the complicated play that Aristotle called for, a play that includes a *peripeteia* and an *anagnōrisis*, demands an action by the hero of a certain seriousness and a certain responsibility. Aristotle's approach was to the total action that the tragedy presents—not directly to the ethical standards of the hero.

But Hegel's view of tragedy begins—and, one is inclined to say, ends—with the ethical problem. Whereas Aristotle was content to make

[1] Cf. *ante* Chapter 17, pp. 372-3.
[2] Cf. *ante* Chapter 17.

hamartia a partly responsible act of error without attempting to define the degree of culpability precisely, Hegel defines the hero's error very precisely: the good chosen by the hero is only a partial good though the hero treats it as though it were an absolute good. The characteristic struggle in tragedy is between rival ethical claims: good is set up against good; and the choice is not between good and evil, but between one good and another.[3]

Hegel considered *Antigone* to be the ideal example of Greek tragedy, probably because in this play we have the maximum of ethical tension. Both Creon and Antigone are right in the sense that the ethical loyalties that they acknowledge are valid. But each is wrong in assuming that the ethical principle exerts an *absolute* claim upon his loyalty. The reconciliation comes in our realization that the claims are but partial and that catastrophe has occurred through the human failure of mistaking the part for the whole. But it is well to notice that the reconciliation as envisaged by Hegel occurs in the mind of the spectator or auditor—not necessarily in the mind of the protagonist. Antigone, one has to suppose, goes to her death without ever realizing that she has mistaken a limited ideal for an absolute ideal.

The spectator perceives that though the conflict is dreadful for the human antagonists caught up in it, it is after all simply a stage in the dialectic through which spirit eternally expresses itself. Indeed, the tragic conflict as Hegel defines it fits comfortably into his massive philosophical system. Tragic conflict proves to be simply another instance of the contradiction of thesis by antithesis, a contradiction to be resolved only in a higher synthesis, where the counter claims of thesis and antithesis are admitted, yet any ultimate contradiction between them is shown to be illusory.

Hegel's is a philosopher's definition of tragedy—not necessarily the worse for that, to be sure—but it has provoked the reaction that it is too "intellectual," and it is certainly part and parcel of a theory of art which regards literature as a primitive, and therefore for the mature mind a limited and defective, kind of philosophy. Benedetto Croce, certainly not the least sympathetic critic of Hegelianism, has put this criticism decisively:

> In a greater degree than any of his predecessors Hegel emphasized the cognitive character of art. But this very merit brought him into a difficulty more easily avoided by the rest. Art being placed in the sphere of absolute Spirit, in company with Religion and Philosophy, how will she be able to hold her own in such powerful and aggressive company, especially in that of Philosophy, which in the Hegelian system stands at the summit

[3] See *The Philosophy of Fine Art*, trans. F. P. B. Osmaston (London, 1920), Vol. IV.

of all spiritual evolution? If Art and Religion fulfilled functions other than the knowledge of the Absolute, they would be inferior levels of the Spirit, but yet necessary and indispensable. But if they have in view the same end as Philosophy and are allowed to compete with it, what value can they retain? None whatever; or, at the very most, they may have that sort of value which attaches to transitory historical phases in the life of humanity. The principles of Hegel's system are at bottom rationalistic and hostile to religion, and hostile no less to art.[4]

Hegel's concept of tragedy does not fit all the extant Greek tragedies. *Oedipus Rex*, Aristotle's ideal tragedy, would have to be pulled and twisted more than a bit to make it answer to Hegel's definition: where in that play, for instance, is an ethical good set over against a rival good? Hegel himself admits that practically none of Euripides' tragedies conform to his notion, a matter which he explains by regarding Euripidean tragedy as "modern" in its concern for character and in its ethical laxity.

II

YET Hegel's concept of tragedy, in spite of its forbidding austerity, has had great and lasting influence. A. C. Bradley, for example, in his *Shakespearean Tragedy* (1904) and in his *Lectures on Poetry* (1909) gave us a somewhat softened, though distinctly Hegelian, view. In setting this forth for the English-speaking reader, Bradley was at some pains to defend Hegel against charges of inflexibility. He maintained that Hegel

> does not teach, as he is often said to do, that tragedy portrays only the conflict of such ethical powers as the family and the state. He adds to these . . . others, such as love and honour, together with various universal ends; and it may even be maintained that he has provided in his general statement for those numerous cases where . . . no substantial or universal ends collide, but the interest is centred on "personalities." [5]

But Bradley conceded that Hegel's treatment of the aspect of reconciliation was inadequate. Hegel did not sufficiently notice that more is involved than acquiescence. As spectators of tragedy we feel a positive exultation along with, and indeed because of, our awareness of the fact that "the hero has never shown himself so great or noble as in the death which seals his failure." [6] Our solace at the fall of the hero is, then, not

[4] *Aesthetic* (1901), trans. Douglas Ainslie (London, 1922), p. 301.
[5] *Lectures* (London, 1909), p. 85, by permission of Macmillan & Company, Ltd., and St. Martin's Press.
[6] *Lectures*, p. 84.

so much a reaffirmation of the moral structure of the universe as a heightened awareness of the greatness of man. Though not every tragedy shows ethical powers in conflict with each other, every tragedy does show, so Bradley argued, "a self-division and self-waste of spirit." [7] We see Macbeth's courage and imagination wasted in his defeat—yet their true grandeur is revealed only by his defeat. Thus, Bradley would broaden Hegel's definition: the typical and essential conflict to be found in tragedy is not that of good against good, but rather a conflict within the self: "*any* spiritual conflict involving spiritual waste is tragic." [8]

Bradley's definition has the merit of fixing attention upon an element that is found in a great deal of literature: not only in a tragedy like *Macbeth,* but in *Don Quixote,* in "Sir Patrick Spens," and even in "An Ode to a Nightingale." But the definition will scarcely help us distinguish tragedy as a genre. The tragic conflict is within the soul: tragedy manifests itself in our sense of spiritual waste. In this essentially "lyric" definition, the tragic becomes a personal and subjective quality.

In rejecting, as a ground for tragedy, Hegel's austere idealism in favor of a milder humanism, Bradley certainly acted in the spirit of the age. He praised tragedy for bringing home to us the spiritual qualities of the hero—his self-assertion, his noble endurance, his magnificent vitality—and nearly all recent writers on the subject have joined Bradley in this emphasis. Bonamy Dobrée, for example, regards tragedy as our prime means for testing man's ultimate strength. "Tragedy," he writes, "is man's trial of his individual strength, a trial becoming increasingly unpopular, indeed incomprehensible, with the advance of democracy." [9]

Prosser Frye's *Romance and Tragedy* (1922) also presented a Hegelian view of tragedy, but Frye retained, as the very center of tragedy, Hegel's insistence upon a problem of ethical choice. Like Hegel, Frye found in Greek tragedy the very type of tragedy, and he refused to soften the edges of his definition to admit more comfortably the Shakespearian masterpieces. Shakespeare, great poet though Frye admitted him to be, was dangerously committed to a modern and "Euripidean" interest in character—to the consequent blurring of a proper ethical focus.

Tragedy, as Frye defined it, rests upon the assertion of a universal moral order. The fall of the hero momentarily disturbs that order: the auditor or the reader is shocked. So great is the disproportion between what we feel ought to happen and what actually does happen that we experience a kind of giddiness—what Frye calls "the moral qualm." In genuine tragedy, however, that qualm is overcome: the very fall of the hero confirms the moral order which it had at first shock seemed to call in question. The tragic writer must stress this ultimate stability of the

[7] *Lectures,* p. 86.
[8] *Lectures,* p. 87.
[9] *Restoration Tragedy* (Oxford, 1929), p. 9.

moral order, for he is interested as a writer, not in a psychological, but in a metaphysical problem. The question that he must put is this: why does evil occur?

Shakespeare's alleged failure to put this question causes Frye to deny that he is a typically tragic poet. The question that Shakespeare characteristically puts seems to be: by what steps, through what process, did this apparently powerful and virtuous creature come to grief? And so we have the "tragedies" of Othello or of Hamlet, with their inordinate interest in character and their blurred focus on the metaphysical problem.

Sophocles, on the other hand, shows us that the fall of the hero is not an "accident" but is inevitable, the consequence of a certain blindness on the part of the hero. *Antigone*—which Frye follows Hegel in regarding as the ideal instance of tragedy—will illustrate. Antigone in her entire devotion to one ethical claim denies the other. But to defy the *polis* was a terrible thing, no matter what the motive, and no matter even that the motive be one which, like Antigone's, elicits a pitying response. The Greek audience, Frye insists, would have felt Antigone to be involved in criminality. This tension between terror and pity in our attitude toward the protagonist is for Frye the one necessary tension in tragedy. When this tension is relaxed—when we can view the protagonist with unqualified sympathy, then we are no longer in the presence of tragedy. The downfall of the hero has indeed become merely an unfortunate accident, a matter of unpropitious environment, or of some failure of adjustment. The tragic protagonist has to be responsible for his act; but if he is responsible, then he is in some sense culpable.

To this important point, Frye bears able and effective testimony, but he out-Hegels Hegel in the sternness of his ethical demands. His tragic writer is frankly a teacher; and he argues that literature, in so far as it is "true to itself and its own character," is concerned not to "image life" but to "commemorate some idea about it—or in other words interpret it." The interpretation that Frye demands is of a specific kind: it is not to be an economic or a sociological or an anthropological interpretation. It is to be a "humane" interpretation, and for Frye this depends upon the "new humanism" of Irving Babbitt and Paul Elmer More.[1] Indeed, Frye's *Romance and Tragedy* must be regarded as one of the ablest documents produced by the New Humanists. But, as in so much of the work of this group, there is a certain note of desperation. Frye is carrying out a stubborn rear-guard action. He gloomily notes that almost from the very birth of tragedy there has been a falling off, with no real recoveries. Even the classical Racine did not accomplish a return to genuine tragedy. The neohumanist scholar did not really hope for better days: he was simply keeping the record straight.

[1] Cf. *ante* Chapter 20.

Most modern writers on tragedy, however, have found such a diet too rich for their blood. They have not been interested in ultimate metaphysical questions. They are thoroughly secular and man-centered. What they see in tragedy is primarily a glorification of man's power to endure. We have already mentioned Dobrée's emphasis upon this theme, and other names might be added. Thus, W. V. O'Connor in his *Climates of Tragedy* (1943) refuses to allow that certain modern plays are tragedies on the ground that they do not sufficiently stress "the strength of man," but instead merely "offer consolation in a dogma." And Joseph Wood Krutch in *The Modern Temper* (1929) makes "faith in the greatness of man" a necessary condition for producing tragedy. A tragic writer, he says, does not have to believe in God, but "he must believe in man." Thus, our modern failure to write tragedies springs, not from our loss of faith in the supernatural, but from our loss of faith in the worth of human nature.

Modern writers—Krutch certainly and even A. C. Bradley probably —did not, however, arrive at the theme of noble, tragic endurance by simply expanding Hegel's formula. They borrowed generously from Hegel's German contemporaries and followers. Thus the theme of man's endurance as stated by Krutch reads like a secularization of A. W. Schlegel's treatment of tragic endurance as a form of human self-assertion, a gesture, as Schlegel would have it, made in the face of fate in order to assert the mind's proud claim to a participation in the divine.[2] Among the 19th-century German aestheticians, however, one may point to a much more direct and obvious source in the work of Arthur Schopenhauer. He was "for a long time unread and unknown," but by the end of the 19th century he had become "the most popular and influential of writers. Even in authors, like Gautier or Flaubert, who probably never set eyes on one of his books, we may fancy we feel a kindred spirit."[3]

In *The World as Will and Idea* (1818), Schopenhauer utterly rejected Hegel's notion that the universe manifests the force of spirit, *Geist*, unfolding itself through a self-ordained dialectic and revealing its reasonable nature more and more fully in history. Instead Schopenhauer conceived the ultimate reality to be a blind energy, which in its aimlessness actually belied the term *Will* by which he would name it. This "Will" objectified itself at various levels, in inorganic matter, in the vegetable and the animal kingdoms, and of course, in Man himself. But Man's reason does not represent a coming into consciousness of the Will, a stage in its *self*-realization, for the Will is irrational.

Man's reason is simply one more instrument at the disposal of the Will's blind striving. Yet it lies in Man's power to refuse to be an instru-

[2] Cf. *ante* Chapter 17.
[3] Gilbert and Kuhn, p. 472.

ment of the Will. He is able to free himself of desire, and at least at moments, stand aside from the struggle and simply contemplate serenely the innermost nature of reality.

Scientific knowledge, Schopenhauer insisted, does not reveal that reality. Scientific knowledge is eminently practical: it describes phenomena so as to put them at our service—which really means, at the service of the Will. But the knowledge that art gives is impractical, and that is its glory. Tragedy gives us an insight into the heart of the mystery, into the nature of evil, which is the nature of reality and hence of the Will. But Schopenhauer reserved a special function to the art of music. Music, unlike the other arts, is not tied to any objective representation of the Will but "speaks of the Will itself." "The composer reveals the inner nature of the world, and expresses the deepest wisdom in a language which his reason does not understand; as a person under the influence of mesmerism tells things of which he has no conception when he wakes." [4]

III

TRAGEDY is profoundly "musical" in just this sense, so argued Friedrich Nietzsche in his brilliant essay on *The Birth of Tragedy* (1872). But in doing so, Nietzsche rejected Schopenhauer's notion that tragedy was to be associated with serene contemplation. Tragedy did not arise among the Greeks out of any withdrawal from life, nor were the spectators of the tragedies of Aeschylus and Sophocles "detached" observers. On the contrary, only a formal and artificial barrier separated them from the dancing chorus, with whom emotionally they were at one.

Nietzsche, accordingly, repudiated the notion that Greek tragedy was developed under the auspices of Apollo, the god of the poised, harmonious, "classical" art that we traditionally associate with the Greeks. Nietzsche conceded a role to Apollo in Greek tragedy, but it was a role finally subordinate to that of Dionysus, the god of wild flute music, of wine and intoxication, of the dancing throng and of the orgy in which men as satyrs were connected with their darker, subterranean selves and with the primordial unity of nature.

The luminous order and tranquillity that are traditionally associated with Greek art were not the expression of a naturally Apollonian spirit. The Greek was naturally Dionysian; and his art thus represents a victory won over his own nature. As Nietzsche put it in a later essay:

> Extravagance, wildness, and Asiatic tendencies lie at the root of the Greeks. Their courage consists in their struggle with their

[4] *The World as Will and Idea,* trans. R. B. Haldane and J. Kemp (London, n.d.), I, 336.

Asiatic nature: they were not given beauty any more than they were given Logic and moral naturalness: in them these things are victories, they are willed and fought for. . . .[5]

Tragedy was thus, for Nietzsche, the product of a fruitful tension between diverse energies. Certain other forms of art contrive to remain relatively pure. For instance, the painter, the sculptor, and the epic poet are characteristically Apollonian: they work under the special patronage of the god of light, of vision, and of dream. And the actor, the dancer, the musician, and the lyric poet are characteristically devotees of Dionysus. They follow a wilder prompting, and create dynamic patterns out of ecstasy and incantation.

To the modern reader imbued with Freud, Nietzsche's association of *dream* with the Apollonian serenity may appear puzzling, even perverse. For the modern reader will be tempted to regard Nietzsche's Apollonian art as that of the conscious mind and the Dionysian as that of the Freudian unconscious, in which case, dream, with its bold violations of space-order and of logic and its connections with the primordial depths of the mind will seem to be Dionysian rather than Apollonian. But Nietzsche uses *dream* primarily in the sense of the seer's vision, the waking dream, an ideal view which represents phenomena not as they are, but as they ought to be. For this very reason the Apollonian dreaming art demands a Dionysian counterbalance. The idealized representation if *too consciously imposed* degenerates into a flaccid and sterile academicism. The detachment proper to great art can come only after passionate involvement.

The timid German bourgeois, Nietzsche scornfully noted, was eager for ideal schemes that flattered his complacency, for solutions that he had not "earned," for harmonies that were trivial because they avoided the very appearance of dissonance. Such a person, Nietzsche insisted, was quite incapable of conceiving what tragic art meant to the audiences that viewed the drama of Aeschylus and Sophocles. To participate in the experience of genuine tragedy, man must put aside the brittle rigidities of his rationality. Man must lose his petty civic identity and become elemental man; he must, before the vision of the god can be vouchsafed to him, become the satyr, the goat-man.

Indeed, according to Nietzsche, this was just what actually happened in the course of history. Ancient Greek tragedy grew out of the worship of Dionysus. The satyr chorus—originally the band of ecstatic worshippers—was "the womb of dialogue." In the plays before Euripides, all the tragic protagonists were types of Dionysus, seen as such by the chorus in their ecstatic state. When Euripides failed to retain the chorus in its primi-

[5] *The Will to Power* (1896), *Complete Works*, XV (trans. A. M. Ludovici, New York, 1910), 417. This and following passages from Nietzsche's works reprinted by permission of the publishers, George Allen & Unwin Ltd.

tive function, he destroyed tragedy. Nietzsche elaborates the point: the "optimistic dialectic" of Euripides—which Nietzsche associates with that of Socrates—"drove *music* out of tragedy." [6] In the Socratic-Euripidean dispensation, there was a "necessary, visible connection between virtue and knowledge"; hence the tragic protagonist necessarily became a dialectician, the dramatist became essentially "an echo of his own conscious knowledge," and the dark, vital wisdom of the chorus was rendered nugatory. In short, Euripidean "tragedy" had moved toward the Apollonian pole.

True tragedy, on the other hand, Nietzsche asserted, could be interpreted only as "a manifestation and illustration of Dionysian states, as the visible symbolization of music, as the dream-world of Dionysian ecstasy." [7] Such a "dream-world" is, of course, in Nietzsche's terms, Apollonian—but in tragedy, Apollo is made to express "Dionysian knowledge."

> . . . the Apollonian illusion is [in the effect of tragedy] found to be what it really is,—the assiduous veiling during the performance of tragedy of the intrinsically Dionysian effect: which, however, is so powerful, that it finally forces the Apollonian drama itself into a sphere where it begins to talk with Dionysian wisdom, and even denies itself and its Apollonian conspicuousness. Thus then the intricate relation of the Apollonian and the Dionysian in tragedy must really be symbolized by a fraternal union of the two deities: Dionysus speaks the language of Apollo; Apollo, however, finally speaks the language of Dionysus; and so the highest goal of tragedy and of art in general is attained. [8]

The spectator of tragedy sees the hero "in epic clearness and beauty" —the epic, we remember, is an "Apollonian" art—nevertheless, wrought up to Dionysian ecstasy, the spectator "delights in [the hero's] annihilation. . . . He feels the actions of the hero to be justified, and is nevertheless still more elated when these actions annihilate their originator." [9]

When Apollo begins to talk with "Dionysian wisdom," he gives us myth, for tragic myth, as Nietzsche defines it, is "a symbolizing of Dionysian wisdom by means of the expedients of Apollonian art." [1] Science, with optimistic belief in "the explicability of nature," destroys myth, and with it, the possibility of tragedy. This notion that tragedy— and by later extension, all art—is grounded in myth was, however, to

[6] *The Birth of Tragedy* (1872), *Complete Works*, I (trans. W. A. Haussmann, London, 1910), 111.
[7] *Birth of Tragedy*, p. 111.
[8] *Birth of Tragedy*, pp. 166–7.
[9] *Birth of Tragedy*, p. 168.
[1] *Birth of Tragedy*, p. 168.

make its main fortune in the next century. Its typical 20th-century modes will be discussed later in Chapter 31.

IV

SCIENCE is optimistic, but tragic wisdom is joyful. The zest for life expresses itself through conflict and tension. Though elements of this view were derived from Schopenhauer, Nietzsche, as time went on, attacked with increasing bitterness Schopenhauer's idea that tragedy begot a mood of resignation. Art is "the great stimulus," the "great will to life," [2] and tragedy springs from exultant strength. Nietzsche charged Aristotle with folly in having supposed that the function of tragedy was to purge us of the emotions of pity and fear. Tragedy is not cathartic but tonic. Even a Zola's preoccupation with the ugly and sordid came about because artists like Zola rejoice in the ugly. The ugliness and disorder of the world constitute a challenge to the artist. The artist does not passively record a beauty that he finds rooted in nature. Beauty is not found—it is made by the artist, who imposes it by his own will, and thus wins a victory over disorder. For in beauty, "contrasts are overcome, the highest sign of power thus manifesting itself in the conquest of opposites." [3] The artist creates out of joy and strength—not out of weakness—and the most convincing artists are precisely those "who make harmony ring out of every discord." [4] The great artist is able to acknowledge "the terrible and questionable character of existence" [5] and still affirm the goodness of life. As a poet of our own time has expressed it:

> All perform their tragic play,
> There struts Hamlet, there is Lear,
> That's Ophelia, that's Cordelia;
> Yet they, should the last scene be there,
> The great stage curtain about to drop,
> If worthy their prominent part in the play,
> Do not break up their lines to weep.
> They know that Hamlet and Lear are gay;
> Gaiety transfiguring all that dread.[6]

And again, as he looked out upon the world moving toward the Second World War:

[2] *Will to Power*, p. 285.
[3] *Will to Power*, p. 245.
[4] *Will to Power*, p. 288.
[5] *Will to Power*, p. 291.
[6] W. B. Yeats, "Lapis Lazuli," *Collected Poems* (New York, 1951), p. 292. This and following passages from Yeats's writings are reprinted by permission of The Macmillan Company.

Irrational streams of blood are staining earth;
Empedocles has thrown all things about;
Hector is dead and there's a light in Troy;
We that look on but laugh in tragic joy.[7]

If all art is an affirmation of life, and if the greatest art is that in which the affirmation is made in the face of the terrible and questionable, then tragic art reveals itself as the greatest art:

> The highest state of Yea-saying to existence is conceived as one from which the greatest pain may not be excluded: the tragico-Dionysian state.[8]

The artist, as Nietzsche conceives him, is a projection of the Nietzschean philosopher. He is a man who is hard and lives dangerously, scorning cowardly generalizations and shop-worn solutions, despising syntheses that he has not "earned," daring to subdue to his purpose the most recalcitrant materials, always "setting his chisel to the hardest stone." Yet the artist does deal in illusion—at least his work can be exploited for the illusory comfort that it may seem to give. And so Nietzsche sometimes praised the artist as the man who truly lives "beyond good and evil," but at other times was moved to reproach the artist because he solaced men with lies. Only a hairline would seem to separate the poet's gift of "metaphysical comfort" from the bogus comfort of soporifics and anodynes.

It is probably idle to try to labor Nietzsche's position into entire consistency: Nietzsche was the deliberate iconoclast, using a rhetoric of overstatement, bold metaphor, exhortation, laconic imperatives, and the like; and moreover his philosophy suffered alteration during the course of his career. In making the value of art depend, not upon the work itself but upon the stress in the soul of the artist who produced it[9] or upon the process, strenuous or easy, by which the spectator apprehended it, Nietzsche provided the basis for endlessly shifting subsequent evaluations.

We have earlier spoken of the pervasive "lyric" quality of the German 19th century: the norm of poetry is consciously or unconsciously sought for in the personal and subjective utterance. The fundamental poetic problem became that of the poet's personal expression, and more

---

[7] "The Gyres," *Collected Poems*, p. 291.
[8] *Will to Power*, p. 291.
[9] Substantially this position is taken in a recent essay by a critic whom one would never think of associating with Nietzsche. Lionel Trilling, at the end of his *Liberal Imagination* (New York, 1950), p. 297, writes: "The aesthetic effect which I have in mind can be suggested by a word that I have used before—activity. We feel that Hemingway and Faulkner [as contrasted with Dos Passos, O'Neill, and Wolfe] are intensely at work upon the recalcitrant stuff of life; when they are at their best they give us the sense that the amount and intensity of their activity are in a satisfying proportion to the recalcitrance of their material."

specifically, the problem of how he might, in the midst of a hostile world, preserve his own individuality and set the seal of his own personality upon the pattern of words that he makes. Tragedy, because of the authority of classical Greek literature, was still spoken of by the Germans as the highest of the literary arts. But the soul of tragedy was no longer to be sought in the plot: it was to be sought in the dramatist's own soul. Nietzsche, as we have seen, conceived of tragedy as "musical": it was the greatest of the arts because it involved a "harmonization" of the greatest possible tensions.

The assimilation of tragedy to a "lyric" form through conceiving of it as a pattern of tensions that are "resolved" or of discords that are ultimately "harmonized" suggests a counterdevelopment that was to appear in later criticism; that is, the tendency to see in even the tiniest lyric a kind of "drama," a pattern of conflicts set up, developed, and then resolved. The "musical" structure of poetry, of which the French symbolists were to make so much, is "musical" in something like this Nietzschean sense. Here again Nietzsche proved himself a forerunner. He anticipated brilliantly the course that the age was to take.

V

TRAGEDY and comedy have always been bracketed together, if only in simple opposition—the laughing mask set off by the weeping mask. Nietzsche's conception of tragedy as a pattern of tensions obviously provides a means for bringing tragedy and comedy much closer together. In German romantic theory we have already [1] called attention to the strong concern to provide a rationale for the comic and to dignify it as an integral side of the serious. Nietzsche's theorizing provides, from the side of tragedy, a powerful answering tendency. By boldly asserting that tragedy is "Dionysian," Nietzsche roots it in impulses immemorially assigned to the comic—that is, in the natural and instinctive impulses which reach their apogee in intoxication, revelry, and wild exuberance.

The celebrated essay *Le Rire* (1900) by Henri Bergson yields a sufficiency of parallels to *The Birth of Tragedy*. Bergson found the basis for the comic in the contrast between the mechanical and the organic. It is intelligence that treats everything mechanically; it is instinct that has an affinity for the organic. Like Nietzsche, Bergson traced art ultimately to the dark, instinctive side of the mind.

He asserts in his *Évolution Créatrice* that it is instinct, not intelligence, that is molded on the very form

> of life. While intelligence treats everything mechanically, instinct proceeds, so to speak, organically. If the consciousness

[1] Cf. *ante* Chapter 17.

that slumbers in it should awake, if it were wound up into knowledge instead of being wound off into action, if we could ask and it could reply, it would give up to us the most intimate secrets of life.[2]

The intellect deals with what Bergson terms "extensive manifolds"; thus the intellect produces science and all the systematizations of knowledge that are so useful to us for the practical ordering of our lives. But the intellect distorts reality—freezes it into abstract patterns—breaks it up into discrete data—and so falsifies the essentially dynamic and changing thing that is reality; that is, the intellect is incapable of dealing with an "intensive manifold." For this we require the more subtle instrument of art. Like Schopenhauer, Bergson finds in art, not in science, the means to the knowledge of reality.

Life presents itself to us, Bergson says, as "evolution in time and complexity in space. . . . [There is a] continual change of aspect, the irreversibility of the order of phenomena, [and] the perfect individuality of a perfectly contained series. . . ."[3] Since such are the characteristic traits that distinguish what is alive from what is mere mechanism, their antitheses—*repetition, inversion,* and *reciprocal interference of series*—are the characteristic patterns of the mechanical; and it is the mechanical that prompts our laughter. We laugh at the failure of human response: the man acting like an automaton, mindlessly following a pattern when the situation calls for change (repetition); the man allowing himself to be victimized by mere things (inversion); the man clumsily falling over himself instead of acting gracefully and effectively (reciprocal interference of series).

Bergson valiantly strove to relate every instance of the comic to one of these three categories of the mechanical. Disguise, for example, was to be regarded as comic because the disguising clothes (as distinguished from our "normal" clothing, which seems at one with the body) appear to us to be a "rigid envelope round the living suppleness of the body." Disguise, in other words, constitutes another instance of the impingement of the mechanical upon the vital and organic. Having stretched his theory sufficiently to make disguise an instance of mechanization, Bergson then stretched the category of disguise:

A man in disguise is comic. A man we regard as disguised is also comic. So, by analogy, all disguise is seen to become comic, not only that of a man, but that of society also, and even the disguise of nature.[4]

[2] *Creative Evolution* (1907), trans. Arthur Mitchell (New York, 1937), p. 165.
[3] *Laughter: an Essay on the Meaning of the Comic,* trans. Brereton and Rothwell (London, 1911), pp. 88–9. Reprinted by permission of Doubleday & Company, Inc.
[4] *Laughter,* p. 42.

Though maintaining that every comic incongruity is an instance of mechanization, Bergson was aware that not every such mechanization produces a comic effect. We do not laugh, for example, at the automatism of a crippled man, even though his hobbling gait is to the last degree mechanical. The comic response demands that we suppress our sympathies: there must be, in Bergson's phrase, an "anesthesia of the heart." Where, as with the crippled man, we cannot suppress our sympathies, there will be no laughter.

The writer of comedy realizes this. He plays down our sympathy for the individual; he appeals to the assumptions of society; he engages our intelligence rather than our emotions. Thus, he achieves the necessary anesthesia. For the function of comedy is corrective; society punishes by laughter the individual's deviation from the social norms.

Bergson's account of the social function of comedy is substantially the orthodox, "classical" account—quite as much as George Meredith's.[5] But Bergson achieved his orthodoxy by a kind of *tour de force*. For comedy's very commitment to society and its association with the play of intelligence forced Bergson to deny that comedy was a genuine art. He denied it in so many words: comedy, he wrote,

> is not disinterested as genuine art is. By *organising* laughter, comedy accepts social life as a *natural* environment, it even obeys an impulse of social life. And in this respect it turns its back upon art, which is *a breaking away from society and a return to pure nature*.[6]

In such a passage, Bergson's romantic bias is fully declared: genuine art is natural and instinctive. Comedy makes the deviations from social life seem mechanical as if they were deviations from nature and therefore comic in their own right. The parallel with Nietzsche's view of tragedy again invites attention. One might say that whereas Nietzsche's tragedy represents the dark and instinctive (the Dionysian) drawing the luminous and rational (the Apollonian) into its orbit, Bergson's comedy represents a countermovement: our ultimate commitment to the instinctive and natural is drawn into the orbit of the self-conscious and artificial.

Bergson makes his case against the aberrancy of comedy from "genuine art" by exhibiting typical comic characters. Though genuine art is always concerned with what is uniquely individual, the characters that appear in comedies are types. A comic character is generality personified—which is why we can so readily speak of "a Tartuffe," Bergson

---

[5] In Chapter 11 *ante*, we have observed that Meredith's essay—one has to remind oneself of its date, 1877—was a kind of anachronism. It is a brilliant summation of an earlier ideal of comedy—French classical comedy of the great period.

[6] *Laughter*, pp. 170–1. The italics are ours.

says, but never of "a Phèdre" or "a Polyeucte." [7] Plausible as this statement sounds, perhaps we may wonder whether it constitutes a decisive
test: it is not altogether clear that we cannot with propriety speak of "a
Hamlet," tragic character though he be; and the great comic character
Falstaff has appeared to many readers to be anything but mere generality personified. Be that as it may, Bergson has called down upon himself
reproaches for what have impressed some critics as strained manipula-
tions of the facts, the better to make them answer to his special theory.
Even his basic tenet that all laughter springs from the contrast between what is mechanical and what is natural has been criticized as much
too narrow and rigid. Yet it must be conceded that Bergson's conception
of the comic as closely connected with the natural and instinctive is fully
in the current of 19th-century ideas.

VI

Much earlier, in 1709, Lord Shaftesbury, in an essay significantly entitled *"Sensus Communis:* an Essay on the Freedom of Wit and Humor"
(I, iv), had observed that

> the natural free spirits of ingenious men, if imprisoned or con-
> trolled, will find out other ways of motion to relieve themselves
> in their constraint; and whether it be in burlesque, mimicry, or
> buffoonery, they will be glad at any rate to vent themselves, and
> be revenged on their constrainers. . . .

During the 19th century, the psychologist Bain, whom Bergson quotes,
developed the theory of laughter as "the rebound of hilarity," a sudden
deliverance from emotional and moral constraints. Charles Renouvier
added the notion that laughter was also a deliverance from the constraints
of rationality itself. And Auguste Penjon published in 1893, several years
before the appearance of Bergson's *Le Rire,* an essay entitled *"Le Rire
et la Liberté"* in which laughter is interpreted as the sudden surging up
of the sense of freedom. Penjon's theory of humor was summed up by
an American psychologist, L. W. Kline, in the following terms:

> The humor stimulus gives glimpses of the world of uncertain-
> ties, of spontaneities and of life, and in so doing creates the sense
> of freedom of which the sense of humor is the obverse side. [8]

The function of humor is to rest and relax the mind. Humor is said to
cut "the surface tension of consciousness" and to increase "the pliancy

[7] *Laughter,* p. 163.
[8] "The Psychology of Humor," *American Journal of Psychology,* XVIII (July,
1907), 437.

of [the mind's] structure to the end that it may proceed on a new and strengthened basis." It "spells" the mind, as Kline put it; it permits it a breathing space on "an uphill pull."

How humor accomplishes this ministry is stated in terms reminiscent of Schopenhauer: humor detaches us "from our world of good and evil, of loss and gain and enable[s] us to see it in proper perspective." And Kline's account of how humor has promoted the very evolution of the race seems to echo Bergson:

> Influences that tend to check mechanization and to incline the mind to grapple with the new and with the ideal prolong the possibilities of spiritual development. Humor and play are two such processes, with the honors in favor of humor. It stands guard at the dividing line between free and mechanized mind, to check mechanization and to preserve and fan the sparks of genius.[9]

The sense in which laughter betokens a freedom from constraint was then interpreted more literally and brutally by Horace Kallen.[1] All laughter reflects a sense of triumph and self-enhancement which may or may not also involve the degradation of an enemy. Having conquered its enemy, "the organism," riding on a tide of released energies, finding itself "again in possession of itself," and now apprehending the "lapsed situation," laughs "spontaneously, instinctively." Kallen remarks that the facial expression of the laughable as in smiling bears "a startling resemblance to [that of] an animal about to rend and devour its prey." But he is able to trace the first dawn of humor to a period before even the teeth appear. For he can find a semblance of the "apprehension of the comic" in "the replete child, repeating the pleasurable act of sucking." [2]

The notion of laughter as the expression of triumphant well-being is as old as the speculations of Thomas Hobbes—as old indeed as the Platonic dialogues; and some readers will prefer Hobbes's account of it to Kallen's, finding Hobbes's brand of behaviorism handled with more dignity and with somewhat less facial contortion.

> *Sudden Glory* [Hobbes writes in his *Leviathan*, I, vi] is the passion which maketh those *Grimaces* called LAUGHTER; and is caused either by some sudden act of their own, that pleaseth them; or by the apprehension of some deformed thing in another, in comparison whereof they suddenly applaud themselves.[3]

[9] Kline, *American Journal of Psychology*, XVIII, 439.
[1] "The Aesthetic Principle in Comedy," *American Journal of Psychology*, XXII (April, 1911), 137–57.
[2] Kallen, *American Journal of Psychology*, XXII, 156.
[3] *Leviathan* (1651).

But perhaps one should not dismiss the facial contortions too summarily. Because of the marked physiological reactions that occur in laughter, comedy has from an early date attracted to itself far more affective theorizing than has tragedy. The development of laboratory techniques in the 19th century produced hundreds of physiological studies bearing on the phenomenon of laughter. Even psychologists not notably behavioristic in approach have been interested in and influenced by the physiological character of laughter. For example, Sigmund Freud writes in a passage that anticipates the phraseology of Kallen, "the grimaces and contortions of the corners of the mouth that characterize laughter appear first in the satisfied and satiated nursling when he drowsily quits the breast." But his *Wit and Its Relations to the Unconscious* (1905) elaborates a far more complex theory of the comic than this particular quotation might suggest.[4] Indeed, Freud will not allow that the "sudden glory" of triumphant well-being is comic laughter at all, insisting that children do not have a sense of the comic. Nevertheless, it is in the happiness of the replete child that Freud finds the key to the pleasure that adults take in the comic. Indeed, his monumental essay concludes with the statement that the methods of wit, comedy, and humor all attempt to return us to the state of the child. They

> strive to bring back from the psychic activity a pleasure which has really been lost in the development of this activity. For the euphoria which we are thus striving to obtain is nothing but the state of a bygone time, in which we were wont to defray our psychic work with slight expenditure. It is the state of our childhood in which we did not know the comic, were incapable of wit, and did not need humor to make us happy.[5]

But to understand why the state of euphoria experienced by the child is characterized by a "slight expenditure" of psychic energy requires further examination of Freud's views on the subject.

VII

EARLY in his study Freud remarks that brevity is indeed the soul of wit, quoting Shakespeare's statement and that of the psychologist Theodor Lipps.[6] The brevity manifests itself through various devices of condensation such as "mixed word-formation" and "double meaning with allu-

---

[4] The passages quoted here and on pp. 573–6 and 611 are taken from *The Basic Writings of Sigmund Freud*, trans. and ed. by A. A. Brill, copyright, 1938, by Random House, Inc. Reprinted by permission of the Trustees of the Brill Estate.

[5] *Basic Writings*, p. 803.

[6] Freud writes: " 'Brevity alone is the body and soul of wit,' declares Jean Paul (*Vorschule der Ästhetik* [1804], I, 45). . . . Lipps' description of the brevity of

sion." Freud distinguishes eleven such devices, all of which he regards as simply variant forms of the principle of condensation. What is common to wit, in Freud's conception, is a principle of parsimony in the expenditure of psychic energy. The verbal economy observable in witty expressions—the "use of few or possibly the same words"—points toward a more important kind of economy, this saving of psychic energy.

What is actually saved and how the saving is effected is most easily illustrated by taking our examples from what Freud calls "tendency" wit, that is, wit that is aggressive, whether hostile or obscene. (Freud holds that all obscene wit represents an act of sexual aggression.)

How such wit serves to economize psychic energy, Freud illustrates in this fashion: When circumstances forbid any direct attack upon an enemy or even directly abusive language, as in retort to superior authority, "wit . . . serves as a resistance against such authority and as an escape from its pressure." For wit provides a means for getting around whatever hinders directly hostile expression and thus allows us to express ourselves after all. Such hindrances to expression need not be outward; they may be inward. "Repressions," for example, forbid the civilized man's enjoyment of the obscene. But a witty obscenity allows him to elude the repression and to enjoy what, if expressed directly, would not be tolerated.

> The only difference between the cases of outer and inner hindrances consists in the fact that here an already existing inhibition is removed, while there the formation of a new inhibition is avoided. . . . a *"psychic expenditure"* is required for the formation as well as the retention of a psychic inhibition. Now if we find that in both cases the use of tendency-wit produces pleasure, then it may be assumed *that such resultant pleasure corresponds to the economy of psychic expenditure.*[7]

So much for the pleasure of wit that has a hostile or obscene tendency. The pleasure that we take in "harmless wit" also arises from an economy of psychic expenditure. The reason is not far to seek. All thinking requires effort: it is "easier to mix up things than to distinguish them; and it is particularly easier to travel over modes of reasoning unsanctioned by logic." Children delight, for example, in word play and nonsense games. One of the pleasures of alcohol is that under its influence the adult can become again a "child who derives pleasure from the free

---

wit is also significant. He states that '. . . [wit] expresses itself in words that will not stand the test of strict logic or of the ordinary mode of thought and expression. In fine, it can express itself by leaving the thing unsaid' [*Komik und Humor*, 1898, *Beiträge zur Ästhetik*, VI, p. 90]." *Basic Writings*, p. 636.

[7] *Basic Writings*, p. 712.

disposal of his mental stream without being restricted by the pressure of logic." [8]

> Ale, man, ale's the stuff to drink
> For fellows whom it hurts to think.

But all of us, Freud would argue, plausibly enough, are fellows whom it hurts to think. Alcohol protects our childish pleasure by dulling the censorship of reason. In harmless wit, the wit-work circumvents this obstacle by offering a sop to reason; that is, the wit-work sees to it that the "senseless combination of words or the absurd linking of thoughts" does "make sense after all." Thus, just as tendency wit circumvents the hindrances set up by suppressions and inhibitions, harmless wit circumvents the hindrances set up by reason and critical judgment. As Freud summarizes the matter, wit

> begins as play in order to obtain pleasure from the free use of words and thoughts. As soon as the growing reason forbids this senseless play . . . , it turns to the jest or joke in order to hold to these sources of pleasure and in order to be able to gain new pleasure from the liberation of the absurd. In the rôle of harmless wit it assists the thoughts and fortifies them against the impugnment of the critical judgment. . . . Finally, it enters into the great struggling suppressed tendencies in order to remove inner inhibitions. . . . Reason, critical judgment, and suppression, these are the forces which it combats in turn.[9]

The semi-automatic reaction of laughter is easily fitted into Freud's scheme, for if wit always involves an economy of psychic energy, it is that "saved" or "gained" energy that is discharged as laughter. Freud borrows, and in the process modifies, Herbert Spencer's view of laughter as the discharge of psychic *irritation*.[1]

VIII

FREUD carefully distinguishes the witty from the comical and the humorous. All three, to be sure, involve a "saving" of psychic energy, and all three discharge the gained energy in laughter. But Freud seeks through a rather intricate argument to differentiate the several ways in which the gain in energy is made and to specify in each case the form of psychic energy that is conserved. In wit, as we have seen, Freud argues that our gain in psychic energy comes about through our not having to expend our energy in sustaining an inhibition. In contemplating the comic, how-

---

[8] *Basic Writings*, p. 719.
[9] *Basic Writings*, p. 726.
[1] Freud also mentions L. M. Dugas's description of laughter as a release from tension and Bain's conception of laughter as a "freedom from restraint."

ever, our gain comes from finding that we have built up expectative tensions that are redundant. For example, we see someone straining to lift a heavy basket and laugh when the basket proves to be unexpectedly light. We compare the expected effort with the actual effort as we imaginatively project ourselves into the lifter's situation. Such a comparison occurs, Freud insists, in all instances of the comic. We always compare, if only unconsciously, the effort that the fumbling clown or the clumsy child makes in order to perform some action with the effort which we should need to exert. Thus Freud's theory of the comic at some points resembles Bergson's, the clumsily wasteful expenditure of energy reminding one of Bergson's stiffly mechanical actions. Like Bergson too, Freud attempts some remarkable extensions of what he regards as the basic comic situation. The comic, he tells us, is always found first in *persons* and is then transferred to objects, situations, and the like.

In dealing with the third member of his triad, humor, Freud is much less intricate and consequently may seem less strained. The psychic energy that we "save" in the humorous situation is the energy that would otherwise go into feelings of sympathy. The most obvious instance is that furnished by "gallows-humor." The prisoner on the way to execution pretends to worry about catching cold, and we laugh. If "he who is most concerned is quite indifferent to the situation," [2] then we can save our sympathy, and it is this sympathy that we expected to expend but did not expend that we discharge pleasurably in laughter.

Freud assigns humor and the comic to the foreconscious, but wit, to the unconscious. Indeed, at one point Freud describes wit as "the contribution to the comic from the sphere of the unconscious." The techniques used in dream work—displacement, representation by opposite, absurdity, indirect expression, and so forth—are the techniques used in wit. Since the aim of the dream is simply to preserve our sleep, the dream does not need to be intelligible. It is an asocial product. Wit, however, has to be intelligible; we feel the need to impart wit. Hence in wit the amount of distortion through displacement and condensation has its limit. Dream serves "preponderantly to guard against pain," but wit serves "to acquire pleasure"; and that pleasure, as Freud has described it in the passage that we quoted earlier, is an approximation to the euphoria of childhood.

IX

ONE of the most vigorous attacks upon Freud's theory of the comic has been made by Max Eastman.[3] Eastman finds it incomprehensible that Freud should deny a sense of the comic to children, who are, of course,

---

[2] *Basic Writings*, p. 799.
[3] *The Enjoyment of Laughter* (New York, 1936).

the "greatest laughers of all." But, of course, Freud does not deny that children laugh. The child laughs, and his motives for laughter, Freud says, are "clear and assignable." Someone slips and falls, and the child laughs "out of a feeling of superiority or out of joy over the calamity of others. [His laughter] amounts to saying: 'You fell, but I did not.' " [4] In short, the child's laughter is an instance of Hobbes's "sudden glory." (And this is precisely why Freud denies that it has a part in the comic.) Balzac can be quoted: "As children only do we laugh, and as we travel onward laughter sinks down and dies out like the light of the oil-lit lamp." So true is this, Eastman goes on to say, that most adults will rarely laugh at "a mere nothing . . . unless it is reinforced and sanctioned by some meaning. . . . They demand, in short, that jokes should have a point." [5] But in writing this, Eastman has blundered squarely upon Freud's central idea. Indeed, when Freud writes that "Certain pleasure motives of the child seem to be lost for us grown-ups . . . ," he might be echoing Balzac. His *Wit and Its Relation to the Unconscious* could be fairly described as a study of the manoeuvers by which the adult endeavors to recover the lost infantile laughter.

A much more competent and informed criticism of Freud's theory of the comic is made by Arthur Koestler in his *Insight and Outlook* (1949). Koestler is able to accept most of what Freud has to say about wit, but he finds Freud's comments upon the comic needlessly intricate. Freud attempts to "reduce differences in the quality of the behaviour patterns involved in a comic situation to differences in quantity." Koestler finds that this preoccupation with mere quantitative difference on occasion leads to absurdities, as when Freud writes: "Chance exposures of the body . . . affect us as comic, because we compare this easy way of enjoying what is offered to the eye with the great effort which would otherwise be necessary to attain the same aim." [6] As if, comments Koestler, this were the way to account for our laughter when the dignified gentleman rips his trouser seat as he executes a sweeping bow.

Koestler locates the principal defect of Freud's theory in what he calls a failure to distinguish between the self-assertive and the self-transcending emotions. Neither Bergson [7] nor Freud recognizes the existence of a self-transcending emotion, and as a consequence neither of them

---

[4] *Basic Writings*, p. 794.

[5] *The Enjoyment of Laughter*, p. 37.

[6] *Insight and Outlook* (New York, 1949), p. 426. Reprinted by permission of The Macmillan Company.

[7] Koestler regards Bergson's theory of the comic as too narrow—Bergson's "comic" is only one sub-category, though a frequently occurring sub-category, of the comic. Bergson also neglects "the emotional dynamics of laughter," but his is "the most stimulating work ever written on the subject" (*Insight and Outlook*, p. 421).

is able to see "the direct connection between the comic and the tragic, between laughter and crying, between humour and art." [8]

In *Insight and Outlook*, Koestler boldly undertakes to demonstrate just these relationships. He would connect not only the comic with the tragic, but the mental processes involved in the creation of wit with those involved in making a scientific discovery. The key to these connections lies in what Koestler calls the "bisociative" treatment of a phenomenon. The comic contrast is bisociative: we see the phenomenon in question under two contrasting aspects. It is linked to two different fields of interest. The phenomenon is regarded as an habitual member of one of these fields, but its affinities with the second field "have hitherto been regarded as adventitious, or have passed unnoticed." [9] This bisociative treatment may be illustrated by the simplest joke ("One swallow does not make a summer, nor quench the thirst"); but it is also illustrated by Archimedes' action when, lying in his bath, he suddenly connected the immersion of a body in water with the problem of measuring the volume of the crown. The pun on "swallow" links two quite different fields through a trivial sound connection; the discovery that sent Archimedes rushing from his bath shouting "Eureka" also connected different fields —and again through a trivial and unimportant link, though the consequences were to be most important. Both wit and the "eureka process" have, as Koestler puts it, the same "intellectual geometry." Metaphor also employs this intellectual geometry: metaphor links up two fields not ordinarily connected and allows us to view the "link" in the perspective of two fields—"bisociatively."

Koestler regards laughter as the discharge of nervous tension, but he gives this notion a twist not to be found in Freud. Emotional processes have greater inertia than cognitive processes. When one line of logic or one chain of association is suddenly intersected by another, our understanding

> does jump from the first field to the second, whereas our emotion, incapable of performing the sudden jump, is spilled. This difference in behaviour implies that emotion tends to persist in the direction of a straight line, like a bull, whereas thought can dance about like a matador; in other words, that emotion has a greater mass momentum.[1]

Laughter is the discharge of the emotion "spilled" when the understanding makes one of its sudden hair-pin turns in traversing the course of the witticism. The emotion suddenly becomes excessive—or to use Freud's

---

[8] *Insight and Outlook*, p. 430.
[9] *Insight and Outlook*, p. 53.
[1] *Insight and Outlook*, p. 60.

term, there is a sudden "gain"—and the now unneeded emotion can gush out as laughter.

Man alone is capable of laughter; his ability to laugh is a mark of his civilization. "All animals are fanatics," since they cannot emancipate themselves "from the fanaticism of the biological urge."

> The sudden realization that one's own emotional state is "Unreasonable" signalizes the emergence of self-criticism. . . . Thus laughter rings the bell of man's departure from the rails of instinct.[2]

The inert emotions discharged in laughter are the self-assertive, aggressive-defensive emotions. They are to be carefully discriminated from the self-transcending, integrative emotions that underlie tragic art. Any tragedy can be turned into a comedy by altering the emotional charge. "Every story of Boccaccio's" can be transformed into a little tragedy without altering its factual content and "Oedipus Rex can be made to appear as a prize fool who kills his father and marries his mother, all by mistake; the tragedy is turned into a French farce without altering its cognitive layout." [3]

Unlike the self-asserting emotions, the self-transcending emotions

> are capable of following the train of thought round any junctional corner. . . . The emotions of participative sympathy attach themselves like a dog to the narrative and do not become detached from it whatever the surprises, jumps, changes of associative climate through which the narrator leads it. . . . When a bisociation occurs, [they] do not become detached from thought, but follow it loyally to the new field.[4]

Since tragedy, like comedy, makes use of a bisociative technique, Koestler requires some such explanation as this to account for the fact that the emotional charge in tragedy is not also "spilled" en route and discharged in laughter. Koestler frankly would not want it spilled, for the self-transcending emotions have their own value, they are integrative; they move man toward a sympathetic participation in the universe about him. They teach loyalty to the larger whole of which man is a part.

Koestler's position here is that of the modern liberal humanist, with all the appropriate political and social implications. Art is a civilizing influence: through comedy it helps us to jettison the assertive emotions: through tragedy it fosters the integrative emotions; it teaches us to live together; and through its cathartic effects it helps the individual to endure what is otherwise without remedy.

[2] *Insight and Outlook*, pp. 69–70.
[3] *Insight and Outlook*, p. 241.
[4] *Insight and Outlook*, p. 277.

The experience of tragedy is of special therapeutic value for modern man, who is confined "to the arid plane of associative routine," the plane of the trivial. His contacts with tragic reality are so infrequent that, "instead of eliciting original adjustments, [they] throw him completely out of gear. . . . Routine has become man's rusty armour which makes the living flesh rot underneath." [5] Modern man, deadened as he is by "associative routine," stands in special need of viewing himself and his situation "bisociatively." He needs to have the trivial plane on which he lives intersected by the tragic plane.

The prominence that Koestler gives to the self-transcending emotions renders his theory of literature strongly reminiscent of that of 18th-century aestheticians like Shaftesbury and Lord Kames who emphasize sympathy.[6] Koestler's tone is, of course, quite different: he levies upon modern biological and neurological research for evidence, pointing to the basic tendency toward integration in even the most primitive organisms. But his stress upon the affective and his assumption that the greatest and most valuable art civilizes man by extending his sympathies connect him unmistakably with figures like Shaftesbury. Like the 18th-century aestheticians, Koestler holds what is ultimately an optimistic view of man and his arts. The self-transcending emotions, even though they are connected with " 'depersonalization' of consciousness," or with "the self becoming dissolved" or with Freud's "oceanic feeling," are *not* connected with Freud's death-instinct.[7] That, Koestler dismisses as having no biological foundation. ". . . biologically Freud's death-and-destruction drive is a myth—the only one," Koestler somewhat startlingly avers, "which his myth-destroying genius embodied into his system." [8] Cultivation of self-transcendence points, then, not toward death but toward the road of evolution and human progress.

A number of tendencies that have developed through the last seventy-five years seem to culminate in Koestler's *Insight and Outlook:* the stress upon conflict, upon tension, and upon the quality of emotional charge; the drawing together of comedy and tragedy, and their subsumption—along with aesthetic illusion and the "eureka" process—under one pattern, a pattern of bifurcation, of resistances acknowledged but transcended.

Koestler's is an ambitious, and in its promise of neat unification, an attractive scheme. That tragedy and comedy do make use of the same *general* intellectual frame-work—the same "intellectual geometry," in

---

[5] *Insight and Outlook*, p. 379.
[6] Cf. *ante* Chapter 14.
[7] Koestler writes (p. 216) that the "pessimistic, antihumanistic bias" in Freud's system may have been determined by "Freud's life-long work on neurotic patients with infantile fixations and regressive tendencies, against the background of the decaying civilization of the Austro-Hungarian Empire."
[8] *Insight and Outlook*, p. 153.

Koestler's phrase—may perhaps without too much difficulty be conceded. But the concession tends to throw great weight upon the character of the "emotional charge" in a literary work: for the quality of that
charge would seem to be the sole means left by which one may differentiate comedy and tragedy. Thus there are difficulties. How one can
alter an emotional charge without also altering the "cognitive layout"
may not be altogether apparent. We have already noted Koestler's claim
that *Oedipus Rex* could be transformed into a French farce without
tampering with the cognitive layout. But Koestler hardly tells us how we
can know that Oedipus is a tragic hero and not a "prize fool" apart from
what Oedipus says and does—apart, that is, from the action of the play.
Koestler takes it for granted that the author could manipulate the reader's attitude toward a character without at the same time altering the
presentation of the character. There is obviously some loose and easy
sense in which an author can do this; otherwise it would not be possible
to produce parodies and ironic paraphrases. But Koestler seems to commit himself to a more questionable proposition—namely, that the emotional charge can in fact be quite sharply and cleanly separated from the
cognitive "layout." He says flatly that "other attitudes can be produced
[by] altering the stimulus . . . in such a way that its cognitive aspect or
ground plan remains unchanged while its emotion-evoking aspects are
altered," [9] and he goes on to say that his distinction between the "cognitive aspect" and the "emotion-evoking aspects" corresponds to the distinction made in *The Meaning of Meaning* [1] by C. K. Ogden and I. A.
Richards between "two uses of language," the referential and the emotive.

This distinction between the referential and the emotive does play
an important part in the theorizing of some of the critics to be discussed
in a later chapter. Ogden and Richards, like Koestler, are conversant with
modern psychology, and again, like him, their theories show a strong affective bias. But just because they are less ambitious to subsume so many
various workings of the mind under one pattern, they will provide us
with a more specifically literary focus for our examination of the problem.

SUPPLEMENT

Thus Satan's character, as Milton presents it, cannot but inspire feelings of
sympathy and admiration. The traditional motive of Satan's fall was pride.
Milton had then to describe the pride of Satan. But, as we have seen, pride

[9] *Insight and Outlook*, p. 240.
[1] *The Meaning of Meaning: a Study of the Influence of Language upon Thought
and of the Science of Symbolism* (London, 1923).

was the ruling passion in his own soul. Consequently, the character of Satan is drawn with a power unique in literature. In reality, Milton pours out his own feelings. Satan's first speeches are pure Miltonic lyricism.

—Denis Saurat, *Milton: Man and Thinker* (New York, 1925), p. 214

. . . any real exposition of the Satanic character and the Satanic predicament is likely to provoke the question "Do you, then, regard *Paradise Lost* as a comic poem?" To this I answer, No; but only those will fully understand it who see that it might have been a comic poem. Milton has chosen to treat the Satanic predicament in the epic form and has therefore subordinated the absurdity of Satan to the misery which he suffers and inflicts. Another author, Meredith, has treated it as comedy with consequent subordination of its tragic elements. But *The Egoist* remains, none the less, a pendant to *Paradise Lost*, and just as Meredith cannot exclude all pathos from Sir Willoughby, so Milton cannot exclude all absurdity from Satan, and does not even wish to do so. That is the explanation of the Divine laughter in *Paradise Lost* which has offended some readers. There is a real offence in it because Milton has imprudently made his Divine Persons so anthropomorphic that their laughter arouses legitimately hostile reactions in us—as though we were dealing with an ordinary conflict of wills in which the winner ought not to ridicule the loser. But it is a mistake to demand that Satan, any more than Sir Willoughby, should be able to rant and posture through the whole universe without, sooner or later, awaking the comic spirit. The whole nature of reality would have to be altered in order to give him such immunity, and it is not alterable. At that precise point where Satan or Sir Willoughby meets something real, laughter *must* arise, just as steam must when water meets fire. And no one was less likely than Milton to be ignorant of this necessity. We know from his prose works that he believed everything detestable to be, in the long run, also ridiculous; and mere Christianity commits every Christian to believing that "the Devil is (in the long run) an ass."

—C. S. Lewis, *A Preface to Paradise Lost* (Oxford, 1942), pp. 92–3, by permission of Oxford University Press, Inc.

A serious analysis of literary art [such as this] with only an occasional, passing mention of Shakespeare may have seemed to many readers a curious innovation. The reason for it, however, is simple enough, and has been suggested above: Shakespeare is essentially a dramatist, and drama is not, in the strict sense, "literature."

Yet it is a poetic art, because it creates the primary illusion of all poetry —virtual history. Its substance is an image of human life—ends, means, gains and losses, fulfillment and decline and death. It is a fabric of illusory experience, and that is the essential product of poesis. But drama is not merely a distinct literary form; it is a special poetic mode, as different from genuine literature as sculpture from pictorial art, or either of these from architecture. That is to say, it makes its own basic abstraction, which gives it a way of its own in making the semblance of history.

Literature projects the image of life in the mode of virtual memory; language is its essential material; the sound and meaning of words, their familiar or unusual use and order, even their presentation on the printed page, create the illusion of life as a realm of events—completed, lived, as words formulate them—events that compose a Past. But Drama presents the poetic illusion in a different light: not finished realities, or "events," but immediate, visible responses of human beings, make its semblance of life. Its basic abstraction is the act, which springs from the past, but is directed toward the future, and is always great with things to come.

—Susanne K. Langer, *Feeling and Form* (New York, 1953), p. 306. Reprinted by permission of Charles Scribner's Sons.

I have gone into this scene [I, v of *Hamlet*] at some length, since it illustrates so perfectly the relationship between psychology and form, and so aptly indicates how the one is to be defined in terms of the other. That is, the psychology here is not the psychology of the *hero*, but the psychology of the *audience*. And by that distinction, form would be the psychology of the audience. Or, seen from another angle, form is the creation of an appetite in the mind of the auditor, and the adequate satisfying of that appetite. This satisfaction—so complicated is the human mechanism—at times involves a temporary set of frustrations, but in the end these frustrations prove to be simply a more involved kind of satisfaction, and furthermore serve to make the satisfaction of fulfilment more intense. If, in a work of art, the poet says something, let us say, about a meeting, writes in such a way that we desire to observe that meeting, and then, if he places that meeting before us—that is form. While obviously, that is also the psychology of the audience, since it involves desires and their appeasements.

—Kenneth Burke, *Counter-Statement* (New York, 1931), p. 40; also Hermes Publications, 1953, pp. 30-1. By permission of the author.

If the difference between tragedy and comedy is a difference between the emotions they express, it is not a difference that can be present to the artist's mind when he is beginning his work; if it were, he would know what emotion he was going to express before he had expressed it. No artist, therefore, so far as he is an artist proper, can set out to write a comedy, a tragedy, an elegy, or the like. So far as he is an artist proper, he is just as likely to write any one of these as any other; which is the truth that Socrates was heard expounding towards the dawn, among the sleeping figures in Agathon's dining room.

—R. G. Collingwood, *The Principles of Art* (Oxford: Clarendon Press, 1938), p. 116, by permission of Oxford University Press, Inc.

SYMBOLISM

§ *Coleridge's wish to destroy the antithesis between words and things: its partial fulfillment in certain modern philosophies of symbolic form—II. Emerson's Transcendentalism: its relation to Coleridge and to German philosophers, its strength and its weakness, Whitman's optimism and Melville's disquieting doubts—III. Edgar Allan Poe's concern for lyric intensity: his efforts to "purify" poetry, the implications of these efforts for subject matter and form, poetry analogized to music—the influence of Poe's ideas upon Baudelaire: Baudelaire's system of "correspondences," tendencies in Baudelaire toward the irrational and the occult—IV. Mallarmé's poetry as a refinement of thing or event to a "Platonic idea" of itself, poetry as evocation and poetry as ritual—V. two side developments of French symbolism: Verlaine and lyric impressionism, and Rimbaud and the systematic disordering of the senses, Rimbaud's conception of the poet as* voyant—*VI. Valéry and his detachment of the poem, as pure meaning, from the realm of reality, his years of silence, the tendency of symbolist poetry to extinguish itself—some attempts to define and summarize the nature of French symbolism—VII. William Butler Yeats as a symbolist poet: his debt to Arthur Symons, the relation of "magic" to poetry, Yeats's attempt to create a personal myth—VIII. Yeats's knowledge of philosophy, his conception of poetry as yielding a peculiar kind of knowledge, parallels between his position and that of R. G. Collingwood—Yeats's saving dualism: his refusal to fall into "angelism"* §

THE DOCTRINE THAT WORDS CREATE KNOWLEDGE IS A PART OF THE romantic theory of the imagination. Coleridge, for example, constantly verges upon such a conception in his speculations upon poetry as a way of mediating between the subject and the object. In a letter to William Godwin (22 September 1800) he writes:

> I wish you to write a book on the power of the words. . . . is *Thinking* impossible without arbitrary signs? And how far is the word "arbitrary" a misnomer? Are not words, etc., parts and germinations of the plant? And what is the law of their growth? In something of this sort I would endeavour to destroy the old antithesis of Words and Things; elevating, as it were, Words into Things and living things too.[1]

Many of the more recent developments in literary theory can be read as attempted answers to the questions which Coleridge puts here to Godwin. Present-day philosophers like Croce, R. G. Collingwood, Ernst Cassirer, and Susanne Langer have concerned themselves with the laws that govern the growth of words and may indeed be said to have gone far to destroy the old antithesis between words and things. Even a theorist like I. A. Richards, who began with the thesis that words were arbitrary signs, in the course of time proceeded toward a correction and modification of that thesis, and in doing so came to argue for a much more organic conception of words, finally arriving at the view that reality itself, as man can know it, is a symbolic construction: "the fabric of our meanings, which is the world," is Richards' way of putting it in 1936.[2] Indeed, the tendency to treat words as things has in our time gone so far as to provoke vehement reactions. Thus, Allen Tate has denounced the

> belief that language itself can be reality, or by incantation can create a reality: a superstition that comes down in French from Lautréamont, Rimbaud, and Mallarmé to the Surrealists, and in English to Hart Crane, Wallace Stevens, and Dylan Thomas.[3]

In Tate's list, the preponderance of French and American names is significant. Though Coleridge prophetically raised the right questions and

---

[1] *Unpublished Letters of S. T. Coleridge*, ed. E. L. Griggs (London, 1932), I, 155–6. A few years later Lord Byron voiced much the same aspiration in his *Childe Harold*.

> I do believe,
> Though I have found them not, that there may be
> Words which are things.
>
> —Canto III, stanza CXIV

[2] Cf. *post* Chapter 28.

[3] *The Forlorn Demon* (Chicago, 1953), p. 61.

even implied some of the answers later to be proposed by the symbolist theoreticians, the most direct line of development does lead through French and American thinkers. Coleridge's American followers, more nearly than his English, entered into direct engagement of the problem of symbolic form. We refer to the American Transcendentalists, Ralph Waldo Emerson, H. D. Thoreau, and Herman Melville.

II

IN HIS essay entitled "The Poet" (1844) Emerson boldly pronounced "Words and deeds" to be "quite indifferent modes of the divine energy. Words are also actions, and actions are a kind of words." [4] The poet is not to be sharply set apart from the "practical" man; nor is his work to be thought of as artful in some sense that cuts it off from nature and the natural. ". . . the poet names the thing because he sees it, or comes one step nearer to it than any other. This expression or naming is not art, but a second nature, grown out of the first, as a leaf out of a tree." [5] The last phrase echoes the metaphor that Coleridge used in his letter to Godwin, and to something like Coleridge's purpose. Emerson is insisting that verbal expression is not a wilful and arbitrary thing—as Coleridge put it elsewhere, not "a pure work of the will"—but natural and organic as the growth of the leaf is organic.

We are not to take too seriously, of course, such parallels of phrasing between Emerson and Coleridge. They may be accidental, and the reader in any case soon learns not to put too much reliance upon the letter of the somewhat rhapsodic language in which Emerson habitually expressed himself. Yet there can be no doubt that Emerson has to be accounted one of the forerunners of the conception of literature as symbolic form. [6]

Emerson drew upon Coleridge's sources in neo-Platonism and German idealistic philosophy, and, of course, he drew directly upon Coleridge himself. But he was apparently affected even more deeply than was Coleridge by a sense of crisis in the problem of knowledge. He was sensitized to feel that problem by a number of circumstances—his provincialism, his lack of a rich and sustaining tradition, his "innocence," and his relatively slight interest in aesthetic forms as such.

The old rationalism in which Emerson had been brought up had been routed. The Cartesian dualism between the objects of the world and the spirit which thought about them had suddenly collapsed. Kant had

[4] *Works* (Fireside Edition, Boston and New York, 1909), III, 14.
[5] *Works*, III, 26.
[6] See the convincing argument made by Charles Feidelson, Jr., in *Symbolism and American Literature* (Chicago, published by The University of Chicago Press, 1953. And copyright 1953 by the University of Chicago.) See especially pp. 119–35.

asserted that the mind was no *tabula rasa* on which external objects scratched their impressions: the mind was an active force, which, by its own forms, moulded our conceptions of reality. Emerson and the other intellectual leaders of his culture, starved after two hundred years of the Puritanic attenuation of symbolism and already more than vaguely dissatisfied with abstractions, were ripe for the discovery that the mind was a transcendental force.[7]

But Emerson was not a thinker systematic enough to work out the implications of the position, either for philosophy or for literary criticism. The fact of the mind's transcendence remained for him a kind of overpowering insight to which he recurred in endless variations in his rather high-pitched and evangelistic essays. Emerson wins his victories of reconciliation over the contradictions of experience a shade too easily. William Butler Yeats might have said of Emerson, as he did say of Shelley, that he lacked the vision of evil. One remembers Carlyle's complaint to Emerson that he took "so little heed of the frightful quantities of *friction* and perverse *impediment* there everywhere are; the reflections upon which in my own poor life made me now and then very sad, as I read you." [8] Emerson reminds one of the protagonist in *The Waste Land,* whose eyes failed him at the vision in the hyacinth garden, and who was neither living nor dead, "Looking into the heart of light, the silence." Emerson's vision of the poem fails under excess of light: he sees little more in any poem than the scintillant fact that it *is* a poem—no mere shadow of external objects and no mere subjective fancy, but a coalescence of man with nature in a union that guarantees the participation of both man and nature in something transcendental.

For Emerson the poetic vision, we may say, is a kind of universal solvent: it brings the most refractory and stubbornly contradictory things into unity. Or, as he put it himself in "The Poet," the poet renders the whole realm of phenomena transparent:

> As the eyes of Lyncæus were said to see through the earth, so the poet turns the world to glass, and shows us all things in their right series and procession. For through that better perception he stands one step nearer to things, and sees the flowing or metamorphosis; perceives that thought is multiform . . . and following with his eyes the life, uses the forms that express that life, and so his speech flows with the flowing of nature.[9]

The difficulty of turning the world to glass, however, is that a really transparent world would be quite invisible. Wishing to see everything,

[7] *Symbolism and American Literature*, p. 129.

[8] Carlyle to Emerson, April 6, 1870. *The Correspondence of Carlyle and Emerson* (Boston, 1894), II, 360–1.

[9] "The Poet," *Works*, III, 25.

we should actually see nothing. It would be unfair to the spirit of his essay to bind Emerson rigidly by the terms of his own metaphor. The fact of *some* transparency—"We are symbols and inhabit symbols,"[1] he says in the same essay—is evidently all that Emerson really meant to claim. Yet the passage quoted does fairly suggest the weakness in Emerson's conception, and it points to a problem that any thoroughgoing system of symbolism has to face: if there are no fixities and definites at all but only symbolic fluidity, then there would appear to be some danger that everything will disappear into froth and bubbles.

Such is the characteristic weakness of the poetic performance of Walt Whitman, the poet upon whom Emerson's transcendental theory registered with most emphatic force. In Whitman's *Song of Myself* the poet and the universe about him merge so effortlessly that the poem threatens to collapse into tautology. The poet discovers with a kind of jaunty wonder that he is a part of nature and indeed is not to be separated from all those things ordinarily thought of as external to man:

> I find I incorporate gneiss, long-threaded moss, fruits,
> grains, esculent roots,
> And am stucco'd with quadrupeds and birds all over. . . .

The typical problem raised by Herman Melville's work, however, is not that of too easy reconciliation. With Melville the question is rather whether there is any reconciliation at all. Even more than Emerson, Melville was shaken by the crisis in epistemology. And Melville possessed the vision of evil. That the universe was not merely an external and mechanical framework, but was plastic, "organic," and alive was for Melville something more than an innocently exhilarating discovery. The discovery also held an element of terror, for the evil in the world was not thereby canceled; indeed, it was rendered more deeply and ineradicably alive. Moreover, to a mind desperate for truth, the very ambiguity of the universe was horrible.

The heroes of Melville's novels are all concerned with the problem of knowledge. Each of them asks whether we can truly *know* anything, or whether we are not actually caught in a quicksand of our own dreams and imaginative projections, a quicksand into which our struggles to reach objective truth can only mire us deeper. In his masterpiece, *Moby Dick* (1851), Melville frankly accepted a "methodological paradox." That is, he accepted the fact that although the "realm of significance" would seem to deny "the dual reality of subject and object," yet in fact the realm of significance rises from and returns to that duality. The realm of significance is allowed to do so in this novel; for example, the whale is "simultaneously the most solid of physical things and the most

[1] *Works*, III, 24.

meaningful of symbols." [2] But in Melville's later novels, the objects are hazy and the heroes become more and more involved in a frustrating struggle with shadows. The failure of Melville's novel *Pierre: or The Ambiguities* (1852) may be imputed to Melville's having become "contemptuous of literary form in general." Melville as author "suspects from the beginning what his hero discovers in the end, that all literature is meretricious." [3]

> He reached not only a personal, but also a technical, impasse. The logic of his career was the logic of his aesthetic premises; his concept of artistic truth was calculated to lead him into a skepticism of art.[4]

Something of the sort seems to have happened to another extreme proponent of symbolist theory, the French poet Arthur Rimbaud. After publishing *Une Saison en Enfer*, Rimbaud apparently came to an impasse, burned his manuscripts, and left Europe to become an ivory-trader and gun-runner in Abyssinia.[5]

III

THERE are good reasons for grouping Edgar Allan Poe with the Transcendentalists, who were, of course, his contemporaries and fellow-countrymen. Poe, to be sure, had some sharp things to say on the topic of Emerson's obscurantism, and he deplored the general bias of New Englanders toward the allegorical and toward the didactic. "We Americans especially," he writes, "have patronised [the heresy of the Didactic]; and we Bostonians, very especially, have developed it in full." [6] But Poe's literary theorizing was in general derived from the same sources as those of the Transcendentalists.

What sets Poe apart from the Transcendentalists is his special aestheticism, aspects of which have already been discussed in our chapter on "Art for Art's Sake." [7] By contrast with Emerson's attitude toward poetry, Poe's is technical and "professional." Poe envisages the poet not as that vague and splendidly democratic creature, "man speaking," but as a craftsman who brings his intelligence fully, and even coldly, to bear upon the problem of organizing words into specific literary struc-

[2] *Symbolism and American Literature*, p. 184.

[3] *Symbolism and American Literature*, p. 201.

[4] *Symbolism and American Literature*, p. 164.

[5] Enid Starkie in her study, *Arthur Rimbaud* (New York, 1947), p. 294, offers among other conjectures, the suggestion that "perhaps [Rimbaud's] new form of poetry led him to a dead end. . . ."

[6] "The Poetic Principle," *Complete Works*, ed. J. A. Harrison (New York, 1902), XIV, 271.

[7] Cf. *ante* Chapter 22.

tures. Poe was prepared to take quite literally Milton's compliment to Lycidas on his knowledge of how "to build the lofty rhyme." A poem had an architecture and it was well built or ill built. Its shape ought not to be a matter of "accident or intuition" but ought to reveal—at least in the ideal case—"the precision and rigid consequence of a mathematical problem." [8] This aspect of Poe's criticism was to prove, as we shall see, most attractive to Baudelaire and the other French symbolist poets. For them it evidently constituted a special way of focusing upon the pure lyric intensity that Poe argued was the essence of poetry.

There could be no such thing as a *long* poem. That phrase, Poe confidently declared, was "simply a flat contradiction in terms." The "degree of excitement" which entitles one to use the term "poem" simply cannot be sustained throughout a long work, for all such excitements are "through a psychal necessity, transient." [9] This stress upon lyric intensity implied a special kind of subject matter and a special kind of form. The subject matter must be an experience of peculiar intensity. The form must be purely functional, with all that is nonfunctional—all that is merely "prose" connective tissue—eliminated. In short a poem should have the intensity that one finds in a waking dream and its elements should contain as little "inert" matter as the notes of a musical composition. It is "in Music, perhaps," Poe writes, "that the soul most nearly attains . . . the creation of supernal Beauty." [1]

Thus dream and music were used by Poe to suggest the special kinds of purity that he demanded of poetry, and this analogizing of poetry to dream and to music was to run all the way through the speculations of the French symbolists. Poe refers in his *Marginalia* to "points of time where the confines of the waking world blend with those of the world of dreams." [2] Nearly a century later, Poe's very phrasing returns to us in a passage of one of W. B. Yeats's last poems, referring to

> . . . forms that are or seem
> When sleepers wake and yet still dream,
> And when it's vanished still declare,
> With only bed and bedstead there,
> That heavens had opened. [3]

This indeed would be to catch a glimpse of the supernal beauty; and if the modern poet's almost aggressive insistence upon the domestic realism of the bedroom furniture seems oddly out of key with the ornate and mannered Gothic decor that Poe usually provides as the setting for

[8] "The Philosophy of Composition," *Works*, XIV, 195.
[9] "The Poetic Principle," *Works*, XIV, 266.
[1] "The Poetic Principle," *Works*, XIV, 274.
[2] *Works*, XVI, 88.
[3] "Under Ben Bulben," *Collected Poems* (New York, 1951), p. 343, by permission of The Macmillan Company.

such experiences, the contrast itself makes a point: it testifies to the vitality of Poe's key ideas and to their ability to suffer translation from one realm of sensibility to another. Yeats's version of the waking dream, of course, reveals the impress of his own personality and also reflects the modifications the notion received in passing through the succession of French symbolists and then back into English again. Like most other British and American poets, Yeats accepted very little from Poe directly. The poetry that enchanted Baudelaire left Yeats cold. He observed to a friend: "Analyse the Raven and you find that its subject is a commonplace and its execution a rhythmical trick. Its rhythm never lives for a moment, never once moves with an emotional life. The whole thing seems to me insincere and vulgar." [4]

But upon Baudelaire Poe's empurpled rhetoric registered with very different effect. In 1846 or 1847 Baudelaire read his first French translations of Poe, and felt immediately a powerful sense of spiritual kinship with the American poet. In an ecstasy of discovery, he took over Poe's whole doctrine of pure poetry. The poet, Poe had said, had nothing to do with the good or the true, but only with the beautiful. His prime task was to "reach the Beauty above," [5] of which the beauty of this world is a reflection. In Chapter 22 *ante* we have already considered the implications of this statement for the doctrine of art for art's sake. It remains to relate it more specifically to the theories of the French symbolists.

To assert that the beauty of this world is but a "reflection" of a "Beauty above" is in itself to imply a symbolist aesthetic of sorts. But Poe makes it quite plain that we can attain to this eternal beauty—even if to no more than "a portion" of it—only by making use of "multiform combinations among the things and thoughts of Time." [6] The general recipe is old enough: but in Poe's formulation it is worth noting that "things and thoughts" are made to lie down beside each other as if any invidious distinction between them had been obliterated.

Poe's "multiform combinations" finds its parallel and development in Baudelaire's more celebrated "system of correspondences." As Baudelaire wrote in 1859 in an article on Théophile Gautier: ". . . it is our instinct for beauty which causes us to consider the earth and its visibilia . . . 'comme une *correspondance* du Ciel.' " [7] In *Les Fleurs du Mal*

[4] The letter, dated 3 September 1899, is addressed to W. T. Horton. See *The Letters of W. B. Yeats*, ed. Allan Wade (New York, 1955), p. 325. This and following passages from Yeats's writings are reprinted by permission of The Macmillan Company. Aldous Huxley has some acute as well as amusing observations on the fact that French men of letters have so much admired Poe whereas English-speaking readers tend to find him vulgar. See his *Vulgarity in Literature* (London, 1930), pp. 26–36.

[5] "The Poetic Principle," *Works*, XIV, 273.

[6] "The Poetic Principle," *Works*, XIV, 274.

[7] Guy Michaud, *Message Poétique du Symbolisme* (Paris, 1947, 3 vols.), I, 70.

(1857), Baudelaire expresses this conception in a sonnet entitled "*Correspondances*," where all nature is viewed as a temple, a natural temple whose living pillars are the trees. As the wind blows through these "forests of symbols," confused words are now and then breathed forth. The poet, because of his special endowment, is able to apprehend these words, for in all things there is a symbolic sense and every object in nature has its special connection with a spiritual reality.[8]

The correspondences are developed upon several planes. The poet asserts that there are equivalences among the data of the various senses— sounds, colors, odors. ("*Les parfums, les couleurs, et les sons se répondent.*") And he speaks of perfumes "fresh as a child's skin, sweet as oboes, green as meadows."

In the second place,

> Since sensuous data can have "the expansion of infinite things," it follows that a desire, a regret, a thought—things of the mind —can awaken a corresponding symbol in the world of images (and vice versa). . . . From the world of the senses the poet takes the material in which to forge a symbolic vision of himself or of his dream; what he asks of the world of the senses is that it give him the means of expressing his soul. [9]

The neo-Platonic flavor of this conception of poetry is sufficiently evident. In Baudelaire's poetry, this general idealistic tendency reinforces, and is reinforced by, special tendencies toward the irrational and the occult. But Baudelaire showed himself the true disciple of Poe [1] in refusing to be guided by instinct alone. He believed in method; he could even refer to inspiration as "the reward of daily effort." He classed himself among those artists who attempt to "discover the obscure laws by virtue of which they have created, and to draw from this study a number of precepts whose divine goal is the infallibility of poetic production." [2]

IV

PREOCCUPATION with method was, however, far more than with Baudelaire the special concern of Stéphane Mallarmé. Mallarmé took very

---

[8] Baudelaire's theory of correspondences also derives in part from the notions of the Swedish mystic, Emanuel Swedenborg. In his article on Victor Hugo (1861), Baudelaire writes: "Moreover Swedenborg . . . has already taught us . . . that everything, form, motion, number, color, scents, in the *spiritual* as well as in the *natural* realm, is significant, reciprocal, converse, corresponding. . . ." See Guy Michaud, *La Doctrine Symboliste: Documents* (Paris, 1947), p. 22.

[9] Marcel Raymond, *From Baudelaire to Surrealism* (Paris, 1933, revised 1940); translated into English by "G.M." *Documents of Modern Art Vol. 10,* New York: George Wittenborn, Inc., 1949, p. 18.

[1] Cf. *ante* Chapter 22.

[2] In an article on Richard Wagner. See *From Baudelaire to Surrealism*, p. 21.

seriously Poe's notion of a poem so carefully organized that it possessed "the precision and rigid consequence of a mathematical problem." One finds Mallarmé writing such a passage as the following:

> The further I go, the more faithful I shall be to those severe ideas which my great master, Edgar Poe, has bequeathed me. The wonderful poem *The Raven* was conceived thus, and the soul of the reader enjoys exactly what the poet wanted it to enjoy.[3]

During the 1870's and the 1880's, Mallarmé came to be regarded as the saint and sage of the symbolist movement. He was not a popular poet; he published little; but his Tuesday receptions at which he talked with his friends about poetry became an institution. To his house there came not only the French poets and critics of the period, but writers in English such as Oscar Wilde, Arthur Symons, George Moore, and W. B. Yeats. With Mallarmé, the cultivation of poetry went far toward becoming a ritual and a cult. It also went farthest toward becoming an enterprise engaging all the powers of the mind—not a matter of blind inspiration or of sudden and inexplicable visitations by the Muse, but a problem of craftsmanship and of philosophical theorizing. It is to Mallarmé that one turns, incidentally, for what is probably the most celebrated observation about symbolic methods. In 1891 he wrote:

> . . . the Parnassians, for their part, take the thing as a whole and show it; that's where they are deficient in mystery. They deprive the mind of the delicious joy of believing that it is creating. To name an object is to do away with three-quarters of the enjoyment of the poem which is derived from the satisfaction of guessing little by little; to suggest it, that is the illusion. It is the perfect handling of the mystery that constitutes the symbol: to evoke an object little by little in order to show a state of mind or inversely to choose an object and to disengage from it a state of mind, by a series of unriddlings.[4]

Someone has described Mallarmé's characteristic poetic activity as that of trying to refine and purify any object or event to the "Platonic idea" of that object or event. There was in him a compulsion to reduce to essences by removing the accidental and adventitious. Mallarmé was concerned that nothing in the poem be the effect of mere chance, that the articulation of every part with every other part should be complete,

[3] *Message Poétique du Symbolisme,* I, 165.
[4] *Réponse à une Enquête* (1891), quoted in *La Doctrine Symboliste: Documents,* p. 74. Mallarmé's reference to the "delicious joy" that the mind experiences in "believing that it is creating" recalls Coleridge's remark that the reader feels Shakespeare to be a poet "inasmuch as for a time he has made you one—an active creative being." For more recent instances of this view, see *post* Chapter 28.

each part implying every other part, and that the meaning of the poem should be inseparable from its formal structure. In the Mallarmean poem the words acquire something of the bulk and density of things; the poem is treated almost as if it were a plastic object with weight and solidity and with even a certain opacity. For the words are not *signs*, transparently redacting ideas. Instead they have acquired something like bulk and mass. The poems have become little mysterious worlds whose meaning is to be read with only somewhat less difficulty than the meaning of the great world of which the poems are in a sense analogical copies.

Words for Mallarmé were then much more than signs. Used evocatively and ritualistically, they are the means by which we are inducted into an ideal world. "Poetry is," as Mallarmé defined it in 1886, "the expression by means of human language restored to its essential rhythm, of the mysterious sense of the aspects of existence: it endows our sojourn with authenticity and constitutes the sole spiritual task." [5]

V

THE main line of succession of the French symbolist movement, it is generally agreed, runs from Baudelaire to Mallarmé and thence to Paul Valéry.[6] But before taking up Valéry, it will be useful to examine briefly two important side developments. The first of these has to do with the career of Paul Verlaine. We have already had occasion to cite Poe's observation that it is in music that the soul most "nearly attains . . . the creation of supernal Beauty." The symbolist movement may be described as the effort to bring poetry to the condition of music—indeed Valéry did so describe it in 1926. Mallarmé's poetry is clearly musical in this sense, words being organized and orchestrated almost as if they were musical notes. But Verlaine's poetry is "musical" in a more direct and literal sense. In his poetry, the words tend to be emptied of their intellectual content. As Michaud puts it, in Verlaine's poetry "the language is vaporized and is reabsorbed into the melody." [7] Raymond says of Verlaine that he was "born to bring to its perfection the intimate and sentimental lyricism founded by Marceline Desbordes-Valmore and Lamartine." [8] Verlaine represents a temperament, a mood, rather than a technique. It will be more accurate to call his poetry impressionistic than to call it symbolist.

Yet if Verlaine has to be excluded from the circle of genuine symbolist poets, he had, nevertheless, much to do with bringing symbolism

[5] *Message Poétique du Symbolisme*, II, 321.
[6] See, for instance, *From Baudelaire to Surrealism*, p. 5.
[7] *Message Poétique du Symbolisme*, I, 123.
[8] *From Baudelaire to Surrealism*, p. 22.

to public notice. In 1884 Verlaine published his *Les Poètes Maudits*. The "accurst" poets discussed were Mallarmé, Tristan Corbière, and Arthur Rimbaud. It is easy to see why Verlaine applied the adjective to Corbière and Rimbaud, poets clearly repulsed by the society in which they lived; it is less easy to see how it applies to Mallarmé, and a recent writer on Mallarmé doubts whether Verlaine ever understood Mallarmé's poetry "in any profound way." [9]

The case of Verlaine provides an opportunity to render more precise the sense in which symbolist poetry may be said to be "musical"; that of Rimbaud allows one to develop a little further the sense in which the symbolist poet may be said to give over the initiative to the words themselves. Mallarmé, though he may be said to have given words their heads,[1] never, as the Surrealists were to do later, dropped the reins completely, abandoning the poem to the latent energies of language. Whether Rimbaud may be fairly said to have "abandoned" all conscious control is debatable; but Rimbaud is clearly a precursor of Surrealism. He deliberately cultivated the unconventional and the irrational.

In Rimbaud's conception, the poet is essentially a *voyant*, a seer. He applauded, as the "first voyant," Baudelaire, that "King of poets, a real God," even though he lamented the fact that Baudelaire lived in "too artistic a *milieu*" and encumbered himself with old literary forms.[2] For the new discoveries demanded new forms. The *voyant* perceives those images that the unconscious reveals only fitfully and accidentally to the ordinary man. Rimbaud's poetry was to be the systematic exploitation of such images. To this end the poet would make use of drugs, alcohol, debauchery—anything that broke down the control of reason and freed the faculties from their ordinary inhibitions. Rimbaud's famous recipe for the poet's activity reads thus: "The poet makes himself *voyant* by a long, vast, reasoned derangement of all the senses" (*Lettres du Voyant*, 1871).[3]

VI

VERLAINE, as we have seen, called Rimbaud and Mallarmé "poètes maudits" and himself gloried in the term *décadent*. Théophile Gau-

---

[9] Wallace Fowlie, *Mallarmé* (Chicago, 1953. Copyright [1953] by the University of Chicago). Fowlie goes on to say (p. 255): "The essay on Mallarmé was Verlaine's opportunity to cast opprobrium on those critics and readers who had considered him insane and ridiculous. Although Mallarmé's personal life would never place him with Poe, Baudelaire, Rimbaud, and Verlaine himself, his fate as poet was that of revolutionary, one cursed by the existing society."

[1] "A pure work, Mallarmé has written, gives over the initiative to the words themselves. The deliberate rhetoric of the poet disappears in them."—Fowlie, *Mallarmé*, p. 269.

[2] See *Message Poétique du Symbolisme*, I, 138, and Starkie's *Rimbaud*, p. 128.

[3] See Starkie, *Rimbaud*, p. 129.

tier had used *décadent* in his preface to Baudelaire's *Les Fleurs du Mal*, and Paul Bourget would call Baudelaire the "theoretician of decadence." The *décadent* was a seeker after rare sensation, a dandy, perhaps a roué, a cultivated dilettante, and, as one critic has phrased it, decadence came "to signify a kind of moral solitude of an artist, coupled with an exasperated and perverse form of mysticism." [4] The fashion of decadence was a way of protecting oneself from bourgeois triviality and all the dullness of a world increasingly given over to industrialism. So defined, the term has pertinence for Rimbaud and Verlaine, but less for a poet like Mallarmé. (Valéry observes that although "Verlaine and Rimbaud continued Baudelaire in the order of sentiment and sensation, Mallarmé carried his work forward in the province of perfection and poetic purity.") [5] At any rate, in 1885 some of the younger *décadent* writers repudiated that term and chose to call themselves "symbolists." The latter term certainly answered more nearly to the idealism of men like Mallarmé and Valéry, to their stress upon the intellectual construct, and above all to their attitude toward language. The symbolists, having discovered the non-notational aspect of language, proceed to explore the rich possibilities of intimation, suggestion, and all the other modes of linguistic indirection. Thus, one might attempt to summarize the history of the movement.

But "symbolism" was a rather loose and vague term, as Valéry himself was well aware. It was used to cover various and sometimes conflicting conceptions of poetry. What had been baptized Symbolism, Valéry was to write in retrospect in 1920, is summed up simply in an "intention of several groups of poets (not always friendly to one another) to recover from music the heritage due to them." [6] In music, there is no dross, no inert residue. Form and content coalesce. It was to this purified wholeness that symbolist poetry aspired. Valéry remarks in his essay on Baudelaire that Poe

> understood that [poetry] could claim to realize its own object and produce itself, to some degree, in a *pure state*.
>
> Thus, by analysing the requirements of poetic delight and defining *absolute poetry* by *exhaustion*, Poe showed a way and taught a very strict and fascinating doctrine in which he united a sort of mathematics with a sort of mysticism. . . . [7]

In Valéry's own work this aspiration to absolute purity finally led

[4] Fowlie, *Mallarmé*, p. 257.

[5] "The Position of Baudelaire" (first published in 1924), *Variety: Second Series*, trans. W. A. Bradley (New York, 1938), p. 98.

[6] Fowlie, *Mallarmé*, p. 268. Valéry's words are: "*Ce qui fut baptisé le Symbolisme, se résume très simplement dans l'intention commune à plusieurs familles de poètes (d'ailleurs ennemies entre elles) de reprendre à la Musique leur bien.*"

[7] *Variety: Second Series*, p. 92.

on past poetry, considered as a realized structure, to a preoccupation with the poetic activity as such. That is why Valéry could say to his friend André Gide: "They take me for a poet! I don't give a damn about poetry. It interests me only by a fluke. It is by accident that I have written verse. It has no importance for me." [8] Poetry, that is, was interesting only in so far as one could make it an exercise in pure creation. Thus symbolist poetry at its apogee threatens to purify itself out of existence. If the pressure for pure meaning is pressed unremittingly, the poem is finally detached from reality and becomes knowledge of *nothing!* Valéry's poetic masterpiece, "*Le Cimitière Marin*," derives its power from a candidly tragic apprehension of some final dichotomy between knowledge and life. It is the dichotomy tirelessly echoed, though of course with a different inflection, in the later poetry of William Butler Yeats:

> For wisdom is the property of the dead,
> A something incompatible with life. . . .[9]

That symbolist poetry should, in its yearning for purity, extinguish itself was much more than a merely academic possibility. Valéry did remain silent for some twenty years before he resumed the writing of poetry. We have already referred to Rimbaud's abandonment of poetry in favor of a life of action in Africa.

Any attempt to summarize symbolist doctrine exposes the vagueness of the pronouncements of the various symbolists and critics, not to mention their frequent contradictions. One might be forgiven for coming to doubt whether the term "symbolism" has any specific meaning at all, and to conclude that it is, like the term "romanticism," simply the name for a bundle of tendencies, not all of them very closely related. A definition may be attempted as follows:

> Whether a real school of symbolism ever existed, remains a problem of speculation. . . . Each poet developed and represented a single aspect of an aesthetic doctrine that was perhaps too vast for one historical group to incorporate. . . . But more than on any other article of belief, the symbolists united with Mallarmé in his statements about poetic language. The theory of the suggestiveness of words comes from a belief that a primitive language, half-forgotten, half-living, exists in each man. It is language possessing extraordinary affinities with music and dreams.[1]

This is a just appraisal; yet the phrasing, "primitive language, half-forgotten, half-living," could be misleading to a modern reader. It could

[8] *Message Poétique du Symbolisme*, III, 572.
[9] "Blood and the Moon," *Collected Poems*, p. 234.
[1] *Mallarmé*, p. 264.

suggest certain special developments of our own time which scarcely existed for Baudelaire and Mallarmé and to which, as the context shows, the words do not refer: that is, the tremendous contemporary interest in the pre-logical and primitive mind, whether of children or savages or neurotics, and as treated typically in anthropology and in depth psychology. With this interest, there has arisen a powerful new interest in myth as a "primitive language, half-forgotten, half-living," and there have been bold and sometimes extravagant speculations about the relation of myth to poetry. Such developments of symbolist and expressionist theory will be dealt with in a subsequent chapter. Suffice it to say that the French symbolists were interested in the magic of the Rosicrucians rather than that of the Trobriand Islanders, and in the ritual practices of the heretical sects of the Middle Ages rather than in those of the present-day tribes of the Congo and Amazon. In short, their interests were "philosophical" rather than "psychological," and "traditional" rather than "anthropological."

VII

SUCH also were the interests of the English-speaking poets and critics who were most powerfully influenced by the French symbolists, men like T. E. Hulme, Ezra Pound, and T. S. Eliot, whose ideas we shall consider in a later chapter, and even men like William Butler Yeats, whose attempt to construct a personal myth in *A Vision* (1925) might seem to argue a different concern. The affinities between Yeats and the French symbolists are numerous, and some of them have already been suggested by our recourse to Yeats in several earlier pages in order to illustrate symbolist ideas. Yet the direct influence of the French poets upon Yeats was slight. Though as early as 1894 Yeats took with him on a visit to Paris a letter of introduction to Mallarmé, he seems to have learned about symbolist ideas largely from his friend Arthur Symons, who dedicated to Yeats his *Symbolist Movement in Literature* (1899). A letter that he wrote many years later in 1937 indicates how slight the direct influence of Mallarmé had been. Yeats writes that he has just been looking at

> Roger Fry's translation of Mallarmé. . . . I find it exciting, as it shows me the road I and others of my time went for certain furlongs. It is not the way I go now, but one of the legitimate roads.[2]

What Yeats learned from Symons about symbolism comes out most plainly in Yeats's essay on "The Symbolism of Poetry" (1900). He re-

[2] Written, May 4, to Dorothy Wellesley: see *Letters of W. B. Yeats*, p. 887.

marks that the scientific movement had tended to bring into literature "externalities of all kinds," and that as a consequence, literature had been in danger of losing itself in

> opinion, in declamation, in picturesque writing, in word-painting, or in what Mr. Symons has called an attempt "to build in brick and mortar inside the covers of a book." [3]

Now, however, "writers have begun to dwell upon the element of evocation, of suggestion." Yeats asserts that "the substance of all style" is a "continuous indefinable symbolism," which he chooses to illustrate, not from one of the new writers, but from one of the 18th-century poets, Robert Burns.

> There are no lines [he writes] with more melancholy beauty than these by Burns—
> "The white moon is setting behind the white wave,
> And Time is setting with me, O!"
> and these lines are perfectly symbolical. Take from them the whiteness of the moon and of the wave, whose relation to the setting of Time is too subtle for the intellect, and you take from them their beauty. But, when all are together, moon and wave and whiteness and setting Time and the last melancholy cry, they evoke an emotion which cannot be evoked by any other arrangement of colours and sounds and forms. [4]

In the same essay Yeats writes that

> All sounds, all colours, all forms, either because of their pre-ordained energies or because of long association, evoke indefinable and yet precise emotions, or, as I prefer to think, call down among us certain disembodied powers, whose footsteps over our hearts we call emotions. [5]

Yeats's deliberate invocation of some kind of supernaturalism by references to "pre-ordained energies" and "disembodied powers" and the general glitter of his rhetoric should not be allowed to distract us from what is the central issue: though the emotions are "indefinable" yet they are nevertheless "precise." That is, the fact that the emotions cannot be defined in logical and scientific terms does not in the least invalidate their claim to precision.

A year later, in an essay entitled "Magic," Yeats trailed his cloak even more vigorously in the face of the naturalist, flaunting his belief

---

[3] W. B. Yeats, *Ideas of Good and Evil* (London, 1903), p. 240, by permission of The Macmillan Company.
[4] *Ideas of Good and Evil*, pp. 241–2.
[5] *Ideas of Good and Evil*, p. 243.

in the "evocation of spirits" (though he was careful to acknowledge that he did "not know what they are"). He recorded in that essay his belief in three doctrines which have been, he declared, "the foundations of nearly all magical practices." The doctrines were:

(1) That the borders of our minds are ever shifting, and that many minds can flow into one another, as it were, and create or reveal a single mind, a single energy.

(2) That the borders of our memories are as shifting, and that our memories are a part of one great memory, the memory of Nature herself.

(3) That this great mind and great memory can be evoked by symbols.[6]

"To show that past times have believed as I do," Yeats cites Joseph Glanvill's story of the Scholar Gipsy, the story upon which Matthew Arnold founded his poem. Yeats seems to take the Scholar Gipsy's powers quite literally; yet the context makes it plain that what interests him especially is what is summed up in the twice-used phrase, "the power of imagination." Yeats quotes the passage in which the Scholar Gipsy tells his Oxford friends that the gipsies

he went with were not such impostors as they were taken for, but that they had a traditional kind of learning among them and could do wonders by the power of imagination. . . . The scholars . . . earnestly desired him to unriddle the mystery. In which he gave them satisfaction, by telling them that what he did was by the power of imagination, his phantasy leading theirs. . . .[7]

That power, Yeats declares, is alive today, and symbols are still the "greatest of all powers whether they are used consciously by the masters of magic, or half unconsciously by their successors, the poet, the musician and the artist."[8]

The contrast with Arnold could hardly be more complete: the Scholar Gipsy, for the great Victorian critic, is obviously a fabulous creature, part of the folklore of a charmingly naive world toward which the sore-beset modern rationalist can turn back no more than a wistful glance. But for Yeats, the power of imagination possessed by the Gipsy is still valid and is to be claimed to its fullest extent. If to assert one's

[6] *Ideas of Good and Evil*, p. 29.
This conception of the great mind and the great memory sounds like an interesting anticipation of Carl Jung's doctrine of the collective unconscious with its repository of archetypal images which on occasion can well up into individual minds. Jung stated his conception first in 1912.
[7] *Ideas of Good and Evil*, pp. 48–9.
[8] *Ideas of Good and Evil*, p. 64.

belief in this kind of power means to make claims for magic as such, Yeats will do so. But it is worth remarking that Yeats seems to swallow the magic for the sake of possessing the imagination and not the other way around.

Our softening of Yeats's assertions of a literal belief in magic may seem overconfident in view of his membership in organizations boasting such titles as the "Order of the Golden Dawn," his association with Madame Blavatsky, and his lifelong interest in table-rapping, spirit mediums, and clairvoyants. But these more lurid stageprops ought not to distract us from Yeats's other interests—such as the philosophy of history as developed by Vico and Hegel and the epistemology of Plato and Plotinus and Bishop Berkeley. Even *A Vision*, that extravagant attempt to set forth a personal mythology, the substance of which Yeats claimed to have received from the "teaching spirits" through the mediumship of his wife, had an intellectual justification which Yeats could state in sober enough terms. Works like Berkeley's *Principles of Human Knowledge*, Yeats wrote, might prove "to our logical capacity" that there is a "transcendental portion of our being that is timeless and spaceless," and yet "our imagination [may] remain subjected to nature as before." It was otherwise for the ancient philosopher, Yeats maintained, for he "had something to reinforce his thought,—the Gods, the Sacred Dead, Egyptian Theurgy, the Priestess Diotime." [9] *A Vision* was to furnish to the modern philosopher a like imaginative reinforcement.

VIII

ALL symbolist doctrines seem to rest either upon some kind of idealism or else to deny the dualism of ideality and materialism altogether by considering these opposed concepts to be abstractions out of a prior and deeper reality in which they lie undifferentiated. The latter alternative has proved historically a difficult one to sustain. The position of those philosophers of symbolic form who, like Ernst Cassirer and Susanne Langer, seek to avoid moving into any kind of pure idealism, we shall discuss in a later chapter. Most symbolist poets and critics, including those already discussed in this chapter, tend to be rather pure idealists. And so did Yeats.

In 1926 Yeats wrote to his friend Sturge Moore that because the "teaching spirits" had forbidden it, he did not read philosophy until he had completed *A Vision*. But then, he writes, "I read for months every day Plato and Plotinus. Then I started on Berkeley and Croce and Gentile." [1] One of the topics canvassed at length in this correspond-

[9] *A Vision* (London, 1925), pp. 251–2.

[1] *W. B. Yeats and T. Sturge Moore: their Correspondence, 1901–1937*, ed. Ursula Bridge (Oxford University Press, Inc.: New York, 1953), p. 83.

ence (published 1953) has to do with the cat that John Ruskin was alleged to have picked up and thrown out of the window with the explanation that it was really a tempting demon. Yeats wanted to know on what basis, if any, the cat could be regarded as "unreal," and specifically how Ruskin could have distinguished the demon cat from the house cat. His choice of the problem is significant. It provided him with an occasion to talk about the topics that had particularly engaged his interest as he read Plato, Berkeley, Kant, Hegel, and Croce. Some of his arguments turn out to be quite fantastic, but, as Yeats wrote to Moore, the "points most of my fantasies and extravagancies were meant to suggest are . . . that images of the mind and images of sense must have a common root . . . and that whatever their cause or substratum that substratum is not fixed at one spot in space." [2]

In general Yeats was a good—if somewhat unconventional—Kantian. He termed "the vast Kantian argument" the "most powerful in philosophy." From it there descended "two great streams of thought," the "philosophy of will in Schopenhauer, Hartmann, Bergsen [sic], James, and that of knowledge in Hegel, Croce, Gentile, Bradley and the like." [3] Of these "two paths to reality," as Yeats elsewhere refers to them, that "of knowledge" proved the more attractive to him.

Poetry yields a special kind of knowledge. Through poetry, man comes to know himself in relation to reality, and thus attains wisdom. On this theme Yeats's own poetry descants tirelessly. The magi seeking the manger in Bethlehem are conceived of as seekers after knowledge, "hoping to find . . . The uncontrollable mystery on the bestial floor." [4] When Yeats imagines the rape of Leda by the swan, the question that he puts is: "Did she put on his knowledge with his power?" [5] In "The Gift of Harun Al-Rashid," the young bride gives unwittingly to her older philosopher husband that precious gift that is "to age what milk is to a child," "A quality of wisdom" which springs from "her love's Particular quality." [6] Even Yeats's account of the fortunes of the soul after death, as detailed in *A Vision*, is the story of a quest for knowledge. The soul must first relive all the passionate experiences of its life until it understands them, and then it must experience the opposite of all that it actually did and suffered in its life so that it may truly complete its knowledge of itself. Only then is it allowed to drink of the cup of Lethe.

The knowledge that poetry confers is obviously something other than a traffic in "opinions," which the poet associates with competition and intellectual hatred. It is not produced by the "levelling, rancorous, ra-

[2] *Yeats and Moore: Correspondence*, p. 92.
[3] *Yeats and Moore: Correspondence*, pp. 122–4.
[4] *Collected Poems*, p. 124.
[5] *Collected Poems*, p. 212.
[6] *Collected Poems*, p. 444.

tional sort of mind That never looked out of the eye of a saint Or out of a drunkard's eye." [7] It is so completely detached from the life of action that Yeats says more than once that only the dead have true wisdom; or else he regards such true wisdom as the living may enjoy to be something so deep and instinctive that its possessor hardly knows that he possesses it—

> Considering that, all hatred driven hence,
> The soul recovers radical innocence
> And learns at last that it is self-delighting,
> Self-appeasing, self-affrighting,
> And that its own sweet will is Heaven's will. . . .[8]

Perhaps we shall appreciate these scattered "poetic" utterances if we set beside them some comparable passages from a systematic aesthetician. The writings of the late R. G. Collingwood, philosopher and one of the English translators of Croce, will serve our purpose well. Collingwood admired Yeats's poetry, his own position is that of an idealist and symbolist, and like Yeats he was even interested in "magic" and found a place for it in his intellectual scheme. In his *Principles of Art*, he comments upon the artist's concern for knowledge as follows:

> Theoretically, the artist is a person who comes to know himself, to know his own emotion. This is also knowing his world, that is, the sights and sounds and so forth which together make up his total imaginative experience. The two knowledges are to him one knowledge, because these sights and sounds are to him steeped in the emotion with which he contemplates them: they are the language in which that emotion utters itself to his consciousness. His world is his language. What it says to him it says about himself; his imaginative vision of it is his self-knowledge.[9]

Compare with this passage what Yeats wrote in 1900:

> Solitary men in moments of contemplation receive . . . the creative impulse from the lowest of the Nine Hierarchies, and so make and unmake mankind, and even the world itself, for does not "the eye altering alter all"? [1]

And in one of his earliest poems:

[7] *Collected Poems*, p. 236.
[8] *Collected Poems*, p. 187.
[9] *The Principles of Art* (Oxford, 1938), p. 291, by permission of Oxford University Press, Inc.
[1] "The Symbolism of Poetry," *Ideas of Good and Evil*, pp. 246–7.

> . . . words alone are certain good:
> Sing, then, for this is also sooth. . . .
> Dream, dream, for this is also sooth.[2]

Collingwood goes on to say:

> But this knowing of himself [by the artist] is a making of himself. . . . The coming to know his emotions is the coming to dominate them, to assert himself as their master. . . .
>
> Moreover, his knowing of this new world is also the making of the new world which he is coming to know. The world he has come to know is a world consisting of language; a world where everything has the property of expressing emotion. In so far as this world is thus expressive or significant, it is he that has made it so. . . .
>
> The aesthetic experience . . . is a knowing of oneself and of one's world. . . . It is also a making of oneself and of one's world, the self which was psyche being remade in the shape of consciousness, and the world, which was crude sensa, being re-made in the shape of language, or sensa converted into imagery and charged with emotional significance.[3]

Beside this passage from the philosopher can be set any number of passages gleaned from the poet, in which he asserts the creative power of man's imagination. Out of "poet's imaginings," out of the "memories of love," out of "Memories of the words of women,"

> Man makes a superhuman
> Mirror-resembling dream. . . .[4]

> From man's blood-sodden heart are sprung
> Those branches of the night and day
> Where the gaudy moon is hung. . . .[5]

More arrogantly still,

> Death and life were not
> Till man made up the whole,
> Made lock, stock and barrel
> Out of his bitter soul,
> Aye, sun and moon and star, all.[6]

And of man's rage for knowledge of what he is, the poet declares:

[2] *Collected Poems*, p. 8.
[3] *The Principles of Art*, pp. 291–2.
[4] *Collected Poems*, p. 197.
[5] *Collected Poems*, p. 247.
[6] *Collected Poems*, p. 196.

> man's life is thought,
> And he, despite his terror, cannot cease
> Ravening through century after century,
> Ravening, raging, and uprooting that he may come
> Into the desolation of reality. . . .[7]

But it is to a letter written by Yeats not long before his death that one turns for what is perhaps the best statement of Yeats's yearning for the "concrete" knowledge that poetry can give, of his sense of the part that man's own expression plays in the determination of that knowledge, and of his recognition of man's limitation with regard to the apprehension of any knowledge:

> . . . I know for certain that my time will not be long. I have put away everything that can be put away that I may speak what I have to speak, and I find "expression" is a part of "study." In two or three weeks—I am now idle that I may rest after writing much verse—I will begin to write my most fundamental thoughts and the arrangement of thought which I am convinced will complete my studies. I am happy, and I think full of an energy, of an energy I had despaired of. It seems to me that I have found what I wanted. When I try to put all into a phrase I say, "Man can embody truth but he cannot know it." I must embody it in the completion of my life. The abstract is not life and everywhere draws out its contradictions. You can refute Hegel but not the Saint or the Song of Sixpence. . . .[8]

An argument is subject to refutation. The noble life, the song, the poem, are none of them subject to refutation. For the poem, like the life of the saint, does not state a proposition but embodies a meaning.

Earlier in this chapter we had occasion to speak of the danger inherent in any thorough-going symbolic system, particularly as held by an idealist: if, as Emerson put it, "the poet turns the world to glass," how shall he be able to show us anything? Will not all shapes and outlines simply disappear into one blur of diffused radiance? Yet this danger, Yeats, in spite of the extravagance of some of his idealistic pronouncements, successfully avoided. Indeed, we have had few poets in history who have stressed more powerfully the density and hard particularity of the objects of the external world. In celebrating the power of words, as all proponents of symbolist-expressionist doctrines must, Yeats did not lose thereby his grip upon things. Or, if we were willing to suppose with the symbolists that we could get at things only through language, then we would still have to say that in Yeats's poetry, language is not de-

[7] *Collected Poems*, p. 287.

[8] Written to Lady Elizabeth Pelham, 4 January 1939: see *Letters of W. B. Yeats*, p. 922.

natured and diluted into a common gray "wordiness." Words retain the
sharp outlines and individual profiles of "things." Yeats's earliest poetry is
indeed vague and dreamy, everything melting imperceptibly into something else; but the poetry of his maturity is angular, precise, and even
shockingly realistic. Because this is true, the poet is able to exploit real
oppositions. The poetry is filled with tensions between stubbornly recalcitrant contraries. Everywhere Yeats finds the drama of the antinomies.

"Donne," Yeats observes in his *Autobiographies* (1916), "could be as
metaphysical as he pleased, and yet never seemed unhuman and hysteri-
cal as Shelley often does, because he could be as physical as he pleased." [9]
Yeats took the lesson to heart. Even in celebrating his hero Bishop Berkeley, in whose clarifying vision "Everything that is not God" was "consumed with intellectual fire," Yeats remembered the lesson. He gives
Berkeley the proud title "God-appointed" because he

> proved all things a dream,
> That this pragmatical, preposterous pig of a world, its farrow
>   that so solid seem,
> Must vanish on the instant if the mind but change its theme.[1]

But the poetry establishes the solidity of the pig. If the intellectual fire
emanating from the Bishop's mind promises to consume pig, bishop, and
all in a blaze that will leave no ash, the poet is too wise to attempt to portray that holocaust in the poem. In the poem, the pig is as real (and for
the poem as necessary) as the bishop.

One can state Yeats's saving physicality in a somewhat different way:
a danger endemic to symbolist doctrine is that of "angelism," the "sin of
a man who rejects human existence and wants to be like God." Raymond,
in his *From Baudelaire to Surrealism*, says that a Catholic would find such
a sin in Mallarmé's poem, "*Les Fenêtres*," where the speaker, unwilling
to accept his limitations as a man, wishing to extend the domain of his
consciousness forever farther, turns his back upon life as a great frustrating force, and facing the casement windows, now "gilded by the chaste
morning of the infinite," exclaims, "I look upon myself and see an angel." [2]
"Angelism" as a sin incurred by Poe is the subject of Allen Tate's essay
entitled "The Angelic Imagination." Tate admits that "strictly speaking,
an *angelic imagination* is not possible. Angels by definition have un-
mediated knowledge of essences." [3] Man, lacking such direct intuition of
essences, is committed to the imagination, for he can take hold of essences
only through analogy—analogy to the natural world. If in his pride, however, he refuses to look at nature, then Tate says, he is "doomed to see

[9] Quoted from *Autobiographies* (New York, 1927), p. 402.
[1] *Collected Poems*, p. 233.
[2] *From Baudelaire to Surrealism*, p. 24.
[3] *The Forlorn Demon*, p. 70.

nothing." Poe "overleaped and cheated the condition of man. The reach of our imaginative enlargement is perhaps no longer than the ladder of analogy. . . . [Poe having kicked the ladder away] sits silent in darkness." [4]

Yeats never scorned the ladder of analogy, and never forgot the relationship of the "masterful images" of his accomplished poetry to the world of "things," even when those images, "because complete," seem to compel the admission that they "Grew in pure mind." In a stanza that is suggestive of Tate's figure of the ladder (and which Tate may unconsciously be recalling), Yeats writes that the "masterful images" began in

> A mound of refuse or the sweepings of a street,
> Old kettles, old bottles, and a broken can,
> Old iron, old bones, old rags, that raving slut
> Who keeps the till. Now that my ladder's gone,
> I must lie down where all the ladders start,
> In the foul rag-and-bone shop of the heart.[5]

These lines may seem too somberly desperate in their acknowledgement of the limitations of the human being. They collide with Yeats's bolder idealistic assertions. They certainly embarrass any attempt to reduce Yeats's critical position to a neat and tidy consistency. But they point to an important fact about Yeats's poetry: there is a real working dualism—real oppositions as distinguished from merely opposed positions in an abstract dialectic. The poetry can aspire to the reduction of all things to "intellectual fire" for the very good reason that the materials to be consumed are not wraiths of uninflammable moonshine. (Like the French symbolists before him, Yeats had learned, in part from Nietzsche, the uses of tension and conflict in art.) The materials that make up the poems have enough substance to resist, and when ignited, to feed, combustion.

SUPPLEMENT

For the poet, language is a structure of the external world. The speaker is *in a situation* in language; he is invested with words. They are prolongations of his meanings, his pincers, his antennae, his eyeglasses. He maneuvers them from within; he feels them as if they were his body; he is surrounded by a verbal body which he is hardly aware of and which extends his action upon the world. The poet is outside of language. He sees words inside out as if he

[4] *The Forlorn Demon,* p. 78.
[5] *Collected Poems,* p. 336.

did not share the human condition, and as if he were first meeting the word as a barrier as he comes toward men. Instead of first knowing things by their name, it seems that first he has a silent contact with them, since, turning toward that other species of thing which for him is the word, touching them, testing them, palping them, he discovers in them a slight luminosity of their own and particular affinities with the earth, the sky, the water, and all created things.

—Jean-Paul Sartre, *What is Literature?*, trans. Bernard Frechtman (New York, 1949), pp. 13–14. Reprinted by permission of the publishers, The Philosophical Library.

It may be well to remind the reader that in the work from which this passage is quoted, Sartre is arguing for an engaged literature—not at all for art-for-art's-sake.

Whereas the Neoclassical writers had been taught to observe particular natural objects carefully and accurately and then abstract the general from them, the Romantics reverse the process. Thus Blake says: "All goodness resides in minute particulars" but "Natural objects always did and now do weaken, deaden and obliterate imagination in me" and Coleridge writes in a letter:

> The further I ascend from animated Nature (i.e., in the embracements of rocks and hills), from men and cattle, and the common birds of the woods and fields, the greater becomes in me the intensity of the feeling of life. Life seems to me then a universal spirit that neither has nor can have an opposite.

As long as images derived from observation of nature had a utility value for decorating the thoughts of the mind, nature could be simply enjoyed, for Nature was not very important by comparison with human reason. But if there is a mysterious relation between them, if

> La Nature est un temple où de vivants piliers
> Laissent parfois sortir de confuses paroles;
> L'homme y passe à travers des forêts de symbols
> Qui l'observent avec des regards familiers.
>
> Comme de longs échos qui de loin se confondent
> Dans une ténébreuse et profonde unité,
> Vaste comme la nuit et comme la clarté,
> Les parfums, les couleurs et les sons se répondent.

—Baudelaire (*Correspondances*)

then the merely visual perception is not the important act, but the intuitive vision of the meaning of the object, and also Nature becomes a much more formidable creature, charged with all the joys, griefs, hopes and terrors of the human soul, and therefore arousing very mixed feelings of love and hatred.

On the one hand, the poets long to immerse in the sea of Nature, to enjoy its endless mystery and novelty, on the other, they long to come to port in some transcendent eternal and unchanging reality from which the unexpected is excluded. Nature and Passion are powerful, but they are also full of grief. True happiness would have the calm and order of bourgeois routine without its utilitarian ignobility and boredom.

Thus the same Baudelaire who writes:

Why is the spectacle of the sea so infinitely and eternally agreeable?

Because the sea presents at once the idea of immensity and of movement . . . Twelve or fourteen leagues of liquid in movement are enough to convey to man the highest expression of beauty which he can encounter in his transient abode.

(Mon Coeur Mis à Nu)

and identifies human nature with the sea:

> *Vous êtes tous les deux ténébreux et discrets*
> *Homme, nul n'a sondé le fond de tes abîmes,*
> *O mer, nul ne connaît tes richesses intimes*
> *Tant vous êtes jaloux de garder vos secrets!*
> *(L'Homme et la Mer)*

also exclaims:

> *Ah! ne jamais sortir des Nombres et des Êtres*

and likens Beauty to a dream of stone (cp. the stone of Wordsworth's dream):

> *Je hais le mouvement qui déplace les lignes,*
> *Et jamais je ne pleure et jamais je ne ris.*

—From *The Enchafèd Flood* by W. H. Auden, pp. 84–6, copyright 1950 by The Rector and Visitors of the University of Virginia. Reprinted by permission of Random House, Inc.

We have entered a universe that only answers to its own laws, supports itself, internally coheres, and has a new standard of truth. Information is true if it is accurate. A poem is true if it hangs together. Information points to something else. A poem points to nothing but itself. Information is relative. A poem is absolute.

—E. M. Forster, *Anonymity: An Enquiry* (London, 1925), p. 14

Symbolism in one form or another has been used by nearly every great European poet and Baudelaire's definition could without violence be applied to their practice. The use of symbols is simply one aspect of language; the mistake lies in trying to invest them with some sort of transcendental significance instead of regarding them as a technical device of the same order as simile or metaphor. A symbol is nothing more than a vehicle for imaginative experience. What is essential is that it should correspond to the emotion evoked, and a great deal of Mallarmé's obscurity is due to the fact that he tried to use symbols to convey experiences which had not been transmuted into poetry. Baudelaire himself cannot be altogether exonerated from the charge of adding to the confusion and it is unfortunate that his *Correspondances* have been used by critics as a text instead of being treated as a piece of muddled psychology.

This does not mean that Baudelaire and his followers did not extend and develop the use of symbols. They undoubtedly did. Now the term has a variety of meanings. It includes the expanded image in *l'Albatros*, the use of the "sea" as a symbol of liberation in the work of both Baudelaire and Mallarmé and Mallarmé's way of "working" words in the *Swan*. These are straightforward examples. What is more interesting is Baudelaire's use of the *néant* and the *gouffre* to symbolize the void behind the façade of contemporary civilization.

—Martin Turnell, "The Heirs of Baudelaire," *Scrutiny*, XI (Summer, 1943), 295–6, by permission of the author.

I. A. RICHARDS:
A POETICS OF TENSION

§ *Affective criticism and laboratory techniques—other forms of psychological criticism: Freud's view of art as "substitute-gratification"—Max Eastman's concept of art as "pure realization," and Santayana's hedonism—II. Richards' evaluation of various psychological views of art: his rejection of hedonism, of the specifically "aesthetic" emotion, of empathy, etc., in favor of synaesthesis—III. synaesthesis defined as the equilibrium of opposed impulses: discriminated from either vacillation on the one hand or simple resolution on the other—synaesthesis characterized as a readiness to take any action we choose—this harmonization of impulses related to the principles of "exclusion" and "inclusion," parallels with Santayana, irony as a character of this "balanced poise"—IV. Ransom's criticism of Richards' notion that the poise is in our response and not in the structure of the "stimulating object"—Ransom's criticism of other art theories that are based upon some notion of tension and fusion, his criticism of Eliot—the resemblances and differences between the theories of Richards and Eliot—V. Richards' series of cleavages: between two kinds of aesthetic failure, between evaluative and technical criticism, his later modification of these views—VI. Richards' separation of two kinds of "truth," truth of reference and truth of coherence, and his solution of the problem of the relation of science and poetry—VII. other dualistic and quasi-dualistic theories of poetry: Ransom's distinction of structure and texture, his doctrine of the irrelevance of the texture to the structure, this notion as criticized by Yvor Winters—Eastman's parallel doctrine of irrelevance: poetic discourse as "impractical," Ransom's psychologism and his appeal to Freud—VIII. Freud's general contribution to criticism reassessed and compared with that of Richards §*

AFFECTIVE CRITICISM IS, AS WE HAVE SEEN, AS OLD AS CRITICISM ITSELF. It appears, for example, in Plato's view that poetry "feeds and waters the passion" and in Aristotle's doctrine of catharsis. But in the 19th century, the decay of metaphysics and the extraordinary growth of the physical sciences gave a special stress to affective theories. Gustav Fechner, for example, took the problems of aesthetics into the laboratory. Fechner set out to construct an aesthetic theory, not *von oben* but *von unten*. The methods of investigation were to be empirical and inductive. There were to be "controlled" experiments to determine what percentage of human beings find the rectangle a more pleasing shape than the square or what percentage prefer rectangles proportioned to the golden section as compared to rectangles of other proportions. But the future of psychologism in criticism was not to lie with this kind of experimentation, whether carried out by Fechner or by such investigators as Zeising, Wundt, or Helmholtz.[1] The great impact of psychology upon 20th-century criticism was to come through introspective psychologists like Theodor Lipps or through students of abnormal psychology like Sigmund Freud and Carl Jung.

Freud's theory of wit and the comic has been discussed in a preceding chapter. Though Freud did not apply his theory of wit directly to literature, certain parallels clearly suggest themselves. The creation of poetry like the creation of wit draws upon the unconscious; poetry and wit are both in some sense "inspired." Many of the techniques of poetry, like those of wit and dream, are evidently to be subsumed under a principle of condensation. "Rhyme, alliteration, refrain, and other forms of repetition of similar sounding words in poetry" afford us pleasure, Freud writes, for the same reason that "harmless wit" yields us pleasure; and that pleasure, as we have seen in the last chapter, is a pleasure gained through economy of psychic expenditure.[2]

When Freud does address himself directly to the subject, his account of art is disappointingly simple: the pleasure of art is quite baldly reduced to that of a "substitute-gratification." Freud lumps the artist and the neurotic together in their reversion to fantasy. Art represents a vicarious fulfilment of wishes denied to the artist by reality. But the artist differs from the neurotic in several very important ways:[3]

---

[1] Adolf Zeising (*Neue Lehre von den Proportionen des menschlichen Körpers*, 1854) actually preceded Fechner in some of Fechner's characteristic experiments; Fechner's *Vorschule der Ästhetik* was published in 1876. Wilhelm Wundt made researches in sensation and feeling. Herman Helmholtz produced works on *Physiological Optics* (1856–66) and *Tone Sensation* (1862).

[2] "Wit and its Relation to the Unconscious," *The Basic Writings*, pp. 712 ff.

[3] From *A General Introduction to Psychoanalysis* by Sigmund Freud, copyright R 1948 Susie Hoch; copyright 1935 Edward L. Bernays, by permission of Liveright Publishers, New York (Permabook Edition, pp. 384–5).

First of all he understands how to elaborate his day-dreams, so that they lose that personal note which grates upon strange ears and become enjoyable to others; he knows too how to modify them sufficiently so that their origin in prohibited sources is not easily detected. Further, he possesses the mysterious ability to mold his particular material until it expresses the ideas of his phantasy faithfully; and then he knows how to attach to this reflection of his phantasy-life so strong a stream of pleasure that, for a time at least, the repressions are outbalanced and dispelled by it. When he can do all this, he opens out to others the way back to the comfort and consolation of their own unconscious sources of pleasure, and so reaps their gratitude and admiration; then he has won—through his phantasy—what before he could only win in phantasy: honor, power, and the love of women.[4]

Freud makes pleasure a specific means used by the artist ("attach . . . so strong a stream of pleasure") as well as the general end of his art; moreover the closing sentence of the passage indicates that he was willing to lump together, quite indiscriminately, the various kinds of pleasure to which art may conduce, including the quite solid and material pleasures which financial success may bring. But Freud, as he himself more than once pointed out, made no pretense to a total literary theory. He was apparently willing to leave the task of discriminating specific aesthetic pleasure or pleasures to the aesthetician and literary critic.

II

BEFORE examining the special positions argued by typical affective critics, however, it may be well to reiterate that the heavy stress upon affectivity in our time is closely related to our preoccupation with science. Thus, a critic like Max Eastman, who regards poetry as a "pure effort to heighten consciousness," [5] counsels the poet "to yield up to science the task of interpreting experience" and "of finding out what we call truth." [6] Eastman instances a poet like Edna St. Vincent Millay as exhibiting the proper stance with reference to science. She is quite well informed about "complexes" and "ductless glands" and yet does not allow that knowledge to inhibit a burning love poetry. She recaptures the language of the Elizabethans, not to recover their "unscientific" world view, but "only to clothe therein her feelings and her fearless will to have them." [7]

[4] Cf. Melvin Rader, *A Modern Book of Esthetics* (1935), pp. 70–2.
[5] *The Literary Mind* (New York, 1932), p. 170, by permission of the publishers, Charles Scribner's Sons.
[6] *The Literary Mind*, p. 239.
[7] *The Literary Mind*, p. 148.

George Santayana had earlier begun with a similar distinction between the emotionally neutral and abstract world as described by science and the emotions that the objects of that world stir within us. The beauty that we attribute to objects is merely, Santayana argued, in *The Sense of Beauty* (1896), the objectification of our own emotions. Though we insist upon regarding beauty as "the quality of a thing," it is really a pleasure within us, and indeed in our normal, common-sense view of the world, it would never occur to us to include in our concept of reality "emotional or passionate elements." This objectification of our feelings in the "sense of beauty" is a survival of an "animistic and mythological habit of thought," once quite universal, as with primitive man, but now banished from the world of pure science and also from "the intermediate realm of vulgar day," where "mechanical science" has influenced our thinking.[8]

> The scientific idea of a thing is a great abstraction from the mass of perceptions and reactions which that thing produces; the esthetic idea is less abstract, since it retains the emotional reaction, the pleasure of the perception, as an integral part of the conceived thing.[9]

The need for clarification of our ideas in this realm was pressed with a special urgency by I. A. Richards, the critic through whose mediation psychology was to make its greatest impact upon literary criticism. Richards asked his readers to purge their critical thinking of all such animistic habits as cause us to make unwarranted connections between our inner feelings and the nature of objective reality. But his specific contribution lay in his account of the way language bears on the problem. He distinguished "two uses of language."

> A statement may be used for the sake of the *reference*, true or false, which it causes. This is the *scientific* use of language. But it may also be used for the sake of the effects in emotion and attitude. . . . This is the *emotive* use of language.[1]

Science makes statements, but poetry makes what Richards calls "pseudo-statements": their referential value is nil. Poetry makes an emotive use of language. That is its specific character. But, of course, not every instance of such emotive use is aesthetically valuable, and Richards indicts both Eastman and Santayana for not discriminating between emotional intensity and valuable emotional experience. Richards' earliest book, *The Foundations of Aesthetics* (1921), written in collaboration with

---

[8] *The Sense of Beauty* (New York, 1896), p. 47.
[9] *The Sense of Beauty*, p. 48.
[1] *The Principles of Literary Criticism* (London, 1924; 4th impression, 1930), p. 267, by permission of the publishers, Harcourt, Brace and Company, Inc.

C. K. Ogden and James Wood, will provide a convenient scheme for summarizing the more typical affective theories of our century and at the same time setting forth the choices and rejections by which Richards arrived at his own special theory. Richards and his colleagues list sixteen meanings of the term *beauty*, the last seven of which they label "psychological views."

The simplest of these defines the beautiful as anything "which excites Emotions." [2] Such a definition, our authors comment, is much too wide. For "it is not easy to ascribe the highest value to emotions in general, merely as emotions. They may often be experienced without particular significance, and have their place without necessarily being the concern of art." [3]

A somewhat more restricted view specifies pleasurable emotions; that is, "Anything is beautiful—which causes Pleasure." Richards and his colleagues choose to refer this definition of beauty to Santayana, its "most accomplished modern advocate." [4] But the great disadvantage of any pleasure view of art, they point out, "is that it offers us too restricted a vocabulary." [5] Criticism exhausts itself in recording that the art work is indeed pleasing. (Such would indeed seem to be the limitation of a really simple hedonism, but it is a question whether Santayana's hedonism is of this kind. His hedonism, as we shall see, has been subjected to a number of complications and refinements.)

Among the writers who have felt constrained to narrow the field of emotions expressed by art to "some unique emotion," Richards and his colleagues cite Clive Bell and Roger Fry. Bell asserts that the work of art gives us a "peculiar emotion," an "aesthetic emotion" as such. Both Bell and Fry specify that the work of art must possess "significant form." "Significant form," however, can be defined only by the "rather uncommon emotion which it causes." [6]

The difficulty with such a peculiar emotion, Richards points out, is that any attempt to define it is bound to be circular: death-dealing things, for example, do not necessarily have any quality in common except that they all can cause death, and by the same token "beautiful" things need have in common only the fact that they can cause someone to avow that they are beautiful. But if the critic proposes to connect beautiful things by nothing further than the assertion that he feels them all to be beautiful,

[2] *Foundations of Aesthetics*, 2nd ed. (New York, 1925), p. 21. The passage refers to what is essentially Eastman's position though Eastman is not mentioned in this book. For Richards's specific comments upon Eastman, see *The Philosophy of Rhetoric* (New York, 1936), pp. 123–4.

[3] *Foundations*, p. 56, by permission of George Allen and Unwin, Ltd., and the authors.

[4] *Foundations*, p. 52.

[5] *Foundations*, p. 53.

[6] *Foundations*, p. 61.

he has not advanced beyond his original assertion: namely, that they provoke in him that "peculiar" emotion.

Richards and his colleagues mention further attempts to characterize the art emotion. The beautiful has been defined as anything that involves the processes of *empathy*. Empathy (*Einfühlung*) was the name that Theodor Lipps gave to a process which he described as "feeling something, namely, oneself, into the esthetic object." [7] In this activity, "the antithesis between myself and the object disappears, or rather does not yet exist." [8]

Vernon Lee (Violet Paget) independently formulated much the same account as that of Lipps. When we say, for example, that the *mountain rises*, we are transferring from ourselves to the looked-at shape of the mountain the idea of rising and the emotions that accompany it.

> . . . it is this complex mental process, by which we (all unsuspectingly) invest that inert mountain, that bodiless shape, with the stored up and averaged and essential modes of our activity— it is this process whereby we make the mountain *raise itself*, which constitutes what . . . I have called *Empathy*.[9]

But since experiences involving empathy are part of the day-by-day experiences of our lives and are by no means confined to aesthetic experiences, Richards points out that we shall have to limit empathic experiences further if we are to distinguish those which are beautiful. Vernon Lee limits the beautiful to those objects which allow empathic projection *and* in which the projection is pleasurable because the process facilitates our vitality. But such a formula is still too vague to represent any real advance over the usual hedonistic account of art.[1]

This review of various affective theories, though not exhaustive, will suggest some of the reasons for Richards' choice of *synaesthesis* as the one affective theory that seemed to him fit to serve as the foundation of an aesthetic. Even projective theories like empathy apply to so much non-artistic experience that they fail to isolate the specific values of art. The element constant to all experiences that have the characteristic of beauty, concludes Richards, is *synaesthesis*—a harmony and equilibrium of our impulses.

[7] *"Einfühlung, innere Nachahmung, und Organempfindungen," Archiv für die gesamte Psychologie*, Vol. I (1903): quoted from Melvin Rader, *A Modern Book of Esthetics* (1935), p. 302.

[8] Rader, p. 294. Here we are evidently dealing with a psychological version of the metaphysics of Fichte or Schelling—cf. *ante* Chapter 17.

[9] *The Beautiful* (Cambridge, 1913), pp. 65-6.

[1] ". . . the experiences we get from successfully riding a bicycle, which presumably cause pleasure and facilitate our vitality, could clearly be recalled by our projecting similar movements into lines and rhythms, and the resultant state would be neither more nor less aesthetic than the original one, except in virtue of its new origin in recall through projection" (*Foundations*, p. 69).

III

ANY experience must involve the arousal and interplay of various impulses, but in the experience of beauty Richards contends that our impulses are organized in a peculiar way. In this peculiar organization which
constitutes synaesthesis, the rivalry of conflicting impulses is avoided, not
by our suppressing the impulses, but, paradoxically, by our giving them
free rein.

> Not all impulses . . . are naturally harmonious, for conflict is
> possible and common. A complete systematization must take the
> form of such an adjustment as will preserve free play to every
> impulse, with entire avoidance of frustration. In any equilibrium
> of this kind, however momentary, we are experiencing beauty.[2]

Such a conception, indeed, presents its difficulties, for an equilibrium
of conflicting impulses is easily confused with the state of "balance" that
one finds in irresolution—that is, an oscillation between two sets of
opposed impulses in which the mind, like the fabled donkey poised between the equally attractive bales of hay, can only remain suspended in
inaction. Richards and his friends warn us that this is not at all what they
mean by synaesthesis. Synaesthesis is no such oscillation but a harmonization: the competing impulses sustain not two states of mind but one. They
do not split the ego in two, but complete and enrich it. In the experience
of synaesthesis, our "interest is not canalised in one direction,"[3] and
there is a sense of detachment and disinterest. Our lack of commitment to
any particular course of action means in reality that we are, like the poised
athlete, in readiness for any kind of action.

For this special kind of "disinterest," a technical psychological explanation is offered. Our authors say that whereas two perfectly simple
impulses must either oscillate or lock, a "more complex initial conflict"
may discharge itself "through its branch connections." Such a complex
conflict may "solve" itself "in the arousal of the other impulses of the
personality."[4] At any rate, whatever the precise nature of the psychological explanation, Richards and his colleagues are confident that the
sense of disinterest in the aesthetic experience means, paradoxically, that
the maximum number of interests is actually involved, and that the feeling
of "impersonality" that synaesthesis induces means that the "whole of
the personality" has been brought into play. By the equilibrium of synaesthesis Richards evidently would suggest, then, not the lifeless balance

[2] *Foundations*, p. 75.
[3] *Foundations*, p. 78.
[4] *Foundations*, p. 77, note.

of deadlock but the vibrant poise of the completely co-ordinated personality.

There is a second state of mind which we are also warned not to confuse with synaesthesis. Our authors remark that the feeling of "lucidity, self-possession and freedom" [5] that characterizes the experience of synaesthesis may also attach to the state of mind that arises when one is possessed by an intense emotion such as anger or joy. In one of his later poems, W. B. Yeats admirably describes this state of "simple resolution":

> Know that when all words are said
> And a man is fighting mad,
> Something drops from eyes long blind,
> He completes his partial mind,
> For an instant stands at ease
> Laughs aloud, his heart at peace. . . . [6]

But since this state of mind gains its "harmony" by having no warring impulses to harmonize, its resemblance to synaesthesis is illusory. Richards and his colleagues offer a test by which it can be distinguished from synaesthesis: synaesthesis "refreshes and never exhausts." [7]

In their theorizing about synaesthesis it is evident that Richards and his colleagues have moved beyond any simple pleasure principle. A few years after the publication of *The Foundations of Aesthetics*, Richards asserted that the pleasure that a competent reader feels is "no more the aim of the activity in the course of which it arises, than, for example, the noise made by a motor-cycle—useful though it is as an indication of the way the machine is running—is the reason in the normal case for its having been started." [8] The main value of literature was to be found in its *after*-effects upon the mind.

One more observation on synaesthesis is pertinent here: though Richards deplored Kant's having created a "phantom problem of the aesthetic mode" through his attempt to define the "judgment of taste" as a judgment "concerning pleasure which is disinterested, universal, unintellectual, and not to be confused with the pleasures of sense or of ordinary emotions," [9] Richards' own doctrine of synaesthesis courts, if it does not actually demand, the same series of adjectives. True, the term synaesthesis has a psychological orientation, not a metaphysical, but synaesthesis is certainly disinterested, and this aspect comes out most plainly when Richards tries to distinguish it from the false equilibrium of irresolution or from that of full emotional commitment.

[5] *Foundations*, p. 77, note.
[6] "Under Ben Bulben," *Collected Poems*, p. 342.
[7] *Foundations*, p. 77, note.
[8] *The Principles of Literary Criticism*, p. 97.
[9] *Principles*, p. 11.

Attitudes, as Richards defines them, are incipient or "imaginal" actions. In synaesthesis, these incipient actions are so ordered and so balanced that the maximum number of them are involved and the minimum number are blocked—but they remain incipient; no action occurs. Synaesthesis is defined as our readiness "to take any direction we choose," but in synaesthesis evidently we do *not* choose. Presumably if we did choose and acted upon that choice, that very fact would indicate that the supposed state of synaesthesis was illusory, not real.

> When works of art produce such action, or conditions which lead to action, they have either not completely fulfilled their function or would in the view of equilibrium here being considered be called not "beautiful" but "stimulative." [1]

Synaesthesis, says Richards, is the ground-plan of all aesthetic experience. Many people obviously have had this experience in the past, but they have confused the experience with a revelation of some sort. The arts, he admits, do seem "to lift away the burden of existence" and we do seem "to be looking into the heart of things," but this state of euphoria, he insists, has actually nothing to do with truth. For truth belongs to science, which represents a "different [principle] upon which impulses may be organized," [2] and which has a very different function from that of the arts.

In his *Principles of Literary Criticism*, Richards never makes use of the key term "synaesthesis." Instead the terms "inclusion" and "synthesis" are used to name the character of the greatest and most valuable poetry. *Synthesis* [3] is, of course, fair coin for synaesthesis, and the key passage in which Richards defines synthesis bears a remarkable resemblance to one of the paragraphs in Santayana's *The Sense of Beauty*. It will be useful to set the two passages side by side.

In a section of his book that he significantly entitled "The Liberation of the Self," Santayana had written:

> Now, it is the essential privilege of beauty to so *synthesize* and bring to a focus the various *impulses of the self*, so to suspend them to a single image, that a great peace falls upon that

---

[1] *Foundations*, p. 77. Stephen Dedalus in *A Portrait of the Artist as a Young Man* (New York, 1916), p. 240, makes a comparable point in denying that "kinesthetic" art (i.e., art that provokes us to a particular action) is truly art at all.

[2] *Principles*, p. 265. Compare with this Santayana's assertion that a great work of art leaves us with the sense that "however tangled the net may be in which we feel ourselves caught, there is liberation beyond, and an ultimate peace" (*The Sense of Beauty*, p. 239).

[3] The term may show the influence of Coleridge's description of the imagination as a "synthetic and magical" power. In any case the adaptation of Coleridge's account of the imagination is frankly acknowledged. See the chapter on "The Imagination," in *Principles*, pp. 239-53.

perturbed kingdom. In the experience of these momentary harmonies we have the basis of the enjoyment of beauty, and of all its mystical meanings. But there are always two methods of securing harmony: one is to unify all the given elements, and another is to reject and expunge all the elements that refuse to be unified. Unity by *inclusion* gives us the beautiful; unity by *exclusion*, opposition, and isolation gives us the sublime. Both are pleasures: but the pleasure of the one is warm, passive, and pervasive; that of the other cold, imperious, and keen. The one identifies us with the world, the other raises us above it.[4]

And now for the passage from Richards:

There are two ways in which *impulses* may be organized; by *exclusion* and by *inclusion*, by *synthesis* and by *elimination*. Although every coherent state of mind depends upon both, it is permissible to contrast experiences which win stability and order through a narrowing of the response with those which widen it. A very great deal of poetry and art is content with the full, ordered development of comparatively special and limited experiences, with a definite emotion, for example, Sorrow, Joy, Pride, or a definite attitude, Love, Indignation, Admiration, Hope, or with a specific mood, Melancholy, Optimism or Longing. And such art has its own value and its place in human affairs. No one will quarrel with "Break, break, break," or with the *Coronach* or with *Rose Aylmer* or with *Love's Philosophy*, although clearly they are limited and *exclusive*. But they are not the greatest kind of poetry; we do not expect from them what we find in the *Ode to the Nightingale*, in *Proud Maisie*, in *Sir Patrick Spens*, in *The Definition of Love* or in the *Nocturnall upon S. Lucie's Day*.[5]

The two kinds of poetry are not, for Richards as they evidently are for Santayana, on the same level. Richards displays no interest in distinguishing the beautiful from the sublime; his interest is rather to distinguish a richer, deeper, and more tough-minded poetry from a more "limited and exclusive" kind of poetry. Furthermore, Santayana's harmonization of the impulses of the self by rejection and expungement of all "the elements that refuse to be unified" could not, in Richards' terms, qualify as a harmonization at all; instead it rather suggests Richards' state of "simple resolution." [6] But the resemblances between the passages are striking enough.

---

[4] *The Sense of Beauty*, pp. 235–6. The italics are ours.
[5] *Principles*, pp. 249–50. The italics are ours.
[6] Cf. *ante* p. 617.

Richards proceeds to give a psychological account of the peculiar kind of stability of this second kind of poetry (the poetry of synthesis) and to use the presence of irony as a kind of touchstone for such poetry.

> The difference comes out clearly if we consider how comparatively unstable poems of the first kind are. They will not bear an ironical contemplation. We have only to read *The War Song of Dinas Vawr* in close conjunction with the *Coronach*, or to remember that unfortunate phrase "Those lips, O slippery blisses!" from *Endymion*, while reading *Love's Philosophy*, to notice this. Irony in this sense consists in the bringing in of the opposite, the complementary impulses; that is why poetry which is exposed to it is not of the highest order, and why irony itself is so constantly a characteristic of poetry which is.
>
> These opposed impulses from the resolution of which such experiences spring cannot usually be analysed. When, as is most often the case, they are aroused through formal means, it is evidently impossible to do so.[7]

I V

RICHARDS' confession of the difficulty—not to mention the impossibility—of analyzing the "opposed impulses" throws an interesting light upon the psychological machinery which he has used to account for the effects of this "poetry of inclusion." When we get ready to use the machinery, it evaporates. The poem is before us and is susceptible to analysis, but the psychological goings-on turn out to be below the surface and out of sight. This curious state of affairs is a main object of attack in John Crowe Ransom's criticism of Richards.[8]

Ransom points out that Richards' account of the relevant poetic structure is not only a mere hypothesis, but that this particular hypothesis, if accepted, would destroy criticism. For if the "balanced poise" is, as Richards says it is, in our "response" and not at all "in the structure of the stimulating object," then the labor of criticism in "analysing the poetic object" is vain. Vain also was the labor of the poet in putting the poem into a particular "shape." On Richards' showing, the

> poem is not needed in that shape; and what the proper shape would be we are not likely to know. I for one feel that I cannot know even what it is in the poem which constitutes its stimulus.[9]

[7] *Principles*, pp. 250–1.
[8] *The New Criticism* (New York, 1941). Copyright 1941 by New Directions and reprinted by permission of the publisher.
[9] *The New Criticism*, p. 32.

It is indeed questionable whether Richards actually succeeds in cutting his desiderated "balanced poise" cleanly off from all relation to "the structure of the stimulating object." Though Richards is careful to point out that such balanced poise is "not peculiar to Tragedy," significantly it is in tragedy, the form of literature in which conflicts and tensions are obvious structural features, that he finds his clearest illustrations. Nietzsche too had found that in tragedy "contrasts are overcome" and "oppositions" are "conquered," [1] and his insistence that the greatest artists are those "who make harmony ring out of every discord" strengthens the notion that Nietzsche anticipated Richards' conception of a "poetry of inclusion," though Nietzsche gave his "inclusion" a clear structural reference. For the discords are in the composition, and the larger harmony in which these momentary disharmonies are finally resolved is obviously to be referred to the total structure. Not the least important of the "musical" characteristics that Nietzsche attributes to tragedy is this conception of a richer and more intricate harmony, achieved by the resolution of apparent discords, as opposed to the "thinner" harmony of less ambitious works.

Richards himself, when he suggests that one may test the stability of such poetry by exposing it to ironical contemplation, seems to regard the differentia of "inclusive" poetry as structural. For, though the reader supplies the ironical squint, the subsequent collapse in the defective poem is a structural collapse.

Richards' insistence that irony is "so constantly" a characteristic of the highest order of poetry reminds one of Solger's claim that irony is "coextensive with art." [2] It also calls for comparison with T. S. Eliot's notion that the function of wit is to provide an "internal equilibrium" for the poem in which it occurs. If Richards' irony is not made to provide the stability of the experience, it is at least a symptom of the stability. Eliot's notion about wit seems to be the complement of Nietzsche's conception of a "harmony" that is rung "out of every discord." For in saying that witty poetry implies "in the expression of every experience" the recognition of the fact that "other kinds of experience . . . are possible," [3] Eliot is saying that wit calls to our attention the potentially discordant; that is, the unity of the witty poem is not a unity easily won by glossing over the discordant elements of human experience.

Such restatements of Richards' conceptions of "inclusion" and of "tension" would, however, scarcely appease a critic like Ransom. He impartially condemns both Richards and Eliot for talking about the reconciliation of what he insists are in fact irreconcilables:

---

[1] Cf. *ante* Chapter 25.
[2] Cf. *ante* Chapter 17.
[3] "Andrew Marvell" (1921), *Selected Essays, 1917–32* (New York, 1932), p. 262, by permission of the publishers, Harcourt, Brace and Company, Inc.

My belief is that opposites can never be said to be resolved or reconciled merely because they have been got into the same poem, or got into the same complex of affective experience to create there a kind of "tension"; that if there is a resolution at all it must be a logical resolution; that when there is no resolution we have a poem without a structural unity; and this is precisely the intention of irony, which therefore is something very special, and ought to be occasional.[4]

This statement is of a piece with Ransom's criticism of Eliot's conception of metaphysical poetry: "The aspiration here is for some sort of fusion of two experiences that ordinarily repel one another," and Ransom warns us not to become "the fools of the shining but impractical ideal of 'unity' or of 'fusion.' "[5] Thus, on the special and limited nature of irony, he firmly takes his stand beside Irving Babbitt and the new Humanists.[6] Far from being a "a constant characteristic" of good poetry, irony signifies for Ransom a failure to unify. "In a pointed form of irony," he writes, "the oppositions produce an indecisive effect, just as in tragedy there is an opposition with a negative effect."[7] Richards had been careful to distinguish the poetry of "harmonious equilibrium" (of which irony is "so constantly a characteristic") from mere "irresolution." Ransom's argument is that ironic poetry can represent only irresolution: that is, the oppositions "produce an indecisive effect."

Ransom is no less firm in dismissing Eliot. Though he has called Eliot "The Historical Critic," he says that Eliot's theory of poetry is "equivalent to some version of Richards' psychologistic theory."[8] There is some psychologism in Eliot; and there are certain conceptions that he shares with Richards. One remembers Eliot's statement that for the poet the noise of the typewriter and the smell of cooking, reading Spinoza or falling in love—experiences which for the ordinary man have nothing to do with one another—"are always forming new wholes."[9] And one places beside it this passage from Richards:

The wheeling of the pigeons in Trafalgar Square may seem to have no relation to the colour of the water in the basins, to the tones of a speaker's voice or to the drift of his remarks. A narrow field of stimulation is all that we can manage, and we overlook the rest. But the artist does not, and when he needs it, he has it at his disposal.[1]

Unless one recognizes the amount of agreement between Richards and Eliot, one will find it difficult to understand the relative ease with

---

[4] *The New Criticism*, p. 95.
[5] *The New Criticism*, p. 183.
[6] Cf. *ante* Chapter 20.
[7] *The New Criticism*, p. 96.

[8] *The New Criticism*, p. 152.
[9] *Selected Essays*, p. 247.
[1] *Principles*, p. 185.

which Richards' influence upon criticism has merged with that of Eliot, and one will find it difficult to account for some of the later developments in Richards' own criticism—see the next chapter. Nevertheless, the differences between Eliot and Richards are very important, and nowhere more so than in their treatment of thought and feeling. In spite of some waverings and confusions encouraged by an occasional use of affective terminology, Eliot stands by his bold assertion that a poem is a *fusion* of thought and feeling. Richards, on the other hand, from the first has endeavored to maintain a careful distinction between the emotional state produced in the reader (the balance of impulses or state of synaesthesis) and the means used to produce this emotional state.

V

RICHARDS' endeavors to distinguish between the emotional effect produced in the reader and the means by which it is produced give rise in his criticism to a whole series of related separations: between value (content) and communication (as conditioned by form); between the "badness" that results from the communication to the reader of a worthless experience and the "badness" that results from the faulty communication of what was presumably a valuable experience; between technical criticism (which Richards defines as dealing with the make-up of the stimulating object) and evaluative criticism (which deals with the value of the experience communicated). An exploration of some of these topics supplies striking instances of the difficulties with which an affective theory burdens a critic who has genuine literary sensitivity and whose deepest allegiance is evidently to poetry rather than to the psychology of reader response.

In *The Principles of Literary Criticism*, Richards illustrated the two kinds of "badness" by using a tiny Imagist poem by H. D. and a rather glib love sonnet by Ella Wheeler Wilcox. H. D.'s scrap of Imagist verse was said to fail because it did not sufficiently communicate the valuable experience that Richards conceded that the poet might have had. The Wilcox sonnet was said to fail because the experience that it communicated—all too clearly—had no value. The sonnet was dominated by an elaborate analogy between Summer and Love and Friendship and Autumn. And Richards pointed out that those readers "who have adequate impulses as regards *any* of the four main systems [of impulses] involved" in this poem are not "appeased" by the poem. "Only for those who make certain conventional, stereotyped maladjustments instead, does the magic work." [2]

Yet it might have been simpler to deal with adequacy of imagery

[2] *Principles*, p. 202.

rather than with adequacy of "impulses." A critic of the poem could simply have said that any reader who attended to the imagery of the poem would find it absurdly confused. If the reader knew anything about autumn, he would know that an autumn day with a "touch of frost . . . in the air" tends to be crisp and sparkling, not hazy with the mellowness of St. Martin's summer. If he knew anything about love, he would hardly be satisfied with the metamorphosis of Love into "large-eyed Friendship" through a kind of fadeout-dissolve of one obviously trumped up allegorical figure into another.[3]

In spite of a certain superficial plausibility, the distinction between defectiveness of communication and the "worthlessness" of the experience communicated cannot in fact be maintained. We can only speculate about values that are not revealed in the poem itself. That there might have been a valuable experience behind H. D.'s "The Pool" is, and must remain, pure hypothesis. On the other hand, one *could* argue that the alleged clarity of the Wilcox sonnet is actually an illusion since what is inextricably confused cannot have "clarity." The "badness" of this poem consists in a pretension to coherence that is not made good; the analogy between Summer-Autumn and Love-Friendship is asserted but never realized dramatically. The essential act in condemning the poem consists therefore in exposing the basic *incoherence*.[4]

The motive for Richards' various "separations" is, of course, rooted in his desire to discuss poetry in terms of stimulus and response. This fact comes out most clearly in his attempt to distinguish "technical" remarks from "critical" (i.e., evaluative) remarks. He regards the distinction as important because, as he writes, the trick of mistaking "the means for the end, the technique for the value, is in fact the most successful of the snares which waylay the critic." [5] Yet on the same page Richards indi-

---

[3] As a measure of the coherence proper to a genuine poem, one might contrast with the Wilcox sonnet, Keats's "To Autumn," in which the "completeness" of an autumn day is made to subsist *with* a note of melancholy, or with Shakespeare's "How Like a Winter hath mine Absence Been," where there is a responsible alignment of the vicissitudes of love with seasonal change, or with Edna St. Vincent Millay's "The Cameo," which gives a *coherent* rendering of something like the specific theme of the Wilcox poem.

[4] Richards' very proper concern for the pernicious social effects of bad art seems to be as well served by this account as by his own: the reader who asks only that certain of his stock responses be titillated, who is content with certain "conventional, stereotyped maladjustments," is a reader who is oblivious to the kind of incoherence that characterizes the Wilcox sonnet. Such a reader will be baffled by the incoherence of H. D.'s "The Pool," but the incoherence of the Wilcox sonnet, because it mirrors his own distortions and oversimplifications, will probably be seen in quite other terms: as a clear and exalted vision of life. His inability to make sense of a poem—any poem—may well be coterminous with his inability to make sense of his own experiences; but with this latter problem we move from the field of criticism proper into a consideration of education, ethics, and the analysis of popular culture.

[5] *Principles*, p. 24.

cates his belief in an *organic* theory of poetry. There are problems: in what sense can a part of a poem be regarded as the means to an end? There is a sense, to be sure, in which all the parts of an organic whole may be regarded as reciprocally means and ends. The head is a "means" to the functioning of the heart and the heart is a "means" to the functioning of the head. But within the poem, it is not clear how there can be ends and means; the correct relation would seem to be that of parts to a whole.

By 1934 Richards himself had become suspicious of this distinction. In *Coleridge on Imagination* he wrote:

> It is with deceptive ease . . . that the inquiry [into poetic mean-ing] divides into questions about the *what* and the *how*. Or into questions about the *methods* a poet uses and the *feats* he thereby achieves. Or into questions about his *means* and his *ends*. Or about the *way* of his work and the *whither*.[6]

Though he regards the division as for some purposes "necessary" and for other purposes "convenient," he warns that it tends to distort the whole meaning of the work by abstracting "some component to be treated as its *whither* and to be set over against the rest as its *way*." [7]

VI

THE best-known and the most radical of Richards' separations is, of course, that which he made between the emotive and the referential "uses of language." [8] Richards denied to poetry any truth of reference and argued that the "truth" as applied to a work of art could mean only the "internal necessity" or "rightness" of the work of art: that is, whereas scientific truth has to do with correspondence to the nature of reality, artistic "truth" is a matter of inner coherence.

> The "Truth" of *Robinson Crusoe* is the acceptability of the things we are told, their acceptability in the interests of the ef-fects of the narrative, not their correspondence with any actual facts involving Alexander Selkirk or another. Similarly the falsity of happy endings to *Lear* or to *Don Quixote*, is their failure to be acceptable to those who have fully responded to the rest of the work. It is in this sense that "Truth" is equivalent to "internal necessity" or rightness. That is "true" or "internally necessary" which completes or accords with the rest of the experience. . . .[9]

[6] *Coleridge on Imagination* (New York, 1934), p. 198.
[7] *Coleridge on Imagination*, p. 199.
[8] *Principles*, pp. 261 ff.
[9] *Principles*, p. 269.

The "truth" of *Robinson Crusoe* or of *King Lear*, in short, has nothing to do with objective truth. The "effects of the narrative" which determine the "acceptability" of the "things we are told" are psychological effects. The happy ending supplied by Nahum Tate for *Lear* is "false" because it is at odds with the rest of the play; the play as a whole is "true" only in virtue of giving rise to the proper psychological effects, in helping us, that is, to "order our attitudes to one another and to the world." That is why "we need no beliefs" in order to read *King Lear*. Indeed, Richards goes much further and writes that "we must have [no beliefs], if we are to read *King Lear*"; [1] for beliefs, with their claims to objective truth, would disturb the self-contained coherence, the "internal necessity" which is the only "truth" that Richards will allow to the play.

Such was Richards' solution to the conflict of science and poetry: it is as drastic as it is neat. There could be no conflict for the good reason that there was no common ground upon which science and poetry (properly understood) could meet. They were held to utilize radically different aspects of language.

There are, to be sure, certain things that Robinson Crusoe cannot do because they would violate our sense of his character as built up in the earlier pages. The happy ending that Nahum Tate clapped onto *King Lear* simply does not accord with the earlier parts of the play. And yet more would seem to be operative in forming our rejections than what is contained in previous chapters or previous scenes of a specific novel or play: we appeal to, and are influenced by, our whole previous acquaintance with human beings. When we decide that Crusoe cannot do this or that, we are relying upon our notions of human psychology—very general notions perhaps—but notions that refer to a world outside the formmal limits of the art work itself. Even the world of Aesop's fables or of the fairy tale or of "science fiction" has not cut all connections with a world of our experience.

There would have been little debate if Richards' severance of poetry from all "reference" had amounted to no more than saying that the reader of Shakespeare did not need to worry about the inaccurate Scottish history in *Macbeth*, or that the reader of Coleridge had no cause to be disturbed by such scientifically impossible descriptions as that which places a star within the nether tip of the moon. On this level, the severance between poetry and history and poetry and science had been made by the ancients. But Richards, going further, seemed to be arguing that poetry was literally nonsense, though, for reasons bound up with his psychologistic theory, a peculiarly valuable kind of nonsense. It was difficult for critics like Allen Tate and John Crowe Ransom to see how one

---

[1] *Science and Poetry* (London, 1925; 2nd ed. 1926), p. 67.

could deny all truth to poetry, and yet at the same time argue in the fashion of Matthew Arnold that "poetry could save us."

VII

YET the temptation to make such severances and separations as Richards makes is stubbornly persistent in modern criticism. A striking instance occurs in the work of Ransom himself. Earlier in this chapter we have referred to Ransom's denial that there can be any "fusion" of "experiences that ordinarily repel one another" [2]—as that notion is held either by Richards or by Eliot.

Ransom drew a crucial distinction between the *texture* and the *structure* of a poem. The texture of a poem is constituted of its rich local values, the quality of things in their "thinginess." The structure is the "argument" of the poem. It gives the poem such shape as it has; it regulates the assemblage of sensory data, providing order and direction. Science has, properly speaking, no texture; it is content with pure structure and exhibits no rich particularity. A poem, on the other hand, has a texture *and* a structure. Though the texture is strictly irrelevant to the logic of the poem, yet it does after all affect the shape of the poem; it does so by *impeding* the argument. The very irrelevance of the texture is thus important. Because of its presence we get, not a streamlined argument, but an argument that has been complicated through having been hindered, and diverted, and having thus had its very success threatened. In the end we have our logic, but only after a lively reminder of the aspects of reality with which logic cannot cope.

A main source of Ransom's dissatisfaction with Richards' theory was its affectivity, and Ransom stressed the cognitive element in his own theory. But his would have to be described as a kind of "bifocal" cognitive theory: poetry gives us through its structure and texture, respectively, knowledge of universals and knowledge of particulars. Poetry is the complement of science which, restricting itself to universals, can mirror only a world of abstractions. Ransom hands over the realm of the universals to science, and in effect retains for poetry no more than an apprehension of particulars.

There are some problems here: are the two knowledges on the same level? Can they be kept from fusing? Or do they function intermittently, and if they do, is there any reason why they should occur in connection with each other? Ransom has rejected any notion of the union of the levels as an impossible oil-and-water mixture: neither component will dissolve into the other. What he proposes would have to be described as

[2] See *ante* p. 622.

a sort of emulsion—the little droplets of local "knowledge" suspended in, and diffused through, the other "knowledge" of universals.

> [The imagination] presents to the reflective mind the particularity of nature; whereas there is quite another organ, working by a technique of universals, which gives us science.[3]

On a strict interpretation, Ransom would seem to confine the imagination to such matters as the reflection of odors, tactile impressions, tone, colors, and other sensations, leaving out larger patterns such as those woven by the "moral" imagination.

The doctrine of the irrelevance of the texture poses another formidable problem. Yvor Winters has asked why, in view of the irrelevance of all texture, one "irrelevant" detail should be preferred to another.[4] Would not one texture do for any given poem as well as another? Marvell's "To his Coy Mistress" is, in terms of Ransom's thesis, the fine poem that it is because the lover's argument runs such an obstacle race before it can come to its conclusion. But Winters conjectures that in terms of such a theory as this, Crashaw's poem "The Weeper" would prove to be a finer poem still, its argument being even more besettingly impeded by the irrelevance of its texture.[5] Irrelevance, he urges, is irrelevance. To argue that some forms of irrelevant detail are more suitable to the poem than other forms of irrelevant detail would be to admit that *irrelevant* was not, after all, the proper term.

Ransom's theory that "impeding" the argument gives poetry's special knowledge of particularity finds a parallel in Eastman's notion that the hyperconsciousness achieved in poetry comes through "obstruction." As was noted earlier in this chapter, Eastman assumes that the function of art is to heighten consciousness. The artist does this by stimulating a response and yet obstructing it. To invoke an analogy: putting on a coat is a largely automatic action; we need not be conscious, and usually are not fully conscious, of what we are doing. But if the lining of the sleeve is torn and the action of thrusting the arm through it proves unexpectedly difficult, we become intensely aware of what we are doing. And so:

> [Art] must arouse a reaction and yet impede it, creating a tension in our nervous systems sufficient and rightly calculated to make us completely aware that we are living something—and no matter what.[6]

[3] *The World's Body* (New York, 1938), p. 156.

[4] *The Anatomy of Nonsense* (1943), included in and reprinted from *In Defense of Reason* by Yvor Winters by permission of the publisher, Alan Swallow. Copyright 1937 and 1947 by Yvor Winters, pp. 537–9.

[5] *In Defense of Reason*, pp. 538–9.

[6] *The Literary Mind*, p. 205. Richards has made considerable play with the careless abandon of Eastman's "and no matter what." He points out that if one ties a man down and then approaches him brandishing a red-hot poker—stimulating and yet

To pursue this parallelism between Ransom and Eastman: Eastman asserts that the "impractical identifications" made by metaphor and the "luxury of surprising and rich adjectives and figurative expressions . . . do not help to explain like maps or illustrations, but rather obscure the meaning of the sentence in which they occur."[7] Ransom has been careful to make his details of texture "impractical," and to show that, from the point of view of prose discourse, they are a "luxury"; yet he insists that it is just because they are impractical, that they force us to take in the rich particularity of experience. But Eastman's theory of poetry is frankly affective and psychologistic.[8]

On closer examination, the function that Ransom accords to "statement" or "structure" in poetry resembles very closely that accorded to statement in poetry by Richards. Richards makes it plain that referential statements in poetry are not important in themselves, though they frequently occur and indeed usually must occur "*as conditions* for, or *stages in*, the ensuing development of attitudes"—the elements that *are* important.[9] Likewise Ransom stresses the fact that a poem cannot do without structure (i.e., a determining argument): the human mind is so constituted that it has to have an argument to follow. But the arguments of most poems, Ransom concedes to be, in themselves, usually dull affairs;[1] we follow the pathway of the argument really for the sake of the details that border the path. We are tempted to pick a daisy or to investigate an oddly shaped bush (the elements of "texture"). We keep returning to the path and eventually arrive at our elected destination, but we arrive having seen the country—as we would not have had we kept to the strait and narrow path of science. The incidental details give the journey its value.[2] For Ransom as well as for Richards, the statements made in the poem are important only in so far as they are a means to something else.

---

impeding a response—one will produce a spectacularly heightened consciousness but scarcely anything that can be called art. See *The Philosophy of Rhetoric* (New York, 1936), p. 124.

[7] *The Literary Mind*, p. 183.

[8] Eastman's praise for Richards amounts to commendation for his serious effort to apply psychology to criticism. Eastman has little patience with the actual results. He finds in Richards' "harmonious equilibrium of impulses" no "foundation of aesthetics." If perchance we do find in a work of art a "reconciliation of our conflicting impulses," then that particular art "besides being art . . . is for us a kind of medicine" (*The Literary Mind*, p. 205). But most art is not, and no art need be, medicinal. In general Eastman deplores Richards' attempt to regard the scientific (the referential) apart from the emotive. A scientific interpretation of an event (e.g., that the snake in the path is not a garter snake but a copperhead) can evoke as much emotion and make the percipient jump as quickly as a merely "emotive" interpretation—besides being a better basis for proper action (*The Literary Mind*, p. 302).

[9] *Principles of Literary Criticism*, p. 267.

[1] The paraphrase of a poem, Ransom writes, "is a fair version of the logical structure," and since the paraphrase of even a fine poem usually reveals an undistinguished and commonplace argument, he concludes that the structure is not the valuable element of the poem.

[2] *The New Criticism*, p. 73, and pp. 184-5.

Ransom's justification of poetic structure, no less than Richards', rests upon an appeal to psychology: that is, human beings demand at least an apparent argument; we will not swallow our local detail neat. Ransom remarks that "it is hard to say what poetry intends by its odd structure," and the makeup of poetry, as he has described it, *is* odd— so odd that one must despair of accounting for it in terms of any entelechy of its own. Only the cravings of the human psyche can account for it, and Ransom, in a later phase of his theory,[3] came to seek for the explanation in Freudian psychology. The conscious and reasonable *ego* flourishes upon neat and tidy orderliness, but the unconscious *id* requires the concrete and unpredictable particulars for its sustenance. Poetry thus ministers to the health of the mind, and Ransom's later position tends to approximate in some features the earlier position of Richards. This fact, taken together with the counter-fact that Richards, in *his* own later criticism, has moved toward a cognitive position, is eloquent testimony to the difficulties inherent in any critical theory which begins by slicing apart value and knowledge—whether it be Richards' cutting the emotive use of language free from the referential or Ransom's cutting the valuable illogical "texture" free from logical "structure." The critic may indeed make refinements that push his theory nearer to a cognitive view, but in so far as the value of the poem is something that cannot be figured forth in the poetic meaning before us, psychology will have to be called in, either at the beginning or at the end, to justify the irrational elements in which the value has been made to reside.

Ransom's appeal to Freud is, however, somewhat startling in view of the embarrassing simplicity of Freud's own theory of literature as offering a kind of surrogate gratification, a theory touched upon briefly earlier in this chapter.[4] But it ought to be observed that Freud's concept of the mind and of its workings has exerted a profound influence, even upon critics who are quite willing to dismiss Freud's specific literary theory as inadequate. Lionel Trilling, for example, who admits that Freud has said "many clumsy and misleading things about art," and remarks that Freud "eventually . . . speaks of art" with "what we must indeed call contempt,"[5] nevertheless has urged us not to underestimate the value of Freud's contribution to literary criticism.

VIII

THERE is a certain propriety in ending this chapter as we began it with some observations upon Freud, the more so since those made in the open-

[3] See in particular two articles in *The Kenyon Review*, IX (Summer and Autumn, 1947), Nos. 3 and 4.
[4] See *ante* p. 611.
[5] *The Liberal Imagination*, p. 42.

ing pages could scarcely do justice to his influence. We owe to Freud a whole new psychological vocabulary—the *Id*, the *Ego*, the *Super-ego*, *transference*, and *repression* are only a few of its terms—a vocabulary which reflects a new conception of the psyche and its functioning. In elucidating the symbolic content of dreams and the way in which the "dream-work" is performed—through *condensation*, *substitution*, and *displacement*—and in calling attention to typical *motifs* (like the Oedipus Complex) which recur in literature, Freud has enlarged our notions of the richness and complexity to which a literary symbol may attain. In his concept of the *overdetermination* or multiple relevance of accurately used language, Freud has paralleled such more specifically literary concepts of ambiguous verbal riches as those which we shall consider in succeeding chapters. Trilling's summary of Freud's accomplishment on this level is probably not overstated:

> In the eighteenth century Vico spoke of the metaphorical, imagistic language of the early stages of culture; it was left to Freud to discover how, in a scientific age, we still feel and think in figurative formations, and to create, what psychoanalysis is, a science of tropes, of metaphor and its variants, synechdoche and metonymy.[6]

The value of the tools with which Freud has supplied the literary critic ought indeed to be acknowledged, even though the tools are at the mercy of the tool-users, and they in turn are at the mercy of whatever literary theory they may hold. A new "science of tropes" does not necessarily provide a new theory of literature. Suffice it to say that up to this time most Freudian critical studies have devoted themselves to psychoanalyses of the artist[7] while making very questionable assumptions about the nature of his accomplished work, or else they have occupied themselves with the effect of the work upon the reader and have thus tended to move off into studies in reader psychology.

The most fruitful and intensive application to literature of something like a new "science of tropes" has in fact come out of the influence of Richards rather than that of Freud, and this fact itself serves to point a difference between Richards' affectivism and Freud's. (That some of the most brilliant "Freudian" critical studies have been written by critics like William Empson, who are even more deeply indebted to Richards,

---

[6] *The Liberal Imagination*, p. 53.

[7] See, for example, Ernest Jones, *Hamlet and Oedipus* (London, 1911), in which he attempts to probe into "the deeper working of Shakespeare's mind." Trilling's criticism of Jones's assumption is to be found in *The Liberal Imagination*, pp. 48–51. See also Daniel E. Schneider, *The Psycho-Analyst and the Artist*, (New York, 1950); and Ernest Kris, *Psychoanalytic Exploration in Art*, (New York, 1952). Dr. Kris makes the comment (p. 286) that "Literary critics seem of late weary of the intrusion of psychoanalysis. However politely, they assert—and rightly so—their independence."

tends to confirm this point.) As Susanne Langer has put it: to make all art a natural self-expressive function like dream and "make-believe" tends to put good art and bad art on a par. "One does not say of a sleeper that he dreams clumsily, nor of a neurotic that his symptoms are carelessly strung together; but a poem may certainly be charged with ineptitude or carelessness."[8] Richards, on the other hand, has from the beginning focused attention upon the problem of discriminating good art from bad and he has to a remarkable degree, sometimes one feels in spite of his own more extravagant theories, stressed the organic structure of the work itself.

SUPPLEMENT

Selection will be sure to take care of itself, for it has a constant motive behind it. That motive is simply experience. As people feel life, so they will feel the art that is most closely related to it. This closeness of relation is what we should never forget in talking of the effort of the novel. Many people speak of it as a factitious, artificial form, a product of ingenuity, the business of which is to alter and arrange the things that surround us, to translate them into conventional, traditional moulds. This, however, is a view of the matter which carries us but a very short way, condemns the art to an eternal repetition of a few familiar *clichés*, cuts short its development, and leads us straight up to a dead wall. Catching the very note and trick, the strange irregular rhythm of life, that is the attempt whose strenuous force keeps Fiction upon her feet. In proportion as in what she offers us we see life *without* rearrangement do we feel that we are touching the truth; in proportion as we see it *with* rearrangement do we feel that we are being put off with a substitute, a compromise and convention. It is not uncommon to hear an extraordinary assurance of remark in regard to this matter of rearranging, which is often spoken of as if it were the last word of art. Mr. Besant seems to me in danger of falling into the great error with his rather unguarded talk about "selection." Art is essentially selection, but it is a selection whose main care is to be typical, to be inclusive. For many people art means rose-coloured window-panes, and selection means picking a bouquet for Mrs. Grundy.

—Henry James, *The Art of Fiction* (New York, 1948), pp. 16–17

Irony arises when one tries, by the interaction of terms upon one another, to produce a *development* which uses all the terms. Hence, from the standpoint of this total form (this "perspective of perspectives"), none of the participating "sub-perspectives" can be treated as either precisely right or precisely wrong. They are all voices, or personalities, or positions, integrally affecting

[8] *Feeling and Form* (New York, 1953), p. 245.

one another. When the dialectic is properly formed, they are the number of characters needed to produce the total development. Hence, reverting to our suggestion that we might extend the synecdochic pattern to include such reversible pairs as disease-cure, hero-villain, active-passive, we should "ironically" note the function of the disease in "perfecting" the cure, or the function of the cure in "perpetuating" the influences of the disease. Or we should note that only through an internal and external experiencing of folly could we possess (in our intelligence or imagination) sufficient "characters" for some measure of development beyond folly.

People usually confuse the dialectic with the relativistic. Noting that the dialectic (or dramatic) explicitly attempts to establish a distinct set of characters, all of which protest variously at odds or on the bias with one another, they think no further. It is certainly relativistic, for instance, to state that any term (as per metaphor-perspective) can be seen from the point of view of any other term. But insofar as terms are thus encouraged to participate in an orderly parliamentary development, the dialectic of this participation produces (in the observer who considers the whole from the participation of all the terms rather than from the standpoint of any one participant) a "resultant certainty" of a different quality, necessarily ironic, since it requires that all the sub-certainties be considered as neither true nor false, but *contributory* (as were we to think of the resultant certainty or "perspective of perspectives" as a noun, and to think of all the contributory voices as necessary modifiers of that noun).

—Reprinted with permission of publishers from *A Grammar of Motives* by Kenneth Burke. Copyright, 1945, by Prentice-Hall, Inc.

It is possible to interpret aesthetic response in a purely subjectivistic manner by denying that aesthetic quality actually characterizes the object of awareness. The subjectivist admits that aesthetic response has psychological characteristics which distinguish it from other types of response. But he denies that some objects of awareness actually possess in greater or less degree an objective aesthetic character of their own. He explains the *apparent* objectivity of aesthetic quality by saying that we unconsciously project our aesthetic feelings into the object of our awareness, and thus ascribe to it a quality which the object itself completely lacks. The subjectivist may admit that some objects occasion this projection more readily than other objects, and that some aesthetic preferences are idiosyncratic, some more general, and some very widespread. But this fact is explained solely in terms of temperamental variations, social habits, and cultural traditions, and not at all in terms of the presence or absence of an aesthetic quality in different objects of awareness. Aesthetic quality is thus asserted to be merely a function of aesthetic evaluation, and evaluation, in turn, is not conceived to be the discovery of an objective quality in things. . . .

Aesthetic quality is, I believe, *as* objective as the secondary qualities of color and sound, and may (following G. E. Moore) be entitled a tertiary quality. It is "objective" in the sense of actually characterizing certain objects of awareness and not others, and therefore as awaiting discovery by the aesthetically sensitive observer. It is correctly described as "objective" because it satisfies the generic criterion of objectivity, namely, coercive order. Aesthetic quality is apprehended by the aesthetically-minded observer as a quality which presents itself to him with compelling power; which characterizes different objects in different degrees and in conformity to certain basic principles; which he can rediscover on different occasions and explore as he explores other objective qualities; and which other aesthetically sensitive observers can also discover and investigate.

I have adopted this position because it seems to me to do full justice to the sensitive layman's and the thoughtful critic's normal interpretation of the aesthetic experience, whereas the subjectivistic interpretation does unnecessary violence to this experience. . . . the burden of proof must rest with the iconoclastic philosopher. And no defense of subjectivism yet formulated seems to me to be compelling or even plausible. I shall therefore presume the objectivity of aesthetic quality in the following analysis.

—Theodore Meyer Greene, *The Arts and the Art of Criticism* (Princeton, 1947), p. 4, by permission of Princeton University Press, Publishers.

THE SEMANTIC PRINCIPLE

RICHARDS' INTEREST IN SEMANTICS [1] HAS BEEN MENTIONED IN THE preceding chapter. In *The Meaning of Meaning*, written in collaboration with C. K. Ogden, the preferred term is "science of Symbolism." Such a science, the authors believed, had now become pos-

---

[1] In Charles W. Morris' terminology (see *Foundations of the Theory of Signs*, Vol. I, no. 2 of *The Encyclopaedia of Unified Science*, Chicago, 1938) *semantics* proper involves the reference of a sign to its object. It is a subdivision of the general

sible largely through developments in psychology.[2] The function of such a science would be to purify thinking of the errors and distortions forced upon it by the "Power of Words."

> . . . words may come between us and our objects in countless subtle ways, if we do not realize the nature of their power. In logic . . . they lead to the creation of bogus entities, the universals, properties and so forth. . . . By concentrating attention on themselves, words encourage the futile study of forms which has done so much to discredit Grammar; by the excitement which they provoke through their emotive force, discussion is for the most part rendered sterile; by the various types of Verbomania and Graphomania, the satisfaction of naming is realized, and the sense of personal power factitiously enhanced.[3]

But the power of words need not be merely negative; it can be positive and beneficent, and to this positive power Richards turns in his *Principles of Literary Criticism*. That book "endeavours to provide for the emotive function of language the same critical foundation" as *The Meaning of Meaning* attempted to provide "for the symbolic [i.e., referential]."[4]

Even in Richards' earliest work his concern for semantic analysis—the subtle and elaborate examination of verbal complexities—is evident. His discussion of Coleridge will show how closely synaesthesis and semantics are in practice associated in Richards' mind. Richards finds in Coleridge's celebrated description of the imagination as a "synthetic and magical" power an early hint of the doctrine of synaesthesis.[5] Coleridge's discussion of concrete instances of the "synthetic and magical power" reveals him to be a *semasiologist*, that is, a man centrally concerned with "the meanings of words," and as part of this concern, anxious to inquire into "the behaviour of words in poetry."[6] Moreover, Coleridge's account of the behavior of words in certain passages of Shakespeare's *Venus and Adonis* provides admirable instances of poetic analysis. For example, Richards quotes Coleridge's commentary upon the lines:

> Look! how a bright star shooteth from the sky,
> So glides he in the night from Venus' eye.

---

study of linguistics signs, which is *semiotic*. (The other subdivisions of semiotic are the *syntactical*, having to do with the relations of linguistic signs to one another, and the *pragmatic*, having to do with the practical effects of such signs.) Richards occasionally makes use of the term *semiology*, and, as we shall see, he refers to Coleridge as a *semasiologist*.

[2] *The Meaning of Meaning* (New York, 1923), p. 8.

[3] *Meaning of Meaning*, p. 45, by permission of the publisher, Harcourt, Brace and Company, Inc.

[4] See the Preface to the second edition of *The Meaning of Meaning* (1926).

[5] *Principles of Literary Criticism*, pp. 242 ff.

[6] *Coleridge on Imagination*, pp. xi–xii.

Coleridge emphasizes the number of "images and feelings" that

> are here brought together without effort and without discord—
> the beauty of Adonis—the rapidity of his flight—the yearning
> yet helplessness of the enamoured gazer. . . .

And Richards, picking up the theme, enlarges further upon the interconnections among the various images.[7]

A great deal of Richards' practical criticism, much of it incidental to the stated topic of discussion and scattered through his various books, is criticism of this kind. For an impressive body of such criticism, however, it is convenient at this point to turn to the work of Richards' pupil, William Empson. Empson's contributions to this kind of criticism are more extensive than those of Richards and they are on the whole more daringly ingenious. They illustrate the substantial achievement of semantic analysis; they also reveal some of the problems that it raises.

II

EMPSON, impressed by the multiplicity of meanings revealed in an analysis by Robert Graves and Laura Riding of Shakespeare's sonnet "The Expense of Spirit in a Waste of Shame," [8] set out to explore the applicability of this kind of analysis to English poetry in general. The result was the publication in 1930 of his brilliant study *Seven Types of Ambiguity*. The choice of the term "ambiguity" was perhaps not altogether happy, for this term reflects the point of view of expository prose, where one meaning, and only one meaning, is wanted. The presence of a second or third meaning creates a puzzle. The man habituated to expository prose asks: which is *the* meaning? [9] Because the term "ambiguity" connotes doubt and puzzlement, Philip Wheelwright has argued that we need a more positive term, and one that will suggest richness of meaning. He proposes *plurisignation*.[1]

---

[7] *Coleridge on Imagination*, pp. 82–3. M. H. Abrams in *The Mirror and the Lamp* (New York, 1953), p. 182, criticizes Richards for translating "the difference between the products of the faculties [of fancy and imagination as distinguished by Coleridge] into that of the number of 'links' or 'cross-connections' between their 'units of meaning.'" Cf. *ante* Chapter 18.

[8] Robert Graves and Laura Riding, *A Survey of Modernist Poetry* (New York, 1929).

[9] So also with the literary theorists of the past, including Aristotle. As W. B. Stanford points out in his *Ambiguity in Greek Literature* (Oxford, 1939), p. 1, Aristotle was "inclined to consider all ambiguity as a perversion or failing of language instead of its natural and valuable quality. . . . he allowed the danger of dialectical dishonesty in ambiguities to obscure their poetic value—and this even in his literary criticism." Yet ambiguity is, in Stanford's words, "a natural, subtle and effective instrument for poetry and dramatic purposes," and for that reason it occurs very frequently in Greek literature.

[1] *The Burning Fountain* (Bloomington, 1954), p. 61.

Whatever the proper term, the phenomenon in question is one of multiple implication, as a typical passage of Empsonian analysis will reveal:

> When a word is selected as a "vivid detail," as particular for general, a reader may suspect alternative reasons why it has been selected; indeed the author might find it hard to say. When there are several such words there may be alternative ways of viewing them in order of importance.

> Pan is our All, by him we breathe, we live,
> We move, we are; . . .
> But when he frowns, the sheep, alas,
> The shepherds wither, and the grass.
> (Ben Jonson, *Pan's Anniversary*)

> *Alas*, the word explaining which of the items in this list we are to take most seriously, belongs to the *sheep* by proximity and the break in the line, to the *grass* by rhyming with it, and to the *shepherds*, humble though they may be, by the processes of human judgment; so that all three are given due attention, and the balance of the verse is maintained. The Biblical suggestions of *grass* as symbolic of the life of man ("in the mornings it is green and groweth up; in the evening it is cut down, dried up, and withered") add to the solemnity; or from another point of view make the passage absurdly blasphemous, because Pan here is James I. The grace, the pathos, the "sheer song" of the couplet is given by an enforced subtlety of intonation, from the difficulty of saying it so as to bring out all the implications.[2]

Empson's classification of ambiguities into *seven* types is not, as he himself makes clear, to be pressed too hard. The types overlap and at points the definitions are highly arbitrary. Some such classification was apparently necessary to allow him to lay out his material and to provide him with a framework for the many acute analyses of particular poems —analyses which brought home to a whole generation of readers the fact of the manysidedness of language. That would be our perhaps biased way of disposing of the scheme itself, and of acknowledging the qualifications of his scheme that Empson himself has made.

Empson has a general psychologistic bias which comes out clearly in such a passage as the following:

> Ambiguities of this sort [he has been discussing Shakespeare's sonnet XVI] may be divided into those which, once understood,

---

[2] Quoted from the second edition of *Seven Types of Ambiguity* (New York, 1947), p. 27. All rights reserved. Reprinted by permission of the publishers, New Directions.

remain an intelligible unit in the mind; those in which the pleasure belongs to the act of working out and understanding, which must at each reading, though with less labour, be repeated; and those in which the ambiguity works best if it is never discovered. Which class any particular poem belongs to depends in part *on your own mental habits and critical opinions.*[3]

This is to classify in terms of the reader rather than the poem. The second kind of ambiguity (in which the "act of working out and understanding . . . must . . . be repeated") would seem to be in fact merely an imperfectly apprehended version of the first kind. That is, if the labor of working out the meaning becomes, on further readings, progressively less, one might plausibly expect that it would eventually disappear. But it is for the third kind of ambiguity that Empson provides a completely baffling definition. Here the reader is required to be *unaware* that he is confronted with an ambiguity, for this third kind is said to work "best if it is never discovered." What Empson has done is to classify three kinds of response—not three kinds of poems, but three grades of reading.

Empson's general psychologistic emphasis has an important negative bearing on the problem of evaluation. His "method" can obviously be applied to a poor poem just as easily as to a good one—a fact of which he himself is well aware. For example, in discussing Eliot's criticism of the first stanzas of Shelley's "Sky Lark," he proceeds to show how the various images which Eliot believed to be unrelated could actually be related; but he goes on to remark of his own analysis:

> At the same time the thought [in Shelley's poem] seems excessively confused; this muddle of ideas clogging an apparently simple lyrical flow may be explained, but it is not therefore justified; and it is evident that a hearty appetite for this . . . type of ambiguity would apologise for, would be able to extract pleasure from, very bad poetry indeed.[4]

In at least one passage in *Seven Types* Empson does attempt to deal explicitly with the problem of value. An ambiguity is valuable, he says, and not merely a bothersome muddle "in so far as [it] . . . sustains intricacy, delicacy, or compression of thought, or is an opportunism devoted to saying quickly what the reader already understands." But ambiguity is a nuisance—Empson's precise phrase is "not to be respected"—in so far as "it is due to weakness or thinness of thought," when it "obscures the matter in hand unnecessarily," or when, because it is so removed from the focus of interest, its presence gives the reader "a general impression of incoherence." A valuable ambiguity is indeed a "plurisignation," add-

[3] *Seven Types* (1947), p. 57. The italics are ours.
[4] *Seven Types* (1947), p. 160.

ing richness and complexity to, but not obscuring, the structure of meaning.

The foregoing justification of ambiguity reflects the strong cognitive tendency that runs throughout Empson's criticism. But he has other passages in which the cognitive element is overshadowed or is suppressed in favor of other interests. Empson's inveterate psychologism constantly makes him put such questions as these: Why would a reader of such and such a kind find this ambiguous? What historical circumstances make the 18th-century reader, say, prone to take this rather than that as the primary meaning? Did the poet put this in by design or by inadvertence? Indeed, Empson's interest sometimes seems to be merely a curiosity as to what could be made of a particular passage if he simply gave his mind to the search for puzzles. His raccoon-like curiosity [5] perhaps goes a long way to account for the hostility toward Empson felt by many scholars and critics who have been able to see in his work only the naughtiness of the little boy who dismembers the clock in order to see what makes it go.

In his latest book, [6] the psychologism continues as a dominant element. In the literary analyses that occupy him here, Empson sometimes works overtly in terms of author psychology, speculating upon the author's unconscious motivations, his private beliefs, his sense of what kind of rhetorical tricks he could play upon his audience; sometimes, in terms of audience response, examining the ideas that the particular audience had inherited, the literary conventions to which it had been conditioned, its sensitivity or its stupidity. In one very important regard, however, *Complex Words* makes a signal advance toward a cognitive position. In his very first chapter, Empson finds it necessary to reject Richards' doctrine that the "Emotions of the words in poetry are independent of the Sense." In fact, Empson argues, whenever you find

> a case where there are alternative ways of interpreting a word's action, of which one can plausibly be called Cognitive and the other Emotive, it is the Cognitive one which is likely to have important effects on sentiment or character, and in general it does not depend on accepting false beliefs. But in general it does involve a belief of some kind . . . so that it is no use trying to chase belief-feelings out of the poetry altogether. [7]

[5] Compare Marianne Moore's lines on Kenneth Burke:

> and Burke is a
> psychologist—of acute, racoon-
> like curiosity.

From "Picking and Choosing," *Selected Poems* (London, 1935). A reviewer of Empson's book complained that: "Quite a number of Mr. Empson's analyses do not seem to have any properly critical conclusion; they are interesting only as a revelation of the poet's, or Mr. Empson's, ingenious mind."—*Criterion*, July, 1931.

[6] *The Structure of Complex Words* (New York, 1951).

[7] *Complex Words*, p. 10.

Empson makes the further observation that by the time Richards had come to write *The Philosophy of Rhetoric*, Richards himself "seems to have dropped the idea that a writer of poetry had better not worry about the Sense"; indeed, in this book he finds Richards arguing "that the only tolerable way to read poetry is to give the full Sense a very sharp control over the Emotion." [8]

III

THE comment upon the shift in Richards' emphasis is just. In his *Philosophy of Rhetoric* (1936), Richards seems to have quietly laid aside the distinction between the referential and the emotive aspects of language and to have devoted himself to an account of a new rhetoric founded upon semantic analysis.

> . . . the old Rhetoric treated ambiguity as a fault in language, and hoped to confine or eliminate it[;] the new Rhetoric sees it as an inevitable consequence of the power of language and as an indispensable means of most of our important utterances— especially in Poetry and Religion. [9]

Richards admits that the ambiguity of words is not absolute; a condition of general conformity among users is a condition of communication. "*That*," he writes, "no one would dream of disputing"; for language is a social fact as well as a part of personal experience. [1] Stable meanings derive from stable contexts. The meaning of a word like *knife* is rather stable, because the situations in which *knife* occurs are much the same. Stability may be imposed artificially. The stability of the meaning of *mass* as a technical term in physics has been established by limiting and specializing the contexts which we will take into account in using the word technically. Scientific terms are thus limited by convention to one "right or good use"—one proper meaning that the term always and invariably bears.

But this tidy arrangement, Richards goes on to say, is impossible outside of the technical language of the sciences, and most of our discourse, including some of our most important discourse, is not technically scientific. In nontechnical discourse, words "must shift their meanings." If they did not, "language, losing its subtlety with its suppleness, would lose also its power to serve us." [2] The last sentence is worth careful inspection. Not only does Richards see ambiguity as normal; he

[8] *Complex Words*, p. 14.
[9] *Philosophy of Rhetoric*, p. 40, by permission of the publishers, Oxford University Press, Inc.
[1] *Philosophy of Rhetoric*, p. 54.
[2] *Philosophy of Rhetoric*, p. 73.

couples "suppleness" of language with "subtlety." Terms that have lost their pliability, their capacity for being stretched or wrenched a little so as to apply to a new context, are no longer subtle terms. As terms become incapable of ambiguous use they become incapable of precise use.

This view runs quite counter to our conventional notions of precision of meaning, which are founded for the most part on the nature of scientific terminology. Richards had written much earlier in the *Principles* that "Words, when used . . . scientifically, not figuratively . . . , are capable of directing thought to a comparatively few features of the more common situations," [3] and he is making the same point here. Scientific language has its own kind of precision; but another kind of precision, or if not precision, then "subtlety," is required for "the topics with which all generally interesting discussion is concerned." [4]

Richards extends this view of meaning to include rhythm. Poetic rhythm, he had already argued in *Practical Criticism* (1929), influences and is influenced by meaning: ". . . the difference between good rhythm and bad is not simply a difference between certain sequences of sounds; it goes deeper, and to understand it we have to take note of the meanings of the words as well." [5]

We commonly think of rhythm as making a direct appeal to the emotions: a vigorous march is stirring, certain minor airs are plaintive. And, it should be pointed out, Richards does not take the extreme position of denying that the rhythm of a poem *as such* may have emotional efficacy. The actual sounds are important. They are the stuff with which the poet works—comparable, one supposes Richards would say, to the "dictionary" meanings of the words that the poet uses. But the "actual sounds . . . do not carry the whole responsibility for the rhythm." And if we want to praise or condemn the rhythm of a particular poem, we shall not be able, except in the loosest sort of way, to deal with rhythm apart from meaning.[6]

Richards exhibits a phonetic dummy in nonsense syllables of Stanza XV of Milton's "On the Morning of Christ's Nativity." He challenges the reader to find in the dummy the aesthetic virtues which are sometimes ascribed to the "mere sound" of Milton's stanza, including its "expressiveness" as mere sound. If the reader of the dummy finds in it as a

---

[3] *Principles*, p. 131.

[4] *Philosophy of Rhetoric*, pp. 72–3.

[5] *Practical Criticism* (New York, 1929), p. 227.

[6] In *Practical Criticism*, p. 229, Richards says that the rhythm that we admire and feel that we detect in the sounds themselves is something that we "ascribe" to them. Later, in *Coleridge on Imagination*, p. 119, he puts the matter in terms nearer those of Coleridge: "The movement of the verse becomes the movement of the meaning; and prosody, as a study of verse-form apart from meaning, is seen to be a product of unwary abstraction. In saying that 'the sense of musical delight . . . is a gift of the imagination,' Coleridge set aside the conventional conception to restore a wholeness to our view of the act of speech. . . ."

mere series of sounds the phonetic virtue characterizing Milton's stanza, then successful verse must be amenable to a formula, for one can make up such dummies *ad infinitum.* If, on the other hand, the reader protests that the dummy is not a phonetic replica of Milton's sonnet, he is in reality arguing that the difference *in sound* between the dummy and original is what deprives the dummy of all merit. "In which case," Richards points out, the reader "will have to account for the curious fact that just those transformations which redeem it as sound, should also give it the sense and feeling we find in Milton. A staggering coincidence, unless the meaning were highly relevant to the effect of the form." [7]

IV

At this point it may be well to summarize some of the consequences of what Richards calls broadly a "context" theory of meaning.

First, words interanimate one another. They are qualified by the whole context in which they figure, and they bring to that context powers derived from other contexts in which they have figured in the past. Much of modern criticism devoted to the "close reading of texts," including that of Empson, illustrates the subtle and rich complex of meaning which a finely wrought poetic context can yield.

Second, the problem of meaning—especially *the* meaning of a poem or drama or piece of fiction—is seen to be a matter not easily and summarily determined. It is not enough to seize upon one or two "statements" as indicating the thesis and to relegate everything else to the role of ornament or detailed illustration. "Statements" (such as "Beauty is truth" or "Ripeness is all") may indeed bear importantly upon the meaning of the whole work and may in some instance summarize that meaning, but not necessarily: they are subject to all the pulls and attractions of the other elements of the work.

Third, the poet necessarily tailor-makes his language as he explores his meaning. He does not (and cannot) "build up the meaning of his sentences as a mosaic is put together of discrete independent tesserae." The senses of the author's words are not such "fixed factors" as these. Instead, what we call the "meanings" of his words "are resultants which we arrive at only through the interplay of the interpretative possibilities of the whole utterance." [8]

[7] *Practical Criticism,* pp. 232-3. T. S. Eliot, following the main line of French symbolist doctrine, affirms the interconnection between rhythm and meaning quite as emphatically. In *The Music of Poetry* (Glasgow, 1942), he writes (p. 13): "the music of poetry is not something which exists apart from the meaning. Otherwise, we could have poetry of great musical beauty which made no sense, and I have never come across such poetry."

[8] *Philosophy of Rhetoric,* p. 55.

Fourth, the reader, like the writer, finds the meaning through a process of exploration. "Inference and guesswork!" Richards exclaims. "What else is interpretation? How, apart from inference and skilled guesswork, can we be supposed ever to understand a writer's or speaker's thought?" [9]

Fifth, in the light of the context theory, metaphor is seen to be a typical instance of the merging of contexts. A metaphor is more than a mere "comparison" that illustrates a point, or recommends a doctrine by lending it an attractive coloring. A metaphor is the linchpin joining two contexts, contexts which may be quite far apart and, in conventional discourse at least, utterly unrelated. The meaning achieved by a metaphor —and certainly by the most vigorous and powerful metaphor—is not simply a prettified version of an already stated meaning, but a new meaning in which imagination pushes itself forward and occupies new ground.

Mere vividness has never been the aspect of imagery that has interested Richards. He has countenanced neither Max Eastman's quest for intense realization, nor even T. E. Hulme's insistence that poetic language should "hand over sensations bodily." Poetry's inveterate concern for concrete particulars has for Richards a very different importance: concrete particularity means heterogeneity; it means difference; and it insures the sort of confrontation of unlike elements that is necessary to prevent discourse from collapsing into literal statement.

In fact, what determines that a given usage is metaphorical rather than literal is this linkage with a second context. As a test case, Richards instances Hamlet's question: "What should such fellows as I do crawling between earth and heaven?" Is *crawling* to be taken literally or metaphorically? Metaphorically, Richards answers. A baby literally crawls, and, on occasion, a man may literally crawl, but here "there is an unmistakable reference to other things that crawl," such things as cockroaches or snakes. If we substitute for *crawling, walking,* or more decisively still, the more general word *moving,* we shut out the context of *crawling* creatures and the use becomes literal. Metaphors die into fixed and literal terms when habitual usage confines them to one context: the *eye* of a needle or the *leg* of a table have lost all metaphoric force. They are no longer what Richards calls metaphor, "a transaction between contexts."

This last definition has a bearing on the problem of triteness, a topic we have touched upon in an earlier chapter.[1] It would be oversimple to conclude that every trite expression has become so through simple repetition. The attrition by repetition is only one, and perhaps not an essential, factor. Some expressions may attain triteness, and some have undoubtedly had triteness forced upon them, but some again are born trite. Even at a first hearing some phrases seem "shopworn." On the other hand, many

[9] *Philosophy of Rhetoric,* p. 53.
[1] Cf. *ante* Chapter 16, pp. 354-60.

readings do not impoverish Shakespeare's *King Lear*. Even passages like Hamlet's "Something is rotten in the state of Denmark," which may be said to have had triteness forced upon them, slough off their triteness at once when set back into the context of the whole play.

W. B. Stanford (whose *Ambiguity in Greek Literature* has been mentioned earlier in this chapter) calls metaphor a "stereoscope of ideas." [2] Stanford offers this definition:

> The term metaphor is fully valid only when applied to a very definite and a rather complicated concept, *viz.* the process and result of using a term (X) normally signifying an object or concept (A) in such a context that it must refer to another object or concept (B) which is distinct enough in characteristics from A to ensure that in the composite idea formed by the synthesis of the concepts A and B and now symbolized in the word X, the factors A and B retain their conceptual independence even while they merge in the unity symbolized by X. . . .[3]

Stanford says that the objects or concepts related by the metaphor must be sufficiently "distinct" to retain conceptual independence. Consider such an example as the following: "The dog raged like a wild beast." This sentence has almost no metaphoric force, for the dog, a tamed beast, is not sufficiently distinct from a wild beast. "The man raged like a wild beast" or "The sea raged like a wild beast" are poor enough as metaphor, but with the substitution of *man* or *sea*, a trace of metaphoric power begins to be perceptible.

Stanford's own metaphor of a stereoscope insists upon this necessary maintenance of difference: only by keeping the two pictures distinct can the stereoscope use them to create a third thing, the depth picture, which is a "synthesis" of the two flat pictures, a picture in which the flat pictures may be said to "merge" but which is in fact a third thing, quite different from either.

Metaphor "means" a third thing, different from the meaning of either of its terms taken in isolation. "The traditional theory," notes Richards, made metaphor seem to be only "a shifting and displacement of words," whereas "fundamentally it is a borrowing between and intercourse of *thoughts*, a transaction between contexts." [4] Metaphor is not merely "a grace or ornament or *added* power of language"; it is "its constitutive form." [5] And again, "*Thought* is metaphoric, and proceeds by comparison, and the metaphors of language derive therefrom."

[2] See his *Greek Metaphor* (Oxford, 1936), p. 105, by permission of the publishers, Oxford University Press, Inc.
[3] *Greek Metaphor*, p. 101.
[4] *Philosophy of Rhetoric*, p. 94.
[5] *Philosophy of Rhetoric*, p. 90.

V

WE ARE invited to apply the contextual theory of meaning as elaborated by Richards in his *Philosophy of Rhetoric* to his earlier distinction between a poetry of "exclusion" and a poetry of "inclusion." [6] That which is "excluded" for the sake of unity, one might argue, is a different "context." A sentimental love poem, to take an easy and obvious example, systematically excludes from its context such matters as doctors' bills, squalling babies, and the odors of the kitchen. Its unity depends upon the reader's viewing it from a certain perspective and in a certain light. When the reader, because of the enlargement of the relevant context, is forced to view such a poem from a different perspective, the essential flimsiness of the poem is revealed. The altered perspective reveals that the recalcitrant and contradictory elements of the experience in question have not been taken into account—they have simply been ignored. The poetry of "inclusion," on the other hand, systematically draws upon other and larger contexts. It has already made its peace with the recalcitrant and the contradictory. That is why it is, as Richards says, "invulnerable" to "ironic contemplation."

Thus might a sympathetic critic be expected to relate certain key terms of Richards' earlier critical theory to the "context" theory elaborated in his *Philosophy of Rhetoric*. Such an interpretation of Richards' views has the merit of implying a conception of irony congenial to that held by many critics of the present and of the recent past. For example, Henry James, in his Preface to *The Lesson of the Master*, declared that "operative" irony "implies and projects the possible other case" [7]—an observation possibly echoed by T. S. Eliot in his definition of wit as involving "a recognition, implicit in the expression of every experience, of other kinds of experience which are possible." [8] Such also is the function of irony described in R. P. Warren's "Pure and Impure Poetry" (1943). The unwillingness to face up to the "other possible case" constitutes for Warren the characteristic weakness of the "pure" poetry that avoids on principle any manifestation of irony and witty intellection.

Why, Warren asks, should a love poem, for instance, include in its make-up "self-contradictions, cleverness, irony, realism—all things which call us back to the world of prose and imperfection"? [9] He answers his

[6] Cf. I. A. Richards, *Principles of Literary Criticism* (New York, 1929), p. 240, the discussion of metaphor as "the supreme agent by which disparate and hitherto unconnected things are brought together in poetry."

[7] *The Art of the Novel*, introduction by R. P. Blackmur (New York, 1953), p. 222.

[8] "Andrew Marvell," *Selected Essays*, p. 262.

[9] "Pure and Impure Poetry," *The Kenyon Review*, V (Spring, 1943); reprinted in R. W. Stallman, *Critiques and Essays in Criticism, 1920–1948* (New York, 1949), p. 86, by permission of the author.

question by making a comparison of three love poems: Tennyson's
"Now sleeps the crimson petal, now the white," Shelley's "Indian Sere-
nade," and *Romeo and Juliet*. The first two poems aspire to purity of
effect: they "exclude" the sordid and the realistic. *Romeo and Juliet* does
not: it "includes" the bawdy jests of Mercutio, just outside the wall of
Juliet's garden, and it includes the earthy and common-sense nurse who
also has her bawdy jests and who will offer her counsel of half-meas-
ures and compromises. It is, as Warren puts it, as if the

> poet seems to say: "I know the worst that can be said on this
> subject, and I am giving fair warning. Read at your own risk."
>   Let us return to one of the other gardens, in which there
> is no Mercutio or nurse, and in which the lady is more sympa-
> thetic. Let us mar its purity by installing Mercutio in the shrub-
> bery, from which the poet was so careful to banish him. You
> can hear his comment when the lover says:
>
>> And a spirit in my feet
>> Hath led me—who knows how?
>> To thy chamber window, Sweet!
>
> And we can guess what the wicked tongue would have to say
> in response to the last stanza.
>   It may be that the poet should have made his peace early
> with Mercutio, and have appealed to his better nature. For Mer-
> cutio seems to be glad to cooperate with a poet. But he must be
> invited; otherwise, he is apt to show a streak of merry vindic-
> tiveness about the finished product.[1]

Warren, for the sake of making his point, has proposed to "install"
Mercutio "in the shrubbery." But in suggesting that poets should always
make their peace with Mercutio, he implies that Mercutio is actually lurking in Shelley's poem all the time—and that he lurks in all poems. Mercutio, the implied argument runs, had best be invited for the simple reason
that it does not lie in the poet's power to keep him away. The many-
sided complexity of reality and the nature of language are facts that have
to be reckoned with: only technical language—that is, language that allows a systematically literal reading—would seem to offer a setting quite
bare of any cover in which a Mercutio might lurk. Looked at in this fashion, the exclusions made by a poetry that strains after purity reveal themselves as failures to develop and exploit latent meanings, meanings which,
since they are in the words, must be brought to bear positively or else
must be neglected in the hope that the neglect will not be noticed. In a
poetry of "inclusion," the metaphoric potentialities have been taken into
account. They have been harnessed to support each other and to sustain

[1] Stallman, p. 88.

the meaning of the whole. In a poetry of exclusion, the unrecognized and unused potentialities are a threat to any superficial unity that the poet has established: a vigorous and imaginative reading brings these elements to life—to the distraction of the poem.[2]

V I

THOUGH Warren's essay seems to invite even a further development along the lines we have just indicated, it is only fair to observe that an exploration in this direction would uncover a series of problems not fully solved in Warren's essay, nor—for they are substantially the same problems—solved in the work of Empson and Richards.

A poetry capable of surviving an ironic contemplation must not, Warren would say, be purged of all "impurities" or, as Richards might put it, draw upon too narrow a context. Thus, these critics would seem to demand a certain complexity as the desideratum of any "good" poem. But, by insisting that poetry is a complex structure capable of richness (ambiguity) and toughness (irony), they have alarmed some readers by seeming to deny any value to simplicity. Their attack—or at least what those readers took to be an attack—upon a virtue so long honored by critics of all schools prompted sharp protests. But before looking directly at such protests, it may be well to notice at this juncture a second, closely related problem. It may be called the problem of relevant context.

This problem may be put as a question: against how wide a context should a given poem be read? A play like *Romeo and Juliet* obviously can appeal to, and make use of, much wider and richer contexts than any lyric can. What, in this connection, is the proper "magnitude" (if we may use Aristotle's term) of an art work? How many competing contexts must be active in a lyric in order for it to be properly and sufficiently complex?

Socially minded critics of our time sometimes dispose of the problem by disposing of simplicity. The Marxist E. B. Burgum, for example, argues[3] that there is no lyric so humble that it need be ashamed of its simplicity. There was nothing wrong with "Empson's method," but only with Empson's "non-social use of it." Burgum's use of the method applies "sociological perspectives" to poetry. Even though the closing choral

[2] What happens in such a case is analogous to what happens sometimes in bad prose when dead or benumbed metaphors, unwanted by the author who has failed to take their potentialities into account, waken into life, to the embarrassment of the whole passage. Such prose fares better under a superficial reading: it dare not invite, and may seriously suffer under, a vigorously imaginative reading.

[3] "The Cult of the Complex in Poetry," *Science and Society*, XV (Winter, 1951), 31–48.

lines of Aeschylus' *Prometheus Bound* [4] present no evident ambiguity, a more careful consideration manages to reveal that they imply two Greek philosophical systems, the religious and the materialistic, in conflict. Complexity enters "when it is recognized that the play is ending with this contradiction . . . unresolved." Burgum urges "the fact that the simplest idea becomes complex when related to human experience." [5]

The show-piece of the essay is Wordsworth's lyric "She dwelt among the untrodden ways." Though this poem, according to Burgum, would have to be regarded "in Empsonian terms" as simple and straightforward, it actually involves all sorts of complexity: the speaker is revealed to be conscious of his moral isolation; Lucy herself turns out to be a neurotic personality; [6] the value system as implied in the poem reveals itself as that of an era of rapid social change, and so forth. But in distinguishing the complexity that he finds in this poem from any complexity "in the phrasing (as Empson would put it)," Burgum, of course, has given over any specific literary problem, or rather he has denied that any specific literary problem exists. He treats Wordsworth's poem about Lucy as merely a document of the manners, morals, and value judgments of its age. The "problem of poetic meaning, like all problems of meaning, is fundamentally sociological." [7]

Burgum, in his exploration of complexity, does not stop with the poem conceived as a unit. By relating it to that grand manifold "human experience," he is able to propose that even a single line of poetry—his example is the Arnoldian touchstone "In his will is our peace"—is "complex." He obviously might have gone further still, for it is evident that by this sort of method one will be able to show just as convincingly that a single word possesses "complexity." For if Dante's line about God's will and our peace is "complex," the word "God," or the word "peace," with its varying and manifold implications, is "complex" also.

VII

MOST protests against Empsonian-Ricardian complexity have, however, stopped short of merging all poetic meaning into general psycho-socio-

[4] 'Tis Zeus who driveth his furies
   To smite me with terror and madness.
   O Mother Earth all-honored,
   O Air revolving thy light
   A common boon to all,
   Behold what wrongs I endure.
[5] *Science and Society*, XV, 43.
[6] Burgum's treatment of this poem makes the examples of the application of the historical method that we observed earlier in Chapter 24 seem very conservative indeed.
[7] *Science and Society*, XV, 37.

logical meaning. The protestants, indeed, have tended, when it came to a matter of the relevant context, to be strict constructionists. They have deplored Empson's method, not because it is "non-social" but because they think it implies a license to read "anything one likes" into the text. Such was the nature of the protest made by F. L. Lucas in his *Decline and Fall of the Romantic Ideal* (1937).[8] Another typical protest was that voiced by Donald Stauffer: critics who insisted upon the complexity of poetry were guilty of partial sympathies: they demanded that all poems be "original, spare, and strange" and thus disparaged verses written "with simplicity and sentiment." [9] What, he asked, would such critics do with the simple lyrics of a Wordsworth or a Blake? Or with the simple eloquence of the Psalms?

There is often latent in such protests the misconception that a complex structure must necessarily reflect an equally complex intention on the writer's part. The poem could not be so complex as Empsonian analysis would make it, for that would argue that the writer was intolerably self-conscious. To this criticism, Richards and Empson would no doubt answer that it is naive to equate a theory of structure with a theory of composition.

A second misconception reveals itself when someone offers a great line or a memorable passage of poetry as an example of how truly *simple* great poetry can be, *forgetting* that it depends for its power upon the great literary context from which it has been taken. Thus Herbert Muller, echoing the method of Matthew Arnold,[1] has quoted brief memorable passages from Shakespeare and Dante as proof of the poetic power to be found in the simple statement of a great master.[2] It may be hard for us to realize how powerfully the context of a great literary work may qualify our reading of a passage that we *believe* we are dealing with in isolation. Shakespeare's "Ripeness is all," for example, may seem movingly eloquent because of its very naked simplicity, but if we repeat "Ripeness is all" to someone who *really* knows nothing of its context, especially if we divorce it from all literary contexts by speaking it casually at a fruit-stand, we shall find that its eloquence has been lost upon our auditor. For him it will not be poetry at all.[3]

[8] "In a recent work with the apocalyptic title, *Seven Types of Ambiguity*, it has been revealed to an admiring public that the more ways a poem can be misunderstood, the better it is" (p. 228).

[9] "The *Mesures* Lectures," *Kenyon Review*, IV (Autumn, 1942), pp. 412–13.

[1] Cf. *ante* Chapter 20.

[2] "The New Criticism in Poetry," *The Southern Review*, VI (Spring, 1941), 823.

[3] The whole matter of context is rightly seen by historical critics to be very important. How much can one poem be isolated from the context of the author's work in general? (Blake's "Lamb" taken in isolation is not quite the same poem as when viewed as a part of a whole which is the *Songs of Innocence*; it becomes a third thing when paired with "The Tiger" and viewed as one half of a double poem.)

The problem of "simplicity" has its complications. They begin to emerge as soon as we notice how little a "simple" lyric differs in its general structure from a "complex" poem. Warren urges this consideration in the essay we have previously cited. He argues there very persuasively for a considerable complexity in "Western wind, when wilt thou blow," a tiny four-line lyric usually celebrated as a pure cry of the heart.[4]

VIII

AN AMUSING illustration of the amount of complexity that may lurk beneath a commonly accepted simplicity is provided by Laura Riding and Robert Graves. In their *Pamphlet Against Anthologies*,[5] published one year before their *Survey of Modernist Poetry* which was to send William Empson out upon his career of semantic analysis,[6] they set forth a detailed discussion of the complications of meaning to be found in Wordsworth's "A Slumber Did My Spirit Seal."

Convinced that William Wordsworth was too "simple" and straightforward to have "meant" the logical contradictions that they found in his little poem, they experimented with a rewriting to correct Wordsworth's mistakes.

> The details [of the poem] are even more illogical than the main argument. Apparently what Wordsworth has in his mind is that "I thought once she was non-human in a spiritual sense, but now she is dead I find her non-human in the very opposite sense." But all the words have got misplaced. "Spirit" has got attached to Wordsworth [A slumber did *my* spirit seal] when it should go with Lucy; "no human" [*I* had no human fears] likewise. There is a false comparison made between "A slumber did my spirit seal" and "She neither hears nor sees." "Trees" is an irrelevant climax to "rocks and stones." "Thing" should not qualify the first Lucy [She seemed a thing that could not feel] but should be with the second Lucy among the rocks and stones. . . . [The poem] would run more logically, something like this:
>
> > A slumber sealed my *human fears*
> >   For her mortality:
> > Methought *her spirit* could withstand
> >   The touch of earthly years.

---

[4] "Pure and Impure Poetry," Stallman, pp. 88–9.
[5] *A Pamphlet Against Anthologies* (London, 1928), by permission of the authors.
[6] See *ante* p. 637.

> Yet now her spirit fails, she is
> Less sentient than a *tree*,
> Rolled round in earth's diurnal course
> With rocks and stones and things.[7]

But the revision reduces the poem to a tidy emptiness: the loss of the rhymes is the very least of the losses incurred. Riding and Graves themselves prefer Wordsworth's own version of the poem, arguing that in spite of its illogical details, it has not a "sublogical" incoherence but a "supra-logical harmony." They justify the form that he has given to his poem by a kind of Longinian argument to the effect that the "inability of the mind to face the actual reality of death" mirrors itself here in the speaker's "inability to get the right words to pair off in a logical prose manner"; [8] i.e., the speaker's very incoherence points to the depth of the emotional shock that he has suffered.

But this would seem to be an unnecessarily desperate line of defense. For it can be argued that Wordsworth's "misplacing" of words is the best placing of them. The apparent contradictions and violations of logic turn out to be in fact refinements of meaning and subtleties of statement. The lover, for example, is saying that Lucy's present strange slumber has waked him out of his—out of that strange slumber in which he, unable to conceive that *she* could ever feel the "touch of earthly years," had been indifferent to the possibility of her death. But now Lucy "feels" the touch of earthly years indeed in her very lack of feeling—in the numbing of hearing, sight, and her other senses at the touch of mortality. "No motion has she now," and yet her inert body is hurled in violent motion, along with the stones and the trees, as the planet spins them all in the empty whirl that measures out each earthly day and each of the "earthly years." [9] Be the proper justification of the poem what it may, Riding and Graves by their proposed revisions, clearly showed how far this "simple" poem departs from straightforward statement and how much it partakes of the ambiguous and the paradoxical.

Semantic analysis such as that associated with Richards and Empson does seem to imply a value in complexity itself. The great poems reveal an organic structure of parts intricately related to each other, and the totality of meaning in such a poem is rich and perhaps operative on several levels. In terms of this view of poetic excellence, a principal task of criticism—perhaps *the* task of criticism—is to make explicit to the reader the implicit manifold of meanings. That this view implies a rejection of any *simpliste* notion of art is quite clear; yet it is only

[7] *Pamphlet Against Anthologies*, pp. 128–9.

[8] *Pamphlet Against Anthologies*, p. 129.

[9] For the detail of such an interpretation, see Cleanth Brooks, "Irony as a Principle of Structure," *Literary Opinion in America* (New York, 1951), pp. 735–7.

fair to observe that there are senses of the term simplicity which the semantic critic does not need, and presumably does not want, to reject. In any case, the problem is not new. It goes back at least to Plotinus and the third century of our era. In an earlier chapter we noted that the term used for "simple" by Plotinus (*haplous*)

> may describe either *absence* of *internal differentiation* (as with the simplicity or unity of a pebble) or precisely the opposite, a high degree of *internal differentiation*—in other words, organic unity (as with the unity of a living body).[1]

For the semanticist, it is no praise to say that poetry is simple in the first sense. The sheer simplicity of the pebble is to be despised; a high degree of "internal differentiation" is praiseworthy. Our modern semantic criticism has insisted upon its debt (as through Richards) to Coleridge, remembering his emphasis upon organic form. But it might properly also pay its respects to one of Coleridge's masters, Plotinus. It might claim still another ancestor in the person of St. Augustine who wrote:

> Any beautiful object whatsoever is more worthy of praise in its totality as a whole than in any one of its parts. So great is the power of integrity and unity that what pleases as a part pleases much more in a unified whole.—*Contra Manichaeos*, I, 32 [2]

SUPPLEMENT

> We, too, had known golden hours
> When body and soul were in tune. . . .
> And would in the old grand manner
> Have sung from a resonant heart.
> But, pawed-at and gossipped-over
> By the promiscuous crowd,
> Concocted by editors
> Into spells to befuddle the crowd,
> All words like peace and love,
> All sane affirmative speech,
> Had been soiled, profaned, debased
> To a horrid mechanical screech:

[1] Cf. *ante* Chapter 7, p. 118.
[2] Cf. *ante* Chapter 7, p. 123.

No civil style survived
That pandaemonium
But the wry, the sotto-voce,
Ironic and monochrome:
And where should we find shelter
For joy or mere content
When little was left standing
But the suburb of dissent.

—"To Reinhold and Ursula Niebuhr," from *Nones* by W. H. Auden, copyright 1951 by W. H. Auden. Reprinted by permission of Random House, Inc.

In the celebrated description of cold weather in the beginning of *The Eve of St. Agnes* [ll. 14–16], the poet intensifies the cold with the added suggestion of silence and immobility. It is not a blustery north-wind that he has described, but the penetrating cold of a still, dead air. In the second stanza of the poem, Keats makes use of three puns, which, *though often unnoticed*, assist in the poetic fusion of ideas.

In the first stanza he begins with the outside world. The sheep are silent; and when the hare moves, it is in a limp, a cataleptic movement from one rigid posture to another. The poet then moves inside to the monk, in the attitude of prayer, or moving down the chapel aisle with the slow shuffle of age, a muffled noise which in the deserted chapel accentuates the stillness and the cold.

Following the first quatrain of the second stanza, however, Keats moves away from all forms of life to the complete immobility of art, "the foster child of silence and slow time." Each of three successive lines contains a pun, but so fused in the imagination are the various suggestions of the three words that *the reader is unaware of the poetic alchemy*. The most obvious perhaps is "freeze" in line 14, which, while establishing the relationship of coldness with the stone figures, at the same time reemphasizes the immobility and imprisonment of the "sculptured dead" by fixing them in a frieze along the chapel walls.

In line 15, in "rails," Keats undoubtedly has in mind a word derived from OE *hrægl*, "garment, dress, cloak," which according to the NED was *last used in this sense in the thirteenth century* in "The Owl and the Nightingale." The more obvious meaning of "rails" as bars strengthens the word "emprison'd" and indeed has a suggestion of coldness; but "purgatorial rails," or the bars which enclose purgatory, a place of punishment and unrest, suggest just the opposite of coldness and immobility, with which Keats is primarily concerned here. The other meaning of "rail" as a garment or a cloak has a subtle influence on the word "purgatory," quieting any suggestion of restlessness and torment, and presenting merely a picture of death and grave clothes.

In line 16, the word "orat'ries" likewise carries a double meaning. In such a poem so particularly concerned with the terminology as well as the atmosphere of the mediaeval church, "orat'ries" suggests other places of devotion, like the cold, deserted chapel Keats has just described, in which the knights and ladies prayed in a dimmer and more distant time. However, with its qualifying adjective "dumb" the word takes on its more obvious meaning in the secular world. The "orat'ries" are the words that might have been spoken in the articulated prayers of the dead figures, but which, frozen in stone, remain "dumb."

In the last two lines of the stanza, Keats returns to the monk to show the effect of the "sculptured dead" on his thin, meagre life. More than before, his weak spirit fails before the idea of death so subtly suggested in the cold silence of the chapel air. The three puns are not only inoffensive *to the point of being unnoticed:* they amplify beyond analysis the fused idea of stillness and cold culminating in death, which Keats wished to establish in the beginning of the poem, as a counterpoint to the happier idea of mobility and warmth leading to life, which in the climax of the poem is expressed in the consummated love of Madeline and Porphyro.

—Elmo Howell, "Keats' The Eve of St. Agnes, 14–16," *The Explicator,* XIV (February, 1956), No. 5, by permission of the editors. The italics are ours—with no real misgivings about the interpretation of them.

Words can be effective only if they have a definite meaning. And what defines the meaning of a word is its undeniable correspondence with certain things, certain feelings, the fact that it necessarily pledges acts. Now this correspondence ceases to be arbitrary only by virtue of a unanimous agreement, which is to say that it can be brought about only in the midst of a living group or community. A common tradition, law, faith and authority alone are capable of defining the meaning of what we call current words. But all these things have disappeared in our century. Then the words that circulate everywhere lead nowhere. Our language is *out of gear.* The more we speak the less we understand one another. Death alone can put everyone into agreement.

The twentieth century will appear in the future as a kind of verbal nightmare, of delirious cacophony: people spoke more often than they had ever spoken (imagine those radio stations which *can* no longer be silent day or night, where words are delivered at so much per minute, whether or not there are listeners, whether or not there are things to say), a time when words wore out faster than in any century of History, a time of prostitution of language, which was to be the measure of the true, and of which the Gospel says that at its source it is "the life and the light of men!"

Alas, what have we done with language! No longer able even to lie in certain mouths, language has fallen lower than the lie, I mean into insignificance. How the Devil rejoices over the pleasant or excited chatter of the radio-speakers! He, the great confusionist, who likes nothing better than flattering equivocation, the drone of official style, the senile incontinence of after-dinner verbiage. He, the romantic, who, when we are stupefied by speeches, suggests to us that the *inexpressible* is perhaps truer than clear, sharp speech! . . . He knows that . . . by . . . debasing the meaning of words he destroys the very basis of our loyalties. He knows that wherever a spade is called a spade, evil recedes and loses something of its prestige; this is why he has invented the language of diplomats and its insane coyness. He knows that nothing in the world can make us be silent, now that we have the radio, and he takes up his post in all the microphones. He finally organizes that verbal inflation, words no longer being "covered" by acts, which he hopes, not without reason, will complete, more effectively than the worst tyrannies, the utter confusion of our moral sense. . . .

I was about to write that the only remedy would be to combat him with *semantics*, which is the science of meanings, of precise and shaded language, guaranteed by a long tradition and by etymologies. A *Ministry of the Meaning of Words*, endowed with discretionary powers—this is what a Democracy needs—since after all it is a regime entirely founded on words.[3] (This ministry was formerly the Church. An analysis of our vocabularies would show that the little common sense which they preserve comes from biblical and liturgical reminiscences.)

—Denis de Rougemont, *The Devil's Share*, trans. Haakon Chevalier (Pantheon Books, 1944), Chapter 64, "The Meaning of Words," pp. 211-13, by permission of the publishers, Pantheon Books, Inc.

---

[3] The parliamentary regime, social contracts, laws, public opinion, free press, meetings, conferences. The monarchy was founded on ritual, consecrated formulae, plastic ceremony. Dictatorship is the regime of blows where speech has ceased to be anything but planned and directed lying.

ELIOT AND POUND:
AN IMPERSONAL ART

§ *Eliot's classicism: discriminated from that of Mat-*
thew Arnold and Irving Babbitt, its relation to the French
symbolists and particularly to Remy de Gourmont—II.
T. E. Hulme's classicism: his association of the classic view
of man with the religious view, his indifference towards
kinds of subject matter, his exaltation of craftsmanship, his
stress upon metaphor and on the organic character of the
poem—III. Pound's insistence that poetry should possess
the virtues of good prose, his interest in the Chinese ideo-
graph as a paradigm of the poetic method, and his stress
upon poetry as a kind of "inspired mathematics"—IV.
Eliot's doctrine of the impersonality of poetry, his associa-
tion of the method of the 17th century "metaphysical"
poets with that of the 19th century French symbolist poets
—Eliot's theory of a "dissociation of sensibility" with its
implications for a poetics of tension—V. his doctrine of the
objective correlative—the attack upon that doctrine by
Eliseo Vivas, and by Yvor Winters—VI. Winters' classi-
cism: his indictment of the "fallacy of imitative form," his
insistence upon the need for a rational structure, and his
attack upon "qualitative progression" as a method for or-
ganizing a poem—VII. Winters' reprehension of irony as
reflecting either the poet's carelessness or his irresponsi-
bility: this view of irony contrasted with that held by
Eliot and by Warren—VIII. Winters' criticism of modern
poetry interpreted as a reassertion of the importance of
"plot" and of dramatic organization—the implications of
this view: the lyric as drama, metaphor as drama—IX.
Eliot's doctrine of the impersonality of poetry reconsid-
ered: the view that the poem has a "life" of its own, as
interpreted by Eliot, and by Allen Tate §

657

WHEN T. S. ELIOT ANNOUNCED IN 1928 THAT HE WAS A ROYALIST in politics, an Anglo-Catholic in religion, and a classicist in literature, the reaction was immediate and noisy. The revelation of his political and religious position elicited most of the cat-calls and solemn protests, but his profession of classicism drew its share too, mingled with expressions of honest bewilderment. For Eliot's own poetry was surely "romantic," was it not? And how could a poet who had obviously derived so much from the French symbolist poets of the 19th century maintain with a straight face that he honored "classicism"?

The line of descent from the classicism of Matthew Arnold to that of Eliot is certainly neither an evident nor an unbroken one. Of Arnold, Eliot has remarked that he "might have become a critic,"[1] but had in fact devoted his energies to "attacking the uncritical." Though Irving Babbitt had been one of his teachers at Harvard, Eliot felt that Babbitt, like Arnold, had confused literary criticism with something else. Neither Babbitt nor his fellow neo-Humanist, Paul Elmer More, Eliot had been forced to conclude, was "primarily interested in art." Primarily they were moralists, and whereas he acknowledged that it was a "worthy and serious thing to be" a moralist, Eliot had had to write down Babbitt and More among his "Imperfect Critics."[2]

Yet Eliot made it plain in his essay entitled "The Perfect Critic" (1920) that he did not consider that the proper alternative to moralization was impressionism. A critic like Arthur Symons, for example, undertook to give us his impressions of the work in hand; but Eliot points out that it is impossible for the critic to rest there; for "the moment you try to put the impressions into words, you either begin to analyse and construct, to 'ériger en lois,' or you begin to create something else."[3] By taking the second alternative, Symons produced, instead of a work of criticism, a prose poem about his own responses.

Eliot had borrowed the phrase *"ériger en lois"*[4] from the French critic, Remy de Gourmont. The sentence from which it is taken serves as an epigraph for Eliot's whole essay, and strikes its keynote: the true critic will strive to build his impressions up into laws. His impressions will be subjective and personal—how could they be otherwise?—but because he will try to refer them to principles he will move away from mere impressionism toward objectivity. Aristotle is for Eliot the classic instance of such critical power, and of "all modern critics," he

[1] "Introduction," *The Sacred Wood* (1920), 2nd ed. (London, 1928), p. xiii, by permission of the author and of the publishers, Methuen and Co., Ltd.
[2] See "Imperfect Critics" (1920), *The Sacred Wood*, pp. 41-4.
[3] *The Sacred Wood*, p. 5.
[4] *"Ériger en lois ses impressions personelles, c'est le grand effort d'un homme s'il est sincère"* occurs in *Lettres à l'Amazone* (1914).

writes, "perhaps Remy de Gourmont [has] had most of the general intelligence of Aristotle." [5]

Eliot's emphasis upon the "generalizing power" and upon the critic's need to objectify gives the clue to his special kind of classicism. Of that we shall have more to say later in this chapter. But his collocation of the symbolist poet and critic, de Gourmont, with Symons, the author of *The Symbolist Movement in Literature*, is in itself significant. It points to the fact that important "classical" elements were to be found in a movement that it has been fashionable to regard as a "second wave" of Romanticism. Ezra Pound, Eliot's friend and fellow literary revolutionist, said flatly: "De Gourmont prepared our era; behind him there stretches a limitless darkness." Despite the fact that he had his beginning "in the symbolistes," de Gourmont becomes for Pound a restorer of "the light of the XVIIIth century." [6]

II

IN THIS general connection one ought to mention another conspicuous champion of the classical virtues, T. E. Hulme, who was a companion of Pound's in London during the years before the first World War, in which Hulme was to die in 1917. When Pound launched "Imagism" in 1912, one of his prime exhibits was a group of five short poems, devised by Hulme to illustrate a point in a literary discussion, and published by Pound half-jokingly as "the complete poetical works of T. E. Hulme." Between Hulme's critical theory and de Gourmont's there are numerous parallels, as René Taupin has shown; [7] and de Gourmont himself has commented upon the Imagist poets with special reference to their debt to the French symbolists:

> The English Imagists obviously proceed from the French Symbolists. One sees that first of all in their horror of the cliché, horror of rhetoric and the grandiose, of every oratorical and facile manner with which the imitators of Victor Hugo have always disgusted us; the precision of the language, the nakedness of vision, the concentration of thought which they love to fuse in a dominant image. [8]

[5] *The Sacred Wood*, p. 13.

[6] "Remy de Gourmont: a Distinction followed by Notes" (1919), *Instigations* (New York, 1920), p. 169.

[7] *L'Influence du Symbolisme Français sur la Poésie Américaine, 1910–1920* (Paris, 1929), pp. 84–5.

[8] *La France*, May 5, 1915; quoted by Taupin, p. 87.

Hulme published very little in his short lifetime. His *Speculations* (the source of all the passages that we shall quote below) did not appear until 1924. Much of his influence upon his contemporaries has therefore to be referred to his lectures and conversations. (He and Eliot, by the way, had no personal contact.) It has been argued that Hulme's actual influence upon his immediate generation was much slighter than our present-day reading of *Speculations* would suggest.[9] Yet the parallels between his position and Eliot's are striking.

Hulme, like Eliot's Harvard teacher, Irving Babbitt, referred romanticism to Jean Jacques Rousseau's notion that "man was by nature good, that it was only bad laws and customs that had suppressed him." In the Romantic view man is "an infinite reservoir of possibilities" and not as in the classical view, a creature "intrinsically limited, but disciplined by order and tradition to something fairly decent." Hulme considered the classical view to be "identical with the normal religious attitude." [1]

The traditionalism of Hulme is thus much more thoroughgoing than that of Babbitt or of Arnold. It goes behind Babbitt's "Humanism" and Arnold's participation in the Victorian Compromise, and thus anticipates almost precisely Eliot's criticism of Babbitt and Arnold. Hulme wanted a return to orthodox doctrine. His concern with religion had nothing to do with recapturing "the sentiment of Fra Angelico."

> What is important, is what nobody seems to realize—the dogmas like that of Original Sin, which are the closest expression of the categories of the religious attitude. That man is in no sense perfect, but a wretched creature, who can yet apprehend perfection. It is not, then, that I put up with the dogma for the sake of the sentiment, but that I may possibly swallow the sentiment for the sake of the dogma.[2]

But the relation of such orthodoxy to Hulme's views about actual works of verbal art might not be hit at first guess by an uninitiated person. Unlike Babbitt and unlike Arnold, Hulme is not marshalling

[9] Ezra Pound, for example, writes: "Without malice toward T. E. H. it now [1938] seems advisable to correct a distortion which can be found even in portly works of reference. The critical LIGHT during the years immediately pre-war in London shone not from Hulme but from Ford (Madox, etc.) in so far as it fell on writing at all. . . . It detracts no jot from the honour due Hulme that he had no monopoly of London literary life and did not crowd out other interests. . . . Hulme's broadside may have come later as a godsend when published. I have no doubt that the bleak and smeary 'Twenties' wretchedly needed his guidance, and the pity is that he wasn't there in person to keep down vermin. . . ." (*The Townsman*, January, 1938). Quoted from *The Poetry of Ezra Pound*, by Hugh Kenner (Norfolk, Conn. 1951), pp. 307–9.

[1] *Speculations* (New York, 1924), pp. 116–17, by permission of the publishers, Harcourt, Brace and Company, Inc.

[2] *Speculations*, p. 71.

ethical or religious views as a frame for a didactic theory of literature. On the contrary the classicism of Hulme is a form of objectivism which insists upon clear distinctions between ethical or religious doctrine and poetic composition. Hulme thought that poetry ought to recognize its limitations. In order to compete with religion poetry has to try to lug in the infinite, and the infinite in poetic form may be somewhat less than satisfactory. We encounter here mainly the *emotions* "that are grouped round the word infinite." We enter the area of "spilt religion," a certain romantic "damp." [3] What Hulme is getting round to saying is that if ethics and religion themselves are firm, art too will enjoy its own kind of "dry hardness" [4]—not as a vehicle for, or simple statement of, ethics or religion, but as a human artifact taking shape in the same universe where ethics and religion are sustaining principles. Certain corollaries of this basic view form a cluster of doctrines which we shall see interacting rather tightly in the logic of the neo-classic criticism.

(1) There is no such thing as a "poetic" subject matter. Hulme wants to knock out both Arnold's high seriousness and the romantic distinction between fancy and imagination. "It doesn't matter an atom," he says, "that the emotion produced is not of dignified vagueness, but on the contrary amusing." [5] The Coleridgean "fixities and definites" are apparently just what the poetic fancy *should* be occupied with. For "the great aim is accurate, precise and definite description." [6] Fancy would be the proper faculty for producing the "cheerful, dry and sophisticated" verse that Hulme predicted was to come.

(2) The business of the poet is not personal expression but craft. Hulme's version of this doctrine is, looking toward the reader, an objection to the "sloppiness" which "doesn't consider that a poem is a poem unless it is moaning or whining about something or other." [7] The proper aim of the poet is to "get the exact curve of what he sees, whether it be an object or an idea in the mind." [8]

(3) Poetry is a matter of images, metaphors. That much is entailed in the advice about accuracy just given. "Visual meanings can only be transferred by the new bowl of metaphor; prose is an old pot that lets them leak out. Images in verse are not mere decoration, but the very essence of an intuitive language." [9] And so we are led to dwell on a distinction between prose and poetry, and, borrowing some logical terms from Henri Bergson, to explain the difference as a difference between the "extensive" and the "intensive." Prose—that is, the mode of intellectual exposition—the use of language properly made by writers of cook

[3] *Speculations*, p. 118.
[4] *Speculations*, p. 126.
[5] *Speculations*, p. 137.
[6] *Speculations*, p. 132.
[7] *Speculations*, p. 126.
[8] *Speculations*, p. 132.
[9] *Speculations*, p. 135.

books and legal constitutions and scientific treatises—deals with "extensive manifolds." Prose makes "diagrams, and diagrams are essentially things whose parts are separate one from another. The intellect always analyses—when there is a synthesis it is baffled." But poetry deals with "intensive" manifolds, and "to deal with the intensive you must use intuition,"[1] and hence "images," which "are the very essence of an intuitive language."[9]

(4) Finally, the complexity with which poetry deals is not mechanical but organic. Each "part" of a poem is "modified by the other's presence, and each to a certain extent is the whole."[1] Hulme is bound to remind us here of the German romantics and Coleridge rather than of any classical or neo-classical source. His central essay, "Romanticism and Classicism," indeed makes extensive reference to Coleridge. Still Hulme does emphasize the art object more cleanly than Coleridge. And as we have seen he has a positive distaste for that expansive "genius," or mind producing the art object, which was Coleridge's chief distraction. Hulme is guilty of a good many references to the poet's sincerity and to the zest which goes into his poetic activity—yet in the end he seems to refer these experiences to the actual poem and to want to find their validation there if anywhere. He is giving us on the whole the classical and objective version of organicity, which to be sure is what appears in the Schlegels and other German "romantics," if not in Coleridge.

III

HULME'S training as a student of philosophy enabled him to provide a rather systematic account of the new classic reaction. By contrast, Ezra Pound's most vigorous and most influential criticism is *ad hoc* and occasional. It has often taken the form of practical advice to other writers. Pound has not aspired to system-building; he has rather been concerned to "discover" a new author; to help him find his appropriate idiom; to preside over the formation of taste (one of his books bears the characteristic title, *The ABC of Reading*); to assist in the final revision of particular poems. (The most celebrated of these was Eliot's *The Waste Land*, which is dedicated to Pound as *Il Miglior Fabbro*.)

Pound's special critical emphasis reveals itself in a letter that he wrote in 1915 to Harriet Monroe: "Poetry," he says, "must be *as well written as prose*," a sentiment to be echoed by Eliot in his Introduction to Samuel Johnson's *The Vanity of Human Wishes*. In the same letter Pound went on to specify the "prose" virtues that he had in mind:

[9] *Speculations*, p. 135.
[1] *Speculations*, p. 139.

There must be no book words, no periphrases, no inversions. It must be as simple as De Maupassant's best prose, and as hard as Stendhal's. . . . Rhythm MUST have meaning. It can't be merely a careless dash off, with no grip and no real hold to the words and sense. . . .

There must be no clichés, set phrases, stereotyped journalese. The only escape from such is by precision, a result of concentrated attention to what [one] is writing. . . . Objectivity and again objectivity, and expression: no hindside-beforeness, no straddled adjectives (as "addled mosses dank"), no Tennysonianness of speech; nothing—nothing that you couldn't, in some circumstance, in the stress of some emotion, actually say." [2]

For Pound, content and expression are coterminous. In a good poem, where every word performs its function, there is no room for an idle ornament or a vague expression or a mechanical and irrelevant rhythm. Form is expressive of meaning: ideally, form *is* meaning.[3] "Great literature," Pound writes, "is simply language charged with meaning to the utmost possible degree." [4]

Pound's ideal poetry has the "simplicity" (the economy) of good prose; and it has the "hardness" of good prose—as opposed to the vague and imprecise feeling that he like Hulme associated with "romantic" poetry. But poetry has in addition its own characteristic devices for rendering its meanings. Principal among them is something which Pound connects with the method of the Chinese ideogram.[5]

Pound was fascinated with the concrete particularity apparently enjoined by the Chinese written character. In reading Chinese, it seemed to him that one was not attending to a mere "juggling [of] mental counters," but was "watching *things* work out their fate." How did the Chinese write "Man sees horse"?

. . . the Chinese method follows natural suggestion. First stands the man on his two legs. Second, his eye moves through space: a bold figure represented by running legs under an eye, a modified picture of an eye, a modified picture of running legs but unforgettable once you have seen it. Third stands the horse on his four legs.[6]

[2] *Letters of Ezra Pound*, ed. D. D. Paige (New York, 1950), pp. 48–9, by permission of the publishers, Harcourt, Brace and Company, Inc. Compare Coleridge's amusingly similar remarks in his *Biographia Literaria*, Chapters I and XVIII.

[3] Cf. Croce's position, *ante* Chapter 23.

[4] "How to Read" (1929), *Polite Essays* (Norfolk, Conn., 1939), p. 167.

[5] By 1913 Pound had encountered the writings of Ernest Fenollosa and in 1919 edited Fenollosa's "The Chinese Written Character as a Medium for Poetry." This work was reprinted in *Instigations* (New York, 1920).

[6] *Instigations*, p. 363.

Whether in any workable language the discrete elements could retain so much of their original integrity may perhaps be questioned. A comparison with English (which is a manifold of dead metaphors that resist all but the most unremitting attempts to resuscitate them) will be hardly reassuring. But in any case the Chinese ideogram provided Pound with a screen upon which to make a vivid projection of his ideal for a poetic language.

In such a language, the grip upon concrete particulars remains firm. The language resists a tendency (to which Pound believes the modern Western reader is particularly prone) either to slip into woolly abstractions or to take abstractions to be themselves *things*. The ideographic method of juxtaposing picturable elements not only seemed to inhibit shallow and oversimple abstractions: it allowed a skilful artist to define with subtlety and precision what he wanted to say: not this, and not that, but precisely *this*.

Pound's ideographic method is, of course, metaphoric in essence and Pound acknowledges as much: "[The ideographic] process is metaphor, the use of material images to suggest immaterial relations." [7] But it is not hard to see why Pound would welcome a new term, one which would avoid the notions of refinement and decoration that adhere to the term *metaphor*, and which would allow him to stress function and structure. The ideograph is an arrangement of concrete particulars; there is a confrontation of these, yielding not a denatured abstraction, but a precise concrete experience. In constructing his ideograph, the poet is as "impersonal" as the scientist. "Poetry," Pound wrote in 1910, "is a sort of inspired mathematics, which gives us equations, not for abstract figures, triangles, spheres, and the like, but equations for the human emotions." [8]

IV

IT WAS Eliot, however, who brought this matter of impersonality squarely to the attention of his generation. In "Tradition and the Individual Talent" (1919), Eliot stated the position with almost shocking emphasis:

> the poet has, not a "personality" to express, but a particular medium, which is only a medium and not a personality, in which impressions and experiences combine in peculiar and unexpected ways. Impressions and experiences which are important for the man may take no place in the poetry, and those which

[7] *Instigations*, p. 376.
[8] *The Spirit of Romance* (London, 1910), p. 5.

become important in the poetry may play quite a negligible part in the man, the personality.[9]

Such an "impersonal" conception of art is almost belligerently "anti-romantic." It focuses attention, "not upon the poet but upon the poetry." It thus emphasizes the art object as such. It represents a return to something like Aristotelian theory. Hardly since the 17th century had a critic writing in English so resolutely transposed poetic theory from the axis of pleasure versus pain to that of unity versus multiplicity.[1]

The relations among the parts that make up the art work become the important matter for critical investigation. That relationship is conceived to be complex. Eliot even suggests that the work of art is to be regarded as an organism, alive with a life of its own. Thus, in the Introduction to the 1928 edition of *The Sacred Wood*, he writes:

> We can only say that a poem, in some sense, has its own life; that its parts form something quite different from a body of neatly ordered biographical data; that the feeling, or emotion, or vision, resulting from the poem is something different from the feeling or emotion or vision in the mind of the poet.[2]

Such an emphasis was bound to bring down upon Eliot the charge that he had reduced the poet to an automaton who secreted his poem in some unconscious and brainless way, and that he had thus committed himself to the most "romantic" theory possible. We shall notice some of these attacks upon Eliot's theory of art a little later in this chapter. But for the moment we are concerned to round out a little further Eliot's "classicism," particularly in its more general aspects. For Eliot, as for Pound, the essence of poetry is metaphor; but the special insights that he brings to metaphor come, not from Chinese picture writing, but from the French symbolist poets of the 19th century and from the English "metaphysical" poets of the 17th.

Eliot refused to be upset by the notorious "conceits" of a Donne or a Herbert; their admitted failures did not impugn their successes. As for Dr. Johnson's criticism that these poets "yoked by violence together" the "most heterogeneous ideas," Eliot remarked that "a degree of heterogeneity of material compelled into unity by the operation of the poet's mind is omnipresent in poetry."[3] He accepted the

[9] *Selected Essays, 1917–1932* (New York, 1932), p. 8. Cf. also from the same essay (p. 11) "The emotion of art is impersonal. And the poet cannot reach this impersonality without surrendering himself wholly to the work to be done," and (p. 10) "Poetry is not a turning loose of emotion, but an escape from emotion; it is not the expression of personality, but an escape from personality." René Taupin has pointed out (pp. 212–15) the derivation of these notions from Remy de Gourmont's *Problème du Style*.

[1] Cf. *ante* Chapter 7, p. 134.

[2] *The Sacred Wood* (1928), p. x.

[3] "The Metaphysical Poets," *Selected Essays*, p. 243.

incongruity of the elements as inevitable: the perennial problem of the poet was to unite what resists unification; the skilful poet was the poet who could turn to positive account the very resistances set up by his materials.

Eliot found in the bold and often strenuous figurative language of the metaphysical poets the necessary means for achieving "a direct sensuous apprehension of thought, or a recreation of thought into feeling." [4] He saw that the problem of "acceptable" metaphor was continuous with the general problem of poetic unity. Thus he writes:

> A thought to Donne was an experience; it modified his sensibility. When a poet's mind is perfectly equipped for its work, it is constantly amalgamating disparate experience; the ordinary man's experience is chaotic, irregular, fragmentary. The latter falls in love, or reads Spinoza, and these two experiences have nothing to do with each other, or with the noise of the typewriter or the smell of cooking; in the mind of the poet these experiences are always forming new wholes. [5]

This power to "amalgamate disparate experience" was not limited to the metaphysical poets. It was possessed by the great Elizabethan dramatists. Dante possessed it. And coming nearer to our own time, Eliot discerned in some of the French symbolist poets "a method curiously similar to that of the 'metaphysical poets'. . . . Jules Laforgue and Tristan Corbière in many of his poems, are," he declared, "nearer to the 'school of Donne' than any modern English poet." [6]

Any lapse of this power to "amalgamate" results in the separation of thought and feeling, the poetic and the unpoetic, form and content. As applied to figurative language, it has the effect of making metaphor non-structural, a mere echo of the thought (illustration) or emotional excess baggage (ornamentation). A high point of his praise of Andrew Marvell is that Marvell's best verse satisfies "the elucidation of Imagination given by Coleridge: 'This power . . . reveals itself in the balance or reconcilement of opposite or discordant qualities. . . .'" [7] In terms reminiscent of Hulme, Eliot speaks of Marvell's "bright, hard precision," which, as achieved by Marvell, does not render his poetry less but more serious. Marvell's poetry, with its serious wit, challenges Coleridge's distinction between the fancy and the imagination, for many of the devices in Marvell's poetry that Coleridge would have to range under

---

[4] *Selected Essays*, p. 246.
[5] *Selected Essays*, p. 247.
[6] *Selected Essays*, pp. 248–9.
[7] "Andrew Marvell," *Selected Essays*, p. 258. In the same essay Eliot remarks that "in the verses of Marvell . . . there is the making of the familiar strange, and the strange familiar, which Coleridge attributed to good poetry."

fancy are actually used to achieve effects that show the full power of the imagination.

V

ELIOT's thoughts about an impersonal art arrived at their most celebrated formulation in an essay entitled "Hamlet and his Problems" (1919). Eliot wrote:

> The only way of expressing emotion in the form of art is by finding an "objective correlative"; in other words, a set of objects, a situation, a chain of events which shall be the formula of that *particular* emotion; such that when the external facts, which must terminate in sensory experience, are given, the emotion is immediately evoked.[8]

The phrase "objective correlative" has gained a currency probably far beyond anything that the author could have expected or intended. With the advantage of hindsight, it is easy to see why; the notion of an objective correlative puts the emphasis firmly upon the work itself as a structure. Since the poet cannot transfer his emotions or his idea from his own mind directly to his readers, there must be some kind of mediation —"a set of objects, a situation, a chain of events." It is through these that the transaction between author and reader necessarily takes place. This is where "what the author has to say" is objectified, and it is with the shape and character of this object that the critic is properly concerned. For this object is the primary source of, and warrant for, the reader's response, whatever that may be; and it is also the primary basis for whatever inferences we may draw about what it is that the "author wanted to say."

Yet the doctrine of the objective correlative is a kind of summation of what Eliot, along with Hulme and Pound, derived from the theory and practice of the French symbolists. The symbolists had argued that poetry cannot express emotion directly; emotions can only be evoked. And their studies had canvassed the various means by which this can be done. Baudelaire maintained that every color, sound, odor, conceptualized emotion, and every visual image has its correspondence in each of the other fields. Mallarmé, insisting that poetry was made, not of ideas, but of words,[9] devoted himself to exploring the potentialities of words

---

[8] *Selected Essays*, pp. 124–5. This notion is perhaps anticipated by Pound's phrase "equations for the human emotions": cf. *ante* p. 664.

[9] Degas tried to write sonnets and complained to Mallarmé that he was unsuccessful, despite all the ideas he had. "You don't write poems with ideas, my dear Degas," said Mallarmé, "but with words." P. Valéry, 'Poésie et Pensée Abstraite," in *Variété* V (Paris, 1945), p. 141.

conceived as gesture or as modes of emotive suggestion, and treated the interplay of words as a kind of ballet or a kind of "musical" organization. To name an object was to destroy three-quarters of the delight proper to a poetic evocation of it. Pound, in making acknowledgement of "the great gifts of 'symbolisme,'" mentions specifically "the doctrine that one should 'suggest' not 'present.'"[1]

The doctrine of the "objective correlative" places a thoroughly anti-Romantic stress upon craftsmanship; but Eliot, in the way in which he argues it, manages to involve himself in the language of expressionism. This expressionism and the "language of the emotions" have come in for a vigorous overhauling by the philosopher Eliseo Vivas.[2]

Eliot has implied that Shakespeare knew in advance the particular emotion for which *Hamlet* was to be the "correlative," and has implied further that the reader (or auditor) ought to feel this particular emotion too, if the play is to be considered successful. But Vivas contends that in fact the poet only discovers his emotion through trying to formulate it in words. What the poet "really felt could only be expressed precisely in and through the poem, which is to say that he had to discover it through the act of composition."[3] It is impossible that the reader should ever feel the same emotion as the poet did, and there is no reason why he should. A poem expresses *less* than the emotion with which the poet began, but it also expresses much more. It expresses "all that which the poet presents objectively in it for apprehension."[4] Among the elements making up the poem-object,

> there are some that we find easier to denote. . . . through the terms which we use to denote emotions. But I see no reason to assume that all else in the poem is put there merely to arouse an emotion in us or to bring about its objective denotation. Surface, formal, and ideational elements are all in their own right of intrinsic interest. And while the emotion expressed is also of interest, it is not, and it should not be, of chief or exclusive interest to the reader.[5]

Vivas is confident that such objections have "devastating" consequences for Eliot's "critical approach"; and with special regard to the theory about *Hamlet*, that judgment may well be correct. As regards Eliot's general position, however, Vivas' criticism is a pruning operation that lops off excrescences but can hardly affect the main branches of the theory set forth in "Tradition and the Individual Talent." "Poetry is

[1] *Make It New* (New Haven, 1935), p. 187.
[2] "The Objective Correlative of T. S. Eliot," *The American Bookman*, Winter, 1944; reprinted in *Creation and Discovery* (New York: The Noonday Press, 1955). Reprinted by permission of the author.
[3] *Creation and Discovery*, p. 184. [5] *Creation and Discovery*, p. 188.
[4] *Creation and Discovery*, p. 188.

not a turning loose of emotion. . . . it is not the expression of personality, but an escape from personality." [6] "Honest criticism and sensitive appreciation are directed not upon the poet but upon the poetry." [7] Eliot is at times inconsistent, but he seems never to subscribe seriously to the notion that the poet's main job is to hand over to the reader some determinate content, whether an emotion or an idea, or that the poet's effectiveness is to be measured by the success of this transaction. On the contrary, the weight of Eliot's prestige has been thrown behind a quite antithetical conception: an anti-Romantic, "impersonal" art, in which the claims of the art-object, with all their complexity and indeterminacy have first consideration. A less vulnerable statement of the objective correlative might be found in another of Eliot's essays, that "On the Metaphysical Poets": "[The metaphysical poets] were, at best, engaged in the task of trying to find the verbal equivalent for states of mind and feeling." [8] The phrase "states of mind and feeling" has the merit of minimizing the notion of some pure emotion, personal to the poet, with which the reader is to be directly infected.

VI

OTHER attacks on Eliot, notably those of Ransom and Yvor Winters, have rested upon more fundamental disagreements. Ransom found Eliot's criticism too psychologistic, too much concerned with affective experience and too little cognitive.[9] Eliot's classicism, in short, was not classical enough. This was in part Winters' criticism; but Winters' classical reaction, which harks back to that of Irving Babbitt, has in it a strong ethical ingredient. Winters castigates romanticism not merely for its murky indefiniteness but for its moral delinquency. Indeed he regards one as an aspect of the other.[1]

In the first place, Eliot's acknowledgement that the poem has in some sense a life of its own seems to Winters a concession that goes far toward making the poet merely an automaton.[2] And this is very bad for poetry.

The artistic process is one of moral evaluation of human experience, by means of a technique which renders possible an evaluation more precise than any other. The poet tries to understand his experience in rational terms, to state his understanding, and

---

[6] *Selected Essays*, p. 10.
[7] *Selected Essays*, p. 7.
[8] *Selected Essays*, p. 248.
[9] Cf. *ante* Chapter 27.
[1] Compare the position of Tolstoy: see *ante* Chapter 21.
[2] Ransom makes the same point: "This is very nearly a doctrine of poetic automatism" (*The New Criticism*, p. 152).

simultaneously to state, by means of the feelings which we attach to words, the kind and degree of emotion that should properly be motivated by this understanding.[3]

Since the poet is making an evaluation, he must remain fully in control of his poem; there must be no French-symbolist nonsense about letting the reins lie loose upon the horse's neck, allowing him to find his own way. Eliot trusts Pegasus too far when he writes: "I do not deny that art may be affirmed to serve ends beyond itself; but art is not required to be aware of these ends. . . ." [4] The poet must be aware of where he is going; it is not enough for him merely to try to "find the verbal equivalent of states of mind and feeling." Those states of mind and feeling must be judged and evaluated.

Winters charges that Eliot was too often content merely to reflect the disorder and incoherence of the age. Instead of mastering his experience and judging it, he simply mirrors it. To do this is to fall into what Winters has called the "fallacy of expressive, or imitative, form; the procedure in which the form succumbs to the raw material of the poem." [5] The modern poet would justify the formlessness of his poem by saying that he is writing about a chaotic and disordered age. But on the basis of such reasoning as this one could argue that the proper way to write a poem about madness is to make the poem itself insanely irrational, and the proper way to write about dulness is for the poet to make his *Dunciad* as dull and sleep-provoking as possible.

Winters has urged his indictment relentlessly. Eliot's *Waste Land* betrays in its "limp" rhythms Mr. Eliot's own "spiritual limpness." [6] Likewise Pound's "Hugh Selwyn Mauberly," St. John Perse's *Anabase*, and Joyce's *Ulysses*—all are found guilty in some degree or other of the fallacy of imitative form. Even a poet like Marianne Moore, whom Winters credits with "unshakeable certainty of intention" [7] as distinguished from the romantic ironist's "moral insecurity," reveals in her poetry some of the weaknesses of imitative form.

Fortunately, one does not have to endorse Winters' applications of his principle in order to endorse the principle itself. Winters is clearly right in pointing out that confusion cannot be rendered by confusion; the negative, by the presentation of a slice of negation. This insight has allowed him to put with special cogency several questions having to do with the structure of poetry: what is the minimum coherence required of a poem and by what structural methods is that coherence to be attained?

[3] *In Defense of Reason*, p. 464.
[4] "The Function of Criticism," *Selected Essays*, p. 13.
[5] *Primitivism and Decadence* (1937), included in *In Defense of Reason*, p. 41.
[6] *In Defense of Reason*, p. 22.
[7] *In Defense of Reason*, p. 71.

The poem must have a rational structure, for it is the rational structure that controls the emotion. The rational statement made by the poem is the "motive" for the emotion. Winters, to be sure, does not demand that the poem have an *explicitly* logical organization: it is enough that it be "implicitly rational." The test is whether the poem "can be paraphrased in general terms." [8] The last phrase does a great deal to remove the rigor from Winters' prescriptions. If the terms of the paraphrase be general enough, then any poem that "makes sense" can be paraphrased, including many poems to which Winters would deny a rational structure. Ezra Pound, for instance, has denied Winters' charge that he has abandoned "logic in the Cantos." Much depends upon what person is to apply the test of paraphrasability.

The rational statement that the poem makes—however necessary in Winters' scheme—is not the essence of the poem. Winters himself cites a poem in which the rational content as such says quite the reverse of what the poem taken as a whole "says." [9] The "moral attitude" that Winters insists the poem shall present is defined not by the "logical content alone" but by the feeling as well, and "the feeling is quite specific and unparaphrasable." Yet however indirect the influence of rational structure, it has its final importance, and Winters' censure of Eliot boils down to the charge that he gives "primacy . . . to the emotions." [1]

Certain structural methods yield poems that cannot be paraphrased. Many of our modern poets, laying aside such time-honored methods for organizing a poem as Repetition, Logical Method, and Narrative, have used what Winters calls "Pseudo-reference" and "Qualitative Progression." Pseudo-reference pretends to rational coherence (by retaining the "syntactic forms and much of the vocabulary of rational coherence") [2] but it is not really coherent. Qualitative Progression goes further and abandons even the pretence of rational progression. It is an attempt to build poetry out of the "connotative" (i.e., the suggestive) aspects of language alone, and it actually results in merely a blur of "reverie."

In Qualitative Progression, the transition from image to image is governed by mood: the principle of coherence is that of feeling. Qualitative Progression occurs in traditional poetry, to be sure, but only as an ancillary to the basic method of progression, not as the basic method itself. For example, in Shakespeare

the qualitative progression . . . is peripheral, the central movement of each play being dependent upon . . . the psychology of the hero, or narrative logic, and so firmly dependent that oc-

[8] *In Defense of Reason*, p. 31.
[9] See his discussion of Allen Tate's "The Subway," *In Defense of Reason*, pp. 19–20.
[1] *In Defense of Reason*, p. 469.
[2] *In Defense of Reason*, p. 40.

casional excursions into the rationally irrelevant can be managed with no loss of force, whereas in [Eliot's] *The Waste Land* the qualitative progression is central: it is as if we should have a dislocated series of scenes from *Hamlet* without the prince himself, or with too slight an account of his history for his presence to be helpful. The difference between Mr. Eliot and Mr. Pound is this: that in *The Waste Land*, the prince is briefly introduced in the footnotes, whereas it is to be doubted that Mr. Pound could manage such an introduction were he so inclined.[3]

Beneath Winters' polemics lurks an important distinction that deserves a clear restatement: emotions may be presented in one of two basic ways. The poet can give the reasons for his hero's emotion, "motivating" the emotion by giving us the events which produced it, or the poet can define the emotion through a symbol or a series of analogies. One method, of course, does not exclude the other. Shakespeare can give us the series of dramatic events that prompt Hamlet's puzzled disgust with himself, but he can also, and does, allow Hamlet to find an analogy for his feelings: "O what a rogue and peasant slave am I!" Winters censures the modern poet for relying too exclusively upon the second method: he moves in an aimless and random reverie from image to image with only a kind of stream-of-consciousness connection between the images. The result is vagueness and obscurity. "The great discovery of the French symbolists," remarks the author of a recent book on Pound, "was the irrelevance, and hence the possibility of abolition, of paraphrasable plot."[4] It is just this abolition that Winters censures.

VII

WINTERS has defined a third structural method that he regards as reprehensible. He calls it progression by Double Mood (i.e., by ironic qualification). He regards Lord Byron as the first poet to use this method on a "pretentious scale," but Jules Laforgue and Tristan Corbière yield striking instances of it in modern poetry. In this kind of progression, the poet alternates moods: he "builds up a somewhat grandiloquent effect only to demolish it by ridicule or by ridiculous anticlimax."[5] Such a method is "the formula for adolescent disillusionment: the unhappily 'cynical' reaction to the loss of a feeling not worth having."[6]

The deflation of the positive mood is accomplished by irony—ro-

[3] *In Defense of Reason*, p. 59.
[4] Hugh Kenner, *The Poetry of Ezra Pound*, p. 91.
[5] *In Defense of Reason*, p. 65.
[6] *In Defense of Reason*, p. 67.

mantic irony,[7] Winters calls it, carefully distinguishing it from the classical irony of a Dryden or a Pope, who was "perfectly secure in his own feelings" [8] and whose irony was used to attack someone else.

The romantic ironist is not morally secure and his irony is thus a reflection of his confusion or of his moral flabbiness or of his lack of concern to focus his poem. It amounts to "an admission of careless feeling, which is to say careless writing." Winters therefore recommends "the waste-basket and a new beginning." [9] For the poet cannot legitimately say: my confused and uncertain poem simply reflects the confusion of the situation which happens to be my subject matter. That would be to embrace the fallacy of imitative form.

Winters' bias toward the logical, the definite, and the unequivocal gives him a certain corrective value. He has refused to be imposed upon by misty and vague meanings, and he has been able to put his finger on tendencies toward incoherence that have escaped the notice of many other modern critics. But one may doubt whether Winters leaves sufficient room for what was once attributed to the superventions and ministering grace bestowed by the Muse. Winters assumes that the poet knows (or ought to know) how to "adjust feeling" [1] to the rational structure of his poem, and that his failure to do so is a kind of moral failure. Thus, he places a great burden upon the poet's conscious intention, more perhaps than it can sustain. For as Vivas, for instance, has pointed out (see p. 668 above) the poet often *discovers* what he has to say in the process of saying it. Furthermore, Winters perhaps needs to be reminded of Mallarmé's dry observation that poetry is written not with ideas, but with words. The poet has to take into account not only the complexities of experience but the recalcitrant qualities of language; he must always depend, to some degree, upon implication and indirection.

Eliot's suggestion that a poem "has its own life" acknowledges its resistance to direct control by the poet. So do Eliot's reiterations that all poetry, even a lyric from the Greek anthology, is *dramatic*.[2] There may be some significance in the fact that Winters defines poetry as a *statement*. (He regards it as a statement of a special kind, to be sure, but a statement, nevertheless.) Winters never quite escapes, nor apparently does he wish to escape, the consequences of this term.

A curious passage in *Primitivism and Decadence* illustrates Winters' suspicion of "dramatic" presentation. He quotes with approval a student's

---

[7] Winters borrows the term from Irving Babbitt (cf. *ante* Chapter 20), whose use of the term was influenced by his unsympathetic response to the German critics' development of irony: cf. *ante* Chapter 17.

[8] *In Defense of Reason*, p. 70.

[9] *In Defense of Reason*, p. 73.

[1] *In Defense of Reason*, p. 367.

[2] "A Dialogue on Dramatic Poetry" (1928), *Selected Essays*, p. 38.

remark that "Laforgue resembles a person who speaks with undue harshness and then apologizes; whereas he should have made the necessary subtractions before speaking." [3] A considered *statement* does indeed require that one make the "subtractions" first, but the mode of *drama* undertakes to give us the very process by which the final attitude is reached: the "subtractions," the conflicts between rival attitudes, the ironic qualifications, the various stages in the dialectic—all of these are of the essence of dramatic presentation. For Winters, however, the issue comes down to this: "the question of how carefully one is willing to scrutinize his feelings and correct them." [4] So it does, and Winters is right in demanding that the poet refrain from "careless feeling, which is to say careless writing." That is to say, the poet should not correct his poem in public as it goes along. For such botching, Winters' recommendation is surely the proper one: "instead of irony as the remedy for the unsatisfactory feelings," the "wastebasket and a new beginning." But it can be argued that irony has other and more respectable functions.

Once the dramatic character of poetry is admitted, we make room for a very different conception of irony. Irony becomes a recognition of the incongruities with which poetry has to deal. It acknowledges the pressure of the total context upon the individual word or image, the slight warping of signification continually made by the poet as he shades the word to its precise meaning in its context. It registers the tensions set up between the disparate elements of the poem which are being compelled into unity. It concedes the element of compulsion.

If one insists in finding in this structural irony an index of the poet's attitude, that attitude is not necessarily one of carelessness or cynicism or moral slovenliness. The irony might rather point to his humility, to his sense of the limitations of the human mind and of the complexity of experience. Such a poet is willing to qualify his more sweeping generalizations and to undercut his more fervent enthusiasms.[5]

Most of what Eliot has had to say on this specific topic occurs in his essay on Marvell under the rubric "wit." Marvell's wit is "a tough rea-

---

[3] *In Defense of Reason*, p. 72.

[4] *In Defense of Reason*, p. 72.

[5] Much turns here upon whether one accepts the view that some measure of indirection is enjoined upon the poet by the very nature of poetry. To the man habituated to the motorboat of logic, the manoeuvers of a sailing vessel forced to tack against the wind will seem wasteful and silly. He may even accuse the skipper of drunkenness or of moral vacillation.

T. E. Hulme definitely found in his "classical" poetry a manifestation of the poet's humility and of his sense of his own limitations. Hulme wrote that even in "the most imaginative flights" of the classical poet, there is "always a holding back, a reservation. The classical poet never forgets this finiteness, this limit of man. . . . If you say an extravagant thing which does exceed the limits inside which you know man to be fastened, yet there is always conveyed in some way at the end an impression of yourself standing outside it, and not believing it, or consciously putting it forward as a flourish" (*Speculations*, pp. 119–20).

sonableness beneath the slight lyric grace"; it "implies a constant inspection and criticism of experience"; [6] it provides for his poetry an
"internal equilibrium." [7] But R. P. Warren will provide a good instance of
the tendency of critics influenced by Eliot to use the term irony itself as
a structural principle. In an essay from which we have already quoted he
tries to answer the argument that poetry ought to be eloquently simple
without ironic tension:

> Poets *have* tried very hard, for thousands of years, to say what
> they mean. But they have not only tried to say what they mean,
> they have tried to prove what they mean. The saint proves his
> vision by stepping cheerfully into the fires. The poet, somewhat
> less spectacularly, proves his vision by submitting it to the fires of
> irony—to the drama of his structure—in the hope that the fires
> will refine it. In other words, the poet wishes to indicate that his
> vision has been earned, that it can survive reference to the com-
> plexities and contradictions of experience. And irony is one such
> device of reference. [8]

VIII

BUT though Winters seems distrustful of "dramatic" presentation, because of its reliance upon implication and the consequent relinquishment
of the poet's control over his "statement," his choice of the term *motive*
("rational statement . . . is . . . motive to emotion") [9] actually points
toward the mode of drama. For if the emotions are "motivated," the
emotion can only be *inferred* from the context of situation and action.
It cannot be stated directly, and the paraphrasable matter that "motivates"
it is not so much a "statement" as a dramatic situation—a narrative, or
a plot.

Indeed it is possible to interpret Winters' criticism as a powerful reassertion of the importance of plot. One might even compare it to Matthew
Arnold's "classical" protest against romantic "confused multitudinous-
ness" and "exuberance of expression." [1] But Eliot's concern with metaphor
and symbol and even with irony represents a like "classical" reaction.
For these, as Eliot treats them, are all aspects of a dramatic presentation
as distinguished from the *personal* expression of the poet. The distinction
is crucial: once we have dissociated the speaker of the lyric from the
personality of the poet, even the tiniest lyric reveals itself as drama. A

[6] *Selected Essays,* p. 262.
[7] *Selected Essays,* p. 263.
[8] "Pure and Impure Poetry," Stallman's *Critiques,* p. 103.
[9] *Anatomy of Nonsense,* p. 13.
[1] Cf. *ante* Chapter 20.

poem is not a "statement about" something, but, as Aristotle said of tragedy, an *action*. Even metaphor is an action is this sense. It is a presentation of discrete entities, and the role of interpreting their relationship is forced upon the hearer or the reader. Since the identification asserted by a metaphor is *literal* nonsense, the interpretation, by implication, directs attention to the situation, the character of the speaker, and the occasion.

If the smallest lyric can be regarded as a drama, conversely the most formidable tragedy can be regarded as symbolic. *Macbeth* is perennially interesting to us, not as a historic incident (even if the history in that play were undistorted history), but because Macbeth is universal, he is in some sense ourselves. If his emotions are "motivated" by the events presented in the play, they are also meaningful symbols of our own emotions. Otherwise we should feel that Macbeth's emotional reactions were indeed "unmotivated": he would seem perverse or incomprehensible.

A realization that Winters' conception of poetry, like Eliot's, is ultimately "dramatic" need not impugn the useful distinction between motive (the reason for an emotion) and objective correlative (the symbol of an emotion). (The perception may indicate, however, why it is difficult to maintain the absolute distinction, especially with reflexive and highly allusive poetry.) It suggests further that Winters' "motive" is itself a kind of objective correlative. If the poet is to "control" emotion by providing "motives" for it, he is indeed compelled to make use of "a set of objects, a situation, or a chain of events." These are objective and can be presented; and since the emotion is generated by these objects and actions and, in so far as it is controlled, is controlled by the selection and rearrangement of these objectified elements, they may fairly be called the "correlative" of the emotion. For whether their "relation" to the emotion is that of cause or of symbolic equivalent, their *cor*relation with the emotion is evident.

IX

THE concern for the poem as an objective thing is the special highlight of the classicism of Eliot. We have mentioned Eliot's observation that the poem possesses a life of its own, and his insistence on the poet's need to extinguish his personality in the poem. Though such remarks as these can be interpreted as an abdication of the poet's proper responsibility, they need not be. Indeed, Eliot's metaphor about the poem's "life" and his suggestion that the poet's primary task is to foster and nurture that life are not incorrigibly irrational. It is possible to argue that the poem, like a growing plant, naturally grows toward the light and unless interfered with tends to grow straight.

This notion that the developing poem furnishes the poet with certain norms for its own nurturing (along with the further implication that poetry gives us a special kind of knowledge) has been spelled out by Allen Tate a little more fully than by Eliot. Tate, rejecting Winters' conception of a poem as a *statement* about something, would define it as an action rendered in its totality. This action is not prescriptive of means (as science is) nor of ends (as religion is). The reader is left to draw his own conclusions: (". . . the vision of the whole," as Tate says, "is not susceptible of logical demonstration.") [2] There can be no *external* verification: the reader grasps it by an act of the imagination or not at all. (The didactic poet, the rhetorician in the service of a cause, the advertising man—all do appeal to some "truth"—some authority, scientific or unscientific—as proof of the case being made.)

But though the poem is not a statement that can be proved, Tate will not allow that it is a whimsical, subjective "projection." He reprehends metaphors and similes that are "imposed upon the material from above," for they should "grow out of the material." [3] The implications of the last clause are significant: the poet, it is implied, does not fashion statements to a prearranged formula. He does not impose his formulas upon experience but reveals the patterns inherent in experience.

As an instance of adequate metaphor Tate adduces "Ripeness is all," as spoken by Edgar in *King Lear*. This figure is not imposed upon the experience "as an explanation" of it. Rather

> the figure rises from the depths of Gloucester's situation. . . .
> Possibly *King Lear* would be as good without Edgar's words;
> but it would be difficult to imagine the play without the passage
> ending in those words. They are implicit in the total structure,
> the concrete quality, of the whole experience that we have
> when we read *King Lear*.[4]

One must be careful in assigning very precise meanings to phrases like "grow out of the material" and "implicit in . . . the whole experience," which are themselves figurative. But surely they seem to discountenance the view that the imagination is merely whimsical. They suggest that the imagination obeys laws implicit in the human psyche. They even seem to demand the assumption that all human experience is finally one.

Tate, it is true, never states these assumptions in so many words, and one supposes that he would have to resist the view that this ultimate

---

[2] "Three Types of Poetry" (1934), *On the Limits of Poetry* (New York, 1948), p. 113.
[3] *On the Limits of Poetry*, p. 92.   [4] *On the Limits of Poetry*, p. 93.

oneness of the human psyche can be formulated in a set of laws which could then be used to determine the goodness or badness of particular poems. But the assumption that man exists and that his fundamental oneness transcends the innumerable differences that set apart individual men and set apart men of various cultures and periods of history seems implicit here. Perhaps it should be brought to light and stated quite flatly. For it may be the necessary assumption if we are to undertake to talk about poetry at all. Unless we can assume it, we necessarily abandon any concept of an aesthetics of poetry in favor of a tabulation of various kinds of social and personal expressions.

SUPPLEMENT

. . . Among the things that dramatic action must burn up are the author's opinions; while he is writing he has no business to know anything that is not a portion of that action. Do you suppose for one moment that Shakespeare educated Hamlet and King Lear by telling them what he thought and believed? As I see it, Hamlet and Lear educated Shakespeare, and I have no doubt that in the process of that education he found out that he was an altogether different man to what he thought himself, and had altogether different beliefs. A dramatist can help his characters to educate him by thinking and studying everything that gives them the language they are groping for through his hands and eyes, but the control must be theirs, and that is why the ancient philosophers thought a poet or dramatist Daimon-possessed.

—W. B. Yeats to Sean O'Casey, *Letters*, ed. Allan Wade (New York, 1955), p. 741, by permission of the publishers, The Macmillan Company.

. . . even Hulme, who, as an anti-romantic, explicitly leads away from the Coleridgean imagination, must, as I shall show, end by returning to a markedly similar theory of poetic creativity.

Hulme feels that the essence of romanticism is located in its idolatry of the individual who, for the romantics, should have unlimited aspirations since he has unlimited powers. . . . For the classicist, according to Hulme, sees man as an extremely limited being who needs all kinds of severely imposed disciplines if he is to function as he should in his proper sphere. Thus Hulme, defending the view of the classicist, rejects a concept of imagination which would substitute a monism for Christian dualism and would make of man a god. For the attribution to man of the power to create absolutely, *ex nihilo*, could mean little less. Thus Hulme explicitly calls for a poetry of fancy rather than the poetry of unbounded imagination which he feels contaminated English verse in the nineteenth and early twentieth centuries. He calls for a poetry that is formally precise and whose pretensions are limited to simple and vivid description. One might say that he calls for a return to a theory of imitation and opposes the reigning theory of expression, the introduction of which was so largely Coleridge's responsibility.

But there is also a quite different side of Hulme. In his essay on Bergson, in which he expounds sympathetically the aesthetic of his master in philosophy, there is a description of the poet's activity that seems nearly as transcendental as Coleridge's. Here Hulme distinguishes between intuition and stock perception and characterizes artistic creativity as the former. It is only the artist, he claims, who can break through the mere static recognition of the world about us which practical life demands; he alone can see through to the dynamic flux which characterizes essential reality. And as artist he makes this vision available to others who, without the artist, could never see beyond the stereotyped world of practicality.

This conception gives the poet a far higher and more romantic function than Hulme has assigned him in his severe "Romanticism and Classicism.". . . For while Hulme, as influenced by Bergson, still wants the poet to be descriptive, he adds a metaphysical dimension to this objective. He would have the poet describe the world about him not merely as it seems to be but rather as it really is behind the veil which hides it from most of us. The poet must not give us as the world "the film of familiarity and selfish solicitude" (note how apt this Coleridgean phrase is here) which our senses normally allow to us; rather he must give us the rare world beyond, which he somehow intuits. Now this is a handsome objective; and the intuitive faculty which is to fulfill it for Hulme seems not far removed from the imagination invoked by Coleridge. Surely we may doubt the power of fancy to operate at these profound levels.

—Murray Krieger, *The New Apologists for Poetry* (Minneapolis, 1956), pp. 33–4, by permission of the University of Minnesota Press.

At this point I shall venture to generalize, and suggest that with this disappearance of the idea of *Original Sin,* with the disappearance of the idea of intense moral struggle, the human beings presented to us both in poetry and in prose fiction to-day, and more patently among the serious writers than in the underworld of letters, tend to become less and less real. It is in fact in moments of moral and spiritual struggle depending upon spiritual sanctions, rather than in those 'bewildering minutes' in which we are all very much alike, that men and women come nearest to being real. If you do away with this struggle, and maintain that by tolerance, benevolence, inoffensiveness and a redistribution or increase of purchasing power, combined with a devotion, on the part of an elite, to Art, the world will be as good as anyone could require, then you must expect human beings to become more and more vaporous.

—T. S. Eliot, *After Strange Gods* (London, 1934), p. 42

[Melville's] letter to Mrs. Hawthorne acknowledging her symbolic interpretation of *Moby-Dick* is remarkable both for what it says and for what it assumes:

> But, then, since you, with your spiritualizing nature, see more things
> than other people, and by the same process, refine all you see, so that

they are not the same things that other people see, but things which while you think you but humbly discover them, you do in fact create them for yourself—therefore, upon the whole, I do not so much marvel at your expressions concern'g Moby Dick. At any rate, your allusion for example to the "Spirit Spout" first showed to me that there was a subtle significance in that thing—but I did not, in that case, *mean* it. I had some vague idea while writing it, that the whole book was susceptible of an allegoric construction, & also that *parts* of it were—but the speciality of many of the particular subordinate allegories, were [*sic*] first revealed to me, after reading Mr. Hawthorne's letter, which, without citing any particular examples, yet intimated the part-&-parcel allegoricalness of the whole.

This is the full-blown doctrine of aesthetic impersonality.

—Charles Feidelson, Jr., *Symbolism and American Literature* (Chicago, 1953), p. 176. Published by the University of Chicago Press, and copyright 1953 by the University of Chicago.

Augustine puts this [argument concerning evil] as succinctly as Pope does: As bad men use to ill purpose the goods of the world, God, who is good, uses bad men to good purpose. The painter knows where to place black in the scheme of his picture, and God knows where to place wicked men in the scheme of his world. (*Sermon* CCCI, 5)

All these abstract pieces of his argument Pope [in the *Essay on Man*] catches up like his predecessors in the metaphor of harmony-from-discord that has influenced Western thinking for more than twenty centuries. It may be that the ultimate appeal of this metaphor has lain in giving imaginative configuration to the average human being's sense that he is, and yet is not, at home in a world he never made. At any rate, it has had the special virtue for theodicy of recognizing the fact of evil while restricting its significance. It enabled one to take account of the observed heterogeneity and conflict of things, but reconcile them; as, for example, in the thought of Heraclitus, its probable inventor, who asserted that the universal discord—"everything happens by strife"—was the ground of the universal union—"as with the bow and the lyre, so with the world: it is the tension of opposing forces that makes the structure one." Thus the image brought together in one perspective man's present suffering and his faith, the partial and the whole views; and in such a way that even its commonest linguistic formulations (*concors discordia rerum*) dramatized the triumph of cosmos over chaos, and its commonest analogies (the world as picture, play, poem, building, etc.) all suggested, like the parent image, that in some higher dialectic than men could grasp the thesis and antithesis of experienced evil would be resolved: "All discord, harmony not understood."

—Maynard Mack, ed. Alexander Pope, *An Essay on Man* (Twickenham Edition, London, 1950), Introduction, pp. xxxiv–xxxv, by permission of Methuen and Co., Ltd.

FICTION AND DRAMA: THE GROSS STRUCTURE

§ *Henry James's concern for the novel as an art form in its own right: his debt to Turgenev and Flaubert—II. the novel conceived as an organic and dramatic structure: the action "rendered" rather than "told"—the problem of the narrator and the point of view—the problem of sequence in time, and of the "time-shift" as theorized by Conrad and Ford Madox Ford—III. the connection between this conception of fiction and the Eliot-Pound conception of poetry: an organic and "impersonal" quality shared by both, with differences only in scope and strategy —IV. the reassertion of the claims of plot as made by some recent critics—Francis Fergusson's denial that drama is "primarily" a composition "in the verbal medium": his definition of "action"—V. his indictment of a "lyric" conception of drama, and his appeal for a return to an Aristotelian theory of "imitation"—Elder Olson's "Aristotelian" poetics of the lyric—Henry James's views on objective values and the organic structure of fiction—VI. Eliot on the relation of poetry and drama—the general problem of the genres—VII. "cold-blooded" critics of poetry and "warm-blooded" critics of fiction* §

THE CONCEPTION OF THE NOVEL AS A SPECIAL ART FORM COMES relatively late. Henry James could complain in 1888 that the English novel "had no air of having a theory, a conviction, a consciousness of itself behind it—of being the expression of an artistic faith, the result of choice and comparison." [1] The French novelist, to be sure,

---

[1] "The Art of Fiction," in *Partial Portraits* (London and New York, 1888), reprinted in *The Art of Fiction and Other Essays by Henry James*, ed. Morris Roberts (New York, 1948), p. 3.

did regard writing as a craft and applied himself to the novel as an art form. But even in France the consciousness of fiction as a craft was relatively new, and James was separated by only one generation from the men whom he regarded as the first serious theorists of the art of fiction to be found anywhere—Ivan Turgenev and Gustave Flaubert. Guy de Maupassant, another of James's conscious artists, was seven years younger than James himself. As a young man James had talked with all of them, and in 1912 he could regard himself as the "last survivor of those then surrounding Gustave Flaubert." [2]

James was willing to concede that the English novel was not "necessarily the worse for" the fact that it proceeded from no special theorizing. But the English novel was "*naif*"; and James was himself too much the artist to rejoice in the "comfortable, good-humoured feeling" so widely held that "a novel is a novel, as a pudding is a pudding, and that our only business with it could be to swallow it." [3] The novel was or ought to be a work of art, and its special potentialities as a form needed to be explored. Flaubert was, for James, "the novelist's novelist," [4] and Flaubert became, especially for novelists like Joseph Conrad and Ford Madox Ford, who derived their theories from James as well as from the 19th-century French novelists, a fountainhead. James disliked, to be sure, the vision of the world that he found in Flaubert and Balzac and Zola. All three saw life as more dreary, more sordid, more mean and limited than James believed the facts to warrant. But whereas Zola conceived himself to be a kind of scientist and Balzac thought of himself as a historian, Flaubert, for all the solidity of his report of human circumstance, had shown himself to be an artist. At any rate, James believed that he could learn from Flaubert's work the principles of fictional construction.

"A novel," James declared in his essay on "The Art of Fiction," "is in its broadest definition a personal, a direct impression of life." [5] It is not clinical and "scientific," since it depends upon the individual artist's imaginative perception; and it is *direct*—not mediated through formulae or general ideas about life. A novel is also to be conceived as an organic thing—"all one and continuous, like any other organism." [6] How fully

---

[2] *The Letters of Henry James*, ed. Percy Lubbock (New York, 1920), II, 258.

[3] In a letter to Hugh Walpole, dated May 19, 1912, James wrote: "Tolstoi and D[ostoevsky] are fluid pudding, though not tasteless, because the amount of their own minds and souls in solution in the broth gives it savour and flavour, thanks to the strong, rank quality of their genius and their experience. But there are all sorts of things to be said of them, and in particular that we see how great a vice is their lack of composition. . . ." See *The Selected Letters of Henry James*, ed. Leon Edel (New York, 1955), p. 171.

[4] "Gustave Flaubert," *The Art of Fiction*, p. 153. He applied the same epithet to Turgenev.

[5] *The Art of Fiction*, p. 8.

[6] *The Art of Fiction*, p. 13.

organic James found Flaubert's best novels to be is well illustrated from a passage in which he discusses Flaubert's attention to the exact phrase:

> It was truly a wonderful success to be so the devotee of the phrase and yet never its victim. Fine as he inveterately desired it should be he still never lost sight of the question Fine for what? It is always so related and associated, so properly part of something else that is in turn part of something other, part of a reference, a tone, a passage, a page, that the simple may enjoy it for its least bearing and the initiated for its greatest.[7]

James praises Turgenev by saying that his work does away with "the perpetual clumsy assumption that subject and style are—aesthetically speaking or in the living work—different and separable things." [8]

II

A VIEW of art so thoroughly organic as this implies as a corollary an impersonal art; that is, that the work grows in accordance with some inner principle of its own being, and is not merely the creature of the writer's ego, either as an expression of his feelings as a man or as an assertion of his opinions. Ford Madox Ford records a conversation in which James said: "There are things that one wants to write all one's life, but one's artist's conscience prevents one. . . . And then . . . perhaps one allows oneself. . . ." [9] James was speaking of one of his failures, "The Altar of the Dead"; and Ford goes on to comment that the bitter lesson that the artist has to learn is "that he is not a man to be swayed by the hopes, fears, consummations or despairs of a man. He is a sensitized instrument, recording to the measure of the light vouchsafed him what is—what *may* be—the Truth." [1]

For the novelist, the problem of securing impersonality for his art has a special connection with management of the point of view. How does the narrator avoid intruding himself into the work? How, when there is information to be conveyed, can he avoid seeming to lecture his reader? How can he avoid spoiling a powerful scene by seeming to bob up before the reader like a prompt-clerk? These were questions that concerned James. But these also were the questions which Ford, and according to Ford, Joseph Conrad, with whom he collaborated on two or three novels, were to give particular attention.

They wished to make the reader forget the writer altogether so

[7] "Gustave Flaubert," *The Art of Fiction*, pp. 143-4.
[8] *The Art of Fiction*, p. 120.
[9] *Thus to Revisit* (London, 1921), p. 49.
[1] *Thus to Revisit*, p. 49.

that the story would seem to tell itself and develop with its own life. The novelist was not to "tell the reader" about what happened but to *render* it as action. Moreover, the action was not to be rendered with photographic fidelity but as it would make its impression upon a human observer. Hence Ford's name for the new art, Impressionism. As Ford put it, "Conrad found salvation not in any machined Form, but in the sheer attempt to produce in words life as it presents itself to the intelligent observer." [2] Or as Conrad himself put it (in his Preface to *The Nigger of the Narcissus*): "before all, to make you see."

The general tendency was back toward drama with the emphasis upon direct presentation rather than the mediation of a special expositor, and with a concomitant reliance upon the reader's power to infer, in Henry James's words, "the unseen from the seen, to trace the implication of things, to judge the whole piece by the pattern." [3]

Percy Lubbock, whose scholarly handbook *The Craft of Fiction* (1929) gives what may be regarded as the standard exposition of the tenets of the Flaubert-James school, distinguishes between panorama (the long-range view of the action) and scene (the close-up view), and describes the design of a novel in terms of the presentation of the action through scenes and panoramas, and the proper disposition of these in relation to each other.

It follows that two matters of special concern for critics of this school were those of the narrator and the point of view from which he "sees" the action. The narrator of the story is frequently a character, whose knowledge is limited to what he himself could have seen and heard, and this narrator may be either a major or a minor character. And even when the narrator is omniscient, possessed of all that the author himself knows about the story, he is scarcely to be thought of as merely the author speaking in his own right. Thus Lubbock interprets the celebrated impersonality of Flaubert's art to mean only "that Flaubert does not announce his opinion in so many words. . . . [The impersonality] of Flaubert and his kind lies only in the greater tact with which they express their feelings—dramatizing them, embodying them in living form, instead of stating them directly." [4]

The question about point of view is, of course, not a new one. In some sense it is as old as literature. Ezra Pound remarks: "I have . . . found also in Homer the imaginary spectator, which in 1918 I still thought was Henry James' particular property." [5] But since Flaubert's time the

[2] *Thus to Revisit*, p. 46.

[3] *The Art of Fiction*, p. 11. James is actually referring in this passage to a power of the novelist, but it is a power which in some measure any writer using a dramatic method must also demand of his reader.

[4] *The Craft of Fiction* (London, 1921), pp. 67–8.

[5] *The ABC of Reading* (1934), reprinted by New Directions (Norfolk, Conn., 1951), p. 43.

problem has come in for more conscious examination than perhaps it had ever received before.

The handling of time sequence is another such problem that comes in for special treatment by these theorists of fiction. Again, it is an old problem, and one that has received very sophisticated practical solutions in the past, including devices so different as the folk-balladist's abrupt juxtaposition of little discrete scenes without intermediate narration and the classic epic-writer's beginning *in medias res*. But such theorizing as it has received in the past has had to do principally with the drama, and under the rubric of the unities of time and place. In the modern novel, the problem, for obvious reasons, arises with special force.

The modern fiction writer's concern with time goes further than the making of a series of scenes and deciding the relative emphasis to be placed upon each of them. The novelist has frequently found it desirable to alter the chronological arrangement of events, sometimes describing an earlier event *after* portraying a later event, and he has sometimes attempted to achieve an effect of simultaneity of events. Flaubert, in discussing the famous incident of the *comices agricoles* in his *Madame Bovary*, wrote:

> Everything should sound simultaneously; one should hear the bellowing of the cattle, the whisperings of the lovers and the rhetoric of the officials all at the same time.[6]

But, as Joseph Frank points out in his "Spatial Form in Modern Literature," [7]

> since language proceeds in time, it is impossible to approach this simultaneity of perception except by breaking up temporal sequence. And this is exactly what Flaubert does: he dissolves sequence by cutting back and forth between the various levels of action in a slowly-rising crescendo until—at the climax of the scene—Rodolphe's Chateaubriandesque phrases are read at almost the same moment as the names of prize winners for raising the best pigs.

This device of incongruous juxtaposition became the "Time-shift" developed by Conrad and Ford. Ford likened the effect of simultaneity gained by the time-shift to the effect experienced by a person looking out of a window "through glass so bright that whilst you perceive through it a landscape or a backyard, you are aware that, on its surface it reflects a face of a person behind you." [8] Joyce, of course, exploited the device to the limit in his *Ulysses*. But it is by no means confined to

[6] Cited by Joseph Frank; see footnote 7.
[7] *The Sewanee Review*, LI (Spring, 1943); reprinted in *Critiques*, p. 322.
[8] "On Impressionism," *Poetry and Drama*, I (June, 1914), 174.

modern fiction. Frank finds it throughout modern poetry—in Pound's *Cantos* and in Eliot's *Waste Land*, where the poet makes use of a "deliberate disconnectedness" and "superimposes one time scheme upon another." [9]

III

THAT modern poetry and fiction should make use of similar devices and should exhibit what is essentially the same kind of organization is not surprising. For the theorists of fiction we have been discussing were the associates of Hulme, Pound, and Eliot—and in the instance of Flaubert and James, moreover, they were sources from whom Hulme, Pound, and Eliot derived much of their theory. Like the theorists of poetry discussed in the preceding chapter they too display, in reaction against romantic inspirationalism, a concern for craftsmanship, and a stress upon form as opposed to the exploitation of privileged "poetic" materials. Indeed theirs too might be called an "impersonal" art. Even those aspects of it which might be thought of as exclusively "fictional"—*e.g.*, concern with point of view and with time sequence—are aspects of dramatic presentation—of the process of *rendering* as distinguished from *telling*. The time-shift also, with its potentiality for incongruous juxtapositions, finds its corresponding devices in the ironic confrontations characteristic of the poetry of Pound and Eliot.

There is no need to claim too much here. Fiction is set off sharply enough from lyric poetry to preclude any serious danger of our ever confusing the two. Fiction, for example, has an appetite for richness of circumstance, for sheer concretion, that sets it well apart from any lyric. Even short stories so far tilted over toward the lyric sensibility as James Joyce's "Clay," "Araby" and "The Sisters" do not seriously challenge this statement. Yet the lyric shares with the novel a common fictionality. If "character" and "sequence of action" seem to be especially the problems for the novelist, a little reflection will reveal that they confront the poet too. Eliot's Prufrock is a character, and Pound's "Mauberley" involves the problem of handling a sequence of time. Both Eliot's poem and Pound's differ in scope and scale, of course, from any novel. But like any novel, they too are organic structures, and they are forced to exploit to the limit such resources as a smaller compass affords—and because it is smaller, demands. Yet the general principle governing the relation of individual word to the total work is not changed simply because these are poems and not novels. As one writer on James remarks:

> James's concern for form in the novel "implies an elaborate art, often close to poetry, the aim of which is the maximum of expression." [1]

[9] Stallman, *Critiques*, p. 321.
[1] Morris Roberts, Introduction to *The Art of Fiction*, p. xix.

I V

A CONCERN for "character" and "action" as they occur in poem or novel has not always, of course, been complemented by an adequate concern for craftsmanship. (In *Thus to Revisit*, Ford Madox Ford comments with amusement and sometimes bitterness on the slovenliness of the English novel of the 19th century.) Matthew Arnold [2] was confident that if one chose a "fitting action" and allowed oneself to become "penetrated" with "the feeling of its situations," then "everything else [would] follow." This prescription for composing a work might even be described as an implicitly "organic" theory inasmuch as Arnold's basic assumption seems to be that details of style and structure must be consonant with, being dictated by, the larger governing principle: these details, that is, have no merit in themselves but only in virtue of giving substantial form to the entelechy of the whole. About the soundness of this principle, neither Ford nor James could possibly have quarreled, though they might have wondered that Arnold should so scant the intricate problem of working out the details of style and structure, and though they might have been puzzled as to how one could be sure that one had chosen a "fitting action" until one had "fitted" it to words.

Arnold, as we have seen, was asserting the primacy of subject matter and plot against what he felt to be an overemphasis upon lyric sensibility and a preoccupation with the verbal medium as such. In our own times, the criticism stemming from Hulme and Eliot has provoked similar reactions and counterclaims for the primacy of plot. One of a group of critics writing recently at the University of Chicago notes that "the criticism of the last two centuries . . . has . . . been marked by a subsidiary interest in plot and its needful agents." [3] Plot and character delineation, so the argument of this group runs, have been slighted and neglected; the tendency has been to reduce literature to the verbal element.[4] Such counterclaims typically derive from the Aristotelian *Poetics* with its focus upon drama and its stress upon plot as "the soul of

[2] Cf. *ante* Chapter 20.

[3] Norman Maclean, in *Critics and Criticism, Ancient and Modern*, p. 414.

[4] A similar conflict occurred in the 17th century, with Thomas Rymer as the worthy champion of plot, "the foundation," as he termed it, in dealing with which the English dramatists had been defective. Dryden conceded the point but argued that they had been able to attain the end of tragedy through complementary means, namely, through their excellent treatment of the "superstructure" (characters, thoughts, and words). See Frank L. Huntley, *The Unity of John Dryden's Dramatic Criticism* (Chicago, 1944).

Charles Gildon also disparaged the critic who reaches "no farther than Words and Sentences; dealing in the very Scraps of Poetry; a Couplet, an Expression is the utmost he pretends to. But for a Design, or a complete Poem, to meddle with it, he accounts Pedantry, or Imposition" (*The Complete Art of Poetry*, 1718).

tragedy." Such also is the general derivation of a book from another quarter, Francis Fergusson's *The Idea of a Theater* (1949), which is one of the most engaging of these reassertions of the primacy of plot.

Fergusson does not regard drama as "primarily a composition in the verbal medium." Drama is a mixed art to which the actor and even the stage designer make their contributions. Yet the presence of such elements as these does not constitute the real basis for Fergusson's separation of drama from fiction and poetry. Remembering Aristotle, who, though naming "song" and "spectacle" as parts of tragedy, yet spends very little time in discussing them,[5] Fergusson gives scant attention to acting and stage effects as such. He is in search of something more ultimate; he is looking for "that dramatic art which, in all real plays, underlies these as well as the more highly developed arts of language."[6]

His basic direction is indicated in his assertion that whereas the lyric is a composition in the verbal medium, in drama "the words result . . . from the underlying structure of incident and character."[7] But it is not clear upon what kind of substructure the words of a lyric are supposed to rest. What supports *them* or do they simply float on the air? If the question should turn out to be a bogus question—like the ancient question as to what the earth rested upon, upon the back of an immense tortoise, or upon that of a fabulous elephant—its unintelligibility might call in question the distinction that Fergusson makes between lyric poetry and the drama. To this possibility we shall have to recur.

At any rate, Fergusson's search for a "dramatic art" that underlies all the "arts of language" takes him down to a stratum deeper even than plot, for he insists that plot itself rests upon "action." But action is something that Fergusson acknowledges it is difficult to define, and which cannot be "abstractly defined"[8] at all. It seems to be both inside and outside the drama, and thus Fergusson sometimes seems to be talking about an element within the play; at other times, about something outside the play which is to be located in the historical culture—a myth, for example. In considering a concrete instance, the action in *Oedipus Rex*, he is willing to describe the action as a theme: he calls it a quest—the search for the culprit in order to purify human life. He goes on to say:

> Sophocles must have seen this seeking action as the real life of
> the Oedipus myth. . . . Moreover, he must have seen this par-
> ticular action as a type, or crucial instance, of human life in

[5] "The 'visual aspect of the staging' [*opsis*], despite its emotional appeal, is the least artistic of all the elements and has least to do with the art of poetry. . . . moreover the production of scenic effects lies more in the province of the 'costumer and stage-manager' [*skeuopoios*] than of the poet." *Poetics* VI: *Aristotle*, trans. Philip Wheelwright (New York, 1951), p. 299.

[6] *The Idea of a Theater* (Princeton, 1949), p. 9, by permission of the publishers, Princeton University Press.

[7] *Idea of a Theater*, p. 8.   [8] *Idea of a Theater*, p. 230.

general; and hence he was able to present it in the form of the ancient ritual which also presents and celebrates the perennial mystery of human life and action. Thus by "action" I do not mean the events of the story but the focus or aim of psychic life from which the events, in that situation, result.[9]

The *Oedipus Rex* is regarded as the expression of a total culture. "The perspectives of the myth, the rituals, and of the traditional *hodos*, the way of life of the City—'habits of thought and feeling' which constitute the traditional wisdom of the race—were all required to make this play possible." [1] The myths and rituals which were Sophocles' heritage and the heritage of the audience for which he wrote were "actions" upon which the dramatist could draw. Such resources are not available to the dispossessed and alienated modern artist. He must rely merely on his *art*—an observation which helps explain Fergusson's curious remark that Racine and Wagner were "purer artists than Sophocles, as the best modern critics have taught us to understand that idea." [2] The implication would seem to be that great art is not *merely* art but something else (art plus religion?).

V

FERGUSSON has made it clear that the "best modern critics" have been concerned with subtle verbal analysis, to the *neglect* of "action." Certain passages in his book, however, suggest that those qualities of drama that the lyric does *not* possess are outside the bounds of art altogether or at least are outside those of "pure art." They would seem to be cultural elements shared by the artist with his fellow citizens and thus would be mythic, ritualistic, religious, and even philosophical patterns.

In discussing the "action" upon which great drama has been based, Fergusson shows a great concern for what was *available* to a Sophocles and to the audience that saw his plays. T. S. Eliot, in his *Dialogue on Dramatic Poetry* (1928) had a speaker remark that

> Aristotle did not have to worry about the relation of drama to religion, about the traditional morality of the Hellenes, about the relation of art to politics . . . he did not have to read the (extremely interesting) works of Miss Harrison or Mr. Cornford, or the translations of Professor Murray, or wrinkle his brow over the antics of the Todas and the Veddahs. Nor did he have to reckon with the theatre as a paying proposition.[8]

[9] *Idea of a Theater*, p. 36.
[1] *Idea of a Theater*, p. 32.
[2] *Idea of a Theater*, p. 3.
[8] *Selected Essays*, p. 32.

But these are just the topics about which Fergusson feels that he must worry. The remark of Eliot's speaker, he says, is wistful because "we cannot escape the unanswerable questions which Aristotle did not have to ask. The analysis of the art of drama leads to the idea of a theater which gives it its sanction, and its actual time and place. And when the idea of a theater is inadequate or lacking, we are reduced to speculating about the plight of the whole culture." [4] Precisely. And Fergusson realizes that much of his book is just such a speculation. He is too intelligent to chide the modern author for what he cannot help. The problem is communal, and the artist can fairly be asked nothing more than that he should recognize that he is alienated and rootless and try to set his own lands in order.

Fergusson also would persuade the modern artist to abandon idealistic expressionism in favor of some theory of art based on "imitation." But the modern artist, "after three hundred years of rationalism and idealism, with the traditional modes of behavior lost or discredited," [5] finds it difficult to imitate or even to "see" any action other than that of his own subjectivity. Eliot, for example, approaches the drama from the standpoint of lyric poetry, and thus begins "with the Idealistic conception of art as formally prior to the theater itself." [6] Fergusson, on the other hand, would "extend Aristotle's definition to subsequent forms [of the drama]," for it presupposes an objective world, knowable but outside the mind that knows it. The "lyric" conception is hopelessly idealistic and subjective. Fergusson admits that

> The phrase "objective equivalent" [for the poet's feeling] seems to support Eliot's announced classicism. Yet it refers, not to the vision of the poet, but to the poem he is making; and it implies that it is only a *feeling* that the poet has to convey. . . . The emphasis on the poem and its form, to the exclusion of what it represents, recognizes only one of the instincts which Aristotle thought were the roots of poetry in general, the "instinct for harmony and rhythm." [7]

In brief, Fergusson, sensing the tendency of theories of symbolic form to become monistic, urges the counterview that the poet's vision must be objective. Sophocles, he says, "must have believed in the objective reality of the human situation which the tragic theater enabled him to mirror and celebrate." [8] Sophocles was not merely expressing himself but imitating something outside himself.

The question as to whether Eliot's objective correlative is merely

[4] *Idea of a Theater*, p. 226.
[5] *Idea of a Theater*, p. 239.
[6] *Idea of a Theater*, p. 8.
[7] *Idea of a Theater*, p. 240.
[8] *Idea of a Theater*, p. 236.

expressionistic has come in for some attention in Chapter 29 (*ante*, p. 668). But in any case, one may wonder whether the only way to avoid the extreme of subjective expressionism is to adopt a theory of "imitation." Fergusson is properly cautious in his speculations as to Sophocles' actual beliefs, and he has to admit that Euripides, though inheriting the "theater of Sophocles," did not believe in the Greek myths at all.[9]

One may come at the matter from the other direction. Fergusson's account of the "action" suggests that it is not an element peculiar to drama but is to be found in all literature, including lyric poetry. For he says action is "the focus or aim of psychic life from which the events . . . result." But every piece of literature is about psychic life in some sense, and the briefest lyric, if it is really a poem and not an aimless farrago, has a focus or an aim. Moreover, though one does not mean to collapse the useful distinction between the song and the drama, the analogies are there. The most fragile lyric has at least one character, that of the implied speaker himself, and it has a "plot"—an arrangement of psychic incidents, with a development, at least of mood.

What Fergusson and Eliot hold in common is the belief that the work of art is an organic whole, and this view of the art work is in some sense more important than the decision to fix our criticism upon the diction or upon the action—upon the "actualization" of the work or upon the "soul" of the work. In an organic work, one implies the other, and we can work from "inner" soul to "outer" manifestation, or *vice versa*. For if the work be truly organic, then each element of structure is a necessary or probable consequence of the larger principle of the whole. But if we do work backwards from the words to the characters who speak them and from the characters on back to the plot in which the characters are involved, small wonder that the final and fundamental governing principle, Fergusson's "action," should prove so difficult to define. Indeed, our only clues to it are its "actualizations," that is, the text of the play itself. If "action" is held to be the most important thing in the work, it yet remains an inference, a hypothesis constructed by the reader. The "action" resembles the Aristotelian *substance*, which is known only through the *accidents* that inhere in it. The *raison d'être* of Fergusson's action would seem to be to provide a ground in which

---

[9] Fergusson thinks that "Sophocles might well have taken myth and ritual as literally 'fictions,' yet still have accepted their deeper meanings—trope, allegory, and anagoge—as valid" (p. 35). This guess may well be correct, but if so, one wonders what to make of the difference between the ancient poet, buoyed up by myth and ritual, and the alienated modern who, "with the traditional modes of behavior lost or discredited," is unable to "see" any action but his own, and is thus unable to "imitate" it. Even William Butler Yeats, it can be claimed, accepted "the deeper meanings" of his *Vision*—"trope, allegory, and anagoge" as "valid." One could claim at least as much, presumably much more, for the symbols of T. S. Eliot's later poetry.

the "accidents" of the play (speeches, characters, gestures) may subsist.

Elder Olson has shown how arbitrary the use of terms taken from an imitative theory of art can be. The occasion is his adjustment of the Aristotelian terms to a poetics of the lyric. Olson arrives at his poetics by remodeling, or perhaps it would be more accurate to say, truncating, the Aristotelian poetics of tragedy. Whereas Aristotle found six parts in a tragedy, Olson requires four in order to deal with the lyric—or rather, to observe his own precision, "that species [of lyric] to which Yeats's *Sailing to Byzantium* belongs."[1] The four necessary parts are choice, character, thought, and diction. "For choice is the activity, and thought and character are the causes of the activity, and diction is the means. The choice, or deliberative activity of choosing, is the principal part for reasons analogous to those which make plot the principal part of tragedy. Next in importance comes character; next thought; and last, diction."

Yet one might argue for "plot" as a fifth necessary part—or at least as a substitute for "choice." Yeats's poem actually has a plot. The speaker in this poem pictures himself as having made the voyage to Byzantium and in excited reverie imagines his visit to St. Sophia and his vision of the holy sages and the prayer that he will utter to them. Conversely, one could argue that the four parts might be reduced to three: *e.g.*, that the term *thought* might be omitted altogether, since there can be neither character nor choice without thought. To conclude, the "four parts" would seem to be more or less convenient terms under which to discuss the poem—not the inevitable and necessary elements of the poem.

The doctrine of imitation has great virtues of its own, and it avoids a difficulty into which expressionist doctrines so easily slip: that of turning the whole work into the subjective fantasies issuing out of the poet's private consciousness. But the doctrine of imitation has its own difficulties. Aristotle himself did not make the artist's "imitation" a literal mirroring. It is in some sense a transformation as well. Fergusson's "action" seems to be at once inside and outside the work of art: sometimes it seems to be the primal structural principle of the drama but, at other times, it is an "aim of psychic life" with mythic antecedents.

Henry James, who was a good enough "Aristotelian" to believe that in his novels he was giving a picture of a real and objective and external world and to declare that "the soul of a novel is its action," faced this problem in his "Art of Fiction." His common sense is refreshing. He writes:

> I cannot see what is meant by talking as if there were a part of a novel which is the story and part of it which for mystical reasons is not. . . . "The story," if it represents anything, repre-

[1] *Critics and Criticism*, p. 563.

sents the subject, the idea, the *donnée* of the novel; and there is surely no "school" . . . which urges that a novel should be all treatment and no subject. There must assuredly be something to treat; every school is intimately conscious of that. The sense of the story being the idea, the starting-point, of the novel, is the only one that I see in which it can be spoken of as something different from its organic whole; and since in proportion as the work is successful the idea permeates and penetrates it, informs and animates it, so that every word and every punctuation-point contribute directly to the expression, in that proportion do we lose our sense of the story being a blade which may be drawn more or less out of its sheath.[2]

We have cited James and Eliot as champions of an organic theory of literature, and we have drawn the inference that for them and their schools the differences between poetry and fiction and drama tend to become less sharp and less radically deep. Whatever the author may owe to an idea as a "starting-point" or to a story as a "subject," informing idea and actualized story become something else in the work itself: they are no longer separable from the work.

VI

But it may be only fair to notice that on occasion Eliot himself can write as if poetry and drama were radically different forms. In *Poetry and Drama* he writes:

> I laid down for myself the ascetic rule to avoid poetry which could not stand the test of strict dramatic utility: with such success, indeed, that it is perhaps an open question whether there is any poetry in the play at all.
> . . . the self-education of a poet trying to write for the theatre seems to require a long period of disciplining his poetry, and putting it, so to speak, on a very thin diet. . . .[3]

But the stylistic problem described in these passages is precisely that described by Ford Madox Ford in his account of the wrestle with style that went on in his collaborations with Conrad.

[2] *The Art of Fiction*, pp. 17–18.
[3] *Poetry and Drama* (Cambridge, Mass., 1951), pp. 39–40, by permission of the publishers, Harvard University Press. In a recently reported interview, Eliot seems to make a distinction between "pure, unapplied" poetry and dramatic poetry as "applied" poetry. Perhaps we may wonder how much we are allowed to press distinctions made in apparently informal conversation. See *The New York Times Book Review*, November 29, 1953.

The trouble . . . with us was this: we could not get our own prose keyed down enough. . . .

Our most constant preoccupation, then, was to avoid words that stuck out of sentences either by their brilliant unusualness or their "amazing aptness." For either sort of word arrests the attention of a reader, and thus "hangs up" both the meaning and the cadence of a phrase.[4]

Even in *Poetry and Drama* Eliot makes it plain that drama in verse is the ideal. Prose dramatists, even the great prose dramatists, have been "hampered in expression by writing in prose." There is a "peculiar range of sensibility" that lies beyond prose but which "can be expressed by dramatic poetry, at its moments of greatest intensity."[5] If we put this late essay beside the earlier "Dialogue on Dramatic Poetry" (1928) we get some such conception as this: poetry is essentially dramatic and the greatest poetry always moves toward drama; drama is essentially poetic and the greatest drama always moves toward poetry.[6]

The moral would seem to be that anyone, including Mr. Eliot, speaking in a special and limited context, is likely to talk as if poetry and drama were two very different things. For here we come up against the ancient and vexing problem of genres. A recent discussion of genre theory[7] indicates how confused and confusing some of these problems are. The notion of genres, as Austin Warren points out, furnishes a principle of order. If, to borrow his phrase, we reduce lyric, epic, and drama to "a common literariness," how shall we distinguish a play from a story? Such reductions are in the interest of nobody. Yet it is proper to glance at the other extreme: if we multiply the genres indefinitely, we shall ultimately have to recognize a special genre for each art work,[8] and if we make the larger genres watertight compartments, we shall end up with at least three separate "literatures," not one.

[4] *Thus to Revisit*, pp. 52-3.

[5] *Poetry and Drama*, p. 43.

[6] "C: Do you mean that Shakespeare is a greater dramatist than Ibsen, not by being a greater dramatist, but by being a greater poet? B: That is precisely what I mean. For, on the other hand, what great poetry is not dramatic? Even the minor writers of the Greek Anthology, even Martial, are dramatic. . . . E: [Archer] was wrong, as you said, in thinking that drama and poetry are two different things." *Selected Essays*, pp. 38-9.

[7] By Austin Warren, in Wellek and Warren's *Theory of Literature* (New York, 1949). See pp. 235-47.

[8] A possibility less remote than one might think. Elder Olson writes that "the beauty of a tragedy is not the same as the beauty of a lyric, any more than the distinctive beauty of a horse is the same as that of a man," but then the beauty of a lyric of "the species to which Yeats's 'Sailing to Byzantium' belongs" is evidently not that of a poem belonging to another subspecies of the lyric. Would Yeats's "Among School Children" require the postulation of another subspecies? And his Crazy Jane poems, still another? See *Critics and Criticism, Ancient and Modern*, p. 563.

VII

CERTAIN academic critics, however, are not alone in their objection to a criticism that seems to deal "only with words" rather than with "character" and "plot." The more frequent objections come from those who care little for the niceties of genre theory and want only to distinguish "mere words" from "life." They often write as if words were a necessary evil—pale limp things, interposing themselves between the reader and the compelling stuff of experience offered him by the author.

Such objectors are by no means always literary journalists. At their best, one may say that these critics take the necessary mediation of words for granted and want to get on to the qualities in the author—his breadth of view, his compassion, his knowledge of the human heart—, or to an exposition of his views—his political sagacity, the relevance of what he says to the cultural situation, and the like.

At their most careless or most trivial, they express the typical Anglo-Saxon distrust of words. *Art* for them means the "artful" and probably also the "artificial." They frequently write as if the author could lay upon the page warm, quivering chunks of life, if he were only gifted enough, and if he only chose to. They are suspicious of any attempt to talk about words and their interaction.

The editor of *The Kenyon Review* has taken cognizance of the contemporary situation in the following terms:

> So in an age of unusual critical achievement we have managed to arrive rather quickly at an excruciating impasse: with cold-blooded critics of poetry working away at what sometimes appear to be the merest exercises with words; and warm-blooded critics of the critics of poetry [he has already said that these are likely to be "critics of fiction"] reproaching their exercises, and perhaps about to reproach their poetry too.
>
> How confidently, twenty years or so past, were some of us offering a new "understanding of poetry"! I will not say, How brashly; for the innovation was real, it was momentous; but it was not complete, and now it has bogged down at a most embarrassing point.[9]

The protest of the warm-bloods is scarcely new; something like it, we have noted, was to be heard in early Victorian England. John Henry Newman and his friend John Keble, author of *The Christian Year*, expressed this same sort of distrust of "art," technique, and execution. Like the modern warm-blooded "critics of fiction," Newman and Keble as-

---

[9] John Crowe Ransom, *The Kenyon Review*, XIV (Winter, 1952), p. 159.

sociated the difference between cold calculation and warm spontaneity with the difference between "plotted" narrative and the plotless lyric.[1] But Newman and Keble just reversed the modern correlation: with them "plot" is associated with cold-blood; the lyric utterance is warm and effusive. This reversed alignment of the contrasted elements reinforces the deeper commitment that both Victorian and modern warm-blooded critic share: a distrust of art and technique—whether the concern in question is that of poet or critic. As for the impasse apparently reached by modern criticism, we are disposed to offer a different metaphor, not that the caravan "has [now] bogged down at a most embarrassing point" in new and unexplored country, but rather that the hunt has circled and that some of the hounds are once again baying on the trail of the Longinian fox.

SUPPLEMENT

She was largish and of a French figure, that is with a noticeable waist and a more noticeable rear, and she had heels too high for her balance in a spurting bus. . . . She had much trouble getting the two fares in the box, and considerably more trouble getting herself from the box down the aisle, hauling from seat to seat by their shining handles against the momentum of the bus, lurching, as she had to, in all directions save the right one. During the whole business—and this is what I am getting at—she managed by sniffs and snorts, by smiles, by sticking her tongue out very sharp, by batting her very blue eyes about, and generally by cocking her head this way and that, she managed to express fully, and without a single word either uttered or wanted, the whole mixed, flourishing sense of her disconcertment, her discomfiture, her uncertainty, together with a sense of adventure and of gaiety, all of which she wanted to share with her companion behind me, who took it I was sure, as I did myself, all smiles. . . .

That is an example of the gesture that comes before language; but reflecting upon it, it seems also an example of the gesture which when it goes with language crowns it, and so animates it as to make it independent of speaker or writer; reflecting upon it, it seems that the highest use of language cannot be made without incorporating some such quality of gesture within it. How without it could the novelist make his dialogue ring? how could the poet make his cry lyric, his incongruity comic, or his perspective tragic? The great part of our knowledge of life and of nature—perhaps all our knowledge of their play and interplay—comes to us as gesture, and we are masters of the skill of that knowledge before we can ever make a rhyme or a pun, or even a simple sentence. Nor can we master language purposefully without re-mastering ges-

[1] Cf. *ante* Chapter 20.

ture within it. Gesture, in language, is the outward and dramatic play of inward and imagined meaning. It is that play of meaningfulness among words
which cannot be defined in the formulas in the dictionary, but which is defined in their use together; gesture is that meaningfulness which is moving, in
every sense of that word: what moves the words and what moves us.

—R. P. Blackmur, *Language as Gesture* (New York, 1952) pp. 5–6, by
permission of the publisher, Harcourt, Brace and Company.

But who am I to offer such a diagnosis of fiction's ailment? Four years
of instruction under the greatest faculty in English, philosophy and history
that Harvard, or any other American university ever assembled, must have
taught me nothing, because the constitutionally academic critics dismiss my
kind as mere journalists, just as they dismiss any writing with the juice of life
in it as mere journalism. The best I can wish for some of these gentlemen is
that they might be exposed for a brief period of their careers to the bracing
winds of human sympathy and understanding which blow through every
newspaper office.
  One trouble with literary criticism in this country today is that too much
of it has been taken over by a group of impenetrably insulated bookworms.
What they have to say about literature interests neither the intelligent public
nor those writers who are worth their salt. Yet they exercise a corrupting influence because many of them are in a position to foist their ideas upon un-
formed, immature minds.

—J. Donald Adams, *The New York Times Book Review* (September 5,
1954). Reprinted by permission of the author and the publishers.

Also, I would hold that a "dramatistic" placement of the lyric is to be
arrived at "deductively" in this sense: one approaches the lyric from the category of *action*, which Aristotle considers the primary element of the drama.
And then by dialectic coaching one looks for a form that will have as its
primary element the moment of *stasis*, or *rest*. We are admonished, however,
to note that there are two concepts of "rest," often confused because we may
apply the same word to both. There is rest as the sheer cessation of motion
(in the sense that a rolling ball comes to rest); and there is rest as the end of action (end as finish or end as aim), the kind of rest that Aristotle conceived
as the *primum mobile* of the world, the ground of motion and action both.
It is proper for the physical sciences, we would grant, to treat experience non-
dramatically, in terms of motion, but things in the realm of the social or human require treatment in terms of action or drama. Or rather, though things
in the realm of the human *may* be treated in terms of motion, the result will
be statements not about the intrinsic, but about the extrinsic (as per our
remarks on an "incongruous" science of the personality).
  A treatment of the lyric in terms of action would not by any means require us merely to look for analogies from the drama. On the contrary, the
state of arrest in which we would situate the essence of the lyric is not analogous to dramatic action at all, but is the dialectical counterpart of action. Con-

sider as an illustration the fourteen Stations of the Cross: The concern with them in the totality of their progression would be dramatic. But the pause at any one of them, and the contemplation and deepening appreciation of its poignancy, in itself, would be lyric.

A typical Wordsworthian sonnet brings out this methodological aspect of the lyric (its special aptitude for conveying a *state* of mind, for erecting a moment into a universe) by selecting such themes as in themselves explicitly refer to the arrest, the pause, the hush. However, this lyric state is to be understood in terms of action, inasmuch as it is to be understood as a state that sums up an action in the form of an attitude.

Thus approached, an attitude is ambiguous in this sense: It may be either an incipient act or the substitute for an act. An attitude of sympathy is incipiently an act, for instance, in that it is the proper emotional preparation for a sympathetic act; or it may be the substitute for an act in that the sympathetic person can let the intent do service for the deed (precisely through doing nothing, one may feel more sympathetic than the person whose mood may be partially distracted by the conditions of action). In either case, an attitude is a state of emotion, or a moment of stasis, in which an act is arrested, summed up, made permanent and total, as with the Grecian Urn which in its summational quality Keats calls a "fair Attitude."

—Kenneth Burke, *A Grammar of Motives* (New York, 1945), pp. 475–6. Reprinted with permission of the publishers, from *A Grammar of Motives* by Kenneth Burke. Copyright, 1945, by Prentice-Hall, Inc.

MYTH AND ARCHETYPE

§ *The increasing modern interest in the symbolization of primitive man: Vico as a pioneer in this field, and modern contributions from anthropology and psychology—Ernst Cassirer's* Philosophy of Symbolic Forms: *the origin of language and the origin of myth, the identification of subject and object in the symbol—II. Cassirer's view of what poetry expresses and of its relation to the language of science—W. M. Urban's* Language and Reality: *metaphysics as a symbolic language mediating among such other symbolic languages as those of science and art—III. Mrs. Langer's* Philosophy in a New Key *and her* Feeling and Form: *the "import" of art as a "pattern of sentience," her account of lyrics and of more complicated poems— the strengths and limitations of the doctrine of symbolic form—IV. the distinction between poetry and myth as maintained by Cassirer and Langer: the assimilation of poetry to myth made today by the new "myth" critics— Northrop Frye and the elevation of literary criticism to a social science—Richard Chase and the equation of poetry and myth—Leslie Fiedler and the return to the poet's biography—V. other applications of myth study to literature: Maud Bodkin and W. H. Auden—VI. Carl Jung's influence upon modern literary criticism: his conception of "purposive" myths and dreams, his application of a "cognitive" criticism to myths and dreams—VII. Jung's distinction between the dream and the work of art—his specification of what the psychologist can contribute to the study of literature—Yeats and the uses of myth* §

ONE CONSEQUENCE OF THE SYMBOLIST DEVELOPMENT IN LITERATURE [1] has been an increasing respect for the symbolism of primitive man, and specifically for the myths and legends through which he characteristically expresses himself. If, as Kant argued, the mind is no passive mirror, merely giving back the world reflected in it, but is

[1] Cf. *ante* Chapter 26.

rather an active force that affects the very shape of reality as perceived by us, then the symbolizations of primitive man are not necessarily childish and absurd, but have their own interest and perhaps make their own contribution to "truth." As we have seen in an earlier chapter,[2] J. G. Herder, who was a younger contemporary of Kant's, boldly derived language from the mythic process and made the special character of poetry reside in the fact that poetry preserves the dynamic quality of myth. Even earlier in his *Scienza Nuova*, the Neapolitan scholar Giambattista Vico had elaborated the theory that myth was a kind of poetic language, the only language that man was capable of in his primitive stage of development, and yet, for all that, a genuine language with its own principle of structure and its own logic.

Vico conjectured that language first began with gesture, then developed through the stages of myth and figurative language to the clarified and ordered language of modern polite societies. Yet if Vico dignified poetry by regarding it as a form of knowledge—and, for the historian of primitive times, an indispensable mode of knowledge—he regarded it as an inferior knowledge which had been superseded as civilization developed.

Vico had very little influence upon the thinkers of his own day. René Wellek writes that "the attempts to prove his influence in France, England, and Germany during the 18th century, especially in aesthetics, have all failed."[3] In our own time, however, Vico has come to exert a very powerful influence. Our modern studies of primitive man have confirmed some of Vico's insights and have, in any case, compelled recognition of his position as a brilliant pioneer. Even some of his more questionable observations find their parallels in those of present-day critics. If, for example, Vico was unable to distinguish poetry from myth, we find modern critics like Richard Chase insisting that myth is only poetry. It is interesting, however, to note that a modern philosopher like Croce, whom Vico influenced directly, displays very little interest in the sort of anthropological speculation in which Herder indulged in the 18th century and of which today Vico is to be regarded as the great pioneer. In spite of his acknowledged debt to the historical empiricism of Vico, Croce developed a rigorous philosophical idealism.

The philosopher of our day who has pushed furthest the concern for the origin of language and the laws that govern the development of primitive ritual and myth is Ernst Cassirer. His *Philosophy of Symbolic Forms* (1923–29) is Kantian in its general orientation, but Cassirer pays high tribute to Herder, calling him "the Copernicus of history."[4] He quarrels, however, with Herder's attempt to derive language from myth,

[2] Cf. *ante* Chapter 17.
[3] *A History of Modern Criticism*, I, 135.
[4] *The Philosophy of Symbolic Forms* (New Haven, 1953), I, 41.

insisting that neither is derivable from the other. We are rather to think of language and myth as "two diverse shoots from the same parent stem," [5] springing from the same impulse of symbolic formulation. This impulse Cassirer calls "a concentration and heightening of simple sensory experience." Cassirer's association of primordial language with intense emotional experience is a matter of some importance for his conception of poetry. We shall return to it. But first it is important to sum up what Cassirer seems to say about the relation of language to reality.

Some of Cassirer's comments promise a great deal. Symbols, he holds, are shaped by man's needs and purposes. The symbol is not an aspect of reality: it *is* reality. In the symbol there is a thoroughgoing identification between subject and object:

> . . . in place of a more or less adequate "expression," we find a relation of identity, of complete congruence between "image" and "object," between the name and the thing.[6]

Indeed, Cassirer insists that we falsify the issues when we describe the symbol as a "meeting-place" of subject and object, for the very concept of the ego and non-ego belong to what is a relatively "late development" of language. Primitive man, Cassirer conjectures, knew no such duality. The distinction between the apprehending self and the apprehended thing required for its recognition the development of the power of reflection and of logic.

In an earlier chapter [7] we remarked upon Coleridge's yearning for the discovery of a realm in which the distinction between words and things should be abolished. But that realm actually exists, Cassirer declares—it exists in the world of the savage mentality. In the mind of primitive man, the flickering mythic perceptions—the "momentary gods" that are generated out of the savage's more vivid experiences—are, through the medium of words, stabilized and given a relative fixity. The word is no mere surrogate. "Often it is the *name* of the deity," Cassirer has observed, "rather than the god himself, that seems to be the real source of efficacy." [8]

Indeed, for Cassirer a local habitation and a name remains even today of the utmost importance; lacking a name, human experience cannot be "stored and stabilized." Only through the habitation afforded by a name can the psychic energy pass over into something like substance—a deposit of meaning that can be contemplated on later occasions, and linked with and related to other such deposits of meaning. The ability

[5] *Language and Myth*, trans. Susanne Langer (New York, 1946), p. 88, by permission of the publishers, Harper and Brothers.
[6] *Language and Myth*, p. 58.
[7] Cf. *ante* Chapter 26.
[8] *Language and Myth*, p. 48.

to make and use such symbols is what renders man a human being: man is the symbol-making animal—the only such animal.[9]

II

But as logic and discursive thought develop, language loses its emotional charge; its quality of concreteness is attenuated; and it approaches the state of the language of science. The process is, on the whole, one of deprivation: language is reduced to "a bare skeleton." There remains one area, however, in which, even for sophisticated modern man, language "recovers the fullness of life."[1] That is the realm of "artistic expression," where the original creative power of language is not only "preserved" but "renewed." Poetry expresses, Cassirer writes,

> neither the mythic word-picture of gods and daemons, nor the logical truth of abstract determinations and relations. . . . The world of poetry stands apart from both, as a world of illusion and fantasy—but it is just in this mode of illusion that the realm of pure feeling can find utterance, and can therewith attain its full and concrete actualization.[2]

Cassirer makes it plain that the "pure" feeling that art expresses is not merely the personal emotions of the poet. The lyric poet, he tells us, is not "just a man who indulges in displays of feeling." This realm of pure feeling has its own claim to objectivity. Since we can know reality only through symbolic forms, art constitutes one of the perspectives by which to view reality. Art is no mere entertainment, no mere diversion, no mere act of play. It is a revelation of a genuine aspect of our life.

> What would we know of the innumerable nuances in the aspect of things were it not for the works of the great painters and sculptors? Poetry is, similarly, the revelation of our personal life. The infinite potentialities of which we had but a dim and obscure presentiment are brought to light by the lyric poet, by the novelist, and by the dramatist. Such art is in no sense mere counterfeit or facsimile, but a genuine manifestation of our inner life.[3]

Cassirer seems to conceive of art as in some sense a counterpoise to science. Art gives us a special knowledge of our "inner" life, as science presumably does of our "outer" life. It restores the dimension of emotion

---

[9] "Hence, instead of defining man as an *animal rationale*, we should define him as an *animal symbolicum*." *An Essay on Man* (New Haven, 1944), p. 26.
[1] *Language and Myth*, p. 98.
[2] *Language and Myth*, p. 99.
[3] *Essay on Man*, p. 169.

and emotional response and thus offsets the attenuation and abstraction necessary to science. One wishes that Cassirer were somewhat clearer on this matter of the relation of one kind of language to another, and specifically with reference to the relation of art to science. He has, to be sure, some interesting and suggestive passages in which he says that language "moves in the middle kingdom between the 'indefinite' and the 'infinite,' " [4] and that the effort to realize a truly *pure* treatment of either being or of self would necessarily take us outside the realm of language altogether into "a world of silence." He tells us too that since we can know reality only through symbolic forms, the question of what reality is apart from such forms becomes irrelevant. The basic philosophical question, he says in his *Language and Myth*, has to do with the "mutual limitation and supplementation" [5] of myth, art, religion, and science— that is, with a mediation among the various accounts of reality given by the various kinds of language.

But by making science the "last step in man's mental development," by frankly calling it the "highest and most characteristic attainment of human culture," [6] Cassirer seems to give it a priority over the other kinds of language. Though he defends the objectivity of the other kinds of language, he leaves the suggestion that science, by paring away the personal and emotional elements that are so much a constitutive part of the languages of myth, religion, and art, does actually give us a wider and deeper aspect of reality—that in some sense, in spite of his general argument, science does have some very superior access to reality. On the whole, therefore, one must agree with a recent critic who writes that:

> Although Cassirer represents poetry as the regeneration of the creative power of the word. . . , he is ultimately loyal to reason. Truth is the province of the "conceptual sign," and poetry, however valuable, is "a world of illusion and fantasy." [7]

Wilbur Urban, who shares many of Cassirer's fundamental views, has been careful to repudiate any implication that art and religion use more "primitive" languages than do science and philosophy. In his *Language and Reality* he points out that all three are relevant to man, and to modern man. [8] He is also concerned to present them as not merely meaningful but true. That is, Urban is concerned to relate to one underlying reality what is "said" by all the kinds of languages. Urban's way

[4] *Language and Myth*, p. 81.
[5] *Language and Myth*, p. 9.
[6] *Essay on Man*, p. 261.
[7] *Symbolism and American Literature*, p. 55. Cf. René Wellek on this aspect of Cassirer, *Rocky Mountain Review*, IX (Summer, 1945), 195.
[8] *Language and Reality* (New York, 1939), *passim*. On pp. 469–70, he writes that it is a fallacy to view the aesthetic symbol "as a mere stage of, or imperfect substitute for, scientific and philosophical knowledge." Reprinted by permission of the publishers, The Macmillan Co.

of solving Cassirer's problem of "mutual limitation and supplementation" is to set up metaphysics as the special discipline whose function it is to interpret what art, religion, and science have "to say" about reality and to mediate their varying "statements."

In a loyal adherence to the doctrine of symbolic form, Urban has to dismiss any hope that we can discover "hypothetical 'pure experience' . . . by stripping [it of] language." [9] But he thinks that there is an approach to some final truth and reality through understanding the "symbolic forms of language" and through becoming "more conscious of the formative principles embodied in these constructions." Urban's deepest difficulty is to penetrate a "symbolic" language fully while respecting the fact that it *is* symbolic. This difficulty comes out especially in his remarks on the problem of art. Like Croce, he holds that a poem is strictly untranslatable.[1] The artistic symbol is not "merely a surrogate for a concept" but is rather the way in which the ideal content is apprehended and expressed. Yet if one wishes to connect what art has to tell us about reality with what science or with what religion has to tell us about reality, one is apparently compelled to make some kind of translation:

> We are apparently faced with a dilemma. If we are to interpret the "sense" of the symbol we must expand it, and this must be in terms of literal sentences. If, on the other hand, we thus expand it we lose the "sense" or value of the symbol *as symbol*. The solution of this paradox seems to me to lie in an adequate theory of interpretation of the symbol. It does not consist in substituting *literal* for symbol sentences, in other words substituting "blunt" truth for symbolic truth, but rather in deepening and enriching the meaning of the symbol.[2]

The fact that Urban ventures such a solution throws some light on our general problem. The autonomy that is conferred upon poetry by a doctrine of symbolic forms is bought at a high price if it leaves that autonomous realm quite isolated from other autonomous realms such as that of science. Yet Urban's solution poses real difficulties; and Mrs. Susanne K. Langer, another philosopher of symbolic form, has had to reject Urban's attempt to "interpret" artistic symbols as not only unsatisfactory but as quite inconsistent with Urban's general position.

III

Mrs. Langer's view appears first in *Philosophy in a New Key*, 1942. The title suggests something of the excitement with which her book is written. She considers that the concept of symbolic transformation, for which

[9] *Language and Reality*, p. 374.   [2] *Language and Reality*, pp. 434–5.
[1] *Language and Reality*, p. 490.

she gives special credit to Cassirer, strikes a new key in philosophy, a key into which all the great questions of our age must now be transposed.

The end of a philosophical epoch, she argues, comes "with the exhaustion of its motive concepts." [3] Now once more the springs of "philosophical thought have run dry." [4] In our own otherwise arid landscape, the principle of symbolic transformation represents a fresh fountainhead, a generative force providing us with new motives and problems. Activities of our day apparently so diverse as symbolic logic and Freudian psychology reveal themselves to be in fact related when one reflects that each has discovered in its own way the importance of this power of symbolization.

Like Cassirer, Mrs. Langer regards myth as the "primitive phase of metaphysical thought, the first embodiment of *general ideas.*" [5] In due course mythic conception gives way when discursive language has been developed. The civilization then moves into a rationalistic period, though Mrs. Langer concedes that a day may come in which, ideas having been "exploited and exhausted, there will be another vision, a new mythology." [6] But Mrs. Langer, though she seems to connect poetry and the arts generally with mythic thinking, is not willing to concede that art is a mere passing phase in man's mental history. On the contrary, art is a "new symbolic form" which is able to live on "side by side with philosophy and science and all the higher forms of thought." [7] Here, of course, Mrs. Langer follows closely Cassirer's statement that poetry presents us with a "world of illusion" in which "the realm of pure feeling can find utterance." In *Philosophy in a New Key* music was her primary example. Music, she says, is "our myth of the inner life—a young, vital, and meaningful myth, of recent inspiration and still in its 'vegetative' growth." [8] In *Feeling and Form*, 1953, she applies her theory of symbolic transformation in detail to the other arts.

All art has meaning, or more precisely, something called "import." Music, for example, has articulated form; it represents an intuition simple or complex, on the part of the composer. It has

> import, and this import is the pattern of sentience—the pattern of life itself, as it is felt and directly known. Let us therefore call the significance of music its "vital import" instead of "meaning," using "vital" not as a vague laudatory term, but as a qualifying adjective restricting the relevance of "import" to the dynamism of subject experience. [9]

[3] *Philosophy in a New Key* (Cambridge, Mass., 1942), p. 9.
[4] *Philosophy in a New Key*, p. 13.   [6] *Philosophy in a New Key*, p. 202.
[5] *Philosophy in a New Key*, p. 201.   [7] *Philosophy in a New Key*, p. 202-3.
[8] *Philosophy in a New Key*, p. 245.
[9] *Feeling and Form* (New York, 1953), pp. 31-2, by permission of the publishers, Charles Scribner's Sons.

A vase, a painting, even an abstract design has its import. We are presented not with actual feeling but with "ideas of feeling" and through
art we come to recognize and know the "life of sentience."

Since the life of feeling is a stream of tensions and resolutions, and
since all vital tension patterns are organic patterns, any work of art must
be essentially organic. But Mrs. Langer warns us not to confuse this
illusion of the life of feeling with anything so crude as a direct copying
of feelings. Indeed, since the artist does not give us a direct copy, he
need not have experienced in actual life the feelings that his work expresses. He may, in articulating the work, even discover new possibilities
of feeling. "For, although a work of art reveals the character of subjectivity, it is itself objective; its purpose is to objectify the life of feeling." [1]

Mrs. Langer's position is in general a sensitive and highly sophisticated exposition of the symbolist view of art. Her highest praise of a
poem is that it should be "entirely expressive"; and in fact her critical
position scarcely allows her to offer more in the way of praise. This fact
is clearly revealed in the detailed analyses of poems which she gives us
in *Feeling and Form*. She is much more convincing when writing on
the short lyrics than on more complicated poems. She is, for example,
quite excellent in discussing a relatively simple and lyrical poem like
William Blake's "The Echoing Green," which she takes to be a symbol
"of life completely lived." "Here," she writes, the artistic form is "completely organic, and therefore able to articulate the great vital rhythms
and emotional overtones and undertones." [2]

But her observations on Wordsworth's "Intimations Ode" suggest
some of the embarrassments to which she is exposed by a poem of greater
complexity. This "philosophical" poem, she points out properly enough,
is not really a very formidable piece of philosophizing. The poet could
not have "elaborated and defended his position." He evidently did not
really believe in the doctrine of Platonic anamnesis to which the poem
seems to commit him. The logical structure "of the thought is really
very loose." [3] What the poem expresses is

> essentially the experience of having so great an idea [as that of
> transcendental remembrance], the excitement of it, the awe, the
> tinge of holiness it bestows on childhood, the explanation of the
> growing commonplaceness of later life, the resigned acceptance
> of an insight. [4]

The poem expresses what it feels like to have so great an idea. But
what of greatness? If the idea seemed trivial to the reader, would

[1] *Feeling and Form*, p. 374.   [3] *Feeling and Form*, p. 220.
[2] *Feeling and Form*, p. 227.   [4] *Feeling and Form*, p. 219.

that fact not make a real difference? It would have been possible for
Mrs. Langer to argue that only two things are required: first, as she has
actually argued, that the idea should have appeared great to the poet,
and second, as her general theory of art implies, that the poet should
have been sufficiently competent as a poet to make the idea seem great
to us; that is, Mrs. Langer might have argued that the poet's failure could
only be the failure of inexpressiveness.[5] But the circular nature of such
an argument scarcely needs pointing out: for the reader to whom the
idea has been rendered great, it *is* great—that is, within the relevant
frame of reference, the experience of the poem.

Mrs. Langer expresses some dissatisfaction with T. S. Eliot's "purer"
poems, and she is rather impatient of some of his literary methods,
particularly his use of literary allusions. Her reference to Eliot's "desperate nostalgia for a vanished culture," [6] makes one wonder, however,
whether her dissatisfaction has to do merely with literary techniques and
not also with Eliot's ideas—which may not seem "true and important" [7]
to her even though one assumes they must have seemed so to the poet.
Yet one may question whether, in terms of her general theory, she is
entitled to say more than that Eliot's poems are sometimes inexpressive.
For elsewhere in *Feeling and Form* she makes such remarks as these:
"Materials [for a poem] are neither good nor bad, strong nor weak"; [8]
"Where a theme comes from makes no difference; what matters is the
excitement it begets, the importance it has for the poet"; [9] and "There is
nothing the matter with an ardent moral idea in poetry, provided the
moral idea is used for poetic purposes." [1]

On the negative side, Mrs. Langer's presentation of the doctrine of
symbolic form is admirable. She puts cogently the warning that we must
not impose our preconceptions on the poem; nor wrench out of context
any "statements" that may be imbedded in the poem; nor demand that
it be a political or philosophical document answering to our own political
or philosophical notions. But as another "answer to science" the doctrine
of symbolic form, even as developed by Mrs. Langer, risks claiming at
once too little and too much.

It risks claiming too little in stressing as the essential pattern of poetry the "life of sentience." Mrs. Langer is much more sophisticated than,
say, Max Eastman. She carefully distinguishes between the pattern of
feelings as articulated in the poem and the poet's own outpouring of
emotions; she avoids the notion that the poet is simply projecting a subjective experience. But on close scrutiny there actually may be little to
differentiate her account of what poetry expresses from Eastman's. He
opines that

[5] *Feeling and Form*, p. 234.   [8] *Feeling and Form*, p. 406.
[6] *Feeling and Form*, p. 248.   [9] *Feeling and Form*, p. 254.
[7] *Feeling and Form*, p. 219.   [1] *Feeling and Form*, p. 5.

George Meredith made poetry of happy passion in "Love in the Valley," and of unhappy pain in "Modern Love," and though he was very intellectual, he had nothing to say to us about either one of them [i.e., those feelings] that we have been able to remember, except that there they were.[2]

At the same time, the doctrine of symbolic form risks claiming too much. Even in Mrs. Langer's treatment, and not merely in the obviously extravagant treatments of an Emerson or a Whitman, there is this risk. If all the cards in the deck are "wild" and can be counted as belonging to whatever suit and constituting whatever value we care to assign them, then the game ends. The possibility of conflict disappears. Perhaps Wordsworth's "great idea," Mrs. Langer has argued, was required only to generate the emotion for Wordsworth's poem, as a grain of sand within the oyster is required to generate a pearl. But the power of the idea to excite the poet's awe is not so easily separated from its ability to elicit the reader's awe: for to assume that the poet could have done quite as well with *any* idea that appealed to him is to conclude that ideas do not matter at all or—what amounts to the same thing—to assume that the poet is a kind of god, capable of making up his meanings out of whole cloth. In either case we are back to Emerson's symbolistic monism. If Mrs. Langer avoids this kind of monism, as on the whole she does, it is because in practise she uses more referential criteria than she is perhaps aware that she is using and more than her theory strictly entitles her to use.

IV

THOUGH both Cassirer and Mrs. Langer are, as we have seen, much interested in the relation of poetry to myth, and though they both levy upon myth to illustrate the theory of symbolic form, they are scrupulously careful to distinguish myth from poetry. Mrs. Langer writes, for instance, "Legend and myth and fairy tale are not in themselves literature, they are not art at all, but fantasies; as such, however, they are the natural materials of art."[3] But many of the critics of our time have, more boldly (or shall one say less scrupulously) seized upon the connection between myth and literature as providing a new key to criticism.

These new "myth" critics, now to be discussed, tend to be more conversant with psychology than with philosophy. They have also been heavily influenced by the anthropological studies of the last fifty years. They have been tremendously impressed by the discovery—or the rediscovery—that myth, ritual, and poetry are to be found at the begin-

[2] *The Literary Mind*, p. 148.   [3] *Feeling and Form*, p. 274.

nings of every culture. The specifically human estate begins, it has been
persuasively argued, with these forms of human expression, and it develops under their influence. The modern myth critic has probably been
even more powerfully impressed by the evidence that primitive man still
lurks within each of us, and that the 20th-century citizen who dutifully
drives to work each morning in an automobile, transacts business by
telephone with a firm three thousand miles away, and gets himself ready
for sleep by watching entertainment relayed to his living-room by the
electronics industry, recreates nightly in his dreams the primordial symbols of ancient myth. Seen in these terms, myth seems to offer to poetry
an inviolable refuge against the incursions of a hostile science.

Myth suggests a fresh means by which to study the "laws of the
imagination." Mrs. Langer herself is willing to agree that, since these
laws are "really just canons of symbolization," the "systematic study of
them" may be justly said to have been "first undertaken by Freud." [4] The
critics who hope to find in myth the key to artistic creation make much
of the number of characteristics that poetry shares with dream. The
process that Freud calls the "dream-work" shows startling similarities
with "poetic work." In both there is "condensation" (the combining
several images in one image), "displacement" (the vesting in some apparently unimportant element the underlying significance of the whole),
and "overdetermination" (several quite different significances focused
upon the same element so that it bears more than one meaning). In both
poetry and dream, logical relationships are frequently evaded or transcended by the mere juxtaposition of images.[5] Not only Freud, but
notably among other psychologists Carl Jung, and the cultural anthropologists in general are regarded as having furnished positive and specific
directives for the study of poetry. Some of our recent critics, under
the stimulus of such studies, write with the excitement of men who have
suddenly envisaged a whole new hemisphere.

For Northrop Frye the discovery points to the possibility of turning
literary criticism for the first time into a true science. No true science,
he argues, can be content to rest in the structural analysis of the object
with which it deals. The poet is only the *efficient* cause of the poem, but
the poem, having form, has a formal cause that is to be sought. On
examination, Frye finds this formal cause to be the archetype.[6]

What Frye calls "total" literary history moves from the primitive to
the sophisticated, and so Frye glimpses the possibility of envisaging lit-

---

[4] *Feeling and Form*, p. 241.

[5] Cf. *ante* Chapter 27 for parallels in the modern "semantic" study of poetic
language.

[6] "My [Critical] Credo," *The Kenyon Review*, XII (Winter, 1951), pp. 92–110.
"Archetype," borrowed from Jung, means a primordial image, a part of the collective
unconscious, the psychic residue of numberless experiences of the same kind, and thus
part of the inherited response-pattern of the race.

erature as the "complication of a relatively . . . simple group of formulas that can be studied in a primitive culture." [7] In the light of this possibility, the search for archetypes becomes a kind of "literary anthropology, concerned with the way that literature is informed by preliterary categories such as ritual, myth and folk tale." [8] Since the quest-myth is central to ritual and myth—and thus to literature—all the literary genres may be derived from it. Groupings under the rubrics of the four seasons emerge. That of spring will illustrate what Frye has in mind:

> The dawn, spring, and birth phase. Myths of the birth of the hero, of revival and resurrection, of creation and . . . of the defeat of the powers of darkness, winter and death. Subordinate characters: the father and mother. The archetype of romance and of most dithyrambic and rhapsodic poetry. [9]

Frye not only envisages criticism's taking its place "among the other social sciences." He has suggestions for bringing this about through what amounts to a production-line technique. The literary specialists who will deal with the text in question are disposed as follows: first the editor ("to clean up the text for us"), then the rhetorician and philologist, the literary psychologist, the literary social historian, the philosopher and the historian of ideas, and finally at the end of the line, the literary anthropologist. Frye consistently refers to the work of art as a "product," an organic commodity that is capable of being sorted, classified, and graded—a notion that receives some support from the way in which Frye chooses to suggest how a poem comes into being:

> The fact that revision is possible, that the poet makes changes not because he likes them better but because they are better, means that poems, like poets, are born and not made. The poet's task is to deliver the poem in as uninjured a state as possible, and

---

[7] *Kenyon Review*, XII, 99.

[8] *Kenyon Review*, XII, 99–100.

[9] *Kenyon Review*, XII, p. 104. Joseph Campbell's *The Hero with a Thousand Faces* (Bollingen Series, XVII, 1949), is one of a number of recent books that treat the quest-myth. Campbell too feels that his mission is to proclaim the new dispensation. He tells us that the "great coordinating mythologies . . . now are known as lies" (p. 388), yet the problems with which they purported to deal remain. We shall solve these problems, he predicts, by learning "to recognize the lineaments of God in all the wonderful modulations of the face of man" (p. 390). Still more extravagant claims for the benefits to spring from our knowledge of the universal myth are made by James K. Feibleman in his *Aesthetics* (New York, 1949). He argues that the future of modern literature is immense: Though we moderns have no legends like that of Troy nor myths like that of the House of Atreus, we do have an extensive knowledge of the master myth, "the myth of the year god" (p. 426). The possession of this myth gives our artists an even greater opportunity than that afforded the Greek artist of the fifth century B.C., for the modern artist not only knows a *greater number* of myths he knows much more about the very nature of myth!

if the poem is alive, it is equally anxious to be rid of him, and screams to be cut loose from his private memories and associations, his desire for self-expression, and all the other navel-strings and feeding tubes of his ego. The critic takes over where the poet leaves off. . . .[1]

In this lively analogy the poem is evidently the babe, the poet the mother, and the critic the midwife and nurse, who ties off the cord, tells the mother the infant is a boy or girl, washes it up for presentation to the outside world, and presumably gives it an anthropological classification and takes its Bertillion measurements. Yet Frye's analogy fails to cover what must finally be the crucial question of whether the poem is still-born and inert, or alive. He merely alludes to this question with the cautionary "if the poem is alive." In some sense this has always been the primary question with which criticism has had to concern itself: is the poem "alive," or is it merely a document, wooden, dead, lifeless, a mere "exhibit," without literary merit? Frye's midwife-critic, in none of the special roles portioned out to him as textual editor, historian of ideas, or even literary anthropologist, can answer that question, and in none of the many roles that Frye assigns him does he need to answer that question. The inert and valueless "document" will submit to the kind of classification that Frye specifies just as well as a valuable poem. The promise that by such means criticism may take its place among the other social sciences justifies pressing the question suggested by Frye's analogy. For it is a matter of some consequence whether criticism, once it has become a social science, will become as chary of making evaluations and rendering normative judgments. In short, is the aim to make criticism a purely descriptive, value-free social science? That eventuality would prove to be simply a new variant on the old historicism.

In the position developed by Richard Chase in *The Quest for Myth*, the term "myth" is clearly a value term. A poem that is vibrantly alive *is* mythic and vice versa; for Chase absolutely identifies poetry and myth. "Myth," he writes, "is only art."[2] The adverb *only* in this context is rather curious. One wants to ask whether Chase is attempting to debunk myth, on the assumption that myth has close affiliations with religion; or whether he is striving to enhance art by suggesting that the important function claimed for myth in past cultures is actually still available through art for our scientific civilization. A reading of Chase's book indicates that he means to do something of both.

Poetry and myth, he argues, arise out of the same human needs, represent the same kind of symbolic structure, succeed in investing experience with the same kind of awe and magical wonder, and perform

[1] *Kenyon Review*, XII, 97–8.
[2] *The Quest for Myth* (Baton Rouge, 1949), p. 110.

the same cathartic function. The last phrase, however, is strictly a misnomer. Here Chase substitutes for Aristotle's metaphor of purgation a figure of his own that has to do with animal taming. We have been made, he says, whether we like it or not, the trustees "of inhumanly powerful forces which were once caged and domesticated by the apparatus of the Christian religion." That cage has been broken and the beasts have escaped and now lurk in the depths of man's unconscious. Ghosts such as haunt the hero in Henry James's "The Beast in the Jungle"

> are terrible and destructive just because they are inadequately projected by their victims. . . . We must do with "the beast" what James himself did: flush it from the jungle so that it may be captured in the texture of aesthetic experience and bent to our will.[3]

The artist is evidently the hound that flushes the beast from the jungle; his art is the cage that holds him when captured, and also, one supposes, the kitchen-chair and whip which the artist lion-tamer uses to force him to take his stand on the pedestal and sit quietly, obedient to the trainer's will. But the complications of Chase's image need not obscure at all the function which he assigns to poetry. It is substantially the role that Matthew Arnold assigned to poetry. The strength of art is that it does not rest upon dogma, and therefore can survive the breakup of dogma. If myth once upon a time tamed the destructive forces within man, and if myth is only art, then art ought to be able to tame them for us now.

The parallel with Arnold will suggest why Chase is so hostile to the proposition that myth originally implied belief. And here, of course, Chase comes into sharp collision with philosophers of symbolic form like Cassirer and Langer, who, as we have seen, firmly insist that in the true "mythical imagination there is always implied an act of *belief*."[4] I. A. Richards once wrote of *The Waste Land* that Eliot had effected a complete severance of poetry and belief, though Eliot himself was to demur. Chase seems to be saying that there never was any effective relation between belief and myth (poetry). The claim is almost heroically desperate. Yet it is easy to see why Chase has to insist upon it. If it could be made good, it would constitute an answer to a question that nowadays is certain to be raised by many voices: namely, how modern man is to profit from the power inherent in myth if in fact no intellectually respectable modern can any longer believe in myth? If, however, myth is "only art," the day is saved.

For Leslie Fiedler, the new perspective now offered by myth leads

[3] *Quest for Myth*, p. 102. [4] *An Essay on Man*, p. 75.

straight back into the study of message and consequently into the study of biography.[5] Fiedler reacts sharply against recent "formalist" trends in criticism: the emphasis upon an "impersonal art," upon the poem itself rather than the study of its background. He wishes to reaffirm the importance of the poet's personality and the relevance of the poet's "intention." It is easy to see why: the theories that he is attacking tend to minimize the ancient distinction between literary form and content. Fiedler is engaged in reasserting a full dualism. For the archetypal materials are really a privileged poetic subject matter in disguise. He argues that any great poem must be an acceptable rendition of this special poetic content.

At the same time, a study of the poet's response—of the way in which he expresses, and by expressing, stamps, his personal "signature" upon the archetype—forces the critic to take full account of the biography of the poet. For in Fiedler's conception, a poem is not an object to be known; it is rather a clue to an event in the poet's psyche. The poet's psyche is the arena in which *Dichtung* and *Wahrheit* become one: the poetic work itself is incidental to this important process:

> In deed as in word, the poet composes himself as maker and mask, in accordance with some contemporaneous *mythos* of the artist. And as we all know, in our day, it is even possible to be a writer without having written anything! [6]

Literature has come a long way since the day of Thomas Gray and his "mute inglorious Miltons." That our poets may be tongue-tied, or too busy with their psychic struggles to stop and put anything down on paper, may or may not endanger their status as real poets. But, of course, Fiedler expects them normally to put themselves on paper, for then the therapeutic benefits of the process of poetic objectification (compare Chase *ante*) become socially available:

> In the Mask of [the poet's] life and the manifold masks of his work, the poet expresses for a whole society the ritual meaning of its inarticulate selves; the artist goes forth not to "recreate the conscience of his race," but to redeem its unconscious. We cannot get back into the primal Garden of the unfallen Archetypes, but we can yield ourselves to the dreams and images that mean paradise regained.[7]

In the same essay Fiedler writes that the poet is able to take us back "to his unconscious core, where he becomes one with us all in the presence of our ancient Gods, the protagonists of fables we think we no

---

[5] "Archetype and Signature," *The Sewanee Review*, LX (Spring, 1952), 253–73. Reprinted by permission of *The Sewanee Review*.
[6] *The Sewanee Review*, LX, 261.   [7] *Sewanee Review*, LX, 273.

longer believe." [8] But never mind what we *think* on these occasions; do we or do we not believe? That will be the question that some readers will want to put. Can we, by taking a firm hold on our bootstraps, actually lift ourselves to a belief in what we do not "really believe"? Or is "believe" being used in a Pickwickian sense? One is aware that the question may not be easy to answer, but eventually it must at least be faced.

V

THE more literary question that is raised by Fiedler and by the myth critics in general may be put as follows: Have they found in their study of myth and the psychology of dreams an authoritative clue to the interpretation of poems? They certainly write with the excitement of men who have found such a key. Yet their claims are a little incoherent and at points contradictory.

The attempt to apply Freudian theory to poetry runs into a similar problem: Mrs. Langer points out that the peculiar weakness of Freud's theory as applied to poetics is that it tends to "put good and bad art on a par, making all art a natural self-expressive function like dream and 'make-believe.' " [9]

It is possible, of course, to argue that one poet uses a myth more "artistically" or more "powerfully" than another; or one may argue that some myths are more powerful or more significant than other myths and therefore yield greater poems. But to take either alternative would seem to reinstate the traditional critical problems in full force. For our attempt to show that Poem A uses Myth X artistically whereas Poem B does not, brings up what Frye has called the "problem of rhetoric." And so does our argument that Myth X is more significant (and therefore makes for a greater poem) than Myth Y. Considerations of this sort suggest that "mythic" and "archetypal" criticism, whatever other contribution it may make, provides no way of circumventing the basic problems of traditional criticism. [1]

In considering some of the recent "myth" criticism, we have seen how various it is in its emphases: with Frye we are asked to assign an almost monstrous "life of its own" to the poem; with Fiedler, on the other hand, the poem is important as an event in the life of the poet; and there is Chase's concern for the audience in his therapeutic emphasis. But the literary use of the study of myths *can* be centered firmly upon the poetic structure itself. Maude Bodkin's *Archetypal Patterns of*

[8] *Sewanee Review*, LX, 273.
[9] *Feeling and Form*, p. 240.
[1] Cf. Fergusson, *Idea of a Theater*, pp. 17, 77.

Poetry is an excellent demonstration of this possibility. Her archetypal patterns are the primordial images that occur in the poetry of both the past and the present. They are such images as that of the mysterious cavern, of the guilt-haunted wanderer, of the fountain, of the buried corn, and so on. She keeps specific passages of the poems that she discusses steadily in view. In her sensitive commentaries on particular poems, Miss Bodkin is for the most part filling out implications, suggesting comparisons between the symbols in the poem and symbols as they occur in tribal and religious life, and in general employing the special findings of psychology and comparative religion in the same way that she employs other fields of knowledge. Such work is always important, but it scarcely invokes a revolutionary technique—nor does Miss Bodkin regard it as doing so. Her very conception of archetypes implies that images endowed with such universal significance—images rooted so deep in the human psyche—must have yielded much of their significance to both poet and reader in the past. The work left to the modern psychologist can be no more than to make explicit in a particular way what was already in some sense intuited by the earlier reader.

> It is with the complete resources of our minds that we must appreciate, if appreciation is to be genuine. If, for instance, we have found certain elements in experience made newly explicit through the teaching of Freud, that new awareness will enter into our apprehension of *Othello*, or of *Hamlet*, though it was not present in Shakespeare's own thought, nor in the audience for whom he wrote.
>
> One can no more bind within the limits of the author's intention the interactions with new minds of a play or poem that lives on centuries after his death, than one can restrict within its parents' understanding the interrelations of the child that goes forth from their bodies to live its own life in the world.[2]

Thus, Miss Bodkin, refusing to allow the "author's intention" to tyrannize over the meaning of the work, recognizes the possibility of a growth of meaning in the constituent elements of a work and therefore a possible development in the meaning of the work itself. But she is as far as she can be from suggesting that a new "archetypal" criticism will now replace criticism as we have known it. Knowledge of archetypes may be regarded as an acquisition of new artistic materials or else as an enrichment of older artistic materials: it constitutes an enlargement of the poet's (and of the reader's) potential resources; but it is not a "new" method of organization or interpretation.

[2] *Archetypal Patterns of Poetry* (Oxford, 1934), p. 334, by permission of the publishers, Oxford University Press, Inc. Another excellent treatment of this sort of imagery is to be found in W. H. Auden's *The Enchaflèd Flood* (1950).

VI

RECENT "myth" criticism, as previous allusions in this chapter indicate, owes more to Carl Jung than to any other man. It may be interesting, therefore, to examine his notions of the relation of the study of myth to literary criticism. There can be no doubt as to the serious role that Jung assigns to myth. One aspect of the seriousness with which he takes the function of myth in our psychic life is his insistence that one must discriminate very carefully among myths and even among dreams. He does not speak of dreaming "skilfully" or "eloquently," but he does assert that one can on occasion dream "significantly." He writes that he is compelled to admit "that the unconscious mind is capable at times of assuming an intelligence and purposiveness which are superior to actual conscious insight." [3] The implications of this statement are large. If the activity of the unconscious in dream and myth is not merely a symptom of psychic disorder but "at times" at least is an intelligent and purposive ordering, then all myths and dreams are not alike; some are evidently more purposive and significant than others. And this judgment, that some are more purposive and significant than others, implies a cognitive criticism and interpretation of myth and dream. Jung means too that the function of "purposive" myths and dreams is not merely or even primarily cathartic; it is knowledge-giving: dreams give us knowledge of ourselves.

This emphasis in Jung perhaps accounts for the fact that he has been more directly influential on recent literary criticism than Freud has been. Miss Bodkin has put the matter very well:

> The difference between the two schools [of Freud and Jung] lies in Jung's belief that a synthetic or creative function does pertain to the unconscious—that within the fantasies arising in sleep or waking life there are present indications of new directions or modes of adaptation, which the reflective self, when it discerns them, may adopt, and follow with some assurance that along these lines it has the backing of unconscious energies.[4]

It may not be too much to say that Jung (in contrast to Freud with his "psychiatric" analysis even of the poem) brings a cognitive criticism to bear even upon the dream.

> The "manifest" dream-picture is the dream itself, and contains the "latent" meaning. If I find sugar in the urine, it is sugar, and not a façade that conceals albumen. When Freud speaks of

[3] *Psychology and Religion* (New Haven, 1938), p. 45.
[4] *Archetypal Patterns*, p. 73.

the "dream-façade," he is really speaking, not of the dream itself, but of its obscurity. . . . We say that a dream has a false front only because we fail to see into it. We would do better to say that we are dealing with something like a text that is unintelligible, not because it is a façade, but simply because we cannot read it.[5]

Some of the dreams that he describes are very elaborate symbolic structures. Their parts are ordered in accordance with a "logic of the imagination" and are therefore, to the proper interpreter, coherent and intelligible. They are in some sense analogous to poems, and the role of the interpreter—if we are to judge from Jung's own procedure in his published analyses—is analogous to that of the literary critic. For example, Jung will write of a particularly elaborate dream that it "speaks of religion and that it means to do so. Since the dream is elaborate and consistent it suggests a certain logic and a certain intention." [6] Moreover the interpretation does not require a secret key: the symbols that it makes use of are remarkably "public" and traditional—not nearly so clandestine as one might have thought. The condensations, juxtapositions and symbolic ambiguities, as Jung interprets this dream, show a remarkable resemblance to those met with in much modern literary criticism.

"A great work of art," Jung writes, "is like a dream." And he specifies two ways in which it is: "for all its apparent obviousness it does not explain itself and is never unequivocal." That is, the poem is not prescriptive; neither the poem nor even the dream says "You ought" or "This is the truth." Moreover, like the dream, the poem requires us to make our own interpretation, for the poem presents an image "in much the same way as nature allows a plant to grow, and we must draw our own conclusions." [7]

VII

IN VERY important ways, Jung's conception of the poem parallels that of the symbolist theorist. A poem is organic; it is filled with implicit meaning; the relation of its parts may transcend that of rational arrangement —may indeed involve the reconciliation of apparent contradictions. This last parallel with certain modern theories of poetry becomes especially apparent if, following up Jung's claim for parallelism between poem and dream, we attribute to poetry on his view the kind of tension which he is emphatic in claiming for dream. Psychic energy in general, he

---

[5] *Modern Man in Search of a Soul* (New York, 1933), p. 15, by permission of the publishers, Harcourt, Brace and Company, Inc.
   [6] *Psychology and Religion*, p. 31.   [7] *Modern Man*, p. 198.

tells us, involves "the play of opposites." The healthy growth of the mind involves a shattering of narrow states of consciousness through "the tension inherent in the play of opposites" and a building up thereby of a state of "wider and higher consciousness."[8]

We have thus far stressed the likeness between poem and dream. Jung in fact draws a very sharp distinction between them. The dream is shaped by the unconscious, but the poem, though it may draw upon the depths of man's being, is "apparently intentional and consciously shaped."[9] Moreover Jung is careful to distinguish the psychologist's study of the poet from his study of the poem:

> The truth is that [Freud's view of art] takes us away from the psychological study of the work of art, and confronts us with the psychic disposition of the poet himself. That the latter presents an important problem is not to be denied, but the work of art is something in its own right, and may not be conjured away.[1]

The psychologist, then, is able (if he wishes) to study the poem and not merely the mind of the man who made it.

If we ask what specific contribution the psychologist can make to the study of literature, Jung first offers us a distinction between two broad classes of literary work. There is what he calls "psychological" literature, which

> always takes its materials from the vast realm of conscious human experience—from the vivid foreground of life, we might say. I have called this mode of artistic creation psychological because in its activity it nowhere transcends the bounds of psychological intelligibility. . . .
>
> In dealing with the psychological mode of artistic creation, we never need ask ourselves what the material consists of or what it means.[2]

But this question does force itself upon us as soon as we come to the visionary mode of creation.

> We are astonished, taken aback, confused, put on our guard or even disgusted—and we demand commentaries and explanations. We are reminded in nothing of everyday, human life,

---

[8] *Modern Man*, p. 117.

[9] *Modern Man*, p. 175. The full context of Jung's discussion makes it quite plain that the intentionality is to be inferred from the work itself and not merely from some statement by the poet. In this matter Jung is emphatic, writing that "the truth is that poets are human beings, and that what a poet has to say about his work is often far from being the most illuminating word on the subject" (p. 186).

[1] *Modern Man*, p. 185.   [2] *Modern Man*, pp. 180–2.

but rather of dreams, night-time fears and the dark recesses of the mind that we sometimes sense with misgiving.[3]

Apparently, the literature of the visionary mode may require the services of the psychologist. What those specific services are, it remains to consider.

In the first place, according to Jung, the psychologist can show us that the kind of experience with which, say, a Dante or a Melville deals is, in spite of its "visionary" nature, important and to be taken seriously. The psychologist can point out that "we must take [the vision] at least as seriously as we do the experiences that underlie the psychological mode of artistic creation," experiences that "no one doubts . . . are both real and serious."[4]

In the second place, the psychologist can point out that however "dark this nocturnal world" with which the visionary artist deals may be, "it is not wholly unfamiliar."[5] The last clause is worth stressing. If what the visionary artist treated were *wholly* unfamiliar, that is, really private and eccentric, its expression might have value for the artist himself and might provide an interesting case-study for the psychologist, but it would cease to be a work of art. The fact is that the nocturnal world is in some sense the world of all of us, and this the psychologist can help us to see.

The work of the psychologist, *qua* psychologist, therefore, turns out to be not so much a work of interpretation as one of vindication. The artist is to be freed from the charge that his vision is merely a symptom of some personal psychic maladjustment and from the charge that his symbols are merely subjective distortions of that world fashioned by those whom Jung calls the "reason-mongers." Actually, as to specific "methods" of interpretation, Jung has in his later writings very little to say. But the clear implication is against the possibility of any special "method" by which the psychologist takes over from, and substitutes himself for, the literary critic. Jung has made it plain that "visionary" literature includes some of the most important literature that we have—*Moby Dick* and even the *Divine Comedy*. But he is careful also to include among instances of "visionary" literature such a work as Rider Haggard's *She*.[6] Jung does not indicate how we know that *She* is not so great a novel as *Moby Dick;* he simply takes it for granted that we do know it. But this judgment of relative literary value is clearly made by the critic, judging by whatever criteria a critic does judge, and not by the psychologist judging as psychologist.

To the question raised earlier as to whether the new "myth" criticism possesses a special key for literary interpretation, the answer of

[3] *Modern Man*, p. 182.   [4] *Modern Man*, p. 185.   [5] *Modern Man*, p. 188.
[6] Jung also says specifically that "Literary products of highly dubious merit are often of the greatest interest to the psychologist" (*Modern Man*, p. 177).

Jung would seem to be an emphatic no. The literary critic will obviously profit by all that he can learn about what human beings are, about how they behave, and especially about the way their minds work.[7] He will also find valuable whatever knowledge he can obtain about the languages in which men express themselves—not only Latin or French or Old Norse, but all those recurrent patterns of symbolism to which the modern anthropologist or the depth psychologist or the student of comparative literature direct our attention. By studying these symbolic languages he will learn again how various is man and yet how much the same man remains. In this area of knowledge Jung furnishes stimulating—even exciting—observations, but by his own confession, his contribution would seem to consist in having added to our knowledge about man's processes of symbolization and the great immemorial symbols—the archetypes—in which man tends to express himself.

So it is also with W. B. Yeats, surely the greatest of the recent poets who have tried to use myth as the basis of their own work. As we have indicated in an earlier chapter,[8] Yeats proposed in writing *A Vision* to create a living myth. But no one knew better than Yeats that this would be literally impossible. We find him saying, therefore, that no mere intellectual revolution can bring back the "old simple celebration of life tuned to its highest pitch." What might be possible for such a revolution to bring about would necessarily have to be "something more deliberate . . . , more systematized, more external, more self-conscious, as must be at a second coming." [9]

Just so. Yeats's own "myth" as embodied in *A Vision* is more fully systematized, more deliberate, more external than any genuine myth can be. *A Vision* is in part a theory of history; in part a psychology of creation, in part—and perhaps most importantly—a dictionary of public and semi-personal symbols—a kind of logbook of the symbols that Yeats had used and was in the future to use in his own poetry. *A Vision* contains some prose wrought almost fully up to the pitch of poetry; and it throws light upon Yeats's own development as a thinker and an artist. But the finest of Yeats's poems do not depend upon it. They transcend it, making use of the "natural" and traditional symbols that he discusses in *A Vision*, or at times ignoring that body of symbols altogether and creating their own symbols. They are poems and their symbols are poetically effective, not because Yeats was a maker of myths but because he was a poet. And we for our part recognize his poems to be poems by whatever means we have for recognizing poetry.

[7] "Psychology and the study of art will always have to turn to one another for help, and the one will not invalidate the other" (*Modern Man*, p. 177).

[8] Cf. *ante* Chapter 26.

[9] *Wheels and Butterflies*, 1934 (New York, 1935), pp. 65–6.

PART FIVE

PART FIVE

EPILOGUE

§ *retrospect: from Plato through the Middle Ages—II. the Renaissance and neo-classic eras—III. the romantic and post-romantic, to about 1940—IV. the historical method as a study of the audience, criticism of gross structure, myth and ritual origins, the century of the common man—V. the correct view of Plato's rhapsode? the critical problem of values and emotions, subject and object, relative and universal, the role of words, accent on experience, light refracted through a crystal, reality of external values, the "naive"—VI. aesthetic emotion and real life, tension and reconciliation, tragic and comic, Plato's Philebus, pure and impure pleasures, aesthetics of "significant form," 18th-century dismal feelings, opposed to analysis of wit and irony, problem of pain and destruction, material concreteness, division, conflict, evil in literature, problem of moral commitment, Manichaean dualism, human substance vs. philosophic melodrama—VII. irony as metaphoric structure, "form," the metaphysical metaphor, metaphor as universality and concreteness, metaphor and historical information, multiple perspectives, Aristotelian mimetic, Ricardian affective, Crocean expressionistic and linguistic, metaphor in criticism, status of the literary "kinds," various focuses—VIII. values sensory, spiritual, and aesthetic (representative and non-representative), reduction up or down, opposing and reconciling terms, "speculative," "practical," "doing," "making," "useful," "fine," various simplifications, the difficult alternative: "A theory of poetic or fine art must keep asserting in various idioms, by various stratagems, in accord with the demands of the dialectic of the time, the special character of poetry as a tensional union of making with seeing and saying"* §

723

THE HISTORY WHICH WE HAVE JUST BROUGHT TO ONE OF ITS MOMEN-tary conclusions in the modern theory of mythic archetypes had one of its remote formal beginnings, we remember, in a Platonic dialogue where an ironic dialectician compelled a naive professor and reciter of poetry, a rhapsode, to make some damaging admissions about the kind of science or wisdom which either the rhapsode or his authority the poet might lay claim to. The upshot of the inquisition appeared to be that neither poet nor rhapsode, so far as they were simply poet or rhapsode, "knew" anything at all. They were prompted to their marvelous utterance by a divinely irrational afflatus; they were out of their minds with a power which came directly to the poet and was passed on by him to the rhapsode and to *his* auditors by a kind of magnetism.

The *Ion* was an early and simple preliminary to Plato's more elaborate attacks on the illusionistic and emotive power of poetry (and of rhetoric) in the *Republic, Phaedrus* and other mature dialogues. Aristotle in his *Poetics* answered that a workout of painful emotions is a good thing, effecting a homeopathic purgation, and as for the allegedly deceptive remove at which poetry stood from the universals, the tragic or epic poem was actually a kind of ethical invention which came much closer than the uncontrived chronicle of history to saying something serious and philosophic and universal about the human protagonist. There were hints about a certain blend of goodness and fault in that protagonist and his experience of disastrous results. A comic poem was more abstract, less mythic, and the mistakes made were less painful and less destructive. In his *Rhetoric* Aristotle made some remarks about verbal tricks and heightened metaphoric ways of speaking, and about the character of a speaker and the emotions of his audience. These were inescapable dimensions of discourse, and as they might be used in one way by the sophist, the honest orator had better look well to their opposite use.

A few hundred years later in Augustan Rome we found the urbane lyric and epistolary poet Horace still talking—in a tradition of Peripatetic codifications—about dramatic and epic poetry and speaking casually about Socratic wisdom as a sufficient source of poetic content. It seemed important to him—or he spoke as if it seemed important—to recognize certain well defined types of poetry, their metres, contents, and rules of decorum. He said that correct usage in words was important and along with that a great deal of care and craft in putting them together. Despite his formal textbook talk about tragedy and comedy (the genres a young aspirant would be expected to try his hand at), Horace himself was a conversational, satiric, and epistolary poet—and through this focus on poetry as a kind of skilled and gentlemanly exercise in talking he makes his shrewdest observations. But then at Rome less than a century later, we have, in the all but anonymous Greek man of letters who wrote the *Peri Hupsous*, almost the direct opposite of Horace. The *Peri Hupsous* is a celebration of ecstasy and inspiration; it now asserts in full earnestness and enthusiasm the view that was framed half playfully in Plato's *Ion*. The educational prestige of declamation and rhetoric was such in first-century Rome that the treatise of Longinus could not but be much preoccupied with certain technical entanglements, figures and kinds of diction and formulas for amplification. But the special and pulsing accent of Longinus is on the great and impassioned soul of the poet, his flashes and spurts of inspiration, the careless and plunging grandeur of his utterance, the bigness of the objects which inspire him, and the corresponding transport of his audience.

And that accent was something far from alien to the full Roman neo-Platonism which appears two centuries later with the metaphysician and visionary Plotinus. The difference is that whereas Longinus rests his case on the flash of inspiration, the quasi-divine illumination, Plotinus, systematic, meditative, profoundly metaphysical and brooding, would integrate the flash into a comprehensive philosophy of divine intelligence and life radiant through and immanent in all the universe and all human souls and minds. A special instance of that intelligence is the artist, who by some superior access to divinity gives us the better and brighter image of Zeus. The ambitious synthetic reasoning of Plotinus produces some interesting emphases, such as those on the beauty and simplicity of light, on the superiority of the ocular sense which meets and appreciates light, and on the likeness and union of knowing organ and subject with object. The same reasoning produces two such difficult problems as that of the double form (form upon form) in the carved stone, and the conflict between the divine principle of unity and the Stoic principle of beauty in the complexity implied by "symmetry." St. Augustine with a geometric and numerical emphasis on unity and harmony, and Aquinas (despite a nearly Platonic assignment of poetry to the area of sophistry) continue the Plotinian accent on order and radiance and on "connaturality" of subject and object.

The long course of the Christian Middle Ages acknowledges and develops without deviation the philosophy of intelligible unity, being, and beauty, with an accent now on numerical harmony, astronomy and music, now on a cosmological principle of visible radiance, and always on the vast and minutely detailed symbolism of God's illuminated book, the universe. Thus one kind of Platonic strain joins with and, from Patristic times on, helps to develop the ancient allegorical reading of poetry, which is freshly and with unprecedented vigor applied to the exegesis of the Hebrew and Christian Scriptures. The Middle Ages and later the Renaissance make a long period of all-out symbolic reading—though scarcely in the more fluid and "creative" sense in which "symbolism" has been understood in times closer to our own. Finally, the Middle Ages is a period of a certain kind of rhetorical poetics— *Poetria Nova* in the 13th century—which means Hellenistic prescriptions for how to use all the figures, and on what occasions.

II

DURING all that period Aristotle was not known as a literary authority, and there was no other authority. But with the 16th century in Italy Aristotle's *Poetics* had to be dealt with (perhaps for the first time directly as a dead system of partly cryptic notes), and Horace too, who became "fused" with Aristotle in a newly completed code. But meanwhile there was the luxuriance of vernacular literature from Dante to Ariosto to be coped with by the theoretical arbiters, vernacular problems of diction and of metrics, and of burlesque and "errant" romance forms of epic. There was the heroic love theme of Tasso, the pastoral mixture innovated by Guarini. Hence a series of denunciations and spirited defences. Romantic freedoms were won, but the classic professors were stout champions too—and from Scaliger and Castelvetro, though for different reasons, emerged the hyper-Aristotelian dramatic unities of action, time and place, destined to become for French dramatists of the next century and for Dryden a theoretical precedent and challenge of great meaning. During the later 16th century in Italy the question about levels of symbolism appears in somewhat simpler forms than in the Middle Ages, and there appears too the grand question, implied in the whole classical debate from Plato and Aristotle on, as to whether poetry is an "icastic" (or literal, or realistic) image, or whether it has some kind of warrant to be imaginative or "fantastic." *Aut prodesse aut delectare* too is much debated—and all possible combinations of the aims of pleasing and teaching are contrived, including in the French mid-17th century at least as early as the Abbé D'Aubignac's *Pratique du Théâtre*, 1657, the notion that poetry is to please *through* instructing —a notable, if somewhat cramped, anticipation of the later famous idea that aesthetic values are one kind of end in themselves. Sir Philip Sidney is the Elizabethan English man of letters who gives us the best epitome of all these continental themes, especially the didactic and moral. His phrase about the poet "ranging within the zodiac of his own wit" and his dictum that the poet "nothing affirmeth and therefore never lieth" are brilliant, if perhaps only incidental, announcements of poetic freedom and might. And beside these may be set Bacon's passage about science buckling and bowing the mind to reality, poetry "submitting the shews of things to the desires of the mind."

In the generation of the Jacobeans, Ben Jonson's more ruggedly assertive didactic and satiric classicism includes a surprisingly severe, almost agelastic, version of Aristotle's meager dictum that the comic is a form of the ugly. Jonson furnishes also a lively demonstration, through free and virile Englishing, how little the classic mind thought that previous realization of an idea could tarnish it.

The most long-lived, productive and important English critic of the 17th century is Dryden, who in his several phases—as the "new" English dramatic theorist against the French norms, as heroic dramatist, court wit and conversationalist, as Shakespearian critic, as satirist or refined executioner of dullness, as translator of the classics, as translator and appreciator of Chaucer—shows us the meaning of such gradually shifting neo-classic debates as those concerning the stage unities and rhyme in drama (matters of intensity and realization disguised as matters of verisimilitude), those concerning verbal decorum, the real, the marvelous and the heroic, and those concerning such various topics as "poetic justice," the serious aims of laughter, the rivalry between ancients and moderns, the possibility and the meaning of translation and imitation. The "heroic" focus (so far as it really was a theoretical focus) was a momentary juncture of Aristotelian ideas about the hero with inflational notions of grandeur and inspiration. Concurrently (in a confused alliance with the heroic) came the quieter and tougher revival of Horatian courtly urbanity—the kind of wit that was destined to succeed "metaphysical" wit (a thing uncelebrated in contemporary theory), the kind of poetry that would persist longest into the severe era of reason that was being ushered in.

The 17th century saw the end of Ciceronian and medieval and early Renaissance rhetorical culture; it was a century of decline in the prestige of words and the mysteries of auditory doctrine, of a soaring new prestige for seeing and diagramming, for the simplifying and classifying spirit of science. We have observed the variations in meaning of the index word "wit"—the gradual discountenancing of the metaphysical and imaginative meaning (one which might be used to describe the poetry of Donne, Herbert, Milton, or Shakespeare) and the evolution of the new concept of "true" wit as only judgment after all, propriety of thought and speech, "nature to advantage dressed"—until literary criticism centered in a highly ambiguous *new* key term. The term "wit" might now be either viewed suspiciously in its older poetic meaning, as by Locke or Addison, or applied in its safer new meaning (by reason of an ingeniously evasive submission to good sense on the part of the best English poets) in a deceptive way to current poetry.

In that crisis of the accomplished dissociation of sensibility, with Cartesian and Newtonian rationality running ahead to apparently limitless conquests of clarity, and with the verbal arts lavishing themselves

on patterns of oratorical trim, on repeated metaphorical recommenda-
tions of a lost sense—was heard the new accent on ocular and auditory
pleasure ("pleasures of the imagination"), on sensation, on the aesthetic,
on landscape, on supposed weddings of the arts in forms like oratorio,
song, and opera. And there was heard also, more and more plainly, the
new accent on feeling, on tender and sympathetic feeling, on the pleasures of painful feeling. The Platonic universal of Samuel Johnson and
Sir Joshua Reynolds was merged in the neo-Longinian sublime. Despite
much stalwart talk about norms and species, Johnson's classic garment
flies in tatters in the strong affective breezes. Yet classical precedents
were always invoked: for the sensational, the Horatian *ut pictura poesis;*
for the emotive, both Longinian ecstasy and sentimentalized versions of
Aristotelian catharsis. In the sublimity of awful and threatening natural
phenomena, in the physiognomy of emotive expressions, the aesthetic
of sensation and the aesthetic of emotion conclusively joined. The new
movement, for all its sources in antiquity, was headlong toward the
future and would be "modern" for at least two centuries to come. Add
the subtly pervasive principle of "association." This was first only a way
of breaking up traditional patterns of expectancy and of value. But in
a second phase (in conjunction with a new fondness for particularity
and especially for picturesque details of nature) it became a principle
of positive, creative, emotionally warm and plastic power—a principle
of imaginative "coalescence."

III

A CERTAIN kind of classicism persisted long in England under the name
and in the actuality of "poetic diction"—that curious species of glossy
ornament which was demolished by Wordsworth in the first phases of
his primitivism and simplism. After that the scene was clear for both
Wordsworth and Coleridge to proceed from "association" in its simpler
Hartleyan and mechanical phase to the more emotive and plastic notion
which, by pushing ahead only a slight distance and by showing in their
mature poems what the fullness of the doctrine could mean, they
established in the glorious (though momentary) status of "imagination." Coleridge added the deepening and fortification of German metaphysics—the epistemology of "object" and "subject," or the imaginative
reconciliation of these two opposites and along with them of art and
nature, emotion and thought, the universal and the particular, and other
satellites. Coleridge and Wordsworth show in a manageable landscape
vignette what the larger and more varied movement of German romanticism, the poetry and theory of Goethe and Schiller and Novalis,
the lectures of the Schlegels, the philosophy of Kant, Schelling and

Fichte, was in process of doing for the whole history of modern poetry and aesthetics in the West.

The romantic theory was in effect a highly ambiguous and double claim—a claim both for poetic freedom and for poetic responsibility. It was thus the cloud-capped starting point for certain quite opposite lines of poetic theory that came down through the 19th century toward our own day. One of these, moving from Kantian disinterest, formality and beauty, through French academic aesthetics and then early symbolist and Parnassian poetics, resulted in what we look back on as Art for Art's Sake—the end-of-the-century gilded celebration of autonomous poetic power. At the level of general aesthetics and linguistic, the philosophy of Benedetto Croce is the voraciously systematic expression of this view. Not so far removed from art-for-art's sake as we might wish to think, and in some phases part of it, was the thing, technically so much more subtle and more interesting to us, which came out of romantic "imagination" and "symbol" and became "symbolism." This seems to have come not so much directly from the German philosophers as through Coleridge and Poe, and Heine and Baudelaire, to the era of Mallarmé and the Wagnerians. Here was a more subtle "music" of "ideas" than the neo-classic theory of painting the passions had conceived—and a new quasi-spiritual reaction against the philosophy of science.

But those kinds of theory, both pure art and symbolism, were directly at odds with three other main kinds which developed the opposite accent of the romantic heritage—not that on autonomous privilege but that on moral and social power and evolutionary responsibility. Here were three versions of didacticism: one, the earliest and most fully romantic—what we may call the rhapsodic, the bardic, the prophetic, as it is brandished for instance in the *Defense of Poetry* by Shelley or the *Heroes and Hero Worship* of Carlyle; a second, the most nearly allied to a proper literary interest, the classical humanism, severity, and loftiness, both German and French in origin, which is fully expressed in English by Matthew Arnold; a third, owing much to Hegelian dialectic, getting under way more slowly, but more modern and more resolute, the Franco-Russian complex of ideas under the heads of the real, the natural, the social or sociological. This last was the most urgently didactic and the most confidently evolutionary of all. Tolstoy is the greatest literary artist who gave himself to this kind of theory. Tolstoy on what is true and telling in literature, on what is effete, jaded, hedonistic, and merely aristocratic, hits hard, and we may have to take him into account in a way that we do not have to take into account Zola on the novel as an experiment in a social science laboratory.

If we look around the critical scene and especially the American critical scene during the first decades of our own century, we see distinct aftermaths of all the 19th-century events which we have just been tracing: For one thing the exotic and flashy tail-ends of the art-for-art's sake tradition, the cosmopolitanism of the *Smart Set* and *Mercury* writers. For another, the continuation of Arnoldian humanism in the long influence of P. E. More and Irving Babbitt and the approximate end of that humanism in the twin detonations of the anthologies for and against it in 1930. There was also a strong socio-real tradition, under the names of naturalism, Responsibilities of the Novelist, and the uglier name of Muck-Raking, and also the coming of age of honest America, a matter of smoke and steel, the Prairie Schooner, and slabs of the sunburnt west. And then the most acutely didactic accent of all, in the Marxist criticism of the 1930's—rampaging until it becomes obvious to the literary intelligences connected with it that this kind of thing will never do.

One of the most novel strains of literary criticism produced by the 20th century has been that which we may roughly sum up under the name of psychologism. On the one hand, and perhaps most conspicuously: the Freudian kind, in the shape of new motivations drawn out of the unconscious for novels and poems, and literary biographies rewritten into case histories and ordeals. (Groping for tragic and comic motives in depth psychology and anthropology goes back through Freud to Nietzschean rhapsody and repose and Hegelian conflict of ethical substance.) And on the other hand: the quieter kind of affectivism, the equipoise, the beautiful harmony of impulses, promoted by Richards and his colleagues in the 'twenties. And this slips back through the exquisitely refined hedonism of Santayana to the affectivism connected with utilitarian ethics during the 19th century. J. S. Mill's two essays on poetry show how this 18th-century heritage could get into criticism. Mill echoes the way it had already done so in Wordsworth and Coleridge.

But by and large the literary discussion of the 19th century, unlike that of the 18th, had not been notable for any systematic affectivism. And when this romantic and aesthetic plea reappeared with Richards in the 1920's, it had so much to say about mere incipience of impulses and their equipoise that it was a new witness for something like a classical disinterest or detachment. With its up-to-date paraphernalia of verbal analysis, Ricardian aesthetic was readily available, or at least convertible, for purposes of cognitive literary discussion.

Richards connected readily enough with the "neo-classicism" which was represented in the same era by the conspicuous figures of Pound and Eliot. Twentieth-century "neo-classicism" derived attitudes from the intuitionist but classical philosopher T. E. Hulme, from the precise grammatical statements of Gourmont, and from the whole tide of the French symbolist and musically ironic poetics. (With Pound there was too the thing called "imagism," and at least a flourish of something supposed or pretended to be due to the fact of Chinese ideographic writing. But that can hardly be important.) Impersonality, craftsmanship, objectivity, hardness and clarity of a kind, a union of emotion with verbal object, a norm of inclusiveness and reconciliation and hence a close interdependence of drama, irony, ambiguity, and metaphor, or the near equivalence of these four—such ideas made up the neo-classic system as it worked its way into practical criticism about 1935 or 1940. And, however far short the system fell of being able to convince old-line historians or to demonstrate beyond appeal or cavil that this or that poem meant this much or that much or was excellent or not, the arrival of this kind of criticism did mean a new technical and objective interest in poetry.

I V

THE past fifteen years on the critical front have seen several new, or newish, large claims making headway. Let us move somewhat more slowly now for a few pages and let us restate and bring together certain themes which have appeared more or less separately in earlier chapters (21, 24, 31). The most academic of the new claims, the most professional, the most scholarly, is that relatively new kind of graduate school study that seeks to substitute for the poem, not the author, as in former more romantic phases of historicism, but precisely and deliberately the audience for which the author may in any sense be proved to have written the poem. If we look back to the mid-18th century and the first clear start of the modern historical method in such documents as Thomas Warton's *Observations on the Faerie Queene*, Bishop Hurd's *Letters on Chivalry and Romance*, or even Samuel Johnson's *Preface to Shakespeare*, we note that their sympathy for the Gothic or the Elizabethan hesitates somewhat between a plea for tolerance of antique authors, despite the barbarous ages in which they wrote, and a plea for appreciation of the inspirational opportunities afforded by those very ages. But the decisive concept for the time was personal "genius." That is, criticism was on the side of Shakespeare in spite of his handicaps. In the 19th century, there were nationalism, folklorism, and cultural determinism, the race, milieu, and moment of Taine's *History*. But literary studies still tended to marshal such interests rather squarely behind the author. That is, they were important because they showed the mind of the author, what made him write the way he did. Sainte-Beuve's profession of intense interest in the author's boyhood, his brothers and sisters, his parents and his grandparents, is an extreme yet typical instance of such Shandean depth in criticism. Despite the somewhat contrary cultural massiveness of Courthope's *History of English Poetry*, it is mainly right to say that English and American literary research (following good continental models) continued until fairly recent years to be a pursuit of the author, his whole history, both internal and external, and his habitat. It requires perhaps only a tilt of the mirror to turn the habitat into the author's audience. And the audience had of course all along received attention. It was clearly one name for the socio-real focus. But to shift the accent of value in academic research (the accent on both the value of poetry itself and the value of research into poetic history) was yet another step, and it has been a fairly recent one. Until recently it was the normal aim of academic research to be able to announce: "And thus we prove what the author was trying to say," "thus we prove his learning and accuracy," "thus we prove his sincerity," or "thus we prove his deep feeling." But the new mode, one which is more comprehensive and difficult, and has yet advanced so little as to have perhaps a large and dangerous future, seems to entertain the aim of announcing: "And thus we prove that the author's poem was addressed to the audience of his day, or to the real audience, or to the audience that mattered." "Thus he knew what he was doing, and thus he was a good author." More and more articles in journals and books from university presses nowadays have titles referring to *Shakespeare's Audience*, to *The Social Mode of Restoration Comedy*, to *Paradise Lost and the Seventeenth Century Reader*, to *Box, Pit, and Gallery, The Theatrical Public in the Time of Garrick*, to the rise of a reading public, to the number of Victorian persons who bought Macaulay's *History of England* or Tennyson's *Maud*.

It is not difficult to suggest sympathies between the new kind of historicism turned toward the audience and a second recent critical trend, the bad conscience which has been developing in some critics with regard to nice verbal analysis. This is being expressed not only in direct misgivings about analysis, or pleas for a more "open" contextual reading, but also partly in the form of proclamations about the need for doing justice to the overall structures of stories and dramas, their motives, plots, actions, tragic rhythms, their deeper, wider, and more bulky symbolism, their bigger meaning—in short, all that part and aspect of them which may be supposed to be too massive and too important to be penetrated by the technique known as verbal criticism. This kind of conscience had a summary and rather impressive exposition about 100 years ago in Matthew Arnold's Preface to his *Poems* of 1853, where he repented of the inaction, or the suicidally limited action, of his *Empedocles*, appealed to the great serious action of the Greek tragedies, and thought that Shakespeare enjoyed such rhetorical virtuosity that he had been a bad influence on romantic poets, notably on Keats. (Keats, like a modern critic summoned before the bar in Chicago, was too much interested in words and images.) Arnold was giving Germanic and post-romantic moral resonance to an older classical plea—heard, for instance, in Rymer, with echoes by Dryden, and in Gildon—that Shakespeare was defective and not to be imitated in the fundamental matter of plot, and that a critic ought indeed to concern himself with the plot, with the whole poem, the grand design, and not be a "criticaster" of words, a "piece-broker." It was a theme heard in the classically severe Lessing too, whose ideas on drama were parallel to his Lockean and Cartesian notion that the colors of painting were unreal and hence inferior to the reality of sculptural mass and shape. The ideas of Arnold were part of his ambitious humanistic and moralistic program for literature. That, as we have been saying, was one branch of post-romantic didacticism. Later on there was a new criticism concerning prose fiction, not the criticism of Zola, but that of Flaubert, James and Ford, and this was not so far from the spirit of symbolist poetics. It does not appear that Henry James was much afraid of being caught in the mesh of words or of piddling away his effort on the texture or surface of things. If a woman put her hand on a table and looked at him in a certain way, that was for James, or for one of his characters, an event. And the event interlocked with every other event in the world. (The artist tried to conjure or pretend some kind of circle around it.) It is not in these great theorists of prose fiction that we find the scruple against dallying with the details of the medium.

. But we do find it again more recently, and not only in the fortifications of a certain kind of academic neo-Aristotelianism but in more momentous campaigns under the standard of myth and the ritual origins. Here metaphor is action, and big action. For the first time since Dryden and Le Bossu the literary gist is supposed to be big enough and solid enough so that you would think it could be rendered essentially from one language to another. The rhythm of the tragic idea—the going out in quest, the confrontation and passion, the discovery or education—is the big thing. We have observed that the book which gives this theory the most persuasive articulation is Francis Fergusson's *Idea of a Theatre*. Here we have the most imposing of the several recent critical trends. Surely the hugest cloudy symbol, the most threatening, of our last ten or fifteen years in criticism is the principle of criticism by myth and ritual origins.

It is true that this new mythologism is not always associated with any strong mistrust of rhetorical inspection. Expression and symbolism can make a ready enough alliance with myth and ritual. For all four are theories of the creative imagination, the fiat of the human spirit as deity or as participating in deity. Herder and Schelling and Cassirer join Lévy-Bruhl and Frazer and the Cambridge classical anthropologists in the secularization of the spirit according to the philosophy of symbolic form. Philip Wheelwright's *Burning Fountain*, the most recent important book in the mythic mode, is a magnificent synopsis of relations between a special semantics on the one hand and on the other ritual anthropology interpreted by the darkness visible of depth psychology. The semantics states the difference between a scientifically bare "steno-language" and

the "plurisignations," the trans-logical "depth-language" common to poetry, myth, religion, and metaphysics. The anthropology dwells on he-
reditary and "preconsciously rooted" symbols, symbols of the "threshold,"
the world view of primitive man, the death and rebirth of the vegetation
god. (The *Fire Sermon* of Buddha, the *Oresteia* of Aeschylus, the *Four
Quartets* of Eliot may be cited to define the infra-red range of illustration.) To a writer who participated strongly in the new yearning for a
gross structural poetics Wheelwright's book might well look like a deplorable re-celebration of imagery and thematic "paraplots."

But myth and ritual are, as we have already said, patterns of action
and of large action. In that way they can have their easy enough connection with an anti-verbal poetics. And both these interests involve a stress
on what is important about poetry in a large and public way, what can
give it religious and social dignity and didactic claims. The validation for
the new myth philosophy is thought to lie in the primitive racial unconsciousness. Thus it eschews the risky appeal to objectivity, but plunges in
the vast reservoir of racial and prelogical unconsciousness for an intersub-
jective base of universality. It arrives at the phase of apocalyptic and prophetic vision. Along with the Greeks and the Hindus (from whom Friedrich Schlegel also once drew inspiration), there is Milton, there is Blake,
there is Melville, there is Yeats, there is Eliot, there is Joyce, and maybe
there is Faulkner. The three main trends of recent criticism which we
have just sketched—that toward the audience, that toward gross structure, and that toward myth—have in common a horizontal or folkways
alignment (in contrast, for instance, to the vertical and aristocratic alignment of the neoclassic formalism). All three show to some degree the
didactic and evangelizing interest which was prepared in the 19th-century
socio-real tradition. Despite the fact that sociology does come out of the
19th century, the humanism and literary theory in English and French
during that century were mainly inspirational, individualistic, and heroic.
It is the present century, as we all know, which is the century of the common man. The literary trends we have named conceive man, whether
common or elite, in large multiples, thinking and responding in classes.
Plato's rhapsode makes a strong bid for the recovery of his weeping
thousands.

V

WHAT is the real status, the correct status, of Plato's rhapsode and of the
poet whose inspired representative the rhapsode is? After Aristotle and
throughout antiquity—in the Peripatetic and Horatian tradition, in the
Isocratean and Ciceronian tradition of wisdom in oratorical eloquence, in
the emotive and mysterious phases of neo-Platonism, the poetic power
enjoyed a certain fairly high prestige, perhaps we may say an approxi-

mately sufficient degree and kind of prestige. During the Middle Ages both for theological reasons and because of the growing, strongly implicit scientific aims of the whole scholastic effort, poetry went through an era of theoretically low esteem. The Renaissance was a rebirth exactly of the humanistic classical literary claim, though this was vastly complicated now by codifications drawn out of the authority of the ancient writings and by the dialectic engendered from literary practice in the emergent spirit of "romance." The waning of the Renaissance into the era of literary neo-classicism and the first centuries of modern science brought a decline in the prestige of verbal power comparable to what Plato, at least in moments of the *Republic* and in the *Ion*, would seem to have thought desirable. The reawakening or German romantic renascence of poetic power drew plentifully enough on the classical heritage, but was also in a new way emotive, subjective, associational, "imaginative," creative, the claimant of a markedly new kind of authority. Since the day of the high romanticizing, literary theory has included perhaps the whole range of possible claims for poetry: the autonomy of various expressionisms, and of art for art's sake, the biographical and environmental substitutions made possible by improved historical methodology, the deterministic and evolutionary aspects of sociological theory, and the varied didacticisms of the 19th century, reappearing in the claims of the 20th-century archetypal myth.

We can study the history of changes in opinion, writes T. S. Eliot in his short history of English criticism, "without coming to the stultifying conclusion that there is nothing to be said but that opinion changes." The present writers have not written this short history of literary opinion without seeing in it a pattern of effort pointed toward at least a certain kind of goal.

The most difficult moment, the most insistently recurring moment under the most varying forms, in the history and dialectic of literary theory is that which touches values and emotions—or what human beings like and dislike and the experience of their liking and disliking. And one of the most sustained trends of modern critical history—paralleling and shadowing the course of modern metaphysics and psychology—has been toward the reduction of values to subjectivity, that is, toward the doctrine that what human beings like and dislike is a question that refers precisely and only to the experience itself of their liking and disliking. It would be difficult, perhaps impossible, for a literary critic or a historian of literary criticism to contrive within the limit of his own idiom and decorum a sufficient account of the difficult metaphysics that make the problem of value. Yet a literary theorist ought to be at least moderately aware of the relation his thoughts may show to that problem.

The great variety of human tastes for pleasure and of emotive responses to experience, the variety even for a single person from moment to moment and under this or that condition, may at times cast a chilly light over our speculations about value. These facts are scarcely matters which the theorist of poetry can dispute as facts. He can scarcely re-verify or re-count them, or balance or redress them by fresh statistics. He may, however, have a deeper or a shallower perspective in the understanding of such facts. A sense of order, of hierarchy, of unity in the universe of our experience—a sense of purpose, if one may whisper the word—can do something to dispel the cold illusion of the neutral substrate, the opaque ground below good and evil.

Let us say first that the situation of the person confronting his world of values is a vastly complicated one. He confronts not any single type and grade of thing constituting an objectively insulated and external "value," but various objects in various kinds of relations to himself. In each value situation there is both an objective and a subjective aspect—but the accent falls now upon one and now upon the other of these, and with various degrees of weight. A man is hurt by a knife or a club, and he feels the hurt and the damage as something that happens to a part of himself—not as a quality of the knife or club, the inflicting external entity. He tastes salt or sugar, and the taste with the liking or disliking of it is a subtle union of that specific new entity from outside both with his own mouth and with whatever may just previously have been tasted. And then, at a third level, he views red or blue, and whatever any theory may tell him about the relation of light to his eye (whatever sophistication in theory of vision he is equal to) he experiences the pleasant or unpleasant quality as a quality outside himself. (Such at least is the "phenomenology" of the event.) He looks at a landscape, and the complexity of the visual pattern and of the meanings inevitably attached to it place the locus of value even more emphatically—and stereoptically—outside. (To tickle one's foot, to "tickle" one's palate, to "tickle" one's fancy—these three grades in the semantics of the word "tickle" will summarize the series of values which we have just sketched.) Finally, suppose that a given man sees or hears of a murder (a knife stuck in another man); here the value implicated exhibits a very distinct and superior kind of external firmness and objectivity—that of the ethical realm. And yet this value is rooted in the pain and destruction inflicted upon a certain subject. To say that a value is relative to a subject is not to say that the value is relative in the sense that anybody's opinion about it may be as correct as anybody else's. Or, to say that a value is not objective, or not purely and simply objective, is not to say that it is not *universal*, or valid in relation to all subjects. Some such term as *inter-subjective* may perhaps be invoked to describe the accent that falls on some universals. It is surely true, for instance, that any human subject whatever will suffer pain and damage from knife wounds—even though this truth is not sufficient to establish a property of evil intrinsic to the knife itself.

But here let us revert, with some insistence, to the fact that the present discussion is concerned not directly with knives and persons, with sensory pleasures or moral values, but with poetry and hence with words. The problem of value which we are sketching is made even more complicated for the poetic theorist—and perhaps a certain distance from the basic value problem is created for him—by the fact that poetry is composed of words. For words introduce a special kind of valuing "subject," the subject who not only responds to values with emotions or feelings but formulates and utters (if only to himself) his awareness of both value and response. Not that such persons are unusual, but by the very fact of utterance a person values in a special way.

And most likely he values in a very subtly mingled way:—by exclamations and by the rhythmic aspects of utterance achieving something like a direct expression at least of vaguer feeling; by the names of pleasures and pains and of emotions and of their correlative values (hate, anger, love, and joy, the good and the bad, the beautiful and the ugly) achieving a firmer if more abstract delineation; by the neutral-sounding names of all sorts of objects, qualities, actions, and relations (of man, animal, and stone, of color, shape, and movement) achieving a deeper substantiation. The words of the last category do not name either responses or values directly, yet in real contexts they may have intense emotive import. For the purpose of poetic criticism it would appear to be significant to divide this large group into two great parts: the names of objects and actions which are causes, or motives, of an emotive response (the characters and the plot of the poem), and the names of the large world of symbols and associations which, though not direct objects of emotion, often fortify emotive interpretation (the black, the white, the crow, and the dove). No one of these classes of words carries very far in creating the expression (or in promoting the contagion) of emotive experience. They operate always by a complex meshing and nowhere more than in the verbal constructions which are poems. The complexity of their operation forbids all the more extreme simplifications of poetic theory—both the simply mimetic (theories of either real or metaphysically ideal imitation of the objective world) and the simply emotive or sentimental (pure theories of emotive expression or pure theories of emotive result).

One of the main lessons of critical history would seem, indeed, to be that the stress of literary theory must fall on the *experience* (subjective and emotive) rather than on the *what*, the object of value so far as that is outside *any* experiencing subject. Yet, for reasons which we have been sketching, this lesson need not be interpreted as relegating the values of poetry to the realm of the whimsical and undebatable. A refraction of light through a crystal tells something about the light, something about the crystal; the refraction itself is a kind of reality, interesting to observe. Let us say that poetry is a kind of reality refracted through subjective responses. This refraction itself is an area of reality. Does the refraction tell us something unique and profound about the reality beyond itself? We need not actually say much about this for the purposes of a workable poetics. (Much will depend on what we conceive the ultimate character of that reality to be.)

The norm of wit and cunning word-play entertained by Horace and centuries later, with a stress on the imitation of gentlemanly polite conversation, by Boileau, Dryden, and Pope, was one version of this important truth:—that if poetry is to "imitate," it will imitate what is alive with the human spirit. And no less relevant to the same truth was the fully self-conscious, creative and expressionist romantic theory. The following resonant statement by Shelley has been partly quoted in an earlier chapter:

> . . . as the lyre trembles and sounds after the wind has died away, so the child seeks, by prolonging in its voice and motions the duration of the effect, to prolong also a consciousness of the cause. In relation to the objects which delight a child, these expressions are, what poetry is to higher objects. The savage . . . expresses the emotions produced in him by surrounding objects in a similar manner; and language and gesture, together with plastic or pictorial imitation, become the image of the combined effect of those objects, and of his apprehension of them. Man in society, with all his passions and his pleasures, next becomes the object of the passions and pleasures of man; an additional class of emotions produces an augmented treasure of expressions; and language, gesture, and the imitative arts, become at once the representation and the medium, the pencil and the picture, the chisel and the statue, the chord and the harmony.

In a more soberly grammatical passage of the *Biographia* (Chapter XXII) Coleridge wrote:

> Be it observed . . . that I include in the *meaning* of a word not only its correspondent object, but likewise all the associations which it recalls. For language is framed to convey not the object alone, but likewise the character, mood and intentions of the person who is representing it.

A capsule symbol of the situation for the theorist might be made out of the *Poetics* of Aristotle, which talks about *mimēsis* or the imitation (through words and music and scenes and an outward story) of certain objects, but the objects are characters, passions, and *praxeis*, that is, actions or farings, adventures, experience—objects of the inner realm of spirit.

Yet we have been implying, and let us now say more plainly, that

to entertain such a theory of poetic value is not to *deny* the reality and
the value of the outer realm, the *what* which is at various levels external
to each valuing subject. The theory cannot make such a denial, even at
what may appear the most superficial levels, without dissolving the
grounds on which it hopes to talk about poetic experience. As we move
into the inner moral and spiritual experience of man in search of our most
clearly absolute, our most securely universal, concepts of value, it may
seem that we leave behind, abandon to an uncertain and merely academic
fate, the values, pleasant or unpleasant, which in a more superficial scheme
we might assign to such external phenomena as the colors red and blue.
Neither the poet nor the theorist, however, is in a good position to leave
these behind. If there were nobody else at all—no metaphysician, moralist, or theologian—who cared to speak in defence of sensory values—yet
the poet, in his indirect and obscure way, would have to go on con-
fessing them, and his theorist would have to think about them. For they
contribute the symbolic, the external, the phenomenological language by
which the poet speaks about the inner and deeper realities of value. And
if they did not constitute at least an inter-subjectively universal and reliable set of values, they could not be used as signs in the poet's communication. Most likely it is not necessary for the theorist of poetry to decide the
nice metaphysical question as to the *locus* of each sensory value—*in* object or *in* subject. Perhaps the very question is illusory. But both poet and
theorist can be sure of one minimum thing: that at least inter-subjective
viability is required for poetic communication. It will not be enough for
a reader to be instructed (by a theorist or by a historian) that once upon
a time, here and there, this meant that, purple was royal, black meant
death, Dorian was martial, Lydian erotic, flutes were sweet, thunder
frightening. If a poem is actually experienced and valued, these things,
no less than (and as a condition for) the deeper poetic meanings of spirit,
must lie somehow within the range of experience.

"We see how . . . [Schiller] plagued himself," says Goethe, "with
the design of perfectly separating sentimental from *naive* poetry. For the
former he could find no proper soil, and this brought him into unspeak-
able perplexity. As if . . . sentimental poetry could exist at all without
the *naive* ground in which, as it were, it has its root." [1] A theorist of
poetry may be driven to be some kind of idealist about the nature of
poetry itself or the area of its operation. But if he remains close to the
objects of his scrutiny—that is, to actual poems—he will be equally
driven to remain a realist in his conception of the universe in which the
poetic area is contained and in which poetry finds its reasons. Theories of
sheer affectivity and subjective valuing have suffered the paradox of
promoting not enthusiasm for value but distance, detachment, cooling,
neutrality. The sterner metaphysical, cognitive theories, talking about

[1] *Conversations*, November 14, 1823.

real right and wrong, real beauty and ugliness, are the theories which actually sustain value and make responses to value possible. For response cannot feed indefinitely on itself.[2]

VI

WHAT is the relation of the poetic or aesthetic emotion to the emotions of real or ordinary life? This difficult question has been implicit in the critical debate from ancient days, with the catharsis of Aristotle or the transport of Longinus, to the recent past, with the incipience and equipoise of Ricardian psychology or the Freudian varieties of worked-off inhibitions. If one has to make a stark choice between the simply realistic theory—that poetry deals with straight emotions of pity, fear, or erotic passion, and that is why we like it—and some theory of artistic modification—that poetry works some distinctive change in real-life emotions, and that is why we like it—one must clearly choose the latter. But then this alternative, the theory of modification, is itself perhaps susceptible of a puzzling refinement into alternatives. Is the emotion which is characteristic of poetry only a modification of real-life emotion (anger toned down, for instance, or anger caught or embodied in an expression), or is the modified and expressed real-life emotion the ground or object of some further distinct emotion, not anger at all, but precisely the aesthetic emotion? Something like the latter would seem to be required if we are to range poetry under the time-honored heading of the "beautiful"—or the aesthetic. The correct response to the beautiful or the aesthetic is presumably not anger, even in an ameliorated form. Yet that correct response is something that can hardly be the proper business of the critic or theorist of poetry, simply because it *is* an ultimate emotive response to the poetic object and not a part of that object. This correct response will have to take care of itself. If it *is* the aim of poetry, it is an aim beyond the direct aim, which is to make an utterance.

[2] The situation of the poet in general is well described in the following recent account of symbolism. "The conscious symbolist will find himself in a curious position. . . . Poetic form presupposes the rational world. . . . And the more thoroughly the symbolist conceives of language as symbol, the more likely it is that he will lose touch with language as sign; to the extent that he attains his aim, it would seem that his sense of direction must waver, since he cannot locate his work with reference to himself or an external world. Deliberate symbolism is hazardous in its quest for a pure poetry, for poetry can be pure only by virtue of the impurities it assimilates. In the degree that the poem shakes loose from the poet himself and from the world of objects, in the degree that the poetic world is free from logical bonds, poetry will be deprived of material; in performing its function, it will destroy its subject matter."—Charles Feidelson, Jr., *Symbolism and American Literature* (Chicago, 1953), pp. 70–1. Published by The University of Chicago Press and copyrighted (1953) by the University of Chicago.

We move thus from the epistemological problem—whether the value expressed by poetry is something objective or something subjective—to a kind of ontological problem arising perhaps precisely out of the specific mixed or half-way epistemology of the poetic act. For if we say poetry is to talk of beauty and love (and yet not aim at exciting erotic emotion or even an emotion of Platonic esteem) and if it is to talk of anger and murder (and yet not aim at arousing anger and indignation)—then it may be that the poetic way of dealing with these emotions will not be any kind of intensification, compounding, or magnification, or any direct assault upon the affections at all. Something indirect, mixed, reconciling, tensional might well be the strategem, the devious technique by which a poet indulged in all kinds of talk about love and anger and even in something like "expressions" of these emotions, without aiming at their incitement or even uttering anything that essentially involves their incitement. This problem has been touched on obliquely all through critical history —in all discussions of the tragic and painful and all hints about the comically defective and about the tragicomic—in all theories of irony, paradox, and reconciled opposites.

One part of the difficulty about the modern myth and ritual claims has all along been their solemnity:—the deep cathartic function and the vast canonical subject matters, the cycles of death and rebirth which they impute to or prescribe for the poetry of serious worth. These ideas may be called unhistorical. Like 18th-century Gothicists and Druidists, the myth critics want to push us back into some prelogical and hence preliterary supposed state of very somberly serious mentality. And hence they are forgetting where they are in history and are overlooking at least two great types of lesson—the lesson of religion, especially that of the Hebrew and Christian religion—which is the lesson of genuine solemnity —and the lesson of accomplished poetry, in Homer, let us say, in Horace, Dante, Shakespeare, Pope—which is surely a different kind of lesson. Let us run the risk of seeming frivolous by saying that it is much less like a lesson of solemnity than a lesson of strife and fun. And to round out our pattern of competing principles, let us add a third modern lesson, that of abstract philosophy.

The ancient division of poetry into tragic and comic, while it is a division, is also an inclusion, and it involves a suggestion that the tragic and the comic may be complementary. On the other hand, there was Plato, in his *Republic*, complaining about the promotion of strife and division by poetry, the feeding and watering of the passions, and in his *Philebus* (or as the recent Cambridge translation calls it, *Plato's Doctrine of Pleasure*) saying that both tragedy and comedy are impure pleasures arising from pain and certain kinds of triumph over pain (like life itself, which is at once tragic and comic), but that a better kind of pleasure is the pure kind arising, for instance, from the knowledge of geometric forms. We can see this kind of Platonism, the numerical and geometric, reappearing here and there down through the centuries, in Augustine and Boethius, for instance (where the orientation is musical), in 18th-century reasoners on order and harmony like Hutcheson (where the orientation again may be visual and geometric). During the early part of our own century the same thing, with frequent appeals to Plato's *Philebus*, has appeared in the aesthetic of "significant" form. The ideas of Bell, Fry, and Wilenski, or of Jay Hambidge, on painting and sculpture, have a clear enough resemblance to art for art's sake in the phase of Whistler and Wilde, and this whole school of formalism (intent on the "significance" of the cube, the "significance" of the cylinder, as well as on the porcelain nicety of certain French verse forms) has contributed a shade of meaning to the term "formalist" when it has been used in an unfriendly way during the more or less recent course of literary debate. Nevertheless, the school of significant form provides us with a sufficiently sharp contrast to the kind of "formalist" criticism which in recent years has been so much concerned with principles of tension, drama, metaphor, paradox, irony, and wit. Another early modern solution to the problem of evil in art was the opposite of the Platonic, and just as extreme. This was the 18th-century resolution by surrender to dismal or to tender feelings. The analysis of wit has been equally an opponent of that. Thus the authors of this history find little difficulty in explaining to themselves a strong sympathy for the contemporary neo-classic school of ironic criticism and for what it has in common with the theory that prevailed in the time of Coleridge and the Germans.

We have observed that the reconciliation of opposites as it was meditated by Schelling and Coleridge had a largely metaphysical bearing. How to get subject and object together and yet explain their distinctness; how to unify inner and outer, general and particular, thought and emotion, art and nature, or a longer series of almost any such opposites one might name—this was the speculation that preoccupied these deeply introspective, transcendentally minded men. An irony of a more darkly moral coloring, a sardonic self-transcendence, was known to Friedrich Schlegel and others. The 20th-century neo-classic irony of poetic inclusiveness, looking back to conversational ironic symbolism, and finding a theoretical hint in quotations from Coleridge by Eliot and Richards, has had a strongly emotive and at times moral accent. There is a direct concern with human affairs and human values here (human "interests"), good and evil, pleasure and pain, rather than with the mysteries of knowledge and creation, the activity of that "synthetic and magical power" the imagination. And so it seems to us that the recent ironists have put a hard problem very compellingly.

Pain and destruction are the two great components of the problem. You can show that pleasure is only an elusive and phantasmal by-product of things and qualities; it cannot be pursued in itself with any success; and you can subsume pleasure under the head of interest, which is the general affective counterpart of knowledge and objects. But pain is not like that; it can sometimes be avoided (that is, it does not always increase through flight; as pleasure diminishes through pursuit); and when it cannot be avoided, we wish it could be. It is one of the most positive experiences we have. (Pain has the two dominant aspects of being a thing we don't like and of being a kind of intensity. The artist, we may speculate, in achieving a certain distance from the aspect of what we don't like is able to take advantage of the intensity.) On the other hand, destruction is clearly enough negative, the termination of experience, being, and interest. The question here is: Why? There is a religious answer that speaks of patience and atonement. This answer is not at odds with poetry, but neither is it available to poetry as a formal solution to the poetic problem.

Of course the reflective and responsible theorist will say that he doesn't call evil itself, or division, or conflict, desirable things. He is sure, however, that facing up to them, facing up to the human predicament, is a desirable and mature state of soul and the right model and source of a mature poetic art. But again, with a certain accent, that may sound somewhat like telling a boy at a baseball game that the *contest* is not really important but only his *noticing* that there *is* a contest.

Let us say that we recognize the fact of material concreteness in human experience, and though matter itself be not evil (as in the Persian scheme), yet it does seem the plausible enough ground for some kind of dualism, division, tension, and conflict, the clash of desires, and evil and pain. Spirit and matter, supernatural and natural, good and evil, these tend to line up as parallel oppositions. Even so refined and geometric a material concept as that of symmetry has its danger for the concept of beauty through unity. How *could* symmetry be part of the definition of beauty? Think, says Plotinus, what that doctrine leads to. "Only a compound can be beautiful, never anything devoid of parts" (I, vi, 1). But parts and composition (and decomposition) seem to be inescapable in the human situation, and on the modern view, art, especially verbal art, confronts this fact. The theorist says that art ought to have the concreteness which comes from recognizing reality and including it. Art ought to have tension, balance, wholeness. Anybody will have to admit that there could never be any drama or story, either comic or tragic, without tension, without conflict, without evil. It may not be at first glance so obvious, but it is nevertheless true, that without some shade of these same elements there could never be any pastoral or idyllic retreat, any didactic or satiric warning, any lyric complaint—or, for that matter, any lyric rejoicing,[3] so far are the springs of human rejoicing buried in the possibility, the threat, the memory of sorrow, so far is human life an experience of mutation, of struggle, of stasis only momentarily and dynamically attained.[4] The great works and the fine works of literature seem to need evil—just as much as the cheap ones, the adventure or detective stories. Evil or the tension of strife with evil is welcomed and absorbed into the structure of the story, the rhythm of the song. The literary spirit flourishes in evil and couldn't get along without it.

The problem can be put succinctly in the following way: Is the unity and order of beauty (and poetry) something that comes about *in spite of* diversity of parts or only *in virtue of* such diversity? The obvious facts in tragedy and comedy and the less obvious facts in other poetic genres would seem to say that the kind of unity required can come about only in virtue of diversity—only in virtue of a certain strife. In certain arts of abstract visual design and perhaps even in some kinds of music, we can see the diversity necessary for the art appearing without much, or without any, idea of strife or painful emotion attached to it. There may well be certain Platonic forms of truly fine art—notably certain forms of drawing and carving, arts which Plato himself was apparently concerned to

---

[3]
> Yet if we could scorn
> Hate and pride and fear;
> If we were things born
> Not to shed a tear,
> I know not how thy joy we ever should come near.
> —P. B. Shelley, *To a Skylark*

Shelley's brief statement concerning pain and poetry in his *Defense* (ed. Cook, p. 35) is much to the point. The following is one of many fine glimpses in Wordsworth's *Prelude*:

> To fear and love,
> To love as prime and chief, for there fear ends,
> Be this [imaginative wisdom] ascribed; to early intercourse,
> In presence of sublime or beautiful forms,
> With the adverse principles of pain or joy—
> Evil as one is rashly named by men
> Who know not what they speak.
> —(1850), XIV, 163

[4] Somewhat more extremely: ". . . it is not possible for imagination to acquaint us with any other world. . . . without the horror we should never focus the beauty; without death there would be no relish for life; without danger, no courage; without savagery, no gentleness; and without the background of our frequent ignominy, no human dignity and pride. (These are excellent and rather Hegelian commonplaces.) . . . there is provided traditionally, betwixt the residence of the soul in one world and its residence in another world, a Lethean bath to bring forgetfulness of that nature which the soul has just lived with; in order that it may adapt to whatever nature may be next in order" (John Crowe Ransom," "The Concrete Universal: Observations on the Understanding of Poetry, II," *The Kenyon Review*, XVII, Summer, 1955, 405–6; also in Ransom's *Poems and Essays*, New York 1955, Vintage Books, Inc.). The Nietzschean version of these commonplaces has been sampled *ante* Chapter 25, pp. 562–4.

purify in the geometric direction, and perhaps certain kinds of music. But as soon as we get into the realm of verbal art, we see the accent of strife in diversity very prominent, and in the major poetic forms, either narrative or dramatic, that element is unmistakable and unavoidable.

One might look on the concept of "poetry" as a kind of central locus where a pull for duality and conflict coming in from the direction of tragedy and comedy encounters and has its own kind of conflict with a pull for harmony coming in from the direction of general aesthetics, "beauty," and beyond that the philosophy of order, being, and the unity of God. "Human interest" confronts Kantian "disinterest" and Thomist "ipsa apprehensio."

Perhaps we face here some kind of problem concerning *The Marriage of Heaven and Hell*. If we take the relatively cautious course of saying that in poetry there has to be an ironic balance of impulses, rather than clear Fourth-of-July choices and celebrations, it will sound to a moralist as if we entertained only wavering beliefs and purposes, no moral commitments.[5] And if we talk more boldly about evil being "reconciled" in poetry, we may sound as if we were actually propitiating evil, giving some dark earth spirit its rightful place in the scheme of things. We may look like a set of Manichaean dualists, some kind of split personalities, or pagans trying to stand on tiptoe.[6]

The lineaments of a response to such difficulties may be discerned in the well-enough-known fact that poetic art is neither the comic-strip melodrama of good and evil as separate agents, hero and villain, nor any kind of philosophic melodrama, truth and falsity disguised as personages and fighting out their duel to one only canonical conclusion, the triumph of truth. For the theater of poetic conflict is human substance itself, ethical substance, as Hegel put it; the conflict is of man with himself or of good and evil in man. Even if the conflict is externally so simple as man against a flood or a forest fire, the poetic conflict is what happens inside the man fighting or the man observing the man fighting. The desire expressed by a few recent theorists for some kind of literary substance as opposed to either Platonic idea or Platonic semblance may be invoked here as a witness. We have alluded in an earlier chapter to what we may call the "no-angelism" of Allen Tate in his volume of "Didactic and Critical Essays" entitled *The Forlorn Demon*. And thus Miss Elizabeth Sewell:

> I have repeated one essential thing about what I conceive to be
> the true life of the imagination, that in it the life of the mind de-
> pends for its liberation upon a kind of submission to the life of
> the body (and the human), and that the two must live together,
> according to the way of man, and not of angels or demons.

[5] Cf. *ante*, Chapter 29, pp. 672–4, the view of Yvor Winters.
[6] Cf. H. M. McLuhan, review of D. E. S. Maxwell on T. S. Eliot in *Renascence*, Spring, 1955.

This submission is, superficially, a scandal, but, more profoundly viewed, it is a way of freedom.[7]

Other writers in this vein have touched more emphatically on the intimacy which obtains between human substance and the fact of evil both as suffering and as division and destruction. Thus Father William Lynch:

> True tragedy has always been a sober calculation of the relation of human energy to existence. Such calculating has always required profound honesty and the rejecting of the cheaper forms of mysticism. St. Paul himself had weighed the matter well and found it impossible to work out the equation. And he therefore cried out: "Who shall deliver me from the body of this death?"[8]

The patristic idea of the "Fortunate Fall," variously expressed by Ambrose, by Augustine, by Gregory the Great, and in the liturgy ("*O felix culpa, quae talem ac tantum meruit habere Redemptorem*")[9] is probably a closer analogue to an adequate literary theory than such neo-Platonic ideas as Augustine entertained about the beauty of the triangle or the circle. The writers of the present history have not been concerned to implicate literary theory with any kind of religious doctrine. It appears to us, however, relevant, as we near our conclusion, at least to confess an opinion that the kind of literary theory which seems to us to emerge the most plausibly from the long history of the debates is far more difficult to orient within any of the Platonic or Gnostic ideal world views, or within the Manichaean full dualism and strife of principles, than precisely within the vision of suffering, the optimism, the mystery which are embraced in the religious dogma of the Incarnation.

And let us say furthermore: that if verbal art has to take up the mixed business of good and evil, its most likely way of success and its peculiar way is a mixed way. And this means not simply a complicated corresponence, a method of alternation, now sad, now happy (as in some neo-classic theories of tragicomedy), but the oblique glance, the vertical unification of the metaphoric smile. To pursue the ironic and tensional theories in the way most likely to avoid the Manichaean heresy will require a certain caution in the use of the solemn and tragic emphasis. Dark feelings, painful feelings, dismal feelings, even tender feelings move readily toward the worship of evil. And they have the further disadvantage that they run readily into pure feeling itself, its indulgence and the theory of that, as in the 18th century. There was a girl in Mrs. Thrale's set at

---

[7] "The Death of the Imagination," *Thought*, XXVIII (Autumn, 1953), 443.
[8] "Confusion in Our Theater," *Thought*, XXVI (Autumn, 1951), 359–60.
[9] Cf. A. O. Lovejoy, *Essays in the History of Ideas* (Baltimore, 1948), pp. 285–94, "Milton and the Paradox of the Fortunate Fall."

Streatham who could weep so prettily that she was sometimes called upon for a parlor demonstration.

It is true that pure laughter too has its limitations. It may be idiotic. There is a certain kind of optimistic writing that sounds like the result of laughing gas. But bright feelings and the smile go with metaphor and wit, and when playing on serious topics, wit generates a certain mimicry of substance which is poetry. There was another member of the Streatham set who in a *Preface to Shakespeare* noticed that "Shakespeare has united the powers of exciting laughter and sorrow not only in one mind, but in one composition." By this line of suggestion and by quoting further authorities of this tenor we might arrive at a theory that sounded too much like the homely formula "Grin and bear it," or perhaps like a prescription for *The Most Lamentable Comedy and Most Cruel Death of Pyramus and Thisbe*. But the theory also could be made to sound like a phrase in Aristotle's *Poetics*—the four words *anōdunon kai ou phthartikon* —not painful and not destructive, a description which Aristotle meant for the comic object as distinguished from the hideously suffering tragic object. But the phrase, even in Aristotle's system, can easily be lifted so as to operate not only at the level of poetic object but at that of poetic utterance, poetry itself, and then it will refer not only to comedy but to tragedy too.

VII

ONE apparently needs to insist nowadays that the term "irony" need not always be taken with a strongly emotive and moral accent. "Irony" may be usefully taken rather as a cognitive principle which shades off through paradox into the general principle of metaphor and metaphoric structure —the tension which is always present when words are used in vitally new ways. The ultimate advantage of the theory of irony and metaphor is that it is a theory that involves both poetic content and poetic "form" and demands the interdependence of these two. There are certain kinds of contentual meaning which can scarcely be discussed except under the aspect of technique, style, "form." These meanings are pre-eminently the ironic-metaphoric.

The term "form," perhaps it will be well to assert briefly at this point, is one which we have been content to use throughout this history in a provisional but convenient Renaissance and modern manner [1] to refer

[1] See, for instance, Gilbert, pp. 202, 470, 492, 500, Dante (*Letter to Can Grande*) and Tasso (*Discorsi*); Gregory Smith, I, 266, William Webbe; René le Bossu, *Traité du poème epique*, 1675, "Livre Second, De la matière du poème epique"; "Livre Troisième, De la Forme du poème epique"; and *ante*, Chapter 22, p. 484, Arnold on Wordsworth; p. 488–9, Gautier on *Emaux et Camées* and Wilde ("Form is everything"). And see Chapter 2, p. 33.

to all those elements of a verbal composition—rhythm, metrics, structure, coherence, emphasis, diction, images—which can more or less readily be discussed as if they were not a part of the poem's "content," message, or doctrine. "Form," as we have suggested by apposition just above, is technique and style. "Form" includes all those elements which an aesthete might conceive as justifying a view of art as pure, non-conceptual, non-didactic. It is all that the old rhetorical theory might call either "disposition" or "elocution." It is what Aristotle in the *Poetics* calls "medium" (diction and music) and "manner" (spectacle). Thus "form" is not identical, at first glance anyway, with *all* the character that a work may have, as in the radical view of monistic expressionism. "Form" in the sense implied by the last three or four hundred years of literary criticism is only a dim analogy of the Aristotelian idea or essence by which "matter" is *formed* into some kind of thing (stone into a statue, or something less identifiable than stone into stone itself). Only a dim or inferior analogy, we say. Yet it is at least as clear and good as the opposed more Platonic analogy (found in Scaliger and more recently in the Chicago critics) by which "matter" is the sheer meaningless phonetics, the physical sound, of words (if such a thing can be conceived) and "form" is the idea of the story or other meaning imposed upon the words. Our exposition has preferred to make use of the readily definable and widely understood convention that "matter" is the content or message of literary works, so far as that may be extricated from their dense formality, and "form" is all that complication and stylization which in past ages has in one way or another been looked on as extraneous to matter—a kind of ornament, recommendation, fortification, dress, or the like. Nevertheless our final view, implicit in our whole narrative and in whatever moments of argument we may have allowed ourselves, has been that "form" in fact embraces and penetrates "message" in a way that constitutes a deeper and more substantial meaning than either abstract message or separable ornament. In both the scientific or abstract dimension and in the practical or rhetorical dimension there *is* both message and the means of conveying message, but the poetic dimension is just that dramatically unified meaning which is coterminous with form. This is true both in the sense that all verbal discourse, no matter how unpoetic, has this poetic aspect, and in the more special sense that certain instances of verbal discourse are almost insusceptible of abstractive message reading, and these are poems (in verse and prose) in the most special and excellent sense.

Poetry is truth of "coherence," rather than truth of "correspondence," as the matter is sometimes phrased nowadays. We have heard Sir Philip Sidney say that the poet "nothing affirmeth and therefore never lieth." And Wilde, in the vein of wit peculiar to him: "After all, what is a fine lie? Simply that which is its own evidence."

A close internal relation exists of course between this kind of "form" and the tension of values and emotions on which we were insisting a few pages back. Such tension can occur at structural levels or in local detail of symbols and metaphors. It can be read as metaphoric meaning here and there in poems or as metaphoric character or dimension extending all through poems and constituting their very "imitative" relation to the world of reality which with their aid and in them we come to know. For excellent reasons the *discordia concors* of the metaphysical metaphor or simile has seemed to some critics of our generation the very type and acme of the poetic structure. Such a figure is at least a small-scale model, a manageable miniature, in which a critic may more or less readily scrutinize certain features: the non-literal confrontation of vehicle and tenor, the pull of opposite values and feelings—the lovers, their sighs and anguish, and the willed control, the restraint, the geometry and the compasses.

Let us speak briefly here in praise of metaphor. Let us observe that metaphor combines the element of necessity or universality (the prime poetic quality which Aristotle noticed) with that other element of concreteness or specificity which was implicit in Aristotle's requirement of the mimetic object. Metaphor is the union of history and philosophy which was the main premise of Sidney's *Defence*. And metaphor would seem to be the only verbal structure which will accomplish this feat. We can have our universals in the full conceptualized discourse of science and philosophy. We can have specific detail lavishly in the newspapers and in records of trials and revelations of psychiatric cases. But it is only in metaphor, and hence it is *par excellence* in poetry, that we encounter the most radically and relevantly fused union of the detail and the universal idea. Detail in itself is contingent on information and it is the characteristic object of the historian's research. Still it gets into poems, and poems start with it and from it, and the historian is in the happy position of not necessarily renouncing criticism. Metaphor is the universal amber for the preservation and enhancement of the scraps and trifles of historic fact. "Pretty! in amber to observe the forms, Of hairs, or straws, or dirt, or grubs, or worms! The things, we know, are neither rich nor rare, But wonder how the devil they got there." For it is not a universal fact and not universally admired that men should wear cork-heeled "shoon." But joined with certain ideas of vanity and frivolity and with salt water (in the ballad of *Sir Patrick Spens*), the shoes make a permanent and important, a universally conceivable, human meaning. A "superannuated" British warship of the year 1838 becomes by modern naval norms a highly vulnerable smallish wooden tub. But in the high slant perspective, the orange and bloody sunset, of Turner's illumination we still have *The Fighting Téméraire*. Metaphors are poetry's permanent and necessary conclusions drawn from variable and contingent premises. Other universals are abstract and to that extent *a priori*, even tautological. (A rose is a rose. . . .) Metaphor is a substantive—or a mock-substantive—universal.

It is true that metaphor in poetry is not the same thing as metaphor in poetic theory. Yet a metaphoric theory of poetry is almost necessarily a theory of multiple focuses and hence a historic theory and a perspective theory. It entertains not historically separate and opaque conceptions but a translucent continuous view of history as vista and development. The theory implicit in our narrative sees three main focuses or three most radical ideas in the history of literary criticism, believes them interrelated and reconcilable, and aspires to discard no one of the three. Thus, we recognize: (1) the mimetic or Aristotelian, which does justice to the world of things and real values and keeps our criticism from being merely idealistic; (2) the emotive (as developed with most subtlety perhaps by Richards), which does justice to human responses to values and keeps criticism from talking too much about either ethics or physics; (3) the expressionistic and linguistic (*par excellence* the Crocean), which does justice to man's knowledge as reflexive and creative and keeps criticism from talking about poetry as a literal recording of either things or responses. Our account of critical history says that the second and the third of these radical ideas are present in Aristotle along with the first, though the third, the expressionistic, is surely the weakest of the three and least explicitly developed. It appears to us that these ideas can be made the main points of reference for an indefinitely variable criticism of *all* poems. That is, there are no poems which, as one academic school of our day would have it, are in some exclusively proper way "mimetic" and which hence should not be permitted an expressionistic or symbolic reading; and conversely, all "symbolic" poems, if they are real poems, are in some important sense "mimetic" and dramatic. It seems to us, finally, that metaphor is not only in a broad sense the principle of all poetry but is also inevitable in practical criticism and will be active there in proportion as criticism moves beyond the historical report or the academic exercise.

These observations imply the principle too by which we evaluate the history of the celebrated, perhaps notorious, "genres," literary "species," "types," or "kinds"—not wishing to adopt either these genres or any modification of them as authoritative points of reference or fixations in our scheme of literary valuing, nor on the other hand to follow the Crocean sweep in refusing to allow any worth at all to or make any use of such technically defined entities. The evolution of criticism has produced four, perhaps five, genre conceptions dominant enough in their eras to serve as focusses for the poetic whole. Each of these (with perhaps one exception) seems to have had its advantages; each has enabled a certain understanding not only of one literary genre but of the whole poetic structure and problem. Aristotle's view was dramatic, or more precisely tragic (with intimations of a twin comic view), and this had the great advantage of opening up the more broadly "dramatic," the ethically

problematic and tensional, aspect of poetry as a whole. *Peri Poiētikēs*—
On the Art of Fiction. Aristotle, if read rightly, has something to say
about all the poetic genres. The next basic view is that of Horace, conversational, epistolary, idiomatic, ironic, satiric—despite all the defunct
doctrines about drama which Horace manages to embalm in his gentlemanly wit. This view has the advantage of opening up the linguistic, the
idiomatic, the metaphoric and in that sense again the "dramatic" aspect
of all poetry. Next is the high, the grand, the ecstatic view of Longinus—
which on the whole opens up more dangers and confusions perhaps than
affective advantage, and is not a view according to literary species (but
just the opposite) unless we look on it as making a large contribution
(via Boileau) to the new genre of the "heroic" in the third quarter of the
17th century. Here was a perspective that was almost altogether inflationary and bad, looking not into the realm of spirit and word, where poetry really is, but into a gigantorama of grossly direct stimulations, of
pageantry, drums, duels, warfare, spectres, loud protestations of lust,
honor, and valor. Meanwhile, in the same essays of Dryden which defend the heroic, a theory of courtly wit and ridicule is asserted, and by
the time of Pope and Swift, this can be considered a second focussing of
the Horatian conversational and satiric ideal. And in close liaison, appears the mocking genre of the anti-heroic or burlesque. (Both these, it
is true, are, as with the original Horatian satire, genre norms more by
the implication of prevalent and successful practice than by any clearly
enunciated theory.) Lastly, the cycle of genres is completed in the era
of the romantics with the now affectionately remembered lyric ideal and
its attendant opinion that a long poem is a contradiction in terms. This
had the advantage of exploiting a new view of "expression," a view of
subjectivity both as cognition and as feeling, and of metaphor as the
small-scale model and touchstone of the whole poetic business. After that
Copernican revolution, from dramatic, epic and satiric forms to the lyric,
there were no new genre theories.[2] Theories after that were returns ei-

---

[2] "Those forms which he [Friedrich Schlegel] finds appropriate to his own
taste and time and which are congenial, above all, to the reflective, ironic temper
of the modern mind are the fragment, the dialogue (*das Gespräch*), the rhapsody,
the arabesque, the ironic comedy, and the speculative, satirical, or polemical
aphorism. All these are 'mixed' forms ('All pure, classical forms,' he says in *Lyceum*
fragment 60, 'are now absurd'). . . . The lyrical soliloquy, so indicative of a later
and different sort of nineteenth-century romanticism, is for Schlegel an enviable
but certainly a primitive and inferior manner. Unlike these forms, which have at
least a sporadic historical character in common, the form of the novel is radically
new and certainly without a continuous history. The novel (*der Roman*) represents
for Schlegel the most significant invention of the modern analytical sensibility. It is
related by its philosophical and discursive purpose not to the classical epic but to
the didactic poem, whose greatest single specimen is the *Divine Comedy.* . . . the
novel is not a consistent art form; it is not, in a strict sense, a genre . . ." (Victor
Lange, "Friedrich Schlegel's Literary Criticism," *Comparative Literature*, VII, Fall,
1955, 299).

ther to the classic idea of bigness, as with Arnold, or to the romantic idea of the lyrically intense moment, as with the imagists of the early 20th century. Or they were more and more subtly and dialectically blended obliterations of the old genre idea, as with the 19th-century dramatic monologues and idylls, and then the varieties of symbolism, post-symbolism, and latterly surrealism. The interlude of the porcelain verse genres with the Parnassians scarcely counts.

VIII

ONE perhaps will look about for some comprehensive issue, some paradoxical junction, that will catch, if only in a precarious and momentary stasis, the whole of the problem. This seems to appear nowadays in the question so often asked or implied: whether a poetic theory should be Platonic (concerned with meanings, even though only with analogical meanings) or Aristotelian, concerned, some critics appear to suppose, only with structures—structures of meaning which are somehow, in themselves, as structures, devoid of any meaning and not a modification or enablement of the meanings which are thought to be structured. Which view should poetic theory lean toward? Or, perhaps better, why should such a question be asked? The reason appears to lie in a kind of three-story pattern of human values which may be expounded roughly as follows: There is (1) easiest and lowest, the level of sensory pleasure and pain, terminal in its own way, unexplainable, more or less opaque. There is—to jump to the other extreme—(3) spiritual value, ethical and religious, terminal too, in a different way, in the sense that there is no higher appeal or sanction. And then in between there is (2) something like what Kant saw (which made him close a gap in his system with the *Critique of Judgment*). That is, there is aesthetic pleasure, pleasure of art, and this divides into two kinds: (A) the non-referential and Platonic, a form of sensory-intellectual pleasure (like wall paper and arabesques), terminal again in its own way—and (B) the referential or symbolic, the anti-Platonic art pleasure, especially the pleasure of poetry. But this kind of aesthetic value is an unstable conception. It almost inevitably invites being reduced—either up or down—to (1) sensory values, pleasure and pain (the portrayal of flowers and perfumes in Eden, says Addison, is more delightful than the portrayal of brimstone and smoke in Hell)—or to (3) conceptualized ethical and religious values (poetry, says the old didactic theory, is to teach correct lessons).

The grand problem for the theorist would appear to be how to evade these temptations, or, perhaps better, how to embrace them both and thus have a double or paradoxical theory. His best chance to do this, we have suggested, is found in the curious fact of metaphor, which is a combi-

nation of concreteness and significance, a reconciliation or simultaneous
embodiment of diverse emotive pulls, a way of facing and even asserting
something serious while at the same time declining the didactic gambit
which nature is always pushing forward—both to artist and to theorist.

A theory of art will not be able to get along without at least two
key terms—to stand in partial opposition to each other and keep the theory from collapsing into tautology or into literalism. At the same time
it will hardly be a theory at all unless it tries to bring these two terms
into a reconciled and necessary relation, or to see each in and through
the other. The two best critical terms, the most simple, inclusive, and unavoidable, are perhaps *making* and *saying* (if the latter be understood
to include its expressionist complement the term *seeing*—"Always the
seer is a sayer"). Or *Creation and Discovery*, as the title of an aesthetic
philosopher's recent book has it. *Making*, the Aristotelian emphasis, and
saying-seeing, the Platonic and romantic. The justification of this polar
arrangement is the impossibility that the two can ever come completely
together without the collapse and loss of poetry, and the equal impossibility of their being taken in strict dichotomy or separation without the
same loss. Under these two complementary but opposed heads we can
marshal an indefinite list of the antitheses that emerge in various phases
of critical argument: drama vs. statement, metaphor vs. literal fact, concrete vs. abstract, whole vs. part, whole structure vs. Longinian or Crocean flash, inclusion vs. exclusion, pleasure *and* pain vs. pleasure *or* pain,
Aristotelian *harmonia* vs. Aristotelian *mimēsis*, art in full vs. either romantic or classical art; finally, and again basically, the work vs. either the
author or the audience. Art or poetry is the peculiar situation where we
see each member of each pair only in or through its opposite: making
through saying and saying through making.

Something can be learned, something perhaps ultimate, from the
most abstract schemes of the philosophers. Let us take a concluding look
at an Aristotelian and scholastic classification of human mental activities
recently readvertised in the aesthetic writings of the neo-scholastic philosopher Jacques Maritain. Systematic mental activities (arts and sciences), says the tradition, are either speculative (like metaphysics and
mathematics) or practical, and the practical are either concerned with doing (ethics and politics) or with making (arts), and then these activities
of making are further divisible into useful arts and fine arts—the last being the category where we find poetry. Perhaps, though we will not urge
this in a quarrelsome way against aestheticians of painting or music, poetry is *the* fine art. Mr. Maritain thinks that something he calls "poetry,"
a principle of subjective communion with objective reality, is the essence
of all the fine arts. And indeed the verbal principle as it works in poetry
more pronouncedly than in other arts does at least put a special emphasis
on the relation of tension which holds between fine art (especially po-

etry) and the other arts and between art in general and the sciences. There is a doubling of art and fine art, in two stages, from their generic non-speculative direction back through the status of *making* (as distinct from doing) to the status of *fine* (as distinct from useful). This last, the status of *fine*, is one where acting takes on in a peculiar way the aspect of speculation (seeing-saying). Let us imagine a tabular arrangement as follows:

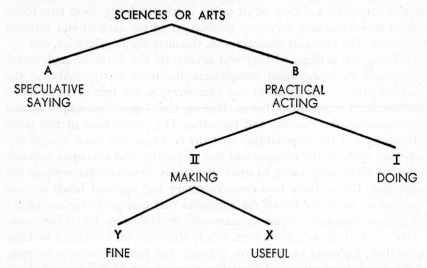

And let us recite thus the broadest lessons of critical history: (1) A pragmatic general philosophy collapses A and B, and hence there is no possibility that a problem about art can really arise. "When we look at a picture, or read a poem, or listen to music," says Richards, "we are not doing something quite unlike what we were doing on our way to the Gallery or when we dressed in the morning." [3] (2) Functionalism in art theory (even in a scholastic frame of general reference) collapses X and Y, echoing and complementing the general pragmatic reduction of A to B. "To make a drainpipe," says Eric Gill, "is as much the work of an artist as it is to make paintings or poems." [4] (3) Platonic versions of art and beauty (including perhaps the neo-scholastic theory of Mr. Maritain) and fully idealist versions of expressionism, like that of Croce, put a transcendental "beauty" somehow specially under Y, though by definition as a transcendental this beauty is also everywhere else and is hence the proper object of the most generalized speculative activity. "If an epigram be art," says Croce, "why not a simple word?" [5] (4) Didactic art theory, from Plato to the present day, completes too in its own way the motion of return (from right to left in our spatial representation) and rules art

[3] *Principles of Literary Criticism* (New York, 1934), p. 16.
[4] Eric Gill, *Art* (London, 1935), p. 4.
[5] *Aesthetic*, trans. Douglas Ainslie (London, 1922), p. 13.

by the straight norms of A, conceptual truth. Poetry, that is, becomes the art of *saying* something *correct* either about God or nature or about some human activity. Would a pilot or a poet know better, asks Socrates, how to steer a boat in a storm?

It remains that a theory of poetic or fine art must do something yet different. It must keep asserting in various idioms, by various strategems, in accord with the demands of the dialectic of the time, the special character of Y (poetry) as a tensional union of making with seeing and saying.

INDEX

A NOTE ON THE TYPE

This book was set on the Linotype in Janson, *a recutting made direct from the type cast from matrices made by Anton Janson some time between 1660 and 1687. Janson's original matrices were, at last report, in the possession of the Stempel foundry, Frankfurt am Main.*

Of Janson's origin nothing is known. He may have been a relative of Justus Janson, a printer of Danish birth who practiced in Leipzig from 1614 to 1635. Some time between 1657 and 1668 Anton Janson, a punch-cutter and type-founder, bought from the Leipzig printer Johann Erich Hahn the type-foundry that had formerly been a part of the printing house of M. Friedrich Lankisch. Janson's types were first shown in a specimen sheet issued at Leipzig about 1675. Janson's successor, and perhaps his son-in-law, Johann Karl Edling, issued a specimen sheet of Janson types in 1689. His heirs sold the Janson matrices in Holland to Wolffgang Dietrich Erhardt, of Leipzig.

Composed, printed, and bound by Kingsport Press, Inc., Kingsport, Tennessee. Paper manufactured by P. H. Glatfelter Company, Spring Grove, Pa. Designed by Harry Ford.